DEATH, DYING, and EUTHANASIA

DEATH, DYING, and EUTHANASIA

Edited By
DENNIS J. HORAN
DAVID MALL

1980
Aletheia Books
University Publicatons of America, Inc.

The quote of T.S. Eliot on page 647 is from "East Coker" in *Four Quartets*, copyright, 1943, by T.S.
Eliot; renewed, 1971 by Esme Valerie Eliot. Reprinted by permission of Harcourt Brace Jovanovich,
Inc.

Acknowledgments

C. Anthony Friloux, Jr.'s "Death, When Does It Occur?" is reprinted with the permission of the author and publisher from the *Baylor Law Review*, Vol. 27, 1975, pp. 10-21.

Alexander Morgan Capron and Leon R. Kass's "A Statutory Definition of the Standards for Determining Human Death: An Appraisal and a Proposal" is reprinted with the permission of the authors and publisher from the *University of Pennsylvania Law Review*, Vol. 121: 87, 1972, pp. 87-118.

Anthony Shaw's "Dilemmas of 'Informed Consent' in Children" is reprinted with the permission of the author and publisher from *The New England Journal of Medicine*, Vol. 289, No. 17, Oct. 25, 1973, pp. 885-890.

Raymond S. Duff and A.G.M. Campbell's "Moral and Ethical Dilemmas in the Special-Care Nursery" is reprinted with the permission of the author and publisher from *The New England Journal of Medicine*, Vol. 289, No. 17, Oct. 25, 1973, pp. 890-894.

Pegeen L. Soare and Anthony J. Raimondi's "Intellectual and Perceptual-Motor Characteristics of Treated Myelomeningocele Children" was supported by the Psychiatric Training and Research Funds of the Illinois Department of Mental Health Grant No. 17-321 and by NINDS Research Grant No. NS09025.

John A. Robertson's "Involuntary Euthanasia of Defective Newborns: A Legal Analysis" is reprinted with the permission of the author and publisher from the *Stanford Law Review*, Vol. 27, 1975, pp. 213-269.

James M. Gustafson's "Mongolism, Parental Desires, and the Right to Life" is reprinted with the permission of the author and publisher from *Perspectives in Biology and Medicine*, Vol. 16, No. 4, Summer 1973, pp. 529-557.

Pope Pius XII's address "The Prolongation of Life" is reprinted with the permission of the author and publisher from *The Pope Speaks*, Vol. 4, No. 4, Spring 1958, pp. 393-398.

Joseph Fletcher's "Ethics and Euthanasia" is reprinted with the permission of the author and publisher from *To Live and to Die: When, Why, and How* (New York: Springer-Verlag, Inc., 1973, pp. 113-122).

Paul Ramsey's "The Indignity of 'Death with Dignity" is reprinted with the permission of the author and publisher from *Hastings Center Studies*, May 1974, Vol. 2, No. 2, pp. 47-62.

Paul Ramsey's "Death's Pedagogy" is reprinted with the permission of the author and publisher from *Commonweal*, 20 September 1974, p. 497-502.

Rabbi Immanuel Jakobovits' "Some Recent Jewish Views on Death and Euthanasia" is reprinted with the permission of the author and publisher from *Jewish Medical Ethics* (New York: Bloch Publishing Company, 1975, pp. 275-276).

Arthur Dyck's "Beneficent Euthanasia and Benemortasia: Alternative Views of Mercy" is reprinted with the permission of the author and publisher from *Beneficent Euthanasia* (ed. Marvin Kohl, Prometheus Books, Inc., Buffalo, N.Y., 1975).

Rev. Kevin D. O'Rourke's "Christian Affirmation of Life" is reprinted with the permission of the author and publisher from *Hospital Progress*, July, 1974.

David W. Louisell's "Euthanasia and Biathanasia: On Dying and Killing" is reprinted with the permission of the author and publisher from the *Catholic University Law Review*, Vol. 22:723, 1973, pp. 723-745.

Yale Kamisar's "Some Non-Religious Views against Proposed 'Mercy-Killing' Legislation" is reprinted with the permission of the author and publisher from the *Minnesota Law Review*, Vol. 42, No. 6, May 1958, pp. 969-1042.

Glanville Williams' "'Mercy-Killing' Legislation—A Rejoinder" is reprinted with the permission of the author and publisher from the *Minnesota Law Review*, Vol. 43:1, 1958, pp. 1-12.

C. Everett Koop's "The Seriously Ill or Dying Child: Supporting the Patient and the Family" is reprinted with the permission of the author and publisher from *Pediatric Clinics of North America*, Vol. 16, No. 3, August, 1969.

Richard Lamerton's "How Hospices Cope" is reprinted with the permission of the author and publisher from *Care of the Dying* (London: Priory Press Limited, 1973, pp. 43-61).

Leo Alexander's "Medical Science Under Dictatorship" is reprinted with the permission of the author and publisher from *The New England Journal of Medicine*, 241:39-47, 1949.

Thomas St. Martin's "Euthanasia: The Three-in-One Issue" is reprinted with the permission of the author and publisher from the *Baylor Law Review*, Vol. 27, No. 1, Winter 1975, pp. 62-67.

Frederic Wertham's "The Geranium in the Window" is reprinted with the permission of the author and publisher from *A Sign for Cain* (New York: Macmilllan Publishing Co., Inc., 1966, pp. 153-191).

Robert M. Byrn's "Compulsory Lifesaving Treatment for the Competent Adult" is reprinted with the permission of the author and publisher from the *Fordham Law Review*, Vol. 44, October 1975.

The editors also wish to acknowledge the following authors for their kind contributions of original essays: Vincent J. Collins, Eugene F. Diamond, Stanley Hauerwas, Marshall McLuhan, Eugene Ionesco, Karen Lebacqz, H. Tristram Engelhardt, Jr., and Germain Grisez.

Finally, the editors extend special thanks to Richard Potts for the cover artwork and to Virginia Reuter for typing the manuscript.

Contents

Introduction

Our era, more than any other, has faced directly the complex of issues—social, legal, medical, moral—surrounding death. We have decided that the subject will be discussed openly, that all aspects of the problem will now be as commonplace in our literature as it once was missing from our literature. We have, in the words of one author in this collection, assaulted the last taboo. Whether or not that assault is in the service of mankind remains to be seen.

Any contemporary discussion of death inevitably means, in addition, a discussion of what is seen as the many other inextricably intertwined issues which usually do more to cause confusion than to shed light. This is nowhere more evident than in the endless struggle with terminology that runs through every discussion of euthanasia. The very word itself causes untold confusion in the discussion of the issue. The purpose of the editors of this volume is to shed some light on these issues and avoid as much confusion as possible. That is a modest enough undertaking. For all of its size, this book is basically a very modest undertaking when one considers the size of the problem itself—individual human life, its progeny and its passing.

The editors have decided that seven issues must be discussed to at least begin seeking some solutions to the problems. Thus, this book is divided into seven parts under appropriate title headings, each part containing relevant essays. In each part, the heading states what the editors conceive the issue to be. The various parts may seem, at first glance, to be disconnected, but we are convinced that they are a unified whole, each of which must be understood by a society which seeks an ultimate answer—a value judgment—to the questions now being posed about human life itself.

DEATH: WHEN DOES IT OCCUR AND
HOW DO WE DEFINE IT?

For many years the problem of defining death was basically one of a simple medical judgment made by a physician at the deathbed in a home or in a hospital. The criteria for determining when death occurred were medical criteria easily applied by physicians and seldom, if ever, questioned by the public. There existed no statutory definitions of death, and the common law considered the issue only in relation to the distribution of property or in determining whether a person who had been the victim of an assault died within a year and a day. The common law defined death as a moment when life had ceased, "defined by physicians as a total stoppage of the circulation of the blood and a cessation of the animal and vital functions consequent therein, such as respiration, pulsation, etc." Any more was not necessary, and so no more was undertaken.

Then, two advancing areas of medicine converged on the deathbed to create one of our current problems. The first of these was the increasing ability of medicine to resuscitate dying patients and to maintain those patients on sophisticated machinery. The second was the ability of medicine to transplant organs from one person to another. Both of these advances depended upon a myriad of factors too complicated to discuss here, but were related to the tremendous growth in medical technology of recent years.

In response to the problems of resuscitation and the modern use of respirators, several states passed new laws redefining death in two ways. One definition is used when the death occurred in the hospital where resuscitative methods were being used. This definition brought in the relatively recent requirement of "brain death." The other definition of death was applicable when resuscitative means were not involved. This definition continued to rely on the traditional grounds of cessation of heartbeat and respiration.

The Kansas statute was the first of these statutes to create such a dichotomy. This statute is discussed at some length by Alexander Morgan Capron and Leon R. Kass in the third article in this volume.

However, even before one reaches a legal definition of death, one must discuss the medical criteria for determining when death has occurred. This has been done by Dr. Vincent Collins, who is a professor of anesthesiology at Northwestern University Medical School and president of the medical staff at Cook County Hospital. In addition, Dr. Collins operates the pain control clinic at Cook County Hospital about which more will be said later.

Dr. Collins' essay discusses not only the physical characteristics of death, but includes a scoring method (similar to the widely used Apgar scoring method) for determining when resuscitative methods should be discontinued. Dr. Collins first determines what it means to be alive—to be an integral functioning individual—and then decides that the lack of those qualities determines when death has occurred. Whether Dr. Collins' dying and recovery score becomes a norm for use by the medical profession remains to be seen.

Once medicine has determined what death is, then the law *may* have some capability of statutorily defining it. These issues are separate and should be understood in that manner. Obviously, physicians have been pronouncing individuals dead for many centuries, and even more obviously there have not existed statutory definitions of death until our modern age. The one is not dependent upon the other. The fact that death remains undefined in state statutes does not mean that doctors will be unable to declare individuals dead. Such a common sense insight into the problem should not be forgotten.

Much of the pressure for the creation of a statutory definition of death has come from those interested in the transplantation of organs. This is unfortunate because it has created an aura of distrust over the entire problem. The issue of organ transplantation is one that should be decided on the basis of a person's ability and willingness to donate organs rather than on the issue of when they are living or when they are dead. Since all of these elements are intertwined, confusion becomes rampant; but the basic issue of when a person is dead should not be confused with the separate issue as to whether or not that person has consented for the donation of his or her organs. Having so consented, the question then arises as to when the organs can be removed. If the organs are necessary to sustain life, then obviously they can only be removed when the person's life has ended. Nonetheless, the determination as to when that life has ended is a medical judgment which should not be clouded by an anxious desire to remove organs, even if done for the laudable reason of providing a better life for someone else. Most state statutes have solved that problem by removing the transplant surgeon from the consultation as to when death has occurred and by prohibiting him from being involved in that decision.

Resuscitation and maintenance on respiratory machines pose many difficult medical problems concerning when such therapy can be discontinued and what are the medical and legal criteria for discontinuing therapy. These will be discussed later in the section dealing with the Quinlan case.

We have concluded the first section of this book with the article written by Professor Capron and Dr. Kass on a proposed statutory definition of the standards for determining human death. The transplant issue has brought to the forefront the concern with cerebral death. The brain has three basic centers of which the cerebrum or cortex is only one. Many persons argue that the death of the cerebrum, or cortical death, is the death of the person. However, the American Bar Association has opted for a definition of brain death which includes "total brain death," meaning all three centers of the brain. Many of the issues surrounding such a choice are elucidated by the Capron and Kass article. Their conclusion and alternative to the Kansas statute is simple and has the great benefit of not trying to statutorily define the parameters of medical practice. No one would think of passing a state statute indicating when a physician should do an appendectomy, and one wonders what hysteria or furor has caused the medical profession to run to state legislatures in an attempt to define death. Putting that aside for the moment, however, the fact of the matter is that state after state has passed a definition of death statute, and, consequently, the subject matter should be discussed and the issues clarified. We now find the same rush to the legislature with regard to the living will.

Professor Richard Stith, J.D., Ph.D., Assistant Professor of Law and of Community Medicine and the Director of the Development of Programs in Biomedical Ethics at St. Louis University, has criticized the Capron-Kass definition of death because it would allow persons who had brain function but lacked spontaneous respiratory and circulatory functions to be declared dead. This definition, he argues, would allow such persons to be declared dead in two ways: 1) prior to the connection of a life support system, his permanent lack of spontaneous circulation might be rapidly ascertainable and he could be declared dead, although his brain would still be not beyond repair; 2) or, much more likely, he could be declared dead while fully conscious and on artificial life supports, if one could simply find a way to determine that he would never again have spontaneous respiratory and circulatory functions.

Although the Capron-Kass definition of death may be deficient in the area which Professor Stith points out, it should also be noted that the Capron-Kass article makes clear that the first portion of their definition of death which is criticized by Professor Stith is based upon the prevailing medical and legal definition of death when artificial means of support are not being used. Under current law, turning off a respiratory support system when the person's brain was undamaged would constitute homicide. Would the Capron-Kass proposal alter this and allow homicide in the two cases discussed by Professor Stith? As a practical matter, no one has suggested that this result was intended or foreseen. What has been suggested by others is that the support systems be terminated when the cerebrum or cortex is dead, but not other portions of the brain. Obviously, in drafting a statute, Professor Stith's objection should be met and dealt with, but does it seem to be a reasonable deterrence to the use of the Capron-Kass definition?

DEATH AS A TREATMENT OF CHOICE?: INVOLUNTARY EUTHANASIA OF THE DEFECTIVE NEWBORN

The Duff and Campbell paper entitled "Moral and Ethical Dilemmas in the Special Care Nursery" has raised the issue concerning the extensive care which our society routinely renders to defective children in the newborn nursery. The argument is made that modern resuscitative methods and the tremendous advances in medicine have enabled medicine to treat these very difficult cases which would have otherwise ended in death shortly after birth. As a result of medicine's ability to maintain the lives of these children, significant issues have been raised concerning the amount of treatment that society should allocate to the newborn nurseries. Some have argued that our society should not allocate otherwise scarce medical resources to the care of defective children whose expected quality of life is extremely low. They argue that the paradigm of the abortion solution should be operative in the newborn nursery also: If the severely defective child is unwanted by its parents, it should remain untreated and be allowed to die. Still others have said that rather than merely allowing such unwanted and severely defective children to die by starvation or lack of treatment, would not the more humane solution be a quiet but dignified death administered by a loving physician and family?

In all, there are eight papers which discuss the various issues raised by the Duff and Campbell paper. John A. Robertson, a professor of law at the University of Wisconsin School of Law, presents a legal analysis which the nontreatment of these children raises. Professor Robertson concludes that withholding ordinary medical care from these children may involve homicide, intentional torts, or wilful neglect. To these views, Duff and Campbell conclude: "If working out these dilemmas in ways such as those we suggest is in violation of the law, we believe the law should be changed."

The issue here involves a difficult problem for our society. When, if ever, is the withholding of ordinary medical means of treatment for defective children justifiable? Is such withholding of ordinary medical treatment a homicide? Under our current law, euthanasia is homicide. As Paul Ramsey indicates, the withholding of ordinary means of medical treatment in the newborn nursery is involuntary euthanasia. John Robertson concludes the same.

Paul Ramsey concludes that society should treat all members of the newborn nursery as equals. If a form of treatment is normative for one child, then it should also be for another, even if that other is a Down's syndrome child. Obviously, such judgments are not easily made, since medical anomalies are usually multiple and the complex of medical problems requires forms of treatment only recently available. The argument is made that the treatment and its success which is only now available has for the first time thrust such life and death issues into medicine. There is some truth and some exaggeration in that view. Medicine has always dealt with dying patients. The difference now is that some medical persons are asking that the law condone death as a treatment of choice—a willed medical intervention made, they argue—for the benefit of the child, the child's family, and our society.

The initial judgment as to whether treatment should be withheld is, and should be, a medical judgment. The issue raised by Duff and Campbell questions whether such medical judgments can instead be made based upon societal factors such as the expected quality of life of the defective child. This decision cannot be made by medicine alone, since it involves a value judgment central to the constituent fabric of our society. We are all involved in making this decision whether we participate or not. Thus, this book.

Societal judgments must be based, first of all, upon the medical evidence. Consequently, we have included the paper by Drs. Soare and Raimondi, showing the intellectual characteristics of treated meningomyelocele children, one of the most difficult of the defective birth problems.

In an age when the courts are for the first time declaring retarded individuals to be of equal worth with other individuals in our society and under our Constitution, it seems anomolous that equal justice under law is being threatened in the newborn nursery.

EUTHANASIA: ETHICAL, RELIGIOUS AND MORAL ASPECTS

Almost every discussion of euthanasia begins with the allocution of Pope Pius XII to the International Congress of Anesthesiologists in 1957, and this book is no exception. In one of the overlooked statements in that address there is a *caveat* worth noting. Pope Pius XII points out that verification of when death occurs in a particular case is beyond the competence of religion or morals and depends upon a medical judgment.

In their recently issued pastoral letter on moral value, the United States Conference of Catholic Bishops stated that, although euthanasia or mercy killing is much discussed and increasingly advocated today and although the discussion is often confused by the ambiguous slogan "death with dignity," that, whatever the word or term, "it is a grave moral evil deliberately to kill persons who are terminally ill or deeply impaired. Such killing is incompatible with respect for human dignity and reverence for the sacredness of life." The Catholic bishops further stated that the issue of euthanasia is distinct from the care and treatment which should be rendered to the terminally ill patient. While euthanasia or direct killing is always gravely wrong, it does not follow, say the bishops, that there is an obligation to prolong the life of a dying person by extraordinary means.

Joseph Fletcher, on the other hand, argues forcefully that religion should not be a consideration in a pluralistic society and that relief of pain leading to a "good death" should be the aim of society. Consequently, Fletcher concludes that voluntary euthanasia should be legalized since either assisted suicide or mercy killing could be the right thing to do in some exigent and tragic circumstances.

Arthur Dyck, Professor of Population Ethics at Harvard University, offers a different point of view. He argues from a purely philosophical point of view and concludes that, even in a pluralistic society, the moral obligation not to kill is mandated to all regardless of religious persuasion. Paul Ramsey, in his inimitable fashion, discusses the concept of "death with dignity" and attempts to place it in its proper perspective.

SUICIDE AND THE PATIENT'S RIGHT TO REJECT MEDICAL TREATMENT

The route toward the legalization of euthanasia is most easily perceived when one realizes that voluntary euthanasia is akin to assisted suicide. The parameters of the moral, legal, and societal issues surrounding assisted suicide are discussed in Section VII of this book by three essays.

In his paper, "Suicide and Euthanasia," Germain Grisez argues that on strictly philosophical grounds suicide and assisted suicide are intrinsically wrong under any circumstances.

Karen Lebacqz and H. Tristram Englehardt, Jr., conclude that suicide may be licit under certain extreme circumstances where relief of intractable pain is sought and no injustice is done to other persons. In view of that opinion, it is important that the medical control of pain be well understood. Richard Lamerton, in his paper in Section V, discusses control of pain; and Dr. Collins, in his work in the pain control clinic at Chicago's Cook County Hospital, has concluded that there is no such thing as uncontrollable, intractable pain.

Law professor Robert M. Byrne treats the suicide issue from a legal point of view as well as the patient's right to refuse medical treatment. His close analysis of the law involved in these areas indicates that things are not as clear as moral medical commentators outside of the legal area would like to think they are, but that, nonetheless, a competent adult ordinarily has a right to refuse medical treatment. What ramification does such a right have? The Quinlan case raised that right to constitutional levels for New Jersey residents. Byrne's paper discusses five models which should be examined in their entirety before concluding what the current law is on the question of suicide, the patient's right to refuse medical treatment, and the rights of other individuals involved in a family and close relationships with that person.

EUTHANASIA: THE LEGAL ASPECTS OF MERCY KILLING

Percy Foreman has said that euthanasia is a high-falutin' word for murder. This is true under our current law, as is discussed by Professors David Louisell and Yale Kamisar. The papers of Glanville Williams and Yale Kamisar present a classic confrontation on the issue of euthanasia—Professor Kamisar arguing that there are valid nonreligious objections to the legalization of euthanasia, and Professor Williams stating the classical case for the legalization of euthanasia.

In addition, we have added the opinion of the New Jersey Supreme Court in the Karen Quinlan case and an editorial discussion of that case. Although the Quinlan case should not be understood in any way as condoning euthanasia or leading toward the legalization of euthanasia, nonetheless the American press viewed the case as falling into that category of societal issues. Consequently, the Quinlan case has had tremendous impact on the public and the courts.

We call attention here again to the *caveat* of Pope Pius XII that these decisions are, first of all, medical decisions which should be based upon sound medical judgment with only the prognosis of the individual patient in mind. We have argued that that prognosis should not include such concepts as "meaningful life," and we hope that the terms used by the Quinlan court—"cognitive life" and "sapient life"—do not become equated in the public's mind with the concept of meaningful life.

The *New England Journal of Medicine* recently published several articles based upon the finding of a study committee on resuscitative methods and stated the medical criterion for determining whether or not such methods should be used or discontinued in any given case. This is good. Society and medicine should face, discuss, and resolve these issues. A disturbing era—the era in which a physician gives verbal orders to a nurse not to employ resuscitative methods yet is unwilling to so indicate in the medical record—is over. Whether or not resuscitative methods are going to be used should be faced. If the medical judgment in a given case is that such methods should not be used, based upon the relevant medical (not societal) factors involved, then such an order should be written in the medical chart after proper consultation with the individual involved and his or her family. Medicine should always follow its ancient adage: "Do no harm." Consistent with that adage, medicine should seek the proper consents for any treatment that is to be rendered. That treatment should be for the patient's benefit and not otherwise. Whether that term "benefit" includes the deliberate destruction of the individual's life is really the subject matter of this entire book and a subject matter which our society will be grappling with for years to come. That issue is nowhere more evident than in the newborn nursery, where many have argued that the term "benefit" does include the deliberate destruction of the patient's life.

HOW SHOULD MEDICINE AND SOCIETY TREAT THE DYING?

Very little, if any, disagreement occurs in this area of society and medicine. All agree that the dying patient should be treated with the utmost love and care. Two papers here by men practicing their art in this area indicate the heights to which good medicine can strive in order to provide the best for individuals who trust themselves to the care of the physician. The tragic case of the dying child is the most difficult to deal with, and the article by Dr. Koop indicates how medicine attempts to handle this problem.

Those who are outside medicine and who continually critique it with their own atomic microscopes should remember that it is one thing to peer in and another thing to be on the inside practicing with individuals who are suffering and dying. No other profession has striven for excellence the way medicine has, and no other profession has continually scrutinized and criticized itself from all points of view as has medicine. True, some practitioners have opted for what may be considered a poor societal result in the abortion issue, yet, nonetheless, the record of medicine in its service to mankind is unequalled by any other profession.

The most important aspect of Richard Lamerton's paper is the high sense of duty in the service of the dying which he holds up to us as a model for all of society. If his model were followed by our society, there would be no discussion of euthanasia, and the ending of life would be as sacred and important as its beginnings. Men would not die alone and estranged from their loved ones, but in the presence and in the comfort and care of their loved ones.

Additionally, Lamerton's paper says something very important about the euthanasia issue. He concludes that the control of pain is not beyond medicine. This is especially true if we remember the humanity of the dying and treat them as such. As we have stated, Dr. Vincent Collins, in the current work that he is doing at the Cook County Hospital pain clinic, has concluded that there is no such thing as intractable pain. Any pain can be controlled, he states, if it is the desire of the treating physician to control it and the aim of society to see that man's last days pass in care and comfort rather than intolerable suffering.

In discussing the legalization of euthanasia, intractable pain and the relief of that agonizing suffering is usually the opening wedge for assisted suicide or the legalization of euthanasia. In considering whether or not society should arrive at that result, we must remember that the control of pain is only now being undertaken as a study and only now being practiced in clinics throughout America. Even so, Dr. Vincent Collins has concluded in these early stages of the development of this new brand of medicine that pain can be controlled, that it is not intractable, and that the last days of a person's life can be made comfortable and loving without the necessity for killing them.

LEGALIZED EUTHANASIA: SOCIAL ATTITUDES AND GOVERNMENTAL POLICIES

The spectre of Nazi Germany hangs over the euthanasia issue. We do not mean to include a discussion of Nazi euthanasia in order to make an *in terrorem* argument. Our point merely is that both a society and the medicine practiced in that society at one time in modern history voluntarily opted for the involuntary destruction of the mentally ill, the unfit, and the social outcast. When proponents of mercy killing ask our contemporary society to legalize mercy killing, they should not hide the facts and circumstances surrounding the Nazi use of involuntary euthanasia of the mentally defective. That issue should be discussed for many reasons, the primary one of which is that legalized euthanasia began in Germany not so much because of pressure from the Nazi government, but because a willing medical community found euthanasia compatible with the way they wished to practice medicine. This point of view is amply stated by both Dr. Leo Alexander and Dr. Frederic Wertham. In particular, Dr. Wertham takes great care to point out that the legalization of euthanasia in Nazi Germany for mental defectives was possible only because the leading practitioners of psychiatric medicine at that time had already accepted the destruction of the mentally ill as a form of good medical practice. This insight by Dr. Wertham should be kept in the mind of every practitioner of medicine. It is only too easy for worthwhile social goals to slip and slide into utilitarian considerations which balance human life as one value on a scale where the cost-benefit ratio is the other value.

DENNIS J. HORAN

I.
Death:
When Does
It Occur
and
How Do We
Define It?

CONSIDERATIONS IN PROLONGING LIFE:
A DYING AND RECOVERY SCORE

Vincent J. Collins, M.D.

SUMMARY

Ethical and scientific considerations in prolonging life and in diagnosing death are reviewed. Death is defined in simplistic terms and is divided into clinical death and biological death. Dying is described as a progressive process, with each organ deteriorating at a different rate. Clinical death is the cessation of integrative action between all organ systems of the body. A multiparameter scoring system assists the physician in defining irreversible coma. It is used in determining when efforts at resuscitation should be abandoned yet when biological life of organs continues. The score helps to quantitate also the stages of recovery from coma and anesthesia.

INTRODUCTION

Phenomenal technological and scientific advances in medical science make it possible to prolong threatened life to an incredible degree. An essential question arises, however, as to whether at times we are dealing with true human life.

When the vital functions are maintained, the integrity of the brain and of other organs, at their particular capacity at that moment, can be sustained and functional recovery will likely occur and a rational human being can be restored. Sometimes, the vital organs are irreparably damaged by injury or disease and recovery or reanimation to a spontaneous level is impossible. Although we may be able to use extraordinary means to sustain the biological activities of organs and provide the semblance of existence, an integrated spontaneously existing rational man may be unattainable.

These considerations have prompted re-examination of the ethics of medical practice. There exist apparent contradictions and dilemmas in the medical, the moral and the legal area. An initial question is what is new about our problems? Or do we have adequate guides or principles to solve the problems of medicine or society? Perhaps what is most new is our assumption that the problems are new. Actually, only the appearances of the problems are new. The circumstances are, indeed, complicated by our science and by our machines, but the guides to their solution are still elemental, sound and true.

THE DILEMMAS

A dilemma in the area of medical practice concerns the recognition of life on the one hand and the decision to conclusively diagnose death on the other. Guided by the ethical principle inherent in the Hippocratic oath is the doctor's obligation to both benefit his patient and at the same time do no harm. Adherence to the two parts of this oath is many times the principle dilemma. To relieve suffering by appropriate drugs or procedures may be a threat to life. Many procedures which aim to preserve life may increase suffering. The terminally ill patient requires careful assessment of dying. When is it justified to withhold or to discontinue therapy in such patients? This is a revealing rhetorical question which has a clear answer: when the therapy is ineffective and without benefit! Note that one must distinguish between the terminally ill patient who is requiring "intense care" and extraordinary measures, who is in the final phases of the dying process, and a patient with a terminal illness or disease who at some later time will be in the final phases of the dying process.

The dilemma of death is summarized in two questions. At what moment is it right to pronounce a patient *clinically dead*, without hope of reanimation to a full human life with a meaningful existence (Collins, 1968), and yet at the same time the individual organs are biologically alive and potentially useful for transplantations? This leads to the next question of "when is it morally right and scientifically correct to remove artificial life supports and to remove organs for transplantation to sustain the life of another (Collins, 1964)?" The answers to these questions lie in correct diagnosis of clinical death—yet, to make this decision at a point in time before the biological death process is operational.

The dilemma actually concerns the recognition of life versus the need to conclusively diagnose death either at the clinical phase or the biological phase. It is asserted that the solution to the dilemmas faced in prolonging life, delaying death, or of recognizing each is the responsibility of the medical profession. The broad guidelines to making the decision are elemental.

THE PRIMARY DETERMINANTS

The basic obligation of the physician is to ensure man's existence as a whole human being with a meaningful life. In confronting the problem of death or of life the physician is challenged by the need for differential diagnoses.

For any course of action there are three determinants. These are: 1) contractual (patient-physician relationship); 2) ethical; and 3) scientific.

PHYSICIAN-PATIENT CONTRACT

The crux of medical practice is, of course, the physician-patient relationship. This is a contract with an implicit and explicit relationship. In the physician-patient relationship medical care is implied. The duties of the physician are correlative to those of the patient. The patient expects the services of the physician to be for his benefit, and therefore permits an invasion of his physical and mental privacy. Incumbent on every physician is the obligation that he must exert individual judgement, self-discipline and a conscientious attitude in his decisions regarding another special human being— his patient. He must respect the patient's rights.

As a "natural right" of man is the right of privacy. "It is the claim of an individual to determine for himself when, how, and to what extent information about himself is communicated to others" (A. Westin). It is never absolute, since society has certain claims and above all, the only absolute authority over our minds or bodies must remain a supernatural one.

One might also state that the right to maintain the privacy of one's personality is part of the right of self-preservation. This is the right that is shared and even surrendered by a patient when he consults a physician. When a patient visits a physician he is reasonably seeking advice and help. There is an implied consent for therapy. In the inter-relationship the physician informs the patient of the state of health and the option to maintain health. It is the duty to educate the patient as to his, the patient's, condition. This has popularly been designated as informed consent, but is better termed an "educated consent."

Some forms of therapy are implicit. Other more serious complex therapies, such as surgery and anesthesia, may be explicit in a written consent form.

Throughout his practice a moral understanding and sensibility to the health problems of the individual must be exercised by the physician.

The contractual relationship is and must be one governed by the moral virtue of Faith and the doctrine of trust.

ETHICAL GUIDES

Since an implicit contract exists between a physician and a patient, we must assess the ethical principles guiding the physician in fulfilling his contract. Every contract has *obligations*. Elements that operate in this personal contract include the *faith* of the patient in the doctor, and the doctor's competence, dependability and expertise; the *hope* of the patient that he will be relieved of his illness and of the physician that his efforts will be fruitful; and *love* of patient and physician as neighbors in society. Hippocrates stated this in the Physician's Oath:

> I will follow that method of treatment which, according to my ability and judgement, I consider for the benefit of my patient, and abstain from whatever is deleterious and wrong. I will give no medicine deadly to anyone, even if asked, nor suggest any such counsel.

Another way of stating the duties of a physician to his patient is that it should be according to the Golden Rule, the Universal Rule found in all religions but stated in various ways. This is a most pertinent guide to regulate human and medical conduct. The words of Christ appear in Luke (6:31):

As you wish that men would do to you, do so to them.

It is also revealed in the Talmud (Shabbat 31a):

What is hateful to you, do not to your fellow man. That is the Law; all else is commentary.

Medical ethics are part of general ethics. These are rules of conduct established between men and women dealing with the rights of man and what is good and beneficial. They are exemplified in the duties and in the habits of doing good deeds. Ethics are principles founded in the moral virtue of Love (charity).

The fulfillment of our humanitarian duties requires a reverance for human life; requires a respect for the sanctity of the body and a recognition of the right to human dignity.

EFFECTIVENESS OF THERAPY
THE SCIENTIFIC DETERMINANT

Based on medical facts and good judgement, the physician does those things in any situation which will benefit his patient. He must do those things which predictably result in improvement of his patient. The techniques of reanimation are proven, sound and legitimate. They can and do prolong life, *but* it must be determined that the nature of the resultant life is not mere biological existence of several organs, but totally integrated functional existence at a human rational level.

To continue an act or procedure of therapy, which produces no improvement, does not achieve or have the potential to achieve "full human life" and is demonstrably ineffective in its objectives, is imprudent, illogical and irrational. This is the essence of medical practice.

When a physician and his team bring together all the knowledge and skill related to sustaining life processes and treating patients with disease, he does so rationally. The effectiveness of his therapeutic skill must be constantly assessed. In artificially maintaining life or in arresting a disease process, the physician buys time. He provides by his assistance time for the patient's natural recovery processes to act, to allow natural restoration of functional organization and return the individual to a spontaneous, personal full life.

If, after some time all measures are obviously not effective and are not reversing the dying process, then the measures are failing. Deterioration may be observed. To persist may produce the appearance of life, but it is most often technical or mechanical life. The final decision will then be made in the face of a late phase or a second endpoint, namely, that of biological life. It is the physician's obligation to cease efforts early when they are determined to be ineffective in the total reanimation process and objectives. The patient should then be allowed to die. He has this right; he should not be cheated of a peaceful death in the face of a physician powerless to restore consciousness.

A vegetating patient, hopeless and irresponsive and showing no spontaneous activity, should be allowed to die peacefully and not in pieces. And physicians should make the dying process dignified.

The scientific determinant is founded in the moral principle of Hope. Science is one of the intellectual virtues denoted by understanding, knowledge and wisdom. The patient hopes that his physician will apply these virtues and expects him to show prudence and respect in the selection of a course of action. To a large extent in modern medical practice the scientific determinant must also be tempered by distributive justice.

COURSES OF ACTION IN TREATMENT

In the unconscious or hopelessly ill patient requiring resuscitation, there are *three* courses of action:

1. *Active Treatment* — Prolonged Dying vs. Reanimation.

2. *Active Intervention to End Life* — Euthanasia.

3. *Passive Management* — Shortening the Dying Process.

Let us address ourselves to these courses of action.

The first problem that poses a dilemma and requires serious examination is entitled "The Problem of Prolonging Life"; this is in reality a problem of therapy. Second, and in contrast, *is a problem of euthanasia*; this is a problem of a deliberate decision to actively end life—it is not a dilemma.

The prolonging of life is the lengthening of life. Euthanasia has its objective, the shortening of life and contrasts with the shortening of the dying process by passive management.

A physician's approach toward the inevitable ending of life may be either passive or active. Death could occur by actively interceding or by passively discontinuing therapy. In the first instance, one directly causes life to end by an overt act, whereas by discontinuing therapy, death is permitted by omission of an act and permitting nature to take its course.

ORDINARY AND EXTRAORDINARY MEANS

A definition of ordinary and extraordinary means is required. Ordinary measures of patient care are recognized as elements of essential care. They represent obligatory, proven and justified therapies and procedures. They are denoted by the fact that the patient himself can obtain them and put them to his own use. They further represent measures which he can reasonably undergo with only minimal or moderate danger and maximal effectiveness. Such measures are also not an impossible or excessive burden.

Extraordinary measures, on the other hand, are complicated methods. They are impossible for the patient to use or apply to himself and present a costly and difficult burden. In addition, they represent a high level of danger and the results expected are not predictable. That is, the effectiveness is minimal or moderate while the dangers are maximal.

Extraordinary measures sustain life artificially at the level it is found. Hopefully, at this point in time, there is no organic deterioration. The measures in resuscitation may then arrest the lethal process. The aim is to gain time in order for natural restorative processes to operate.

ASPECTS OF PROLONGING LIFE

But the more complicated question is that of prolonging life. Can we reconcile our scientific decisions to prolong life or let a patient die with our ethics and morality? Yes! But we must continue to clearly distinguish between letting a patient die and euthanasia.

Every physician is liable for his actions, but every action of a physician requires medical judgment. In saving a life, in preventing death, and then in prolonging the life, the question must repeatedly be asked as to whether the end result is inevitable or irrevocable. Is the end result, death, inevitable—or is the end result of the sustained immediate life mere organic existence?

When one permits death by not continuing therapy, the harm that is done is done by *nature acting*. This is passive management based on reason and judgement—and shortening the act of dying. It is rational. Therapy is discontinued when the efforts to maintain sound life are manifestly ineffective.

Thus, the problem is a challenge in therapy. It is possible for the doctor to artificially support life, at least the traditional vital functions of respiration and circulation. He must know what to do, when to do it and when to stop. In his therapeutic approach, the doctor will employ both simple or ordinary means as well as extraordinary means to support life.

EUTHANASIA

When one actively intercedes to end life, one is, in fact, causing harm to the individual. Even though this harm may apparently have a good. This course of action is abhorrent and prohibited.

Another apparent dilemma is that of motives. Behind every good deed is a motive. Motives can be colored. When man is the direct instrument to death, the law has historically related this to his intention. And two intentions are evident, an intention with malice or the intention with mercy. Regardless of the reason, whether malice or mercy, the end is murder.

The withdrawal of ineffective therapy and of special life supports in irreversible coma is NOT euthanasia—passive or otherwise. It is therapeutic rationalism. This is also the alternative to euthanasia. The only valid argument for euthanasia is the relief of suffering. But this can be accomplished by concerned and appropriate therapy and pain control services. Euthanasia can be characterized as an act of commission which achieves relief by destroying the sufferer. It is non-therapeutic; involves total harm and is abandonment of the patient. As such it is misguided mercy. The act of killing is the proximate cause of death.

We should now dispose of this question immediately: Shall we perform a deliberate act to positively end a life—that is, euthanasia? From the legal standpoint, from the moral codes and from the guidelines of ethical practice, we find applied the general law that no one is permitted to actively kill —regardless of the intent.

NEWER DEFINITIONS OF LIFE—DEATH

Because of the new dilemmas, standards of practice must be reassessed and re-established. The medical profession must confront the problems of death and its present definition, as well as it confronts the problem of understanding life.

The challenge is to apply human and moral customary principles to the dilemmas.

In examining the subject of prolonging life (by artificial mechanical means—by organ transplantation) the medical profession is faced with the fundamental need and, indeed, an obligation to formulate:

1. Clearer criteria of life.
2. Clearer standards of death.

Nature of Life. To identify the nature of human life is the first obligation. Fundamentally, life is the *integration* of the biological functions of at least nine organ systems (Angrist, 1958). The integration of these systems is emphasized. Life is not the mere function of these organs independently, nor is human life represented by the independent simple biological life processes in each organ. Blood cells, organ tissues, and even a whole organ may be maintained alive *in vitro* but such independent existence does not represent a human being.

It is whole organism representing the sum of the structural parts, all integrated functionally which when present establish the existence of life. To these are added a supreme integrative action by the central nervous system manifested by the capacity to reason and abstract. This capacity identifies human life as against all other forms of life. Thus by the total integrative process, there emerges a being greater than the parts called man.

Definition of Death. It is worthwhile that we define death and refer to the kinds of death which in different professional areas may be appropriately identified. Death in its simplest and broadest sense is the irreversible cessation of life functions. There are three forms of death to be recognized: clinical death; biological or cell death; and theological death (Collins, 1968). Of importance to our text is clinical death, which is the permanent cessation of integrated life functions.

Biological death refers to the cessation of the simple life processes of organs, tissues and cells. Theological death may designate the time when the soul is no longer present.

The Nature of Dying. Dying is a progressive process. Each part of the body or each organ system deteriorates progressively at different rates. Each organ has a *vulnerability index* and a revival time. Thus, the brain has a high degree of vulnerability to lack of oxygen and/or nutrition. It is more sensitive in this regard than the next most vulnerable organ, namely, the heart. The time during which the brain may recover if restoration of circulation is achieved is approximately 4 minutes (Sugar and Gerald, 1938). This is a period of relative vulnerability and deterioration. Recovery is probable, but after 4 minutes becomes improbable, and after 8 minutes is usually impossible. The heart can withstand loss of circulation upwards of 8 minutes but thereafter the revival of the heart becomes improbable, if not impossible. *The revival period* to which we refer is therefore dependent upon several factors: 1) time; 2) temperature; 3) perfusion; 4) oxygen tension; 5) total circulation. (A reduction in total cardiac output to 12% is critical for the brain).

The Dying Process. Three phases of deterioration leading to absolute clinical death can be recognized. These are modified from Kramer (1966) and are designated as: 1) disordered function (disequilibration); 2) distintegration; and 3) deanimation.

In the first phase, disordered function, each organ system or part of the body deteriorates functionally, insofar as it is integrated with, and coordinated with, other organ systems of the body. This may be considered as a period of early clinical death. It is reversible if resuscitation measures are immediately instituted and complete recovery is not only possible, but probable, if direct injury with destruction of the tissues has not occurred at the brain or heart levels.

The second phase of intrinsic disintegration represents deterioration of an organ itself with regard to its capacity to respond. In a sense this is the loss of extrinsic regulation and leaves only an automatic vegetative or intrinsic cellular autoregulation. This is a critical period, and revival—indeed, complete reanimation—is still possible. This is a period of intermediate clinical death.

The third phase of deanimation is actually one of structural and tissue disintegration. It is the period of progressive deanimation in which structural damage begins and has been referred to as annihilation as evidenced by the isoelectric electroencephalogram. During this time there is a progressive loss of organ autoregulation by different organs; this is accompanied by cellular changes and damage and subsequent necrosis.

Some injuries or causative factors, however, may be directly and immediately destructive of cellular integrity. This is not a reversible situation. Complete reanimation is not possible. A semblance of life may be attained artificially from 24 to 72 hours. But this is vegetative existence. Human life, or, indeed, an organized life, is not possible. However, some organs may be kept alive at the cellular or biological level, if the resuscitation technics are applied effectively, and before complete loss of autoregulation occurs. Individual organs may be alive at this simple tissue level, but the sum of all these does not result in an integrated whole.

Cessation of life functions or clinical death at the organ-system level leads to cellular death or what is more appropriately called biological death.

Some cells may be kept alive in a primitive sense by perfusion technics. This is done *in vitro* in the laboratory but can occur clinically by artificial means and represents a heart-lung preparation.

As a consequence of late institution of resuscitation procedures, many organs and tissues may show cellular dissolution or complete structural destruction when examined post mortem. With respect to the brain, a tissue-culture preparation may in fact exist, when the artificial methods of resuscitation are continued long after clinical death has occurred and after any hope of restoration to spontaneous function or total reanimation is possible. Such a period of time during which cellular autolysis is progressing is often called the incubation-brain and produces the phenomenon of respirator brain syndrome (Kimura, Gerber and McCormick, 1968).

Diagnosis of Death. The imminence of death or a conclusive set of circumstances leaving no alternative or hope is a medical decision (Fletcher, 1968). The law cannot make a determination of death but it can designate the person who is competent to do so. The first skillful statutory definition of death in the history of Common Law has been drafted by the State of Kansas. It leaves the determination of death in the hands of the attending physician at the scene of death (Curran, 1971).

The *recognition* of death is one of diagnosis based on logical thinking. The diagnosis of conclusive death and the decision that there is no likelihood of recovery must be established on customary medical-scientific observations and tests. This may be done in consultation or by a "Committee on Reanimation" of two or three physicians in a hospital with expertise in these matters. Such a group might well consist of an anesthesiologist, neurologist, cardiologist and cardiac surgeon.

As with any diagnosis, the patient must be examined by a physician. Death is dependent upon the observations made —the signs and symptoms or lack thereof. Five principal physiologic components must be assessed and indeed tested, namely: mental, sensory, motor, reflex and autonomic activity. These are the criteria and determinants. No single clinical factor, indeed, no single observations such as stoppage of respiration or stoppage of cardiac action or cessation of nervous system activity can today be considered sufficient or adequate by itself to establish a diagnosis of death. No single factor can stand alone in the differential diagnosis of any disease and be the final determinant. To arrive at a point in time when it must be considered that all efforts are hopeless and should therefore be abandoned must rest on many signs and observations. To be sure, the diagnosis of decision is initially presumptive. But with current technics the decision can be made conclusive.

ESTABLISHING CLINICAL DEATH

The task is to establish the fact of death. The pronounce-ment of this will then identify the time when *clinical death* is certain or conclusive and the resuscitation procedures have no possibility of reanimating the life processes of the organ systems to an integrated whole with a full human potential. And Biological Death is imminent. Yet the individual life processes of many organs may be present. The diagnosis of clinical death must then be stated by the Physician of the chart; only thereafter may extraordinary measures of resuscitation be withdrawn or abandoned.

One should not consider any other factor but the medical status in reaching a decision. When the virtues of continuing life-sustaining measures are questioned the physician must make the decision and inform the family—for who else can weigh the pros and cons.

The Dying Score. To assist the physician in this serious matter of determining the end point of life (vital and biologic) the concept of a score to determine death is proposed. To a degree this score parallels the Apgar Score, or living score for newborn babies (Apgar, Holaday, James, Weisbrot and Berrient, 1958).

It is asserted as a basic premise that no single sign or function can or should be used to assess the capacity to live nor establish the state of death. No single sign is adequate to determine total capability for human existence or the lack thereof. Patients should be evaluated according to several signs of life.

Therefore, five physiologic functions have been selected to be assessed as to their presence, their potential, or their absence. An arbitrary scoring system of 0, 1, and 2 is used. The physiologic functions selected are all of critical and vital importance. However, they are not all of equal importance but are interdependent for spontaneous life (Table III). Nor are they listed in their order of importance, but to some degree there is an increasing order of dependence of one function upon the other. These functions are:

1. Cerebral
2. Reflex
3. Respiratory
4. Circulatory
5. Cardiac

The irrevocable absence of one of these functions or the lack of capacity to perform spontaneously precludes the ability of the others to perform spontaneously.

In applying the score, an initial value is obtained as soon as the artificial resuscitation procedures have been instituted and the requirements of emergency care satisfied. It is then recommended that serial determinations of a score be made at least every 15 minutes over a period of at least 1 to 6 hours. Such a working plan will show a trend and be of predictive value. A score of 5 or more points represents potential life. A score of under 5 points represents impending or presumptive death. A score of 0 is conclusive death. It is further noted that an increasing score over a period of 2 hours indicates effective therapy and patient recovery; while a decreasing score over a period of 1 to 2 hours indicates failing therapy and patient deterioration.

To the clinical observations, there may be added laboratory, pharmacologic and monitoring tests of function and responsiveness.

[1] Cerebral Function. In the absence of consciousness, one assumes a depression or the loss of cortical function. Initially this may be reversible and during this reversible period sensory stimulation may evoke responses. At first, these are somatic in nature but later only the visceral or neurovegetative type of responses will be evoked and one may define a state of irreversible coma (Beecher, 1968).

Muscular movements may be observed and if noted to be purposeful, coordinated, and spontaneous, a score of 2 would be assigned. When such movements are altered, incoordinate, and without purpose, and are only observed when induced by strong stimulation, a score of 1 would be assigned. When such movements are absent and cannot be evoked by strong stimulation a score of 0 would be assigned.

It is emphasized that the electroencephalogram reflects cortical function only! It does not indicate total brain (cerebral) function. Special reliance on this type of study can be misleading since it is not the single key to the determination of death or life.

The electroencephalogram may show progressive deterioration (Kimura, et al., 1968); (Beecher, 1968).

When spike bursts alternate with periods of suppression, depression of cortical functions is evident. This pattern would represent a score of 1. When complete silence and an isoelectric potential is observed and there is a loss of evoked potentials, a score of 0 is assigned. The method of electroencephalographic study reveals primarily changes in cortical function and may be highly suggestive of cortical dysfunction; it does not necessarily reflect the capacity of the organism to be revived, nor does it reflect the existence of cellular life throughout the cerebral axis. The actual patterns of electrical activity should be assessed when the amplification is maximal (Kimura, et al., 1968). Rather than a flat pattern one should speak of an isoelectric pattern. These cortical patterns may be easily silenced by many stresses, drugs, shock, trauma; yet the body can be brought back to full life.

An isoelectric pattern without evoked responses over 2-6 hours is highly suggestive of cortical death and cerebral disorganization. But it is not conclusive and must be assessed concurrently with the other clinical signs and responses of other organs.

[2] Reflex Excitability. This function is evaluated by the observation of several responses. First, the size of the pupils is observed. Constricted pupils are evidence of good central nervous control at the diencephalic level and a score of 2 is warranted. Dilated pupils indicate a loss of such control. However, the testing of the dilated pupil of light stimulus and evoking some constriction indicates the capacity to recover and dictates a score of one. Many other sensitive reflexes may be stimulated in sequence. One can progress from the eyelid reflex to the pupillary light reflex to the pharyngeal, laryngeal, and carinal reflexes. Stimulating the larynx, trachea and carina usually evokes a modified cough or "buck." In deep coma no response occurs and a score of zero is indicated.

[3] Respiration. The presence of respiratory efforts which are spontaneous and adequate dictates a score of 2. When breathing becomes abnormal and requires assistance, a score of 1 is assigned. If spontaneous respiration is absent, but the administration of a respirogenic drug (i.e. doxapram) evokes a spontaneous respiratory effort, then a score of 1 is assigned. When respiration is absent, complete artificial control is required and the drug challenge to the respiratory center and to the pulmonary apparatus does not evoke a response, a score of 0 is indicated.

[4] Circulation. The presence of the circulation can be determined by detection of peripheral pulse, estimation of a

pressure and the observation of the capillary refill phenomenon in the skin or nail bed. A more sophisticated method of assessment of circulatory function is the observation of retinal vessels by opthalmoscopy. The presence of a measurable blood pressure, of a palpable pulse and good capillary refill suggests a score of 2.

The absence of an estimable blood pressure and the absence of a peripheral pulse with no capillary refill, but the presence of a detectable large artery pulsation indicates a score of 1. The score is verified by evoking a pressure response with a peripheral-acting vasopressor. A sluggish movement of blood in the eye grounds is of further help. This state can be designated by a score of 1 for the circulation.

When no pulsation is detected in large arteries and there is no evoked response to a vasopressor, a score of 0 is justified.

[5] Cardiac Action. For a score of 2, a spontaneous palpable cardiac thrust over the chest wall should be present and a peripheral pulse detected. Auscultation should reveal a regular heart beat, with the ECG of normal configuration.

When the heart beat is not detected by palpation and weak, ineffective contractions exist as evidenced by normal heart sounds coupled with an incoordinate bizarre pattern in the ECG, a score of 1 is assigned. Cardiac resuscitation measures should be needed and cardiac assistance indicated.

When a score of 1 is considered a pharmacologic stimulus to the heart, such as the injection of isoproterenol or epinephrine should evoke a response. In addition, at this critical time an intravenous cardiac pacemaker may be employed. If either should produce an effective cardiac contraction and response, a score of 1 is assigned.

The absence of any spontaneous cardiac activity and no ECG electrical activity demands artificial circulation by cardiac compression ("massage"). The failure to respond to a pharmacologic stimulus or for the electrical pacemaker to produce an effective cardiac contraction determines a zero cardiac score.

SECONDARY CONSIDERATIONS

Other factors than the medico-scientific may and do operate in our complex and pluralistic society. Such aspects as the economic, social, family, emotion, and indeed, the legal as well as religious must not operate determinatively. Indeed, the physician must remain aloof from these and pursue his art to the best of his reasonable ability. Economic and especially family considerations must not dominate his logic; for, if this logic and the science of medicine operate clearly and unencumbered so that a proper decision is reached in regard to the patient, then the best interests of all will be served, whether they be economic, family, legal or religious. Whatever reasonable and rational course of action is best for the patient will inevitably coincide with the best interests of the family if the care is humane and personalized.

WHOSE RESPONSIBILITY?

The solution of the dilemmas or contradictions faced in prolonging life or delaying death or of recognizing one or the other is the responsibility of the medical profession.

In reaching a decision one should not consider any other factor but the *medical* status of the patient and his welfare. When the virtues of continuing life-sustaining measures and the relief of pain, or the determination of futility of the therapy and the establishment of the presence of death are under consideration—who else can weigh the pros and cons but the physician?

WHAT ABOUT THE LEGAL RESPONSIBILITY?

Under no circumstances can the law determine death. Physicians must do this for society and then provide the common law grounds for action. The law clearly recognizes that the pronouncement and certification of death is that of a physician. The responsibility of decision rests squarely on the shoulder of the physician. The old definitions in law and even in medicine, emanating from long practice, are now inadequate.

It is now necessary for medicine to recognize determinants of death, to recognize a time for decision and a time to make decisions.

The law is only secondarily involved, once death is certified by the physician; then the law operates to dispose of a decedent's estate. It is understood that the law also operates to prevent a physician from performing unscientific therapies or to challenge him for negligence.

In the eyes of the law, the traditional signs of death are those consisting of a person whose "breathing has stopped" and who has "no pulse." This provides the layman with a basis to decide by common sense. Perhaps one might add for general purposes the observation of "no response" to stimulation and the impossibility of successful resuscitation. But something more scientific and conclusive than this is needed.

Perhaps the most lucid exposition of the subject of "Prolonging Life" and the legal aspects of any medical decision regarding death is that of Law Professor George P. Fletcher of the University of Washington. He states:

> The responsibility for the patient's expectations lies with the medical profession as a whole.
> The medical profession (not the legal profession) confronts the challenge of developing human and sensitive customary standards for guiding decisions to prolong the lives of terminal patients.
> They should have a clear standard for deciding when to render aid or not to the dying patient.

WHAT ABOUT THE RELIGIOUS RESPONSIBILITY?

Major religious leaders have clearly indicated that it is the doctor's responsibility to conclusively establish that death does, in fact, exist. I should only quote from Pope Pius XII in this regard. In answer to the question "When does death occur?," proposed at the International Congress of Anesthesiologists in Rome, November 24, 1957, Pope Pius XII stated:

> Human life continues for as long as its vital

functions, distinguished from the simple life (biologic) of the organs, manifest themselves spontaneously without the help of artificial processes.

The task of determining the exact instant of death is that of the physician.

SUMMARY OF RESPONSIBILITY

In summary, it is evident that in the area of prolonging life and determining death it is not a theological or legal responsibility. It is clearly a medical responsibility. There are three *primary* determinants regarding the limits of medical responsibility. These are fundamental. They are, first, the physician-patient contract. This involves a surrendering of certain features both physical and psychological of the natural rights of privacy of the individual to the doctor. Second, the ethical guidance and motivation of the physician by his code of ethics—as established by the Universal Rule of Love of Neighbor. And, third, the science and art of the physician as exemplified in his wise application of knowledge and diagnostic ability.

SUMMARY

It is the purpose of this paper to present the concept of "multiparameter scoring," to provide an end-point defining irreversible clinical death at a time when biological organ death has not occurred. As the technology of prolonging life and the science of organ transplantation has progressed, the need for such an end-point has become increasingly apparent.

A "model" score sheet currently being utilized is presented; this will undoubtedly be modified as experience is gained in multiparameter scoring.

At least three objectives may be realized by such a scoring system:

The physician can decide when efforts at resuscitation in an attempt to prolong life are no longer successful and should be abandoned; and this will allow the patient to die peacefully and not in pieces (Westin, 1968).

The score permits the anesthesiologists and the intense care physician to quantitate the stages of recovery from anesthesia or assess the recovery from coma.

A precise scoring system, based on sound medical and scientific principles will protect any potential donor from even the possibility of precipitous removal of organs. Death can be pronounced without the shadow of doubt before artificial and extraordinary supports are terminated and any organ removed for purposes of transplantation.

Thus, the question of homicide would not be raised and the interests of patient, physician and public will all be served.

TABLE I

Life—Integration of Physiological Functions (After Angrist)

Locomotion—Musculoskeletal System
Digestion—Gastrointestinal
Metabolism—All Cells
Excretion—Renal
Endocrine—Glands
Coordination—Nervous System
Respiration—Pulmonary
Circulation—Cardiocirculatory
Reproduction—Genital System

TABLE II

Factors Influencing Determination of Death

1. Nature of Human Being
2. State of Unconsciousness
3. Prognosis—Decision
4. Means to Manage
5. Patient's Rights—Wishes of Patient
6. Physician's Responsibility
7. Economics
8. Emotional—Sentimentality and Pity
9. Society's Demands
10. Legal Implications
11. Morality
12. Nature of Death

TABLE III

RECOVERY AND DYING SCORE IN COMATOSE PATIENT

SIGN	NORMAL	ABNORMAL	ABSENT
CEREBRAL FUNCTION	NORMAL	DEPRESSED	ABSENT
EEG	Alpha	Spikes	Isoelectric
STIMULUS— Light Temp		EVOKED RESPONSE	NO EVOKED RESPONSE
REFLEX ACTION Eyes Laryngeal Tendon Reflexes Nerve Stimulus	PRESENT Constricted Pupils Pharyngeal Reflex	DIMINISHED Pupillary Response Laryngeal—Carinal AN EVOKED RESPONSE	ABSENT Dilated NO EVOKED RESPONSE
RESPIRATION Doxapram Test	NORMAL Spontaneous Adequate	ABNORMAL Assisted EVOKED RESPONSE	ABSENT Controlled NO RESPONSE
CIRCULATION Vasopressor Test	NORMAL Pulse Pressure	DEPRESSED No Pulse No Pressure Artificial Support EVOKED RESPONSE	ABSENT NO EVOKED RESPONSE
CARDIAC Action	NORMAL Heart Sounds	INEFFECTIVE Assisted	ABSENT
ECG	Normal	Abnormal	Isoelectric
Pacemaker	Not needed	EVOKED RESPONSE	NO EVOKED RESPONSE

1. Initial evaluation as soon as artificial resuscitation procedures have been instituted.
2. Serial determinations at least every 15 minutes.
3. A score of 5 or more indicates potential life. A score of under 5 indicates *impending* or presumptive death.
4. A score of 0 is *conclusive* death.
5. An increasing score over a period of 1 hour represents effective therapy and patient recovery.
6. A decreasing score over a period of 1 hour represents failing therapy and patient deterioration.

Model Form

THE VIABILITY SCORE

*For differentiation between clinical and
biologic death for evaluation of
recovery potential of*

_____

PATIENT

FUNCTION	PRESENT (Value: 2)	ABNORMAL (Value: 1)	ABSENT (Value 0)
I. CEREBRAL			
Stimulus:			
(1) Light	_____	_____	_____
(2) Temperature	_____	_____	_____
(3) Pain	_____	_____	_____
EEG	_____	_____	_____
II. REFLEXIVE			
1. Ocular	_____	_____	_____
2. Laryngeal	_____	_____	_____
3. Tendinal	_____	_____	_____
4. Neuro-muscular	_____	_____	_____
III. RESPIRATORY			
1. Doxapram	_____	_____	_____
IV. CIRCULATORY			
1. Vasopressor	_____	_____	_____
V. CARDIAC			
1. Auscultation	_____	_____	_____
2. ECG	_____	_____	_____
3. Pacemaker	_____	_____	_____

Check the various signs:

TOTAL SCORE:

_____   _____M.D.

Witness

_____   _____M.D.

_____M.D.

_____

Date

To be made a part of patient's chart.

REFERENCES

1. Angrist A. "Certified Cause of Death-Analysis and Recommendations." *J.A.M.A.* 166: 2148-2153, 1958.

2. Apgar, V., Holaday, D.A., James, L.S., Weisbrot, I.M., and Berrient, C. "Evaluation of the Newborn Infant. Second Report." *J.A.M.A.* 168: 1985-1988, 1958.

3. Beecher, H.K. "A Definition of Irreversible Coma." *J.A.M.A.* 205: 337-340, 1968.

4. Collins, V.J. "Limits of Medical Responsibility in Prolonging Life—Guides to Decisions." *J.A.M.A.* 206: 389-392, 1968.

5. Collins, V.J. "Human Experimentation—The Mathematics of Danger." *Linacre Quarterly* 31: 179-184, 1964.

6. Curran, W.F. "Legal and Medical Death—Kansas Takes The First Step." *New Eng. J. Med.* 284: 260, 1971.

7. DeBakey, M.D. "Medical Research and the Golden Rule." *J.A.M.A.* 203: 574-576, 1968.

8. Fletcher, G.P. "Legal Aspects of the Decision Not To Prolong Life." *J.A.M.A.* 203: 65-68 (Jan. 1), 1968.

9. Kimura, J., Gerber, H.W., and McCormack, W.F. "The Isoelectric Encephalogram. Significant in Establishing Death in Patients Maintained on Mechanical Respirators." *Arch. Intern. Med.* 121: 515-517 (June), 1968.

10. Kramer, W. "Extensive Necrosis of the Brain: Development During Reanimation." Proc. Fifth International Congress of Neuropathology. New York. Excerpta Medica Foundation. Page 33-35, 1966.

11. Sugar, O., and Gerald, R.W. "Anoxia and Brain Potentials." *J. Neurophysiology* 1: 558-572, 1938.

12. Westin, Alan F. *Privacy and Freedom.* Atheneum Press, 1968.

DEATH, WHEN DOES IT OCCUR?

C. ANTHONY FRILOUX, JR.*

INTRODUCTION

Death is an event where medicine, religion, and law surround a human being in his last minutes of life. Medicine has done its share as physical life has come to an end. Religion claims the soul in the very moment it become separated from the body. When a somebody is dead, he no longer is "somebody." The responsibility for his rights is taken over by the law. At that moment medicine has no more to offer and respectfully steps aside, while religion continues to support the departed soul, and law perpetuates the abstract intentions of somebody, who is no more.[1]

Recent advances in the medical field have not been followed by correspondingly satisfactory advances in the medico-legal determination of death (when it occurs).

It is into the vacuum created by the recent advances in medical capability in artificial support systems, and the unique problems created by the advent of organ transplants, that a few pilot states have taken legislative steps to define "death" and to try to enact a specific "definition" of death, and the criteria to make such a determination.

Unlike the legal profession, the medical profession looks upon death as a continuing process and not an "instant" or "moment" in time as the law believes.[2]

The declaration of Sydney, adopted by the Twenty-Second World Medical Assembly in August, 1968 stated: "[D]eath is a gradual process at the cellular level with tissues varying in their ability to withstand deprivation of oxygen supply."[3]

The inflexibility of the law in relation to progressive medical and scientific advances is visible in the controversy involving the determination of the time of death, and/or the definition of "death."

In the legal sphere, "death" occurs precisely when life ceases and

---

*J.D., partner in the firm of Friloux & Woolf, Houston. Presently serving as the dean of the National College of Criminal Defense Lawyers and Public Defenders. Charter member and former president of the Texas Criminal Defense Lawyers Association. Member of the Criminal Justice Council of the American Bar Association.

[1]Corday, *Life-Death in Human Transplant*, 55 A.B.A.J. 629 (1969) ; 205 J.A.M.A. (1968) ; Biörck, *When is Death?*, 1968 WIS. L. REV. 484, 497 (1968).

[2]Mueller, *Legal Medicine and Determination of Death*, 14 WORLD MED. J. 140 (1967).

[3]Wecht & Arauson, *Medical-Legal Ramifications of Human Tissue Transplantation*, 18 DEPAUL L. REV. 488, 493 (1969) ; Kutner, *Due Process of Human Transplant: A Proposal*, 24 U. MIAMI L. REV. 782 (1970).

does not occur until the heart stops beating and respiration ends. Death is *not* a continuing event and is an event that takes place at a precise time.[4]

The divergence of traditional heart death and modern "brain death" theories pose significant legal ramifications. Ability to artificially maintain circulation and respiration confuses the issue and consequently the surgeon (in transplant cases) assumes the onerous burden of balancing medical success with possible legal repercussions.

When the brain damaged patient is subjected to life supportive techniques there might be a choice of establishing death from cessation of brain activity, or cardio-respiratory activity, and the time interval may extend to hours or occasionally, days.

This can have judicial consequences and it goes to the heart of the death concept itself.[5] Certain authorities within the medical society argue that there are multiple kinds of death occurring at different times;[6] these include organismal death, psychic death and vegetive death.

All of these obviously divergent views, coupled with the uncertainty of assuming a single medically accepted definition of "death," places the question of when death occurs from a legal sense, in its present unacceptable unresolved posture.

DECISIONAL OPINIONS—STATUTORY EVALUATION

In discussing the "legal" time of death, or "legal definition of death," recognition must be given to the fact that within the various disciplines in the medical field, medical standards for determining death are not singular, simple or universally accepted. Numerous common medical standards have been used to approximate the time of death; these include:[7]

The development and degree of:
1) Post mortem lividity,
2) Post mortem rigidity,
3) Loss of body heat,
4) Lysis of rigidity,
5) Clouding of cornea, and
6) Use of enzyme essay.

---

[4]Thomas v. Anderson, 96 Col. App.2d 371, 215 P.2d 478 (1968). *See also* Sauger v. Butler, 101 S.W. 459 (Tex. Civ. Auu. 1907, *n.w.h.*); Griegel's Adm'r. v. Orth's Ex'r., 236 S.W.2d 460 (Ky. Ct. App. 1950).
[5]Biörck, *When is Death?*, 18 Wis. L. Rev. 494 (1968).
[6]*Legal Levels of Life and Death*, Sill, M.D., MP.H.
[7]Majoska, *The Determination of Time of Death in a Case of Suspected Infanticides*, 5 J. For. Sci. 33 (1966). *See* Curley, *Role of the Forensic Pathologist in the Medico-Legal Certification of Modes of Death*, 13 J. For. Sci. 163 (1960).

In clinical circumstances the traditional standards, cessation of heart beat and respiratory functions, have been expanded to include the newly acceptable (among a growing number of medico-legal scholars) "brain-death" standards.

Before discussing the newly emerging statutory attempts at defining death, it must be understood that any such attempts to determine "time of death" or to "define death" must be written to encompass the clinical death occurrences as well as the non-clinical death situation.

From a legal standpoint, the historic traditionalist view widely recognized throughout the United States was based in whole or in part on the definition of death set forth in Black's Law Dictionary.

Black's states:

> Death—The cessation of life; the ceasing to exist; defined by physicians as a total stoppage of the circulation of the blood, and a cessation of the animal and vital functions consequent thereon, such as respiration, pulsation, etc. . . .[8]

In searching the reported cases in an attempt to discover the general approach taken by the trial courts to date, one is immediately aware of the scarcity of attempts to define the term (death). With the exception of a few criminal cases, the recorded cases deal with civil controversies involving survivorship, heirship, and related legal determinations.

In the cases of survivorship, the courts generally have looked to the medical profession for the definition. In *Thomas v. Anderson,*[9] *Smith v. Smith,*[10] and *Schmidt v. Pierce,*[11] the courts cited the traditional definition found in Black's Law Dictionary as authority.

A prime example of the use of this definition as a basis for determining when death occurred is *Gray v. Sawyer,*[12] in which the court adopted the definition given by the doctors who testified in the case. The doctors told the court in *Gray* as follows:

> A body is not dead so long as there is a heart beat. . . . This is so though the brain may have quit functioning.[13]

In *Vaegemont v. Hess,*[14] the court simply alluded to the traditional medical definition: "[D]eath takes place upon cessation of the vital functions of respiration and ciruclation."[15]

---

[8]BLACK'S LAW DICTIONARY 488 (4th ed. 1959).
[9]96 Cal. App.2d 371, 215 P.2d 478 (1950).
[10]299 Ark. 579, 317 S.W.2d 275 (1958).
[11]344 S.W.2d 120 (Mo. 1961).
[12]247 S.W.2d 496 (Ky. 1952).
[13]*Id.,* at 497.
[14]203 Minn. 207, 280 N.W. 641 (1938).
[15]*Id.,* at 643.

A review of the cases involving this issue quickly reflects that most courts neither define, nor allude to the medical definition, but merely rely upon the evidence of who the survivor was. If unable to do this, the court applies either the common law or statutory provisions relating to death by common disaster.

Until the advent of statutory definitions of death, the controversy was largely an intra-disciplinary dispute within the medical profession. The proponents of the clinical death and biological death further fragmented into those whose views were even more divergent. The medical terms "medical death," "clinical death," "molecular death," "sematic death," "systematic death," "brain death," etc. all combined to create an irreconcilable conflict when these divergent views were then presented to lay juries who were deliberating. The traditional common law determination of death and the time it occurs are fact questions for a jury. To say that such a state of the law was acceptable or workable would be a distortion of reality.

Smith v. Smith[16] is particularly significant since it was one of the first cases in which an attempt was made to induce a court to recognize the brain death concept, later written into law in the codes of Kansas,[17] Virginia,[18] Maryland,[19] and California.[20] One additional judicial pronouncement in *Smith* which is worthy of note was the trial court's statement: "[W]e take judicial notice that one breathing, though unconscious is not dead."[21]

In Arkansas, it is likely, in the absence of statutory enactment, that the same result and view as stated in *Smith* would result today, in spite of the growing reliance on more objective medical determinators.

A Texas court in *Sanger v. Butler*[22] was interpreting a will which contained the provision, "in the case of the death of my wife, Mary Butler and myself at the same time." The court ruled:

> Doubtless the word "death," in the majority of instances in which it is ordinarily employed, means "the act of dying." This however, we regard as a restrictive meaning. In its broader sense, the word "death" imports "the state or condition of being dead."[23]

Such a redundancy does not help the situation.

A similar result was reached in *Finch v. Edwards*[24] wherein the

---

16Note 2, *supra*.
17§ 77 - 202 Kan. Stat. Ann. (1973).
18§ 32 - 364,3 :1 Vir. Ann. Code (1974).
19Art. 43, § 54F Md. Ann. Code (1974).
20California Code—Enacted Oct. 1, 1974, not reported to date, Assembly Bill No. 3560.
21Note 2, *supra*.
22101 S.W. 459 (Tex. Civ. App. 1907, *n.w.h.*).
23*Id.*, at 461.
24239 Mo. App. 788, 198 S.W2.d 665 (1947).

Missouri court ruled that "death" when used with respect to a person is commonly and ordinarily understood to mean "departure from life."[25]

Amazingly enough, the United States Government has thus far not undertaken to define death, even though opportunities to do so have been numerous. The report of the Secretary's Commission on Medical Malpractice resulted in a conclusion that the question of the legal definition should be enacted into law only by the Congress of the United States.[26]

Many concerned legal and medical scholars may well have serious reservations about the resolution of this important issue by throwing it into the Congressional cauldron which has historically been somewhat less than effective in solving these type problems.

Because of the totally unexpected condition now existing in Texas and forty-three other states, where statutory determinations are absent, it must be conceded by the writer that legislative (state) action in determining "the instant of death" or definition of "death" would probably solve more problems than it would leave unresolved. Only in this way would the divergent views within the medical profession, as well as the equally divergent views within the legal profession, have an opportunity to assist in the formulation of compromise determiners which would be acceptable to both disciplines in meeting this very difficult determination.

Texas, like most states, has not met this problem head on; the new Penal Code does not define time of death, nor does it give any directional guidelines to the legal and medical professions in this state.

The "time of death," or the "instant death occurs," or the definition of "when a person is dead," are still questions to be determined according to the facts in the case. It is a "fact question" for determination by the courts, or the lay jury based on medical and lay testimony relevant to the facts surrounding the death of the particular person whose demise is the center of the controversy.

In the field of criminal law several cases are worthy of note. In the criminal case, the cause of death is inexorably tied to the "time of death" or "instant of death," particularly in heart or organ transplant cases. A graphic example is reflected in the California case of *People v. Lyons*[27] where the jury was confronted with determining whether the bullet from defendant's gun caused the death of the victim, or whether the death occurred as a result of the removal of organs from the deceased's body by physicians.

---

[25]*Id.*, at 470.

[26]U.S. Dept. of Health, Education and Welfare, Pub. No. 73-89 at 13-32 (1973).

[27]Cal. Sup. Ct., Oakland, Cal., May 21, 1974 (before enactment of new California statute defining death, Sept., 1974).

The trial court resolved the jury's dilemma by ruling, as a matter of law, that the death of the victim occurred *before* the removal of organs for transplant, and that the jury was instructed that the victim was legally dead when his heart was removed for transplant purposes.

The court's instruction and judicial ruling included, in part, the following:

> Death is the cessation of life. A person may be pronounced dead if, based on the usual and customary standards of medical practice, it has been determined that the person has suffered an irreversible cessation of brain function . . . and since that the deceased Samuel Moore was dead, before the removal of his heart, there was no issue of fact as to the cause of death.[28]

A factor of importance to legal and medical scholars is the reliance of the trial court on the medical testimony of Dr. Norman Shumway and Dr. Folkert Bilzer of the University of California Medical Transplant Center, who are (as you are aware) strong proponents of the "brain death" concept as a legal-medical determiner of death. These two physicians were instrumental in influencing the California legislature to adopt its present code using "brain death" as a primary determiner of when death occurs. The pre-occupation with the clinical (transplant) cases is reflected in the California codes failing to address itself to the totality of the problem (non-clinical death as well as the clinical death occurrences).

In *Tucker v. Lower*[29] the same issue of the "moment of death" and the "cause of death" confronted the court and jury. At the conclusion of the trial the court gave an alternate charge to the jury which included, in essence, the traditional definition (Black's), and as an alternative, "the loss of brain function test" or criterion.

Unfortunately, neither *Tucker* nor *Lyons* resulted in appellate review, thus leaving the legal status to conjecture and not definitive from a legal standpoint.

It was in the aftermath of the *Lyons* case in California that the legislature enacted the new California statute dealing with the definition of death; it was signed into law by the Governor in late September, 1974, and it is yet unpublished in the codes (see Appendix).

The California statute utilized the "total and irreversible cessation of brain function," or "brain death" test. Indications are the California code is similar to the Kansas, Virginia and Maryland statutes in using the brain death as one of the criteria for death approach but does not attempt alternative definitions.

---

[28]*Id.*
[29]Civil No. 2831 (Court of Law and Equity, Richmond, Va., 1972).

Reviewing these pilot statutes, which are generally similar, it becomes apparent the present legislative trend is toward adoption of some phase or variance of the general "brain death" theory. The "brain death" criterion as a determiner or criteria can be very helpful in clinical circumstances, particularly when transplants are contemplated, but cannot eliminate the nebulous area where death occurs outside clinical control, such as in an accident or violent death circumstance. The determination of death in these cases will inevitably result in a "fact determination" based on medically accepted criteria and lay testimony.

Many times, a lay jury will find that death occurred at a certain time in order to achieve a desired result. This obviously occurred in the *Estate of Rowley,*[30] where the fact question was which of two persons survived the other in a simultaneous death circumstance. The jury's unbelievable finding that one survived the other by 1/500,000 of a second is a graphic example of this objective. Obviously the finding was based, not on medical facts, but on the jury's desire to allow inheritance to go the way they felt it should go.

The recent ability of physicians to control the functions of organs by external devices over which the patient has no control, and the recognition of limitations on the cessation of heart beat and respiration as signs of death, force a re-evaluation and re-examination of the entire concept of "medical death."

With external devices supplementing vital organ functions, death must be defined in physical, social, and moral terms.

Various studies by medical committees have resulted in divergent views on resolution of this problem; however, it is apparent that the "brain death" proponents have substantially influenced the legislators of the pilot states and the legislators in other states who are grappling with this problem at this time.

The realistic fact of life is that, except in clinical cases, it appears difficult, if not impossible, to determine the medical testimony, scientific evidence, and lay testimony as a foundation for a legal determination of approximately when death occurred in such a case.[31]

In *Schmidt's Estate,*[32] the California appellate court (prior to the new statute) adhered to the concept of death as "the cessation of all vital signs" as the legal definition of death. In discussing its opinion, the court noted a variance in the medical opinion expressed and stated, "[F]or the purpose of this decision this court considers death as defined in Black's Dictionary, Third Edition."[33]

---

[30]257 Cal. App.2d 324, 65 Cal. Rep. 1939 (1967).
[31]4 AM. JR. PROOF OF FACTS—DEATH § 4-6 (1960).
[32]261 Cal. App.2d 262, 67 Cal. Rptr. 847 (1968).
[33]*Id.,* at 268.

In enacting the Uniform Anatomical Gift Act, forty-one states, including Texas,[34] adopted the act as drafted by the National Conference of Commissioners on Uniform State Laws, and approved by the American Medical Association and the American Bar Association. The act, unfortunately, does not define death or the determiners for ascertaining the "instant of death." The only legal significance of the act in this area is the act's placing upon the attending physician, or treating physician, the responsibility for determining the time of death, and allows civil immunity for the physician who acts in good faith in accordance with the act's criteria.

The Code does have a legal significance in relation to the transplant problem as it states that the physician (treating) charged with determining time of death "shall not participate in the procedures for the removing or transplanting a part."[35]

One further confusing factor resulted from the testimony of the technical consultants to the Acts Special Committee in its hearings before the United States Senate Committee which arose by *implication*, that the physician can make a determination of death using unconventional criteria based on the "brain death" concept rather than solely rely upon traditional cessation of all vital functions criteria, and still be judged by the reasonableness of the medical criteria and not by prior judicial precedents.[36]

STATUTORY EVOLUTION

The first attempt at a legislative resolution of the problems related to defining "death" and the "moment of death" was made in 1970 by the Kansas legislature when it adopted a statute entitled "[A]n act relating to and defining death."[37]

This first legislative step into the medico-legal morass appears to create almost as many problems as it resolves. The Kansas statute has come under criticism as an attempt to resolve too many collateral issues, as well as defining "death," and in so doing alternate definitions of death were created. The best analysis of the shortcomings of the Kansas statute appear in a 1972 law review article by Capron and Kass, A Statutory Definition of Standards for Determining Human Death.[38]

---

[34]Art. 4590-2, TEX. REV. CIV. STAT. (1974).

[35]*Id.*, at § 8.

[36]Hearing on § 2999 before the Senate Committee in the District of Columbia, 91st Cong., 2nd Sess., at 43 (1970); *see also, Sadler v. Sadler, The Uniform Anatomical Gift Act, A Model for Reform,* 206 J.A.M.A. 2502 (1968).

[37]Note 17, *supra.*

[38]Capron & Kass, *A Statutory Definition of the Standards for Determining Human Death: An Appraisal and a Proposal.* 121 U. PENN. L. REV. 87 (1972).

One unique approach for determining death as set out by the Kansas statute is that death occurs at two distinct points in time during the process of dying.[39] Kansas also enacted measures concerning resuscitation, i.e. when it is needed, when it can terminate, etc.

The Maryland and Minnesota statutes are somewhat identical to the Kansas statute and obviously modeled thereon, and are subject to the same criticism as their progenitor (Kansas).

Bills are currently pending in other states, including Florida, Illinois and Wisconsin, which seem to be following the same pattern used by Kansas in enacting their code.

California, recognizing some basic problems inherent in the pilot codes, attempted to legislate under a different approach. California did not attempt a unitary definition of death, or multiple death definitions, but concentrated instead on establishing the legality of the "concept of brain death" as an additional acceptable medical criteria. Until the enactment of the California statute, the great stumbling block has been the necessity to feel that a "brain death statute" must be an explicit definition, whereas California felt that the only real need was to establish the *legality* of the concept of "brain death," rather than attempt a definitive and restrictive definition as has Kansas.

With the passage of the California statute, the legality of "brain death," however it may be established, will not be litigable. This approach does not lock in the existing criteria (for both clinical and non-clinical death determinations) for determining when "irreversible cessation of brain function" has occurred, and leaves ample room for scientific and medical change. Yet, it permits judicial scrutiny of these criteria. Thus, under the California statute, when a physician pronounces a person dead on the basis of "brain death," his action will be legally acceptable *provided* he employs currently acceptable criteria.

It will be conceded that statutory approval of brain death has not been accepted by the American Medical Society nor by a number of state medical associations to date.

CONCLUSIONS

Death is not instantaneously determinable under present medical criteria; it is a staged process which a person goes through. Clinical death and death under non-clinical circumstances require employment of divergent criteria in arriving at a decision of when a person is legally dead.

---

[39] *Kennedy 1M: The Kansas Statue of Death: An Appraisal*, 285 N. ENGL. J. MED. 946 (1971); *see also* Mills, *Statutory Brain Death*, 229 J.A.M.A. (Aug. 26, 1974).

Statutorily inflexible definitions of death are more confusing to the medico-legal disciplines than they are enlightening. The purpose of a definition is to make a complex and obscure term more definite and understandable by analysis and restatement in terms which are simple and better understood. Attempts at definition by statute to date have resulted in the exact opposite result.[40]

It would appear that the long accepted conventional (traditional) evidences or criteria, enhanced by the new criteria developing today in medical acceptability, including the concept of "brain death," appear basically adequate both medically and legally.

Rigid criteria and definitions are as troublesome as the total absence of such criteria.

Some thought should be given to providing the parameter within which the physician can determine death by the medically accepted criteria for both clinical and non-clinical episodes as opposed to the head long rush to statutory rigidity. This is the challenge facing the medico-legal disciplines today.

---

[40]Hirsch, *Death, A Medical Status or Legal Definition,* 78 CASE AND COM. 30.

APPENDIX A
CALIFORNIA

Chapter 3.7 Death.

Provides that a person shall be pronounced dead if it is determined by a physician that the person has suffered a total and irreversible cessation of brain function. Requires independent confirmation of the death by another physician.

Specifies that nothing in the act shall prohibit a physician from using other usual and customary procedures for determining death as the exclusive basis for pronouncing a person dead.

Requires independent confirmation of the death of the donor, when a part is used for direct transplantation pursuant to the Uniform Anatomical Gift Act, by another physician when the death is determined by determining that the donor has suffered a total and irreversible cessation of brain function. Prohibits *both the physician making the determination of death and* the physician making the independent confirmation from participating in part removal or transplant procedures.

Requires that complete patient medical records meeting prescribed requirements be kept, maintained, and preserved with respect to the requirements of the act when a person is pronounced dead by determining that the person has suffered a total and irreversible cessation of brain function.

7180. A person shall be pronounced dead if it is determined by a physician that the person has suffered a total and irreversible cessation of brain function. There shall be independent confirmation of the death by another physician.

Nothing in this chapter shall prohibit a physician from using other usual and customary procedures for determining death as the exclusive basis for pronouncing a person dead.

7881. When a part of the donor is used for direct transplantation pursuant to the Uniform Anatomical Gift Act (Chapter 3.5 [commencing with Section 7150]) and the death of the donor is determined by determining that the person has suffered a total and irreversible cessation of brain function, there shall be an independent confirmation of the death by another physician. *Neither the physician making the determination of death under Section 7155.5 nor the* physician making the independent confirmation shall participate in the procedures for removing or transplanting a part.

7182. Complete patient medical records required of a health facility pursuant to regulations adopted by the department in accordance with Section 1275 shall be kept, maintained, and preserved with respect to the requirements of this chapter when a person is pronounced dead by determining that the person has suffered a total irreversible cessation of brain function.

Sec. 2. This act is an urgency statute necessary for the immediate preservation of the public peace, health, or safety within the meaning of Article IV of the Constitution and shall go into immediate effect. The facts constituting such necessity are:

In order that the dramatic decline in the availability of human kidney donors can be reversed, it is necessary that this act take effect immediately.

APPENDIX B
VIRGINIA

Chapter 19.2—U.A.G.A.

§ 32-364.3:1. When person deemed medically and legally dead.—A person shall be medically and legally dead if, (a) in the opinion of a physician duly authorized to practice medicine in this State, based on the ordinary standards of medical practice, there is the absence of spontaneous respiratory and spontaneous cardiac functions and, because of the disease or condition which directly or indirectly caused these functions to cease, or because of the passage of time since these functions ceased, attempts at resuscitation would not, in the opinion of such physician, be successful in restoring spontaneous life-sustaining functions, and, in such event, death shall be deemed to have occurred at the time these functions ceased; or (b) in the opinion of a consulting physician, who shall be duly licensed and a specialist in the field of neurology, neurosurgery, or electroencephlography, when based on the ordinary standards of medical practice, there is the absence of spontaneous brain functions and spontaneous respiratory functions and, in the opinion of the attending physician and such consulting physician, based on the ordinary standards of medical practice and considering the absence of the aforesaid spontaneous brain functions and spontaneous respiratory functions and the patient's medical record, further attempts at resuscitation or continued supportive maintenance would not be successful in restoring such spontaneous functions, and, in such event, death shall be deemed to have occurred at the time when these conditions first coincide. Death, as defined in subsection (b) hereof, shall be pronounced by the attending physician and recorded in the patient's medical record and attested by the aforesaid consulting physician.

Notwithstanding any statutory or common law to the contrary, either of these alternative definitions of death may be utilized for all purposes in the Commonwealth, including the trial of civil and criminal cases.

APPENDIX C

MARYLAND

54F U.A.G.A.—When is a person considered medically and legally dead?

(a) A person will be considered medically and legally dead if, based on ordinary standards of medical practice, there is the absence of spontaneous respiratory and cardiac function and, because of the disease or condition which caused, directly or indirectly, these functions to cease, or because of the passage of time since these functions ceased, attempts at resuscitation are considered hopeless; and, in this event, death will have occurred at the time these functions ceased; or

(b) A person will be considered medically and legally dead if, in the opinion of a physician, based on ordinary standards of medical practice *and because of a known disease or condition,* there is the absence of spontaneous brain function; and if based on ordinary standards of medical practice, during reasonable attempts to either maintain or restore spontaneous circulatory or respiratory function in the absence of spontaneous brain function, it appears that further attempts at resuscitation or supportive maintenance will not succeed, death will have occurred at the time when these conditions first conicide. Death is to be pronounced before artificial means of supporting respiratory and circulatory function are terminated and before any vital organ is removed for purposes of transplantation.

(c) These alternative definitions of death are to be utilized for all purposes in this State, including the trials of civil and criminal cases, any laws to the contrary notwithstanding.

APPENDIX D

KANSAS

77-202. Definition of death. A person will be considered medically and legally dead if, in the opinion of a physician, based on ordinary standards of medical practice, there is the absence of spontaneous respiratory and cardiac function and, because of the disease or condition which caused, directly or indirectly, these functions to cease, or because of the passage of time since these functions ceased, attempts at resuscitation are considered hopeless; and, in this event, death will have occurred at the time these functions ceased; or

A person will be considered medically and legally dead if, in the opinion of a physician, based on ordinary standards of medical practice, there is the absence of spontaneous brain function; and if based on ordinary standards of medical practice, during reasonable attempts to either maintain or restore spontaneous circulatory or respiratory function in the absence of aforesaid brain function, it appears that further attempts at resuscitation or supportive maintenance will not succeed, death will have occurred at the time when these conditions first coincide. Death is to be pronounced before artificial means of supporting respiratory and circulatory function are terminated and before any vital organ is removed for purposes of transplantation.

These alternative definitions of death are to be utilized for all purposes in this state, including the trials of civil and criminal cases, any laws to the contrary notwithstanding.

77-203. Notice; certified mail in lieu of registered mail; sufficiency. In lieu of giving notice by registered mail as provided for by specific statutes of this state, any party may give notice required by certified mail and notice so given by certified mail shall constitute and be sufficient notice the same as though such notice was made pursuant to specific statutes requiring registered mail.

EDITORS' COMMENT

As of 1977 at least twelve state legislatures had enacted new definition of death laws: Kansas, Maryland, Virginia, California, Oregon, Georgia, Michigan, New Mexico, Alaska, Louisiana, Illinois, and Tennessee.

The wording of the new proposed statutes can vary considerably, but in general the new definitions propose that cessation of brain function be entered as a new and separate criteria for death, with great variation in the specific definition of brain death and in the conditions attendant on the determination of death.

The American Bar Association (ABA) definition reads: "For all *legal* purposes, a human body with irreversible cessation of total brain function, according to usual and customary standards of medical practice, shall be considered dead" (Resolution adopted February 24, 1975). It is customary for such ABA definitions to be forwarded to the commission of Uniform State Laws as a basis for drafting a recommended bill. However, the American Medical Association is on record in opposition to a statutory definition of death (resolutions 1973, 1974 and earlier).

By 1974 the Uniform Anatomical Gift Act, proposed by the National Conference of Commissioners on Uniform State Laws in 1968, had been adopted by virtually all the states. This Act does not define death. It leaves the determination of death to the physician. "The time of death shall be determined by a physician who tends the donor at his death, or, if none, the physician who certifies the death. The physician shall not participate in the procedures for removing or transplanting a part" (Sec. 7(b)).

A STATUTORY DEFINITION OF THE STANDARDS FOR DETERMINING HUMAN DEATH: AN APPRAISAL AND A PROPOSAL*

ALEXANDER MORGAN CAPRON[†]

AND

LEON R. KASS[‡]

In recent years, there has been much discussion of the need to refine and update the criteria for determining that a human being has died.[1] In light of medicine's increasing ability to maintain certain signs of life artificially[2] and to make good use of organs from newly dead

* This Article grew out of discussions held by the Research Group (formerly Task Force) on Death and Dying of the Institute of Society, Ethics and the Life Sciences, a nonprofit organization engaged in interdisciplinary analysis of the issues generated by biomedical advances. The Research Group has been investigating various practical and philosophical problems in the "meaning" of death and the care of dying patients. Earlier drafts of the Article were discussed at meetings of the Research Group, and, although not the subject of formal approval by the group, the Article reflects the conclusions of the Research Group's members, who include Henry K. Beecher, M.D., Harvard University; Eric Cassell, M.D., Cornell University Medical College; Daniel Callahan, Ph.D., Institute of Society, Ethics and the Life Sciences; Renée C. Fox, Ph.D., University of Pennsylvania; Michael Horowitz, LL.B., New York, N.Y.; Hans Jonas, Ph.D., New School for Social Research; Irving Ladimer, S.J.D., American Arbitration Association; Marc Lappé, Ph.D., Institute of Society, Ethics and the Life Sciences; Robert Jay Lifton, M.D., Yale University; William F. May, Ph.D., Indiana University; Robert S. Morison, M.D., Cornell University; Paul Ramsey, Ph.D., Princeton University; Elisabeth Kübler-Ross, M.D., Chicago, Ill.; Alfred Sadler, M.D., Yale University; Blair Sadler, J.D., Yale University; Jane Schick, Ph.D., M.D., Cornell University Medical College; Robert Stevenson, Ph.D., Bionetics, Inc., Frederick, Md.; Robert Veatch, Ph.D., Institute of Society, Ethics and the Life Sciences. The work of the Research Group has been supported in part by a grant from the New York Foundation. The authors thank the members of the Research Group for their valuable suggestions and critical review of the manuscript and Sharmon Sollito, B.A., Institute of Society, Ethics and the Life Sciences, for her assistance in research.

† Assistant Professor of Law, University of Pennsylvania. B.A. 1966, Swarthmore College; LL.B. 1969, Yale University. Member, District of Columbia Bar.

‡ Executive Secretary, Committee on the Life Sciences and Social Policy, National Research Council—National Academy of Sciences. B.S. 1958, University of Chicago; M.D. 1962, University of Chicago; Ph.D. 1967, Harvard University.

1 See, e.g., P. RAMSEY, THE PATIENT AS PERSON 59-112 (1970); Louisell, Transplantation: Existing Legal Constraints, in ETHICS IN MEDICAL PROGRESS: WITH SPECIAL REFERENCE TO TRANSPLANTATION 91-92 (G. Wolstenholme & M. O'Connor eds. 1966) [hereinafter cited as MEDICAL PROGRESS]; Discussion of Murray, Organ Transplantation: The Practical Possibilities, in id. 68 (comments of Dr. G. E. Schreiner), 71 (comments of Dr. M. F. A. Woodruff); Wasmuth & Stewart, Medical and Legal Aspects of Human Organ Transplantation, 14 CLEV.-MAR. L. REV. 442 (1965); Beecher, Ethical Problems Created by the Hopelessly Unconscious Patient, 278 NEW ENG. J. MED. 1425 (1968); Wasmuth, The Concept of Death, 30 OHIO ST. L.J. 32 (1969); Note, The Need for a Redefinition of "Death," 45 CHI.-KENT L. REV. 202 (1969).

2 A dramatic increase over the past twenty years in the use of extraordinary means of support such as artificial respirators for terminal patients is generally assumed by physicians, on the basis of observational and anecdotal evidence, but no quantitative studies of this phenomenon have been done. Telephone interview with Dr. Claude L'Enfant, Director, Division of Lung Diseases, National Heart and Lung Institute, Bethesda, Md., Oct. 16, 1972. For this reason it is not possible to offer any detailed estimate of the impact that the proposed statute, see text accompanying note 86 infra, would have on the resources allocated to patient care.

bodies, new criteria of death have been proposed by medical authorities.[3] Several states have enacted or are considering legislation to establish a statutory "definition of death,"[4] at the prompting of some members of the medical profession who apparently feel that existing, judicially-framed standards might expose physicians, particularly transplant surgeons, to civil or criminal liability.[5] Although the leading statute in this area[6] appears to create more problems than it resolves,[7] some legislation may be needed for the protection of the public as well as the medical profession, and, in any event, many more states will probably be enacting such statutes in the near future.[8]

---

[3] *See, e.g.*, Ad Hoc Committee of the Harvard Medical School to Examine the Definition of Brain Death, *A Definition of Irreversible Coma*, 205 J.A.M.A. 337 (1968) [hereinafter cited as *Irreversible Coma*]; *Discussion* of Murray, *Organ Transplantation: The Practical Possibilities*, in MEDICAL PROGRESS, *supra* note 1, at 69-74 (remarks of Drs. G. P. J. Alexandre, R. Y. Calne, J. Hamburger, J. E. Murray, J. P. Revillard & G. F. Schreiner) *When Is a Patient Dead?*, 204 J.A.M.A. 1000 (1968) (editorial); *Updating the Definition of Death*, MED. WORLD NEWS, Apr. 28, 1967, at 47.

In an earlier article, our Research Group appraised the proposed new medical criteria for the determination of death and discussed some of the sources of public concern. Task Force on Death and Dying, Institute of Society, Ethics and the Life Sciences, *Refinements in Criteria for the Determination of Death: An Appraisal*, 221 J.A.M.A. 48 (1972) [hereinafter cited as *Refinements in Criteria*]. In discussing the procedures used to establish the new criteria, the article concluded:

Clearly, these matters of decisionmaking and the role of law need further and widespread discussion. The acceptability of any new concept or criteria of death will depend at least as much on the acceptability of the procedure by which they are adopted as on their actual content.

Id. 53.

[4] KAN. STAT. ANN. § 77-202 (Supp. 1971); MARYLAND SESSIONS LAWS ch. 693 (1972). Bills are presently pending in Florida, H. 551, 2d Fla. Legis. (n.s.) (1971), Illinois, H. 1586, 77th Gen. Assemb., 1st Sess. (1971), and Wisconsin, S. 550, Biennial Sess. (1971).

Section IV of this Article argues that terms such as "defining death" and "definition of death" are extremely ambiguous, and that the ambiguity is an important cause of misunderstanding and confusion regarding the propriety of legislation in this area. Though it would be desirable not to use such terms, they are too well established in professional and public discourse on these matters to be eliminated. For convenience, and often deliberately to emphasize the problem of ambiguity, we occasionally use these terms in quotation marks. For an explanation of four different levels of specificity which may be intended when the term "definition of death" is employed, see notes 57-60 *infra* & accompanying text.

[5] *See, e.g.*, Taylor, *A Statutory Definition of Death in Kansas*, 215 J.A.M.A. 296 (1971) (letter to the editor), in which the principal draftsman of the Kansas statute states that the law was believed necessary to protect transplant surgeons against the risk of "a criminal charge, for the existence of a resuscitated heart in another body should be excellent evidence that the donor was not dead [under the "definition" of death then existing in Kansas] until the operator excised the heart." *Cf.* Kapoor, *Death & Problems of Transplant*, 38 MAN. B. NEWS 167, 177 (1971); Baker, *Liability and the Heart Transplant*, 6 HOUSTON L. REV. 85, 97-101 (1968). The specter of civil liability was raised in *Tucker v. Lower*, a recent action brought by the brother of a heart donor against the transplantation team at the Medical College of Virginia. *See* notes 42-50 *infra* & accompanying text.

[6] KAN. STAT. ANN. § 77-202 (Supp. 1971); see notes 74-88, 98-101 *infra* & accompanying text for a discussion of this statute.

[7] *See* notes 74-85 *infra* & accompanying text.

[8] In addition to the state medical societies, *see* Taylor, *supra* note 5, others have advocated a statutory definition of death. "Medical researchers and M.D.'s involved in transplants must break with their traditional reluctance to seek statutory changes in the definition of death or find themselves floundering in a morass of court suits in coming years." 15 DRUG RESEARCH REP., June 7, 1972, at 1. Moreover, once a statute is enacted

I.   BACKGROUND

Courts and physicians can no longer assume that determining whether and when a person has died is always a relatively simple matter. The development and use of sophisticated machinery to maintain artificially both respiration and circulation has introduced difficulties in making this determination in some instances. In such cases, the use of a cardiac pacemaker or a mechanical respirator renders doubtful the significance of the traditional "vital signs" of pulse, heartbeat, and respiratory movements as indicators of continuing life. Similarly, the ability of an organ recipient to go on living after his own heart has been removed and replaced by another's has further undermined the status of the beating heart as one of the most reliable—if not *the* most reliable—signs that a person is still alive. In addition, the need of transplant surgeons to obtain organs in good condition from cadavers has stimulated the search for tests that would permit the death of the organism as a whole to be declared before the constituent organs have suffered extensive deterioration. Consequently, new criteria for judging a person dead have been proposed and are gaining acceptance among physicians. The most prominent are those formulated in 1968 by the Harvard Medical School's Ad Hoc Committee to Examine the Definition of Brain Death, chaired by Dr. Henry K. Beecher.[9]

The Harvard Committee described in considerable detail three criteria of "irreversible coma": (1) "unreceptivity and unresponsivity" to "externally applied stimuli and inner need"; (2) absence of spontaneous muscular movements or spontaneous respiration; and (3) no elicitable reflexes.[10] In addition, a flat (isoelectric) electroencephalogram was held to be "of great confirmatory value" for the clinical diagnosis.[11] Although generally referred to as criteria for "cerebral

on a new subject in one state, there seem to be direct and indirect pressures for it to be viewed as a model for adoption in other states. *Cf. id.* 5, which notes that the Virginia statute allowing a medical examiner to provide a decedent's organs for transplantation is "the first of its kind in the nation" and terms it "a model for other states to emulate," when it is in fact poorly conceived and nearly incomprehensible.

[9] *See Irreversible Coma, supra* note 3. In addition to Dr. Beecher, the committee consisted of nine other physicians, an historian, a lawyer, and a theologian, all Harvard University faculty members. *Id.*

[10] *Id.* 337-38.

[11] The Harvard committee spelled out its central conclusions as follows:

An organ, brain or other, that no longer functions and has no possibility of functioning again is for all practical purposes dead. Our first problem is to determine the characteristics of a *permanently* nonfunctioning brain.

A patient in this state appears to be in deep coma. The condition can be satisfactorily diagnosed by points 1, 2, and 3 to follow. The electroencephalogram (point 4) provides confirmatory data, and when available it should be utilized. In situations where for one reason or another electroencephalographic monitoring is not available, the absence of cerebral function has to be determined by purely clinical signs, to be described, or by absence of circulation as judged by standstill of blood in the retinal vessels, or by absence of cardiac activity.

death" or "brain death," these criteria assess not only higher brain functions but brainstem and spinal cord activity and spontaneous respiration as well. The accumulating scientific evidence indicates that patients who meet the Harvard criteria will not recover and on autopsy will be found to have brains which are obviously destroyed,[12]

---

1. *Unreceptivity and Unresponsitivity.*—There is a total unawareness to externally applied stimuli and inner need and complete unresponsiveness—our definition of irreversible coma. Even the most intensely painful stimuli evoke no vocal or other response, not even a groan, withdrawal of a limb, or quickening of respiration.

2. *No Movements or Breathing.*—Observations covering a period of at least one hour by physicians is [*sic*] adequate to satisfy the criteria of no spontaneous muscular movements or spontaneous respiration or response to stimuli such as pain, touch, sound, or light. After the patient is on a mechanical respirator, the total absence of spontaneous breathing may be established by turning off the respirator for three minutes and observing whether there is any effort on the part of the subject to breathe spontaneously. (The respirator may be turned off for this time provided that at the start of the trial period the patient's carbon dioxide tension is within the normal range, and provided also that the patient has been breathing room air for at least 10 minutes prior to the trial.)

3. *No reflexes.*—Irreversible coma with abolition of central nervous system activity is evidenced in part by the absence of elicitable reflexes. The pupil will be fixed and dilated and will not respond to a direct source of bright light. Since the establishment of a fixed, dilated pupil is clear-cut in clinical practice, there should be no uncertainty as to its presence. Ocular movement (to head turning and to irrigation of the ears with ice water) and blinking are absent. There is no evidence of postural activity (decerebrate or other). Swallowing, yawning, vocalization are in abeyance. Corneal and pharyngeal reflexes are absent.

As a rule the stretch of tendon reflexes cannot be elicited; i.e., tapping the tendons of the biceps, triceps, and pronator muscles, quadriceps and gastrocnemius muscles with the reflex hammer elicits no contraction of the respective muscles. Plantar or noxious stimulation gives no response.

4. *Flat Electroencephalogram.*—Of great confirmatory value is the flat or isoelectric EEG. We must assume that the electrodes have been properly applied, that the apparatus is functioning normally, and that the personnel in charge is competent. We consider it prudent to have one channel of the apparatus used for an electrocardiogram. This channel will monitor the ECG so that, if it appears in the electroencephalographic leads because of high resistance, it can be readily identified. It also establishes the presence of the active heart in the absence of the EEG. We recommend that another channel be used for a noncephalic lead. This will pick up space-borne or vibration-borne artifacts and identify them. The simplest form of such a monitoring noncephalic electrode has two leads over the dorsum of the hand, preferably the right hand, so the ECG will be minimal or absent. Since one of the requirements of this state is that there be no muscle activity, these two dorsal hand electrodes will not be bothered by muscle artifact. The apparatus should be run at standard gains $10\mu v/mm$, $50\mu v/5$ mm. Also it should be isoelectric at double this standard gain which is $5\mu v/mm$ or $25\mu v/5$ mm. At least ten full minutes of recording are desirable, but twice that would be better.

It is also suggested that the gains at some point be opened to their full amplitude for a brief period (5 to 100 seconds) to see what is going on. Usually in an intensive care unit artifacts will dominate the picture, but these are readily identifiable. There shall be no electroencephalographic response to noise or to pinch.

All of the above tests shall be repeated at least 24 hours later with no change.

The validity of such data as indications of irreversible cerebral damage depends on the exclusion of two conditions: hypothermia (temperature below 90 F. [32.2 C.]) or central nervous system depressants, such as barbiturates. *Irreversible Coma, supra* note 3, at 337-38.

[12] In the largest single study of patients with flat E.E.G.'s of twenty-four hours'

and supports the conclusion that these criteria may be useful for determining that death has occurred. The Harvard Committee's views were apparently well received in the medical community.[13] Not all physicians have been enthusiastic, however. Professor David Rutstein of the Harvard Medical School, for example, expressed concern over "this major ethical change [which] has occurred right before our eyes . . . with little public discussion of its significance."[14]

Not surprisingly, disquiet over the change in medical attitude and practice arose in lay as well as medical circles.[15] The prospect of physicians agreeing amongst themselves to change the rules by which life is measured in order to salvage a larger number of transplantable organs met with something short of universal approval.[16] Especially with increasing disenchantment over heart transplantation (the procedure in which the traditional criteria for determining death posed the most difficulties), some doubt arose whether it was wise to adopt measures which encouraged a medical "advance" that seemed to have gotten ahead of its own basic technology. Furthermore, many people —doctors included—found themselves with nagging if often unarticulated doubts about how to proceed in the situation, far more com-

---

duration, which involved 2639 comatose patients without anesthetic doses of c.n.s. depressants, not one recovered. Silverman, Masland, Saunders & Schwab, *Irreversible Coma Associated with Electrocerebral Silence*, 20 NEUROLOGY 525 (1970). In an unreported study on 128 individuals who fulfilled the Harvard clinical criteria, postmortem examinations showed their brains to be destroyed. Unpublished results of E. Richardson, reported in *Refinements in Criteria*, *supra* note 3, at 50-51.

13 One member of the committee has observed that "since the publication of the report, the clinical recommendations have been accepted and followed on a worldwide basis in a most gratifying fashion." Curran, *Legal and Medical Death—Kansas Takes the First Step*, 284 NEW ENG. J. MED. 260 (1971). Dr. Beecher recently noted that legal doubts have prevented uniform acceptance of the Harvard Committee's views. "Almost every (doctor) on the East Coast has accepted irreversible brain damage as the criterion for death, whereas most West Coast physicians do not for fear of suits." Ross, *Death with Dignity*, The Washington Post, Aug. 9, 1972, at B-15, col. 1 (quoting Dr. Beecher); for a fuller account of the testimony, see *Hearings on Death with Dignity Before the Senate Special Comm. on Aging*, 92d Cong., 2d Sess. (1972).

14 Rutstein, *The Ethical Design of Human Experiments*, 98 DAEDALUS 523, 526 (1969). Leaders of the Netherlands Red Cross Society's Organ Transplantation Committee argue that only "total absence of the brain's functional capacity" and not "irreversible coma" indicates that death has occurred and state the Dutch position that the Harvard criteria "are grounds for stopping treatment and letting the patient die," but not for declaring death. Rot & van Till, *Neocortical Death after Cardiac Arrest*, 2 LANCET 1099-100 (1971) (letter to the editor).

15 *See, e.g.*, Arnold, Zimmerman & Martin, *Public Attitudes and the Diagnosis of Death*, 206 J.A.M.A. 1949 (1968) [hereinafter cited as Arnold]; Biörck, *When is Death?*, 1968 WIS. L. REV. 484, 490-91; N.Y. Times, Sept. 9, 1968, at 23, col. 1 (quoting Drs. F. C. Spencer & J. Hardy); *The Heart: Miracle in Cape Town*, NEWSWEEK, Dec. 18, 1967, at 86-87.

16 [C]ertain actions by transplant surgeons in establishing time of death on death certificates and hospital records have shaken public confidence. Coroners have denounced them in the press for signing a death certificate in one county when the beating heart was removed a day later in a far-off city. The public wonders what the "item" was that was transplanted across the state line and later registered as a person in the operating room record.
Corday, *Life-Death in Human Transplantation*, 55 A.B.A.J. 629, 632 (1969).

mon than transplantation, in which a long-comatose patient shows every prospect of "living" indefinitely with artificial means of support.[17] As a result of this growing public and professional concern, elected officials,[18] with the encouragement of the medical community,[19] have urged public discussion and action to dispel the apprehension created by the new medical knowledge and to clarify and reformulate the law. Some commentators, however, have argued that public bodies and laymen in general have no role to play in this process of change.[20] Issue is therefore joined on at least two points: (1) ought the public to be involved in "defining" death? and (2) if so, how ought it to be involved—specifically, ought governmental action, in the form of legislation, be taken?[21]

II. PUBLIC INVOLVEMENT OR PROFESSIONAL PREROGATIVE?

In considering the possible need for and the desirability of public involvement, the central question appears to be to what extent, if at all, the "defining" of death is a medical matter, properly left to physicians because it lies within their particular sphere of competence. The belief that the matter of "defining death" is wholly medical is frequently expressed, and not only by physicians.[22] Indeed, when a

---

17 [M]any people are now maintained in a sort of twilight state by the use of machines which do the work of their lungs or their heart while they are completely unconscious . . . . Many of these people will never resume an independent existence away from the machines . . . . One has to decide therefore when to switch off the machines, and this question arises quite independently of considerations about transplants.
Discussion of Murray, *Organ Transplantation: The Practical Possibilities*, in MEDICAL PROGRESS, *supra* note 1, at 71 (comments of Dr. M. F. A. Woodruff).

18 *See, e.g.*, Mondale, *Health Science and Society*, 117 CONG. REC. S3708 (daily ed. Mar. 24, 1971); H. Res. 2830, 2d Fla. Legis. (n.s.) (1971) (resolution introduced by Rep. Sackett, M.D., to create a commission to study death).

19 *See, e.g.*, Taylor, *supra* note 5, at 296; Arnold, *supra* note 15, at 1954; Corday, *Definition of Death: A Double Standard*, HOSPITAL TRIBUNE, May 4, 1970, at 8; Halley & Harvey, *On an Interdisciplinary Solution to the Legal-Medical Definitional Dilemma in Death*, 2 INDIANA LEGAL F. 219, 227 (1969).

20 *See, e.g.*, Kennedy, *The Kansas Statute on Death: An Appraisal*, 285 NEW ENG. J. MED. 946 (1971); *What and When is Death?*, 204 J.A.M.A. 539, 540 (1968) (editorial).

21 To some extent this formulation of the problem is, of course, unrealistic, since "public action" (*i.e.*, action by an official public body), in the form of a court decision, can come about at the instance of a private litigant regardless of any policy reasons in favor of public inaction. Although it may therefore be impossible to avoid creating "law" on the subject, there might still be no significant public involvement if the courts restricted themselves merely to endorsing conclusions reached by private groups, such as those representing physicians. Kennedy's support for judicial involvement in "defining" death seems to operate on that premise. *See* Kennedy, *supra* note 20, at 947. *See also* note 36 *infra* & accompanying text.

22 *See, e.g.*, Kennedy, *supra* note 20, at 947; Berman, *The Legal Problems of Organ Transplantation*, 13 VILL. L. REV. 751, 754 (1968); Sanders & Dukeminier, *Medical Advance and Legal Lag: Hemodialysis and Kidney Transplantation*, 15 U.C.L.A.L. REV. 357, 409 (1968) [hereinafter cited as Sanders]; NATIONAL CONFERENCE OF COMMISSIONERS ON UNIFORM STATE LAWS, HANDBOOK AND PROCEEDINGS OF THE ANNUAL CON-

question concerning the moment at which a person died has arisen in litigation, common law courts have generally regarded this as "a question of fact" for determination at trial on the basis (partially but not exclusively) of expert medical testimony.[23] Yet the standards which are applied in arriving at a conclusion, although based on medical knowledge, are established by the courts "as a matter of law."[24]

Thus while it is true that the application of particular criteria or tests to determine the death of an individual may call for the expertise of a physician, there are other aspects of formulating a "definition" of death that are not particularly within medical competence. To be sure, in practice, so long as the standards being employed are stable and congruent with community opinion about the phenomenon of death,

---

FERENCE 192 (1968); cf. Sadler, Sadler & Stason, *The Uniform Anatomical Gift Act: A Model for Reform*, 206 J.A.M.A. 2501 (1968). The ad hoc Harvard Committee, composed largely of physicians, came to the same conclusion. *See Irreversible Coma, supra* note 3, at 339.

23 *See* Thomas v. Anderson, 96 Cal. App. 2d 371, 215 P.2d 478 (1950). In that appeal, the court was called upon to decide whether the trial judge had erred in holding inapplicable to the case a provision of the California Probate Code based on the Uniform Simultaneous Death Act which provided for the equal distribution of the property of two joint tenants "[w]here there is no sufficient evidence that [they] have died otherwise than simultaneously . . . ." The court cited the definition in *Black's Law Dictionary* that "death is the cessation of life; the ceasing to exist; defined by physicians as a total stoppage of the circulation of the blood, and a cessation of the animal and vital functions consequent thereon, such as respiration, pulsation, etc.," and went on to observe that "death occurs precisely when life ceases and does not occur until the heart stops beating and respiration ends. Death is not a continuing event and is an event that takes place at a precise time." *Id.* at 375, 215 P.2d at 482. It concluded that the "question of fact" as to which of the two deceased men died first had been correctly determined by the trial court in light of "sufficient evidence" given by nonmedical witnesses concerning the appearance of the men on the evening in question.

24 Smith v. Smith, 229 Ark. 579, 587, 317 S.W.2d 275, 279 (1958) (quoting 41 AM. JUR. *Husbands and Wives* § 244 (1938)). The Smiths, a childless couple who by will had each left his or her estate to the other, were involved in an automobile accident. Mr. Smith apparently died immediately, but when assistance arrived Mrs. Smith was unconscious, and she remained so in the hospital for seventeen days. Thereafter, Mr. Smith's administrator petitioned for the construction of the wills, alleging:

> That as a matter of modern medical science, your petitioner . . . will offer the Court competent proof that the [Smiths] lost their power to will at the same instant, and that their demise as earthly human beings occurred at the same time in said automobile accident, neither of them ever regaining any consciousness whatsoever.

Id. at 582, 317 S.W.2d at 277. The Supreme Court of Arkansas upheld the trial court's dismissal of the petition as a matter of law on the ground that "it would be too much of a strain on credulity for us to believe any evidence offered to the effect that Mrs. Smith was dead, scientifically or otherwise, unless the conditions set out in the [*Black's Law Dictionary* (4th ed.)] definition existed." *Id.* at 586-87, 317 S.W.2d at 279. The court took "judicial notice that one breathing, though unconscious, is not dead," *id.* at 589, 317 S.W.2d at 281, and concluded that Mrs. Smith's death was therefore not simultaneous with her husband's.

Cf. In re Estate of Schmidt, 261 Cal. App. 2d 262, 67 Cal. Rptr. 847 (1968). *Schmidt*, like *Thomas* and *Smith*, involved an inheritorship issue under the Uniform Simultaneous Death Act. The court of appeals found that there was sufficient eyewitness testimony by laymen to support the trial court's conclusion that Mrs. Schmidt survived her husband by some minutes, and it found no fault in the use of the *Black's Law Dictionary* "definition of death" despite the argument that it "is an anachronism in view of the recent medical developments relating to heart transplants," since there was no evidence that the deceased were resuscitable. *Id.* at 273, 67 Cal. Rptr. at 854 (dictum).

most people are content to leave the matter in medical hands.[25] But the underlying extra-medical aspects of the "definition" become visible, as they have recently, when medicine departs (or appears to depart) from the common or traditional understanding of the concept of death. The formulation of a concept of death is neither simply a technical matter nor one susceptible of empirical verification. The idea of death is at least partly a philosophical question, related to such ideas as "organism," "human," and "living." Physicians *qua* physicians are not expert on these philosophical questions, nor are they expert on the question of which physiological functions decisively identify a "living, human organism." They, like other scientists, can suggest which "vital signs" have what significance for which human functions. They may, for example, show that a person in an irreversible coma exhibits "total unawareness to externally applied stimuli and inner need and complete unresponsiveness,"[26] and they may predict that when tests for this condition yield the same results over a twenty-four hour period there is only a very minute chance that the coma will ever be "reversed."[27] Yet the judgment that "total unawareness . . . and complete unresponsiveness" are the salient characteristics of death, or that a certain level of risk of error is acceptable, requires more than technical expertise and goes beyond medical authority, properly understood.

The proposed departure from the traditional standards for determining death not only calls attention to the extra-medical issues involved, but is itself a source of public confusion and concern. The confusion can perhaps be traced to the fact that the traditional signs of life (the beating heart and the expanding chest) are manifestly accessible to the senses of the layman, whereas some of the new criteria require sophisticated intervention to elicit latent signs of life such as brain reflexes. Furthermore, the new criteria may disturb the layman by suggesting that these visible and palpable traditional signs, still useful in most cases, may be deceiving him in cases where supportive machinery is being used. The anxiety may also be attributable to the apparent intention behind the "new definition," which is, at least in part, to facilitate other developments such as the transplantation of cadaver organs. Such confusion and anxiety about the standards for determining death can have far-reaching and distressing consequences for the patient's family, for the physician, for other patients, and for

---

[25] *See* Arnold, *supra* note 15, at 1950, in which the public's "nearly complete acceptance" of professional practice in this century until cardiac transplantation began is contrasted with the great concern manifested in the 19th century and earlier, before embalming became routine, largely because of the fear of premature burial.

[26] *Irreversible Coma, supra* note 3, at 337.

[27] *See* note 12 *supra*.

the community at large.[28] If the uncertainties surrounding the question of determining death are to be laid to rest, a clear and acceptable standard is needed. And if the formulation and adoption of this standard are not to be abdicated to the medical fraternity under an expanded view of its competence and authority, then the public and its representatives ought to be involved.[29] Even if the medical profession takes the lead—as indeed it has—in promoting new criteria of death, members of the public should at least have the opportunity to review, and either to affirm or reject the standards by which they are to be pronounced dead.

III. WHAT MANNER OF PUBLIC INVOLVEMENT?

There are a number of potential means for involving the public in this process of formulation and review, none of them perfect. The least ambitious or comprehensive is simply to encourage discussion of the issues by the lay press, civic groups, and the community at large. This public consideration might be directed or supported through the efforts of national organizations such as the American Medical Association, the National Institutes of Health, or the National Academy of Sciences.[30] A resolution calling for the establishment of an ad hoc body to evaluate public attitudes toward the changes wrought by biomedical advances has been sponsored by Senator Mondale since 1967 and was adopted by the Senate in December 1971.[31] Mondale's proposed National Advisory Commission on Health Science and Society,

---

[28] See Sanders, supra note 22, at 407-09; 3 M. HOUTS & I.H. HAUT, COURTROOM MEDICINE §§ 1.02(3)(a)-(g) (1971). As long as the legal standard is ambiguous, the possibility exists that the processes of criminal, as well as civil, justice will be impeded. See, e.g., D. MEYERS, THE HUMAN BODY AND THE LAW 116-18 (1970) (discussing an unreported British case, Regina v. Potter, in which a manslaughter defendant was convicted of common assault upon proof that surgeons had removed a kidney from the decedent while he was being maintained on a respirator and before he had been found to be "dead"); Trial to Test M.D.'s Role in Death of Heart Donor, A.M.A. News, Nov. 11, 1968, at 2 (man charged with manslaughter raised as defense surgeons' removal of victim's heart when he was kept alive by artificial means).

[29] Matte, Law, Morals, and Medicine: A Method of Approach to Current Problems, 13 J. FOR. SCI. 318, 331-32 (1968). See also note 19 supra.

A theoretical risk of illegal conduct exists in the present state of the law. The law is apparently waiting for a social and theological consensus on this point [of "defining" death] . . . . The theologians, the philosophers and the physicians will have to formulate the judgment of propriety here before it is crystallized into a definite statutory rule.

Discussion of Louisell, Transplantation: Existing Legal Constraints, in MEDICAL PROGRESS, supra note 1, at 99 (comments of Prof. D. W. Louisell).

[30] For example, early in the debate over heart replacement the Board on Medicine of the National Academy issued a "Statement on Cardiac Transplantation," but addressed itself primarily to the need for caution in the spread of the operation to medical centers which were not suited to carrying it out scientifically. 18 NEWS REPORT OF THE NATIONAL ACADEMY OF SCIENCES 1 (Mar. 1968).

[31] S.J. Res. 75, 92d Cong., 1st Sess. (1971), in 117 CONG. REC. S20,089-93 (daily ed. Dec. 2, 1971). See also note 18 supra. The joint resolution is now in the House Committee on Interstate Commerce.

under the direction of a board of fifteen members of the general public and professionals from "medicine, law, theology, biological science, physical science, social science, philosophy, humanities, health administration, government, and public affairs," would conduct "seminars and public hearings" as part of its two-year study.[32] As important as it is to ventilate the issues, studies and public discussions alone may not be adequate to the task. They cannot by themselves dispel the ambiguities which will continue to trouble decisionmakers and the public in determining whether an artificially-maintained, comatose "patient" is still alive.

A second alternative, reliance upon the judicial system, goes beyond ascertaining popular attitudes and could provide an authoritative opinion that might offer some guidance for decisionmakers. Reliance on judge-made law would, however, neither actively involve the public in the decisionmaking process nor lead to a prompt, clear, and general "definition." The courts, of course, cannot speak in the abstract prospectively, but must await litigation, which can involve considerable delay and expense, to the detriment of both the parties and society. A need to rely on the courts reflects an uncertainty in the law which is unfortunate in an area where private decisionmakers (physicians) must act quickly and irrevocably. An ambiguous legal standard endangers the rights—and in some cases the lives—of the participants. In such circumstances, a person's choice of one course over another may depend more on his willingness to test his views in court than on the relative merits of the courses of action.[33]

Once called upon to "redefine" death—for example, in a suit brought by a patient's relatives or, perhaps, by a revived "corpse" against the physician declaring death—the judiciary may be as well qualified to perform the task as any governmental body. If the issue could be resolved solely by a process of reasoning and of taking "judicial notice" of widely known and uncontroverted facts, a court could handle it without difficulty. If, on the other hand, technical expertise is required problems may arise. Courts operate within a limited compass —the facts and contentions of a particular case—and with limited expertise; they have neither the staff nor the authority to investigate

---

[32] S.J. Res. 75, 92d Cong., 1st Sess. (1971), in 117 CONG. REC. S20,090 (daily ed. Dec. 2, 1971).

[33] For example, suppose that transplant surgeons were willing to employ a neurological definition of death, although most other physicians continued to use the "traditional" definition because of the unsettled nature of the law. If (*ex hypothesis*) those surgeons were less averse to the risks of testing their position in litigation, because of their temperament, training, values and commitments, or desire for success, their "courage" could lead to patients being declared dead prematurely according to the traditional standard.

or to conduct hearings in order to explore such issues as public opinion or the scientific merits of competing "definitions."[34] Consequently, a judge's decision may be merely a rubberstamping of the opinions expressed by the medical experts who appear before him.[35] Indeed, those who believe that the "definition of death" should be left in the hands of physicians favor the judicial route over the legislative on the assumption that, in the event of a law suit, the courts will approve "the consensus view of the medical profession"[36] in favor of the new standards. Leaving the task of articulating a new set of standards to the courts may prove unsatisfactory, however, if one believes, as suggested previously, that the formulation of such standards, as opposed to their application in particular cases, goes beyond the authority of the medical profession.[37]

Uncertainties in the law are, to be sure, inevitable at times and are often tolerated if they do not involve matters of general applicability or great moment. Yet the question of whether and when a person is dead plainly seems the sort of issue that cannot escape the need for legal clarity on these grounds. Therefore, it is not surprising that although they would be pleased simply to have the courts endorse their views, members of the medical profession are doubtful that the judicial mode of lawmaking offers them adequate protection in this area.[38] There is currently no way to be certain that a doctor would not be liable, criminally or civilly, if he ceased treatment of a person found to be dead according to the Harvard Committee's criteria but not according to the "complete cessation of all vital functions" test presently employed by the courts. Although such "definitions" were adopted in cases involving inheritors' rights and survivorship[39] rather than a doctor's liability for exercising his judgment about when a person has died, physicians have with good reason felt that this affords

[34] See, e.g., Repouille v. United States, 165 F.2d 152, 153 (2d Cir. 1947) (L. Hand, J.), 154 (Frank, J., dissenting).

[35] Because of the adversary nature of the judicial process, testimony is usually restricted to the "two sides" of an issue and may not fairly represent the spectrum of opinion held by authorities in the field.

[36] Kennedy, supra note 20, at 947. Kennedy's reliance on a medical "consensus" has a number of weaknesses, which he himself seems to acknowledge: (1) there may be "a wide range of opinions" held by doctors, so that "there need not necessarily be only one view" on a subject which is supported by the medical community, in part because (2) the "usual ways" for these matters to be "discussed and debated" are not very clear or rigorous since (3) the "American medical profession is not all that well regulated" unlike its British counterpart and (4) is not organized to give "official approval" to a single position or (5) to give force to its decision, meaning (6) that "the task will be assumed by some other body, most probably the legislature." Id.

[37] Cf. Blocker v. United States, 288 F.2d 853, 860 (D.C. Cir. 1961) (en banc) (Burger, J., concurring in the result) (criticizing psychiatrists' attempt to alter legal definition of "mental disease").

[38] See note 19 supra.

[39] See notes 23-24 supra; cf. Gray v. Sawyer, 247 S.W.2d 496 (Ky. 1952).

them little assurance that the courts would not rely upon those cases as precedent.[40] On the contrary, it is reasonable to expect that the courts would seek precedent in these circumstances. Adherence to past decisions is valued because it increases the likelihood that an individual will be treated fairly and impartially; it also removes the need to relitigate every issue in every case. Most importantly, courts are not inclined to depart from existing rules because to do so may upset the societal assumption that one may take actions, and rely upon the actions of others, without fear that the ground rules will be changed retroactively.[41]

Considerations of precedent as well as other problems with relying on the judicial formulation of a new definition were made apparent in *Tucker v. Lower*,[42] the first case to present the question of the "definition of death" in the context of organ transplantation. Above all, this case demonstrates the uncertainty that is inherent in the process of litigation, which "was touch and go for the medical profession"[43] as well as the defendants. *Tucker* involved a $100,000 damage action against Drs. David Hume and Richard Lower and other defendant doctors on the Medical College of Virginia transplant team, brought by William E. Tucker, whose brother's heart was removed on May 25, 1968, in the world's seventeenth human heart transplant. The plaintiff claimed that the heart was taken without approval of the next of kin and that the operation was commenced before his brother had died. On the latter point, William Tucker offered evidence that his brother was admitted to the hospital with severe head injuries sustained in a fall and that after a neurological operation he was placed on a respirator. At the time he was taken to the operating room to have his organs removed "he maintained vital signs of life, that is, . . . normal body temperature, normal pulse, normal blood

---

[40] *See* Taylor, *supra* note 5, at 296. *But cf.* Kennedy, *supra* note 20, at 947.

[41] "[R]ules of law on which men rely in their business dealings should not be changed in the middle of the game . . ." Woods v. Lancet, 303 N.Y. 349, 354, 102 N.E.2d 691, 695 (1951). It must be admitted, however, that such principles usually find their most forceful articulation when the court is about to proceed on the counter-principle that when necessary the common law will change with the times to achieve justice. (In *Woods*, for example, the New York Court of Appeals overruled its prior decision in Drobner v. Peters, 232 N.Y. 220, 133 N.E. 567 (1921), in order to permit a child to sue for prenatal injuries.) Although in this country, at least, strict adherence to precedent has been less true on the civil side than on the criminal (where the courts hold closer to the doctrine of *nullum crimen sine lege* than do English courts), it is probably fair to state that judges are more likely to depart from precedent in order to *create* a new cause of action than they are to reject an existing standard and thereby destroy a cause; to adjust the "definition of death" to the perhaps changing views of the medical profession would be to derogate the rights of those litigants injured by declarations of death which departed from previously accepted standards.

[42] Tucker v. Lower, No. 2831 (Richmond, Va., L. & Eq. Ct., May 23, 1972).

[43] 15 DRUG RESEARCH REP., June 7, 1972, at 1.

pressure and normal rate of respiration."[44] Based on the neurologist's finding that the brother was dead from a neurological standpoint, the respirator was turned off and he was pronounced dead. The defendants moved to strike the plaintiff's evidence and for summary judgment in their favor, but the trial judge denied the motions.

> The function of This Court is to determine the state of the law on this or any other subject according to legal precedent and principle. The courts which have had occasion to rule upon the nature of death and its timing have all decided that death occurs at a precise time, and that it is defined as the cessation of life; the ceasing to exist; a total stoppage of the circulation of the blood, and a cessation of the animal and vital functions consequent thereto such as respiration and pulsation.[45]

The court adhered to "the legal concept of death" and rejected "the invitation offered by the defendants to employ a medical concept of neurological death in establishing a rule of law."[46] The court ruled that the jury would be allowed to assess damages if it concluded "that the decedent's life was terminated at a time earlier than it would ordinarily have ended had all reasonable medical efforts been continued to prolong his life."[47]

When he sent the case to the jurors, however, the judge permitted them to consider all possible causes of death, including injury to the brain as well as cessation of breathing or heartbeat, and a verdict was returned for the defendants. Unfortunately, the discrepancy between the initial ruling and the subsequent instructions to the jury did little to resolve the legal uncertainty. The plaintiff has announced that he plans to appeal to the Supreme Court of Virginia,[48] and the creation of a clear and binding rule will depend on the action of that court.[49]

In declining the defendants' suggestion that he adopt a standard

---

[44] Tucker v. Lower, No. 2831, at 4 (Richmond, Va., L. & Eq. Ct., May 23, 1972).

[45] *Id.* at 8 (citations omitted).

[46] *Id.*

While it is recognized that none of the cases cited above involved transplants, to employ a different standard in this field would create chaos in other fields of the law and certainly it cannot be successfully argued that there should be one concept of death which applies to one type of litigation while an entirely different standard applies in other areas.

Id. at 8-9.

[47] *Id.* at 11.

[48] N.Y. Times, May 27, 1972, at 15, col. 5; *id.*, June 4, 1972, § 4, at 7, col. 1.

[49] As one medical journal, which favors legislative formulation of a "definition," said of the decision of the Richmond court: "It applies only to cases coming before that court and can be reversed on appeal or overriden by contrary decisions handed down in higher courts." 15 DRUG RESEARCH REP., June 7, 1972, at 1.

based on neurological signs, the judge stated that application for "such a radical change" in the law should be made "not to the courts but to the legislature wherein the basic concepts of our society relating to the preservation and extension of life could be examined and, if necessary, reevaluated."[50] A statutory "definition" of death would have notable advantages as an alternative to a judicial promulgation. Basically, the legislative process permits the public to play a more active role in decisionmaking and allows a wider range of information to enter into the framing of criteria for determining death. Moreover, by providing prospective guidance, statutory standards could dispel public and professional doubt, and could provide needed reassurance for physicians and patients' families, thereby reducing both the fear and the likelihood of litigation for malpractice (or even for homicide).

The legislative alternative also has a number of drawbacks, however. Foremost among these is the danger that a statute "defining" death may be badly drafted. It may be either too general or too specific, or it may be so poorly worded that it will leave physicians or laymen unsure of its intent. There is also the danger that the statutory language might seem to preclude future refinements that expanding medical knowledge would introduce into the tests and procedures for determining death. The problem of bad draftsmanship is compounded by the fact that a statute once enacted may be difficult to revise or repeal, leaving to the slow and uncertain process of litigation the clarification of its intent and meaning.[51] By contrast, although judges usually espouse the doctrine of stare decisis, flexibility over time is a hallmark of the common law. An additional practical problem is the possibility that the statutes enacted may reflect primarily the interests of powerful lobbying groups—for example, state medical societies or transplant surgeons. This possibility—similar to the danger of judicial "rubberstamping" of medical experts' opinions—may be avoided by legislatures' holding open and well-publicized hearings at which sociologists, lawyers, theologians, and representatives of various viewpoints are also called upon to testify.

Professor Ian Kennedy has suggested the further danger that a statutory "definition," rather than protecting the public may leave it vulnerable to physicians who through "liberal interpretation and clever argument" might take actions "just within the letter if not the spirit of the law."[52] Kennedy would rely instead on the medical profession's

---

[50] Tucker v. Lower, No. 2831, at 10 (Richmond, Va., L. & Eq. Ct., May 23, 1972).

[51] The general durability of statutes has the backhanded advantage, however, of emphasizing for the public as well as for legislators the importance of a thorough thrashing out of the issues in hearings and legislative debates.

[52] Kennedy, *supra* note 20, at 947.

generalized "consensus view"[53] of the proper "definition of death." It is, however, far from clear why physicians who would violate a statute are unlikely to depart from such an informal "consensus," which may or may not eventually be sanctioned by the courts. Legislation will not remove the need for reasoned interpretation—first by physicians and perhaps then by judges—but it can restrict the compass within which they make their choices to one which has been found acceptable by the public.

Finally, the legislative route may reduce the likelihood that conflicting "definitions" of death will be employed in different jurisdictions in this country. Theoretically, uniformity is also possible in judicial opinions, but it occurs infrequently. If the formulation and reception of the Uniform Anatomical Gift Act provide any precedent, the Commissioners on Uniform State Laws appear to be well situated to provide leadership in achieving an intelligent response to changes in medical procedure.[54]

In sum, then, official action, as opposed to mere discussion of the issues, is needed if the conflict between current medical practice and present law is to be eliminated. A reformulation of the standards for determining death should thus be undertaken by either courts or legislatures. There are strengths and weaknesses in both law-creating mechanisms, but on balance we believe that if legislators approach the issues with a critical and inquiring attitude, a statutory "definition" of death may be the best way to resolve the conflicting needs for definiteness and flexibility, for public involvement and scientific accuracy.[55] Moreover, since pressures for a legislative response to the problem appear to be mounting,[56] careful examination of the proper scope and content of such a statute seems to be called for.

---

[53] *Id.*

[54] Completed in July 1968 by the Commissioners on Uniform State Laws and approved by the American Bar Association in August of that year, the Uniform Anatomical Gift Act was adopted with only minor changes in 40 jurisdictions including the District of Columbia in 1969; by the end of 1971, the Act had been adopted in the remaining 11 states. For a detailed discussion of the national acceptance of the Act see Sadler, Sadler & Stason, *Transplantation and the Law: Progress Toward Uniformity*, 282 NEW ENG. J. MED. 717 (1970). *See also* Brickman, *Medico-Legal Problems with the Question of Death*, 5 CALIF. W.L. REV. 110, 122 (1968) (urging Commissioners to draft uniform act on "the procedures for determining death").

[55] This is, of course, not to say that a judge faced with a case to decide should hold back from engaging in the sort of analysis, or reaching the conclusions about a proper "definition," presented here. As Professor Clarence Morris once observed, the age-old argument that a legislature has a "superior opportunity" to frame general rules should not foreclose judicial reform of the law where the legislature has failed to act. A judge has, after all, "no reliable way of knowing" that legislative action will ever be forthcoming, and if he acts in a way the legislature finds erroneous, his mistake can be set right by statute. Morris, *Liability for Pain and Suffering*, 59 COLUM. L. REV. 476, 482 (1959).

[56] *See* note 8 *supra.* It would certainly be preferable for state legislatures and the Uniform Act Commissioners to begin work on laws now, rather than risking the enactment

IV. What Can and Should Be Legislated?

Arguments both for and against the desirability of legislation "defining" death often fail to distinguish among the several different subjects that might be touched on by such legislation. As a result, a mistaken impression may exist that a single statutory model is, and must be, the object of debate. An appreciation of the multiple meanings of a "definition of death" may help to refine the deliberations.

Death, in the sense the term is of interest here, can be defined purely formally as the transition, however abrupt or gradual, between the state of being alive and the state of being dead.[57] There are at least four levels of "definitions" that would give substance to this formal notion; in principle, each could be the subject of legislation: (1) the basic concept or idea; (2) general physiological standards; (3) operational criteria; and (4) specific tests or procedures.[58]

The *basic concept* of death is fundamentally a philosophical matter. Examples of possible "definitions" of death at this level include "permanent cessation of the integrated functioning of the organism as a whole," "departure of the animating or vital principle," or "irreversible loss of personhood." These abstract definitions offer little concrete help in the practical task of determining whether a person has died but they may very well influence how one goes about devising standards and criteria.

In setting forth the *general physiological standard(s)* for recognizing death, the definition moves to a level which is more medico-technical, but not wholly so. Philosophical issues persist in the choice to define death in terms of organ systems, physiological functions, or recognizable human activities, capacities, and conditions. Examples of possible general standards include "irreversible cessation of spontaneous respiratory and/or circulatory functions," "irreversible loss of

---

of "emergency legislation hastily contrived in response to public pressure and emotional reaction to [a] particular medical calamity." Matte, *supra* note 29, at 332; *cf.* Woodside, *Organ Transplantation: The Doctor's Dilemma and the Lawyer's Responsibility*, 31 Ohio St. L.J. 66, 96 (1970).

[57] For a debate on the underlying issues see Morison, *Death: Process or Event?*, 173 Science 694 (1970); Kass, *Death as an Event: A Commentary on Robert Morison*, 173 Science 698 (1971).

[58] To our knowledge, this delineation of four levels has not been made elsewhere in the existing literature on this subject. Therefore, the terms "concept," "standard," "criteria," and "tests and procedures" as used here bear no necessary connection to the ways in which others may use these same terms, and in fact we recognize that in some areas of discourse, the term "standards" is more, rather than less, operational and concrete than "criteria"—just the reverse of our ordering. Our terminology was selected so that the category we call "criteria" would correspond to the level of specificity at which the Ad Hoc Harvard Committee framed its proposals, which it called and which are widely referred to as the "new *criteria*" for determining death. We have attempted to be consistent in our use of these terms throughout this Article. Nevertheless, our major purpose here is not to achieve public acceptance of our terms, but to promote awareness of the four different levels of a "definition" of death to which the terms refer.

spontaneous brain functions," "irreversible loss of the ability to respond or communicate," or some combination of these.

Operational criteria further define what is meant by the general
physiological standards. The absence of cardiac contraction and lack
of movement of the blood are examples of traditional criteria for
"cessation of spontaneous circulatory functions," whereas deep coma,
the absence of reflexes, and the lack of spontaneous muscular movements and spontaneous respiration are among criteria proposed for
"cessation of spontaneous brain functions" by the Harvard Committee.[59]

Fourth, there are the *specific tests and procedures* to see if the
criteria are fulfilled. Pulse, heart beat, blood pressure, electrocardiogram, and examination of blood flow in the retinal vessels are among
the specific tests of cardiac contraction and movement of the blood.
Reaction to painful stimuli, appearance of the pupils and their responsiveness to light, and observation of movement and breathing
over a specified time period are among specific tests of the "brain
function" criteria enumerated above.

There appears to be general agreement that legislation should not
seek to "define death" at either the most general or the most specific
levels (the first and fourth). In the case of the former, differences of
opinion would seem hard to resolve, and agreement, if it were possible, would provide little guidance for practice.[60] In the case of the
latter, the specific tests and procedures must be kept open to changes
in medical knowledge and technology. Thus, arguments concerning
the advisability and desirability of a statutory definition of death are
usually confined to the two levels we have called "standards" and
"criteria," yet often without any apparent awareness of the distinction
between them. The need for flexibility in the face of medical advance
would appear to be a persuasive argument for not legislating any specific operational criteria. Moreover, these are almost exclusively technical matters, best left to the judgment of physicians. Thus, the kind
of "definition" suitable for legislation would be a definition of the
general physiological standard or standards. Such a definition, while
not immutable, could be expected to be useful for a long period of time
and would therefore not require frequent amendment.

There are other matters that could be comprehended in legislation
"defining" death. The statute could specify who (and how many) shall
make the determination. In the absence of a compelling reason to

---

[59] *See* notes 3, 10 *supra*.

[60] *Cf.* Robertson, *Criteria of Death*, 175 Science 581 (1972) (letter to the editor).

change past practices, this may continue to be set at "a physician,"[61] usually the doctor attending a dying patient or the one who happens to be at the scene of an accident. Moreover, the law ought probably to specify the "time of death." The statute may seek to fix the precise time when death may be said to have occurred, or it may merely seek to define a time that is clearly after "the precise moment," that is, a time when it is possible to say "the patient is dead," rather than "the patient has just now died." If the medical procedures used in determining that death has occurred call for verification of the findings after a fixed period of time (for example, the Harvard Committee's recommendation that the tests be repeated after twenty-four hours), the statute could in principle assign the "moment of death" to either the time when the criteria were first met or the time of verification. The former has been the practice with the traditional criteria for determining death.[62]

Finally, legislation could speak to what follows upon the determination. The statute could be permissive or prescriptive in determining various possible subsequent events, including especially the pronouncement and recording of the death, and the use of the body for burial or other purposes.[63] It is our view that these matters are best handled outside of a statute which has as its purpose to "define death."[64]

V. PRINCIPLES GOVERNING THE FORMULATION OF A STATUTE

In addition to carefully selecting the proper degree of specificity for legislation, there are a number of other principles we believe should guide the drafting of a statute "defining" death. First, the phenomenon of interest to physicians, legislators, and laymen alike is human death. Therefore, the statute should concern the death of a human being,

---

[61] *Cf.* UNIFORM ANATOMICAL GIFT ACT § 7(b).

[62] *See* note 99 *infra* & accompanying text.

[63] If . . . sound procedures for stating death are agreed to and carried out, then theologians and moralists and every other thoughtful person should agree with the physicians who hold that it is *then* permissible to maintain circulation of blood and supply of oxygen in the corpse of a donor to preserve an *organ* until it can be used in transplantation. Whether one gives the body over for decent burial, performs an autopsy, gives the cadaver for use in medical education, or uses it as a "vital organ bank" are all alike procedures governed by decent respect for the bodies of deceased men and specific regulations that ensure this. The ventilation and circulation of organs for transplant raises no question not already raised by these standard procedures. None are life-and-death matters. P. RAMSEY, THE PATIENT AS PERSON 72 (1970).

[64] Nevertheless, a statutory "definition" of death would most appropriately be codified with the provisions on the procedures to be followed to certify death, undertake post-mortem examinations, and so forth. For the reasons given below, the statute "defining" death ought not to be appended to the Uniform Anatomical Gift Act or other "special purpose" laws, however. *See* notes 65, 79-80 *infra* & accompanying text.

not the death of his cells, tissues or organs, and not the "death" or cessation of his role as a fully functioning member of his family or community. This point merits considerable emphasis. There may be a proper place for a statutory standard for deciding when to turn off a respirator which is ventilating a patient still clearly alive, or, for that matter, to cease giving any other form of therapy.[65] But it is crucial to distinguish this question of "when to allow to die?" from the question with which we are here concerned, namely, "when to declare dead?" Since very different issues and purposes are involved in these questions, confusing the one with the other clouds the analysis of both. The problem of determining when a person is dead is difficult enough without its being tied to the problem of whether physicians, or anyone else, may hasten the death of a terminally-ill patient, with or without his consent or that of his relatives, in order to minimize his suffering or to conserve scarce medical resources.[66] Although the same set of social and medical conditions may give rise to both problems, they must be kept separate if they are to be clearly understood.

Distinguishing the question "is he dead?" from the question "should he be allowed to die?" also assists in preserving continuity with tradition, a second important principle. By restricting itself to

---

[65] *See* Potter, *The Paradoxical Preservation of a Principle*, 13 VILL. L. REV. 784, 791 (1968):

What type of questions are entailed in the debate concerning when a comatose patient should be declared dead? Medical questions and answers are only one element of the decisionmaking process. Medical skill may be used to establish that a patient has now entered and is likely to remain in a certain condition. But medical personnel along with the other members of the community must then ask: "What are we to do with patients in this condition?" The answer to that question does not flow directly from any medical knowledge. It is a question of social policy which must be decided by the entire community. Implementation of the communal policy may be left in the hands of physicians, but they act as agents of the communal conscience.

See generally Note, *Death with Dignity: A Recommendation for Statutory Change*, 22 U. FLA. L. REV. 368 (1970); Fletcher, *Legal Aspects of the Decision Not to Prolong Life*, 203 J.A.M.A. 65 (1968); Sharpe & Hargest, *Lifesaving Treatment for Unwilling Patients*, 36 FORDHAM L. REV. 695 (1968); Note, *The Dying Patient: A Qualified Right to Refuse Medical Treatment*, 7 J. FAM. L. 644 (1967); Elkinton, *The Dying Patient, The Doctor and the Law*, 13 VILL. L. REV. 740 (1968); Biörck, *supra* note 15, at 488-90.

[66] The ease with which the two questions can become confused is demonstrated by the following "general definition of human death" proposed in Halley & Harvey, *Medical vs. Legal Definitions of Death*, 204 J.A.M.A. 423, 425 (1968):

Death is irreversible cessation of *all* of the following: (1) total cerebral function, (2) spontaneous function of the respiratory system, and (3) spontaneous function of the circulatory system.

Special circumstances may, however, justify the pronouncement of death when consultation consistent with established professional standards have been obtained and when valid consent to withhold or stop resuscitative measures has been given by the appropriate relative or legal guardian.

The authors seem to have realized the mistake in making the state of being dead (rather than the acceptance of imminent death) depend on the "consent" of a relative or guardian, and this aspect of the "definition of death" is absent from their subsequent writings. *See, e.g.*, Halley & Harvey, *Law-Medicine Comment: The Definitional Dilemma of Death*, 37 J. KAN. B. ASS'N 179, 185 (1968); *cf.* D. MEYERS, *supra* note 28, at 135-36 (criticizing Halley and Harvey's second definition for its internal inconsistency).

the "is he dead?" issue, a revised "definition" permits practices to move incrementally, not by replacing traditional cardiopulmonary standards for the determination of death but rather by supplementing them. These standards are, after all, still adequate in the majority of cases, and are the ones that both physicians and the public are in the habit of employing and relying on. The supplementary standards are needed primarily for those cases in which artificial means of support of comatose patients render the traditional standards unreliable.

Third, this incremental approach is useful for the additional and perhaps most central reason that any new means for judging death should be seen as just that and nothing more—a change in method dictated by advances in medical practice, but not an alteration of the meaning of "life" and "death." By indicating that the various standards for measuring death relate to a single phenomenon legislation can serve to reduce a primary source of public uneasiness on this subject.[67] Once it has been established that certain consequences —for example, burial, autopsy, transfer of property to the heirs, and so forth—follow from a determination of death, definite problems would arise if there were a number of "definitions" according to which some people could be said to be "more dead" than others.

There are, of course, many instances in which the law has established differing definitions of a term, each framed to serve a particular purpose. One wonders, however, whether it does not appear somewhat foolish for the law to offer a number of arbitrary definitions of a natural phenomenon such as death. Nevertheless, legislators might seek to identify a series of points during the process of dying, each of which might be labelled "death" for certain purposes. Yet so far as we know, no arguments have been presented for special purpose standards except in the area of organ transplantation. Such a separate "definition of death," aimed at increasing the supply of viable organs, would permit physicians to declare a patient dead before his condition met the generally applicable standards for determining death if his organs are of potential use in transplantation. The adoption of a special standard risks abuse and confusion, however. The status of prospective organ donor is an arbitrary one to which a person can be assigned by relatives[68] or physicians and is unrelated to anything about the extent to which his body's functioning has deteriorated. A special "definition" of death for transplantation purposes would thus need

---

[67] See notes 15, 16 supra. The way in which cardiopulmonary and brain functions relate to each other and to the phenomenon of death is explored in note 89 infra.

[68] UNIFORM ANATOMICAL GIFT ACT § 2(c). For example, if a special standard were adopted for determining death in potential organ donors, relatives of a dying patient with limited financial means might feel substantial pressure to give permission for his organs to be removed in order to bring to a speedier end the care given the patient.

to be surrounded by a set of procedural safeguards that would govern
not only the method by which a person is to be declared dead but
also those by which he is to be classified as an organ donor.[69] Even
more troublesome is the confusion over the meaning of death that
would probably be engendered by multiple "definitions."[70] Consequently, it would be highly desirable if a statute on death could avoid
the problems with a special "definition." Should the statute happen
to facilitate organ transplantation, either by making more organs
available or by making prospective donors and transplant surgeons
more secure in knowing what the law would permit, so much the better.[71]

If, however, more organs are needed for transplantation than can
be legally obtained, the question whether the benefits conferred by
transplantation justify the risks associated with a broader "definition"
of death should be addressed directly[72] rather than by attempting to
subsume it under the question "what is death?" Such a direct con-

---

[69] The Uniform Anatomical Gift Act, which establishes procedures for the donation
of organs by an individual or his relatives, appears to operate on the premise that
"death" will be determined by standards which are generally accepted and applied in
the ordinary course of events; it does not undertake to "define" death. *But cf.* note 100
infra.

[70] For instance, suppose that Mr. Smith, a dying patient in University Hospital,
is found to be immunologically well matched with Mr. Jones, a University Hospital
patient awaiting a heart transplant. Under the special transplantation "definition" Smith
is then declared dead, but just as the surgeons are about to remove Smith's heart,
Jones suddenly dies. The doctors then decide that Smith is no longer needed as an
organ donor. His condition does not meet the standards for declaring death in non-
donors. Is Smith "dead" or "alive"?

[71] This would be the case if the generally applicable standards for determining
death permit organs to be removed at a time when they are still useable for transplantation purposes. The "definition" suggested by the Article meets this objective, we
believe.

[72] Much of the public's fear of premature excision arises from the failure to
distinguish the general practitioner's and the transplant surgeon's meaning of the
term 'death'. It would be desirable to distinguish the two formally, and use
different terms.
Hillman & Aldridge, *Towards a Legal Definition of Death*, 116 SOL. J. 323, 324 (1972)
[hereinafter cited as Hillman]. These British medical-legal commentators suggest that
"irreversible brain damage," which would include patients with no higher brain activity
but continued spontaneous respiration, be recognized as a ground for removal of organs
prior to ordinary death. They contemplate that certain "essential safeguards" be incorporated into a statute on "irreversible brain damage" to avoid abuse of this category. *Id.*
325.
Prior to the first heart transplant in France, a special "definition" was enacted to
remove any uncertainty about the permissibility of removing a beating heart from a
"dead" donor. In April 1968 the government decreed a "definition of clinical death" for
use with organ donors, based on a flat electroencephalogram of ten minutes duration
which was taken to show that an artificially maintained patient lacks "function in the
higher nervous centers." D. MEYERS, *supra* note 28, at 113. Meyers seems to question this
approach; he believes that the public must be shown
    not just that the brain has been irreparably damaged, but also that the extent of
    this damage is absolutely inconsistent with continued maintenance of independent
    life in the individual. If electro-enphalograph testing can in fact show this, then it
    is a valuable definitional tool in ascertaining clinical death; but the medical profes-
    sion as yet appears somewhat divided on its reliability. In such circumstances, the
    public cannot be expected to accept the evidence of an electro-encephalographic
    reading as part of a legislative definition of death.
Id. 135.

frontation with the issue could lead to a discussion about the standards and procedures under which organs might be taken from persons near death, or even those still quite alive, at their own option[73] or that of relatives, physicians, or representatives of the state. The major advantage of keeping the issues separate is not, of course, that this will facilitate transplantation, but that it will remove a present source of concern: it is unsettling to contemplate that as you lie slowly dying physicians are free to use a more "lenient" standard to declare you dead if they want to remove your organs for transplantation into other patients.

Fourth, the standards for determining death ought not only to relate to a single phenomenon but should also be applied uniformly to all persons. A person's wealth or his "social utility" as an organ donor should not affect the way in which the moment of his death is determined.

Finally, while there is a need for uniformity of application at any one time, the fact that changes in medical technology brought about the present need for "redefinition" argues that the new formulation should be flexible. As suggested in the previous section, such flexibility is most easily accomplished if the new "definition" confines itself to the general standards by which death is to be determined and leaves to the continuing exercise of judgment by physicians the establishment and application of appropriate criteria and specific tests for determining that the standards have been met.

VI. THE KANSAS STATUTE

The first attempt at a legislative resolution of the problems discussed here was made in 1970 when the State of Kansas adopted "An Act relating to and defining death."[74] The Kansas statute has

---

[73] *See, e.g.*, Blachly, *Can Organ Transplantation Provide an Altruistic-Expiatory Alternative to Suicide?*, 1 LIFE-THREATENING BEHAVIOR 6 (1971); Scribner, *Ethical Problems of Using Artificial Organs to Sustain Human Life*, 10 TRANS. AM. SOC. ARTIF. INTERNAL ORGANS 209, 211 (1964) (advocating legal guidelines to permit voluntary euthanasia for purpose of donating organs for transplantation).

[74] Law of Mar. 17, 1970, ch. 378, [1970] Kan. Laws 994 (codified at KAN. STAT. ANN. § 77-202 (Supp. 1971)). It provides in full:
A person will be considered medically and legally dead if, in the opinion of a physician, based on ordinary standards of medical practice, there is the absence of spontaneous respiratory and cardiac function and, because of the disease or condition which caused, directly or indirectly, these functions to cease, or because of the passage of time since these functions ceased, attempts at resuscitation are considered hopeless; and, in this event, death will have occurred at the time these functions ceased; or
A person will be considered medically and legally dead if, in the opinion of a physician, based on ordinary standards of medical practice, there is the absence of spontaneous brain function; and if based on ordinary standards of medical practice, during reasonable attempts to either maintain or restore spontaneous circulatory or respiratory function in the absence of aforesaid brain

received a good deal of attention; similar legislation was enacted in the spring of 1972 in Maryland and is presently under consideration in a number of other jurisdictions.[75] The Kansas legislation, which was drafted in response to developments in organ transplantation and medical support of dying patients, provides "alternative definitions of death,"[76] set forth in two paragraphs. Under the first, a person is considered "medically and legally dead" if a physician determines "there is the absence of spontaneous respiratory and cardiac function and . . . attempts at resuscitation are considered hopeless."[77] In the second "definition," death turns on the absence of spontaneous brain function if during "reasonable attempts" either to "maintain or restore spontaneous circulatory or respiratory function," it appears that "further attempts at resuscitation or supportive maintenance will not succeed."[78] The purpose of the latter "definition" is made clear by the final sentence of the second paragraph:

> Death is to be pronounced before artificial means of supporting respiratory and circulatory function are terminated and *before any vital organ is removed for the purpose of transplantation.*[79]

The primary fault with this legislation is that it appears to be based on, or at least gives voice to, the misconception that there are two separate phenomena of death. This dichotomy is particularly unfortunate because it seems to have been inspired by a desire to establish a special definition for organ transplantation, a definition which physicians would not, however, have to apply, in the drafts-

---

function, it appears that further attempts at resuscitation or supportive maintenance will not succeed, death will have occurred at the time when these conditions first coincide. Death is to be pronounced before artificial means of supporting respiratory and circulatory function are terminated and before any vital organ is removed for purposes of transplantation.

These alternative definitions of death are to be utilized for all purposes in this state, including the trials of civil and criminal cases, any laws to the contrary notwithstanding.

[75] *See* note 4 *supra.* In the Maryland law, which is nearly identical to its Kansas progenitor, the phrase "in the opinion of a physician" was deleted from the first paragraph, and the phrase "and because of a known disease or condition" was added to the second paragraph following "ordinary standards of medical practice." MARYLAND SESSIONS LAWS ch. 693 (1972). Interestingly, Kansas and Maryland were also among the first states to adopt the Uniform Anatomical Gift Act in 1968, even prior to its official revision and approval by the National Conference of Commissioners on Uniform State Laws.

[76] Note 74 *supra.*

[77] *Id.* In using the term "hopeless," the Kansas legislature apparently intended to indicate that the "absence of spontaneous respiratory and cardiac function" must be irreversible before death is pronounced. In addition to being rather roundabout, this formulation is also confusing in that it might be taken to address the "when to allow to die?" question as well as the "is he dead?" question. *See* note 85 *infra* & accompanying text.

[78] Note 74 *supra.*

[79] *Id.* (emphasis added).

man's words, "to prove the irrelevant deaths of most persons."[80] Although there is nothing in the Act itself to indicate that physicians will be less concerned with safeguarding the health of potential organ donors, the purposes for which the Act was passed are not hard to decipher, and they do little to inspire the average patient with confidence that his welfare (including his not being prematurely declared dead) is of as great concern to medicine and the State of Kansas as is the facilitation of organ transplantation.[81] As Professor Kennedy cogently observes, "public disquiet [over transplantation] is in no way allayed by the existence in legislative form of what appear to be alternative definitions of death."[82] One hopes that the form the statute takes does not reflect a conclusion on the part of the Kansas legislature that death occurs at two distinct points during the process of dying.[83] Yet this inference can be derived from the Act, leaving open the prospect "that X at a certain stage in the process of dying can be pronounced dead, whereas Y, having arrived at the same point, is not said to be dead."[84]

The Kansas statute appears also to have attempted more than the "definition" of death, or rather, to have tried to resolve related questions by erroneously treating them as matters of "definition." One supporter of the statute praises it, we think mistakenly, for this reason: "Intentionally, the statute extends to these questions: When can a physician avoid attempting resuscitation? When can he terminate resuscitative efforts? When can he discontinue artificial main-

---

80 Taylor, *supra* note 5, at 296.

81 *Cf.* Kass, *A Caveat on Transplants*, The Washington Post, Jan. 14, 1968, § B, at 1, col. 1; *Discussion* of Murray, *Organ Transplantation: The Practical Possibilities*, in MEDICAL PROGRESS, *supra* note 1, at 67 (comments of Dr. T. E. Starzl): "[T]he new risk is introduced [by the use of cadaver organs] that the terminal care of such potential donors may be adversely influenced by the events which are expected to follow after death, which might conceivably remove whatever small chance there might have been for survival."

82 Kennedy, *supra* note 20, at 947.

83 General use of the term "resuscitation" might suggest the existence of a common notion that a person can die once, be revived (given life again), and then die again at a later time—in other words, that death can occur at two or more distinct points in time. But resuscitation only restores life "from *apparent* death or unconsciousness." WEBSTER'S THIRD NEW INTERNATIONAL DICTIONARY 1937 (1966) (emphasis added). The proposed statute, text accompanying note 88 *infra*, takes account of the possibility of resuscitation by providing that death occurs only when there has been an *irreversible* cessation of the relevant vital bodily functions. *Cf.* 3 M. HOUTS & I.H. HAUT, COURTROOM MEDICINE § 1.01 (3)(d) (1971):

The ability to resuscitate patients after apparent death, coupled with observations that in many cases the restoration was not to a state of consciousness, understanding and intellectual functioning, but merely to a decerebrate, vegetative existence, and with advances in neurology that have brought greater, though far from complete, understanding of the functions of the nervous system, has drawn attention to the role of the nervous system in maintaining life.

84 Kennedy, *supra* note 20, at 948.

tenance?"[85] To be sure, "when the patient is dead" is one obvious answer to these questions, but by no means the only one. As indicated above, we believe that the question "when is the patient dead?" needs to be distinguished and treated separately from the questions "when may the doctor turn off the respirator?" or "when may a patient —dying yet still alive—be allowed to die?"

VII. A STATUTORY PROPOSAL

As an alternative to the Kansas statute we propose the following:

> A person will be considered dead if in the announced opinion of a physician, based on ordinary standards of medical practice, he has experienced an irreversible cessation of spontaneous respiratory and circulatory functions. In the event that artificial means of support preclude a determination that these functions have ceased, a person will be considered dead if in the announced opinion of a physician, based on ordinary standards of medical practice, he has experienced an irreversible cessation of spontaneous brain functions. Death will have occurred at the time when the relevant functions ceased.

This proposed statute provides a "definition" of death confined to the level of *general physiological standards*, and it has been drafted in accord with the five principles set forth above in section V. First, the proposal speaks in terms of the *death* of a *person*. The determination that a person has died is to be based on an evaluation of certain vital bodily functions, the permanent absence of which indicates that he is no longer a living human being. By concentrating on the death of a human being as a whole, the statute rightly disregards the fact that some cells or organs may continue to "live" after this point,[86] just as others may have ceased functioning long before the determination of death. This statute would leave for resolution by other means the question of when the absence or deterioration of certain capacities, such as the ability to communicate, or functions, such as the cerebral, indicates that a person may or should be allowed to die without further medical intervention.

Second, the proposed legislation is predicated upon the single phenomenon of death. Moreover, it applies uniformly to all persons,[87]

---

[85] Mills, *The Kansas Death Statute: Bold and Innovative,* 285 NEW ENG. J. MED. 968 (1971).

[86] *Cf.* F. MOORE, TRANSPLANT 27-36 (1972).

[87] Differences in the exact mode of diagnosing death will naturally occur as a result of differing circumstances under which the physician's examination is made. Thus, the techniques employed with an automobile accident victim lying on the roadside at

by specifying the circumstances under which each of the standards is to be used rather than leaving this to the unguided discretion of physicians. Unlike the Kansas law, the model statute does not leave to arbitrary decision a choice between two apparently equal yet different "alternative definitions of death."[88] Rather, its second standard is applicable only when "artificial means of support preclude" use of the first. It does not establish a separate kind of death, called "brain death." In other words, the proposed law would provide two standards gauged by different functions, for measuring different manifestations of the same phenomenon. If cardiac and pulmonary functions have ceased, brain functions cannot continue; if there is no brain activity and respiration has to be maintained artificially, the same state (*i.e.*, death) exists.[89] Some people might prefer a single standard, one based either on cardiopulmonary or brain functions. This would have the advantage of removing the last trace of the "two

---

night may be less sophisticated than those used with a patient who has been receiving treatment in a well-equipped hospital.

[88] KAN. STAT. ANN. § 77-202 (Supp. 1971).

[89] [L]ife is supported by the smooth and integrated function of three principal systems: circulatory, respiratory and nervous . . . . So long as the integrated function of these three systems continues, the individual lives. If any one of them ceases to function, failure of the other two will shortly follow, and the organism dies. In any case it is *anoxia*, or deprivation of oxygen, that is the ultimate cause of death of cells: in central nervous system failure, because the impulses which maintain respiration cease; in cardiac failure, because oxygenated blood is not moved to the cells; and in respiratory failure, because the blood, although circulating, is not releasing carbon dioxide nor replenishing oxygen in the lungs. Although other organs, such as the liver and kidneys, perform functions essential to life, their failure does not *per se* result in immediate death; it results, rather, in the eventual failure of one of the three systems described, and is thus only an indirect cause of death.

3 M. HOUTS & I.H. HAUT, COURTROOM MEDICINE § 1.01(2)(a) (1971).

It has long been known that, even when a patient loses consciousness and becomes areflexive, he may recover if heartbeat and breathing continue, but if they do not there is no hope of recovery. Thus, death came to be equated with the absence of these two "vital signs," although what was being detected was really the permanent cessation of the integrated functioning of the circulatory, respiratory, and nervous systems. In recent years, the traditional concept of death has been departed from, or at least severely strained, in the case of persons who were dead according to the rationale underlying the traditional standards in that they had experienced a period of anoxia long enough to destroy their brain functions, but in whom respiration and circulation were artificially re-created. By recognizing that such artificial means of support may preclude reliance on the traditional standards of circulation and respiration, the statute proposed here merely permits the logic behind the long-existing understanding (*i.e.*, integrated trisystemic functioning) to be served; it does not create any "new" type of death. Practically, of course, it accomplishes this end by articulating the "new" standard of "irreversible cessation of spontaneous brain functions," as another means of measuring the existing understanding. Dr. Jean Hamburger has observed, "After the guillotine has cut off a criminal's head, it is possible now to keep the heart and lungs going on for days. Do you think that such a person is dead or alive?" *Discussion* of Louisell, *Transplantation: Existing Legal Constraints*, in MEDICAL PROGRESS, *supra* note 1, at 100. The purpose of the "new" standard is to make it clear that the answer to Hamburger's question is unequivocally that the person is dead. *Cf.* Gray v. Sawyer, 247 S.W.2d 496 (Ky. 1952) (newly discovered evidence that blood was gushing from decedent's decapitated body is significant proof that she was still alive following an accident); Biörck, *supra* note 15, at 485; Note, *supra* note 1, at 206.

deaths" image, which any reference to alternative standards may still leave. Respiratory and circulatory indicators, once the only touchstone, are no longer adequate in some situations. It would be possible, however, to adopt the alternative, namely that death is *always* to be established by assessing spontaneous brain functions. Reliance only on brain activity, however, would represent a sharp and unnecessary break with tradition. Departing from continuity with tradition is not only theoretically unfortunate in that it violates another principle of good legislation suggested previously, but also practically very difficult, since most physicians customarily employ cardiopulmonary tests for death and would be slow to change, especially when the old tests are easier to perform,[90] more accessible and acceptable to the lay public, and perfectly adequate for determining death in most instances.

Finally, by adopting standards for death in terms of the cessation of certain vital bodily functions but not in terms of the specific criteria or tests by which these functions are to be measured, the statute does not prevent physicians from adapting their procedures to changes in medical technology.[91]

A basic substantive issue remains: what are the merits of the proposed standards? For ordinary situations, the appropriateness of the traditional standard, "an irreversible cessation of spontaneous respiratory and circulatory functions,"[92] does not require elaboration. Indeed, examination by a physician may be more a formal than a real requirement in determining that most people have died. In addition

---

[90] The clinical signs of irreversible loss of brain functions are probably not a great deal more difficult to elicit than the traditional signs of death are to detect, although the former are less accessible since they require active intervention to be educed and are not susceptible of mere observation. Aside from the taking of an electroencephalogram, the tests involved (such as tickling the cornea, irrigating the ear with ice water, and tapping the tendons with a reflex hammer) are fairly simple, but unlike the customary tests (such as listening for heartbeat with a stethoscope, seeing if a mirror held by the nose and mouth is clouded by breathing, and measuring pulse), they require equipment which a physician may be less likely to have at hand.

[91] For example, it remains to be determined whether an electroencephalographic reading is necessary for an accurate diagnosis, as many now hold, or whether it should be regarded as having only "confirmatory value," as urged by the Harvard Committee. *See* note 11 *supra*.

[92] This language, taken from the proposed statute, is intended as a succinct summary of the standard now employed in ordinary circumstances. Of course, the requirement that the cessation of these functions be *irreversible* cannot be emphasized too strongly. A physician may be needed to make this determination in some cases—and to apply the means necessary to reverse a temporary cessation caused by a heart attack or the like. But laymen are also aware of the significance of the requirement as is indicated by the common practice of giving "first aid," in the form of artificial respiration, to restore breathing in victims of mishaps, particularly drowning, electric shock, and poisoning.

Two British commentators suggest that legislation "defining" death also prescribe the resuscitative efforts required to be made before death may be declared. Hillman, *supra* note 72, at 325. We believe it is enough to demand "irreversibility," as a consequence of which whatever attempts at resuscitation are established by current standards of good medical practice would be compelled.

to any obvious injuries, elementary signs of death such as absence of heartbeat and breathing, cold skin, fixed pupils, and so forth, are usually sufficient to indicate even to a layman that the accident victim, the elderly person who passes away quietly in the night, or the patient stricken with a sudden infarct has died.[93] The difficulties arise when modern medicine intervenes to sustain a patient's respiration and circulation. As we noted in discussing the Harvard Committee's conclusions, the indicators of brain damage appear reliable, in that studies have shown that patients who fit the Harvard criteria have suffered such extensive damage that they do not recover.[94] Of course, the task of the neurosurgeon or physician is simplified in the common case where an accident victim has suffered such gross, apparent injuries to the head that it is not necessary to apply the Harvard criteria in order to establish cessation of brain functioning.

The statutory standard, "irreversible cessation of spontaneous brain functions," is intended to encompass both higher brain activities and those of the brainstem. There must, of course, also be no spontaneous respiration; the second standard is applied only when breathing is being artificially maintained. The major emphasis placed on brain functioning, although generally consistent with the common view of what makes man distinctive as a living creature, brings to the fore a basic issue: What aspects of brain function should be decisive? The question has been reframed by some clinicians in light of their experience with patients who have undergone what they term "neocortical death" (that is, complete destruction of higher brain capacity, demonstrated by a flat E.E.G.). "Once neocortical death has been unequivocally established and the possibility of any recovery of consciousness and intellectual activity [is] thereby excluded, . . . al-

---

[93] The statute provides that the determination of death depends on "the announced opinion of a physician." This raises two distinct sorts of questions. First, which physician's opinion is decisive? As previously observed, text accompanying note 64 *supra*, under "ordinary standards of medical practice" the physician declaring death would be the patient's own attending physician; this is particularly true of a patient who is receiving cardiopulmonary support in a hospital. Since, however, circumstances such as an automobile accident may arise in which death will have to be determined by a physician who had not previously attended the decedent, it was thought best to cast the language in terms of "a physician."

Second, questions may arise concerning the determination of death by nonphysicians. In an emergency, laymen may sometimes have to decide whether death has occurred, and to act on that determination, as in deciding whether to attempt to rescue someone who may or may not have already died. The proposed statute does nothing to change that practice or to alter any liability that might result under such circumstances, but merely specifies that an official determination must rest on "the opinion of a physician." This is consistent with existing state laws on the procedures by which death is "certified." These provisions, as well as ordinary medical practices, make it unnecessary to spell out in the model statute the exact manner in which the physician's opinion should be recorded or certified in the medical files or official documents.

[94] *See* note 12 *supra* & accompanying text.

though [the] patient breathes spontaneously, is he or she alive?"[95] While patients with irreversible brain damage from cardiac arrest seldom survive more than a few days, cases have recently been reported of survival for up to two and one-quarter years.[96] Nevertheless, though existence in this state falls far short of a full human life, the very fact of spontaneous respiration, as well as coordinated movements and reflex activities at the brainstem and spinal cord levels, would exclude these patients from the scope of the statutory standards.[97] The condition of "neocortical death" may well be a proper justification for interrupting all forms of treatment and allowing these patients to die, but this moral and legal problem cannot and should not be settled by "defining" these people "dead."

The legislation suggested here departs from the Kansas statute in its basic approach to the problem of "defining" death: the proposed statute does not set about to establish a special category of "brain death" to be used by transplanters. Further, there are a number of particular points of difference between them. For example, the proposed statute does not speak of persons being "medically and legally dead," thus avoiding redundancy and, more importantly, the mistaken implication that the "medical" and "legal" definitions could differ.[98]

---

[95] Brierley, Adams, Graham & Simpsom, *Neocortical Death After Cardiac Arrest*, 2 LANCET 560, 565 (1971) [hereinafter cited as Brierley]. In addition to a flat (isoelectric) electroencephalogram, a "neuropathological examination of a biopsy specimen . . . from the posterior half of a cerebral hemisphere" provides further confirmation. *Id.* The editors of a leading medical journal question "whether a state of cortical death can be diagnosed clinically." Editorial, *Death of a Human Being*, 2 LANCET 590 (1971). *Cf.* note 14 *supra*.

[96] Brierley and his colleagues report two cases of their own in which the patients each survived in a comatose condition for five months after suffering cardiac arrest before dying of pulmonary complications. They also mention two unreported cases of a Doctor Lewis, in one of which the patient survived for 2¼ years. Brierley, *supra* note 95, at 565.

[97] The exclusion of patients without neocortical function from the category of death may appear somewhat arbitrary in light of our disinclination to engage in a philosophical discussion of the basic concepts of human "life" and "death." *See* text accompanying notes 57-60 *supra*. Were the "definition" contained in the proposed statute a departure from what has traditionally been meant by "death," such a conceptual discussion would clearly be in order. But, as this Article has tried to demonstrate, our intention has been more modest: to provide a clear restatement of the traditional understanding in terms which are useful in light of modern medical capabilities and practices. *See* note 89 *supra*.

A philosophical examination of the essential attributes of being "human" might lead one to conclude that persons who, for example, lack the mental capacity to communicate in any meaningful way, should be regarded as "not human" or "dead." It would nevertheless probably be necessary and prudent to treat the determination of that kind of "death" under special procedures until such time as medicine is able routinely to diagnose the extent and irreversibility of the loss of the "central human capacities" (however defined) with the same degree of assurance now possible in determining that death has occurred. Consequently, even at the conceptual level, we are inclined to think that it is best to distinguish the question "is he dead?" from such questions as "should he be allowed to die?" and "should his death be actively promoted?"

[98] The use of the word "legally" (as in "a person will be considered legally dead") in a law defining death is redundant. Besides, if there were a distinction between a

Also, the proposed legislation does not include the provision that "death is to be pronounced before" the machine is turned off or any organs removed. Such a *modus operandi*, which was incorporated by Kansas from the Harvard Committee's report, may be advisable for physicians on public relations grounds, but it has no place in a statute "defining" death. The proposed statute already provides that "Death will have occurred at the time when the relevant functions ceased."[99] If supportive aids, or organs, are withdrawn after this time, such acts cannot be implicated as having caused death. The manner in which, or exact time at which, the physician should articulate his finding is a matter best left to the exigencies of the situation, to local medical customs or hospital rules, or to statutes on the procedures for certifying death or on transplantation if the latter is the procedure which raises the greatest concern of medical impropriety. The real safeguard against doctors killing patients is not to be found in a statute "defining" death. Rather, it inheres in physicians' ethical and religious beliefs, which are also embodied in the fundamental professional ethic of *primum non nocere* and are reinforced by homicide and "wrongful death" laws and the rules governing medical negligence applicable in license revocation proceedings or in private actions for damages.

The proposed statute shares with the Kansas legislation two features of which Professor Kennedy is critical. First, it does not require that two physicians participate in determining death, as recommended by most groups which set forth suggestions about transplantation. The reasons for the absence of such a provision should be obvious. Since the statute deals with death in general and not with death in relation to transplantation, there is no reason for it to establish a general rule which is required only in that unusual situation. If particular dangers lurk in the transplantation setting, they should be dealt with in legislation on that subject, such as the Uniform Anatomical

---

"medical" and a "legal" standard of death, a statute could only legislate the legal standard. Consequently, the adjectives "medical" and "legal" are unnecessary as well as potentially misleading. *Cf.* Halley & Harvey, *Medical vs. Legal Definition of Death*, 204 J.A.M.A. 423 (1968).

99 It is necessary to state a standard for judging *when* death occurred for disputes, typically concerning inheritance or rights of survivorship, in which the exact time of death is a decisive factor. The proposed statute, in accordance with existing practice, *see* text accompanying note 62 *supra*, fixes the time of death as the point at which the person actually dies, not the point at which the diagnosis is confirmed. This approach conforms to the commonsense understanding that both a man who dies in a coal mine and cannot be found for 24 hours and one who dies in a hospital where the practice is to require confirmation of the diagnosis by repeating the tests after 24 hours have been dead for a day before their deaths can be pronounced with certainty. The statutory phrase "relevant functions" refers to whichever functions are being measured: cardiopulmonary functions in the usual case, or brain functions where the others are obscured by the artificial means being employed.

Gift Act.[100] If all current means of determining "irreversible cessation of spontaneous brain functions" are inherently so questionable that they should be double-checked by a second (or third, fourth, etc.) physician to be trustworthy, or if a certain means of measuring brain function requires as a technical matter the cooperation of two, or twenty, physicians, then the participation of the requisite number of experts would be part of the "ordinary standards of medical practice" that circumscribe the proper, non-negligent use of such procedures. It would be unfortunate, however, to introduce such a requirement into legislation which sets forth the general standards for determining who is dead, especially when it is done in such a way as to differentiate between one standard and another.

Kennedy's second objection, that a death statute ought to provide "for the separation and insulation of the physician (or physicians) attending the patient donor and certifying death, from the recipient of any organ that may be salvaged from the cadaver," is likewise unnecessary.[101] As was noted previously, language that relates only to transplantation has no place in a statute on the determination of death.

VIII. CONCLUSION

Changes in medical knowledge and procedures have created an apparent need for a clear and acceptable revision of the standards for determining that a person has died. Some commentators have argued that the formulation of such standards should be left to physicians. The reasons for rejecting this argument seem compelling: the "definition of death" is not merely a matter for technical expertise, the uncertainty of the present law is unhealthy for society and physicians alike, there is a great potential for mischief and harm through the possibility of conflict between the standards applied by some physicians and those assumed to be applicable by the community at

[100] In fact, § 7(b) of the Uniform Anatomical Gift Act calls only for one physician: "The time of death [of a donor] shall be determined by a physician who attends the donor at his death, or, if none, the physician who certifies the death."

In *Tucker v. Lower* (*see* notes 42-50 *supra* & accompanying text) the defendants argued that this provision amounted to a "definition" of death (death is when a physician says you're dead), although Virginia had not adopted the Act until 1970, two years after the transplantation of the plantiff's brother's heart. The court rejected this argument since "neither the decedent nor anyone acting on his behalf had made a gift of any part of his body" and the Act was therefore inapplicable. The reasons for rejecting the defendant's suggestion seem to us to go deeper; they have been presented throughout this Article and are summarized in the concluding section.

[101] Kennedy, *supra* note 20, at 949. Again, § 7(b) of the Uniform Anatomical Gift Act covers this point adequately: "The physician [who declares death] shall not participate in the procedures for removing or transplanting a part."

large and its legal system, and patients and their relatives are made uneasy by physicians apparently being free to shift around the meaning of death without any societal guidance. Accordingly, we conclude the public has a legitimate role to play in the formulation and adoption of such standards. This Article has proposed a model statute which bases a determination of death primarily on the traditional standard of final respiratory and circulatory cessation; where the artificial maintenance of these functions precludes the use of such a standard, the statute authorizes that death be determined on the basis of irreversible cessation of spontaneous brain functions. We believe the legislation proposed would dispel public confusion and concern and protect physicians and patients, while avoiding the creation of "two types of death," for which the statute on this subject first adopted in Kansas has been justly criticized. The proposal is offered not as the ultimate solution to the problem, but as a catalyst for what we hope will be a robust and well-informed public debate over a new "definition." Finally, the proposed statute leaves for future resolution the even more difficult problems concerning the conditions and procedures under which a decision may be reached to cease treating a terminal patient who does not meet the standards set forth in the statutory "definition of death."

II.
Death as a Treatment of Choice?: Involuntary Euthanasia of the Defective Newborn.

DILEMMAS OF "INFORMED CONSENT" IN CHILDREN

ANTHONY SHAW, M.D.

ABSTRACT

If parents have the "right" to give "informed consent" regarding surgery on their minor children, does this mean that they also have the "right" to deny consent when such denial means death for their child? Some ethical, moral and legal questions about the rights and obligations of physicians, hospital staffs, parents and society arise when parents decide to withhold consent for treatment of critically ill minor children. Specific examples are severely retarded or severely deformed infants whose parents refuse surgical correction of a lethal gastrointestinal or genitourinary anomaly, and children in need of lifesaving surgery whose parents refuse treatment for religious or social reasons, or merely out of fear or ignorance. My response in these situations has been individualized and has ranged from supporting parental decisions to seeking court intervention under the child-neglect laws. (N Engl J Med 289:885-890, 1973)

Numerous articles have been written about "rights" of patients. We read about "right to life" of the unborn, "right to die" of the elderly, "Bill of Rights" for the hospitalized, "Declaration of Rights" for the retarded, "right of privacy" for the pregnant and, of course, "right to medical care" for us all.

Whatever the legitimacy of these sometimes conflicting "rights" there is at present general agreement that patients have at least one legal right: that of "informed consent"—i.e., when a decision about medical treatment is made, they are entitled to a full explanation by their physicians of the nature of the proposed treatment, its risks and its limitations. Once the physician has discharged his obligation fully to inform* an adult, mentally competent patient, that patient may then accept or reject the proposed treatment, or, indeed, may refuse any and all treatment, as he sees fit. But if the patient is a minor, a parental decision rejecting recommended treatment is subject to review when physicians or society disagree with that decision.

The purpose of this paper is to consider some of the moral and ethical dilemmas that may arise in the area of "informed consent" when the patient is a minor. The following case reports, all but two from my practice of pediatric surgery, raise questions about the rights and obligations of physicians, parents and society in situations in which parents decide to withhold consent for treatment of their children.

Instead of presenting a full discussion of these cases at the end of the paper, I have followed each case presentation with a comment discussing the points I wish to make, relating the issues raised by that case to those raised in some of the other cases, and posing the very hard questions that I had to ask myself in dealing with the patients and parents. At present the questions are coming along much faster than the answers.

CASE REPORTS

Case A.

Baby A was referred to me at 22 hours of age with a diagnosis of esophageal atresia and tracheoesophageal fistula. The infant, the firstborn of a professional couple in their early thirties, had obvious signs of mongolism, about which they were fully informed by the referring physician. After explaining the nature of the surgery to the distraught father, I offered him the operative consent. His pen hesitated briefly above the form and then as he signed, he muttered, "I have no

*I agree with Ingelfinger[1] that "educate" is a better concept here than "inform."

choice, do I?" He didn't seem to expect an answer, and I gave him none. The esophageal anomaly was corrected in routine fashion, and the infant was discharged to a state institution for the retarded without ever being seen again by either parent.

Comment

In my opinion, this case was mishandled from the point of view of Baby A's family, in that consent was not truly informed. The answer to Mr. A's question should have been, "You *do* have a choice. You might want to consider not signing the operative consent at all." Although some of my surgical colleagues believe that there is no alternative to attempting to save the life of every infant, no matter what his potential, in my opinion, the doctrine of informed consent should, under some circumstances, include the right to withhold consent. If the parents do have the right to withhold consent for surgery in a case such as Baby A, who should take the responsibility for pointing out that fact to them—the obstetrician, the pediatrician or the surgeon?

Another question raised by this case lies in the parents' responsibility toward their baby, who has been saved by their own decision to allow surgery. Should they be obligated to provide a home for the infant? If their intention is to place the baby after operation in a state-funded institution, should the initial decision regarding medical and surgical treatment for their infant be theirs alone?

Case B.

Baby B was referred at the age of 36 hours with duodenal obstruction and signs of Down's syndrome. His young parents had a 10-year-old daughter, and he was the son they had been trying to have for 10 years; yet, when they were approached with the operative consent, they hesitated. They wanted to know beyond any doubt whether the baby had Down's syndrome. If so, they wanted time to consider whether or not to permit the surgery to be done. Within 8 hours a geneticist was able to identify cells containing 47 chromosomes in a bone-marrow sample. Over the next 3 days the infant's gastrointestinal tract was decompressed with a nasogastric tube, and he was supported with intravenous fluids while the parents consulted with their ministers, with family physicians in their

home community and with our geneticists. At the end of that
time the B's decided not to permit surgery. The infant died 3
days later after withdrawal of supportive therapy.

Comment

Unlike the parents of Baby A, Mr. and Mrs. B realized
that they did have a choice—to consent or not to consent to the
intestinal surgery. They were afforded access to a wide range
of resources to help them make an informed decision. The infant's deterioration was temporarily prevented by adequate
intestinal decompression and intravenous fluids.

Again, some of the same questions are raised here as with
Baby A. Do the parents have the right to make the decision to
allow their baby to die without surgery?

Can the parents make a reasonable decision within hours
or days after the birth of a retarded or brain-damaged infant?
During that time they are overwhelmed by feelings of shock,
fear, guilt, horror and shame. What is the proper role of the
medical staff and the hospital administration? Can parents
make an intelligent decision under these circumstances, or are
they simply reacting to a combination of their own instincts
and fears as well as to the opinions and biases of medical staff?
Rickham[2] has described the interaction of physician and parents in such situations as follows:

> Every conscientious doctor will, of course,
> give as correct a prognosis and as impartial an
> opinion about the possible future of the child as
> he can, but he will not be able to be wholly im-
> partial, and, whether he wants it or not, his
> opinion will influence the parents. At the end it
> is usually the doctor who has to decide the is-
> sue. It is not only cruel to ask the parents wheth-
> er they want their child to live or die, it is dis-
> honest, because in the vast majority of cases,
> the parents are consciously or unconsciously
> influenced by the doctor's opinion.

I believe that parents often *can* make an informed decision if,
like the B's, they are afforded access to a range of resources
beyond the expertise and bias of a single doctor and afforded

sufficient time for contemplation of the alternatives. Once the parents have made a decision, should members of the medical staff support them in their decision regardless of their own feelings? (This support may be important to assuage recurrent feelings of guilt for many months or even years after the parents' decision.)

When nutritional and fluid support was withdrawn, intestinal intubation and pain medication were provided to prevent suffering. To what extent should palliative treatment be given in a case in which definitive treatment is withheld? The lingering death of a newborn infant whose parents have denied consent for surgery can have disastrous effect on hospital personnel, as illustrated last year by the well publicized Johns Hopkins Hospital case, which raised a national storm of controversy. In this case, involving an infant with mongoloidism and duodenal atresia, several of the infant's physicians violently disagreed with the parents' decision not to allow surgery. The baby's lingering death (15 days) severely demoralized the nursing and house staffs. In addition, it prolonged the agony for the parents, who called daily to find out if the baby was still alive. Colleagues of mine who have continued to keep such infants on gastrointestinal decompression and intravenous fluids for weeks after the parents have decided against surgery have told me of several cases in which the parents have finally changed their minds and given the surgeon a green light! Does such a change of heart represent a more deliberative decision on the part of the parents or merely their capitulation on the basis of emotional fatigue?

After the sensationalized case in Baltimore, Johns Hopkins Hospital established a committee to work with physicians and parents who are confronted by similar problems. Do such medical-ethics committees serve as a useful resource for physicians and families, or do they, in fact, further complicate the decision-making process by multiplying the number of opinions?

Finally, should a decision to withhold surgery on an infant with Down's syndrome or other genetically determined mental-retardation states be allowed on clinical grounds only, without clear-cut chromosomal evidence?

Case C.

I was called to the Newborn Nursery to see Baby C, whose father was a busy surgeon with three teen-age children. The diagnoses of imperforate anus and microcephalus were obvious. Doctor C called me after being informed of the situation by the pediatrician. "I'm not going to sign that op permit," he said. When I didn't reply, he said, "What would you do, doctor, if he were your baby?" "I wouldn't let him be operated on either," I replied. Palliative support only was provided, and the infant died 48 hours later.

Comment

Doctor C asked me bluntly what I would do were it my baby, and I gave him my answer. Was my response appropriate? In this case I simply reinforced his own decision. Suppose he had asked me for my opinion before expressing his own inclination? Should my answer in any case have simply been, "It's not my baby"—with a refusal to discuss the subject further? Should I have insisted that he take more time to think about it and discuss it further with his family and clergy, like the parents of Baby B? Is there a moral difference between withholding surgery on a baby with microcephalus and withholding surgery on a baby with Down's syndrome?

Some who think that all children with mongolism should be salvaged since many of them are trainable, would not dispute a decision to allow a baby with less potential such as microcephalic Baby C to die. Should, then, decisions about life and death be made on the basis of IQ? In a recent article,[3] Professor Joseph Fletcher outlined criteria for what he calls "humanhood"—minimal standards by which we could judge whether a living organism is or is not a human being. These criteria (further defined in Dr. Fletcher's article) include minimal intelligence, self-awareness, self-control, a sense of time, a sense of futurity, a sense of the past, the capability to relate to others, concern for others, communication, control of existence, curiosity, change and changeability, balance of rationality and feeling, idiosyncrasy and neocortical function. Dr. Fletcher also offers a shorter list of what a human being is not. By trying to arrive at a definition of what we call "human," Doctor Fletcher has, of course, stirred up a hornet's nest. But in so doing, he is not laying down a set of rigid standards but is issuing a challenge that should be a particularly attractive one to the medical profession. Is it possible that physicians and philosophers can agree on a "profile of man" that might afford more rational grounds for approaching problems in biomedical ethics?

Case D.

In 1972 I wrote a piece published by the New York Times, "Parents of mongoloids have the legal (and I believe, the moral) responsibility of determining if their child with a potentially deadly but surgically correctable defect should live or die."[4] After reading this article, Mr. D called me for advice concerning his 2-week-old grandson. This infant had been born in a New York hospital with Down's syndrome and with bilateral hydroureteronephrosis secondary to urethral valves, for the correction of which the family had refused surgery. Since the infant was becoming increasingly uremic, the family was being strongly pressured by the medical staff to consent to surgery. After an absolute refusal to sign, the family was ordered to take the infant home immediately despite the wish for the baby to die in the hospital. At my last conversation with the infant's grandfather, the family and the hospital had reached an impasse about discharge and the infant was dying slowly of uremia.

Comment

In threatening to discharge the dying infant, the medical staff was trying to coerce the family into signing consent for surgery. Aside from the issue of coercion here, is providing facilities for dying patients a proper role for a hospital? The parents refused to take the infant home because of the devastating emotional impact that the dying baby would have on the entire family. The hospital wanted to discharge the infant partly because of the devastating emotional impact that the dying infant was having on the hospital staff. Can we prepare hospital, medical and paramedical personnel to accept the death of infants under these circumstances without the destruction of morale? Can we realistically expect hospital staff to be able to make such an emotional accommodation no matter how they view the situation from an intellectual standpoint? Finally, if the decision is not to operate, where does one draw the line between palliation of the infant's suffering and active shortening of the infant's life? This, of course, is one of the areas where the question of euthanasia has been raised. To my knowledge, the question of whether Baby D died at home or in the hospital finally became a legal matter to be resolved between the hospital's legal counsel and the family's attorney.

If the medical staff felt strongly that allowing Baby D to die for lack of simple surgery was immoral, why did they not obtain a court order permitting them to operate?

Case E.

A court order *was* obtained for Baby E who was "reported" in Life Magazine two years ago. This infant, with Down's syndrome, intestinal obstruction and congenital heart disease, was born in her mother's car on the way to the hospital. The mother thought that the retarded infant would be impossible for her to care for and would have a destructive effect on her already shaky marriage. She therefore refused to sign permission for intestinal surgery, but a local child-welfare agency, invoking the state child-abuse statute, was able to obtain a court order directing surgery to be performed. After a complicated course and thousands of dollars worth of care, the infant was returned to the mother. The baby's continued growth and development remained markedly retarded because of her severe cardiac disease. A year and a half after the baby's birth, the mother felt more than ever that she had been done a severe injustice.

Comment

Is the crux of this case parental rights versus the child's right to life? Can the issue in this case be viewed as an extension of the basic dilemma in the abortion question? Does this case represent proper application of child-abuse legislation —i.e., does the parents' refusal to consent to surgery constitute neglect as defined in child-abuse statutes? If so, under these statutes does a physician's concurrence in a parental decision to withhold treatment constitute failure to report neglect, thereby subjecting him to possible prosecution?

Baby E's mother voluntarily took the baby home, but had she not done so, could the state have forced her to take the baby? Could the state have required her husband to contribute to the cost of medical care and to the subsequent maintenance of the infant in a foster home or institution?

If society decides that the attempt must be made to salvage every human life, then, as I have written, ". . . society *must* provide the necessary funds and facilities to meet the continuing medical and psychological needs of these unfortunate children."[4]

Case F.

Baby F was conceived as the result of an extramarital relation. Mrs. F had sought an abortion, which she had been denied. F was born prematurely, weighing 1600 g and in all respects normal except for the presence of esophageal atresia and tracheoesophageal fistula. Mrs. F signed the operative consent, and the surgery was performed uneventfully. Mrs F fears that her husband will eventually realize that the baby is not his and that her marriage may collapse as a result of this discovery.

Comment

Like those of Mrs. E, Mrs. F's reasons for not wanting her baby were primarily psychosocial. However, Mrs F never raised the question of withholding consent for surgery even though the survival of her infant might mean destruction of her marriage. Does the presence of mental retardation or severe physical malformation justify withholding of consent for psychosocial reasons (Babies B, C, D and E), whereas the absence of such conditions does not (Baby F)? If she had decided to withhold consent there is no doubt in my mind that I would have obtained a court order to operate on this baby, who appeared to be normal beyond her esophageal anomaly. Although I personally would not have objected to an abortion in this situation for the sociopsychologic reasons, I would not allow an otherwise normal baby with a correctable anomaly to perish for lack of treatment for the same reasons. Although those who believe that all life is sacred, no matter what its level of development, will severely criticize me for the apparent inconsistency of this position, I believe it to be a realistic and humane approach to a situation in which no solution is ideal.

Although my case histories thus far have dealt with the forms of mental retardation most common in my practice, similar dilemmas are encountered by other physicians in different specialties, the most obvious being in the spectrum of hydrocephalus and meningomyelocele. Neurosurgeons are still grappling unsuccessfully and inconsistently with indications for surgery in this group, trying to fit together what is practical, what is moral, and what is humane. If neurosurgeons disagree violently over criteria for operability on infants with meningomyelocele, how can the parents of such a child decide whether to sign for consent? Who would say that they *must* sign if they don't want a child whose days will be measured by operations, clinic visits and infections? I have intentionally omitted from discussion in this paper the infant with crippling deformities and multiple anomalies who does not have rapidly lethal lesions. Infants with such lesions may survive for long periods and may require palliative procedures such as release of limb contractures, ventriculoperitoneal shunts, or colostomies to make their lives more tolerable or to simplify their management. The extent to which these measures are desirable or justifiable moves us into an even more controversial area.

I must also point out that the infants discussed in the preceding case reports represent but a small percentage of the total number of infants with mental-retardation syndromes on whom I have operated. Once the usual decision to operate has been made I, of course, apply the same efforts as I would to any other child.

Case G.

Six-year-old boy G was referred to me because of increasing shortness of breath due to a large mediastinal mass. The parents had refused diagnostic procedures and recommended treatment until the child had become cachectic and severely dyspneic. His liver was enlarged. A thorough in-hospital work-up, including liver biopsy, bone-marrow aspiration, thoracentesis and mediastinal tomography failed to establish a diagnosis. The child was obviously dying of progressive compromise of his respiratory tract and vena-cava obstruction. His family belonged to a fundamentalist religious sect and firmly believed that the child would be healed by God. They refused to sign permission for exploratory thoracotomy. We spent 2 weeks trying to convince them that, although the boy's chances were slim in any case, his only hope lay in the possibility of our encountering a resectable tumor. When the parents refused to sign permission for surgery, a court order was obtained from the Juvenile Court Judge permitting surgery. The next day exploratory thoracotomy was carried out, and a non-resectable neuroblastoma was found. The child died a respiratory death 3 days later. Members of the family subsequently threatened the lives of the physicians and of the judge. A letter of inquiry was subsequently sent to me by their lawyer, implying an intention to sue. However, it was not followed up.

Comment

Some of the same questions are raised here as in the Jehovah's Witness cases. Does the parents' right to practice their religion include the right to deny their child medical or surgical treatment? The fact that I allowed a two-week delay before obtaining the court order indicates my strong feeling that a court order should be the last resort used to obtain parents' co-operation on behalf of their child. We persisted as long as we thought we might obtain such co-operation.

Should a court order be obtained by physicians only when they think their treatment will certainly save the child, or should they obtain an order so long as there is any possibility of helping the child? Were we justified in obtaining the court order and putting the parents and ourselves through such an ordeal when the odds against us of finding a curable lesion were so long? I believe the answer is yes. In making a decision to obtain a court order directing surgery, the physician must balance the risk for the child if surgery is withheld against the risk of surgery itself coupled with the demoralizing consequences for the family if the surgery fails. In G's case, in which his life expectancy without treatment appeared to be measurable in days, I believe that the decision to obtain a court order was appropriate.

Statutes on child abuse and neglect have on occasion been invoked to give a hospital or a physician temporary custody of a child whose parents' religion prevents lifesaving medical care. At the same time some states have worded their child-abuse statutes to avoid appearance of interfering with constitutional guarantees of freedom of religion. For example, in Virginia's child-abuse law,[5] the following statement appears ". . . that a child who is being furnished Christian Science treatment by a duly accredited Christian Science practitioner shall not be considered for that reason alone a physically neglected child for the purposes of this section." However, the law may be invoked when, as a result of the practice of his parents' religion, a child's health can be demonstrated to be in jeopardy. For this reason, such religious exclusion clauses as the one just cited would not, in my opinion, be held applicable in G's case.

Several new questions arise when a child is an adolescent who himself refuses surgery on the basis of his sincere religious conviction. Then, one has to ask whether minors should be allowed to make life-and-death decisions about their own treatment. Should it depend on the degree of maturity of the child, or can one try to write into law an age at which a child's wishes should be seriously taken into consideration in medical decision making? In a sensitively written article Schowalter et al.[6] recently discussed the "agonizing dilemma" created for a hospital staff by a 16-year-old girl with uremia who, with her parents' consent, chose death over continued therapeutic efforts. The authors concluded that ". . . there are instances when a physician should honor an adolescent patient's wish to die." The case in point, although not terminal, had a poor prognosis. Suppose the patient had been a 16-year-old Jehovah's Witness with a ruptured spleen, who appeared to be mature and in full possession of his faculties and who, although he understood he would die without blood, refused to accept it?

Case H.

Ten-year-old H was brought to the surgical clinic by her mother for removal of some cysts from the scalp. The family is well known to our hospital since most of its members have Gardner's syndrome and most of the senior family members either have enterostomies or have died of cancer of the gastrointestinal tract. H's mother has had rectal bleeding for the past year but has not permitted herself to be examined by a physician. She also would not permit H to have a barium-enema examination or sigmoidoscopy when this question was first raised. However, when excision of the scalp cysts was made contingent upon the mother's permitting evaluation of the child's colon, she consented. The barium-enema study and a proctosigmoidoscopy were negative. The cysts were excised. Since more cysts tend to form, we expect to be able to arrive at a regular quid pro quo that will enable us to continue evaluating the child's colon until such time as the premalignant polyps are detected. We do not know what we will do if polyps begin to proliferate, making colectomy advisable before H achieves legal maturity. In all likelihood, the mother will not willingly permit us to perform major surgery on her child.

Comment

Here we found a substitute for judicial intervention. We called it "making a deal." If the mother had not consented to this bargain, would we have been justified in obtaining a court order for a diagnostic procedure? Would it not then be necessary to put the mother under long-term court supervision so that she would be forced to bring the child for regular diagnostic examinations and for resection when deemed necessary? It seems to me that such judicial intervention is proper when one is dealing with a potentially lethal condition in a young child and would be, I believe, fully sanctioned by the child-neglect laws of most states. Note that there is no question of religious freedom involved here. Should court orders also be sought in situations in which parents refuse treatment for children with diseases or deformities that, if untreated, will result in permanent physical or emotional damage but not death?

DISCUSSION

If an underlying philosophy can be gleaned from the vignettes presented above, I hope it is one that tries to find a solution, humane and loving, based on the circumstances of each case rather than by means of dogmatic formula approach. (Fletcher has best expressed this philosophy in his book, Situation Ethics,[7] and in subsequent articles[3,8]) This outlook contrasts sharply with the rigid "right-to-life" philosophy, which categorically opposes abortion, for example. My ethic holds that all rights are not absolute all the time. As Fletcher points out, ". . . all rights are imperfect and may be set aside

if human *need* requires it."[3] My ethic further considers quality
of life as a value that must be balanced against a belief in the
sanctity of life.

Those who believe that the sanctity of life is the overriding consideration in all cases have a relatively easy time
making decisions. They say that all babies must be saved; no
life may be aborted from the womb, and all attempts to salvage newborn life, whatever its quality and whatever its human and financial costs to family and society, must be made.
Although many philosophies express the view that "heroic"
efforts need not be made to save or prolong life, yesterday's
heroic efforts are today's routine procedures. Thus, each year
it becomes possible to remove yet another type of malformation from the "unsalvageable" category. All pediatric surgeons, including myself, have "triumphs"—infants who, if
they had been born 25 or even five years ago, would not have
been salvageable. Now with our team approaches, staged surgical technics, monitoring capabilities, ventilatory support
systems and intravenous hyperalimentation and elemental
diets, we can wind up with "viable" children three and four
years old well below the third percentile in height and weight,
propped up on a pillow, marginally tolerating an oral diet of
sugar and amino acids and looking forward to another operation.

Or how about the infant whose gastrointestinal tract has
been removed after volvulus and infarction? Although none of
us regard the insertion of a central venous catheter as a "heroic" procedure, is it right to insert a "lifeline" to feed this
baby in the light of our present technology, which can support him, tethered to an infusion pump, for a maximum of
a year and some months?

Who should make these decisions? The doctors? The
parents? Clergymen? A committee? As I have pointed out, I
think that the parents must participate in any decision about
treatment and that they must be fully informed of the consequences of consenting and of withholding consent. This is a
type of informed consent that goes far beyond the traditional
presentation of possible complications of surgery, length of
hospitalization, cost of the operation, time lost from work,
and so on.

It may be impossible for any general agreement or guide-lines for making decisions on cases such as the ones presented here to emerge, but I believe we should bring these problems out into public forum because whatever the answers may be, they should not be the result of decisions made solely by the attending physicians. Or should they?

1. Ingelfinger, F. J.: Informed (but uneducated) consent. N. Engl. J. Med., 287:465-466. 1972.

2. Rickham, P. P.: The Ethics of Surgery on Newborn Infants. Clin. Pediatr. 8:251-253. 1969.

3. Fletcher, J.: Indicators of Humanhood: A Tentative Profile of Man. The Hastings Center Report, Vol. 2., No. 5. Hastings-on-Hudson, New York. Institute of Society. Ethics and Life Sciences, November, 1972. pp. 1-4.

4. Shaw, A.: Doctor, Do We Have a Choice? New York Times Magazine. January 30, 1972, pp. 44-54.

5. Virginia Code. Sect. 16.1-217.1 through 16.1-217.4.

6. Schowalter, J. E., Ferholt, J. B., Mann, N. M.: The Adolescent Patient's Decision to Die. Pediatrics 51:97-103, 1973.

7. Fletcher, J. F.: Situation Ethics: The New Morality. Philadelphia. Westminster Press. 1966.

8. *Idem.* Ethical Aspects of Genetic Controls: Designed Genetic Changes in Man. N. Engl. J. Med. 285:776-783, 1971.

MORAL AND ETHICAL DILEMMAS IN THE SPECIAL-CARE NURSERY

RAYMOND S. DUFF, M.D.

AND

A.G.M. CAMPBELL, M.B., F.R.C.P. (EDIN.)

ABSTRACT

Of 299 consecutive deaths occurring in a special-care nursery, 43 (14 percent) were related to withholding treatment. In this group were 15 with multiple anomalies, eight with trisomy, eight with cardiopulmonary disease, seven with meningomyelocele, three with other central-nervous-system disorders, and two with short-bowel syndrome. After careful consideration of each of these 43 infants, parents and physicians in a group decision concluded that prognosis for meaningful life was extremely poor or hopeless, and therefore rejected further treatment. The awesome finality of these decisions, combined with a potential for error in prognosis, made the choice agonizing for families and health professionals. Nevertheless, the issue has to be faced, for not to decide is an arbitrary and potentially devastating decision of default. (N Engl J Med 289:890-894, 1973)

Between 1940 and 1970 there was a 58 percent decrease in the infant death rate in the United States.[1] This reduction was related in part to the application of new knowledge to the care of infants. Neonatal mortality rates in hospitals having infant intensive-care units have been about ½ those reported in hospitals without such units.[2] There is now evidence that in many conditions of early infancy the long-term morbidity may also be reduced.[3] Survivors of these units may be healthy, and their parents grateful, but some infants continue to suffer from such conditions as chronic cardiopulmonary disease, short-bowel syndrome or various manifestations of brain damage; others are severely handicapped by a myriad of congenital malformations that in previous times would have resulted in early death. Recently, both lay and professional persons have expressed increasing concern about the quality of life for these severely impaired survivors and their families.[4,5] Many pediatricians and others are distressed with the long-term results of pressing on and on to save life at all costs and in all circumstances. Eliot Slater[6] stated, "If this is one of the consequences of the sanctity-of-life ethic, perhaps our formulation of the principle should be revised."

The experiences described in this communication document some of the grave moral and ethical dilemmas now faced by physicians and families. They indicate some of the problems in a large special-care nursery where medical technology has prolonged life and where "informed" parents influence the management decisions concerning their infants.

BACKGROUND AND METHODS

The special-care nursery of the Yale-New Haven Hospital not only serves an obstetric service for over 4000 live births annually but also acts as the principal referral center in Connecticut for infants with major problems of the newborn period. From January 1, 1970, through June 30, 1972, 1615 infants born at the Hospital were admitted, and 556 others were transferred for specialized care from community hospitals. During this interval, the average daily census was 26, with a range of 14 to 37.

For some years the unit has had a liberal policy for parental visiting, with the staff placing particular emphasis on helping parents adjust to and participate in the care of their infants with special problems. By encouraging visiting, attempting to create a relaxed atmosphere within the unit, exploring carefully the special needs of the infants, and familiarizing parents with various aspects of care, it was hoped to remove much of the apprehension—indeed, fear—with which parents at first view an intensive-care nursery.[7] At any time, parents may see and handle their babies. They commonly observe or participate in most routine aspects of care and are often present when some infant is critically ill or moribund. They may attend, as they choose, the death of their own infant. Since an average of two to three deaths occur each week and many infants are critically ill for long periods, it is obvious that the concentrated, intimate social interactions between personnel, infants and parents in an emotionally charged atmosphere often make the work of the staff very difficult and demanding. However, such participation and recognition of parents' rights to information about their infant appear to be the chief foundation of "informed consent" for treatment.

Each staff member must know how to cope with many questions and problems brought up by parents, and if he or she cannot help, they must have access to those who can. These requirements can be met only when staff members work closely with each other in all the varied circumstances from simple to complex, from triumph to tragedy. Formal and informal meetings take place regularly to discuss the technical and family aspects of care. As a given problem may require, some or all of several persons (including families, nurses, social workers, physicians, chaplains and others) may convene to exchange information and reach decisions. Thus, staff and parents function more or less as a small community in which a concerted attempt is made to ensure that each member may participate in and know about the major decisions that concern him or her. However, the physician takes appropriate initiative in final decision making, so that the family will not have to bear that heavy burden alone.

For several years, the responsibilities of attending pediatricians have been assumed chiefly by ourselves, who, as a result, have become acquainted intimately with the problems of infants, the staff, and the parents. Our almost constant availability to staff, private pediatricians and parents has resulted in the raising of more and more ethical questions about various aspects of intensive care for critically ill and congenitally deformed infants. The penetrating questions and challenges, particularly of knowledgeable parents (such as physicians, nurses, or lawyers), brought increasing doubts about the wisdom of many of the decisions that seemed to parents to be predicated chiefly on technical considerations. Some thought their child had a right to die since he could not live well or effectively. Others thought that society should pay the costs of care that may be so destructive to the family economy. Often, too, the parents' or siblings' rights to relief from the seemingly pointless, crushing burdens were important considerations. It seemed right to yield to parent wishes in several cases as physicians have done for generations. As a result, some treatments were withheld or stopped with the knowledge that earlier death and relief from suffering would result. Such options were explored with the less knowledgeable parents to ensure that their consent for treatment of their defective children was truly informed. As Eisenberg[8] pointed out regarding the application of technology, "At long last, we are beginning to ask, not *can* it be done, but *should* it be done?" In lengthy, frank discussions, the anguish of the parents was shared, and attempts were made to support fully the reasoned choices, whether for active treatment and rehabilitation or for an early death.

To determine the extent to which death resulted from withdrawing or withholding treatment, we examined the hospital records of all children who died from January 1, 1970, through June 30, 1972.

RESULTS

In total, there were 299 deaths; each was classified in one of two categories; deaths in Category 1 resulted from pathologic conditions in spite of the treatment given; 256 (86 percent) were in this category. Of these, 66 percent were the result of respiratory problems or complications associated with extreme prematurity (birth weight under 1000 g.) Congenital heart disease and other anomalies accounted for an additional 22 percent (Table 1).

Deaths in Category 2 were associated with severe impairment, usually from congenital disorders (Table 2): 43 (14 percent) were in this group. These deaths or their timing were associated with discontinuance or withdrawal of treatment. The mean duration of life in Category 2 (Table 3) was greater than that in Category 1. This was the result of a mean life of 55 days for eight infants who became chronic cardiopulmonary cripples but for whom prolonged and intensive efforts were made in the hope of eventual recovery. They were infants who were dependent on oxygen, digoxin and diuretics, and most of them had been treated for idiopathic respiratory-distress syndrome with high oxygen concentrations and positive-pressure ventilation.

Some examples of management choices in Category 2 illustrate the problems. An infant with Down's syndrome and intestinal atresia, like the much-publicized one at Johns Hopkins Hospital,[9] was not treated because his parents thought that surgery was wrong for their baby and themselves. He died several days after birth. Another child had chronic pulmonary disease after positive-pressure ventilation with high oxygen concentrations for treatment of severe idiopathic respiratory-distress syndrome. By five months of age, he still required 40 percent oxygen to survive, and even then, he was chronically dyspneic and cyanotic. He also suffered from cor pulmonale, which was difficult to control with digoxin and diuretics. The nurses, parents and physicians considered it cruel to continue, and yet difficult to stop. All were attached to this child, whose life they had tried so hard to make worthwhile. The family had endured high expenses (the hospital bill exceeding $15,000), and the strains of the illness were believed to be threatening the marriage bonds and to be causing sibling behavioral disturbances. Oxygen supplementation was stopped, and the child died in about three hours. The family settled down and 18 months later had another baby, who was healthy.

A third child had meningomyelocele, hydrocephalus and major anomalies of every organ in the pelvis. When the parents understood the limits of medical care and rehabilitation, they believed no treatment should be given. She died at five days of age.

We have maintained contact with most families of children in Category 2. Thus far, these families appear to have experienced a normal mourning for their losses. Although some have exhibited doubts that the choices were correct, all appear to be as effective in their lives as they were before this experience. Some claim that their profoundly moving experience has provided a deeper meaning in life, and from this they believe they have become more effective people.

Members of all religious faiths and atheists were participants as parents and as staff in these experiences. There appeared to be no relation between participation and a person's religion. Repeated participation in these troubling events did not appear to reduce the worry of the staff about the awesome nature of the decisions.

DISCUSSION

That decisions are made not to treat severely defective infants may be no surprise to those familiar with special-care facilities. All laymen and professionals familiar with our nursery appeared to set some limits upon their application of treatment to extend life or to investigate a pathologic process. For example, an experienced nurse said about one child, "We lost him several weeks ago. Isn't it time to quit?" In another case, a house officer said to a physician investigating an aspect of a child's disease, "For this child, don't you think it's time to turn off your curiosity so you can turn on your kindness?" Like many others, these children eventually acquired the "right to die."

Arguments among staff members and families for and against such decisions were based on varied notions of the rights and interests of defective infants, their families, professionals and society. They were also related to varying ideas about prognosis. Regarding the infants, some contended that individuals should have a right to die in some circumstances such as anencephaly, hydranencephaly, and some severely deforming and incapacitating conditions. Such very defective individuals were considered to have little or no hope of achieving meaningful "humanhood."[10] For example, they have little or no capacity to love or be loved. They are often cared for in facilities that have been characterized as "hardly more than dying bins,"[11] an assessment with which, in our experience, knowledgeable parents (those who visited chronic-care facilities for placement of their children) agreed. With institutionalized well children, social participation may be essentially nonexistent, and maternal deprivation severe; this is known to have an adverse, usually disastrous, effect upon the child.[12] The situation for the defective child is probably worse, for he is restricted socially both by his need for care and by his defects. To escape "wrongful life,"[13] a fate rated as worse than death, seemed right. In this regard, Lasagna[14] notes, "We may, as a society, scorn the civilizations that slaughtered their infants, but our present treatment of the retarded is in some ways more cruel."

Others considered allowing a child to die wrong for several reasons. The person most involved, the infant, had no voice in the decision. Prognosis was not always exact, and a few children with extensive care might live for months, and occasionally years. Some might survive and function satisfactorily. To a few persons, withholding treatment and accepting death was condemned as criminal.

Families had strong but mixed feelings about management decisions. Living with the handicapped is clearly a family affair, and families of deformed infants thought there were limits to what they could bear or should be expected to bear. Most of them wanted maximal efforts to sustain life and to rehabilitate the handicapped; in such cases, they were supported fully. However, some families, especially those having children with severe defects, feared that they and their other children would become socially enslaved, economically deprived, and permanently stigmatized, all perhaps for a lost cause. Such a state of "chronic sorrow" until death has been described by Olshansky.[15] In some cases, families considered the death of the child right both for the child and for the family. They asked if that choice could be theirs or their doctors.

As Feifel has reported,[16] physicians on the whole are reluctant to deal with the issues. Some, particularly specialists based in the medical center, gave specific reasons for this disinclination. There was a feeling that to "give up" was disloyal to the cause of the profession. Since major research, teaching and patient-care efforts were being made, professionals expected to discover, transmit and apply knowledge and skills; patients and families were supposed to co-operate fully even if they were not always grateful. Some physicians recognized that the wishes of families went against their own, but they were resolute. They commonly agreed that if they were the parents of defective children, withholding treatment would be the most desirable for them. However, they argued that aggressive management was indicated for others. Some believed that allowing death as a management option was euthanasia and must be stopped for fear of setting a "poor ethical example" or for fear of personal prosecution or damage to their clinical departments or to the medical center as a whole. Alexander's report on Nazi Germany[17] was cited in some cases as providing justification for pressing the effort to combat disease. Some persons were concerned about the loss through death of "teaching material." They feared the training of professionals for the care of defective children in the future and the advancing of the state of the art would be compromised. Some parents who became aware of this concern thought their children should not become experimental subjects.

Practicing pediatricians, general practitioners and obstetricians were often familiar with these families and were usually sympathetic with their views. However, since they were more distant from the special-care nursery than the specialists of the medical center, their influence was often minimal. As a result, families received little support from them, and tension in community-medical relations was a recurring problem.

Infants with severe types of meningomyelocele precipitated the most controversial decisions. Several decades ago, those who survived this condition beyond a few weeks usually became hydrocephalic and retarded, in addition to being crippled and deformed. Without modern treatment, they died earlier.[18] Some may have been killed or at least not resuscitated at birth.[19] From the early 1960's, the tendency has been to treat vigorously all infants with meningomyelocele. As advocated by Zachary[20] and Shurtleff,[21] aggressive management of these children became the rule in our unit as in many others. Infants were usually referred quickly. Parents routinely signed permits for operation though rarely had they seen their children's defects or had the nature of various management plans and their respective prognoses clearly explained to them. Some physicians believed that parents were too upset to understand the nature of the problems and the options for care. Since they believed informed consent had no meaning in these circumstances, they either ignored the parents or simply told them that the child needed an operation on the back as the first step in correcting several defects. As a result, parents often felt completely left out while the activities of care proceeded at a brisk pace.

Some physicians experienced in the care of these children and familiar with the impact of such conditions upon families had early reservations about this plan of care.[22] More recently, they were influenced by the pessimistic appraisal of vigorous management schemes in some cases.[5] Meningomyelocele, when treated vigorously, is associated with higher survival rates,[21] but the achievement of satisfactory rehabilitation is at best difficult and usually impossible for almost all who are severely affected. Knowing this, some physicians and some families[23] decide against treatment of the most severely affected. If treatment is not carried out, the child's condition will usually deteriorate from further brain damage, urinary-tract infections and orthopedic difficulties, and death can be expected much earlier. Two thirds may be dead by three months, and over 90 percent by one year of age. However, the quality of life during that time is poor, and the strains on families are great, but not necessarily greater than with treatment.[24] Thus, both treatment and nontreatment constitute unsatisfactory dilemmas for everyone, especially for the child and his family. When maximum treatment was viewed as unacceptable by families and physicians in our unit, there was a growing tendency to seek early death as a management option, to avoid that cruel choice of gradual, often slow, but progressive deterioration of the child who was required under these circumstances in effect to kill himself. Parents and the staff then asked if his dying needed to be prolonged. If not, what were the most appropriate medical responses?

Is it possible that some physicians and some families may join in a conspiracy to deny the right of a defective child to live or die? Either could occur. Prolongation of the dying process by resident physicians having a vested interest in their careers has been described by Sudnow.[25] On the other hand, from the fatigue of working long and hard some physicians may give up too soon, assuming that their cause is lost. Families, similarly, may have mixed motives. They may demand death to obtain relief from the high costs and the tensions inherent in suffering, but their sense of guilt in this thought may produce the opposite demand, perhaps in violation of the sick person's rights. Thus the challenge of deciding what course to take can be most tormenting for the family and the physician. Unquestionably, not facing the issue would appear to be the easier course, at least temporarily; no doubt many patients, families, and physicians decline to join in an effort to solve the problems. They can readily assume that what is being done is right and sufficient and ask no questions. But pretending there is no decision to be made is an arbitrary and potentially devastating decision of default. Since families and patients must live with the problems one way or another in any case, the physician's failure to face the issues may constitute a victimizing abandonment of patients and their families in times of greatest need. As Lasagna[14] pointed out, "There is no place for the physician to hide."

Can families in the shock resulting from the birth of a defective child understand what faces them? Can they give truly "informed consent" for treatment or withholding treatment?

Some of our colleagues answer no to both questions. In our opinion, if families regardless of background are heard sympathetically and at length and are given information and answers to their questions in words they understand, the problems of their children as well as the expected benefits and limits of any proposed care can be understood clearly and in practically all instances. Parents *are* able to understand the implications of such things as chronic dyspnea, oxygen dependency, incontinence, paralysis, contractures, sexual handicaps and mental retardation.

Another problem concerns who decides for a child. It may be acceptable for a person to reject treatment and bring about his own death. But it is quite a different situation when others are doing this for him. We do not know how often families and their physicians will make just decisions for severely handicapped children. Clearly, this issue is central in evaluation of the process of decision making that we have described. But we also ask, if these parties cannot make such decisions justly, who can?

We recognize great variability and often much uncertainty in prognoses and in family capacities to deal with defective newborn infants. We also acknowledge that there are limits of support that society can or will give to assist handicapped persons and their families. Severely deforming conditions that are associated with little or no hope of a functional existence pose painful dilemmas for the layman and professionals who must decide how to cope with severe handicaps. We believe the burdens of decision making must be borne by families and their professional advisers because they are most familiar with the respective situations. Since families primarily must live with and are most affected by the decisions, it therefore appears that society and the health professions should provide only general guidelines for decision making. Moreover, since variations between situations are so great, and the situations themselves so complex, it follows that much latitude in decision making should be expected and tolerated. Otherwise, the rules of society or the policies most convenient for medical technologists may become cruel masters of human beings instead of their servants. Regarding any "allocation of death"[26] policy we readily acknowledge that the extreme excesses of Hegelian "rational utility" under dictatorships must be avoided.[17] Perhaps it is less recognized that the uncontrolled application of medical technology may be detrimental to individuals and families. In this regard, our views are similar to those of Waitzkin and Stoekle.[27] Physicians may hold excessive power over decision making by limiting or controlling the information made available to patients and families. It seems appropriate that the profession be held accountable for presenting fully all management options and their unexpected consequences. Also, the public should be aware that professionals often face conflicts of interest that may result in decisions against individual preferences.

What are the legal implications of actions like those described in this paper? Some persons may argue that the law has been broken, and others would contend otherwise. Perhaps more than anything else, the public and professional silence on a major social taboo and some common practices has been broken further. That seems appropriate, for out of the ensuing dialogue perhaps better choices for patients and families can be made. If working out these dilemmas in ways such as those we suggest is in violation of the law, we believe the law should be changed.

TABLE 1

PROBLEMS CAUSING DEATH IN CATEGORY 1

Problem	No. of Deaths	Percentage
Respiratory	108	42.2
Extreme prematurity	60	23.4
Heart disease	42	16.4
Multiple anomalies	14	5.5
Other	32	12.5
TOTALS:	256	100.0

TABLE 2

PROBLEMS ASSOCIATED WITH DEATH IN CATEGORY 2

Problem	No. of Deaths	Percentage
Multiple anomalies	15	34.9
Trisomy	8	18.6
Cardiopulmonary	8	18.6
Meningomyelocele	7	16.3
Other central-nervous-system defects	3	7.0
Short-bowel syndrome	2	4.6
TOTALS:	43	100.0

TABLE 3

SELECTED COMPARISONS OF 256 CASES IN CATEGORY 1
AND 43 IN CATEGORY 2

Attribute	Category 1	Category 2
Mean length of life	4.8 days:	7.5 days:
Standard deviation	8.8	34.3
Range	1-69	1-150
Portion living for < 2 days	50.0%	12.0%

1. Wegeman, M.E.: "Annual Summary of Vital Statistics—1970." *Pediatrics,* 48:979-983, 1971.

2. Swyer, P. R.: "The Regional Organization of Special Care for the Neonate." *Pediatr. Clin. North Am.,* 17:761-776. 1970.

3. Rawlings, G., Reynold, E.O.R., Stewart, A., et al: "Changing Prognosis for Infants of Very Low Birth Weight." *Lancet,* 1:516-519. 1971.

4. Freeman, E.: "The God Committee." *New York Times Magazine,* May 21, 1972, pp. 84-90.

5. Lorber, J.: "Results of Treatment of Myelomeningocele." *Dev. Med. Child Neurol.* 13:279-303. 1971.

6. Slater, E.: "Health Service or Sickness Service." *Br. Med. J.* 4:734-736. 1971.

7. Klaus, M. H., Kennell, J. H.: "Mothers Separated From Their Newborn Infants." *Pediatr. Clin. North Am.* 17:1015-1037. 1970.

8. Eisenberg, L: "The Human Nature of Human Nature." *Science.* 176:123-128. 1972.

9. Report of the Joseph P. Kennedy Foundation International Symposium on Human Rights. Retardation and Research. Washington, D.C., The John F. Kennedy Center for the Performing Arts. October 16, 1971.

10. Fletcher, J.: "Indicators of Humanhood: A Tentative Profile of Man." The Hastings Center Report, Vol. 2, No. 5. Hastings-on-Hudson, New York. Institute of Society, Ethics and the Life Sciences, November, 1972, pp. 1-4.

11. Freeman, H.E., Brim, O.G., Jr., Williams, G.: New Dimensions of Dying. The Dying Patient. Edited by O.G. Brim, Jr., New York. Russell Sage Foundation, 1970, pp. xiii-xxvi.

12. Spitz, R.A.: "Hospitalism: An Inquiry into the Genesis of Psychiatric Conditions in Early Childhood." *Psychoanal. Study Child.* 1:53-74. 1945.

13. Engelhardt, H. T., Jr.: "Euthanasia and Children: The Injury of Continued Existence." *J. Pediatr.* 83:170-171. 1973.

14. Lasagna, L.: *Life, Death and the Doctor.* New York. Alfred A. Knopf, 1968.

15. Olshansky, S.: "Chronic Sorrow: A Response to Having a Mentally Defective Child." *Soc. Casework,* 43:190-193. 1962.

16. Feifel, H.: "Perception of Death." *Acad. Sci.* 164:669-677. Ann, N.Y., 1969.

17. Alexander, L.: "Medical Science Under Dictatorship." *N. Engl. J. Med.* 241:39-47, 1949.

18. Laurence, K. M. and Tew, B. J.: "Natural History of Spina Bifida Cystica and Cranium Bifidum Cysticum: Major Central Nervous System Malformations in South Wales. Part IV." *Arch. Dis. Child.* 46:127-138. 1971.

19. Forrest, D.M.: "Modern Trends in the Treatment of Spina Bifida: Early Closure in Spina Bifida—Results and Problems." *Proc. R. Soc. Med.* 60:763-767, 1967.

20. Zachary, R. B.: "Ethical and Social Aspects of Treatment of Spina Bifida." *Lancet,* 2:274-276. 1968.

21. Shurtleff, D. B.: Care of the Myelodysplastic Patient. Ambulatory Pediatrics. Edited by M. Green, R. Haggerty. Philadelphia, W.B. Saunders Company, 1968, pp. 726-741.

22. Matson, D. D.: "Surgical Treatment of Myelomeningocele." *Pediatrics.* 42:225-227. 1968.

23. MacKeith, R. C.: "A New Look at Spina Bifida Aperta." *Dev. Med. Child Neurol.* 13:277-278. 1971.

24. Hide, D.W., Williams, H.P., Ellis, H.L.: "The Outlook for the Child with a Myelomeningocele for Whom Early Surgery was Considered Inadvisable." *Dev. Med. Child. Neurol.* 14:304-307. 1972.

25. Sudnow, D.: *Passing On.* Engelwood Cliffs, New Jersey, Prentice Hall. 1967.

26. Manning, B.: Legal and Policy Issues in the Allocation of Death. The Dying Patient. Edited by O. G. Brim, Jr., New York, Russell Sage Foundation, 1970. pp. 253-274.

27. Waitzkin, H., Stoeckle, J. D.: "The Communication of Information About Illness." *Adv. Psychosom. Med.* 8:180-215, 1972.

INTELLECTUAL AND PERCEPTUAL-MOTOR CHARACTERISTICS OF TREATED MYELOMENINGOCELE CHILDREN

Pegeen L. Soare, M.A.
AND
Anthony J. Raimondi, M.D.

ABSTRACT

This is a prospective study of 173 treated myelomeningocele children, 133 of whom developed hydrocephalus (and were shunted) and 40 who did not. The hydrocephalus was diagnosed neuroradiologically. Eighty siblings were tested as a control group. Sixty-three percent of myelomeningoceles with hydrocephalus had IQ's above 80, whereas 87% of those without hydrocephalus had IQ's above 80. Myelomeningoceles with hydrocephalus were significantly less intelligent than their siblings, whereas myelomeningoceles without hydrocephalus were not significantly different. When myelomeningoceles and their siblings were matched by age and IQ, the former scored significantly lower on a test of perceptual-motor functioning. When myelomeningoceles with and without hydrocephalus were similarly matched, those with hydrocephalus scored lower. Hypotheses as to the etiology of the perceptual-motor deficit were discussed. The inverse relationships between site of the sac and IQ, and sensory level and IQ, were found to be dependent upon the association of higher level sacs and sensory loss with hydrocephalus. Patients' IQ was related to family income and education.

INTRODUCTION

With few exceptions,[1,2,3,4,5,6,7] published reports of the intelligence of myelomeningocele children with (mm/h) and without (mm) hydrocephalus have limited themselves to analyzing the natural history of non-operatively treated hydrocephalus. By and large, these studies have been retrospective, based upon accumulation of varying numbers of survivors and have been wanting in valid norms. Similary, the appraisals of survival, quality of survival, and impact of the mm and mm/h child on his home and environment have been made from analyses of groups of children whose management has not been described.

As a first step in studying these children we established the criteria for diagnosing hydrocephalus in the myelomeningocele child, determining precisely when a shunt is no longer functioning, comparing intellectual quotients with the presence or absence of hydrocephalus (treated, in the former event), using the sibs as the norm, and identifying (neuroradiologically) the nature and degree of brain dysplasia.[8,9,10,11,12,13]

There is, at the present time, considerable interest in the matter of whether to treat mm children and, if so, whether they should all be treated . . . or whether treatment should be offered only to those children who may be expected to "live a meaningful life." Criteria upon which such a decision may be based are wanting, though some rather arbitrary findings at birth (such as level of the myelomeningocele sac, paraplegia, hydrocephalus) have been suggested. In fact, one author has carried prediction to an extreme, reporting such a poor prognosis for myelomeningocele children with a thoraco-lumbar lesion, for example, irrespective of the presence of hydrocephalus, that he recommends withholding all forms of treatment.[1,2]

It is the purpose of this paper to present the results of our prospective study of the intellectual development of 173 myelomeningocele children—133 shunted for hydrocephalus (mm/hs) and 40 who never developed hydrocephalus (mm)— data which should be compared to the nontreated (mm/h) and to siblings of all myelomeningocele children, since intellectual and social potentials are two important parameters by which the quality of survival may be evaluated. It is desirable that this information be presented now that we are all attempting to establish criteria upon which to base a decision to treat, or not to treat. We identified four goals:

(1) To determine whether mm/hs perform better on IQ tests if the hydrocephalus is diagnosed early, treated immediately the diagnosis is made, and then followed closely for malfunctioning of the shunt system . . . considering "arrested" hydrocephalus a pathologic condition.

2) To explore the inter-relationships between the site of the sac, hydrocephalus, and IQ.

3) To establish meaningful norms for our sample, giving due consideration to what might be expected of each child according to his socio-economic background.

4) To determine whether perceptual-motor deficits are present and, if so, in mm, mm/hs or both groups.

SUBJECTS

This series consists of 173 children with myelomeningocele, 133 of whom are mm/hs and 40 mm. Those children with hydrocephalus, therefore, make up 77% of the total sample. These cases were selected only on the basis of survival to the time of testing. Since patients were not routinely tested until 16-18 months of age, children who were too young (5), who are scheduled to be seen for the first time in the next six months (18), and who had died before they were old enough to be tested (68) are not included. We have also necessarily excluded 73 myelomeningocele children who were lost to follow-up before we could test them the first time (almost all had moved). Therefore, the 173 tested myelomeningocele children represent slightly more than half (51%) of the total number managed by us.

Since Children's Memorial Hospital receives many referrals from outside the immediate vicinity, our sample is quite heterogeneous. The racial and ethnic composition of our sample is: white, 78%; Spanish-American, 11%; black, 11%. Our research design called for the testing of a sibling of each patient. Thus far we have tested 61 siblings (2 half-sibs) of mm/hs and 19 siblings of mm.

Seven of the mm/hs patients are currently without shunts, 2 following a posterior fossa decompression and the others following ventriculitis. Five mm/hs died since they were initially tested. The mean IQ of those 5 was 60. The average age at the time of death was 3 years, 3 months.

Regarding closure of the myelomeningocele sac, if it was covered with skin, no surgery was recommended at birth. If it was not covered with skin, repair was routinely performed within 24 hours of birth. If, for reasons such as delayed referral, the child could not be operated on during the first day of life, the sac was treated with 10 minute surgical scrubs every 6 hours (daily cultures were taken) until the area was negative for bacterial growth for five consecutive days, at which time the sac was closed surgically. There was no correlation between surgical closure of the sac and survival, the onset of hydrocephalus, or neurological deficit.

The diagnosis of hydrocephalus, and the distinction between aqueductal occlusion and constrictive hydrocephalus, was made neuroradiologically in all children, as was the identification of the Arnold-Chiari II anomaly, associated tentorial dysplasia, mesencephalic hyperplasia, microgyri, and buckling of the medulla oblongata on the medulla spinalis.[8,9] All children diagnosed as having hydrocephalus were shunted immediately the diagnosis was made, and then followed closely thereafter . . . with revisions being performed on an emergency basis whenever indicated.

METHODS

The instruments used to evaluate these children were: 1) the Stanford-Binet Intelligence Scale, From L-M; 2) the Cattell Infant Intelligence Scale, a downward extension of the Stanford-Binet; 3) the Vineland Social Maturity Scale, which measures self-help skills; 4) the Goodenough-Harris Draw-a-Man test and, 5) the Beery-Buktenica Developmental Test of Visual-Motor Integration, or V.M.I.,[14] which measures perceptual-motor skills. The latter was chosen over other perceptual-motor tests because it may be applied to the widest age ranges.

The two tests involving drawing, the VMI and the Draw-a-Man, cannot be given until the child has the fine motor skills to make a reasonable attempt (in average children at about the age of 4 to 4½ years). The average chronological age at the time of the first psychological test for the mm/hs was 3.9 years with a range from 11 months to 12 years and 4 months. For the 40 mm patients the average chronological age was 7.3 years, with a range from 10 months to 18 years and 11 months.

We obtained information from the families of our patients relevant to the following variables: 1) size of family; 2) occupation of the breadwinner; 3) income; 4) age of parents at birth of patient; and, 5) education of the parents. As part of the research design the parents were requested to bring in for testing the next older sibling of the patient. It is generally accepted that there is a correlation of about .50 between the IQ's of full siblings in a family.[15] It has been shown that a child's socioeconomic status correlates with IQ at the level of about .20 to .40.[16] Thus, the rationale for getting the sibling's IQ and the socioeconomic data was to try to determine as accurately as possible the patient's potential for development outside the disease entity.

In order to assess the effects of socioeconomic variables, an index or composite score, based on the mother's education and the family income was developed. The U.S. Bureau of the Census classification system was used so that our sample could be compared to national averages. Data on education and family income were based upon figures for the year 1969. These composite scores were then split at the sample median, and the IQ's of those above the median were compared to those below the median.

The Developmental Test of Visual-Motor Integration[14] was used as an indicator of perceptual-motor functioning. This test yields an age equivalency score which for normal children should be equivalent to the chronological age. Fifty-nine of the 133 mm/hs had VMI scores. Thirty-eight siblings of these patients were the control group. Twenty-nine of the 40 mm had VMI scores. Twelve of their siblings were the control group. The children who did not have VMI scores were either too young or too retarded.

In order to assess the effect of length of hospitalization upon perceptual-motor functioning, the 10 children with the greatest perceptual-motor disabilities were compared to the 10 with the least perceptual-motor disabilities as to days spent in the hospital during the first three years. The mm/hs were excluded so as to reduce the obvious bias from length of stay due to the shunting procedure(s).

Information concerning the site of the myelomeningocele sac was taken from each child's medical record. Based upon this information, the following groups were formed: 1) occipito-cervical and cervical; 2) thoraco-lumbar and thoraco-lumbo-sacral. Also obtained from each child's medical record was the most recent sensory level. All patients with sensory levels at T12 and above were combined into one group, and those with "no sensory loss" into another. Based on the IQ scores, an *a posteriori* decision was made to combine levels L1 through L4 into one group and levels L5 through S5 into another.

RESULTS

Children whose myelomeningocele was repaired on the day of birth, or the following day, were classified as being repaired within the first 24 hours. As may be seen from Table 1, 43% of all myelomeningocele children were operated upon within the first 24 hours.

The mean age at the time of initial shunt placement for mm/hs was 2.6 months (standard deviation 6.2 months). In a previous study we showed that IQ is not related to the number of shunt revisions.[13] For the sample of 133 mm/hs reported here, the mean number of revisions per child was 3.6 (standard deviation 3.6).

Table 2 shows the distribution of shunt revisions over time after the initial shunt placement for the mm/hs. All patients who were at least 2 years of age at the time the analysis was done were included in the "2-5 year" groups. Only 75 patients were over 5 years of age and included in that group.

Since this is a longitudinal study, each child is re-examined at approximately yearly intervals. New patients are added continuously. Thus far, 2 patients have been seen 5 times, 9 have been seen 4 times, 23 have been seen 3 times, 56 have been seen twice, and 82 have been seen once. Between the first and most recent tests, 41 patients increased in IQ, 45 decreased, and 4 showed no change. The average change over all patients was only +.33 IQ points. Of those tested more than once, 52% showed a change of ± 10 points and 26% increased or decreased from 11 to 20 points. Only 11, or 12%, changed by more than 20 points and, of these, 7 were in a positive direction. All results discussed in this paper are based on the most recent IQ score obtained. The mean IQ's for the mm and mm/hs patients and their siblings are presented in Table 3.

A t test was done between the means of mm and mm/hs groups. The results showed a significant difference at the .001 level ($t = 3.61$), indicating that the mm group was significantly brighter than the mm/hs. Of the mm/hs, 63% had IQ's above 80 and of the mm, 87% had IQ's above 80.

Sixty-one siblings of mm/hs were tested as controls. The IQ's of the 61 patient-sib pairs were examined. The means were significantly different, $t = 5.50$, $p < .01$. A correlation was done between sib IQ and patient IQ. In the normal populations such a correlation should be about .50. For our 61 pairs the correlation was .21, which was not significant. Nineteen sibs of mm children were tested as controls and IQ's compared. A t test showed no significant difference between the two. The correlation between the 2 groups was .52, which was significant ($p < .01$).

A socioeconomic index based upon mother's education and family income was devised for our total sample and these index scores split at the median. The mean IQ of those patients above the median was 100.6 (standard deviation 20.0), $n = 85$, and those below the median 79.8 (standard deviation 24.8), $n = 85$. The difference between the two means was significant at the .001 level ($t = 6.0$), indicating that the group above the median had higher IQ's. Approximately equal numbers of mm and mm/hs were above and below the median.

We were interested in determining how the perceptual-motor age scores compared with the actual chronological age scores (Table 4). A t test for related means showed a significant difference between VMI ages and chronological ages for the mm/hs ($t = 9.21$, $p < .001$) and mm ($t = 4.41$, $p < .001$), with the VMI ages lower. However, a t test between chronological ages and VMI ages for the siblings was also significant ($t = 3.08$, $p < .01$). It seemed logical that VMI scores should be related to chronological ages, since the VMI scores are not age standardized. The correlation between VMI age and chronological age for all myelomeningocele children was .70, $n = 88$, $p < .001$. It was also logical to investigate the possibility of a relationship between VMI scores and IQ. A partial correlation was done between VMI age and IQ with chronological age partialled out. The correlation was .51, $n = 88$, which was significant at the .001 level, indicating that those patients with high IQ's tended also to have high VMI scores.

A different statistical procedure had to be used to compare patients with sibs on the VMI since differences in IQ and chronological age between the patient and sibs would bias the results (as indicated by the correlations in the preceeding paragraph).

A selection of patients and sibs was made on the basis of those who could be matched *both* according to chronological age (within ±2 years of each other) and IQ (within ±15 points of each other). This procedure provided 14 pairs. The difference scores (chronological age minus VMI age) of both groups were then compared. Table 5 shows that the matching procedure was successful in that the mean C.A. and IQ for the patients and sibs were very close.

A *t* test for related means showed that there was a significant difference between patients and sibs (Table 5), indicating that the patients did more poorly on the perceptual-motor tests than did their siblings.

In order to compare the perceptual-motor skills of mm and mm/hs, the same type of matching procedure was used. Patients were selected from 2 groups and matched according to the criteria of age and IQ (the means are presented in Table 6). This resulted in 26 pairs. The difference scores (CA minus VMI) were then compared. A *t* test for related means showed that there was a significant difference between mm and mm/hs (Table 6), indicating that the mm/hs had more perceptual-motor difficulties than did the mm.

The ten children with the greatest perceptual-motor difficulties were compared to the 10 with the least difficulties as to days spent in hospital during the first 3 years of life. The difference between the two groups was not significant. When the 2 groups were compared as to days spent in hospital during the first five years of life, the groups were significantly different (p <.05) with the "least difficulties" group having spent fewer days in the hospital.

The relationship between perceptual-motor deficit and level of the sac was then studied. Only one of the 10 children with the most difficulties had a lesion within the lumbosacral area. All others were within the lumbar or thoracic area. Of the children with the least difficulties, 6 had lesions within the lumbosacral area and 4 within the lumbar and thoracic areas. The Fisher Exact Probability Test[17] showed that there was a significant association between higher lesions and greater perceptual-motor difficulties (p < .05, one-tailed).

Another area of interest was to determine whether there was a relationship between the level of the myelomeningocele sac, sensory level, and IQ, *independent of the effects of hydrocephalus.* In order to test for this, we analyzed the mm and mm/hs groups separately. The mean IQ scores for mm and mm/hs, listed according to the site of the myelomeningocele sac, are presented in Table 7.

Excluded from Table 7 were three mm/hs with a thoracic level (IQ's: 94, 106, 84) and 3 mm with a thoracic level (IQ's: 64, 114, 77). The group with lesions within the occipitocervical areas was excluded from the analysis of variance because the requirement of homogeneity of variance was not met (the standard deviation was too different from the others). The deletion of this group does not affect the impact of the relationship. An analysis of variance was done on the IQ scores of the mm/hs and was found not to be significant, indicating that the mean IQ's of patients within the three different levels were not significantly different from each other.

For the mm, a *t* test was done between the lumbar groups and the lumbosacral and sacral groups and was also found not to be significant. When an analysis of variance was done on the means for both groups together, it was significant at the .01 level, indicating that the IQ's of the myelomeningoceles differ significantly according to the level of the sac.

As a method of comparison, groups were formed on the basis of the sensory level. These data are presented in Table 8.

An analysis of variance was done on the mean IQ scores for the mm/hs and was not significant, indicating that the mean IQ's of the patients within the four sensory levels were not significantly different from each other. An analysis of variance was done on the mm group (excluding T4-T12, which had only one person). It, also, was not significant, indicating that the mean IQ's of the patients within the three sensory levels were not significantly different from each other. When the means of both groups were analyzed together, a significant difference was found, p < .05, indicating that the IQ's of the groups based upon sensory level were significantly different from each other.

DISCUSSION

Our results, showing mm/hs performing at a significantly lower level than mm, support a trend in the literature[16,18,19,20] in untreated hydrocephalic myelomeningoceles, although our differences are of a lesser magnitude. In fact, our data show that 63% of the mm/hs have IQ's above 80, while Merrill et al.[6] reported 10% and Stephen[18] 40% above 80 for mm/h (untreated hydrocephalic myelomeningoceles). Although it is difficult to compare results with treated (mm/hs) and untreated (mm/h) hydrocephalics because of the different survival rates, it is true that the presence of hydrocephalus in a child with myelomeningocele decreases his chances for normal intelligence. Though surgical treatment of the hydrocephalus increases the chances for normal intelligence, myelomeningoceles with hydrocephalus, as a group, are still significantly less intelligent than their normal siblings and also less intelligent than myelomeningoceles without hydrocephalus. This is particularly significant since 23% of our myelomeningocele children do not become hydrocephalic!

The percentage of mm/hs with IQ's above 80 (63%) is higher than that reported by Lorber[1] of 52% and 57% for two series, Ames and Schut[4] of 48% and Spain[3] of about 33% . . . who were considered "normal." Lorber's percentages of mm with IQ's above 80 are also lower than those reported here (83% and 83% vs. our 87%). The mm we are reporting have higher IQ's than most of the other groups cited,[6,18,21] with the exception of Ames and Schut who reported 90% with an IQ of 80 or above.

We wish to discuss briefly our results with regard to two of Lorber's prognostic criteria.[1,2] First, the thoracolumbar lesion: he found that one-half of the survivors were of normal intelligence, although none had an IQ over 100 and 14% had an IQ of 60 or less. We, also, found that about one-half of our patients with a thoracolumbar lesion attain normal intelligence, that one had an IQ over 100 . . . but that *only* one had an IQ of less than 60. Aside from the fact that our patients are not doing so poorly as Lorber's, it seems that a criterion which abandons children with a 50% chance of normal intelligence is not a very sound one. The second criterion is gross enlargement of the head, defined as at least two centimeters above the 90th percentile, corrected for birth-weight. He recommends no treatment for those with severe hydrocephalus at birth, but would treat those with mild hydrocephalus. We found no correlation between the degree, or severity, of hydrocephalus prior to initial shunt, and IQ. Our results indicate that those children with severe hydrocephalus prior to shunting have just as good a chance to develop normally as those with mild hydrocephalus, provided the hydrocephalus is treated promptly.[13]

Ames and Schut[4] have stated: "We have been unable to determine at birth which of the children will be competitive and ambulatory. We have, therefore, adopted the program of operating on all children to close the defect and relieve the hydrocephalus, individualizing the time of the procedure to each patient." We agree with this approach.

The question arises as to why the patients in this study seem to be doing better than those reported in other studies. One explanation may be that we insist upon angiographic evidence of ventricular enlargement and increased intraventricular pressure before diagnosing hydrocephalus.[8] Thus, those children shunted are those definitely determined to have both increased intraventricular size and intracranial pressure. Newborn with myelomeningocele are not shunted prophylactically. They are kept under close observation and shunted only if, and when, hydrocephalus is diagnosed neuroradiologically. We do not consider "arrested" hydrocephalus to be a nonpathogenic process. Consequently, the child who may be designated elsewhere as having "arrested" hydrocephalus, and thus not shunted, is shunted by us.

Our results with the VMI indicate that the perceptual-motor age equivalences for mm and mm/hs are significantly below the chronological ages. Since the mean IQ's of the mm and mm/hs were 101.4 and 95 respectively (Table 4), one should not seek an explanation in the positive correlation between VMI and IQ. The emphasis of the results may seem to be attenuated by the fact that the sibs also were found to be functioning below expected levels on the VMI. This may be explained by a ceiling effect operating with 9 sibs . . . that is, the test was not able to measure the upper limits of their ability. Even with this artificial restriction, however, the sibs averaged only .8 years behind, while the mm/hs averaged 2.3 years and the mm 1.9 years behind (Table 4). Our data lend support to other studies showing perceptual-motor problems in children with spina bifida,[7,19,20,22] although it has not been clear in the literature exactly which groups suffered from these problems. Badell-Ribera et al.[19] reported indications of such problems only for mm/h while we found discrepancies for both mm and mm/hs. Miller and Sethi[22] did not include mm in their study and Sand et al.[20] did not report whether either mm or mm/h were significantly different from normal, although they were different from each other.

There are at least three possible explanations for the apparent perceptual-motor deficit. One is that it is a function of the disease entity: a form of brain damage associated with the Arnold-Chiari malformation. The specific effects of cerebral dysplasia, heterotopia, and vascular changes remain to be determined. Another is that the deficit is related to the decreased stimulation resulting from prolonged hospital stays and reduced opportunities for exploration. The third is that it is a combination of the two. Beery[14] has hypothesized that "form copy may be a relatively sensitive measure of lack of neurological integrity, whether this is disorganization resulting from damage or failure of organization resulting from inadequate experience."

Shepherd[23] found that normally intelligent children, having a history of chronic illness, performed below expected levels on visual-motor perception tasks. His observations were made on 47 second-graders each of whom had been confined to bed for a period of at least three consecutive months between the ages of 1 and 6 years. The nature of the illness was not stated. Shepherd's study lends some support to the hypothesis of experiential and sensory deprivation.

Our results concerning perceptual-motor difficulties were examined in an attempt to support or reject the hypothesis. Mm/hs were found to have more perceptual-motor problems than mm: an obvious explanation would be that the difference is due to brain damage caused by hydrocephalus. However, that would not explain why mm have perceptual-motor problems. It has been shown that the presence of hydrocephalus is associated with the higher lesions. Thus, our group of mm/hs was distinguished from the mm by having higher level lesions as well as by having hydrocephalus. Since it was found that greater perceptual-motor problems were associated with the higher level lesions within the group with hydrocephalus, it may be that the differences between the two groups are along the "level of lesion" dimension rather than the "hydrocephalus" dimension. Since higher lesions are associated with hydrocephalus, they may also be associated with greater damage

due to the Arnold-Chiari malformation. A study of the relationship between the Arnold-Chiari malformation and both
IQ and perceptual-motor functioning has now been undertaken by us.

Because of the greater incidence of hydrocephalus in children with higher lesions, it may be that these children, as a
consequence of the greater physical involvement and restricted
mobility, are more deprived in their early learning experiences.
They are also more likely to spend more time in hospital.

We noted that children with greater perceptual-motor
problems spent more time in hospital during the first five years
of life. Time in hospital may be seen as either a causative or
resulting factor. The greater amount of time in hospital may
be a cause of perceptual-motor dysfunction, in that it contributes to experiential deprivation. It may also be the consequence of brain damage, however, since children with higher level lesions (and more perceptual-motor problems) tend to
have more surgical procedures requiring hospitalization. The
fact that there were no differences in time spent in hospital
during the first three years is inconclusive with regard to
either hypothesis. Realistically, "days in hospital" is only a
gross indicator of experiential or sensory deprivation: the
child's family interactions and home influences are probably
much more important in determining how "deprived" his experiences are within the limits of his physical capabilities.

One might ask whether these perceptual-motor deficits
represent a developmental lag rather than a true dysfunction.
Forty-one percent of our myelomeningocele children who had
VMI scores were nine years or older, and there seems to be no
indication that, as a group, they are catching up by that age.
However, since this is a longitudinal study, we hope to be
able to answer this question empirically.

Our results, indicating the presence of perceptual-motor
deficits in all myelomeningocele children (mm and mm/hs),
should be of use in advising and assisting the parents in the
performance of a full range of exercise activities on the children and in planning educational programs. Teachers should
be informed that normal IQ scores do not necessarily indicate
normal perceptual-motor development. Perhaps special programs could be developed to maximize strengths and minimize weaknesses.

The relationship between socio-economic status and IQ seems clear from our results. The children who come from families with more education and income are doing significantly better than those who come from families with lower education and income. Family background is a good predictor of IQ. The correlation between sib and patient IQ indicated that the sib IQ was not a good predictor for mm/hs (.21), but that it was for mm (.53). The low correlation for mm/hs is probably explained by the greater variability in IQ.

An association between high lesions and lower IQ has been reported,[1,2,4] but it has not heretofore been clear whether this association was independent or attributable to the relationship between high lesions and hydrocephalus. In analyzing the mm and mm/hs groups separately, we found that neither sensory level nor level of the myelomeningocele sac were significantly related to IQ. When the two groups were combined, however, there was a significant relationship between the two independent variables and IQ, children with high lesions and sensory levels having lower IQ's. This suggests that knowledge of the level of the sac or the sensory level is not a reliable predictor of IQ.

TABLE 1

Age of Repair of the Myelomeningocele

	24 hours	1 day-1 wk.	8 days-1 mo.	1 mo.*
With hydro.	60 (45%)	23 (17%)	29 (23%)	20 (15%)
Without hydro.	15 (38%)	9 (22%)	7 (18%)	9 (22%)
TOTAL:	75 (43%)	32 (18%)	36 (21%)	29 (17%)

*One child with hydro. was never repaired.

TABLE 2

Mean Number of Shunt Revisions Over Time

For 133 mm/hs

Time After Initial Shunt

	<6 mos.	6 mos.-1 yr.	1-2 yrs.	2-5 yrs.	>5 yrs.
Mean no. of revisions	1.4	.59	.61	1.04	.47
Mean cumulative no. of revisions	1.4	1.73	2.34	3.38	3.63

Of the total number of patients with shunts, 24% had no revisions, 38% had 1 to 3 revisions, 20 % had 4 to 6 revisions, and 19 % had more than 6 revisions.

TABLE 3

IQ Scores of Myelomeningoceles With and Without
Hydrocephalus and Their Sibs

Group

	mm/hs	Sibs	mm	Sibs
Mean	87.7	109.5	102.3	119.9
s.d.	24.8	17.4	19.9	13.6
n	133	61	40	19

TABLE 4

Mean IQ, Chronological Age, and VMI Scores for Myelomeningoceles

With and Without Hydrocephalus and Their Sibs

	mm/hs (n=59)	mm (n=29)	All sibs (n=50)
Scores			
IQ			
Mean	95.0	101.4	109.0
s.d.	20.1	20.0	15.4
Chronological age (yrs.)			
Mean	8.0	9.6	10.0
s.d.	2.4	3.5	3.2
V.M.I. (yrs.)			
Mean	5.7	7.7	9.2
s.d.	1.8	2.5	2.2

TABLE 5

Mean CA, IQ & Different Scores for Patients (mm/hs and mm) and Sibs

(N = 14 pairs)

	CA (yrs.)	IQ	Diff. Score (CA minus VMI)
Patients	9.3	105.5	2.1 yrs.
Sibs	9.0	106.2	.2 yrs.
			t = 3.73, p < .01

TABLE 6

Mean CA, IQ and Difference Scores for mm and mm/hs

(N = 26 pairs)

	CA (yrs.)	IQ	Diff. Score (CA minus VMI)
mm/hs	8.7	101.6	2.0 yrs.
mm	8.8	101.0	1.4 yrs.
			t = 2.26, p < .05

TABLE 7

Mean IQ Scores of mm/hs and mm by Site of the Sac*

	Occipito-cervical and Cervical	Thoraco-lumbar and Thora-columbo-sacral	Lumbar	Lumbro-sacral and Sacral
mm/hs				
Mean	72.6	84.2	84.0	92.5
s.d.	41.0	17.3	24.9	22.4
n	8	16	48	55
mm				
Mean			99.8	106.3
s.d.			14.0	21.2
n	0	0	10	25
Total				
Mean	72.6	84.2	86.7	96.8
s.d.	41.0	17.3	24.0	22.8
n	8	16	58	80

*Information not available on all patients.

TABLE 8

Mean IQ Scores of mm/hs and mm by Sensory Level

Sensory Level*

	T_4-T_{12}	L_1-L_4	L_5-S_5	Normal (excl. encephaloceles)
mm/hs				
Mean	82.9	86.9	98.8	88.8
s.d.	21.9	21.6	21.0	33.0
n	28	52	28	12
mm				
Mean	77.0	101.0	107.7	112.0
s.d.	0	19.1	24.1	18.3
n	1	20	7	8
Total				
Mean	82.7	91.0	98.9	98.1
s.d.	21.5	21.9	21.7	29.8
n	29	72	35	20

*Information not available on all patients.

REFERENCES

1. Lorber, J. "Results of treatment of myelomeningocele." *Develop. Med. Child Neurol.* 13:279-303, 1971.

2. Lorber, J. "Spina bifida cystica: results of treatment of 270 consecutive cases with criteria for selection for the future." *Arch. Dis. Childh.*, 47:854-873, 1972.

3. Spain, B. "Verbal and performance ability in preschool spina bifida children." *Develop. Med. Child Neurol. Suppl. 27,* 14:155, 1972.

4. Ames, M.D. and Schut, L. "Results of treatment of 171 consecutive myelomeningoceles—1963 to 1968." *Pediatrics,* 50, no. 3, 466-470, 1972.

5. Tew, B. and Laurence, K. "The ability and attainments of spina bifida patients born in South Wales between 1956-1962." *Develop. Med. Child Neurol. Suppl. 27,* vol. 14, no. 6, 124-131, 1972.

6. Merrill, R.E., Isom, J.B., Anslow, R.M., and Pinkerton, J.A. "Hydrocephalus and meningocele: the course of 100 patients." *Pediatrics,* 30:809-814, 1962.

7. Parsons, J. "Assessments of aptitudes in young people of school-leaving age handicapped by hydrocephalus and spina bifica cystica." *Develop. Med. Child Neurol.,* Suppl. 27, vol. 14, no. 6, 101-108, 1972.

8. Raimondi, A.J. *Pediatric Neuroradiology.* W.B. Saunders and Company, Philadelphia, Penn., Nov., 1972.

9. Raimondi, A.J. and White, H. "Cerebral angiography in the newborn and infant. I. General Principles." *Ann. Radiol.* 10:146-165, 1967.

10. Raimondi, A.J., Torres, H. and Yarzagaray, L. "Angiographic diagnosis of hydrocephalus in the newborn." *J. of Neurosurg.* 31:550, 1969.

11. Raimondi, A.J., Samuelson, G. and Yarzagaray, L. "Positive contrast (Conray 60) serial ventriculography in the normal and hydrocephalic infant." *Annales de Radiologie* 12:377-392, 1969.

12. Raimondi, A.J. "Hydrocephalus and the congenital anomalies associated with it: angiographic diagnosis." *Seminars in Roentgenology* 67:111-125, 1971.

13. Raimondi, A.J. and Soare, P. "Intellectual development in shunted hydrocephalic children." *Amer. J. Dis. Child,* 127:664-680, 1974.

14. Beery, K. *Visual-Motor Integration Monograph.* Chicago, Follet Co., 1967.

15. Fuller, J., and Thompson, W. *Behavior Genetics.* New York: John Wiley & Sons, Inc., 1960.

16. Deutsch, M., Katz, I., and Jensen, A. *Social Class, Race and Psychological Development.* New York: Holt, Rinehart, and Winston, Inc., 1968.

17. Siegel, S. *Nonparametric Statistics: For the Behavioral Sciences.* New York: McGraw-Hill, Inc., 1956.

18. Stephen, E. "Intelligence levels and educational status of children with meningomyelocele." *Develop. Med. Child Neurol.* 5:572-576, 1963.

19. Badell-Ribera, A., Shulman, K. and Paddock, N. "The relationship of non-progressive hydrocephalus to intellectual functioning in children with spina bifida cystica." *Pediatrics* 37:787-793, 1966.

20. Sand, P., Taylor, N., Rawlings, M., and Chitnis, S. "Performance of children with spina bifida manifesta on the Frostig Developmental Test of Visual Perception." *Percep. Mot. Skills* 37:539-546, 1973.

21. Kolin, I., Scherzer, A., New, B., and Garfield, M. "Studies of the school-age child with meningomyelocele: Social and emotional adaptation." *J. Pediat.*, 78:1013-1019, 1971.

22. Miller, E., and Sethi, L. "The effect of hydrocephalus on perception." *Develop. Med. Child Neurol., Suppl. 25*, vol. 13, no. 6, 77-81, 1971.

23. Shepherd, C., Jr. "Childhood chronic illness and visual motor perceptual development." *Excep. Child.* 36:39-42, 1969.

THE DEFORMED CHILD'S RIGHT TO LIFE

EUGENE F. DIAMOND, M.D.

This paper will consider the medical and moral issues concerning euthanasia in the special care nursery. For purposes of this analysis, we will consider the following case:

CASE DISCUSSION

A two-day-old full term male infant, second-born to a married middle-class, middle-income Protestant couple in their twenties, who have a normal 2-year-old girl. The pregnancy was uneventful except for excess amniotic fluid accumulation. Delivery was normal. Greenish vomiting began shortly after birth. There was slight abdominal distension and moderate dehydration. There was no evidence of cardiac abnormalities. The infant had mongoloid facies and features. X-ray of the abdomen showed intestinal obstruction. The clinical impression was Down's Syndrome and Duodenal Atresia.

After discussion with the parents, a decision was made not to operate to repair the obstruction due to the Duodenal Atresia. All feeding and fluids were withheld and the child eventually died, after fifteen days, from starvation and dehydration.

This case report is that of an actual case from Johns Hopkins hospital and has been dramatized in a movie by the Kennedy Foundation. As if to further desensitize the public to the occurrence of such management in medical circles, the Yale-New Haven Medical Center reported a series of 43 similar cases on their newborn service, in the *New England Journal of Medicine*.

It is important to examine the rationalization involved in such medical management in order to understand the implication of this new development in medical ethics and its significance for the profession and the society as a whole. The rationale is not easy to understand and a short 10 years ago would have been considered monstrous and unacceptable. Perhaps we can begin to understand if we break the elements of the physical problem down.

1. *Patients with Neither Down's Syndrome nor Duodenal Atresia.* Obviously the physician cannot kill the child and the nursery personnel cannot fail to feed it. Of relevance, here is a consideration of the parents' dominion over the child. I served on the Child Health Committee of the Illinois Medical Society during the time it was considering its Model Child Abuse Law. Implicit in the development of such laws is the concept that the parents' control of the child is limited; that they cannot injure him or kill him. This is a departure from the Roman right of "Pater Familias" which gave the father unlimited rights over his children even to the extent of killing them if he so chose. These limits on parental control were always implicit but they are now codified into law.

2. *No Down's Syndrome but Duodenal Atresia.* Here we are talking about a defect which can be corrected by an operative procedure with about a 98% survival rate. The mortality of acute appendicitis in the newborn period is higher than that of duodenal atresia. The surgeon cannot fail to operate in such a case and cannot fail to recommend an operation. Parents who refuse to consent to such an operation would almost certainly be compelled to do so by legal action.

3. *Down's Syndrome Without Duodenal Atresia.* Here most would agree that medical personnel would certainly be obligated to nourish and treat the child. Indeed if nurses or physicians were to concur in a decision of the parents not to feed such a child, they would be guilty of active participation in a killing act and not just an omission.

4. *Both Down's Syndrome and Duodenal Atresia.* Here for some reason, there is a change in the rules and a physician's duty is also said to change. The physician's duty

obviously derives from the physician-patient relationship. Traditional medical ethics has obviously had exquisite difficulty in making a distinction between one's duty to a retarded child and one's duty to a normal child. It has held, if anything, that there was a greater obligation to the retarded. If I have the obligation to care for a child without Down's Syndrome, out of the physician-patient relationship, how can I avoid my obligation to the child with Down's Syndrome. If I have a clear obligation to care for the child with Down's Syndrome, does not that obligation compel me *not to omit* a duty which I am physically capable of performing. In this case, I am not obligated *not to omit* a virtually risk-free operation. These would seem like rhetorical questions expecting the answer "yes" and yet, as I listen, I do not hear a strong affirmative reply from my profession and I wonder why. Is it because of a judgment that I have passed on the child with Down's Syndrome which places him in a disadvantaged position as he tries to incur my obligation to him? If so, then I should ask, first, "who is the Mongoloid child" and secondly "what are his rights."

The incidence of Down's Syndrome is about 1 per 600 live births. This would include the classical 47 chromosome trisomy 21, translocation trisomys and 47/46 mosaics. The average IQ of the trisomy 21 child would be 35, and the average IQ of the Mosaic 47/46 would be 62. I have personal knowledge of three children who are pure trisomys and have IQ's between 80 and 90. Mongoloid children would typically fall into the Trainable Mentally Handicapped category and could be expected to fit into settings where they could be taught socialization and self-help. Indeed some can be taught simple industrial disciplines and can become somewhat self-supporting. In the Zurich sheltered workshop, for example, Mongoloid children are employed repairing telephone equipment. Children with Down's Syndrome do far better at home and only a small percentage should ever be institutionalized. It costs about $12,000 per bed per year to institutionalize a child. This means that if all of the 5,000 children with Down's Syndrome who were born last year were institutionalized, we would be spending each year on their care about 1/10 of what we spend as a nation on dogfood.

In fact, however, these children should not be placed away from home and will not be if the pediatrician and obste-

trician perform properly. The Mongoloid child was has broken
his mother's heart will usually mend it again in 2-3 years.

There is no avoiding, of course, the initial reaction of
grief. The parents should be allowed active grief without detachment. They should, however, recognize the baby as their
own and should have physical contact with it. One of the recurrent mistakes made is that of the obstetrician who says,
"Don't take him home or you will become attached to him."
First of all, becoming attached to your own child is not necessarily a bad development. Secondly, this attachment does not
begin with taking the baby home. The mother has already
been "attached" to this baby for 9 months. He was a presence
within her from the earliest weeks and a more profound and
intimate presence as he began to move, to grow, to accompany her to bed, to go literally everywhere with her.

If parents see the physician treat the Down's child as he
would any other child, they draw their strength from him.
One disadvantage for the physician is that the descriptive
terminology used in describing the features of the child with
Down's Syndrome is often pejorative. Such children are described as having a "Simian" foot or a "Simian" crease, a
"Mongoloid" facies, a "saddle" nose, a "spade" hand and so
on. When the doctor describes her baby in terms usually reserved for foreigners or monkeys, it is not surprising that the
mother will hesitate to welcome it into her home. (I once asked
Dr. Myong Sun Moon, who collaborated with me in a study on
Down's Syndrome at the Misericordia Home, what they called
"Mongoloid" children in China. It turned out to be something
like "a not-too-bright Chinaman.") We should remember that
the term "Cretin" to describe children with congenital hypo-
thyroidism is probably derived from the French word for Christian—Christians were also supposed to be funny-looking people.

What are the rights of the child with Down's Syndrome?
If there was ever a doubt that the retarded have equal rights
those doubts have been categorically removed. A French-
sponsored resolution in the U.N. General Assembly on December 20, 1971 stated that "The mentally retarded person has to
the maximum degree of feasibility the same rights as other
human beings" i.e. the right to proper medical care, economic
security, legal safeguards, a meaningful occupation, freedom
from abuse or abridgement and all other assistance to enable
him to develop to his maximum potential. A series of United

States court decisions in recent years have underscored the need for a "bill of rights" for the retarded in this country. In the 1965 St. Elizabeth's hospital case in Washington, D.C., it was ruled that "the retarded must be cared for and trained, not just kept in custody." This standard was also applied in the Pennhurst case in Pennsylvania in 1971. In an Alabama case, Federal Judge Frank Johnson held that these rights "are present ones and must not only be declared but secured at the earliest practicable time."

How is it possible, then, that these rights were so clearly violated and abridged in this case. What were the factors which conditioned public acceptance of the fact that medical personnel chose to starve this baby to death rather than to go to court to compel restorative surgery?

1. The most important, to my mind, has been the development of large amniocentesis programs funded by the March of Dimes or by federal agencies. The recognition of chromosomal disorders during prenatal life has had the effect of the establishment of a "free-fire zone" during the late-middle and last trimester. There are no restrictions on aborting Mongoloid children even after viability. Recently a pediatric journal published an article entitled "The Prevention of Mongolism through Amniocentesis." I wrote a letter to the editor pointing out that the only way to *prevent* Mongolism was at conception by preventing the fertilization of a 24 chromosome gamete by a 23 chromosome gamete or better yet, by preventing non-disjunction during meiosis. Aborting a Mongoloid child only prevents his birth. The editor refused to publish the letter calling me a "religious fanatic." Presumably he was referring to genetics as a religion which it well may become.

2. Just as the sacrifice of newborn infants with Down's Syndrome is the logical extension of the abortion of viable infants with Down's Syndrome, the rationalization of withholding care for newborns establishes a precedent for neglecting older children with Down's Syndrome. In the Florida state legislature, Representative Sackett, who is also a physician, introduced a Death with Dignity bill (H.B. 407) ostensibly aimed at allowing individuals to execute a "living will." Representative Sackett, however, in his testimony before Senator Church's U.S. Sen-

ate Select Committee on Aging, betrayed an underlying motive in proposing his bill. This motive was what he described as "a major change in American law." He disclosed that the "first step" of allowing individuals to execute their own living wills was to be followed by a "second step" of allowing next of kin to execute living wills on behalf of individuals and a "third step" of allowing physicians to execute the "living will" when next of kin were not available. He suggested that as many as 90% of institutionalized mental defectives in Florida might qualify for elimination under the provisions of steps two and three. One might, for example, withhold therapy of a Down's Syndrome child with pneumonia in a state institution, allowing the pneumonia to become fatal by omission. The American Civil Liberties Union and the Florida Medical Society remained strangely silent about this horrible proposal but the Florida Association for Retarded Children recognized his intentions. The Association unanimously adopted a resolution at its September 15, 1973 meeting which read as follows:

WHEREAS, there has been introduced into the Florida Legislature and espoused throughout the United States a proposed law entitled "Death With Dignity," and;

WHEREAS, in truth and fact the proposed law does not propose death with dignity, but instead proposes the intentional ending of life of persons who are disabled, physically and/or mentally and who are limited in their ability to function, and;

WHEREAS, the sponsor for the proposed law has been guilty of misrepresentation to the public nationally, the purpose of the law, misrepresenting alleged facts about the number of disabled persons in Florida and their cost of public assistance, and misrepresenting that he has support for such a law from various public groups; when in fact there is no such support;

THEREFORE, the Florida Association for Retarded Children, at its September 1973 Annual Meeting, does resolve as follows:

(1) It condemns the proposed law which is deceitfully entitled "Death With Dignity";

(2) It condemns the misrepresentation of its author;

(3) It requests the National Association for Retarded Children to study the proposed law and its inhumane ramifications, and to repudiate publicly on a national scale, the proposed law and the philosophy which gives rise to it.

The second factor of importance is the attempt to substitute the "quality of life" ethic for the "sanctity of life" ethic in medicine. Applying this ethic to the child with Down's Syndrome and Duodenal Atresia, we need only declare that life is not worth living unless it can be lived without handicaps or that "Vita is not vita unless it can be La Dolce Vita." From this cult of perfection, then, we derive a new definition of death. Atresia would only prolong the "living death" of Down's Syndrome.

It is quite possible that this alleged compassion for the handicapped may be entirely misplaced. There is no evidence that the handicapped child would rather not go on living. As a matter of fact, handicapped persons commit suicide far less often than normal persons. An interesting study was done at the Ana Stift in Hanover, Germany, a center where a large number of children with phocomelia, due to thalidomide, are cared for. Psychological testing on these children indicated that they do indeed value their lives, that they are glad that they were born and they look forward to the future with hope and pleasant anticipation.

3. A third important factor is the intrusion of government economists into medical care and planning, and their preoccupation with cost-benefit analysis. A recurring theme is the notion of "the finite health dollar." One is told that if we could only divert the money spent on the custodial care of retarded children into research and nutrition, that we would soon have both a cure for cancer and sirloin for every family in the inner city. Caring for retarded children and research and nutrition are not mutually exclusive. Who says, that in a trillion dollar economy, we can not do all three by shifting our priorities? We can probably do, as a country, whatever we want to do as the space program amply indicates. Look around this country at what we have done to retarded children in the re-

cent past. We have hidden them in human warehouses like Willowbrook; we have built state hospitals in remote areas like Lincoln and Dixon, Illinois far from medical and academic centers. President Kennedy started us on the road back from Bedlam. If we accept death as a modern solution to mental retardation, then we have left Bedlam in order to journey to Dachau.

4.   We are listening to the wrong "experts." I have taken my own poll on this case and have come up with some interesting statistics. When left with the choice between surgery and starvation, the parents, grandparents, and siblings of children with Down's Syndrome vote overwhelmingly for surgery as do pediatricians who subspecialize in the care of the retarded. Nurses and other primary physicians cast a majority vote for surgery and only surgeons and educators are unsure. One surgeon described the withholding of food and water for two weeks as "conservative management."

       Make no mistake about what effect a case like this has on the medical profession or our relationship with the public. Every time we let something like this happen, we all lose something. What we lose is a little of what sustains us, a little of what holds us together. We become more as technocrats, less of a learned profession. If a physician becomes pre-occupied with the social and public good, who will protect the individual rights of the patient. I remember the nurse from Decatur, Illinois who described having gone into the room of a Mongoloid child during his twelfth day without nourishment. She described having to conceal water on her person which she could use to moisten the baby's eyes so that he could, at least, close his dessicated eyelids. No doctor will ever have status with her again.

What should we do as a profession in order to maintain our standing as ethical professionals? It would seem that, under the law, we have very limited choices. Under the law, parents can only consent to what will help the child. They cannot consent to an injury or an illegal act committed against the child. It would seem, then, that the parents' consent to the withholding of food and drink would be worthless and that the hospital instructing its personnel to starve any infant would be guilty of malpractice at the least. It is more likely, however, that the failure to feed a child is not merely a civil misdemeanor but rather a criminal act. Since the starvation is intended in these cases, it possesses malice and the criminal act is probably murder. If I know that parents intend to starve their child, I probably have an affirmative obligation as the child's physician to compel the removal of the child from the parents' care. Not to operate on *any* child with Duodenal Atresia is probably both malpractice and murder. The engagement in pedantic discussions about the alleged "appropriateness" of starving such a child becomes incredible against this background.

Certain ethical decisions do not involve "obligations" so much as "higher callings." If I cannot swim, I am not *obligated* to try to rescue someone I see drowning but it would be noble of me to attempt such a rescue. The ethics of obligation, however, are germane to the care of the Mongoloid child with Duodenal Atresia. The performance of corrective surgery is not merely something I ought to do to be magnanimous but rather something that I *must* do to be an ethical physician.

On one extreme, Joseph Fletcher (1) reasons that a decision to abort a defective fetus (which he would define as "subhuman life") is logically the same as the decision to end a senile "subhuman life in extremis." He abhors moral distinctions between acts of commission and omission, at either end of the life cycle. He not only advocates abortion of viable defective children after diagnosis by amniocentesis, but also advocates eliminating traditional restraints against euthanasia for defective infants. His reasoning is that if one would perform abortions based on prenatal diagnosis, we should actively end the lives of infants born with the same condition. He considers it to be morally evasive to condemn positive acts of euthanasia while approving negative strategies such as starvation which achieve the same purpose. To him, the end of preventing the human harm justifies the means of a positive killing act through the reasoning of consequentialism. Paul Ramsey (2), however, would disagree with this rationale and would hold that there are means which are wrong regardless of the good ends that may be achieved. He would apply this standard both to genetically indicated abortions and to infanticide of defective newborns. To Ramsey (3), both the fetus and the newborn possess humanhood of irreducible dignity received as a free gift of God. To Fletcher, humanhood is conferred by other humans upon fulfillment of certain qualitative and quantitative standards (4).

Between these two polar views, there are others who would vary their judgment along lines based on different views of humanhood and euthanasia. John Fletcher (5) would accept abortion of a defective unborn. He arrives at this conclusion on the basis of the fact that the infant is 1) separate from the mother after birth, 2) that it is more available to treatment, and 3) that parental acceptance of the infant as a person is "more developed." If John Fletcher's reasoning seems brutal and based on a jaded view of human nature, it at least has more logical consistency than that of John Fletcher. Most genetic abortions will be done on viable infants. The separation of a viable infant from its mother is a change of location and not of substance. Many infants with biochemical defects are protected by maternal function *in utero* and are *less* available to treatment after birth. The view that the newborn's rights derive from a parental acceptance of those rights is the fundamental fallacy of the Supreme Court decision on abortion which John Fletcher, predictably, uses as one of his ethical sources.

McCormick (6) attempts to steer a course between dogmatism and relativism by applying a principle of proportionality to the defective child. He properly defines life as a relative rather than an absolute value but then rather arbitrarily decides that a "potentiality for human relationships" be the standard for the preservation of life.

It is not clear how he would apply this principle. He uses as an example the child with anencephaly. Such an example is inappropriate and offers no clarification since there is no real choice in the case of anencephaly. The anencephalic will die no matter what you do or do not do for him. In the case of the child with Down's Syndrome and Duodenal Atresia, the surgical procedure will save the child's life but will not improve his potentiality for human relationships. Father McCormick is not inclinced to apply his principle to the Mongoloid child but the management of the case at Johns Hopkins could not be said to be inconsistent with his principles as broadly stated. Lorber warns against euthanasia as "an extremely dangerous weapon in the hands of unscrupulous individuals" (7). Bok (8) has dramatically illustrated the brutalization of a society which condones euthanasia. Both McCormick and Ramsey abhor and condemn euthanasia but Ramsey's guidelines seem much better defined and less susceptible to misuse in real world situations.

A recent trend in the evaluation of care in the newborn nursery has been a suggestion that all should withdraw except the parents and the physician (9). Everyone else would be consigned to the peculiar isolation of "outsiders" since only the parents and the attending neonatologist could claim real insight into a particular situation. Shaw (10) describes such a situation:

> When surgery is denied, (the doctor) must try to keep the infant from suffering while *natural forces* sap the baby's life. As a surgeon whose natural inclination is to use the scalpel to fight off death, standing by and watching a salvagable baby die is the most emotionally exhausting experience I know. It is easy at a conference, in a theoretical discussion, to decide that such infants should be allowed to die. It is altogether different to stand by in the nursery and watch as dehydration and infection wither a tiny being over hours and days. This is a terrible ordeal *for me and the hospital staff*, much more so than for the parents who never set foot in the nursery.

One would never guess from the foregoing that starvation was a terrible ordeal for the infant who is being starved. I would suggest that most Down's Syndrome children obliged to watch a surgeon starve would feel sorry for the surgeon and not for themselves. The infant who is the victim of starvation needs other advocates in the nursery beside the doctors and the parents, since such decision-making terms have demonstrated a willingness and even a propensity to decide for starvation.

BIBLIOGRAPHY

1. Fletcher, Joseph. "Ethics and Euthanasia." *Am. J. Nursing,* 73: 670, 1973.

2. Ramsey, P. "Abortion." *Thomist,* 37:174, 1973.

3. Ramsey, P. "Feticide/Infanticide Upon Request." *Religion in Life,* 39: 170, 1970.

4. Fletcher, Joseph. "Indicators of Humanhood." *Hastings Center Report,* 2 (5):1, 1972.

5. Fletcher, John. "Abortion, Euthanasia, and Care of Defective Newborns." *N. Eng. J. Med.* 292:75, 1975.

6. McCormick, R. "To Save or Let Die." *J.A.M.A.,* 229: 172, 1974.

7. Lorber, J. "Selective Treatment of Meningomyelocele." *Pediatrics,* 53:307, 1974.

8. Bok, S. "Ethical Problems of Abortion." *Hastings Center Studies,* 2:33, 1974.

9. Duff, R.S. et al. "Moral and Ethical Dilemmas in the Special Care Nursery." *N. Eng. J. Med.* 289:890, 1973.

10. Shaw, A. "Doctor, Do We Have a Choice?" *New York Times Magazine,* January 30, 1972, p. 54.

INVOLUNTARY EUTHANASIA OF DEFECTIVE NEWBORNS: A LEGAL ANALYSIS*

JOHN A. ROBERTSON†

One of the most perplexing dilemmas of modern medicine concerns whether "ordinary"[1] medical care justifiably can be withheld from defective newborns. Infants with malformations of the central nervous system[2] such as anencephaly,[3] hydrocephaly,[4] Down's syndrome,[5] spina bifida,[6] and

---

* I am indebted to the Program in Medical Ethics of the University of Wisconsin Medical School for providing research support for this Article. I owe particular thanks to Norman Fost, George Annas, and Mark Tushnet for many helpful comments on an earlier draft, and to David Hancock and Lise Gammeltoft for research assistance.

† A.B. 1964, Dartmouth College; J.D. 1968, Harvard University. Assistant Professor of Law, University of Wisconsin.

1. Few persons would argue that "extraordinary" care must be provided a defective newborn, or indeed, to any person. The difficult question, however, is to distinguish "ordinary" from "extraordinary" care. See notes 141–48 infra and accompanying text. In this Article "ordinary" care refers to those medical and surgical procedures that would normally be applied in situations not involving physically or mentally handicapped persons.

2. The need for ordinary treatment will also arise with noncentral nervous system malformations such as malformations of the cardiovascular, respiratory, orogastrointestinal, urogenital, muscular and skeletal systems, as well as deformities of the eye, ear, face, endocrine glands, and skin. See generally J. WARKANY, CONGENITAL MALFORMATIONS (1971). Often these defects will accompany central nervous system malformations. The medical-ethical dilemma discussed in this Article has arisen chiefly with regard to central nervous system problems, perhaps because the presence of such defects seriously affects intelligence, social interaction, and the potential for development and growth, and will be discussed only in the context of the major central nervous system malformations. Parents of physically deformed infants with normal intelligence might face the same choice, but because of the child's capacity for development, pressure to withhold ordinary treatment will be less severe.

3. Anencephaly is partial or total absence of the brain. J. WARKANY, supra note 2, at 189–99.

4. Hydrocephaly is characterized by an increase of free fluid in the cranial cavity which results in a marked enlargement of the head. Id. at 217. It is a symptom of many diverse disorders, and is associated with hereditary and chromosomal syndromes. Id. at 217–18. Warkany describes the symptoms as follows: "Bulging of the forehead, protrusion of the parietal areas and extension of the occipital region are characteristic changes . . . . The skin of the scalp is thin and stretched and its veins are dilated . . . . The head cannot be held up, and walking and talking are delayed. The legs are spastic, the tendon reflexes increased and convulsions may occur. Anorexia, vomiting and emaciation complicate severe cases. As a rule, hydrocephalic children are dull and lethargic. Blindness can develop, but hearing and the auditory memory may be good. Physical and mental development depend on several factors, such as rapidity of onset, intracranial pressure, compensatory growth of the head, nature of the basic malformations and progress or arrest of the process. Such variability makes the prognosis and evaluation of therapeutic measures difficult. Pressure on the hypothalamic area can cause obesity or precocious puberty in exceptional cases." Id. at 226–27.

5. Down's syndrome or mongolism is a chromosomal disorder producing mental retardation caused by the presence of 47 rather than 46 chromosomes in a patient's cells, and marked by a distinctively shaped head, neck, trunk, and abdomen. Id. at 311–12, 324. For summary of clinical and pathological characteristics, see id. at 324–31.

6. Spina bifida refers generally to midline defects of the osseous spine. The defect usually appears in the posterior aspects of the vertebral canal, and may be marked by an external saccular protrusion (spina bifida cystica). Id. at 272. Spina bifida is often seriously involved with urinary tract deficiency, hydrocephaly, and may involve paralysis of the lower extremities. Id. at 286–88. While there are important differences between spina bifida, meningoceles, and myelomeningocele, the terms will be used interchangeably in discussing and evaluating the duty to treat.

myelomeningocele[7] often require routine surgical or medical attention[8] merely to stay alive. Until recent developments in surgery and pediatrics, these infants would have died of natural causes. Today with treatment many will survive for long periods, although some will be severely handicapped and limited in their potential for human satisfaction and interaction. Because in the case of some defective newborns, the chances are often slim that they will ever lead normal human lives, it is now common practice for parents to request, and for physicians to agree, not to treat such infants. Without treatment the infant usually dies.

Nontreatment of defective newborns has occurred throughout history, but only recently has the medical profession openly acknowledged the scope and alleged desirability of the practice. In 1973, Doctors Raymond S. Duff and A. G. M. Campbell documented 43 cases of withholding care from defective infants at the Yale–New Haven Hospital,[9] thereby breaking what they characterized as "public and professional silence on a major social taboo."[10] Subsequently, similar cases across the country have received widespread public attention.[11] Recently, the Senate Subcommittee on Health held hearings at which eminent physicians attempted to justify the practice.[12] Pediatric textbooks discuss clinical indicators for withholding treatment,[13] and physicians writing in medical journals have advocated nontreatment in certain situations.[14] Thus, nontreatment of defective infants, now occurring in hospitals throughout the United States and England, is rapidly gaining status as "good medical practice."[15]

This development is significant because it represents the only large-scale instance of involuntary euthanasia[16] now being practiced by the

---

7. The saccular enlargements of spina bifida cystica protruding through osseous defects of the vertebral column that contain anomalous meninges and spinal fluid but do not have neural elements affixed to their walls are called meningoceles. If the spinal cord or nerves are included in the formation of the sac, the anomaly is called myelomeningocele. *Id.* at 272. As with spina bifida, myelomeningocele may substantially interfere with locomotion, sphincter and bladder control, and may be accompanied by kyphoscoliosis and hydrocephaly leading to mental retardation. For a description of symptoms and treatment alternatives, *see* Lorber, *Results of Treatment of Myelomeningocele*, 13 DEVELOP. MED. & CHILD NEUROL. 279–303 (1971).

8. The infant might suffer from duodenal atresia and need surgery to connect the stomach to the intestine; or need an appendectomy; or antibiotics to fight pneumonia; or suffer from Respirator Distress Syndrome and need breathing assistance. In some cases the question is whether to begin or continue feeding.

9. Duff & Campbell, *Moral and Ethical Dilemmas in the Special-Care Nursery*, 289 NEW ENG. J. MED. 890 (1973).

10. *Id.* at 894.

11. *See* Boston Globe, Feb. 25, 1974, at 1, col. 1; Newark Star Ledger, Oct. 3, 1973, at 32, col. 8; notes 27 & 185 *infra. See also* R. TRUMBO, AN ACT OF MERCY 145 (1973); TIME, Mar. 25, 1974, at 84.

12. N.Y. Times, June 12, 1974, at 18, col. 4.

13. F. INGRAHAM & D. MATSON, NEUROSURGERY OF INFANCY AND CHILDHOOD 35–39 (1954).

14. *See, e.g.,* Gimbel, *Infanticide: Who Makes the Decision*, WIS. MED. J., Vol. 73, No. 5, at 10 (1974); Lorber, *supra* note 7, at 279.

15. Although some reservations have been expressed, *see, e.g.,* Cooke, *Whose Suffering?*, 80 J. OF PEDIATRICS 906 (1972), public furor as evidenced in anti-abortion campaigns has yet to erupt. *See* Grunberg, *Who Lives and Who Dies?*, N.Y. Times, Apr. 22, 1974, at 35, col. 2.

16. The term "involuntary euthanasia" is used here to denote the absence of consent of the

medical profession, at a time when most physicians and the public retain strong opposition to involuntary euthanasia in other circumstances.[17] This does not imply that the decision to withhold care is lightly made. The clash between the norms of preventing suffering and preserving life is too great to ignore, and has engendered much soul searching and ethical analysis on the part of parents, physicians, and nursing staffs. Duff and Campbell, for instance, described in detail their efforts to help parents reach informed choices: "In lengthy frank discussion, the anguish of parents was shared and attempts were made to support fully the reasoned choices, whether for active treatment and rehabilitation or for an early death."[18]

Indeed, no sensitive person can fail to sympathize with the plight of the parents, or blithely pass judgment on the choice they make. After months of expectancy, they are informed that the newborn infant has serious mental and physical defects and will never know a normal existence. The shock of learning that one's child is defective overwhelms parents with grief, guilt, personal blame, and often hopelessness.[19] They are suddenly confronted with an uncertain future of financial and psychological hardship, with potentially devastating effects on their marriage, family, and personal aspirations. If asked to approve a medical or surgical procedure necessary to keep the child alive, it is perhaps understandable that the parents view a life capable only of minimal interaction and development as the greater evil and refuse to provide consent.[20]

person from whom treatment is withheld, as opposed to "voluntary euthanasia," where the subject gives full, knowing consent to another person's causing his death. Involuntary and voluntary euthanasia can also be distinguished on the following grounds: Involuntary euthanasia is passive and indirect, as where care or sustenance is withheld; voluntary euthanasia is active and direct as where the act that causes death is actually performed rather than omitted. This Article deals only with issues arising from involuntary, passive euthanasia of defective newborns. Although "involuntary" may be redundant in the case of newborns who are in any case incapable of consent, the term is retained to emphasize the absence of consent from the subject.

17. The only situation calling forth a comparable consensus for withholding ordinary medical care arises in the case of the moribund, particularly the elderly moribund, where treatment would at best prolong the dying process or maintain a life with little chance of social interaction or development. *See* Fletcher, *Ethics and Euthanasia*, 73 Am. J. of Nursing 670 (1973); Fletcher, *Legal Aspects of the Decision Not to Prolong Life*, 203 J.A.M.A. 65 (1968); Fletcher, *Prolonging Life*, 42 Wash. L. Rev. 999 (1967); Williams, *Euthanasia and Abortion*, 38 U. Colo. L. Rev. 38 (1966). This practice may often be correctly described as involuntary euthanasia, for the patient may be unconscious or not have previously consented to the cessation of ordinary medical care, and undoubtedly involves more patients than nontreatment of defective newborns.

18. Duff & Campbell, *supra* note 9, at 891.

19. Cohen, *The Impact of the Handicapped Child on the Family*, 43 Social Casework 137 (1962); Fletcher, *Attitudes Toward Defective Newborns*, Hastings Center Studies, Vol. 2, No. 1, at 21 (1974); Goodman, *Continuing Treatment of Parents With Congenitally Defective Infants*, Social Work, Vol. 9, No. 1, at 92 (1964); Mandelbaum & Wheeler, *The Meaning of a Defective Child to Parents*, 41 Social Casework 360 (1960).

20. In the curious manner in which art often prefigures life, Franz Kafka anticipated the emotional and ethical dilemma of parents of the defective newborn in his short story, *The Metamorphosis*, more than 50 years ago. Kafka, *The Metamorphosis*, in The Metamorphosis and Other Stories 67–135 (Shocken ed. 1961). While the story concerns Gregor Samsa, an adult commercial traveller, the situation dramatized by Kafka captures most of the pressures facing parents of defective children. The middle-class Samsa family awakes one morning to find that their son, Gregor, sole support of the family, has been transformed into an insect-like monstrosity. They are shocked by this strange trick

But, while one may empathize with the parents of a defective infant one cannot forget that the innocent life of an untreated child is also involved. Like any infant, the deformed child is a person with a right to life —a right that is the basis of our social order and legal system. In fact, the plight of the infant is probably greater than that of the parents. Handicapped at birth, it stands to lose ameliorative treatment, loving care, and probably life itself. Moreover, with the parents' rejection, no one remains to protect or even articulate its interests. Whatever the morality of the ultimate choice, it seems unfair to subject the life of a helpless infant to the unguided discretion of parent and physician, particularly when they may have conflicting interests.[21] Indeed, in other circumstances, the right of parents to injure their children, even if done benevolently, is sharply limited,[22] and the rights of physical and mental defectives are now strenuously protected.[23] From the infant's perspective withdrawing care would appear to be a serious infringement of a basic right.

In resolving the emotional and ethical dilemmas that confront parents of defective infants, it is surprising that law and legal values have rarely been invoked. The law's long experience with protecting minority rights[24] and its concern with procedure and decisionmaking processes may offer a path out of this troublesome thicket. Yet, Duff and Campbell, while attempting to aid parents in making an informed choice, neglected to advise as to legal duties and the legal ramifications of withholding medical care.[25] Per-

---

of fate and recoil in horror, attempting to hide their shame by isolating Gregor in his room. His sister and mother feel sympathy. They leave him milk and bread, and sometimes sit with him. But revulsion soon takes over. As the psychic and economic burdens mount, the family sinks into depression and lethargy. Gregor realizes their embarrassment, and to save them from further grief decides to die. On his death, the Samsa family suddenly awakes, dismissing the charwoman and boarders who knew of their shame, and begins life anew.

21. *See* notes 262–65 *infra* and accompanying text.

22. Thus, Jehovah's Witness parents, who believe that blood transfusions are a transgression of God's law and hence not in their children's best interests, may generally not prevent a child from receiving a transfusion if essential to prevent substantial harm to the child. *See* Jehovah's Witnesses v. Kings County Hosp., 278 F. Supp. 488 (W.D. Wash. 1967), *aff'd*, 390 U.S. 598 (1968); People *ex rel.* Wallace v. Labrenz, 411 Ill. 618, 104 N.E. 2d 769, *cert. denied*, 344 U.S. 824 (1952); State v. Perricone, 37 N.J. 463, 181 A.2d 751, *cert. denied*, 371 U.S. 890 (1962). Similarly, parents who believe that a public school education is not in the best interests of their child are limited in the educational alternatives that they may select, because of the state's judgment that the absence of certain forms of education will harm the child. *Cf.* Wisconsin v. Yoder, 406 U.S. 205 (1972).

23. *See* Jackson v. Indiana, 406 U.S. 715 (1972); Lessard v. Schmidt, 349 F. Supp. 1078 (E.D. Wis. 1972), *vacated and remanded*, 414 U.S. 473 (1974); Mills v. Board of Educ., 348 F. Supp. 866 (D.D.C. 1972).

24. For example, the law has been solicitous of the rights of indigent defendants, Griffin v. Illinois, 351 U.S. 12 (1956); the rights of racial minorities, Brown v. Board of Educ., 347 U.S. 483 (1954); the rights of aliens, Takahashi v. Fish & Game Comm'n, 334 U.S. 410 (1948) and the rights of pregnant women, Cleveland Bd. of Educ. v. LaFleur, 414 U.S. 632 (1974). For a more general discussion and applications in many other areas, *see Developments in the Law—Equal Protection*, 82 HARV. L. REV. 1069 (1969).

25. One may question whether parents in a legal sense provide informed consent to withhold treatment when they have not been informed that they risk criminal liability. This raises a serious issue of medical ethics that Duff and Campbell apparently ignored. *See* Roberts v. Young, 369 Mich. 113, 119 N.W.2d 627 (1963); Walz & Scheuneminn, *Informed Consent to Therapy*, 64 Nw. U.L. REV. 628 (1969).

haps the most appropriate solution to this problem is, as they suggest, to allow parents and physicians wide latitude in decisionmaking.[26] This decision, however, can be reasonably made only after we understand and evaluate existing legal policy, and consider how law can best resolve the dilemma.

This Article analyzes the criminal liability of the parties involved in the decision to withhold treatment from defective infants and attempts a reasoned evaluation of current legal policy. It takes the position that under existing law, parents, physicians, and hospital staff commit several crimes in withholding care, and that on the whole, with few exceptions, criminal liability may be both desirable and morally compelled. It argues further that a principled case for nonliability can be made only if we are prepared to establish a legislative definition of a narrow class of persons from whom care justifiably can be withheld, and if procedural safeguards to limit the possibility of arbitrary decisions are instituted. Depending on one's view on this issue, present criminal sanctions should be enforced more fully, or legislation permitting nontreatment should be enacted.

I. Criminal Liability Under Existing Laws

Although the courts have not yet ruled directly on the criminal liability of persons who refuse ordinary lifesaving medical care for defective infants,[27] under traditional principles of criminal law the omission of such care by parents, physicians, and nurses creates criminal liability. The crimes committed may include murder, involuntary manslaughter, conspiracy, and child abuse or neglect. This Part analyzes the legal theories upon which prosecution can be based, and then considers the defenses available to a defendant.

A. *Liability of the Parents*

1. *Homicide.*

Generally a person is criminally liable for homicide by omission if: (1) he has a legal duty to protect another; (2) with knowledge or gross negligence he fails to act; and (3) such failure proximately causes the death of the other.[28] If the omission is intentional the person can be prose-

---

26. Duff & Campbell, *supra* note 9, at 894.

27. But parents have been prosecuted for direct killing of defective offspring. *See* United States v. Repouille, 165 F.2d 152 (2d Cir. 1947). In addition, a recent Arizona case, in which parents of a newborn myelomeningocele child had agreed with their physician to withhold sustenance from the baby, created considerable publicity and led to the calling of a coroner's jury after the baby died. The jury ruled that the baby had died from natural causes (meningitis) and not from the parents' decision to withhold food and liquids. The Arizona Attorney General's office, which still had the option to prosecute, declined to do so, because the coroner's jury reached a "reasoned verdict." Telephone interview with James Schaefer, Assistant Attorney General, Ariz., Aug. 19, 1974.

28. W. LaFave & A. Scott, Handbook of Criminal Law 182–91 (1st ed. 1972); J. Turner, Russell on Crime 402 (12th ed. 1964); G. Williams, Criminal Law: The General Part 4–8 (2d

cuted for first- or second-degree murder depending on the extent of his premeditation and deliberation.[29] If, on the other hand, the omission is the result of the person's gross carelessness or disregard of the consequences of failing to act, the homicide is involuntary manslaughter.[30] The parental decision to refuse consent to a medical or surgical procedure necessary to maintain the life of a defective infant quite clearly falls within the bounds of homicide by omission.[31]

a. *The parents' duty to the defective infant.*

Parents undoubtedly have a legal duty to provide necessary medical assistance to a helpless minor child.[32] The duty was recognized at common law and is now imposed by statute in every state.[33] In addition the case law has generally upheld homicide liability of parents whose failure to procure needed medical assistance causes the death of minor children, and these cases clearly apply to the defective infant situation.[34]

ed. 1968); Frankel, *Criminal Omissions: A Legal Microcosm,* 11 WAYNE L. REV. 367 (1965); Glazebrook, *Criminal Omissions: The Duty Requirement in Offenses Against the Person,* 76 L.Q. REV. 386 (1960); Hughes, *Criminal Omissions,* 67 YALE L.J. 590 (1958); Perkins, *Negative Acts in Criminal Law,* 22 IOWA L. REV. 659 (1937); Rudolph, *The Duty to Act: A Proposed Rule,* 44 NEB. L. REV 499 (1965).

29. Gibson v. Commonwealth, 106 Ky. 360, 50 S.W. 532 (1889); Commonwealth v. Hall, 322 Mass. 523, 78 N.E.2d 644 (1948); State v. Barnes, 141 Tenn. 469, 212 S.W. 100 (1919); Biddle v. Commonwealth, 206 Va. 14, 141 S.E.2d 710 (1965).

30. *See* note 29 *supra.*

31. In the case of the defective infants in the Duff and Campbell study, doctors informed the parents that death would result from a failure to treat and that their decision to withhold treatment was expressly made to cause the death of the child. *See* Duff & Campbell, *supra* note 9, at 891. This presents a prima facie case of first-degree murder, subject, of course, to the defenses to be analyzed subsequently and to the discretion of the prosecution. *See* notes 141–80 *infra* and accompanying text.

32. *See, e.g.,* State v. Stehr, 92 Neb. 755, 139 N.W. 676, *aff'd on rehearing,* 142 N.W. 670 (1913). *See also* Paulsen, *The Legal Framework for Child Protection,* 66 COLUM. L. REV. 679 (1956).

33. *See, e.g.,* CAL. PENAL CODE § 270 (West 1970); N.J. STAT. ANN. tit. 9, § 6–1 (West 1960).

34. *See* notes 41–51 *infra* and accompanying text.

Nevertheless, some courts have refused to impose such liability where, for example, a mother in labor failed to obtain medical assistance that could have saved her child's life. Their decision stems from the refusal of the trial judges in two English cases to submit a manslaughter charge in such circumstances to the jury. In the first, Regina v. Knights, 175 Eng. Rep. 952 (1860), the judge found no authority for the prosecution's nonfeasance theory and, therefore, refused to submit the case. Forty-four years later in Rex v. Izod, 20 Cox Crim. Cas. 690 (Oxford Cir. 1904), the trial judge held that a mother's duty to provide medical care and to care for a child commenced only after birth.

Although *Knights* and *Izod* were the rulings of trial judges and never scrutinized by an appellate court, the Wyoming Supreme Court relied on them in reversing the manslaughter conviction of a mother whose male infant had died shortly after birth. State v. Osmus, 73 Wyo. 183, 276 P.2d 469 (1954). While there was considerable conflict in the evidence as to whether the child was born alive and died shortly after birth, *id.* at 193–94, 276 P.2d at 472–73, the court characterized the state's case as based on defendant's failure to fulfill an alleged duty of providing medical care to a child about to be born. Finding no case in opposition to *Knights* and *Izod,* and wishing to avoid unfair imposition of liability on women in the throes of childbirth, the court affirmed the rule that an infant must be born before a duty of care commences. *Id.* at 201, 209, 276 P.2d 475, 479.

This distinction, however, between omissions occurring after rather than before birth does not withstand critical scrutiny. A better approach, applied in State v. Shepherd, 255 Iowa 1218, 124 N.W.2d 712 (1963) (baby died from lack of oxygen induced from shock of being placed on cold floor), is whether, with birth imminent, a reasonable person would have obtained medical care. Where circumstances make the possible need for medical care clear, failure to obtain care that leads to the infant's death should be culpable. But even if an exception from the parental duty of providing medical care were recognized in this situation, it would not be applicable to the case of the defective infant who is born alive and is then refused available medical care.

The parental duty of care also arises when a lawfully aborted viable fetus dies because medical care is withheld after removal from the mother's body. Although a mother has not yet been prosecuted for such omission[35] her duty to care for the live abortus can be found on two grounds.[36] First, if the infant is alive after removal, a human being has been born and the parental duty to provide medical care attaches, until parental rights and obligations are terminated.[37] Second, even if the direct parental duty is inapplicable, the mother has a legal duty to act on the theory that one who places another in peril, however innocently, has a legal duty of rescue.[38] While after delivery the mother can reasonably be expected to do very little, one reasonably can expect steps to assume care of the infant to be taken before birth.[39] If a woman is fully informed of the alternative outcomes of a late-term abortion by hysterotomy, including the possibility of a live abortus, she would be under a duty to assure that the child would be cared for. At the minimum she cannot request preoperatively that the infant be refused treatment and allowed to die.

b. *The parents' knowing or grossly negligent failure to act.*

Since the duty of parents to care for their children is well established in most instances,[40] cases that have dealt with the question of a parent's liability for failure to provide his child with the necessary medical assis-

---

35. A physician, however, has been prosecuted for allegedly cutting off the blood supply of a viable fetus before removal from the uterus during a lawfully performed abortion by hysterotomy. *See* Robertson, *Medical Ethics in the Courtroom*, Hastings Center Report, Vol. 4, No. 4, at 1–3 (1974); N.Y. Times, Apr. 13, 1973, at 1, col. 2; note 185 *infra*.

36. A physician's duty of care following an abortion will be explored in a later section. While several states are considering or have recently passed legislation specifically requiring physicians to treat and care for lawfully aborted viable fetuses, *see* N.Y. Times, June 16, 1974, at 1, col. 3, this Article argues that such a duty exists even without a specific statute. *See* notes 72–106 *infra* and accompanying text.

37. Most states have some procedure by which parents may voluntarily divest themselves of legal rights to and legal obligations to provide for their children. Wisconsin and Delaware, for example, provide explicitly for a voluntary termination of all parental rights and obligations. 13 Del. Code § § 1103–08 (Additional Supp. 1970); Wis. Stat. § 48.40 (West 1957). Other jurisdictions, such as Massachusetts, provide that upon application of a parent, the Department of Public Welfare "may accept a temporary delegation of certain rights and responsibilities regarding a child." Mass. Laws Ann. ch. 119, § 23 (1973 Supp.). Other provisions of Massachusetts law suggest that a parent wishing to relinquish rights and responsibilities toward a child can successfully do so, although a formal right to termination is less clear. *See* Mass. Laws Ann. ch. 119, § 23(B), (C), (E) (Additional Supp. 1973). Some states have statutes authorizing parents to apply to the Department of Welfare "for such care or custody of such child as the circumstances may require." N.J. Stat. 30:4C–11 (West 1964). Although most statutes speak only to the issue of involuntary termination, "this omission . . . has been criticized for the reasons, among others, that without the guidance of a statute and a judicial determination, the natural parent will be less likely to understand the implications of termination and secondly, the clarity and finality of a judicial determination will be absent." Gordon, *Terminal Placements of Children and Permanent Termination of Parental Rights: The New York Permanent Neglect Statute*, 46 St. John's L. Rev. 215, 216 (1971). In practice, however, under any of the above or similar statutes, parents are generally able to divest themselves of parental rights and obligations, although parents with means may have to pay a reasonable sum toward the care of the child.

38. *See* notes 101–106 *infra* and accompanying text.

39. *See* note 34 *supra*.

40. *See* notes 32–38 *supra* and accompanying text.

tance have often turned on the question of whether the parent's failure to act was culpable. This question is particularly troublesome when parents claim that they refused to provide their child with medical care because of their religious beliefs.

In the leading case of *Regina v. Senior*,[41] a "good and kind father in all other respects" with an "excellent character for general good conduct" failed to provide medical aid or medicine to an 8- or 9-month-old infant suffering from diarrhea and pneumonia.[42] He belonged to a sect called the "Peculiar People" who relied on prayer rather than doctors and drugs in times of sickness. In upholding the defendant's manslaughter conviction, which was based on an English statute making it a misdemeanor for any person having the custody, charge, or care of any child under 16 to "wilfully . . . neglect . . . such child . . . in a manner likely to cause such child unnecessary suffering, or injury to its health,"[43] the Queen's Bench rejected the religious motives of the defendant and held that the evidence and trial instructions were sufficient to sustain his conviction. *Senior* thereby overruled two earlier cases[44] that suggested that religious motivation might offer a defense to such criminal prosecution, and has been influential in English,[45] Canadian,[46] and American[47] courts.

Similarly, courts have generally upheld manslaughter convictions of parents whose poverty and ignorance have been offered to excuse their otherwise grossly negligent conduct. *Stehr v. State*[48] involved the manslaughter conviction of a German immigrant who allegedly was criminally negligent in providing medical care to his 2-year-old stepson, whose feet froze during a severe blizzard and coldspell.[49] The Nebraska Supreme Court, rejecting defendant's contention that he was not responsible for the child's neglect because he was unable to speak English and lacked the means to procure medical assistance,[50] upheld his conviction. Moreover, although

---

41. [1899] 1 Q.B. 283.
42. *Id.*
43. Prevention of Cruelty to Children Act, 57 & 58 Vict., c. 41, § 1 (1894).
44. Regina v. Hines, 80 Central Crim. Ct. Cas. 309 (1874); Regina v. Wagstaffe, 10 Cox Crim. Cas. 530 (Central Crim. Ct. 1868).
45. *See, e.g.*, Rex v. Jones, 19 Cox Crim. Cas. 678 (Oxford Cir. 1901).
46. *See, e.g.*, Rex v. Lewis, 6 Ont. L.R. 132 (C.A. 1903).
47. *See, e.g.*, State v. Chenoweth, 163 Ind. 94, 71 N.E. 197 (1904); Craig v. State, 220 Md. 590, 155 A.2d 684 (1959); State v. Watson, 77 N.J.L. 299, 71 A. 1113 (1909); State v. Barnes, 141 Tenn. 469, 212 S.W. 100 (1919).
48. 92 Neb. 755, 139 N.W. 676, *aff'd on rehearing*, 142 N.W. 670 (1913).
49. When the defendant saw grey and green spots on the boy's feet, he treated them with hot water and vaseline, but did not call a physician until 11 days later, when the stench from the child's decomposing feet had become unbearable. Two doctors were called, but each declined the case because the defendant had no money. The city physician finally amputated the gangrenous feet. Sepsis, however, had already occurred, and the child died. *Id.* at 760, 139 N.W. at 677.
50. The evidence showed that the defendant was an intelligent man who was aware that the child's feet were decomposing and in need of medical assistance. Although he spoke only German, he was surrounded by friends and neighbors who could assist him in procuring aid. In addition, the defendant's lack of money could not excuse his inaction since "poor laws" and other aid could provide financial assistance. *Id.* at 760–61, 139 N.W. at 677–78.

the *Stehr* decision is more than 60 years old, other cases suggest the continuing viability of the court's reasoning.[51] Thus, it is clear that courts generally will not excuse parents' intentional or negligent failure to provide medical care to their children even under the most difficult circumstances.

c. *The parents' failure to act is the cause of death.*

Although it is readily apparent that parents have a legal duty to provide medical assistance to their minor children,[52] and that a failure to fulfill this duty will not be lightly excused,[53] parents who refuse to provide ordinary lifesaving medical care to defective infants are not guilty of homicide unless it can be shown that their failure to act is the proximate cause of the child's death.[54]

In *Bradley v. State*,[55] the father of a minor, epileptic daughter was convicted of manslaughter when he refused to obtain medical care for burns she suffered by falling in a fire during a seizure.[56] Refusing all offers of medical care on religious grounds, the father kept her at home in severe pain for 34 days. Finally he brought her to a hospital where she died 22 days later. Although ostensibly holding that a Florida statute that defined manslaughter as the "killing of a human being by the act, procurement, or culpable negligence of another . . ." did not pertain to the father's refusal of medical attention,[57] the court placed a great deal of emphasis on the absence of evidence of a causal relation between the father's omission and the death of the child. According to the court, the death of the child manifestly was caused by the accidental burning in which the father had no part, and even if medical attention would have prevented the child's death and the father's omission was culpable negligence within the intent

---

51. *See, e.g.,* Eaglen v. State, 249 Ind. 144, 231 N.E.2d 147 (1967). In this case, a husband and wife were convicted of involuntary manslaughter of a 5-month-old infant who died from pneumonia and malnutrition. Proper medical care would have saved the child. The father appealed on the ground that he had fulfilled his parental duty by furnishing sufficient support money, and thus should not be held responsible for the mother's failure to use the money to obtain food and medical care. Citing an Indiana statute that imposed a duty of providing "sufficient food, clothing, maintenance, . . . medical attendance or surgical treatment" on any person having "the care, custody and control" of a child, and finding that the defendant was living with his wife and children at the time, the court held that the father's duty was not discharged merely by entrusting the care of his child to his wife. He must have been aware of the child's condition, for he admitted playing with the baby during the evenings, and for several weeks before death the child's flesh was lying in folds on his legs, bleeding sores covered the lower body, and pus covered his penis. Lack of actual knowledge of the condition, however, provided no defense, since the exercise of ordinary care would have revealed the child's need. *Id.* at 146, 150, 231 N.E.2d at 148, 150.

52. *See* notes 32–38 *supra* and accompanying text.

53. *See* notes 40–51 *supra* and accompanying text.

54. Craig v. State, 220 Md. 590, 155 A.2d 684 (1959). However, the parent probably could be convicted under a state's neglect statute. *See* notes 61–71 *infra* and accompanying text.

55. 79 Fla. 651, 84 So. 677 (1920).

56. *Id.* at 654, 84 So. at 678.

57. *Id.* at 655, 84 So. at 679. In State v. Staples, 126 Minn. 396, 148 N.W. 283 (1914), the Minnesota Supreme Court interpreted a similarly worded statute to include parental omissions of needed medical care.

of the statute, his omission of care did not "cause the 'killing' of the child."[58]

However, this view of causation, under which no omission ever causes death, does not withstand analysis,[59] and has not been followed in other jurisdictions.[60] Were other courts to subscribe to the *Bradley* court's reasoning, parents who withheld "ordinary" medical care from defective newborn children would never be guilty of homicide since the child's deformity rather than the parents' omission would always be the cause of death. Nevertheless, even under *Bradley*, as the following section demonstrates, parents who follow this course of "inaction" still risk serious criminal liability.

2. *Neglect.*

In addition to homicide liability, parents may be prosecuted under statutes that punish the withholding of necessary medical care from minor children. The failure to provide medical care to minors is cognizable under various statutory formulations, ranging from requirements of child support and provision of necessaries,[61] to prohibitions of maltreatment, cruelty, or endangering the life or health of minors.[62] Moreover, several states specifically punish the failure to furnish medical assistance.[63] However, even where the duty to provide medical aid is not expressly mentioned, and statutes generally prohibit neglect, endangering health, cruelty, or maltreatment, courts have interpreted these terms to include medical assistance.[64]

Although the neglect statutes are clearly applicable when a parent's refusal to provide medical care causes or could cause death or serious injury,[65] such a finding is not necessary to a finding of neglect liability. The omission of ameliorative care, if medically recommended, is sufficient to

---

58. 79 Fla. at 655, 84 So. at 679.

59. *See, e.g.,* J. Hall, General Principles of Criminal Law 196–97 (2d ed. 1960).

60. *See, e.g.,* State v. Staples, 126 Minn. 396, 148 N.W. 283 (1914); State v. Pickles, 46 N.J. 542, 218 A.2d 609 (1965). However, even in these jurisdictions, causation is still a tricky problem and is asserted frequently as a defense. This Article will deal with these other problems of causation later when it considers defenses that may be interposed against prosecution. *See* notes 149–56 *infra* and accompanying text.

61. *See, e.g.,* N.Y. Penal Law § 260.05 (McKinney 1967), *as amended,* (Supp. 1972).

62. *See, e.g.,* Conn. Gen. Stat. Ann. tit. 53, ch. 939, § 53–21 (1960); Ill. Ann Stat. ch. 23, § 2354 (1968); N.Y. Penal Law § 260.10 (McKinney 1967), *as amended,* (Supp. 1970); Consol. Penn. Stat. Ann. tit. 18, § 4304 (1973). *See also* Paulsen, *supra* note 32, at 681.

63. *See, e.g.,* N.J. Stats. § 9:6–3 (West 1960), and the definition of "neglect" at *id.* § 9:6–1.

64. *See, e.g.,* State v. Clark, 5 Conn. 699, 261 A.2d 294 (Cir. Ct. 1969).

65. Matthews v. State, 240 Miss. 189, 126 So. 2d 245 (1961) (parents prosecuted for neglecting to provide digitalis for a child left in care of nursery); State v. Perricone, 35 N.J. 463, 181 A.2d 751 (1962) (parents prosecuted for refusing blood transfusion). *See also* Maine Medical Center v. Houle, Civil No. 74–145 (Super. Ct., Cumberland C'ty, Feb. 14, 1974) (parents' refusal to permit surgery to correct a tracheal esophageal fistula that prevented normal feeding and breathing in a deformed infant constituted neglect).

establish neglect in a civil proceeding,[66] and arguably will support a criminal prosecution as well. In such cases parents could argue that when neither death nor serious physical injury is threatened, they have an absolute prerogative to determine whether a child should undergo merely elective or ameliorative procedures. A few cases have, in fact, held that a parent's refusal to permit corrective but not lifesaving surgery does not constitute the type of neglect that warrants the appointment of a guardian.[67] These cases can be distinguished from the case of the spina bifida or myelomeningocele child whose parents refuse corrective surgery that is not strictly essential to preserve life. The surgical procedures that were at issue in these cases carried a high risk of death,[68] while the minors' defects impaired only their social existence and did not subject them to the threat of death. In addition, the judges in some of the cases relied heavily on the wishes of the minors who opposed treatment.[69] In myelomeningocele, however, the corrective procedures carry a much lower risk of death and are necessary to prevent high-risk infection, pain, and retardation.[70] Moreover,

66. *In re* Sampson, 65 Misc. 2d 658, 317 N.Y.S.2d 641 (Fam. Ct. 1970), *aff'd*, 37 App. Div. 2d 688, 323 N.Y.S.2d 253 (3d Dept. 1971), *aff'd*, 29 N.Y.2d 900, 278 N.E.2d 918, 328 N.Y.S.2d 686 (1972), held that a 15-year-old boy suffering from neurofibromatosis, which caused a massive deformity on the right side of his face and neck, giving him a grotesque and repulsive appearance that "must inevitably exert a most negative effect upon his personality development, his opportunity for education and later employment and upon every phase of his relationship with peers and others," 65 Misc. 2d at 661, 317 N.Y.S.2d at 644, was neglected when his mother, a Jehovah's Witness, refused to consent to blood transfusions necessary for corrective surgery, even in the absence of an immediate threat to his health from the condition.

67. *See In re* Seiferth, 309 N.Y. 80, 127 N.E.2d 820 (1955) (parents refused corrective surgery for a harelip and cleft palate in a 15-year-old boy); *In re* Green, 448 Pa. 338, 292 A.2d 387 (1972) (parents refused surgery to correct a severe curvature of the spine in a 17-year-old boy); *In re* Tuttendario, 21 Pa. Dist. 561 (1911) (parents refused surgery that would prevent a 7-year-old boy from becoming crippled from rickets); *In re* Hudson, 13 Wash. 673, 126 P.2d 765 (1942) (parents refused to amputate a grossly malformed left arm that weighed several times more than the other arm and interfered with the child's psychosocial development).

68. The parents in *Tuttendario*, 21 Pa. Dist. 561 (1911), objected to the surgery out of fear that the boy would die in what was necessarily a major surgical procedure. The parents had previously lost 7 of their 10 children. Since medical science could not assure an absolutely correct diagnosis or prognosis, the court held that the fear of the parents was a reasonable one and did not constitute neglect. 21 Pa. Dist. at 563. In *Hudson*, 13 Wash. 673, 126 P.2d 765 (1942), although the monstrous arm made the child more susceptible to infection, the court found sufficient risk of death in the amputation procedure to justify the objections of the mother. The choice of whether the child should go through life handicapped by an enlarged, deformed arm or undergo the risks and benefits of amputation was one for the mother to make.

69. In *Seiferth*, 309 N.Y. 80, 127 N.E.2d 820 (1955), the minor and his father objected to surgery, even after being fully informed of the prognosis of a corrective procedure. Ordering surgery against the child's wishes would diminish its benefits, for the child would be less likely to participate in postoperative speech therapy essential for its success. *Id.* at 85, 127 N.E.2d at 823. In *Green*, 448 Pa. 338, 292 A.2d 387 (1972), the court remanded the case for an evidentiary hearing on the question whether the boy objected to receiving blood transfusions necessary for the corrective surgery. The court strongly implied that if the child had no objections, the procedure would be ordered, or at least could legally occur, even without parental consent. *Id.* at 348–50, 292 A.2d at 392. For a differently focused analysis of the medical neglect cases discussed in this section, *see* Note, *State Intrusion into Family Affairs: Justifications and Limitations*, 26 STAN. L. REV. 1383, 1399–1401 (1974).

70. Rickham & Mawdsley, *The Effect of Early Operation on the Survival of Spina Bifida Cystica*, DEVELOP. MED. & CHILD NEUROL. 20 (Supp. 11, 1966).

the minor's consent is unascertainable, and the risk of surgery is less than the risk of not treating the defect, which frequently must be remedied immediately if it is to benefit the child.[71]

B. *Liability of the Physician and Hospital*

The practice of withholding ordinary lifesaving treatment from defective infants exposes physicians and hospitals as well as parents to extensive criminal liability. The attending physician, hospital interns, residents, consultants, nurses, chiefs of staff, and even the hospital itself may be guilty of crimes ranging from homicide to failure to conform to child-abuse reporting laws. Since the theories upon which the criminal liability of these parties is based are basically the same, this section will primarily confine its analysis to the attending physician who does not administer lifesaving treatment to a defective infant; for it is he who faces the greatest potential liability.

The attending physician plays an influential role when parents decide to provide or withhold lifesaving treatment from a defective infant. The physician informs the parents of the child's defects, explains the prognosis, and discusses the need for medical or surgical intervention. The parents look to him both as an authoritative source of painful information and as a counsel during a difficult moment.[72] When the parents refuse treatment, the physician faces a difficult choice. He can acquiesce, thereby leading to the child's death and conflicting with ethical norms; or he can protect the infant by seeking judicial authority for the treatment or by informing public authorities who can initiate neglect proceedings.[73] While intervening against the parents' wishes is an uncomfortable step for a physician, the physician who accepts the parents' decision and does nothing further may be guilty of several crimes.[74]

1. *Homicide.*

The attending physician who withholds lifesaving treatment from a defective infant may be found culpable of homicide on two separate the-

---

71. *See* Sharrard, Zachary, Lorber & Bruce, *A Controlled Trial of Immediate and Delayed Closure of Spina Bifida Cystica*, 38 ARCHIVES DISEASE CHILDHOOD 18 (1963); note 70 *supra*.

72. Duff & Campbell, *supra* note 9, at 892–93. *See also* Shaw, *Dilemmas of 'Informed Consent' in Children*, 289 NEW ENG. J. MED. 885 (1973). But in some cases, physicians have not informed parents of the entire situation and its various alternatives, or have emphasized only the worst aspects of the problem, thereby encouraging a decision against treatment. *See* Duff & Campbell, *supra* note 9, at 893.

73. Most states have a procedure whereby the question of whether a child is neglected can be brought before a court, which will appoint a guardian, if necessary, to consent to the medical procedure. *See, e.g.,* WIS. STAT. § 48.35 (West 1957).

74. If the physician performed the procedure during a nonemergency without the consent of the parent or legal guardian, he might be liable in tort for a battery to the child. Bonner v. Moran, 126 F.2d 121 (D.C. Cir. 1941). Although the chances of a suit and recovery against the physician are slim because the intervention is presumably for the child's benefit, it is preferable, time per-

ories. First if his withholding of care or failure to report the case to appropriate public authorities violates state neglect[75] or child-abuse reporting[76] statutes, and the child dies, he may be guilty of involuntary manslaughter under the misdemeanor-manslaughter rule.[77] The second theory imposes liability for a knowing or grossly negligent failure to provide care, thereby proximately causing the death of the person to whom the duty is owed.[78] Under this second theory, the physician is liable for homicide only if he has a *legal*, as opposed to a moral, duty to act to protect the child.[79]

Physicians incur a legal duty to treat a patient only by their consent in undertaking his care.[80] The physician who declines to aid the injured accident victim commits no crime.[81] However, the physician who has contracted with the parents to deliver and treat their newborn infant has assumed an obligation to act on the infant's behalf.[82] The question that arises is whether the physician remains obligated to care for the infant if the parents either refuse to consent to a procedure that he advises is essential to maintain the child's life, or discharge him altogether. The following discussion explores three different grounds that demonstrate that the parents in this situation cannot extinguish the physician's duty of care toward the infant.[83]

a. *Contract.*

The legal duty to provide medical care, the omission of which supports a homicide conviction, may be created by contract.[84] While no appellate

mitting, to seek a determination that the child is neglected because of lack of medical care and that a guardian should be appointed to consent to the procedure.

75. *See* notes 115–23 *infra* and accompanying text. *See also* notes 61–71 *supra* and accompanying text.

76. *See* notes 124–36 *infra* and accompanying text.

77. W. LaFave & A. Scott, *supra* note 28, at 594–601. *See also* notes 41–43, 48–51 *supra* and accompanying texts.

78. *See* note 28 *supra* and accompanying text. As was true of the criminal liability of parents, if the breach of duty is intentional, first- or second-degree murder is a possible charge. *See* notes 29–30 *supra* and accompanying text. However, proving intention in this situation may be difficult, and thus involuntary manslaughter based on a grossly negligent or reckless breach of the physician's duty to care for the child is the crime more likely to be prosecuted.

79. W. LaFave & A. Scott, *supra* note 28, at 182–91; G. Williams, *supra* note 28, at 7–8.

80. *See* notes 84–106 *infra* and accompanying text.

81. Agnew v. Parks 172 Cal. App. 2d 756, 343 P.2d 118 (2d Dist. 1959); Butterworth v. Swint, 53 Ga. App. 602, 186 S.E. 770 (1936); Hurley v. Eddingfield, 156 Ind. 416, 59 N.E. 1058 (1901).

82. Moreover, supervisory or administrative physicians such as the hospital's chief of staff, the chief of surgical service, and the director of the pediatric intensive-care unit also may have assumed a contractual obligation to act on the infant's behalf in certain circumstances. As employees of the hospital, the supervisors are under a contractual obligation with the hospital to assure that the health and safety of patients are protected, and the patients are considered third-party beneficiaries of this arrangement. *See* notes 91–93 *infra* and accompanying text. Similarly, a nurse employed by the hospital to provide nursing services to infants in her ward also has assumed a contractual obligation to care for the child, with the child being an intended third-party beneficiary to the contract. *Id.*

83. A similar analysis reveals that the contractual obligations that nurses and supervisory physicians assume with regard to the defective infant, *see* note 82 *supra*, cannot be extinguished by the hospital or its agents.

84. *See* Jones v. United States, 308 F.2d 307 (D.C. Cir. 1962); J. Turner, *supra* note 28, at 410–12.

case deals directly with the criminal liability of a physician for failure to perform a contract for medical services, his civil liability in such cases is well established in the doctrine of abandonment.[85] Abandonment, with roots both in tort and contract, recognizes that once the physician-patient relationship has been established, the physician, in the absence of a special agreement, is under an obligation to attend the case as long as it requires attention.[86] Moreover, the criminal consequences of abandonment have been clearly recognized with persons other than physicians who assume care of children. In one case,[87] for example, a woman who contracted with a mother to care for a 17-month-old baby was convicted of manslaughter when she failed to provide the baby with proper food, medicine, and medical attendance, causing its death.[88] Similarly, another court[89] stated that manslaughter is supportable if the defendant accepted a contractual arrangement to care for the deceased child and failed to provide medical care.[90]

In addition to the doctrine of abandonment, the courts may regard the newborn infant as an intended third-party beneficiary of a contract between the parents and physician.[91] According to the law that governs third-party beneficiary contracts, the promisee is generally free to modify or release the promisor up until the moment that the third party's rights or benefits under the contract vest.[92] In the case of infants, who lack legal or actual capacity to assent or rely on a contract made for their benefit, the law presumes that their rights vest as soon as the contract is made.[93] Thus,

---

85. "It consists of a failure by the physician to continue to provide service to the patient when it is still needed in a case for which the physician has assumed responsibility and from which he has not been properly relieved." D. LOUISELL & H. WILLIAMS, MEDICAL MALPRACTICE 217 (1960). *See* McGulpin v. Bessmer, 241 Iowa 1119, 43 N.W.2d 121 (1950); Fortner v. Koch, 272 Mich. 273, 261 N.W. 762 (1935); Cazzell v. Schofield, 319 Mo. 1169, 85 S.W.2d 580 (1928); Burnett v. Laymen, 133 Tenn. 323, 181 S.W. 157 (1915); Vann v. Harden, 187 Va. 555, 47 S.E.2d 314 (1948).

86. D. LOUISELL & H. WILLIAMS, *supra* note 85, at 219. The case may cease to require attention if the patient discharges the physician, or the physician informs the patient that he intends to discontinue his services with notice adequate to enable the patient to find another physician. *See also* Amer. Med. Ass'n, *Principles of Medical Ethics*, in W. CURRAN & E. SHAPIRO, LAW, MEDICINE, AND FORENSIC SCIENCE 524–25 (2d ed. 1970).

87. Rex v. Jones, 19 Cox Crim. Cas. 678 (1901).

88. The defendant's claim that she lacked money to provide medical care was rejected because she had received a lump sum from the mother, which, if properly allocated, would have furnished sufficient means. *Id.*

89. Jones v. United States, 308 F.2d 307 (D.C. Cir. 1962).

90. *See also* People v. Montecino, 66 Cal. App. 2d 85, 152 P.2d 5 (2d Dist. 1944); State v. Lowe, 66 Minn. 296, 68 N.W. 1094 (1896).

91. The contract between parents and physician is intended primarily for the benefit of a third party—the infant. Thus, he is regarded as an intended third-party beneficiary of the contract. Under older classifications of third-party beneficiary law, the child is a creditor as opposed to a donee beneficiary, for he receives a benefit—medical care—which the parents are legally obligated to provide. *See generally* A. CORBIN, THE LAW OF CONTRACTS §§ 772–79C (1952); L. SIMPSON, CONTRACTS 241–49 (1965).

92. A. CORBIN, *supra* note 91, §§ 812–16; L. SIMPSON, *supra* note 91, at 256–57; RESTATEMENT (SECOND) OF CONTRACTS § 142 (Tent. Drafts Nos. 1–7, 1973).

93. *See* Rhodes v. Rhodes, 266 S.E.2d 790 (Ky. Ct. App. 1954) (father who designated his infant son as beneficiary under corporate annuity plan with no provision to change beneficiary could not designate another beneficiary in derogation of son's rights); Plunkett v. Atkins, 371 P.2d 727

with regard to the parent-physician contract, the parents as promisees cannot modify or rescind the contractual duty of the physician as promisor to provide needed medical services to the infant.[94]

Where parents request that the physician stop treatment of the infant, and compliance with that request would jeopardize the patient's health, the physician nevertheless may be required to provide medical services without parental consent. But since such action could conceivably expose the physician to tort liability for battery,[95] the better practice in nonemergency cases would be to seek judicial authority for the procedure or to notify public authorities who could bring a neglect proceeding that would lead to the appointment of a guardian empowered to consent to the procedure.[96]

b. *Assumption of care.*

A legal duty to act, the omission of which will support homicide liability, is also recognized when one not otherwise under a duty to act has voluntarily assumed or undertaken the care of another.[97] Thus, whether

---

(Okla. Sup. Ct. 1962) (father contracted with mother to pay for support and education of his illegitimate infant son and later, when mother remarried, attempted to reduce the payments; court held that without son's consent parents cannot modify original contract). The only situation in which parents have the power to modify or rescind the contract made for the benefit of the child is when they expressly reserved that right at the time of entering into the original contract. *See* Rhodes v. Rhodes, *supra.* In many defective-infant situations, however, the contract for care of the child is made while the child is *in utero.* Although one may question whether a third-party beneficiary's rights may vest when it is not yet in existence, these rights would vest upon birth. Thus, the parents' power to modify the contract for the child's medical services remains only until the moment of birth.

In many cases these metaphysical subtleties will be of slight concern, for the physician confronted with the parental decision not to treat will often be a pediatrician whose contract to provide general care for the child takes effect only upon the child's birth. In this case no problem concerning the vesting of third-party beneficiary rights in a fetus arises.

94. This argument that the physician is under a nonextinguishable contractual duty to provide care for the newborn is based on the assumption that parents and physicians commonly enter into agreements to provide general, as opposed to special, medical care for the child. For example, parents normally contract with an obstetrician or general practitioner for delivery of the child and all care needed by the newborn until another physician, such as a pediatrician, assumes care of the child. Similarly, an agreement with a pediatrician to care for the child after delivery will ordinarily be an agreement to provide general care for the child. However, physicians could avoid a contractual duty to treat defective newborns if their agreement for postnatal or perinatal care was specifically limited to cases of nondeformed children, or stated that they were not undertaking to keep a deformed infant alive in all circumstances. Similarly, the physician's duty of general care might be extinguishable where the parents have expressly reserved the right to modify the services that they expect to be provided. *See* Antley v. New York Life Ins. Co., 139 S.C. 23, 139 S.E. 199 (1927); RESTATEMENT (SECOND) OF CONTRACTS § 142 (Tent. Drafts Nos. 1–7, 1973). But resort to either of these arrangements to avoid a contractual duty would seem unlikely, since parents and physicians probably will not have considered the possibility of giving birth to a defective child thoroughly enough to plan ahead until the event occurs. Of course, if prosecutions began to occur, one might expect to see precautionary changes in the contractual arrangements between parents and physicians.

95. *See* note 74 *supra.*

96. *See* notes 73–74 *supra* and accompanying text. Moreover, under child-abuse reporting laws, the physician may have a separate statutory duty to report such incidents. *See* notes 124–36 *infra* and accompanying text.

97. *See* W. LaFave & A. Scott, *supra* note 28, at 185–86. This rule of law is very similar to the doctrine of abandonment. See notes 85–90 *supra* and accompanying text. For example, in the leading case on this point of law, Regina v. Instan, 17 Cox Crim. Cas. 602 (1893), the Queen's Bench affirmed the manslaughter conviction of a niece whose failure to provide food and medical assistance caused the death of an elderly aunt with whom she was living. The defendant, an un-

or not the physician enters a formal contractual arrangement with parents to provide care for the child, his voluntary assumption of the child's care imposes a legal duty to continue to provide such care as long as the child's health is endangered.[98] Although there are no cases directly on point, the

---

married woman without income, was supported by her aunt. Until a few weeks before her death the deceased was healthy and able to care for herself. She then contracted gangrene in her leg, which rendered her incapable of attending to her needs or procuring assistance. The defendant, the sole person with knowledge of the aunt's condition, continued to live in the house at the deceased's expense, and took in food supplied by tradespeople, but neither gave nor procured medical or nursing assistance although there was ample opportunity to do so. The cause of death was "exhaustion" from "gangrene" substantially accelerated by neglect, want of food, and lack of nursing and medical attendance during the several days preceding death. The trial judge instructed the jury that if they found that the defendant had implicitly undertaken to attend the deceased and that failure to do so substantially accelerated death, they might find her guilty of manslaughter. Lord Coleridge, speaking for three judges, affirmed the conviction on the ground that the defendant had a "clear duty at common law to supply [food] to the deceased," which rested on "taking upon herself the performance of the moral obligation" to care for the aunt. *Id.* at 604.

98. Under this approach, only the attending physician employed to care for the child incurs a legal duty to protect it when the parents reject treatment. A physician specially employed as a consultant who does not undertake to provide general care is not so obligated. However, nurses, supervisory physicians, and even the hospital itself probably could be viewed as having undertaken to care for particular patients and thus may be under an obligation to protect the defective newborn infant.

Nurses just as clearly as attending physicians frequently voluntarily undertake the care of a child. However, since nurses and physicians fulfill different professional roles, it could be argued that their duties of care are not commensurate. Physicians diagnose, treat, and prescribe; nurses observe and record symptoms and administer treatments and medications prescribed by the physician. E. SPRINGER, NURSING AND THE LAW 62 (1970). Since the nurse's care of a patient is subordinated or pursuant to the orders of a physician, her duty of care arguably is fulfilled when she employs the skills and techniques within her training, and reports all other needs of the patient to the attending physician. *See, e.g.,* Cooper v. National Motor Bearing Co., 136 Cal. App. 2d 229, 288 P.2d 581 (1st Dist. 1955). Thus, under this view, if the physician concurs in or acquiesces in the parental decision to withhold treatment, the nurse has no legal duty to take any other steps to protect the patient.

However, neither the ethics of the nursing profession, public policy considerations, nor case law supports such a narrow view of the nursing role. Nursing is a separately licensed profession with its own set of norms and ethical commitments. E. SPRINGER, *supra,* at 57–60. These norms clearly indicate a duty and relationship to the patient independent of the physician. Like the physician, the nurse is under a legal duty not to abandon her patient in situations endangering his health. *See* notes 84–90 *supra* and accompanying text. While a nurse generally administers the treatment prescribed by the physician, her primary duty is to the patient. If a physician orders an obviously negligent or dangerous treatment, a nurse is legally liable if she administers it. *See* Hubuda v. Trustees of Rex Hosp. Inc., 3 N.C. App. 11, 164 S.E.2d 17 (Ct. App. 1968); Byrd v. Marion Gen. Hosp., 202 N.C. 337, 162 S.E. 738 (1932); Monogue v. Rutland Hosp., 119 Vt. 336, 125 A.2d 796 (1956). *See also* Goff v. Doctors Gen. Hosp., 166 Cal. App. 2d 314, 333 P.2d 29 (1958). Similarly, a nurse has a legal duty to take steps to protect an infant whom the attending physician and parents have decided to let die. At the very least this duty requires that the nurse notify either the public welfare authorities or the appropriate child-welfare personnel within the hospital.

Supervisory or administrative physicians, such as the hospital's chief of staff and the director of the pediatric intensive-care unit also may be viewed as having undertaken to perform supervisory duties, including assuring the safe care of hospital patients. Having assumed this supervisory role, they are charged by law with exercising due care in the discharge of their duties, and are not free to omit supervision that could endanger patient health and safety. Thus, if they are aware of a case in which a physician acquiesces in a parent's decision to withhold treatment from a defective infant, they should be legally obligated to take action to protect that infant's life and to prevent similar situations in the future.

It is even possible that the hospital itself could be held liable for an intentional or grossly negligent failure to take reasonable steps to protect the health and safety of infant patients whose care it implicitly assumed. In civil cases, hospitals have been held liable for "abandoning a patient," *see, e.g.,* Bonregeois v. Dade County, 99 So. 2d 575 (Fla. 1957), as well as for dereliction in not restricting staff privileges of nonemployee physicians whom they had reason to know were negligent, *see, e.g.,* Purcell v. Zimbelman, 18 Ariz. App. 75, 500 P.2d 335 (Ct. App. 1972). Thus, it is possible that a hospital could be found criminally liable under a similar corporate-negligence argument. The rationale of the assumption-of-care doctrine[99] compels the conclusion that parents' refusal to consent to a procedure necessary to save the life of the infant cannot limit or extinguish the duty incurred by the physician in choosing to care for the child. Again, the minimum act that satisfies the physician's duty is the notification of public authorities of the grave danger facing the infant so that neglect proceedings leading to the appointment of a guardian may be commenced.[100]

c. *Creation of peril.*

A third basis for imposing a legal duty on the physician to act to save the infant's life is the physician's role in creating the child's peril. When *A* has placed *B* in a position of harm, *A* incurs a legal duty to act to protect *B*.[101] Justice Holmes put the point succinctly: "If a surgeon from benevolence cuts the umbilical cord of a new-born child he cannot stop there and watch the patient bleed to death. It would be murder wilfully to allow death to come to pass in that way."[102]

Although the attending physician is in most cases not the cause of the defective child's malformities,[103] he may be said to be responsible for its present peril in two senses. First, if the attending physician delivered the baby, he is an immediate (though by no means the sole) cause of its present peril; but for his act, the child would not be facing the prospect of nontreatment. In this sense having placed the child in danger, the physician is legally obligated to protect it.[104] Second, without information provided by the

easiest case would be where the hospital, acting through its trustees or medical staff, explicitly adopted a policy (1) prohibiting house staff and nurses from treating defective infants, or (2) delegating the treatment decision to parents and attending physicians. Such policies could constitute an intentional failure of the hospital to perform its duty of care to defective infant patients. But where the hospital has merely been derelict in preventing the omission of care by attending physicians and staff, liability would exist only if the dereliction were gross or reckless. A high degree of negligence is more likely to be found if supervisory personnel fail to act when such cases are brought to their attention than if they merely have been negligent in keeping abreast of such cases. However, once a defective infant is allowed to die, failure to keep informed may become gross negligence. *See id.* Since the hospital acts through the agency of the medical staff, including chiefs of staff and services, criminal liability of the hospital is likely to be coextensive with that of supervisory personnel. Whether either actually is likely to be prosecuted is another question that will be explored later. *See* notes 181–85 *infra* and accompanying text.

99. Assumption-of-care liability is based on the rationale that persons who might have come to the rescue of an endangered individual will no longer perceive the necessity of doing so once another has assumed his care. *See* W. LaFave & A. Scott, *supra* note 28, at 185.

100. *See* note 96 *supra* and accompanying text.

101. W. LaFave & A. Scott, *supra* note 28, at 186; *see Jones v. State,* 220 Ind. 384, 43 N.E.2d 1017 (1942); King v. Commonwealth, 285 Ky. 654, 148 S.W.2d 1044 (1941); Depue v. Flateau, 100 Minn. 299, 111 N.W.2d 1 (1907). This duty to act arises even if the defendant innocently or unintentionally creates the situation of danger. *Cf.* Commonwealth v. Calli, 247 Mass. 20, 141 N.E. 510 (1923).

102. O. Holmes, The Common Law 278 (1881).

103. Unless he negligently prescribed a drug that created the deformities, failed to advise the mother of risk and of the possibility of amniocentesis, or failed to perform *in utero* screening with due care.

104. One may, however, argue that this view distorts the ordinary meaning of "cause" or "place in peril," by confusing being born with being placed in danger, and by treating the agent

physician concerning the infant's defects, prognosis, and need for surgery, the parents might not even consider withholding care, or even be aware that such an option exists. Just as the physician's delivering a baby may be said to cause its birth, the physician's discussing treatment options with the parents of a defective infant may be the immediate cause of its not being treated.[105] The importance of this doctrine of "creation of peril" clearly is evidenced by the case of a viable fetus lawfully aborted by hysterotomy. It is difficult to conceive that a physician who removes the fetus alive and breathing from its mother's womb is free to place it on a table and do nothing to protect or treat it. If the infant dies from want of care, the physician would appear to be guilty of homicide by omission. The omitted legal duty, however, is not contractual, for the physician has made no contract with the mother to provide medical services to the newborn; rather, the contract is to perform an abortion. Nor has the physician undertaken to care for the infant; the very purpose of the abortion is to remove the fetus from its life-support system in the mother's womb. The physician's duty not to omit needed care could only derive from the doctrine of "creation of peril."[106]

2. *Accessory before-the-fact.*

Even if the courts were to hold that in some cases a physician's legal duty to save the life of the child can be extinguished and, therefore, that a physician is not guilty of homicide for failure to act, he may still be punished for murder or manslaughter if his actions make him an accessory before-the-fact to a homicide by the parents. An accessory before-the-fact is one who orders, counsels, encourages, or aids and abets another to commit a felony, and who is not present at the commission of the offense.[107]

---

of the birth as a cause or instrumentality of the child's peril. Moreover, it can be argued that the physician's duty in such a case is dependent on the mere fortuity that he rather than another delivered the child—hardly a sound basis for a legal duty.

In response to these objections, one may reply that legal determinations of cause always involve a selection of one necessary condition for an occurrence among many, even though all conditions are necessary for the occurrence, and none alone is sufficient. *See* Weinreb, *Comment on Basis of Criminal Liability; Culpability; Causation: Chapter 3, Section 610,* in WORKING PAPERS OF THE NATIONAL COMMISSION ON REFORM OF FEDERAL CRIMINAL LAW 105, 142–43 (1970). The proper question then is not whether other causes also exist, but whether social policy justifies selecting the physician's act as the one imperiling the child. Since the physician's actions can be influenced by social judgments and sanctions, and thus ameliorate or limit the impact of the child's defects, it is appropriate to view his actions as causing the child's peril, at least for the limited purpose of creating in him a duty to act. Moreover, the fortuitous nature of the situation is not distinguishable from other fortuities that lead to legal responsibilities. One who accidentally hits another automobile incurs a duty to aid others, even though the collision was the result of the fortuity of coming upon an invisible icy patch in the road.

105. While the consultant physician normally would not assume a legal duty to care for the child on a contractual or assumption-of-care basis, *see* note 98 *supra,* a consultant physician whose role is to provide information and who knew or had reason to know that the information he provided is likely to lead to a refusal of treatment potentially could incur liability under this theory.

106. *See* note 35 *supra*; note 185 *infra.*

107. W. LaFave & A. Scott, *supra* note 28, at 498. This common law formulation largely has been superseded by state statutes creating accomplice liability for such acts as "aiding," "abetting,"

Accomplice or accessorial liability does not require actual physical aid, and may arise from actions long before the crime itself is committed.[108] Direct communication between principal and accessory is not necessary; nor is a showing that the accessory's aid or encouragement played an actual part in the commission of the crime.[109] In essence, one is an accomplice merely if he intentionally acts to induce, aid, or encourage the commission of a crime that subsequently is committed. Moreover, in some jurisdictions one also may be liable if, lacking an actual intention to facilitate or commit the crime, he gives assistance or encouragement with the knowledge that it may have that effect.[110]

The attending or consultant physician may incur accessorial liability in his role as adviser and counselor to the parents. Since the physician presents information to the parents concerning defects, prognosis, and treatment, often with great persuasiveness or authority, he may induce or influence the decision the parents reach concerning treatment. The clearest case is one in which the physician feels the child should not live, and consequently advises, counsels, induces, or otherwise encourages the parents to withhold consent. If omission of care by the parent is criminal, then the physician's liability as an accessory clearly follows. Moreover, if the physician had intentionally sought to have the child die, and its parents were merely "reckless" in refusing consent for treatment, the physician could conceivably be held as an accessory to first-degree murder, although the parents would only be guilty of manslaughter.[111]

The more difficult case arises when the physician is personally indifferent to the child's fate, or would prefer that it live, but feels obligated to provide the parents with all the facts and allow them to make the decision; thus, he provides information that he knows may encourage or lead them to refuse consent. While the rule that knowledge without intent suffices for accessorial liability can be seen as consistent with criminal law objectives, it conflicts with the physician's legal and ethical duty to disclose all relevant information to the parental decisionmaker.[112] Moreover,

---

"advising," "assisting," "causing," "counseling," "encouraging," "hiring," "inducing," and "procuring." *Id.* at 502.

108. *Id.* at 503.

109. People v. Wright, 26 Cal. App. 2d 197, 79 P.2d 102 (3d Dist. 1938) (no direct communication needed); Skidmore v. State, 80 Neb. 698, 115 N.W. 288 (1908) (accessory need not play an active part in crime).

110. W. LaFave & A. Scott, *supra* note 28, at 508; *see* Backun v. United States, 112 F.2d 635 (4th Cir. 1940).

111. W. LaFave & A. Scott, *supra* note 28, at 507.

112. The duty to disclose is recognized in the concept of informed consent; however, it is not absolute, and it is likely that a privilege to withhold information from the parents might apply. *See* Canterbury v. Spence, 464 F.2d 772 (D.C. Cir. 1972); Cobbs v. Grant, 8 Cal. 3d 229, 502 P.2d 1, 104 Cal. Rptr. 505 (1972); Wilkinson v. Vesey, 110 R.I. 606, 295 A.2d 676 (1972). The situation does, however, create a difficult choice for the physician, who must decide to withhold from the parents relevant information or disclose and endanger the child.

to base accomplice liability on these grounds also would be unfair since physicians cannot consistently be expected to know how parents will react to information. Thus, while some earlier cases have reached contrary results,[113] in most jurisdictions and in recent cases generally, knowing aid or facilitation without actual intent to procure the commission of a crime is insufficient to create accessorial liability.[114]

3. Neglect.

The physician who acquiesces in the parental refusal to treat a defective child also may violate child-neglect laws. While typically these offenses are only misdemeanors,[115] they should nevertheless be of serious concern to a physician.[116]

A physician's liability under the neglect statutes depends in the first instance on the precise wording of the statute applied to his conduct. Although some 40 states have what may be termed cruelty-to-children or neglect statutes,[117] the conduct prohibited and the persons obligated thereunder vary widely. The statutes fall into two groups. Most statutes are addressed to the parents or a person having "care or custody or legal control" of a child.[118] While a strict reading of such language arguably might exclude the attending physician, it is reasonable to consider the attending physician as being in loco parentis or otherwise having custody or legal control of the hospitalized infant.[119] The ambiguity of such language is lessened further when the words "any person having care . . ." are employed.[120]

In contrast to statutes addressed to parents or those in care or custody, many states simply prohibit "any person" from using cruelty or maltreating children,[121] with cruelty or maltreatment often defined to include the absence of necessary medical care.[122] Under these formulations the physician can hardly argue that he is not within the class of persons to whom

---

113. See, e.g., Jindra v. United States, 69 F.2d 429 (5th Cir. 1934); Vukich v. United States, 28 F.2d 666 (9th Cir. 1928).

114. Nye & Nissen v. United States, 336 U.S. 613 (1949); Hicks v. United States, 150 U.S. 442 (1893); Baker v. United States, 395 F.2d 368 (8th Cir. 1968); United States v. Garguilo, 310 F.2d 249 (2d Cir. 1962); Morei v. United States, 127 F.2d 827 (6th Cir. 1942); United States v. Peoni, 100 F.2d 401 (2d Cir. 1938); United States v. Dellaro, 99 F.2d 781 (2d Cir. 1938); United States v. Nearing, 252 F. 223 (S.D.N.Y. 1918).

115. See, e.g., N.J. STAT. §§ 9:6-3, 9:6-1 (West 1960).

116. If the physician violates the child-neglect laws, and the child dies, he may be guilty of involuntary manslaughter under the "misdemeanor-manslaughter" rule. See notes 41–43, 48–51 & 77 supra and accompanying texts.

117. See Paulsen, supra note 32, at 681.

118. See, e.g., ARK. STAT. ANN. § 41-1105 (1964); HAWAII REV. LAWS § 577-12 (1968).

119. Cf. Ybarra v. Spangard, 25 Cal. 2d 486, 154 P.2d 687 (1944) (a patient undergoing an operation is in the care and custody of doctors and nurses, and if he receives injuries while under their control, he is entitled to rely on the doctrine of res ipsa loquitur and is not required to prove which doctor or nurse is responsible for his injuries).

120. See, e.g., 23 ILL. ANN. STAT. § 2354 (1968).

121. See, e.g., CAL. PENAL CODE § 273a (West 1970); N.Y. PENAL LAW § 260.10 (McKinney 1967).

122. See note 64 supra and accompanying text.

the prohibition is addressed, for the statute specifies "any person." Hence, except for states having no neglect statute or those that expressly limit their reach to parents or others within a narrow definition of legal custody,[123] physicians risk criminal liability for neglect in refusing to act to save a defective infant.

4. *Child-abuse reporting laws.*

A physician also may be criminally liable for failure to notify public authorities when a child is neglected or injured by the parents' denial of ordinary medical care. In the early and middle 1960's, 44 states imposed a mandatory duty on physicians to report to public authorities cases of battered, neglected, or injured children;[124] 27 of these statutes carry criminal penalties for failure to report, running the gamut from Vermont's "not more than $25.00"[125] to California's "not less than 1 year nor more than 10 years."[126]

The child-abuse reporting laws have an important legal significance for physicians confronting parents of defective infants. Even in states that prescribe no criminal penalty for failure to report, the effect of such statutes is to create a statutory reporting duty independent of a duty arising from contract, undertaking care, or placing in peril.[127]

While the scope and specific requirements of the child-abuse statutes vary, the language is generally broad enough to impose criminal liability for failure to report on the attending physician, consultants, nurses, and hospital administrators or supervisors. A model reporting statute proposed by the Children's Bureau of the United States Department of Health, Education, and Welfare—and essentially embraced in 22 jurisdictions[128]— requires

> any physician, including any licensed osteopathic physician, intern and resident having reasonable cause to suspect that a child . . . brought to him or coming before him for examination, care or treatment has had some physical injury or injuries inflicted upon him other than by accidental means by a parent or other person responsible for his care, shall report or cause reports to be made in accordance with the provisions of this act . . . .[129]

---

123. Massachusetts, for example, would not impose neglect liability on the physician in these circumstances. *See* Mass. Gen. Laws Ann. ch. 119, § 39; ch. 273 § 1 (Supp. 1973).

124. See J. Waltz & F. Inbau, Medical Jurisprudence 320–21 (1971).

125. Vt. Stat. Ann. tit. 13, § 1304 (1974).

126. Cal. Penal Code § 273a (1) (West 1970).

127. *See* notes 84–106 *supra* and accompanying text. Moreover, while a contract or assumption of care approach creates duties solely in the physician caring for the child, *see* notes 84–100 *supra* and accompanying text, the child-abuse reporting laws impose a reporting duty on all physicians, including consultants, residents, and interns, who may examine or treat the child.

128. *See* Paulsen, *Child Abuse Reporting Laws: The Shape of the Legislation,* 67 Colum. L. Rev. 1, 8 (1967).

129. J. Waltz & F. Inbau, *supra* note 124, at 321.

Another 20 states add to this list varying classes of nurses, although some obligate the nurse only if a physician is not present.[130]

In the case of the neglected, defective infant, the main determinant of physician or nurse liability is whether the injury resulting from the denial of ordinary care is the type of injury or abuse that the statute requires to be reported. The Children's Bureau Model Act, for example, requires reporting if the child has "had serious physical injury or injuries inflicted on him other than by accidental means."[131] Other statutes require the reporting of "physical harm due to neglect,"[132] or "gross physical neglect or injury."[133] Under any of these formulations, the physician (and nurse in an applicable state) should have a duty to report the withholding of ordinary medical care that causes an infant's death.

The other requirements for liability under the reporting laws are easily met. No serious question of accidental death will arise;[134] nor can a physician in this situation easily argue that he lacked "a reasonable cause to believe" or "suspect" that a reportable injury had occurred.[135] Thus, the child-abuse reporting laws clearly impose a reporting duty on the physician that can independently lead to criminal prosecution in 27 states.[136]

5. *Conspiracy.*

In addition to potential homicide and accessory liability, a physician also may be guilty of a conspiracy with the parents and hospital personnel to kill the child through omission of necessary medical care. Conspiracy is an agreement or combination to achieve an unlawful objective.[137] Many jurisdictions require, in addition to proof of intent or agreement, an overt act in furtherance of the conspiracy.[138] Hence, if the parents and doctors agree that the child should die, and take any step to achieve that end, a conspiracy to commit murder may lie. Similarly, if physicians and nurses, in discussing the case, agree that the infant should die, and agree to encourage or persuade the parents to withhold treatment, a conspiracy may be charged.

Policy or guidelines for treating defective infants that are developed by the medical staff, or directors of pediatric services or intensive-care units, could be taken as evidence of a conspiracy to commit murder, neglect, and failure to report under the child-abuse laws. Conceivably, the mere provi-

---

130. *See* Paulsen, *supra* note 128, at 6–7 n.21, for citations.
131. J. WALTZ & F. INBAU, *supra* note 124, at 321.
132. D.C. CODE tit. 2, § 161 (1973).
133. PA. STAT. ANN. tit. 11, § 2103 (1967).
134. *See* text accompanying note 129 *supra*.
135. *Id.*
136. *See* text accompanying notes 125–26 *supra*.
137. W. LaFAVE & A. SCOTT, *supra* note 28, at 453.
138. *Id.* at 476.

sion of information to the parents may make a physician, whatever his intention, a conspirator, though the cases on this issue are in conflict.[139] Furthermore, liability for a conspiracy may also impose liability for the substantive crimes committed in pursuance thereof, even if there is no personal participation in the commission of the substantive offense.[140] Hence, a physician who himself is under no legal duty to act to protect the child may be prosecuted for murder or for neglect arising from the parents' denial of treatment if he has conspired to withhold care.

C. Defenses

A party prosecuted for any of the above crimes, in addition to disputing that a duty exists to provide medical care or report its absence, may assert three affirmative defenses. This section analyzes these defenses and assesses the chances of their success.

1. Ordinary versus extraordinary means.

A defendant parent, physician, or nurse may argue that the duty owed to the infant encompasses only ordinary means of care, and that the level of necessary care becomes extraordinary in the case of infants who are born with major defects and deformities. The distinction between ordinary and extraordinary care has not been expressly recognized in case or statutory law, or adequately analyzed in the legal literature.[141] A cogent argument can be made for such a distinction and an appellate court faced, for example, with a case in which a physician has been convicted of homicide for turning off a respirator on a terminally ill patient in a coma might hold that the physician's duty of care does not extend to extraordinary means.[142]

The legal basis for the distinction derives from the scope of the duty owed by a parent, a physician, or one who undertakes the care of another. While the duty varies, each individual is required to provide only the level of care that society may reasonably expect, given the risk, available means, and likelihood of benefit in the precise circumstances facing the actor.[143]

---

139. *Compare* United States v. Falcone, 311 U.S. 205 (1940), *and* People v. Lauria, 251 Cal. App. 2d 471, 59 Cal. Rptr. 628 (2d Dist. 1967), *with* Direct Sales Co. v. United States, 319 U.S. 703 (1943).

140. W. LaFave & A. Scott, *supra* note 28, at 478–82.

141. *But see* N. St. John-Stevas, Life, Death and the Law 275–76 (1961); Gurney, *Is There a Right to Die?—A Study of the Law of Euthanasia*, 3 Cumberland-Samford L. Rev. 235, 243–46 (1972); Louisell, *Euthanasia and Biothanasia*, 22 Cath U.L. Rev. 723, 735–36 (1973); Note, *Euthanasia: Criminal, Tort, Constitutional and Legislative Considerations*, 48 Notre Dame Law. 1202, 1207–10 (1973).

142. A Swedish doctor who, after receiving the family's consent, discontinued intravenous feeding of an elderly patient who had suffered a cerebral hemorrhage was acquitted in a prosecution for professional neglect. *See* Note, *supra* note 141, at 1209–10. For a definition of "extraordinary means," *see* text accompanying note 145 *infra*.

143. The Restatement (Second) of Torts (1965) formulates the point:
"§291. . . . Where an act is one which a reasonable man would recognize as involving a risk of

The law does not demand the unreasonable or extraordinary, for few people could live up to such a standard, and fewer would try. Thus, just as a parent is not obligated to attempt to save a drowning child if the parent cannot swim,[144] neither is he obligated to incur enormous expense in providing treatment with a slight chance of success. Parental duty is limited by what can reasonably be expected of parents, given their protective relationship to a child. Similarly, a physician's duty to undertake a medical procedure is determined by what can reasonably be expected in light of customary medical practice, the likelihood of success, and the available alternatives. Of course, physicians may often employ extraordinary means in particular cases, but they are not legally obligated to do so.

Assuming, then, a legal as well as moral distinction between the ordinary or reasonable and the extraordinary, the difficulty arises in distinguishing between these two levels of care. In the medical situation, the distinction has been phrased as follows:

> Ordinary means are all medicines, treatments, and operations, which offer a reasonable hope of benefit and which can be obtained and used without excessive expense, pain, or other inconvenience.
>
> Extraordinary means are all medicines, treatments, and operations, which cannot be obtained or used without excessive expense, pain, or other inconvenience, or which, if used, would not offer a reasonable hope of benefit.[145]

Yet even if accepted by a court, this distinction does not appear to provide a winning defense for a defendant who is prosecuted for violating a duty to treat a defective infant. In many cases, such as an appendectomy for a Down's baby, the procedure itself does not involve "excessive pain, expense, or other inconvenience," although survival of the infant might have that effect on his family or on society. When the procedure entails great expense or inconvenience to the family, or pain to the infant, there is lack of "a reasonable hope of benefit" only if life itself is not deemed a benefit for the child.

---

harm to another, the risk is unreasonable and the act is negligent if the risk is of such magnitude as to outweigh what the law regards as the utility of the act or of the particular manner in which it is done.

"§292. . . . In determining what the law regards as the utility of the actor's conduct for the purpose of determining whether the actor is negligent, the following factors are important:

"(a) the social value which the law attaches to the interest which is to be advanced or protected by the conduct;

"(b) the extent of the chance that this interest will be advanced or protected by the particular course of conduct;

"(c) the extent of the chance that such interest can be adequately advanced or protected by another and less dangerous course of conduct . . . ."

144. *See* Port Huron v. Jenkinson, 77 Mich. 414, 43 N.W. 923 (1889) (holding unconstitutional an ordinance that had the effect of imposing a penalty on who omits to do an impossible act); W. LaFave & A. Scott, *supra* note 28, at 188.

145. Kelly, *The Duty to Preserve Life*, 12 Theol. Studies 550 (1951). *See also* N. St. John-Stevas, *supra* note 141, at 275.

The case of lifesaving treatment for the defective infant is thus distinguished from the cases of terminal illness where resuscitation, surgery, or medication, although possibly prolonging life, are considered extraordinary procedures. The terminally ill patient will soon die, with or without the procedure. Thus, treatment merely prolongs dying.[146] The defective infant, on the other hand, if treated, can normally live for significant periods. Unless the quality of his life affects its value, a judgment for which there is no legal precedent,[147] the likelihood that treatment means life should justify the procedure. But, where the medical procedure has no reasonable prospect, given the state of the art, of substantially prolonging the child's life, the procedure may be extraordinary and thus not required.[148]

2. Causation.

In a homicide prosecution arising out of a failure to provide medical care to a defective infant, the state has the burden of proving that the omission caused the infant's death. A defendant to such a prosecution may raise two defenses based on lack of a causal relation between his omission and the child's death. He could contend that, even with the omitted medical care, the child would have died—the lack of care thus not being causally related to the death. This issue turns on empirical medical proof and must be decided ultimately by the trier of fact. In certain cases, such as that of a 5- or 6-month-old fetus which, after removal from the mother, is not taken to the nursery, it might be quite easy to show that even with care the infant would not have lived.

In many instances, however, the omitted care might have prolonged the infant's life. Technically, intentionally accelerating an already certain or imminent death is murder.[149] In most cases of omission, the requisite care probably could have prolonged life several days, weeks, or months, if not longer. As the period shortens, however, the distinction between ordinary and extraordinary duties of care[150] becomes relevant. If the care would not reasonably enhance the prospects for life—if only a few days or hours of existence would result from treatment—then its omission is not culpable even though accelerating death, for such care would be extraordinary and thus not legally (or morally) required.

---

146. *See* P. RAMSEY, THE PATIENT AS PERSON 125 (1967); Louisell, *supra* note 141, at 736–39.

147. *See* Gleitman v. Cosgrove, 49 N.J. 22, 227 A.2d 689 (1967).

148. For example, the defense of extraordinary means probably could succeed in the extreme situation of a person in an irreversible coma, with no chance of recovering consciousness or with no spontaneous reaction to stimuli. Treatment considered ordinary in other contexts, such as antibiotics or routine surgery, might be deemed extraordinary and no longer required.

149. W. LaFAVE & A. SCOTT, *supra* note 28, at 250. Thus, a person who cuts the throat of a terminally ill cancer patient, or a physician who injects an air bubble into his vein, is guilty of homicide even if death from cancer would have occurred shortly. *See* People v. Ah Fat, 48 Cal. 61 (1874); State v. Mally, 139 Mont. 599, 366 P.2d 868 (1961).

150. *See* notes 141–48 *supra* and accompanying text.

A second defense based on causation is that the omission of a particular defendant should not legally be considered the cause of the infant's death because the infant would not have died had the other persons with a duty of care fulfilled their obligations to him. Just as a person who inflicts a nonmortal wound is not guilty of homicide if the victim dies through the gross negligence of the hospital or physician,[151] a parent or physician should not be liable when, but for another's intentional or grossly negligent omission, the child would have been saved.[152] The omission of another could be viewed as a sufficiently independent intervening cause to break the causal link between the defendant's act and the resulting death.[153]

There are two major problems with such an argument. First, although the defendant's omission may not be a sufficient condition of the child's death, it clearly is a *necessary* condition. The child would not have died *but for* the defendant's omission, even if the omission alone is not sufficient to cause the death. Treating defendant's omission as a legal cause is thus no different from the assignment of legal causation in other situations. The legal cause is never actually sufficient to cause the result, but is always one of many necessary conditions to the occurrence.[154] Determinations of cause thus always involve policy judgments and must be evaluated on that basis. The law selects one or more necessary conditions as the legal cause when there is a reasonable likelihood that human actions can prevent future occurrences of that necessary condition and thus the prohibited result. A bullet fired from a gun is only one of many conditions that must exist for a human death from shooting. Although firing the gun is a necessary but not sufficient condition of the death, the law justifiably selects that act as the legal cause because the shooting is a point at which social interventions may effectively prevent future deaths by gunfire. Similarly, a social policy of keeping defective infants alive would reasonably label the omission of each party as a legal cause of the death, even though no omission alone would have caused the child to die.

Second, if the defendant reasonably foresees or expects that others with a duty to act will not intervene, the argument that their omissions are independent intervening causes that break the chain of causation fails.[155] Since the parent, or physician, or nurse generally knows whether the others' actions will be forthcoming, the likelihood that the defendant's omission

---

151. *See* Parsons v. State, 21 Ala. 300 (1852); State v. Murphy, 33 Iowa 270 (1871); W. LaFave & A. Scott, *supra* note 28, at 259.

152. *See* People v. Hebert, 228 Cal. App. 2d 514, 39 Cal. Rptr. 539 (2d Dist. 1964).

153. *Cf.* Doss v. Town of Big Stone Gap, 145 Va. 520, 134 S.E. 563 (1920). *See generally* Williams, *Causation in Homicide*, 1957 Crim. L. Rev. 429, 510.

154. *See* note 104 *supra*.

155. Whether an intervening cause breaks a chain of causation depends on whether in light of the actor's conduct it was both independent and unforeseeable. *See* J. Hall, *supra* note 59, at 261–70.

will lead to the infant's death is reasonably foreseeable. Moreover, even if one person failed to act, thinking that the others would then take care of the child, the others' omission might not be sufficiently independent, even if unforeseeable, to break the causal chain and absolve the first omitter of liability. This is clearest in the case of the parents. The doctor's and nurse's omissions arise only because of the parents' failure to act, and thus are initiated or caused by it. Similarly, a nurse's failure to act is not independent of the parents' and physician's forbearance, but in an important sense is occasioned by it. Thus, the omission of the nurse may not be a sufficiently independent act to break the chain of causation as to the parents and doctor.[156]

3. Necessity.

A defendant may also argue that his failure to act was necessary because refusing treatment avoided psychological, economic, and physical suffering by the infant, its family, and society that clearly outweighs the harm that ensued from the death of the infant. The legal doctrine of necessity, recognized at common law,[157] and by statute in New York,[158] Illinois[159] and Wisconsin,[160] provides a defense when committing a crime is the only means of avoiding imminent harm that clearly exceeds the harm that the law aims to prevent, and the emergency is not the fault of the defendant.[161] Traditionally, the doctrine refers to an imminent harm caused by overwhelming physical danger, but not to situations of duress or self-defense when another person is the source of the threat.[162] It recognizes the futility of expecting persons in certain emergency situations to conform to the law. Its existence is a "tacit admission" of man's impotence against some of the greatest evils that assail him, apart from its providing a measure of his moral obligation even in extremis.[163]

---

156. The few statutory formulations of common law principles of causation support this analysis and seem to hold that the omission of one individual is a legal cause, despite the omissions of others legally obligated to act. For example, the MODEL PENAL CODE § 2.03(1)(a) (Tent. Draft No. 4, 1955), states that "conduct is the cause of a result when: (a) it is an antecedent but for which the result in question would not have occurred." This reaches the omission of all individuals involved in a situation, for the conduct of each is a necessary "but for" condition of the result. Alternative formulations also reach the conduct of all persons, even when all are viewed as concurrent causes. The Proposed Federal Criminal Code, for example, denies legal causality to a concurrent cause if other concurrent causes are "clearly sufficient to produce the result and the conduct of the accused clearly insufficient." FED. CRIM. CODE § 305 (Proposed Draft 1971).

157. See W. LaFave & A. Scott, supra note 28, at 381–82; J. Turner, supra note 28, at 92–93; G. Williams, supra note 28, § 173, at 124–28.

158. N.Y. Penal Law § 35.05(2) (McKinney 1967).

159. Ill. Ann. Stat. ch. 38, § 7.13 (1972).

160. Wis. Stat. § 939.47 (1969).

161. See generally J. Hall, supra note 59, at 416–48.

162. Id. The Illinois and New York statutes, however, are not limited to threats from natural forces, as is the Wisconsin statute.

163. Id. at 416.

Because necessity excuses the infliction of harm on the person or interests of an innocent third party, the need must indeed be compelling, and the emergency situation cannot have been created by the actor.[164] Thus sailors may mutiny to compel the captain to return a leaky vessel to port during a gale,[165] and cargo may be jettisoned in a storm to save life.[166] Similarly, the defense of necessity may excuse crimes against the person as well as against property. For example, in *Woods v. State*,[167] the court reversed a conviction for failing to stop and render aid to another motorist with whom the defendant had collided, on the grounds that the failure to stop could have been necessitated by the need to obtain medical aid for the defendant's companion who also was injured in the collision. Indeed, the defendant would have been justified in not stopping even if he had negligently caused the collision and was himself the injured party.[168]

The doctrine of necessity may even justify the killing of another innocent human being in certain circumstances, although English and American courts have split on this point. In the famous shipwreck case of *United States v. Holmes*,[169] crew members in a crowded longboat filled with survivors of a collision with an iceberg threw single male passengers overboard to avert immediate sinking. The following day the survivors were rescued.

---

164. For example, in Bice v. State, 109 Ga. 117, 34 S.E. 202 (1899), the defendant's need to carry alcohol as a medicine for his wife's heart condition was held no defense to a prosecution for having liquor near a church. The harm was not imminent and could have been avoided by her staying home. Similarly, unemployed demonstrators could not justify breaking into a storehouse and taking food, because there was no showing that the defendants were near starvation, or even hungry, much less that food could not be obtained elsewhere by lawful means. State v. Moe, 174 Wash. 303, 24 P.2d 630 (1933). Cases have also held that neither unsanitary and unsafe prison conditions, People v. Whipple, 100 Cal. App. 261, 279 P. 1008 (2d Dist. 1929), nor the threats of other inmates to rape the defendant or kill him for refusal to participate in homosexual activities, People v. Richards, 269 Cal. App. 2d 768, 75 Cal. Rptr. 597 (1st Dist. 1969), are sufficient to invoke the necessity defense in prosecutions for escape. The courts generally find that the harm from permitting escape (increased number of escapes, disruption of prison discipline, attack on guards) outweighs the harm suffered by the prisoner, State v. Palmer, 45 Del. 308, 310, 72 A.2d 442, 444 (Ct. Gen. Sess. 1950); that other alternatives such as petitions through legal channels would suffice, People v. Noble, 18 Mich. App. 300, 170 N.W.2d 916 (Ct. App. 1969); or that the threat of harm to the defendant is not so imminent that escape is the sole alternative, State v. Green, 470 S.W.2d 565 (Mo.), *cert. denied*, 405 U.S. 1073 (1971). *But see* People v. Harmon, 15 Crim. L. Rptr. 2425–26 (Mich. Ct. App. 1974). Likewise, Vietnam War protestors were not excused by the necessity of preventing further war deaths when they refused to leave the offices of a war contractor, State v. Morley, 509 P.2d 1095 (Hawaii 1973), or destroyed draft files, United States v. Kroncke, 459 F.2d 607 (8th Cir. 1972). Not only were alternative means of protest available, but the crime was in no way reasonably calculated to avert the greater evil of war. Finally, in State v. Johnson, 289 Minn. 196, 183 N.W.2d 541 (1971), the court rejected the necessity defense by a person charged with driving a snowmobile on a state highway, because the defendant could have avoided the emergency by taking advance precautions.

165. United States v. Ashton, 24 F. Cas. 873 (No. 14,470) (C.C.D. Mass. 1834).

166. *See* J. HALL, *supra* note 59, at 425–26; W. LaFAVE & A. SCOTT, *supra* note 28, at 384; MODEL PENAL CODE § 3.02, Comment (Tent. Draft No. 8, 1958).

167. 135 Tex. Crim. 540, 121 S.W.2d 604 (Crim. App. 1938).

168. *Id.* at 542, 121 S.W.2d at 606. But where the defendant drove in an intoxicated state to a hospital, seeking care for an injury he suffered while drinking, the Texas court refused to accept a necessity defense on the theory that the emergency resulted from defendant's own actions. Butterfield v. State, 167 Tex. Crim. 64, 317 S.W.2d 943 (Crim. App. 1938). *See also* Sansom v. State, 390 S.W.2d 279 (Tex. Crim. App. 1965).

169. 26 F. Cas. 360 (No. 15,383) (C.C.E.D. Pa. 1842).

Although the court refused to take the case from the jury or grant a new trial on a defense of necessity, it recognized that the sacrifice of a few lives to save many is legally justified if those sacrificed are chosen by a fair procedure, such as lot.[170] However, since single male passengers, but none of the crew, were arbitrarily chosen as victims, the action was unjustifiable.[171]

Thirty years later, in the equally famous case of *The Queen v. Dudley & Stephens*,[172] the Queen's Bench rejected the *Holmes* court's narrow circumscription of circumstances in which necessity could justify the taking of life. Three men and a 17-year-old youth were near starvation after being shipwrecked for several days. Two of the men killed the boy, who was in a more feeble condition, and with the third ate his flesh, enabling them to survive for 4 additional days until they were rescued. Lord Coleridge rejected the defense of necessity on the ground that "there is [no] absolute or unqualified necessity to preserve one's life,"[173] and that "it may be the plainest and highest duty to sacrifice [life]."[174] Moreover, the court saw no objective way of determining when the necessity existed and who was to be sacrificed:

> Who is to be the judge of this sort of necessity? By what measure is the comparative value of lives to be measured? Is it to be strength or intellect or what? It is plain that the principle leaves to him who is to profit by it to determine the necessity which will justify him in deliberately taking another's life to save his own. In this case the weakest, the youngest, the most unresisting, was chosen. Was it more necessary to kill him than any of the grown men?[175]

The foregoing description of the law of necessity makes clear its inapplicability to the omissions of parents, physicians, and nurses confronted with a defective child who will die if not provided ordinary medical care. Although the child and the family may indeed suffer if treatment is provided, the elements of necessity are not met in two respects. First, the evil to be averted is not sufficiently imminent or immediate to constitute an emergency. The suffering of the child and family, if it does occur, looms over time, and does not immediately threaten as in *Holmes* and *Dudley & Stephens*. Moreover, the parents always have the option of terminating their parental rights and obligations, and relinquishing the child to the care and custody of the state.[176] Hence, it is inconceivable that parents have no immediate choice but to withhold care.

Secondly, the gravity of the harm to be avoided does not clearly out-

---

170. *Id.* at 363.
171. *Id.*
172. 14 Q.B.D. 273 (1884).
173. *Id.* at 287.
174. *Id.*
175. *Id.* at 287–88.
176. *See* note 37 *supra*.

weigh the harm of killing another human being. For unlike the decision facing the survivors in *Holmes,* the alternative to killing the defective child is not the death of other persons. The harm sought to be avoided is the inconvenience, shame, and psychological pressure of caring for a sickly, abnormal child, as well as the economic burden on family members and possibly on society. These harms would not justify the withholding of care by parents who always retain the option of institutionalizing the child or terminating parental obligations.[177]

A stronger case can be made where an infant is anencephalic, experiencing incessant, unmanageable pain, and certain to be profoundly retarded and nonambulatory for life. Here it could be argued that it is necessary to withhold treatment in order to save the infant from the horrible existence that would follow from caring for his many defects. But lacking precedents for making such a quality-of-life judgment,[178] it is unlikely that a court would be willing to deviate from respecting the value of human life.[179]

The case of a defective infant, in short, does not provide the overpowering necessity of committing a crime because a clearly higher value is at stake. Indeed, the parents and doctor make rational choices after considering the alternative costs and benefits available to them, and are not overwhelmed by immediate physical forces, as in the decided cases.[180] Moreover,

---

177. Even potential financial ruin would not constitute an economic necessity that justifies withholding care. *See* notes 48–50 *supra* and accompanying text.

178. *See* note 147 *supra* and accompanying text.

179. Moreover, recent cases have explicitly recognized the equal protection and due process rights of the mentally ill and retarded. *See* Mills v. Board of Educ., 348 F. Supp. 866 (D.D.C. 1972) (failure to provide publicly supported specialized education to children labeled as behavioral problems, mentally retarded, emotionally disturbed, or hyperactive violated statutes and school board regulations and denied these children and the class they represented equal protection and due process of law). *See also* Wyatt v. Stickney, 344 F. Supp. 387 (M.D. Ala. 1972).

In addition, the statutory formulations of the necessity defense are particularly unhelpful to a defendant in such a case. Wisconsin requires that his conduct be "the only means of preventing imminent public disaster, or imminent death or great bodily harm to himself or another and which causes him so to act . . . ." WIS. STAT. § 939.47 (1969). Thus psychological, economic, and other nonbodily harms do not even enter into the calculus of costs and benefits of omitting care. Moreover, necessity in Wisconsin is not a complete defense to murder, but only reduces murder to manslaughter. New York law stresses imminence and emergency, requiring that a "public or private injury . . . [be] about to occur," and that the harm in question be "of such gravity that, according to ordinary standards of intelligence and morality, the desirability and urgency of avoiding such injury clearly outweigh the desirability of avoiding the injury sought to be prevented by the statute defining the offense in issue." N.Y. PENAL LAW § 35.05(2) (McKinney 1967). The New York statute also contains a provision that specifically excludes the defense when considerations pertaining only to morality are claimed to make application of the criminal statute inadvisable. *Id.* The legislative history suggests that this language was included to prevent mercy killing, and thus its relevance here is clear. *See* People v. Brown, 70 Misc. 2d 224, 229–30, 333 N.Y.S.2d 342, 349 (Sup. Ct. 1972).

180. There is, however, a conceivable situation in which necessity might successfully be interposed as a defense to withholding care from a defective newborn. Suppose the only available pediatric intensive-care unit has no place available for an otherwise normal infant who has just undergone surgery to correct a defective heart valve. If intensive-care services are available, the chances are great that the surgery will be successful, and that the child will recover to lead a fully normal life. To enable the normal infant to live, the doctor removes the defective infant to the general nursery, where it dies.

Clearly, the case for a necessity defense is stronger. The necessity compelling the homicide is the life of another human being, rather than psychosocial or economic harm. The difficulty, however,

the necessity defense has even less applicability when a viable abortus is denied care. If not defective, the claim of preventing suffering to the infant is not applicable. Nor is the financial and psychological suffering of the family involved, for they have clearly decided to give up the child; the only harm that lack of care may prevent is the harm that occurs in adoption, or failure to adopt. But this clearly cannot justify infanticide.

D. *A Note on Prosecution*

Although a clear basis for prosecution exists, no parent or physician has to date been criminally prosecuted for withholding ordinary medical care from a defective infant. Parents have been prosecuted for direct killing of defective offspring,[181] but these cases involve children who have survived the neonatal period. The closest parallel is the recent manslaughter indictment of a Boston physician who allegedly killed a viable fetus during a lawful abortion.[182]

This enforcement pattern suggests that the legal liability facing parents and physicians is actually quite different from what a formal analysis of the criminal law indicates. One might, for example, better describe the situation as one in which prosecuting authorities, through the exercise of their discretion, have informally delegated authority to parents and physicians to decide the fate of defective newborns.[183] While some prosecutors may have decided that these decisions are best left to parents and physicians, other factors suggest that prosecuting authorities have *not* made explicit policy decisions to tolerate the views of parents and physicians concerning treatment of the defective newborn.

Another explanation of nonenforcement is the extremely low visibility of the practice. In many cases of nontreatment no one complains to a district attorney because the parties involved agree that the best course of action has been taken. Nor do district attorneys customarily read the medical journals in which these issues have been discussed. Without doctors, nurses, and hospital authorities complying with reporting statutes, a district attorney has little chance to learn of the practice. Of course, on occasion

---

lies in showing that by ordinary moral standards the value of the life of the normal child *clearly outweighs* the value of the life of the defective child. An analogy in the lifeboat situation might arise if the lifeboat were full, and swimming alongside was a famous violinist or a young man who was the sole support of his family. To make room for the swimmer the occupants of the boat throw a crippled, elderly, or feebleminded individual overboard. It is doubtful that ordinary moral standards could approve such an act, for it is difficult to balance the worth of human lives, *cf.* text accompanying note 170 *supra*, even if the ultimate social benefit derived from one person's activities is greater than that derived from another's. *Cf.* C. FRIED, AN ANATOMY OF VALUES 200–06 (1970).

181. *See* cases summarized in Sanders, *Euthanasia: None Dare Call It Murder*, 60 J. CRIM. L.C. & P.S. 351, 355 n.36 (1969).

182. *See* note 35 *supra*; note 185 *infra*.

183. Such a policy has its appeal and is discussed in a later section. *See* notes 261–71 *infra* and accompanying text.

a particular case is widely publicized. But as in Maine and elsewhere,[184] these situations usually have involved neglect proceedings that have seemed outside the prosecutor's bailiwick.

Another reason for nonprosecution is the unique and somewhat exceptional nature of the crimes involved. If a reasonable case for criminal liability can be made, it is also true that some novel and complicated points of law are at issue, particularly concerning liability of parties other than the parents. Without having undertaken research, prosecuting offices probably are not familiar with the law. In addition, some prosecutors may know of the practice but decide for other reasons not to proscute. They too may feel that withholding treatment is the most desirable practice. Or prosecution may appear politically unpopular, or unfeasible because of lack of manpower.

Thus, one cannot conclude that parents and physicians have nothing to fear when they decide not to treat a defective newborn. Rather, as the practice is more openly acknowledged and debated, some criminal prosecutions are likely to occur, at least while the legal issues are still being clarified. Although the right-to-life groups have focused on abortion and not yet entered this area, they may rechannel their efforts in the future, particularly as they suffer defeat on the abortion issue. In many instances complaints by a few citizens, who find involuntary euthanasia of defective newborns to be morally repulsive, might suffice to focus the district attorney's awareness on the issue and possibly engender prosecution.[185]

II. Evaluation of Alternative Legal Arrangements

A. *The Issue*

It is reasonably clear that parents who withhold ordinary care from a defective infant, as well as physicians, nurses, and hospital officials who acquiesce in this decision, risk liability for crimes ranging from homicide

---

184. *See* note 11 *supra* and accompanying text.

185. The events leading up to the Boston abortion prosecution are instructive in showing the forces that might lead to prosecutions. On June 7, 1973, an article describing research at the City Hospital in Boston involving fetal tissue from 33 therapeutic abortions was published. *See* Philipson, Sabath & Charles, *Transplacental Passage of Erythromycin and Clindamycin*, 288 NEW ENG. J. MED. 1219 (1973). An anti-abortion group noted the article and complained of experimentation on live fetuses to the mayor, attorney general, and several legislators, and called a press conference to publicize the issue. *See* Scheckan, *BCH Fetus Case: Research at Stake*, Boston Globe, June 2, 1974, at 1, col. 1. The Boston City Council, which has authority over the hospital, began an investigation and held a public hearing. The hearing brought the issue to the attention of Suffolk County District Attorney, Garret Byrne, who also began receiving information from sources within the hospital concerning certain types of activities by some doctors. *Id.* His office investigated and learned of two dead fetuses for whom no death certificates had been filed, as required by state law. While the abortions had been lawfully performed, evidence indicated that either the fetus had been intentionally killed during the procedure, or had been removed alive from the mother and then allowed to die. This information was presented to a grand jury and an indictment resulted. *Id.*

to neglect and violation of the child-abuse reporting laws. The chance of prosecution at the present time, however, is small.

One may ask whether either full or partial enforcement of the law is a desirable mode of regulation, or whether some alternative legal arrangement would better resolve the conflicting values in the defective-infant situation. Duff and Campbell, for instance, argue that "[i]f working out these dilemmas in ways such as [we] suggest is in violation of the law, . . . the law should be changed,"[186] an opinion apparently shared by many other physicians.[187] Other persons consider withholding care from the newborn as morally unjustifiable, and presumably prefer to see the law fully enforced. Still others suggest that new laws be enacted to handle the situation. Possible modifications include amending the homicide and neglect statutes and creating a separate offense of withholding treatment from defective newborns; subjecting to further review the decision not to treat an infant; or designating a decisionmaker wholly independent of parents and physicians to make these decisions.[188]

The appropriate legal response to the defective-infant situation depends on our expectations of what law can and should accomplish. A minimum requirement should guarantee certainty of rule and rule enforcement, thereby informing people of the limits of their discretion and enhancing freedom by permitting them to take legal rules into account. In addition to certainty, however, the law should create a system of expectations that resolves conflicting interests consistent with prevailing morality and our sense of what is just and right. An arrangement exacting too heavy a cost in the values of life; personal, parental and professional autonomy; scarce resources; or other strongly held values will be unacceptable.

What legal rule best comports with dominant values, while doing minimal violence to conflicting interests and providing certainty of application? This question can be answered only by considering two other questions that are at the core of the defective-infant dilemma. The first is whether there is a definable class of beings, such as defective newborns, from whom, under prevailing moral standards, ordinary medical care may be withheld without their consent. If withholding care can never be justified, the sole policy question then is whether existing legal categories best implement that goal or whether a new offense and penalty structure should be created. The second question arises if we conclude that withholding care in some instances is morally justified or socially desirable and asks who among parents, physicians, or other decisionmakers is best equipped

---

186. Duff & Campbell, *supra* note 9, at 894.
187. *See* note 14 *supra*.
188. *See generally* notes 261–277 *infra* and accompanying text.

to decide when care is to be withheld. Legal rules in this regard must focus on criteria, procedures, and decisionmaking processes for implementing a social policy of involuntary passive euthanasia. Until we thoroughly canvass these questions, decisions about legal policy cannot reasonably be made.

This Part first considers two arguments in favor of withholding necessary but ordinary medical care from defective infants, and concludes that neither is persuasive. It then considers whether, given the appropriateness of failing to treat some infants, parents and physicians should be given discretion to make such decisions, and suggests an alternative solution to the issue of who should decide.

B. *Arguments in Favor of Withholding Ordinary Medical Care from Defective Infants*

1. *Defective infants are not persons.*

Children born with congenital malformations may lack human form and the possibility of ordinary, psychosocial development. In many cases mental retardation is or will be so profound, and physical incapacity so great, that the term "persons" or "humanly alive"[189] have odd or questionable meaning when applied to them. In these cases the infant's physical and mental defects are so severe that they will never know anything but a vegetative existence, with no discernible personality, sense of self, or capacity to interact with others.[190] Withholding ordinary medical care in such cases, one may argue, is justified on the ground that these infants are not persons or human beings in the ordinary or legal sense of the term, and therefore do not possess the right of care that persons possess.

Central to this argument is the idea that living products of the human uterus can be classified into offspring that are persons, and those that are not. Conception and birth by human parents does not automatically endow one with personhood and its accompanying rights. Some other character-

---

189. Commentary, *The Ethics of Surgery in Newborn Infants*, 8 CLINICAL PEDIATRICS 251 1969); *cf.* Grunberg, *Who Lives and Dies?*, N.Y. Times, Apr. 22, 1974, at 35, col. 2.

190. *Id.* While the proposition appears to draw some support from Bracton's statement in a noncriminal context that a monster is not a human being, "Quia partus monstruosus est cum non nascatur ut homo," *cited* in G. WILLIAMS, THE SANCTITY OF LIFE AND THE CRIMINAL LAW 20–21 (1957), no case has ever held that a live human offspring is not a human being because of certain physical or mental deficits, and therefore may be killed. *See* G. WILLIAMS, *supra*, at 20–24. The state, in the exercise of its *parens patriae* power to protect persons incapacitated by infancy, neglect, or mental incompetence, recognizes that many "persons" incapable of leading an ordinary or normal life are nevertheless persons with rights and interests to be protected. *See, e.g.*, Herr, *Retarded Children and the Law: Enforcing the Constitutional Rights of the Mentally Retarded*, 23 SYR. L. REV. 995 (1972). Even a slave was protected by the law of homicide even though incapable of full social interaction. *See, e.g.*, Fields v. State, 1 Yager's Rep. 156 (Tenn. 1829). Thus, a judge in Maine recently had little difficulty in concluding that a deformed child with multiple anomalies and brain damage was "at the moment of live birth . . . a human being entitled to the fullest protection of the law." Maine Medical Center v. Houle, No. 74–145, at 4 (Super. Ct., Cumberland Cty., Feb. 14, 1974).

istic or feature must be present in the organism for personhood to vest,[191] and this the defective infant arguably lacks. Lacking that property, an organism is not a person or deserving to be treated as such.

Before considering what "morally significant features" might distinguish persons from nonpersons, and examining the relevance of such features to the case of the defective infant, we must face an initial objection to this line of inquiry. The objection questions the need for any distinction among human offspring because of

> the monumental misuse of the concept of 'humanity' in so many practices of discrimination and atrocity throughout history. Slavery, witchhunts and wars have all been justified by their perpetrators on the grounds that they held their victims to be less than fully human. The insane and the criminal have for long periods been deprived of the most basic necessities for similar reasons, and been excluded from society . . . .
>
> . . . Even when entered upon with the best of intentions, and in the most guarded manner, the enterprise of basing the protection of human life upon such criteria and definitions is dangerous. To question someone's humanity or personhood is a first step to mistreatment and killing.[192]

Hence, according to this view, human parentage is a necessary and sufficient condition for personhood, whatever the characteristics of the offspring, because qualifying criteria inevitably lead to abuse and untold suffering to beings who are unquestionably human. Moreover, the human species is sufficiently different from other sentient species that assigning its members greater rights on birth alone is not arbitrary.

This objection is indeed powerful. The treatment accorded slaves in the United States, the Nazi denial of personal status to non-Aryans, and countless other incidents, testify that man's inhumanity to man is indeed greatest when a putative nonperson is involved.[193] Arguably, however, a distinction based on gross physical form, profound mental incapacity, and the very existence of personality or selfhood, besides having an empirical basis in the monstrosities and mutations known to have been born to women,[194] is a basic and fundamental one. Rather than distinguishing among the particular characteristics that persons might attain through the contingencies of race, culture, and class, it merely separates out those who lack the potential for assuming any personal characteristics beyond breathing and consciousness.

This reply narrows the issue: should such creatures be cared for, protected, or regarded as "ordinary" humans? If such treatment is not war-

---

191. *See* Tooley, *Abortion and Infanticide*, 2 PHIL. & PUB. AFFAIRS 37, 51 (1972).
192. Bok, *Ethical Problems of Abortion*, 2 HASTINGS CENTER STUDIES, Jan. 1974, at 33, 41.
193. *See* Alexander, *Medical Science under Dictatorship*, 241 NEW ENG. J. MED. 39 (1949).
194. T. BECK & J. BECK, ELEMENTS OF MEDICAL JURISPRUDENCE 422 (11th ed. 1960).

ranted, they may be treated as nonpersons. The arguments supporting care in all circumstances are based on the view that all living creatures are sacred, contain a spark of the divine, and should be so regarded. Moreover, identifying those human offspring unworthy of care is a difficult task and will inevitably take a toll on those whose humanity cannot seriously be questioned. At this point the argument becomes metaphysical or religious and immune to resolution by empirical evidence, not unlike the controversy over whether a fetus is a person.[195] It should be noted, however, that recognizing all human offspring as persons, like recognizing the fetus to be a person,[196] does not conclude the treatment issue.[197]

Although this debate can be resolved only by reference to religious or moral beliefs, a procedural solution may reasonably be considered. Since reasonable people can agree that we ordinarily regard human offspring as persons, and further, that defining categories of exclusion is likely to pose special dangers of abuse, a reasonable solution is to presume that all living human offspring are persons. This rule would be subject to exception only if it can be shown beyond a reasonable doubt that certain offspring will never possess the minimal properties that reasonable persons ordinarily associate with human personality. If this burden cannot be satisfied, then the presumption of personhood obtains.

For this purpose I will address only one of the many properties proposed as a necessary condition of personhood—the capacity for having a sense of self—and consider whether its advocates present a cogent account of the nonhuman. Since other accounts may be more convincingly articulated, this discussion will neither exhaust nor conclude the issue. But it will illuminate the strengths and weaknesses of the personhood argument and enable us to evaluate its application to defective infants.

Michael Tooley has recently argued that a human offspring lacking the capacity for a sense of self lacks the rights to life or equal treatment possessed by other persons.[198] In considering the morality of abortion and infanticide, Tooley considers "what properties a thing must possess in order to have a serious right to life,"[199] and he concludes that:

> [h]aving a right to life presupposes that one is capable of desiring to continue existing as a subject of experiences and other mental states. This in turn presupposes both that one has the concept of such a continuing entity and that one believes that one is oneself such an entity. So an entity that lacks such a consciousness of itself as a continuing subject of mental states does not have a right to life.[200]

---

195. *See* Tribe, *Foreword—Toward a Model of Roles in the Due Process of Life and Law*, 87 HARV. L. REV. 1, 18–20 (1973).
196. *See* Thomson, *A Defense of Abortion*, 1 PHIL. AND PUB. AFFAIRS 47 (1971).
197. *See* notes 210–259 *infra* and accompanying text.
198. Tooley, *supra* note 191, at 49.
199. *Id.* at 37.
200. *Id.* at 49.

However, this account is at first glance too narrow, for it appears to exclude all those who do not presently have a desire "to continue existing as a subject of experiences and other mental states." The sleeping or unconscious individual, the deranged, the conditioned, and the suicidal do not have such desires, though they might have had them or could have them in the future. Accordingly, Tooley emphasizes the capability of entertaining such desires, rather than their actual existence.[201] But it is difficult to distinguish the capability for such desires in an unconscious, conditioned, or emotionally disturbed person from the capability existing in a fetus or infant. In all cases the capability is a future one; it will arise only if certain events occur, such as normal growth and development in the case of the infant, and removal of the disability in the other cases. The infant, in fact, might realize its capability[202] long before disabled adults recover emotional balance or consciousness.

To meet this objection, Tooley argues that the significance of the capability in question is not solely its future realization (for fetuses and infants will ordinarily realize it), but also its previous existence and exercise.[203] He seems to say that once the conceptual capability has been realized, one's right to desire continued existence permanently vests, even though the present capability for desiring does not exist, and may be lost for substantial periods or permanently. Yet, what nonarbitrary reasons require that we protect the past realization of conceptual capability but not its potential realization in the future? As a reward for its past realization? To mark our reverence and honor for someone who has realized that state? Tooley is silent on this point.

Another difficulty is Tooley's ambiguity concerning the permanently deranged, comatose, or conditioned. Often he phrases his argument in terms of a temporary suspension of the capability of conceptual thought.[204] One wonders what he would say of someone permanently deranged, or with massive brain damage, or in a prolonged coma. If he seriously means that the past existence of a desire for life vests these cases with the right to life, then it is indeed difficult to distinguish the comatose or deranged from the infant profoundly retarded at birth. Neither will ever possess the conceptual capability to desire to be a continuing subject of experiences. A distinction based on reward or desert seems arbitrary, and protection of life applies equally well in both cases. Would Tooley avoid this problem by holding that the permanently comatose and deranged lose their rights after a certain point because conceptual capacity will never be regained?

---

201. *Id.* at 50.
202. Tooley concedes that the infant attains this capacity in the first year of life, though further research is necessary to identify the exact time. *Id.* at 64.
203. *Correspondence*, 2 PHIL. & PUB. AFFAIRS 419 (1973).
204. *Id.* at 421–23.

This would permit killing (or at least withholding of care) from the insane and comatose—doubtless an unappealing prospect.[205] Moreover, we do not ordinarily think of the insane, and possibly the comatose, as losing personhood before their death. Although their personality or identity may be said to change, presumably for the worse, or become fragmented or minimal, we still regard them as specific persons. If a "self" in some minimal sense exists here then the profoundly retarded, who at least is conscious, also may be considered a self, albeit a minimal one. Thus, one may argue that Tooley fails to provide a convincing account of criteria distinguishing persons and nonpersons. He both excludes beings we ordinarily think of as persons—infants, deranged, conditioned, possibly the comatose—and fails to articulate criteria that convincingly distinguish the nonhuman.[206] But, even if we were to accept Tooley's distinction that beings

---

205. A somewhat similar approach to the definition of personhood by Richard McCormick also fails to cogently distinguish the case of the deranged. McCormick argues that if the potential for human relationships "is simply nonexistent or would be utterly submerged and undeveloped in the mere struggle to survive, that life has achieved its potential" and ordinary care need not be provided. McCormick, *To Save or Let Die—The Dilemma of Modern Medicine*, 229 J.A.M.A. 172, 175 (1974). But would we sanction withholding antibiotics from an insane person suffering a serious infection simply because his capacity to enter into human relationships had become minimal?

206. John Rawls makes a similar argument for the proposition that not all human offspring are entitled to "equal basic rights" of liberty or "the guarantees of justice," *see* J. Rawls, A Theory of Justice 504–10 (1971), and is equally unsuccessful in articulating convincing criteria. His argument arises in the course of a discussion of the features of human beings which entitle them, as opposed to plants, animals, and machines, to be treated in accordance with the principles of justice. To be owed or entitled to equal justice one must possess a certain capacity not present in all human organisms. The capacity is moral personality: "Moral persons are distinguished by two features: First, they are capable of having (and are assumed to have) a conception of their good (as expressed by a rational plan of life); and second they are capable of having (and are assumed to acquire) a sense of justice, a normally effective desire to apply and to act upon the principles of justice, at least to a certain minimum degree." *Id.* at 505. Moral personality qualifies one to be treated with justice, because the principles of justice are derived from the choices which moral persons in the original position desiring to maximize their own (but unknown) good would make: "We use the characterization of the person in the original position to single out the kinds of beings to whom the principles chosen apply. After all, the parties are thought of as adopting those criteria to regulate their common institutions and their conduct toward one another: and the description of their nature enters into the reasoning by which these principles are selected. Thus equal justice is owed to those who have the capacity to take part in and to act in accordance with the public understanding of the initial situation." *Id.*

Rawls, unlike Tooley, accepts the potential rather than present or soon-to-be-assumed capability for moral personality, which includes infants and those "who could take part in the initial agreement, were it not for fortuitous circumstances . . . ." *Id.* at 504. Although he is hesitant in describing moral personality as both a necessary and sufficient condition for justice, he does distinguish those "who have lost their realized capacity temporarily through misfortune, accident, or mental stress" from those "more or less permanently deprived of moral personality," who "may present a difficulty." *Id.* at 510. However, even if creatures lacking this capacity are not entitled to strict justice, "it does not follow that there are no requirements at all in regard to them, [n]or in our relations with the natural order. Certainly it is wrong to be cruel to animals and the destruction of a whole species can be a great evil. The capacity for feelings of pleasure and pain and for the forms of life of which animals are capable clearly imposes duties of compassion and humanity in their case." *Id.* at 512.

Rawls' position, however, is not strictly necessary for the "natural completion of justice as fairness." While Rawls needs to distinguish human claims from those of machines, plants, and animals, such a distinction can stand without dividing human organisms into two classes—the privileged and nonprivileged to enjoy justice. The need for persons in the original position to have certain capacities does not necessarily entail that the principles chosen apply only to those blessed in the natural lottery with the capacity to choose in the original position. Surely those whose capacity for justice or a life plan has been ended by accident or mental disturbance do not lose equal liberty. Why then

lacking the potential for desire and a sense of self are not persons who are owed the duty to be treated by ordinary medical means, this would not appear to be very helpful in deciding whether to treat the newborn with physical or mental defects. Few infants, it would seem, would fall into this class.[207] First, those suffering from malformations, however gross, that do not affect mental capabilities would not fit the class of nonpersons. Second, frequently even the most severe cases of mental retardation cannot be reliably determined until a much later period;[208] care thus could not justifiably be withheld in the neonatal period, although this principle would permit nontreatment at the time when nonpersonality is clearly established.[209] Finally, the only group of defective newborns who would clearly qualify as nonpersons is anencephalics, who altogether lack a brain, or those so severely brain-damaged that it is immediately clear that a sense of self or personality can never develop. Mongols, myelomeningoceles, and other defective infants from whom ordinary care is now routinely withheld would not qualify as nonpersons. Thus, even the most coherent and cogent criteria of humanity are only marginally helpful in the situation of the defective infant. We must therefore consider whether treatment can be withheld on grounds other than the claim that such infants are not persons.

2. *No obligation to treat exists when the costs of maintaining life greatly outweigh the benefits.*

If we reject the argument that defective newborns are not persons, the question remains whether circumstances exist in which the consequences of treatment as compared with nontreatment are so undesirable that the omission of care is justified. As we have seen, the doctrine of necessity permits one to violate the criminal law when essential to prevent the occurrence of a greater evil.[210] The circumstances, however, when the death of a nonconsenting person is a lesser evil than his continuing life are narrowly circumscribed, and do not include withholding care from defective infants.[211]

should incapacity at birth disqualify one? If I understand Rawls correctly those in the original position would protect themselves against such a contingency by deriving principles which apply to all human offspring, whatever their capacity for a sense of justice or a life plan at any stage of life. Thus Rawls' statement that "[t]hose who can give justice are owed justice," *id.* at 510, need not exclude those who by accident or natural infirmity are incapable of giving justice.

207. Warkany, for example, reports the incidence of anencephaly, the absence of all or most of an infant's brain, as approximately 1 in 1,000 for children born in hospital wards, but notes that "remarkable variations have been reported from different areas." J. WARKANY, *supra* note 2, at 189.

208. *Id.* at 39.

209. But other factors might lead to treatment at this later point in time. For example, if care and nurturing occur immediately after birth, a strong mother-child bond is built, which might prevent mothers from deciding to withhold care when a serious defect is discovered weeks later. Barnett, Leiderman, Globstein & Klaus, *Neonatal Separation: The Maternal Side of Interactional Deprivation*, 45 PEDIATRICS 197, 197–99 (1970); Kennel & Klaus, *Care of the Mother of the High Risk Infant*, 14 CLIN. OBSTET. & GYNECOL. 926, 930–36 (1971).

210. *See notes* 157–64 *supra* and accompanying text.

211. *See* notes 169–80 *supra* and accompanying text.

Yet many parents and physicians deeply committed to the loving care of the newborn think that treating severely defective infants causes more harm than good, thereby justifying the withholding of ordinary care.[212] In their view the suffering and diminished quality of the child's life do not justify the social and economic costs of treatment. This claim has a growing commonsense appeal, but it assumes that the utility or quality of one's life can be measured and compared with other lives, and that health resources may legitimately be allocated to produce the greatest personal utility. This argument will now be analyzed from the perspective of the defective patient and others affected by his care.

a. *The quality of the defective infant's life.*

Comparisons of relative worth among persons, or between persons and other interests, raise moral and methodological issues that make any argument that relies on such comparisons extremely vulnerable. Thus the strongest claim for not treating the defective newborn is that treatment seriously harms the infant's own interests, whatever may be the effects on others. When maintaining his life involves great physical and psychosocial suffering for the patient, a reasonable person might conclude that such a life is not worth living. Presumably the patient, if fully informed and able to communicate, would agree. One then would be morally justified in withholding lifesaving treatment if such action served to advance the best interests of the patient.[213]

---

212. *See* Duff & Campbell, *supra* note 9.

213. The perspective that the mere saving of life is not enough unless the lives are worth saving" is well represented in the medical literature. Lorber, in discussing the process of selecting spina bifida infants for treatment, states: "Severe degree of paralysis is the most generally adopted reason for withholding treatment, but incontinence, severe hydrocephalus, gross deformities and social conditions are also taken into account. . . . There is no doubt that the future quality of life of many patients with myelomeningocele depends at least partly on the speed, efficiency and comprehensiveness of treatment from birth onwards—and often throughout their lives. Nevertheless, there are large numbers who are so severely handicapped at birth that those who survive are bound to suffer from a combination of major physical defects. In addition, many will be retarded in spite of everything that can be done for them. It is not necessary to enumerate all that this means to the patient, the family and the community in terms of suffering, deprivation, anxiety, frustration, family stress and financial cost. The large majority surviving at present have yet to reach the most difficult period of adolescence and young adult life and the problems of love, marriage and employment." Lorber, *supra* note 7, at 279, *citing* Rickham & Mawdsley, *supra* note 70, at 20. He summarizes the results of treating 524 cases of myelomeningocele on an unselected basis: "In summary, at the most 7 per cent of those admitted have less than grossly crippling disabilities and may be considered to have a quality of life not inconsistent with self-respect, earning capacity, happiness and even marriage. The next 20 per cent are also of normal intelligence and some may be able to earn their living in sheltered employment, but their lives are full of illness and operations. They are severely handicapped and are unlikely to live a full life-span. They are at a risk of sudden death from shunt complications or are likely to die of renal failure at an early age. The next 14 per cent are even more severely handicapped because they are retarded. They are unlikely to earn their living and their opportunities in life will be severely restricted. They will always be totally dependent on others." *Id.* at 286. He concludes that "[i]t is unlikely that many would wish to save a life which will consist of a long succession of operations, hospital admissions and other deprivations, or if the end result will be a combination of gross physical defects with retarded intellectual development." *Id.* at 300.

Congenital malformations impair development in several ways that lead to the judgment that deformed retarded infants are "a burden to themselves."[214] One is the severe physical pain, much of it resulting from repeated surgery that defective infants will suffer.[215] Defective children also are likely to develop other pathological features, leading to repeated fractures, dislocations, surgery, malfunctions, and other sources of pain. The shunt, for example, inserted to relieve hydrocephalus, a common problem in defective children, often becomes clogged, necessitating frequent surgical interventions.[216]

Pain, however, may be intermittent and manageable with analgesics. Since many infants and adults experience great pain, and many defective infants do not, pain alone, if not totally unmanageable, does not sufficiently show that a life is so worthless that death is preferable. More important are the psychosocial deficits resulting from the child's handicaps. Many defective children never can walk even with prosthesis, never interact with normal children, never appreciate growth, adolescence, or the fulfillment of education and employment, and seldom are even able to care for themselves. In cases of severe retardation, they may be left with a vegetative existence in a crib, incapable of choice or the most minimal response to stimuli. Parents or others may reject them, and much of their time will be spent in hospitals, in surgery, or fighting the many illnesses that beset them. Can it be said that such a life is worth living?

There are two possible responses to the quality-of-life argument. One is to accept its premises but to question the degree of suffering in particular cases, and thus restrict the justification for death to the most extreme cases. The absence of opportunities for schooling, career, and interaction may be the fault of social attitudes and the failings of healthy persons, rather than a necessary result of congenital malformations. Psychosocial suffering occurs because healthy, normal persons reject or refuse to relate to the defective, or hurry them to poorly funded institutions. Most nonambulatory, mentally retarded persons can be trained for satisfying roles. One cannot assume that a nonproductive existence is necessarily unhappy; even social rejection and nonacceptance can be mitigated.[217] Moreover, the psychosocial ills of the handicapped often do not differ in kind from those experienced by many persons. With training and care, growth, development,

---

214. Smith & Smith, *Selection for Treatment in Spina Bifida Cystica*, 4 Brit. Med. J. 189, 195 (1973).

215. *See* Lorber, *supra* note 7, at 284.

216. Ames & Schut, *Results of Treatment of 171 Consecutive Myelomeningoceles—1963 to 1968*, 50 Pediatrics 466, 469 (1972); Shurtleff & Foltz, *A Comparative Study of Meningomyelocele Repair or Cerebrospinal Fluid Shunt As Primary Treatment in Ninety Children*, Develop. Med. & Child Neuro. 57 (Supp. 13, 1967).

217. *See* E. Goffman, Stigma: Notes on the Management of Spoiled Identity 57–129 (1963).

and a full range of experiences are possible for most people with physical and mental handicaps. Thus, the claim that death is a far better fate than life cannot in most cases be sustained.

This response, however, avoids meeting the quality-of-life argument on its strongest grounds. Even if many defective infants can experience growth, interaction, and most human satisfactions if nurtured, treated, and trained, some infants are so severely retarded or grossly deformed that their response to love and care, in fact their capacity to be conscious, is always minimal. Although mongoloid and nonambulatory spina bifida children may experience an existence we would hesitate to adjudge worse than death, the profoundly retarded, nonambulatory, blind, deaf infant who will spend his few years in the back-ward cribs of a state institution is clearly a different matter.

To repudiate the quality-of-life argument, therefore, requires a defense of treatment in even these extreme cases. Such a defense would question the validity of any surrogate or proxy judgments of the worth or quality of life when the wishes of the person in question cannot be ascertained. The essence of the quality-of-life argument is a proxy's judgment that no reasonable person can prefer the pain, suffering, and loneliness of, for example, life in a crib at an IQ level of 20, to an immediate, painless death.

But in what sense can the proxy validly conclude that a person with different wants, needs, and interests, if able to speak, would agree that such a life were worse than death? At the start one must be skeptical of the proxy's claim to objective disinterestedness. If the proxy is also the parent or physician, as has been the case in pediatric euthanasia, the impact of treatment on the proxy's interests, rather than solely on those of the child, may influence his assessment. But even if the proxy were truly neutral and committed only to caring for the child, the problem of egocentricity and knowing another's mind remains. Compared with the situation and life prospects of a "reasonable man," the child's potential quality of life indeed appears dim. Yet a standard based on healthy, ordinary development may be entirely inappropriate to this situation. One who has never known the pleasures of mental operation, ambulation, and social interaction surely does not suffer from their loss as much as one who has. While one who has known these capacities may prefer death to a life without them, we have no assurance that the handicapped person, with no point of comparison, would agree. Life, and life alone, whatever its limitations, might be of sufficient worth to him.[218]

---

218. *Cf.* Gleitman v. Cosgrove, 49 N.J. 22, 227 A.2d 689 (1967). The court denied plaintiff's right to collect damages for being born with deformities when a defendant physician was allegedly negligent in informing the plaintiff's mother of rubella, which would have led her to seek an abortion.

One should also be hesitant to accept proxy assessments of quality-of-life because the margin of error in such predictions may be very great. For instance, while one expert argues that by a purely clinical assessment he can accurately forecast the minimum degree of future handicap an individual will experience,[219] such forecasting is not infallible,[220] and risks denying care to infants whose disability might otherwise permit a reasonably acceptable quality-of-life. Thus given the problems in ascertaining another's wishes, the proxy's bias to personal or culturally relative interests, and the unreliability of predictive criteria, the quality-of-life argument is open to serious question. Its strongest appeal arises in the case of a grossly deformed, retarded, institutionalized child, or one with incessant unmanageable pain, where continued life is itself torture. But these cases are few, and cast doubt on the utility of any such judgment. Even if the judgment occasionally may be defensible, the potential danger of quality-of-life assessments may be a compelling reason for rejecting this rationale for withholding treatment.[221]

b. *The suffering of others.*

In addition to the infant's own suffering, one who argues that the harm of treatment justifies violation of the defective infant's right to life usually relies on the psychological, social, and economic costs of maintaining his existence to family and society. In their view the minimal benefit of treatment to persons incapable of full social and physical development does not justify the burdens that care of the defective infant imposes on parents, sib-

---

The court stated: "It is basic to the human condition to seek life and hold on to it however heavily burdened. If Jeffrey could have been asked as to whether his life should be snuffed out before his full term of gestation could run its course, our felt intuition of human nature tells us he would almost surely choose life with defects as against no life at all." *Id.* at 30, 227 A.2d at 693.

Similarly, in the case of *In re* Hudson, 13 Wash. 2d. 673, 126 P.2d 765 (1942), a child was held not to be neglected when her parent refused to consent to life-endangering surgery to correct a gross deformity that made normal development and interaction impossible: "As we read the evidence, it is admitted by all concerned that . . . the child may not survive the ordeal of amputation; nevertheless, every one except the child's mother is willing, desirous, that the child be required to undergo the operation. Implicit in their position is their opinion that it would be preferable that the child die instead of going through life handicapped by the enlarged, deformed left arm. That may be to some today the humane, and in the future it may be the generally accepted, view. However, we have not advanced or retrograded to the stage where, in the name of mercy, we may lawfully decide that one shall be deprived of life rather than continue to exist crippled or burdened with some abnormality. That right of decision is a prerogative of the Creator." *Id.* at 684, 126 P.2d at 771. *See also* Cooke, *supra* note 15, at 906–08.

219. *See* Lorber, *supra* note 7, at 299.

220. In Lorber's series, 20% of 110 infants "with major adverse criteria at birth were of normal intellectual development at 2–4 years of age, though all [had] severe physical handicaps and their life expectation [was] short." *Id.* at 300. Moreover, other researchers question the adequacy of Lorber's selection criteria. Ames and Shut, for example, in a report on unselected treatment cases of myelomeningocele find "it is not always possible to determine potential at birth," and report success with infants that Lorber would not have selected. *See* Ames & Schut, *supra* note 216, at 469–70.

221. If this judgment is to be made, it is essential that the circumstances in which nontreatment may be said to be in a patient's best interests be specified beforehand by an authoritative body, and that procedures which assure that a particular case falls within such criteria be followed. *See* notes 272–77 *infra* and accompanying text.

lings, health professionals, and other patients. Matson, a noted pediatric neurosurgeon, states:

> [I]t is the doctor's and the community's responsibility to provide [custodial] care and to minimize suffering; but, at the same time, it is also their responsibility not to prolong such individual, familial, and community suffering unnecessarily, and not to carry out multiple procedures and prolonged, expensive, acute hospitalization in an infant whose chance for acceptable growth and development is negligible.[222]

Such a frankly utilitarian argument raises problems. It assumes that because of the greatly curtailed orbit of his existence, the costs or suffering of others is greater than the benefit of life to the child. This judgment, however, requires a coherent way of measuring and comparing interpersonal utilities, a logical-practical problem that utilitarianism has never surmounted.[223] But even if such comparisons could reliably show a net loss from treatment, the fact remains that the child must sacrifice his life to benefit others. If the life of one individual, however useless, may be sacrificed for the benefit of any person, however useful, or for the benefit of any number of persons, then we have acknowledged the principle that rational utility may justify any outcome.[224] As many philosophers have demonstrated, utilitarianism can always permit the sacrifice of one life for other interests, given the appropriate arrangement of utilities on the balance sheet.[225] In the absence of principled grounds for such a decision, the social equation involved in mandating direct, involuntary euthanasia[226] becomes a difference of degree, not kind, and we reach the point where protection of life depends solely on social judgments of utility.

These objections may well be determinative.[227] But if we temporarily bracket them and examine the extent to which care of the defective infant subjects others to suffering, the claim that inordinate suffering outweighs the infant's interest in life is rarely plausible. In this regard we must examine the impact of caring for defective infants on the family, health professions, and society-at-large.

The family. The psychological impact and crisis created by birth of a defective infant is devastating.[228] Not only is the mother denied the normal

---

222. Matson, *Surgical Treatment of Myelomeningocele*, 42 PEDIATRICS 225, 226 (1968).
223. J. RAWLS, *supra* note 206, at 90–91.
224. *Cf.* Silving, *Euthanasia: A Study in Comparative Criminal Law*, 103 U. PA. L. REV. 350, 356 (1954).
225. *See, e.g.*, J. RAWLS, *supra* note 206, at 22–27.
226. Alexander, *supra* note 193, at 39.
227. The New Jersey Supreme Court, for example, would clearly reject a balancing test in such situations. *See* Gleitman v. Cosgrove, 49 N.J. 22, 227 A.2d 689 (1967).
228. "The experience of learning that your child is defective immediately after birth can still be categorized among the most painful and stigmatizing experiences of modern people. It is as if the parents' raison d'etre were called into question before an imagined parental bar of justice and an ontological blow dealt to their hopes of continuing their identities." Fletcher, *supra* note 19, at 24.

tension release from the stresses of pregnancy,[229] but both parents feel a crushing blow to their dignity, self-esteem and self-confidence.[230] In a very short time, they feel grief for the loss of the normal expected child, anger at fate, numbness, disgust, waves of helplessness, and disbelief.[231] Most feel personal blame for the defect, or blame their spouse. Adding to the shock is fear that social position and mobility are permanently endangered.[232] The transformation of a "joyously awaited experience into one of catastrophe and profound psychological threat"[233] often will reactivate unresolved maturational conflicts. The chances for social pathology—divorce, somatic complaints, nervous and mental disorders—increase and hard-won adjustment patterns may be permanently damaged.[234]

The initial reactions of guilt, grief, anger, and loss, however, cannot be the true measure of family suffering caused by care of a defective infant, because these costs are present whether or not the parents choose treatment. Rather, the question is to what degree treatment imposes psychic and other costs greater than would occur if the child were not treated. The claim that care is more costly rests largely on the view that parents and family suffer inordinately from nurturing such a child.

Indeed, if the child is treated and accepted at home, difficult and demanding adjustments must be made. Parents must learn how to care for a disabled child, confront financial and psychological uncertainty, meet the needs of other siblings, and work through their own conflicting feelings. Mothering demands are greater than with a normal child, particularly if medical care and hospitalization are frequently required.[235] Counseling or professional support may be nonexistent or difficult to obtain.[236] Younger siblings may react with hostility and guilt, older with shame and anger.[237] Often the normal feedback of child growth that renders the turmoil of childrearing worthwhile develops more slowly or not at all. Family resources can be depleted (especially if medical care is needed), consumption patterns altered, or standards of living modified.[238] Housing may have to

---

229. See Goodman, *supra* note 19. See generally Kennel & Klaus, *supra* note 209.

230. Bentovim, *Emotional Disturbances of Handicapped Pre-School Children and Their Families—Attitudes to the Child*, 3 BRIT. MED. J. 579, 580 (1972); Giannini & Goodman, *Counseling Families During the Crisis Reaction to Mongolism*, 67 AM. J. MENTAL DEFICIENCY 740, 740–41 (1962); Goodman, *supra* note 19; Mandelbaum & Wheeler, *The Meaning of A Defective Child to Parents*, 41 SOCIAL CASEWORK 360 (1960); Schild, *Counselling with Parents of Retarded Children Living at Home*, 9 SOCIAL WORK 86 (1964); Zachary, *Ethical and Social Aspects of Treatment of Spina Bifida*, THE LANCET, Aug. 3, 1968, at 274–75.

231. *See* note 230 *supra*.

232. *See* Giannini & Goodman, *supra* note 230, at 743.

233. Goodman, *supra* note 19, at 92.

234. *Id.* at 93.

235. *See* Hunt, *Implications of the Treatment of Myelomeningocele for the Child and his Family*, THE LANCET, Dec. 8, 1973, at 1308, 1309–10; Zachary, *supra* note 230, at 275.

236. Hunt, *supra* note 235, at 1310.

237. *Id.* at 1309; Bentovim, *supra* note 230, at 581.

238. Zachary, *supra* note 230, at 275.

be found closer to a hospital, and plans for further children changed.[239]
Finally, the anxieties, guilt, and grief present at birth may threaten to recur
or become chronic.[240]

Yet, although we must recognize the burdens and frustrations of raising
a defective infant, it does not necessarily follow that these costs require nontreatment, or even institutionalization. Individual and group counseling
can substantially alleviate anxiety, guilt, and frustration, and enable parents
to cope with underlying conflicts triggered by the birth and the adapta-
tions required.[241] Counseling also can reduce psychological pressures on
siblings, who can be taught to recognize and accept their own possibly
hostile feelings and the difficult position of their parents. They may even
be taught to help their parents care for the child.[242]

The impact of increased financial costs also may vary.[243] In families

239. Hunt, *supra* note 235, at 1310.

240. "At each stage there may be a fresh feeling of loss: the precarious balance is once more
shattered, rage, depression, rejecting feelings, fear of battering, strain, somatic aches and pains, may
be the result. Problems such as financial difficulties, poor housing, marital strain, pressure from
siblings can compound such problems. Social life can be severely restricted and the handicapped
child then has to cope with the additional handicap of a withdrawn, preoccupied, depressed, angry
and hopeless parent, as well as the effect of the handicap itself." Bentovim, *supra* note 230, at 581.

241. *See, e.g.,* Cohen, *supra* note 19; Giannini & Goodman, *supra* note 230; Schild, *supra* note
230, at 86.

242. *See* citations in note 241 *supra.*

243. The financial impact of caring for the defective child is difficult to estimate and varies
with the seriousness of the defect, the resultant medical costs, health insurance coverage, and state
assistance programs. For example, it may cost the parents of a child born with spina bifida from
$5,000 to more than $40,000 to pay for the necessary operations, hospital care, medication, doctor's
checkups, and braces. Interview with Peggy Miezio, Wis. Spina Bifida Ass'n, Aug. 24, 1974.

Since almost 180 million Americans in 1971 were covered by some form of health insurance,
HEALTH INSURANCE INSTITUTE, 1972–73 SOURCE BOOK OF HEALTH INSURANCE DATA 19 (1972),
many parents find that insurance covers at least some of the costs. Until recently many policies excluded coverage for disorders commencing before the age of 15 days, and thus did not cover such
congenital disorders as spina bifida, Down's syndrome, or cystic fibrosis. *See, e.g.,* Kissil v. Beneficial
Nat'l Life Ins., 64 N.J. 555, 319 A.2d 67 (1974). Recently, several states have passed legislation requiring health insurance policies to cover newborn children from the day of birth. *See, e.g.,* CAL. INS.
CODE § 10119 (West 1972). In addition, even if the policy lawfully excludes coverage of deformed
newborns, indications are that in many cases, because of "social pressures," insurance companies
cover newborn infants from the day of birth. Interview with Roy Anderson, Office of Comm'r of Ins.,
Madison, Wis., Aug. 22, 1974.

In addition to the availability of coverage, two other problems face parents of defective newborns. One is the limits of such coverage. If the medical expenses of the child are high, and the
coverage limits of the policy low, parents may have to resort to use of savings or income, or seek
state aid. Second, even if a parent were covered by a group policy, the coverage does not transfer
if the primary insured leaves the business from which he obtained his policy. Availability of insurance coverage depends on "insurability," and as it is virtually impossible for a family to obtain
new coverage for a handicapped child after birth, the families are, in effect, "locked into" their group
policy, with a resulting decrease in mobility.

For families with inadequate or no insurance coverage and who lack the means to absorb high
expenditures for care of a deformed newborn, the availability of state assistance becomes crucial.
In general, fairly adequate state aid is available to parents who do not wish to institutionalize
their child. In California, for example, the state Crippel Children Services offers extensive aid
for families with deformed children. When a deformed child requires medical attention that the
parents are unable to afford, the parents, hospital, or family doctor may contact the local health
department, which will then determine if the child is "medically eligible" for the services of the
Crippled Children Department. A diagnostic evaluation of the child's condition is performed and
an estimate is made of the cost of care. The Crippled Children Services then determines if the
family is financially eligible for aid. An allowable income level is set according to several factors,

with high income or adequate health insurance, the financial costs are manageable. In others, state assistance may be available.[244] If severe financial problems arise or pathological adjustments are likely, institutionalization, although undesirable for the child, remains an option.[245] Finally, in many cases, the experience of living through a crisis is a deepening and enriching one, accelerating personality maturation, and giving one a new sensitivity to the needs of spouse, siblings, and others. As one parent of a defective child states: "In the last months I have come closer to people and can understand them more. I have met them more deeply. I did not know there were so many people with troubles in the world."[246]

Thus, while social attitudes regard the handicapped child as an unmitigated disaster, in reality the problem may not be insurmountable, and often may not differ from life's other vicissitudes. Suffering there is, but seldom is it so overwhelming or so imminent that the only alternative is death of the child.[247]

Health professionals. Physicians and nurses also suffer when parents give birth to a defective child, although, of course, not to the degree of the parents. To the obstetrician or general practitioner the defective birth may be a blow to his professional identity. He has the difficult task of informing the parents of the defects, explaining their causes, and dealing with the par-

---

and below a certain level (presently $6,300 for a family of four), all expenses are paid by the state. Above this level, the families pay an amount not greater than one-half of the difference between their income and the cost-of-living allowance level. Hospital expenses, medication, braces, nursing care—all the needs of the deformed child—are provided, and the only limit on aid is the agency's budget. Telephone interview with Darleen Gibben, State Crippled Children Services, Sacramento, Cal., Aug. 22, 1974.

For retarded children without serious physical defects, state aid, whether the child is institutionalized or not, is available depending on parental income. Telephone interview with Robert Baldo, Regional Center for Developmentally Disabled, Sacramento, Cal., Aug. 22, 1974.

Similar systems of aid for both physical and mental handicaps, and special education needs, are available in Illinois, Telephone interview with Dr. Graham Blanton, Director of Developmental Disabilities, Dep't of Mental Health and Developmental Disabilities, Springfield, Ill., Aug. 22, 1974; and in Wisconsin, Telephone interview with Elie Asleson, Bureau of Handicapped Children, Dep't of Health and Social Services, Madison, Wis., Aug. 27, 1974; and presumably in other states, since much of the state budget for these services is federally funded.

Although the data is too incomplete to conclude that care of a defective newborn will never severely drain a family's financial resources, it seems clear that the impact can be cushioned or minimized by institutionalization of the child, health insurance, or state aid. Obviously, if legislative policy remains committed to the value of life, a strong argument may be made that the taxpayers as a whole rather than individual families or insurance holders should bear the cost of care.

I am indebted to Marsha Peckham for clarification of the financial issues involved in the care of the defective newborn.

244. *See* note 243 *supra.*

245. Moreover, parental rights and obligations can be terminated. *See* note 37 *supra.*

246. *Quoted in* Johns, *Family Reactions to the Birth of a Child with a Congenital Abnormality,* 26 Obstet. & Gynecol. Survey 635, 637 (1971).

247. Since parents and physicians now view treatment and acceptance of a defective child as discretionary with the parents, acceptance may be viewed as a gift on the part of the parents to the child. Because of the child's defects, however, the debt or obligation owed to the donor by the recipient of a gift cannot be repaid, and few substitutions for that debt seem available. Given the frequency with which families donate organs to ailing members, it may be that the defective infant situation is not structured to maximize the chance of parental giftgiving. *See* R. Fox & J. Swayze, The Courage To Fail: A Social View of Organ Transplants and Dialysis 20–27 (1974).

ents' resulting emotional shock. Often he feels guilty for failing to produce a normal baby.[248] In addition, the parents may project anger or hostility on the physician, questioning his professional competence or seeking the services of other doctors.[249] The physician also may feel that his expertise and training are misused when employed to maintain the life of an infant whose chances for a productive existence are so diminished. By neglecting other patients, he may feel that he is prolonging rather than alleviating suffering.

Nurses, too, suffer role strain from care of the defective newborn. Intensive-care-unit nurses may work with only one or two babies at a time. They face the daily ordeals of care—the progress and relapses—and often must deal with anxious parents who are themselves grieving or ambivalent toward the child. The situation may trigger a nurse's own ambivalence about death and mothering, in a context in which she is actively working to keep alive a child whose life prospects seem minimal.[250]

Thus, the effects of care on physicians and nurses are not trivial, and must be intelligently confronted in medical education or in management of a pediatric unit. Yet to state them is to make clear that they can but weigh lightly in the decision of whether to treat a defective newborn. Compared with the situation of the parents, these burdens seem insignificant, are short term, and most likely do not evoke such profound emotions. In any case, these difficulties are hazards of the profession—caring for the sick and dying will always produce strain. Hence, on these grounds alone it is difficult to argue that a defective person may be denied the right to life.

Society. Care of the defective newborn also imposes societal costs, the utility of which is questioned when the infant's expected quality-of-life is so poor. Medical resources that can be used by infants with a better prognosis, or throughout the health-care system generally, are consumed in providing expensive surgical and intensive-care services to infants who may be severely retarded, never lead active lives, and die in a few months or years. Institutionalization imposes costs on taxpayers and reduces the resources available for those who might better benefit from it,[251] while reduc-

---

248. Kennel & Klaus, *supra* note 209, at 946. This is particularly true if a physician identifies with the family and its values. "The physician may feel a sense of having failed the family with whom he has a relationship—and his own emotions and feelings come into play—seemingly to a greater extent than with lower class families. His recommendations may be influenced unconsciously by his discomfort with the situation and his strong desire to 'save' the family." Giannini & Goodman, *supra* note 230, at 744.

249. Cohen, *supra* note 19, at 138.

250. Author's observations at conference concerning treatment of a defective newborn at St. Mary's Hospital, Madison, Wis., Apr. 15, 1974.

251. "It may be true that further advances should improve the outlook for many, but unfortunately the basic defect is usually so severe that the children will always be severely handicapped in spite of any advances which can be foreseen today. Meanwhile it may be best to concentrate our therapeutic efforts on those who can truly benefit from treatment. If all the most severe cases are treated, the pressure of work will be such that adequate time cannot be devoted to the less severely affected who would benefit most." Lorber, *supra* note 7, at 300.

ing further the quality of life experienced by the institutionalized defective.

One answer to these concerns is to question the impact of the costs of caring for defective newborns. Precise data showing the costs to taxpayers or the trade-offs with health and other expenditures do not exist. Nor would ceasing to care for the defective necessarily lead to a reallocation within the health budget that would produce net savings in suffering or life;[252] in fact, the released resources might not be reallocated for health at all.[253] In any case, the trade-offs within the health budget may well be small. With advances in prenatal diagnosis of genetic disorders, many deformed infants who would formerly require care will be aborted beforehand.[254] Then, too, it is not clear that the most technical and expensive procedures always constitute the best treatment for certain malformations.[255] When compared with the almost seven percent of the GNP now spent on health,[256] the money in the defense budget, or tax revenues generally, the public resources required to keep defective newborns alive seem marginal, and arguably worth the commitment to life that such expenditures reinforce. Moreover, as the Supreme Court recently recognized,[257] conservation of the taxpayer's purse does not justify serious infringement of fundamental rights. Given legal and ethical norms against sacrificing the lives of nonconsenting others, and the imprecisions in diagnosis and prediction concerning the eventual outcomes of medical care,[258] the social-cost argument does not compel nontreatment of defective newborns.[259]

---

252. For example, the resources instead might be used to increase physicians' salaries or the profits of drug or medical supply industries.

253. Resources presently consumed in the care of the defective may have been appropriated for that purpose only, and if not so utilized, will be withdrawn.

254. For instance, amniocentesis carried out on pregnant women over 35—the most risky age for Down's syndrome—should reduce the incidence of mongolism and the attendant problems of care. *Cf.* Smith, *On Letting Some Babies Die*, HASTINGS CENTER STUDIES, Vol. 2, No. 2, at 37, 45 (1974).

255. *See* Ames & Schut, *supra* note 216, at 467–70, which emphasizes the counseling and shunting of spina bifida babies rather than more elaborate and expensive intervention. *See also* C. FRIED, *supra* note 180, at 200–06.

256. Mechanic, *Problems in the Future Organization of Medical Practice*, 35 LAW & CONTEMP. PROB. 233, 234 (1970).

257. Memorial Hosp. v. Maricopa County, 415 U.S. 250 (1974).

258. *See* note 220 *supra* and accompanying text.

259. Moreover, although the case is unlikely to arise in medically developed nations, imagine, for example, that two myelomeningocele infants both need a shunt, orthopedic surgery, and other services, but resources are so limited that either complete care can be given to one and custodial care to the other, or both can be given only minimal care. Complete care for Baby *A* would lead to ambulation and normal intelligence, while complete care for Baby *B* would still leave him severely retarded and nonambulatory. Minimal care for both would leave both nonambulatory and retarded. Or suppose that resources would permit only one surgical procedure to correct duodenal atresia, but both a Down's syndrome and a normal baby need the operation. In either situation one may argue that physicians should be able to allocate scarce medical resources on the basis of their perception of which allocation will produce the most "good." Presumably, an outcome where the normal infant survives would be chosen. However, one may question whether, in situations of scarcity, distributive justice is satisfied by anything but a random or a first-come-first-served allocation, or an allocation system indifferent to the personal characteristics of each infant. To allocate health resources on the basis of prospective quality of life or social utility would raise in all but a few extreme cases the difficult task of (1) determining and measuring quality, and (2) specifying criteria for a nonarbitrary conclusion that quality *X* is better than quality *Y*. As David Smith observes: "Such an approach leads

C. *The Decisionmaking Process*

Assuming that the above arguments are rejected and we conclude that defective infants are either nonpersons, or persons from whom care justifiably can be withheld in certain cases, the question of procedure remains. Should parents and physicians have final discretion to determine whether a particular infant is treated, or should this power vest in a formally designated decisionmaking body? Should criteria and procedures for nonselection be promulgated? Should broad guidelines suffice? Since parents always may decide to treat and care for their child,[260] whatever its characteristics, the procedural question arises only when they have rejected treatment, and the attending physician concurs. The issue then posed is whether their decision should be determinative.

1. *Who should decide?*

a. *Final authority with parents and physicians.*

Duff and Campbell present the argument for granting parents and physicians final discretion to decide whether a defective infant should be treated, and hence live or die:

> We believe the burdens of decisionmaking must be borne by families and their professional advisers because they are most familiar with the respective situations. Since families primarily must live with and are most affected by the decisions, it therefore appears that society and the health professions should provide only general guidelines for decisionmaking. Moreover, since variations between situations are so great, and the situations themselves so complex, it follows that much latitude in decisionmaking should be expected and tolerated.[261]

The logic of this argument, however, is unpersuasive. It rests on the assumption that parents have but two options—to withhold care or to be burdened with the care of the child throughout their lives. But a third op-

---

one to think that the ideal result is either a 'perfect' baby or a dead baby. And the root problems of this way of looking at the issue are that both the human rights of defectives and the imperfections of all babies are glossed over." Smith, *supra* note 254, at 46 (footnote omitted).

Thus, one may argue that even here qualitative or utilitarian judgments are out of place, for they depend on nonobjective, culturally relative standards of quality. The lot of some is improved by making others worse off, yet the reasons for preferring one group are not compelling on nonarbitrary grounds. Unless one were willing to accept the principle that medical decisionmakers may opt to maximize social utility when limited resources require a selection among patients, then the defective newborn could not be denied treatment because of his defects alone. Fortunately, this dilemma, which arose frequently when hemodialysis resources were in short supply, does not yet seem to have arisen in the case of defective newborns. *See* C. FRIED, *supra* note 180, at 200–06; Katz, *Process Design for Selection of Hemodialysis and Organ Transplant Recipients*, 22 BUFF. L. REV. 373 (1973).

260. It is clear that parents have the right to retain and raise their offspring. Unless there exists a clear possibility that the offspring are or will be neglected, a statute depriving the parents of custody would be unconstitutional. *Cf.* Wisconsin v. Yoder, 406 U.S. 205 (1972); Pierce v. Society of Sisters, 268 U.S. 510 (1925); Meyer v. Nebraska, 262 U.S. 390 (1923).

261. Duff & Campbell, *supra* note 9, at 894.

tion exists—termination of parental rights and obligations.[262] However, while parental discretion to terminate the parental relationship may be justified,[263] it does not follow that parents should also have the right to decide whether the child lives or dies. Clearly, discretion to terminate a relationship of dependency does not mandate that one have the power to impose death on the terminated party. Furthermore, a central element of procedural justice is impartial decisionmaking after full consideration of relevant information.[264] Yet, neither parents nor physicians are impartial or disinterested; both have a strong personal interest in the outcome of their decision. Parents face the decision with the guilt, grief, and damaged image that birth of a defective child brings.[265] They have a strong interest in maintaining previous life plans, and adjustment patterns, and in avoiding the psychic and financial costs of adjusting to care of a defective infant. Moreover, the treatment decision arises in highly emotional circumstances, when their rational faculties are weakest and full information concerning the defect and prognosis is wanting.[266] In addition, the physician's objectivity may be compromised. The obstetrician, for example, may feel guilt or responsibility for the defect, and prefer that the problem be eliminated as soon as possible.[267] He may think that the least he can do for the parents is to relieve them of a potential lifelong burden. Similarly, though less involved, the advice of a pediatrician or consultant is likely to be influenced by his own values concerning care for defective infants. In short, since parents and physicians face the treatment decision with conflicting interests and the pressure of strong emotions, giving them final, unguided discretion to decide whether defective infants live will often lead to hasty, biased choices.

A glaring example of this danger is the 1971 Johns Hopkins case in which doctors did not operate on a Down's syndrome baby with duodenal atresia who died 15 days later of starvation.[268] The parents decided that they did not want to be burdened with a child who would be retarded and in-

---

262. In most states parents are empowered to terminate parental obligations, thereby leading to adoption or state custody. *See* note 37 *supra*.

263. *See* notes 228–40 *supra* and accompanying text.

264. Taylor v. Hayes, 94 S. Ct. 2697 (1974); Ward v. Village of Monroeville, 409 U.S. 57 (1972); Tumey v. Ohio, 273 U.S. 510 (1927).

265. *See* notes 228–34 *supra* and accompanying text.

266. Some physicians argue that patients or their guardians are incapable of rationally deciding for or against treatment in most circumstances, and some empirical evidence supports this view. *See* Fellner & Marshall, *Kidney Donors—The Myth of Informed Consent*, 126 AM. J. PSYCH. 79 (1970). Duff and Campbell claim, however, that if there is open sharing of information and decisionmaking with parents, a rational, informed choice will result. *See* note 18 *supra* and accompanying text. While the extent of their counseling is unclear (and hence we cannot assess to what degree the parents have worked through the emotional trauma of birth), the practices of Yale–New Haven Hospital's special nursery may be the exception rather than the rule. *See also* notes 229–40 *supra* and accompanying text.

267. *See* note 248 *supra* and accompanying text.

268. *See* Gustafson, *Mongolism, Parental Desires, and the Right to Life*, 16 PERSPECTIVES IN BIOL. & MED. 529, 529–33 (1973).

capable of full human development, and rejected surgery. The physicians acquiesced in their decision, even though allowing the baby to starve to death created great consternation among the staff. The death of this child appears particularly unnecessary since mongols can interact, be trained, and lead a reasonably comfortable or happy existence. Moreover, the child was otherwise healthy and would not have required constant medical care. The absence of a convincing case for death in this case illustrates the dangers of Duff's and Campbell's suggestion of having "only general guidelines" and allowing "much latitude" in this type of decisionmaking.[269]

However, arguably we can depend on the ethical commitments of the medical profession to prevent parental abuses. Physicians perhaps are better equipped than parents to consider these judgments and can intervene when parents misjudge the interests of society and child, thus operating as a check on parental decisionmaking. If the physician challenges the parental choice, as occurred recently in Maine, he can seek judicial protection for the child.[270] There is some merit to this claim, but one cannot reliably base a rule on the contingency that physicians will intervene in particularly egregious cases. There is no guarantee that physicians can adequately strike the most socially desirable balance. While nearness to extreme situations often requires physicians to make such judgments, nothing in their training or background qualifies them to identify, assess, and balance all interests involved—in short, to "play judge."[271] In addition, decisions by physicians are likely to reflect specific class, economic, ethical, and cultural biases or interests arising out of prior relationships with the parents. Perhaps the Johns Hopkins example is atypical of medical ethics, but that case and the now widespread practice of involuntary pediatric euthanasia hardly attest to physicians' ability to check questionable decisions of parents.

b. *A decisionmaking body.*

An alternative that seeks to avoid the inherent bias of parents and attending physicians is the designation of a person or group of persons to decide whether a parental decision to terminate treatment, when acquiesced in by the attending physician, should be final. For example, such a decision could be made final only when approved by a judge, or a specially designated committee. In either case, the infant, through appointment of an advocate, could present evidence, confront witnesses, request a hearing, and seek review of the board's decision. Such a decisionmaker would be better equipped to examine and evaluate dispassionately all the interests involved, and reach a socially more desirable decision.

The main problems with this proposal are obvious: it adds another com-

---

269. *See* note 261 *supra* and accompanying text.
270. *See* note 73 *supra* and accompanying text.
271. Potter, *The Paradoxical Preservation of Principle*, 13 VILL. L. REV. 784, 788 (1968).

mittee to a hospital setting already filled with committees; it is cumbersome and easily bureaucratized; it provides for a body that may be no better equipped to weigh social values than the ad hoc decisionmaking process of parents and physicians.[272] Moreover, a committee, while more likely to achieve impartiality than physicians and parents, is vulnerable to pressures to accept the decisions of attending physicians. Thousands of such committees are unlikely to achieve uniform results or even implement equivalent criteria for nontreatment. Other problems may arise if the committees are judicialized with counsel, hearings, and appeals. This will extend the decisionmaking process and, accordingly, the agony of parents. Simply finding competent persons for such a committee in every hospital may be a tremendous task.

Beyond these practical concerns is the broader question of the wisdom of constituting citizen committees to mete out life or death. While society is fairly callous about saving lives when seen as statistics, to sanction directly the taking of identifiable lives on social-cost grounds is a step of a radically different order. We have, for example, very different attitudes toward a mining company's failure to install mine safety devices than toward its failure to undertake rescue of trapped miners. Calabresi observes:

> It should be clear that the foregoing does not mean that individual human life is not valued highly. Nor, certainly, does it suggest that we are indifferent to when and how society should choose to sacrifice lives. Quite the contrary; it indicates that there is a deep conflict between our fundamental need constantly to reaffirm our belief in the sanctity of life and our practical placing of some values (including future lives) above an individual life. That conflict suggests, at the very least, the need for a quite complex structuring to enable us *sometimes* to sacrifice lives, but hardly ever to do it blatantly and as a society, and above all to allow this sacrifice only under quite rigorous controls . . . . The consequence is that collective societal action seems always to be directed toward preserving the individual life rather than taking it, and our commitment is further strengthened.[273]

Hence, such a committee structure risks losing society's pervasive symbolic commitment to the value of individual life, as well as embarking on the slippery path of rational-utility assessments of personal worth.[274]

2. How should the decision be made?

a. Criteria for decisionmaking.

The difficulty of choosing an appropriate decisionmaker can be lessened by identifying the class of infants for whom treatment may lawfully be

---

272. The unspectacular success of human experimentation committees is illustrative of these problems. *See* B. BARBER, J. LALLY, J. MAKARUSHKA & D. SULLIVAN, RESEARCH ON HUMAN SUBJECTS 166–67 (1973).

273. Calabresi, *Reflections on Medical Experimentation in Humans*, 98 DAEDLUSA 387, 389–90 (1969).

274. *See* notes 223–26 *supra* and accompanying text.

withheld and by specifying applicable clinical indicators. Any decision-making alternative runs the risk of leading to unfettered discretion, arbitrary unprincipled decisions, and unjustified deaths. But, just as authoritative and specific criteria have eased the physician's determination of when brain death has occurred,[275] the risks of delegating treatment discretion to parents, physicians, or committees can be similarly lessened if specific criteria are developed to describe defective characteristics and the familial or institutional situations in which tratment may be withheld from defective infants.

If recognized by the courts or legislature,[276] such criteria would represent a collective social judgment, rather than idiosyncratic choices of parents and committees, as to when social costs outweigh individual benefits. To achieve legislative consensus, the criteria for death necessarily should be narrow, reaching only the most extreme cases. Further protection can be gained by a procedure that assures that the required clinical findings are accurately assessed, for example, by certification by two nonattending physicians before treatment is withheld.

But can criteria that lend themselves to reliable identification of a justifiable nontreated class be articulated? Many thoughtful physicians and parents believe such a class exists, for on the basis of implicit or explicit standards, they approve withholding care in particular cases.[277] Hence, if

---

275. See Capron & Kass, *A Statutory Definition of the Standards for Determining Human Death: An Appraisal and A Proposal*, 121 U. PA. L. REV. 87 (1972). But in practice such mechanisms may not provide as much protection as desired because of the intrahospital familiarity and informal professional norms that often make fellow physicians reluctant to criticize or override the wishes of other physicians. See STAFF REPORT OF SENATE COMM. ON FINANCE, MEDICARE AND MEDICAID: PROBLEMS, ISSUES, AND ALTERNATIVES, 91st Cong., 1st Sess. 105-12 (1970).

276. While explicit legislative approval of the criteria would be helpful, it would not be necessary for the legislature to draft or enact the criteria. A better solution might be to constitute formally a decisionmaking body with medical, community, and lay representation along the lines of the National Commission for the Protection of Human Subjects of Biomedical and Behavioral Research, created by the National Research Service Award Act of 1947, 42 U.S.C. § 289l, and delegate to it the development of the appropriate criteria and relevant clinical indicators. To prevent obsolescence in the criteria, and to monitor the extent of nontreatment and the effectiveness of developed standards, the body could be permanently constituted and perform similar functions with regard to other biomedical problems. Alternatively, the courts could give judicial recognition to criteria developed by authoritative medical or professional groups. In either case it is essential that the criteria be perceived as the expression of a community consensus concerning the limits of protecting human life.

277. McCormick, in arguing for a definition of personhood based on a capacity for human relationships, also argues for explicit formulation of criteria for identifying defective newborns from whom treatment may justifiably be withheld: " 'Broad guidelines,' 'substantive standards.' There is the middle course, and it is the task of a community broader than the medical community. A guideline is not a slide rule that makes the decision. It is far less than that. But it is far more than the concrete decision of the parents and physician, however seriously and conscientiously this is made. It is more like a light in a room, a light that allows the individual objects to be seen in the fullness of their context. Concretely, if there are certain infants that we agree ought to be saved in spite of illness or deformity, and if there are certain infants that we agree should be allowed to die, then there is a line to be drawn. And if there is a line to be drawn, there ought to be some criteria, even if very general, for doing this. Thus, if nearly every commentator has disagreed with the Hopkins decision, should we not be able to distill from such consensus some general wisdom that will inform

considered thought produces a consensus that, for example, profoundly retarded, nonambulatory hydrocephalics who are blind and deaf or infants who are unlikely to survive beyond a year are not owed ordinary treatment, a basis for developing criteria exists. Initially a common law approach might serve to identify certain categories of defects, with cases added or removed by their similarity to clear-cut categories. On the other hand, a common-law-like evolution may be less desirable than a forthright statement of the standards implicit in our considered judgments of clear-cut cases. The venture is risky, but considerable light may be shed by attempting to frame standards based on minimal capacity for social interaction, personality development, consciousness, and the like.

Perhaps acceptable criteria cannot be articulated, because factual variations are too many and justifiable ethical judgments cannot always be rationally explained. Nevertheless, the attempt should be made because the process of developing such criteria will at least reveal whether the judgments by which we presently decide to withhold care are principled or arbitrary, and thus whether they deserve to be honored at all.

b. *Specified procedures.*

If we grant the impossibility of articulating reliable and useful criteria for decisionmaking, the danger of arbitrary decisions by parents and physicians still may be reduced by mandating procedures that assure access to all relevant information and time for reflection. If decisionmaking could be structured so that all considerations enter into the calculus, the risk of arbitrariness by parents and physicians would lessen. Thus, if the postpartum hours are fraught with emotion, no treatment should be withheld for, say, 7 days. Alternatively, the parents' decision could be disregarded until they have one or more counseling sessions with a social worker or some other suitable adviser. Similar measures could assure exposure to the widest range of information relevant to their decision: for example, the parents expressly can be made aware of the benefits and costs of institutional care and the availability of state aid for home care.

Attending physicians also can be required to follow specified procedures before giving effect to parental choice. They can be required to state in writing their reasons for withholding treatment. A post hoc review, along the lines of a tissue committee or other forms of peer review, could be established. As we proliferate ideas for assuring impartial consideration of relevant factors, we move toward a committee structure. If we can achieve those advantages without undue bureaucracy, such an approach has appeal.

---

and guide future decisions?" McCormick, *supra* note 205, at 172, 173. *See also* Carney, *Medical Standards for Deformed Newborns*, Wash. Post, Mar. 20, 1974, at A15, col. 1.

III. CONCLUSION

The pervasive practice of withholding ordinary medical care from defective newborns demonstrates that we have embarked on a widespread program of involuntary euthanasia. This practice has not resulted from a careful consideration of public policy alternatives, nor has it been arrived at by a public or collective decision. Formal public policy, in fact, condemns the practice, and until recently, the medical profession rarely acknowledged its existence. But now, as a result of new-found technological skills and perhaps changing attitudes toward social-utility assessments of human life, the practice has come to be accepted in the interstices of medical and legal practice. Given this situation, the crucial question is whether nontreatment of defective neonates is the opening wedge in expanding involuntary euthanasia, or whether its scope and impact can be limited. How we practice involuntary euthanasia thus becomes as important as the practice itself.

The problem of treating defective newborns may usefully be viewed as a problem of the proper limits of discretion, and is therefore amenable to traditional legal controls on discretion—rules, procedures, and review. Nonenforcement of existing criminal laws grants parents and physicians effective discretion to decide the fate of infants born with a range of defects. Their decisions inevitably reflect their perception of the child's, the family's, and perhaps society's interests. In short, they implicitly or explicitly constitute judgments as to when social costs outweigh the benefits of treatment. But these criteria are rarely articulated, and their judgments do not undergo the close scrutiny that decisions of such magnitude warrant. In nearly all cases in which the attending physician concurs in the parental decision to withhold care, neither parents nor physicians are required to justify their choice, nor is the decision reviewed by a disinterested party. The absence of due process for the infant is all the more striking given the emotional circumstances of the parental decision and the lack of publicly certified guidelines or criteria for withholding care. We thus have a situation in which interests other than the infants can dominate, and in which arbitrary and unjustified killings can and have occurred.

It is highly unlikely that full enforcement of present laws can correct the imbalances of the present situation. Some prosecutors might begin to enforce the law as the practice is more widely publicized. Yet if such enforcement occurs at all, it is likely to be scattered or sporadic. Although the law clothes the defective infant with a right to life, and a corresponding duty of care from those in certain relations with him, many people think that that right ends when it conflicts with the interests of parents, the medical profession, and the infant's own potential for full development. The law in action is likely to reflect this view, and, if the law in theory differs, this difference probably will be ignored.

If the nontreatment of defective newborns has become deeply engrained in medical practice, one can only hope that it will be confined to those cases in which the clearest and most indisputable grounds for withholding care exist. The attending physician is a partial check on parents who would unjustifiably deny treatment, even if the criminal law is not. But the peculiarities of his role, the risk of conflicting interests, and the lack of special ethical skill or training, make the physician an unreliable protector of the infant. In fact, granting the physician this authority may only foster present tendencies of the medical profession to assume decisionmaking authority over issues that are not theirs by law, training, or expertise to make. Unless physicians are to be final arbiters of all social policy and ethical issues with a medical component, they should not have such authority here.

By requiring that certain procedures be followed in deciding whether parents' nontreatment decision is to be final, the exercise of discretion can be structured to maximize the possibility of providing a disinterested decisionmaker who is equipped with relevant information and is sensitive to all interests. However, enforcing these procedures may present major problems, and even if administratively feasible, undoubtedly will require a relatively unfocused judgment as to whether care can be justifiably withheld.

Thus, in addition to procedures, the decisionmaking should be confined or limited by specific criteria, identifying the cases in which treatment can be justifiably withheld. Drafting criteria creates problems and difficult ethical choices, but these are no more significant than those that faced the Harvard Medical School committee that produced a definition of brain death. Rather, the problem will be in deciding whether rules such as "no anencephalics need be treated" or "no hydrocephalic can be denied treatment for this defect alone" provide justifiable differentiations in deciding the need for treatment.

The use of criteria thus confronts us with the question of whether there are classes of infants who may justifiably be allowed to die when parents so choose, and whether we can openly acknowledge the criteria which inform our decisionmaking. For while we may save lives and limit discretion by formalizing decisionmaking, we risk establishing a precedent that once loosed, is not easily cabined. Given the current acceptance of involuntary euthanasia of defective newborns, further danger from formalizing the precedent appears small. Indeed, subjecting the nontreatment decision to rules and procedures may demonstrate the solemn nature of a difficult situation. Since the power to cause the death of a defective newborn is an awesome one, it is essential that such decisions be carefully confined by law.

EUTHANASIA AS A FORM OF
MEDICAL MANAGEMENT

DENNIS J. HORAN

In their paper in the *New England Medical Journal*, **Duff** and Campbell have raised the question of allowing children to die in the special care nursery as a form of "medical management."[1] Although the paper discusses 299 deaths, only 43 were related to withholding medical treatment, and of the 43 only a handful (perhaps 9 or 10) involve what I would classify as a medical-moral problem. I say this because the paper itself does not make the very necessary distinction between treatable cases and non-treatable cases, i.e. cases where the available treatment can lead to good medical prognosis in the physical sense. I say this not to be critical, but in order to better define the problem the paper raises.

The issue of death intentionally willed as a management option in the care of the defective newborn is only now being widely discussed, although some have contended that the practice is common in our culture. It is surprising to see how seldom the effect of legal or constitutional personhood is considered by those commentators anxious to allow death as a treatment of choice. For example, H. Tristram Engelhardt, Jr., in opting for euthanasia of the defective newborn, concludes:

> Since children are not persons strictly but exist in and through their families, parents are the appropriate ones to decide whether or not to treat a deformed child when (a) there is not only little likelihood of full human life but also great likelihood of suffering if the life is prolonged, or (b) when the cost of prolonging life is very great.[2]

True, parents pay the bills and raise the children, but to conclude that a child's dependency on a parent means that a child is a non-legal person or a non-constitutional person is pure legal balderdash. As on commentator said:

> In resolving the emotional and ethical dilemmas that confront parents of defective infants, it is surprising that law and legal values have rarely been invoked. The law's long experience with protecting minority rights and its concern with procedure and decision-making processes may offer a path out of this troublesome thicket. Yet, Duff and Campbell, while attempting to aid parents in making an informed choice, neglected to advise as to legal duties and the legal ramifications of withholding medical care.[3]

Where medical treatment is not available, such as in the case of short bowel syndrome, the "withholding" of unavailable treatment hardly amounts to the creation of a moral-medical problem. So, too, where the anomalies are multiple and add up to a hopeless condition, our moral sense is not aroused by "allowing death as a management option." However, where the treatment is withheld for social reasons, such as in the one case stated in the body of the Duff and Campbell paper involving Down's syndrome, then our concern becomes one of death not as a management option in the medical sense, but as an alternative choice in the social sense: involuntary euthanasia in the nursery. The similarity to the abortion problem is stunning:

> An infant with Down's syndrome and intestinal atresia, like the much publicized one at Johns Hopkins Hospital, was not treated because his parents thought that surgery was wrong for their baby and themselves. He died seven days after birth.[4]

There is no statement in their paper concerning treatment during the seven days, but in similar cases, such as at Johns Hopkins and the Decatur case,[5] not only treatment but allegedly also all sustenance was withheld until the children died.[6] In short, once the decision is made that the atresia will not be repaired, the decision is made that death will be allowed. Usually this is done by starvation, which took some 15 days in Johns Hopkins and even longer in Decatur.[7]

The importance of these cases lies in the fact that the atresia problems involved are usually treatable and the prognosis good. In short, the real reason the treatment was withheld was because the child was a mongoloid.

Of even more significance than the Duff and Campbell paper is the paper which has recently appeared summarizing the findings and conclusions of a conference on moral issues in the newborn nursery.[8]

In this paper one sees in print for the first time the analogy being drawn between abortion and infanticide. Of one of the legal papers presented, the article stated:

> He [the author of the legal paper] maintained that the dilemma facing the parents, doctors, and society in neonatal intensive care units is similar to that faced and resolved by the United States Supreme Court in the abortion decision. A defective child, like a fetus, may be unwanted. The maintenance of a defective child, like carrying a fetus to term, may involve not only broad social costs but a threat to its family's viability.[9]

The similarity to *Roe* v. *Wade*, and the application of legal personhood based on medical indications of quality of life, is further clearly stated:

> Marks argued for a social policy that would withhold legal personhood from certain carefully defined categories of high-risk infants until a clear diagnosis and prognosis can be made concerning them and until their parents have made an informed decision whether or not they want to keep and nurture these infants.[10]

The participants faced the moral dilemmas directly and responded to a questionnaire on the basic issues involved. Of the 20, 17 answered "yes" to active euthanasia in some circumstances; 2 answered "no"; and 1 was uncertain.[11]

The conference paper concluded with a statement of nine ethical propositions to be applied as a public moral policy in the neonatal intensive care unit:

Ethical Propositions

(1) Every baby born possesses a *moral value*

which entitles it to the medical and social care necessary to effect its well-being.

(2) Parents bear the principal *moral responsibility* for the well-being of their newborn infant.

(3) Physicians have the *duty* to take medical measures conducive to the well-being of the baby in proportion to their fiduciary relationships to the parents.

(4) The State has an *interest* in the proper fulfillment of responsibilities and duties regarding the well-being of the infant, as well as an interest in ensuring an equitable apportionment of limited resources among its citizens.

(5) The responsibility of the parents, the duty of the physician, and the interests of the State are conditioned by the medico-moral principle, "do no harm, without expecting compensating benefit for the patient."

(6) Life-preserving intervention should be understood as doing harm to an infant who cannot survive infancy, or will live in intractable pain, or cannot participate even minimally in human experience.

(7) If the court is called upon to resolve disagreements between parents and physicians about medical care, prognosis about quality of life for the infant should weigh heavily in the decision as to whether or not to order life-saving intervention.

(8) If an infant is judged beyond medical intervention, and if it is judged that its continued brief life will be marked by pain or discomfort, it is permissible to hasten death by means consonant with the moral value of the infant and the duty of the physician.

(9) In cases of limited availability of neonatal intensive care, it is ethical to terminate therapy for an infant with poor prognosis in order to provide care for an infant with a much better prognosis.[12] (emphasis in original)

Obviously, numbers 6 and 8 are of most concern to us, although number 1 contains the source of the problem, for it finds *moral* value in a born baby but is entirely silent on *legal* values. Those who argue for a completely permissive abortion policy also find moral value in the fetus, but moral value only, and that outweighed by moral problems of the women; more significantly, however, completely outweighed by the legal value of the woman's right of privacy, vis-a-vis the non-legal personhood of the unborn. These nine propositions require that the born child be treated as a non-legal person, i.e. a something with no intrinsic legal value of its own right unless it has attained the required quality of life.

In the creation of these principles, was any thought given to the constitutional rights of the child involved? The born child, no matter what its condition of health, is, under current law, a constitutional person entitled to be treated as such not only by the courts but also by its parents and its physician.[13]

That, however, is not the basic problem with the approach of this paper. One cannot quarrel with the thoughtfulness, the moral sensitivity and the concern shown by the participants in this conference and the writers of this paper. Any child in their hands would undoubtedly receive as much consideration as a human can in the difficult problem area of the neonatal intensive care unit.

However, the nine criteria must be recognized for what they are: just as much a non-legal life and death screening program as they are a sensitive moral answer to difficult moral questions. These criteria do not set the standard only for letting life in, but also for excluding certain lives out. If this is a medical conclusion, I have no quarrel with it. If this is a societal conclusion, I have very grave concerns.

I have another basic concern with the paper. The argument is usually given that such conferences are held because of the advances in medicine which only now, they say, create these medical-moral dilemmas. It seems to me, however, that the present is really not that different than the past; but only now since *Roe* v. *Wade* has the way been shown to a new method of solving the problem. True, technology has brought these problems to the special care nursery, but aren't they the same problems that always existed in other wards of the hospital? As medicine and technology advance, they leave behind the old problems, but, in medicine especially, isn't the problem really one of life and death, the same problem medicine has always faced? And isn't the axiom "I should do no harm" the same axiom that was applied to every person under a physicians's care? Why *now* the special consideration for the problem? The answer, of course, is that now there is another option: Death as a treatment of choice, the profound paradigm of the abortion solution.

The Jonsen paper indicates that a Down's syndrome child fulfills the criteria for having the required quality of life, but a trisomy 18 child does not.[14] But Duff and Campbell seem to disagree with that, and ask that the law be changed to accomodate other than life-saving solutions.[15]

How does one translate these principles into law? It seems to me that this can only be done by asking the prosecutor to keep his nose out of the nursery, which requires seeing the child as something other than a legal person with constitutional rights in his or her own right. The parents and the doctor will decide. Sounds very much like *Roe* v. *Wade*, doesn't it?

What do we say about principle 8 which allows active euthanasia? I suppose that it's no different than abortion anyway. The logic seems inescapable but, nonetheless, very troublesome. The fact that euthanasia is murder under our law shouldn't trouble anyone.[16] Abortion was illegal at one time also.

In a recent paper on this subject Paul Ramsey said:

> Ethically, the benign neglect of defective infants should be called by its proper name: involuntary euthanasia.[17]

With rare exception, Professor Ramsey concludes that the principle operative in the special care nursery should be "to always treat the defective newborn as we would treat the normal child." He finds Lesch-Nyhan disease as such an exception,[18] but primarily because it cannot be treated. As to the inclusion of societal indicators when confronting the medical problems, he concludes:

> One can understand—even appreciate—the motives of a physician who factors in an unhappy marriage or family poverty when weighing the tragedy facing one child against that facing another; and rations his help accordingly. Nevertheless, that surely is a species of injustice. Physicians are not appointed to remove all life's tragedy, least of all by lessening medical care now and letting infants die who for social

reasons seem fated to have less care in the future than others. That's one way to remove
every evening the human debris that has accumulated since morning.[19]

I will now direct this paper to a very abbreviated discussion of the traditional moral[20] analysis that has been applied
to these special care nursery cases, and the more "modern"
approach used by Fr. Richard McCormick.[21]

I will commence by pointing out that perhaps in these
difficult times where Christian witness to life is more important than ever before, compromise is even less possible than
ever before. I do not mean by that that Christian moralists
ever compromised before, but I do mean that perhaps in these
times the norm for conduct in a Christian hospital should not
be the minimally acceptable conduct of a rational human, but
rather of a Christian.[22]

In the Decatur case the chaplain analyzed the problem
using the traditional moral approach of ordinary and extraordinary means.[23] Like the Johns Hopkins case, this case involved a child with both Down's Syndrome and esophegeal
atresia. It was alleged that in addition to refusing the corrective operation, all sustenance was withheld from the child,
who subsequently died on approximately the 21st day of life.[24]

The chaplain made a thorough analysis of the case and
concluded:

> Nevertheless in view of the principles stated and
> the examples cited, I judge that in the St.
> Mary's case the parents of the child do not need
> to undertake the extraordinary means that sur-
> gical procedures would demand.[25]

The examples cited referred to a standard moral text
once used widely in Catholic seminaries to teach moral theology.[26] This book has been "criticized" by some moral theologians for its liberality on the euthanasia issue.[27]

The fallacy in applying the traditional analysis of extraordinary vs. ordinary means to the problem involving the
special care nursery is that *usually it is the decision not to
render medical treatment which makes the case terminal.* The
death process is commenced only because we have decided to
withhold treatment. Consequently, it is illogical to use an
analysis derived from the nature of man about the natural
end of his life at a time when only a decision not to treat or

feed has brought about the death process. This is even more true when one realizes that the unspoken assumption on which such a decision rests is that the child is a mongoloid who will not live a meaningful life.

This is not to deny the importance of the very valid moral distinction between ordinary and extraordinary means, but only to point out that its use in the special care nursery cases makes Catholic teaching on euthanasia (read Youthanasia) seem as "liberal" as the cost benefit analyses of Walter Sacket.[28]

Ordinarily, when we end the extraordinary means of maintaining life, or do not use the extraordinary means to save life, the patient dies as a result of the natural condition of ill-being from which he is suffering. He is already in the dying process and our analysis refers only to the use of extraordinary medical means to prolong his life. We are usually never discussing the medical means which would cure the condition. But in the nursery we are almost always speaking of exactly that. The esophegeal repair will cure the problem, not just prolong the life of an already terminally ill patient.

In the Johns Hopkins and Decatur cases the children were not dying—they were *caused to die* because (1) they were not given the corrective surgery they needed, and (2) they were not given sustenance. The two situations (the special care nursery and the terminal illness) are not similar, and consequently the same principles should not be applied.

In his papers Fr. McCormick applies the principle of proportionality, which principle, I note in passing, appears explicitly stated in seven of the Catholic Hospital Ethical Directives.[29] There is a line to be drawn, he says, between dogmatism and pure concretism and pure relativism.[30] The problem, of course, is where to draw the line, and what principles do we use in drawing it.

Unfortunately, Fr. McCormick chooses a relativism mired in an arbitrary quicksand: ". . . it seems to follow that life is a value to be preserved only insofar as it contains some potentiality for human relationships."[31] I say unfortunately, because there is no way that this relational principle can be less than the death warrant for some retardates, except in the hands of Fr. McCormick himself. Just as Daniel Callahan's solution to the abortion dilemma was wonderfully humane for him, so, too, there was only one Daniel Callahan to apply it; and, oddly enough, he was probably not asked by one woman caught in the dilemma to apply the principle. So, too, Fr. McCormick will not be asked in the majority of cases to apply the principle, but, nonetheless, if adopted it will be applied countless number of times and applied in order to withhold the very treatment which would cure, but would not add to the child's relational capabilities. The decision is being made not because of the medical condition under scrutiny, but because of the expected quality of the child's mental life.

During the abortion debate, those of us who were lawyers involved in the debate had this tremendous communications gap with the theologians. The translation of their subtle moral principles into law could not be accomplished without disaster to both their ideas and the population at risk, namely, the unborn, and now the retardate. To say that the right to life of the retardate depends on relational values is fine in the classroom of the moral theologian, but to translate that into civil law means disaster for the mentally retarded, as we have learned by experience that it has for the unborn. In our society it means that many mentally retarded will one day be allowed to die in the nursery. We are not debating these issues in a vacuum, but for the purpose of enshrining the principles in law. If, for example, we decide in agreement with Fr. McCormick that relational potentiality is the correct moral principle to be applied, then we should be ready to change our law accordingly. That change would mean that the parents and the doctor, unfettered by the law, will decide if the child is to live or die. How do we reach the theologians to make them understand this?

The real danger in the McCormick thesis is similar to the definitional danger in the Callahan approach to the abortion problem. Both define life as that capable of having potential relationships.[32] This implies that legal personhood is an endowment which depends on the quality of life for its right, for obviously McCormick, like Callahan, must be saying that where the parents and the physician have made the decision that no potential for human relationships exists, then legal personhood does not exist, and we may decree the withdrawal of medical treatment and sustenance.

The similarity between this and the *Roe* v. *Wade* solution is apparent, the only difference being that since the child is born and is now, presumably, a constitutional person, the father also participates in the decision with the physician.

Thus, the child may be allowed to die without fear of the law.

The significance of this approach is best understood once we realize that the decision based on relational potential is not a medical one, but a societal one. (It is assumed even by Fr. McCormick that we are discussing a principle applicable to those medical conditions we can cure. If this were not the case, there would be no argument.) This implies an absence of legally protected personhood until the test is made (relational potential) and the child passes, consequently the decision does not seek to give or withhold treatment because of the medical problem under consideration, but rather the whole penumbra of potentialities for relational life which the child will have *if we cure him of this medical problem, which we can.*

In my opinion, neither the traditional approach of ordinary vs. extraordinary means, nor the modern approach of relational humanism, answers the problems posed in the special care nursery in this era when Christians have been called upon to defend life. Certainly there are difficult medical judgments to be made, but I do not perceive an adequate solution in the sources I have searched.

My great fear is that this problem will go the same way as the abortion problem, i.e. while moral theologians argue about when ensoulment occurs, the world slaughters the unborn because it doesn't particularly care even if there is a soul.

Let us make one more shift in our approach to this problem, and consider our analysis strictly on the basis of the current state of the law applicable to the Johns Hopkins and Decatur cases. We will assume that the hospital administrator has just learned of a situation similar to the Johns Hopkins one which is now developing in his own hospital. The question is now asked: Morality aside, what is the *potential legal liability* for the physicians and the hospital? Obviously the administrator is not morally insensitive, but as a prudent man of business he has, in addition, a moral responsibility to know the potential for legal liability that exists. He must, as a prudent administrator, guide his institution to a solution of this vexing problem.

John Robertson has written a comprehensive and excellent legal analysis of involuntary euthanasia of defective newborns. He concludes, as I had,[33] that the parents who withhold ordinary care from a defective infant, as well as physicians, nurses and hospital officials who acquiesce in the decision, risk liability for crimes ranging from homicide to neglect and violation of child abuse laws.[34] In addition, the physician, hospital and involved hospital personnel risk civil liability through malpractice damage suits.[35]

In analyzing the euthanasia issue, Prof. David Louisell makes this vital point:

> The distinction between affirmative killing and allowing one to die according to nature's order without extraordinary effort to "stretch him out longer" continues to be valid, viable, and meaningful.[36]

The distinction, of course, has many sources, but one which has received much attention recently, particularly by those promoting euthanasia of the fuzzy brand which fails to make even the most elemental common sense distinctions, such as between voluntary and involuntary.[37] This source is the allocution by Pius XII given in November, 1957. There is an overlooked phrase in that allocution:

> On the other hand, one is not forbidden to take more than the strictly necessary steps to preserve life and health, *as long as he does not fail in some more serious duty.*[38]

In analyzing this difficult legal problem—the current legal ramifications of failure to treat and/or feed a mongoloid child with intestinal obstructions—the law constantly reminds those involved in this tragic situation of a higher duty.

The higher duty which may have been referred to by Pius, and which is referred to by our common law traditions, is the duty that one man has toward another who is incompetent, and more particularly a parent for a child, a guardian for his ward, or a hospital for a minor child in its custody.

Under the law there is a particular legal relationship that exists between a parent and child which matures and changes as the child matures, until the roles ultimately reverse themselves. For example, on the one hand a parent is responsible for the payment of medical bills for care and treatment to a minor child; on the other hand, an adult child may become responsible under certain circumstances for medical treatment to an elderly parent. The criterion is usually one of dependency.

The relationship that concerns us is that—dependency: the dependency of the child on its parent, of the incompetent on its guardian, of the abandoned neonate on the one who has custody of it.

In April of 1973 I was rather rudely shaken in some of my assumptions when notified of a case taking place in a Catholic hospital in Decatur, which on the surface seemed substantially similar to the Johns Hopkins case. "The infant was born without the normal esophagus. Cannot ingest food or drink. There are indications that she has Downs [sic] Syndrome. Intravenous feeding or the employment of a gavage may prolong the infant's life. Surgery may correct the condition, also may not. May the infant be permitted to die?"[39]

The chaplain after very careful consideration of the applicable moral principles, concluded that "the parents of the . . . child do not need to undertake the extraordinary means that surgical procedures would demand."[40]

All well and good. I quote from the opinion once again in order to give us a point of departure *only*, and in no sense to be critical, for the questions which I now raise are the ones that concern the medical and hospital personnel today. Given that judgment by the moralist and the parent, what is the duty that *is now created* for the doctor, the hospital, and other hospital personnel?

To understand the extremely difficult legal situation in which each of these classes of individuals now find themselves, we will have to discuss certain aspects of criminal law, civil law, the law of medical consent, and the peculiar problems of persons having unwilling custody of a minor incompetent child. Each of these areas of the law finds as high a duty now existing on each of these groups of persons (doctor, hospital and nurse) as previously existed for the *natural parents*.

In analyzing this problem, there are two significant aspects of the Decatur case to be kept in mind: (1) That the operation was, in fact, not done; and (2) Those of us on the periphery acted (or reacted) toward the problem on the basis of our understanding that, as in the Johns Hopkins case, the child was not being fed.

CRIMINAL LAW: AFFIRMATIVE ACTS OF KILLING

The Illinois homicide statute, which is typical of most, provides that "a person who kills an individual without lawful justification commits murder, if, in performing the acts which caused the death: (1) He either intends to kill or do great bodily harm to that individual or another, or knows that such acts will cause death to that individual or another; or (2) He knows that such acts create a strong probability of death or great bodily harm to that individual or another . . ."[41]

Although some commentators have argued that the fact situation common to most mercy killings does not fit or should not fit the common law definition of murder or manslaughter,[42] it is clear from an examination of case law that a mercy killing is no different from any other form of murder.[43] The layman's conception of murder normally includes a requirement of malice aforethought, or a hazy conception of some sort of "evil intent." A legal definition of malice, however, includes no requirement of a "black heart," but merely a design to take life. The courts have repeatedly found that the requirement of legal malice is present in a mercy killing.[44]

There is little case law on the subject of active euthanasia, *per se*.[45] Prosecutions for active euthanasia are still rare, and convictions rarer still. Juries have been more than willing to find that a defendant on trial for a mercy killing was temporarily insane.[46] This does not mean, however, that the law regarding euthanasia is nebulous or embryonic. Despite the small number of written decisions, the common law attitude toward active euthanasia is clear—*it is murder*.[47]

Every civilized legal system considers euthanasia a crime. The law of England and America may consider it to be a more serious crime than any other legal system.[48] The reason for this is rooted in Anglo-American common law which has traditionally placed the highest value on human life, regarding life as sacred and inalienable. The criminal law reflects this basic philosophy. Any unjustified killing is regarded as murder, no matter how kindly the motive. In a very recent American case concerning euthanasia the court clearly addressed itself to this common law tradition when it stated:

> Thus, one who commits euthanasia bears no ill
> will towards his victim and believes his act is
> morally justified, but he nonetheless acts with

malice if he is able to comprehend that society prohibits his act regardless of his personal belief.[49]

Many other American cases involving euthanasia have clearly rejected the defense that the motive, albeit seemingly "altruistic," can protect the perpetrator from the criminal sanctions required. For example, in *State* v. *Ehlers*, the New Jersey court stated:

> If the proved facts established that the defendant in fact did the killing wilfully, that is, with intent to kill . . . and as a result of premeditation and deliberation, therapy implying preconsideration and determination, this is *murder* in tho first degree, *no matter what the defendant's motive may have been . . .*"[50]

In fact, the common law similarly doesn't hold an actor blameless even if the homicide is committed at the request of the victim.[51] In *Turner* v. *State*, the Supreme Court of Tennessee stated:

> Murder is no less murder because a homicide is committed at the desire of the victim. He who kills another upon (the other's) desire or command is, in the judgment of the law, as much a murderer as if he had done it merely of his own volition."[52]

Further, the common law philosophy that life is inalienable precludes any individual from giving permission for his own destruction.[53] The common law and statutory sanctions against suicide were universal. The common law belief in the sacredness of life is so strong and pervasive that there is no doubt that it protects those whose death is imminent.

The Anglo-American legal tradition is clear—as long as the least spark of life remains, a positive act which extinguishes it is criminal. As some commentators have said: "Thus, those special factors which may be said to distinguish euthanasia from more reprehensible forms of killing—a humanitarian motive, possible consent of the victim, the victim's hopeless condition—*are irrelevant* in the eyes of the law. The common law makes no exception for euthanasia, but jealously guards the life of every individual, however grotesque it may be. One who acts to shorten such a life, for any reason whatever, is guilty of murder in the first degree."[54]

AFFIRMATIVE ACTS: CIVIL LIABILITY

In addition, one who acted positively to end a life would be guilty of a civil tort which may take various forms. The action may be an assault or battery, but typically would lie in the area of an intentional tort for wrongful death. A physician so sued probably would not be covered by his malpractice insurance policy since intentional or criminal acts are not ordinarily covered.[55]

CRIMINAL LAW: OMISSION TO ACT

This is a murky area indeed. Few criminal cases can be found predicated upon a refusal to act.[56] There is no known criminal case against physicians or hospitals for a refusal to render treatment.[57] I do not think much time or concern should be spent here because it is unnecessary to our analysis, as will be shown hereafter. However, one commentator has said of this area:

> The more general framework of the law sets out specific guidelines within which decisions as to the treatment that a defective newborn should receive must be made. The law defines a newborn as a person from the moment of birth. As a person, he or she cannot be killed by, or at the request of, anyone, not even his or her parents. The law has always equated with active killing a narrow category of predictably fatal omissions to aid persons who are helpless or dependent—omissions by those who have previously assumed or been charged with the responsibility of providing care. Included in this narrow category are the omissions of one charged by family law with a duty of care (the parent), or one who has agreed to provide care (the doctor), or one who is required by a special statute to take certain protective actions (the doctor or hospital personnel in the case of "child neglect" laws). But the omission must be a failure to take ordinary and reasonable actions.[58]

Consequently, whether murky or not, there is no doubt in the minds of many that criminal prosecution for a failure to provide ordinary medical treatment may be a homicide and the doctor and nurses could be prosecuted. A hospital administrator could also be prosecuted as an accessory, aider or abettor.

CIVIL LIABILITY: OMISSION TO ACT

The law imposes civil liability for an omission to act only where there is a legal duty to do so; therefore, any discussion of a physician's liability for an omission to act should begin with an examination of that duty. If there is no duty, there is no liability.

The relationship between a physician and patient is basically contractual.[59] Although a doctor is under no obligation to treat all comers, once a doctor has undertaken to render treatment the law imposes a *duty* on him to continue such treatment as long as the case requires, in the absence of agreement to the contrary.[60] On the basis of duty, it is usually said that a physician must take all ordinary means necessary to treat his patient. If he does not do so, he may violate the standard of care and be liable for civil damages. The law requires the physician to possess and exercise the skill and judgment of an ordinarily well-qualified physician in the same locale and under similar circumstances.[61] The requirement that he possess only ordinary skills can easily be translated into the concommitant duty that he is therefore only required to exercise ordinary means in exercising that ordinary skill.

The attending physician is not a volunteer, he is bound to the standards of medical performance common to the profession, including the duty to perform affirmative acts, under the sanction of malpractice liability. An attending physician cannot justify his failure to perform up to this standard of medical care on the ground that his failure was "inaction" rather than "affirmative action."

I know of no case where a medical malpractice claim has ever been filed against a physician who, in a terminal situation, and with the consent of the family, ended the extraordinary means that were being used to prolong the life of an already terminally ill patient who is in the death process.[62]

For that matter, I know of no criminal action filed against a physician under similar circumstances.[63]

The situation, of course, is different when the physician is charged with active intervention to end life. Under those circumstances either criminal liability or civil liability (malpractice) can attach.[64] However, there are no known tort cases arising out of active euthanasia situations.[65]

Applying these same principles to the beginning of life is another problem, especially where the result is clearly colored by the mental condition of the patient involved. When that patient is a mongoloid neonate then an even more complicated legal analysis is required.

EXTRAORDINARY VS. ORDINARY MEANS

The difference between ordinary and extraordinary or heroic means of medical treatment is one which the medical profession must delineate, since the physician is legally obligated to proffer treatment which is consistent with customary medical practice—a continually changing standard. A physician is not legally obligated to sustain life by heroic or extraordinary means.[66] He is obligated, however, to obtain informed consents for the termination of any medical treatment unless the treatment itself is useless.[67]

Extraordinary means has been defined as "all medicines, treatments, and operations, which can't be obtained or used without excessive expense, pain, or other inconvenience, or which, if used, would not offer a reasonable hope or benefit."[68]

What is ordinary or extraordinary is very difficult to determine, especially with the rapid advance of medical science and technology. The suggestion has been made that the ordinary vs. extraordinary distinction can retain its viability with but a few more further distinctions. One of these distinctions is that the criterion be viewed from the subjective point of view where the competent adult is concerned, and from the objective or prudent man point of view where the newborn or other legally incompetent person is concerned. This analysis would allow the parent or guardian of the newborn to consent on behalf of the child to refusal of medical treatment if the consent, viewed objectively or from the outside, would be what any prudent person would have done under like or similar circumstances.[69]

However appealing such analysis might otherwise be, it must be pointed out that the law has not yet allowed a parent or guardian to consent to medical treatment to the child, or its lack, which is not for the child's benefit.[70] In fact, child abuse laws which exist in almost every state make such parental conduct a felony. Obviously one can argue that letting a Down's Syndrome child die is beneficial to the child, but enshrining such a principle in the law is fraught with the most grave consequences. It would allow the parents alone the right to decide whether this defective child should live or die. The analogy to the abortion decision is obvious, but its application to born persons is frightening.[71]

The removal of an intestinal obstruction may be an ordinary means of sustaining life of the otherwise normal patient, where the operation offered a reasonable hope of benefit as it usually does. Certainly a physician would feel obligated to recommend removal of the intestinal obstruction if the patient were not a mongoloid. The choice of whether or not to use ordinary means of sustaining a patient's life should not depend on the mental quality of that patient's life.

The standard of "ordinary means" will change with the advance of the state of the healing art. What is now considered extraordinary will become required treatment when it offers a reasonable hope of benefit. That standard will define the extent of a physician's legal obligation to a terminally ill patient, or to any patient, for that matter.

A Missouri judge ruled recently that "Missouri courts cannot order doctors to unhook respirators and other artificial life-supporting machines from otherwise 'dead' patients." The court apparently decided that it did not have jurisdiction to immunize a physician from civil or criminal liability if he, in fact, did turn off the respirator. The article pointed out the similarities to the famous Karen Quinlan case, but made little other comment.[72]

With the Missouri judge's narrow holding I would agree. American courts do not ordinarily have jurisdiction to entertain suits without controversy where someone is merely asking for what lawyers term an advisory opinion.[73]

Tort liability in a euthanasia situation, or, in other words, liability for money damages for a civil as opposed to a criminal wrong, is just now developing as an area of study for legal commentators and in case law.[74] Tort liability for euthanasia may be based on one of several theories; battery, assault and wrongful death. Most frequently, a cause of action which could have alleged euthanasia has been filed under a more euphemistically acceptable theory such as child abuse or malpractice. In any event, whether a tort action expressly alleges euthanasia or not, the physician, his assistant, the spouse or friend of the decedent are all potentially liable. The liability looms greater as medical science increases longevity and techniques and procedures are developed of recognized efficacy for the prolonging of life.[75]

Such liability may exist even if the perpetrator or perpetrators act with humanitarian motives, and even if they have retained the consent of the victim and/or his spouse or next of kin or legal guardian.[76]

As I suggested before, there is an important legal distinction between actively seeking the death of a terminally ill patient and a calculated "benign neglect" toward a patient. This should not be confused with the physician's duty to act. There is a difference between omitting the use of extraordinary means to keep a terminally ill patient alive, on the one hand, and the distinction recognized in the law, on the other, between a physician's responsibility for his actions or his inaction. There is a common law notion that despite the relative ease of rescue, a stranger may ignore a person in a dire predicament with legal impunity. In other words, there is no legal obligation placed on a stranger to rescue a drowning child. However, the law holds a person who attempts to rescue that drowning child to a standard of "ordinary care."[77] Likewise, a physician has no obligation to take on a patient. If a doctor does begin to treat a patient he is held to the standard of ordinary care common to the medical profession. He is then under a legal duty to provide that standard of care. He is not required to provide extraordinary care, but once provided he may not omit it without the proper consents. Consent is a crucial issue in the case of the newborn, since the newborn can never be considered competent to give a legal consent. Ramsey correctly concludes his analyses of this problem with a rejection of the use of the extraordinary, ordinary means analyses in the nursery:

> It seems reasonable to conclude at this point that if the meaning of the distinction between ordinary and extraordinary means is to be found in only actively caring for the dying and in a

patient's right to refuse treatment, that distinction cannot be invoked in the case of defective newborn infants. "Benign" motives may be behind the practice of neglect, but the practice itself is morally the same as involuntary euthanasia. This judgment is reflected in our law of negligent homicide.[78]

Whatever viability the doctrine has elsewhere, its use in the special care nursery has led consistently to the starvation deaths of defective children who, had they been normal, but for the Down's Syndrome, would have received the life-saving treatment. In short, the use of the ordinary vs. extraordinary means distinction may have led to immoral killings which are actionable at law both civilly and criminally. In addition, it has led to the deprivation of the civil rights of these mentally defective newborns. Whether such conduct is actionable under the Civil Rights Act[79] is questionable, since it does not ordinarily involve state action.[80] The conspiracy argument may be available if it can be shown that the prosecutor acted in concert with the hospital and physicians in a conspiracy to deprive the child of constitutional rights, such as the right to life. Such actions may be maintained against private individuals without regard to state action.[81]

I have no quarrel with the use of the ordinary vs. extraordinary means analysis where it is used with competent adults or persons already in the dying process. I seriously question its use in the newborn nursery where its primary effect is to allow the withholding of otherwise effective medical treatment because of the child's otherwise mental quality of life.

CONSENT

Ordinarily a parent can consent on behalf of the child for the receipt of medical treatment.[82] Treatment without consent and without the presence of an emergency would amount to a legal battery.[83] However, in the manner in which our law has developed it is understood that the parents' ability to consent for the child is limited to consenting for actions that are *beneficial* to the child.[84]

The consent must be obtained either from an adult of sound mind, or in the case of incapacity or infancy from the spouse, next of kin, authorized guardian or conservator.

There are a few cases which appear to sustain an individual refusing treatment. However, this has occurred only in those cases involving treatments previously termed "extraordinary means,"[85] although some decisions have recognized an individual's capacity to refuse seemingly ordinary treatment such as a blood transfusion.[86] It is highly doubtful that those few courts which have recognized the individual's capacity to refuse *ordinary* treatment would also impute this capacity to a guardian or spouse.[87] The cases permitting the refusal of ordinary means of sustaining life have only involved conscious, competent individuals refusing treatment on themselves.[88]

Emergency aside, a minor does not have the capacity to consent to an operation.[89] The guardian, parent or person *in loco parentis* must consent.[90] May the parent, guardian or person *in loco parentis* consent to the withdrawal of life-saving treatment? That really is the subject matter of this entire paper and, indeed, this entire section of this book. We have been seeking to maintain the viability of the distinction between ordinary and extraordinary medical treatment because of the value such a distinction has in analyzing all of the various life/death problems involved with medical care. Consequently, we desire to answer that question in this fashion.

Yes, the parent may so give consent when the medical treatment is extraordinary, but not when the treatment is ordinary. We are constrained from doing so, however, by the complexity and difficulty facing the delineation of ordinary from extraordinary. However, we do not maintain that all efforts must be used to prolong life. Prolonging life may be as great an act of despair as premature termination for unjust societal reasons.

What we prefer to say is that the parent may consent to termination of useless means of prolonging death. This is a distinction not of the higher order, vis-a-vis our problem, but rather of a different order altogether. We are not giving parents the right to refuse ordinary or even extraordinary medical means, but are instead focusing on the reasonably expected results of the treatment. If the treatment is beneficial to life, then the parents may not consent to its withdrawal. However, where the "treatment" amounts to a mere prolongation of the death process, parental consent to termination should be allowed.

Consequently, in most cases under consideration in this chapter, the parent may not consent to withdrawal of treatment since that consent constitutes the beginning of the death process, not its natural termination. For example, in the Down's Syndrome case under consideration, the refusal to consent to the esophageal repair means the child will die because it cannot be fed by mouth and intravenous feeding with gavage becomes useless. We will speak more of the feeding problem hereafter.

Consequently, such a consent by the guardian would be *void* and subject the guardian, the administrator and the physician to liability.[91] In recently proposed legislation one bill has advocated allowance of refusal of artificial or extraordinary means of sustaining life even where children are concerned.[92]

Even more chilling to those who might be held potentially liable both criminally and for money damages is the fact that the situations surrounding the obtaining of consents have often been given very strict judicial examination, and courts have turned a sympathetic ear to complaints that the consent was obtained through a mistake, duress or fraud.

Another chilling thought is that even in the event it could be determined that the consent was properly obtained from the proper guardian, such a void consent would not necessarily bar a suit by other relatives of the deceased under the Wrongful Death Act.

FAILURE TO FEED

Does that analysis help us here? I submit yes and no. Because the decision of whether to give or refrain from giving certain medical treatment is a medical question. However, the decision of whether to feed or not, is *not*.

When the atresia is not repaired, it is said that feeding becomes useless. Nothing can be taken by mouth, but intravenous feeding with gavage could maintain life optimally. But what kind of life can a human have hooked up to an IV? Consequently, the decision not to operate becomes the deci-

sion to kill, since it must of necessity be followed with a refusal to give any sustenance even by intravenous feeding. In
a recent *Newsweek* article on the Karen Quinlan case, this
was said:

> The decision to withhold treatment from a pa-
> tient unable to express his wishes—a patient
> like Karen Quinlan—is the most difficult of all,
> and it is particularly controversial in the case of
> the infant born with severe mental or physical
> defects. The matter is easiest to decide in babies
> with anencephaly, the complete absence of the
> cerebral cortex. "With the best of care they live
> for only a few months," notes Dr. John Free-
> man of Johns Hopkins, "so many of us believe
> it is acceptable to withhold feeding and treat-
> ment of infections.[93]

Other comments by physicians on the problem in the
newborn nursery are equally interesting:

> In some cases, the matter has been taken to
> court and judges have ordered the life-saving
> surgery. No matter how well intended, how-
> ever, such decisions should not be left to the
> courts alone, in the view of some doctors. "I'd
> tell the judge: You ordered the surgery to be
> done," says Dr. Jordan Weitzman of the Uni-
> versity of Southern California, "now you find
> the surgeon."
> Weitzman recalls the case of a baby born with
> a malformed brain and severe facial deformities,
> whose unmarried mother left the hospital and
> abandoned the child. Since the baby couldn't
> eat except through a tube, the doctors decided,
> wisely in Weitzman's opinion, to let him die.
> But on a tip from someone at the hospital, the
> *Los Angeles Times* published a heart-rending
> feature about the baby's plight and doctors
> were pressured into continuing treatment.[94]

Let us assume that surgical repair of an esophageal atresia is an extraordinary operation and one that can be morally
and legally rejected even by a parent, guardian or conservator. I submit that the decision *not to feed* or not to give sustenance does not partake of the same dimension, and it is not
even permissible for a parent or anyone else having custody
of the child to intentionally refuse to feed the child.[95] If the

child dies as a result of this failure to feed, I submit the case becomes murder.[96]

This becomes particularly clear when one understands that any person who even so much as unnecessarily exposes a child to the cold, or in any manner injures the child in health or limb, is guilty of a class-4 felony.[97] In order to be a person so charged one need not be a parent. One only has to be the perpetrator of the act or the aider or abettor.

Consequently, no doctor, hospital or hospital personnel can stand passively by while a child in the hospital is allowed to starve to death. A typical child abuse statute requires the following:

> Any *physician, surgeon*, dentist, osteopath, chiropractor, podiatrist, or Christian Science practitioner having reasonable cause to believe that a child brought to him or coming before him for examination, care or treatment has suffered injury or disability from physical abuse, or neglect inflicted upon him or shows evidence of malnutrition, other than by accidental means, and *any hospital to which a child comes*, or *is brought suffering from injury, physical abuse, or neglect apparently* inflicted upon him or shows evidence of malnutrition, other than by accidental means, shall promptly report or cause reports to be made in accordance with this Act. This Section applies to cases of children whose death occurs from apparent injury, neglect or malnutrition, other than by accident means, before found or brought to a hospital.[98] (Emphasis added)

This statute places an affirmative duty on physicians and hospital personnel to report such cases to the proper authorities or become participants in the act.

You may ask: Supposing if the operation is not done, does not the feeding become useless? This may be true, but our analysis holds. The failure to feed is a crime, and if it causes death the crime is murder. Remember, we are not dealing with a terminally ill patient except as a consequence of our refusal to act. The feeding has only become useless as a result of our refusal to act. You may argue that this analysis has led us to the position that the repair *must* be done in the first place. This may be true and illustrates the difficulty of applying principles to a difficult medical situation where the mental retardation hangs like a spectre brooding over the problem.

The reality of this situation is that if the child was mentally adequate then our analysis would be entirely unnecessary because repair would be "considered" ordinary means, and even extraordinary means would be willingly used to keep the child alive.

Paul Ramsey points out that "In the reported cases of the benign neglect of defective infants it is quite obvious that few were born *dying* and certainly none were competent to refuse medical treatment."[99] He then concludes: "That means that the standard for letting die must be the same for the normal child as for the defective child. If an operation to remove a bowel obstruction is indicated to save the life of a normal infant, it is also the indicated treatment of a mongoloid infant. The latter is certainly not dying of Down's Syndrome. Like any other child with an obstruction in its intestinal tract, it will starve to death unless an operation is performed to remove the obstruction to permit normal feeding."[100] Ramsey concludes:

> Ordinarily, the neglected infants are not born dying. They are only born defective and in need of help. The question whether no treatment is the indicated treatment cannot legitimately be raised. The comparison should be among treatments measured to the need. As God is no respecter of persons of high degree, neither should we be. The proper form of the question to be asked is: Should we not close the wound in a newborn expected to be normal? Should we not provide him with devices correcting his incontinence? Should not physical conditions likely to impair any child's mental capacity be stopped if possible; or, if not, subdued?[101]

In another perceptive moral analysis of this problem, James Gustafson has said:

> I have tried to make a persuasive case to indicate why the claim of the infant constitutes a moral obligation on the parents and the physicians to keep the child alive. The intrinsic value or rights of a human being are not qualified by any given person's intelligence or capacities for

productivity, potential consequences of the sort that burden others. Rather, they are constituted by the very existence of the human being as one who is related to others and dependent upon others for his existence. The presumption is always in favor of sustaining life through ordinary means; the desires of persons that run counter to that presumption are not sufficient conditions for abrogating that right.[102]

The reality of this book is the growing willingness of our society to terminate those lives found not worthy of continued existence. This is a hard fact, but true.

CONCLUSION

The higher duty that we spoke of is one that the law thrusts upon the shoulders of any doctor, hospital or hospital employee to render care and treatment for a child abandoned into their care and who will die without their care. They may feel aggrieved at, once again, the unfairness of a society that thrusts this problem on their shoulders, and one can hardly blame them. Nonetheless, the problem is there, and the only prudent course of conduct that I can see for the physician and hospital under these circumstances is the fulfillment of their duty to preserve the child's life.

1. Duff, Raymond S., M.D.; Campbell, A.G.M., M.D., F.R.C.P. (Edin) "Moral and Ethical Dilemmas in the Special Care Nursery", The New England Journal of Medicine, Vol. 289, No. 17, Oct., 1973, pp. 890-894.

2. Engelhardt, H. Tristram, Jr., "Aiding the Death of Young Children" in Beneficent Euthanasia ed. by Marvin Kohl, Prometheus Books, N.Y. at p. 189.

3. Robertson, John A., "Involuntary Euthanasia of Defective Newborns: A Legal Analysis" in The Stanford Law Review, Vol. 27, Jan. 1975, pp. 213-269 at p. 216. See also Smith, David H., "On Letting Some Babies Die" in Facing Death, Vol. 2, No. 2, May, 1974 issue of The Hastings Center Studies, pp. 37-46, at p. 37, 38.

4. Duff & Campbell, Op. Cit. at p. 891.

5. Miner, Michael, Chicago Sun-Times, April 27, 1973, p. 8.

6. Report of the Joseph P. Kennedy Foundation's International Symposium on Human Rights, Retardation and Research, Washington, D.C., The John F. Kennedy Center for the Performing Arts, Oct. 16, 1971. See also: Gustafson, James A., "Mongolism, Parental Desires and the Right to Life" in Perspectives in Biology and Medicine, Summer 1973, pp. 529-557 at p. 530.

7. Miner, Michael, Chicago Sun-Times, April 27, 1973, p. 8; Ob-Gyn News 1/1/73, p. 8.

8. Jonsen, A.R., S.J., Ph. D.; Phibbs, R.H., M.D.; Tooley, W.H., M.D. and Garland, M.J., Ph. D., "Critical Issues in Newborn Intensive Care: A Conference Report and Policy Proposal", in Pediatrics, Vol. 55, No. 6, June, 1975, pp. 756-768.

9. Ibid, p. 758.

10. Ibid.

11. The appendix of the paper gives another figure: 12 yes, 2 no, 2 uncertain.

12. Ibid, pp. 760-761.

13. Hodgson v. Spannus, 378 F. Supp. 1008 (D.C. Minn. 1974), Appeal Dismissed on Other Grounds, 43 U.S.L.W. 3415 (1974), where this Three-Judge Federal Court said in speaking of a born child, that he/she ". . . becomes a person—protected by the usual constitutional rights."

14. Ibid, ft. 6, p. 762.

15. Duff & Campbell, Op. Cit., ft. 67.

16. Kamisar, Yale, "Some Non-Religious Views Against Proposed 'Mercy Killing' Legislation", 42 Minn. L. Rev., No. 6, May, 1958, pp. 969-1042.

17. Ramsey, Paul, "The Benign Neglect of Defective Infants", unpublished paper given at Illinois Right to Life Committee dinner, Chicago, Illinois, Sept. 20, 1975.

18. Ibid, Prof. Ramsey says: "Lesch-Nyhan disease is a genetic defect, identified and described in a series of cases in 1964, which is passed on only to male children. Its victims are unable to walk or sit up unassisted; they suffer uncontrollable spasms; and suffer mental retardation. So far, I should say, care can and should always be conveyed to such victims, though as yet no cure. When, however, the babies' teeth appear they will gnaw through their lips, gnaw their hands and shoulders, they often bite off a finger, and mutilate any part of their own bodies they can reach. There they sit, bloody and unremediable. Is this not a close approximation to the case of undefeatable pain which in the terminal adult patient

places him beyond human caring action and abolishes the moral significance of the distinction between always continuing to care and direct dispatch? When care cannot be conveyed, it need not be extended."

19. Ibid.

20. Apparently, the most common analysis and that which was actually used in both the Johns Hopkins and Decatur cases is the traditional use of ordinary vs. extraordinary means. At the recent symposium on this issue at the Stritch School of Medicine, Rev. Joseph Mangan, S.J., indicated some concern with this traditional approach as applied to the special care nursery.

21. McCormick, Richard; To Save or Let Die, America Magazine, July 13, 1974, pp. 6-10; McCormick, Richard; The New Medicine and Morality, Theology Digest, Vol. 21 No. 4, Winter 1973, pp. 308-321.

22. Enunciated very clearly by Dr. Bart Heffernan and Dr. Eugene Diamond at Stritch School of Medicine, Pediatric Roundtable, Sept., 1974. For a discussion of Christian ethics as a moral norm see Gustafson, James; *Can Ethics Be Christian?*, Univ. of Chicago Press (1975).

23. See the unpublished paper: Casus Conscientiae, a Solution Proposed by Father Kruger, Chaplain of St. Mary's Hospital, Re· Patterson Infant, April, 1973.

24. Decatur Herald, Monday, April 30, 1973.

25. Op. Cit. ft. 21 at p. 5.

26. Healy, Edwin F., S.J., "Medical Ethics", Loyola Univ. Press, Chicago, Illinois, 1956.

27. See, e.g. Dedek, John F., "Human Life; Some Moral Issues," Sheed & Ward, New York, p. 128, 129.

28. Sackett, Walther W., M.D., Testimony at the Hearings before the Special Committee on Aging, of the United States Senate, second session, Part I, "Death with Dignity—An Inquiry into Related Public Issues", U. S. Govt. Printing Office, Washington, D.C., 1972, Doc. 83-683, pp. 29-39, where at p. 30, Dr. Sackett discussed a Cost-Benefit Analysis of the euthanasia question and concludes: "Now, where is the benefit in these 1,500 severely retarded, who never had a rational thought, and still we are going to let 125 people whose lives could be prolonged in a useful state . . . and yet we are going to let 125 of these people die [people who used dialysis] because we are putting all this money into these huge institutions" [for the severely retarded].

29. Ethical and Religious Directives for Catholic Health Facilities, Dept. of Health Affairs, United States Catholic Conference, Sept.-Oct., 1971, 1312 Massachusetts Ave., N.W., Washington, D.C., 20005, see Directives 5, 6, 13, 23, 26, 30, 33; in other Directives the principle is applied but not stated, see e.g. Directive 17, 20.

30. McCormick, Richard A., "To Save or Let Die", America, July 13, 1974, pp. 6-10, at p. 8; (Also printed in JAMA Vol. 229, No. 2, July 8, 1974, pp. 172-176.

31. Ibid at p. 9.

32. Callahan, Daniel, "Abortion: Law, Choice and Morality", New York; MacMillan, 1972, pp. 497, 498.

33. Horan, Dennis J.; "Euthanasia, Medical Treatment and the Mongoloid Child: Death As a Treatment of Choice", Baylor Law Review, Vol. 27, No. 1, Winter 1975, pp. 76-86. This article (Euthanasia As a Form of Medical Management) is an enlargement of the article which appeared in the Baylor Law Review.

34. Robertson, John A., "Involuntary Euthanasia of Defective Newborns: A Legal Analysis", Stanford Law Review, Vol. 27, Jan., 1975, pp. 213-269.

35. Ibid, at p. 244, 245.

36. Louisell, David, Pope John XXIII Lecture, Catholic University Law School, 1972, The Catholic Univ. L. Rev., Vol. 22, pp. 723-745, (1973).

37. The importance of making some elemental distinctions and definitions before discussing the morality of euthanasia and related problems cannot be overestimated. Prof. Louisell in his article (ft. 31 supra) and Prof. Dyck ("Beneficent Euthanasia and Benemortosia: Alternative Views of Mercy" in *Beneficent Euthanasia*, ed. Marvin Kohl, Prometheus Books, Buffalo, New York, 1975, pp. 117-130) have shown clearly that much of the problem in arriving at solutions to these vexing problems is the inadequate thought structure and definitional beginnings employed. Indeed, one author has concluded that careful analysis leads to the conclusion that "The euthanasia controversy is more one of semantics than of substance. As it is now constituted, the controversy does not exist." Vodiga, Bruce, "Euthanasia and the Right to Die—Moral, Ethical and Legal Perspectives", in IIT/Chicago Kent Law Rev., Vol. 51, No. 1, Summer 1974, pp. 1-40.

38. Pope Pius XII, Address to Anesthesiologists, November 13, 1957.

39. Casus Conscientiae, Kruger, Charles F., S.J., Unpublished paper, April 24, 1973, pp. 1-4, at p. 1.

40. Ibid at p. 4.

41. Illinois Revised Statutes, Chapter 38, Section 9-1.

42. Mannes, Marya, *Last Rights, A Case for the Good Death*, a Signet Book, New American Library, New York, New York (1973); Maguire, Daniel, *Death by Choice*, Doubleday and Co., Inc., Garden City, New York (1974); Wilson, Jerry B., *Death by Decision*, The Westminster Press, Philadelphia (1975).

43. Kamisar, Yale, "Some Non-Religious Views Against Proposed 'Mercy-Killing' Legislation", 42 Minn. L. Rev. 969, 970 at f. 9 (1958); Note, "Euthanasia: Criminal, Tort, Constitutional and Legislative Considerations", Notre Dame Law Rev., Vol. 48, June, 1973, pp. 1202-1260, at p. 1203.

44. Idem.

45. The Student Survey noted above (ft. 37) says, "Only one reported decision has used the term, and then only in dictum. *People* v. *Conley*, 49 Cal. Rptr. 815, 822, 411 P 2d 911, 918 (1966)." At footnote 1.

46. Meyers, David W., "The Legal Aspects of Voluntary Medical Euthanasia" in *The Dilemmas of Euthanasia*, edited by John A. Behnke and Sissela Bok, Anchor Press/Doubleday, Garden City, New York (1975), pp. 51-67, at p. 54.

47. Kamisar, Op. Cit. ft. 37 supra.

48. Note, Op. Cit. ft. 37 supra, at p. 1203.

49. *People* v. *Conley*, 49 Cal. Rptr. 815, 822, 411 P 2d 911, 918 (1966).

50. *State* v. *Ehlers*, 98 N.J.L. 236, 240 (1922).

51. See ft. 37 supra.

52. *Turner* v. *State*, 119 Tenn. 663, 671, 108 S.W. 1139, 1141 (1908).

53. See ft. 37 supra.

54. Survey, ft. 37 supra at p. 1205.

55. Horan, Dennis J., Weithers, Thomas J., Hamm, Jean, Erb, John C., "Insurance Coverages: Products Liability, Comprehensive General Liability and Professional Liability" in Liability Insurance Handbook, published by Illinois Institute for Continuing Legal Education, 1976, 2395 West Jefferson St., Springfield, Illinois, 62702.

56. See Robertson, John A., Op. Cit. ft. 30B, pp. 224-235 for applicable legal theories.

57. See Note, ft. 37 supra, at p. 1215, and at p. 1207 footnote 43 which cites: Gurney, "Is There a Right to Die?—A Study of the Law of Euthanasia", 3 Cumberland-Samford L. Rev., 235, 248 (1972); Kamisar, supra ft. 37 at p. 983; and Silving, Helen, "Euthanasia: A Study in Comparative Criminal Law", 103 U. Pa. L. Rev. 350, at p. 360 (1954).

58. Heymann, Philip B. and Holtz, Sara, "The Severely Defective Newborn: The Dilemma and the Decision Process", in Public Policy, Vol. 23, No. 4, Fall 1975, pp. 382-417, at p. 385, 386.

59. Waltz, Jon R., and Inbau, Fred E., Medical Jurisprudence, The MacMillan Company, New York (1971) at pp. 40-41; For an excellent and intriguing analysis of that contractual relationship and its effect on malpractice, see Epstein, Richard A., "Medical Malpractice: The Case for Contract", American Bar Foundation Research Journal, Vol. 1976, No. 1, pp. 87-149.

60. Waltz, Idem.

61. Waltz, Op. Cit. ft. 49 at pp. 38-58.

62. See Note, ft. 37 supra, p. 1215 and ft. 48 supra.

63. Idem.

64. Robertson, ft. 30B supra.

65. Note, ft. 37 supra, at p. 1217.

66. Heymann, Op. Cit. ft. 48A at p. 386. This is a necessary corollary of the physician's duty under tort law. He is obligated to provide ordinary and reasonable treatment and his omission to do so renders him civilly liable. The difficulty comes in trying to determine what treatment is ordinary and what is extraordinary. The cases are not helpful at all in making this determination, either. Probably a more reasonable way of analyzing the problem lies in the area of medical prognosis: will the treatment, if given ordinarily and reasonably, provide a better prognosis for life (not meaningful life) in the circumstances of this case? If the answer is "no", then the treatment can be discontinued regardless of whether it is called extraordinary or ordinary.

67. Horan, Dennis J., "Authority for Medical Treatment: Consent", pp. 7-1 through 7-31, in Medical Malpractice, published by Illinois Institute of Continuing Legal Education (1975), 2395 West Jefferson, Springfield, Illinois.

68. N. St. John-Stevas, "Euthanasia," in Life, Death and the Law, at p. 275; Dedek, John E., Human Life, Some Moral Issues, Sheed & Ward, New York, 1972, at p. 126; The definition is usually taken from: Kelly, Medico-Moral Problems at p. 129.

69. Such consents are sometimes referred to as "Substituted Judgment". The doctrine has been used to substantiate the consent of a parent for the donation of an organ by an incompetent to an ill brother. Strunk v. Strunk, (Ct. of Appeals, Kentucky) 445 SW 2d 145, 35 ALR 3d 683. It is obviously wrong to extend that doctrine to our present concern in such a way as to allow a parent to give consent for the death of a defective child. All legal authorities seem to agree. (See e.g.

Sanders, David, and Dukeminies, Jr., "Medical Advance and Legal Lag: Hemodialysis and Kidney Transplantation", 15 UCLA L. Rev. 357-413 at footnote 103 and 104; Grad, Frank P., "Legislative Responses to the New Biology: Limits and Possibilities", 15 UCLA L. Rev. 480 [1968] at footnote 58.) Yet, that is the position Richard McCormick espoused in an editorial recently published in the Journal of the American Medical Association on the Karen Quinlan case.

70. In *Strunk* v. *Strunk*, ft. 58A supra, the court reasoned that giving consent for the removal of the kidney of the incompetent brother was for that brother's benefit since he would not want to see his brother die because of inability to obtain a donor. In addition, the risk to the donor is minimal and "has been estimated at 0.07 percent" (Hamburger, et al., 1964). The dissent vigorously disagreed. More importantly, for our purposes a 0.07 percent statistical risk bears no relationship to a 100% risk of death, about which we are speaking in the case of refusing ordinary treatment to the mongoloid.

71. This is not to say that such an analogy is not being regularly made and argued. See, e.g. ft. 6 supra.

72. Chicago Daily Law Bulletin, Vol. 121, No. 210, p. 1, October 28, 1975.

73. *Aetna Life Insurance Company of Hartford* v. *Haworth*, 300 U.S. 227 (1937).

74. See Note, ft. 37 supra, pp. 1216-1226.

75. Robertson, Op. Cit. ft. 30B.

76. See Note, ft. 37 supra, pp. 1219-1222.

77. As far as physicians are concerned, see Waltz, ft. 49 supra, pp. 124-130.

78. Ramsey, Paul, Unpublished talk to Illinois Right to Life Committee, 1975.

79. 28 U.S.C. 1981 et seq.

80. *Doe* v. *Bellin* (7th Cir. 1973) 479 F 2d 757. However, public institutions would not be so insulated.

81. 28 U.S.C. 1985.

82. Horan, Op. Cit. ft. 57 supra.

83. *Pratt* v. *Davis*, 224 Ill. 300, 79 NE 562 (1906); *Mohr* v. *Williams*, 95 Minn. 261, 104 NW 12 (1905); *Schloendorff* v. *Society of New York Hospital*, 211 NY 125, 105 NE 92 (Ct. App. NY, 1914, opinion by Justice Cardozo).

84. See ft. 58A and 58B supra.

85. Byrn, Robert, "Compulsory Life Saving Treatment for the Competent Adult", 44 Fordham L. Rev. 1 (1975). See also: Schwartz, Brian M., "In the Name of Treatment: Autonomy, Civil Commitment and Right to Refuse Treatment", Notre Dame Lawyer, Vol. 50, June, 1975, pp. 808-842.

86. *In re Estate of Brooks*, 32 Ill. 2d 361, 205 NE 2d, 435 (Supreme Court of Illinois sustained first amendment right of Jehovah's Witnesses to refuse treatment.) However, the courts universally refuse a parent's attempt to exercise that right for their child. Waltz, ft. 49 supra, at pp. 172, 173.

87. *In re Karen Quinlan*, Superior Court of New Jersey, Chancery Division, Morris County, Docket No. C-201-75, Opinion C by Judge Muir, Nov. 10, 1975. There was testimony in the *Quinlan* case that a respirator was ordinary medical care.

88. *United States* v. *George*, 239 F. Supp. 752 (D. Conn. 1965); *In re Osborne*, 294 A. 2d 372 (D.C. Ct. App. 1972); *In re Brooks Estate*, ft. 67 supra; See also ft. 66 supra. See also Note, Op. Cit. ft. 37 supra, pp. 1220-1221; See also discussion of J. Muir, ft. 68 supra

89. Horan, Op. Cit. ft. 57 supra.

90. Idem.

91. Idem.

92. S.B. 670 Wisconsin Legislature (1971).

93. Newsweek Magazine, November 3, 1975, pp. 58-69, at p. 67.

94. Idem.

95. See the typical child abuse statute. See: Robertson, Op. Cit. ft. 30B supra, p. 222.

96. Ibid, p. 224, 225.

97. See e.g. Illinois Revised Stats., Ch. 23, Sec. 2042 et seq.

98. Idem.

99. Ramsey, Paul, unpublished talk to Illinois Right to Life Committee, 1975.

100. Idem.

101. Idem.

102. Gustafson, James, "Mongolism, Parental Desires and the Right to Life", Perspectives in Biology and Medicine, Summer 1973, Vol. 16, No. 4, pp. 529-557, at p. 552, 553.

SELECTING CHILDREN TO LIVE OR DIE: AN ETHICAL ANALYSIS OF THE DEBATE BETWEEN DR. LORBER AND DR. FREEMAN ON THE TREATMENT OF MENINGOMYELOCELE

STANLEY HAUERWAS

1. THE ETHICAL ISSUES

Should children suffering from meningomyelocele (manifesta) receive medical care? Should children born with Down's Syndrome complicated by duodenal atresia be operated on to save their lives? These and similar questions have recently become the focus for raising the broader question of whether parents or society has the responsibility of doing everything medically possible to save and sustain the life of every child born regardless of their disabilities (Duff and Campbell, 1973). We will, however, make little headway on this latter question if we answer it directly. Rather what we must do is enter the kind of discussion Drs. Freeman and Lorber have begun concerning the treatment of children suffering from meningomyelocele. Unless we are willing to deal with the specifics of the issue we will run the danger of doing ethics over unreal choices.

It is extremely important that we see a decisive difference between the meningomyelocele cases and the Down's Syndrome cases mentioned above. Both cases, of course, raise some of the same broad ethical issues, but on analysis their difference is more important than the similarity. This difference is not simply that people tend to have an immediate moral reaction for or against operating on the child with Down's Syndrome but remain ambiguous about whether meningomyelocele children should be treated. Nor is it just that the retardation of the Down's Syndrome child is generally more prejudicial than the less well known attending complications of spina bifida. Rather the difference is that the multiple disabilities associated with meningomyelocele make prognosis more difficult and yet the meningomyelocele child does not force an immediate life or death decision. As I will try to show the moral issues involved in decisions affecting the Down's Syndrome child are perhaps more immediately dramatic but not nearly as complex as those involved in the continuing care of the child with spina bifida.

1.1 Selection

There are at least three primary issues involved in the debate between Drs. Lorber and Freeman. The first and most prominent concerns Dr. Lorber's policy of selective treatment of spina bifida in terms of his carefully developed criteria of selection (Lorber, 1973; Lorber, 1974). It is Dr. Lorber's contention that it is cruel to subject all children born with spina bifida to surgery when their prognosis is so poor that they can be expected to attain only the most minimal levels of human existence. Those children selected out of surgery are therefore spared years of unnecessary suffering as they usually die with the first year of life.

Dr. Freeman, however, argues that such a selection policy cannot be free from error and thereby unnecessarily endangers the child who may live when we thought he would die. For not to operate on such a child means that the attending conditions associated with meningomyelocele will be worse than if the child had the operation early. Thus since we cannot be sure which will die and which will live we are obligated to give every child optimal care (Freeman, 1974a, 13-21; Freeman, 1974b).

It should be noted that neither Drs. Freeman or Lorber are particularly happy with their "solution." As Dr. Lorber suggests, "Everyone realizes that the solution offered by 'selection' is not a good one. There is no 'good solution,' to a desperate, insoluble problem, merely a 'least bad solution,' which is being offered" (Lorber, 1973, 204). And Dr. Freeman only recommends "optimal care" in "an ambivalent fashion," which I take it denotes his discomfort with his own position. Such ambivalence suggests an important clue to the grammar of the ethical problem involved—namely what we are dealing with is a case where the only appropriate description is the "lesser evil." This I think helps illuminate why we are uneasy about raising such issues explicitly; for most of our moral lives are lived under the metaphor of doing good. We feel extremely uncomfortable at having to embody in our moral character the "lesser evil." For we fear the possible implications for other aspects of our moral life if such a description became a policy.

1.2 Who Should Decide

As the debate now stands, selection is the most prominent issue. However, there are two other important matters. First, who shall make the decision to treat or not to treat. Dr. Freeman argues that "the ultimate decision rests with the physician," (Freeman, 1974a, 14) while Dr. Lorber seems to think the decision must be made in consultation with the parents even if it is necessary to repeat the interview (Lorber, 1973, 202). I assume that consultation means that the parents' attitudes do not just "heavily influence" the physician's decision as Dr. Freeman would have it, but that the parents' decision can have veto power even over the physician's wishes. [I am a little suspicious of Dr. Lorber's claim that the "risks and complications are explained without bias" but it is not proper to analyze this at this point. My suspicion of being able to give a description is based on my general opinion of the "neutrality" of medical description. For example, before the development of treatment of spina bifida 40% of children born with meningomyelocele in London were born "dead." After 1962 that number dropped to zero (Freeman, 1974a, 16)].

1.3 Euthanasia

The other issue involved in these cases is of course the question of euthanasia and in particular childhood euthanasia. Dr. Freeman's position is quite clear. "It is time that society and medicine stopped perpetuating the fiction that withholding treatment is ethically different from terminating life. It is time that society began to discuss mechanisms by which we can alleviate the pain and suffering for those individuals whom we cannot help." (Freeman, 1972, 905). Indeed, Dr. Freeman thinks that active euthanasia might be the most humane course for the most severely affected infants, but since it is illegal he is forced to give all optimal care since without euthanasia he cannot be sure they will die. Dr. Lorber, on the other hand, while admitting the logic of recommending euthanasia in these cases disagrees with such a policy because it would be a "dangerous weapon in the hands of the State or ignorant or unscrupulous individuals" (Lorber, 1973, 204).

My remarks in this essay will primarily concentrate on the ethical issues associated with whether selection is or is not the most morally viable policy. I will deal with the other two issues only as they bear on the issue of selection. However, it should be clearly noted that it may be that these latter issues are more important for any ultimate determination of the kind of care that should be given for children suffering from spina bifida.

2. THE INABILITY OF ETHICS TO PROVIDE AN ETHICAL SOLUTION

It has now become a ritual for those of you who have participated in interdisciplinary exchanges between doctors and ethicists that ethicists begin by saying that ethics cannot provide a solution or advocate what should be done in such a circumstance. This declaration of incompetence is not because the ethicist, in the face of such hard problems, does not think he can have a solution. Rather, his hesitancy grows out of the very nature of ethics itself. As David Sidorsky has recently pointed out "A central characteristic of modern ethical theory has been a systematic and principled effort to deny for philosophy any special competence in moral decision-making. Most contemporary ethicists defend that plea of incompetency with aggressive rigor. They draw a sharp distinction between the legitimacy of philosophical theories in ethics, which provide an analysis of the concepts and language of morality, and the pretentiousness of those philosophical theories in ethics that assert normative values or lay claims to a knowledge of moral principles that can guide decision-making" (Sidorsky, 1974, 8).

2.1 The Ethicist as Advocate

Yet there continues to prevail among doctors the view that ethicists are special people who have a better idea of the moral good than most people—we are the new popes of what should be done. For example Dr. Freeman says that even though Dr. Lorber's figures show that even with the best that medicine can do the end results of the enormous time, money, and effort spent on these children is disappointing, ethicists "still contend that it is better for the child to be severely handicapped than to be dead" (Freeman, 1974a, 20). But I must ask what ethicists, surely not all. Moreover it is not a question of what they contend, but why and what kind of reasons they can give for such a contention. The point is simply that the ethicists properly conceived should be more concerned about the argument than he is about the conclusion.

2.2 Ethics Is Not a Decision Procedure

Yet I am in sympathy with Dr. Freeman's concern that the doctor receive guidance on these issues from people other than doctors. Moreover, I disagree with that ethical tradition represented by Sidorsky above as I do not think that the ethicists can analyze an issue without assuming normative alternatives. However, it is important to see that such normative commitments involve more than the ethicist arguing that one decision rather than another is correct. It is fundamentally misleading to assume that the moral life is primarily made up of the decisions we make or that ethics only begins its work when we have a conflict of values situation. For example, Dr. Freeman suggests that when "a parent strongly desires therapy, no ethical decision is involved," but that is patently false (Freeman, 1974a, 14). Extraordinary ethical commitments are involved in deciding to care for such a child that are no less real even if it seems one did not have to agonize over the decision. Such situations may well be one of the dramatic places that the ethical life is manifested, but that should not lead us to forget that generally decisions are what we do when everything else has been lost. The habits, virtues, fundamental convictions and beliefs that form our character make up our moral life much more than our decision. Consider the moral significance of the fact that we continue to assume that a child with spina bifida is still a child—having spina bifida does not defeat that notion with all its attending moral expectations. This should remind us that at least as important as the decision we make is the language we use to describe the situation at all. For example, the Nuer tribe in Africa simply assumes that infants born with deformities or other anomalies are really hippopotamuses born to humans by accident. In this case the prescribed action is clear: put them in the river where they belong (Hauerwas, 1974b).

2.3 Rules and Decisions

In this connection there is also the very troublesome assumption that if you have a rule concerning these kinds of cases then you no longer have an ethical problem. For example, Dr. Freeman suggests "Each child, and each family, is a unique problem. Blanket rules that every child should be operated upon, are easier for the physician to live with, for they evade the ethical and moral dilemmas and necessity for decisions" (Freeman, 1974a, 15). But not to develop guidelines is to leave ourselves at the mercy of ethics done by slogan—i.e., that every child must be operated on because it has a "right to life" or that we should not make "quality of life" judgments. But as McCormick has recently suggested the problem with slogans is that they "are not tools for analysis and enlightenment; they are weapons for ideological battle" (McCormick, 1974). Moreover statements like Dr. Freeman's make it appear that the only "ethical alternatives are narrowed to dogmatism (which imposes a formula that prescinds from circumstances) and pure concretism (which denies the possibility or usefulness of any guidelines)" (McCormick, 1974, 173).

But guidelines or rules do not make a decision—people do that. A slavish dependence on rules of course can be morally destructive, but without rules all moral discourse becomes but a shadow play for deeper games of arbitrary power and of one man's domination of another. As McCormick suggests, "A guideline is not a slide rule that makes the decision. It is far less than that. But it is far more than the concrete decision of the parents and physician, however seriously and conscientiously this is made. It is more like a light in a room, a light that allows the individual objects to be seen in the fulness of their context" (McCormick, 1974, 173).

2.4 My Own Position

Having said this perhaps it would be wise for me to say
that I simply do not know which side I favor in this debate.
Because I think our humanity is fundamentally bound up
with our willingness to care for the weak (Hauerwas, 1973a;
Hauerwas, 1974c) I tend to think that parents and doctors
ought to be willing to care for children suffering from spina
bifida. But I am ambivalent about whether "care" in this
context means subjecting the child to all the medical skill at
our disposal. For kindness can become demonic when it is
magnified by a technological skill which draws its moral force
from a promethean view of man that thinks this existence
should be free from suffering. I shall say more about this at
the end, but generally I see this problem involving the assumption that care today means "all that medicine can do for
you," and I think that may be wrong. In other words the issue determining this care of spina bifida may not be what
kind of obligation we have to the child, but when do we have
the right to refuse medical care for ourselves and for another.

3. DOES SELECTION RAISE AN ETHICAL PROBLEM?

After having given this extended introduction into what
ethics is and is not and what it can and cannot do, it may be
that all this is irrelevant. For on the face of it the dispute between Drs. Freeman and Lorber appears not to be an ethical
issue at all, but a factual one. Thus Dr. Lorber states, "Those
who are against selection often state that it is not possible to
withhold treatment from any infant with meningomyelocele,
as one can never tell what the outlook is for an individual case.
The data presented here make such an opinion untenable. *It
is possible to forecast* from a purely clinical assessment with
accuracy the *minimum degree of future handicap* in an individual even if it is impossible to *forecast the maximum degree
of disability* which he may suffer, if he survives" (Lorber,
1971, 300). Thus the issue seems to be whether carefully selected spina bifida children who are not treated will soon die.
As an empirical matter I have no special competency to decide one way or the other. (I must admit I am extremely interested in the whole idea of "statistical lives" as it seems to
play a part in these kinds of decisions; I wonder if a utilitarian

bias is not built into the very idea of "statistical lives." This can be seen as soon as one asks what happens if your care is dictated by the results in 70% of such and such cases, but you happen to be in the remaining 30%. Should your care be determined by what "usually" happens? By becoming a "statistical life," have you already been treated like a means rather than an end?)

However, I think on examination it is clear the dispute between Drs. Lorber and Freeman involves much more than simply whether Dr. Lorber is right that all non-treated severe cases will soon die. Dr. Lorber admits there is no way to avoid the occasional properly "selected" patient who will survive longer (Lorber, 1974, 308). But the ethical issues in the dispute are more fundamental than even this admission, as can be illustrated by pointing out the ambiguity involved in Dr. Lorber's position.

(There is, of course, a practical problem involved in Dr. Lorber's criteria that is not strictly ethical but may have ethical significance. One may agree that selection is a good thing and that Dr. Lorber's criteria are the most appropriate but still have difficulty in applying them. Must a child meet all six criteria before we select them out of treatment or is three or four enough. For example, should a child with gross paralysis of the legs and thoracolumbar lesion, but without nyphosis, gross hydrocephalus, and further congenital defects be treated.)

3.1 What Is the Function of the Criteria of Selection?

I have no competency to judge how adequate Dr. Lorber's criteria of selection are to determine the future prognosis of the child. However, I am extremely unclear as to what the criteria are intended to do: (1) are they intended to show that the child cannot live long?; (2) or are they intended to show that even if the child lives with proper care he or she will never be able to reach a high level of human development. If the criteria are meant to perform the first function then one must still ask what does it mean to live "long." How long do you have to live to be a "liver" rather than a "dier"? Thus even if the criteria of selection are meant to determine the child's prognosis for sheer physical survival, that is not a non-ethical decision, as it involves fundamental assumptions about when the dying process begins (Illich, 1974).

However, if the criteria are meant to perform the second function then it must be asked what is taken to be an acceptable level of human development. For if it is the second function the criteria are meant to determine, then what we are saying is that this child will never be able to do X, Y, and Z, and therefore we hope by withholding care it will die. In certain contexts this seems to be what Dr. Lorber is arguing as he suggests "At best not more than 10% of all survivors (with and without hydrocephalus) were likely to have a chance of earning a living in competitive employment." Because of this he suggests that "the ethical validity of prolongation of profoundly handicapped lives, consisting of frequent operation, hospital admissions, and absence from home and school and with no prospect of marriage or employment, became less and less tenable. The cost of maintaining each such child is now about 3,000 pounds a year" (Lorber, 1973, 201).

3.2 Selection and the "Fully Human"

These criteria are open to challenge. For surely if we only operated on those people who would be capable of marrying or holding a job, that would apply to many more patients than those just suffering from spina bifida. In other words these criteria seem extremely arbitrary to be used to locate what constitutes "fully human development" or even "acceptable minimum human development."

It should be noted there are two separate issues here: (1) whether to have a selection policy at all; and (2) if you have a selection policy which criteria are the most appropriate. Of course Dr. Freeman is arguing there should be no selection, but even if you think Dr. Freeman wrong then it is not clear which criteria give you the kind of child you desire. Put differently it is not clear what the relation is between Dr. Lorber's carefully worked out empirical criteria and his criteria of function. For in terms of the latter (i.e., marriage and employment) it seems that it might be just as rational to let all these children die.

Perhaps another way of making this clear is by trying to think of an analogous case. (It is fortunate that I have no medical knowledge as this allows me to construct a case completely indifferent to its medical possibility.) Suppose a man is brought to a hospital from an automobile accident. He has a back injury that clearly has affected the spine. Both legs are severely crushed, there is possible brain damage, and it is suspected that he may have internal injuries affecting his ability to defecate. Moreover unless an operation on his back is performed soon his condition may become worse, but if you do not operate he may die but there is the equal possibility he may continue to live for some time. I suspect that the assumption is that we have more reason to operate in this case than for the child born with spina bifida. But why is that the case—because this man already has a history; because he exists in a network of relations that have built up certain expectations of what he can count on if he is in trouble; that even if he cannot marry or hold a job after this he can still find some forms of satisfying activity; or that he will not have that long to live anyway so he does not have untold years of suffering ahead of him. Such a thought experiment provides a means of testing if we would be as willing to apply Dr. Lorber's criteria to an adult as a child. For if our decision is relative to the patient being a child, then perhaps we should ask if we should not especially protect children from our adult prejudices about what constitutes "human development."

3.3 Selection and the Costs of Repair

Of course this may be a misleading interpretation of Dr. Lorber's position since he does offer another reason why certain of these children should be selected out of care—namely, that some of these children will consume thousands of dollars in medical care with little or no result. Put crudely it appears that Dr. Lorber is suggesting we should weigh the value of this severely affected child against the future costs of maintaining its life. When put in this manner there is always the response that life and dollars are not comparable. This is a fine ideology, but in fact we know that Dr. Lorber's suggestion in this respect cannot be avoided. However, if the dollar value tradeoff is done in the name of providing care for others, then it must be shown this will in fact occur—a condition that I suspect is very difficult to fulfill. The money saved from refusing to care for one child suffering from spina bifida can just as easily go to buy more gasoline as it can to other forms of patient care. However, the concern with expenses may be relative to the well-being of the child's family, which raises a different kind of issue to be discussed below.

Moreover, Dr. Lorber's suggestion that in sustaining these children's lives we do so with no idea of the ultimate cost is a bit misleading, insofar as it makes it appear that it is a problem unique to these children. But in effect we all sustain our lives with no idea of what it is going to cost; and in particular we sustain every child's life with no estimate of the cost. What is different about the child born with spina bifida is that we *know* to some extent that the costs are going to be great, but then the question becomes how much we should let this knowledge weigh against the child's continued existence.

3.4 Selection and Normal Care

There is one other issue that is directly involved in Dr. Lorber's account of selection that needs to be raised. He suggests that the children selected not to be treated should only be given "normal" care. By normal care he means they "were fed on demand. Analgesics were given as required, but no other treatment was offered: no oxygen, tube feeding, antibiotic drugs, or resuscitation" (Lorber, 1973, 203). But one must surely wonder if this is "normal care." If the child were "normal" he would certainly receive antibiotics and vaccinations. Dr. Lorber's "normal" care seems to be a euphemism for minimal.

But if what is meant *is* minimal care then surely Dr. Freeman's concern expressed earlier about the difficulty of drawing a meaningful distinction between acting and refraining in these cases is a matter with which Dr. Lorber must deal. As I have argued elsewhere (Hauerwas, 1974d) the language of letting die or "letting nature take its course" assumes wrongly that refraining from action is conceptually different from acting. Of course Dr. Lorber may make recourse to the traditional distinction between ordinary and extraordinary care, but on analysis I think this distinction is fraught with as many, if not more, difficulties as that between acting and refraining. For example, to suggest as McCormick has that financial costs would constitute extraordinary means (if crushing to the family) is actually verbal legislation to avoid saying that the child's life is a relative good in comparison to the overall well-being of the family (McCormick 1974, 174-175). (See also Reich, 1973, 9-10 for a treatment of spina bifida using the distinction between ordinary and extraordinary). It seems to me that this position may well be viable, but, if so, we will be much more honest to argue that we are under no obligation to care for children if we cannot afford it rather than use the misleading language of extraordinary care.

Moreover, if Dr. Lorber's sense of "normal care" is specifically designed to see that the child should die soon, it must be asked why he thinks this policy is less dangerous than the active euthanasia he so fears. Indeed it seems that the exact opposite is the case since the policy of refraining from care encourages the illusion that we have really not ceased to care for the child. Moreover it seems that the unscrupulous would even be less able to be checked in this use of "normal care" since they could claim that they were not in fact trying to put the child to death.

4. THE ETHICAL FOCUS OF THE DISPUTE

The analysis of the ambiguities involved in Dr. Lorber's selection policy has been used only to establish that the dispute between him and Dr. Freeman is ethical. However, we still have no clear sense in what the fundamental disagreement is between them. For it is to be noted that Drs. Freeman and Lorber share more in common than they disagree about. Neither thinks that these children should be saved because of some ideology such as "life under all circumstances should be sustained." We have already noted that Dr. Freeman might well agree with Dr. Lorber if euthanasia were legal.

4.1 Life as a Relative Value

I suspect that though neither Drs. Lorber nor Freeman explicitly articulate it they both assume a position concerning the preservation of life much like Rev. McCormick's recent statement—namely that human life is not an absolute good, but is relative to the other goods for whose attainment it is the necessary condition. This suggests that it is not inhuman to see that there is a point where an individual's condition represents the negation of any human potential even to himself. Thus life is not a value to be preserved in and for itself, but rather "is a value to be preserved only insofar as it contains some potentiality for human relationship. When in human judgment this potentiality is totally absent or would be, because of the condition of the individual, totally subordinated to the mere effort of survival, that life can be said to have achieved its potential" (McCormick, 1974, 175. See also my chapter on death and dying, Hauerwas, 1974c).

Yet even with this clearly stated we are still far from being sure what kind of ethical issue is involved. For it is very well to say that life is relative to other considerations, but the crucial question is what those considerations are. At times Dr. Lorber seems to suggest that the good of the child should be balanced against the harm done to the family or society by the child's continued existence. However, that kind of balancing is not invited by McCormick as he suggests the value that must be weighed is the child's own value to himself.

4.2 Who Is the Patient?

In this respect it must be asked who Dr. Lorber and Dr. Freeman see as their primary patient—the child or the child's family. Traditionally it has been assumed that the doctor's primary patient is the child. Of course the doctor may be concerned about the parents insofar as their condition will affect the condition of his patient. But that is quite a different thing than the suggestion that the question of the continued existence of the child is determined by the effect that the child will have on the family. If this is what is meant there is little to prevent the perversion of medicine, for the practice of medicine would be open to the will of the most corrupt parents and society.

4.3 The Doctor and the Relief of Suffering

In this respect I think the modern doctor tends to think of himself as being too responsible for the alleviation of suffering. It is one of our peculiar human traits to think that if we do the morally right thing it should work out to everyone's best interests. But the plain fact is that we may do the right thing, with tragic results. A child may be saved—a right and perhaps even dutiful act—and yet tragically it may destroy the family. That does not indicate that we need to change our ethics, but rather that we must be people and doctors who are substantive enough to know how to go on acting morally in such a world.

4.4 The Doctor or the Family as Decision Maker

I am extremely interested in some of the reasons that are given as to why doctors should make these kind of decisions rather than the parents. I think this may partly be due to doctors' built-in paternalistic assumptions toward their patients. However, I take it there are also some issues involved that are more important than those kind of ethically unsupportable assumptions of the doctors' moral superiority. Even if such assumption by the doctor is interpreted in the most favorable moral light, doctors must realize to choose to take another's moral burdens on oneself may at times be immoral.

I take it that the reason that some doctors feel they must make the decision is that they think the parents cannot really understand the technical medical issues involved (Freeman, 1974a, 14). That may well be the case, but I suggest that it is not decision enough to justify preventing the parents from being the primary decision makers. For one does not need to know the etiology of a disease in order to know its effects. Informed consent is a difficult matter, but I would suggest that being informed to make a decision does not mean the patient must know everything that the doctor knows about the disease, but rather he must know about the disease in terms of its effects on him. (Or Freeman does say the doctor must let the parents' wishes "heavily influence" his decision, but I have no idea what or how he does that.)

Of course, one may respond that is exactly what parents in this situation cannot know—they cannot imagine what it would be like to raise a child with such serious problems year after year. I think this is probably true, but I do not think it is a consideration decisive enough to rob them of the right of making the decision. They should not only have the situation described, they should also be given the opportunity to meet parents and children who have lived with such a malady. None of us knows I suspect, what problems we take on when we raise any child, but I am sure that our innocence on this respect does not defeat our right to make the decision to have or not have children.

I think one of the reasons that doctors think that they must make the decision is that they have become very conscious of the fact that there is no neutral way to present the "facts"—alternatives. Indeed we know that to present even the possibility of non-treatment is already to take an ethical stance toward these cases. Therefore the doctor, recognizing that he cannot avoid a moral role, becomes a willing participant in the decision. I think that this is fine as long as the doctor does not finally try to usurp the rightful role of the parents.

Dr. Randolph has suggested that the doctor should do this partly because once the parents feel supported by the doctor they can "then make an objective decision with less guilt than if you send them home and say, 'If you wish, we will withhold treatment that is available and your baby will not survive for very long'" (Randolph, 1973, 269). But I see no reason why it should be the doctor's task to help parents avoid guilt. Morally the question is never whether we should be guilty or not guilty, but whether we should be guilty over the right kind of thing. It may be that our penchant for describing what evil we do as good in order to avoid guilt is exactly one of the most dangerous forms of immorality, as it reinforces our penchant to self-deception (Hauerwas, 1974b).

4.5 Act Always to Produce the Least Suffering

Even though both Drs. Lorber and Freeman sound like they are at times qualifying the child's life by other societal or familial values, they actually tend (and Dr. Lorber explicitly states [Lorber, 1971, 299]) to make the decision in terms of what will finally produce the least suffering for these children in themselves. In other words I think both Drs. Lorber and Freeman are primarily guided by the moral principle that they should act to produce the less suffering for these kind of children irrespective of the effect on their family or society. However, this agreement I think hides what I take to be the most significant ethical disagreement between Dr. Lorber and Dr. Freeman.

Dr. Lorber, in defending his selective policy, admits that some "properly 'selected' untreated patients will survive longer. Their handicaps will not necessarily be graver than the thousands who survive with all the operations. Occasionally hard cases should not sway the discerning physician to do what he considers the best for his patient and his patient's family" (Lorber, 1974, 308). Dr. Lorber seems to assume that it is better to have one suffer in order to spare others the many years of suffering due to being treated unwisely. Thus by selection we have less suffering both in terms of the years involved and the quality of suffering of those who have been aided.

Dr. Freeman is no less interested in preventing suffering, but his perspective is determined by the one case that is not treated but lives. In order to avoid this one case he is willing to give life to the many who admittedly will increase the sum total of suffering in the class of people with spina bifida.

The disagreement so stated puts us very close to locating the basic ethical dispute involved in this debate. For Lorber is taking what I would call a classical negative utilitarian position by attempting to reduce the amount of suffering for the greatest number of individuals born with spina bifida. (The qualifying clause "born with spina bifida" is important as it makes clear that Lorber is not necessarily committed to a thorough utilitarian position where he would be required to balance the suffering of others against that of those with spina bifida.) In other words Lorber's basic ethical principle is to act to produce the least amount of suffering for the greatest number in the class of humans with spina bifida.

Dr. Freeman's position, on the other hand, tends to be more Kantian as he assumes that you should never use one man for the good of others. In this context, however, this would be more properly stated as never increase one man's suffering in order to reduce the suffering of the many, for to do so violates the basic ethical imperative to always treat others as ends never as means. Therefore Dr. Freeman's willingness to entertain euthanasia is not to reduce the burden on society or even on the family, but rather it is to reduce the burden of the child on himself—that is it is to save him unnecessary suffering.

If I am right in how I have construed the ethical issue between Dr. Freeman and Dr. Lorber then we have made some progress. For what this allows us to do is see that this dispute is not unique to the problems of spina bifida, but rather involves a classical ethical disagreement that reaches to the fundamental assumptions of what we consider the moral life to be. There may simply be no way finally of settling the kind of disagreement. However, we at least now know the proper kind of questions to ask each position in order to determine which we consider the most valid. For example Dr. Lorber, or one holding a position like Dr. Lorber's, must find some way to counter the recurrent criticism that utilitarianism, even of his negative kind, fails to account for some of our fundamental intuitions about the nature of justice (Williams, 1972; Williams, 1973).

Moreover once we have these alternatives clearly stated we can also test them in terms of which does the most justice to traditional assumptions about the ethos that should inform medicine. As I suggested earlier the moral viability of medicine, its very nature as a profession, is dependent on the doctor's fundamental commitment to the health of each patient irregardless of the patient's worth to others (Ramsey, 1972). All our strictures involving human experimentation and the concern for informed consent rest on this moral conviction. Dr. Lorber must therefore show how his call to balance the life of some of these children against others (in a non-triage situation) can be justified in relation to these traditional commitments of medicine.

4.6 Care and the Power of Medicine

Since I have directed my criticism at Dr. Lorber it may appear I am in total agreement with Dr. Freeman. This however is not the case as the same kind of commitment to the patient also suggests that the patient has a moral standing prior to his relation to the doctor. Modern medicine seems to confront us with a seamless web of care that enmeshes us from the beginning to the end of our lives. To be alive is to be under the care of medicine until the doctor can no longer do anything for us. Indeed, natural death now means "when the doctor can no longer cure" (Illich, 1974).

This attitude I think also helps account for the doctor's assumption that once you start any medical procedure on a patient then every available medical procedure must be employed. In other words medicine seems to carry with it some kind of moral imperative that once you do anything you must do everything. But that embodies a far too intimate relationship between medicine and human life that leaves us as men far too manipulable by the latest medical "advance."

What we must begin is a new reclaiming of our life and our death from medicine. We need to see the possibility of choosing our death apart from medicine's power to keep us alive. I would suggest at least a way to begin on such a project is to reconsider the possibility of refusal of suggested therapy. What the doctor suggests is not necessarily what morally we must do. We may well have an obligation to keep ourselves healthy, but such an obligation is not the same as doing everything our doctor says. For the health of the person is not necessarily the same as the health that modern medicine brings.

These very general considerations do not however apply directly to the case of the child suffering from spina bifida. For in such a case it is simply not a matter of our choosing to refuse treatment, but of choosing for another. This indeed complicates the issue, just as there is a deep moral difference between choosing euthanasia for oneself and choosing it for another. But it at least makes clear that perhaps what is involved is not choosing to "kill" the child, or even choosing to "let it die." Rather, what we are doing is choosing not to have the therapy the doctor suggests. That does not mean we have ceased to care for such a child, but rather that we reembody ways of caring for dying children rather than substituting for such care modern medical therapy.

I think that we are not ready to know how such refusal of therapy can be ethically viable. I am fairly certain we must first start learning what it might mean for us, before we start applying it to children. Therefore I am not offering this as a new way to get us out of our dilemma of how to treat children with meningomyelocele, but rather as a proper way to start thinking about our own health that may provide a clue as to how we might think about theirs.

5. *THE MORAL ASSUMPTIONS BEHIND PARENTING*

In closing I would like to raise what I regard as some of the background beliefs that help to highlight this issue. For involved in the care of such children are fundamental attitudes that we all share about the kind of care and obligation that we have toward our children. It is my hunch that we have failed to notice a subtle, but extremely significant, shift in our parental attitudes and assumptions about why we have children at all. This shift I think has affected in a fundamental way how we view childhood death. Modern medicine has been influenced by this shift.

In the past it was not possible to decide to have or not have children. In such a situation children were viewed as a gift of God which to be sure brought special obligation and duties. However, it was assumed that the child had a standing in the universe that was separate from the parents' valuing of the child. Children were cared for by God in a special sense—such care did not mean that they were less subject to the dangers of disease and death—but rather that God had a special place in his heart for them. The death of the child was no less tragic, but the tragedy was bounded by hope.

It is interesting to note that the Catholic and Jewish view of the obligation of their people to have children had much the same moral implications. Each in its own way transformed the unavoidability to have children into the freedom to have children by understanding it as an obligation. Children were brought into the world, not because we cannot avoid them, not because we like them, not because we must keep the species going, but to assure the continuation of the people of God. The death of the child is therefore not an unmitigated disaster, because the child was not brought into this world in the first place to exist but to serve the purpose of God. New life was willed not to break the eternal boredom of living in a world where nothing is worth dying for but exactly because there is something worth dying for.

I am aware that these notions strike us as extraordinary, and perhaps even morally perverse. But if we take them seriously they may help us to feel the oddness of our own assumptions about children. For we see children neither as gifts nor as obligations, rather we choose to have children. We call this freedom, but in fact it places us as parents under the most stringent slavery, for we feel since it is our choice to have children we must be responsible for them from conception (thus mothers who worry about having intercourse at the right time for the "best" conceptus) to vocation. We try to raise our children sheltered from the dangers and threats we know to be present in this world. We feel uniquely threatened if our children would die, for we take it to be our bedrock duty to keep our children alive under all circumstances—it is our responsibility.

We therefore call upon modern medicine's amazing arsenal of skills to keep our children alive under all circumstances. I am of course aware that such skills are partly developed simply as a result of the scientific curiosity of the doctor. More over, the power of such skill often becomes magnified as the skill begins with tentative first steps to help one patient, but when combined with the skills of other doctors becomes a power to help some patients who were before thought beyond all help. However, I suspect that medicine's new power to cure children is part and parcel of doctors' willing acquiescence to the desires of parents to keep their children alive at all costs.

In conclusion I am therefore going to be bold enough to suggest that underlying these cruel dilemmas of pediatric medicine is a much more fundamental perversion: That we have lost the moral basis to know how to accept the death of children because we claim unwarranted responsibility for our children's lives. I suspect that we will not know how to deal with these issues until we learn to live, and we learn to raise our children with the assumption that there are some things worth dying for.

REFERENCES

Duff and Campbell. "Moral and Ethical Dilemma in the Special Care Nursery." *New England Journal of Medicine,*
289 (1973), 890-894.

Freeman, John. "Is There a Right to Die?" *The Journal of
Pediatrics,* 80 (May, 1972), 904-905.

Freeman, John. *Practical Management of Meningomyelocele.*
Baltimore: University Park Press, 1974a.

Freeman, John. "The Shortsighted Treatment of Myelomeningocele: A Long Term Case Report." *The Journal
of Pediatrics,* 53 (March, 1974b), 311-313.

Illich, Ivan. "The Political Uses of Natural Death." *Hastings
Center Studies,* 2 (January, 1974), 1-20.

Hauerwas, Stanley. "The Retarded and the Criteria for the
Human." *The Finacre Quarterly,* 40 (November, 1973),
217-222.

_____, "Must We Relieve Suffering?" *Pediatric News,*
8 (March, 1974a), 54-55.

_____, "Self-Deception and Autobiography: Theological
and Ethical Reflection on Speer's *Inside the Third Reich.*"
Journal of Religious Ethics, 2, 1 (May, 1974b), 99-118.

_____, *Vision and Virtue: Essays in Christian Ethical
Reflection.* Notre Dame: Fides, 1974c.

_____, "The Demands and Limits of Care: Ethical Re-
flections on the Moral Dilemmas of Neonatal Intensive
Care." *The American Journal of the Medical Sciences,*
269 (March-April, 1975), 222-236.

Lorber, J. "Results of Treatment of Myelomeningocele."
Development: Medical Child Neurology, 13 (1971), 279-
303.

_____, "Early Results of Selective Treatment of Spinal Bifida Cyctica." *British Medical Journal,* 27 (October, 1973), 201-204.

_____, "Selective Treatment of Myelomeningocele: To Treat or not to Treat." *Journal of Pediatrics,* 53 (March, 1974), 307-388.

McCormick, Richard. "To Save or Let Die: The Dilemma of Modern Medicine." *Journal of American Medical Association,* 229 (July 8, 1974), 172-176.

Ramsey, Paul. *The Patient or Person.* New Haven: Yale, 1971.

Randolph, Judson. "The Right to Life: Can We Decide?" *Clinical Proceedings of Children's Hospital National Medical Center,* XXIX (December, 1973), 268-269.

Reich, Warren. "On the Birth of a Severely Handicapped Infant." *Hastings Center Report,* 9 (1973), 10-11.

Sidorsky, David. "Health Care and Human Values: A Care Preventative." *Seminar Reports: Columbia University,* 8 (May 15, 1974), 8-11.

Smart, J.J.C., and Williams, Bernard. *Utilitarianism For and Against.* Cambridge University Press, 1973.

Williams, Bernard. *Morality: An Introduction to Ethics.* New York: Harper Torchbooks, 1972.

MONGOLISM, PARENTAL DESIRES, AND THE RIGHT TO LIFE*

JAMES M. GUSTAFSON†

The Problem

THE FAMILY SETTING.

Mother, 34 years old, hospital nurse.
Father, 35 years old, lawyer.
Two normal children in the family.

In late fall of 1963, Mr. and Mrs. —— gave birth to a premature baby boy. Soon after birth, the child was diagnosed as a "mongoloid" (Down's syndrome) with the added complication of an intestinal blockage (duodenal atresia). The latter could be corrected with an operation of quite nominal risk. Without the operation, the child could not be fed and would die.

At the time of birth Mrs. —— overheard the doctor express his belief that the child was a mongol. She immediately indicated she did not want the child. The next day, in consultation with a physician, she maintained this position, refusing to give permission for the corrective operation on the intestinal block. Her husband supported her in this position, saying that his wife knew more about these things (i.e., mongoloid children) than he. The reason the mother gave for her position—"It would be unfair to the other children of the household to raise them with a mongoloid."

The physician explained to the parents that the degree of mental retardation cannot be predicted at birth—running from very low mentality to borderline subnormal. As he said: "Mongolism, it should be stressed, is one of the milder forms of mental retardation.

* This paper was written at the request of the Joseph P. Kennedy, Jr., Foundation in response to the "case study" included and additional information, for its Symposium on Human Rights, Retardation, and Research, October 16, 1971. It is an extended version of The Johns Hopkins case study.

† University Professor of theological ethics, University of Chicago.

That is, mongols' IQs are generally in the 50–80 range, and sometimes a little higher. That is, they're almost always trainable. They can hold simple jobs. And they're famous for being happy children. They're perenially happy and usually a great joy." Without other complications, they can anticipate a long life.

Given the parents' decision, the hospital staff did not seek a court order to override the decision (see "Legal Setting" below). The child was put in a side room and, over an 11-day period, allowed to starve to death.

Following this episode, the parents undertook genetic counseling (chromosome studies) with regard to future possible pregnancies.

THE LEGAL SETTING

Since the possibility of a court order reversing the parents' decision naturally arose, the physician's opinion in this matter—and his decision not to seek such an order—is central. As he said: "In the situation in which the child has a known, serious mental abnormality, and would be a burden both to the parents financially and emotionally and perhaps to society, I think it's unlikely that the court would sustain an order to operate on the child against the parents' wishes." He went on to say: "I think one of the great difficulties, and I hope [this] will be part of the discussion relative to this child, is what happens in a family where a court order is used as the means of correcting a congenital abnormality. Does that child ever really become an accepted member of the family? And what are all of the feelings, particularly guilt and coercion feelings that the parents must have following that type of extraordinary force that's brought to bear upon them for making them accept a child that they did not wish to have?"

Both doctors and nursing staff were firmly convinced that it was "clearly illegal" to hasten the child's death by the use of medication.

One of the doctors raised the further issue of consent, saying: "Who has the right to decide for a child anyway? . . . The whole way we handle life and death is the reflection of the long-standing belief in this country that children don't have any rights, that they're not citizens, that their parents can decide to kill them or to let them live, as they choose."

THE HOSPITAL SETTING

When posed the question of whether the case would have beer taken to court had the child had a normal IQ, with the parents re fusing permission for the intestinal operation, the near unanimous opinion of the doctors: "Yes, we would have tried to override their decision." Asked why, the doctors replied: "When a retarded child presents us with the same problem, a different value system comes in; and not only does the staff acquiesce in the parent's decision to let the child die, but it's probable that the courts would also. That is, there is a different standard. . . . There is this tendency to value life on the basis of intelligence. . . . [It's] a part of the American ethic."

The treatment of the child during the period of its dying was also interesting. One doctor commented on "putting the child in a side room." When asked about medication to hasten the death, he replied: "No one would ever do that. No one would ever think about it, because they feel uncomfortable about it. . . . A lot of the way we handle these things has to do with our own anxieties about death and our own desires to be separated from the decisions that we're making."

The nursing staff who had to tend to the child showed some resentment at this. One nurse said she had great difficulty just in entering the room and watching the child degenerate—she could "hardly bear to touch him." Another nurse, however, said: "I didn't mind coming to work. Because like I would rock him. And I think that kind of helped me some—to be able to sit there and hold him. And he was just a tiny little thing. He was really a very small baby. And he was cute. He had a cute little face to him, and it was easy to love him, you know?" And when the baby died, how did she feel?—"I was glad that it was over. It was an end for him."

The Resolution

This complex of human experiences and decisions evokes profound human sensibilities and serious intellectual examination. One sees in and beyond it dimensions that could be explored by practitioners of various academic disciplines. Many of the standard questions about the ethics of medical care are pertinent, as are questions that have been long discussed by philosophers and theologians. One would have to write a full-length book to plow up, cultivate, and bring to fruition the implications of this experience.

I am convinced that, when we respond to a moral dilemma, the way in which we formulate the dilemma, the picture we draw of its salient features, is largely determinative of the choices we have. If the war in Vietnam is pictured as a struggle between the totalitarian forces of evil seeking to suppress all human values on the one side, and the forces of righteousness on the other, we have one sort of problem with limited choice. If, however, it is viewed as a struggle of oppressed people to throw off the shackles of colonialism and imperialism, we have another sort of problem. If it is pictured as more complex, the range of choices is wider, and the factors to be considered are more numerous. If the population problem is depicted as a race against imminent self-destruction of the human race, an ethics of survival seems to be legitimate and to deserve priority. If, however, the population problem is depicted more complexly, other values also determine policy, and our range of choices is broader.

One of the points under discussion in this medical case is how we should view it. What elements are in the accounts that the participants give to it? What elements were left out? What "values" did they seem to consider, and which did they seem to ignore? Perhaps if one made a different montage of the raw experience, one would have different choices and outcomes.

Whose picture is correct? It would not be difficult for one moral philosopher or theologian to present arguments that might undercut, if not demolish, the defenses made by the participants. Another moralist might make a strong defense of the decisions by assigning different degrees of importance to certain aspects of the case. The first might focus on the violation of individual rights, in this case the rights of the infant. The other might claim that the way of least possible suffering for the fewest persons over the longest range of time was the commendable outcome of the account as we have it. Both would be accounts drawn by external observers, not by active, participating agents. There is a tradition that says that ethical reflection by an ideal external observer can bring morally right answers. I have an observer's perspective, though not that of an "ideal observer." But I believe that it is both charitable and intellectually important to try to view the events as the major participants viewed them. The events remain closer to the confusions of the raw experience that way; the passions, feelings, and emotions have some echo of vitality remaining. The parents were not without feeling, the nurses not without anguish. The experiences could become a case in which x represents the rights of the infant to life, y represents the consequences of continued life as a mongoloid person, and z represents the consequences of his continued life for the family and the state. But such abstraction has a way of oversimplifying experience.

One would "weigh" x against y and z. I cannot reproduce the drama even of the materials I have read, the interviews with doctors and nurses, and certainly even those are several long steps from the thoughts and feelings of the parents and the staff at that time. I shall, however, attempt to state the salient features of the dilemma for its participants; features that are each value laden and in part determinative of their decisions. In the process of doing that for the participants, I will indicate what reasons might justify their decisions. Following that I will draw a different picture of the experience, highlighting different values and principles, and show how this would lead to a different decision. Finally, I shall give the reasons why I, an observer, believe they, the participants, did the wrong thing. Their responsible and involved participation, one must remember, is very different from my detached reflection on documents and interviews almost a decade later.

THE MOTHER'S DECISION

Our information about the mother's decision is secondhand. We cannot be certain that we have an accurate account of her reasons for not authorizing the surgery that could have saved the mongoloid infant's life. It is not my role to speculate whether her given reasons are her "real motives"; that would involve an assessment of her "unconscious." When she heard the child was probably a mongol, she "expressed some negative feeling" about it, and "did not want a retarded child." Because she was a nurse she understood what mongolism indicated. One reason beyond her feelings and wants is given: to raise a mongoloid child in the family would not be "fair" to the other children. That her decision was anguished we know from several sources.

For ethical reflection, three terms I have quoted are important: "negative feeling," "wants" or "desires," and "fair." We need to inquire about the status of each as a justification for her decision.

What moral weight can a negative feeling bear? On two quite different grounds, weight could be given to her feelings in an effort to sympathetically understand her decision. First, at the point of making a decision, there is always an element of the rightness or wrongness of the choice that defies full rational justification. When we see injustice being done, we have strong negative feelings; we do not need a sophisticated moral argument to tell us that the act is unjust. We "feel" that it is wrong. It might be said that the mother's "negative feeling" was evoked by an intuition that it would be wrong to save the infant's life, and that feeling is a reliable guide to conduct.

Second, her negative response to the diagnosis of mongolism suggests that she would not be capable of giving the child the affection and the care that it would require. The logic involved is an extrapolation from that moment to potential consequences for her continued relationship to the child in the future. The argument is familiar; it is common in the literature that supports abortion on request—"no unwanted child ought to be born." Why? Because unwanted children suffer from hostility and lack of affection from their mothers, and this is bad for them.

The second term is "wants" or "desires." The negative feelings are assumed to be an indication of her desires. We might infer that at some point she said, "I do not want a retarded child." The status of "wanting" is different, we might note, if it expresses a wish before the child is born, or if it expresses a desire that leads to the death of the infant after it is born. No normal pregnant woman would wish a retarded child. In this drama, however, it translates into: "I would rather not have the infant kept alive." Or, "I will not accept parental responsibilities for a retarded child." What is the status of a desire or a want as an ethical justification for an action? To discuss that fully would lead to an account of a vast literature. The crucial issue in this case is whether the existence of the infant lays a moral claim that supersedes the mother's desires.

If a solicitor of funds for the relief of refugees in Bengal requested a donation from her and she responded, "I do not want to give money for that cause," some persons would think her to be morally insensitive, but none could argue that the refugees in Bengal had a moral claim on her money which she was obligated to acknowledge. The existence of the infant lays a weightier claim on her than does a request for a donation. We would not say that the child's right to surgery, and thus to life, is wholly relative to, and therefore exclusively dependent upon, the mother's desires or wants.

Another illustration is closer to her situation than the request for a donation. A man asks a woman to marry him. Because she is asked, she is under no obligation to answer affirmatively. He might press claims upon her—they have expressed love for each other; or they have dated for a long time; he has developed his affection for her on the assumption that her responsiveness would lead to marriage. But none of these claims would be sufficient to overrule her desire not to marry him. Why? Two sorts of reasons might be given. One would refer to potential consequences: a marriage in which one partner does not desire the relationship leads to anxiety and suffering. To avoid needless suffering is obviously desirable. So in this case, it might be said that the mother's desire is to avoid needless suffering and anxiety: the undesirable consequences can be avoided by permitting the child to die.

The second sort of reason why a woman has no obligation to marry her suitor refers to her rights as an individual. A request for marriage does not constitute a moral obligation, since there is no prima facie claim by the suitor. The woman has a right to say no. Indeed, if the suitor sought to coerce her into marriage, everyone would assert that she has a right to refuse him. In our case, however, there are some differences. The infant is incapable of expressing a request or demand. Also, the relationship is different; the suitor is not dependent upon his girl friend in the same way that the infant is dependent upon his mother. Dependence functions in two different senses; the necessary conditions for the birth of the child were his conception and *in utero* nourishment—thus, in a sense the parents "caused" the child to come into being. And, apart from instituting adoption procedures, the parents are the only ones who can provide the necessary conditions for sustaining the child's life. The infant is dependent on them in the sense that he must rely upon their performance of certain acts in order to continue to exist. The ethical question to the mother is, Does the infant's physical life lay an unconditioned moral claim on the mother? She answered, implicitly, in the negative.

What backing might the negative answer be given? The most persuasive justification would come from an argument that there are no unconditioned moral claims upon one when those presumed claims go against one's desires and wants. The claims of another are relative to my desires, my wants. Neither the solicitor for Bengal relief nor the suitor has an unconditioned claim to make; in both cases a desire is sufficient grounds for denying such a claim. In our case, it would have to be argued that the two senses of dependence that the infant has on the mother are not sufficient conditions for a claim on her that would morally require the needed surgery. Since there are no unconditioned claims, and since the conditions in this drama are not sufficient to warrant a claim, the mother is justified in denying permission for the surgery.

We note here that in our culture there are two trends in the development of morality that run counter to each other: one is the trend that desires of the ego are the grounds for moral and legal claims. If a mother does not desire the fetus in her uterus, she has a right to an abortion. The other increasingly limits individual desires and wants. An employer might want to hire only white persons of German ancestry, but he has no right to do so.

The word "fair" appeals to quite different warrants. It would not be "fair" to the other children in the family to raise a mongoloid with them. In moral philosophy, fairness is either the same as justice or closely akin to it. Two traditional definitions of justice might show how fairness could be used in this case. One is "to each his due." The other children would not get what is due them because of the inordinate requirements of time, energy, and financial resources that would be required if the mongoloid child lived. Or, if they received what was due to them, there would not be sufficient time, energy, and other resources to attend to the particular needs of the mongoloid; his condition would require more than is due him. The other traditional definition is "equals shall be treated equally." In principle, all children in the family belong to a class of equals and should be treated equally. Whether the mongoloid belongs to that class of equals is in doubt. If he does, to treat him equally with the others would be unfair to him because of his particular needs. To treat him unequally would be unfair to the others.

Perhaps "fairness" did not imply "justice." Perhaps the mother was thinking about such consequences for the other children as the extra demands that would be made upon their patience, the time they would have to give the care of the child, the emotional problems they might have in coping with a retarded sibling, and the sense of shame they might have. These consequences also could be deemed to be unjust from her point of view. Since they had no accountability for the existence of the mongoloid, it was not fair to them that extra burdens be placed upon them.

To ask what was due the mongoloid infant raises harder issues. For the mother, he was not due surgical procedure that would sustain his life. He was "unequal" to her normal children, but the fact of his inequality does not necessarily imply that he has no right to live. This leads to a matter at the root of the mother's response which has to be dealt with separately.

She (and as we shall see, the doctors also) assumed that a factual distinction (between normal and mongoloid) makes the moral difference. Factual distinctions do make moral differences. A farmer who has no qualms about killing a runt pig would have moral scruples about killing a deformed infant. If the child had not been mongoloid and had an intestinal blockage, there would have been no question about permitting surgery to be done. The value of the infant is judged to be relative to a quality of its life that is predictable on the basis of the factual evidences of mongolism. Value is relative to quality: that is the justification. Given the absence of a certain quality, the value is not sufficient to maintain life; given absence of a quality, there is no right to physical life. (Questions about terminating life among very sick adults are parallel to this instance.)

What are the qualities, or what is *the* quality that is deficient in this infant? It is not the capacity for happiness, an end that Aristotle and others thought to be sufficient in itself. The mother and the doctors knew that mongoloids can be happy. It is not the capacity for pleasure, the end that the hedonistic utilitarians thought all men seek, for mongoloids can find pleasure in life. The clue is given when a physician says that the absence of the capacity for normal intelligence was crucial. He suggested that we live in a society in which intelligence is highly valued. Perhaps it is valued as a quality in itself, or as an end in itself by some, but probably there is a further point, namely that intelligence is necessary for productive contribution to one's own well-being and to the well-being of others. Not only will a mongoloid make a minimal contribution to his own well-being and to that of others, but also others must contribute excessively to his care. The right of an infant, the value of his life, is relative to his intelligence; that is the most crucial factor in enabling or limiting his contribution to his own welfare and that of others. One has to defend such a point in terms of the sorts of contributions that would be praiseworthy and the sorts of costs that would be detrimental. The contribution of a sense of satisfaction to those who might enjoy caring for the mongoloid would not be sufficient. Indeed, a full defense would require a quantification of qualities, all based on predictions at the point of birth, that would count both for and against the child's life in a cost-benefit analysis.

The judgment that value is relative to qualities is not implausible. In our society we have traditionally valued the achiever more than the nonachievers. Some hospitals have sought to judge the qualities of the contributions of patients to society in determining who has access to scarce medical resources. A mongoloid is not valued as highly as a fine musician, an effective politician, a successful businessman, a civil rights leader whose actions have brought greater justice to the society, or a physician. To be sure, in other societies and at other times other qualities have been valued, but we judge by the qualities valued in our society and our time. Persons are rewarded according to their contributions to society. A defense of the mother's decision would have to be made on these grounds, with one further crucial step. That is, when the one necessary condition for productivity is deficient (with a high degree of certitude) at birth, there is no moral obligation to maintain that life. That the same reasoning would have been sufficient to justify overtly taking the infant's life seems not to have been the case. But that point emerges later in our discussion.

The reliance upon feelings, desires, fairness, and judgments of qualities of life makes sense to American middle-class white families, and anguished decisions can very well be settled in these terms. The choice made by the mother was not that of an unfeeling problem-solving machine, nor that of a rationalistic philosopher operating from these assumptions. It was a painful, conscientious decision, made apparently on these bases. One can ask, of course, whether her physicians should not have suggested other ways of perceiving and drawing the contours of the circumstances, other values and ends that she might consider. But that points to a subsequent topic.

THE FATHER'S DECISION

The decision of the father is only a footnote to that of the mother. He consented to the choice of not operating on the infant, though he did seek precise information about mongolism and its consequences for the child. He was "willing to go along with the mother's wishes," he "understood her feelings, agreed with them," and was not in a position to make "the same intelligent decision that his wife was making."

Again we see that scientific evidence based on professional knowledge is determinative of a moral decision. The physician was forthright in indicating what the consequences would be of the course of action they were taking. The consequences of raising a mongoloid child were presumably judged to be more problematic than the death of the child.

THE DECISION OF THE PHYSICIANS

A number of points of reference in the contributions of the physicians to the case study enable us to formulate a constellation of values that determined their actions. After I have depicted that constellation, I shall analyze some of the points of reference to see how they can be defended.

The constellation can be stated summarily. The physicians felt no moral or legal obligation to save the life of a mongoloid infant by an ordinary surgical procedure when the parents did not desire that it should live. Thus, the infant was left to die. What would have been a serious but routine procedure was omitted in this instance on two conditions, both of which were judged to be necessary, but neither of which was sufficient in itself: the mongolism and the parents' desires. If the parents had desired the mongoloid infant to be saved, the surgery would have been done. If the infant had not been mongoloid and the parents had refused permission for surgery to remove a bowel obstruction, the physicians would at least have argued against them and probably taken legal measures to override them. Thus, the value-laden points of reference appear to be the desires of the parents, the mongolism of the infant, the law, and choices about ordinary and extraordinary medical procedures.

One of the two most crucial points was the obligation the physicians felt to acquiesce to the desires of the parents. The choice of the parents not to operate was made on what the physicians judged to be adequate information: it was an act of informed consent on the part of the parents. There is no evidence that the physicians raised questions of a moral sort with the parents that they subsequently raised among themselves. For example, one physician later commented on the absence of rights for children in our society and in our legal system and on the role that the value of intelligence seems to have in judging worthiness of persons. These were matters, however, that the physicians did not feel obligated to raise with the distressed parents. The physicians acted on the principle that they are only to do procedures that the patient (or crucially in this case, the parents of the patient) wanted. There was no overriding right to life on the part of a mongoloid infant that led them to argue against the parents' desires or to seek a court order requiring the surgical procedure. They recognized the moral autonomy of the parents, and thus did not interfere; they accepted as a functioning principle that the parents have the right to decide whether an infant shall live.

Elaboration of the significance of parental autonomy is necessary in order to see the grounds on which it can be defended. First, the physicians apparently recognized that the conscientious parents were the moral supreme court. There are grounds for affirming the recognition of the moral autonomy of the principal persons in complex decisions. In this case, the principals were the parents: the infant did not have the capacities to express any desires or preferences he might have. The physicians said, implicitly, that the medical profession does not have a right to impose certain of its traditional values on persons if these are not conscientiously held by those persons.

There are similarities, but also differences, between this instance and that of a terminal patient. If the terminally ill patient expresses a desire not to have his life prolonged, physicians recognize his autonomy over his own body and thus feel under no obligation to sustain his life. Our case, however, would be more similar to one in which the terminally ill patient's family decided that no further procedures ought to be used to sustain life. No doubt there are many cases in which the patient is unable to express a preference due to his physical conditions, and in the light of persuasive medical and familial reasons the physician agrees not to sustain life. A difference between our case and that, however, has to be noted in order to isolate what seems to be the crucial point. In the case of the mongoloid infant, a decision is made at the beginning of his life and not at the end; the effect is to cut off a life which, given proper care, could be sustained for many years, rather than not sustaining a life which has no such prospects.

Several defenses might be made of their recognition of the parents' presumed rights in this case. The first is that parents have authority over their children until they reach an age of discretion, and in some respects until they reach legal maturity. Children do not have recognized rights over against parents in many respects. The crucial difference here, of course, is the claimed parental right in this case to determine that an infant shall not live. What grounds might there be for this? Those who claim the moral right to an abortion are claiming the right to determine whether a child shall live, and this claim is widely recognized both morally and legally. In this case we have an extension of that right to the point of birth. If there are sufficient grounds to indicate that the newborn child is significantly abnormal, the parents have the same right as they have when a severe genetic abnormality is detected prenatally on the basis of amniocentesis. Indeed, the physicians could argue that if a mother has a right to an abortion, she also has a right to determine whether a newborn infant shall continue to live. One is simply extending the time span and the circumstances under which this autonomy is recognized.

A second sort of defense might be made: that of the limits of professional competence and authority. The physicians could argue that in moral matters they have neither competence nor authority. Perhaps they would wish to distinguish between competence and authority. They have a competence to make a moral decision on the basis of their own moral and other values, but they have no authority to impose this upon their patients. Morals, they might argue, are subjective matters, and if anyone has competence in that area, it is philosophers, clergymen, and others who teach what is right and wrong. If the parents had no internalized values that militated against their decision, it is not in the province of the physicians to tell them what they ought to do. Indeed, in a morally pluralistic society, no one group or person has a right to impose his views on another. In this stronger argument for moral autonomy no physician would have any authority to impose his own moral values on any patient. A social role differentiation is noted: the medical profession has authority only in medical matters—not in moral matters. Indeed, they have an obligation to indicate what the medical alternatives are in order to have a decision made by informed consent, but insofar as moral values or principles are involved in decisions, these are not within their professional sphere.

An outsider might ask what is meant by authority. He might suggest that surely it is not the responsibility (or at least not his primary responsibility) or the role of the physician to make moral decisions, and certainly not to enforce his decisions on others. Would he be violating his role if he did something less determinative than that, namely, in his counseling indicate to them what some of the moral considerations might be in choosing between medical alternatives? In our case the answer seems to be yes. If the principals desire moral counseling, they have the freedom to seek it from whomsoever they will. In his professional role he acknowledges that the recognition of the moral autonomy of the principals also assumes their moral self-sufficiency, that is, their capacities to make sound moral decisions without interference on his part, or the part of any other persons except insofar as the principals themselves seek such counsel. Indeed, in this case a good deal is made of the knowledge-ability of the mother particularly, and this assumes that she is moral-ly, as well as medically, knowledgeable. Or, if she is not, it is still not the physician's business to be her moral counselor.

The physicians also assumed in this case that the moral autonomy of the parents took precedence over the positive law. At least they felt no obligation to take recourse to the courts to save the life of this infant. On that issue we will reflect more when we discuss the legal point of reference.

Another sort of defense might be made. In the order of society, decisions should be left to the most intimate and smallest social unit involved. That is the right of such a unit, since the interposition of outside authority would be an infringement of its freedom. Also, since the family has to live with the consequences of the decision, it is the right of the parents to determine which potential conse-quences they find most desirable. The state, or the medical pro-fession, has no right to interfere with the freedom of choice of the family. Again, in a formal way, the argument is familiar; the state has no right to interfere with the determination of what a woman wishes to do with her body, and thus antiabortion laws are infringe-ments of her freedom. The determination of whether an infant shall be kept alive is simply an extension of the sphere of autonomy properly belonging to the smallest social unit involved.

In all the arguments for moral autonomy, the medical fact that the infant is alive and can be kept alive does not make a crucial difference. The defense of the decision would have to be made in this way: if one grants moral autonomy to mothers to determine whether they will bring a fetus to birth, it is logical to assume that one will grant the same autonomy after birth, at least in instances where the infant is abnormal.

We have noted in our constellation of factors that the desire of the parents was a necessary but not a sufficient condition for the de-cisions of the physicians. If the infant had not been mongoloid, the physicians would not have so readily acquiesced to the parents' de-sires. Thus, we need to turn to the second necessary condition.

The second crucial point is that the infant was a mongoloid. The physicians would not have acceded to the parents' request as readily if the child had been normal; the parents would have authorized the surgical procedure if the child had been normal. Not every sort of abnormality would have led to the same decision on the part of the physicians. Their appeal was to the consequences of the abnormality of mongolism: the child would be a burden financially and emotionally to the parents. Since every child, regardless of his capacities for intelligent action, is a financial burden, and at least at times an emotional burden, it is clear that the physicians believed that the quantity or degree of burden in this case would exceed any benefits that might be forthcoming if the child were permitted to live. One can infer that a principle was operative, namely, that mongoloid infants have no inherent right to life; their right to life is conditional upon the willingness of their parents to accept them and care for them.

Previously we developed some of the reasons why a mongoloid infant was judged undesirable. Some of the same appeals to consequences entered into the decisions of the physicians. If we are to seek to develop reasons why the decisions might be judged to be morally correct, we must examine another point, namely, the operating definition of "abnormal" or "defective." There was no dissent to the medical judgment that the infant was mongoloid, though precise judgements about the seriousness of the child's defect were not possible at birth.

Our intention is to find as precisely as possible what principles or values might be invoked to claim that the "defectiveness" was sufficient to warrant not sustaining the life of this infant. As a procedure, we will begin with the most general appeals that might have been made to defend the physician's decision in this case. The most general principle would be that any infant who has any empirically verifiable degree of defect at birth has no right to life. No one would apply such a principle. Less general would be that all infants who are carriers of a genetic defect that would have potentially bad consequences for future generations have no right to life. A hemophiliac carrier would be a case in point. This principle would not be applicable, even if it were invoked with approval, in this case.

Are the physicians prepared to claim that all genetically "abnormal" infants have no claim to life? I find no evidence that they would. Are they prepared to say that where the genetic abnormality affects the capacity for "happiness" the infant has no right to live? Such an appeal was not made in this case. It appears that "normal" in this case has reference to a capacity for a certain degree of intelligence.

A presumably detectable physical norm now functions as a norm in a moral sense, or as an ideal. The ideal cannot be specified in precise terms, but there is a vague judgment about the outer limits beyond which an infant is judged to be excessively far from the norm or ideal to deserve sustenance. Again, we come to the crucial role of an obvious sign of the lack of capacity for intelligence of a certain measurable sort in judging a defect to be intolerable. A further justification of this is made by an appeal to accepted social values, at least among middle- and upper-class persons in our society. Our society values intelligence; that value becomes the ideal norm from which abnormality or deficiencies are measured. Since the infant is judged not to be able to develop into an intelligent human being (and do all that "normal" intelligence enables a human being to do), his life is of insufficient value to override the desires of the parents not to have a retarded child.

Without specification of the limits to the sorts of cases to which it could be applied, the physicians would probably not wish to defend the notion that the values of a society determine the right to life. To do so would require that there be clear knowledge of who is valued in our society (we also value aggressive people, loving people, physically strong people, etc.), and in turn a procedure by which capacities for such qualities could be determined in infancy so that precise judgments could be made about what lives should be sustained. Some members of our society do not value black people; blackness would obviously be an insufficient basis for letting an infant die. Thus, in defense of their decision the physicians would have to appeal to "values generally held in our society." This creates a different problem of quantification: what percentage of dissent would count to deny a "general" holding of a value? They would also have to designate the limits to changes in socially held values beyond which they would not consent. If the parents belonged to a subculture that value blue eyes more than it valued intelligence, and if they expressed a desire not to have a child because it had hazel eyes, the problem of the intestinal blockage would not have been a sufficient condition to refrain from the surgical procedure.

In sum, the ideal norm of the human that makes a difference in judging whether an infant has the right to life in this case is "the capacity for normal intelligence." For the good of the infant, for the sake of avoiding difficulties for the parents, and for the good of society, a significant deviation from normal intelligence, coupled with the appropriate parental desire, is sufficient to permit the infant to die.

A third point of reference was the law. The civil law and the courts figure in the decisions at two points. First, the physicians felt no obligation to seek a court order to save the life of the infant if the parents did not want it. Several possible inferences might be drawn from this. First, one can infer that the infant had no legal right to life; his legal right is conditional upon parental desires. Second, as indicated in the interviews, the physicians believed that the court would not insist upon the surgical procedure to save the infant since it was a mongoloid. Parental desires would override legal rights in such a case. And third (an explicit statement by the physician), if the infant's life had been saved as the result of a court order, there were doubts that it would have been "accepted" by the parents. Here is an implicit appeal to potential consequences: it is not beneficial for a child to be raised by parents who do not "accept" him. The assumption is that they could not change their attitudes.

If the infant had a legal right to life, this case presents an interesting instance of conscientious objection to law. The conscientious objector to military service claims that the power of the state to raise armies for the defense of what it judges to be the national interest is one that he conscientiously refrains from sharing. The common good, or the national interest, is not jeopardized by the granting of a special status to the objector because there are enough persons who do not object to man the military services. In this case, however, the function of the law is to protect the rights of individuals to life, and the physician-objector is claiming that he is under no obligation to seek the support of the legal system to sustain life even when he knows that it could be sustained. The evidence he has in hand (the parental desire and the diagnosis of mongolism) presumably provides sufficient moral grounds for his not complying with the law. From the standpoint of ethics, an appeal could be made to conscientious objection. If, however, the appropriate law does not qualify its claims in such a way as to (a) permit its non-applicability in this case or (b) provide for exemption on grounds of conscientious objection, the objector is presumably willing to accept the consequences for his conscientious decision. This would be morally appropriate. The physician believed that the court would not insist on saving the infant's life, and thus he foresaw no great jeopardy to himself in following conscience rather than the law.

The second point at which the law figures is in the determination of how the infant should die. The decision not to induce death was made in part in the face of the illegality of overt euthanasia (in part, only, since also the hospital staff would "feel uncomfortable" about hastening the death). Once the end or purpose of action (or inaction) was judged to be morally justified, and judged likely to be free from legal censure, the physicians still felt obliged to achieve that purpose within means that would not be subject to legal sanctions. One can only speculate whether the physicians believed that a court that would not order an infant's life to be saved would in turn censure them for overtly taking the life, or whether the uncomfortable feelings of the hospital staff were more crucial in their decision. Their course of decisions could be interpreted as at one point not involving obligation to take recourse to the courts and at the other scrupulously obeying the law. It should be noted, however, that there is consistency of action on their part; in neither instance did they intervene in what was the "natural" course of developments. The moral justification to fail to intervene in the second moment had to be different from that in the first. In the first it provides the reasons for not saving a life; in the second, for not taking a life. This leads to the last aspect of the decisions of the physicians that I noted, namely, that choices were made between ordinary and extraordinary means of action.

There is no evidence in the interviews that the language of ordinary and extraordinary means of action was part of the vocabulary of the medical staff. It is, however, an honored and useful distinction in Catholic moral theology as it applies to medical care. The principle is that a physician is under no obligation to use extraordinary means to sustain life. The difficulty in the application of the principle is the choice of what falls under ordinary and what under extraordinary means. Under one set of circumstances a procedure may be judged ordinary, and under another extraordinary. The surgery required to remove the bowel obstruction in the infant was on the whole an ordinary procedure; there were no experimental aspects to it, and there were no unusual risks to the infant's life in having it done. If the infant had had no other genetic defects, there would have been no question about using it. The physicians could make a case that when the other defect was mongolism, the procedure would be an extraordinary one. The context of the judgment about ordinary and extraordinary was a wider one than the degree of risk to the life of the patient from surgery. It included his other defect, the desires of the family, the potential costs to family and society, etc. No moralists, to my knowledge, would hold them culpable if the infant were so deformed that he would be labeled (nontechnically) a monstrosity. To heroically maintain the life of a monstrosity as long as one could would be most extraordinary. Thus, we return to whether the fact of mongolism and its consequences is a sufficient justification to judge the lifesaving procedure to be extraordinary in this instance. The physicians would argue that it is.

The infant was left to die with a minimum of care. No extraordinary means were used to maintain its life once the decision not to operate had been made. Was it extraordinary not to use even ordinary procedures to maintain the life of the infant once the decision not to operate had been made? The judgment clearly was in the negative. To do so would be to prolong a life that would not be saved in any case. At that point the infant was in a class of terminal patients, and the same justifications used for not prolonging the life of a terminal patient would apply here. Patients have a right to die, and physicians are under no moral obligation to sustain their lives when it is clear that they will not live for long. The crucial difference between a terminal cancer patient and this infant is that in the situation of the former, all procedures which might prolong life for a goodly length of time are likely to have been exhausted. In the case of the infant, the logic of obligations to terminal patients takes its course as a result of a decision not to act at all.

To induce death by some overt action is an extraordinary procedure. To justify overt action would require a justification of euthanasia. This case would be a good one from which to explore euthanasia from a moral point of view. Once a decision is made not to engage in a life-sustaining and lifesaving procedure, has not the crucial corner been turned? If that is a reasonable and moral thing to do, on what grounds would one argue that it is wrong to hasten death? Most obviously it is still illegal to do it, and next most obviously people have sensitive feelings about taking life. Further, it goes against the grain of the fundamental vocation of the medical profession to maintain life. But, of course, the decision not to operate also goes against that grain. If the first decision was justifiable, why was it not justifiable to hasten the death of the infant? We can only assume at this point traditional arguments against euthanasia would have been made.

THE DECISIONS OF THE NURSES

The nurses, as the interviews indicated, are most important for their expressions of feelings, moral sensibilities, and frustrations. They demonstrate the importance of deeply held moral convictions and of profound compassion in determining human responses to ambiguous circumstances. If they had not known that the infant could have survived, the depth of their frustrations and feelings would have not been so great. Feelings they would have had, but they would have been compassion for an infant bound to die. The actual range of decision for them was clearly circumscribed by the role definitions in the medical professions; it was their duty to carry out the orders of the physicians. Even if they conscientiously believed that the orders they were executing were immoral, they could not radically reverse the course of events; they could not perform the required surgery. It was their lot to be the immediate participants in a sad event but to be powerless to alter its course.

It would be instructive to explore the reasons why the nurses felt frustrated, were deeply affected by their duties in this case. Moral convictions have their impact upon the feelings of persons as well as upon their rational decisions. A profound sense of vocation to relieve suffering and to preserve life no doubt lies behind their responses, as does a conviction about the sanctity of human life. For our purposes, however, we shall leave them with the observation that they are the instruments of the orders of the physicians. They have no right of conscientious objection, at least not in this set of circumstances.

Before turning to another evaluative description of the case, it is important to reiterate what was said in the beginning. The decisions by the principals were conscientious ones. The parents anguished. The physicians were informed by a sense of compassion in their consent to the parents' wishes; they did not wish to be party to potential suffering that was avoidable. Indeed, in the way in which they formulated the dilemma, they did what was reasonable to do. They chose the way of least possible suffering to the fewest persons over a long range of time, with one exception, namely, not taking the infant's life. By describing the dilemma from a somewhat different set of values, or giving different weight to different factors, another course of action would have been reasonable and justified. The issue, it seems to me, is at the level of what is to be valued more highly, for one's very understanding of the problems he must solve are deeply affected by what one values most.

THE DILEMMA FROM A DIFFERENT MORAL POINT OF VIEW

Wallace Stevens wrote in poetic form a subtle account of "Thirteen Ways of Looking at a Blackbird." Perhaps there are 13 ways of looking at this medical case. I shall attempt to look at it from only one more way. By describing the dilemma from a perspective that gives a different weight to some of the considerations that we have already exposed, one has a different picture, and different conclusions are called for. The moral integrity of any of the original participants is not challenged, not because of a radical relativism that says they have their points of view and I have mine, but out of respect for their conscientiousness. For several reasons, however, more consideration ought to have been given to two points. A difference in evaluative judgments would have made a difference of life or death for the infant, depending upon: (1) whether what one ought to do is determined by what one desires to do and (2) whether a mongoloid infant has a claim to life.

To restate the dilemma once again: If the parents had "desired" the mongoloid infant, the surgeons would have performed the operation that would have saved its life. If the infant had had a bowel obstruction that could be taken care of by an ordinary medical procedure, but had not been a mongoloid, the physicians would probably have insisted that the operation be performed.

Thus, one can recast the moral dilemma by giving a different weight to two things: the desires of the parents and the value or rights of a mongoloid infant. If the parents and the physicians believed strongly that there are things one ought to do even when one has no immediate positive feelings about doing them, no immediate strong desire to do them, the picture would have been different. If the parents and physicians believed that mongoloid children have intrinsic value, or have a right to life, or if they believed that mongolism is not sufficiently deviant from what is normatively human to merit death, the picture would have been different.

Thus, we can redraw the picture. To be sure, the parents are ambiguous about their feelings for a mongoloid infant, since it is normal to desire a normal infant rather than an abnormal infant. But (to avoid a discussion of abortion at this point) once an infant is born its independent existence provides independent value in itself, and those who brought it into being and those professionally responsible for its care have an obligation to sustain its life regardless of their negative or ambiguous feelings toward it. This probably would have been acknowledged by all concerned if the infant had not been mongoloid. For example, if the pregnancy had been accidental, and in this sense the child was not desired, and the infant had been normal, no one would have denied its right to exist once it was born, though some would while still *in utero,* and thus would have sought an abortion. If the mother refused to accept accountability for the infant, alternative means of caring for it would have been explored.

To be sure, a mongoloid infant is genetically defective, and raising and caring for it put burdens on the parents, the family, and the state beyond the burdens required to raise a normal infant. But a mongoloid infant is human, and thus has the intrinsic value of humanity and the rights of a human being. Further, given proper care, it can reach a point of significant fulfillment of its limited potentialities; it is capable of loving and responding to love; it is capable of realizing happiness; it can be trained to accept responsibility for itself within its capacities. Thus, the physicians and parents have an obligation to use all ordinary means to preserve its life. Indeed, the humanity of mentally defective children is recognized in our society by the fact that we do not permit their extermination and do have policies which provide, all too inadequately, for their care and nurture.

If our case had been interpreted in the light of moral beliefs that inform the previous two paragraphs, the only reasonable conclusion would be that the surgery ought to have been done.

The grounds for assigning the weights I have to these crucial points can be examined. First, with reference simply to common experience, we all have obligations to others that are not contingent upon our immediate desires. When the registrar of my university indicates that senior grades have to be in by May 21, I have an obligation to read the exams, term papers, and senior essays in time to report the grades, regardless of my negative feelings toward those tasks or my preference to be doing something else. I have an obligation to my students, and to the university through its registrar, which I accepted when I assumed the social role of an instructor.

The students have a claim on me; they have a right to expect me to fulfill my obligations to them and to the university. I might be excused from the obligation if I suddenly became too ill to fulfill it; my incapacity to fulfill it would be a temporarily excusing condition. But negative feelings toward that job, or toward any students, or a preference for writing a paper of my own at that time, would not constitute excusing conditions. I must consider, in determining what I do, the relationships that I have with others and the claims they have on me by virtue of those relationships.

In contrast to this case, it might be said that I have a contractual obligation to the university into which I freely entered. The situation of the parents is not the same. They have no legal contractual relationship with the infant, and thus their desires are not bound by obligations. Closer to their circumstances, then, might be other family relationships. I would argue that the fact that we brought our children into being lays a moral obligation on my wife and me to sustain and care for them to the best of our ability. They did not choose to be; and their very being is dependent, both causally and in other ways, upon us. In the relationship of dependence, there is a claim of them over against us. To be sure, it is a claim that also has its rewards and that we desire to fulfill within a relationship of love. But until they have reached an age when they can accept full accountability (or fuller accountability) for themselves, they have claims upon us by virtue of our being their parents, even when meeting those claims is to us financially costly, emotionally distressing, and in other ways not immediately desirable. Their claims are independent of our desires to fulfill them. Particular claims they might make can justifiably be turned down, and others can be negotiated, but the claim against us for their physical sustenance constitutes a moral obligation that we have to meet. That obligation is not conditioned by their IQ scores, whether they have cleft palates or perfectly formed faces, whether they are obedient or irritatingly independent, whether they are irritatingly obedient and passive or laudably self-determining. It is not conditioned by any predictions that might be made about whether they will become the persons we might desire that they become. The infant in our case has the same sort of claim, and thus the parents have a moral obligation to use all ordinary means to save its life.

An objection might be made. Many of my fellow Christians would say that the obligation of the parents was to do that which is loving toward the infant. Not keeping the child alive was the loving thing to do with reference both to its interests and to the interests of the other members of the family. To respond to the objection, one needs first to establish the spongy character of the words "love" or "loving." They can absorb almost anything. Next one asks whether the loving character of an act is determined by feelings or by motives, or whether it is also judged by what is done. It is clear that I would argue for the latter. Indeed, the minimal conditions of a loving relationship include respect for the other, and certainly for the other's presumption of a right to live. I would, however, primarily make the case that the relationship of dependence grounds the claim, whether or not one feels loving toward the other.

The dependence relationship holds for the physicians as well as the parents in this case. The child's life depended utterly upon the capacity of the physicians to sustain it. The fact that an infant cannot articulate his claim is irrelevant. Physicians will struggle to save the life of a person who has attempted to commit suicide even when the patient might be in such a drugged condition that he cannot express his desire—a desire expressed already in his effort to take his life and overridden by the physician's action to save it. The claim of human life for preservation, even when such a person indicates a will not to live, presents a moral obligation to those who have the capacity to save it.

A different line of argument might be taken. If the decisions made were as reliant upon the desires of the parents as they appear to be, which is to say, if desire had a crucial role, what about the desire of the infant? The infant could not give informed consent to the non-intervention. One can hypothesize that every infant desires to live, and that even a defective child is likely to desire life rather than death when it reaches an age at which its desires can be articulated. Even if the right to live is contingent upon a desire, we can infer that the infant's desire would be for life. As a human being, he would have that desire, and thus it would constitute a claim on those on whom he is dependent to fulfill it.

I have tried to make a persuasive case to indicate why the claim of the infant constitutes a moral obligation on the parents and the physicians to keep the child alive. The intrinsic value or rights of a human being are not qualified by any given person's intelligence or capacities for productivity, potential consequences of the sort that burden others. Rather, they are constituted by the very existence of the human being as one who is related to others and dependent upon others for his existence. The presumption is always in favor of sustaining life through ordinary means; the desires of persons that run counter to that presumption are not sufficient conditions for abrogating that right.

The power to determine whether the infant shall live or die is in the hands of others. Does the existence of such power carry with it the moral right to such determination? Long history of moral experience indicates not only that arguments have consistently been made against the judgment that the capacity to do something constitutes a right to do it, or put in more familiar terms, that might makes right. It also indicates that in historical situations where persons have claimed the right to determine who shall live because they have the power to do so, the consequences have hardly been beneficial to mankind. This, one acknowledges, is a "wedge" argument or a "camel's nose under the tent" argument. As such, its limits are clear. Given a culture in which humane values are regnant, it is not likely that the establishment of a principle that some persons under some circumstances claim the right to determine whether others shall live will be transformed into the principle that the right of a person to live is dependent upon his having the qualities approved by those who have the capacity to sustain or take his life. Yet while recognizing the sociological and historical limitations that exist in a humane society, one still must recognize the significance of a precedent. To cite an absurd example, what would happen if we lived in a society in which the existence of hazel eyes was considered a genetic defect by parents and physicians? The absurdity lies in the fact that no intelligent person would consider hazel eyes a genetic defect; the boundaries around the word defect are drawn by evidences better than eye color. But the precedent in principle remains; when one has established that the capacity to determine who shall live carries with it the right to determine who shall live, the line of discussion has shifted from a sharp presumption (of the right of all humans to live) to the softer, spongier determination of the qualities whose value will be determinative.

Often we cannot avoid using qualities and potential consequences in the determination of what might be justifiable exceptions to the presumption of the right to life on the part of any infant—indeed, any person. No moralist would insist that the physicians have an obligation to sustain the life of matter born from human parents that is judged to be a "monstrosity." Such divergence from the "normal" qualities presents no problem, and potential consequences for its continued existence surely enter into the decision. The physicians in our case believed that in the absence of a desire for the child on the part of the parents, mongolism was sufficiently removed from an ideal norm of the human that the infant had no overriding claim on them. We are in a sponge. Why would I draw the line on a different side of mongolism than the physicians did? While reasons can be given, one must recognize that there are intuitive elements, grounded in beliefs and profound feelings, that enter into particular judgments of this sort. I am not prepared to say that my respect for human life is "deeper," "profounder," or "stronger" than theirs. I am prepared to say that the way in which, and the reasons why, I respect life orient my judgment toward the other side of mongolism than theirs did.

First, the value that intelligence was given in this instance appears to me to be simplistic. Not all intelligent persons are socially commendable (choosing socially held values as the point of reference because one of the physicians did). Also, many persons of limited intelligence do things that are socially commendable, if only minimally providing the occasion for the expression of profound human affection and sympathy. There are many things we value about human life; that the assumption that one of them is the *sine qua non,* the necessary and sufficient condition for a life to be valued at all, oversimplifies human experience. If there is a *sine qua non,* it is physical life itself, for apart from it, all potentiality of providing benefits for oneself or for others is impossible. There are occasions on which other things are judged to be more valuable than physical life itself; we probably all would admire the person whose life is martyred for the sake of saving others. But the qualities or capacities we value exist in bundles, and not each as overriding in itself. The capacity for self-determination is valued, and on certain occasions we judge that it is worth dying, or taking life, for the sake of removing repressive limits imposed upon persons in that respect. But many free, self-determining persons are not very happy; indeed, often their anxiety increases with the enlargement of the range of things they must and can determine for themselves. Would we value a person exclusively because he is happy? Probably not, partly because his happiness has at least a mildly contagious effect on some other persons, and thus we value him because he makes others happy as well. To make one quality we value (short of physical life itself, and here there are exceptions) determinative over all other qualities is to impoverish the richness and variety of human life. When we must use the sponge of qualities to determine exceptions to the presumption of the right to physical life, we need to face their variety, their complexity, the abrasiveness of one against the other, in the determination of action. In this case the potentialities of a mongoloid for satisfaction in life, for fulfilling his limited capacities, for happiness, for providing the occasions of meaningful (sometimes distressing and sometimes joyful) experience for others are sufficient so that no exception to the right to life should be made. Put differently, the anguish, suffering, embarrassment, expenses of family and state (I support the need for revision of social policy and practice) are not sufficiently negative to warrant that a mongoloid's life not be sustained by ordinary procedures.

Second, and harder to make persuasive, is that my view of human existence leads to a different assessment of the significance of suffering than appears to be operative in this case. The best argument to be made in support of the course of decisions as they occurred is that in the judgment of the principals involved, they were able to avoid more suffering and other costs for more people over a longer range of time than could have been avoided if the infant's life had been saved. To suggest a different evaluation of suffering is not to suggest that suffering is an unmitigated good, or that the acceptance of suffering when it could be avoided is a strategy that ought to be adopted for the good life, individually and collectively. Surely it is prudent and morally justifiable to avoid suffering if possible under most normal circumstances of life. But two questions will help to designate where a difference of opinion between myself and the principals in our drama can be located. One is, At what cost to others is it justifiable to avoid suffering for ourselves? On the basis of my previous exposition, I would argue that in this instance the avoidance of potential suffering at the cost of that life was not warranted. The moral claims of others upon me often involve emotional and financial stress, but that stress is not sufficient to warrant my ignoring the claims. The moral and legal claim of the government to the right to raise armies in defense of the national interest involves inconvenience, suffering, and even death for many; yet the fact that meeting that claim will cause an individual suffering is not sufficient ground to give conscientious objection. Indeed, we normally honor those who assume suffering for the sake of benefits to others.

The second question is, Does the suffering in prospect appear to be bearable for those who have to suffer? We recognize that the term "bearable" is a slippery slope and that fixing an answer to this question involves judgments that are always hypothetical. If, however, each person has a moral right to avoid all bearable inconvenience or suffering that appears to run counter to his immediate or long-range self-interest, there are many things necessary for the good of other individuals and for the common good that would not get done. In our case, there appear to be no evidences that the parents with assistance from other institutions would necessarily find the raising of a mongoloid child to bring suffering that they could not tolerate. Perhaps there is justifying evidence to which I do not have access, such as the possibility that the mother would be subject to severe mental illness if she had to take care of the child. But from the information I received, no convincing case could be made that the demands of raising the child would present intolerable and unbearable suffering to the family. That it would create greater anguish, greater inconvenience, and greater demands than raising a normal child would is clear. But that meeting these demands would cause greater suffering to this family than it does to thousands of others who raise mongoloid children seems not to be the case.

Finally, my view, grounded ultimately in religious convictions as well as moral beliefs, is that to be human is to have a vocation, a calling, and the calling of each of us is "to be for others" at least as much as "to be for ourselves." The weight that one places on "being for others" makes a difference in one's fundamental orientation toward all of his relationships, particularly when they conflict with his immediate self-interest. In the Torah we have that great commandment, rendered in the New English Bible as "you shall love your neighbour as a man like yourself" (Lev. 19:18). It is reiterated in the records we have of the words of Jesus, "Love your neighbor as yourself" (Matt. 22:39, and several other places). Saint Paul makes the point even stronger at one point: "Each of you must regard, not his own interests, but the other man's" (1 Cor. 10:24, NEB). And finally, the minimalist saying accredited both to Rabbi Hillel and to Jesus in different forms, "Do unto others as you would have others do unto you."

The point of the biblical citations is not to take recourse to dogmatic religious authority, as if these sayings come unmediated from the ultimate power and orderer of life. The point is to indicate a central thrust in Judaism and Christianity which has nourished and sustained a fundamental moral outlook, namely, that we are "to be for others" at least as much as we are "to be for ourselves." The fact that this outlook has not been adhered to consistently by those who professed it does not count against it. It remains a vocation, a calling, a moral ideal, if not a moral obligation. The statement of such an outlook does not resolve all the particular problems of medical histories such as this one, but it shapes a bias, gives a weight, toward the well-being of the other against inconvenience or cost to oneself. In this case, I believe that all the rational inferences to be drawn from it, and all the emotive power that this calling evokes, lead to the conclusion that the ordinary surgical procedure should have been done, and the mongoloid infant's life saved.

III.
Euthanasia:
Ethical,
Religious,
and
Moral
Aspects.

THE PROLONGATION OF LIFE

AN ADDRESS OF POPE PIUS XII TO AN
INTERNATIONAL CONGRESS OF
ANESTHESIOLOGISTS

Dr. Bruno Haid, chief of the anesthesia section at the surgery clinic of the University of Innsbruck, has submitted to Us three questions on medical morals treating the subject known as "resuscitation" (*la réanimation*).

We are pleased, gentlemen, to grant this request, which shows your great awareness of professional duties, and your will to solve in the light of the principles of the Gospel the delicate problems that confront you.

According to Dr. Haid's statement, modern anesthesiology deals not only with the problems of analgesia and anesthesia properly so-called, but also with those of "resuscitation." This is the name given in medicine, and especially in anesthesiology, to the technique which makes possible the remedying of certain occurrences which seriously threaten human life, especially asphyxia, which formerly, when modern anesthetizing equipment was not yet available, would stop the heart-beat and bring about death in a few minutes. The task of the anesthesiologist has therefore extended to acute respiratory difficulties, provoked by strangulation or by open wounds of the chest. The anesthesiologist intervenes to prevent asphyxia resulting from the internal obstruction of breathing passages by the contents of the stomach or by drowning, to remedy total or partial respiratory paralysis in cases of serious tetanus, of poliomyelitis, of poisoning by gas, sedatives, or alcoholic intoxication, or even in cases of paralysis of the central respiratory apparatus caused by serious trauma of the brain.

In the practice of resuscitation and in the treatment of persons who have suffered headwounds, and sometimes in the case of persons who have undergone brain surgery or of those who have suffered trauma of the brain through anoxia and remain in a state of deep unconsciousness, there arise a number of questions that concern medical morality and involve the principles of the philosophy of nature even more than those of analgesia.

It happens at times—as in the aforementioned cases of accidents and illnesses, the treatment of which offers reasonable hope of success—that the anesthesiologist can improve the general condition of patients who suffer from a serious lesion of the brain and whose situation at first might seem desperate. He restores breathing either through manual intervention or with the help of special instruments, clears the breathing passages, and provides for the artificial feeding of the patient.

Thanks to this treatment, and especially through the administration of oxygen by means of artificial respiration, a failing blood circulation picks up again and the appearance of the patient improves, sometimes very quickly, to such an extent that the anesthesiologist himself, or any other doctor who, trusting his experience, would have given up all hope, maintains a slight hope that spontaneous breathing will be restored. The family usually considers this improvement an astonishing result and is grateful to the doctor.

If the lesion of the brain is so serious that the patient will very probably, and even most certainly, not survive, the anesthesiologist is then led to ask himself the distressing question as to the value and meaning of the resuscitation processes. As an immediate measure he will apply artificial respiration by intubation and by aspiration of the respiratory tract; he is then in a safer position and has more time to decide what further must be done. But he can find himself in a delicate position, if the family considers that the efforts he has taken are improper and opposes them. In most cases this situation arises, not at the beginning of resuscitation attempts, but when the patient's condition, after a slight improvement at first, remains stationary and it becomes clear that only automatic artificial respiration is keeping him alive. The question then arises if one must, or if one can, continue the resuscitation process despite the fact that the soul may already have left the body.

The solution to this problem, already difficult in itself, becomes even more difficult when the family—themselves Catholic perhaps—insist that the doctor in charge, especially the anesthesiologist, remove the artificial respiration apparatus in order to allow the patient, who is already virtually dead, to pass away in peace.

Out of this situation there arises a question that is fundamental from the point of view of religion and the philosophy of nature. When, according to Christian faith, has death occurred in patients on whom modern methods of resuscitation have been used? Is Extreme Unction valid, at least as long as one can perceive heartbeats, even if the vital functions properly so-called have already disappeared, and if life depends only on the functioning of the artificial-respiration apparatus?

The problems that arise in the modern practice of resuscitation can therefore be formulated in three questions:

First, does one have the right, or is one even under the obligation, to use modern artificial-respiration equipment in all cases, even those which, in the doctor's judgment, are completely hopeless?

Second, does one have the right, or is one under obligation, to remove the artificial-respiration apparatus when, after several days, the state of deep unconsciousness does not improve if, when it is removed, blood circulation will stop within a few minutes? What must be done in this case if the family of the patient, who has already received the last sacraments, urges the doctor to remove the apparatus? Is Extreme Unction still valid at this time?

Third, must a patient plunged into unconsciousness through central paralysis, but whose life—that is to say, blood circulation—is maintained through artificial respiration, and in whom there is no improvement after several days, be considered *"de facto"* or even *"de jure"* dead? Must one not wait for blood circulation to stop, in spite of the artificial respiration, before considering him dead?

We shall willingly answer these three questions. But before examining them We would like to set forth the principles that will allow formulation of the answer.

Natural reason and Christian morals say that man (and whoever is entrusted with the task of taking care of his fellowman) has the right and the duty in case of serious illness to take the necessary treatment for the preservation of life and health. This duty that one has toward himself, toward God, toward the human community, and in most cases toward certain determined persons, derives from well ordered charity, from submission to the Creator, from social justice and even from strict justice, as well as from devotion toward one's family.

But normally one is held to use only ordinary means—according to circumstances of persons, places, times, and culture—that is to say, means that do not involve any grave burden for oneself or another. A more strict obligation would be too burdensome for most men and would render the attainment of the higher, more important good too difficult. Life, health, all temporal activities are in fact subordinated to spiritual ends. On the other hand, one is not forbidden to take more than the strictly necessary steps to preserve life and health, as long as he does not fail in some more serious duty.

Where the administration of sacraments to an unconscious man is concerned, the answer is drawn from the doctrine and practice of the Church which, for its part, follows the Lord's will as its rule of action. Sacraments are meant, by virtue of divine institution, for men of this world who are in the course of their earthly life, and, except for baptism itself, presuppose prior baptism of the recipient. He who is not a man, who is not yet a man, or is no longer a man, cannot receive the sacraments. Furthermore, if someone expresses his refusal, the sacraments cannot be administered to him against his will. God compels no one to accept sacramental grace.

When it is not known whether a person fulfills the necessary conditions for valid reception of the sacraments, an effort must be made to solve the doubt. If this effort fails, the sacrament will be conferred under at least a tacit condition (with the phrase *"Si capax est,"* "If you are capable,"—which is the broadest condition). Sacraments are instituted by Christ for men in order to save their souls. Therefore, in cases of extreme necessity, the Church tries extreme solutions in order to give man sacramental grace and assistance.

The question of the fact of death and that of verifying the fact itself (*"de facto"*) or its legal authenticity (*"de jure"*) have, because of their consequences, even in the field of morals and of religion, an even greater importance. What We have just said about the presupposed essential elements for the valid reception of a sacrament has shown this. But the importance of the question extends also to effects in matters of inheritance, marriage and matrimonial processes, benefices (vacancy of a benefice), and to many other questions of private and social life.

It remains for the doctor, and especially the anesthesiologist, to give a clear and precise definition of "death" and the "moment of death" of a patient who passes away in a state of unconsciousness. Here one can accept the usual concept of complete and final separation of the soul from the body; but in practice one must take into account the lack of precision of the terms "body" and "separation." One can put aside the possibility of a person being buried alive, for removal of the artificial respiration apparatus must necessarily bring about stoppage of blood circulation and therefore death within a few minutes.

In case of insoluble doubt, one can resort to presumptions of law and of fact. In general, it will be necessary to presume that life remains, because there is involved here a fundamental right received from the Creator, and it is necessary to prove with certainty that it has been lost.

We shall now pass to the solution of the particular questions.

1. Does the anesthesiologist have the right, or is he bound, in all cases of deep unconsciousness, even in those that are considered to be completely hopeless in the opinion of the competent doctor, to use modern artificial respiration apparatus, even against the will of the family?

In ordinary cases one will grant that the anesthesiologist has the right to act in this manner, but he is not bound to do so, unless this becomes the only way of fulfilling another certain moral duty.

The rights and duties of the doctor are correlative to those of the patient. The doctor, in fact, has no separate or independent right where the patient is concerned. In general he can take action only if the patient explicitly or implicitly, directly or indirectly, gives him permission. The technique of resuscitation which concerns us here does not contain anything immoral in itself. Therefore the patient, if he were capable of making a personal decision, could lawfully use it and, consequently, give the doctor permission to use it. On the other hand, since these forms of treatment go beyond the ordinary means to which one is bound, it cannot be held that there is an obligation to use them nor, consequently, that one is bound to give the doctor permission to use them.

The rights and duties of the family depend in general upon the presumed will of the unconscious patient if he is of age and *"sui juris."* Where the proper and independent duty of the family is concerned, they are usually bound only to the use of ordinary means.

Consequently, if it appears that the attempt at resuscitation constitutes in reality such a burden for the family that one cannot in all conscience impose it upon them, they can lawfully insist that the doctor should discontinue these attempts, and the doctor can lawfully comply. There is not involved here a case of direct disposal of the life of the patient, nor of euthanasia in any way: this would never be licit. Even when it causes the arrest of circulation, the interruption of attempts at resuscitation is never more than an indirect cause of the cessation of life, and one must apply in this case the principle of double effect and of *"voluntarium in causa."*

2. We have, therefore, already answered the second question in essence: "Can the doctor remove the artificial respiration apparatus before the blood circulation has come to a complete stop? Can he do this, at least, when the patient has already received Extreme Unction? Is this Extreme Unction valid when it is administered at the moment when circulation ceases, or even after?"

We must give an affirmative answer to the first part of this question, as We have already explained. If Extreme Unction has not yet been administered, one must seek to prolong respiration until this has been done. But as far as concerns the validity of Extreme Unction at the moment when blood circulation stops completely or even after this moment, it is impossible to answer "yes" or "no."

If, as in the opinion of doctors, this complete cessation of circulation means a sure separation of the soul from the body, even if particular organs go on functioning, Extreme Unction would certainly not be valid, for the recipient would certainly not be a man anymore. And this is an indispensable condition for the reception of the sacraments.

If, on the other hand, doctors are of the opinion that the separation of the soul from the body is doubtful, and that this doubt cannot be solved, the validity of Extreme Unction is also doubtful. But, applying her usual rules: "The sacraments are for men" and "In case of extreme necessity one tries extreme measures," the Church allows the sacrament to be administered conditionally in respect to the sacramental sign.

3. "When the blood circulation and the life of the patient who is deeply unconscious because of a central paralysis are

maintained only through artificial respiration, and no improvement is noted after a few days, at what time does the Catholic Church consider the patient "dead," or when must he be declared dead according to natural law (questions 'de facto' and 'de jure')?"

(Has death already occurred after grave trauma of the brain, which has provoked deep unconsciousness and central breathing paralysis, the fatal consequences of which have nevertheless been retarded by artificial respiration? Or does it occur, according to the present opinion of doctors, only when there is complete arrest of circulation despite prolonged artificial respiration?)

Where the verification of the fact in particular cases is concerned, the answer cannot be deduced from any religious and moral principle and, under this aspect, does not fall within the competence of the Church. Until an answer can be given, the question must remain open. But considerations of a general nature allow us to believe that human life continues for as long as its vital functions—distinguished from the simple life of organs—manifest themselves spontaneously or even with the help of artificial processes. A great number of these cases are the object of insoluble doubt, and must be dealt with according to the presumptions of law and of fact of which We have spoken.

May these explanations guide you and enlighten you when you must solve delicate questions arising in the practice of your profession. As a token of divine favors which We call upon you and all those who are dear to you, We heartily grant you Our Apostolic Blessing.

EDITORS' COMMENT

In their recent pastoral letter on moral values, the National Conference of Catholic Bishops discussed the question of euthanasia and treatment of the terminally ill as follows:

The Aged

The adventure of marriage and family is a continuing one in which elderly people have important lessons to teach and learn. Contemporary American society tends to separate the aging from their families, isolating kin in ways that are more than physical, with the result that the wisdom of experience is often neither sought, imparted nor further developed.

Families should see the story of loving reciprocity through its closing chapters. Where possible, the elderly should be welcomed into their own families. Moreover, children have an obligation of human and Christian justice and love to keep closely in touch with aging parents and do what lies in their power to care for them in their old age. "If anyone does not provide for his own relatives and especially for members of his immediate family, he has denied the faith; he is worse than an unbeliever." The community should provide for those who lack families and, in doing so, attend to all their needs, not just physical ones. Here the church has played and can continue to play a special role. The elderly must be cherished, not merely tolerated, and the church community, through parishes and other agencies should seek to mediate the loving concern of Jesus and the Father to them.

Euthanasia or mercy killing is much discussed and increasingly advocated today, though the discussion is often confused by ambiguous use of the slogan "death with dignity." Whatever the word or term, it is a grave moral evil deliberately to kill persons who are terminally ill or deeply impaired. Such killing is incompatible with respect for human dignity and reverence for the sacredness of life.

Something different is involved, however, when the question is whether hopelessly ill and painfully afflicted people must be kept alive at all costs and with the use of every available medical technique. Some seem to make no distinction between respecting the dying process and engaging in direct killing of the innocent. Morally there is all the difference in the world. While euthanasia or direct killing is gravely wrong, it does not follow that there is an obligation to prolong the life of a dying person by extraordinary needs. At times the effort to do so is of no help to the dying and is even contrary to the compassion due them. People have a right to refuse treatment which offers no reasonable hope of recovery and imposes excessive burdens on them and perhaps also their families. At times it may even be morally imperative to discontinue particular medical treatments in order to give the dying the personal care and attention they really need as life ebbs. Since life is a gift of God we treat it with awesome respect. Since death is part and parcel of human life, indeed the gateway to eternal life and the return to the Father, it too, we treat with awesome respect.[1]

---

[1] "To Live in Christ Jesus: A Pastoral Reflection on the Moral Life", A Pastoral letter on moral values adopted by the National Conference on Catholic Bishops, The New World, Vol. 84, No. 47, pp. 17, 18, Nov. 19, 1976.

One Catholic hospital has devised the following procedure for discontinuing extraordinary means of sustaining life:

PROCEDURE FOR
DISCONTINUING EXTRAORDINARY MEANS
OF SUSTAINING LIFE

It is not inconsistent with the hospital's philosophy to discontinue extraordinary means of prolonging life. To insure that such a decision is the wish of the family of the patient, the following procedure is recommended.

1. Request must be made by next of kin to discontinue extraordinary means.

2. Decision of family must be consistent with attending doctors prognosis and must have his approval.

3. Hospital chaplain should review the situation to determine that the action is morally and ethically acceptable.

4. A second physician should review the situation and must likewise agree that there is no hope for recovery of the patient.

5. It will be necessary to have two EEG's one hour apart to prove death.

   Death has been defined by Illinois State law as the irreversible cessation of total brain function according to the usual and customary standards of medicine.

6. The next of kin must sign the permit to discontinue the treatment. This form must be signed by the attending physician and chaplain also.

NEXT OF KIN

1. In case of a child—the parents (both)

2. In case of unmarried adult—
   a. the parents
   b. siblings

3. In case of married adult—
   a. spouse

    b. children (if of age)
    c. parents
    d. siblings

4. In a case that does not fit into any of the above it will be handled on an individual basis by Administration in consultation with the hospital's attorney.

The hospital also adopted the following consent form as part of the procedure:

REQUEST TO DISCONTINUE EXTRAORDINARY MEANS OF SUSTAINING LIFE

I, ... ,hereby authorize St. Francis Hospital and Dr. . . . . to discontinue the following treatment and equipment:

on . . . . ,Relationship . . . .

It has been explained to me by my doctor that the continuation of these treatments will not improve the patient's condition. I realize that when these treatments are discontinued, it will lead to cessation of biological functions of the patient.

I make this decision of my own free will without coercion.

                       Signed . . . .

                       . . . .

I, ... , the physician of this patient, agree with the decision of the family and have witnessed the family's decision.

Signed. . . . .

. . . .

It is against neither the laws of good nor the moral principles under which this hospital functions for the family of . . . . to request the doctor in charge to discontinue all extraordinary (i.e., mechanical) means in the treatment of . . . .

date. . . . .   Signed. . . . .

Witness. . . . .

. . . .

The Editors do not cite either the procedure or the consent form as legally definitive, but merely as an illustration of how one Catholic hospital copes with this difficult problem.

ETHICS AND EUTHANASIA

JOSEPH FLETCHER

It is harder to morally justify letting somebody die a slow and ugly death, dehumanized, than it is to justify helping him to escape from such misery. This is the case at least in any code of ethics which is humanistic or personalistic, i.e., in any code of ehtics which has a value system that puts humanness and personal integrity above biological life and function. It makes no difference whether such an ethics system is grounded in a theistic or a naturalistic philosophy. We may believe that God wills human happiness or that man's happiness is, as Protagoras thought, a self-validating standard of the good and the right. But what counts *ethically* is whether human needs come first—not whether the ultimate sanction is transcendental or secular.

What follows is a moral defense of euthanasia. Primarily I mean active or positive euthanasia, which helps the patient to die; not merely the passive or negative form of euthanasia which "lets the patient go" by simply witholding life-preserving treatments. The plain fact is that negative euthanasia is already a fait accompli in modern medicine. Every day in a hundred hospitals across the land decisions are made clinically that the line has been crossed from prolonging genuinely human life to only prolonging subhuman dying, and when that judgment is made respirators are turned off, life-perpetuating intravenous infusions stopped, proposed surgery canceled, and drugs countermanded. So-called "Code 90" stickers are put on many record-jackets, indicating "Give no intensive care or resuscitation." Arguing pro and con about negative euthanasia is therefore merely flogging a dead horse. Ethically, the issue whether we may "let the patient go" is as dead as Queen Anne.

Straight across the board of religious traditions there is substantial agreement that we are not morally obliged to preserve life in *all* terminal cases. (The religious-ethical defense of negative euthanasia is far more generally accepted by ministers and priests than medical people recognize or as yet even accept.) Humanist morality shows the same nonabsolutistic attitude about preserving life. Indeed, not only Protestant, Catholic, and Jewish teaching take this stance; but it is also true of Buddhist, Hindu, and Moslem ethics. In short, the claim that we ought always to do everything we can to preserve any patient's life as long as possible is now discredited. The last serious advocate of this unconditional pro-vitalist doctrine was David Karnofsky—the great tumor research scientist of the Sloan-Kettering Institute in New York. The issue about *negative* euthanasia is settled ethically.

Given modern medicine's capabilities always to do what is technically possible to prolong life would be morally indefensible on any ground other than a vitalistic outlook; that is, the opinion that biological survival is the first-order value and that all other considerations, such as personality, dignity, well-being, and self-possession, necessarily take second place. Vestigal last-ditch pro-vitalists still mumble threateningly about "what the Nazis did," but in fact the Nazis never engaged in euthanasia or mercy killing; what they did was merciless killing, either genocidal or for ruthless experimental purposes.

THE ETHICAL AND THE PRE-ETHICAL

One way of putting this is to say that the traditional ethics based on the sanctity of life—which was the classical doctrine of medical idealism in its prescientific phases—must give way to a code of ethics of the *quality* of life. This comes about for humane reasons. It is a result of modern medicine's successes, not failures. New occasions teach new duties, time makes ancient good uncouth, as Whittier said.

There are many pre-ethical or "metaethical" issues that are often overlooked in ethical discussions. People of equally good reasoning powers and a high respect for the rules of inference will still puzzle and even infuriate each other. This is because they fail to see that their moral judgments proceed from significantly different values, ideals, and starting points. If God's will (perhaps "specially revealed" in the Bible or "generally revealed" in his Creation) is against any responsible human initiative in the dying process, or if sheer life is believed to be, as such, more desirable than anything else, then those who hold these axioms will not find much merit in any case we might make for either kind of euthanasia—positive or negative. If, on the other hand, the highest good is personal integrity and human well-being, then euthanasia in either form could or might be the right thing to do, depending on the situation. This latter kind of ethics is the key to what will be said in this chapter.

Let's say it again, clearly, for the sake of truly serious ethical discourse. Many of us look upon living and dying as we do upon health and medical care, as person-centered. This is not a solely or basically biological understanding of what it means to be "alive" and to be "dead." It asserts that a so-called "vegetable," the brain-damaged victim of an auto accident or a microcephalic newborn or a case of massive neurologic deficit and lost cerebral capacity, who nevertheless goes on breathing and whose midbrain or brain stem continues to support spontaneous organ functions, is in such a situation no longer a human being, no longer a person, no longer really alive. It is *personal* function that counts, not biological function. Humanness is understood as primarily rational, not physiological. This "doctrine of man" puts the *homo* and *ratio* before the *vita*. It holds that being human is more "valuable" than being alive.

All of this is said just to make it clear from the outset that biomedical progress is forcing us, whether we welcome it or not, to make fundamental *conceptual* changes as well as scientific and medical changes. Not only are the conditions of life and death changing, because of our greater control and in consequence our greater decision-making responsibility; our *definitions* of life and death also have to change to keep pace with the new realities.

These changes are signaled in a famous surgeon's remark recently: "When the brain is gone there is no point in keeping anything else going." What he meant was that with an end of cerebration, i.e., the function of the cerebral cortex, the *person* is gone (dead) no matter how many other spontaneous or artificially supported functions persist in the heart, lungs, and vascular system.* Such noncerebral processes might as well be turned off, whether they are natural or artificial.

This conclusion is of great philosphical and religious interest because it reaffirms the ancient Christian-European belief that the core of humanness, of the *humanum*, lies in the *ratio*—man's rational faculty. It is not the loss of brain function in general but of cerebral function (the synthesizing "mind") in particular that establishes that death has ensued.

Using the old conventional conceptual apparatus, we naturally thought about both life and death as events, not as processes, which, of course, they are. We supposed that these events or episodes depended on the accidents of "nature" or on some kind of special providence. It is therefore no surprise to hear people grumbling that a lot of the decision making that has to be carried out in modern medical care is "playing God." And given that way of thinking the only possible answer to the charge is to accept it: "Yes, we *are* playing God." But the real question is: Which or whose God are we playing?

The old God who was believed to have monopoly control of birth and death, allowing for no human responsibility in either initiating or terminating a life, was a primitive "God of the gaps"—a mysterious and awesome deity, who filled in the gaps of our knowledge and of the control which our knowledge gives us. "He" was, so to speak, an hypothecation of human ignorance and helplessness.

In their growing up spiritually, men are now turning to a God who is the creative principle behind things, who is behind the test tube as much as the earthquake and volcano. This God can be believed in, but the old God's sacralistic inhibitions on human freedom and research can no longer be submitted to.

We must rid ourselves of that obsolete theodicy according to which God is not only the cause but also the builder of nature and its works, and not only the builder but even the manager. On this archaic basis it would be God himself who is the efficient as well as the final cause of earthquake and fire, of life and death, and by logical inference any "interference with nature" (which is exactly what medicine is) is "playing God." That God, seriously speaking, is dead.

*The "brain death" definition of the Harvard Medical School's *ad hoc* committee is far too imprecise, effecting no real difference from the traditional clinical definition. The recent Kansas statute (Ann. Supp., 77-262, 1971) which is based upon it changes nothing since it requires absence of *brain* function, whereas what is definitive is cerebration, not just any or all brain functions regardless of whether they are contributory to personal quality.

ELECTIVE DEATH

Most of our major moral problems are posed by scientific discoveries and by the subsequent technical know-how we gain, in the control of life and health and death. Ethical questions jump out at us from every laboratory and clinic. May we exercise these controls at all, we wonder—and if so, then when, where, how? Every advance in medical capabilities is an increase in our moral responsibility, a widening of the range of our decision-making obligations.

Genetics, molecular biology, fetology, and obstetrics have developed to a point where we now have effective control over the start of human life's continuum. And therefore from now on it would be irresponsible to leave baby-making to mere chance and impulse, as we once *had* to do. Modern men are trying to face up in a mature way to our emerging needs of quality control—medically, ecologically, legally, socially.

What has taken place in birth control is equally imperative in death control. The whole armory of resuscitation and prolongation of life forces us to be responsible decision makers about death as much as about birth; there must be quality control in the terminating of life as in its initiating. It is ridiculous to give ethical approval to the positive ending of subhuman life in utero, as we do in therapeutic abortions for reasons of mercy and compassion, but refuse to approve of positively ending a subhuman life in extremis. If we are morally obliged to put an end to a pregnancy when an amniocentesis reveals a terribly defective fetus, we are equally obliged to put an end to a patient's hopeless misery when a brain scan reveals that a patient with cancer has advanced brain metastases.

Furthermore, as I shall shortly explain, it is morally evasive and disingenuous to suppose that we can condemn or disapprove positive acts of care and compassion but in spite of that approve negative strategies to achieve exactly the same purpose. This contradiction has equal force whether the euthanasia comes at the fetal point on life's spectrum or at some terminal point post-natally.

Only man is aware of death. Animals know pain, and fear it, but not death. Furthermore, in humans the ability to meet death and even to regard it sometimes as a friend is a sign of manliness. But in the new patterns of medicine and health care patients tend to die in a moribund or comatose state, so that death comes without the patient's knowledge. The Elizabethan litany's petition, ". . . from sudden death, good Lord, deliver us," has become irrelevant much if not most of the time.

It is because of this "incompetent" condition of so many of the dying that we cannot discuss the ethical issues of elective death only in the narrow terms of voluntary, patient-chosen euthanasia. A careful typology of elective death will distinguish at least *four* forms—ways of dying which are not merely willy-nilly matters of blind chance but of choice, purpose, and responsible freedom (historical ethics and moral theology are obviously major sources of suggestion for these distinctions):

(1) Euthanasia, or a "good death," can be *voluntary and direct*, i.e., chosen and carried out by the patient. The most familiar way is the overdose left near at hand for the patient. It is a matter of simple request and of personal liberty. If it can be held in the abortion debate that compulsory pregnancy is unjust and that women should be free to control their own bodies when other's lives (fetuses) are at stake, do not the same moral claims apply to control of the lives and bodies of people too? In any particular case we might properly raise the question of the patient's competence, but to hold that euthanasia in this category is justifiable entails a rejection of the simplistic canard that all suicide victims are mentally disordered.

Voluntary euthanasia is, of course, a form of suicide. Presumably a related issue arises around the conventional notion of consent in medical ethics. The codes (American Medical Association, Helsinki, World Medical Association, Nuremberg) all contend that valid consent to any surgery or treatment requires a reasonable prospect of benefit to the patient. What, then, is benefit? Could death in some situations be a benefit? My own answer is in the affirmative.

(2) Euthanasia can be *voluntary but indirect*. The choice might be made either in situ or long in advance of a terminal illness, e.g., by exacting a promise that if and when the "bare bodkin" or potion cannot be self-administered somebody will do it for the patient. In this case the patient gives to others— physicians, lawyers, family, friends—the discretion to end it all as and when the situation requires, if the patient becomes comatose or too dysfunctioned to make the decision pro forma.

There is already a form called the Living Will, sent upon request to thousands by the Euthanasia Educational Fund (although its language appears to limit it to merely negative methods). This perfectly reasonable "insurance" device is being explored by more and more people, as medical prolongation of life tends to make them more afraid of senescence than of death.

Since both the common law tradition and statute law are caught practically unequipped to deal with this medical-legal lag, the problem is being examined worriedly and behind the scenes by lawyers and legislators. They have little or no case law to work with. As things stand now the medieval outlook of the law treats self-administered euthanasia as suicide and when effected by a helping hand as murder.

(3) Euthanasia may be *direct but involuntary*. This is the form in which a simple "mercy killing" is done on a patient's behalf without his present or past request. Instances would be when an idiot is given a fatal dose or the death of a child in the worst stages of Tay-Sachs disease is speeded up, or when a man trapped inextricably in a blazing fire is shot to end his suffering, or a shutdown is ordered on a patient deep in a mindless condition, irreversibly, perhaps due to an injury or an infection or some biological breakdown. It is in this form, as directly involuntary, that the problem has reached the courts in legal charges and indictments.

To my knowledge Uruguay is the only country that allows it. Article 37 of the *Codiga Penal* specifically states that although it is a "crime" the courts are authorized to forego any penalty. In time the world will follow suit. Laws in Colombia and in the Soviet Union (Article 50 of the Code of Criminal Procedure) are similar to Uruguay's, but in their codes freedom from punishment is exceptional rather than normative. In Italy, Germany, and Switzerland the law provides for a reduction of penalties when it is done upon the patient's request.

The conflict and tension between the stubborn prohibitionism on the one hand and a humane compassion on the other may be seen in the legal history of the issue in the United States. Eleven cases of "mercy killing" have actually reached the courts: one was on a charge of voluntary manslaughter, with a conviction and penalty of three to six years in prison and a $500 fine; one was for first-degree murder, resulting in a conviction, which was promptly reduced to a penalty of six years in jail with immediate parole. All of the other nine cases were twisted into "temporary insanity" or no-proof judgments—in short, no convictions.

(4) Finally, euthanasia might be *both indirect and involuntary*. This is the "letting the patient go" tactic which is taking place every day in our hospitals. Nothing is done for the patient positively to release him from his tragic condition (other than "trying to make him comfortable"), and what is done negatively is decided *for* him rather than in response to his request.

As we all know, even this passive policy of compassion is a grudging one, done perforce. Even so, it remains at least theoretically vulnerable to malpractice suits under the lagging law—brought, possibly, by angry or venal members of the family or suit-happy lawyers. A sign of the times was the bill to give negative euthanasia a legal basis in Florida, introduced by a physician member of the legislature.

But *ethically* regarded, this indirect-involuntary form of euthanasia is manifestly superficial, morally timid, and evasive of the real issue. I repeat: it is harder morally to justify letting somebody die a slow and ugly death, dehumanized, than it is to justify *helping* him to avoid it.

MEANS AND ENDS

What, then, is the real issue? In a few words, it is whether we can morally justify taking it into our own hands to hasten death for ourselves (suicide) or for others (mercy killing) out of reasons of compassion. The answer to this in my view is clearly Yes, on both sides of it. Indeed, *to justify either one, suicide or mercy killing, is to justify the other.*

The heart of the matter analytically is the question of whether the end justifies the means. If the end sought is the patient's death as a release from pointless misery and dehumanization, then the requisite or appropriate means is justified. Immanuel Kant said that if we will the end we will the means. The old maxim of some moral theologians was *finis sanctificat media*. The point is that no act is anything but random and *meaningless* unless it is purposefully related to some end or object. To be moral an act must be seeking an end.

However, to hold that the end justifies the means does not entail the absurd notion that *any* means can be justified by *any* end. The priority of the end is paired with the principle of "proportionate good"; any disvalue in the means must be outweighed by the value gained in the end. In systems analysis, with its pragmatic approach, the language would be: the benefit must repay the cost or the trade-off is not justified. It comes down to this, that in some situations a morally good end can justify a relatively "bad" means, on the principle of proportionate good.

The really searching question of conscience is, therefore, whether we are right in believing that *the well-being of persons* is the highest good. If so, then it follows that either suicide or mercy killing could be the right thing to do in some exigent and tragic circumstances. This could be the case, for instance, when an incorrigible "human vegetable," whether spontaneously functioning or artificially supported, is progressively degraded while constantly eating up private or public financial resources in violation of the distributive justice owed to others. In such cases the patient is actually already departed and only his body is left, and the needs of others have a stronger claim upon us morally. The fair allocation of scarce resources is as profound an ethical obligation as any we can imagine in a civilized society, and it arises very practically at the clinical level when triage officers make their decisions at the expense of some patients' needs in favor of others.

Another way of putting this is to say that the crucial question is not whether the end justifies the means (what else could?) but *what justifies the end?* And this chapter's answer is, plainly and confidently, that human happiness and well-being is the highest good or *summum bonum*, and that therefore any ends or purposes which that standard or ideal validates are just, right, good. This is what humanistic medicine is all about; it is what the concepts of loving concern and social justice are built upon.

This position comes down to the belief that our moral acts, including suicide and mercy killing, are right or wrong depending on the consequences aimed at (we sometimes fail, of course, through ignorance or poor reasoning), and that the consequences are good or evil according to whether and how much they serve humane values. In the language of ethics this is called a "consequential" method of moral judgment.

I believe that this code of ethics is both implicit and explicit in the morality of medical care and biomedical research.
Its reasoning is inductive, not deductive, and it proceeds empirically from the data of each actual case or problem, choosing the course that offers an optimum or maximum of desirable consequences. Medicine is not a-prioristic or *prejudiced*
in its ethos and modalities, and therefore to proscribe either
suicide or mercy killing is so blatantly nonconsequential that
it calls for critical scrutiny. It fails to make sense. It is un-
clinical and doctrinaire.

The problem exists because there is another kind of ethics,
radically different from consequential ethics. This other kind
of ethics holds that our actions are right or wrong according
to whether they follow universal rules of conduct and absolute
norms: that we ought or ought not to do certain things no
matter how good or bad the consequences might be foreseeably. Such rules are usually prohibitions or taboos, expressed
as thou-shalt-nots. Whereas this chapter's ethics is teleological or end-oriented, the opposite approach is "deontological"
(from the Greek *deonteis,* meaning duty); i.e., it is duty-ethics,
not goal-ethics. Its advocates sometimes sneer at any determination of obligation in terms of consequences, calling it "a
mere morality of goals."

In duty-ethics what is right is whatever act obeys or ad-
heres to the rules, even though the foreseeable result will be
inhumane. That is, its highest good is not human happiness
and well-being but obedience to a rule—or what we might call
a prejudiced or predetermined decision based not on the clinical variables but on some transcending generality.

For example, the fifth of the Ten Commandments, which
prohibits killing, is a no-no rule for nonconsequentialists when
it comes to killing in the service of humane values like mercy
and compassion, and yet at the same time they ignore their
"moral law" when it comes to self-defense. The egocentricity
and solipsism in this moral posture, which is a very common
one, never ceases to bemuse consequentialists. You may end
your neighbor's life for your own sake but you may not do it
for his sake! And you may end your own life for your neighbor's sake, as in an act of sacrificial heroism, but you may
not end your life for your own sake. This is a veritable mare's
nest of nonsense!

The plain hard logic of it is that the end or purpose of
both negative and positive euthanasia is exactly the same: to

contrive or bring about the patient's death. Acts of deliberate omission are morally not different from acts of commission. But in the Anglo-American *law*, it is a crime to push a blind man off the cliff. It is not, however, a crime to deliberately not lift a finger to prevent his walking over the edge. This is an unpleasant feature of legal reasoning which is alien to ethics and to a sensitive conscience. Ashamed of it, even the courts fall back on such legal fictions as "insanity" in euthanasia cases, and this has the predictable effect of undermining our respect for the law.

There is something obviously evasive when we rule motive out in charging people with the crime of mercy killing, but then bring it back in again for purposes of determining punishment! It is also a menacing delimitation of the concepts of culpability, responsibility, and negligence. No *ethically* disciplined decision maker could so blandly separate right and wrong from motives, foresight, and consequences. (Be it noted, however, that motive is taken into account in German and Swiss law, and that several European countries provide for recognition of "homicide when requested" as a special category.)

It is naïve and superficial to suppose that because we don't "do anything positively" to hasten a patient's death we have thereby avoided complicity in his death. Not doing anything is doing something; it is a decision to act every bit as much as deciding for any other deed. If I decide not to eat or drink any more, knowing what the consequence will be, I have committed suicide as surely as if I had used a gas oven. If physicians decide not to open an imperforate anus in a severely 21-trisomy newborn, they have committed mercy killing as surely as if they had used a poison pellet!

Let the reader at this point now ask himself if he is a consequentialist or an a priori decision maker; and again, let him ask himself if he is a humanist, religious or secular, or alternatively has something he holds to be better or more obliging than the well-being of the patient. (Thoughtless religious people will sometimes point out that we are required to love God as well as our neighbors, but can the two loves ever come into conflict? Actually, is there any way to love God other than through the neighbor? Only mystics imagine that they can love God directly and discretely.)

Occasionally I hear a physician say that he could not resort to positive euthanasia. That may be so. What anybody would do in such tragic situations is a problem in psychology, however, not in ethics. We are not asking what we would do but what we should do. Any of us who has an intimate knowledge of what happens in terminal illnesses can tell stories of rational people—both physicians and family—who were quite clear ethically about the rightness of an overdose or of "turning off the machine," and yet found themselves too inhibited to give the word or do the deed. That is a phenomenon of primary interest to psychology, but of only incidental interest to ethics.

Careful study of the best texts of the Hippocratic Oath shows that it says nothing at all about preserving life, as such. It says that "so far as power and discernment shall be mine, I will carry out regimen for the benefit of the sick and will keep them from harm and wrong." The case for euthanasia depends upon how we understand "benefit of the sick" and "harm" and "wrong." If we regard dehumanized and merely biological life as sometimes real harm and the opposite of benefit, to refuse to welcome or even introduce death would be quite wrong morally.

In most states in this country people can and do carry cards, legally established (by Anatomical Gift Acts), which explain the carrier's wish that when he dies his organs and tissue should be used for transplant when needed by the living. The day will come when people will also be able to carry a card, notarized and legally executed, which explains that they do not want to be kept alive beyond the *humanum* point, and authorizing the ending of their biological processes by any of the methods of euthanasia which seems appropriate. Suicide may or may not be the ultimate problem of philosophy, as Albert Camus thought it is, but in any case it is the ultimate problem of medical ethics.

THE INDIGNITY OF "DEATH WITH DIGNITY"

PAUL RAMSEY

Never one am I to use an ordinary title when an extra-ordinary one will do as well! Besides, I mean to suggest that there is an additional insult besides death itself heaped upon the dying by our ordinary talk about "death with dignity." Sometimes that is said even to be a human "right"; and what should a decent citizen do but insist on enjoying his rights? That might be his duty (if there is any such right), to the commonwealth, to the human race or some other collective entity; or at least, embracing that "right" and dying ration-ally would exhibit a proper respect for the going concept of a rational man. So the "The Indignity of Death" would not suf-fice for my purposes, even though all I shall say depends on understanding the contradiction death poses to the unique worth of an individual human life.

The genesis of the following reflections may be worth noting. A few years ago,[1] I embraced what I characterized as the oldest morality there is (no "new morality") concerning responsibility toward the dying: the acceptance of death, stop-ping our medical interventions for all sorts of good, human reasons, *only* companying with the dying in their final pas-sage. Then suddenly it appeared that altogether too many people were agreeing with me. That caused qualms. As a Southerner born addicted to lost causes, it seemed I now was caught up in a triumphal social trend. As a controversialist in ethics, I found agreement from too many sides. As a general-ly happy prophet of the doom facing the modern age, unless there is a sea-change in norms of action, it was clear from these premises that anything divers people agree to must necessarily be superficial if not wrong.

Today, when divers people draw the same warm blanket of "allowing to die" or "death with dignity" close up around their shoulders against the dread of that cold night, their various feet are showing. Exposed beneath our growing agreement to that "philosophy of death and dying" may be significantly different "philosophies of life"; and in the present age that agreement may reveal that these interpretations of human life are increasingly mundane, naturalistic, antihumanistic when measured by *any* genuinely "humanistic" esteem for the individual human being.

These "philosophical" ingredients of any view of death and dying I want to make prominent by speaking of "The Indignity of 'Death with Dignity'." Whatever practical agreement there may be, or "guidelines" proposed to govern contemporary choice or practice, these are bound to be dehumanizing unless at the same time we bring to bear great summit points and sources of insight in mankind's understanding of mankind (be it Christian or other religious humanism, or religiously-dependent but not explicitly religious humanism, or, if it is possible, a true humanism that is neither systematically nor historically dependent on any religious outlook.)

DEATH WITH DIGNITY IDEOLOGIES

There is nobility and dignity in caring for the dying, but not in dying itself. "To be a therapist to a dying patient makes us aware of the uniqueness of each individual in this vast sea of humanity."[2] It is more correct to say that a therapist brings to the event, from some other source, an awareness of the uniqueness, the once-for-allness of an individual life-span as part of an "outlook" and "on-look" upon the vast sea of humanity. In any case, that is the reflected glory and dignity of caring for the dying, that we are or become aware of the unique life here ending. The humanity of such human caring is apt to be more sensitive and mature if we do not lightly suppose that it is an easy thing to convey dignity to the dying. That certainly cannot be done simply by withdrawing tubes and stopping respirators or not thumping hearts. At most, those omissions can only be prelude to companying with the dying in their final passage, if we are fortunate enough to share with them—they in moderate comfort—those interchanges that are in accord with the dignity and nobility of mankind. Still, however noble the manifestations of caring called for, however unique the individual life, we finally must come to the reality of death, and must ask, what can possibly be the meaning of "death with dignity"?

At most we convey only the liberty to die with human dignity; we can provide some of the necessary but not sufficient conditions. If the dying die with a degree of nobility it will be mostly their doing in doing their own dying. I fancy their task was easier when death as a human event meant that special note was taken of the last words of the dying— even humorous ones, as in the case of the Roman Emperor who said as he expired, "I Deify." A human countenance may be discerned in death accepted with serenity. So also there is a human countenance behind death with defiance. "Do not go gentle into that good night," wrote Dylan Thomas. "Old age should rage and burn against the close of day; Rage Rage against the dying of the light." But the human countenance has been removed from most modern understandings of death.

We do not begin to keep human community with the dying if we interpose between them and us most of the current notions of "death with dignity." Rather do we draw closer to them if and only if our conception of "dying with dignity" encompasses—nakedly and without dilution—the final indignity of death itself, whether accepted or raged against. So I think it may be profitable to explore "the indignity of 'death with dignity'." "Good death" (euthanasia) like "Good grief!" are ultimately contradictions in terms, even if superficially, and before we reach the heart of the matter, there are distinctions to be made; even if, that is to say, the predicate "good" still is applicable in both cases in contrast to worse ways to die and worse ways to grieve or not to grieve.

"Death is simply a part of life," we are told, as a first move to persuade us to accept the ideology of the entire dignity of dying with dignity. A singularly unpersuasive proposition, since we are not told what sort of part of life death is. Disease, injury, congenital defects are also a part of life, and as well murder, rapine, and pillage.[3] Yet there is no campaign for accepting or doing those things with dignity. Nor, for that matter, for the contemporary mentality which would enshrine "death with dignity" is there an equal emphasis on "suffering with dignity," suffering as a "natural" part of life, etc.

All those things, it seems, are enemies and violations of human nobility while death is not, or (with a few changes) need not be. Doctors did not invent the fact that death is an enemy, although they may sometimes use disproportionate means to avoid final surrender. Neither did they invent the fact that pain and suffering are enemies and often indignities, although suffering accepted may also be ennobling or may manifest the nobility of the human spirit of any ordinary person.

But, then, it is said, death is an evolutionary necessity and in that further sense a part of life not to be denied. Socially and biologically, one generation follows another. So there must be death, else social history would have no room for creative novelty and planet earth would be glutted with humankind. True enough, no doubt, from the point of view of evolution (which—so far—never dies). But the man who is dying happens not to be evolution. He is a part of evolution, no doubt: but not to the whole extent of his being or his dying. A crucial testimony to the individual's transcendence over the species is man's problem and his dis-ease in dying. Death is a natural fact of life, yet no man dies "naturally," nor do we have occasions in which to practice doing so in order to learn how. Not unless the pursuit of philosophy is a practice of dying (as Plato's *Phaedo* teaches); and that I take to be an understanding of the human being we moderns do not mean to embrace when we embrace "death with dignity."

It is small consolation to tell mortal men that as long as you are, the death you contribute to evolution is not yet; and when death is, you are not—so why fear death? That is the modern equivalent to the recipe offered by the ancient Epicureans (and some Stoics) to undercut fear of death and devotion to the gods: as long as you are, death is not; when death is, you are not; there's never a direct encounter between you and death; so why dread death? Indeed, contrary to modern parlance, those ancient philosophers declared that death is *not a part of life;* so why worry?

So "death is not a part of life" is another declaration designed to quiet fear of death. This can be better understood in terms of a terse comment by Wittgenstein: "Our life has no limit in just the way in which our visual field has no limit."[4] We cannot see beyond the boundary of our visual field; it is more correct to say that beyond the boundary of our visual field *we do not see*. Not only so. Also, we do not see the boundary, the limit itself. There is no seeable bound to the visual field. *Death is not a part of life* in the same way that the boundary is not a part of our visual field. Commenting on this remark by Wittgenstein, James Van Evra writes: "Pressing the analogy, then, if my life has no end in *just the same way* that my visual field has no limit, then it must be in the sense that I can have no experience of death, conceived as the complete cessation of experience and thought. That is, if life is considered to be a series of experiences and thoughts, then it is impossible for me to experience death, for to experience something is to be alive, and hence is to be inside the bound formed by death."[5] This is why death itself steadfastly resists conceptualization.

Still, I think the disanalogy ought also to be pressed, against both ancient and contemporary analytical philosophers. That notion of death as a limit makes use of a visual or spatial metaphor. Good basketball players are often men naturally endowed with an unusually wide visual field; this is true, for example, of Bill Bradley. Perhaps basketball players, among other things, strive to enlarge their visual fields, or their habitual use of what powers of sight they have, if that is possible. But ordinarily, everyone of us is perfectly happy within the unseeable limits of sight's reach.

Transfer this notion of death as a limit from space to time as the form of human perception, from sight to an individual's inward desire, effort and hope, and I suggest that one gets a different result. Then death as the temporal limit of a life-span is something we live toward. That limit still can never be experienced or conceptualized; indeed death is *never* a part of life. Moreover, neither is the boundary. Still it is a limit we conative human beings know we live *up against* during our life-spans. We do not live toward or up against the side-limits of our visual-span. Instead, within that acceptable visual limit (and other limits as well) as channels we live toward yet another limit which is death.

Nor is the following analogy for death as a limit of much help in deepening understanding. ". . . The importance of the limit and virtually *all* of its significance," writes Van Evra, "derives from the fact that the limit serves as an ordering device"—just as absolute zero serves for ordering a series; it is not *just* a limit, although nothing can exist at such a temperature. The analogy is valid so far as it suggests that we conceive of death not in itself but as it bears on us while still alive. As I shall suggest below, death teaches us to "number our days."

But that may not be its only ordering function for conative creatures. Having placed death "out of our league" by
showing that it is not a "something," or never a part of life,
and while understanding awareness of death as awareness of
a limit bearing upon us only while still alive, one ought not
forthwith to conclude that this understanding of it "exoner-
ates death as the purported snake in our garden." Death as a
limit can disorder no less than order the series. Only a dis-
embodied reason can say, as Van Evra does, that "the bound,
not being a member of the series, cannot defile it. The series
is what it is, happy or unhappy, good or bad, quite independently of any bound as such." An Erik Erikson knows better than that when writing of the "despair and often unconscious fear of death" which results when "the one and only
life cycle is not accepted as the ultimate life." Despair, he
observes, "expresses the feeling that the time is short, too
short for the attempt to start another life and to try out alternate roads to integrity."[6]

It is the temporal flight of the series that is grievous (not
death as an evil "something" within life's span to be balanced,
optimistically or pessimistically, against other things that are
good). The reminder that death is *not a part of life,* or that it
is only a boundary never encountered, is an ancient recipe
that can only increase the threat of death on any profound
understanding of human life. The dread of death is the dread
of oblivion, of there being only empty room in one's stead.
Kubler-Ross writes that for the dying, death means the loss
of every loved one, total loss of everything that constituted
the self in its world, separation from every experience, even
from future possible, replacing experiences—nothingness beyond. Therefore, life is a time-intensive activity and not only
a goods-intensive or quality-intensive activity. No matter
how many "goods" we store up in barns, like the man in Jesus'
parable we know that this night our soul may be required of
us (Luke 12:13-21). No matter what "quality of life" our lives
have, we must take into account the opportunity-costs of
used time. Death means the conquest of the time of our lives
—even though we never experience the experience of the nothingness which is natural death.

"Awareness of dying" means awareness of *that;* and
awareness of that constitutes an experience of ultimate indignity in and to the awareness of the self who is dying.

We are often reminded of Koheleth's litany: "For everything there is a season, and a time for every matter under heaven: a time to be born and a time to die; a time to plant, and a time to pluck up what is planted," etc. (Eccles. 3:1,2). Across those words of the narrator of Ecclesiastes the view gains entrance that only an "untimely" death should be regretted or mourned. Yet we know better how to specify an untimely death than to define or describe a "timely" one. The author of Genesis tells us that, at 180 years of age, the patriarch Isaac "breathed his last; and he died and was gathered to his people, old and full of years . . ." (Gen. 35:29). Even in the face of sacred Scripture, we are permitted to wonder what Isaac thought about it; whether he too knew how to apply the category "fullness of years" *to himself* and agreed his death was nothing but timely.

We do Koheleth one better and say that death cannot only be timely; it may also be "beautiful." Whether such an opinion is to be ascribed to David Hendin or not (a "fact of life" man he surely is, who also unambiguously subtitled his chapter on euthanasia "Let There Be Death"),[7] that opinion seems to be the outlook of the legislator and physician, Walter Sackett, Jr., who proposed the Florida "Death with Dignity" Statute. All his mature life his philosophy has been, "Death, like birth, is glorious—let it come easy."[8] Such was by no means Koheleth's opinion when he wrote (and *wrote* beautifully) about a time to be born and a time to die. Dr. Sackett also suggests that up to 90 percent of the 1,800 patients in state hospitals for the mentally retarded should be allowed to die. Five billion dollars could be saved in the next half century if the state's mongoloids were permitted to succumb to pneumonia, a disease to which they are highly susceptible.[9] I suggest that the physician in Dr. Sackett has atrophied. He has become a public functionary, treating taxpayers' pocketbooks under the general anesthesia of a continuous daytime soap opera entitled "Death Can Be Beautiful!"

"Death for an older person should be a beautiful event. There is beauty in birth, growth, fullness of life and then, equally so, in the tapering off and final end. There are analogies all about us. What is more beautiful than the spring budding of small leaves; then the fully-leaved tree in summer; and then in the beautiful brightly colored autumn leaves gliding gracefully to the ground? So it is with humans." Those are the words from a study document on Euthanasia drafted by the Council for Christian Social Action of the United Church of Christ in 1972. An astonishing footnote at this point states that "the naturalness of dying" is suggested in the funeral services when the minister says "God has called" the deceased, or says he has "gone to his reward," recites the "dust to dust" passage, or notes that the deceased led a full life or ran a full course!

Before that statement was adopted by that Council on February 17, 1973, more orthodox wording was inserted: "Transformation from life on earth to life in the hereafter of the Lord is a fulfillment. The acceptance of death is our witness to faith in the resurrection of Jesus Christ (Rom. 8). We can rejoice." The subdued words "we can rejoice" indicate a conviction that *something* has been subdued. The words "acceptance of death" takes the whole matter out of the context of romantic naturalism and sets it in proper religious context —based on the particular Christian tenet that death is a conquered enemy, to be accepted in the name of its Conqueror. More than a relic of the nature mysticism that was so luxurient in the original paragraph, however, remains in the words, "Death for an older person should be a beautiful event. There is beauty in birth, growth, fullness of life and then, *equally so*, in the tapering off and final end. (Italics added.) I know no Christian teaching that assures us that our "final end" is "equally" beautiful as birth, growth, and fullness of life. Moreover, if revelation disclosed any such thing it would be contrary to reason and to the human reality and experience of death. The views of our "pre-death morticians" are simply discordant with the experienced reality they attempt to beautify. So, in her recent book, Marya Mannes writes "the name of the oratorio is euthanasia." And her statement "dying is merely suspension within a mystery," seems calculated to induce vertigo in face of a fascinating abyss in prospect.[10]

No exception can be taken to one line in the letter people are being encouraged to write and sign by the Euthanasia Societies of Great Britain and America. That line states: "I do not fear death as much as I fear the indignity of deterioration, dependence and hopeless pain." Such an exercise in analyzing *comparative indignities* should be given approval. But in the preceding sentence the letter states: "Death is as much a reality as birth, growth, maturity, and old age—it is the one certainty." That logically leaves open the question what sort of "reality," what sort of "certainty," death is. But by placing death on a parity with birth, growth, maturity—and old age in many of its aspects—the letter beautifies death by association. To be written long before death when one is thinking "generally" (i.e. "rationally"?) about the topic, the letter tempts us to suppose that men can think generally about their own deaths. Hendin observes in another connection that "there is barely any relation between what people think that they think about death and the way they actually feel about it when it must be faced."[11] Then it may be that "the heart has its reasons that reason cannot know" (Pascal)—beforehand—and among those "reasons," I suggest, will be an apprehension of the ultimate (noncomparative) indignity of death. Talk about death as a fact or a reality seasonally recurring in life with birth or planting, maturity and growth, may after all not be very rational. It smacks more of whistling before the darkness descends, and an attempt to brainwash one's contemporaries to accept a very feeble philosophy of life and death.

Birth and death (our *terminus ad quo* and our *terminus ad quem*) are not to be equated with any of the qualities or experiences, the grandeur and the misery, in between, which constitutes "parts" of our lives. While we live toward death and can encompass our own dying in awareness, no one in the same way is aware of his own birth. We know that we were born in the same way that we know *that* we die. Explanations of whence we came do not establish conscious contact with our individual origin; and among explanations, that God called us from the womb out of nothing is as good as any other; and better than most. But awareness of dying is quite another matter. That we may have, but not awareness of our births. And while awareness of birth might conceivably be the great original individuating experience (if we had it), among the race of men it is awareness of dying that is uniquely individuating. To encompass one's own death in the living and dying of one's life is more of a task than it is a part of life. And there is something of indignity to be faced when engaging in that final act of life. Members of the caring human community (doctors, nurses, family) are apt to keep closer company with the dying if we acknowledge the loss of all worth by the loss of him in whom inhered all worth in this world. Yet ordinary men may sometimes nobly suffer the ignobility of death.

By way of contrast with the "A Living Will" framed by the Euthanasia Society, the Judicial Council of the AMA in

its recent action on the physician and the dying patient had
before it two similar letters. One was composed by the Connecticut Delegation:

> *To my Family, my Physician*
> *my Clergyman, my Lawyer—*

If the time comes when I can no longer actively
take part in decisions for my own future, I wish
this statement to stand as the testament of my
wishes. If there is no reasonable expectation of
my recovery from physical or mental and spirit-
ual disability, I, ..., request that
I be allowed to die and not be kept alive by artificial means or heroic measures. I ask also that
drugs be mercifully administered to me for terminal suffering even if in relieving pain they
may hasten the moment of death. I value life
and the dignity of life, so that I am not asking
that my life be directly taken, but that my dying not be unreasonably prolonged nor the dignity of life be destroyed. This request is made,
after careful reflection, while I am in good health
and spirits. Although this document is not legally binding, you who care for me will, I hope,
feel morally bound to take it into account. I recognize that it places a heavy burden of responsibility upon you, and it is with the intention of
sharing this responsibility that this statement
is made.

A second letter had been composed by a physician to express
his own wishes, in quite simple language:

> *To my Family, To my Physician—*

Should the occasion arise in my lifetime when
death is imminent and a decision is to be made
about the nature and the extent of care to be giv-
en to me and I am not able at that time to express
my desires, let this statement serve to express
my deep, sincere, and considered wish and hope
that my physician will administer to me simple,
ordinary medical treatment. I ask that he not
administer heroic, extraordinary, expensive, or
useless medical care or treatment which in the final analysis will merely delay, not change, the
ultimate outcome of my terminal condition.

A comparison of these declarations with "A Living Will" circulated by the Euthanasia Society reveals the following signal differences: neither of the AMA submissions engages in any superfluous calculus of "comparative indignities";[12] neither associates the reality of death with such things as birth or maturation; both allow death to be simply what it is in human experience; both are in a general sense "pro-life" statements, in that death is neither reified as one fact among others nor beautified even comparatively.[13]

Everyone concerned takes the wrong turn in trying either to "thing-ify" death or to beautify it. The dying have at least this advantage, that in these projects for dehumanizing death by naturalizing it the dying finally cannot succeed, and death makes its threatening visage known to them before ever there are any societal or evolutionary replacement values or the everlasting arms or Abraham's bosom to rest on. Death means *finis*, not in itself *telos*. Certainly not a telos to be engineered, or to be accomplished by reducing both human life and death to the level of natural events.

"Thing-ifying" death reaches its highest pitch in the stated preference of many people in the present age for *sudden* death,[14] for death from unanticipated internal collapse, from the abrupt intrusion of violent outside forces, from some chance occurrence due to the natural law governing the operation of automobiles. While for a comparative calculus of indignities sudden *unknowing* death may be preferred to suffering knowingly or unknowingly the indignity of deterioration, abject dependence, and hopeless pain, how ought we to assess in human terms the present-day absolute (noncomparative) preference for sudden death? Nothing reveals more the meaning we assign to human "dignity" than the view that sudden death, death as an eruptive natural event, could be a prismatic case of death with dignity or at least one without indignity. Human society seems about to rise to the moral level of the "humane" societies in their treatment of animals. What is the principled difference between their view and ours about the meaning of dying "humanely"? By way of contrast, consider the prayer in the Anglican prayer book: "From perils by night and perils by day, perils by land and perils by sea, and *from sudden death*, Lord, deliver us." Such a petition bespeaks an age in which dying with dignity was a gift and a task (*Gaube und Aufgaube*), a liberty to encompass dying as a final act among the actions of life, to enfold awareness of dying as an

ingredient into awareness of one's self dying as the finale of
the self's relationships in this life to God or to fellowman — in
any case to everything that was worthy.

MAN KNOWS THAT HE DIES

Before letting Koheleth's "a time to be born and a time
to die" creep as a gloss into *our* texts, perhaps we ought to
pay more attention to the outlook on life and death expressed
in the enchantment and frail beauty of those words,[15] and ask
whether that philosophy can possibly be a proper foundation
for the practice of medicine or for the exercise of the most
sensitive care for the dying.

That litany on the times for every matter under heaven
concludes with the words, "What gain has the worker from
his toil?" (Eccles. 3:9). In general, the author of Ecclesiastes
voices an unrelieved pessimism. He has "seen everything that
is done under the sun," in season and out of season. It is altogether "an unhappy business that God has given to the sons
of men to be busy with" — this birthing and dying, planting
and uprooting; "all is vanity and seeking after wind" (Eccles.
1:3b, 14). So, he writes with words of strongest revulsion, "I
hated life, because what is done under the sun was grievous
to me"; "I hated all my toil and gave myself up to despair . . ."
(Eccles. 2:17, 18a, 20).

After that comes the litany "for everything there is a
season" — proving, as Kierkegaard said, that a poet is a man
whose heart is full of pain but whose lips are so formed that
when he gives utterance to that pain he makes beautiful
sounds. Koheleth knew, as later did Nietzsche, that the eternal recurrence of birth and death and all things else was simply "the spirit of melancholy" unrelieved, even though there
is nothing else to believe since God died.[16] (The Pope knows:
he was at the bedside.)

"Death with dignity" because death is a "part" of life, one
only of its seasonal realities? If so, then the acceptable death
of all flesh means death with the same signal indignity that
brackets the whole of life and its striving. Dying is worth as
much as the rest; it is no more fruitless.

"For the fate of the sons of men and the fate of the beasts
is the same; as one dies so dies the other. They all have the

same breath, and man has no advantage over the beasts; for all is vanity" (Eccles. 3:19). "Death with dignity" or death a part of life based on an equilibration of the death of a man with the death of a dog? I think that is not a concept to be chosen as the foundation of modern medicine, even though both dogs and men are enabled to die "humanely."

Or to go deeper still: "death with dignity" because the dead are better off than the living? "I thought the dead who are already dead," Koheleth writes in unrelieved sorrow over existence, "more fortunate than the living who are still alive; and better than both is he who has not yet been, and has not seen the evil deeds that are done under the sun" (Eccles. 4:2,3). Thus the book of Ecclesiastes is the source of the famous interchange between two pessimistic philosophers, each trying to exceed the other in gloom: First philosopher: More blessed are the dead than the living. Second philosopher: Yes, what you say is true; but more blessed still are those who have never been born. First philosopher: Yes, wretched life; but few there be who attain to that condition!

But Koheleth thinks he knows some who have attained to the blessed goal of disentrapment from the cycles in which there is a time for every matter under heaven. ". . . An untimely birth [a miscarriage] is better off [than a living man], for it [a miscarriage] comes into vanity and goes into darkness, and in darkness its name is covered, moreover it has not seen the sun or known anything; yet it finds rest rather than he [the living]" (Eccles. 6:3b, 4,5). So we might say that death can have its cosmic dignity if untormented by officious physicians, because the dying go to the darkness, to Limbo where nameless miscarriages dwell, having never seen the sun or known anything. Thus, if dying with dignity as a part of life's natural, undulating seasons seems not to be a thought with much consolation in it (being roughly equivalent to the indignity besetting everything men do and every other natural time), still the dying may find rest as part of cosmic order, from which, once upon a time, the race of men arose to do the unhappy business God has given them to be busy with, and to which peaceful darkness the dying return.

Hardly a conception that explains the rise of Western medicine, the energy of its care of the dying, or its war against the indignity of suffering and death—or a conception on which to base its reformation! Dylan Thomas' words were directed against such notions: "The wise men at their end know dark is right,/Because their words had forked no lightning."

There is finally in Ecclesiastes, however, a deeper strand than those which locate men living and dying as simply parts of some malignly or benignly neglectful natural or cosmic order. From these more surface outlooks, the unambiguous injunction follows: Be a part; let there be death—in its time and place, of course (whatever that means). Expressing a deeper strand, however, Koheleth seems to say: Let the natural or cosmic order be whatever it is; men are different. His practical advice is: Be what you are, in human awareness apart and not a part. Within this deeper understanding of the transcendent, threatened nobility of a human life, the uniqueness of the individual human subject, there is ground for awareness of death as an indignity yet freedom to encompass it with dignity.

Now it is that Koheleth reverses the previous judgments he decreed over all he had seen under the sun. Before, the vale of the sunless not-knowing of a miscarriage having its name covered by darkness seemed preferable to living; and all man's works a seeking after wind. So, of course, there was "a time for dying." But now Koheleth writes, ". . . there is no work or thought or knowledge or wisdom in Sheol, to which you are going" (Eccles. 9:10b). While the fate of the sons of men and the fate of the beasts are the same, still "a living dog is better than a dead lion"; and to be a living man is better than either, because of what Koheleth means by "living." "He who is joined with all the living has hope" (Eccles. 9:4), and that is hardly a way to describe dogs or lions. Koheleth, however, identifies the grandeur of man not so much with hope as with awareness, even awareness of dying, and the misery of man with the indignity of dying of which he, in his nobility, is aware. "For the living know that they will die," he writes, "but the dead know nothing . . ." (Eccles. 9:5). Before, the dead or those who never lived had superiority; now, it is the living who are superior precisely by virtue of their awareness of dying and of its indignity to the knowing human spirit.

Therefore, I suggest that Koheleth probed the human condition to a depth to which more than twenty centuries later Blaise Pascal came. "Man is but a reed, the feeblest in nature, but he is a thinking reed. . . . A vapour, a drop of water, is sufficient to slay him. But were the universe to crush him, man would still be nobler than that which kills him, for *he knows that he dies,* while the universe knows nothing of the advantage it has over him. Thus our whole dignity consists in thought."[17] (Italics added.)

So the grandeur and misery of man are fused together in the human reality and experience of death. To deny the indignity of death requires that the dignity of man be refused also. The more acceptable in itself death is, the less the worth or uniqueness ascribed to the dying life.

TRUE HUMANISM AND THE DREAD OF DEATH

I always write as the ethicist I am, namely, a Christian ethicist, and not as some hypothetical common denominator. On common concrete problems I, of course, try to elaborate analysis at the point or on a terrain where there may be convergence of vectors that began in other ethical outlooks and onlooks. Still one should not pant for agreement as the hart pants for the waterbrooks, lest the substance of one's ethics dissolve into vapidity. So in this section I want, among other things, to exhibit some of the meaning of "Christian humanism" in regard to death and dying, in the confidence that this will prove tolerable to my colleagues for a time, if not finally instructive to them.

In this connection, there are two counterpoised verses in the First Epistle of St. John that are worth pondering. The first reads: "Perfect love casts out fear" (which being interpreted means: Perfect care of the dying casts out fear of one's own death or rejection of their dying because of fear of ours). The second verse reads: "Where fear is, love is not perfected" (which being interpreted means: Where fear of death and dying remains, medical and human care of the dying is not perfected). That states nothing so much as the enduring dubiety and ambiguity of any mortal man's care of another through his dying. At the same time there is here applied without modification a standard for unflinching care of a dying fellow-man, or short of that of any fellow mortal any time. That standard is cut to the measure of the perfection in benevolence believed to be that of our Father in Heaven in his dealings with mankind. So there is "faith-ing" in an ultimate righteousness beyond the perceptible human condition presupposed by those verses that immediately have to do simply with loving and caring.

Whatever non-Christians may think about the *theology* here entailed, or about similar foundations in any religious ethics, I ask that the notation upon or penetration of the human condition be attended to. Where and insofar as fear is, love and care for the dying cannot be perfected in moral agents or the helping professions. The religious traditions have one way of addressing that problematic. In the modern age the problematic itself is avoided by various forms and degrees of denial of the tragedy of death which proceeds first to reduce the unique worth and once-for-all-ness of the individual life-span that dies.

Perhaps one can apprehend the threat posed to the dignity of man (i.e., in an easy and ready dignifying of death) by many modern viewpoints, especially those dominating the scientific community, and their superficial equivalents in our culture generally, by bringing into view three states of consciousness in the Western past.

The burden of the Hebrew Scriptures was man's obedience or disobedience to covenant, to Torah. Thus sin was the problem, and death came in only as a subordinate theme; and, as one focus for the problematic of the human condition, this was a late development. In contrast, righteousness and disobedience (sin) was a subordinate theme in Greek religion. The central theme of Greek religious thought and practice was the problem of death—a problem whose solution was found either by initiation into religious cults that promised to extricate the soul from its corruptible shroud or by belief in the native power of the soul to outlast any number of bodies. Alongside these, death was at the heart of the pathos of life depicted in Greek tragical drama, against which, and against the flaws of finitude in general, the major character manifested his heroic transcendence. So sin was determinative for the Hebrew consciousness; death for the Greek consciousness.

Consciousness III was Christianity, and by this, sin and death were tied together in Western man's awareness of personal existence. These two foci of man's misery and of his need for redemption—sin and death—were inseparably fused. This new dimension of man's awareness of himself was originally probed most profoundly by St. Paul's Letter to the Romans (5-7). Those opaque reflections, I opine, were once understood not so much by the intellect as along the pulses of ordinary people in great numbers, in taverns and market places; and it represents a cultural breakdown without parallel that these reflections are scarcely understandable to the greatest intelligences today. A simple night school lesson in them may be gained by simply pondering a while the two verses quoted above from St. John's Epistle.

The point is that according to the Christian saga the Messiah did not come to bring boors into culture. Nor did he bear epilepsy or psychosomatic disorders to gain victory over them in the flesh before the interventions of psychoneurosurgery. Rather is he said to have been born *mortal* flesh to gain for us a foretaste of victory over sin and death where those two twin enemies had taken up apparently secure citadel.

Again, the point for our purposes is not to be drawn into agreement or disagreement with those theological affirmations, and it is certainly not to be tempted into endless speculation about an after-life. Crucial instead is to attend to the notation on the human condition implied in all that. Death is an enemy even if it is the last enemy to be fully conquered in the Fulfillment, the eschaton; meanwhile, the sting of death is sin. Such was the new consciousness-raising that Christianity brought into the Western world. And the question is whether in doing so it has not grasped some important experiential human realities better than most philosophies, whether it was not attuned to essential ingredients of the human condition vis-a-vis death—whatever the truth or falsity of its theological address to that condition.

The foregoing, I grant, may be an oversimplification; and I am aware of needed corrections more in the case of Hebrew humanism than in the case of Greek humanism. The New Testament word, "He will wipe away every tear from their eyes, and death shall be no more, neither shall there be mourning nor crying nor pain any more, for the former things have passed away," (Rev. 21:3,4) has its parallel in the Hebrew Bible: "He will swallow up death forever, and the Lord God will wipe away tears from all faces . . ." (Isa. 25:8). Again, since contemplating the Lord God may be too much for us, I ask only that we attend to the doctrine of death implied in these passages: it is an enemy, surely, and not simply an acceptable part of the natural order of things. And the connection between dread of death and sin, made most prominent in Christian consciousness, was nowhere better stated than in Ecclesiastes: "This is the root of the evil in all that happens under the sun, that one fate comes to all. Therefore, men's minds are filled with evil and there is madness in their hearts while they live, for they know that afterward—they are off to the dead!"

One can, indeed, ponder that verse about the source of all evil in the apprehended evil of death together with another verse in Ecclesiastes which reads: "Teach us so to number our days that we may apply our hearts unto wisdom." The first says that death is an evil evil: it is experienced as a threatening limit that begets evil. The second says that death is a good evil: that experience also begets good. Without death, and death perceived as a threat, we would also have no reason to "number our days" so as to ransom the time allotted to us, to receive life as a precious gift, to drink the wine of gladness in toast to every successive present moment. Instead, life would be an endless boredom and boring because endless; there would be no reason to probe its depths while there is still time. Some there are who number their days so as to apply their hearts unto eating, drinking and being merry—for tomorrow we die. Some there are who number their days so as to apply their hearts unto wisdom—for tomorrow we die. Both are life-spans enhanced in importance and in individuation under the level of the beasts of the field are both enhanced because of death, the horizon of human existence. So, debarment from access to the tree of life was on the horizon and a sequence of the events in the Garden of Paradise; the temptation in eating the fruit of the tree of knowledge of good and evil was because that seemed a way for mortal creatures to become like gods. The punishment of that is said to have been death; and no governor uses as a penalty something that anyone can simply choose to believe to be a good or simply receive as a neutral or dignified, even ennobling, part of life. So I say death may be a good evil or an evil evil, but it is perceived as an evil or experienced indignity in either case. Existential anxiety or general anxiety (distinguishable from particular fears or removable anxieties) means anxiety over death toward which we live. That paradoxically, as Reinhold Niebuhr said, is the source of all human creativity and of all human sinfulness.

Of course, the sages of old could and did engage in a calculus of comparative indignities. "O death, your sentence is welcome," wrote Ben Sira, "to a man worn out with age, worried about everything, disaffected and beyond endurance" (Eccles. 41:2,3). Still death was a "sentence," not a natural event acceptable in itself. Moreover, not every man grows old gracefully in the Psalms; instead, one complains:

Take pity on me, Yahweh,
I am in trouble now.

Grief wastes away my eye,
My throat, my inmost parts.
For my life is worn out with sorrow,
My years with sighs;
My strength yields under misery,
My bones are wasting away.
To every one of my oppressors
I am contemptible,
Loathsome to my neighbors,
To my friends a thing of fear.
Those who see me in the street
Hurry past me.
I am forgotten, as good as dead, in their hearts,
Something discarded. (Ps. 31:9-12)

What else is to be expected if it be true that the madness in men's hearts while they live, and the root of all evil in all that happens under the sun, lies in the simple fact that every man consciously lives toward his own death, knowing that afterward he too is off to the dead? Where fear is—fear of the properly dreadful—love and care for the dying cannot be perfected.

Unless one has some grounds for respecting the shadow of death upon every human countenance—grounds more ultimate than perceptible realities—then it makes good sense as a policy of life simply to try to outlast one's neighbors. One can, for example, *generalize*, and so attenuate our neighbors' irreplaceability. "If I must grieve whenever the bell tolls," writes Carey McWilliams, "I am never bereft: some of my kinsmen will remain. Indeed, I need not grieve much—even, lest I suggest some preference among my brethren, should not grieve much—for each loss is small compared to what remains."[18] But that solace, we know, is denied the dead who have lost everything making for worth in this their world. Realistic love for another irreplaceable, non-interchangeable individual human being means, as Unamuno wrote, care for another "doomed soul."

In this setting, let us now bring into consideration some empirical findings that in this day are commonly supposed to be more confirmatory than wisdom mediated from the heart.

In the second year anatomy course, medical students clothe with "gallows humor" their encounter with the cadaver which once was a human being alive. That defense is not to be despised; nor does it necessarily indicate socialization in shallowness on the students' part. Even when dealing with the remains of the long since dead, there is special tension involved—if I mistook not a recent address by Renée Fox—when performing investigatory medical actions involving the face, the hands, and the genitalia. This thing-in-the-world that was once a man alive we still encounter as once a communicating human being, not quite as an object of research or instruction. Face and hands, yes; but why the genitalia? Those reactions must seem incongruous to a resolutely biologizing age. For a beginning of an explanation, one might take up the expression "carnal knowledge"—which was the best thing about the movie bearing that title—and behind that go to the expression "carnal *conversation*," an old, legal term for adultery, and back of both to the Biblical word "knew" in "And Adam *knew* his wife and begat. . . ." Here we have an entire anthropology impacted in a word, not a squeamish euphemism. In short, in those reactions of medical students can be discerned a sensed relic of the human being bodily experiencing and communicating, and the body itself uniquely speaking.

Notably, however, there's no "gallows humor" used when doing or observing one's first autopsy, or in the emergency room when a D.O.A. (Dead on Arrival) is brought in with his skull cleaved open. With regard to the "newly dead" we come as close as we possibly can to experiencing the incommensurable contrast between life and death. Yet those sequential realities—life and death—here juxtaposed never *meet* in direct encounter. So we never have an impression or experience of the measure and meaning of the two different worlds before which we stand in the autopsy and the emergency room. A cadaver has over time become almost a thing-in-the-world from which to gain knowledge of the human body. While *there* a little humor helps, to go about acquiring medical knowledge from autopsies requires a different sort of inward effort to face down or live with our near-experience of the boundary of life and death. The cleavage in the brain may be quite enough and more than enough to *explain* rationally why this man was D.O.A. But, I suggest, there can be no gash deep enough, no physical event destructive enough to account for the felt difference between life and death that we face here. The physician or medical student may be a confirmed materialist. For him the material explanation of this death may be quite sufficient rationally. Still the heart has its reasons that the reason knows not of; and, I suggest, the awakening of these feelings of awe and dread should not be repressed in anyone whose calling is to the human dignity of caring for the dying.

In any case, from these empirical observations, if they be true, let us return to a great example of theological anthropology in order to try to comprehend why death was thought to be the assault of an enemy. According to some readings, Christians in all ages should be going about bestowing the gift of immortality on one another posthaste. A distinguished Catholic physician, beset by what he regarded as the incorrigible problems of medical ethics today, once shook his head in my presence and wondered out loud why the people who most believe in an afterlife should have established so many hospitals! That seems to require explanation, at least as against silly interpretations of "otherworldliness." The answer is that none of the facts or outlooks cited ever denied the reality of death, or affirmed that death ever presents a friendly face (except comparatively). The explanation lies in the vicinity of Christian anthropology and the Biblical view that death is an enemy. That foundation of Western medicine ought not lightly to be discarded, even if we need to enliven again the sense that there are limits to man's struggle against that alien power.

Far from the otherworldliness or body-soul dualism with which he is often charged, St. Augustine went so far as to say that "the body is not an extraneous ornament or aid, but a part of man's very nature."[19] Upon that understanding of the human being, Augustine could then express a quite realistic account of "the dying process":

> Wherefore, as regards bodily death, that is, the separation of the soul from the body, it is good to none while it is being endured by those whom we say are in the article of death [dying]. For the very violence with which the body and soul are wrenched asunder, which in the living are conjoined and closely intertwined, brings with it a harsh experience, jarring horribly on nature as long as it continues, till there comes a total loss of sensation, which arose from the very interpenetration of flesh and spirit.[20]

From this Augustine correctly concludes: "Wherefore death is indeed . . . good to none while it is actually suffered, and

while it is subduing the dying to its power. . . ." His ultimate
justifications attenuate not at all the harshness of that alien
power's truimph. Death, he only says, is "meritoriously endured for the sake of winning what *is* good. And regarding
what happens after death, it is no absurdity to say that death
is good to the good, and evil to the evil."[21] But that is not to
say that death as endured in this life, or as life's terminus, is
itself in any way good. He even goes so far as to say:

> For though there can be no manner of doubt
> that the souls of the just and holy lead lives in
> peaceful rest, yet so much better would it be for
> them to be alive in healthy, well-conditioned
> bodies, that even those who hold the tenet that
> it is most blessed to be quit of every kind of
> body, condemn this opinion in spite of them-
> selves.[22]

Thus, for Biblical or later Christian anthropology, the only
possible form which human life in any true and proper sense
can take here or hereafter is "somatic." That is the Pauline
word; we today say "psychosomatic." Therefore, for Christian theology death may be a "conquered enemy"; still it was
in the natural order—and as long as the generations of mankind endure will remain—an enemy still. To pretend otherwise adds insult to injury—or, at least, carelessness.

There are two ways, so far as I can see, to reduce the
dreadful visage of death to a level of inherently acceptable
indifference. One way is to subscribe to an interpretation of
"bodily life" that reduces it to an acceptable level of indifference to the person long before his dying. That—if anyone can
believe it today, or if it is not a false account of human nature
—was the way taken by Plato in his idealized account of the
death of Socrates. (It should be remembered that we know
not whether Socrates' hands trembled as he yet bravely drank
the hemlock, no more than we know how Isaac experienced
dying when "fullness of years" came upon him. Secondary
accounts of these matters are fairly untrustworthy.)

Plato's dialogue *The Phaedo* may not "work" as a proof
of the immortality of the soul. Still it decisively raises the
question of immortality by its thorough representation of the
incommensurability between mental processes and bodily
processes. Few philosophers today accept the demonstration
of the mind's power to outlast bodies because the mind itself
is not material, or because the mind "plays" the body like a

musician the lyre. But most of them are still wrestling with the mind-body problem, and many speak of two separate languages, a language for mental events isomorphic with our language for brain events. That's rather like saying the same thing as Socrates (Plato) while claiming to have gone beyond him (Soren Kierkegaard).

I cite *The Phaedo* for another purpose: to manifest one way to render death incomparably welcomed. Those who most have mature manhood in exercise—the lovers of wisdom—have desired death and dying all their life long, in the sense that they seek "in every sort of way to dissever the soul from the communion of the body"; "thought is best when the mind is gathered into herself and none of the things trouble her—neither sounds nor sights nor pain nor any pleasure—when she takes leave of the body. . . ." That life is best and has nothing to fear that has "the habit of the soul gathering and collecting herself into herself from all sides out of the body." (Feminists, note the pronouns.)

Granted, Socrates' insight is valid concerning the self's transcendence, when he says: "I am inclined to think that these muscles and bones of mine would have gone off long ago to Megara and Boeotia—by the dog, they would, if they had been moved only by their own idea of what was best. . . ." Still Crito had a point, when he feared that the impending dread event had more to do with "the same Socrates who has been talking and conducting the argument" than Socrates is represented to have believed. To fear the loss of Socrates, Crito had not to fancy, as Socrates charged, "that I am the other Socrates whom he will soon see, a dead body." Crito had only to apprehend, however faintly, that there is not an entire otherness between those two Socrates *now*, in this living being; that there was unity between, let us say, Socrates the conductor of arguments and Socrates the gesticulator or the man who stretched *himself* because his muscles and bones grew weary from confinement.

The other way to reduce the dreadful visage of death is to subscribe to a philosophy of "human life" that reduces the stature, the worth, and the irreplaceable uniqueness of the individual person (long before his dying) to a level of acceptable transiency or interchangeability. True, modern culture is going this way. But there have been other and better ways of stipulating that the image of death across the human countenance is no shadow. One was that of Aristotelian philosophy.

According to its form-matter distinction, reason, the formal principle, is definitive of essential humanity. That is universal, eternal as logic. Matter, however, is the individuating factor. So when a man who bears a particular name dies, only the individuation disintegrates—to provide matter for other forms. Humanity goes on in other instances. Anything unique or precious about mankind is not individual. There are parallels to this outlook in Eastern religions and philosophies, in which the individual has only transiency, and should seek only that, disappearing in the Fulfillment into the Divine pool.

These then are two ways of denying the dread of death. Whenever these two escapes are *simultaneously* rejected— i.e., if the "bodily life" is neither an ornament nor a drag but a part of man's very nature; and if the "personal life" of an individual in his unique life-span is accorded unrepeatable, noninterchangeable value—then it is that Death the Enemy again comes into view. Conquered or Unconquerable. A true humanism and the dread of death seem to be dependent variables. I suggest that it is better to have the indignity of death on our hands and in our outlooks than to "dignify" it in either of these two possible ways. Then we ought to be much more circumspect in speaking of death with dignity, and hesitant to—I almost said—thrust that upon the dying! Surely, a proper care for them needs not only to know the pain of dying which human agency may hold at bay, but also care needs to acknowledge that there is grief over death which no human agency can alleviate.

1. Paul Ramsey, "On (Only) Caring for the Dying," *The Patient as Person* (New Haven: Yale University Press, 1971).

2. Elisabeth Kübler-Ross, *On Death and Dying* (New York: Macmillan, 1969), p. 247.

3. Schopenhauer's characterization of human history: If you've read one page, you've read it all.

4. Wittgenstein, *Tractatus*, 6.4311.

5. James Van Evra, "On Death as a Limit," *Analysis* 31 [5] (April, 1971), 170-76.

6. Erik Erikson, "Identity and the Life Cycle," *Psychological Issues*, I, [1] (New York: International University Press, 1959).

7. David Hendin, *Death as a Fact of Life* (New York: W. W. Norton, 1973).

8. Reported in *ibid.*, p. 89.

9. *The Florida Times-Union*, Jacksonville, Fla., Jan. 11, 1973.

10. Marya Mannes, *Last Rights* (New York: William Morrow, 1973), p. 6, (cf. 80, 133).

11. Hendin, *Death as a Fact of Life*, p. 103.

12. What, after all, is the point of promoting, as if it were a line of reasoning, observations such as that said to be inscribed on W. C. Field's tombstone: "On the whole I'd rather be here than in Philadelphia"?

13. I may add that while the House of Delegates did not endorse any particular form to express an individual's wishes relating prospectively to his final illness, it recognized that individuals have a right to express them. While it encouraged physicians to discuss such matters with patients and attend to their wishes, the House nevertheless maintained a place for the conscience and judgment of a physician in determining indicated treatment. It did not subsume every consideration under the rubric of the patient's right to refuse treatment (or to have refused treatment). That sole action-guide can find no medical or logical reason for distinguishing, in physician actions, between the dying and those who simply have a terminal illness (or have this "dying life," Augustine's description of all of us). It would also entail a belief that wishing or autonomous choice makes the moral difference between life and death decisions which then are to be imposed on the physician-technician; and that, to say the least, is an ethics that can find no place for either reason or sensibility.

14. Cf. the report of a Swedish survey by Gunnar Biörck, M.D., in *Archives of Internal Medicine*, October, 1973; news report in *The New York Times*, Oct. 31, 1973.

15. In the whole literature on death and dying, there is no more misquoted sentence, or statement taken out of context, than Koheleth's "time to be born and a time to die"—unless it be "Nor strive officiously to keep alive." The latter line is from an ironic poem by the nineteenth century poet Arthur Hugh Clough, entitled "The Latest Decalogue":

> "Thou shalt not kill; but need'st not strive
> Officiously to keep alive.
> Do not adultery commit;
> Advantage rarely comes of it:
> Thou shalt not steal; an empty feat,
> When it's so lucrative to cheat:
> Bear not false witness; let the lie
> Have time on its own wings to fly:
> Thou shalt not covet; but tradition
> Approves all forms of competition.

> The sum of all is, thou shalt love
> If anybody, God above:
> At any rate, shalt never labor
> More than myself to love thy neighbor."

16. Nietzsche, *Thus Spake Zarathustra,* especially XLVI and LXVI.

17. Pascal. *Pensees,* p. 347.

18. Wilson Carey McWilliams, *The Idea of Fraternity in America* (Berkeley: University of California Press, 1973), p. 48.

19. Augustine, *City of God,* Book I, Chapter XIII.

20. *Ibid.,* Book XIII, Chapter VI.

21. *Ibid.,* Book XIII, Chapter VIII.

22. *Ibid.,* Book XIII, Chapter XIX.

DEATH'S PEDAGOGY

The Assault on the Last Taboo

Paul Ramsey

As a teacher, death is a stern disciplinarian. She manifests more than a little "over-againstness" in relation to her pupils. Because of this, we who know we are mortal have the opportunity to learn "so to number our days that we may get a heart of wisdom."

Many a contemporary view of life and death encourages us to avoid that tutelage. "Pre-death morticians" are telling us how to "manage death" so as to avoid facing that threatening, bracing Other. We had rather die in rational control of our dying, we contemplate insuring that we do so rather than risk the instruction in facing death as an alien power. Such is the outlook, I believe, of Marya Mannes' recent book, *Last Rights* (William Morrow, $5.95).

The word "rights" in the title says it all. In the moment and mood of insisting on rights, one is hardly forming oneself in the wisdom of acknowledged limitations. Mannes can write that "the name of the oratorio is euthanasia"—thus banishing with a phrase all engagement in what John Donne called "Death's Duell." And her statement that "dying is merely suspension within a mystery" seems calculated to induce vertigo in face of a fascinating abyss in prospect. Mannes is playing truant.

Moreover, there is a philosophy of human life entailed in that view of death. There may be some truth in saying that "those who give us the most profound insights into death are those who have most fully lived the life of the spirit: the creators among us." Even so, her illustrations are mainly drawn from those whose passion for a full life turns suddenly into an embrace of death. That's a fair proof that neither true life nor real dying has been the instructor.

In the full scope of her book, veneration for the free spirits and the creators among us turns into an elitist practical philosophy of the insightful or rational *versus* the dumb, the brave *versus* (understandably, of course) the cowards. "We continue to call suicide 'irrational,' " Mannes writes, "on the extraordinary assumption that the millions of people in this world who continue to live miserable lives are 'rational.'" A rather condescending and contemptible attitude, I should say, toward the miserable among earth's persevering inhabitants. This is qualified, of course, by the author's recognition that they may have in some ways the better part, and we the worse. Such people often take death in stride with ritual and chant; perhaps "the privacy so dear to the civilized and economically secure has, in banishing communal ritual and common experience, made acceptance of death intolerable."

Among us, however, the brightest and the best in increasing numbers are choosing a still higher way; and here we come to the crux of the book. Contemplating this nation full of half-lives in wards and nursing homes, sustained by tenacity, Mannes takes up a very definite attitude toward that tenacity (not toward the misery as such) as morally second-rate. "The inference here might be," she writes when first insinuating the point, "that those who opt for life on any terms have never known life in its fullest terms." She then observes, seemingly, descriptively, "Millions have never lived to their fullest capacities. And because of this, they would settle rather for a minimal life than no life at all. Their dread of death supersedes all else." Then on the next page she fully endorses the moral judgment underlying those statements: "I believe that the will to die is the direct reflection of the quality of life." "If we have lived to the fullest of our capacities, dying is merely suspension within a mystery. If our lives have seemed wasted or futile, death is more reprieve than reprimand," the author writes just before introducing her own "Living Will" with its specification of many conditions under which she would choose death.

Therefore the reader should reevaluate earlier vignettes that were part of Mannes' accumulation of indignities. For example, her report with obvious distaste of the hospital attendant who cheerily described a patient who "said just yesterday, 'I want to die,' and then right away, 'Can I have two eggs?' "; or the author's report (her rightful distaste this time made explicit in parentheses) of a nursing home supervisor who "said tartly, 'Y' know, they keep on living, they just cling on . . .' (as if this were a nuisance, like incontinence)."

Of course, such tenacity is not a mere nuisance to Marya
Mannes. Still, despite the growing euthanasia movement (con-
fusedly, that means active or passive, and even the use of pain-
relieving drugs!), she believes that a solution must be devised
for those who cannot escape the cake of custom or church. The
"independent spirit" is rare; most of us "fear single action"; it
is easier to do what others do; think what others think." So in
a penultimate chapter the author speaks of "alternative";
these "avenues must be kept open for those who cannot, or will
not, bring themselves to join" the euthanasia movement.

Alternatives

Astonishingly, examples of the alternative devised for the
groundlings are Youville, a Roman Catholic Hospital in Cambridge, Mass. [". . . You should do more to help him be a part
of life as long as he is with us"]; Calvary Hospital in New
York, founded over 70 years ago by a group of Catholic women
[". . . The sense of peace and light and—very palpably—love,
is pervasive"; "There was no smell of death in this place where
it claimed many, so soon. Only compassion, and recognition
long withheld"]; St. Christopher's Hospice in London created
and run by Cicely Saunders; and the Hospice to be built in
New Haven under the leadership of Florence Wald. These alternatives are movingly described by Marya Mannes. They are
among the most graced and graceful institutionalizations of
care for the dying that exist in the modern Western world. Yet,
if I have not entirely misread this book, they are second-best.
The brightest, the best and truly brave will take the high road
to rationalized or administered dying.

By way of contrast, Stewart Alsop, in the written record
he left behind, had not yet wrestled from death more than a
glimpse of its friendly face; nor for him did the human problematic in facing death vary "accordingly as the candidate/pre-
liminary was" (Emily Dickinson). *Ecclesiastes'* talk about the
"times" gain entrance as only a reference in the last lines of Alsop's remarkable account of his own *Stay of Execution* (J. P.
Lippincott, $8.95). "There is a time to live, but there is a time
to die," the book concludes. "That time has not yet come for
me. But it will. It will come for us all." That time came for
Stewart Alsop on May 26, 1974. *Stay of Execution* is a remarkable personal document, a rich heritage of wisdom for his family and friends and for the rest of us who read it with some sensitivity to death's tuition for the still living.

The "fact" that death comes to everyone in time obviously was no replacement for and was little assistance in Alsop's own task of dying.

All along, of course, there is a remarkable "distancing" from death not only to keep it at bay but to entice its friendly features. Alsop converses, as it were, with "the man in the white nightgown" (W.C. Fields), with "Uncle Thanatos," once with "dear old Uncle Thanatos." Two lessons he has learned: "that most people are nicer than they seem to be" and "that, although it can be hard at first, in time one becomes accustomed to living with Uncle Thanatos"—the "strange unconscious, indescribable process . . . of adjustment whereby one comes to terms with death." The abundant life he had lived made little difference in that engagement. There was not the slightest tendency to suppose that lesser clods cling to life because they are lesser. Alsop gained both in solidarity with humankind and in appreciation for the uniqueness of his own and others' individual existence.

There was also a musical metaphor that seemed appropriate to Alsop's experience—but it was not, as for Mannes, the "oratorio of euthanasia." A musical analogy comes in when Alsop, mixing metaphors, speaks of the "little pea of fear at the back of my mind," the fear of death. "It was always present, like a kind of background music. Sometimes it receded almost to inaudibility, and then sometimes it would come blaring back, accompanied by a sense of incredibility, 'My God, I really do have cancer, and I really am going to die.'" While his first reaction was to pounce upon a single ominous phrase in his doctor's report of the results of a test, he found he could tune the music down. "The background music, the music of death, blared high again for a moment. But I put John's remark out of my mind—an essential art for one in fear of death—and the background music—or rather background cacaphony—not exactly a headache but a kind of murmuring unpleasantness. . . . The page would blur, and the cacaphony in my head would mount from a murmur to a shout."

Having begun a "journal" early in his illness, Alsop later observes that in many disguises "the fear leaps out, every fourth page or so, from my notebooks." Bad test-results he dreaded only "second most"; "what I dread most is getting very sick and dying." He came even to believe that he could tell his own symptoms for a really low count of platelets (which physicians say is impossible for a patient to feel) because then "I do not feel at all well in my skin. There is a constant sense of uneasiness."

There was nothing whatsoever about death that in itself was good or could have been timely; not his very own dying. A person's particular death had to be "learned" (as the uneducated sometimes ungrammatically say for "taught") to be good for him. And in the same instructive dialogue Alsop had also to be "learned" the irreplaceable uniqueness and importance of Stewart Alsop's life-span in the vast sea of humanity. Only the grim Reaper "learns us" that. That, I suppose, is one thing past theologians and philosophers (e.g. Bernard Bosanquet) alike have meant by saying that life is a "vale of soul making."

Alsop, of course, was a lucky man; he had the consolations of philosophy and quotations remembered in untranquility as he probed to find behind the masks of death its true *persona*, or its nature manifest (showing forth) in more than one *personae*. But these were not cheerful poems like the one Mannes quotes from Walt Whitman:

> Dark Mother always gliding near with soft feet,
> Have none chanted for thee a chant of fullest welcome?
> Then I chant it for thee; I glorify thee above all:
> I bring thee a song, that when thou must indeed come,
> Come unfalteringly.

Rather more to the point for Alsop were T.S. Eliot's lines:

> I have seen the moment of my greatness flicker.
> I have seen the eternal Footman hold my coat and snicker,
> And in short, I was afraid.

Also he writes, "I was never 'half in love with easeful death,' and I suspect John Keats wasn't either." Consolation and commonality in the human condition were, I judge, conveyed by remembering the words, "On pain of death, name not death to me. It is a word infinitely terrible" (from John Webster, *The Duchess of Malfi*, Alsop thought); and in recalling words from a children's game, "Heavy, heavy [hangs over your head], what hangs over?"—and even in the "horrid little poem": "The worms crawl in and the worms crawl out/They crawl all over your face and snout/ They make a helluva mess of you." There was nothing maudlin or excessively self-pitying in such thoughts, it seems to me, but rather instruction in the truth *pro nobis*.

Following tests, "bad counts were bad news—much worse news than the gloomiest headlines in the newspapers." So much for the consolations of "social immortality" or Jay Lifton's "surrogates for immortality" needed in the modern age, and for what Robert Morrison thinks the continuation of Cornell is going to do for him. What matters to a dying patient is simply "how far he is away from death." So Alsop himself distanced from it as much as he could. He called himself and was called "Dr. Alsop." To a perception of the "odd sense of unreality: that it was *my* death we were discussing," he adds an additional layer of consciousness: "This is a most interesting experience," he twice observes, "although one wishes one were not so personally involved." Even the one "personally" involved is the impersonal pronoun "one" and not quite yet "I myself." He was aware of the need for "papering over misery," that "a man can't be afraid all the time" and can only talk about it when it is over.

The constant tribute to his wife Tish is not for articulated understanding but for silence mutually shared and for "the squeeze of a warm hand in time of darkness and fear." *Dreadful* is the mysterious power of fate" (italics added), Alsop twice comments, once when reviewing the notebook record of his recent experience, and again when remembering what might have been or not been if in Great Britain during World War I a comrade in the King's Royal Rifle Corps called "Plowboy" had not been ordered to guard duty and Alsop gone instead to a party where he first met Tish: "my six children would not exist," he writes. Not that six other children might exist instead. The singularity of the reference to those non-interchangeable human beings is worth pondering, and applying as well to the life-span here ending by the dreadful verdict of death. The grim Instructor was "learning" Stewart Alsop a thing or two.

Death is nothing but dreadful to any human being; it is not a fact of life negotiable or manageable like other facts. Quite naturally, then, Alsop thinks of experiences of combat in war, "the first sudden shock of realizing that the people on the other side are really trying to kill you"—after which "an unhappy inner stolidity takes over." That is all that is meant by an understanding of death as always an Enemy, that there are "people" on the other side who are trying to kill you and that in the case of death in the end "they" are going to succeed. So Alsop thinks of his children: while glad that none of his boys has been in war, he wonders whether they may not have missed something all the same. They may have missed finding out more about themselves; it might have been useful for them to face the chance of death when they were young; that "helps to prepare you to face death when you are old." In any case, Alsop "did not realize, until I got sick, how much the war had meant to me."

Combat Imagery

Applying the combat-imagery to his own case he composed in Churchillian periods the following expression of his personal stance toward the Enemy: "We will fight amongst the platelets. We will fight in the bone marrow. We will fight in the peripheral blood. We will never surrender."

Having written *that* in a letter to a friend, Alsop began to cry for "the first time in about fifty years," and in order to get away from his hospital roommate he went into the bathroom and "cried my heart out" and felt a good deal better. There are little ritual "prayers" which he repeats: "Thank you God, thank you Mother, thank you Father, thank you Aggie" or "Please God, please Mother [who is thought maybe to be in the vicinity of God the Father interceding for him as she once did with Franklin Delano Roosevelt!], please Father, Please Aggie"—the latter petition because "one wants to put a chip on the double zero, just in case." That, too, explains the "inexplicable" ease with which he decided to go to NIH from the Georgetown University Hospital: "A man who knows his life is in danger . . . instinctively tries to better the odds."

To understand death to be always an alien power does not mean that it is sensed to crouch and lurk behind every door; it is rather a constant theme or background music: the background of all backgrounds. Combat is aroused only by the blasts or the cacaphony. Most of the time, like Alsop in an acute sense, one is "waiting for the disease to declare itself"—the disease life was born with.

Of course, from time to time in the experience of encountering the prospect of his own dying, Alsop thought of resort to the "bare bodkin," while chatting intermittently with his wife Tish "about things that didn't interest us." Literary man that he was, he wonders "who would fardels bare, to

grunt and sweat under a weary life?'' He refers to Sir William
Osler's suggestion that it might be a good idea to chloroform
everybody on his sixteenth birthday; and observes, "In fact,
chloroform might be appropriate as soon as a person has to
wear reading glasses; that is where the downhill trail really
starts." He thinks of the convenience of an overdose of sleeping pills. Concerning the latter alternative to chemotherapy
and the laminar flow room (where the air comes in one way an
goes out the other, and most of the patients do likewise), he
writes, "I think I'd choose the pills"; but then wonders whether so: ". . . When you're near death you grasp for life." Perhaps one would not then really want to be so "rational"—or
in *that* way rational. "Perhaps I'd simply refuse to take chemotherapy and let nature, in the shape of infection, take its
course."

Finally Alsop expressed another set of dependent variables—different from those of Marya Mannes, who, as we
have seen, seems to believe that the fuller the life, the higher
the "quality" of life that is experienced, then the more acceptance and the less fear of death there will be. Alsop's dependent variables have nothing to do with richness of life or with
a "timeliness" ascribed to the approaching death. His is a
simple, and more universalizable, functional relation: ". . .
When sick the thought of death was more easeful, and far less
terrible than it had been. Afterward, when I felt well again
and believed I was cured, the thought became very terrible."
If true, that means that acceptance of one's own death remains in the end a judgment of comparative indignities still.

The foregoing functional variables—felt sickness, with
the thought of easeful death—are associated with another set
of variables. Hunting and fishing were joyful activities to
Stewart Alsop, sports without which he believed his children
were missing something. Yet he writes that "when I was really
sick—when I was in close fear of Thanatos—I had no desire
at all to kill anything." " 'Neither will I again smite any more
every thing living,' God told Noah, and the phrase kept coming back to me." That formed feeling is quite enough to provide a foundation for the views of some theologians that the
whole creation groans and is in travail, and must needs be
included in the final Redemption—if there is one. Alternatively and with something of a comic spirit, one can try to
imagine one of our pre-death morticians, in Stewart Alsop's
dying presence, lecturing the fishes and the birds on the "naturalness" of dying.

We should not be surprised, therefore, to find no impulse in Alsop toward an elite of courageous free spirits in contrast to other miserables on earth in regard to dying, such as we saw in Mannes. Concerning an ordinary housewife and mother, back in NIH after a relapse, he discerned that she truly had lived a "normal" life in the interim between treatments and "seemed quite unbothered by the sword of Damocles she must have known was hanging over her," not because she was dumb or because death is no evil but because—as in war—"the bravest men were rarely intellectuals or sensitive souls." The woman had learned to live with the background music, subdued or cacophonous, and that requires (death was "learning" Alsop to his platelets) first of all a recognition that the theme of death throughout lived or dying life is no simple tune to dance to. It is always too untimely for that.

"Would it really be worthwhile to spend a month or more cooped up all alone in a laminar flow room, losing my hair and my flesh, either to die in the room or to emerge a bald skeleton and wait for death?" To ask that question and suchlike questions is to ask about comparative medical indignities or comparatively painful or insulting or embarrassing states of human affairs that are, at least, commensurate with one another. Such problems are intrinsically solvable—even if no one knows the answers and there are none given in the back of the book. Even if not quantifiable along a scale, the comparands (if there is such a word) are on the same plane. A logically appropriate class name for *all possible answers* to suchlike questions might be "euthanasia"—although that term is ordinarily used in a sense restricted to only some possible answers, narrowing down to such things as Hamlet's "bare bodkin." (*That* Alsop thought of when he asked himself that question.) But whether the term encompasses all possible answers to such questions, or only some, "euthanasia" is the name for judgments concerning comparative indignities; it is the name for choices made only because there is worse still in the alternative.

A "better death" would be better to say than a "good death." "Euthanasia" is a term as appropriate for all possible answers as it is for some or any answers to questions of that sort. Would it be better to die this way or that? today or tomorrow?—with the medical details and manner of dying to be filled in. Yet the term is really appropriate to *none* of the possible answers. A "better dying," however, is very often a fitting expression. Alas! To the misleading or falsifying term "euthanasia," the expression "death with dignity" adds only cosmetics and an expansive and dubiously persuasive rhetoric. It should be wholly jettisoned from all our talk about death and dying.

From that question Alsop went deeper to ask himself another; not however in the interrogative mood. Rather did the "disease" of dying "declare" itself. It questioned Stewart Alsop; within his conversation with himself, I should say, he felt himself addressed. ". . . Then a sense of the reality of death crowded in on me—the end of a pleasant life, never to see Tish again or Andrew or Nicky or the four other children again, never to go to Needwood again, or laugh with friends, or see the spring again. There came upon me a terrible sense of aloneness, of vulnerability, of nakedness, of helplessness. I got up, and fumbled in my shaving kit, and found another sleeping pill and at last dozed off."

The same experience is recounted on a day among many days he walked with Tish toward the NIH building to be "marrowed." They observed "a well-tended little triangle of roses"; and Alsop wondered why they don't have Japanese beetles against which nothing works at Needwood. Suddenly silence, "and then I knew I wouldn't see the roses next year. . . . I reached out my hand for Tish's. 'I have just run out of my small store of courage.' I said. She squeezed my hand and said nothing."

If he did not know it before or sense it deeply along his bone marrow, death was saying to Stewart Alsop "I'll learn ye" the meaning of being the transient center of a whole world of worth, his one and only world of worth. Not Tish or the children or their home in the country or the roses or the generations of an old and honored Connecticut Yankee family until now close to centers of political power or the world-historical significance of doing columns for *Newsweek* or getting briefings from Kissinger; not these not yet but *he* was passing away. If Alsop's world of concrete values seems to anyone too narrow, let him expand it however much he will, let him also add realized "qualities of life" however much richer, then let him give all that a history however long, and the result is the same.

The death of him who is the center of all that world of worth—and, not to be sentimental, let us add the cessation of the center of all the evil as well as the good that may comprise an experienced life—cannot fail to be for him an irrepparable loss, an unquenchable grief, the threat of all threats, a dread that is more than all fears aggregated together, an approaching "evil" which annuls every ordinary distinction between good and evil, the background of every background that has foregrounds, a murmuring music rising to a cacophony and then receding which, not written in the score, we hear behind all themes of life whether well or poorly sung. If he knew it not from some philosophy of life and death more profound than that which unfolds the banner of "death with dignity," Stewart Alsop was being "learned" by the final "indignity of death" (if anything, that is too mild an expression) to know the meaning of treading water over a thousand fathoms (or, is it twenty thousand?), of his life's course as a trajectory, and the unrepeatable, non-interchangeable significance of an individual life-span. The most faithful stern teacher of that lesson—and there are others—exacts a high tuition, the highest tuition exacted over all the earth. The more "life" (unique, individual human life) becomes a pro-word, the more death is an enemy; the more death is an anti-word, the more pro we should be and will be in respect for any of our companions in this dying life of ours.

Tolstoy's *The Death of Ivan Ilych* is often read as an attack upon the triviality and superficiality with which death is treated by the people round about a dying man, and as a complaint over the awful isolation of the dying under those circumstances. Or as a testimony to the goodness or acceptability of a natural death apart from such "socialization." These things are true, of course. But one has first of all to bring into view the awfulness and awe-fullness of death itself in order to grasp Tolstoy's understanding of the very meaning of that demeaning superficiality painted over the face of death in civilization today. *Ivan Ilych* must not have been on the reading list at Groton; Alsop never refers to that work. Still I venture to say that Alsop was schooled to many of the same insights.

"Beneath the isolation and superficiality he felt suppressed in [Tolstoy writes] because those who came to see him did not wish 'to admit what they all knew and what he knew' was *a sense of the awfulness and uniqueness of dying:* 'Those lies—*lies enacted over him* on the eve of his death and destined to *degrade this awful solemn act* to the level of visitations, their curtains, their sturgeon for dinner—were a terrible agony to Ivan Ilych. . . . The *awful, terrible act of dying was,* he could see, *reduced* by those about him *to the level of a casual, unpleasant, and almost indecorous incident* (as if someone entered a drawing room diffusing an unpleasant odor)" (italics added).

And what was so special about Ivan Ilych's death that prevented his taking toward it—at least as an ideal—the stance of "a rational man," if not the stance of these men, then some others, perhaps the outlook of a compassionate Ideal Observer who views his death as one among others? What so precious was at stake in excepting his death from the visitation of those "lies enacted over him" that had first to remove the taste of it? Ivan Ilych had always been persuaded of the correctness of the logical syllogism, "Caius is a man, man is mortal, therefore Caius is mortal." That was "correct as applied to Caius but certainly not as applied to himself. That Caius—man in the abstract—was mortal was perfectly correct, but he was not Caius, not an abstract man, but a creature quite separate from all others."

Why, separate from all others? And why would he particularly be degraded by any degradation of the awful, unique, terrible, solemn act of dying? Because of who he was that was dying. Not simply *assertedly* no abstraction. But a human being in bodily identity with that dying process. Not simply a self-centered collection of specific memories: "He had been little Vanya, with toys, a coachman and a nurse." That would seem individuation enough—all elements, doubtless, not without sense and touch. But one in particular strikes me as suggestive of the memory saturated with sense—the smell of leather and the feel of roundness and bodily agility in play— that here was dying. "What did Caius," Ivan Ilych asks, "know of the smell of that striped leather ball Vanya had been so fond of?" Someone should pay attention to what here is forever to be no more when Ivan Ilych dies. He was comprised of that. At least *he* must pay attention. None do, who treat him and that ball as an incident, one among the many. Rather like Stewart Alsop's roses at NIH; or better still his country home to him, and Tish and his children.

In any case, the humanity of mankind is at stake in how, after sex, we go about assaulting the last taboo: death. It is not simply that we hoped to improve matters in the first instance by chatting about sex all day long for the last three decades, and now propose to do the same about death. That policy was foredoomed to failure, and foreseeably so without

a sound understanding of *the human* that can be either enhanced or violated by at least some opinions or actions in the
realm of sexuality. Still largely without that normative guide
to action and for social approval, we now have "calisthenic
sexuality," and 12-hours of consecutive pornographic movies
for the purpose to utterly "desensitize" patients in a poor
people's Masters and Johnson "therapeutic" program at certain medical schools, thereafter to begin their reconstruction
as desiring bodily beings.

The same outlook and program addressed to "the last
taboo" can only lead eventually and logically to the same
thing: to "calisthenic dying," i.e. deliberate death, administered death; and submission to the power of a widespread
chatter that tells us again and again fables about "death with
dignity," good deaths. That, indeed, spells the end of "intensive *care*" for the dying! Such consequences come from first
turning mysteries to be contemplated and deepened altogether into problems to be solved. Can human beings be utterly desensitized and then reconstructed in their attitudes
toward death—at least operationally toward the deaths of the
useless—according to the requirements of instrumental social
rationalism? It remains to be seen whether trepidation, awe
and respect in the face of encounters with death because of
the unique human beings therein made manifest, can withstand dissolution in this civilization any more than sexual
relations between human embodied persons withstood reduction to "sturgeon for dinner."

SOME RECENT JEWISH VIEWS ON DEATH AND EUTHANASIA

RABBI IMMANUEL JAKOBOVITS

1. EUTHANASIA

On euthanasia, as on abortion, the immediate past has witnessed a considerable shift of public opinion. But although the destruction of life before birth and before death is now fairly common, the agitation for legalising these practices has so far been less successful among the advocates of euthanasia than among the abortionists. On the other hand, the steady advance of medical science and technological skills toward the often indefinite prolongation of lingering life has progressively accentuated the problem, whether by reason of the mounting costs and suffering imposed on terminal patients, their families and society alike, or by the inevitable denial of the limited facilities to other patients with a better chance of recovery. The painful conflict between this dilemma and the inviolable sanctity of human life finds some recognition in the latest spate of rabbinical writings on euthanasia.

As we have seen in earlier chapters, while Jewish law rates the mitigation of a patient's suffering, especially in the ordeal prior to death, above virtually any other consideration, if necessary even his ability to make his spiritual and temporal preparations for death, what it cannot do is to purchase relief from pain and misery at the cost of life itself. This is based on Judaism's attribution of *infinite* value to human life. Infinity being indivisible, any fraction of life, however limited its expectancy or its health, remains equally infinite in value. Accordingly, even under the prevailing conditions of medical progress, several authorities have again reiterated the unqualified condemnation of euthanasia proper, that is, any active and deliberate hastening of death, branding such action as sheer murder.[1] This applies whether the physician acts with or without the patient's consent; for Judaism rates suicide as even worse than murder in some respects, since there can be no atonement by repentance for self-destruction.[2] A patient must not shrink from spiritual distress by refusing ritually forbidden services or foods if necessary for his healing; how much less may he refuse treatment to escape from physical suffering.[3]

But this uncompromising stance is limited to any direct attack on human life, in however lingering a state of animation. Quite different is the problem of indirect euthanasia, when the patient's death is merely the unpremeditated result of some medication given only to relieve pain or consequent on the withdrawal of treatment.

Analgesics may be administered, even at the risk of possibly shortening the patient's life, so long as they are given solely for the purpose of rendering him insensitive to acute pain.[4] Some authorities also sanction the removal from a dying patient of medications or machines which only serve to prolong his agony, so long as no *natural* means of subsistence (such as food, blood, and oxygen) are withdrawn.[5] Another view goes even further, holding that there is no obligation to maintain the life of a patient in a permanent coma, and with no prospect of recovery, by medical treatment or the provision of food.[6]

But others will not tolerate any relaxation of efforts, however artificial and ultimately hopeless, to prolong life.[7]

2. THE DEFINITION OF DEATH AND RESUSCITATION

The question of defining the moment of death with precision has exercised the minds of Jewish jurists since Talmudic times, mainly in connection with the suspension of the Sabbath laws for the saving of life and the insistence on speedy burial.[8] But lately the problem has been rendered both more difficult and more critically acute by the advance in resuscitation techniques and by the demand for viable cadaver organs for transplant purposes. The lapse of only a few minutes may spell the difference between success and failure in such operations; on the other hand, the premature removal of organs from the dying may hasten death and constitute murder.

The classic Jewish definition, establishing death by the definite cessation of breathing and pulsation, remains essentially valid in principle and for most practical purposes.[9] But in certain cases the prospect of restoring life even after the pulse and respiration have stopped clearly demonstrates the inadequacy of this definition as an invariable rule.

The rule remains firmly fixed to the extent that Jewish law cannot accept the concept of "clinical death". So long as any spontaneous life action by the heart or lungs persists, even "irreversible brain damage" or a flat electro-encephalogram (EEG) reading does not legally establish death. Any action, even at that stage, which would precipitate the patient's final demise is to be regarded as homicide and strictly condemned.[10] In fact, the Israel Chief Rabbinate issued an official declaration in 1971 specifically opposing "brain death" as decisive in determining the thin line of demarcation between life and death.[11] Indeed, if apparent death occurred suddenly or under an anesthetic, one should wait another 20-30 minutes before treating the patient as dead.[12] However, in an article on the subject by a rabbi and a doctor, the joint authors are prepared to regard death as established (a) on a flat EEG reading and in the absence of any other signs of life (unless caused by a faint or drugs), and (b) on the severance of any vital organs or the fracture of the body into two parts, provided consciousness has been lost.[13] But another religious physician, who has written extensively in this field, advocates a stricter view, since "brain death" itself can never be the legal determinant of death.[14]

On the other hand, the general rule of relying simply on the stoppage of breathing and pulsation now requires some modification in the light of the considerable progress in modern resuscitation methods. Since 80% of unconscious patients have their respiration restored by first-aid means of resuscitation,[15] efforts to revive patients must obviously be made and continued even after these signs of life have disappeared, so long as there is any hope of revival.[16] Such patients must be treated as live persons, though one need not apply artificial methods in hopeless cases at the terminal stage.[17] In such cases, it may indeed be wrong to prolong the suffering by artificially maintaining lingering life.[18] But if resuscitation fails, the patient is considered as retroactively dead from the time breathing ceased.[19]

1. E. Waldenberg, *Sepher Ramat Rachel (Kuntres Bikkur Holim)*, end of r*Tzitz Eliezer*, vol. 5, pp. 38 f.; Y. M. Tuczinsky, *Sepher Gesher Hahayim*, Jerusalem, 1960, 1:44; and N. Z. Friedman, r*Netzer Mata'ai*, 1:30.

2. Friedman, *loc. cit.*; N. Telushkin, "A Person's Right Over His Life", in *Or Hamizrach*, Nisan 5721, pp. 20 ff.

3. Telushkin, *loc. cit.*

4. I. J. Unterman, in *No'am*, 13:3 ff.; and M. D. Wollner, "The Physician's Rights and Qualifications", in *Hatorah Vehamedinah*, Jerusalem, vols. 7-8, 5716-7, pp. 319 f.

5. Wollner, *loc. cit.*; see I. Jakobovits, in *No'am*, 6:271, and *Journal*, p. 166.

6. G. A. Rabinowitz and M. Konigsberg, in *Hadarom*, Tishri 5731, p. 75.

7. Friedman and Telushkin, *loci cit.*

8. See *supra*, pp. 126 ff.

9. r*Tzitz Eliezer*, 9:46; and 10:25:4.

10. r*Tzitz Eliezer*, *loc. cit.*; r*Minchat Yitzchak*, 3:7; I. J. Unterman, in *No'am*, 13:3 f. See also *No'am*, 16 (*K.H.*):5 ff.; and Rosner, pp. 130 f.

11. Letter dated 3 Nisan 5731; see also *She'arim*, 19 Shevat 5731; cited in *No'am*, 16 (*K.H.*):10.

12. See sources in note 90 above.

13. Rabinowitz and Konigsberg, *loc. cit.*

14. J. Levy, in *Asya*, no. 3, Shevat 5731, pp. 40 f.; and in *Hama'yan*, Nisan 5732; see *No'am*, 16 (*K.H.*):9 f.

15. J. Levy in *No'am*, 12:300 ff., and 15:294 f.; and in *Hama'yan*, Tishri 5729, Tishri 5730, and Nisan 5732.

16. Unterman, *loc. cit.*; and r*Igrot Mosheh*, vol. 5, *Even Ha'ezer*, no. 146.

17. Unterman, *loc. cit.*

18. r*Lev Aryeh*, 2:37.

19. S. Z. Auerbach, cited in *Hama'yan*, Tishri 5729; see *No'am*, 16 (*K.H.*)X:10.

BENEFICENT EUTHANASIA AND BENEMORTASIA: ALTERNATIVE VIEWS OF MERCY

ARTHUR DYCK

Debates about the rightness or wrongness of mercy killing generate heated displays of emotion. There are those who consider it so cruel deliberately to end the lives of relatively powerless individuals who are dying that they tend to imagine that only people who are merciless, like the prototypical Nazi agent, could sanction such acts. At the same time, there are others who find it so cruel to wait for death if a dying person is suffering that they tend to regard opponents of mercy killing as insensitive moral legalists, willing to be inhuman for the sake of obedience to absolute rules. Both the proponents and opponents of mercy killing think of themselves as merciful, but each finds it virtually impossible to think of the other as merciful. Perhaps the reader holds the view that moral debates generally engage our deepest emotions. Regardless of our views on that topic, I would like to examine some of the reasons for the strong disagreements that exist between proponents and opponents of mercy killing.

The debate over mercy killing involves different understandings of what it means to show mercy. Indeed, *Webster's New World Dictionary*[1] attaches at least two quite different meanings to the word *mercy*. On the one hand, mercy refers to a constraint against acting in certain ways. Mercy defined in this way is "a refraining from harming or punishing offenders, enemies, persons in one's power, etc." To kill someone is a commonly recognized form of harm, so that refraining from killing someone, particularly someone in one's power, can be seen as being merciful. The association of "mercy" and "failing to kill or be killed" is rendered explicit when the dictionary further defines mercy as "a fortunate thing; thing to be grateful for; blessing (a *mercy* he wasn't killed)."

On the other hand, the dictionary defines mercy as "a disposition to forgive, pity, or be kind" and as "kind or compassionate treatment; relief of suffering." Those who advocate mercy killing under certain circumstances emphasize this meaning of mercy. For them, killing can be justified when it is done out of kindness for the relief of suffering. Because proponents of mercy killing wish to observe and uphold the general prohibition against killing, they limit relief of suffering to instances where suffering can no longer be seen as serving any useful purpose. They speak, therefore, of needless or unnecessary suffering.

So far I have used the term *mercy killing* where many now use the word *euthanasia*. Originally the Greek word *euthanasia* meant painless, happy death. This meaning still appears as one definition of the term. However, a second meaning is now usually added that specifies euthanasia as an "act or method of causing death painlessly, so as to end suffering: advocated by some as a way to deal with persons dying of incurable, painful diseases."[2] Increasingly, euthanasia has come to be equated with mercy killing. For the purposes of this essay, therefore, I will use *mercy killing* and *euthanasia* as synonyms referring to the deliberate inducement of a quick, painless death.

The problem I wish to pose in this essay is whether or not the desire and obligation to be merciful or kind commits us to a policy of euthanasia. Some have claimed that there is a moral obligation to be kind or beneficent and that beneficent euthanasia is, therefore, not only morally justified but morally obligatory. This is a claim that deserves the careful scrutiny of any morally conscientious person. Having examined the arguments for beneficent euthanasia, I will then consider the possibility of an alternative notion of what mercy or kindness requires in those situations where mercy killing would appear to be morally justified or even obligatory.

One of the most compelling cases for beneficent euthanasia has been offered by Marvin Kohl.[3] According to Kohl, all of us have a prima facie obligation to act kindly. For the purposes of indicating when euthanasia would be an act of kindness, he specifies the following sense in which an act can be described as kind: ". . . an act is kind if it (a) is intended to be helpful; (b) is done so that, if there be any expectation of receiving remuneration (or the like), the individual would nonetheless act even if it became apparent that there was little chance of his expectation being realized; and (c) results in beneficial treatment for the intended recipient. The Boy or Girl Scout helping an elderly man or woman cross the street, or the proverbial Good Samaritan, are paradigm cases of kindness."[4] From this definition of kindness, Kohl argues that "the necessary, and perhaps sufficient, conditions for beneficent euthanasia are that the act must involve a painless inducement to a quick death; that the act must result in beneficial treatment for the intended recipient; and that, aside from the desire to help the recipient, no other considerations are relevant [a combination of conditions a and b]."[5]

To further clarify what he means by beneficent euthanasia, Kohl offers the reader two paradigm cases. The first case involves a patient (1) who is suffering from an irremediable condition such as cancer (disseminated carcinoma metastasis); (2) who has severe pain; (3) who has to die as a result of his or her condition; (4) who voluntarily favors some means of "easy death"; and (5) no other relevant circumstances, apart from the desire to help the patient. Kohl cites another case as a paradigm, that of a child severely handicapped, but who is not suffering pain and for whom death is not imminent. These two cases are quite different in Kohl's mind, except insofar as they both involve serious and irremediable physical conditions as well as the arousal in others of a wish to help. However, the most important feature that they share in Kohl's thinking is that induced death would probably be considered an act of kindness by most persons. Kohl underlines the importance of this claim because "if true it means that considerations of free choice, the imminence of death, and/or the existence of pain are not always relevant, at least not to judgments of kindness."[6]

With these paradigms in mind and on the assumption that societies and their individual members have a prima facie obligation to treat one another kindly, Kohl infers quite logically that beneficent euthanasia, because it is a species of kindness, is a prima facie obligation. This conclusion seems so obvious to Kohl that he believes that, were it not for some of the objections that have been raised against euthanasia, no further argument on behalf of beneficent euthanasia would be needed. Kohl, however, is concerned with the possible cogency of objections to his arguments for beneficent euthanasia and therefore adds three more arguments on behalf of it. (1) Over against "edge of the wedge" arguments, he asserts that a policy of beneficent euthanasia will result in minimizing suffering and maximizing kindly treatment. (2) Over against those who claim that homicide is intrinsically unjust, he argues that beneficent euthanasia satisfies a fundamental need for human dignity. And (3) over against those who argue that we are not obligated to kill, even out of kindness, he argues that failure to give help in the form of beneficent euthanasia is a failure to live up to the Good Samaritan ideal.

1. *The "wedge" argument*. Kohl interprets the "wedge" as claiming that if beneficent euthanasia is morally justified, then euthanasia that cannot be considered to be beneficent will come to be practiced and justified. He sees wedge arguments as based upon two assumptions: first, that all theories of euthanasia ultimately rest upon a principle of utility, and second, that all theories of utility are the same as those held by the Nazis, the implication being that great cruelties rather than kindness will result from such theories.

Kohl disassociates himself from any view that would advocate euthanasia for economic reasons. He distinguishes utility from beneficence. The duty of beneficence is in his view the duty to minimize suffering and maximize kindly treatment. If there is a "slippery slide" that results from policies of beneficent euthanasia, it will be in the direction of minimizing suffering and maximizing kindly treatment. Secondly, he distinguishes between the kindest way of doing X and the kindest way of treating a human being as a human being. Beneficent euthanasia has for its objective not merely death with dignity but living and dying with dignity. Again the goal is to minimize suffering and to maximize kindness.

In dealing with the wedge argument, Kohl has not yet confronted it in its most powerful form. A wedge argument does not have to predict that certain practices will follow from another. A wedge argument is concerned with the form or logic of moral justifications.

Consider, for example, Kohl's point that it is morally justifiable and obligatory to practice beneficent euthanasia in some cases where the person to be killed does not choose death, is not dying, and is not in pain. It is difficult to see why this would not justify involuntary euthanasia. Suppose, however, that Kohl is not bothered by this, as indeed he should not be. The next question is that of procuring agreement on the narrowness or broadness of the categories of persons to be appropriate candidates for mercy killing. Presumably the criterion that would for Kohl keep the category of cases narrowly defined is that of preserving the dignity of human beings. A child born without limbs, sight, hearing, or a functioning cerebral cortex, while not in pain and not dying, is for Kohl lacking in dignity, or in any event, will be treated with dignity if painlessly put to death.

Some people have argued that mongoloids, however happy or educable, are also lacking in dignity, so that their lives

need not always be sustained, even when they could be. What
the wedge argument is saying is that there is no logical or
easily agreed upon reason why the range of cases should be
restricted to Kohl's paradigm or why it would not be beneficial to extend the range even beyond the retarded. For example, we have instances where quadriplegics who are fully conscious and rational are not asked whether they wish to live
but are drugged and deprived of life support so that they die.
The justification for this is logically the same as the justification for beneficent euthanasia in the case of the severely retarded. The physician considers the life of a quadriplegic to
be undignified or one of suffering or, at least, a life not worth
living. Such physicians certainly see themselves as acting out
of kindness.

The point of the wedge argument is very simple. Since
killing is generally wrong, it should be kept to as narrow a
range of exceptions as possible. But the argument for beneficent euthanasia, unlike arguments for killing in self-defense,
applies logically to a wide range of cases, and the reasons for
keeping the range of cases narrow are not reasons on which
people will easily agree. In short, arguments for beneficent
euthanasia apply logically to either a narrow or a wide range
of cases. Whether beneficent euthanasia will be applied to a
narrow range of cases does not depend simply on how kind a
society is. It will depend also on the various notions that are
held about what constitutes a dignified or meaningful human
life. About this there will be widespread differences of opinion,
many of them based on implicit or explicit theological assumptions.

Furthermore, the wedge argument warns against adopting a principle of minimizing suffering and maximizing kindness. It sounds right, but its logical implications go far beyond the intentions of a Marvin Kohl. If minimizing suffering
is linked with killing, we have the unfortunate implication
that killing is a quicker, more painless way to alleviate suffering than is the provision of companionship for the lonely and
long-term care for those who are either dying or recuperating
from illnesses.

Clearly, Kohl does not want to minimize suffering by resort to killing, but only by resort to killing out of kindness.
The question remains, then, whether killing out of kindness
can be maximized without involving a much wider range of
cases than Kohl envisages. I shall come back to the question

about whether mercy killing restricted to a narrow range of cases in accord with Kohl's paradigms is something that should be justified despite the very telling difficulties raised by the wedge argument.

2. *Euthanasia as unjust.* Kohl argues that beneficent euthanasia is consistent with justice because it meets a basic need for dignity and self-respect. Such dignity is clearly exercised when people ask for a quick and painless death in circumstances where they see only pain and suffering as their lot. But Kohl does not want to restrict euthanasia to instances where consent can be obtained. Sometimes, he contends, neither justice nor dignity is served when the misery of an individual increases and consent is not possible.

Here again we see that there are instances in which Kohl would claim the inducement of a painless, quick death confers dignity where otherwise there is none. As was noted previously, however, it is difficult to know how wide a range of cases should be included among those where dignity is obtained through a nonvoluntarily induced, painless death. Those who induce this death will no doubt have varying notions as to what kind of misery and how much of it renders a life undignified. This is precisely the problem that the wedge argument points to. If euthanasia were practiced on others by someone like Kohl, it would be used as a last resort. If, however, there were a general policy of considering beneficient euthanasia as a moral obligation and accompanying laws that permitted people to live up to that obligation, its practice might be quite different from what Kohl envisages and sanctions. This would be true not because killing is contagious (Kohl has quite properly objected to that argument) but because the notion of dignity is open to a wide range of meanings. It is also true, as was noted previously, that agreement on what confers dignity is difficult to obtain. In any event, those who advocate beneficent euthanasia should clearly specify what they mean by dignity and how they justify their invocation of that term.

3. *The obligation to avoid killing.* Kohl recognizes that there are some who argue that one is not obligated to help the suffering in every way possible, particularly if such help entails killing. On Kohl's view an important assumption in that argument is that cruelty is to be avoided. Kohl contends that beneficent euthanasia also seeks to avoid cruelty. The difference between opponents and proponents of euthanasia here is

over the meaning of what constitutes cruelty and whether or not avoidance of cruelty is morally sufficient. Kohl argues that those who oppose euthanasia on grounds that it is cruel interpret cruelty in a narrow sense to mean deliberately causing unnecessary pain or harm. They do not use the broader sense of the term, which refers to deliberately causing or allowing needless pain or harm. As a consequence, Kohl maintains, these opponents of euthanasia are too prone to tolerate or excuse human misery.

Kohl calls this desire to avoid cruelty a "taboo" morality. It tells us what not to do, but not what to do. A society that avoids cruelty is admittedly better than one that does not. However, this "taboo" morality is contrary to the ideal of the Good Samaritan, who unlike those who walk past the injured or the sick, seeks to help. Aversion to cruelty may not harm anyone, but it is not, he argues, a sufficient principle of action if it does not include the obligation to help and be beneficent to others.

These arguments by Kohl are not consistent with his usual fairness to opponents. Those who oppose euthanasia because it is an act of killing, and as such is cruel, are trying to prevent death where possible. Those who share with the Good Samaritan the concern to keep somebody from dying do substitute care for killing or letting die. That is surely one of the major reasons for opposing euthanasia, namely, to help people stay alive even when that may not appear to be something they devoutly wish. Kohl would seem to qualify the ideal of the Good Samaritan, so that if the dying man on the road to Jericho had asked the Good Samaritan to help him by making his death painless and quick, presumably the Good Samaritan would have had the obligation to do so, depending upon whether he felt that the injured man was indeed dying.

We see then how we have come full circle. In effect, Kohl is taking the position that only proponents of euthanasia wish positively to exercise mercy, whereas opponents of euthanasia are simply trying to avoid doing something wrong and are so bent on that that they are not willing or able to be merciful. Whether or not one favors euthanasia and whether or not it is considered an obligation would seem, then, to depend on one's notion of what is merciful. Another significant ground for differences between proponents and opponents of euthanasia lies in opposing or sometimes unexamined notions of human dignity.

It is not possible here to do more than sketch some of the main contours of a policy that accepts mercy as a moral obligation but rejects beneficent euthanasia or mercy killing. Such a sketch will, however, clarify the different conceptions of mercy and human dignity that distinguish an ethic of benemortasia from an ethic of beneficent euthanasia.

Because euthanasia no longer functions as a merely descriptive term for a happy or good death, it is necessary to invent another term for this purpose. I have chosen the word "benemortasia," which is derived from two familiar Latin words, *bene* (good) and *mors* (death). What *bene* in benemortasia means depends upon the ethical framework that one adopts in order to interpret what it is to experience a good death, or at least what would be the most morally responsible way to behave in the face of death, either one's own or that of others. The ethic of benemortasia suggested in this essay is concerned with how we ought to behave toward those who are dying or whose death would appear to be a merciful event. It is not necessarily the only ethic one might or should adopt, nor is it complete in scope as presented here.

The ethic of benemortasia that I wish to argue for recognizes mercy or kindness as a moral obligation. Mercy is understood in at least two ways: first, it is merciful not to kill; second, it is merciful to provide care for the dying and the irremediably handicapped where consent is obtained without coercion. (Instances where voluntary consent to care being offered cannot be obtained from its intended recipients, as in cases of comatose or severely retarded patients, raise special issues that will be discussed later.)

The injunction not to kill is part of a total effort to prevent the destruction of human beings and of the human community. It is an absolute prohibition in the sense that no society can be indifferent about the taking of human life. Any act, insofar as it is an act of taking a human life, is wrong; that is to say, taking a human life is a wrong-making characteristic of actions.

To say, however, that killing is prima facie wrong does not mean that an act of killing may never be justified.[7] For example, a person's effort to prevent someone's death may lead to the death of the attacker. However, we can morally justify that act of intervention because it is an act of saving a life, but not because it is an act of taking a life. If it were simply an act of taking a life, it would be wrong.

Advocates of beneficent euthanasia would generally agree that one should not kill innocent people, particularly those who are as powerless to defend themselves as the dying and the handicapped. However, restraint against harming people is not enough. What about positive actions to relieve pain and suffering?

For our ethic of benemortasia, at least the following kind of care can be given to patients who are considered to be imminently dying: (1) relief of pain, (2) relief of suffering, (3) respect for a patient's right to refuse treatment, and (4) universal provision of health care.

1. *Relief of pain.* There is widespread agreement among those who oppose beneficent euthanasia but who believe in mercy that pain relief can be offered to patients even when it means shortening the dying process. This is not considered killing or assisting in a killing because the cause of death is the terminal illness of the patient, and the shortening of the dying process has to do with a choice on the part of the patient to live with less pain during his last days. All of us make choices about whether we will seek pain relief. When we are not terminally ill we also make choices about the kind of care we do or do not seek. There is no reason to deny such freedom to someone who is dying. Indeed, there is every reason to be especially solicitous of a person who is terminally ill. There is no legal or moral objection to the administration of pain relief provided it is for that purpose and not for the purpose of killing someone. This means that one does not knowingly give an overdose of a pain reliever, but rather concentrates on dosages that are sufficient for relief of pain, knowing that at some point the dose administered will be final. Indeed the official regulations of Roman Catholic hospitals in this country explicitly permit hastening the dying process through the administration of pain relief.

2. *Relief of suffering.* Suffering is not the same as pain, although in instances where pain is extremely excruciating, it is virtually impossible to avoid suffering. We know, for example, that physicians can relieve suffering in a variety of ways. There is some evidence that patients who know they are dying generally suffer less and are less inclined to ask for pain relief than those who do not know that they are dying. We know also that one of the major sources of suffering for dying people is loneliness and lack of companionship. Our ethic of benemortasia would consider it not only merciful but

part of good care in the strictest medical sense to make provision for companionship, whether with medical, paramedical, or other kinds of persons brought to the hospital expressly for this purpose. Churches and other voluntary organizations often assist in this way. Note also the splendid care provided by someone like Elisabeth Kubler-Ross, who is an opponent of beneficent euthanasia but a staunch proponent and practitioner of mercy in the form of relief of suffering.[8]

3. *A patient's right to refuse treatment.* Dying patients are also living patients. They retain the same right as everyone else voluntarily to leave the hospital or to refuse specific kinds of care. Indeed, the right to refuse care is legally recognized. No new law is required to allow patients to exercise their rights. One of the important good effects of the whole discussion of euthanasia is that all of us, including health professionals, are becoming more sensitive to this right to refuse care. Given the concern not to kill, one would continue to expect that physicians who hold out some hope of saving a life would usually presuppose consent to try to save patients who in a desperate state may be expressing a wish to die.

Those who are irreversibly comatose or those who, as in Kohl's paradigm, have no functioning of the cerebral cortex, no use of muscles, and so forth, pose special difficulties, both for an ethic of beneficent euthanasia and an ethic of benemortasia. In such instances we are dealing with very tragic circumstances. No decision we make is totally satisfactory from a moral point of view. From the standpoint of our ethic of benemortasia, there is a strong presumption to continue supporting the irreversibly comatose and the severely brain-damaged until there is virtually no reasonable hope of sustaining life, apart from measures that go far beyond ordinary care. There comes a point when the decision to let die can be made out of mercy and also out of the recognition that for the irreversibly comatose death is inevitable and that for the severely brain-damaged child it would be merciful to withhold more than ordinary care in the face of the next serious bout of illness, recognizing also that such episodes of illness will be frequent and devastating. The difference between beneficent euthanasia and our ethic of benemortasia is that, whereas the former would deliberately induce death, the latter, as a last resort after making every effort to save and repair life, mercifully retreats in the face of death's inevitability.

4. *Universal health care.* In order to be merciful as well
as just in the provision of care for dying and severely handicapped people, no single person or family should have to bear
alone the burden of extensive medical costs. It is notorious
that poor people are more often and much sooner let go as
dying persons than those who have ample financial resources.
Those concerned with mercy should also bear in mind that the
much higher rates of maternal and infant death suffered by
blacks is one of the more subtle, systemic ways in which society can permit euthanasia. It is difficult to imagine that
anyone could call such subtle forms of euthanasia in any sense
merciful or beneficent. Discussions of beneficent euthanasia
should not overlook these subtle forms of injustice to people
in need of care.

So far, in discussing an ethic of benemortasia, I have
stressed the ways in which mercy can be extended to patients
without inducing death. However, the proponents of beneficent euthanasia would not be completely satisfied in all cases
with the form that mercy takes in our ethic of benemortasia.
Kohl emphasizes a quick, painless death. Our ethic of benemortasia emphasizes erring on the side of the protection of
life, while still minimizing suffering. In order to understand
this remaining difference between beneficent euthanasia and
our ethic of benemortasia, it is necessary to see that they differ with respect to their notions of what constitutes human
dignity.

Proponents of beneficent euthanasia, including Kohl,
tend to rest their case on the following kinds of presuppositions: (1) that the dignity that attaches to personhood by reason of the freedom to make moral choices demands also the
freedom to take one's own life or to have it taken when this
freedom is absent or lost; (2) that there is such a thing as a
life not worth living, a life that lacks dignity, whether by reason of distress, illness, physical or mental handicaps, or even
sheer despair for whatever reason; (3) that what is sacred or
supreme in value is the "human dignity" that resides in the
rational capacity to choose and control life and death.

Our ethic of benemortasia as outlined here rests on the
following kinds of presuppositions about human dignity: (1)
that the dignity that attaches to personhood by reason of the
freedom to make moral choices includes the freedom to refuse
noncurative, life-prolonging interventions when one is dying,
but does not extend to taking one's life or causing the death

of someone who is dying, because that would be unjustified killing; (2) that every life has some worth; (3) that notions of dignity are judged on the basis of what is right, merciful, and just, obligations that the dying and those who care for them share. Being less than perfect, humans require constraints on their decisions regarding the dying. No human being or human community can presume to know who deserves to live or die. From a religious perspective, some would leave that kind of decision to God.[9]

There are two critical differences between these two sets of presuppositions. Whereas in the ethic of beneficent euthanasia, life of a certain kind, or life having dignity, is what has value, in our ethic of benemortasia, life as such retains some value whatever form it takes. This does not mean that an opponent of beneficent euthanasia cannot let die or administer pain relief that may hasten death. What it means is that life as a value is always a consideration; that is one reason why the onus is on those who believe a person should be allowed to die to give stringent and compelling reasons for their belief.

Another critical difference between these two ethical views is that the notion of mercy in our ethic of benemortasia is controlled by what is considered right, particularly the injunction not to kill, on which a wide moral and social consensus exists. The notion of mercy in an ethic of beneficent euthanasia as depicted, for example, by Kohl and Joseph Fletcher[10] is controlled by the conception of human dignity. One of the reasons that Kohl and Fletcher insist upon including quick death is their belief that certain lives are quite undignified and only become dignified in death. It is for this reason that Fletcher can speak of a right to die.

It is precisely this appeal to some notion of dignity to justify killing that evokes "wedge" arguments. As I indicated previously, there are serious and widespread differences among people about what constitutes human dignity. If who shall live and who shall die is made contingent upon these widely divergent views of human dignity, moral and legal policies that justify mercy killing can in principle justify a very narrow and/or a very wide range of instances in which it will be claimed that we as a society are obligated to kill someone. No one using "wedge" arguments against beneficent euthanasia need predict whether at a given moment in history a country like the United States will or will not, if euthanasia becomes lawful, use such laws to indulge in widespread killing of helpless people. The point of the wedge argument is that logically and actually there is no provision made by proponents of beneficent euthanasia for limiting in principle the notion of human dignity and for guaranteeing some kind of consensus about what constitutes human dignity. In the absence of such a consensus, it is understandable that some people having certain notions of human dignity will welcome a policy of beneficent euthanasia, whereas others will be fearful of their lives should euthanasia be legalized.

The debate concerning what constitutes human dignity cannot be easily resolved. There are deep philosophical and religious differences that divide people on that issue. However, the injunction not to kill is not divisive in this way. Much of the emotion generated by the debate over euthanasia finds its source precisely in the understandable and deep uneasiness that many individuals feel when they are asked to move away from a stringent notion of refrainig from acts of killing, regarding which there is widespread agreement, and to make judgments about who shall live and who shall die on the basis of conceptions of human dignity, regarding which there are deep religious, ethnic, philosophical, and other differences. Anyone who would argue for beneficent euthanasia needs to confront this difficult and divisive aspect of his proposal. Kohl and those who share his point of view will either have to present a notion of human dignity on which widespread agreement can be obtained or make a case for beneficent euthanasia that does not depend on such a complex set of assumptions about human dignity. Until one or the other of these cases is rendered plausible by proponents of beneficent euthanasia, many of us will continue to work out and try to refine an ethic of benemortasia.

1. *Webster's New World Dictionary* (Second College Edition), ed. David B. Guralnik (Englewood Cliffs, N.J.: Prentice-Hall, and New York: World Publishing Co., 1970). p. 889.

2. *Ibid.*, p. 484.

3. See Marvin Kohl, "Understanding the Case for Beneficent Euthanasia," *Science, Medicine and Man*, 1 (1973), pp. 111-121; and "Beneficent Euthanasia," *The Humanist* (July/August 1974), pp. 9-11.

4. Marvin Kohl, "Understanding the Case for Beneficent Euthanasia," p. 112.

5. *Ibid.*, pp. 112-113.

6. *Ibid.*, p. 113.

7. W.D. Ross, *The Right and the Good* (London: Oxford Univ. Press, 1930).

8. Elisabeth Kubler-Ross, *On Death and Dying* (New York: Macmillan, 1970).

9. See Arthur J. Dyck, "An Alternative to the Ethic of Euthanasia," in R.H. Williams, ed., *To Live and To Die: When, Why and How?* (New York: Springer-Verlag, 1973), pp. 98-112, for a fuller discussion of the way in which these presuppositions emerge.

10. See the articles by Marvin Kohl listed in note 3 and Joseph Fletcher, "The Patient's Right to Die," in A.B. Downing, ed., *Euthanasia and the Right to Death* (New York: Humanities Press, 1971).

CHRISTIAN AFFIRMATION OF LIFE

Rev. Kevin D. O'Rourke, OP

Recently, when answering a question sent in by a reader, Abigail Van Buren, the "Dear Abby" columnist, printed a copy of a document known as the Living Will. Within six weeks, the Euthanasia Educational Council, which publishes one version of the Living Will, received 40,000 requests for copies. Even a person who also disagrees with the aims of the Euthanasia Educational Council must admit that the publication of the Council's Living Will aroused the interest of many people.

WHAT IS IT?

The Living Will is a document "by which a person while of sound mind and after careful consideration can signify his wishes to those concerned with his terminal illness."[1] Briefly, the Will states:

> If there is no reasonable expectation of my recovery from physical or mental disability, I request that I be allowed to die and not be kept alive by artificial or heroic measures. . . . I ask that medication be mercifully administered to me for terminal suffering even if it hastens the moment of death. . . . I am not asking that my life be directly taken, but that my dying be not unreasonably prolonged.[2]

Morally speaking, there is nothing wrong with the basic ideas of the Living Will. Christian teaching requires that we use ordinary means to prolong life, but it allows us to refuse extraordinary means if we so desire. Moreover, if the primary purpose is to alleviate pain, pain relieving medication can be administered to a dying person even though the medication would hasten death. Allowing a person to die in this manner is *passive* euthanasia; it is entirely different from taking a positive action that causes a person's death, or *active* euthanasia.

Since the Living Will must be signed well before death, it has the advantage of prompting people to face death before it occurs. Psychologically, this confrontation is beneficial; confronting death and discussing it in a realistic manner when death is not imminent will help individuals accept death more readily whon it occurs.[3] The Living Will could also lessen the possibility of useless, painful, and expensive medical treatment as death approaches. Perhaps this is its strongest appeal. At present, the Will is not accepted as a legal document in any state, but bills have been introduced in many states that would recognize it before the law. If it is legalized, physicians and families of those who are terminally ill would be required to follow the stipulations of the document. They could be prosecuted if they did not. Proponents of the Will maintain that it would impose a moral obligation irrespective of legal recognition.

SHORTCOMINGS

In spite of the fact that the Living Will is not contrary to traditional Christian teaching, that it prompts people to prepare for death, and that it might limit prolonged treatment and expense, it has several drawbacks. First, it gives the impression that decisions concerning the means used to prolong life in danger of death can be made in a routine, abstract, or impersonal manner. These decisions are not automatic; they cannot be made according to a general rule that applies to all individuals regardless of age or illness. They must be particular decisions which take into account a person's total situation. If at all possible, the wishes of the person involved must be observed. A person could change his mind between the time he signed a Living Will and the time he is in danger of death. If an elderly or infirm patient had signed a living will, would his family and physicians later consult him concerning the decision to prolong life?

Decisions as to what constitutes ordinary and extraordinary means of prolonging life must depend upon the person and the circumstances of each case. Specific treatments or drugs cannot be designated as ordinary or extraordinary unless the details and the conditions of the case are known. Penicillin is not an ordinary means to prolong life for people who are allergic to it. Usually oxygen is considered an ordinary means, but a patient confined to a respirator for many years may not consider it ordinary. If the Living Will becomes legal and mandatory, the delicate, individualized care necessary when making decisions concerning the prolongation of life, even when patients are not conscious, would be endangered if not eliminated. Hence, though the basic notion and wording of the Living Will may not be faulted, were it to become legalized its application would be problematic. Proper care and concern often would be sacrificed.

PHYSICIANS' OPINIONS

Objections to the Living Will also have been expressed by leading physicians. The Living Will implies that all physicians will try any and all means to keep dying patients alive as long as possible. Several physicians have testified that this is not proper to their ethos. They are not interested in prolonging terminal cases through extraordinary means. But the simple fact of the matter is that it is often difficult to judge when a patient's illness is truly terminal. As one expert, Lawrence Foye, Jr., director of Education Service, Veterans Administration, explains:

> Such approaches as legalized euthanasia and the Living Will are based upon the misconception that the point of hopelessness can be known with accuracy and that the physician may uselessly prolong suffering beyond that point unless forbidden by law or similarly excused from his obligations. I fear that unless people understand the false reasoning behind these concepts the physician's hands may be tied in just those cases where his skill and modern technology can make the greatest contribution to the saving of lives and the control of disease.[4]

Dr. Andre Hellegers, Director of the Kennedy Institute of Bioethics, has declared that legalizing the Living Will would be extremely dangerous. He warns that the Will "acknowledges that doctors have a right of ownership unless you write a living will. I would be afraid that the person who doesn't have such a will would be presumed to be the doctor's property, and there would be cases where those who did have it would not be resuscitated when they should be."[5] Consider as well the lack of trust between physician and patient that would develop if every patient in danger of death thought his physician would be as likely to let him die as to try to save his life.

Another shortcoming of the Living Will, more subtle but nonetheless serious, is the atmosphere it creates. A mercenary, cold, and pagan atmosphere surrounds the Will itself and the literature supporting its legalization. One of the main arguments in favor of legalizing passive euthanasia emphasizes the cost of keeping the elderly and infirm alive. This argument conceives of the elderly and infirm as a financial burden upon society; it seldom mentions the contribution they may be making or have made. Furthermore, the Living Will never refers to love, hope for life after death, responsibility to God as Lord and Creator, the value of suffering and death, or the love of our Saviour, Jesus Christ, for us. Removing death from the context of love, life, and salvation makes it meaningless and a rather dismal and fear-filled event.

A MORE SERIOUS PROBLEM

If these two shortcomings are not sufficiently disturbing, a third fault is decidedly more serious. The drive to recognize the Living Will as a legal document appears to be but one step in the drive to legalize active euthanasia of the retarded, elderly, and infirm.[6] The most active sponsors of the Living Will, especially those associated with the Euthanasia Educational Council, are also active proponents of abortion on demand and of legalized active euthanasia. It is a small step from making mandatory the withholding of care to legalizing the taking of life. Walter Sackett, MD, a member of the legislature in the State of Florida, several times has introduced a bill which would give legal recognition to the Living Will. However, when he testified before the Special Committee on Aging of the U.S. Senate, he associated his bill with the need to make lawful the elimination of severely retarded people so that the money used in their behalf could be applied to other health needs.[7] Morally speaking, passive euthanasia and elimination of the severely retarded for financial reasons are as different as night and day, but Dr. Sackett seems to place them in the same category. If one is made lawful and mandatory, would legalization of the other be far behind?

Other evidence could be introduced to illustrate the connection between the drive to legalize the Living Will (passive euthanasia) and active euthanasia. But the words of the most renowned expert in the psychology of death and dying will suffice. When testifying before the Senate Committee on Aging concerning Dr. Sackett's bill, Elisabeth Kubler-Ross, MD, declared that she feared legalization of such bills because their loop-holes would allow "elimination" of those lives that are too costly or too much of a "burden."[8]

Although the Living Will offers some potential benefits, its potential hazards are far greater, and hence it should not have the force of law. Is there any way to reap the benefits and eliminate the hazards? I think there is. We can oppose the efforts which would legalize and make mandatory the provisions of the Living Will, thus avoiding its threat to the practice of medicine and lessening the possibility of ultimate legalization of active euthanasia. If people wish to express in writing the desire to avoid unnecessary treatment, suffering, and prolongation of life at the time of terminal illness, we can provide a document of reference and reflection which allows them to express their wish in a context that affirms Christian values. Toward that end I offer the Christian Affirmation of Life.

Christian Affirmation of Life*

To my family, friends, physician, lawyer, and clergyman:

I believe that each individual person is created by God our Father in love and that God retains a loving relationship to each person throughout human life and eternity.

I believe that Jesus Christ lived, suffered, and died for me and that his suffering, death, and resurrection prefigure and make possible the death-resurrection process which I now anticipate.

*This document was approved by the Board of Trustees of the Catholic Hospital Association in June 1974.

I believe that each person's worth and dignity derives from the relationship of love in Christ that God has for each individual person and not from one's usefulness or effectiveness in society.

I believe that God our Father has entrusted to me a shared dominion with him over my earthly existence so that I am bound to use ordinary means to preserve my life but I am free to refuse extraordinary means to prolong my life.

I believe that through death life is not taken away but merely changed, and though I may experience fear, suffering, and sorrow, by the grace of the Holy Spirit, I hope to accept death as a free human act which enables me to surrender this life and to be united with God for eternity.

Because of my belief:

I request that I be informed as death approaches so that I may continue to prepare for the full encounter with Christ through the help of the sacraments and the consolation and prayers of my family and friends.

I request that, if possible, I be consulted concerning the medical procedures which might be used to prolong my life as death approaches. If I can no longer take part in decisions concerning my own future and if there is no reasonable expectation of my recovery from physical and mental disability, I request that no extraordinary means be used to prolong my life.

I request, though I wish to join my suffering to the suffering of Jesus so I may be united fully with him in the act of death-resurrection, that my pain, if unbearable, be alleviated. However, no means should be used with the intention of shortening my life.

I request, because I am a sinner and in need of reconciliation and because my faith, hope, and love may not overcome all fear and doubt, that my family, friends, and the whole Christian community join me in prayer and mortification as I prepare for the great personal act of dying.

Finally, I request that after death, my family, my friends, and the whole Christian community pray for me, and rejoice with me because of the mercy and love of the Trinity, with whom I hope to be united for all eternity.

Signed:_____ Date:_____

1. Euthanasia Educational Council, "Euthanasia," June, 1973.

2. Euthanasia Educational Council, "A Living Will," June, 1973.

3. Elisabeth Kubler-Ross, MD., *Death and Dying,* Macmillan, New York City, 1969.

4. Lawrence Foye, Jr., "Death with Dignity," *Hearings Before a Special Committee on Aging,* August 7, 1972, p. 20, 23; Frank Ayd, *Medical-Moral Newsletter,* February, 1974, p. 24.

5. "Euthanasia Divides Doctors," *Washington Post,* March 12, 1974.

6. James F. Toole, MD, "The Neurologist and the Concept of Brain Death," *Perspectives in Biology and Medicine,* Summer, 1971, p. 602.

7. Walter Sackett, "Death with Dignity," *Hearings,* p. 30.

8. Elisabeth Kubler-Ross, "Death with Dignity," *Hearings,* p. 43.

EDITOR'S COMMENT ON THE LIVING WILL

Dennis J. Horan

One of the legal dilemmas of our electronic age is too much unnecessary legislation enacted too soon and in response to too many non-problems. This is especially true in the legal-medical area where physicians are slowly being hemmed in by such legislation and finding themselves unable to practice their art and to exercise their best judgment in doing so. The Living Will is a typical example of that phenomenon.

California recently passed a living will provision entitled the Natural Death Act. A copy of the Act follows this comment. Although hailed by many as a necessary and important piece of legislation giving another fundamental freedom to persons and protection to physicians, in fact, it gives nothing to persons which they do not already possess under the law, nor does it add any additional legal protection to doctors which they do not already possess. If anything, it adds officious burdens to the death bed, encumbers medical decisions with unnecessary additional consultations and creates rather than clarifies legal problems.

The California Act does not allow or hasten mercy killing, which is strictly prohibited either by active means or by mere omission. Some have argued that living will legislation is the opening wedge towards the ultimate legalization of euthanasia. Since this legislation, in itself, adds nothing to the legal rights people already possess under the law, nor gives physicians additional protections not already possessed, there may be some truth in this charge. For example, Prof. Kamisar points out in his article in this book the position taken by the Euthanasia Society that the living will is the first step towards the ultimate legislation of mercy killing. On the other hand, however, one can also argue that since this legislation adds nothing which does not already exist in the law it cannot, therefore, be considered such an opening wedge but is, rather, a mere codification for clarification purposes of existing laws. Between these extremes lies the truth.

Adult persons of sound mind have a right to refuse medical treatment unless some equal and countervailing rights of other persons would be substantially jeopardized by such a refusal. For example, it has been consistently held by the courts that the right of pregnant women to refuse medical treatment must give way to the unborn child's right to life. Under those circumstances courts have consistently overruled the mother's right to refuse medical treatment even when it may flow from a First Amendment protection—namely, the free exercise of religion.

While the act itself seems to follow the law in this manner, there is an ambiguity. The only reference to pregnancy is contained in Section 7188. But this reference is not in a section of the act mandating a norm of conduct and legislating standards pursuant thereto, but rather appears only as a portion of the form which is to be executed by the declarant. Section 3 of the required form says that "This directive shall have no force and effect during the course of my pregnancy," thus presumably ruling out the form as allowing euthanasia of an unborn child. The act says that this language concerning pregnancy "shall be" in the form. However, the word "shall" has often been interpreted in the law to mean "may," depending on how a court reads the legislative intent. Consequently it is possible that a court would approve a form of living will which omits reference to pregnancy. Section 7191(a) requires the physician to determine that the directive complies with Section 7188, but states no penalty if he does not. In addition, Section 7193 says that the act does not impair or supersede any legal right or responsibility which any person may have to effect the withholding or withdrawal of life-sustaining procedures in any lawful manner. Consequently a physician who has the right and obligation to withdraw life-sustaining procedures may do so under Section 7193 without regard to the form of the will.

A far more important problem created by the act and one which would probably surprise its sponsors is that the act will inhibit rather than increase the physician's ability to solve with dignity and grace the problem of the dying patient. Anytime a statute is passed regulating conduct and creating rewards and punishments for non-compliance, such an act has the effect of chilling or inhibiting similar conduct otherwise legal but now not in conformity with the act. Consequently even though Section 7193 is in the act, still the effect of the act will be to chill and inhibit otherwise lawful conduct of a physician in withdrawing life-sustaining means unless such a living will has been made by the patient. The physician will probably assume that he cannot now withdraw life-sustaining measures unless he has a directive from the patient in compliance with the act.

A better approach of the legislature would have been to pass an act stating that life-sustaining measures may be withdrawn when it may be done in the judgment of the attending physician under usual and customary standards of medicine. Here is an example:

> Life-sustaining measures may be terminated by the attending physician when, in his judgment, based upon a reasonable degree of medical certainty according to usual and customary standards of medicine, it is proper to do so.

It is understood that hospital aids, nurses or technicians who act upon a lawful order of a physician are not liable for doing so, and it is not necessary to say so in the statute. If the order itself constitutes malpractice, mayhem or murder and should have been known to be so by the aid or nurse, or is carried out by them negligently, then that is another matter.

In addition, customary methods and standards in medicine change continuously. There is no way that particularized medical practice can be legislated. Will we pass statutes saying when and under what circumstances an appendix may or must be removed? The physician's judgment must be relied upon by society in these matters. Elements of that judgment can be controlled by statutes prohibiting unwanted conduct such as Section 7188 of the California act which "prohibits" mercy killing. But the homicide laws do this anyway. It is a misunderstanding of the current status of medical-legal principles which causes the confusion. Unfortunately the California Natural Death Act has compounded those problems rather seriously.

Whether or not a physician obtains a consent from the family or next of kin for terminating life-sustaining measures is a separate problem from the exercise of the physician's judgment in determining that the life-sustaining method should be terminated. As a matter of prudence he should obviously do so when the patient is unable to voluntarily consent. Such a consent at least precludes those who gave such a consent from maintaining an action.

Voluntary consent is the difficult problem and the California statute does not make that problem any easier. In fact, it compounds it by 1) using in Section 7186 language that conditions the validity of the directive to a voluntary consent given *when the patient was of sound mind* (How in the world can a physician know that?), and 2) not clarifying in Section 7191(b) that the conclusive presumption may *not* be rebutted by evidence of the unsound mind of the declarant *at the time the directive was executed.* In addition, Section 7190 conditions its immunity grant on compliance with the act. Presumably, failure to follow the act vitiates the immunity.

Section 7191(c) aggravates the problem further by only giving "weight" to the directive as evidence of the patient's directions, but then indicates that he "may" (read must now) consider other factors such as information from the family and even the totality of the circumstances. This section [7191(c)] destroys the entire utility of the act in its present form as far as the apparent intent of the legislature is concerned. This section is the one that will probably be applicable to most patients dying in a hospital. That is, most of these will be patients who have executed the directive previously, but have not re-executed it since becoming a qualified patient. For all these patients the directive will merely be a piece of paper indicating the desires of a patient with little or no legal significance. That is no more (and less effective) than what the patient could have accomplished anyway with a hand written letter to a loved one. Such a letter would probably mean more to the attending physician anyway, rather than a formalized directive which will cause him endless worry and frustration wondering whether the declarant was of sound mind when the directive was executed; worrying about whether the directive has ever been revoked; calling his personal attorney for an opinion; conferring with the hospital attorneys and discovering that they disagree with his personal attorney (or vice versa); conferring with the hospital ethics committee only to discover that they disagree with the lawyers; and last but not least learning to his chagrin that the statute requires him to consider the totality of the circumstances surrounding execution of the document so that he can "justify effectuating the directive."

In addition, Section 7191(a) mandates that the *physicians* determine that the directive complies with the law and if, but only if, the patient is mentally competent and the action to be taken is in "accord with the desires of the qualified patient" may the action be taken. In plain language this means that if the patient is competent and alert the doctor should disregard the directive and obtain an informed consent from the patient to terminate the treatment. If the patient is not competent and alert, then 7191(c) requires the physician to make an inordinate investigation into the surrounding circumstances concerning the execution of that directive. Who needs such a statute? Certainly not doctors.

The provisions of the California statute follow:

The people of the State of California do enact as follows:

SECTION 1. Chapter 3.9 (commencing with Section 7185 is added to Part 1 of Division 7 of the Health and Safety Code, to read:

CHAPTER 3.9 NATURAL DEATH ACT

7185. This act shall be known and may be cited as the Natural Death Act.

7186. The Legislature finds that adult persons have the fundamental right to control the decisions relating to the rendering of their own medical care, including the decision to have life-sustaining procedures withheld or withdrawn in instances of a terminal condition.

The Legislature further finds that modern medical technology has made possible the artificial prolongation of human life beyond natural limits.

The Legislature further finds that, *in the interest of protecting individual autonomy*, such prolongation of life for persons with a terminal condition may cause loss of patient's dignity *and* unnecessary pain and suffering, while providing nothing medically necessary or beneficial to the patient.

The Legislature further finds that there exists considerable uncertainty in the medical and legal professions as to the legality of terminating the use or application of life-sustaining procedures where a patient has voluntarily and in sound mind evidenced a desire that such procedures be withheld or withdrawn.

In recognition of the dignity and privacy which patients have a right to expect, the Legislature hereby declares that the laws of the State of California shall recognize the right of an adult person to make written directive instructing his physician to withhold or withdraw life-sustaining procedures in the event of a terminal condition.

7187 The following definitions shall govern the construction of this chapter:

(a) "Attending physician" means the physician selected by, or assigned to, the patient who has primary responsibility for the treatment and care of that patient.

(b) "Directive" means a written document voluntarily executed by the declarant in accordance with the requirements of Section 7188. The directive, or a copy of the directive, shall be made part of the patient's medical records.

(c) "Life-sustaining procedure" means any medical procedure or intervention which utilizes mechanical or other artificial means to sustain, restore, or supplant a vital function, which, when applied to a qualified patient, would serve only to artificially prolong the moment of death and where, in the judgment of the attending physician, death is imminent whether or not such procedures are utilized. "Life-sustaining procedure" shall not include the administration of medication or the performance of any medical procedure deemed necessary to alleviate pain.

(d) "Physician" means a physician and surgeon licensed by the Board of Medical Quality Assurance or the Board of Osteopathic Examiners.

(e) "Qualified patient" means a patient diagnosed and certified in writing to be afflicted with a terminal condition by two physicians, one of whom shall be the attending physician, who have personally examined the patient.

(f) "Terminal condition" means an incurable condition caused by injury, disease, or illness, which, regardless of the application of life-sustaining procedures, would, within reasonable medical judgment, produce death, and where the application of life-sustaining procedures serve only to postpone the moment of death of the patient.

7188. Any adult person may execute a directive directing the withholding or withdrawal of life-sustaining procedures in a terminal condition. The directive shall be signed by the declarant in the presence of two witnesses not related to the declarant by blood or marriage and who would not be entitled to any portion of the estate of the declarant upon his decease under any will of the declarant or codicil thereto then existing or, at the time of the directive, by operation of law then existing. In addition, a witness to a directive shall not be the attending physician, an employee of the attending physician or a health facility in which the declarant is a patient, or any person who has a claim against any portion of the estate of the declarant upon his decease at the time of the execution of the directive. The directive shall be in the following form:

DIRECTIVE TO PHYSICIANS

Directive made this _____ day of _____ (month, year).

I _____, being of sound mind, willfully, and voluntarily make known my desire that my life shall not be artificially prolonged under the circumstances set forth below, do hereby declare:

1. If at any time I should have an incurable injury, disease, or illness certified to be a terminal condition by two physicians, and where the application of life-sustaining procedures would serve only to artificially prolong the moment of my death and where my physician determines that my death is imminent whether or not life-sustaining procedures are utilized, I direct that such procedures be withheld or withdrawn, and that I be permitted to die naturally.

2. In the absence of my ability to give directions regarding the use of such life-sustaining procedures, it is my intention that this directive shall be honored by my family and physician(s) as the final expression of my legal right to refuse medical or surgical treatment and accept the consequences from such a refusal.

3. If I have been diagnosed as pregnant and that diagnosis is known to my physician, this directive shall have no force or effect during the course of my pregnancy.

4. I have been diagnosed and notified at least 14 days ago as having a terminal condition by _____, M.D., whose address is _____, and whose telephone number is _____. I understand that if I have not filled in the physician's name and address, it shall be presumed that I did not have a terminal condition when I made out this directive.

5. This directive shall have no force or effect five years from the date filled in above.

6. I understand the full import of this directive and I am emotionally and mentally competent to make this directive.

Signed _____

City, County and State of Residence _____

The declarant has been personally known to me and I believe him or her to be of sound mind.

Witness _____

Witness _____

7188.5 A directive shall have no force or effect if the declarant is a patient in a skilled nursing facility as defined in subdivision (c) of Section 1250 at the time the directive is executed unless one of the two witnesses to the directive is a patient advocate or ombudsman as may be designated by the State Department of Aging for this purpose pursuant to any other applicable provision of law. The patient advocate or ombudsman shall have the same qualifications as a witness under Section 7188.

The intent of this section is to recognize that some patients in skilled nursing facilities may be so insulated from a voluntary decisionmaking role, by virtue of the custodial nature of their care, as to require special assurance that they are capable of willfully and voluntarily executing a directive.

7189. (a) A directive may be revoked at any time by the declarant, without regard to his mental state or competency, by any of the following methods:

(1) By being canceled, defaced, obliterated, or burnt, torn, or otherwise destroyed by the declarant or by some person in his presence and by his direction.

(2) By a written revocation of the declarant expressing his intent to revoke, signed and dated by the declarant. Such revocation shall become effective only upon communication to the attending physician by the declarant or by a person acting on behalf of the declarant. The attending physician shall record in the patient's medical record the time and date when he received notification of the written revocation.

(3) By a verbal expression by the declarant of his intent to revoke the directive. Such revocation shall become effective only upon communication to the attending physician by the declarant or by a person acting on behalf of the declarant. The attending physician shall record in the patient's medical record the time, date, and place of the revocation and the time, date, and place, if different, of when he received notification of the revocation.

(b) There shall be no criminal or civil liability on the part of the person for failure to act upon a revocation made pursuant to this section unless that person has actual knowledge of the revocation.

7189.5 A directive shall be effective for five years from the date of execution thereof unless sooner revoked in a manner prescribed in Section 7189. Nothing in this chapter shall be construed to prevent a declarant from reexecuting a directive at any time in accordance with the formalities of Section 7188, including reexecution subsequent to a diagnosis of a terminal condition. If the declarant has executed more than one directive, such time shall be determined from the date of execution of the last directive known to the attending physician. If the declarant becomes comatose or is rendered incapable of communicating with the attending physician, the directive shall remain in effect for the duration of the comatose condition or until such time as the declarant's condition renders him or her able to communicate with the attending physician.

7190. No physician or health facility which, acting in accordance with the requirements of this chapter, causes the withholding or withdrawal of life-sustaining procedures from a qualified patient, shall be subject to civil liability therefrom. No licensed health professional, acting under the direction of a physician, who participates in the withholding or withdrawal of life-sustaining procedures in accordance with the provisions of this chapter shall be subject to any civil liability. No physician, or licensed health professional acting under the direction of a physician, who participates in the withholding or withdrawal of life-sustaining procedures in accordance with the provisions of this chapter shall be guilty of any criminal act or of unprofessional conduct.

7191. (a) Prior to effecting a withholding or withdrawal of life-sustaining procedures from a qualified patient pursuant to the directive, the attending physician shall determine that the directive complies with Section 7188, and, if the patient is mentally competent, that the directive and all steps proposed by the attending physician to be undertaken are in accord with the desires of the qualified patient.

(b) If the declarant was a qualified patient at least 14 days prior to executing or reexecuting the directive, the directive shall be conclusively presumed, unless revoked, to be the directions of the patient regarding the withholding or withdrawal of life-sustaining procedures. No physician, and no licensed health professional acting under the direction of a physician, shall be criminally or civilly liable for failing to effectuate the directive of the qualified patient pursuant to this subdivision. A failure by a physician to effectuate the directive of a qualified patient pursuant to this division shall constitute unprofessional conduct if the physician refuses to make the necessary arrangements, or fails to take the necessary steps, to effect the transfer of the qualified patient to another physician who will effectuate the directive of the qualified patient.

(c) If the declarant becomes a qualified patient subsequent to executing the directive, and has not subsequently reexecuted the directive, the attending physician may give weight to the directive as evidence of the patient's directions regarding the withholding or withdrawal of life-sustaining procedures and may consider other factors, such as information from the affected family or the nature of the patient's illness, injury, or disease, in determining whether the totality of circumstances known to the attending physician justify effectuating the directive. No physician, and no licensed health professional acting under the direction of a physician, shall be criminally or civilly liable for failing to effectuate the directive of the qualified patient pursuant to this subdivision.

7192. (a) The withholding or withdrawal of life-sustaining procedures from a qualified patient in accordance with the provisions of this chapter shall not, for any purpose, constitute a suicide.

(b) The making of a directive pursuant to Section 7188 shall not restrict, inhibit, or impair in any manner the sale, procurement, or issuance of any policy of life insurance, nor shall it be deemed to modify the terms of an existing policy of life insurance. No policy of life insurance shall be legally impaired or invalidated in any manner by the withholding or withdrawal of life-sustaining procedures from an insured qualified patient, notwithstanding any term of the policy to the contrary.

(c) No physician, health facility, or other health provider, and no health care service plan, insurer issuing disability insurance, self-insured employee welfare benefit plan, or nonprofit hospital service plan, shall require any person to execute a directive as a condition for being insured for, or receiving, health care services.

7193. Nothing in this chapter shall impair or supersede any legal right or legal responsibility which any person may have to effect the withholding or withdrawal of life-sustaining procedures in any lawful manner. In such respect the provisions of this chapter are cumulative.

7194. Any person who willfully conceals, cancels, defaces, obliterates, or damages the directive of another without such declarant's consent shall be guilty of a misdemeanor. Any person who, except where justified or excused by law, falsifies or forges the directive of another, or willfully conceals or withholds personal knowledge of a revocation as provided in Section 7189, with the intent to cause a withholding or withdrawal of life-sustaining procedures contrary to the wishes of the declarant, and thereby, because of any such act, directly causes life-sustaining procedures to be withheld or withdrawn and death to thereby be hastened, shall be subject to prosecution for unlawful homicide as provided in Chapter 1 (commencing with Section 187) of Title 8 of Part 1 of the Penal Code.

7195. Nothing in this chapter shall be construed to condone, authorize, or approve mercy killing, or to permit any affirmative or deliberate act or omission to end life other than to permit the natural process of dying as provided in this chapter.

SEC. 2. If any provision of this act or the application thereof to any person or circumstances is held invalid, such invalidity shall not affect other provisions or applications of the act which can be given effect without the invalid provision or application, and to this end the provisions of this act are severable.

SEC. 3. Notwithstanding Section 2231 of the Revenue and Taxation Code, there shall be no reimbursement pursuant to this section nor shall there be any appropriation made by this act because the Legislature recognizes that during any legislative session a variety of changes to laws relating to crimes and infractions may cause both increased and decreased costs to local government entities and school districts which, in the aggregate, do not result in significant identifiable cost changes.

IV.
Euthanasia:
The Legal
Aspects
of
"Mercy Killing."

EUTHANASIA AND BIATHANASIA:
ON DYING AND KILLING

DAVID W. LOUISELL*

In its precise meaning, "euthanasia" is the desideratum of religion as well as of any morally or ethically based social policy that has to do with death. Coming from the Greek words meaning "good" and "death," it specifies the kind of a death that must be as much the ideal of the moral theologian as it is of the philosopher and secular humanist—a happy death. Yet its corruption seems pervasive in popular usage.[1] It has come to mean the

---

* B.S.L., 1935 University of Minnesota; J.D., 1938 University of Minnesota. Professor of Law, University of California, Berkeley.

Professor David W. Louisell returned to the Catholic University Law School after a 22-year absence (he taught Evidence here 1947-50 while practicing in Washington), as the 1972 Pope John XXIII guest lecturer. Professor Louisell departed from both his outstanding work on Evidence and Procedure and the usual substance of law review commentary to provide a fresh and deft handling of what he sees as, and we agree, a coming enigma with which the legal profession must come to grips. We of the Catholic University Law Review take great pleasure in publishing the 1972 Pope John XXIII Lecture, *Euthanasia and Biathanasia: On Dying and Killing.*

1. Not long ago one of the country's great financial houses sponsored a television show called "The Very Personal Death of Elizabeth Schell Holt-Hartford." It starkly dramatized one of the saddest phases of the human condition, perhaps especially cruel quantitatively and qualitatively in our generation: the loneliness, sense of uselessness and abandonment, and bitterness of many old people. The subject of the story was a lady living alone, who had been divorced and finally died at the age of 82, leaving no known survivors. She often spoke of her dire need for but lack of human companionship. The sense of her unhappiness can almost be touched from her own words—"It's such a grim life;" "The only thing you can do is to bear it until someone shoots you." Her physician tells her "You do not know what is on the other side" and she answers "What I know is on this side and I don't want any more of it." That she remains rational and indeed intellectual even after she broke her hip and was immobilized— pointing out for example that she knows she is lucky compared to the aged poverty-stricken of India—seems only to exacerbate the tragedy by emphasizing the felt pain.

At the beginning the announcer had said: "Because of the sensitive nature of this program [the sponsor] has relinquished all commercial messages." But its generous impulses had little counterpart in the public's reaction, which evidenced a bitterness not unlike that of Mrs. Holt-Hartford's own declining years. In a word, the sponsor was charged with advocating euthanasia. The reactions ranged from the frenetic to the thoughtful, one writer pointing out that what was reprehensible about the program was (according to his interpretation) that the only solution to the problem of old age that was suggested was euthanasia. One who did not view the program will withhold

deliberate, intended painless putting to death of one human person by another, the willed termination of human life, which is a euphemism for murder as defined by our law. It would have been better to adhere to the original meaning of "euthanasia" and use another word, perhaps "biathanasia" for deliberate, affirmative killing in the mercy-death context. But so pervasive and universal is the terminological corruption that scholars, too, seem to have relinquished any notion of restoring original usage and have accepted the modern meaning of euthanasia. Thus, Professor Arthur J. Dyck, in using "euthanasia" in the modern sense, would adopt as a synonym for its original meaning the Latin expression, *benemortasia*.[2]

The Definitional Problem: Voluntary and Involuntary Euthanasia

Taking "euthanasia," in accordance with modern usage, to mean deliberate, intentional painless killing is only the beginning of the definitional problem. Does this include such a killing only when it is sought and requested by the euthanatee or one imposed upon him without regard to his consent—the elimination of defective or hopelessly ill or senile persons, such as Hitler's "useless eaters?" In a word, is the definition directed against only voluntary, or also involuntary, euthanasia?

On the surface, the dichotomy would appear clean-cut. If so, the precise thinker would have cause to resent the countering of argument for voluntary euthanasia, with argument pertinent only to the involuntary kind. For example, during a debate on a 1936 bill in Parliament for voluntary euthanasia, one of the prominent proponents invoked two dramatic and appealing cases, one where a man had drowned his four year old daughter who had contracted tuberculosis and had developed gangrene on the face, the other where a woman had killed her mother who was suffering from general paralysis of the insane. Obviously these were instances of compulsory, or involuntary, euthanasia, yet, although the proponent acknowledged that the cases were not covered by the proposed bill for voluntary euthanasia, they were the only specifice cases he described.[3]

Looking below the surface of the voluntary-involuntary dichotomy may

appraisal of the accuracy of this essentially artistic judgment of the theme. The interesting thing for our purposes was the universal use of the word "euthanasia" to characterize the theme.

Based on program of KNXT-TV, Los Angeles, April 23, 1972, and ensuing unpublished information. For a comparable story, *see On the Occasion of a Death in Boston*, N.Y. Times, Oct. 23, 1972, at 31, col. 2.

2. Saltonstall, Professor of Population at Harvard, in a remarkable paper, *Religion: Aid or Obstacle to Life and Death Decisions in Modern Medicine?*, furnished me in manuscript form by the Joseph P. Kennedy, Jr., Foundation, Washington, D.C.

3. Kamisar, *Some Non-Religious Views Against Proposed "Mercy-Killing" Legislation*, 42 MINN. L. REV. 969, 1016 (1958).

render the purist more understanding of the reasons for the confusion and more tolerant of the confused; a page of history may be worth a chapter of linguistic analysis.

Among some primitive people, the abandonment or killing of the aged or helpless apparently was an accepted practice. The Hottentots carried their elderly parents into the bush to die. The Lapp who became too infirm to trek over the mountains with their families were left behind to die unattended, their frozen corpses to be buried on the family's return. But it is easy to over generalize about customs of euthanasia among primitives, for many societies have actually been shown to have had elaborate codes protective of their senior members. "Instances of this are seen in hospitality customs, property rights, food taboos reserving certain choice dishes for the aged [ostensibly as harmful to the young] and other usages."[4]

Doubtless, the settled agricultural communities showed the highest level of solicitude for the elderly, as witness the laws of the Old Testament Hebrews forbidding the killing of the innocent and just. In classical Greece, there does not seem to have been abandonment of elderly or helpless adults. In ancient Rome, largely under the influence of the Stoics, suicide was an accepted form of death as an escape from disgrace at the hands of an enemy, as, indeed, it was until recently in Japan under the form of hara-kiri. Yet Cicero—who wrote that "The God that rules within us forbids us to depart hence unbidden"—abided his conviction and declined to play the "Roman fool" when pursued to death by the revenge of Antony.[5] Jewish, Christian, and Islamic teachings alike have always maintained that deliberate killing in case of abnormality or incurable illness is wrong. The apparent exception in St. Thomas More's *Utopia* is often interpreted to imply his personal endorsement.[6]

The modern interest in euthanasia is usually dated from the 1870's, but the formal movement did not begin in Britain until the 1930's with the organization of the group now known as the Voluntary Euthanasia Society in 1935. The first bill on euthanasia was brought before the British Parliament in 1936. To be eligible for euthanasia, the patient had to be over twenty-one years of age, suffering from an incurable and fatal illness, and sign a form in the presence of two witnesses asking to be put to death. The

---

4. YOUR DEATH WARRANT (Gould & Craigmyle ed. 1971) [hereinafter cited as DEATH WARRANT]. This book, frequently cited, is the product of a Study Group on Euthanasia set up as a joint venture by the Catholic Union of Great Britain and the Guild of Catholic Doctors. The members of the group were Cicely Clarke, Lord Craigmyle, Charles Dent, J.G. Frost, J.E. McA. Glancy, MD, Jonathan Gould, F.J. Herbert, Joseph Molony, QC, G.E. Moriarty, R.A.G. O'Brien, K.F.M. Pole, Hugh Rossi, MP, P.S. Tweedy and William T. Wells, QC.

5. *Id.* at 21.

6. *Id.* at 22. N. ST. JOHN-STEVAS, LIFE, DEATH AND THE LAW 270 (1961).

bill embraced relatively complicated legal proceedings including investigation by a euthanasia referee and a hearing before a special court. In 1950 there was further debate in the House of Lords on a motion in favor of voluntary euthanasia.[7]

In his classic, *The Sancity of Life and the Criminal Law*,[8] Professor Glanville Williams, realizing the practical necessity of countering the contention that too much formality in the sick room would destroy the doctor-patient relationship, proposed a simple formula quite different from the 1936 attempt. He suggested the uncomplicated provision that no medical practitioner should be guilty of an offense in respect of an act done intentionally to accelerate the death of a patient who is seriously ill, unless it is proved that the act was not done in good faith *and* for the purpose of saving him from severe pain in an illness believed to be of an incurable and fatal character.[9] This proposal formed the basis of the 1968 draft bill which, with changes, was debated in the House of Lords in 1969. The most recent parliamentary euthanasia debate was in the House of Commons in April, 1970, on a motion for leave to introduce a bill.[10] But to date no statute has been enacted.

The Euthanasia Society of America was constituted in 1938 and a bill, following the 1936 British model, was introduced that year in the Nebraska Assembly but lost. A similar attempt failed in the New York Assembly.[11]

> The Euthanasia Society of America had at first proposed to advocate the compusory "euthanasia" of monstrosities and imbeciles, but as a result of replies to a questionnaire addressed to physicians in the State of New York in 1941, it decided to limit itself to propaganda for voluntary euthanasia.[12]

In any event, there is today no country in the world whose law permits euthanasia either of the voluntary or involuntary type.[13]

In view of the facial restrictions of the current euthanasia movement to the voluntary type, why does confusion persist as to what precisely is being proposed? Why has Glanville Williams protested:

> The [English Society's] bill [debated in Lords in 1936 and 1950] excluded any question of compulsory euthanasia, even for hopelessly

---

7. DEATH WARRANT 23-26.

8. G. WILLIAMS, THE SANCTITY OF LIFE AND THE CRIMINAL LAW, Ch. VIII (1957) [hereinafter cited as THE SANCTITY OF LIFE]. *See also* Williams, *"Mercy Killing" Legislation—a Rejoinder*, 43 MINN. L. REV. 1 (1958); Williams, *Euthanasia and Abortion*, 38 U. COLO. L. REV. 178 (1966).

9. THE SANCTITY OF LIFE 340. *See also* C. RICE, THE VANISHING RIGHT TO LIVE 54 (1969) [hereinafter cited as THE VANISHING RIGHT].

10. *See* DEATH WARRANT 24-67.

11. *Id.* at 26, 30.

12. *Id.* at 26.

13. French and Swiss permissiveness whereby a physician may provide, but may not administer, poison at the request of a dying patient, is to be distinguished. DEATH WARRANT 27. Apparently the law of Texas is in accord. *See* R. PERKINS, CRIMINAL LAW 67 (1957).

defective infants. Unfortunately, a legislative proposal is not assured of success merely because it is worded in a studiously moderate and restrictive form. The method of attack, by those who dislike the proposal, is to use the "thin edge of the wedge" argument . . . . There is no proposal for reform of any topic, however conciliatory and moderate, that cannot be opposed by this dialectic.[14]

At least several observations are pertinent in explanation of the persisting terminological confusion. Some pertain only to subjective appraisal of the good faith of discussants, but others proceed from the reality that voluntary euthanasia is not as intrinsically severable from the involuntary as the clean-cut verbal distinction suggests.

First, the problem of the rights of minors always lurks to compound the difficulties of human forays into life-death decisions unless application to minors is explicitly precluded. Normally, decisions respecting serious medical procedures on minors must await parental or guardian approval, although historically there have been exceptions for emergencies and even further exceptions under the impetus of permissive abortion laws. If euthanasia is right, should it be withheld from an intelligent and knowledgeable minor, one whose judgment might be highly pertinent to judicial decision respecting child custody in divorce cases? And if the minor and parent differ on acceleration of the former's death, whose judgment controls? Confronted with this dilemma, apparently the best that Glanville Williams could argue, was: "The use that may be made of my proposed measure [euthanasia] in respect of patients who are minors is best left to the good sense of the doctor, taking into account, as he always does, the wishes of the parents as well as those of the child."[15] Those skeptical about the vagaries and nebulosity of judicial "discretion" should take note![16]

Second, voluntary euthanasia by definition would be available only to those who freely, intelligently, and knowingly request it. This presupposes mental competence. Might the test of competence be as intangible and uncertain as it may be with respect to the execution of a will; or commitment as potentially dangerous; or responsibility for criminal conduct—whether

---

14. THE SANCTITY OF LIFE, 333-34. Note how simply the voluntary-involuntary distinction is put in J. DEDEK, HUMAN LIFE: SOME MORAL ISSUES 133 (1972).

15. THE SANCTITY OF LIFE 340, n.8. The proposed 1969 British bill excludes minors by providing that "qualified patient" means a patient over the age of majority. DEATH WARRANT, App., at 139.

16. Regarding the assumed exclusive medical competence of physicians to make moral value judgment in the biological area, see Louisell, *Abortion, the Practice of Medicine, and the Due Process of Law*, 16 U.C.L.A. L. REV. 233, 245-46 (1969); LOUISELL AND NOONAN, CONSTITUTIONAL BALANCE, IN THE MORALITY OF ABORTION 220, 256-57 (J. Noonan ed. 1970). See JAKOBOVITS, *Jewish View on Abortion*, ABORTION AND THE LAW 124, 125-26 (D. Smith ed. 1967); Hellegers, *Law and the Common Good*, COMMONWEAL, June 30, 1967, at 418.

under the M'Naghten,[17] Durham,[18] Model Penal Code,[19] or diminished responsibility test;[20] or capacity to stand trial.[21] The determination of competence in such a context might be even more emergent and difficult than its conventional determinations and the significance of error even more dire in its irreversability. Moreover difficulties might be compounded by the inhibition on free choice inherent in subjection to pain-killing drugs.[22]

Third, quite independently of the effect of narcotics on consciousness, pain itself, the toxic effects of desease, and the repercussions of surgical procedures may substantially undermine the capacity for rational and independent thought. As Professor Yale Kamisar asks: "If . . . a man in this plight [throes of serious pain or disease] were a criminal defendant and he were to decline the assistance of counsel would the courts hold that he had 'intelligently and understandingly waived the benefit of counsel?' "[23] Would a confession made in such circumstances be admissible?

Fourth, what of the proposed euthanatee who is unable to communicate for himself? Would another, possibly a spouse or next of kin, be presumed to be a competent speaker for him? Those who have inquired into the authority of one to bear for another the decisional burden in the more conventional medical dilemmas[24] know how difficult it is to construct an adequate juridical basis for placement of the patient's burden of decision on another, even a loving spouse.[25] After all, an adult under no legal disability has no natural guardian. The 1969 British bill partially avoids this dilemma by providing that a declaration for euthanasia shall come into force 30 days after being made, shall remain in force, unless revoked, for three years, and a declaration re-executed within the 12 months preceding its expiration date shall remain in force, unless revoked, during the lifetime of the declarant.[26] Even so, the continuing effectiveness of a declaration might raise the afore-

---

17. M'Naghten's Case, 10 Clark & F. 200, 8 Eng. Rep. 718 (1843).

18. Durham v. United States, 214 F.2d 826 (D.C. Cir. 1954); *compare* United States v. Brawner, 471 F.2d 909 (D.C. Cir. 1972).

19. § 4.01; *see also* United States v. Currens, 290 F.2d 751 (1961); Diamond, *From M'Naghten to Currens, and Beyond*, 50 CALIF.L. REV. 189 (1962).

20. People v. Wells, 33 Cal. 2d 330, 202 P.2d 53 (1949); People v. Gorshen, 51 Cal. 2d 716, 336 P.2d 492 (1959); *see* Louisell & Hazard, *Insanity as a Defense: The Bifurcated Trial*, 49 CALIF. L. REV. 805, 816 (1961). For brief summary of St. Thomas Aquinas' prescription of criteria relevant to responsibility for acts, *see* Louisell & Diamond, *Law and Psychiatry: Detente, Entente, or Concomitance?* 50 CORN. L.Q. 217, 218 n. 8 (1965).

21. For criteria of responsibility in the criminal area, *see* generally W. CLARK AND W. MARSHALL, CRIMES § 6.01 (7th ed. 1967); Diamond, *Criminal Responsibility of the Mentally Ill*, 14 STAN. L. REV. 59 (1961).

22. Kamisar, *supra* note 3, at 986-87.

23. *Id.* at 987-88.

24. Such as, for example, the decision of a spouse as to when the respirator should be turned off when it has failed to resuscitate the dying spouse.

25. LOUISELL & WILLIAMS, 2 MEDICAL MALPRACTICE ¶ 22.09 (Rev. ed. 1971).

26. DEATH WARRANT, App., at 140.

suggested imponderables of a life-death decision made by one for another, during, for example, a declarant's long coma with a spouse claiming its revocation—a psychologically traumatic context.

Lastly, Glanville Williams' resentment of the "thin edge of the wedge" opposition to euthanasia, however justified in the abstract, loses cogency in the actual context of the movement's strategy and tactics. Yale Kamisar has convincingly demonstrated that the movement's purpose and method substantially has been utilization of the "wedge" principle.[27] This conviction is fortified by the effectiveness of the "wedge" principle as used in the movement for permissive abortion. The public protests of the proponents for abortion seeking "only a moderate statute"—as they characterize the California law,[28] permitting abortion when the mother's physical or mental health is threatened and in case of felonious sexual assault—have given way to their real goal: abortion on demand.[29] A physician has drawn a meaningful parallel: "I don't think that human consciousness and psychology as it exists in our society today could tolerate euthanasia. Yet 20 years ago our society wouldn't have tolerated extensive abortion. Our mores change."[30]

The "thin edge of the wedge" danger is real; the camel's nose does get under the tent; once opened, the movement of the door to death by human choice may be constantly widening, and likely a never narrowing movement. It seems pertinent to remember the Hitlerian eugenic euthanasia— the elimination of "useless eaters"—which preceded his wholesale racial genocide, was supported by "humanitarian petitions" to him by parents of malformed children requesting authority for "mercy deaths." It is perhaps the supreme irony that Jews were initially excluded from the program of eugenic euthanasia in Nazi Germany on the ground that they did not deserve the benefit of such psychiatric care.[31] Whether the distinction between voluntary and involuntary euthanasia is as meaningful and abiding as its facile verbal formulation would suggest is open to debate. This article takes the proponents at their present word and limits the discussion chiefly to so-called "voluntary" euthanasia.[32] The definition of voluntary euthanasia that puts the affirmative case in the strongest possible terms is Professor Kamisar's

---

27. Kamisar, *supra* note 3, at 1014-41.
28. CAL. HEALTH & SAFETY CODE §§ 25951-25952 (West Supp. 1972).
29. N.Y. PENAL LAW § 125.05 (McKinney Supp. 1972).
30. Dr. Michael Kaback, as quoted in Freeman, *The "God Committee,"* N.Y. Times, May 21, 1972, § 6 (Magazine), at 89. [Since this paper was delivered, Roe v. Wade, 93 S. Ct. 705 (1973) and Doe v. Bolton, 93 S. Ct. 739 (1973) have been decided.]
31. THE VANISHING RIGHT 62-63; Kamisar, *supra* note 3, at 1033.
32. In doing so, of course we put outside our ambit one of life's most agonizing dilemmas, crippling infant deformities which at extremity—in terminology as in actuality—produce monsters. The current attention focuses sharply on meningomyelocele, spina bifida, spina aperta, or open spine. *See* E. Freeman, *supra* note 30, at 85.

definition, which assumes:

> [A person] . . . *in fact* (1) presently incurable, (2) beyond the
> aid of any respite which may come along in his life expectancy,
> suffering (3) intolerable and (4) unmitigatable pain and of a (5)
> fixed and (6) rational desire to die . . . .[33]

But before applying that definition to our problem, a few more preliminary
delineations are in order.

More Definitional Problems:
(i) Euthanasia v. Extraordinary Means to Preserve Life;
(ii) Euthanasia v. Alleviation of Pain by Drugs.

The word "euthanasia" does not include the withholding of extraordinary
means to preserve life. To call the mere withholding of extraordinary means
"indirect voluntary euthanasia" is, taking into account the currently accepted
meaning of "euthanasia" as deliberate killing, a confusion of terms that
cannot conduce to precision of thought.[34] Putting aside for the moment
the difficulties in adequately articulating the difference between "extraordinary" and "ordinary" means of preserving life, the soundness of the distinction in principle is central to the main thesis of this article. If the distinction between affirmative killing and letting die is only a quibble, as some
have characterized it,[35] my thesis here fails.

When studying this problem, one inured to common law thinking must be
careful lest he assimilate the "extraordinary—ordinary" means distinction to
our law's classic differentiation between "action" and "inaction." The
common law notion that despite the relative ease of rescue a stranger may
safely ignore a person in dire predicament—a drowning child, for example—
whereas if he undertakes rescue he is held to the standard of due care,[36]
does not govern in the typical application of the "extraordinary"—"ordinary"
means distinction. Under the common law rule (which by no means is
universally accepted),[37] a physician may refuse aid to the stranger-victim of
an emergency without incurring legal liability, while in voluntarily rendering

---

33. Kamisar, *supra* note 3, at 1042.

34. P. RAMSEY, THE PATIENT AS PERSON 152-53 (1970); THE VANISHING RIGHT 68-
69.

35. J. FLETCHER, EUTHANASIA AND ANTI-DYSTHANASIA IN MORAL RESPONSIBILITY
(*The Patient's Right to Die*) 141-60 (1967).

36. "The result of all this is that the Good Samaritan who tries to help may find
himself mulcted in damages, while the priest and the Levite who pass by on the other
side go on their cheerful way rejoicing." PROSSER, LAW OF TORTS 339 (3rd ed.
1964). Of course, this assumes the absence of a relationship that may impose a duty,
e.g., teacher-pupil, carrier-passenger, innkeeper-guest, etc.

37. German Criminal Code § 330c; French Penal Code Art. 63. *See* 2 LOUISELL
AND WILLIAMS, MEDICAL MALPRACTICE ¶ 21.42 at 594.40 (Rev. ed. 1971) [hereinafter
cited as MEDICAL MALPRACTICE].

aid he incurs the obligation of using due care.[38] The important point is that the *attending* physician is not a volunteer; he is bound to the standards of medical performance, including affirmative acts, under the sanction of malpractice liability,[39] as well as other sanctions.[40] Therefore, an attending physician's attempted justification for failure to fulfill the standards of medical practice, on the sole ground that his failure was "inaction" rather than "affirmative action" would be preposterous.[41] But a failure to use "extraordinary" means is a different matter and, in a given context, may be legally justifiable.

Similarly, the use of drugs to alleviate pain, even though that use in fact may hasten death, is not "euthanasia" in the modern meaning of direct, deliberate killing, because even if in both cases death may be "willed" in the sense of desired, there is a difference in means of abiding significance in the realities of the human condition. Thus a provision in the British euthanasia bill of 1969 works a disservice to clarity of analysis when it couples a provision authorizing true euthanasia with one declaring that a patient suffering from an irremediable condition, reasonably thought in his case to be terminal, shall be entitled to the administration of whatever quantity of drugs may be required to keep him free from pain.[42] There is no serious practical question of the present legality of such use of drugs[43] nor any genuine problem with its ethicality.[44] Daniel Maguire's recent question

---

38. MEDICAL MALPRACTICE ¶ 21.35, at 594.24.
The way this caused Good Samaritan statutes, exculpating the physician who follows his conscience rather than his convenience, to sweep the country like prairie fire, is a story I have tried to tell elsewhere. *Id.* ¶ 21.01, at 594.3.

39. Mason v. Ellsworth, 3 Wash. App. 298, 474 P.2d 909 (1970).

40. MEDICAL MALPRACTICE, Ch. VIII.

41. MEDICAL MALPRACTICE, Ch. VIII; Kamisar, supra Note 3, at 982, n.41; D. MEYERS, THE HUMAN BODY AND THE LAW 147-48 (1970).

42. DEATH WARRANT, App., at 141.

43. It is true that good motive conventionally does not per se preclude criminality in homicide. CLARK AND MARSHALL, CRIMES 263-65 (7th ed. 1967); PERKINS, CRIMINAL LAW 721 (1957); *but cf. Id.* 723. Thus it remains arguable that the good motivation of alleviating pain per se would not relieve from murder a physician who injected a heavy dose of drugs with knowledge that it certainly would cause death, any more than one would be relieved who injected with the specific purpose of killing. But the requisite proof of certain "causation," when death was in process in any event, would in the typical case seem as theoretically impossible as it would be practically unavailable. *Compare* G. Fletcher, *Prolonging Life*, 42 WASH. L. REV. 999 (1967). In the trial of Dr. Adams for murder in Britain in 1957, the jury was instructed: "If the first purpose of medicine, the restoration of health, can no longer be achieved there is still much for a doctor to do, and he is entitled to do all that is proper and necessary to relieve pain and suffering, even if the measures he takes may incidentally shorten human life." MEYERS, *supra* note 41, at 146-47. *See also* Recent Decisions, 48 MICH. L. REV. 1199 (1950); Recent Decisions, 34 NOTRE DAME LAWYER 460 (1959).

44. Whether my conclusion that it is ethical for the physician to administer drugs to alleviate pain even to an extent that may shorten life is any more viable than the principle of double effect, or whether indeed that principle is enough to sustain the distinction between such administration and intended killing, let us put aside for

equating "positive action" and "calculated benign neglect" has a similar defect, although in his instance there is at least the justification of an ensuing explicit confrontation with the question's innuendo.[45]

The Ethics of Voluntary Euthanasia

Had this article been written fifteen years ago, its gist almost necessarily would have been an inquiry into the ethics of euthanasia. But in the meantime such inquiry, acutely engendered at one stage by the running debate between Glanville Williams[46] and his opponents, has been richly productive. Whatever the diminution of moral reprehensibility by the facts of a given case, euthanasia in principle is unethical, as well as illegal, killing; this viewpoint has already been essentially presented by Yale Kamisar,[47] Charles E. Rice,[48] David Daube,[49] Norman St. John-Stevas, M.P.,[50] and others.[51] Therefore, only a brief comment regarding the ethics of voluntary euthanasia itself— the deliberate, affirmative, intentional act of effecting a mercy death—is necessary.

In discussing the ethics of euthanasia, a warning immediately comes to mind. Except as Scripture, or extrapolations therefrom, or from received Christian tradition, formulate reasons for opposing euthanasia, in what way do "religious" reasons differ from "non-religious" ones?[52]

---

the moment. But I should candidly note here that I am not among those inclined to emphasize the moral value of pain. Sometimes the writers, particularly some of the more ancient theologians, seem almost to be arguing that it is, after all, human suffering that makes this the best of all possible worlds! Amidst such mock heroics it is refreshing to turn to the common sense of Pius XII who in his February, 1957 address to the Italian anesthesiologists, after pointing out that the growth in the love of God does not come from suffering itself but from the intention of the will, candidly concluded that instead of assisting toward expiation and merit, suffering can also furnish occasion for new faults. Surely there must be a midground between the exaltation of human suffering as glorious, and the attitude often lived by today that it is the ultimate evil, reflected in the automatic gulp for the aspirin bottle at the mere hint of a headache.

45. *The Freedom to Die*, 96 COMMONWEAL (August 11, 1972), at 423-24.
46. *See* note 8 *supra* and accompanying text.
47. *See* note 3 *supra*.
48. *See* THE VANISHING RIGHT, Ch. 4.
49. Daube, *Sanctity of Life*, 60 PROC. ROY. SOC. MED. 1235 (1967).
50. N. ST. JOHN-STEVAS, LIFE, DEATH, AND THE LAW (1961).
51. *See, e.g.*, DEATH WARRANT; P. RAMSEY, THE PATIENT AS PERSON, Ch. 3 (1970). *Compare* D. MEYERS, THE HUMAN BODY AND THE LAW (1970) *with* A. Dyck, Religion: Aid or Obstacle to Life and Death Decisions in Modern Medicine (unpublished manuscript).
52. Apparently to characterize reasons as "religious" is to diminish their significance:
　　It is a great mistake to let people know that moral issues involve religion.
　　If you talk about religion you might just as well talk about politics. Everyone agrees that politics and religion are a matter of opinion. You can take your pick. . . .
　　Let this be clear. When we talk about moral problems we are not talking about religious beliefs—which we can take or leave. Stealing, lying, killing, fornicating would be wrong even if no church condemned them. Hijacking

Are not the following reasons for opposing voluntary euthanasia both "religious" and "non-religious?" Ascertainment of a sick person's abiding desire for death and persistent and true intention affirmatively to seek it, is intrinsically difficult and often impossible. The difficulties inhere in illness with its pain and distraction, and are compounded by narcotics and analgesics. Anything like the legal standard for voluntariness in other contexts would be hard to achieve. Would minors of knowledgeable age and discretion be allowed to elect it, and with or without parental consent? A decision made before illness to elect euthanasia conditionally, would have morbid aspects and would leave lingering doubts as to the continuity of intention, especially with intervening coma. Euthanasia, if legally formalized by procedural restrictions, would threaten to convert the sick room into an adjudicative tribunal. The consequences of required decisions and procedures might be harsher for the family, especially young children, than for the dying person. If left essentially to the discretion of the physician, administration of euthanasia would be as variable as the tremendous variation in medical competence. But not even the best physician is infallible and mistakes, necessarily irretrievable, would have the odious flavor of avoidable tragedy. Moreover, the history of science and medicine increasingly demonstrates that yesterday's incurable disease is the subject matter of today's routine treatment. Even "incurable" cancer is sometimes subject to remissions.[53] In medicine, as in life itself, there is no absolute hopelessness.

Euthanasia would even threaten the patient-physician relationship; confidence might give way to suspicion. Would a patient who had intended to revoke his declaration for euthanasia have faith that his second word would be heeded? Can the physician, historic battler for life, become an affirmative agent of death without jeopardizing the trust of his dependants? Indeed, would not his new function of active euthanator tend psychologically to undermine the physician's acclimation to the historic mandate of the Hippocratic Oath? And what would acceptance of the psychology of euthanasia do to the peace of mind of the mass of the so-called incurables?

How long would we have voluntary euthanasia without surrendering to pressures for the involuntary? Would not the pressures be truly inexorable?

Merely to ask such questions and state these points seems to belie a dichotomy between "religious" and "non-religious" reasons for opposing voluntary euthanasia. They are essentially human reasons.[54]

---

aircraft, tossing bombs into crowded shopping centers and selling drugs to your children are not sins mentioned in the bible. Nor is euthanasia. So keep religion out of this . . . .
DEATH WARRANT, Preface, at 13.

53. *Supra* note 3, at 996-1005.

54. *See* notes 46-50 *supra*. The problem of additional moral sanctions behind reasons formally taught by a religion according to its principles of revelation, or other-

There Is No Obligation "Officiously to Keep Alive" the Dying.

"Thou shalt not kill, but need'st not strive Officiously to keep alive."

It is about as clear as human answers can be in such matters that there is
no moral obligation to keep alive by artificial means those whose lives nature
would forfeit and who wish to die.   Further, the law, in no manner, seeks
to set at nought this moral truth.   The moral idea was put this way by Pius
XII when, in November 1957, he answered questions for the International
Congress of Anesthesiologists:

> Natural reason and Christian morals say that man [and whoever
> is entrusted with the task of taking care of his fellowman] has the
> right and the duty in case of serious illness to take the necessary
> treatment for the preservation of life and health.   This duty that one
> has toward himself, toward God, toward the human community,
> and in most cases toward certain determined persons, derives from
> well ordered charity, from submission to the Creator, from social
> justice and even from strict justice, as well as from devotion toward
> one's family.

> But normally one is held to use only ordinary means—according
> to circumstances of persons, places, times, and culture—that is to
> say, means that do not involve any grave burden for oneself or
> another.   A more strict obligation would be too burdensome for
> most men and would render the attainment of the higher, more im-
> portant good too difficult.   Life, health, all temporal activities are
> in fact subordinated to spiritual ends.   On the other hand, one is
> not forbidden to take more than the strictly necessary steps to
> preserve life and health, as long as he does not fail in some more
> serious duty.[55]

Although Pius XII did not use the expression "extraordinary means,"
it has become customary to capture his thought in the shorthand phrase

---

wise, is of course another matter.   For a contemporary analysis of teaching authority
of the Church, *see* D. Maguire, Moral Absolutes and the Magisterium 14 (Corpus
Papers, 1970).

55. 4 THE POPE SPEAKS 393, 395-96 (Spring, 1958).   Compare the condemnation
of euthanasia by Pius XII, both compulsory, in his encyclical Mystici Corporis, A.A.S.
35:239 (1943), and voluntary, Address of May 23, 1948, to International Congress of
Surgeons.   L'Osservatore Romano, May 23, 1948 at 1, col. 1.   *See* N. ST. JOHN-STEVAS,
LIFE, DEATH, AND THE LAW 270-71; III B. HÄRING, C.S.S.R., THE LAW OF CHRIST, at
239-41 (1966).

In March, 1972, a physician's withdrawal of food from a new-born infant with a
seriously defective brain because "the best thing to do was to let him die 'mercifully'"
aroused wide-spread interest.   The withdrawal of food was countermanded by another
physician in the hospital before the baby died.   H. Nelson, *Life or Death for Brain-
damaged Infant?*, Los Angeles Times, March 17, 1972, at 1 col. 4.   Apparently the
legitimacy of such conduct was in serious dispute among physicians at the August, 1972
hearings before the special U.S. Senate Committee on Aging, although the distinction between withholding extraordinary means and affirmative euthanasia seems not always to
have been acknowledged or even perceived.   The New York Times, August 8, 1972, at
15, col. 1.

"distinction between ordinary and extraordinary means." It is a convenient condensation but, as with short names generally, may mislead unless clarified. For one thing, there seems to be considerable difference between the significance typically given the "ordinary and extraordinary means" distinction by physicians on the one hand and moral theologians on the other. Physicians seem to take the distinction as equivalent to that between *customary* and *unusual* means as a matter of medical practice. Theologians pour into the distinction all factors relevant to appropriate moral decision however nonmedical they may be: the patient's philosophic preference, the conditions of the family including the economic facts, and the relative hardships on a realistic basis of one course of conduct as contrasted with another.[56] Even means that are "ordinary" from the viewpoint of medical practice may be "extraordinary" in the totality of life's dilemmas.[57]

Take the case of a three-year old child, one of whose eyes had already been removed surgically because of malignant tumor. The other eye later became infected in the same way, and medical prognosis offered only the dilemma of either certain death without further surgery or a considerable probability of saving the child's life by a second opthalmectomy. From the medical viewpoint, such surgery represents an ordinary means of saving life. I take it to be the prevailing theological view that one is not obliged to save his life when that entails a lifetime of total blindness. In other words, under the circumstances, the surgery would be an extraordinary, and morally not required, way of saving life.[58]

Thus an artificial means, however ordinary in medical practice, may be morally extraordinary and not obligatory. Also, it may be non-obligatory, even though ordinary, because it is likely to be useless. It should be noted that this does include *artificial* means, such as surgery, but not natural things, such as furnishing of food, drink, and the means of rest. To save the convenient distinction between ordinary and extraordinary means, while at the same time promoting its accuracy, theologians have wisely incorporated into the definitions qualifications necessitated by such cases as the three-year old's,

---

56. P. RAMSEY, THE PATIENT AS PERSON 118-24; DEATH WARRANT 82; Decisions about Life and Death, A Problem in Modern Medicine, App. 4, at 56 (Church Assembly Board for Social Responsibility, Church Information Office, Westminster, 1965).
57. *Id.*
58. J. Lynch, S.J., *Notes on Moral Theology*, 19 THEOLOGICAL STUDIES 165, 176 (1958). Hopefully the increasing faculties afforded by science and technology in substitution for eye-sight, may render this judgment obsolescent. *Compare* the discussion in G. Kelly, S.J., *The Duty of Using Artificial Means of Preserving Life*, 11 THEOLOGICAL STUDIES 203 (1950), as to whether it is obligatory for a diabetic patient on insulin who develops very painful and inoperable cancer to continue to use insulin (*Id.* at 208, 215), or for a cancer victim to submit to intravenous feeding (*Id.* at 210). Where the patient is not legally competent, e.g., a minor, there are of course the additional problems. *Cf.* Prince v. Massachusetts, 321 U.S. 158, 170 (1944).

as well as the common-sense requirement that, to be obligatory, an artificial means must be of potential usefulness. Thus:

> *Ordinary means* are all medicines, treatments, and operations, which offer a reasonable hope of benefit and which can be obtained and used without excessive expense, pain, or other inconvenience.
> *Extraordinary means* are all medicines, treatments, and operations, which cannot be obtained or used without excessive expense, pain, or other inconvenience, or which, if used, would not offer a reasonable hope of benefit.[59]

Of course, the physician cannot be blamed for emphasizing the purely medical considerations in his appraisal of the appropriateness of the means for staving off death. Necessarily this is the trend of his training and competence, perhaps sometimes fortified by the potentiality of malpractice liability. On a practical level, the reconciliation of the physician's and moralist's views on extraordinary means is in the reality that the decision as to how hard and far to push to keep life going by artificial means ultimately belongs to the patient, not to the physician. Although the patient may be morally entitled to reject it as extraordinary, the physician may be legally obligated to proffer what is customary medical practice.[60] Conversely, where it is his final hope because lesser efforts afford no promise, presumably the patient is entitled to have means that the physician regards as medically unusual or extraordinary.

While discussing physicians' participation in the life-death decisional process, it is pertinent to note an apparent tendency among them to regard as more significant, and more hazardous, the stopping of extaordinary means compared to failure to start them in the first place.[61] There is more hesitancy to turn off the resuscitator than to decide originally not to turn it on. From the moral viewpoint, this distinction is only a quibble. Indeed, might there not be more justification in ceasing after a failing effort has been made, than in not trying in the first place? The medical attitude in this regard seems more psychologically than rationally based. Perhaps the physician has been excessively influenced by the common law's historic distinction between "action" and "inaction." From the legal viewpoint it is worth noting that Professor Kamisar's careful research failed to reveal by 1958 a single case where there had been an indictment, let alone a conviction, for a "mercy-killing" by omission.[62] It seems legally far-fetched to convert "omission" into "commission" by the mere fact that the machine is turned off

---

59. Kelly, S.J., *The Duty to Preserve Life*, 12 THEOLOGICAL STUDIES 550 (1951) [emphasis added].
60. MEDICAL MALPRACTICE, Ch. VIII.
61. P. RAMSEY, THE PATIENT AS PERSON 121-22; G. Fletcher, *Prolonging Life*, 42 WASH. L. REV. 999, 1005 et seq. (1967).
62. *Supra* note 3, at 983 n.41.

when it fails to be effective, rather than not turned on in the first place.[63] Civil liability is another matter; but is there really much danger of malpractice because a physician ceases to continue to use an apparently hopeless medical technique, just because he has tried it out? Certainly not so where the patient declines further use; and when he is beyond personal decision, because for example unconscious, clearance from a spouse or family member seems to help, although as previously noted it is hard to find a juridical basis for letting one adult decide for another.[64] Estoppel might become a relevant defense in a suit for wrongful death.

The frenetic efforts to resuscitate or just to keep going often are an affront to human dignity. Those who make such efforts do not have as their objective the prolongation of life as much as the maintenance of the process of dying. Can one doubt that Shakespeare has perceived the moral as well as psychological reality when, in King Lear, he put it: "Vex not his ghost: O, let him pass! he hates him That would upon the rack of this tough world Stretch him out longer."[65]

Since the case for not stretching out longer seems so self-evident, how does one explain the countervailing motives and practices of so many physicians and families? In the case of the former, is it sometimes sheer professional pride, human ego, the thrill of the game, perhaps akin to the lawyer's will to win? As to the families, there is no need to look further than to the traumatic shock of threatened death of a beloved. But is a sense of guilt over past neglect, rather than love, sometimes at least a partial explanation? In such an area, one should not speak abstractly: each threatened death is unique and very personal. Who, however-much in agreement with what is said here, would not applaud the most persistent and heroic efforts imaginable to succor the youthful victim of a casualty such as an automobile accident? Who would deny that, in such a case, every intendment of the presumption of the will to live should be indulged by the physicians and all concerned?

Perhaps these frantic efforts to prolong the earthly life of the aged that nature would forfeit go hand in hand with the materialism of modern society. Hilaire Belloc observed:

> Of old when men lay sick and sorely tried,
> The doctors gave them physic and they died.
> But here's a happier age, for now we know
> Both how to make men sick and keep them so![66]

The willingness to let pass those who are ready and wish to pass seems as much an act of Christian faith as of reconciliation with nature's way. In this sense perhaps there is as much of Christian hopefulness about death as

---

63. *Supra* note 43.
64. *Supra* note 25 with text.
65. W. SHAKESPEARE, KING LEAR, Act V, sc. iii.
66. *Supra* note 58, at 174.

of pagan acceptance of dissolution in the poet's invocation of the concept of *conquering* "the fever called 'Living.' "[67]

That it is permissible to withhold extraordinary means seems so clear that future discussion is likely to focus instead on whether and under what circumstances there is a duty to do so. Recall the ending of the quoted allocution of Pius XII: "[O]ne is not forbidden to take more than the strictly necessary steps to preserve life and health, as long as he does not fail in some more serious duty."[68] Doubtless that is the starting point of the relevant analysis and doubtless, too, the decision typically is for the patient, not the physician. But what are the more serious duties that should preponderate for example in the mind of the head of the family, over extravagant efforts to preserve his own life? It certainly seems relevant that profligate expense may deprive the children of education. Hardly less so is the mental torture that may be imposed on the family by indefinite prolongation of the physical dissolution of its head. And possibly, if medical facilities and services increasingly become of lesser availability in relation to the demand, society's needs may some day be held to supersede the personal requests for extraordinary means even by those financially able to pay.

No sooner has one thus spoken of the right, even possibly the duty, of withholding extraordinary means than he wonders if his message tends to undermine the medical professional's proudest boast and happiest claim— its historic bulldogged defense of human life. For in result, even when not in motivation, there is more than professional pride and human ego in the physician's strugglings. As Gerald Kelley put it:

> By working on even the smallest hope doctors often produce wonderful results, whereas a defeatist attitude would in a certain sense "turn back the clock" of medical progress. Also, this professional ideal is a sure preventive of a euthanasian mentality.[69]

---

67. Edgar Allan Poe, For Annie, first and sixth verses:
Thank Heaven! the crisis—
   The danger is past,
And the lingering illness
   Is over at last—
And the fever called "Living"
   Is conquered at last.
   . . .
And oh! of all tortures
   That torture the worst
Has abated—the terrible
   Torture of thirst,
For the naphthaline river
   Of Passion accurst:—
I have drank of a water
   That quenches all thirst:—
68. *See* note 56 *supra* with text; DEATH WARRANT 69.
69. Kelly, *The Duty of Using Artificial Means of Preserving Life*, 11 THEO. STUDIES 203, 216-17 (1950).

Our last, and hardest question, essentially becomes: Is the distinction between letting die and killing sound enough to preclude the euthanasian mentality?

The Distinction between Killing, and Letting Die, Continues to be Viable, Valid and Meaningful

If it is permissible to let die a patient direly afflicted and sorely suffering, why is it wrong affirmatively to help him die with loving purpose and kindly means? The question poses stark challenge to philosopher, theologian, ethician, moralist, physician, and lawyer.

Let us put onto the scales our conclusions to the moment, on the one side the permissible things, on the other those forbidden. Note that on each side there is a negative and an affirmative thing. It is permissible to withhold extraordinary means, and also to give drugs to relieve pain even to the point of causing death. It is not permissible to withhold ordinary means, or affirmatively and intentionally to cause death. Certainly the fact that our distinctions are fine does not of itself condemn them. Biology, psychology and morality, like life itself, are filled with close questions, narrow definitions, and fine distinctions.[70] The margin between pain and pleasure may be as imprecise as that between love and hate.[71] Nor is universal certainty and equality of application of principle to the facts of cases necessarily a test of the principle's validity. Appellate judges are, wont to say that much must be left to the discretion of trial judges, and moralists must concur that much must be left to the judgment of those who apply principle to hard facts. As Gerald Vann put it:

> [M]oral action presupposes science but is itself an art, the art of living. Moral science concerns itself first of all with general principles, as indeed being a science it must; but the subject of morality is not human action in general, but this or that human action, in this or that set of circumstances, and emanating from this or that personality. Hence the fact, remarked upon by Aristotle, that ethics cannot be an exact science. There is no set of ready-made rules to be applied to each individual case; the principles have to be applied, but this is the function of the virtue of prudence, and with prudence as with art, as Maritain paints out, each new case is really a new

---

70. Compare the fine distinctions in French and Swiss law whereby a physician may provide, but may not administer, poison at the request of a dying patient. This is because suicide is not a crime, and therefore to be an accessory to it cannot be criminal; but directly to kill another even from humane motives is still murder. DEATH WARRANT 27-28. In 1961 the illegality of attempted suicide was abolished in English law, but it remains a serious crime for a person to incite or assist another to commit suicide. *See* note 13 *supra* and accompanying text.

71. MONTAIGNE'S ESSAYS, Vol. 2, Ch. XX, *We Taste Nothing Purely* 607, 608 (Florio trans., Modern Library ed.)

and unique case, each action is a unique action. What constitutes
the goodness of an action is the relation of the mind not to moral
principles in the abstract but to this individual moral action.
Hence an essential element of quasi-intuition is at least implicit
in every willed and chosen action.[72]

Common law lawyers have admirable instruments by which to effectuate
the moralist's acknowledgment of the necessity of accommodation of principle
to fact. There are at the intellectual or formal level the institutions of equity
and on the pragmatic level trial by jury. The accommodation by a jury
may be radical indeed, as Dryden observed centuries ago:

> Who laugh'd but once to see an ass,
> Mumbling to make the cross grain'd thistles pass;
> Might laugh again, to see a jury chaw
> The prickles of an unpalatable law.[73]

---

72. G. VANN, O.P., MORALS AND MAN 83 (1960).

73. Quoted in BOTEIN, TRIAL JUDGE 182 (1952). See Repouille v. United States,
165 F.2d 152, 153 (2d Cir. 1947) (Hand, J.). Sioux City & Pacific Railroad
Co. v. Stout, 84 U.S. (17 Wall.) 657 (1873) remains a leading case on the jury's authority to fix standards in ambiguous areas. Compare HOLMES, THE COMMON LAW
123-24 (1881). One wonders how much of Stout's meaning is forgotten in the
movement to the smaller jury. Williams v. Florida, 399 U.S. 78 (1970); Colgrove v.
Battin, 41 L.W. 5025 (1973). See also Apodaca v. Oregon, 406 U.S. 404 (1972).
And quaere, as to the meaning of the death penalty cases, Furman v. Georgia, 408
U.S. 238 (1972), especially the opinions of White and Stewart, JJ., in respect of the
significance our society accords jury ascertainment of its value judgments. Note the
caveat in the dissenting opinion of Burger, C.J., for himself and Blackmun, Powell,
and Rehnquist, JJ.:

> The selectivity of juries in imposing the punishment of death is properly
> viewed as a refinement on rather than a repudiation of the statutory authoriza-
> tion for that penalty. Legislatures prescribe the categories of crimes for
> which the death penalty should be available, and, acting as "the conscience of
> the community," juries are entrusted to determine in individual cases that the
> ultimate punishment is warranted. Juries are undoubtedly influenced in this
> judgment by myriad factors. The motive or lack of motive of the perpetrator,
> the degree of injury or suffering of the victim or victims and the degree of
> brutality in the commission of the crime would seem to be prominent among
> these factors. Given the general awareness that death is no longer a routine
> punishment for the crimes for which it is made available, it is hardly sur-
> prising that juries have been increasingly meticulous in their imposition of
> the penalty. But to assume from the mere fact of relative infrequency that
> only a random assortment of pariahs are sentenced to death, is to cast grave
> doubt on the basic integrity of our jury system.
>
> It would, of course, be unrealistic to assume that juries have been perfectly
> consistent in choosing the cases where the death penalty is to be imposed,
> for no human institution performs with perfect consistency. There are doubt-
> less prisoners on death row who would not be there had they been tried
> before a different jury or in a different State. In this sense their fate has
> been controlled by a fortuitous circumstance. However, this element of for-
> tuity does not stand as an indictment either of the general functioning of
> juries in capital cases or of the integrity of jury decisions in individual cases.
> There is no empirical basis for concluding that juries have generally
> failed to discharge in good faith the responsibility described in Wither-
> spoon—that of choosing between life and death in individual cases according
> to the dictates of community values. 408 U.S. at 388-89.

With such means of accommodation, we do not need, I think, formal provisions of law to mitigate the potential harshness in applying homicide principles to mercy deaths. But whether we do need them, is certainly a legitimate and open question; some will argue for statutes authorizing lesser penalties in case of euthanasia, as in Norway.[74] I think such a formal provision for mitigation might do more harm educationally by way of undermining the distinction between letting die and killing, than good, substantively.[75] This presupposes the validity of the distinction.

Daniel Maguire in Commonweal recently concluded:

> [I]t can be said that in certain cases, direct positive intervention to bring on death may be morally permissible. . . . The absolutist stance opposed to this conclusion must assume the burden of proof—an impossible burden, I believe.[76]

This conclusion on burden of proof might astound the proceduralist, certainly one of historical orientation, as much as the moralist. For centuries, medical ethics has drawn sharp and firm distinction between "positive action" and "calculated benign neglect," to use Maguire's own terms.[77] The theologian's principle of double effect is an ancient one. In the face of the historical realities, why, suddenly, this reversal of the burden of proof? Hardly because today's logic is sharper; the principle of double effect has been reexamined and criticized by able minds for generations. Do the new psychological insights justify such reversal of the field? Quite the contrary!

The principle of double effect has four criteria. They are:

(i)   the act itself must be morally good, or at least neutral;

(ii) the purpose must be to achieve the good consequence, the bad consequence being only a side effect;

(iii) the good effect must not be achieved by way of the bad, but both must result from the same act;

(iv) the bad result must not be so serious as to outweigh the advantage of the good result.[78]

Admittedly application of these criteria may produce nuances so delicate that the decision of one able and conscientious mind may be at odds with another equally able and conscientious. Take, for example, the distinction between

See also Witherspoon v. Illinois, 391 U.S. 510 (1968); McGautha v. California, 402 U.S. 183 (1971).

74. DEATH WARRANT 28.

75. Compare Silving, Euthanasia: A Study in Comparative Criminal Law, 103 U. PA. L. REV. 350, 352-54 (1954); Recent Decisions, 34 NOTRE DAME LAW, 460-64 (1959). See note 73, supra.

76. The Freedom to Die, COMMONWEAL, August 11, 1972, at 423.

77. P. RAMSEY, THE PATIENT AS PERSON 118-119.

78. DEATH WARRANT 80. For a contemporary discussion of the principle of double effect, see C. Curran, Medicine and Morals 5-7 (Corpus Papers 1970).

the administration of drugs to kill, on the one hand, and the administration to relieve pain even though death may be hastened, on the other. Conceding *arguendo* that a principle of such ambivalent potential may have logical deficiencies, is not the ultimate question of its justification not one of dry logic but of its psychological validity? Let us suppose a physician, faced with his patient's intolerable pain unmitigable by lesser doses and his urgent plea for relief, decides on a dose of analgesic likely to cause death. (You may substitute "certainly to cause death" if you wish, but, in the physiological realities, it may always remain doubtful whether the pain itself might have been as death-producing.)

Contrast the attitude and manner which the motive of relieving pain engenders, with those likely consequent upon a grim determination to kill. If the purpose explicitly were to kill, would there not be profound difference in the very way one would grasp the syringe, the look in the eye, the words that might be spoken or withheld, those subtle admixtures of fear and hope that haunt the death-bed scene? And would not the consequences of the difference be compounded almost geometrically at least for the physician as he killed one such patient after another? And what of the repercussions of the difference on the nurses and hospital attendants? How long would the quality and attitude of mercy survive death-intending conduct? The line between the civilized and savage in men is fine enough without jeopardizing it by euthanasia. History teaches the line is maintainable under the principle of double effect; it might well not be under a regime of direct intentional killing.

There would be adverse effects on the family if law—sometimes the great teacher of our society—were to start to teach the legitimacy of direct killing. David Daube relates a telling illustration of the validity of this concern. There was at Oxford one of the great historians of the century who was totally paralyzed up to the shoulders, with all that implies by way of dependence and suffering. A loving wife and family nurtured and sustained him, at no mean cost. The visit of this profound scholar and scintilating conversationalist to All Souls College were a weekly delight to all who could share the coffee hour with him, even as he sipped with a tube from the cup. Immobile in his wheel chair, he nevertheless gave a final memorable lecture. Under a regime of euthanasia's legitimacy, would not cultivated, sensitive, and selfless spirits such as this feel an obligation to spare their families the burden? Certainly in this case, as Professor Daube concludes, scholarship, family life, and All Souls College might have paid a heavy price in a euthansiac regime for an act that might have been coerced by a sense of obligation.[79] To the sensitive and selfless especially, what the law

---

79. Daube, *Sanctity of Life,* 60 PROC. R. SOC. MED. 1235, 1336 (1967). In his

would permit might well become the measure of obligation to family and friends.[80]

---

paper, *supra* note 2, Professor Dyck asks:

Why are these distinctions [between permitting to die and causing death] important in instances where permitting to die or causing death have the same effect—namely, that a life is shortened? In both instances there is a failure to try to prolong the life of one who is dying. It is at this point that one must see why consequential reasoning is in itself too narrow, and why it is important also not to limit the discussion of euthanasia to the immediate relationship between a single patient and a single physician.

Answering, he states in part:

. . . If a dying person chooses for the sake of relieving pain drugs administered in potent does, this is not primarily an act of shortening life, although it may have that effect, but it is a choice of how the patient wishes to live while dying. Similarly, if a patient chooses to forego medical interventions that would have the effect of prolonging his or her dying without in any way promising release from death, this also is a choice as to what is the most meaningful way to spend the remainder of life, however short that may be. The choice to use drugs to relieve pain and the choice not to use medical measures that cannot promise a cure for one's dying are no different in principle from the choices we make throughout our lives as to how much we will rest, how hard we will work, how little and how much medical intervention we will seek or tolerate and the like.

80. *See* Death Warrant 83-84; J. Dedek, Human Life: Some Moral Issues 121, 127 (1972). Compare the euthanasiac death of Sigmund Freud as told by his physician, Max Schur, Freud: Living and Dying (1972). Freud's cancer of the oral cavity was discovered in April, 1923, when he was about 67 years old. Schur became his personal physician in 1928 and served until Freud's death in 1939, both in Vienna and London. *Id.* at 347. When he first engaged Schur, Freud obtained the promise of euthanasia:

. . . Mentioning only in a rather general way "some unfortunate experiences with your predecessors," he expressed the expectation that he would always be told the truth and nothing but the truth. My response must have reassured him that I meant to keep such a promise. He then added, looking searchingly to me: "Versprechen Sie mir auch noch: Wenn es mal so weit ist, werden Sie mich nicht unnötig quälen lassen." ["Promise me one more thing: that when the time comes, you won't let me suffer unnecessarily."] All this was said with the utmost simplicity, without a trace of pathos, but also with complete determination. We shook hands at this point.

Id. at 408. Thus doctor and patient were under euthanasiac commitment during approximately the last 11 years of Freud's life. Schur relates the final scene:

On the following day, September 21, while I was sitting at his bedside, Freud took my hand and said to me: "Leiber Schur, Sie erinnern sich wohl an unser erstes Gespräch. Sie haben mir damals versprochen mich nicht im Stiche zu lassen wenn es so weit ist. Das ist jetzt nur noch Quälerei und hat keinen Sinn mehr." [My dear Schur, you certainly remember our first talk. You promised me then not to forsake me when my time comes. Now it's nothing but torture and makes no sense any more."]

I indicated that I had not forgotten my promise.

He sighed with relief, held my hand for a moment longer, and said: "Ich danke Ihnen" ["I thank you,"] and after a moment of hesitation he added: "Sagen Sie es der Anna" ["Tell Anna about this."] All this was said without a trace of emotionality or self-pity, and with full consciousness of reality.

I informed Anna of our conversation, as Freud had asked. When he was again in agony I gave him a hypodermic of two centigrams of morphine. He soon felt relief and fell into a peaceful sleep. The expression of pain and suffering was gone. I repeated this dose after about twelve hours. Freud

The principle mischief with such life-interfering proposals as euthanasia is their undue deprecation of the importance of the natural order in human affairs. As a principle heresy of the 19th Century was that progress lay in human domination of the environment, perhaps the heresy of this century will prove to be that biological evolution must be dominated by human will.[81] Certainly the freedom and integrity of the human person should not be as much ravaged and stripped as have been the forests and fields and waters of the world. As a physician puts it:

> [W]e are possessed with a technologic spirit in which power over nature is the predominant theme. We ignore the fact that there is an intrinsic despair and disparity in looking to technology for a solution. We forget that our problem is not to master nature, but to nurture nature. We also forget that technological achievements are, at best, ameliorative, and, at worst, dehumanizing.[82]

The additional dilemmas that a regime of mercy deaths would impose—such problems as ascertainment of true and abiding consent—would seem of themselves reasons for avoiding the creation of more unlighted pathe.[83] Is not the preferred choice continuing progress in the alleviation of pain, loving care of the dying among our neighbors, rather than killing? We are only mortal, and in this area a grand attempt to restructure the natural order seems more dangerous than hopeful. Nature can be harsh and cruel, but it is never corrupt. Human will can be all three.

Conclusion

The distinction between affirmative killing and allowing one to die according to nature's order without extraordinary effort to "stretch him out longer" continues to be valid, viable, and meaningful.[84] The line of demarcation

---

was obviously so close to the end of his reserves that he lapsed into a coma and did not wake up again. He died at 3:00 A.M. on September 23, 1939. Freud had said in his THOUGHTS FOR THE TIMES ON WAR AND DEATH: Towards the actual person who has died we adopt a special attitude: something like admiration for someone who has accomplished a very difficult task. *Id.* at 529.

81. *See* Louisell, *Biology, Law and Reason: Man as Self-Creator*, 16 AM. J. JURIS. 1 (1971). During my recent visit at the University of Minnesota, Mark Graubard, professor of the history of science (now emeritus), indicated a possible incursion into the areas suggested in this paragraph of the text. I hope it is forthcoming!

82. H. Ratner, M.D., Editorial, 7 CHILD AND FAMILY 99 (1968).

83. While I have often thought that permissive abortion is more morally reprehensible than voluntary euthanasia for the aged in that the former cuts off life before it has had its chance, it must be conceded that the self-centered fears and anxieties a euthanasiac regime might engender among the elderly (or those in the process of becoming elderly—as we all are) have no exact counterpart in the case of abortion.

84. There is disturbing language in John F. Kennedy Memorial Hospital v. Heston, 279 A.2d 670 (N.J. 1971). In upholding the subjection of a Jehovah's Witness, age 22 and unmarried, who had sustained severe injuries in an automobile accident, to a

may be fine, but so are many other lines that men must draw in their fallible perception and limited wisdom.   Application of the principled distinction between ordinary and extra-ordinary means of prolonging life occasions difficulties, but hardly any different in quality from various other decisions in applying a general principle to particular facts.   The distinction between the use of drugs to kill and their use to alleviate pain even though death may thereby be hastened is likewise valid.

When the question becomes one for the legal system, fortunately our law has time-tested devices for accommodating principle and facts, notably the jury.   It seems hardly necessary or wise for us to attempt articulation of formal legal standards of lesser liability in cases of euthanasia than for other criminal homicides in the manner of Norwegian law.   The harm of the educative effects of formalization of lesser penalties for euthanasia probably would outweigh the values thereby gained by way of certainty of legal consequence and surer guarantee of equal protection of the law.

Our era is one that seeks, and often for good reason, a constant expansion of a juridical order in human affairs.   But not every human relationship stands to profit from complete juridicalization.   The refusal so far of legislatures to intrude into the mercy-death area has been prudent and in the interest of sound social policy.

---

blood transfusion necessary to save her life, the· Court *per* Weintraub, C.J., said: "It seems correct to say there is no constitutional right to choose to die." *Id.* at 672. Replying to the patient's contention that there is a difference between passively submitting to death and actively seeking it, the Court said: "If the State may interrupt one mode of self-destruction [suicide] it may with equal authority interfere with the other." *Id.*, at 673.   It acknowledges that "It is arguably different when an individual, overtaken by illness, decides to let it run a fatal course." *Id.* Pretermitting the question of the free exercise of religion, it seems unfortunate that the Court did not confront more directly the extent of the obligation to use artificial means to sustain life.   One of the cases cited by the court, Raleigh Fitkin-Paul Morgan Memorial Hospital v. Anderson, 201 A.2d 537, *cert. denied*, 377 U.S. 985 (1964) is distinguishable, in that there the woman involved was bearing a child.   Thus another life was involved, and the court there correctly concluded that an unborn child is entitled to the law's protection when a transfusion is necessary to save its life.   *See* Louisell, *Abortion, the Practice of Medicine and the Due Process of Law*, 16 U.C.L.A. L. REV. 233, 244 (1969).

SOME NON-RELIGIOUS VIEWS AGAINST
PROPOSED "MERCY-KILLING" LEGISLATION

YALE KAMISAR*

> *At the Crystal Palace Aquarium not long
> ago I saw a crab euthanatising a sickly fish,
> doubtless from the highest motives.*[1]

A recent book, Glanville Williams' *The Sanctity of Life and
the Criminal Law,*[2] once again brings to the fore the controversial
topic of euthanasia,[3] more popularly known as "mercy killing". In
keeping with the trend of the euthanasia movement over the past
generation, Williams concentrates his efforts for reform on the
voluntary type of euthanasia, for example, the cancer victim beg-
ging for death; as opposed to the *involuntary variety,* that is, the
case of the congenital idiot, the permanently insane or the senile.

*Associate Professor of Law, University of Minnesota Law School. This
paper was aided by a research grant from the Graduate School of the University of Minnesota. The author acknowledges the constructive criticism of
Professor Kenneth Culp Davis of the University of Minnesota Law School
and the valuable assistance of Dr. Eugene Bernstein, Fellow, University of
Minnesota Medical School.
    1.   Anonymous letter to the editor, 46 The Spectator 241 (1873).
    2.   (1957) (This book is hereinafter referred to as "Williams").
    The book is an expanded and revised version of the James S. Carpentier
lectures delivered by Professor Williams at Columbia University and at the
Association of the Bar of the City of New York in the Spring of 1956. "The
connecting thread," observes the author, "is the extent to which human life,
actual or potential, is or ought to be protected under the criminal law of the
English-speaking peoples," Preface, p. vii. The product of his dexterous
needlework, one might add, is a coat of many colors: philosophical, medical,
ethical, religious, social, as well as legal. *The Un-Sanctity of Life* would
seem to be a more descriptive title, however, since the author presents
cogent reasons for de-criminalizing ·infanticide and abortion at one end of
man's span, and "unselfish abetment of suicide and the unselfish homicide
upon request," *id.* at 310, at the other.
    The book was recently lauded by Bertrand Russell, 10 Stan. L. Rev. 382
(1958). For more restrained receptions see the interesting and incisive reviews by Professor William J. Curran, 71 Harv. L. Rev. 585 (1958) and
Professor Richard C. Donnelly, 67 Yale L.J. 753 (1958).
    3.   Euthanasia has a Greek origin: *eu* (easy, happy, painless), *thanatos*
(death). The term apparently first appeared in the English language in the
early seventeenth century in its original meaning—a gentle, easy death. The
term then came to mean the *doctrine* or *theory* that in certain circumstances
a person should be painlessly killed, and, more recently has come to mean
the *act* or *practice* of bringing about a gentle and easy death. In its broad
sense, euthanasia embraces a variety of situations, some where the patient
is capable of consenting to his death, others where he obviously is not. Thus,

When a legal scholar of Williams' stature[4] joins the ranks of such formidable criminal law thinkers as America's Herbert Wechsler and the late Jerome Michael,[5] and England's Hermann Mannheim[6] in approving voluntary euthanasia, at least under certain circumstances, a major exploration of the bases for the euthanasia prohibition seems in order.[7] This need is underscored by the fact that Williams' book arrives on the scene so soon after the stir caused by a brilliant Anglican clergyman's plea for voluntary euthanasia.[8]

The Law On The Books condemns all mercy-killings.[9] That this

two generations ago, H. J. Rose defined the euthanasia circumstances as "when owing to disease, senility, or the like, a person's life has ceased to be either agreeable or useful". 7 Encyclopedia of Religion and Ethics 598 (Hastings ed. 1912). In the 1930's there sprung up organizations in both England and America which dramatized the plight of the patient in "unnecessary" pain and urged euthanasia for the incurable and suffering patient who wanted to die. Consequently, a current popular meaning of the term is painless death "releasing" the patient from severe physical suffering. An advocate of euthanasia has been called a "euthanasiast"; to subject to euthanasia has been called to "euthanatize." These terms will be so used throughout this paper. See generally Fletcher, Morals and Medicine 172-73 (1954) Sullivan, The Morality of Mercy Killing 1-3 (1950) (originally a dissertation entitled Catholic Teaching on the Morality of Euthanasia); Banks, *Euthanasia*, 161 Practitioner 101 (1948).

4. Williams' admirable treatise, Criminal Law: The General Part (1953), stamps him as one of the giants in the field.

5. Wechsler and Michael, *A Rationale of the Law of Homicide: I*, 37 Colum. L. Rev. 701, 739-40 (1937). Since the article was written before the Nazi euthanasia venture, it is conceivable that Prof. Wechsler, who had ample opportunity to study the Nazi experience as Technical Adviser to American Judges, International Military Tribunal, would come out somewhat differently today.

6. Mannheim, Criminal Justice and Social Reconstruction 13-17 (1946).

7. Since the proposals for reform which have commanded the greatest attention have urged complete immunization of voluntary euthanasia, this paper is concerned with whether or not such killings should be legalized, not whether or not they should be regarded as murder, which is now the case, see note 9 *infra*, or some lesser degree of criminal homicide. One way to achieve mitigation would be to give recognition to "good motive" generally; another would be to make a specific statutory reduction of penalty for voluntary euthanasia alone. For a discussion of these alternatives, see Kalven, *A Special Corner of Civil Liberties: A Legal View I*, 31 N.Y.U.L. Rev. 1223, 1235-36 (1956); Silving, *Euthanasia: A Study In Comparative Criminal Law*, 103 U. of Pa. L. Rev. 350, 386-89 (1954). The Royal Commission on Capital Punishment (1949-53) took the position that "mercy killings" could not feasibly be reduced in penalty. See text at note 34 and note 34 *infra*.

8. Fletcher, *op. cit. supra*, note 3 at 172-210 (1954). The book is quite similar to Williams in that it deals with the moral and legal issues raised by contraception, artificial insemination, sterilization and right of the patient to know the truth. It is the subject of an interesting and stimulating symposium review, 31 N.Y.U.L. Rev. 1160-1245 (1956) by two lawyers, Prof. Harry Kalven and Judge Morris Ploscowe; two theologians, Emanuel Rackman and Paul Ramsey; two philosophers, Horace M. Kallen and Joseph D. Hasset; and a physician, I. Phillips Frohman.

9. In Anglo-American jurisprudence a "mercy-killing" is murder. In theory, neither good motive nor consent of the victim is relevant. See, *e.g.*, 2 Burdick, Law of Crimes §§ 422, 447 (1946); Miller, Criminal Law 55,

has a substantial deterrent effect, even its harshest critics admit.[10] Of course, it does not stamp out all mercy-killings, just as murder and rape provisions do not stamp out all murder and rape, but presumably it does impose a substantially greater responsibility on physicians and relatives in a euthanasia situation and turns them away from significantly more doubtful cases than would otherwise be the practice under any proposed euthanasia legislation to date. When a mercy-killing occurs, however, The Law In Action is as malleable as The Law On The Books is uncompromising. The high incidence of failures to indict,[11] acquittals,[12] suspended sentences[13] and reprieves[14] lend considerable support to the view that—

> If the circumstances are so compelling that the defendant ought to violate the law, then they are compelling enough for the jury to violate their oaths. The law does well to declare these homicides unlawful. It does equally well to put no more than the sanction of an oath in the way of an acquittal.[15]

The complaint has been registered that "the prospect of a sentimental acquittal cannot be reckoned as a certainty."[16] Of course not. The defendant is not always *entitled* to a sentimental acquittal. The few American convictions cited for the proposition that the present state of affairs breeds "inequality" in application may be cited as well for the proposition that it is characterized by

---

172 (1934); Perkins, Criminal Law 721 (1957); 1 Wharton, Criminal Law and Procedure § 194 (Anderson 1957); Orth, *Legal Aspects Relating to Euthanasia,* 2 Md. Med. J. 120 (1953) (symposium on euthanasia); 48 Mich. L. Rev. 1199 (1950); Anno., 25 A.L.R. 1007 (1923).

In a number of countries, *e.g.,* Germany, Norway, Switzerland, a compassionate motive and/or "homicide upon request" operate to reduce the penalty. See generally Helen Silving's valuable comparative study, *supra* note 7. However, apparently only Uruguayan law completely immunizes a homicide characterized by both of the above factors. *Id.* at 369 and n. 74. The Silving article only contains an interesting and fairly extensive comparative study of assisted suicide and the degree to which it is treated differently from a direct "mercy-killing." In this regard see also Friedman, *Suicide, Euthanasia and the Law,* 85 Med. Times 681 (1957).

10. See Williams, p. 342.

11. See, *e.g.,* the case of Harry C. Johnson, who asphyxiated his cancer-stricken wife, apparently at her urging. N.Y. Times, Oct. 2, 1938, p. 1, col. 3; Oct. 3, 1938, p. 34, col. 3. Various psychiatrists reported that Johnson was "temporarily insane" at the time of the killing, but was "now sane", N.Y. Times, Oct. 12, 1938, p. 30, col. 4. A week later, a Nassau County grand jury refused to indict him. N.Y. Times, Oct. 19, 1938, p. 46, col. 1.

12. See, e.g., the *Sander, Paight* and *Braunsdorf* cases discussed at notes 172-176, 183, *infra.*

13. See *e.g.,* the *Repouille* case discussed at note 181, *infra.*

14. See *e.g.,* the *Brownhill* and *Long* cases discussed at notes 178-179, *infra.*

15. Curtis, It's Your Law 95 (1954).

16. Williams, p. 328.

elasticity and flexibility.[17] In any event, if inequality of application suffices to damn a particular provision of the criminal law, we might as well tear up all our codes—beginning with the section on chicken-stealing.[18]

17. Both Williams, at 328, and Prof. Harry Kalven, *supra* note 7 at 1235, cite a single authority for the proposition that the prevailing system does not afford equality of treatment of mercy killers. That single authority is Helen Silving's study, *supra* note 7. Silving in turn relies on a single case, that of Harold Mohr, who was convicted of voluntary manslaughter and sentenced to from three to six years in prison, for the slaying of his blind, cancer-stricken brother. Unlike other mercy killing cases which resulted in acquittals, Mohr's victim had apparently made urgent and repeated requests for death. *Id.* at 354 and n. 15. Silving fails to note however, that Mohr's defense that he "blacked out" just before the shooting was likely to be received with something less than maximum sympathy in light of the fact, pressed hard by the prosecution, that immediately prior to shooting his brother he made a round of taprooms and clubs for *seven* hours and consumed *ten* to *twelve* beers in the process. N.Y. Times, April 8, 1950, p. 26, col. 1. Nor was the jury likely to consider it insignificant that two other brothers of Mohr testified on behalf of the state. *Ibid.* So far as I know, this is the only mercy killing case where relatives testified against the defendant.

In Repouille v. United States, 165 F. 2d 152, 153 (2d cir. 1947) (denying citizenship to alien on ground that chloroforming of idiot son impaired "good moral character"), Judge Learned Hand noted that while Repouille had received a suspended sentence, a "similar offender in Massachusetts" had been imprisoned for life. This, evidently, is a reference to the case of John F. Noxon, who, less than two years after Repouille's mercy-killing, was sentenced to death for electrocuting his idiot son. The sentence was then commuted to life. See note 182, *infra.* But Noxon banked all on the defense that the electrocution had been just an accident, a gamble entailing the risk that the jury would be quite unsympathetic to him if it disbelieved his story. Certainly, a full presentation of the appealing "mercy killing" circumstances would be more difficult under the theory Noxon adopted than under the typical "temporary insanity" defense. That different legal tactics lead to "inequality of treatment" on similar facts is obvious.

Furthermore, the jury might well have been revolted by the manner in which the act was perpetrated: electrocuting the infant by wrapping wire around him, dressing him in wet diapers, and placing him on a silver serving tray. Then, too, whereas Repouille's son was a thirteen-year-old with the mentality of a two-year-old and Greenfield's son, to draw upon another leading case of this type, see note 180, *infra,* was a seventeen-year-old with the mentality of a two-year-old, Noxon's son was only a six-month infant who apparently *would never develop* the mentality of an adult—a situation the jury might well view as less pathetic, at least less provoking. Finally, it should be noted that even in the *Noxon* case, the Law In Action was not without effect. His death sentence was commuted to life and, a year after Judge Hand's apparent reference to him, further commuted to six years. He was paroled less than five years after his conviction of first degree murder. See note 182, *infra.*

In any event, the legislation urged by Williams, Fletcher and the English and American euthanasia societies would in no way relieve the plight of a "mercy-killer" such as Noxon, for his was an act of *involuntary* euthanasia and hence beyond the scope of present proposals.

18. "Not a great many years ago, upon the Norfolk circuit, a larceny was committed by two men in a poultry yard, but only one of them was apprehended; the other having escaped into a distant part of the country, had eluded all pursuit. At the next assizes the apprehended thief was tried and convicted; but Lord Loughborough, before whom he was tried, thinking the offence a very slight one, sentenced him only to a few months imprisonment. The news of this sentence having reached the accomplice in his retreat,

The criticism is also made that "public confidence in the administration of criminal justice is hardly strengthened when moral issues are shifted instead of being solved, or when the law relegates to juries the function of correcting its inequities."[19] But there are many, many occasions on which the jury wrestles with moral issues, and there is certainly substantial support for this practice.[20]

---

he immediately returned, and surrendered himself to take his trial at the next assizes. The next assizes came; but, unfortunately for the prisoner, it was a different judge who presided; and still more unfortunately, Mr. Justice Gould, who happened to be the judge, though of a very mild and indulgent disposition, had observed, or thought he had observed, that men who set out with stealing fowls, generally end by committing the most atrocious crimes; and building a sort of system upon this observation, had made it a rule to punish this offence with very great severity, and he accordingly, to the great astonishment of this unhappy man, sentenced him to be transported. While one was taking his departure for Botany Bay, the term of the other's imprisonment had expired; and what must have been the notions which that little public, who witnessed and compared these two examples, formed of our system of criminal jurisprudence?"

Romilly, Observations on the Criminal Law of England 18-19 (1810). The observations constitute a somewhat revised and expanded version of a famous speech delivered in the House of Commons in support of bills to repeal legislation making it a capital offence to commit certain petty thefts. A substantial portion of the speech, including the extract above, is reprinted in Michael and Wechsler, Criminal Law and its Administration 252-55 (1940). For recent instances of disparities and erraticism in sentencing, see Glueck, *The Sentencing Problem*, Fed. Prob., Dec. 1956, p. 15.

19. Silving, *supra* note 7, at 354.

20. For example, in the famous case of Durham v. United States, 214 F. 2d 862 (D.C. Cir. 1954) regarded by many as a triumph over the forces of darkness in the much-agitated area of mental responsibility, the Court concluded (214 F. 2d at 876) :
Finally, in leaving the determination of the ultimate question of fact to the jury, we permit it to perform its traditional function which . . . is to apply 'our inherited ideas of moral responsibility to individuals prosecuted for crime. . . .' Juries will continue to make moral judgments, still operating under the fundamental precept that 'our collective conscience does not allow punishment where it cannot impose blame.'
To take another example, the difficult area of criminal law dealing with causal relationship between conduct and result, "as has often been said, the question usually presented is not whether there is cause in fact, but rather whether there should be liability for results in fact caused." Wechsler and Michael, *supra* note 5, at 724. Herbert Wechsler, the Chief Reporter of the Model Penal Code, favors the "culpability" rather than "causality" approach, 32 ALI proceedings 162-63 (1955), and this view may very well be ultimately adopted. See section 2.03 (2) (b) of the Model Penal Code (Tent. Draft No. 4, 1955) and the appropriate comment to this section, *id.* at 135, for a discussion of the advantages and disadvantages "of putting the issue squarely to the jury's sense of justice." To take still another example, the elusive distinction between first and second degree murder has well been described as "merely a privilege offered to the jury to find the lesser degree when the suddenness of the intent, the vehemence of the passion, seems to call irresistibly for the exercise of mercy." Cardozo, *What Medicine Can Do For Law*, in Law and Literature 100 (1931). This view is buttressed by the subsequent disclosure that of some 700 cases, every homicide case contained in the New York reports at that time, "only *three* cases have been found where on a murder charge, the indictment was for second degree murder." New York Revision Commission, Communication and Study Relating to Homicide 82 n. 202 (1937). Cardozo pointed out that he had "no objection

The existing law on euthanasia is hardly perfect. But if it is not too good, neither, as I have suggested, is it much worse than the rest of the criminal law. At any rate, the imperfections of the existing law are not cured by Williams' proposal. Indeed, I believe adoption of his views would add more difficulties than it would remove.

Williams strongly suggests that "euthanasia can be condemned only according to a religious opinion."[21] He tends to view the opposing camps as Roman Catholics versus Liberals. Although this has a certain initial appeal to me, a non-Catholic and a self-styled liberal, I deny that this is the only way the battle lines can, or should, be drawn. I leave the religious arguments to the theologians. I share the view that "those who hold the faith may follow its precepts without requiring those who do not hold it to act as if they did."[22] But I do find substantial utilitarian obstacles on the high road to euthanasia.[23]

---

to giving them [the jury] this dispensing power, but it should be given to them directly and not in a mystifying cloud of words." From the frequency with which the dispensing power is exercised, and the manner in which it is viewed by the press and public generally, it seems fairly clear that nobody is mystified very much in the mercy-killing cases.

21. Williams, p. 312. This seems to be the position taken by Bertrand Russell in his review of Williams' book (*supra* note 2 at 382):

> The central theme of the book is the conflict in the criminal law between the two divergent systems of ethics which may be called respectively utilitarian and taboo morality. . . . Utilitarian morality in the wide sense in which I am using the word, judges actions by their effects. . . . In taboo morality . . . forbidden actions are sin, and they do not cease to be so when their consequences are such as we should all welcome.

I trust Russell would agree, if he should read this paper, that the issue is not quite so simple. At any rate, I trust he would agree that I stay within the system of utilitarian ethics.

22. Wechsler and Michael, *supra* note 5 at 740. *But see* Denning, *The Influence of Religion,* in The Changing Law 99 (1953) ("without religion there can be no morality; and without morality there can be no law"). Lord Justice Denning's assertion is the motif of Fitch, Harding, Katz and Quillian, Religion, Morality and Law (1956).

23. I am aware that the arguments I set forth, however "reasonable" or "logical" some of them may be, were not the reasons which first led to the prohibition against mercy-killings. I realize, too, that those who are inexorably opposed to any form of euthanasia on religious grounds do not always limit their arguments to religious ones. See, *e.g.,* Martin, *Euthanasia and Modern Morality,* 10 The Jurist 437 (1950) which views the issue as a conflict between Christianity and paganism, and, in addition raises many non-religious objections. I risk, therefore, the charge that I am but another example of "the tendency of the human mind to graft upon an actual course of conduct a justification or even a duty to observe this same course in the future." Stone, The Province and Function of Law 673-74 (1946). I would meet this charge with the observation that "ordinary experience seems to indicate quite clearly that the reasons people give for their religious, political, economic and legal policies do influence the development of these policies, and that the 'good reasons' professed by our fathers yesterday are among the real reasons of the life of today" M. R. Cohen, The Faith of a Liberal 70 (1946).

After all, that the criminal law itself arose to fill the need to regulate

As an ultimate philosophical proposition, the case for voluntary euthanasia is strong. Whatever may be said for and against suicide generally,[24] the appeal of death is immeasurably greater when it is sought not for a poor reason or just any reason, but for "good cause," so to speak; when it is invoked not on behalf of a "socially useful" person, but on behalf of, for example, the pain-racked "hopelessly incurable" cancer victim. *If* a person is *in fact* (1) presently incurable, (2) beyond the aid of any respite which may come along in his life expectancy, suffering (3) intolerable and (4) unmitigable pain and of a (5) fixed and (6) rational desire to die, I would hate to have to argue that the hand of death should be stayed. But abstract propositions and carefully formed hypotheticals are one thing; specific proposals designed to cover everyday situations are something else again.

In essence, Williams' specific proposal is that death be authorized for a person in the above situation "by giving the medical

---

and obviate self-help and private vengeance, see, *e.g.*, 2 Holdsworth, History of English Law 43-47 (4th ed. 1936); Holmes, The Common Law 2-3, 40 (1881); Maine, Ancient Law 391-401 (Pollock ed. 1930); to say nothing of a possible point of origin in "a religious institution of sacrificing an impious wrongdoer to an offending god who might else inflict his wrath upon the whole communty," Pound, Criminal Justice in America 54 (1930), renders deterrence, incapacitation and rehabilitation no less the "real reasons" of today and no less the real bases for drafting new codes or amending old ones.

I would meet the charge, too, by pointing out that I am not enamored of the status quo on mercy-killing. But while I am not prepared to defend it against all comers, I am prepared to defend it against the proposals for change which have come forth to date.

24. Unlike Professor Williams, even many proponents of voluntary euthanasia appear to shrink from suicide as a general proposition. Consider, for example, the following statements made by vice-presidents of England's Voluntary Euthanasia Legalisation Society:

> The act of the suicide is wrong because he takes his own life solely on his own judgment. It may be that he does so in a mood of despair or remorse and thus evades the responsibility of doing what he can to repair the wrong or improve the situation. He flings away his life when there is still the possibility of service and when there are still duties to be done. The proposals for Voluntary Euthanasia have nothing in common with suicide. They take the decision out of the hands of the individual. The case is submitted to the objective judgment of doctors and specially appointed officials whose duty it would be to enquire whether the conditions which constitute the sinfulness of suicide are present or not.

Matthews, *Voluntary Euthanasia: The Ethical Aspects* 4-5 (Address by the Very Rev. W. R. Matthews, Dean of St. Paul's, Voluntary Euthanasia Legalisation Society Annual Meeting, May 2, 1950) (distributed by the American and English Societies).

> [I]n respect of each of its citizens, the State has made an investment of a substantial amount, and as a mere matter of business it is entitled to demand an adequate return. If a useful citizen, by taking his life, diminishes that return, he does an anti-social act to the detriment of the community as a whole. We cannot carry the doctrine of isolation to the extent of saying that we live unto ourselves. Hence it appears 'on purely rationalistic grounds that the State is entitled to discountenance suicide.

Earengey, *Voluntary Euthanasia,* 8 Medico-Legal Rev. 91, 92 (1940).

practitioner a wide discretion and trusting to his good sense."[25]
This, I submit, raises too great a risk of abuse and mistake to warrant a change in the existing law. That a proposal entails risk of mistake is hardly a conclusive reason against it. But neither is it irrelevant. Under any euthanasia program the consequences of mistake, of course, are always fatal. As I shall endeavor to show, the incidence of mistake of one kind or another is likely to be quite appreciable. If this indeed be the case, unless the need for the authorized conduct is compelling enough to override it, I take it the risk of mistake *is* a conclusive reason against such authorization. I submit too, that the possible radiations from the proposed legislation, *e.g.,* involuntary euthanasia of idiots and imbeciles (the typical "mercy-killings" reported by the press) and the emergence of the legal precedent that there are lives not "worth living," give additional cause to pause.

I see the issue, then, as the need for voluntary euthanasia versus (1) the incidence of mistake and abuse; and (2) the danger that legal machinery initially designed to kill those who are a nuisance to themselves may someday engulf those who are a nuisance to others.[26]

The "freedom to choose a merciful death by euthanasia" may well be regarded, as does Professor Harry Kalven in a carefully measured review of another recent book urging a similar proposal,[27] as "a special area of civil liberties far removed from the familiar concerns with criminal procedures, race discrimination and freedom of speech and religion."[28] The civil liberties angle is definitely a part of Professor Williams' approach:

25. Williams, p. 339.
26. *Cf.* G. K. Chesterton, *Euthanasia and Murder,* 8 Am. Rev. 486, 490, (1937).
27. See Fletcher, *op. cit. supra,* note 8.
28. Kalven, *supra* note 7. I would qualify this statement only by the suggestion that to some extent this freedom may be viewed as an aspect of the freedom of religion of the non-Believer. For a consideration of the problems raised by organizations which claim to be "religious" but do not require their adherents to believe in a Supreme Being, see Washington Ethical Soc'y v. District of Columbia, 249 F.2d 127 (D.C. Cir. 1957); Fellowship of Humanity v. County of Alameda, 315 P.2d 394 (Cal. App. 1957), 58 Colum. L. Rev. 417 (1958).

Undoubtedly the most extreme expression of this view is the bitter comment of Viscount Esher, upon concluding from the run of the speeches that he and his allies would be overwhelmed in the House of Lords debate on the question (169 H.L. Deb. [5th ser.] 551, 574-76 [1950]):

[Voluntary euthanasia] is certainly an evolutionary extension of liberty of great importance, giving to the individual new rights to which, up till now, he has not had access. . . . What we propose this afternoon is, in point of fact, a new freedom, and undoubtedly it will antagonize the embattled forces of the official world. . . . I believe that posterity will look back on this refusal you are going to make this afternoon . . . as

If the law were to remove its ban on euthanasia, the effect
would merely be to leave this subject to the individual conscience.
This proposal would . . . be easy to defend, as restoring personal
liberty in a field in which men differ on the question of conscience. . . .

On a question like this there is surely everything to be said
for the liberty of the individual.[29]

I am perfectly willing to accept civil liberties as the battlefield,
but issues of "liberty" and "freedom" mean little until we begin to
pin down *whose* "liberty" and "freedom" and for *what* need and at
what price. This paper is concerned largely with such questions.

It is true also of journeys in the law that the place you reach
depends on the direction you are taking. And so, where one
comes out on a case depends on where one goes in.[30]

So it is with the question at hand. Williams champions the "personal liberty" of the dying to die painlessly. I am more concerned
about the life and liberty of those who would needlessly be killed in
the process or who would irrationally choose to partake of the
process. Williams' price on behalf of those who are *in fact* "hopeless
incurables" and *in fact* of a fixed and rational desire to die is the
sacrifice of (1) some few, who, though they know it not, because
their physicians know it not, need not and should not die; (2) others,
probably not so few, who, though they go through the motions of
"volunteering", are casualties of strain, pain or narcotics to such
an extent that they really know not what they do. My price on behalf of those who, despite appearances to the contrary, have some
relatively normal and reasonably useful life left in them, or who
are incapable of making the choice, is the lingering on for awhile
of those who, if you will, *in fact* have no desire and no reason to
linger on.

---

people look now on the burning of witches—as a barbarous survival of
mediaeval ideas, an example of that high-minded cruelty from the
entanglement of which it has taken mankind so many centuries to emerge.
In that day we few, we five or six shall, I believe, be remembered.
At the end, the euthanasiasts avoided a vote by withdrawing the question, *id.*
at 598. In an earlier House of Lords debate, proposed voluntary euthanasia
legislation was defeated by a 35-14 vote. 103 H. L. Deb. (5th ser.) 466, 506
(1936).

29. Williams, pp. 341, 346.

30. Frankfurter, J., dissenting in United States v. Rabinowitz, 339 U.S.
56, 69 (1950).

Perhaps as good an example as any may be taken from Glanville Williams' own text, Criminal Law: The General Part § 180 (1953). With a deep
concern for the *parents'* "freedom not to conform" as his starting point,
Williams makes a strong policy argument for immunizing from criminal
law sanctions those "peculiar people" who for sincere religious reasons fail
to summon medical aid to their sick children. One who takes the health and
welfare of *children* as his starting point might well reach a somewhat different conclusion.

I. A CLOSE-UP VIEW OF VOLUNTARY EUTHANASIA

A. The Euthanasiast's Dilemma and Williams' Proposed Solution.

As if the general principle they advocate did not raise enough difficulties in itself, euthanasiasts have learned only too bitterly that specific plans of enforcement are often much less palatable than the abstract notions they are designed to effectuate. In the case of voluntary euthanasia, the means of implementation vary from (1) the simple proposal that mercy-killings by anyone, typically relatives, be immunized from the criminal law; to (2) the elaborate legal machinery contained in the bills of the Voluntary Euthanasia Legalisation Society (England) and the Euthanasia Society of America for carrying out euthanasia.

The English Society would require the eligible patient, *i.e.*, one over twenty-one and "suffering from a disease involving severe pain and of an incurable and fatal character," [31] to forward a specially prescribed application — along with two medical certificates, one signed by the attending physician, and the other by a specially qualified physician — to a specially appointed Euthanasia Referee "who shall satisfy himself by means of a personal interview with the patient and otherwise that the said conditions shall have been fulfilled and that the patient fully understands the nature and purpose of the application"; and, if so satisfied, shall then send a euthanasia permit to the patient; which permit shall, seven days after receipt, become "operative" in the presence of an official witness; unless the nearest relative manages to cancel the permit by persuading a court of appropriate jurisdiction that the requisite conditions have not been met.

The American Society would have the eligible patient, *i.e.*, one over twenty-one "suffering from severe physical pain caused by a disease for which no remedy affording lasting relief or recovery is at the time known to medical science," [32] petition for euthanasia in the presence of two witnesses and file same, along with the certificate of an attending physician, in a court of appropriate jurisdiction; said court to then appoint a committee of three, of whom at least two must be physicians, "who shall forthwith examine the patient and such other persons as they deem advisable or as the court may direct and within five days after their appointment, shall report to

---

31. Section 2(1) of the English Bill. The full text is set forth in Roberts, Euthanasia and Other Aspects of Life and Death 21-26 (1936).

32. Section 301 of the American Bill. The full text is set forth in Sullivan, The Morality of Mercy Killing 25-28 (1950). Fletcher, *op. cit. supra* note 3, at 187, regards this bill as "perhaps the model legislation." Such bills have been unsuccessfully introduced in the legislatures of Nebraska, N.Y. Times, Feb. 3, 1937, p. 7, col. 1; Feb. 14, 1937, p. 17, col. 1; and, some ten years later, New York, Fletcher at 184-85.

the court whether or not the patient understands the nature and purpose of the petition and comes within the [act's] provisions"; whereupon, if the report is in the affirmative, the court shall — "unless there is some reason to believe that the report is erroneous or untrue" — grant the petition; in which event euthanasia is to be administered in the presence of the committee, or any two members thereof.

As will be seen, and as might be expected, the simple negative proposal to remove "mercy-killings" from the ban of the criminal law is strenuously resisted on the ground that it offers the patient far too little protection from not-so-necessary or not-so-merciful killings. On the other hand, the elaborate affirmative proposals of the euthanasia societies meet much pronounced eye-blinking, not a few guffaws,[33] and sharp criticism that the legal machinery is so drawn-out, so complex, so formal and so tedious as to offer the patient far too little solace.

---

33. I venture to say there are few men indeed who will not so much as smile at the portion of the American Society's Bill, Sullivan *op. cit. supra,* note 3 at 28, which provides that if the petition for euthanasia shall be denied by a Justice of the Supreme Court, "an appeal may be taken to the appellate division of the supreme court, and/or to the Court of Appeals".

34. Royal Commission on Capital Punishment, Report, Cmd. No. 8932, at para. 179 (1953). *Cf.* Bentham, The Theory of Legislation 256 (Ogden ed. 1931) :

Let us recollect that there is no room for considering the motive except when it is manifest and palpable. It would often be very difficult to discover the true or dominant motive, when the action might be equally produced by different motives, or where motives of several sorts might have cooperated in its production. In the interpretation of these doubtful cases it is necessary to distrust the malignity of the human heart, and that general disposition to exhibit a brilliant sagacity at the expense of good nature. We involuntarily deceive even ourselves as to what puts us into action. In relation even to our own motives we are wilfully blind, and are always ready to break into a passion against the oculist who desires to remove the cataract of ignorance and prejudice.

Cf. Roberts, *op. cit. supra* note 31, at 10-11 :

Self-deception as to one's motives, what the psychologists call 'rationalization', is one of the most powerful of man's self-protective mechanisms. It is an old observation of criminal psychologists that the day-dreamers and the rationalizers account for a very large proportion of the criminal population; whilst, in murderers, this habit of self-deception is often carried to incredible lengths.

It should be noted, however, that the likelihood of faked mercy-killings would seem to be substantially reduced when such acts are not completely immunized but only categorized as a lesser degree of criminal homicide. If mercy killings were simply taken out of the category of murder, a second line of defense might well be the appearance of a mercy-killing but in planned murders generally the primary concern of the murderer must surely be to escape all punishment whatever, not to give a serious, but not the most serious, appearance to his act, not to substitute a long period of imprisonment for execution. *Cf.* the discussion of faked suicide pacts in Royal Commission, *supra,* Minutes of Evidence, paras. 804-07. As was stated at the outset, however, see note 7, *supra,* this paper deals with proposals to completely legalize mercy-killings, not with the advisability of taking it out of the category of murder.

The naked suggestion that mercy-killing be made a good defense against a charge of criminal homicide appears to have no prospect of success in the foreseeable future. Only recently, the Royal Commission on Capital Punishment "reluctantly" concluded that such homicides could not feasibly be taken out of the category of murder, let alone completely immunized:

> [Witnesses] thought it would be most dangerous to provide that 'mercy killings' should not be murder, because it would be impossible to define a category which could not be seriously abused. Such a definition could only be in terms of the motive of the offender ... which is notoriously difficult to establish and cannot, like intent, be inferred from a person's overt actions. Moreover it was agreed by almost all witnesses, including those who thought that there would be no real difficulty in discriminating between genuine and spurious suicide pacts, that, even if such a definition could be devised, it would in practice often prove extremely difficult to distinguish killings where the motive was merciful from those where it was not. How, for example, were the jury to decide whether a daughter had killed her invalid father from compassion, from a desire for material gain, from a natural wish to bring to an end a trying period of her life, or from a combination of motives?[34]

While the appeal in simply taking "mercy-killings" off the books is dulled by the liklihood of abuse, the force of the idea is likewise substantially diminished by the encumbering protective features proposed by the American and English Societies. Thus, Lord Dawson, an eminent medical member of the House of Lords and one of the great leaders of the English medical profession, protested that the English Bill "would turn the sick room into a bureau," that he was revolted by "the very idea of the sick chamber being visited by officials and the patient, who is struggling with this dire malady, being treated as if it was a case of insanity." [35] Dr. A. Leslie Banks, then Principal Medical Officer of the Ministry of Health, reflected that the proposed machinery would "produce an atmosphere quite foreign to all accepted notions of dying in peace." [36] Dr. I. Phillips Frohman has similarly objected to the American Bill as one whose "whole procedure is so lengthy that it does not seem consonant either with the 'mercy' motive on which presumably it is based, or with the 'bearableness' of the pain." [37]

The extensive procedural concern of the euthanasia bills have repelled many, but perhaps the best evidence of its psychological misconception is that it has distressed sympathizers of the move-

35. 103 H.L. Deb. (5th ser.) 484-85 (1936).
36. Banks, *Euthanasia*, 161 Practitioner 101, 104 (1948).
37. Frohman, *Vexing Problems in Forensic Medicine: A Physician's View*, 31 N.Y.U.L. Rev. 1215, 1222 (1956).

ment as well. The very year the English Society was organized and
a proposed bill drafted, Dr. Harry Roberts observed:

> We all realize the intensified horror attached to the death-penalty
> by its accompanying formalities — from the phraseology of the
> judge's sentence, and his black cap, to the weight-gauging visit
> of the hangman to the cell, and the correct attendance at the
> final scene of the surpliced chaplain, the doctor, and the prison
> governor. This is not irrelevant to the problem of legalized
> euthanasia . . .[38]

After discussing the many procedural steps of the English Bill Dr.
Roberts observed: "I can almost hear the cheerful announcement:
'please, ma'am, the euthanizer's come.' "

At a meeting of the Medico-Legal Society, Dr. Kenneth Mc-
Fadyean, after reminding the group that "some time ago he stated
from a public platform that he had practiced euthanasia for twenty
years and he did not believe he was running risks because he had
helped a hopeless sufferer out of this life," commented on the
English Bill:

> There was no comparison between being in a position to make
> a will and making a patient choose his own death at any stated
> moment. The patient had to discuss it — not once with his own
> doctor, but two, three, or even four times with strangers, which
> was no solace or comfort to people suffering intolerable pain.[39]

Nothing rouses Professor Williams' ire more than the fact
that opponents of the euthanasia movement argue that euthanasia
proposals offer either inadequate protection or overelaborate safeguards. Williams appears to meet this dilemma with the insinuation
that because arguments are made in the antithesis *they must each
be invalid, each be obstructionist, and each be made in bad faith.*[40]

It just may be, however, that each alternative argument is quite
valid, that the trouble lies with the enthanasiasts themselves in
seeking a goal which is *inherently inconsistent:* a procedure for

---

38. Roberts, *op. cit. supra* note 31, at 14-15.
39. Earengey, *Voluntary Euthanasia*, 8 Medico-Legal & Crim. Rev. 91,
106 (1940) (discussion following the reading of Judge Earengey's paper).
40. Williams, p. 334:

> The promoters of the bill hoped that they might be able to mollify the
> opposition by providing stringent safeguards. Now, they were right in
> thinking that if they had put in no safeguards—if they had merely said
> that a doctor could kill his patient whenever he thought it right—they
> would have been passionately opposed on this ground. So they put in
> the safeguards.
>
> *   *   *
>
> Did the opposition like these elaborate safeguards? On the contrary, they
> made them a matter of complaint. The safeguards would, it was said,
> bring too much formality into the sick-room, and destroy the relationship
> between doctor and patient. So the safeguards were wrong, but no one
> of the opposition speakers said that he would have voted for the bill
> without the safeguards.

death which *both* (1) provides ample safeguards against abuse and mistake; and (2) is "quick" and "easy" in operation. Professor Williams meets the problem with more than bitter comments about the tactics of the opposition. He makes a brave try to break through the dilemma:

> [T]he reformers might be well advised, in their next proposal, to abandon all their cumbrous safeguards and to do as their opponents wish, giving the medical practitioner a wide discretion and trusting to his good sense.
> [T]he essence of the bill would then be simple. It would provide that no medical practitioner should be guilty of an offense in respect of an act done intentionally to accelerate the death of a patient who is seriously ill, unless it is proved that the act was not done in good faith with the consent of the patient and for the purpose of saving him from severe pain in an illness believed to be of an incurable and fatal character. Under this formula it would be for the physician, if charged, to show that the patient was seriously ill, but for the prosecution to prove that the physician acted from some motive other than the humanitarian one allowed to him by law.[41]

---

41. *Id.* at 339-40. The desire to give doctors a free hand is expressed numerous times:
[T]here should be no formalities and . . . everything should be left to the discretion of the doctor (p. 340). . . . the bill would merely leave this question to the discretion and conscience of the individual medical practitioner. (p. 341). . . . It would be the purpose of the proposed legislation to set doctors free from the fear of the law so that they can think only of the relief of their patients (p. 342). . . . It would bring the whole subject within ordinary medical practice. (*Ibid.*)
Williams suggests that the pertinent provisions might be worded as follows (345):
1. For the avoidance of doubt, it is hereby declared that it shall be lawful for a physician whose patient is seriously ill—
* * *
b. to refrain from taking steps to prolong the patient's life by medical means;
—unless it is proved that . . . the omission was not made, in good faith for the purpose of saving the patient from severe pain in an illness believed to be of an incurable and fatal character.
2. It shall be lawful for a physician, after consultation with another physician, to accelerate by any merciful means the death of a patient who is seriously ill, unless it is proved that the act was not done in good faith with the consent of the patient and for the purpose of saving him from severe pain in an illness believed to be of an incurable and fatal character.
The completely unrestricted authorization to kill by omission may well be based on Williams' belief, at 326, that under existing law " 'mercy-killing' by omission to prolong life is probably lawful" since the physician is "probably exempted" from the duty to use reasonable care to conserve his patient's life "if life has become a burden." And he adds—as if this settles the legal question—that "the morality of an omission in these circumstances is conceded even by Catholics." *Ibid.*
If Williams means, as he seems to, *that once a doctor has undertaken treatment and the patient is entrusted solely to his care* he may sit by the bedside of the patient whose life has "become a burden" and let him die, *e.g.*, by not replacing the oxygen bottle, I submit that he is quite mistaken.

The outerlimits of criminal liability for inaction are hardly free from doubt, but it seems fairly clear under existing law that the special and traditional relationship of physician and patient imposes a "legal duty to act," particularly where the patient is helpless and completely dependent on the physician, and that the physician who withholds life-preserving medical means of the type described above commits criminal homicide by omission. In this regard, see 2 Burdick, Crimes § 466c (1946) ; Hall, Principles of Criminal Law 272-78 (1947) ; Kenny, Outlines of Criminal Law 14-15, 107-09 (16th ed. Turner 1952) ; Perkins, Criminal Law 513-27 (1957) ; 1 Russell, Crime 449-66 (10th ed. Turner 1950) ; Hughes, *Criminal Omissions,* 67 Yale L.J. 590, 599-600, 621-26, 630 n. 142 (1958) ; Kirchheimer, *Criminal Omissions,* 55 Harv. L. Rev. 615, 625-28 (1942) ; Wechsler and Michael, *supra* note 5 at 724-25.

Nor am I at all certain that the Catholics do "concede" this point. Williams' reference is to Sullivan, *op. cit. supra* note 3, at 64. But Sullivan considers therein what might be viewed as relatively remote and indirect omissions, *e.g.,* whether to call in a very expensive specialist, whether to undergo a very painful or very drastic operation.

The Catholic approach raises nice questions and draws fine lines. *E.g.,* how many limbs must be amputated before an operation is to be regarded as a non-obligatory "extraordinary," as opposed to "ordinary" means, but they will not be dwelt upon herein. Suffice to say that apparently there has never been an indictment, let alone a conviction, for a "mercy-killing" by omission, not even one which directly and immediately produces death.

This, of course, is not to say that no such negative "mercy-killings" have ever occurred. There is reason to think that not too infrequently this is the fate of the defective newborn infant. Williams, at 22, simply asserts that the "beneficient tendency of nature [in that "monsters" usually die quickly after birth] is assisted, in Britain at any rate, by the practice of doctors and nurses, who, when an infant is born seriously malformed, do not 'strive officiously to keep alive.' " Fletcher, at 207 n. 54, makes a similar and like- wise undocumented observation that "it has always been a quite common practice of midwives and, in modern times doctors simply to fail to respirate monstrous babies at birth." A supposition to the same effect was made twenty years earlier in Gregg, *The Right To Kill,* 237 No. Am. Rev. 239, 242 (1934). A noted obstetrician and gynecologist, Dr. Frederic Loomis, has told of occasions where expectant fathers have, in effect, asked him to destroy the child, if born abnormal. Loomis, Consultation Room 53 (1946). For an eloquent presentation of the problem raised by the defective infant see *id.* at 53-64.

It is difficult to discuss the consultation feature of Williams' proposal for affirmative "mercy-killing" because Williams himself never discusses it. This fact, plus the fact that Williams' recurrent theme is to give the general practitioner a free hand indicates that he himself does not regard consulta- tion as a significant feature of his plan. The attending physician need only consult another general practitioner and there is no requirement that there be any concurrence in his diagnosis. There is no requirement of a written report. There is no indication as to what point in time there need be con- sultation. Probably there need be consultation only as to diagnosis of the disease and from that point on the extent and mitigatory nature of the pain, and the firmness and rationality of the desire to die is to be judged solely by the attending physician. For the view that even under rather elaborate consultation requirements, in many thinly staffed communities the con- sulted doctor would merely reflect the view of the attending physician see *Life and Death,* Time, March 13, 1950, p. 50. After reviewing eleven case histories of patients wrongly diagnosed as having advanced cancer, diag- noses that stood uncorrected over long periods of time and after several admissions at leading hospitals, Doctors Laszlo, Colmer, Silver and Standard conclude: [*Errors in Diagnosis And Management of Cancer,* 33 Annals Int. Med. 670 (1950)] :

> [I]t became increasingly clear that the original error was one easily made, but that the continuation of that error was due to an acceptance of the original data without exploring their verity and completeness.

Evidently, the presumption is that the general practitioner is a sufficient buffer between the patient and the restless spouse or over-wrought or overreaching relative, as well as a depository of enough general scientific know-how and enough information about current research developments and trends, to assure a minimum of error in diagnosis and anticipation of new measures of relief. Whether or not the general practitioner will accept the responsibility Williams would confer on him is itself a problem of major proportions.[42]

42. In taking the Hippocratic Oath, the oldest code of professional ethics, the physician promises, of course, to "give no deadly medicine to any one if asked, nor suggest any such counsel." Many doctors have indicated they would not accept the role in which legalized euthanasia would cast them. See, e.g., Frohman, supra note 37, at 1221 ("I could never deliberately choose the time of another's dying. The preservation of human life is not only the primary but the all-encompassing general law underlying the code of the physician. . . . Do not ask life's guardian to be also its executioner.") ; Gumpert, A False Mercy, 170 The Nation 80 (1950). ("As a physician, I feel I would have to reject the power and responsibility of the ultimate decision") ; Lord Haden-Guest, 169 H.L. Deb. [5th ser.] 551, 586 [1950]) ("You are asking the medical profession to do it. Ask somebody else."), Kennedy, Euthanasia: To Be or Not To Be, Colliers, May 20, 1939, pp. 15, 57, reprinted in Colliers, April 22, 1950, pp. 13, 50 ("Who is going to carry out the sentence of death? I am sure not I. . . . too grisly a notion for the profession of medicine to stomach"). In 1950, a banner year for mercy-killing trials (see the Mohr case, supra note 17, and the Sander, Paight and Braunsdorf cases at notes 172-176, 183 infra and accompanying text) the General Assembly of the World Medical Association approved a resolution recommending to all national associations that they "condemn the practice of euthanasia under any circumstances." New York Times, Oct. 18, 1950, p. 22, col. 4. Earlier that year, the Medical Society of the State of New York went on record as being "unalterably opposed to euthanasia and to any legislation which will legalize euthanasia." New York Times, May 10, 1950, p. 29, col. 1.

On the other hand, euthanasiasts claim their movement finds great support in the medical profession. The most impressive and most frequently cited piece of evidence is the formation, in 1946, of a committee of 1,776 physicians for the legalization of voluntary euthanasia in New York. See Williams at 331; Fletcher, op. cit. supra note 3, at 187. Williams states that of 3,272 physicians who replied to a questionnaire in New York State in 1946, 80 per cent approved voluntary euthanasia and the Committee of 1,776 came from among this favorable group. I have been unable to find any authority for the 80 per cent figure, and Williams cites none. Some years ago, Gertrude Anne Edwards, then editor of the Euthanasia Society Bulletin, claimed 3,272 physicians—apparently all who replied—favored legalizing voluntary euthanasia. Edwards, Mercy Death For Incurables Should Be Made Legal, The Daily Compass, Aug. 24, 1949, p. 8, col. 1 (issue of the day). Presumably, as in the case of the recent New Jersey questionnaire discussed below, every physician in New York was sent a questionnaire. If so, then the figures cited, whether Williams or Edwards, would mean a great deal more (and support the euthanasiasts a great deal less) if it were added that 88 or 89 per cent of the physicians in the state did not reply at all. In 1940, there were over 26,000 physicians in the State of New York, U.S. Department of Commerce, Bureau of the Census, The Labor Force, Part 4 at 366; in 1950 there were over 30,000, U.S. Dep't of Commerce, Bureau of the Census, Characteristics of the Population, Part 32 at 260.

The most recent petition of physicians for legalized euthanasia was that signed by 166 New Jersey physicians early in 1957 urging in effect the adoption of the American Society's Bill. See Anderson, Who Signed for

Putting that question aside, the soundness of the underlying premises of Williams' "legislative suggestion" will be examined in the course of the discussion of various aspects of the euthanasia problem.

B. The "Choice."

Under current propoals to establish legal machinery, elaborate or otherwise, for the administration of a quick and easy death, it is not enough that those authorized to pass on the question decide that the patient, in effect, is "better off dead." The patient must concur in this opinion. Much of the appeal in the current proposal lies in this so-called "voluntary" attribute.

But is the adult patient[43] really in a position to concur? Is he truly able to make euthanasia a "voluntary" act? There is a good deal to be said, is there not, for Dr. Frohman's pithy comment that

Euthanasia? 96 America 573 (1957). According to this article, the American Society had sent a letter to *all* the doctors in the state asking them to sign such a petition. The doctors were asked to check either of two places, one indicating that their name could be used, the other that it could not. The 1950 census records over 7,000 physicians in New Jersey. Characteristics of the Population, Part 30 at 203. Thus, about 98 per cent of the state medical profession *declined* to sign such a petition. The Medical Society of New Jersey immediately issued a statement that "euthanasia has been and continues to be in conflict with accepted principles of morality and sound medical practice." See Anderson, *supra*. When their names were published in a state newspaper, many of the 166 claimed they had not signed the petition or that they had misunderstood its purpose or that, unknown to them, some secretary had handled the matter in a routine manner. See Anderson, *supra*.

Cf. Paragraph 27 of the Memorandum submitted by the Council of the British Medical Association (Royal Commission, Minutes of Evidence at p. 318):

In the opinion of the Association, no medical practitioner should be asked to take part in bringing about the death of a convicted murderer. The Association would be most strongly opposed to any proposal to introduce, in place of judicial hanging, a method of execution which would require the services of a medical practitioner, either in carrying out the actual process of killing or in instructing others in the technique of the process.

Examination of medical witnesses disclosed that they opposed execution by intravenous injection as "a matter of professional ethics" since "under oath we are bound to promote life . . . whereas any action which has as its object the termination of life, even directly, we feel is undesirable." *Id.* at para. 4041 (Feb. 3, 1950). See also para. 4 of the Memorandum of the Association of Anaesthetists to the effect that if intravenous injection is adopted as an alternative method of execution "the executioner should have no connection or association with the medical profession." *Id.* at p. 678A. For a general discussion of the problem and the views of the medical profession on the matter, see Royal Commission Report at paras. 737-748. Apparently the American medical profession has the same reluctance to participate in execution by intravenous injection. See Weihofen, The Urge to Punish 168 (1956).

43. It should be noted that under what might be termed the "family plan" feature of Williams' proposal, minors may be euthanatized, too. Their fate is to be "left to the good sense of the doctor, taking into account, as he always does, the wishes of the parents as well as those of the child." Williams, p. 340, n. 8. The dubious quality of the "voluntariness" of euthanasia in these circumstances need not be labored.

the "voluntary" plan is supposed to be carried out "only if the victim is both sane and crazed by pain."[44]

By hypothesis, voluntary euthanasia is not to be resorted to until narcotics have long since been administered and the patient has developed a tolerance to them. *When,* then, does the patient make the choice? While heavily drugged?[45] Or is narcotic relief to

44. Frohman, *Vexing Problems In Forensic Medicine: A Physician's View,* 31 N.Y.U.L. Rev. 1215, 1222 (1956).

45. The disturbing mental effects of morphine, "the classic opiate for the relief of severe pain," Schiffrin and Gross, *Systematic Analgetics,* in Management Of Pain In Cancer p. 22 (Schiffrin ed. 1956) and "still the most commonly used potent narcotic analgesic in treatment of cancer pain," Bonica, *The Management of Cancer Pain,* G.P., Nov. 1954, pp. 35, 39, have been described in considerable detail by Drs. Wolff, Hardy and Goodell in *Studies on Pain: Measurement of the Effect of Morphine, Codeine, and other Opiates on the Pain Threshold and an Analysis of their Relation to the Pain Experience,* 19 J. Clinical Investig. 659, 664 (1940). It is not easy to generalize about the psychological effects of drugs for there is good reason to believe that the type of drug reaction is correlated with "differential personality dynamics, primarily in terms of the balance of mature, socially oriented controls over impulsive, egocentric emotionality," von Felsinger, Lasagna and Beecher, *Drug-Induced Mood Changes in Man,* 157 A.M.A.J. 1113, 1119 (1955), that for example, persons with atypical reactions to drugs are likely to be those with pre-existing immaturity, anxiety and hostility, *id.* at 1116. See also Lindemann and Clark, *Modifications In Ego Structure and Personality Reactions Under the Influence of the Effects of Drugs,* 108 Am. J. Psychiatry 561 (1952). It would seem, however, that the severely ill person would be likely to experience substantially more pronounced effects than those described by Wolff, Hardy and Goodell, *supra,* because in that instance the "subjects" studied were the authors themselves, representing both sexes and different body types, experiencing various degrees of pain by exposing portions of their skin surfaces to thermal radiation, but in the case of an illness due to a malignancy or suspected malignancy, we *start* with a situation where "all kinds of irrational attitudes come to the fore". Zarling, *Psychological Aspects of Pain In Terminal Malignancies,* in Management of Pain in Cancer 205 (Schiffrin ed. 1956).

The increasing use of ACTH or cortisone therapy in cancer palliation, see notes 98-101, *infra* and accompanying text, presents further problems. Such therapy "frequently" leads to a "severe degree of disturbance in capacity for rational, sequential thought." Lindemann and Clark, *supra* at 566. Clark, *et. al., Preliminary Observations On Mental Disturbances Occurring In Patients under Therapy With Cortisone and ACTH,* 246 N. Eng. J. Med. 205, 215 (1952) describe six case histories of "major disturbances" where "delusions of depressive, paranoid and grandiose types occurred" and "affective disturbances, also invariably present, varied from depression to hypomania and from apathy to panic; they included ill-defined states that might be described as bewilderment or turmoil." In a subsequent paper, the authors conclude, Clark, *et. al., Further Observations On Mental Disturbances Associated With Cortisone and ACTH Therapy,* 249 N. Eng. J. Med. 178, 182 (1953) that the clinical course of psychoses associated with ACTH and cortisone is "more remarkable for its variability and unpredictability than any other feature," that, for example, mental disturbances may be separated by "intervals of relative lucidity," that "patients may have tolerated previous courses of ACTH or cortisone without complications and yet become psychotic during a subsequent course of treatment with comparable or even smaller doses."

For an extensive review of the many hypotheses purporting to explain mental disturbances associated with ACTH and cortisone see Quarton, *et. al., Mental Disturbances Associated with ACTH and Cortisone: A Review of*

be withdrawn for the time of decision? But if heavy dosage no longer deadens pain, indeed, no longer makes it bearable, how overwhelming is it when whatever relief narcotics offer is taken away, too?

"Hypersensitivity to pain after analgesia has worn off is nearly always noted."[46] Moreover, "the mental side-effects of narcotics, unfortunately for anyone wishing to suspend them temporarily without unduly tormenting the patient, appear to outlast the analgesic effect" and "by many hours."[47] The situation is further complicated by the fact that "a person in terminal stages of cancer who had been given morphine steadily for a matter of weeks would certainly be dependent upon it physically and would probably be addicted to it and react with the addict's response."[48]

The narcotics problem aside, Dr. Benjamin Miller, who probably has personally experienced more pain than any other commentator on the euthanasia scene,[49] observes:

> Anyone who has been severely ill knows how distorted his judgment became during the worst moments of the illness. Pain and the toxic effect of disease, or the violent reaction to certain surgical procedures may change our capacity for rational and courageous thought.[50]

If, say, a man in this plight were a criminal defendant and he were to decline the assistance of counsel would the courts hold that he had

---

Explanatory Hypotheses, 34 Med. 13 (1955). The authors emphasize the inadequacy of present knowledge of mental disturbances associated with this therapy, but believe, "because of the clinical and experimental studies which suggest it," that "it is useful to assume" "cortisone and ACTH produce a ['probably reversible'] specific pattern of modified nervous system function which is invariably present when a gross mental disturbance occurs," *id.* at 41.

46. Goodman and Gilman, The Pharmacological Basis of Therapeutics 235 (2d ed. 1955). To the same effect is Seevers and Pfeiffer, *A Study of the Analgesia, Subjective Depression, and Euphoria Produced by Morphine, Heroine, Dilaudid and Codeine In the Normal Human Subject,* 56 J. Pharm. & Exper. Therap. 166, 182, 187 (1936).

47. Sharpe, *Medication As A Threat To Testamentary Capacity,* 35 N.C. L. Rev. 380, 392 (1957) and medical authorities cited therein.

In the case of cortisone or ACTH therapy, the situation is complicated by the fact that "a frequent pattern of recovery" from psychoses induced by such therapy is "by the occurrence of lucid intervals of increasing frequency and duration, punctuated by relapses into psychotic behavior." Clark, et. al., *Further Observations On Mental Disturbances Associated With Cortisone and ACTH Therapy,* 249 N. Eng. J. Med. 178, 183, (1953).

48. Sharpe, *supra,* note 47, at 384. Goodman and Gilman, *op. cit., supra,* note 46 at 234, observe that while "different individuals require varying periods of time before the repeated administration of morphine results in tolerance, . . . as a rule . . . after about two to three weeks of continued use of the same dose of alkaloid the usual depressant effects fail to appear" whereupon "phenomenally large doses may be taken." For a discussion of "the nature of addiction," see Maurer and Vogel, Narcotics and Narcotic Addiction 20-31 (1954).

49. See note 77 *infra* and accompanying text.

50. Miller, *Why I Oppose Mercy Killings,* Woman's Home Companion, June 1950, pp. 38, 103.

"intelligently and understandingly waived the benefit of counsel?"[51]

Undoubtedly, some euthanasia candidates will have their lucid moments. How they are to be distinguished from fellow-sufferers who do not, or how these instances are to be distinguished from others when the patient is exercising an irrational judgment is not an easy matter. Particularly is this so under Williams' proposal, where no specially qualified persons, psychiatrically trained or otherwise, are to assist in the process.

Assuming, for purposes of argument, that the occasion when a euthanasia candidate possesses a sufficiently clear mind can be ascertained and that a request for euthanasia is then made, there remain other problems. The mind of the pain-racked may occasionally be clear, but is it not also likely to be uncertain and variable? This point was pressed hard by the great physician, Lord Horder, in the House of Lords debates:

> During the morning depression he [the patient] will be found to favour the application under this Bill, later in the day he will think quite differently, or will have forgotten all about it. The mental clarity with which noble Lords who present this Bill are able to think and to speak must not be thought to have any counterpart in the alternating moods and confused judgments of the sick man.[52]

The concept of "voluntary" in voluntary euthanasia would have a great deal more substance to it if, as is the case with voluntary admission statutes for the mentally ill,[53] the patient retained the right to reverse the process within a specified number of days after he gives written notice of his desire to do so — but unfortunately this cannot be. The choice here, of course, is an irrevocable one.

The liklihood of confusion, distortion or vacillation would appear to be serious draw-backs to any voluntary plan. Moreover, Williams' proposal is particularly vulnerable in this regard, since, as he admits, by eliminating the fairly elaborate procedure of the American and English Societies' plans, he also eliminates a time period which would furnish substantial evidence of the patient's

---

51. Moore v. Michigan, 355 U.S. 155, 161 (1957).

52. 103 H. L. Deb. (5th ser.) 466, 492-93 (1936). To the same effect is Lord Horder's speech in the 1950 debates, 169 H. L. Deb. (5th ser.) 551, 569 (1950). See also Gumpert, *A False Mercy*, 170 The Nation 80 (1950):
Even the incapacitated, agonized patient in despair most of the time, may still get some joy from existence. His mood will change between longing for death and fear of death. Who would want to decide what should be done on such unsafe ground?
For a recent layman's account of the self-pity and fluctuating desires for life and death of a seriously ill person, see the reflections of the famous sports broadcaster Ted Husing in *My Friends Wouldn't Let Me Die*, Look, Feb. 4, 1958, p. 64.

53. See Guttmacher and Weihofen, Psychiatry and the Law 307 (1952).

settled intention to avail himself of euthanasia.[54] But if Williams does not always choose to slug it out, he can box neatly and parry gingerly:

> [T]he problem can be exaggerated. Every law has to face diffi-culties in application, and these difficulties are not a conclusive argument against a law if it has a beneficial operation. The measure here proposed is designed to meet the situation where the patient's consent to euthanasia is clear and incontrovertible. The physician, conscious of the need to protect himself against malicious accusations, can devise his own safeguards appropriate to the circumstances; he would normally be well advised to get the patient's consent in writing, just as is now the practice before operations. Sometimes the patient's consent will be particularly clear because he will have expressed a desire for ultimate euthan-asia while he is still clear-headed and before he comes to be racked by pain; if the expression of desire is never revoked, but rather is reaffirmed under the pain, there is the best possible proof of full consent. If, on the other hand, there is no such settled frame of mind, and if the physician chooses to administer euthanasia when the patient's mind is in a variable state, he will be walking in the margin of the law and may find himself un-protected.[55]

If consent is given at a time when the patient's condition has so degenerated that he has become a fit candidate for euthanasia, when, if ever, will it be "clear and incontrovertible?" Is the suggested al-ternative of consent in advance a satisfactory solution? Can such a consent be deemed an informed one? Is this much different from holding a man to a prior statement of intent that if such and such an employment opportunity would present itself he would accept it, or if such and such a young woman were to come along he would marry her? Need one marshal authority for the proposition that many an "iffy" inclination is disregarded when the actual facts are at hand?[56]

Professor Williams states that where a pre-pain desire for "ulti-mate euthanasia" is "reaffirmed" under pain, "there is the best

---

54. Williams, pp. 343-44.
55. *Id.* at 344.
56. Dr. James J. Walsh in *Life Is Sacred,* 94 The Forum, 333, 333-34, recalls the following Aesop's fable:
> It was a bitter-cold day in the wintertime, and an old man was gathering broken branches in the forest to make a fire at home. The branches were covered with ice, many of them were frozen and had to be pulled apart, and his discomfort was intense. Finally the poor old fellow be-came so thoroughly wrought up by his suffering that he called loudly upon death to come. To his surprise, Death came at once and asked what he wanted. Very hastily the old man replied, 'Oh, nothing; nothing ex-cept to help me carry this bundle of sticks home so that I may make a fire.'

possible proof of full consent." Perhaps. But what if it is alternately renounced and reaffirmed under pain? What if it is neither affirmed or renounced? What if it is only renounced? Will a physician be free to go ahead on the ground that the prior desire was "rational", but the present desire "irrational"? Under Williams' plan, will not the physician frequently "be walking in the margin of the law" — just as he is now? Do we really accomplish much more under this proposal than to put the euthanasia principle on the books?

Even if the patient's choice could be said to be "clear and incontrovertible," do not other difficulties remain? Is this the kind of choice, assuming that it can be made in a fixed and rational manner, that we want to offer a gravely ill person? Will we not sweep up, in the process, some who are not really tired of life, but think others are tired of them; some who do not really want to die, but who feel they should not live on, because to do so when there looms the legal alternative of euthanasia is to do a selfish or a cowardly act? Will not some feel an obligation to have themselves "eliminated" in order that funds allocated for their terminal care might be better used by their families or, financial worries aside, in order to relieve their families of the emotional strain involved?

It would not be surprising for the gravely ill person to seek to inquire of those close to him whether he should avail himself of the legal alternative of euthanasia. Certainly, he is likely to wonder about their attitude in the matter. It is quite possible, is it not, that he will not exactly be gratified by any inclination on their part — however noble their motives may be in fact — that he resort to the new procedure? At this stage, the patient-family relationship may well be a good deal less than it ought to be:

> Illness, pain and fear of death tend to activate the dependent longings [for the family unit]. Conflict can easily arise, since it may be very difficult for the individual to satisfy his need for these passive dependent needs and his previous concept of the necessity for a competitive, constructive individuality. Our culture provides few defenses for this type of stress beyond a suppression of the need. If the individual's defenses break down, he may feel angry toward himself and toward the members of his family.[57]

And what of the relatives? If their views will not always influence the patient, will they not at least influence the attending physician? Will a physician assume the risks to his reputation, if not his pocketbook, by administering the *coup de grace* over the

---

57. Zarling, *supra* note 45, at 215.

objection — however irrational — of a close relative?[58] Do not the relatives, then, also have a "choice?" Is not the decision on their part to do nothing and say nothing *itself* a "choice?"[59] In many families there will be some, will there not, who will consider a stand against euthanasia the only proof of love, devotion and gratitude for past events? What of the stress and strife if close relatives differ — as they did in the famous *Sander* case[60] — over the desirability of euthanatizing the patient?

At such a time, as the well-known *Paight* case clearly demonstrates,[61] members of the family are not likely to be in the best state of mind, either, to make this kind of decision. Financial stress and conscious or unconscious competition for the family's estate aside:

> The chronic illness and persistent pain in terminal carcinoma may place strong and excessive stresses upon the family's emotional ties with the patient. The family members who have strong emotional attachment to start with are most likely to take the patient's fears, pains and fate personally. Panic often strikes them. Whatever guilt feelings they may have toward the patient emerge to plague them.
>
> If the patient is maintained at home, many frustrations and physical demands may be imposed on the family by the advanced illness. There may develop extreme weakness, incontinence and bad odors. The pressure of caring for the individual under these

---

58. The medical profession is apparently already quite sensitive about the "sue consciousness" on the part of the public. See Caswell, *A Surgeon's Thoughts on Malpractice*, 30 Temple L.Q. 391 (1957) (symposium). There is good reason to think that "the greater incidence of suits and claims against physicians alleging medical malpractice and a greater financial success in prosecuting these" has led to "insecurity" on the part of many physicians, and "the insecure physician is going to play it safe." Wachowski and Stronach, *The Radiologist and Professional Medical Liability*, 30 Temple L.Q. 398 (1957). Apparently, in some fields fear of claims and litigation has already set "the psychological stage for undertreatment." *Id.* at 399.

59. *Cf.* the examination of Sir Harold Scott, Commissioner of Police of the Metropolis by the Royal Commission on Capital Punishment, Minutes of Evidence 151 (Oct. 7, 1949):

1599. Nobody at present, except the law, has to decide that a particular person should be sentenced to death, no individual?—No individual at present, except the Home Secretary, has to decide that a particular person sentenced to death must hang.

1600. The Home Secretary is in a different position, is he not? He does not primarily prescribe the death penalty; the law does that. The Home Secretary says whether or not he deems it right to interfere with the course of the law?—Yes, that is the legal position. It is a different position, technically, but it seems to me that morally there really is no difference. The responsibility upon the Home Secretary is really to decide whether this man shall die or not die. The machinery may be by interference or non-interference with the law, but the responsibility to me seems the same.

60. See note 172, *infra*. See also the *Mohr* case; *supra* note 17, where two brothers testified against a third who had euthanatized a fourth.

61. See note 176, *infra*.

circumstances is likely to arouse a resentment and, in turn, guilt feelings on the part of those who have to do the nursing.[62]

Nor should it be overlooked that while Professor Williams would remove the various procedural steps and the various personnel contemplated in the American and English Bills and bank his all on the "good sense" of the general practitioner, no man is immune to the fear, anxieties and frustrations engendered by the apparently helpless, hopeless patient. Not even the general practitioner:

> Working with a patient suffering from a malignancy causes special problems for the physician. First of all, the patient with a malignancy is most likely to engender anxiety concerning death, even in the doctor. And at the same time, this type of patient constitutes a serious threat or frustration to medical ambition. As a result, a doctor may react more emotionally and less objectively than in any other area of medical practice.... His deep concern may make him more pessimistic than is necessary. As a result of the feeling of frustration in his wish to help, the doctor may have moments of annoyance with the patient. He may even feel almost inclined to want to avoid this type of patient.[63]

The only Anglo-American prosecution involving an alleged mercy-killing physician seems to be the case of Dr. Herman Sander. The state's testimony was to the effect that, as Sander had admitted on various occasions, he finally yielded to the persistent pleas of his patient's husband and pumped air into her veins "in a weak moment."[64] Sander's version was that he finally "snapped" under the strain of caring for the cancer victim,[65] bungled simple tasks,[66] and became "obsessed" with the need to "do something" for her — if

---

62. Zarling, *supra,* note 45 at 211-12.

63. *Id.* at 213-14. See also Dr. Benjamin Miller to the effect that cancer "can be a 'horrible experience' for the doctor too" and that "a long difficult illness may emotionally exhaust the relatives and physician even more than the patient." Miller, *supra* note 50, at 103; and Stephen, *Murder from the Best of Motives,* 5 L.Q. Rev. 188 (1889), commenting on the disclosure by a Dr. Thwing that he had practiced euthanasia: "The boldness of this avowal is made particularly conspicuous by Dr. Thwing's express admission that the only person for whom the lady's death, if she had been allowed to die naturally, would have been in any degree painful was not the lady herself, but Dr. Thwing."

64. N.Y. Times, Feb. 24, 1950, p. 1, col. 6.

65. "As I looked at her face and all of the thoughts of the past went through my mind, something snapped in me, and I felt impelled or possessed to do something, and why I did it, I can't tell. It doesn't make sense." N.Y. Times, March 7, 1950, p. 19, col. 1.

66. "I didn't use a tourniquet, which is also rather a ridiculous thing, because ordinarily in a normal patient we put on a tourniquet to bring up the vein so that we can see it. Her veins were collapsed anyhow and I couldn't have been thinking the way I ordinarily do at the time. Otherwise I wouldn't have acted this way." *Ibid.*

only to inject air into her *already* dead body.[67] Whichever side one believes — and the jury evidently believed Dr. Sander[68] — the case well demonstrates that at the moment of decision the tired practitioner's "good sense" may not be as good as it might be.

Putting aside the problem of whether the good sense of the general practitioner warrants dispensing with other personnel, there still remains the problems posed by *any* voluntary euthanasia program : the aforementioned considerable pressures on the patient and his family. Are these the kind of pressures we want to inflict on any person, let alone a very sick person? Are these the kind of pressures we want to impose on any family, let alone an emotionally-shattered family? And if so, why are they not also proper considerations for the crippled, the paralyzed, the quadruple amputee, the iron lung occupant and their families?

Might it not be said of the existing ban on euthanasia, as Professor Herbert Wechsler has said of the criminal law in another connection :

> It also operates, and perhaps more significantly, at anterior stages in the patterns of conduct, the dark shadow of organized disapproval eliminating from the ambit of consideration alternatives that might otherwise present themselves in the final competition of choice.[69]

C. *The "Hopelessly Incurable" Patient and the Fallible Doctor.*

Professor Williams notes as "standard argument" the plea that "no sufferer from an apparently fatal illness should be deprived of his life because there is always the possibility that the diagnosis is wrong, or else that some remarkable cure will be discovered in time."[70] But he does not reach the issue until he has already dismissed it with this prefatory remark :

---

67. "[J]ust the appearance of her face and the combination of all the thoughts of her long suffering and of her husband's suffering also—this expression on her face might have just touched me off and made me feel obsessed that I had to do something and what I did does not make sense." *Ibid.*

68. See note 172 *infra,* and accompanying text.

69. Wechsler, *The Issues of the Nuremberg Trial,* 62 Pol. Sci. Q. 11, 16 (1947). *Cf.* Cardozo, *What Medicine Can Do for Law,* in Law and Literature 88-89 (1931) :

> Punishment is necessary, indeed, not only to deter the man who is a criminal at heart, who has felt the criminal impulse, who is on the brink of indecision, but also to deter others who in our existing social organization have never felt the criminal impulse and shrink from crime in horror. Most of us have such a scorn and loathing of robbery or forgery that the temptation to rob or forge is never within the range of choice; it is never a real alternative. There can be little doubt, however, that some of this repugnance is due to the ignominy that has been attached to these and like offenses through the sanctions of the criminal law. If the ignominy were withdrawn, the horror might be dimmed.

70. Williams, p. 318.

It has been noticed before in this work that writers who object to a practice for theological reasons frequently try to support their condemnation on medical grounds. With euthanasia this is difficult, but the effort is made.[71]

Does not Williams, while he pleads that euthanasia not be theologically prejudged, at the same time invite the inference that nontheological objections to euthanasia are simply camouflage?

It is no doubt true that many theological opponents employ medical arguments as well, but it is also true that the doctor who has probably most forcefully advanced medical objections to euthanasia of the so-called incurables, Cornell University's world-renowned Foster Kennedy, a former president of the Euthanasia Society of America, *advocates* euthanasia in other areas where error in diagnosis and prospect of new relief or cures are much reduced, *i.e.*, the "congenitally unfit".[72] In large part for the same reasons, Great Britain's Dr. A. Leslie Banks, then Principal Medical Officer of the Ministry of Health, maintained that a better case could be made for the destruction of congenital idiots and those in the final stages of dementia, particularly senile dementia, than could be made for the doing away of the pain-stricken incurable.[73]

---

71. *Id.* at 317-18.

72. "What to do with the hopelessly unfit? I had thought at a younger time of my life that the legalizing of euthanasia—a soft gentle-sounding word—was a thing to be encouraged; but as I pondered, and as my experience in medicine grew, I became less sure. Now my face is set against the legalization of euthanasia for any person, who, having been well, has at last become ill, for however ill they be, many get well and help the world for years after. But I *am* in favor of euthanasia for those hopeless ones who should never have been born—Nature's mistakes. In this category it is, with care and knowledge, impossible to be mistaken in either diagnosis or prognosis." Kennedy, *The Problem of Social Control of the Congenital Defective*, 99 Am. J. Psychiatry, 13, 14 (1942).

"We doctors do not always know when a disease in a previously healthy person has become entirely incurable. But there are thousands and tens of thousands of the congenitally unfit, about whom no diagnostic error would be possible. . . . with nature's mistakes . . . there can be, after five years . . . of life, no error in diagnosis, nor any hope of betterment." Kennedy, *Euthanasia: To Be or Not To Be*, Colliers, May 20, 1939, pp. 15, 58; reprinted in Colliers, April 22, 1950, pp. 13, 51.

At the February, 1939, meeting of the Society of Medical Jurisprudence, Charles E. Nixdorff, treasurer and board chairman of the Euthanasia Society of America stated that the case of a 19-year-old girl in Bellevue, with a broken back and paralyzed legs, who "prayed for death every night" was sufficient reason for the Euthanasia Society "to carry on the fight." "Dr. [Foster] Kennedy [then President of the Euthanasia Society], in conversation, said later he did not think that was a particularly good example. He said he had known many such cases where the patients 'got around' and only recently he had 'danced with one.'" N.Y. Times, Feb. 14, 1939, p. 2, col. 6.

73. Banks, *Euthanasia*, 161 Practitioner 101, 106 (1948). According to him, neither "pain" nor "incurability" "is capable of precise and final definition, and indeed if each case had to be argued in open court there would be conflict of medical opinion in practically every instance." *Id.* at 104.

Surely, such opponents of voluntary euthanasia cannot be accused of wrapping theological objections in medical dressing!

Until the euthanasia societies of England and America had been organized and a party decision reached, shall we say, to advocate euthanasia only for incurables on their request, Dr. Abraham L. Wolbarst, one of the most ardent supporters of the movement, was less troubled about putting away "insane or defective people [who] have suffered mental incapacity and tortures of the mind for many years" than he was about the "incurables".[74] He recognized the "difficulty involved in the decision as to incurability" as one of the "doubtful aspects of euthanasia."

> Doctors are only human beings, with few if any supermen among them. They make honest mistakes, like other men, because of the limitations of the human mind.[75]

He noted further that "it goes without saying that, in recently developed cases with a possibility of cure, euthanasia should not even be considered," that "the law might establish a limit of, say, ten years in which there is a chance of the patient's recovery."[76]

Dr. Benjamin Miller is another who is unlikely to harbor an ulterior theological motive. His interest is more personal. He himself was left to die the death of a "hopeless" tuberculosis victim only to discover that he was suffering from a rare malady which affects the lungs in much the same manner but seldom kills. Five years and sixteen hospitalizations later, Dr. Miller dramatized his point by recalling the last diagnostic clinic of the brilliant Richard Cabot, on the occasion of his official retirement:

> He was given the case records [complete medical histories and results of careful examinations] of two patients and asked to diagnose their illnesses. . . . The patients had died and only the hospital pathologist knew the exact diagnosis beyond doubt, for he had seen the descriptions of the postmortem findings. Dr. Cabot, usually very accurate in his diagnosis, that day missed both.
>
> The chief pathologist who had·selected the cases was a wise person. He had purposely chosen two of the most deceptive to remind the medical students and young physicians that even at the end of a long and rich experience one of the greatest diagnosticians of our time was still not infallible.[77]

---

74. Wolbarst, *Legalize Euthanasia!*, 94 The Forum 330, 332 (1935). *But see* Wolbarst, *The Doctor Looks at Euthanasia*, 149 Medical Record, 354 (1939).
75. Wolbarst, *Legalize Euthanasia!*, 94 The Forum 330, 331 (1935).
76. *Id.* at 332.
77. Miller, *supra* note 50, at 39.

Richard Cabot was the John W. Davis, the John Lord O'Brian, of his profession. When one reads the account of his last clinic, one cannot help but think of how fallible the *average* general practitioner must be, how fallible the *young doctor just starting practice* must be—and this, of course, is all that some small communities have in the way of medical care—how fallible the *worst* practitioner, young or old, must be. If the range of skill and judgment among licensed physicians approaches the wide gap between the very best and the very worst members of the bar—and I have no reason to think it does not—then the minimally competent physician is hardly the man to be given the responsibility for ending another's life.[78] Yet, under Williams' proposal at least, the marginal physician, as well as his more distinguished brethren, would have legal authorization to make just such decisions. Under Williams' proposal, euthanatizing a patient or two would all be part of the routine day's work.[79]

Perhaps it is not amiss to add as a final note, that no less a euthanasiast than Dr. C. Killick Millard[80] had such little faith in the average general practitioner that as regards the *mere administering* of the *coup de grace,* he observed:

> In order to prevent any likelihood of bungling, it would be very necessary that only medical practitioners who had been specially licensed to euthanise (after acquiring special knowledge and skill) should be allowed to administer euthanasia. Quite possibly, the work would largely be left in the hands of the official euthanisors, who would have to be appointed specially for each area.[81]

True, the percentage of correct diagnosis is particularly high in cancer.[82] The short answer, however, is that euthanasiasts most emphatically do not propose to restrict mercy-killing to cancer cases. Dr. Millard has maintained that "there are very many diseases be-

---

78. As to how bad the bad physician can be, see generally, even with a grain of salt, 3 Belli, Modern Trials §§ 327-353 (1954). See also Regan, Doctor and Patient and the Law 17-40 (3d ed. 1956).

79. See note 41 *supra,* and accompanying text.

80. As Williams points out, p. 330, Dr. Millard introduced the topic of euthanasia into public debate in 1932 when he advocated that mercy-killing should be legalized in his presidential address to the Society of Medical Officers of Health. In moving the second reading of the voluntary euthanasia bill, Lord Ponsonby stated that "the movement in favour of drafting a Bill" had "originated" with Dr. Millard. 103 H.L. Deb. 466-67 (1936).

81. Millard, *The Case For Euthanasia,* 136 Fortnightly Review 701, 717 (1931). Under his proposed safeguards (two independent doctors, followed by a "medical referee") Dr. Millard viewed error in diagnosis as a non-deterrable "remote possibility." *Ibid.*

82. Euthanasia opponents readily admit this. See *e.g.,* Miller, *supra* note 50, at 38.

sides cancer which tend to kill 'by inches', and where death, when it does at last come to the rescue, is brought about by pain and exhaustion."[83] Furthermore, even if mercy-killings were to be limited to cancer, however relatively accurate the diagnosis in these cases, here, too, "incurability of a disease is never more than an estimate based upon experience, and how fallacious experience may be in medicine only those who have had a great deal of experience fully realize."[84]

Dr. Daniel Laszlo, Chief of Division of Neoplastic Diseases, Montefiore Hospital, New York City, and three other physicians have observed:

> The mass crowding of a group of patients labeled 'terminal' in institutions designated for that kind of care carries a grave danger. The experience gathered from this group makes it seem reasonable to conclude that a fresh evaluation of any large group in mental institutions, in institutions for chronic care, or in homes for the incurably sick, would unearth a rewarding number of salvageable patients who can be returned to their normal place in society. . . . For purposes of this study we were especially interested in those with a diagnosis of advanced cancer. In a number of these patients, major errors in diagnosis or management were encountered.[85]

The authors then discuss in considerable detail the case histories of eleven patients admitted or transferred to Montefiore Hospital alone with the diagnosis of *"advanced cancer in its terminal stage,"* none of whom had cancer at all. In three cases the organ suspected to be the primary site of malignancy was unaffected; in the other eight cases it was the site of some nonmalignant disease. The impact of these findings may be gleaned from a subsequent comment by Doctors Laszlo and Spencer: "Such cases [of mistaken diagnosis of advanced cancer] are encountered even in large medical centers and probably many more could be found in areas poorly provided with medical facilities."[86]

Only recently, Dr. R. Ger, citing case histories of false cancer

---

83. Millard, *supra* note 81, at 702.
84. Frohman, *Vexing Problems in Forensic Medicine: A Physician's View*, 31 N.Y.U.L. Rev. 1215, 1216 (1956). Dr. Frohman added:
We practice our art with the tools and information yielded by laboratory and research scientists, but an ill patient is not subject to experimental control, nor are his reactions always predictable. A good physician employs his scientific tools whenever they are useful, but many are the times when intuition, chance, and faith are his most successful techniques.
85. Laszlo, *et. al., Errors In Diagnosis And Management Of Cancer*, 33 Annals Int. Med. 670 (1950).
86. Laszlo and Spencer, *Medical Problems In The Management Of Cancer*, 37 Med. Clin. N.A. 869, 873 (1953).

diagnoses to buttress his point, had occasion to warn his colleagues:

> Students are often told, and one is exhorted repeatedly in textbooks to do so, to regard signs and symptoms appearing over the age of 40 years as due to carcinoma [malignant epithelial tumor] until proved otherwise. While it is true that carcinoma should take first place on grounds of commonness, it must not be forgotten that there are other conditions which may mimic carcinoma clinically, radiologically and at operation, and which are essentially benign. There is danger, moreover, when presented with a case simulating carcinoma to assume it to be carcinoma without proving or disproving the diagnosis. This may give rise to unnecessary fatalities by either denying treatment because of a hopeless prognosis or carrying out unnecessary procedures.[87]

Even more recently, Doctors De Vet and Walder scored the "extremely dangerous" tendency on the part of general practitioners and specialists alike "when a neoplasm becomes manifest in a patient previously operated on for a malignant tumour . . . to presume that the new growth is a metastasis [a transfer of the malignant disease]."[88] Their studies demonstrated that it is "by no means a rare occurrence" for patients to develop "another, benign tumour after having been operated upon for a malignant one."[89] De Vet and Walder also stress the "remarkable similarity" in symptoms, including "violent pain" in both cases, between metastases and benign processes of the spinal column and the spinal cord.[90]

Faulty diagnosis is only one ground for error. Even if the diagnosis is correct, a second ground for error lies in the possibility that some measure of relief, if not a full cure, may come to the fore within the life expectancy of the patient. Since Glanville Williams does not deign this objection to euthanasia worth more than a pass-

---

87. Ger, *Diagnosis and Misdiagnosis of Carcinoma*, 28 So. Afr. Med. J. 670 (1954).

88. De Vet and Walder, *Pseudo-Metastases*, 7 Archivium Chirurgicum Neerlandicum 78 (1955).

89. *Id.* at 83.

90. *Id.* at 82. Consider also the following: At the 1951 annual meeting of the American Cancer Society, devoted to cytologic diagnosis of cancer, Dr. Henry M. Lemon noted: *Proceedings, Symposium on Exfoliative Cytology* at 106 (Oct. 23-24, 1951):

> The problem of false positive diagnoses has always been a difficult one. About 5 per cent of the 541 non-cancer patients in whom cancer secretions have been studied in the past had false positive diagnosis made, and in our experience, gastritis has been a common cause of false positive diagnosis.

At the same meeting, Dr. William A. Cooper told of "fifteen misses" in X-ray gastric cancer diagnosis out of one hundred cases (*id.* at 102):

> Four of the twenty-five cases of cancer were said to have benign lesions, while eleven of the seventy-five benign lesions were said to have cancer.

ing reference,[91] it is necessary to turn elsewhere to ascertain how it has been met.

One answer is:

It must be little comfort to a man slowly coming apart from multiple sclerosis to think that, fifteen years from now, death might not be his only hope.[92]

To state the problem this way is of course, to avoid it entirely. How do we know that fifteen *days* or fifteen *hours* from now, "death might not be [the incurable's] only hope?"

A second answer is:

[N]o cure for cancer which might be found 'tomorrow' would be of any value to a man or woman 'so far advanced in cancerous toxemia as to be an applicant for euthanasia'.[93]

As I shall endeavor to show, this approach is a good deal easier to formulate than it is to apply. For one thing, it presumes that we know today *what* cures will be found tomorrow. For another, it overlooks that if such cases can be said to exist, the patient is likely to be *so far* advanced in cancerous toxemia as to be no longer capable of understanding the step he is taking and hence *beyond* the stage when euthanasia ought to be administered.[94]

A generation ago, Dr. Haven Emerson, then President of the American Public Health Association, made the point that "no one can say today what will be incurable tomorrow. No one can predict what disease will be fatal or permanently incurable until medicine becomes stationary and sterile." Dr. Emerson went so far as to say that "to be at all accurate we must drop altogether the term 'in-

---

91. See Williams, p. 318.

92. *Pro & Con: Shall We Legalize "Mercy Killing"?*, Readers Digest, Nov. 1938, pp. 94, 96.

93. James, *Euthanasia—Right or Wrong?*, Survey Graphic, May, 1948, pp. 241, 243; Wolbarst, *The Doctor Looks at Euthanasia*, 149 Medical Record, 354, 355 (1939).

94. Thus, Doctor Millard, in his leading article, *supra* note 81, at 710, states:

A patient who is too ill to understand the significance of the step he is taking has got beyond the stage when euthanasia ought to be administered. In any case his sufferings are probably nearly over.

Glanville Williams similarly observes (pp. 342-44):

Under the bill as I have proposed to word it, the consent of the patient would be required, whereas it seems that some doctors are now accustomed to give fatal doses without consulting the patient. I take it to be clear that no legislative sanction can be accorded to this practice, in so far as the course of the disease is deliberately anticipated. The essence of the measures proposed by the two societies is that euthanasia should be voluntarily accepted by the patient.

. . . The measure here proposed is designed to meet the situation where the patient's consent to euthanasia is clear and incontrovertible.

curables' and substitute for it some such term as 'chronic illness'."[95]

That was a generation ago. Dr. Emerson did not have to go back more than a decade to document his contention. Before Banting and Best's insulin discovery, many a diabetic had been doomed. Before the Whipple-Minot-Murphy liver treatment made it a relatively minor malady, many a pernicious anemia sufferer had been branded "hopeless." Before the uses of sulfanilimide were disclosed, a patient with widespread streptococcal blood poisoning was a condemned man.[96]

Today, we may take even that most resolute disease, cancer, and we need look back no further than the last decade of research in this field to document the same contention.[97]

Three years ago, Dr. William D. McCarthy presented the results to date, of an effort begun in 1950 to open a new approach in cancer palliation,[98] a report whose findings of "remarkable improvement" in nearly a third of the cases invoked strong editorial comment in the *New England Journal of Medicine*.[99] At the time of Dr. McCarthy's report, 100 "hopeless" patients with a wide variety of neoplasms had been treated with a combination of nitrogen mustard and ACTH or cortisone. "All patients in the series were in advanced or terminal phases of disease, and were accepted for treatment only after the disease was determined to be progressive after adequate surgery or radiation therapy."[100] Dr. McCarthy summarizes the results:

> In several of these cases there was associated tumor regression or arrest, with definite prolongation of life in increased comfort. This group constituted 15 per cent of the series. Reserved for the classification as excellent response were 16 additional patients (16 per cent) whose subjective and objective remissions were striking, often accompanied with tumor regression or arrest, and whose improvement persisted for six months or longer. These patients represent the true temporary remissions of the series. They are, however, temporary remissions and not

---

95. Emerson, *Who Is Incurable? A Query and Reply*, N.Y. Times, Oct. 22, 1933, § 8, p. 5, col. 1.

96. *Ibid.*, Miller, *supra* note 50, at 39.

97. This is not to say that progress in the treatment of cancer cases has been limited to the last decade. Over twenty years ago, Lord Horder, 103 H.L. Deb. 466, 492 (1936), opposing the euthanasia bill in the House of Lords debates, observed:

> [A]lthough it is common knowledge that the essential causative factors of cancer still elude us, there are patients to-day suffering from this disease, not only living but free from pain, who would not have been living ten years ago, and this as the result of advances made in treatment.

98. McCarthy, *The Palliation and Remission of Cancer With Combined Corticosteroid and Nitrogen Mustard Therapy*, 252 N. Eng. J. Med. 467 (1955).

99. *Treatment of Advanced Cancer*, 252 N Eng. J. Med. 502 (1955).

100. McCarthy, *supra* note 98 at 468.

permanent remissions or so called 'cures.' Nevertheless, as a group originally considered hopeless, each has been afforded longer life, acceptable health and freedom from pain. Fortunately, prolongation of life appeared to occur only in patients who received good palliation. . . .

Unusual temporary remissions for intervals as long as three years were obtained. . . .[101]

Needless to say, a number of those who received substantial benefits from this particular therapy were suffering from great pain and appeared to be leading candidates for voluntary euthanasia. In 1950, the year the new combination therapy investigation was initiated, a swift death appeared to be their only hope. Instead they resumed full and useful lives for a considerable period of time.[102]

Since February, 1951, in a new effort to inhibit certain cancer growth,[103] a number of advanced cancer patients at the Memorial Center for Cancer and Allied Disease have had their adrenal glands removed.[104] Of a total of ten patients with cancer of the prostate adrenalectomized at the time of the 1952 report, three died in the immediate postoperative period of various causes, leaving seven

101. *Id.* at 470, 475. Some of the results were little short of spectacular. See *e.g.,* Case 1, *id.* at 470, the case of a woman whose reticulum-cell sarcoma "was considered too disseminated for radiation therapy" who responded so well to therapy that she returned to employment as a nurse for three years; Case 3, *ibid.,* that of a man taken to the hospital "in a terminal state" with "a massive lymphosarcoma of the pelvis" which had received X-ray therapy and which was increasing rapidly in size, who returned to his occupation and but for a short interval when he underwent a second course of therapy "continued working up to the time of his death . . . eighteen months after the 1st course of combination therapy"; Case 11, *id.* at 472-73, that of a stomach-cancer victim "in a terminal condition, unable to retain solids or fluids" who, after three months of the therapy, regained her normal weight, returned to her occupation and enjoyed excellent health for a full year.

On the other hand, some 40 per cent of the group were considered failures (those who died within a month and those who survived longer but received little benefit); 29 per cent were classed as fair in response (moderate but brief palliation). *Id.* at 470.

102. See also Ravich, *Euthanasia and Pain In Cancer,* 9 Unio Internationalis Contra Cancrum 397 (1953), a report of the promising experimental chemotherapeutic measures (*n*-Butanol, glycerine and sodium thirosulfate) of Dr. Emanuel Revici and the staff of the Institute of Applied Biology. A number of patients whose cancers "had advanced beyond the point where any help was to be anticipated from surgery, X-ray or radium, according to the opinions of the attending physicians," *id.* at 398, returned to their normal occupations after the onset of treatment and remained on the job for several years.

103. Drs. Huggins and Scott had reported the first total bilateral adrenalectomies in patients with prostatic carcinoma in 1945, but since cortisone was not then available all patients died in adrenal insufficiency. The authors therefore concluded at that time that the operation was not practical and temporarily abandoned this approach. See Huggins and Scott, *Bilateral Adrenalectomy In Prostatic Cancer: Clinical Features and Urinary Excretion of 17 Ketosteroids and Estrogen,* 122 Annals of Surgery 1031 (1945).

104. West, *et. al., The Effect of Bilateral Adrenalectomy Upon Neoplastic Disease in Man,* 5 Cancer 1009 (1952).

effective cases for evaluation :

> The most striking beneficial response to adrenalectomy was relief of pain. Three of the patients were confined to bed with pain prior to surgery and were taking narcotics frequently. . . . All three had striking relief of pain postoperatively and became ambulatory. One (J.W.) was in a stuporous condition pre-operatively, confined to bed, and unable to feed himself. Following adrenalectomy his general condition improved remarkably. He became ambulatory and was able to return home to live a relatively normal life. This improvement has been maintained until the present, 218 days after surgery. . . .
>
> Summarizing the prostatic cancer cases, all seven effective cases had striking subjective improvement. Only two cases showed objective improvement. Improvement was temporary in all cases.[105]

From all indications "J.W." was a most attractive target for the euthanasiasts. He was suffering from "severe pain requiring frequent injections of narcotics for relief . . . was extremely lethargic and relatively unresponsive . . . had to be fed by the nursing staff."[106] If he, to use Dr. Wolbarst's words, was not "so far advanced in cancerous toxemia as to be an applicant for euthanasia," when will anybody be? I am not at all sure that at this point J.W. was still *capable* of consenting to his death. If he were, he certainly had reached the very brink. As it turned out, however, to have put J.W. out of his misery at the time would have been to deprive him of over seven months of a "relatively normal life."[107] Adequate quantities of cortisone and other active corticoids had just become available. The postoperative problem of adrenal insufficiency had just been solved.

Breast cancer, the most common cancer in woman,[108] has also yielded substantially to adrenalectomy. A recent five-year evaluation of 52 consecutive patients with metastatic mammary cancer who underwent adrenalectomy disclosed that significant objective

---

105. *Id.* at 1012-13. Dr. M. P. Reiser of the University of Minnesota Medical School and his colleagues have planted radon-filled seeds of gold into the prostate area in an effort to save patients with "inoperable" cancer of the prostate gland. As a result, thirteen of twenty-five patients have lived at least a year; six have lived from three to seven years. Radon is the gas of radium. See Cohn, *'U' Reports Victories Over Cancer,* Minneapolis Morning Tribune, April 4, 1958, p. 13, col. 4.

106. West, *supra* note 104 at 1010.

107. An addendum to the report discloses that J.W.'s post-operative "subjective improvement" lasted 220 days and that he survived for 294 days, *id.* at 1016-17. What pain J. W. suffered in his last days is not revealed, but in general discussion the authors state that ". . . [I]n the majority of the cases, the pain never did return to its preoperative intensity even though the patient later died of cancer." *Id.* at 1015.

108. American Cancer Society, *1958 Cancer Facts and Figures* 17.

remissions of varying lengths of time occurred in 20 patients.[109] Prolonged survival—from three years to 68 months—occurred in seven of these patients, all of whom had been suffering from advanced stages of the disease, had failed to respond to various other types of therapy and were incapacitated. After treatment, "all of them were able to resume their normal physical activities."[110] One of the seven had had such extensive metastases that she "appeared to be moribund," but she survived, with great regression of the neoplasm, more than five years after adrenalectomy.[111]

The pituitary gland, as well as the adrenal glands, has had an increasing apparent role in the control of breast cancer. Since 1951, the availability of ACTH and cortisone has allowed an intensive investigation of the effects of hypophysectomy, *i.e.*, surgical removal of the pituitary body. The results have been most gratifying. A recent report, for example, discloses that of twenty-eight patients with advanced breast cancer who underwent total hypophysectomy, "eighteen . . . have demonstrated striking objective clinical regressions" up to twenty months while an additional four who showed no objective evidence of regression experienced "striking relief of pain."[112]

The dynamic state of current cancer research would appear to be amply demonstrated by the indication, already, that in the treatment of advanced breast cancer, adrenalectomy, itself still in the infant stages, may yield to hypophysectomy.[113]

---

109.   Dao and Huggins, *Metastatic Cancer of the Breast Treated by Adrenalectomy*, 165 A.M.A.J. 1793 (1957).
Furthermore, an additional nine patients who underwent no demonstrable regression experienced marked objective improvement in relief of bone pain, disappearance of respiratory symptoms and return of a sense of well-being. An earlier report on adrenalectomy disclosed that of five "effective" breast carcinoma cases, a sixth having died of other causes a short time after undergoing the operation, "all had severe pain preoperatively, and all had either partial or complete relief of pain following adrenalectomy." West, *supra* note 104, at 1014.
110.   *Id.* at 1796.
111.   *Ibid.*
112.   Kennedy, French and Peyton, *Hypophysectomy in Advanced Breast Cancer*, 255 N. Eng. J. Med., 1165, 1171 (1956). See also Kennedy, *The Present Status of Hormone Therapy in Advanced Breast Cancer*, 69 Radiology 330, 333-34 (1957).
For earlier reports, see Luft and Olivecrona, *Hypophysectomy In Man: Experiences in Metastatic Cancer of the Breast*, 8 Cancer 261 (1955) (13 of 37 patients showed subjective or objective improvement for from 3 to 27 months); Pearson, *et. al., Hypophysectomy in Treatment of Advanced Cancer*, A.M.A.J. 17 (1956) (over half of 41 patients who could be evaluated underwent objective remissions).
113.   "In view of the favorable responses after hypophysectomy,.the concomitant adrenal atrophy and the ease in managing the patient, it appears that hypophysectomy is to be preferred over adrenalectomy in the treatment of advanced breast cancer." Kennedy, French and Peyton, *supra* note 112, at 1171.

True, many types of cancer still run their course virtually unhampered by man's arduous efforts to inhibit them. But the number of cancers coming under some control is ever increasing. With medicine attacking on so many fronts with so many weapons who would bet a man's life on when and how the next type of cancer will yield, if only just a bit?[114]

True, we are not betting much of a life. For even in those areas where gains have been registered, the life is not "saved," death is only postponed. Of course, in a sense this is the case with every "cure" for every ailment. But it may be urged that after all there is a great deal of difference between the typical "cure" which achieves an indefinite postponement, more or less, and the cancer respite which results in only a brief intermission, so to speak, of rarely more than six months or a year. Is this really long enough to warrant all the bother?

Well, how long *is* long enough? In many recent cases of cancer respite, the patient, though experiencing only temporary relief, underwent sufficient improvement to retake his place in society.[115] Six or twelve or eighteen months is long enough to do most of the

114. In addition to the various approaches to the cancer problem discussed *supra,* consider, *e.g.,* the following items which have appeared in the daily newspapers the past few months:

(1). In April of 1958, scientists uncovered a new chemical compound—fluorine combined with a body compound used by cancer cells for growth—which inhibits the growth of cancer cells. The discovery was hailed as a major step in the search for a medical "magic bullet" which can kill cancer cells outright. New York Times, April 4, 1958, p. 23, col. 7; Minneapolis Morning Tribune, April 4, 1958, p. 14, col. 5.

(2). Neutron radiation on brain cancer patients has led to "significant" increases in length of life, according to Dr. William H. Sweet of the Harvard Medical School. This September, Dr. Sweet will use an atomic reactor in an unprecedented effort to remove all remnants of brain cancer from a patient. Cohn, *Brain Cancer Surgeons Will Use Atomic Reactor,* Minneapolis Morning Tribune, March 30, 1958, p. 1, col. 1.

(3). There is reason to think that neurosonic surgery, sound waves focussed on precise spots inside the brain, may prove valuable in treating brain cancers—with a dosage devised to kill only cancer cells. Palsy victims for as long as 35 years have been relieved by such treatment. New York Times, April 2, p. 33, col. 8; Minneapolis Morning Tribune, April 2, 1958, p. 8, col. 5.

(4). Dr. Roy Hertz, an expert of the National Cancer Institute, has disclosed that a drug called methotrexate has suppressed all evidence of a type of cancer occurring in woman during pregnancy, but the "full value of the treatment remains to be determined." New York Times, Feb. 29, 1958, p. 62, col. 4.

(5). Dr. L. M. Tocantins of Jefferson Medical College has been conducting experiments to combat leukemia with whole-body X-ray doses calculated to kill the sick bone marrow cells that are producing the illness. Good marrow, taken from the bones of volunteers, is then injected into the patients. Such a technique has reversed leukemia's course in mice and given some of them normal life spans. Cohn, *They Give Ribs to Fight Leukemia,* Minneapolis Morning Tribune, March 26, 1958, p. 1, col. 4.

115. See notes 101, 102, 105, 109 *supra.*

things which socially justify our existence, is it not? Long enough
for a nurse to care for more patients, a teacher to impart learning to
more classes, a judge to write a great opinion, a novelist to write a
stimulating book, a scientist to make an important discovery and,
after all, for a factory hand to put the wheels on another year's
Cadillac.

D. "Mistakes Are Always Possible".

Under Professor Williams' "legislative suggestion" a doctor
could "refrain from taking steps to prolong the patient's life by
medical means" solely on his own authority. Only when disposition
by affirmative "mercy-killing" is a considered alternative need he do
so much as, and only so much as, consult another general practitioner.[116] There are no other safeguards. No "euthanasia referee,"
no requirement that death be administered in the presence of an
official witness, as in the English society's bill. No court to petition,
no committee to investigate and report back to the court, as in
the American society's bill. Professor Williams' view is:

> It may be allowed that mistakes are always possible, but this is
> so in any of the affairs of life. And it is just as possible to make
> a mistake by doing nothing as by acting. All that can be expected
> of any moral agent is that he should do his best on the facts as
> they appear to him.[117]

That mistakes are always possible, that mistakes are always
made, does not, it is true, deter society from pursuing a particular
line of conduct—if the line of conduct is *compelled* by needs which
override the risk of mistake. A thousand *Convicting the Innocent's*[118] or *Not Guilty's*[119] may stir us, may spur us to improve the
administration of the criminal law, but they cannot and should not
bring the business of deterring and incapacitating dangerous criminals or would-be dangerous criminals to an abrupt and complete
halt.

Professor Williams points to capital punishment, as proponents of euthanasia are fond of doing,[120] but defenders of this
practice do not—as, of course, they cannot—rest on the negative
argument that "mistakes are always possible." Rightly or wrongly,

---

116. For a discussion of the legal significance of "mercy-killing" by
omission and Williams' consultation feature for affirmative "mercy-killing,"
see note 41 *supra*.
117. Williams, p. 318.
118. Borchard, Convicting the Innocent (1932).
119. Frank and Frank, Not Guilty (1957).
120. See, *e.g.*, Fletcher, Morals and Medicine, 181, 195-96 (1954); Millard, *The Case For Euthanasia*, 136 Fortnightly Review 701, 717 (1931);
Potter, *The Case for Euthanasia*, Reader's Scope, May 1947, pp. 111, 113.

they contend that the deterrent value of the death penalty so exceeds
that of life-imprisonment or long-term imprisonment that it is required for the protection of society, that it results in the net gain of a
substantial number of human lives.[121] This is generally regarded
as the "central" or "fundamental" question in considering whether
the death penalty should be abolished or retained.[122] This, as Viscount St. Davids said of a House of Lords debate on capital punishment which saw him advocate abolition, "was what the whole debate was about."[123]

Presumably, when and if it can be established to the satisfaction
of all reasonable men that the deterrent value of capital punishment
as against imprisonment is nil or *de minimus*, mistakes will no
longer be tolerated and the abolitionists will have prevailed over
the few remaining retentionists who would still defend capital
punishment on other grounds.[124] In any event, it is not exactly a
show of strength for euthanasiasts to rely on so battered and shaky
a practice as capital punishment.[125]

---

121. See generally Royal Commission on Capital Punishment, Report,
Cmd. No. 8932, paras. 55-68 (1949-53) ; Michael and Wechsler, Criminal
Law And Its Administration, 235-62 (1940).
122. H. L. A. Hart, *Murder And The Principle Of Punishment:
England And The United States,* 52 N.W. U. L. Rev. 433, 446, 455 (1957).
See also, *e.g.,* Bye, Capital Punishment in the United States 31 (1919) ;
Gardiner, Capital Punishment as a Deterrent: And the Alternative 17, 22
(1956) ; Caldwell, *Why Is the Death Penalty Retained?* 284 Annals Am.
Acad. Pol. & Soc. Sci. 45, 50 (1952).
123. "I believed that the figures showed that if you abolish capital
punishment you do not, in fact, lose more human lives. Other noble Lords
took the opposite view ; they believed that if capital punishment were abolished we should lose more lives. Both sides, however, believed that there is
an ultimate value in human life. That was what the whole debate was about."
169 H.L. Deb. (5th ser.) 551, 591 (1950).
124. The remaining pockets of resistance would be manned by those
who would utilize the death penalty as an instrument of vengeance, as a device
for placing a special stigma on certain crimes, and as a means of furnishing
the criminal with an extraordinary opportunity to repent before execution.
See the discussion in the Royal Commission Report, *supra* note 121, at paras.
52-54.
125. Books attacking the utilization of the death penalty include Bye,
Capital Punishment In the United States (1919) ; Calvert, Capital Punishment In The Twentieth Century (4th ed. 1930) ; Frank and Frank, Not
Guilty 248 (1957) ; Gardiner, Capital Punishment As A Deterrent: And the
Alternative (1956) ; Koestler, Reflections on Hanging (1956) ; Lawes,
Twenty Thousand Years In Sing Sing, 291-337 (1932) ; Weihofen, The
Urge To Punish 146-70 (1956).
In February, 1956, the House of Commons on a free vote of 292 to 246
passed a resolution calling for the abolition or suspension of the death
penalty which stated in part that "the death penalty for murder no longer
accords with the needs or true interests of a civilized society" 548 H.C. Deb.
(5th ser.) 2556, 2652, 2655, (1956). The House of Lords, however, rejected
the legislation passed in the spirit of this resolution. See H.L.A. Hart, *supra*
note 122, at 434. Bertrand Russell recently commented (*supra* note 2, at 385) :
  I have not the relevant statistics, but I think if a poll had been taken [of
  the House of Lords in 1936] it would have been found that most of those
  who objected to euthanasia favoured capital punishment, the dominant

A relevant question, then, is what is the need for euthanasia which leads us to tolerate the mistakes, the very fatal mistakes, which will inevitably occur? What is the compelling force which requires us to tinker with deeply entrenched and almost universal[126] precepts of criminal law?

Let us first examine the qualitative need for euthanasia:

Proponents of euthanasia like to present for consideration the case of the surgical operation, particularly a highly dangerous one: risk of death is substantial, perhaps even more probable than not; in addition, there is always the risk that the doctors have misjudged the situation and that no operation was needed at all. Yet it is not unlawful to perform the operation.[127]

The short answer is the witticism that whatever the incidence of death in connection with different types of operations "no doubt, it is in all cases below 100 per cent, which is the incidence rate for euthanasia."[128] But this may not be the full answer. There are occasions where the law permits action involving about a 100 per cent incidence of death, for example, self-defense. There may well be other instances where the law should condone such action, for example, the "necessity" cases illustrated by the overcrowded life-boat,[129] the starving survivors of a ship-wreck,[130] and—perhaps best of all—by Professor Lon Fuller's penetrating and fascinating tale of the trapped cave explorers.[131]

In all these situations, death for some may well be excused, if not justified, yet the prospect that some deaths will be unnecessary is a real one. He who kills in self-defense may have misjudged the facts. They who throw passengers overboard to lighten the load may no sooner do so than see "masts and sails of rescue . . . emerge out of the fog".[132] But no human being will ever find himself in a situation where he knows for an absolute certainty that one

consideration in each case being faithfulness to tradition.

Perhaps, but I would speculate further that if such a poll had been taken, it may well have been found that most of those who *favored* euthanasia *objected* to capital punishment. And on such grounds as the irrevocability of the death sentence and the inevitable incident of error in the selection of its victims, the insufficient showing that such a drastic method is needed, and, perhaps, the sanctity of life.

126. See Silving, *supra* note 7.

127. See, *e.g.*, Fletcher, *op. cit. supra* note 3, at 198; Euthanasia Society of America, Merciful Release, art. 7; Millard, *supra* note 81 at 717.

128. Rudd, *Euthanasia*, 14 J. Clin. & Exper. Psychopath. 1, 4 (1953).

129. See United States v. Holmes, 26 Fed. Cas. No. 15,383 (C.C.E.D. Pa. 1842).

130. See Regina v. Dudley & Stephens, 14 Q.B.D. 273 (1884).

131. Fuller, *The Case of the Speluncean Explorers*, 62 Harv. L. Rev. 616 (1949).

132. Cardozo, *What Medicine Can Do For Law*, in Law and Literature 113 (1931).

or several must die that he or others may live. "Modern legal systems . . . do not require divine knowledge of human beings."[133]

Reasonable mistakes, then, may be tolerated if as in the above circumstances and as in the case of the surgical operation, these mistakes are the inevitable by-products of efforts to save one or more human lives.[134]

The need the euthanasiast advances, however, is a good deal less compelling. It is only to ease pain.

Let us next examine the quantitative need for euthanasia:

No figures are available, so far as I can determine, as to the number of say, cancer victims, who undergo intolerable or overwhelming pain. That an appreciable number do suffer such pain, I have no doubt. But that anything approaching this number whatever it is, need suffer such pain, I have—viewing the many sundry

133. Hall, General Principles of Criminal Law, 399 (1947). Cardozo, on the other hand, seems to say that absent such certainty it is wrong for those in a "necessity" situation to escape their plight by sacrificing any life. Cardozo, supra note 132, at 113. On this point, as on the whole question of "necessity," his reasoning, it is submitted, is paled by the careful and intensive analyses found in Hall, supra, at 377-426, and Williams, op. cit. supra note 4, at 577-586.

See also Cahn, The Moral Decision (1955). Although he takes the position that in the Holmes' situation, "if none sacrifice themselves of free will to spare the others—they must all wait and die together," Cahn rejects Cardozo's view as one which "seems to deny that we can ever reach enough certainty as to our factual beliefs to be morally justified in the action we take." Id. at 70-71.

Some time after this paper was in galley, Section 3.02 of the Model Penal Code (Tent. Draft No. 8, 1958) made its appearance. This section provides (unless the legislature has otherwise spoken) that certain "necessity" killings shall be deemed justifiable so long as the actor was not "reckless or negligent in bringing about the situation requiring a choice of evils or in appraising the necessity for his conduct." The section only applies to a situation where "the evil sought to be avoided by such conduct is greater than that sought to be prevented by the law," e.g., killing one that several may live. The defense would not be available, e.g., "to one who acted to save himself at the expense of another, as by seizing a raft when men are shipwrecked." Comment to Section 3.02, id. at 8. For "in all ordinary circumstances lives in being must be assumed . . . to be of equal value, equally deserving the protection of the law." Ibid.

134. Cf. Macauley, Notes on the Indian Penal Code, Note B, p. 131 (1851), reprinted in 7 The Miscellaneous Works of Lord Macauley 252 (Bibliophile ed.):

It is often the wisest thing that a man can do to expose his life to great hazard. It is often the greatest service that can be rendered to him to do what may very probably cause his death. He may labor under a cruel and wasting malady which is certain to shorten his life, and which renders his life, while it lasts, useless to others and a torment to himself. Suppose that under these circumstances he, undeceived, gives his free and intelligent consent to take the risk of an operation which in a large proportion of cases has proved fatal, but which is the only method by which his disease can possibly be cured, and which, if it succeeds, will restore him to health and vigor. We do not conceive that it would be expedient to punish the surgeon who should perform the operation, though by performing it he might cause death, not intending to cause death, but knowing himself to be likely to cause it.

palliative measures now available[135]—considerable doubt. The whole field of severe pain and its management in the terminal stage of cancer is, according to an eminent physician, "a subject neglected far too much by the medical profession."[136] Other well-qualified commentators have recently noted the "obvious lack of interest in the literature about the problem of cancer pain"[137] and have scored "the deplorable attitude of defeatism and therapeutic inactivity found in some quarters."[138]

The picture of the advanced cancer victim beyond the relief of morphine and like drugs is a poignant one, but apparently no small

135. The management of intractable pain in cancer may be grouped under two main categories: (1) measures which check, decrease or eliminate the growth itself, (2) symptomatic treatment, *i.e.*, control of the pain without affecting the growth. In the first category are palliative operations for cancers no longer curable; radiation, roentgen and X-ray therapy; administration of endocrine substances, steroids, nitrogen mustards, and radioactive iodine and iron. See text, at notes 98-113 *supra*. In the second category are non-narcotic analgesics such as cobra venom, hypnotics and sedatives; narcotic analgesics, such as morphine, codeine, methadone and, recently, chlorproma-zine; neurosurgical operations, such as rhizotomy, the technique of choice in the management of cancer pain of the head and neck, spinothalmic tractotomy and chordotomy, for relief of pain at or below the nipple line; and pre-frontal lobotomy.

The various measures sketched above are discussed at considerable length in Bonica and Backup, *Control of Cancer Pain*, 54 Nw. Med. 22 (1955); Bonica, *The Management of Cancer Pain*, G. P., Nov. 1954, p. 35, and more extensively by Doctors Schiffrin and Gross *(Systematic Analgetics)*, Sadove and Balogot *(Nerve Blocks For Pain In Malignancy)*, Sugar *(Neurosurgical Aspects of Pain Management)*, Taylor and Schiffrin *(Humoral and Chemical Palliation of Malignancy)* Schwarz *(Surgical Pro-cedures In Control Of Pain In Advanced Cancer)* and Carpender *(Radiation Therapy In The Relief Of Pain In Malignant Disease)* in The Management Of Pain In Cancer (Schiffrin ed. 1956).

Relief of pain by nerve blocking "has a great deal more to offer than prolonged narcotic therapy. Effective blocks produce adequate relief of pain and enable these sufferers to receive more intensive radiation therapy and other forms of medical treatment which otherwise could not be tolerated." Bonica and Backup, *supra* at 27; Bonica, *supra*, at 43. "A recent analysis of cases reported in the literature revealed that of the many patients treated by alcohol nerve blocking, 63 per cent obtained complete relief, 23.5 per cent obtained partial relief, and only 13.5 per cent received no benefits from the blocks." Bonica, *supra*, at 43.

"Chordotomy is perhaps the most useful and most effective neurosurgical operation for the relief of cancer pain. When skillfully carried out in prop-erly selected patients, it produces complete relief in about 65 per cent of the patients, partial relief in another 25 per cent, and no relief in approximately 10 per cent." Bonica and Backup, *supra* at 25.

Prefrontal lobotomy is a radical procedure which many regard as a last resort. Bilateral prefrontal lobotomy almost always produces striking changes in the patient's personality, frequently impairing judgment and causing apathy; the mental changes produced by unilateral lobotomy are much less marked, but pain is likely to recur if the patient survives more than several months. See Sugar, *supra*, at 101-104; Bonica, *supra* at 41-42.

136. Foreword by Dr. Warren H. Cole in Management of Pain In Cancer (Schiffrin ed. 1956).

137. Bonica and Backup, *supra* note 135, at 22; Bonica, *supra* note 135, at 35.

138. *Ibid.*

number of these situations may have been brought about by premature or excessive application of these drugs.[139] Psychotherapy "unfortunately . . . has barely been explored"[140] in this area, although a survey conducted on approximately 300 patients with advanced cancer disclosed that "over 50 per cent of patients who had received analgesics for long periods of time could be adequately controlled by placebo medication."[141] Nor should it be overlooked that nowadays drugs are only one of many ways—and by no means always the most effective way—of attacking the pain problem. Radiation, roentgen and X-ray therapy; the administration of various endocrine

139. "The efficacy of *narcotics analgesics,* particularly opiates, in managing pain of terminal malignancy, is too well known to warrant discussion. . . . Unfortunately their effectiveness, low cost, and ease of administration—very desirable qualities in any drug—are conducive to improper use by the busy practitioner. He may have neither time nor the interest to study and consider each case individually so that the pharmacologic properties of the various narcotic drugs are fully exploited to the advantage of the patient. The attitude and practice of some physicians to "snow the patient under because the end is inevitable" denotes lack of understanding of the problem. Because it is very difficult to estimate the length of life in each individual case, such sense of mistaken humanitarianism may be productive of an unnecessarily premature addiction with consequent stupefication, respiratory depression, headache, anorexia, nausea, vomiting, and will bring on a state of cachexia more rapidly. Moreover, because tolerance develops rapidly, the patient may not obtain adequate relief in the latter stages of the disease, when comfort is so essential, even with massive doses, and he may also develop withdrawal symptoms when the amount administered is no longer effective."
Bonica and Backup, *supra* note 135, at 24-25; to the same effect is Bonica, *supra* note 135, at 38.
See also Schiffrin and Gross, *supra* note 135, at 17:
"Factors facilitating the development of tolerance include the administration of the drug at frequent, regular intervals and the use of successively larger doses. The appearance of clinically significant tolerance can be delayed by using the minimal effective dose as infrequently as possible and by limiting the use of addicting drugs to their primary characteristic, analgesia, and not to secondary properties such as sedation. The writing of such an order as '¼ gr. morphine q. 4 h.' is to be deplored. Addicting analgetics are to be ordered on the basis of pain, not according to the clock or nursing habits."
140. "The opinion appears to prevail in the medical profession that severe pain requiring potent analgesics and narcotics frequently occurs in advanced cancer. Fortunately, this does not appear to be the case. Fear and anxiety, the patient's need for more attention from the family or from the physician, are frequently mistaken for expressions of pain. Reassurance and an unhesitating approach in presenting a plan of management to the patient are well known patient 'remedies,' and probably the clue to success of many medical quackeries. Since superficial psychotherapy as practiced by physicians without psychiatric training is often helpful, actual psychiatric treatment is expected to be of more value. Unfortunately, the potential therapeutic usefulness of this tool has barely been explored." Laszlo and Spencer, *Medical Problems In The Management Of Cancer,* 37 Med. Clinics of N. A. 869, 875 (1953).
141. *Ibid.* "Placebo" medication is medication having no pharmacologic effect given for the purpose of pleasing or humoring the patient. The survey was conducted on patients in Montefiore Hospital, N.Y.C. One clear implication is that "analgesics should be prescribed only after an adequate trial of placebos."

substances; intrathecal alcohol injections and other types of nerve blocking; and various neurosurgical operations such as spinothalmic chordotomy and spinothalmic tractomy, have all furnished striking relief in many cases.[142] These various formidable non-narcotic measures, it should be added, are conspicuously absent from the prolific writings of the euthanasiasts.

That of those who do suffer and must necessarily suffer the requisite pain, many *really* desire death, I have considerable doubt.[143] Further, that of those who may desire death at a given moment, many have a fixed and rational desire for death, I likewise have considerable doubt.[144] Finally, taking those who may have such a desire, again I must register a strong note of skepticism that many cannot do the job themselves.[145] It is not that I condone suicide. It is simply that for reasons discussed in subsequent sections of this paper I find it easier to prefer a *laissez-faire* approach in such matters over an approach aided and sanctioned by the state.

The need is only one variable. The incidence of mistake is another. Can it not be said that although the need is not very great it is great enough to outweigh the few mistakes which are likely to

---

142. See note 135, *supra*.

143. The one thing agreed upon by the eminent physicians Abraham L. Wolbarst, later an officer of the Euthanasia Society of America, and James J. Walsh in their debate on "Tne Right To Die" was that very, very few people ever really want to die.

Dr. Walsh reported that in all the time he worked at Mother Alphonsa's Home for Incurable Cancer he never heard one patient express the wish that he "would be better off dead" and "I know, too, that Mother Alphonsa had very rarely heard it." "On the other hand," adds Walsh, "I have often heard neurotic patients wish that they might be taken out of existence because they could no longer bear up under the pain they were suffering. . . . They were overcome mainly by self-pity. Above all, they were sympathy seekers . . . of physical pain there was almost no trace, but they were hysterically ready, so they claimed to welcome death. . . . Walsh, *Life Is Sacred,* 94 The Forum 333 (1935). Walsh's opponent, Dr. Wolbarst, conceded at the outset that "very few incurables have or express the wish to die. However great their physical suffering may be, the will to live, the desire for life, is such an overwhelming force that pain and suffering become bearable and they prefer to live." Wolbarst, *Legalize Euthanasia!,* 94 The Forum 330 (1935).

The first "lesson" the noted British physician, A. Leslie Banks, learned as Resident Officer to cancer wards at the Middlesex Hospital was that "the patients, however ill they were and however much they suffered, never asked for death." Banks, *Euthanasia,* 26 Bull. N.Y. Acad. Med. 297, 301 (1950).

144. See text at notes 49 and 52 *supra*.

145. In *Euthanasia—Right or Wrong,* Survey Graphic, May, 1948, p. 241, Selwyn James makes considerable hay of the Euthanasia Society of America's claim that numerous cancer patients phone the society and beg for a doctor who will give them euthanasia. If a person retains sufficient physical and mental ability to look up a number, get to a phone and dial, does he really have to ask *others* to deal him death? That is, if it is death he really desires, and not, say, attention or pity.

occur? I think not. The incidence of error may be small in euthanasia, but as I have endeavored to show, and as Professor Williams
has not taken pains to deny, under our present state of knowledge
appreciable error is inevitable. *Some,* no matter how severe the
pain, no matter how strikingly similar the symptoms, will not be
cancer victims or other qualified candidates for euthanasia. Furthermore, among those who are in fact so inflicted, there are bound to
be *some* who no matter how "hopeless" their plight at the moment,
would be able to benefit from some treatment. That is, they would
have been able to lead relatively normal, reasonably useful lives for,
say, six months or a year, if death had not come until it came in its
own way in its own time.

How many are *"some"*? I do not know, but I think they are a
good deal more than *de minimus.* The business of predicting what
cures or temporary checks or measures of relief from pain are
around the corner is obviously an inexact science. And as for error
in diagnosis, doctors, as a rule, do not contribute to *True Confes-
sions.*[146] But I venture to say that the percentage and the absolute
figures would not be as small, certainly not any smaller, than the
grants of federal habeas corpus petitions to set aside state convictions. Federal habeas corpus so operates that only a handful of
petitions are granted and only a small fraction of these cases are
ultimately discharged.[147] Yet its continued existence has been ably

---

146. See, *e.g., Proceedings, Symposium on Exfoliative Cytology* at 58
(Oct. 23-24, 1951):
    Dr. Mortimer Benioff: Dr. [Peter] Herbert is to be congratulated on
    showing you particularly some of the cases which were operated on and
    did not have cancer. Most of the time we have a tendency in our en-
    thusiasm not to talk about things like that. . . .

147. During the nine years from 1946 through 1954, only 79 or 1.6%
of 4,849 federal habeas corpus applications were granted. In 1954, the per-
centage was down to 1.3; in 1955 it had fallen below 1 per cent: 5 out of 688
cases. See Baker, *Federal Judicial Control of State Criminal Justice,* 22 Mo.
L. Rev. 109, 140 (1957); Pollak, *Proposals to Curtail Federal Habeas
Corpus for State Prisoners: Collateral Attack on the Great Writ,* 66 Yale
L. J. 50, 53 (1956); Ribble, *A Look at the Policy Making Powers of the
United States Supreme Court and the Position of the Individual,* 14 Wash. &
Lee L. Rev. 167, 178-9 (1957); Schaefer, *Federalism and State Criminal
Procedure,* 70 Harv. L. Rev. 1, 19 (1956). Of course, these figures do not
necessarily reflect the actual proportion of meritorious cases. Professor
Pollak suggests that the very low measure of success is due in no small
degree to the difficulties of proof involved in reconstructing trials of the
distant past and the ineptness of prisoners handling their own past-conviction
litigation, 66 Yale L. J. at 54, while Professor Baker takes the contrary position that "if even the federal courts themselves must admit that the state
tribunals have been correct at least 98.6 [98.4?] per cent of the time when
their convictions have been challenged, it is not completely amiss to surmise
that the state courts may have been right in those few cases where the writs
were granted and the prisoners discharged," 22 Mo. L. Rev. at 140. I, for
one, find Pollak's reasoning more persuasive, but I think it fair to say that

defended as but another example of the recurrent theme that it is
better that many guilty go free than one innocent be convicted.[148]
So long as this is the vogue, I do not hesitate—although Williams
evidently thinks it is "no contest"—to pit the two or three or four
who might be saved against the hundred who cannot be.

Even if the need for voluntary euthanasia could be said to outweigh the risk of mistake, this is not the end of the matter. That
"all that can be expected of any moral agent is that he should do
his best on the facts as they appear to him"[149] may be true as far as
it goes, but it would seem that where the consequence of error is so
irreparable it is not too much to expect of society that there be *a
good deal more than one moral agent* "to do his best on the facts as
they appear to him." It is not too much to expect for example, that
something approaching the protection thrown around one who appears to have perpetrated a serious crime be extended to one who
appears to have an incurable disease. Williams' proposal falls far
short of this mark.

---

most defenders of the writ are willing to take the figures as they find them.
    Yet, of the handful whose petitions were granted, how many actually
get relief? In 1953, Mr. Justice Frankfurter noted that "during the last four
years five state prisoners, all told, were discharged by federal district courts,"
Brown v. Allen, 344 U.S. 443, 510 (1953) (dissenting opinion), "the minis-
cule figure of .15 per cent", as one of the writ's staunchest friends has put it.
Pollak, *supra,* at 53.

148. It is not surprising that the cry has gone out that federal habeas
corpus is not worth it, that "one swallow does not make a summer", Baker,
supra note 147 at 1042, and that "he who must search a haystack for a needle
is likely to end up with the attitude that the needle is not worth the search."
Jackson, J., concurring in Brown v. Allen, 344 U.S. 443, 537 (1953). But
these views have not prevailed. As Illinois Supreme Court Justice Walter
Schaefer recently observed in his Holmes lecture:

> Even with the narrowest focus it is not a needle we are looking for in
> these stacks of paper, but the rights of a human being. And if the per-
> spective is broadened, even the significance of that single human being
> diminishes, and we begin to catch a glimpse of the full picture. The
> aim which justifies the existence of habeas corpus is not fundamentally
> different from that which informs our criminal law in general, that it is
> better that a guilty man go free than that an innocent one be punished.
> To the extent that the small numbers of meritorious petitions shows that
> the small numbers of meritorious petitions shows that the standards of
> due process are being honored in criminal trials we should be gratified;
> but the continuing availability of the federal remedy is in large part
> responsible for that result. What is involved, however, is not just the
> enforcement of defined standards. It is also the creative process of writ-
> ing specific content into the highest of our ideals. So viewed, the burden-
> some test of shifting the meritorious from the worthless appears less
> futile. . . .

Schaefer, *supra* note 147 at 25-26.
    I think Justice Schaefer would agree that his thought is more often
articulated in terms of "it is better to let a *hundred* guilty men go free than
to convict one innocent." See Kadish, *Methodology and Criteria in Due
Process Adjudication—A Survey and Criticism,* 66 Yale L.J. 319, 346 (1957).

    149. Williams, p. 318.

II. A LONG-RANGE VIEW OF EUTHANASIA

A. Voluntary v. Involuntary Euthanasia.

Ever since the 1870's, when what was probably the first euthanasia debate of the modern era took place,[150] most proponents of the movement—at least when they are pressed—have taken considerable pains to restrict the question to the plight of the unbearably suffering incurable who *voluntarily seeks* death while most of their opponents have striven equally hard to frame the issue in terms which would encompass certain involuntary situations as well, *e.g.*, the "congenital idiots," the "permanently insane," and the senile.

Glanville Williams reflects the outward mood of many euthanasiasts when he scores those who insist on considering the question from a broader angle:

> The [English Society's] bill [debated in the House of Lords in 1936 and 1950] excluded any question of compulsory euthanasia, even for hopelessly defective infants. Unfortunately, a legislative proposal is not assured of success merely because it is worded in a studiously moderate and restrictive form. The method of attack, by those who dislike the proposal, is to use the 'thin edge of the wedge' argument. . . . There is no pro-

---

150. L. A. Tollemache—and not since has there been a more persuasive euthanasiast—made an eloquent plea for voluntary euthanasia, *The New Cure for Incurables,* 19 Fortnightly Review 218 (1873), in support of a similar proposal the previous year, S. D. Williams, *Euthanasia* (1872), (a book now out of print, but a copy of which is at the British Museum). Tollemaches's article was bitterly criticized by the editors of The Spectator, *Mr. Tollemache on The Right To Die,* 46 The Spectator 206 (1873) who stated in part:
> [I]t appears to be quite evident, though we do not think it is expressly stated in Mr. Tollemache's article, that much the strongest arguments to be alleged for putting an end to human sufferings apply to cases where you cannot by any possibility have the consent of the sufferer to that course.
> In a letter to the editor, *The Limits of Euthanasia,* 46 The Spectator 240 (1873), Mr. Tollemache retorted:
> I tried to make it clear that I disapproved of such relief ever being given without the dying man's express consent. . . . But it is said that all my reasoning would apply to cases like lingering paralysis, where the sufferer might be speechless. I think not . . . where these safeguards cannot be obtained, the sufferer must be allowed to linger on. Half a loaf, says the proverb, is better than no bread; one may be anxious to relieve what suffering one can, even though the conditions necessary for the relief of other (and perhaps worse) suffering may not exist. . . . I have stated my meaning thus fully, because I believe it is a common misunderstanding of Euthanasia, that it must needs involve some such proceedings as the late Mr. Charles Buxton advocated (not perhaps quite seriously),—namely, the summary extinction of idiots and of persons in their dotage.
> I give this round to the voluntary euthanasiasts.

posal for reform on any topic, however conciliatory and moderate, that cannot be opposed by this dialectic.[151]

Why was the bill "worded in a studiously moderate and restrictive form?" If it were done as a matter of principle, if it were done in recognition of the ethico-moral-legal "wall of separation" which stands between voluntary and compulsory "mercy-killings," much can be said for the euthanasiasts' lament about the methods employed by the opposition. But if it were done as a matter of political expediency—with great hopes and expectations of pushing through a second and somewhat less restrictive bill as soon as the first one had sufficiently "educated" public opinion and next a third still less restrictive bill—what standing do the euthanasiasts then have to attack the methods of the opposition? No cry of righteous indignation could ring more hollow, I would think, than the protest from those utilizing the "wedge" principle themselves that their opponents are making the wedge objection.

In this regard the words and action of the euthanasiasts are not insignificant.

No sooner had the English Society been organized and a drive to attain "easy death" legislation launched than Dr. Harry Roberts, one of the most distinguished sympathizers of the movement, disclosed some basis for alarm as to how far the momentum would carry:

So far as its defined objects go, most informed people outside the Catholic Church will be in general sympathy with the new Society; but lovers of personal liberty may feel some of that suspicion which proved so well justified when the Eugenics movement was at its most enthusiastic height.
In the course of the discussion at the [1935] Royal Sanitary Institute Congress, two distinguished doctors urged the desirability of legalizing the painless destruction of 'human mental monstrosities' in whom improvement is unattainable; and at the inaugural meeting of the Euthanasia Legislation Society, the Chairman of the Executive Committee said that 'they were concerned to-day only with voluntary euthanasia; but, as public opinion developed, and it became possible to form a truer estimate of the value of human life, further progress along preventive lines would be possible. . . . The population was an ageing one, with a larger relative proportion of elderly persons—individuals who had reached a degenerative stage of life. Thus the total amount of suffering and the number of useless lives must increase.'
We need to discriminate very carefully between facilitating the death of an individual at his own request and for his own relief,

151. Williams, pp. 333-34.

and the killing of an individual on the ground that, for the rest of us such a course would be more economical or more agreeable than keeping him alive.[152]

In the 1936 debate in the House of Lords, Lord Ponsonby of Shulbrede, who moved the second reading of the voluntary euthanasia bill, described two appealing actual cases, one where a man drowned his four-year-old daughter "who had contracted tuberculosis and had developed gangrene in the face,"[153] another where a woman killed her mother who was suffering from "general paralysis of the insane."[154] Both cases of course were of the compulsory variety of euthanasia. True, Lord Ponsonby readily admitted that these cases were not covered by the proposed bill, but the fact remains that they were the *only* specific cases he chose to describe.

In 1950, Lord Chorley once again called the voluntary euthanasia bill to the attention of the House of Lords. He was most articulate, if not too discreet, on excluding compulsory euthanasia cases from coverage:

> Another objection is that the Bill does not go far enough, because it applies only to adults and does not apply to children who come into the world deaf, dumb and crippled, and who have a much better cause than those for whom the Bill provides. That may be so, but we must go step by step.[155]

In 1938, two years after the English Society was organized and its bill had been introduced into the House of Lords, the Euthanasia Society of America was formed.[156] At its first annual meeting the following year, it offered proposed euthanasia legislation:

> Infant imbeciles, hopelessly insane persons . . . and any person not requesting his own death would not come within the scope of the proposed act.
> Charles E. Nixdorff, New York lawyer and treasurer of the society, who offered the bill for consideration, explained to some of the members who desired to broaden the scope of the proposed law, that it was *limited purposely to voluntary euthanasia because public opinion is not ready to accept the broader principle*. He said, however, that *the society hoped eventually to legalize the putting to death of nonvolunteers* beyond the help of medical science.[157]

---

152. Roberts, Euthanasia and other Aspects of Life and Death 7-8 (1936).
153. 103 H.L. Deb. 466, 471 (1936).
154. *Ibid.*
155. 169 H.L. Deb. 551, 559 (1950).
156. N.Y. Times, Jan. 17, 1938, p. 21, col. 8.
157. N.Y. Times, Jan. 27, 1939, p. 21, col. 7 (emphasis added). That the report is accurate in this regard is underscored by Mr. Nixdorff's letter to the editor, N.Y. Times, Jan. 30, 1939, p. 12, col. 7, wherein he complained only that "the patient who petitions the court for euthanasia should not be

About this time, apparently, the Society began to circulate literature in explanation and support of voluntary euthanasia, as follows:

> The American and English Euthanasia Societies, after careful consideration, have both decided that more will be accomplished by devoting their efforts at present to the measure which will probably encounter the least opposition, namely *voluntary euthanasia*. The public is readier to recognize the right to *die* than the right to *kill*, even though the latter be in mercy. To take someone's life without his consent is a very different thing from granting him release from unnecessary suffering at his own express desire. The freedom of the individual is highly prized in democracies.[158]

The American Society's own "Outline of the Euthanasia Movement in the United States and England" states in part:

> 1941. A questionnaire was sent to all physicians of New York State asking (1) Are you in favor of legalizing voluntary euthanasia for incurable adult sufferers? (2) Are you in favor of legalizing euthanasia for congenital monstrosities, idiots and imbeciles? Because only ⅓ as many phyisicians answered 'yes' to question 2 as to question 1, we decided that we would limit our program to voluntary euthanasia.[159]

At a meeting of the Society of Medical Jurisprudence held several weeks after the American Society voluntary euthanasia bill had been drafted, Dr. Foster Kennedy, newly elected president of the Society, "urged the legalizing of euthanasia primarily in cases of born defectives who are doomed to remain defective, rather than for normal persons who have become miserable through incurable illness" and scored the "absurd and misplaced sentimental kindness" that seeks to preserve the life of a "person who is not a person." "If the law sought to restrict euthanasia to those who could speak out for it, and thus overlooked these creatures who cannot speak, then, I say as Dickens did, 'The law's an ass' ".[160] As pointed out elsewhere, *while president* of the Society, Dr. Kennedy not only eloquently advocated involuntary euthanasia but strenuously *opposed* the voluntary variety.[161] Is it any wonder that opponents of

---

described as a 'volunteer'" and that "the best definition of euthanasia is 'merciful release'" rather than "mercy 'killing' or even mercy 'death'" because "being killed is associated with fear, injury and the desire to escape" and "many people dislike even to talk about death."

158. Dr. Frank Hinman of the University of California Medical School quotes such literature in *Euthanasia*, 99 J. Nerv. & Mental Diseases 640, 643 (1944).

159. Distributed by the Euthanasia Society of America.

160. N.Y. Times, Feb. 14, 1939, p. 2, col. 6.

161. See note 72 *supra* and accompanying text.

the movement do not always respect the voluntary-involuntary dichotomy?

. At the same time that Dr. Kennedy was disseminating his "personal" views, Dr. A. L. Wolbarst, long a stalwart in the movement, was adhering much more closely to the party line. In a persuasive address to medical students published in a leading medical journal he pointed out that "a bill is now in preparation for introduction in the New York State Legislature authorizing the administration of euthanasia to incurable sufferers on their own request"[162] and stressed that "the advocates of voluntary euthanasia do not seek to impose it on any one who does not ask for it. It is intended as an act of mercy for those who need it and demand it."[163] What were Dr. Wolbarst's views before the English and American societies had been organized and substantial agreement reached as to the party platform? Four years earlier, in a debate on euthanasia, he stated:

> The question as usually submitted limits the discussion of legal euthanaisa to those 'incurables whose physical suffering is unbearable to themselves.' That limitation is rather unfortunate, because the number of incurables within this category is actually and relatively extremely small. Very few incurables have or express the wish to die. However great their physical suffering may be . . . they prefer to live.
> If legal euthanasia has a humane and merciful motivation, it seems to me the entire question should be considered from a broad angle. There are times when euthanasia is strongly indicated as an act of mercy even though the subject's suffering is not 'unbearable to himself,' as in the case of an imbecile.
> It goes without saying that, in recently developed cases with a possibility of cure, euthanasia should not even be considered; but when insane or defective people have suffered mental incapacity and tortures of the mind for many years—forty-three years in a case of my personal knowledge—euthanasia certainly has a proper field.[164]

In his 1939 address, Dr. Wolbarst also quoted in full the stirring suicide message of Charlotte Perkins Gilman, "described as one of the twelve greatest American women [who] had been in failing health for several years and chose self-euthanasia rather than endure the pains of cancer."[165] He would have presented Mrs. Gilman's views more fully if he had quoted as well from her last article, left

---

162. Wolbarst, *The Doctor Looks at Euthanasia,* 149 Medical Record 354, 355 (1939).
163. *Id.* at 354.
164. Wolbarst, *Legalize Euthanasia!,* 94 The Forum 330-32 (1935).
165. Wolbarst, *supra* note 162 at 356.

with her agent to be published after her death, where she advocates euthanasia for "incurable invalids", "hopeless idiots", "helpless paretics", and "certain grades of criminals".[166] Citing with approval the experience of "practical Germany", Miss Gilman's article asserted that "the dragging weight of the grossly unfit and dangerous could be lightened" by legalized euthanasia, "with great advantage to the normal and progressive. The millions spent in restraining and maintaining social detritus should be available for the safeguarding and improving of better lives."[167]

In 1950, the "mercy killings" perpetrated by Dr. Herman N. Sander on his cancer-stricken patient and by Miss Carol Ann Paight on her cancer-stricken father put the euthanasia question on page one.[168] In the midst of the fervor over these cases, Dr. Clarence Cook Little, one of the leaders in the movement and a former president of the American Society, suggested specific safeguards for a law legalizing "mercy killings" for the "incurably ill but mentally fit" *and* for "mental defectives."[169] The Reverend Charles Francis Potter, the founder and first president of the American Society hailed Dr. Sander's action as "morally right" and hence that which "should be legally right."[170] Shortly thereafter, at its annual meeting, the American Society "voted to continue support" of both Dr. Sander and Miss Paight.[171]

Now, one of the interesting, albeit underplayed, features of these cases—and this was evident all along—was that both were *involuntary* "mercy killings". There was considerable conflict in the testimony at the Sander Trial as to whether or not the victim's *husband* had pleaded with the doctor to end her suffering,[172] but

166. Gilman, *The Right to Die*, 94 The Forum 297-300 (1935).
167. *Ibid*.
168. See notes 172-176 *infra*. More than 100 reporters, photographers and broadcasters attended the Sander trial. In ten days of court sessions, the press corps filed 1,600,000 words. *Not Since Scopes?* Time, March 13, 1950, p. 43.
169. N.Y. Times, Jan. 12, 1950, p. 54, col. 1.
170. N.Y. Times, Jan. 9, 1950, p. 40, col. 2.
171. N.Y. Times, Jan. 18, 1950, p. 33, col. 5.
172. N.Y. Times, Feb. 24, 1950, p. 1, col. 6; Feb. 28, 1950, p. 1, col. 2, *"Similar to Murder,"* Time, March 6, 1950, p. 20. Although Dr. Sander's own notation was to the effect that he had given the patient "ten cc of air intravenously repeated four times" and that the patient "expired within ten minutes after this was started," N.Y. Times, Feb. 24, 1950, p. 15, col. 5; *"Similar To Murder,"* Time, March 6, 1950, p. 20, and the attending nurse testified that the patient was still "gasping" when the doctor injected the air, N.Y. Times, Feb. 28, 1950, p. 1, col. 2, the defendant's position at the trial was that the patient was dead before he injected the air, N.Y. Times, March 7, 1950, p. 1, col. 1; *The Obsessed,* Time, March 13, 1950, p. 23; his notes were not meant to be taken literally, "it's a casual dictation . . . merely a way of closing out the chart," N.Y. Times, March 7, 1950, p. 19, col. 2. Dr. Sander was acquitted, N.Y. Times, March 10, 1950, p. 1, col. 6. The alleged mercy-killing

nobody claimed that the victim herself had done such pleading. There was considerable evidence in the *Paight* case to the effect that the victim's *daughter* had a "cancer phobia," the cancer deaths of two aunts having left a deep mark on her,[173] but nobody suggested that the victim had a "cancer phobia."

It is true that Mother Paight said approvingly of her mercy-killing daughter that "she had the old Paight guts,"[174] but it is no less true that Father Paight had no opportunity to pass judgment on the question. He was asleep, still under the anesthetic of the exploratory operation which revealed the cancer in his stomach when his daughter, after having taken one practice shot in the woods, fired into his left temple.[175] Is it not just possible that Father Paight would have preferred to have had the vaunted Paight intestinal fortitude channelled in other directions, *e.g.*, by his daughter bearing to see him suffer?[176]

The *Sander* and *Paight* cases amply demonstrate that to the press, the public, and many euthanasiasts, the killing of one who does not or cannot speak is no less a "mercy killing" than the killing of one who asks for death. Indeed, the overwhelming majority of known or alleged "mercy killings" have occurred without the consent of the victim. If the *Sander* and *Paight* cases are atypical at all, they are so only in that the victims were not ill or retarded children, as in the *Simpson*,[177] *Brownhill*[178] and *Long*[179] English

---

split the patient's family. The husband and one brother sided with the doctor; another brother felt that the patient's fate "should have been left to the will of God." *40 cc of Air*, Time, Jan. 9, 1950, p. 13. Shortly afterwards, Dr. Sander's license to practice medicine in New Hampshire was revoked, but was soon restored. N.Y. Times, June 29, 1950, p. 31, col. 6. He was also ousted from his county medical society, but after four years of struggle gained admission to one. N.Y. Times, Dec. 2, 1954, p. 25, col. 6.

173. N.Y. Times, Jan. 28, 1950, p. 30, col. 1, Feb. 1, 1950, p. 54, col. 3, Feb. 2, 1950, p. 22, col. 5; *For Love or Pity*, Time, Feb. 6, 1950, p. 15; *The Father Killer*, Newsweek, Feb. 13, 1950, p. 21. Miss Paight was acquitted on the ground of "temporary insanity" N.Y. Times, Feb. 8, 1950, p. 1, col. 2.

174. *The Father Killer*, Newsweek, Feb. 13, 1950, p. 21.

175. See note 173, *supra*. Miss Paight was obsessed with the idea that "daddy must never know he had cancer," N.Y. Times, Jan. 28, 1950, p. 30, col. 1.

176. " 'I had to do it. I couldn't bear to see him suffering.' . . . Once, when she woke up from a strong sedative, she said: 'Is daddy dead yet? I can't ever sleep until he is dead.' " *The Father Killer*, Newsweek, Feb. 13, 1950, p. 21.

177. Rex v. Simpson, 11 Crim. App. R. 218, 84 L.J.K.B. 1893 (1915) dealt with a young soldier on leave, who, while watching his severely ill child and waiting for his unfaithful wife to return home, cut the child's throat with a razor. His statement was as follows:

The reason why I done it was I could not see it suffer any more than what it really had done. She was not looking after the child, and it was lying there from morning to night, and no one to look after it, and I could not see it suffer any longer and have to go away and leave it.

Simpson was convicted of murder and his application for leave to appeal

cases, and the *Greenfield*,[180] *Repouille*,[181] *Noxon*[182] and *Braunsdorf*[183] American cases.

---

dismissed. The trial judge was held to have properly directed the jury that they were not at liberty to find a verdict of manslaughter, though the prisoner killed the child "with the best and kindest motive."

178. Told to undergo a serious operation, and worried about the fate of her 31-year-old imbecile son if she were to succumb, 62-year-old Mrs. May Brownhill took his life by giving him about 100 aspirins and then placing a gas tube in his mouth. The Times (London), Oct. 2, 1934, p. 11, col. 2; N.Y. Times, Dec. 2, 1934, p. 25, col. 1, Dec. 4, 1934, p. 15, col. 3. Her family doctor testified that the boy's life had been "a veritable living death" The Times (London), Dec. 3, 1934, p. 11, col. 4. She was sentenced to death, with a strong recommendation for mercy, The Times (London), Dec. 3, 1934, p. 11, col. 4; N.Y. Times, Dec. 2, 1934, p. 25, col. 1, but she was reprieved two days later, The Times (London), Dec. 4, 1934, p. 14, col. 2; and pardoned and set free three months later, The Times (London), March 4, 1935, p. 11, col. 3; *Mother May's Holiday*, Time, March 11, 1935, p. 21. According to the N.Y. Times, March 3, 1935, p. 3, col. 2, the Home Office acted "in response to nation-wide sentiment." The Chicago Tribune report of the case is reprinted in Harno, Criminal Law and Procedure 36 n. 2 (4th ed. 1957.

Incidentally, Mrs. Brownhill's operation was quite successful. The Times (London), Dec. 3, 1934, p. 11, col. 4.

179. Gordon Long gassed his deformed and imbecile 7-year-old daughter to death, stating he loved her "more so than if she had been normal." *"Goodbye,"* Time, Dec. 2, 1946, p. 32. He pleaded guilty and was sentenced to death, but within a week the sentence was commuted to life imprisonment. The Times (London), Nov. 23, 1946, p. 2, col. 7, Nov. 29, 1946, p. 2, col. 7; N.Y. Times, Nov. 29, 1946, p. 7, col. 2.

180. For 17 years, Louis Greenfield, a prosperous Bronx milliner, had washed, dressed and fed his son, an "incurable imbecile" with the mentality of a two-year-old who spoke in a mumble understandable only by his mother. N.Y. Times, Jan. 13, 1939, p. 3, col. 1, May 12, 1939, p. 1, col. 6. Finally, after considering killing him for several years, Greenfield sent his wife out of the house, lest she interfere with his plans, and chloroformed his son to death. He is reported to have told members of the emergency squad: "Don't revive him, he's better off dead", N.Y. Times, May 9, 1939, p. 48, col. 1. See also *"Better Off Dead,"* Time, Jan. 23, 1939, p. 24.

At the trial Greenfield testified that he killed his son because "I loved him, it was the will of God." He insisted that he was directed by an "unseen hand" and by an "unknown voice" N.Y. Times, May 11, 1939, p. 10, col. 2 and was acquitted of first degree manslaughter, N.Y. Times, May 12, 1939, p. 1, col. 6. Some psychiatrists were reported to have condemned Greenfield as "a murderer who had simply grown tired of caring for his imbecile son." *"Better Off Dead,"* supra.

181. This case is quite similar to the *Greenfield* case which preceded it by several months. In fact, Louis Repouille said he had read the newspaper accounts of the Greenfield case and:

It made me think about doing the same thing to my boy. I think Mr. Greenfield was justified. They didn't punish him for it. But I am not looking for sympathy. N.Y. Times, Oct. 14, 1939, p. 21, col. 2.

Repouille was an elevator operator who had spent his life's earnings trying to cure his "incurably imbecile" thirteen-year-old son who had been blind for five years and bedridden since infancy. Repouille is reported to have put it this way: "He was just like dead all the time. . . . He couldn't walk, he couldn't talk, he couldn't do anything." N.Y. Times, Oct. 13, 1939, p. 25, col. 7. He testified at the trial that the idea of putting his son out of his misery "came to me thousands of times," N.Y. Times, Dec. 6, 1941, p. 34, col. 2. Finally, one day when his wife stepped out of the house for a while, he chloroformed his son to death. N.Y. Times, Oct. 13, 1939, p. 25, col. 7.

Repouille kept a number of canaries and lovebirds in his home. When a neighbor found the Repouille boy with a chloroform-soaked rag over his face, he removed the rag and was about to throw it on the floor when

Repouille is reported to have said: "Don't, can't you see I have some birds here." *Ibid.*

Repouille was found guilty of manslaughter in the second degree, N.Y. Times, Dec. 10, 1941, p. 27, col. 7, and freed on a suspended sentence of 5-10 years. N.Y. Times, Dec. 25, 1941, p. 44, col. 1.

Subsequently, Repouille's petition for naturalization was dismissed on the ground that he had not possessed "good moral character" within the five years preceding the filing of the petition. In an opinion which makes *Repouille* the "mercy killing" perhaps best known to lawyers today, Judge Learned Hand said in part:

It is reasonably clear that the jury which tried Repouille did not feel any moral repulsion at his crime. Although it was inescapably murder in the first degree, not only did they bring in a verdict that was flatly in the face of the facts and utterly absurd—for manslaughter in the second degree presupposes that the killing has not been deliberate—but they coupled even that with a recommendation which showed that in substance they wished to exculpate the offender. Moreover, it is also plain, from the sentence which he imposed, that the judge could not have seriously disagreed with their recommendation.

* * *

Left at large as we are, without means of verifying our conclusion, and without authority to substitute our individual beliefs, the outcome must needs be tentative; and not much is gained by discussion. We can say no more than that, . . . we feel reasonably secure in holding that only a minority of virtuous persons would deem the practise morally justifiable, while it remains in private hands, even when the provocation is as overwhelming as it was in this instance.

Repouille v. United States, 165 F.2d 152, 153 (2d Cir. 1947).

182. John F. Noxon, a 46-year-old well-to-do lawyer, was charged with electrocuting his 6-month-old mongoloid son by wrapping a frayed electric light cord about him and placing him—in wet diapers—on a silver serving tray to form a contact. Noxon claimed it was all an accident. N.Y. Times, Sept. 28, 1943, p. 27, col. 2; Sept. 29, 1943, p. 23, col. 7; Oct. 29, 1943, p. 21, col. 7; Jan. 14, 1944, p. 21, col. 3; July 7, 1944, p. 30, col. 2; July 8, 1944, p. 24, col. 1. After a mistrial because a juror became ill, N.Y. Times, March 10, 1944, Noxon was convicted of first degree murder, N.Y. Times, July 7, 1944, p. 30, col. 2. His death sentence was commuted to life, but in granting the clemency, Gov. M. J. Tobin of Massachusetts did not explain the "extenuating circumstances" other than to caution that a "mercy-killing, so-called," could not be considered an extenuating circumstance and was not a factor in his decision. N.Y. Times, Aug. 8, 1946, p. 42, col. 4. To make parole possible, Noxon's sentence was further commuted to 6 years to life with the proviso that he would live under parole supervision for life upon release from prison. N.Y. Times, Dec. 30, 1948, p. 13, col. 5. Shortly thereafter, Noxon was paroled, N.Y. Times, Jan. 4, 1949, p. 16, col. 3; Jan. 8, 1949, p. 30, col. 4. He was disbarred the following year. N.Y. Times, May 30, 1950, p. 2, col. 7.

183. Virginia Braunsdorf was a spastic-crippled 29-year-old "helpless parody of womanhood," who could not hold her head upright and who talked in gobbling sounds which only her father could understand. At one time, to keep her home and well attended, her father, Eugene, a symphony musician, had held down four jobs simultaneously, but he finally resigned himself to leaving her at a private sanitarium. Worried about his health and the fate of his daughter if he should die, Braunsdorf took her from the sanitarium on a pretense, stopped his car, put a pillow behind her head, and shot her dead. He then attempted suicide. He was found not guilty by reason of temporary insanity. *Murder or Mercy?*, Time, June 5, 1950, p. 20; N.Y. Times, May 23, 1950, p. 25, col. 4.

The prosecution argued that the girl was "human" and "had a right to live" and accused Braunsdorf of slaying her because she was a "burden on his pocketbook." N.Y. Times, May 23, 1950, p. 25, col. 4. The prosecution failed to explain, however, why a person furthering his own financial interests by killing his daughter would then fire two shots into his own chest, and, on reviving, shoot himself twice more.

These situations are all quite moving. So much so that two of the strongest presentations of the need for *voluntary* euthanasia, free copies of which may be obtained from the American Society, lead off with sympathetic discussions of the *Brownhill* and *Greenfield* cases.[184] This, it need hardly be said, is not the way to honor the voluntary-involuntary boundary. Not the way to ease the pressure to legalize at least this type of involuntary euthanasia as well if any changes in the broad area are to be made at all.

Nor, it should be noted, is Williams free from criticism in this regard. In his discussion of "the present law," apparently a discussion of voluntary euthanasia, he cites only one case, *Simpson,* an involuntary situation.[185] In his section on "the administration of the law" he describes only the *Sander* case and the "compassionate acquittal" of a man who drowned his four-year-old daughter, a sufferer of tuberculosis and gangrene of the face.[186] Again, both are involuntary cases. For "some other" American mercy-killing cases, Williams refers generally to an article by Helen Silving,[187] but two of the three cases he seems to have in mind are likewise cases of involuntary euthanasia.[188]

That the press and general public are not alone in viewing an act as a "mercy killing," lack of consent on the part of the victim notwithstanding, is well evidenced by the recent deliberations of the

184. In *The Doctor Looks At Euthanasia,* 149 Medical Record 354 (1939), Dr. Wolbarst describes the *Brownhill* case as an "act of mercy, based on pure mother-love" for which, thanks to the growth of the euthanasia movement in England, "it is doubtful that this poor woman even would be put on trial at the present day."

In *Taking Life Legally,*—Magazine Digest—(1947), Louis Greenfield's testimony that what he did "was against the law of man, but not against the law of God" is cited with apparent approval. The article continues:

The acquittal of Mr. Greenfield is indicative of a growing attitude towards euthanasia, or 'mercy killing', as the popular press phrases it. Years ago, a similar act would have drawn the death sentence; today, the mercy killer can usually count on the sympathy and understanding of the court—and his freedom.

185. Williams, p. 319 and n. 9. For a discussion of the *Simpson* case, see note 177 *supra.*

186. Williams, p. 328. For a discussion of the *Sander* case, see note 172 *supra.* The other case as Williams notes, p. 328 n. 5, is the same one described by Lord Ponsonby in the 1936 House of Lords debate. See text at note 153 *supra.*

187. Williams, p. 328. Williams does not cite to any particular page of the thirty-nine page Silving article, *Euthanasia: A Study In Comparative Criminal Law,* 103 U. of Pa. L. Rev. 350 (1954), but in context he appears to allude to pp. 353-54 of the article.

188. In addition to the *Sander* case, the cases Williams makes apparent reference to are the *Paight* case, see notes 173-76 *supra* and accompanying text; the *Braunsdorf* case, see note 183 *supra*; and the *Mohr* case, see note 17 *supra.* Only in the *Mohr* case was there apparently euthanasia by request.

Royal Commission on Capital Punishment.[189] The Report itself described "mercy killings" as "for example, where a mother has killed her child or a husband has killed his wife from merciful motives of pity and humanity."[190] The only specific proposal to exclude "mercy killings" from the category of murder discussed in the Report is a suggestion by the Society of Labour Lawyers which disregards the voluntary-involuntary distinction:

> If a person who has killed another person proves that he killed that person with the compassionate intention of saving him physical or mental suffering he shall not be guilty of murder.[191]

Another proposal, one by Hector Hughes, M. P., to the effect that only those who "maliciously" cause the death of another shall be guilty of murder,[192] likewise treated the voluntary and involuntary "mercy killer" as one and the same.

Testimony before the Commission underscored the great appeal of the *involuntary* "mercy killings." Thus, Lord Goddard, the Lord Chief Justice, referred to the famous *Brownhill* case, which he himself had tried some fifteen years earlier, as "a dreadfully pathetic case."[193] "The son," he pointed out, "was a hopeless imbecile, more than imbecile, a mindless idiot."[194]

Mr. Justice Humphreys recalled "one case that was the most pathetic sight I ever saw,"[195] a case which literally had the trial judge, Mr. Justice Hawkins, in tears. It involved a young father

---

189. According to the Royal Warrant, the Commission was appointed in May, 1949, "to consider and report whether liability under the criminal law in Great Britain to suffer capital punishment for murder should be limited or modified," but was precluded from considering whether capital punishment should be abolished. Royal Commission on Capital Punishment, Report, Cmd. No. 8932, at p. iii (1953) (called henceforth the Royal Commission Report). For an account of the circumstances which led to the appointment of the Commission, see Prevezer, *The English Homicide Act: A New Attempt to Revise the Law of Murder*, 57 Colum. L. Rev. 624, 629 (1957).

190. "It was agreed by almost all witnesses" that it would "often prove extremely difficult to distinguish killings where the motive was merciful from those where it was not". Royal Commission Report, at Para. 179 (1953). Thus the Commission "reluctantly" concluded that "it would not be possible" to frame and apply a definition which would satisfactorily cover these cases. *Id.*, at para. 180.

191. Royal Commission Report at para. 180 (1953).

192. Minutes of Evidence, pp. 219-20 (Dec. 1, 1949) Mr. Hughes, however, would try the apparent "mercy killer" for murder rather than for manslaughter "because the evidence should be considered not *in camera* but in open court, when it may turn out that it was not manslaughter." *Id.*, at para. 2825. "[T]he onus should rest upon the person so charged to prove that it was not a malicious, but a merciful killing." *Id.*, at para. 2826.

193. Minutes of Evidence, para. 3120 (Jan. 5, 1950). The Lord Chief Justice did not refer to the case by name, but his reference to *Brownhill* is unmistakable. For an account of this case, see note 178 *supra*.

194. Minutes of Evidence, para. 3120 (Jan. 5, 1950).

195. *Id.* at para. 3315.

who smothered his infant child to death when he learned the child had contracted syphilis from the mother (whose morals turned out to be something less than represented) and would be blind for life. "That," Mr. Justice Humphreys told the Commission, "was a real 'mercy killing'."[196]

The boldness and daring which characterizes most of Glanville Williams' book dims perceptibly when he comes to involuntary euthanasia proposals. As to the senile, he states:

> At present the problem has certainly not reached the degree of seriousness that would warrant an effort being made to change traditional attitudes toward the sanctity of life of the aged. Only the grimmest necessity could bring about a change that, however cautious in its approach, would probably cause apprehension and deep distress to many people, and inflict a traumatic injury upon the accepted code of behaviour built up by two thousand years of the Christian religion. It may be however, that as the problem becomes more acute it will itself cause a reversal of generally accepted values.[197]

To me, this passage is the most startling one in the book. On page 348 Williams invokes "traditional attitudes towards the sanctity of life" and "the accepted code of behaviour built up by two thousand years of the christian religion" to check the extension of euthanasia to the senile, but for 347 pages he had been merrily rolling along debunking both. Substitute "cancer victim" for "the aged" and Williams' passage is essentially the argument of many of his *opponents* on the voluntary euthanasia question.

The unsupported comment that "the problem [of senility] has certainly not reached the degree of seriousness" to warrant euthanasia is also rather puzzling, particularly coming as it does after an observation by Williams on the immediately preceding page that "it is increasingly common for men and women to reach an age of 'second childishness and mere oblivion,' with a loss of almost all adult faculties except that of digestion."[198]

How "serious" does a problem have to be to warrant a change in these "traditional attitudes"? If, as the statement seems to indicate, "seriousness" of a problem is to be determined numerically, the problem of the cancer victim does not appear to be as substantial as the problem of the senile.[199] For example, taking just the 95,837

196. *Ibid.*
197. Williams, p. 348.
198. *Id.* at 347.
199. Of all first admissions to New York State Civil Hospitals for mental disorders in 1950, some 5,818 patients—*or more than one third*—were classified as cerebral arteriosclerosis or senile cases. There were 3,379

first admissions to "public prolonged-care hospitals" for mental diseases in the United States in 1955, 23,561—or one fourth—were cerebral arteriosclerosis or senile brain disease cases.[200] I am not at all sure that there are 20,000 cancer victims per year who die *unbearably painful* deaths. Even if there were, I cannot believe that among their ranks are some 20,000 per year who, when still in a rational state, so long for a quick and easy death that they would avail themselves of legal machinery for euthanasia.[201]

If the problem of the incurable cancer victim "has reached the degree of seriousness that would warrant an effort being made to change traditional attitudes toward the sanctity of life," as Williams obviously thinks it has, then so has the problem of senility. In any event, the senility problem will undoubtedly soon reach even Williams requisite degree of seriousness:

> A decision concerning the senile may have to be taken within the next twenty years. The number of old people are increasing by leaps and bounds. Pneumonia, 'the old man's friend' is now checked by antibiotics. The effects of hardship, exposure, starvation and accident are now minimized. Where is this leading us? . . . What of the drooling, helpless, disorientated old man or the doubly incontinent old woman lying log-like in bed? Is it here that the real need for euthanasia exists?[202]

If, as Williams indicates, "seriousness" of the problem is a major criterion for euthanatizing a category of unfortunates, the sum total of mentally deficient persons would appear to warrant high priority, indeed.[203]

---

psychoses with cerebral arteriosclerosis and 2,439 senile psychoses. In the case of cerebral arteriosclerosis this represented a 600% numerical increase and a 300% increase in the proportion of total first admissions since 1920. The senile psychoses constituted almost a 400% numerical increase and a 155% increase in the proportion of total first admissions since 1920. Malzberg, *A Statistical Review of Mental Disorders in Later Life,* in Mental Disorders in Later Life 13 (Kaplan ed. 1956). Dr. George S. Stevenson classes both psychoses together as "mental illness of aging": "As a rule these patients have very limited prospect of recovery. In fact, they die on the average within fifteen months after admission to a mental hospital." Stevenson, Mental Health Planning For Social Action 41 (1956).

200. U.S. Dep't of Health, Education and Welfare, Patients in Mental Institutions 1955, Part II, Public Hospital for the Mentally Ill 21. Some 13,972 were cerebral arteriosclerosis cases; 9,589 had senile brain diseases.

201. See note 143 *supra.*

202. Banks, *Euthanasia,* 26 Bull. N.Y. Acad. Med. 297, 305 (1950).

203. "Mental diseases are said to be responsible for as much time lost in hospitals as all other diseases combined." Boudreau, *Mental Health: The New Public Health Frontier,* 286 Annals Am. Acad. Pol. & Soc. Sci. 1 (1953). As of about ten years ago, there were "over 900,000 patients under the care and supervision of mental hospitals." Felix and Kramer, *Extent of the Problem of Mental Disorders, id.* at 5, 10. Taking only the figures of persons sufficiently ill to warrant admission into a hospital for long-term care of psychiatric disorders, "at the end of 1950 there were 577,000 patients . . . in all long-term mental hospitals." *Id.* at 9. This figure represents 3.8

When Williams turns to the plight of the "hopelessly defective infants," his characteristic vim and vigor are, as in the senility discussion, conspicuously absent:

> While the Euthanasia Society of England has never advocated this, the Euthanasia Society of America did include it in its original program. The proposal certainly escapes the chief objection to the similar proposal for senile dementia: it does not create a sense of insecurity in society, because infants cannot, like adults, feel anticipatory dread of being done to death if their condition should worsen. Moreover, the proposal receives some support on eugenic grounds, and more importantly on humanitarian grounds—both on account of the parents, to whom the child will be a burden all their lives, and on account of the handicapped child itself. (It is not, however, proposed that any child should be destroyed against the wishes of its parents.) Finally, the legalization of euthanasia for handicapped children would bring the law into closer relation to its practical administration, because juries do not regard parental mercy-killing as murder. For these various reasons the proposal to legalize humanitarian infanticide is put forward from time to time by individuals. They remain in a very small minority, and the proposal may at present be dismissed as politically insignificant.[204]

It is understandable for a reformer to limit his present proposals for change to those with a real prospect of success. But it is hardly reassuring for Williams to cite the fact that only "a very small minority" has urged euthanasia for "hopelessly defective infants" as the *only* reason for not pressing for such legislation now. If, as Williams sees it, the only advantage voluntary euthanasia has over the involuntary variety lies in the organized movements on its behalf, that advantage can readily be wiped out.

In any event, I do not think that such "a very small minority" has advocated "humanitarian infanticide." Until the organization of the English and American societies led to a concentration on the voluntary type, and until the by-products of the Nazi euthanasia program somewhat embarrassed, if only temporarily, most proponents of involuntary euthanasia, about as many writers urged one type as another.[205] Indeed, some euthanasiasts have taken consider-

---

per 1,000 population, and a "fourfold increase in number of patients and a twofold increase in ratio of patients to general population since 1903." *Ibid.*
 "During 1950, the state, county and city mental hospitals spent $390,-000,000 for care and maintenance of their patients. *Id.* at 13.
 204. Williams, pp. 349-50.
 205. In Turano, *Murder by Request*, 36 Am. Mercury 423 (1935), the author goes considerably beyond the title of his paper. He scores the "barbarous social policy" which nurtures "infant monstrosities and hopelessly injured children for whom permanent suffering is the sole joy of living" and "old men and women awaiting slow extinction from the accumulated

able pains to demonstrate the superiority of defective infant euthanasia over incurably ill euthanasia.[206]

---

ailments of senility," *id.* at 424, and notes in his discussion of "permissive statutes" that "when the sufferer is not mentally competent, the decision could be left to near relatives," *id.* at 428.

In *Should They Live?*, 7 American Scholar 454 (1938) Dr. W. G. Lennox refers to the congenital idiots, the incurably sick, the mentally ill and the aged as "that portion of our population which is a heavy and permanent liability," *id.* at 457, and agrees with others that "there is *somewhere* a biological limit to altruism, even for man," *id.* at 458. Dr. Lennox would presently eliminate "only the idiots and monsters, the criminal permanently insane and the suffering incurables who themselves wish for death," *id.* at 464. W. W. Gregg similarly advocates euthanasia for all "criminally or hopelessly insane," *The Right to Kill*, 237 No. Am. Rev. 239, 247 (1934) and concludes (*id.* at 249):

> With the coming of a more rational social order . . . it is possible to foresee the emergence of a socialized purpose to eliminate such human life as shows itself conspicuously either inhuman, or unhuman, or unable to function happily; in order thereby to help bring about a safer and fuller living for that normal humanity which holds the hope of the future.

W. A. Shumaker, in *Those Unfit to Live*, 29 L.N. 165, 166-67 (1925) comments:

> Could we but devise an acceptable formula, ten thousand idiots annually put to death by state boards of health would mean no more to us than ten thousand pedestrians annually put to death by automobilists do now.

* * *

> It is impossible to give a common sense reason why an absolute idiot should be permitted to live. His life is of no value to him or to anyone else, and to maintain its existence absorbs a considerable part of the life of a normal being. Of course one shrinks at the thought of putting him to death. But why is it that we shrink? And why, though we shrink from such an act, do we find it possible to excuse him who does it?

* * *

> Is the balance swinging too far toward overconsideration not only for the idiot but for the moron and the lunatic and too little consideration for the normality on which civilization must rest?

In 1935, Dr. Alexis Carrel, the Rockefeller Institute's famed Nobel Prize winner, took the position that "not only incurables but kidnapers, murderers, habitual criminals of all kinds, as well as the hopelessly insane, should be quietly and painlessly disposed of." Newsweek, Nov. 16, 1935, p. 40; Time, Nov. 18, 1935, p. 53; *Pro and Con: Right and Wrong of Mercy Killing*, 1 The Digest 22 (1937).

Another debate on mercy killing, *Pro & Con: Shall We Legalize "Mercy Killing"*, 33 Readers Digest, Nov. 1938, p. 94 similarly embraced involuntary situations. The "question presented" was:

> Should physicians have the legal privilege of putting painlessly out of their sufferings *unadjustably defective infants*, patients suffering from painful and incurable illness and the *hopelessly insane and feeble-minded* provided, of course, that maximum legal and professional safeguards against abuse are set up, *including the consent of the patient when rational and adult?* (Emphasis added.)

The proponents of euthanasia made the pitch for voluntary euthanasia, then shifted (p. 95):

> Euthanasia would also do away with our present savage insistence that some of us must live on incurably insane or degraded by the helplessness of congenital imbecility.

For the results of a 1937 national poll on the question which covered the problem of "infants born permanently deformed or mentally handicapped" as well as "persons incurably and painfully ill" see note 207 *infra*, and accompanying text.

206. Dr. Foster Kennedy believes euthanasia of congenital idiots has two major advantages over voluntary euthanasia (1) error in diagnosis and

As for dismissing euthanasia of defective infants as "politically insignificant," the only poll that I know of which measured the public response to both types of euthanasia revealed that 45% *favored euthanasia for defective infants under certain conditions while only 37.3% approved euthanasia for the incurably and painfully ill under any conditions.*[207] Furthermore, of those who favored the mercy killing cure for incurable adults, some 40% would require only family permission or medical board approval, but not the patient's permission.[208]

Nor do I think it irrelevant that while public resistance caused Hitler to yield on the adult euthanasia front, the killing of malformed and idiot children continued unhindered to the end of the war, the definition of "children" expanding all the while.[209] Is it the embarrassing experience of the Nazi euthanasia program which has rendered destruction of defective infants presently "politically insignificant"? If so, is it any more of a jump from the incurably and painfully ill to the unorthodox political thinker than it is from the hopelessly defective infant to the same "unsavory character?"

possibility of betterment by unforseen discoveries are greatly reduced; (2) there is not mind enough to hold any dream or hope which is likely to be crushed by the forthright statement that one is doomed, a necessary communication under a voluntary euthanasia program. Kennedy's views are contained in *Euthanasia: To Be Or Not To Be,* Colliers, May 20, 1939, p. 15, reprinted, with the notation that his views remain unchanged, in Colliers, April 22, 1950, p. 13; *The Problem of Social Control of the Congenital Defective,* 99 Am. J. Psychiatry 13 (1942). See also text at notes 72-74 *supra.*

Dr. Wolbarst also indicates that error in diagnosis and possibilities of a cure are reduced in the case of insane or defective people. See text at notes 74-76, *supra.*

207. *The Fortune Quarterly Survey:* IX, Fortune, July 1937, pp. 96, 106. Actually, a slight *majority* of those who took a position on the defective infants favored euthanasia under certain circumstances since 45% approved under certain circumstances, 40.5% were unconditionally opposed, and 14.5% were undecided. In the case of the incurably ill, only 37.3% were in favor of euthanasia under any set of safeguards, 47.5% were flatly opposed, and 15.2% took no position.

Every major poll taken in the United States on the question has shown popular opposition to voluntary euthanasia. In 1937 and 1939 the American Institute of Public Opinion polls found 46% in favor, 54% opposed. A 1947 poll by the same group found only 37% in favor, 54% opposed and 9% of no opinion. For a discussion of these and other polls by various newspapers and a breakdown of the public attitude on the question in terms of age, sex, economic and educational levels see Note, *Judicial Determination of Moral Conduct In Citizenship Hearings,* 16 U. of Chi. L. Rev. 138, 141-42 and n. 11 (1948).

As Williams notes, however, at 332, a 1939 British Institute of Public Opinion poll found 68% of the British in favor of some form of legal euthanasia.

208. *The Fortune Quarterly Survey,* note 207, *supra,* at 106.

209. Mitscherlich and Mielke, Doctors of Infamy 114 (1949). The Reich Committee for Research on Hereditary Diseases and Constitutional Susceptibility to Severe Diseases" originally dealt only with child patients up to the age of three, but the age limit was later raised to eight, twelve, and apparently even sixteen or seventeen years. *Id.* at 116.

Or is it not so much that the euthanasiasts are troubled by the Nazi experience as it is that they are troubled that the public is troubled by the Nazi experience?

I read Williams' comments on defective infants for the proposition that there are some very good reasons for euthanatizing defective infants, but the time is not yet ripe. When will it be? When will the proposal become politically significant? After a voluntary euthanasia law is on the books and public opinion is sufficiently "educated?"

Williams' reasons for not extending euthanasia — once we legalize it in the narrow "voluntary" area — to the senile and the defective are much less forceful and much less persuasive than his arguments for legalizing voluntary euthanasia in the first place. I regard this as another reason for not legalizing voluntary euthanasia in the first place.

B. The Parade of Horrors.

Look, when the messenger cometh, shut the door, and hold him fast at the door; is not the sound of his master's feet behind him?[210]

This is the "wedge principle," the "parade of horrors" objection, if you will, to voluntary euthanasia. Glanville Williams' peremptory retort is:

This use of the 'wedge' objection evidently involves a particular determination as to the meaning of words, namely the words 'if raised to a general line of conduct.' The author supposes, for the sake of argument, that the merciful extinction of life in a suffering patient is not in itself immoral. Still it is immoral, because if it were permitted this would admit 'a most dangerous wedge that might eventually put all life in a precarious condition.' It seems a sufficient reply to say that this type of reasoning could be used to condemn any act whatever, because there is no human conduct from which evil cannot be imagined to follow if it is persisted in when some of the circumstances are changed. All moral questions involve the drawing of a line, but the 'wedge principle' would make it impossible to draw a line, because the line would have to be pushed farther and farther back until all action became vetoed.[211]

I agree with Williams that if a first step is "moral" it is moral wherever a second step may take us. The real point, however, the

---

210. II *Kings*, VI, 32, quoted and applied in Sperry, *The Case Against Mercy Killing*, 70 Am. Mercury 271, 276 (1950).
211. Williams, p. 315. At this point, Williams is quoting from Sullivan, Catholic Teaching on the Morality of Euthanasia 54-55 (1949). This thorough exposition of the Catholic Church's position on euthanasia was originally published by the Catholic University of America Press, then republished by the Newman Press as The Morality of Mercy Killing (1950).

point that Williams sloughs, is that whether or not the first step is
precarious, is perilous, is worth taking, rests in part on what the
second step is likely to be.

It is true that the "wedge" objection can always be advanced,
the horrors can always be paraded. But it is no less true that on some
occasions the objection is much more valid than it is on others. One
reason why the "parade of horrors" cannot be too lightly dismissed
in this particular instance is that Miss Voluntary Euthanasia is not
likely to be going it alone for very long. Many of her admirers, as I
have endeavored to show in the preceding section, would be neither
surprised nor distressed to see her joined by Miss Euthanatize the
Congenital Idiots and Miss Euthanatize the Permanently Insane
and Miss Euthanatize the Senile Dementia. And these lasses—
whether or not they themselves constitute a "parade of horrors"—
certainly make excellent majorettes for such a parade:

> Some are proposing what is called euthanasia; at present only a
> proposal for killing those who are a nuisance to themselves; but
> soon to be applied to those who are a nuisance to other people.[212]

Another reason why the "parade of horrors" argument cannot
be too lightly dismissed in this particular instance, it seems to me,
is that the parade *has* taken place in our time and the order of
procession has been headed by the killing of the "incurables" and
the "useless":

> Even before the Nazis took open charge in Germany, a propa-
> ganda barrage was directed against the traditional compas-
> sionate nineteenth-century attitudes toward the chronically ill,
> and for the adoption of a utilitarian, Hegelian point of view. . . .
> Lay opinion was not neglected in this campaign. Adults were
> propagandized by motion pictures, one of which, entitled 'I
> Accuse', deals entirely with euthanasia. This film depicts the
> life history of a woman suffering from multiple sclerosis; in it
> her husband, a doctor, finally kills her to the accompaniment of
> soft piano music rendered by a sympathetic colleague in an ad-
> joining room. Acceptance of this ideology was implanted even
> in the children. A widely used high-school mathematics text . . .
> included problems stated in distorted terms of the cost of caring
> for and rehabilitating the chronically sick and crippled. One of
> the problems asked, for instance, how many new housing units
> could be built and how many marriage-allowance loans could be
> given to newly wedded couples for the amount of money it cost
> the state to care for 'the crippled, the criminal and the insane. . . .'
> The beginnings at first were merely a subtle shift in emphasis
> in the basic attitude of the physicians. *It started with the ac-*

---

212. Chesterton, *Euthanasia and Murder*, 8 Am. Rev. 486, 490 (1937).

ceptance of the attitude, basic in the euthanasia movement, that there is such a thing as life not worthy to be lived. This attitude in its early stages concerned itself merely with the severely and chronically sick. Gradually the sphere of those to be included in this category was enlarged to encompass the socially unproductive, the ideologically unwanted, the racially unwanted and finally all non-Germans. But it is important to realize that the infinitely small wedged-in lever from which this entire trend of mind received its impetus was the attitude toward the non-rehabilitatable sick.[213]

213. Alexander, *Medical Science Under Dictatorship,* 241 New England Journal of Medicine 39, 44, 40 (1949) (emphasis added). To the same effect is Ivy, *Nazi War Crimes of a Medical Nature,* 139 J.A.M.A. 131, 132 (1949), concluding that the practice of euthanasia was a factor which led to "mass killing of the aged, the chronically ill, 'useless eaters' and the politically undesirable," and Ivy, *Nazi War Crimes of a Medical Nature,* 33 Federation Bulletin 133, 142 (1947), noting that one of the arguments the Nazis employed to condone their criminal medical experiments was that "if it is right to take the life of useless and incurable persons, which as they point out has been suggested in England and the United States, then it is right to take the lives of persons who are destined to die for political reasons."

Doctors Leo Alexander and A. C. Ivy were both expert medical advisors to the prosection at the Nuremberg Trials.

See also the November 25, 1940 entry to Shirer, *Berlin Diary* 454, 458-59 (1941):

I have at last got to the bottom of these 'mercy killings'. It's an evil tale. The Gestapo, with the knowledge and approval of the German government, is systematically putting to death the mentally deficient population of the Reich. . . .

X, a German told me yesterday that relatives are rushing to get their kin out of private asylums and out of the clutches of the authorities. He says the Gestapo is doing to death persons who are merely suffering temporary derangement or just plain nervous breakdown.

What is still unclear to me is the motive for these murders. Germans themselves advance three:

*   *   *

3. That they are simply the result of the extreme Nazis deciding to carry out their eugenic and sociological ideas.

*   *   *

The third motive seems most likely to me. For years a group of radical Nazi sociologists who were instrumental in putting through the Reich's sterilization laws have pressed for a national policy of eliminating the mentally unfit. They say they have disciples among many sociologists in other lands, and perhaps they have. Paragraph two of the form letter sent the relatives plainly bears the stamp of the sociological thinking: 'In view of the nature of his serious, incurable ailment, his death, which saved him from a lifelong institutional sojourn, is to be regarded merely as a release.'

This contemporaneous report is supported by evidence uncovered at the Nuremberg Medical Trial. Thus, an August, 1940 form letter to the relatives of a deceased mental patient states in part: "Because of her grave mental illness life was a torment for the deceased. You must therefore look on her death as a release." This form letter is reproduced in Mitscherlich and Mielke, Doctors of Infamy 103 (1949). Dr. Alexander Mitscherlich and Mr. Fred Mielke attended the trial as delegates chosen by a group of German medical societies and universities.

According to the testimony of the chief defendant at the Nuremberg Medical Trial, Karl Brandt, Reich Commissioner for Health and Sanitation and personal physician to Hitler, the Fuhrer has indicated in 1935 that if

The apparent innocuousness of Germany's "small beginnings" is perhaps best shown by the fact that German Jews were at first excluded from the program. For it was originally conceived that "the blessing of euthanasia should be granted only to [true] Germans."[214]

Relatively early in the German program, Pastor Braune, Chairman of the Executive Committee of the Domestic Welfare Council of the German Protestant Church, called for a halt to euthanasia measures "since they strike sharply at the moral foundations of the nation as a whole. The inviolability of human life is a pillar of any social order."[215] And the pastor raised the same question which euthanasia opponents ask today, as well they might, considering the disinclination of many in the movement to stop at voluntary "mercy killings": Where do we, how do we, draw the line? The good pastor asked:

> How far is the destruction of socially unfit life to go? The mass methods used so far have quite evidently taken in many people who are to a considerable degree of sound mind. . . . Is it intended to strike only at the utterly hopeless cases—the idiots and imbeciles? The instruction sheet, as already mentioned, also lists senile diseases. The latest decree by the same authorities requires that children with serious congenital disease and malformation of every kind be registered, to be collected and processed in special institutions. This necessarily gives rise to grave apprehensions. Will a line be drawn at the tubercular? In the case of persons in custody by court order euthanasia measures have evidently already been initiated. Are other abnormal or anti-social persons likewise to be included? Where is the borderline? Who is abnormal, antisocial, hopelessly sick?[216]

Williams makes no attempt to distinguish or minimize the Nazi Germany experience. Apparently he does not consider it worthy of mention in a euthanasia discussion. There are, however, a couple of obvious arguments by which the Nazi experience can be minimized.

---

war came he would effectuate the policy of euthanasia since in the general upheaval of war the open resistance to be anticipated on the part of the church would not be the potent force it might otherwise be. Mitscherlich and Mielke *supra* at 91.

Certain petitions to Hitler by parents of malformed children requesting authority for "mercy deaths" seem to have played a part in definitely making up his mind. *Ibid.*

214. Defendant Viktor Brack, Chief Administrative Officer in Hitler's private chancellory, so testified at the Nuremberg Medical Trial, 1 Trials of War Criminals Before the Nuremberg Military Tribunal Under Control Council Law No. 10, 877-80 (1950) ("The Medical Case").

215. Mitscherlich and Mielke, *op. cit. supra* note 213, at 107.

216. *Ibid.* According to testimony at the Nuremberg Medical Trial, although they were told that "only incurable patients, suffering severely, were involved," even the medical consultants to the program were "not quite clear on where the line was to be drawn." *Id.* at 94.

One goes something like this: It is silly to worry about the prospects of a dictatorship utilizing euthanasia "as a pretext for putting inconvenient citizens out of the way. Dictatorships have no occasion for such subterfuges. The firing squad is less bother."[217] One reason why this counter argument is not too reassuring, however, if again I may be permitted to be so unkind as to meet speculation with a concrete example to the contrary, is that Nazi Germany had considerable occasion to use just such a subterfuge.

Thus, Dr. Leo Alexander observes:

It is rather significant that the German people were considered by their Nazi leaders more ready to accept the exterminations of the sick than those for political reasons. It was for that reason that the first exterminations of the latter group were carried out under the guise of sickness. So-called 'psychiatric experts' were dispatched to survey the inmates of camps with the specific order to pick out members of racial minorities and political offenders from occupied territories and to dispatch them to killing centers with specially made diagnoses such as that of 'inveterate German hater' applied to a number of prisoners who had been active in the Czech underground.

*   *   *

A large number of those marked for death for political or racial reasons were made available for 'medical experiments involving the use of involuntary human subjects.'[218]

The "hunting season" in Germany officially opened when, Hitler signed on his own letterhead, a secret order dated September 1, 1939, which read:

Reichsleiter Bouhler and Dr. Brandt, M.D., are charged with the responsibility of enlarging the authority of certain physicians, to be designated by name, in such a manner that persons who, according to human judgment, are incurable can, upon a more careful diagnosis of their condition of sickness, be accorded a mercy death.[219]

---

217. *Pro & Con: Shall We Legalize "Mercy Killing"*, 33 Readers Digest, Nov. 1938, p. 94 at 96.
218. Alexander, *supra* note 213, at 41. Dr. Alexander Mitscherlich and Mr. Fred Mielke similarly note:
The granting of 'dying aid' in the case of incurable mental patients and malformed or idiot children may be considered to be still within the legitimate sphere of medical discussion. But as the 'winnowing process' continued, it moved more and more openly as purely political and ideological criteria for death, whether the subjects were considered to be 'undesirable racial groups,' or whether they had merely become incapable of supporting themselves. The camouflage around these murderous intentions is revealed especially by proof that in the concentration camps prisoners were selected by the same medical consultants who were simultaneously sitting in judgment over the destiny of mental institution inmates. Mitscherlich and Mielke, *op. cit. supra* note 213 at 41.
219. This is the translation rendered in the judgment of Military Tribunal 1, 2 Trials of War Criminals Before The Nuremberg Military Tri-

Physicians asked to participate in the program were told that
the secrecy of the order was designed to prevent patients from becoming "too agitated" and that it was in keeping with the policy
of not publicizing home front measures in time of war.[220]

About the same time that aged patients in some hospitals were
being given the "mercy" treatment,[221] the Gestapo was also "systematically putting to death the mentally deficient population of
the Reich.[222]

The courageous and successful refusal by a Protestant pastor to
deliver up certain cases from his asylum[223] well demonstrates that
even the most totalitarian governments are not always indifferent
to the feelings of the people, that they do not always feel free to
resort to the firing squad. Indeed, vigorous protests by other ecclesiastical personalities and some physicians, numerous requests of
various public prosecutors for investigation of the circumstances
surrounding the mysterious passing away of relatives, and a generally aroused public opinion finally caused Hitler to yield, if only
temporarily, and in August of 1941 he verbally ordered the dis-

bunals Under Control Council Law No. 10, 196 (1950) ("The Medical
Case"). A slightly different but substantially identical translation appears in
Mitscherlich and Mielke, op. cit. supra note 213 at 92. The letter, Document
630-PS, Prosecution Exhibit 330, as written in the original German, may be
found in 26 Trial of Major War Criminals Before the International Military
Tribunal 169 (1947). For conflicting views on whether or not the order was
back-dated, compare Mitscherlich and Mielke, op. cit. supra with Koessler,
Euthanasia In The Hadamar Sanatorium and International Law, 43 J.
Crim. L., C. & P.S. 735, 737 (1953).
    220. Mitscherlich and Mielke, op. cit. supra note 213, at 93-94.
    221. In the fall of 1940, Catholic priests at a large hospital near Urach
"notices that elderly people in the hospital were dying in increasing numbers, and dying on certain days." Straight, Germany Executes Her "Unfit",
104 New Republic 627 (1941). Such incidents led a German bishop to ask
the Supreme Sacred Congregation whether it is right to kill those "who,
although they have committed no crime deserving death, yet, because of
mental or physical defects, are no longer able to benefit the nation, and are
considered rather to burden the nation and to obstruct its energy and
strength." Ibid. The answer was, of course, in the negative, ibid., but "it is
doubtful if the mass of German Catholics, even if they learned of this statement from Rome, which is improbable, understood what it referred to. Only
a minority in Germany knew of the 'mercy deaths'." Shirer, op. cit. supra
note 213, at 459 n. 1.
    222. Shirer, op. cit. supra note 213, at 454.
    223. "Late last summer, it seems Pastor von Bodelschwingh was asked
to deliver up certain of his worst cases to the authorities. Apparently he got
wind of what was in store for them. He refused. The authorities insisted.
Pastor von Bodelschwingh hurried to Berlin to protest.
    Pastor von Bodelschwingh returned to Bethel. The local Gauleiter
ordered him to turn over some of his inmates. Again he refused. Berlin then
ordered his arrest. This time the Gauleiter protested. The pastor was the
most popular man in his province. To arrest him in the middle of war would
stir up a whole world of unnecessary trouble. He himself declined to arrest
the man. Let the Gestapo take the responsibility; he wouldn't. This was
just before the night of September 18, [1940]. The bombing of the Bethel·
asylum followed. Now I understand why a few people wondered as to who
dropped the bombs." Shirer, op. cit. supra note 213 at 454-55.

continuance of the adult euthanasia program. Special gas chambers in Hadamar and other institutions were dismantled and shipped to the East for much more extensive use of Polish Jews.[224]

Perhaps it should be noted, too, that even dictatorships fall prey to the inertia of big government:

It is . . . interesting that there was so much talk against euthanasia in certain areas of Germany, particularly in the region of Wiesbaden, that Hitler in 1943 asked Himmler to stop it. But, it had gained so much impetus by 1943 and was such an easy way in crowded concentration camps to get rid of undesirables and make room for newcomers, that it could not be stopped. The wind had become a whirlwind.[225]

Another obvious argument is that it just can't happen here. I hope not. I think not.

But then, neither did I think that tens of thousands of perfectly loyal native-born Americans would be herded into prison camps without proffer of charges and held there for many months, even years, because they were of "Japanese blood"[226] and, although the

---

224. Mitscherlich and Mielke, *op. cit. supra* note 213, at 113-114; Koessler, *supra* note 219, at 739.

225. Ivy, *Nazi War Crimes of a Medical Nature,* 33 Federation Bulletin 133, 134 (1947).

226. As Justice Murphy pointed out in his dissenting opinion in Korematsu v. United States, 323 U.S. 214, 241-42 (1944) :

No adequate reason is given for the failure to treat these Japanese Americans on an individual basis by holding investigations and hearings to separate the loyal from the disloyal, as was done in the case of persons of German and Italian ancestry. It is asserted merely that the loyalties of this group 'were unknown and time was of the essence.' Yet nearly four months elapsed after Pearl Harbor before the first exclusion order was issued; nearly eight months went by until the last order was issued; and the last of these 'subversive' persons was not actually removed until almost eleven months had elapsed. Leisure and deliberation seem to have been more of the essence than speed. And the fact that conditions were not such as to warrant a declaration of martial law adds strength to the belief that the factors of time and military necessity were not as urgent as they have been represented to be.

Moreover, there was no adequate proof that the Federal Bureau of Investigation and the military and naval intelligence services did not have the espionage and sabotage situation well in hand during this long period. Nor is there any denial of the fact that not one person of Japanese ancestry was accused or convicted of espionage or sabotage after Pearl Harbor while they were still free, a fact which is some evidence of the loyalty of the vast majority of these individuals and of the effectiveness of the established methods of combatting these evils. It seems incredible that under these circumstances it would have been impossible to hold loyalty hearings for the mere 112,000 persons involved—or at least for the 70,000 American citizens—especially when a large part of this number represented children and elderly men and women.

Justice Murphy then went on to note that shortly after the outbreak of World War II the British Government examined over 70,000 German and Austrian aliens and in six months freed 64,000 from internment and from any special restrictions. 354 U.S. 242 n. 16.

See generally Rostow, *The Japanese American Cases—A Disaster,* 54 Yale L.J. 489 (1945), a tale well calculated to keep you in anger and shame.

general who required these measures emitted considerable ignorance
and bigotry,[227] his so-called military judgment would be largely
sustained by the highest court of the land. The Japanese American
experience of World War II undoubtedly fell somewhat short of
first-class Nazi tactics, but we were getting warm. I venture to say
it would not be too difficult to find American citizens of Japanese
descent who would maintain we were getting very warm indeed.

In this regard, some of Justice Jackson's observations in his
Korematsu dissent[228] seem quite pertinent:

> All who observe the work of courts are familiar with what Judge
> Cardozo described as 'the tendency of a principle to expand it-
> self to the limit of its logic.' [Nature of the Judicial Process,
> p. 51.] A military commander may overstep the bounds of con-
> stitutionality, and it is an incident. But if we review and ap-
> prove, that passing incident becomes the doctrine of the Con-
> stitution. There it has a generative power of its own, and all
> that it creates will be in its own image. Nothing better illus-
> trates this danger than does the Court's opinion in this case.

> It argues that we are bound to uphold the conviction of Kore-
> matsu because we upheld one in *Hirabayashi v. United States*,
> 320 U.S. 81, when we sustained these orders in so far as they
> applied a curfew requirement to a citizen of Japanese ancestry.
> I think we should learn something from that experience.

> In that case we were urged to consider only the curfew feature,
> that being all that technically was involved, because it was the
> only count necessary to sustain Hirabayashi's conviction and
> sentence. We yielded, and the Chief Justice guarded the opinion
> as carefully as language will do. . . . However, in spite of our

---

227. See, e.g., General J. L. Dewitt's Final Recommendation to the
Secretary of War, *U.S. Army, Western Defense Command, Final Report,
Japanese Evacuation From the West Coast,* 1942 (1943) at 32 ("The Japanese race is an enemy race and while many second and third generation
Japanese born on United States soil, possessed of United States citizenship,
have become 'Americanized,' the racial strains are undiluted. . . ."), and his
subsequent testimony, *Hearings Before Subcommittee of House Committee
on Naval Affairs on H.R. 30,* 78th Cong., 1st Sess. (1943) at 739-40 ("You
needn't worry about the Italians at all except in certain cases. Also, the
same for the Germans except in individual cases. But we must worry about
the Japanese all the time until he is wiped off the map. Sabotage and espionage will make problems as long as he is allowed in this area—problems which
I don't want to have to worry about".) After a careful study, Professor
(now Dean) Rostow took this position:

> The dominant factor in the development of this policy was not a military
> estimate of a military problem, but familiar West Coast attitudes of race
> prejudice. The program of excluding all persons of Japanese ancestry
> from the coastal area was conceived and put through by the organized
> minority whose business it has been for forty-five years to increase and
> exploit racial tensions on the West Coast. The Native Sons and
> Daughters of the Golden West and their sympathizers, were lucky in their
> general, for General DeWitt amply proved himself to be one of them
> in opinion and values.

Rostow, *supra* note 226, at 496.
228. See note 226, *supra.*

limiting words we did validate a discrimination on the basis of ancestry for mild and temporary deprivation of liberty. Now the principle of racial discrimination is pushed from support of mild measures to very harsh ones, and from temporary deprivations to indeterminate ones. And the precedent which it is said requires us to do so is *Hirabayashi*. The Court is now saying that in *Hirabayashi* we did decide the very things we there said we were not deciding. Because we said that these citizens could be made to stay in their homes during the hours of dark, it is said we must require them to leave home entirely; and if that, we are told they may also be taken into custody for deportation; and if that, it is argued they may also be held for some undetermined time in detention camps. How far the principle of this case would be extended before plausible reasons would play out, I do not know.[229]

It can't happen here. Well, maybe it cannot, but no small part of our Constitution and no small number of our Supreme Court opinions stem from the fear that *it can happen here unless we darn well make sure that it does not* by adamantly holding the line, by swiftly snuffing out what are or might be small beginnings of what we do not want to happen here. To flick off, as Professor Williams does, the fears about legalized euthanasia as so much nonsense, as a chimerical "parade of horrors," is to sweep away much of the ground on which all our civil liberties rest.

Boyd,[230] the landmark search and seizure case which paved the way for the federal rule of exclusion,[231] a doctrine which now prevails in over twenty state courts as well,[232] set the mood of our day in treating those accused of crime:

> It may be that it is the obnoxious thing in its mildest and least repulsive form; but illegitimate and unconstitutional practices get their first footing in that way, namely, by silent approaches and slight deviations from legal modes of procedure. . . . It is the duty of courts to be watchful for the constitutional rights of the citizen, and against any stealthy encroachments thereon. Their motto should be *obsta principiis*. . . .[233]

---

229. 323 U.S. at 246-47.
230. Boyd v. United States, 116 U.S. 616 (1886).
231. See e.g., Weeks v. United States, 232 U.S. 283 (1914); Gouled v. United States, 255 U.S. 298 (1921); McDonald v. United States, 335 U.S. 451 (1948); United States v. Jeffers, 342 U.S. 48 (1951).
232. See Anno., 50 A.L.R. 2d 531, 536, 556-560 (1956).
233. 116 U.S. 616, 635. The search and seizure cases contain about as good an articulation of the "wedge principle" as one can find anywhere, except, perhaps if one turns to the recent *Covert* and *Krueger* cases, where Mr. Justice Black quotes the *Boyd* statement with approval and applies it with vigor:

> It is urged that the expansion of military jurisdiction over civilians claimed here is only slight, and that the practical necessity for it is very great. The attitude appears to be that a slight encroachment on the Bill

Recent years have seen the Supreme Court sharply divided on search and seizure questions. The differences, however, have been over *application,* not over the *Boyd-Weeks* "wedge principle"; not over the view, as the great Learned Hand, hardly the frightened spinster type, put it in an oft-quoted phrase, "that what seems fair enough against a squalid huckster of bad liquor may take on a very different face, if used by a government determined to suppress political opposition under the guise of sedition."[234] And when the dissenters have felt compelled to reiterate the reasons for the principle, lest its force be diminished by the failure to apply it in the particular case, and they have groped for the most powerful arguments in its behalf, where have they turned, what have they done? Why, they have employed the very arguments Glanville Williams dismisses so contemptuously. They have cited the Nazi experience. They have talked of the police state, the Knock at the Door, the suppression of political opposition under the guise of sedition. They have trotted out, if you will, the "parade of horrors."[235]

---

of Rights and other safeguards in the Constitution need cause little concern. But to hold that these wives could be tried by the military would be a tempting precedent. Slight encroachments create new boundaries from which legions of power can seek new territory to capture.
Reid v. Covert, 354 U.S. 1, 39-40 (1957).

234. United States v. Kirschenblatt, 16 F.2d 202, 203 (2d cir. 1926).

235. Thus, in Brinegar v. United States, 338 U.S. 160 (1949), it was Jackson the Chief Counsel of the United States at the Nuremberg Trials as well as Jackson the Supreme Court Justice who warned (338 U.S. at 180-81):

> Among deprivations of rights, none is so effective in cowing a population, crushing the spirit of the individual and putting terror in every heart. Uncontrolled search and seizure is one of the first and most effective weapons in the arsenal of every arbitrary government. And one need only briefly to have dwelt and worked among a people possessed of many admirable qualities but deprived of these rights to know that the human personality deteriorates and dignity and self-reliance disappear where homes, persons and possessions are subject at any hour to unheralded search and seizure by the police.

In United States v. Rabinowitz, 339 U.S. 56, 82 (1950), Justice Frankfurter cautioned:

> By the Bill of Rights the founders of this country subordinated police action to legal restraints, not in order to convenience the guilty but to protect the innocent. Nor did they provide that only the innocent may appeal to these safeguards. They know too well that the successful prosecution of the guilty does not require jeopardy to the innocent. The knock at the door under the guise of a warrant of arrest for a venial or spurious offense was not unknown to them. . . . We have had grim reminders in our day of their experience. Arrest under a warrant for a minor or a trumped-up charge has been familiar practice in the past, is a commonplace in the police state of today, and too well known in this country. . . . The progress is too easy from police action unscrutinized by judicial authorization to the police state.

In Harris v. United States, 331 U.S. 145 (1947), four Justices dissented in three separate opinions. The first dissent asked (331 U.S. at 163):

> How can there be freedom of thought or freedom of speech or freedom of religion, if the police can, without warrant, search your house and mine from garret to cellar merely because they are executing a warrant

The lengths to which the Court will go in applying the "wedge principle" in the First Amendment area is well demonstrated by instances where those who have labeled Jews "slimy scum" and likened them to "bedbugs" and "snakes"[236] or who have denounced them "as all the garbage that . . . should have been burnt in the incinerators"[237] have been sheltered by the Court so that freedom of speech and religion would not be impaired. Perhaps the supreme example is the *Barnette* case.[238]

There, in striking down the compulsory flag salute and pledge, Justice Jackson took the position that "those who begin coercive elimination of dissent soon find themselves exterminating dissenters. Compulsory unification of opinion achieves only the unanimity of the graveyard."[239] "The First Amendment," he pointed out, "was de-

of arrest? How can men feel free if all their papers may be searched, as an incident to the arrest of someone in the house, on the chance that something may turn up, or rather be turned up? Yesterday the justifying document was an illicit ration book, tomorrow it may be some suspect piece of literature.

The second dissent voiced fears of "full impact of today's decision" (331 U.S. at 194):

The principle established by the Court today can be used as easily by some future government determined to suppress political opposition under the guise of sedition as it can be used by a government determined to undo forgers and defrauders. . . . [It] takes no stretch of the imagination to picture law enforcement officers arresting those accused of believing, writing or speaking that which is proscribed, accompanied by a thorough ransacking of their homes as an 'incident' to the arrest in an effort to uncover 'anything' of a seditious nature.

The third dissent pointed out (331 U.S. at 198):

In view of the readiness of zealots to ride roughshod over claims of privacy for any ends that impress them as socially desirable, we should not make inroads on the rights protected by this Amendment.

236. Terminello v. Chicago, 337 U.S. 1 (1949), striking down an ordinance which imposed a fine of not more than two hundred dollars for a "breach of peace," defined by the trial court as misbehavior which "stirs the public to anger, invites dispute, brings about a condition of unrest, or creates a disturbance, or if it molests the inhabitants in the enjoyment of peace and quiet by arousing alarm." (337 U.S. at 3.) The Court ruled, per Douglas, J., that a conviction on *any* of the grounds charged could not stand. "There is no room under our Constitution for a more restrictive view. For the alterative would lead to standardization of ideas either by legislatures, courts, or dominant political or community groups" 337 U.S. at 4-5. The dissenting opinion by Jackson, 337 U.S. 13-21, culls long passages from the speech in question.

237. Kunz v. New York, 340 U.S. 290 (1951), overturning a conviction and ten dollar fine for holding a religious meeting without a permit, defendant's permit having been revoked after a hearing by the police commissioner on evidence that he had ridiculed and denounced other religious beliefs at prior meetings. Samples of Kunz's prior preachings may be found in Jackson's dissenting opinion, 340 U.S. at 296. Kunz displayed a certain flair for bipartisanship; he also denounced Catholicism as "a religion of the devil" and the Pope as "The anti-Christ". *Ibid.*

238. Board of Education v. Barnette, 319 U.S. 624 (1943).

239. 319 U.S. at 641. There was no majority opinion. Chief Justice Stone and Justice Rutledge concurred in Justice Jackson's opinion; Justices Black and Douglas wrote a concurring opinion; and Justice Murphy wrote a separate concurring opinion.

signed to avoid these ends by avoiding these beginnings."[240] Justices Black and Douglas kept in step in their concurring opinion by advancing the view that "the ceremonial, when enforced against conscientious objectors . . . is a handy implement for disguised religious persecution."[241]

What were these pernicious "beginnings" again? What was this danger-laden ceremonial again? Why, requiring public school pupils "to participate in the salute honoring the Nation represented by the Flag."[242] Talk about "parades of horror"! This one is an extravaganza against which anything euthanasia opponents can muster is drab and shabby by comparison. After all, whatever else Williams and his allies make "mercy-killings" out to be, *these* beginnings are not "patriotic ceremonies."

The point need not be labored. If the prospects of the police state, the knock on Everyman's door, and wide-spread political persecution are legitimate considerations when we enter "opium smoking dens,"[243] when we deal with "not very nice people" and "sordid little cases"[244] then why should the prospects of the police state and the systematic extermination of certain political or racial minorities be taken any less seriously when we enter the sickroom or the mental institution, when we deal with not very healthy or not very useful people, when we discuss "euthanasia" under whatever trade name?

If freeing some rapist or murderer is not too great a price to pay for the "sanctity of the home", then why is allowing some cancer victim to suffer a little longer too great a price to pay for the "sanctity of life"? If the sheltering of purveyors of "hateful and hate-stirring attacks on races and faiths"[245] may be justified in the name of a transcendent principle, then why may not postponing the death of the suffering "incurable" be similarly justified?

A Final Reflection

There have been and there will continue to be compelling circumstances when a doctor or relative or friend will violate The Law On The Books and, more often than not, receive protection

---

240. *Ibid.*
241. 319 U.S. at 644.
242. 319 U.S. at 626.
243. See, *e.g.*, Johnson v. United States, 333 U.S. 10 (1948). The point is made in rather homey fashion in Houts, From Gun to Gavel: The Courtroom Recollections of James Mathers of Oklahoma 213-17 (1954).
244. The phrases are those of Mr. Justice Frankfurter, dissenting in United States v. Rabinowitz, 339 U.S. 56, 68-69 (1950).
245. The phrase is Justice Jackson's dissenting in Kunz v. New York, 340 U.S. 290, 295 (1951).

from The Law In Action. But this is not to deny that there are other occasions when The Law On The Books operates to stay the hand of all concerned, among them situations where the patient is in fact (1) presently incurable, (2) beyond the aid of any respite which may come along in his life expectancy, suffering (3) intolerable and (4) unmitigable pain and of a (5) fixed and (6) rational desire to die. That any euthanasia program may only be the opening wedge for far more objectionable practices, and that even within the bounds of a "voluntary" plan such as Williams' the incidence of mistake or abuse is likely to be substantial, are not much solace to one in the above plight.

It may be conceded that in a narrow sense it is an "evil" for such a patient to have to continue to suffer—if only for a little while. But in a narrow sense, long-term sentences and capital punishment are "evils," too.[246] If we can justify the infliction of imprisonment and death by the state "on the ground of the social interests to be protected"[247] then surely we can similarly justify the postponement of death by the state. The objection that the individual is thereby treated not as an "end" in himself but only as a "means" to further the common good was, I think, aptly disposed of by Holmes long ago. "If a man lives in society, he is likely to find himself so treated."[248]

---

246. Perhaps this would not be true if the only purpose of punishment was to reform the criminal. But whatever *ought to be* the case, this obviously *is not*. "If it were, every prisoner should be released as soon as it appears clear that he will never repeat his offence, and if he is incurable he should not be punished at all." Holmes, The Common Law 42 (1881).

247. Michael and Adler, Crime, Law and Social Science 351 (1933). The authors continue (at 352):

> The end of the criminal law must be the common good, the welfare of a political society determined, of course, by reference to its constitution. Punishment can be justified only as an intermediate means to the ends of deterrence and reformation which, in turn, are means for increasing and preserving the welfare of society. . . .

248. Holmes, The Common Law 44 (1881).

"MERCY-KILLING" LEGISLATION—
A REJOINDER

GLANVILLE WILLIAMS*

I welcome Professor Kamisar's reply [1] to my argument for voluntary euthanasia, because it is on the whole a careful, scholarly work, keeping to knowable facts and accepted human values. It is, therefore, the sort of reply that can be rationally considered and dealt with.[2] In this short rejoinder I shall accept most of Professor Kamisar's valuable footnotes, and merely submit that they do not bear out his conclusion.

The argument in favour of voluntary euthanasia in the terminal stages of painful diseases is quite a simple one, and is an application of two values that are widely recognised. The first value is the prevention of cruelty. Much as men differ in their ethical assessments, all agree that cruelty is an evil—the only difference of opinion residing in what is meant by cruelty. Those who plead for the legalization of euthanasia think that it is cruel to allow a human being to linger for months in the last stages of agony, weakness and decay, and to refuse him his demand for merciful release. There is also a second cruelty involved—not perhaps quite so compelling, but still worth consideration: the agony of the relatives in seeing their loved one in his desperate plight. Opponents of euthanasia are apt to take a cynical view of the desires of relatives, and this may sometimes be justified. But it cannot be denied that a wife who has

* Fellow of Jesus College, Cambridge University.

1. Kamisar, *Some Non-Religious Views Against Proposed "Mercy-Killing" Legislation*, 42 MINN. L. REV. 969 (1958).

2. Professor Kamisar professes to deal with the issue from a utilitarian point of view and generally does so. But he lapses when he says that "the need the euthanasiast advances . . . is a good deal less compelling [than the need to save life]. It is only to ease pain." Kamisar, *supra* note 1, at 1008. This is, of course, on Benthamite principles, an inadmissible remark.

to nurse her husband through the last stages of some terrible disease may herself be so deeply affected by the experience that her health is ruined, either mentally or physically. Whether the situation can be eased for such a person by voluntary euthanasia I do not know; probably it depends very much on the individuals concerned, which is as much as to say that no solution in terms of a general regulatory law can be satisfactory. The conclusion should be in favour of individual discretion.

The second value involved is that of liberty. The criminal law should not be invoked to repress conduct unless this is demonstrably necessary on social grounds. What social interest is there in preventing the sufferer from choosing to accelerate his death by a few months? What positive value does his life still possess for society, that he is to be retained in it by the terrors of the criminal law?

And, of course, the liberty involved is that of the doctor as well as that of the patient. It is the doctor's responsibility to do all he can to prolong worth-while life, or, in the last resort, to ease his patient's passage. If the doctor honestly and sincerely believes that the best service he can perform for his suffering patient is to accede to his request for euthanasia, it is a grave thing that the law should forbid him to do so.

This is the short and simple case for voluntary euthanasia, and, as Kamisar admits, it cannot be attacked directly on utilitarian grounds. Such an attack can only be by finding possible evils of an indirect nature. These evils, in the view of Professor Kamisar, are (1) the difficulty of ascertaining consent, and arising out of that the danger of abuse; (2) the risk of an incorrect diagnosis; (3) the risk of administering euthanasia to a person who could later have been cured by developments in medical knowledge; (4) the "wedge" argument.

Before considering these matters, one preliminary comment may be made. In some parts of his Article Kamisar hints at recognition of the fact that a practice of mercy-killing exists among the most reputable of medical practitioners. Some of the evidence for this will be found in my book.[3] In the first debate in the House of Lords, Lord Dawson admitted the fact, and claimed that it did away with the need for legislation. In other words, the attitude of conservatives is this: let medical men do mercy-killing, but let it continue to be called murder, and be treated as such if the legal machinery is by some unlucky mischance made to work; let us, in other words, take no steps to translate the new morality into the concepts of the law. I find this attitude equally incomprehensible in a doctor, as Lord Dawson was, and in a lawyer, as Professor Kamisar is. Still more

---

3. THE SANCTITY OF LIFE AND THE CRIMINAL LAW 334–39 (1957).

baffling does it become when Professor Kamisar seems to claim as
a virtue of the system that the jury can give a merciful acquittal
in breach of their oaths.[4] The result is that the law frightens some
doctors from interposing, while not frightening others — though
subjecting the braver group to the risk of prosecution and possible
loss of liberty and livelihood. Apparently, in Kamisar's view, it is a
good thing if the law is broken in a proper case, because that relieves
suffering, but also a good thing that the law is there as a threat in
order to prevent too much mercy being administered; thus, whichever result the law has is perfectly right and proper. It is hard to
understand on what moral principle this type of ethical ambivalence
is to be maintained. If Kamisar does approve of doctors administering euthanasia in some clear cases, and of juries acquitting them if
they are prosecuted for murder, how does he maintain that it is an
insuperable objection to euthanasia that diagnosis may be wrong
and medical knowledge subsequently extended?

However, the references to merciful acquittals disappear after
the first few pages of the Article, and thenceforward the argument
develops as a straight attack on euthanasia. So although at the beginning Kamisar says that he would hate to have to argue against
mercy-killing in a clear case, in fact he does proceed to argue against
it with some zest.

In my book I reported that there were some people who opposed
the Euthanasia Bill as it stood, because it brought a ridiculous
number of formalities into the sickroom, and pointed out, without
any kind of verbal elaboration, that these same people did not say
that they would have supported the measure without the safeguards.
I am puzzled by Professor Kamisar's description of these sentences
of mine as "more than bitter comments."[5] Like his references to my
"ire," my "neat boxing" and "gingerly parrying," it seems to be justified by considerations of literary style. However, if the challenge is
made, a sharper edge can be given to the criticism of this opposition than I incorporated in my book.

The point at issue is this. Opponents of voluntary euthanasia say
that it must either be subject to ridiculous and intolerable formalities, or else be dangerously free from formalities. Kamisar accepts
this line of argument, and seems prepared himself to ride both horses
at once. He thinks that they present an ordinary logical dilemma,
saying that arguments made in antithesis may each be valid. Perhaps
I can best explain the fallacy in this opinion, as I see it, by a parable.

In the State of Ruritania many people live a life of poverty and
misery. They would be glad to emigrate to happier lands, but the

---

4. Kamisar, *supra* note 1, at 971–72.
5. *Id.* at 982.

law of Ruritania bans all emigration. The reason for this law is that
the authorities are afraid that if it were relaxed there would be too
many people seeking to emigrate, and the population would be
decimated.

A member of the Ruritanian Senate, whom we will call Senator
White, wants to see some change in this law, but he is aware of the
power of traditional opinion, and so seeks to word his proposal in a
modest way. According to his proposal, every person, before being
allowed to emigrate, must fill up a questionnaire in which he states
his income, his prospects and so on; he must satisfy the authorities
that he is living at near-starvation level, and there is to be an Official
Referee to investigate that his answers are true.

Senator Black, a member of the Government Party, opposes the
proposal on the ground that it is intolerable that a free Ruritanian
citizen should be asked to write out these humiliating details of
his life, and particularly that he should be subject to the investigation of an Official Referee.

Now it will be evident that this objection of Senator Black may be
a reasonable and proper one *if* the Senator is prepared to go further
than the proposal and say that citizens who so wish should be entitled to emigrate without formality. But if he uses his objections to
formality in order to support the existing ban on emigration, one
can only say that he must be muddle-headed, or self-deceptive, or
hypocritical. It may be an interesting exercise to decide which of
these three adjectives fit him, but one of them must do so. For any
unbiased mind can perceive that it is better to be allowed to emigrate on condition of form-filling than not to be allowed to emigrate
at all.

I should be sorry to have to apply any of the three adjectives to
Professor Kamisar, who has conducted the debate on a level which
protects him from them. But, although it may be my shortcoming,
I cannot see any relevant difference between the assumed position
of Senator Black on emigration and the argument of Kamisar on
euthanasia. Substitute painful and fatal illness for poverty, and
euthanasia for emigration, and the parallel would appear to be
exact.

I agree with Kamisar and the critics in thinking that the procedure of the Euthanasia Bill was over-elaborate, and that it would
probably fail to operate in many cases for this reason. But this is no
argument for rejecting the measure, if it is the most that public
opinion will accept.

Let me now turn to the proposal for voluntary euthanasia permitted without formality, as I have put it forward in my book.

Kamisar's first objection, under the heading of "The Choice," is that there can be no such thing as truly voluntary euthanasia in painful and killing diseases. He seeks to impale the advocates of euthanasia on an old dilemma. Either the victim is not yet suffering pain, in which case his consent is merely an uninformed and anticipatory one — and he cannot bind himself by contract to be killed in the future — or he is crazed by pain and stupified by drugs, in which case he is not of sound mind. I have dealt with this problem in my book; Kamisar has quoted generously from it, and I leave the reader to decide. As I understand Kamisar's position, he does not really persist in the objection. With the laconic "Perhaps," he seems to grant me, though unwillingly, that there are cases where one can be sure of the patient's consent. But having thus abandoned his own point, he then goes off to a different horror, that the patient may give his consent only in order to relieve his relatives of the trouble of looking after him.

On this new issue, I will return Kamisar the compliment and say: "Perhaps." We are certainly in an area where no solution is going to make things quite easy and happy for everybody, and all sorts of embarrassments may be conjectured. But these embarrassments are not avoided by keeping to the present law: we suffer from them already. If a patient, suffering pain in a terminal illness, wishes for euthanasia partly because of this pain and partly because he sees his beloved ones breaking under the strain of caring for him, I do not see how this decision on his part, agonizing though it may be, is necessarily a matter of discredit either to the patient himself or to his relatives. The fact is that, whether we are considering the patient or his relatives, there are limits to human endurance.

The author's next objection rests on the possibility of mistaken diagnosis. There are many reasons why this risk cannot be accurately measured, one of them being that we cannot be certain how much use would actually be made of proposed euthanasia legislation. At one place in his Article the author seems to doubt whether the law would do much good anyway, because we don't know it will be used. ("Whether or not the general practitioner will accept the responsibility Williams would confer on him is itself a problem of major proportions."[6]) But later, the Article seeks to extract the maximum of alarm out of the situation by assuming that the power will be used by all and sundry — young practitioners just starting in practice, and established practitioners who are minimally competent.[7] In this connection, the author enters in some detail into examples of mistaken diagnosis for cancer and other diseases. I agree with him that, before deciding on euthanasia in any particular

6. *Id.* at 984.
7. *Id.* at 996.

case, the risk of mistaken diagnosis would have to be considered.[8] Everything that is said in the Article would, therefore, be most relevant when the two doctors whom I propose in my suggested measure come to consult on the question of euthanasia; and the possibility of mistake might most forcefully be brought before the patient himself. But have these medical questions any real relevance to the legal discussion?

Kamisar, I take it, notwithstanding his wide reading in medical literature, is by training a lawyer. He has consulted much medical opinion in order to find arguments against changing the law. I ought not to object to this, since I have consulted the same opinion for the opposite purpose. But what we may well ask ourselves is this: is it not a trifle bizarre that we should be doing it at all? Our profession is the law, not medicine; how does it come about that lawyers have to examine medical literature to assess the advantages and disadvantages of a medical practice?

If the import of this question is not immediately clear, let me return to my imaginary State of Ruritania. Many years ago, in Ruritania as elsewhere, surgical operations were attended with great risk. Pasteur had not made his discoveries, and surgeons killed as often as they cured. In this state of things, the legislature of Ruritania passed a law declaring all surgical operations to be unlawful in principle, but providing that each specific type of operation might be legalized by a statute specially passed for the purpose. The result is that, in Ruritania, as expert medical opinion sees the possibility of some new medical advance, a pressure group has to be formed in order to obtain legislative approval for it. Since there is little public interest in these technical questions, and since, moreover, surgical operations are thought in general to be inimical to the established religion, the pressure group has to work for many years before it gets a hearing. When at last a proposal for legalization is seriously mooted, the lawyers and politicians get to work upon it, considering what possible dangers are inherent in the new operation. Lawyers and politicians are careful people, and they are perhaps more prone to see the dangers than the advantages in a new departure. Naturally they find allies among some of the more timid or traditional or less knowledgeable members of the medical profession, as well as among the priesthood and the faithful. Thus it is small wonder that

---

8. The author is misleading on my reference to capital punishment, which I did not mention in connection with the occurrence of mistakes. See Kamisar, *supra* note 1, at 1005. I merely pointed out the inconsistency of the theological position which admits capital punishment and war as exceptions from the Sixth Commandment although not expressed therein, and says that they are not "murder," while maintaining that a killing done with a man's consent and for his benefit as an act of mercy is "murder." Whatever moral distinction may be found between these rules, they cannot by any feat of ingenuity be deduced from the text of the Commandment.

whereas appendicectomy has been practised in civilised countries since the beginning of the present century, a proposal to legalize it has still not passed the legislative assembly of Ruritania.

It must be confessed that on this particular matter the legal prohibition has not been an unmixed evil for the Ruritanians. During the great popularity of the appendix operation in much of the civilised world during the twenties and thirties of this century, large numbers of these organs were removed without adequate cause, and the citizens of Ruritania have been spared this inconvenience. On the other hand, many citizens of that country have died of appendicitis, who would have been saved if they had lived elsewhere. And whereas in other countries the medical profession has now learned enough to be able to perform this operation with wisdom and restraint, in Ruritania it is still not being performed at all. Moreover, the law has destroyed scientific inventiveness in that country in the forbidden fields.

Now, in the United States and England we have no such absurd general law on the subject of surgical operations as they have in Ruritania. In principle, medical men are left free to exercise their best judgment, and the result has been a brilliant advance in knowledge and technique. But there are just two — or possibly three — operations which are subject to the Ruritanian principle. These are abortion,[9] euthanasia, and possibly sterilization of convenience. In these fields we, too, must have pressure groups, with lawyers and politicians warning us of the possibility of inexpert practitioners and mistaken diagnosis, and canvassing medical opinion on the risk of an operation not yielding the expected results in terms of human happiness and the health of the body politic. In these fields we, too, are forbidden to experiment to see if the foretold dangers actually come to pass. Instead of that, we are required to make a social judgment on the probabilities of good and evil before the medical profession is allowed to start on its empirical tests.

This anomaly is perhaps more obvious with abortion than it is with euthanasia. Indeed, I am prepared for ridicule when I describe euthanasia as a medical operation. Regarded as surgery it is unique, since its object is not to save or prolong life but the reverse. But euthanasia has another object which it shares with many surgical operations — the saving of pain. And it is now widely recognised, as Lord Dawson said in the debate in the House of Lords, that the saving of pain is a legitimate aim of medical practice. The question whether euthanasia will effect a net saving of pain and distress is, perhaps, one that can be only finally answered by trying it. But it is

---

9. Lawful everywhere on certain health grounds, but not on socio-medical grounds (the overburdened mother), eugenic grounds, ethical grounds (rape, incest, etc.), or social and libertarian grounds (the unwanted child).

obscurantist to forbid the experiment on the ground that until it is performed we cannot certainly know its results. Such an attitude, in any other field of medical endeavor, would have inhibited progress.

The argument based on mistaken diagnosis leads into the argument based on the possibility of dramatic medical discoveries. Of course, a new medical discovery which gives the opportunity of remission or cure will almost at once put an end to mercy-killings in the particular group of cases for which the discovery is made. On the other hand, the discovery cannot affect patients who have already died from their disease. The argument based on mistaken diagnosis is therefore concerned only with those patients who have been mercifully killed just before the discovery becomes available for use. The argument is that such persons may turn out to have been "mercy-killed" unnecessarily, because if the physician had waited a bit longer they would have been cured. Because of this risk for this tiny fraction of the total number of patients, patients who are dying in pain must be left to do so, year after year, against their entreaty to have it ended.

Just how real is the risk? When a new medical discovery is claimed, some time commonly elapses before it becomes tested sufficiently to justify large-scale production of the drug, or training in the techniques involved. This is a warning period when euthanasia in the particular class of case would probably be halted anyway. Thus it is quite probable that when the new discovery becomes available, the euthanasia process would not in fact show any mistakes in this regard.

Kamisar says that in my book I "did not deign this objection to euthanasia more than a passing reference." I still do not think it is worth any more than that.

The author advances the familiar but hardly convincing argument that the quantitative need for euthanasia is not large. As one reason for this argument, he suggests that not many patients would wish to benefit from euthanasia, even if it were allowed. I am not impressed by the argument. It may be true, but it is irrelevant. So long as there are *any* persons dying in weakness and grief who are refused their request for a speeding of their end, the argument for legalizing euthanasia remains. Next, the Article suggests that there is no great need for euthanasia because of the advances made with pain-killing drugs. Kamisar has made so many quotations from my book that I cannot complain that he has not made more, but there is one relevant point that he does not mention. In my book, recognising that medical science does manage to save many dying patients from the extreme of physical pain, I pointed out that it often fails to save them from an artificial, twilight existence, with nausea, giddiness, and extreme restlessness, as well as the long hours of consciousness of a hopeless condition. A dear friend of mine, who died of cancer of the bowel, spent his last months in just this state, under the influence of morphine, which deadened pain, but vomiting incessantly, day in and day out. The question that we have to face is whether the unintelligent brutality of such an existence is to be imposed on one who wishes to end it.

The Article then makes a suggestion which, for once, really is a new one in this rather jaded debate. The suggestion appears to be that if a man really wants to die he can do the job himself.[10] Whether the author seriously intends this as advice to patients I cannot discover, because he adds that he does not condone suicide, but that he prefers a *laissez-faire* approach. Whatever meaning may be attached to the author's remarks on this subject, I must say with deep respect that I find them lacking in sympathy and imagination, as well as inconsistent with the rest of his approach. A patient may often be unable to kill himself when he has reached the last and terrible stage of the disease. To be certain of committing suicide, he must act in advance; and he must not take advice, because then he might be prevented. So this suggestion multiplies the risks of false diagnosis on which the author lays such stress. Besides, has he not considered what a messy affair the ordinary suicide is, and what a shock it is for the relatives to find the body? The advantage that the author sees in suicide is that it is not "an approach aided and sanctioned by the state." This is another example of his ambivalence, his failure to make up his mind on the moral issue. But it is also a mistake, for under my legislative proposal the state would not aid and sanction euthanasia. It would merely remove the threat of punishment from euthanasia, which is an altogether different thing. My proposal is, in fact, an example of that same *laissez-faire* approach which the author himself adopts when he contemplates suicide as a solution.

The last part of the Article is devoted to the ancient "wedge" argument which I have already examined in my book. It is the trump card of the traditionalist, because no proposal for reform, however strong the arguments in favour, is immune from the wedge objection. In fact, the stronger the arguments in favour of a reform, the more likely it is that the traditionalist will take the wedge objection — it is then the only one he has. C. M. Cornford put the argument in its proper place when he said that the wedge objection means this, that you should not act justly today, for fear that you may be asked to act still more justly tomorrow.

We heard a great deal of this type of argument in England in the nineteenth century, when it was used to resist almost every social

---

10. Kamisar, *Some Non-Religious Views Against Proposed "Mercy-Killing" Legislation*, 42 MINN. L. REV. 969, 1011 (1958).

and economic change. In the present century we have had less of it, but (if I may claim the hospitality of these columns to say so) it seems still to be accorded an exaggerated importance in American thought. When lecturing on the law of torts in an American university a few years ago, I suggested that just as compulsory liability insurance for automobiles had spread practically through the civilised world, so we should in time see the law of tort superseded in this field by a system of state insurance for traffic accidents, administered independently of proof of fault. The suggestion was immediately met by one student with a horrified reference to "creeping socialism." That is the standard objection made by many people to any proposal for a new department of state activity. The implication is that you must resist every proposal, however admirable in itself, because otherwise you will never be able to draw the line. On the particular question of socialism, the fear is belied by the experience of a number of countries which have extended state control of the economy without going the whole way to socialistic state regimentation.

Kamisar's particular bogey, the racial laws of Nazi Germany, is an effective one in the democratic countries. Any reference to the Nazis is a powerful weapon to prevent change in the traditional taboo on sterilization as well as euthanasia. The case of sterilization is particularly interesting on this; I dealt with it at length in my book, though Kamisar does not mention its bearing on the argument. When proposals are made for promoting voluntary sterilization on eugenic and other grounds, they are immediately condemned by most people as the thin end of a wedge leading to involuntary sterilization; and then they point to the practices of the Nazis. Yet a more persuasive argument pointing in the other direction can easily be found. Several American states have sterilization laws, which for the most part were originally drafted in very wide terms, to cover desexualisation as well as sterilization, and authorizing involuntary as well as voluntary operations. This legislation goes back long before the Nazis; the earliest statute was in Indiana in 1907. What has been its practical effect? In several states it has hardly been used. A few have used it, but in practice they have progressively restricted it until now it is virtually confined to voluntary sterilization. This is so, at least, in North Carolina, as Mrs. Woodside's study strikingly shows. In my book I summed up the position as follows:

> The American experience is of great interest because it shows how remote from reality in a democratic community is the fear — frequently voiced by Americans themselves — that voluntary sterilization may be the 'thin end of the wedge,' leading to a large-scale violation of human rights as happened in Nazi Germany. In fact, the American experience is the precise

opposite — starting with compulsory sterilization, administrative practice has come to put the operation on a voluntary footing.

But it is insufficient to answer the "wedge" objection in general terms; we must consider the particular fears to which it gives rise. Kamisar professes to fear certain other measures that the Euthanasia societies may bring up if their present measure is conceded to them. Surely, these other measures, if any, will be debated on their merits? Does he seriously fear that anyone in the United States is going to propose the extermination of people of a minority race or religion? Let us put aside such ridiculous fancies and discuss prac tical politics.

The author is quite right in thinking that a body of opinion would favour the legalization of the involuntary euthanasia of hopelessly defective infants, and some day a proposal of this kind may be put forward. The proposal would have distinct limits, just as the proposal for voluntary euthanasia of incurable sufferers has limits. I do not think that any responsible body of opinion would now propose the euthanasia of insane adults, for the perfectly clear reason that any such practice would greatly increase the sense of insecurity felt by the borderline insane and by the large number of insane persons who have sufficient understanding on this particular matter.

Kamisar expresses distress at a concluding remark in my book in which I advert to the possibility of old people becoming an overwhelming burden on mankind. I share his feeling that there are profoundly disturbing possibilities here; and if I had been merely a propagandist, intent upon securing agreement for a specific measure of law reform, I should have done wisely to have omitted all reference to this subject. Since, however, I am merely an academic writer, trying to bring such intelligence as I have to bear on moral and social issues, I deemed the topic too important and threatening to leave without a word. I think I have made it clear, in the passages cited, that I am not for one moment proposing any euthanasia of the aged in present society; such an idea would shock me as much as it shocks Kamisar and would shock everybody else. Still, the fact that we may one day have to face is that medical science is more successful in preserving the body than in preserving the mind. It is not impossible that, in the foreseeable future, medical men will be able to preserve the mindless body until the age, say, of 1000, while the mind itself will have lasted only a tenth of that time. What will mankind do then? It is hardly possible to imagine that we shall establish huge hospital-mausolea where the aged are kept in a kind of living death. Even if it is desired to do this, the cost of the undertaking may make it impossible.

This is not an immediately practical problem, and we need not yet face it. The problem of maintaining persons afflicted with senile dementia is well within our economic resources as the matter stands at present. Perhaps some barrier will be found to medical advance which will prevent the problem becoming more acute. Perhaps, as time goes on, and as the alternatives become more clearly realised, men will become more resigned to human control over the mode of termination of life. Or the solution may be that after the individual has reached a certain age, or a certain degree of decay, medical science will hold its hand, and allow him to be carried off by natural causes.[11] But what if these natural causes are themselves painful? Would it not be better kindness to substitute human agency?

In general, it is enough to say that we do not have to know the solutions to these problems. The only doubtful moral question on which we have to make an immediate decision in relation to involuntary euthanasia is whether we owe a moral duty to terminate the life of an insane person who is suffering from a painful and incurable disease. Such a person is left unprovided for under the legislative proposal formulated in my book. The objection to any system of involuntary euthanasia of the insane is that it may cause a sense of insecurity. It is because I think that the risk of this fear is a serious one that a proposal for the reform of the law must leave the insane out.

---

11. An interesting pronouncement, on which there would probably be a wide measure of agreement, was made recently by Pope Pius XII before an international audience of physicians. The Pope said that reanimation techniques were moral, but made it clear that when life was ebbing hopelessly, physicians might abandon further efforts to stave off death, or relatives might ask them to desist "in order to permit the patient, already virtually dead, to pass on in peace." On the time of death, the Pope said that "Considerations of a general nature permit the belief that human life continues as long as the vital functions — as distinct from the simple life of organs — manifest themselves spontaneously or even with the help of artificial proceedings." By implication, this asserts that a person may be regarded as dead when all that is left is "the simple life of organs." The Pope cited the tenet of Roman Catholic doctrine that death occurs at the moment of "complete and definitive separation of body and soul." In practice, he added, the terms "body" and "separation" lack precision. He explained that establishing the exact instant of death in controversial cases was the task not of the Church but of the physician. N. Y. Times, November 25, 1957, p. 1, col. 3.

In The

SUPREME COURT OF NEW JERSEY

September Term, 1975

Docket No. A-116

IN THE MATTER OF KAREN QUINLAN, AN ALLEGED INCOMPETENT

ON CERTIFICATION TO THE SUPERIOR COURT, CHANCERY DIVISION, WHOSE OPINION IS REPORTED AT 137 *N.J. Super.* 227 (1975).

OPINION
Argued January 26, 1976 — Decided March 31, 1976

MR. PAUL W. ARMSTRONG and MR. JAMES M. CROWLEY, a member of the New York Bar, argued the cause for appellant Joseph T. Quinlan (*Mr. Paul W. Armstrong, attorney*).

MR. DANIEL M. COBURN argued the cause for respondent Guardian adLitem Thomas R. Curtin.

MR. WILLIAM F. HYLAND, Attorney General of New Jersey, argued the cause for respondent State of New Jersey (*Mr. Hyland, attorney; Mr. David S. Baime* and *Mr. John DeCicco,* Deputy Attorneys General, of counsel; *Mr. Baime, Mr. DeCicco, Ms. Jane E. Deaterly, Mr. Daniel Louis Grossman,* and *Mr. Robert E. Rochford,* Deputy Attorneys General, on the brief).

MR. DONALD G. COLLESTER, JR., Morris County Prosecutor, argued the cause for respondent County of Morris. [1]

MR. RALPH PORZIO argued the cause for respondents Arshad Javed and Robert J. Morse (*Messrs. Porzio, Bromberg* and *Newman,* attorneys; *Mr. Porzio* and *Mr. E. Neal Zimmerman,* on the brief).

MR. THEODORE E.B. EINHORN argued the cause for respondent Saint Clare's Hospital.

MR. EDWARD J. LEADEM filed a brief on behalf of *Amicus Curiae* New Jersey Catholic Conference.

— The opinion of the Court was delivered by HUGHES, C.J. —

THE LITIGATION

The central figure in this tragic case is Karen Ann Quinlan, a New Jersey resident. At the age of 22, she lies in a debilitated and allegedly moribund state at Saint Clare's Hospital in Denville, New Jersey. The litigation has to do, in final analysis, with her life,—its continuance or cessation,—and the responsibilities, rights and duties, with regard to any fateful decision concerning it, of her family, her guardian, her doctors, the hospital, the State through its law enforcement authorities, and finally the courts of justice.   [2]

The issues are before this Court following its direct certification of the action under the rule, R.2:12-1, prior to hearing in the Superior Court, Appellate Division, to which the appellant (hereafter "plaintiff") Joseph Quinlan, Karen's father, had appealed the adverse judgment of the Chancery Division.

Due to extensive physical damage fully described in the able opinion of the trial judge, Judge Muir, supporting that judgment, Karen allegedly was incompetent. Joseph Quinlan sought the adjudication of that incompetency. He wished to be appointed guardian of the person and property of his daughter. It was proposed by him that such letters of guardianship, if granted, should contain an express power to him as guardian to authorize the discontinuance of all extraordinary medical procedures now allegedly sustaining Karen's vital processes and hence her life, since these measures, he asserted, present no hope of her eventual recovery. A guardian *ad litem* was appointed by Judge Muir to represent the interest of the alleged incompetent.

By a supplemental complaint, in view of the extraordinary nature of the relief sought by plaintiff and the involvement therein of their several rights and responsibilities, other parties were added. These included the treating physicians and the hospital, the relief sought being that they be restrained from interfering with the carrying out of any such extraordin-   [3] ary authorization in the event it were to be granted by the court. Joined, as well, was the Prosecutor of Morris County (he being charged with responsibility for enforcement of the criminal law), to enjoin him from interfering with, or projecting a criminal prosecution which otherwise might ensue in the event of cessation of life in Karen resulting from the exercise of such extraordinary authorization were it to be granted to the guardian.

The Attorney General of New Jersey intervened as of right pursuant to *R*.4:33-1 on behalf of the State of New Jersey, such intervention being recognized by the court in the pretrial conference order (*R*.4:25-1 *et seq.*) of September 22, 1975. Its basis, of course, was the interest of the State in the preservation of life, which has an undoubted constitutional foundation.[1]   [4]

The matter is of transcendent importance, involving questions related to the definition and existence of death, the prolongation of life through artificial means developed by medical technology undreamed of in past generations of the practice of the healing arts;[2] the impact of such durationally indeterminate and artificial life prolongation on the rights   [5] of the incompetent, her family and society in general; the bearing of constitutional right and the scope of judicial responsibility, as to the appropriate response of an equity court of justice to the extraordinary prayer for relief of the plaintiff. Involved as well is the right of the plaintiff, Joseph Quinlan, to guardianship of the person of his daughter.

Among his "factual and legal contentions" under such Pretrial Order was the following:

> I. Legal and Medical Death
>
> (a) Under the existing legal and medical definitions of death recognized by the State of New Jersey, Karen Ann Quinlan is dead.

This contention, made in the context of Karen's profound and allegedly irreversible coma and physical debility, was discarded during trial by the following stipulated amendment to the Pretrial Order:

> Under any legal standard recognized by the State of New Jersey and also under standard medical practice, Karen Ann Quinlan is presently alive.

Other amendments to the Pretrial Order made at the time of trial expanded the issues before the court. The Prosecutor of Morris County sought a declaratory judgment as to the effect any affirmation by the   [6] court of a right in a guardian to terminate life-sustaining procedures would have with regard to enforcement of the criminal laws of New Jersey with reference to homicide. Saint Clare's Hospital, in the face of trial testimony on the subject of "brain death," sought declaratory judgment as to:

> Whether the use of the criteria developed and enun-
> ciated by the Ad Hoc Committee of the Harvard Medi-
> cal School on or about August 5, 1968, as well as simi-
> lar criteria, by a physician to assist in determination of
> the death of a patient whose cardio-pulmonary func-
> tions are being artificially sustained, is in accordance
> with ordinary and standard medical practice.[3]

It was further stipulated during trial that Karen was indeed incompetent and guardianship was necessary, although there exists a dispute as
to the determination later reached by the court that such guardianship
should be bifurcated, and that Mr. Quinlan should be appointed as
guardian of the trivial property but not the person of his daughter.

After certification the Attorney General filed as of right (R.2:3-4) a
cross-appeal challenging the action of the trial court in admitting evidence of prior statements made by Karen while competent as to her dis-   [7]
taste for continuance of life by extraordinary medical procedures, under
circumstances not unlike those of the present case. These quoted statements were made in the context of several conversations with regard to
others terminally ill and being subjected to like herioc measures. The
statements were advanced as evidence of what she would want done in
such a contingency as now exists. She was said to have firmly evinced her
wish, in like circumstances, not to have her life prolonged by the otherwise futile use of extraordinary means. Because we agree with the conception of the trial court that such statements, since they were remote
and impersonal, lacked significant probative weight, it is not of consequence to our opinion that we decide whether or not they were admissible
hearsay. Again, after certification, the guardian of the person of the incompetent (who had been appointed as a part of the judgment appealed
from) resigned and was succeeded by another, but that too seems irrelevant to the decision. It is, however, of interest to note the trial court's
delineation (in its supplemental opinion of November 12, 1975) of the extent of the personal guardian's authority with respect to medical care of
his ward: [8]

> Mr. Coburn's appointment is designed to deal with
> those instances wherein Dr. Morse[4], in the process of
> administering care and treatment to Karen Quinlan,
> feels there should be concurrence on the extent or na-
> ture of the care or treatment. If Mr. and Mrs. Quin-
> lan are unable to give concurrence, then Mr. Coburn
> will be consulted for his concurrence.

Essentially then, appealing to the power of equity, and relying on claimed constitutional rights of free exercise of religion, of privacy and of protection against cruel and unusual punishment, Karen Quinlan's father sought judicial authority to withdraw the life-sustaining mechanisms temporarily preserving his daughter's life, and his appointment as guardian of her person to that end. His request was opposed by her doctors, the hospital, the Morris County Prosecutor, the State of New Jersey, and her guardian *ad litem.*

THE FACTUAL BASE

An understanding of the issues in their basic perspective suggests a brief review of the factual base developed in the testimony and documented in greater detail in the opinion of the trial judge. *In re Quinlan,* 137 *N.J. Super.* 227 (Ch. Div. 1975).   [9]

On the night of April 15, 1975, for reasons still unclear, Karen Quinlan ceased breathing for at least two 15 minute periods. She received some ineffectual mouth-to-mouth resuscitation from friends. She was taken by ambulance to Newton Memorial Hospital. There she had a temperature of 100 degrees, her pupils were unreactive and she was unresponsive even to deep pain. The history at the time of her admission to that hospital was essentially incomplete and uninformative.

Three days later, Dr. Morse examined Karen at the request of the Newton admitting physician, Dr. McGee. He found her comatose with evidence of decortication, a condition relating to derangement of the cortex of the brain causing a physical posture in which the upper extremities are flexed and the lower extremities are extended. She required a respirator to assist her breathing. Dr. Morse was unable to obtain an adequate account of the circumstances and events leading up to Karen's admission to the Newton Hospital. Such initial history or etiology is crucial in neurological diagnosis. Relying as he did upon the Newton Memorial records and his own examination, he concluded that prolonged lack of oxygen in   [10] the bloodstream, anoxia, was identified with her condition as he saw it upon first observation. When she was later transferred to Saint Clare's Hospital she was still unconscious, still on a respirator and a tracheotomy had been performed. On her arrival Dr. Morse conducted extensive and detailed examinations. An electroencephalogram (EEG) measuring electrical rhythm of the brain was performed and Dr. Morse characterized the result as "abnormal but it showed some activity and was consistent with her clinical state." Other significant neurological tests, including a brain scan, an angiogram, and a lumbar puncture were normal in result. Dr. Morse testified that Karen has been in a state of coma, lack of consciousness, since he began treating her. He explained that there are basically two types of coma, sleep-like unresponsiveness and awake unresponsiveness. Karen was originally in a sleep-like unresponsive condition but soon developed "sleep-wake" cycles, apparently a normal improvement for comatose patients occurring within three to four weeks. In the awake cycle she blinks, cries out and does things of that sort but is still totally unaware of anyone or anything around her.

Dr. Morse and other expert physicians who examined her characterized Karen as being in a "chronic persistent vegetative state." Dr. Fred Plum, one of such expert witnesses, defined this as a "subject who [11] remains with the capacity to maintain the vegetative parts of neurological function but who *** no longer has any cognitive function."

Dr. Morse, as well as the several other medical and neurological experts who testified in this case, believed with certainty that Karen Quinlan is not "brain dead." They identified the Ad Hoc Committee of Harvard Medical School report (*infra*) as the ordinary medical standard for determining brain death, and all of them were satisfied that Karen met none of the criteria specified in that report and was therefore not "brain dead" within its contemplation.

In this respect it was indicated by Dr. Plum that the brain works in essentially two ways, the vegetative and the sapient. He testified:

> We have an internal vegetative regulation which controls body temperature which controls breathing, which controls to a considerable degree blood pressure, which controls to some degree heart rate, which controls chewing, swallowing and which controls sleeping and waking. We have a more highly developed brain which is uniquely human which controls our relation to the outside world, our capacity to talk, to see, to feel, to sing, to think. Brain death necessarily must mean the death of both of these functions of the brain, vegetative and the sapient. Therefore, the presence of any function which is regulated or governed or controlled by the deeper parts of the brain which in laymen's terms might be considered purely vegetative would mean that the brain is not biologically dead. [12]

Because Karen's neurological condition affects her respiratory ability (the respiratory system being a brain stem function) she requires a respirator to assist her breathing. From the time of her admission to Saint Clare's Hospital Karen has been assisted by an MA-1 respirator, a sophisticated machine which delivers a given volume of air at a certain rate and periodically provides a "sigh" volume, a relatively large measured volume of air designed to purge the lungs of excretions. Attempts to "wean" her from the respirator were unsuccessful and have been abandoned.

The experts believe that Karen cannot now survive without the assistance of the respirator; that exactly how long she would live without it is unknown; that the strong likelihood is that death would follow soon after its removal, and that removal would also risk further brain damage and would curtail the assistance the respirator presently provides in warding off infection.

It seemed to be the consensus not only of the treating physicians but also of the several qualified experts who testified in the case, that removal from the respirator would not conform to medical practices, standards and traditions.   [13]

The further medical consensus was that Karen in addition to being comatose is in a chronic and persistent "vegetative" state, having no awareness of anything or anyone around her and existing at a primitive reflex level. Although she does have some brain stem function (ineffective for respiration) and has other reactions one normally associates with being alive, such as moving, reacting to light, sound and noxious stimuli, blinking her eyes, and the like, the quality of her feeling impulses is unknown. She grimaces, makes stereotyped cries and sounds and has chewing motions. Her blood pressure is normal.

Karen remains in the intensive care unit at Saint Clare's Hospital, receiving 24-hour care by a team of four nurses characterized, as was the medical attention, as "excellent." She is nourished by feeding by way of a nasal-gastro tube and is routinely examined for infection, which under these circumstances is a serious life threat. The result is that her condition is considered remarkable under the unhappy circumstances involved.

Karen is described as emaciated, having suffered a weight loss of at least 40 pounds, and undergoing a continuing deteriorative process. Her posture is described as fetal-like and grotesque; there is extreme flexion-rigidity of the arms, legs and related muscles and her joints are severely [14] rigid and deformed.

From all of this evidence, and including the whole testimonial record, several basic findings in the physical area are mandated. Severe brain and associated damage, albeit of uncertain etiology, has left Karen in a chronic and persistent vegetative state. No form of treatment which can cure or improve that condition is known or available. As nearly as may be determined, considering the guarded area of remote uncertainties characteristic of most medical science predictions, she can *never* be restored to cognitive or sapient life. Even with regard to the vegetative level and improvement therein (if such it may be called) the prognosis is extremely poor and the extent unknown if it should in fact occur.

She is debilitated and moribund and although fairly stable at the time of argument before us (no new information having been filed in the meanwhile in expansion of the record), no physician risked the opinion that she could live more than a year and indeed she may die much earlier. Excellent medical and nursing care so far has been able to ward off the constant threat of infection, to which she is peculiarly susceptible because of the respirator, the tracheal tube and other incidents of care in her vulnerable condition. Her life accordingly is sustained by the respira-   [15] tor and tubal feeding, and removal from the respirator would cause her death soon, although the time cannot be stated with more precision.

The determination of the fact and time of death in past years of medical science was keyed to the action of the heart and blood circulation, in turn dependent upon pulmonary activity, and hence cessation of these functions spelled out the reality of death.[5]

Developments in medical technology have obfuscated the use of the traditional definition of death. Efforts have been made to define irreversible coma as a new criterion for death, such as by the 1968 report of the Ad Hoc Committee of the Harvard Medical School (the Committee comprising ten physicians, an historian, a lawyer and a theologian), which asserted that:

> From ancient times down to the recent past it was clear that, when the respiration and heart stopped, the brain would die in a few minutes; so the obvious criterion of no heart beat as synonymous with death was sufficiently accurate. In those times the heart was considered to be the central organ of the body; it is not surprising that its failure marked the onset of death. This is no longer valid when modern resuscitative and supportive measures are used. These improved activities can now restore "life" as judged by the ancient standards of persistent respiration and continuing heart beat. This can be the case even when there is not the remotest possibility of an individual recovering consciousness following massive brain damage. ["A Definition of Irreversible Coma," 205 *J.A.M.A.* 337, 339 (1968)].

[16]

The Ad Hoc standards, carefully delineated, included absence of response to pain or other stimuli, pupilary reflexes, corneal, pharyngeal and other reflexes, blood pressure, spontaneous respiration, as well as "flat" or isoelectric electroencephalograms and the like, with all tests repeated "at least 24 hours later with no change." In such circumstances, where all of such criteria have been met as showing "brain death," the Committee recommends with regard to the respirator:

> The patient's condition can be determined only by a physician. When the patient is hopelessly damaged as defined above, the family and all colleagues who have participated in major decisions concerning the patient, and all nurses involved, should be so informed. Death is to be declared and *then* the respirator turned off. The decision to do this and the responsibility for it are to be taken by the physician-in-charge, in consultation with one or more physicians who have been directly involved in the case. It is unsound and undesirable to force the family to make the decision. [205 *J.A.M.A.*, *supra* at 338 (emphasis in original)].   [17]

But, as indicated, it was the consensus of medical testimony in the instant case that Karen, for all her disability, met none of these criteria, nor indeed any comparable criteria extant in the medical world and representing, as does the Ad Hoc Committee report, according to the testimony in this case, prevailing and accepted medical standards.

We have adverted to the "brain death" concept and Karen's disassociation with any of its criteria, to emphasize the basis of the medical decision made by Dr. Morse. When plaintiff and his family, finally reconciled to the certainty of Karen's impending death, requested the withdrawal of life support mechanisms, he demurred. His refusal was based upon his conception of medical standards, practice and ethics described in the medical testimony, such as in the evidence given by another neurologist, Dr. Sidney Diamond, a witness for the State. Dr. Diamond asserted that no physician would have failed to provide respirator support at the outset, and none would interrupt its life-saving course thereafter, except in the case of cerebral death. In the latter case, he thought the respirator would in effect be disconnected from one already dead, entitling the physician under medical standards and, he thought, legal concepts, to terminate the supportive measures. We note Dr. Diamond's distinction of major surgical or transfusion procedures in a terminal case not involv-   [18]
ing cerebral death, such as here:

> The subject has lost human qualities. It would be incredible, and I think unlikely, that any physician would respond to a sudden hemorrhage, massive hemorrhage, or a loss of all her defensive blood cells, by giving her large quantities of blood. I think that ***

major surgical procedures would be out of the question even if they were known to be essential for continued physical existence.

This distinction is adverted to also in the testimony of Dr. Julius Korein, a neurologist called by plaintiff. Dr. Korein described a medical practice concept of "judicious neglect" under which the physician will say:

> Don't treat this patient anymore, *** it does not serve either the patient, the family, or society in any meaningful way to continue treatment with this patient.

Dr. Korein also told of the unwritten and unspoken standard of medical practice implied in the foreboding initials DNR (do not resuscitate), as applied to the extraordinary terminal case:

> Cancer, metastatic cancer, involving the lungs, the liver, the brain, multiple involvements, the physician may or may not write: Do not resuscitate. *** [I]t could be said to the nurse: if this man stops breathing don't resuscitate him. *** No physician that I know personally is going to try and resuscitate a man riddled with cancer and in agony and he stops breathing. They are not going to put him on a respirator. *** I think that would be the height of misuse of technology.   [19]

While the thread of logic in such distinctions may be elusive to the non-medical lay mind, in relation to the supposed imperative to sustain life at all costs, they nevertheless relate to medical decisions, such as the decision of Dr. Morse in the present case. We agree with the trial court that that decision was in accord with Dr. Morse's conception of medical standards and practice.

We turn to that branch of the factual case pertaining to the application for guardianship, as distinguished from the nature of the authorization sought by the applicant. The character and general suitability of Joseph Quinlan as guardian for his daughter, in ordinary circumstances, could not be doubted. The record bespeaks the high degree of familial love which pervaded the home of Joseph Quinlan and reached out fully to embrace Karen, although she was living elsewhere at the time of her collapse. The proofs showed him to be deeply religious, imbued with a morality so sensitive that months of tortured indecision preceded his belated conclusion (despite earlier moral judgments reached by the other family members, but unexpressed to him in order not to influence him) to seek the termination of life-supportive measures sustaining Karen. A   [20]
communicant of the Roman Catholic Church, as were other family

members, he first sought solace in private prayer looking with confidence, as he says, to the Creator, first for the recovery of Karen and then, if that were not possible, for guidance with respect to the awesome decision confronting him.

To confirm the moral rightness of the decision he was about to make he consulted with his parish priest and later with the Catholic chaplain of Saint Clare's Hospital. He would not, he testified, have sought termination if that act were to be morally wrong or in conflict with the tenets of the religion he so profoundly respects. He was disabused of doubt, however, when the position of the Roman Catholic Church was made known to him as it is reflected in the record in this case. While it is not usual for matters of religious dogma or concepts to enter a civil litigation (except as they may bear upon constitutional rights, or sometimes, familial matters; cf. In re Adoption of E, 59 N.J. 36 (1971)), they were rightly admitted in evidence here. The judge was bound to measure the character and motivations in all respects of Joseph Quinlan as prospective guardian; and insofar as these religious matters bore upon them, they were properly scrutinized and considered by the court.

Thus germane, we note the position of that Church as illuminated by the record before us. We have no reason to believe that it would be at all [21] discordant with the whole of Judeo-Christian tradition, considering its central respect and reverence for the sanctity of human life. It was in this sense of relevance that we admitted as *amicus curiae* the New Jersey Catholic Conference, essentially the spokesman for the various Catholic bishops of New Jersey, organized to give witness to spiritual values in public affairs in the statewide community. The position statement of Bishop Lawrence B. Casey, reproduced in the *amicus* brief, projects these views:

(a)   The verification of the fact of death in a particular case cannot be deduced from any religious or moral principle and, under this aspect, does not fall within the competence of the church;—that dependence must be had upon traditional and medical standards, and by these standards Karen Ann Quinlan is assumed to be alive.

(b)   The request of plaintiff for authority to terminate a medical procedure characterized as "an extraordinary means of treatment" would not involve euthanasia. This upon the reasoning expressed by Pope Pius XII in his *allocutio* (address) to anesthesiologists on Novem- [22] ber 24, 1957, when he dealt with the question:

> Does the anesthesiologist have the right, or is he
> bound, in all cases of deep unconsciousness, even in
> those that are completely hopeless in the opinion of

the competent doctor, to use modern artificial respiration apparatus, even against the will of the family?

His answer made the following points:

1. In ordinary cases the doctor has the right to act in this manner, but is not bound to do so unless this is the only way of fulfilling another certain moral duty.

2. The doctor, however, has no right independent of the patient. He can act only if the patient explicitly or implicitly, directly or indirectly, gives him the permission.

3. The treatment as described in the question constitutes extraordinary means of preserving life and so there is no obligation to use them nor to give the doctor permission to use them.

4. The rights and the duties of the family depend on the presumed will of the unconscious patient if he or she is of legal age, and the family, too, is bound to use only ordinary means.

5. This case is not to be considered euthanasia in any way; that would never be licit. The interruption of attempts at resuscitation, even when it causes the arrest of circulation, is not more than an indirect cause of the cessation of life, and we must apply in this case the principle of double effect.   [23]

So it was that the Bishop Casey statement validated the decision of Joseph Quinlan:

Competent medical testimony has established that Karen Ann Quinlan has no reasonable hope of recovery from her comatose state by the use of any available medical procedures. The continuance of mechanical (cardiorespiratory) supportive measures to sustain continuance of her body functions and her life constitute extraordinary means of treatment. *Therefore, the decision of Joseph *** Quinlan to request the discontinuance of this treatment is, according to the teachings of the Catholic Church, a morally correct decision.* (Emphasis in original.)

And the mind and purpose of the intending guardian were undoubtedly influenced by factors included in the following reference to the interrelationship of the three disciplines of theology, law and medicine as exposed in the Casey statement:

> The right to a natural death is one outstanding area in which the disciplines of theology, medicine and law overlap; or, to put it another way, it is an area in which these three disciplines convene.

> Medicine with its combination of advanced technology and professional ethics is both able and inclined to prolong biological life. Law with its felt obligation to protect life and freedom of the individual seeks to assure each person's right to live out his human life until its natural and inevitable conclusion. Theology with its acknowledgment of man's dissatisfaction with biological life as the ultimate source of joy *** defends the sacredness of human life and defends it from all direct attacks.   [24]

> These disciplines do not conflict with one another, but are necessarily conjoined in the application of their principles in a particular instance such as that of Karen Ann Quinlan. Each must in some way acknowledge the other without denying its own competence. The civil law is not expected to assert a belief in eternal life; nor, on the other hand, is it expected to ignore the right of the individual to profess it, and to form and pursue his conscience in accord with that belief. Medical science is not authorized to directly cause natural death; nor, however, is it expected to prevent it when it is inevitable and all hope of a return to an even partial exercise of human life is irreparably lost. Religion is not expected to define biological death; nor, on its part, is it expected to relinquish its responsibility to assist man in the formation and pursuit of a correct conscience as to the acceptance of natural death when science has confirmed its inevitability beyond any hope other than that of preserving biological life in a merely vegetative state.

And the gap in the law is aptly described in the Bishop Casey statement:

> In the present public discussion of the case of Karen Ann Quinlan it has been brought out that responsible people involved in medical care, patients and families have exercised the freedom to terminate or withhold certain treatments as extraordinary means in cases judged to be terminal, i.e., cases which hold no realistic hope for some recovery, in accord with the expressed or implied intentions of the patients themselves. To   [25]

whatever extent this has been happening it has been
without sanction in civil law. Those involved in such
actions, however, have ethical and theological literature to guide them in their judgments and actions.
Furthermore, such actions have not in themselves
undermined society's reverence for the lives of sick and
dying people.

It is both possible and necessary for society to have
laws and ethical standards which provide freedom for
decisions, in accord with the expressed or implied intentions of the patient, to terminate or withhold extraordinary treatment in cases which are judged to be
hopeless by competent medical authorities, without at
the same time leaving an opening for euthanasia. Indeed, to accomplish this, it may simply be required that
courts and legislative bodies recognize the present standards and practices of many people engaged in medical
care who have been doing what the parents of Karen
Ann Quinlan are requesting authorization to have done
for their beloved daughter.

Before turning to the legal and constitutional issues involved, we feel
it essential to reiterate that the "Catholic view" of religious neutrality in
the circumstances of this case is considered by the Court only in the aspect of its impact upon the conscience, motivation, and purpose of the
intending guardian, Joseph Quinlan, and not as a precedent in terms of
the civil law.

If Joseph Quinlan, for instance, were a follower and strongly influenced by the teachings of Buddha, or if, as an agnostic or atheist, his
moral judgments were formed without reference to religious feelings, but
were nevertheless formed and viable, we would with equal attention and [26]
high respect consider these elements, as bearing upon his character,
motivations and purposes as relevant to this qualification and suitability
as guardian.

It is from this factual base that the Court confronts and responds to
three basic issues:

1. Was the trial court correct in denying the specific relief requested
by plaintiff, *i.e.*, authorization for termination of the life-supporting apparatus, on the case presented to him? Our determination on
that question is in the affirmative.

2. Was the court correct in withholding letters of guardianship from
the plaintiff and appointing in his stead a stranger? On that issue our
determination is in the negative.

3. Should this Court, in the light of the foregoing conclusions, grant declaratory relief to the plaintiff? On that question our Court's determination is in the affirmative.

This brings us to a consideration of the constitutional and legal issues underlying the foregoing determinations.   [27]

CONSTITUTIONAL AND LEGAL ISSUES

At the outset we note the dual role in which plaintiff comes before the Court. He not only raises, derivatively, what he perceives to be the constitutional and legal rights of his daughter, Karen, but he also claims certain rights independently as parent.

Although generally a litigant may assert only his own constitutional rights, we have no doubt that plaintiff has sufficient standing to advance both positions.

While no express constitutional language limits judicial activity to cases and controversies, New Jersey courts will not render advisory opinions or entertain proceedings by plaintiffs who do not have sufficient legal standing to maintain their actions. *Walker* v. *Stanhope*, 23 *N.J.* 657, 660 (1957). However, as in this case, New Jersey courts commonly grant declaratory relief. Declaratory Judgments Act, *N.J.S.A.* 2A:16-50 *et seq.* And our courts hold that where the plaintiff is not simply an interloper and the proceeding serves the public interest, standing will be found. *Walker* v. *Stanhope, supra,* 23 *N.J.* at 661-66; *Koons* v. *Atlantic City Bd. of Comm'rs*, 135 *N.J.L.* 329, 338-39 (Sup. Ct. 1946), *aff'd*, 135 *N.J.L.* 204 (E. & A. 1947). In *Crescent Park Tenants Ass'n* v. *Realty Equities Corp.*, 58 *N.J.* 98 (1971), Justice Jacobs said: [28]

> *** [W]e have appropriately confined litigation to those situations where the litigants concerned with the subject matter evidenced a sufficient stake and real adverseness. In the overall we have given due weight to the interests of individual justice, along with the public interest, always bearing in mind that throughout our law we have been sweepingly rejecting procedural frustrations in favor of 'just and expeditious determinations on the ultimate merits.' [58 *N.J.* at 107-08 (quoting from *Tumarkin* v. *Friedman*, 17 *N.J. Super.* 20, 21 (App. Div. 1951), *certif. den.*, 9 *N.J.* 287 (1952))].

The father of Karen Quinlan is certainly no stranger to the present controversy. His interests are real and adverse and he raises questions of surpassing importance. Manifestly, he has standing to assert his daughter's constitutional rights, she being incompetent to do so.

I.

The Free Exercise of Religion

We think the contention as to interference with religious beliefs or rights may be considered and dealt with without extended discussion, given the acceptance of distinctions so clear and simple in their precedential definition as to be dispositive on their face. [29]

Simply stated, the right to religious beliefs is absolute but conduct in pursuance thereof is not wholly immune from governmental restraint. *John F. Kennedy Memorial Hosp.* v. *Heston*, 58 *N.J.* 576, 580 81 (1971). So it is that, for the sake of life, courts sometimes (but not always) order blood transfusions for Jehovah's Witnesses (whose religious beliefs abhor such procedure), *Application of President & Directors of Georgetown College, Inc.* 331 *F.*2d 1000 (D.C. Cir.), *cert. den.*, 377 *U.S.* 978, 84 *S.Ct.* 1883, 12 *L.Ed.* 2d 746 (1964); *United States* v. *George*, 239 *F. Supp.* 752 (D. Conn. 1965); *John F. Kennedy Memorial Hosp.* v. *Heston, supra*; *Powell* v. *Columbia Presbyterian Medical Center*, 49 *Misc.* 2d 215, 267 *N.Y.S.* 2d 450 (Sup. Ct. 1965); *but see In re Osborne*, 294 *A.*2d 372 (D.C. Ct. App. 1972); *In re Estate of Brooks*, 32 *Ill.* 2d 361, 205 *N.E.* 2d 435 (Sup. Ct. 1965); *Erickson* v. *Dilgard*, 44 *Misc.* 2d 27, 252 *N.Y.S.* 2d 705 (Sup. Ct. 1962); *see generally* Annot., "Power Of Courts Or Other Public Agencies, In The Absence Of Statutory Authority, To Order Compulsory Medical Care for Adult," 9 *A.L.R.* 3d 1391 (1966); forbid exposure to death from handling virulent snakes or ingesting poison (interfering with deeply held religious sentiments in such regard), *e.g., Hill* v. *State*, 38 *Ala. App.* 404, 88 *So.* 2d 880 (Ct. App.), *cert. den.*, 264 *Ala.* 697, 88 *So.* 2d 887 (Sup. Ct. 1956); *State* v. *Massey*, [30] 229 *N.C.* 734, 51 *S.E.* 2d 179 (Sup. Ct.), appeal dismissed *sub nom., Bunn* v. *North Carolina*, 336 *U.S.* 942, 69 *S.Ct.* 813, 93 *L.Ed.* 1099 (1949); *State ex rel. Swann* v. *Pack*, ____ *Tenn.* ____, 527 *S.W.* 2d 99 (Sup. Ct. 1975), *cert. den.*, ____ *U.S.* ____, ____ *S.Ct.* ____, ____ *L.Ed.* 2d ____ (44 *U.S.L.W.* 3498, No. 95-956, (March 8, 1976)); and protect the public health as in the case of compulsory vaccination (over the strongest of religious objections), *e.g., Wright* v. *DeWitt School Dist. 1*, 238 *Ark.* 906, 385 *S.W.* 2d 644 (Sup. Ct. 1965); *Mountain Lakes Bd. of Educ.* v. *Maas*, 56 *N.J. Super.* 245 (App. Div. 1959), *aff'd* o.b., 31 *N.J.* 537 (1960), *cert. den.*, 363 *U.S.* 843, 80 *S.Ct.* 1613, 4 *L.Ed.* 2d 1727 (1960); *McCartney* v. *Austin*, 57 *Misc.* 2d 525, 293 *N.Y.S.* 2d 188 (Sup.

Ct. 1968). The public interest is thus considered paramount, without essential dissolution of respect for religious beliefs.

We think, without further examples, that, ranged against the State's interest in the preservation of life, the impingement of religious belief, much less religious "neutrality" as here, does not reflect a constitutional question, in the circumstances at least of the case presently before the Court. Moreover, like the trial court, we do not recognize an independent parental right of religious freedom to support the relief requested. 137 *N.J. Super.* at 267-68.   [31]

II.

Cruel and Unusual Punishment

Similarly inapplicable to the case before us is the Constitution's Eighth Amendment protection against cruel and unusual punishment which, as held by the trial court, is not relevant to situations other than the imposition of penal sanctions. Historic in nature, it stemmed from punitive excesses in the infliction of criminal penalties.[6] We find no pre- [32] cedent in law which would justify its extension to the correction of social injustice or hardship, such as, for instance, in the case of poverty. The latter often condemns the poor and deprived to horrendous living conditions which could certainly be described in the abstract as "cruel and unusual punishment." Yet the constitutional base of protection from "cruel and unusual punishment" is plainly irrelevant to such societal ills which must be remedied, if at all, under other concepts of constitutional and civil right.

So it is in the case of the unfortunate Karen Quinlan. Neither the State, nor the law, but the accident of fate and nature, has inflicted upon her conditions which though in essence cruel and most unusual, yet do not amount to "punishment" in any constitutional sense.

Neither the judgment of the court below, nor the medical decision which confronted it, nor the law and equity perceptions which impelled its action, nor the whole factual base upon which it was predicated, inflicted "cruel and unusual punishment" in the constitutional sense.

III.

The Right of Privacy[7]

It is the issue of the constitutional right of privacy that has given us most concern, in the exceptional circumstances of this case. Here a loving [33] parent, *qua* parent and raising the rights of his incompetent and profoundly damaged daughter, probably irreversibly doomed to no more than a biologically vegetative remnant of life, is before the court. He seeks authorization to abandon specialized technological procedures which can only maintain for a time a body having no potential for resumption or continuance of other than a "vegetative" existence.

We have no doubt, in these unhappy circumstances, that if Karen were herself miraculously lucid for an interval (not altering the existing prognosis of the condition to which she would soon return) and perceptive of her irreversible condition, she could effectively decide upon discontinuance of the life-support apparatus, even if it meant the prospect of natural death. To this extent we may distinguish *Heston, supra,* which concerned a severely injured young woman (Delores Heston), whose life depended on surgery and blood transfusion; and who was in such extreme shock that she was unable to express an informed choice (although the Court apparently considered the case as if the patient's own religious decision to resist transfusion were at stake), but most importantly a pa- [34] tient apparently salvable to long life and vibrant health;—a situation not at all like the present case.

We have no hesitancy in deciding, in the instant diametrically opposite case, that no external compelling interest of the State could compel Karen to endure the unendurable, only to vegetate a few measurable months with no realistic possibility of returning to any semblance of cognitive or sapient life. We perceive no thread of logic distinguishing between such a choice on Karen's part and a similar choice which, under the evidence in this case, could be made by a competent patient terminally ill, riddled by cancer and suffering great pain; such a patient would not be resuscitated or put on a respirator in the example described by Dr. Korein, and *a fortiori* would not be kept *against his will* on a respirator.

Although the Constitution does not explicitly mention a right of privacy, Supreme Court decisions have recognized that a right of personal privacy exists and that certain areas of privacy are guaranteed under the Constitution. *Eisenstadt* v. *Baird*, 405 *U.S.* 438, 92 *S.Ct.* 1029, 31 *L.Ed.* 2d 349 (1972); *Stanley* v. *Georgia*, 394 *U.S.* 557, 89 *S.Ct.* 1243, 22 *L.Ed.* 2d 542 (1969). The Court has interdicted judicial intrusion into many [35] aspects of personal decision, sometimes basing this restraint upon the conception of a limitation of judicial interest and responsibility, such as with regard to contraception and its relationship to family life and decision. *Griswold* v. *Connecticut*, 381 *U.S.* 479, 85 *S.Ct.* 1678, 14 *L.Ed.* 2d 510 (1965).

The Court in *Griswold* found the unwritten constitutional right of privacy to exist in the penumbra of specific guarantees of the Bill of

Rights "formed by emanations from those guarantees that help give them life and substance." 381 *U.S.* at 484, 85 *S.Ct.* at 1681, 14 *L.Ed.* 2d at 514. Presumably this right is broad enough to encompass a patient's decision to decline medical treatment under certain circumstances, in much the same way as it is broad enough to encompass a woman's decision to terminate pregnancy under certain conditions. *Roe* v. *Wade*, 410 *U.S.* 113, 153, 93 *S.Ct.* 705, 727, 35 *L.Ed.* 2d 147, 177 (1973).

Nor is such right of privacy forgotten in the New Jersey Constitution. *N.J. Const.* (1947), Art. I, par. 1.

The claimed interests of the State in this case are essentially the preservation and sanctity of human life and defense to the right of the physician to administer medical treatment according to his best judgment. In this case the doctors say that removing Karen from the respirator will conflict with their professional judgment. The plaintiff answers that Karen's present treatment serves only a maintenance function; that the [36] respirator cannot cure or improve her condition but at best can only prolong her inevitable slow deterioration and death; and that the interests of the patient, as seen by her surrogate, the guardian, must be evaluated by the court as predominant, even in the face of an option *contra* by the present attending physicians. Plaintiff's distinction is significant. The nature of Karen's care and the realistic chances of her recovery are quite unlike those of the patients discussed in many of the cases where treatments were ordered. In many of those cases the medical procedure required (usually a transfusion) constituted a minimal bodily invasion and the chances of recovery and return to functioning life were very good. We think that the State's interest *contra* weakens and the individual's right to privacy grows as the degree of bodily invasion increases and the prognosis dims. Ultimately there comes a point at which the individual's rights overcome the State interest. It is for that reason that we believe Karen's choice, if she were competent to make it, would be vindicated by the law. Her prognosis is extremely poor,—she will never resume cognitive life. And the bodily invasion is very great,—she requires 24-hour intensive nursing care, antibiotics, and the assistance of a respirator, a catheter and feeding tube.   [37]

Our affirmance of Karen's independent right of choice, however, would ordinarily be based upon her competency to assert it. The sad truth, however, is that she is grossly incompetent and we cannot discern her supposed choice based on the testimony of her previous conversations with friends, where such testimony is without sufficient probative weight. 137 *N.J. Super.* at 260. Nevertheless we have concluded that Karen's right of privacy may be asserted on her behalf by her guardian under the peculiar circumstances here present.

If a putative decision by Karen to permit this non-cognitive, vegetative existence to terminate by natural forces is regarded as a valuable incident of her right of privacy, as we believe it to be, then it should not be discarded solely on the basis that her condition prevents her conscious exercise of the choice. The only practical way to prevent destruction of the right is to permit the guardian and family of Karen to render their best judgment, subject to the qualifications hereinafter stated, as to whether she would exercise it in these circumstances. If their conclusion is in the affirmative this decision should be accepted by a society the overwhelming majority of whose members would, we think, in similar circumstances, exercise such a choice in the same way for themselves or [38] for those closest to them. It is for this reason that we determine that Karen's right of privacy may be asserted in her behalf, in this respect, by her guardian and family under the particular circumstances presented by this record.

Regarding Mr. Quinlan's right of privacy, we agree with Judge Muir's conclusion that there is no parental constitutional right that would entitle him to a grant of relief *in propria persona. Id.* at 266. Insofar as a parental right of privacy has been recognized, it has been in the context of determining the rearing of infants and, as Judge Muir put it, involved "continuing life styles." *See Wisconsin* v. *Yoder,* 406 *U.S.* 205, 92 *S.Ct.* 1526, 32 *L.Ed.* 2d 15 (1972); *Pierce* v. *Society of Sisters,* 268 *U.S.* 510, 45 *S.Ct.* 571, 69 *L.Ed.* 1070 (1925); *Meyer* v. *Nebraska,* 262 *U.S.* 390, 43 *S.Ct.* 625, 67 *L.Ed.* 1042 (1923). Karen Quinlan is a 22 year old adult. Her right of privacy in respect of the matter before the Court is to be vindicated by Mr. Quinlan as guardian, as hereinabove determined. [39]

IV.

The Medical Factor

Having declared the substantive legal basis upon which plaintiff's rights as representative of Karen must be deemed predicated, we face and respond to the assertion on behalf of defendants that our premise unwarrantably offends prevailing medical standards. We thus turn to consideration of the medical decision supporting the determination made below, conscious of the paucity of pre-existing legislative and judicial guidance as to the rights and liabilities therein involved.

A significant problem in any discussion of sensitive medical-legal issues is the marked, perhaps unconscious, tendency of many to distort what the law is, in pursuit of an exposition of what they would like the law to be. Nowhere is this barrier to the intelligent resolution of legal controversies more obstructive than in the debate over patient rights at the end of life. Judicial refusals to order lifesaving treatment in the face of contrary claims of bodily self-determination or free religious exercise are too often cited in support of a preconceived 'right to die,' even though the patients, wanting to live, have claimed no such right. Conversely, the assertion of a religious or other objection to lifesaving treatment is at times condemned as attempted suicide, even though suicide means something quite different in the law. [Byrn, "Compulsory Lifesaving Treatment For The Competent Adult," 44 *Fordham L. Rev.* 1 (1975)].   [40]

Perhaps the confusion there adverted to stems from mention by some courts of statutory or common law condemnation of suicide as demonstrating the state's interest in the preservation of life. We would see, however, a real distinction between the self-infliction of deadly harm and a self-determination against artificial life support or radical surgery, for instance, in the face of irreversible, painful and certain imminent death. The contrasting situations mentioned are analogous to those continually faced by the medical profession. When does the institution of life-sustaining procedures, ordinarily mandatory, become the subject of medical discretion in the context of administration to persons *in extremis*? And when does the withdrawal of such procedures, from such persons already supported by them, come within the orbit of medical discretion? When does a determination as to either of the foregoing contingencies court the hazard of civil or criminal liability on the part of the physician or institution involved?

The existence and nature of the medical dilemma need hardly be discussed at length, portrayed as it is in the present case and complicated as it has recently come to be in view of the dramatic advance of medical technology. The dilemma is there, it is real, it is constantly resolved in accepted medical practice without attention in the courts, it pervades the issues in the very case we here examine. The branch of the dilemma [41] involving the doctor's responsibility and the relationship of the court's duty was thus conceived by Judge Muir:

Doctors *** to treat a patient, must deal with medical tradition and past case histories. They must be guided by what they do know. The extent of their training, their experience, consultation with other physicians,

must guide their decision-making processes in providing care to their patient. The nature, extent and duration of care by societal standards is the responsibility of
a physician. The morality and conscience of our society places this responsibility in the hands of the physician. What justification is there to remove it from control of the medical profession and place it in the hands
of the courts? [137 *N.J. Super.* at 259].

Such notions as to the distribution of responsibility, heretofore generally entertained, should however neither impede this Court in deciding
matters clearly justiciable nor preclude a re-examination by the Court as
to underlying human values and rights. Determinations as to these must,
in the ultimate, be responsive not only to the concepts of medicine but
also to the common moral judgment of the community at large. In the
latter respect the Court has a non-delegable judicial responsibility.

Put in another way, the law, equity and justice must not themselves
quail and be helpless in the face of modern technological marvels presenting questions hitherto unthought of. Where a Karen Quinlan, or a [42]
parent, or a doctor, or a hospital, or a State seeks the process and response of a court, it must answer with its most informed conception of
justice in the previously unexplored circumstances presented to it. That is
its obligation and we are here fulfilling it, for the actors and those having
an interest in the matter should not go without remedy.

Courts in the exercise of their *parens patriae* responsibility to protect
those under disability have sometimes implemented medical decisions
and authorized their carrying out under the doctrine of "substituted
judgment." *Hart* v. *Brown*, 29 *Conn. Super.* 368, 289 *A.* 2d 386, 387-88
(Super. Ct. 1972); *Strunk* v. *Strunk*, 445 *S.W.* 2d 145, 147-48 (Ky. Ct.
App. 1969). For as Judge Muir pointed out:

> "As part of the inherent power of equity, a Court of
> Equity has full and complete jurisdiction over the per-
> sons of those who labor under any legal disability ***.
> The Court's action in such a case is not limited by any
> narrow bounds, but it is empowered to stretch forth its
> arm in whatever direction its aid and protection may be
> needed. While this is indeed a special exercise of equity
> jurisdiction, it is beyond question that by virtue there-
> of the Court may pass upon purely personal rights."
> [137 *N.J. Super.* at 254 (quoting from *Am.Jur.* 2d,
> Equity § 69 (1966))].   [43]

But insofar as a court, having no inherent medical expertise, is called
upon to overrule a professional decision made according to prevailing

medical practice and standards, a different question is presented. As mentioned below, a doctor is required

> "to exercise in the treatment of his patient the degree of care, knowledge and skill ordinarily possessed and exercised in similar situations by the average member of the profession practicing in his field." *Schueler* v. *Strelinger*, 43 *N.J.* 330, 344 (1964). If he is a specialist he "must employ not merely the skill of a general practitioner, but also that special degree of skill normally possessed by the average physician who devotes special study and attention to the particular organ or disease or injury involved, having regard to the present state of scientific knowledge." *Clark* v. *Wichman*, 72 *N.J. Super.* 486, 493 (App. Div. 1962). This is the duty that establishes his legal obligations to his parents. [137 *N.J. Super.* at 257-58].

The medical obligation is related to standards and practice prevailing in the profession. The physicians in charge of the case, as noted above, declined to withdraw the respirator. That decision was consistent with the proofs below as to the then existing medical standards and practices.

Under the law as it then stood, Judge Muir was correct in declining to authorize withdrawal of the respirator.   [44]

However, in relation to the matter of the declaratory relief sought by plaintiff as representative of Karen's interests, we are required to reevaluate the applicability of the medical standards projected in the court below. The question is whether there is such internal consistency and rationality in the application of such standards as should warrant their constituting an ineluctable bar to the effectuation of substantive relief for plaintiff at the hands of the court. We have concluded not.

In regard to the foregoing it is pertinent that we consider the impact on the standards both of the civil and criminal law as to medical liability and the new technological means of sustaining life irreversibly damaged.

The modern proliferation of substantial malpractice litigation and the less frequent but even more unnerving possibility of criminal sanctions would seem, for it is beyond human nature to suppose otherwise, to have bearing on the practice and standards as they exist. The brooding presence of such possible liability, it was testified here, had no part in the decision of the treating physicians. As did Judge Muir, we afford this testimony full credence. But we cannot believe that the stated factor has not had a strong influence on the standards, as the literature on the subject plainly reveals. (See footnote 8, *infra*). Moreover our attention is drawn not so much to the recognition by Drs. Morse and Javed of the extant practice and standards but to the widening ambiguity of those standards themselves in their application to the medical problems we are discussing.

The agitation of the medical community in the face of modern life prolongation technology and its search for definitive policy are demonstrated in the large volume of relevant professional commentary.[8] [45]

The wide debate thus reflected contrasts with the relative paucity of legislative and judicial guides and standards in the same field. The medical profession has sought to devise guidelines such as the "brain death" concept of the Harvard Ad Hoc Committee mentioned above. But it is perfectly apparent from the testimony we have quoted of Dr. Korein, and indeed so clear as almost to be judicially noticeable, that humane decisions against resuscitative or maintenance therapy are frequently a [46] recognized *de facto* response in the medical world to the irreversible, terminal, pain-ridden patient, especially with familial consent. And these cases, of course, are far short of "brain death."

We glean from the record here that physicians distinguish between curing the ill and comforting and easing the dying; that they refuse to treat the curable as if they were dying or ought to die; and that they have sometimes refused to treat the hopeless and dying as if they were curable. In this sense, as we were reminded by the testimony of Drs. Korein and Diamond, many of them have refused to inflict an undesired prolongation of the process of dying on a patient in irreversible condition when it is clear that such "therapy" offers neither human nor humane benefit. We think these attitudes represent a balanced implementation of a profoundly realistic perspective on the meaning of life and death and that they respect the whole Judeo-Christian tradition of regard for human life. No less would they seem consistent with the moral matrix of medicine, "to heal," very much in the sense of the endless mission of the law, "to do justice."

Yet this balance, we feel, is particularly difficult to perceive and apply in the context of the development by advanced technology of sophisticated and artificial life-sustaining devices. For those possibly curable, such devices are of great value, and, as ordinary medical proce- [47] dures, are essential. Consequently, as pointed out by Dr. Diamond, they are necessary because of the ethic of medical practice. But in light of the situation in the present case (while the record here is somewhat hazy in distinguishing between "ordinary" and "extraordinary" measures), one would have to think that the use of the same respirator or like support could be considered "ordinary" in the context of the possibly curable patient but "extraordinary" in the context of the forced sustaining by cardio-respiratory processes of an irreversibly doomed patient. And this dilemma is sharpened in the face of the malpractice and criminal action threat which we have mentioned.

We would hesitate, in this imperfect world, to propose as to physicians that type of immunity which from the early common law has surrounded judges and grand jurors, *see, e.g., Grove* v. *Van Duyn*, 44 *N.J.L.* 654, 656-57 (E. & A. 1882); *O'Regan* v. *Schermerhorn*, 25 *N.J. Misc.* 1, 19-20 (Sup. Ct. 1940), so that they might without fear of personal retaliation perform their judicial duties with independent objectivity. In *Bradley* v. *Fisher*, 80 *U.S.* (13 *Wall.*) 335, 347, 20 *L.Ed.* 646, 649 (1872), the Supreme Court held:

[48]

> [I]t is a general principle of the highest importance to the proper administration of justice that a judicial officer, in exercising the authority vested in him, shall be free to act upon his own convictions, without apprehension of personal consequences to himself.

Lord Coke said of judges that "they are only to make an account to God and the King [the State]." 12 *Coke Rep.* 23, 25, 77 *Eng. Rep.* 1305, 1307 (S.C. 1608).

Nevertheless, there must be a way to free physicians, in the pursuit of their healing vocation, from possible contamination by self-interest or self-protection concerns which would inhibit their independent medical judgments for the well-being of their dying patients. We would hope that this opinion might be serviceable to some degree in ameliorating the professional problems under discussion.

A technique aimed at the underlying difficulty (though in a somewhat broader context) is described by Dr. Karen Teel, a pediatrician and a director of Pediatric Education, who writes in the *Baylor Law Review* under the title "The Physician's Dilemma: A Doctor's View: What The Law Should Be." Dr. Teel recalls:

> Physicians, by virtue of their responsibility for medical judgments are, partly by choice and partly by default, charged with the responsibility of making ethical judgments which we are sometimes ill-equipped to make. We are not always morally and legally authorized to make them. The physician is thereby assuming a civil and criminal liability that, as often as not, he does not even realize as a factor in his decision. There is little or no dialogue in this whole process. The physician assumes that his judgment is called for and, in good faith, he acts. Someone must and it has been the physician who has assumed the responsibility and the risk.

[49]

I suggest that it would be more appropriate to provide a regular forum for more input and dialogue in
individual situations and to allow the responsibility of
these judgments to be shared. Many hospitals have established an Ethics Committee composed of physicians, social workers, attorneys, and theologians, ***
which serves to review the individual circumstances of
ethical dilemma and which has provided much in the
way of assistance and safeguards for patients and their
medical caretakers. Generally, the authority of these
committees is primarily restricted to the hospital setting and their official status is more that of an advisory body than of an enforcing body.

The concept of an Ethics Committee which has this
kind of organization and is readily accessible to those
persons rendering medical care to patients, would be, I
think, the most promising direction for further study at
this point. ***

*** [This would allow] some much needed dialogue regarding these issues and [force] the point of exploring
all of the options for a particular patient. It diffuses the
responsibility for making these judgments. Many physicians, in many circumstances, would welcome this
sharing of responsibility. I believe that such an entity   [50]
could lend itself well to an assumption of a legal status
which would allow courses of action not now undertaken because of the concern for liability. [27 *Baylor L.
Rev.* 6, 8-9 (1975)].

The most appealing factor in the technique suggested by Dr. Teel
seems to us to be the diffusion of professional responsibility for decision,
comparable in a way to the value of multi-judge courts in finally resolving on appeal difficult questions of law. Moreover, such a system would
be protective to the hospital as well as the doctor in screening out, so to
speak, a case which might be contaminated by less than worthy motivations of family or physician. In the real world and in relationship to the
momentous decision contemplated, the value of additional views and diverse knowledge is apparent.

We consider that a practice of applying to a court to confirm such
decisions would generally be inappropriate, not only because that would
be a gratuitous encroachment upon the medical profession's field of
competence, but because it would be impossibly cumbersome. Such a
requirement is distinguishable from the judicial overview traditionally required in other matters such as the adjudication and commitment of [51]

mental incompetents. This is not to say that in the case of an otherwise justiciable controversy access to the courts would be foreclosed; we speak rather of a general practice and procedure.

And although the deliberations and decisions which we describe would be professional in nature they should obviously include at some stage the feelings of the family of an incompetent relative. Decision-making within health care if it is considered as an expression of a primary obligation of the physician, *primum non nocere*, should be controlled primarily within the patient-doctor-family relationship, as indeed was recognized by Judge Muir in his supplemental opinion of November 12, 1975.

If there could be created not necessarily this particular system but some reasonable counterpart, we would have no doubt that such decisions, thus determined to be in accordance with medical practice and prevailing standards, would be accepted by society and by the courts, at least in cases comparable to that of Karen Quinlan.

The evidence in this case convinces us that the focal point of decision should be the prognosis as to the reasonable possibility of return to cognitive and sapient life, as distinguished from the forced continuance of that biological vegetative existence to which Karen seems to be doomed.

In summary of the present Point of this opinion, we conclude that the state of the pertinent medical standards and practices which guided the attending physicians in this matter is not such as would justify this [52] Court in deeming itself bound or controlled thereby in responding to the case for declaratory relief established by the parties on the record before us.

V.

Alleged Criminal Liability

Having concluded that there is a right of privacy that might permit termination of treatment in the circumstances of this case, we turn to consider the relationship of the exercise of that right to the criminal law. We are aware that such termination of treatment would accelerate Karen's death. The County Prosecutor and the Attorney General stoutly maintain that there would be criminal liability for such acceleration. Under the statutes of this State, the unlawful killing of another human being is criminal homicide. *N.J.S.A.* 2A:113-1, 2, 5. We conclude that there would be no criminal homicide in the circumstances of this case. We believe, first, that the ensuing death would not be homicide but rather expiration from existing natural causes. Secondly, even if it were to be regarded as homicide, it would not be unlawful.

These conclusions rest upon definitional and constitutional bases. The termination of treatment pursuant to the right of privacy is, within the limitations of this case, *ipso facto* lawful. Thus, a death resulting [53] from such an act would not come within the scope of the homicide statutes proscribing only the unlawful killing of another. There is a real and in this case determinative distinction between the unlawful taking of the life of another and the ending of artificial life-support systems as a matter of self-determination.

Furthermore, the exercise of a constitutional right such as we have here found is protected from criminal prosecution. *See Stanley* v. *Georgia, supra*, 394 *U.S.* at 559, 89 *S.Ct.* at 1245, 22 *L.Ed.* 2d at 546. We do not question the State's undoubted power to punish the taking of human life, but that power does not encompass individuals terminating medical treatment pursuant to their right of privacy. *See id.* at 568, 89 *S.Ct.* at 1250, 22 *L.Ed.* 2d at 551. The constitutional protection extends to third parties whose action is necessary to effectuate the exercise of that right where the individuals themselves would not be subject to prosecution or the third parties are charged as accessories to an act which could not be a crime. *Eisenstadt* v. *Baird, supra*, 405 *U.S.* at 445-46, 92 *S.Ct.* at 1034-35, 31 *L.Ed.* 2d at 357-58; *Griswold* v. *Connecticut, supra*, 381 *U.S.* at 481, 85 *S.Ct.* at 1679-80, 14 *L.Ed.* 2d at 512-13. And, under the circumstances of this case, these same principles would apply to and negate a valid prosecution for attempted suicide were there still such a [54] crime in this State.[9]

VI.

The Guardianship of the Person

The trial judge bifurcated the guardianship, as we have noted, refusing to appoint Joseph Quinlan to be guardian of the person and limiting his guardianship to that of the property of his daughter. Such occasional division of guardianship, as between responsibility for the person and the property of an incompetent person, has roots deep in the common law and was well within the jurisdictional capacity of the trial judge. *In re Rollins*, 65 *A.*2d 667, 679-82 (N.J. Cty. Ct. 1949).   [55]

The statute creates an initial presumption of entitlement to guardianship in the next of kin, for it provides:

> In any case where a guardian is to be appointed, letters of guardianship shall be granted *** to the next of kin, or if *** it is proven to the court that no appointment from among them will be to the best interest of

the incompetent or his estate, then to such other proper person as will accept the same. [*N.J.S.A.* 3A:6-36. *See In re Roll*, 117 *N.J. Super.* 122, 124 (App. Div. 1971)].

The trial court was apparently convinced of the high character of Joseph Quinlan and his general suitability as guardian under other circumstances, describing him as "very sincere, moral, ethical and religious." The court felt, however, that the obligation to concur in the medical care and treatment of his daughter would be a source of anguish to him and would distort his "decision-making processes." We disagree, for we sense from the whole record before us that while Mr. Quinlan feels a natural grief, and understandably sorrows because of the tragedy which has befallen his daughter, his strength of purpose and character far outweighs these sentiments and qualifies him eminently for guardianship of the person as well as the property of his daughter. Hence we discern no valid reason to overrule the statutory intendment of preference to the next of kin.   [56]

DECLARATORY RELIEF

We thus arrive at the formulation of the declaratory relief which we have concluded is appropriate to this case. Some time has passed since Karen's physical and mental condition was described to the Court. At that time her continuing deterioration was plainly projected. Since the record has not been expanded we assume that she is now even more fragile and nearer to death than she was then. Since her present treating physicians may give reconsideration to her present posture in the light of this opinion, and since we are transferring to the plaintiff as guardian the choice of the attending physician and therefore other physicians may be in charge of the case who may take a different view from that of the present attending physicians, we herewith declare the following affirmative relief on behalf of the plaintiff. Upon the concurrence of the guardian and family of Karen, should the responsible attending physicians conclude that there is no reasonable possibility of Karen's ever emerging from her present comatose condition to a cognitive, sapient state and that the life-support apparatus now being administered to Karen should be discontinued, they shall consult with the hospital "Ethics Committee" or like body of the institution in which Karen is then hospitalized. If that consultative body agrees that there is no reasonable possibility of Karen's [57] ever emerging from her present comatose condition to a cognitive, sapient state, the present life-support system may be withdrawn and said action shall be without any civil or criminal liability therefor on the part of any participant, whether guardian, physician, hospital or others.[10] We herewith specifically so hold.

CONCLUSION

We therefore remand this record to the trial court to implement (without further testimonial hearing) the following decisions:

1. To discharge, with the thanks of the Court for his service, the present guardian of the person of Karen Quinlan, Thomas R. Curtin, Esquire, a member of the Bar and an officer of the court.

2. To appoint Joseph Quinlan as guardian of the person of Karen Quinlan with full power to make decisions with regard to the identity of her treating physicians.

We repeat for the sake of emphasis and clarity that upon the concurrence of the guardian and family of Karen, should the responsible attending physicians conclude that there is no reasonable possibility of Karen's ever emerging from her present comatose condition to a cognitive, sapient state and that the life-support apparatus now being administered to Karen should be discontinued, they shall consult with the hospital "Ethics Committee" or like body of the institution in which Karen is then hospitalized. If that consultative body agrees that there is no reasonable possibility of Karen's ever emerging from her present comatose condition to a cognitive, sapient state, the present life-support system may be withdrawn and said action shall be without any civil or criminal liability therefor, on the part of any participant, whether guardian, physician, hospital or others. [58]

By the above ruling we do not intend to be understood as implying that a proceeding for judicial declaratory relief is necessarily required for the implementation of comparable decisions in the field of medical practice.

Modified and remanded. [59]

— NOTES —

¹The importance of the preservation of life is memorialized in various organic documents. The Declaration of Independence states as self-evident truths "that all men *** are endowed by their Creator with certain unalienable Rights, that among these are Life, liberty and the pursuit of happiness." This ideal is inherent in the Constitution of the United States. It is explicitly recognized in our Constitution of 1947 which provides for "certain natural and unalienable rights, among which are those of enjoying and defending life *** ." *N.J. Const.* (1947), Art. I, par. 1. Our State government is established to protect such rights, *N.J. Const.* (1947), Art. I, par. 2, and, acting through the Attorney General (*N.J.S.A.* 52:17A-4(h)), it enforces them.

²Dr. Julius Korein, a neurologist, testified:

A. *** [Y]ou've got a set of possible lesions that prior to the era of advanced technology and advances in medicine were no problem inasmuch as the patient would expire. They could do nothing for themselves and even external care was limited. It was—I don't know how many years ago they couldn't keep a person alive with intravenous feedings because they couldn't give enough calories. Now they have these high caloric tube feedings that can keep people in excellent nutrition for years so what's happened is these things have occurred all along but the technology has now reached a point where you can in fact start to replace anything outside of the brain to maintain something that is irreversibly damaged.

Q. Doctor, can the art of medicine repair the cerebral damage that was sustained by Karen?

A. In my opinion, no. ***

Q. Doctor, in your opinion is there any course of treatment that will lead to the improvement of Karen's condition?

A. No.

³The Harvard Ad Hoc standards, with reference to "brain death," will be discussed *infra*.

⁴Dr. Robert J. Morse, a neurologist, and Karen's treating physician from the time of her admission to Saint Clare's Hospital on April 24, 1975 (reference was made *supra* to "treating physicians" named as defendants; this term included Dr. Arshad Javed, a highly qualified pulmonary internist, who considers that he manages that phase of Karen's care with primary responsibility to the "attending physician," Dr. Morse).

⁵DEATH. The cessation of life; the ceasing to exist; defined by physicians as a total stoppage of the circulation of the blood, and a cessation of the animal and vital functions consequent thereon, such as respiration, pulsation, etc. *Black's Law Dictionary* 488 (rev. 4th ed. 1968).

⁶It is generally agreed that the Eighth Amendment's provision of "[n]or cruel and unusual punishments inflicted" is drawn verbatim from the English Declaration of Rights. *See* 1 Wm. & M., sess. 2, c. 2 (1689). The prohibition arose in the context of excessive punishments for crimes, punishments that were barbarous and savage as well as disproportionate to the offense committed. *See generally* Granucci " 'Nor Cruel and Unusual Punishments Inflicted:' The Original Meaning," 57 *Calif. L. Rev.* 839, 844-60 (1969); Note, "The Cruel and Unusual Punishment Clause and the Substantive Criminal Law," 79 *Harv. L. Rev.* 635, 636-39 (1966). The principle against excessiveness in criminal punishments can be traced back to Chapters 20-22 of the *Magna Carta* (1215). The historical background of the Eighth Amendment was examined at some length in various opinions in *Furman* v. *Georgia*, 408 *U.S.* 238, 92 *S.Ct.* 2726, 33 *L.Ed.* 2d 345 (1972).

The Constitution itself is silent as to the meaning of the word "punishment." Whether it refers to the variety of legal and nonlegal penalties that human beings endure or whether it must be in connection with a criminal rather than a civil proceeding is not stated in the document. But the origins of the clause are clear. And the cases construing it have consistently held that the "punishment" contemplated by the Eighth Amendment is the penalty inflicted by a court for the commission of a crime or in the enforcement of what is a criminal law. *See, e.g., Trop* v. *Dulles*, 356 *U.S.* 86, 94-99, 78 *S.Ct.* 590, 594-97, 2 *L.Ed.* 2d 630, 638-41 (1957). *See generally* Note, "The Effectiveness of the Eighth Amendment: An Appraisal of Cruel and Unusual Punishment," 36 *N.Y.U.L. Rev.* 846, 854-57 (1961). A deprivation, forfeiture or penalty arising out of a civil proceeding or otherwise cannot be "cruel and unusual punishment" within the meaning of the constitutional clause.

[7]The right we here discuss is included within the class of what have been called rights of "personality." *See* Pound, "Equitable Relief against Defamation and Injuries to Personality," 29 *Harv. L. Rev.* 640, 668-76 (1916). Equitable jurisdiction with respect to the recognition and enforcement of such rights has long been recognized in New Jersey. *See, e.g., Vanderbilt* v. *Mitchell*, 72 *N.J. Eq.* 910, 919-20 (E. & A. 1907).

[8]*See, e.g., Downing, Euthanasia and the Right to Death* (1969); *St. John-Stevas, Life, Death and the Law* (1961); *Williams, The Sanctity of Human Life and the Criminal Law* (1957); Appel, "Ethical and Legal Questions Posed by Recent Advances in Medicine," 205 *J.A.M.A.* 513 (1968); Cantor, "A Patient's Decision To Decline Life-Saving Medical Treatment: Bodily Integrity Versus The Preservation of Life," 26 *Rutgers L. Rev.* 228 (1973); Claypool, "The Family Deals with Death," 27 *Baylor L. Rev.* 34 (1975); Elkington, "The Dying Patient, The Doctor and The Law," 13 *Vill. L. Rev.* 740 (1968); Fletcher, "Legal Aspects of the Decision Not to Prolong Life," 203 *J.A.M.A.* 65 (1968); Foreman, "The Physician's Criminal Liability for the Practice of Euthanasia," 27 *Baylor L. Rev.* 54 (1975); Gurney, "Is There A Right To Die?—A Study of the Law of Euthanasia," 3 *Cumb.—Sam. L. Rev.* 235 (1972); Mannes, "Euthanasia vs. The Right To Life," 27 *Baylor L. Rev.* 68 (1975); Sharp & Crofts, "Death with Dignity and The Physician's Civil Liability," 27 *Baylor L. Rev.* 86 (1975); Sharpe & Hargest, "Lifesaving Treatment for Unwilling Patients," 36 *Fordham L. Rev.* 695 (1968); Skegg, "Irreversibly Comatose Individuals: 'Alive' or 'Dead'?," 33 *Camb. L.J.* 130 (1974); Comment, "The Right to Die," 7 *Houston L. Rev.* 654 (1970); Note, "The Time of Death—A Legal, Ethical and Medical Dilemma," 18 *Catholic Law.* 243 (1972); Note, "Compulsory Medical Treatment: The State's Interest Re-evaluated," 51 *Minn. L. Rev.* 293 (1966).

[9]An attempt to commit suicide was an indictable offense at common law and as such was indictable in this State as a common law misdemeanor. 1 *Schlosser, Criminal Laws of New Jersey* § 12.5 (3d ed. 1970); *see N.J.S.A.* 2A:85-1. The legislature downgraded the offense in 1957 to the status of a disorderly persons offense, which is not a "crime" under our law. *N.J.S.A.* 2A:170-25.6. And in 1971, the legislature repealed all criminal sanctions for attempted suicide. *N.J.S.A.* 2A:85-5.1. Provision is now made for temporary hospitalization of persons making such an attempt. *N.J.S.A.* 30:4-26.3a. We note that under the proposed New Jersey Penal Code (Oct. 1971) there is no provision for criminal punishment of attempted suicide. *See* Commentary, § 2C:11-6. There is, however, an independent offense of "aiding suicide." § 2C:11-6b. This provision, if enacted, would not be incriminatory in circumstances similar to those presented in this case.

[10]The declaratory relief we here award is not intended to imply that the principles enunciated in this case might not be applicable in divers other types of terminal medical situations such as those described by Drs. Korein and Diamond, *supra*, not necessarily involving the hopeless loss of cognitive or sapient life.

THE QUINLAN CASE

Dennis J. Horan

Although its importance cannot be overestimated, the decision of the New Jersey Supreme Court in the matter of Karen Quinlan[1] bears little or no resemblance to the newspaper accounts of the case. Its importance is related more to the impact of the media than the logic of the opinion. In its opinion of March 31, 1976 the New Jersey Supreme Court really addressed two rather diverse topics: (1) The Karen Quinlan case, and (2) The right of privacy in terminal illness. Whether it was necessary to discuss the latter in order to decide the former is questionable, and is a question which will be debated in the law reviews.

The judgment in the case is very narrow and is in sharp contrast to the wide breadth of issues discussed in the opinion. The judgment is contained in the last three pages of the opinion entitled "Declaratory Relief." In those pages the Court declared that upon the concurrence of the guardian and family of Karen the life support apparatus being administered to her (a Bennett Respirator) could be discontinued, but on certain conditions. These conditions were: (1) The concurrence of the responsible attending physicians who must conclude that there is no reasonable possibility of Karen's ever emerging from here present comatose condition to a cognitive, sapient state; and (2) The concurrence and agreement by a hospital ethics committee that there is no reasonable possibility of Karen's ever emerging from her present comatose condition to a cognitive, sapient state.

Thereafter, withdrawal of the life support systems under those conditions shall be without any civil or criminal liability on the part of any participant, whether guardian, physician, hospital or others.

The Court then remanded the case to the trial court for implementation of certain narrow decisions: (1) To discharge the present guardian, and (2) To appoint the father, Joseph Quinlan, as guardian with full power to make decisions with regard to the identity of Karen's treating physicians.

The narrowness of the actual Declaratory Relief is to be contrasted with the breadth of the body of opinions which addresses itself to a whole series of issues, the discussion of which were not essential or even necessary for the determination of the case. I contend that the same decision as was reached by the Court could have also been reached by the Court merely by applying current medical-legal law, without the necessity of introducing such issues as the right of privacy or substitute judgment. The mischief these concepts will create remains to be seen.[2] In view of the post-decretal history of the case, and in view of Karen's survival for a lengthy period of time after removal from the respirator, my conclusions seem even more apt.[3]

The Court brushed aside Mr. Quinlan's contention that his First Amendment rights of religious belief were impinged. Nor did the Court recognize an independent parental right of religious freedom to support the relief requested. Similarly the Court disposed of the Quinlan's argument based upon cruel and unusual punishment.

The Court did find in the constitutional right of privacy a right to reject medical treatment. Because of Karen's incompetency and her inability to exercise that right, the Court concluded that Karen's right of privacy may be asserted on her behalf by her guardian "under the peculiar circumstances here present."[4] The Court thus chose to decide the case on constitutional grounds rather than attempting a resolution of the issues on current legal-medical principles. My thesis is that the case could have been decided and the same result reached without resorting to constitutional rights, and in particular the right of privacy.

Resorting to constitutional grounds means that the Court's holding cannot be changed or altered by the legislature. A constitutional amendment would be required. This can be a most difficult state of affairs in the resolution of legal-moral-medical problems, since it forecloses further social experimentation through legislation of other solutions to the legal dilemmas which resuscitation poses. Alternative solutions to profound legal problems such as these should not be foreclosed by the premature use of constitutional grounds. For the same reasons, resort should first be had by the Court to legal-medical precedents rather than constitutional principles. The law is only now beginning to cope with these profound medical-legal problems, and haste in decision making which may produce constitutional solutions which are, practically speaking, henceforth unalterable, should be avoided.

The right to refuse medical treatment does not need constitutional support. A physician may not render treatment without consent except in emergency situations. The fact that consent is necessary has never been considered to need statutory or constitutional support. The right to reject medical treatment exists as a corollary to the necessity for consent to any touching. A competent person has the right to refuse medical treatment, not as a constitutional right of privacy, but as a corollary of the common law tort rule that no one may treat him or her without that consent. This aspect of the right of privacy (refusal of medical treatment) is not constitutional in scope under the federal constitution. It obviously exists now as a constitutional right in New Jersey as a result of the opinion in the Quinlan case.

In an attempt to limit the breadth of many of the comments made, the Court concluded several paragraphs of the opinion with the statement, "under the peculiar circumstances here present."[5] Why this should be repeatedly stated by the Court is unclear. Perhaps there was fear of the real nature of the issues which the Court knew the public thought was being decided.

The Court stated that if a putative decision by Karen to permit this non-cognitive, vegetative existence to terminate by natural forces is regarded as a valuable incident of her right of privacy (i.e., she has a constitutional right to reject medical treatment), then it should not be discarded solely on the basis that her condition prevents her conscious exercise of that choice. Speaking in practicalities, the Court felt that the only way to prevent destruction of this right was to permit the guardian and family of Karen to render their best judgment as to whether she would exercise it in these circumstances. The Court then found that Karen's right of privacy to terminate medical treatment could be asserted in her behalf by her guardian and family "under the peculiar circumstances presented by this record."[6]

Except in emergency situations where it is presumed, consent is a condition precedent for the giving of medical treatment. For minors and incompetents consent must be sought from the parent or guardian. The consent may be given by them where the treatment is beneficial, but not otherwise. For termination of therapy the rules are similar, but not the same. All treatment requires consent, but the termination of therapy for medical reasons does not as long as the patient is not being abandoned by the physician. As applied to the situation at hand, these principles mean that resuscitation therapy may be terminated where the prognosis for life (not meaningful life) is very poor and in the medical judgment of the attending physician continuation of the therapy is unwarranted. Consequently, the New Jersey Supreme Court need not have discussed the case as one requiring the application of constitutional principles. Indeed, in doing so it has seemingly placed another burden on the shoulders of the physician. Presumably he now cannot terminate resuscitative therapy without the consent of the parent or guardian.

The Court next discusses what it labels "the medical factor." Under this heading is placed the most far-reaching and unsettling aspect of the case. Accepting the statement by the physicians in the case that their decision not to terminate the use of the respirator as a form of medical treatment was made according to prevailing medical practice and standards, the Court nonetheless determined that *it* should reevaluate the applicability of the medical standards themselves.[7] The Court specifically indicated that the decision of the physicians in charge of the case was consistent with the proofs below as to the "then"[8] existing medical standards and practices. It even indicated that Judge Muir was correct in declining to authorize withdrawal of the respirator as the law then stood. Then, the Court addressed this, the most profound issue of the case, in a classic of unintelligible legal jargon:

> The question is whether there is such internal consistency and rationality in the application of such standards as should warrant their constituting an ineluctable bar to the effectuation of substantive relief for plaintiff at the hands of the Court. We have concluded not.[9]

In my opinion, this section of the Quinlan case will have the most profound effect on medical practice in future years. For here the Court held that it could overrule the medical and moral standards prevailing in the profession of medicine. Judge Muir had held to the contrary, i.e., that the medical standards must be determined by the medical profession and could not be overruled by the Court.[10] But the New Jersey Supreme Court took particular pains to address this issue in a manner which indicates that it, the New Jersey Supreme Court, would determine what the moral, medical, and legal standard is as applicable to the termination of resuscitative methods. Less there be any doubt about that conclusion, the Court reiterates:

> In summary of the present point of this opinion, we conclude that the state of the pertinent standards and practices which guided the attending physicians in this matter is not such as would justify this Court in deeming itself bound or controlled thereby in responding to the case for declaratory relief established by the parties on the record before us.[11]

It would be much simpler if the Court had said that the attending physicians were wrong in their understanding of the prevailing standard. But the Court says they were right.[12] We must remember that courts have not heretofore dictated to physicians as to how they will conduct the practice of their profession. Even a judicial finding of malpractice usually requires the testimony of another physician that the applicable standard of medical practice has been breached. Where expert testimony is not necessary it is because the standard is self-evident or proved without oral testimony. Here, however, a state supreme court has decreed that a medical standard which, on the record below, was apparently accepted by all as the prevailing standard, can be discarded and replaced by another seemingly contrary standard. Yet, even that pronouncement seems to be at odds with the holding in the judgment that the attending physicianss cannot turn off the respirator until both they and a hospital committee have decided that the treatment is hopeless. Such inconsistencies do not persuade a careful reader of the efficacy of the opinion. Under malpractice laws, what courts say is the prevailing medical standard becomes normative for the physician and mandates his future course of conduct.

The Court also holds that terminating the respirator in this case would not be criminal homicide because death would be from existing natural causes. However, even if it were to be regarded as homicide, the Court says it would not be unlawful because "a death resulting from such an act would not come within the scope of the homicide statutes proscribing only the unlawful killing of another."[13] The Court brings the person who turns off the respirator under the protection of the constitution by declaring that the one who exercises the constitutional right of privacy for another under these circumstances cannot be the subject matter of prosecution if the other individual himself would not be subject to prosecution for refusing medical treatment.

Then, in a most extraordinary statement, the Court states: "and under the circumstances of this case these same principles would apply to and negate a valid prosecution for attempted suicide were there still such a crime in this state."[14] Such a crime, "aiding suicide," is a crime under the proposed New Jersey Penal Code. The Court points out that even if the new criminal code becomes law, "this provision, if enacted, would not be incriminatory in circumstances similar to those presented in this case."[15] I have not before seen a court render a declaratory judgment on a statute not yet in existence.

The case must be considered in the light of the facts as presented to the trial court and to the Supreme Court of New Jersey. At that time it was assumed by all participants that turning off the respirator meant almost immediate death for Karen Quinlan. Consequently, the case was argued in the trial court and on appeal as though the act of terminating a form of medical treatment constituted voluntary or involuntary euthanasia. The subsequent history of the case, and the fact that Karen Quinlan continues to survive without the aid of the respirator, has put the case in its proper perspective. That perspective is this: The Karen Quinlan case concerned a medical decision as to whether or not a certain type of medical therapy should be continued in the case. That judgment should first of all be a medical judgment made by the physicians on the case. If the family concurs with that judgment, well and good. If, however, the family opts for a different form of medical treatment than the physicians on the case, the only practical answer is for the physicians to resign or to fire the physicians and replace them with other physicians. This, however, can be most difficult, as anyone who has been involved in such a case knows. Few physicians will involve themselves in taking over a case under those circumstances. This is seemingly what has occurred since the Court's opinion of March 31, 1976. The disagreement between the attending physicians and the family precipitated this litigation. In their judgment the attending physicians felt that the case was not medically hopeless, and they refused to terminate the use of the respirator. Since the opinion, the same treating physicians have successfully weaned Karen from the respirator and she has been transferred to a nursing home. Given these basic disagreements between physician and family, who prevails?

Ordinarily one would expect the physician to resign in the face of such disagreement. How can he resign, however, without arranging for follow-up care (or be accused of abandonment), and what other physician wants to step into such a situation? The Supreme Court of New Jersey solved this dilemma by giving the guardian (the father) the right to select the physician, even to the extent of firing the current physicians.

But on the important issue—the disagreement—it still held that the successor physicians must first agree that the case is hopeless before therapy can be discontinued. The Court then added another layer to the problem by requiring a hospital committee to do the same. This is the most puzzling aspect of the case. Presumably the Court assumed that other physicians would be found after publication of the opinion who would take the case and would agree with the Court's opinion that the mere existence of a non-cognitive state or non-sapient state (whatever the Court means) is adequate grounds to stop therapy.

Under current medical-legal principles, the Court had only to examine the facts and declare that a physician is authorized under the standards of medical practice to discontinue a form of therapy which in his medical judgment is useless. He is not mandated by the law to render useless treatment, nor does the standard of medical care require useless treatment. Under those circumstances if the treating physicians have determined that continued use of the respirator was useless, then they could decide to discontinue it without fear of civil or criminal liability. Thereafter reappointing the parent as guardian with the obvious power to discharge the physicians if they disagreed with the family, was the only required solution. Whether the family can then find physicians who agree with them and will take the case is a separate issue.

By "useless" is meant that the continued use of the therapy cannot and does not improve the prognosis for recovery. Even if the therapy is necessary to maintain stability, such therapy should not be mandatory where the ultimate prognosis is hopeless. This does not mean that ordinary means of life supports, such as food and drink, can be discontinued merely because the ultimate prognosis is hopeless. It does mean, however, that physicians can use good practical common medical sense in determining whether or not treatment is efficacious and, if it is not, then cease the treatment.

By "hopeless" is meant that the prognosis for life (not meaningful life) is very poor. The fact that someone may not return to "sapient or cognitive life" may or may not fulfill the requirement, depending on other medical factors, but in and of itself it does not. As was said by the Supreme Court of West Germany:

> Where human life exists, human dignity is present to it; it is not decisive that the bearer of this dignity himself be conscious of it and knows personally how to preserve it.[16]

It seems that in the Quinlan case all participants assumed that just as night follows day, death would follow the termination of the respirator. Subsequent facts have proved this to be incorrect and have undermined the force of this decision. Perhaps, however, subsequent facts have placed this decision in its proper perspective. Where the issue is a medical one, namely the termination of useless therapy, that question is one which should be decided by the physicians—not by the courts. All the Court here had to do was find that such a medical decision does not violate the law.

The problem with the Quinlan case is that, according to the lower court, all the physicians agreed that the case was not hopeless. If this is a reasonable medical judgment, then one can only conclude that, in the collective mind of the New Jersey Supreme Court, and although unsaid, either the doctors were factually wrong in their conclusion or medically hopeless means "non-sapient or non-cognitive." What does this mean for the retardate?

If there is a lesson to be learned from the Quinlan case, it seems to me that one lesson is for the court to interfere less with medicine and to spend more time analyzing the legal issues involved, and in particular the impact those legal issues will have on other areas of the law.

Already we see the movement for the legalization of voluntary and involuntary euthanasia. Duff and Campbell have stated their case for the legalization of involuntary euthanasia in the special care nursery.[17] In its provisional report of December 16, 1975, the Council of Europe draft recommendation by the Committee on Social and Health Questions opts for both voluntary and involuntary euthanasia of the incurably ill, or even those whose cerebral functions have irreversibly ceased.[18] Certainly the Quinlan case should not be considered as a step inthat direction since the Court takes great pains to distinguish between the substituted judgment of a parent or guardian to terminate medical treatment for an incompetent and the deliberate intentional taking of another's life. However, one cannot but express the concern previously stated by Prof. Yale Kamisar in his famous article that the slippery slope once begun is indeed difficult to terminate, and where it will terminate is anyone's guess.[19]

The second and more important lesson should be learned by the medical profession. If that profession wants to avoid interference by the courts it ought to liaison with the bar to seek cooperation on these difficult issues long before litigation begins. Such liaison should be permanently institutionalized by the creation of a standing and funded committee composed of physicians, lawyers, and moralists. This committee should be funded by the American Bar Association and the American Medical Association, although totally independent of either. It should have adequate staff.

The committee's main function should be the issuance of legal-moral-medical "opinions" on these and similar issues. Such "opinions" can be the result of study, research, and even testimony before the committee by interested persons. The moral persuasiveness of such "opinions" will depend on the prestige and impartiality of the committee. Certainly any such committee will experience the usual problems such institutions are heir to, but its existence seems imperative to the current and future needs of both medicine and law.

1. In the Matter of Karen Quinlan, Supreme Court of New Jersey, A-116, Sept. term 1975 decided 3/31/76, Slip Opinion pp. 1-59. (Hereafter all citations will be to the Slip Opinion.)

2. The doctrine of substituted judgment is being used in the special care nursery to allow parents the right to refuse consent to even ordinary means of treatment for defective children. See Duff and Campbell, ft. 16 infra.

3. It is reported that Karen was transferred to a nursing home "to spend her last days." Chicago Daily News, June 9, 1976, p. 2.

4. Op. cit. ft. 1 at p. 38.

5. Idem; see also p. 33 ("in the exceptional circumstances of this case"); p. 38, p. 39.

6. Op. cit. ft. 1 at p. 39.

7. Ibid. at p. 13 where the court said: "It seems to be the consensus not only of the treating physicians but also of the several qualified experts who testified in the case, that removal from the respirator would not conform to medical practices, standards and traditions."

8. This ominous word appears twice on page 44: "The physicians in charge of the case, as noted above, declined to withdraw the respirator. That decision was consistent with the proofs below as to the *then* existing medical standards and practices. Under the law as it *then* stood, Judge Muir was correct in declining to authorize withdrawal of the respirator."

9. Op. cit. ft. 1 at p. 45.

10. See Judge Muir's opinion.

11. Op. cit. ft. at p. 52, 53.

12. Op. cit. ft. 1 at p. 13.

13. Ibid. at p. 54.

14. Ibid. at p. 54, 55.

15. Ibid. in court's footnote 9 at p. 55.

16. Gorby, John, and Jonas, Robert E., "West German Abortion Decision: A Contrast to *Roe* v. *Wade*," The John Marshall Journal of Practice and Procedure, Vol. 9, No. 3, Spring 1976, pp. 551-684 at p. 559, 560.

17. Duff and Campbell, "Moral and Ethical Dilemmas in the Special-Care Nursery, 289 New Eng. J. Med. 890 (1973).

18. Draft Recommendation presented by the Committee on Social and Health Questions, Council of Europe, Doc. 3699, Provisional Report of 12/16/75.

19. Kamisar, Yale, "Some Non-Religious Views Against Proposed 'Mercy Killing Legislation'," Minnesota Law Review, Vol. 42, No. 6, May 1958, pp. 669-1042.

V.
How Should
Medicine
and Society
Treat
the Dying?

THE SERIOUSLY ILL OR DYING CHILD: SUPPORTING THE PATIENT AND THE FAMILY

C. Everett Koop, M.D., Sc.D.

No one enters the medical profession skillful in handling the problems that are generated in the hospital, in the family, and in the community by the seriously ill or dying child. The physician who understands well his role in the treatment of disease and the postponement of death for as long a time as possible, frequently does not understand his role in making the serious illness of a child, his impending death, or his actual death as bearable as possible for all of those concerned. Those affected frequently comprise a wider circle than seems to be the case at first glance. One can never escape the tragedy that these circumstances bring to the family of the patient. Less often, the physician may be aware of the impact of a dying child upon hospital personnel, the community, and the child himself.

While it is true that no one enjoys the management of the emotional problems surrounding the dying child, there is, nevertheless, a satisfaction to the one who serves as guide through difficult times to the end that the family is salvaged, the community is able to get on without bitterness toward the hospital or the medical profession, and the hospital staff is able to return to the routines of care knowing that they have played a positive role in an unpleasant situation.

TYPES OF PATIENTS

From the surgeon's point of view, there are four general classes of patients whose emotional management requires almost as much planning as does specific therapy.

In the care of neonatal surgical patients, in whom operative procedures and congenital anomalies incompatible with life still claim a high mortality, the stresses can be considerable. This is true although the family does not know the patient as an individual, and in spite of the fact that the physician does not know the parents as a family. The mother particularly faces a difficult situation: frequently she has never seen her newborn infant, because it has been whisked away to another part of the hospital, or perhaps to a hospital in a distant city, to have a major congenital anomaly, such as an omphalocele, diaphragmatic hernia, or imperforate anus, cared for by those best able to achieve a happy end result. She not only feels deprived of her infant, but usually receives her knowledge of the child's defect from someone other than the surgeon, who is logically the best person to explain it to her. Not uncommonly, she harbors a certain hostility to those unknown members of the medical team who have deprived her of her infant, even though, at the same time, she knows that their motivation is of the best and the situation unavoidable. When she wakes from her analgesia or anesthesia, the whole situation smacks of unreality. Frequently her husband, on whom she would like to lean at this particular time, has accompanied the infant to a medical center and returns to support his wife overwhelmed by the seriousness of the situation and the speed with which his outlook has so recently changed.

The surgeon's obligation begins with a full explanation to the father, who ideally should be kept on hand until the close of the emergency operative procedure. In the discussion, the surgeon would do well to repeat such statements as "Reassure your wife that . . ." or "Be sure that you do assure Mrs J. that we will do thus and so" and especially, "I will call your wife tomorrow and give her a first-hand report on where things stand, unless you think you would rather do it." If he chooses the latter course, the surgeon should be available for back-up explanation. Some facility in the hospital should be activated (social service, nursing staff, house staff) to provide current information when it is requested.

It has frequently been my experience that the referring physician minimizes the risk and gravity of the procedure, and particularly the cosmetic result. He may advise the mother not to visit her infant because the trip might prove too much for her—even though under ordinary circumstances she would be expected to be up and around and caring for her child. Not only is the surgeon and his hospital placed at a disadvantage because of this, but I believe it is a disservice to the mother. She should understand the gravity of the situation, so that if the outcome is not favorable, she will realize what the odds were from the beginning, rather than to assume that things did not go as well as predicted because of a failure of optimal care somewhere along the line. She will be better able to face the reality of the situation if she is able to see her infant and more particularly to touch it. Anyone who has watched a mother deprived of her newborn child immediately after delivery make her first acquaintance with the youngster (particularly if it is her first born) knows what a tremendous reward she receives from seeing and handling her child. Her natural hostility disappears: she becomes an understanding participant in the care of her child and a cooperative member of the team seeking a successful outcome.

In dealing with the neonatal surgical emergency after the operative procedure for the lesion in question has been accomplished, it is well to introduce the family to the possible occurrence of multiple congenital defects. A conversation or two with the father concerning, for example, the fact that heart lesions may not make themselves evident for a few days, places him somewhat on his guard against future difficulties, but also establishes a rapport between patient and physician which is much easier to achieve before than after the occurrence of a stressing complication.

The child who is in dire straits and who faces imminent death because of an accident presents special problems in emotional management with reference to the family. No accident is planned upon, and in addition to all of those things which are built into the stressful situation surrounding serious illness and impending death is the element of shock and disbelief. Frequently, more than one member of the family has been involved in the accident; indeed, one may already be dead. The surgeon in these circumstances has little time to prepare the family for anything. He must be as truthful as possible without removing all hope, and his frequent attendance upon the patient or the constant care of his deputy will support the family as much as any overture in their time of acute crisis.

The acutely ill surgical patient, like the accident victim, usually has provided his family with no warning of an impending catastrophe, and he falls in the field of management somewhere between the accident patient and the chronically ill child.

But it is around the care of the chronically ill child, whose eventual death seems inevitable, that most of our concerns will center. He is the child whose diagnosis carries an almost inevitable death warrant. His is the family that loses the child twice—once when the diagnosis and prognosis is explained, and again when the child actually dies. Both of these losses can be assuaged to a great degree by the physician who makes it his business to deal with these problems adequately. The interval between the two episodes is the time in which he has the opportunity to build into the family, the community, and the hospital those supports which will stand the test of crisis at the time of actual death and thereafter.

WORKING WITH THE FAMILY IN CHRONIC ILLNESS

The process of relating to the family and to the child should begin at the very first contact with the surgeon, who must project his integrity, capacity for compassion, and understanding in such a way that the family will be assured during the time of diagnostic studies that when the eventual diagnosis is known, the surgeon will not only be honest in his dealings with them, but will, to the best of his ability, help them to understand and bear their situation. This does not mean that the surgeon must share *all* of his concerns with the family before an exact diagnosis is reached. Even though there may be relief at times, it is cruel to put a family through the possibility of facing a hopeless prognosis before the surgical procedure that "proves it," even though the diagnosis seems unavoidable in the surgeon's mind. Usually, the family is keyed to a high pitch at the time the unpleasant news must be broken, because the news commonly rests upon the result of a biopsy, an exploratory procedure, or a series of diagnostic tests.

When the moment comes for the surgeon to share his knowledge with the family, attention to a number of seemingly unimportant details will pay great dividends in days to come. First of all, the news should be given to a family in the best of all possible surroundings, such as a room designed for that purpose, the surgeon's office, a quiet lounge, or some other suitable location. It should not be told on the ward, in the corridor, in the outpatient clinic, in the lobby of the hospital, or in any place where a family cannot let their emotions be demonstrated in any way that they see fit without embarrassment. Secondly, if at all possible, both parents should be together at this time, but if anyone else is to be present, the surgeon should be certain that it is a stable member of the family who will supply support, rather than an unstable member who will add to the emotional strain that the family is about to face. Under no circumstances should this be an announcement to a "gathering of the clan."

I have used the word surgeon here not only because I am one, but also because I think this is the surgeon's responsibility. All too frequently the surgeon who supports an adult magnificently turns his juvenile patients and their families over to the pediatrician, who, although attuned to problems of children and their families, is not always able to answer questions which are so frequently surgically oriented.

The actual wording of the announcement will have to fit the physician's personality, but it should be gentle rather than abrupt, compassionate while factual, and free of scientific terms that are not understood as well as free of double talk that will leave the family uncertain and permit the physician to escape to more pleasant tasks.

The situation in which the family has waited for several tension-filled hours, only to have the surgeon return from the operating room and reveal that the diagnosis is a malignant tumor which carries a high mortality, is sometimes more than they can immediately take in. I have found it valuable to announce first of all that the youngster is in the recovery room and that the operation is over and that all concerned with his care are satisfied with his condition. I then proceed to say that as we suspected, the diagnosis was confirmed as being so and so. This indicates to the family that the diagnosis was not an overwhelming surprise and they therefore have reason to believe that being prepared for the diagnosis, the management was also prepared. I usually keep talking about relatively unimportant things while the family absorbs the first shock of this revelation and then begin to describe the immediate steps that we will take to bring about as satisfactory a solution as possible to the terrible problem that we all face. At about the same time, I remind the family that this is a lot to take at one sitting and that I will repeat it all to them in a day or so and am always available to answer questions that come to their mind. No matter what the prognosis, hope should not be totally eliminated from the picture, and assurance should be given that no matter what the outcome, everything will be done to support the patient.

The physician should also be aware of the fact that there are families who hear only what they want to hear. It is usually possible to get some inkling of this, and the physician can check it out by asking the family questions. If he finds that he is indeed dealing with a family that is screening out all of the factual information that is unpleasant, then he must spell it out exceedingly carefully and perhaps do so in the presence of another member of the family, who is able to understand and emotionally interpret it.

As the reality of the situation is grasped by the family, their first questions usually center around suffering and the duration of life. The question of suffering can always be answered with assurance of a positive nature, but it is best to hedge the timing of death, not only because it is unknown, but because so many therapeutic factors may alter the situation.

One can usually tell whether this is a time when the family would like to be alone, or whether they would prefer to have the continuing support of a stranger who is obviously trying to be a friend. This is the time when the surgeon must be all things to all men. A kindly gesture such as an arm around the father or holding the hands of both parents as they sit facing you may seem at times like an embarrassing gesture to the surgeon, but is frequently remembered in days to come as an outstanding act of support. Some families indicate that they would like to talk further at this time; others are too shocked to absorb much more until another day. At some time there are a number of things that I think have to be gotten across that are important to the future.

If one knows the problems the family is going to face in the community, I think it is well to discuss these problems before they present themselves to the family. Parents cannot help but share their tragic news with their friends and relatives. Almost inevitably, some well-meaning individual is so certain that he understands the situation better than the child's doctors or has such faith in his own physician that he will not rest until the family has had either a change of management or at least another opinion. Not because I fear another opinion, but because I am concerned about the family's emotional stability, I tell them that they have no idea how many well-meaning friends they will have who are also amateur physicians or quasi-experts in their child's diagnosis. I also tell them that many people have been duped by cancer quacks and fraudulent cancer remedies. I assure them that bonafide therapy is never the property of one man or one clinic, but is available to all reputable physicians. I further say that if there were anything unique that could be offered their child in another center, I would see that the referral was made and the economic burden eased if such were a problem. Indeed, all of us who deal with dying children occasionally do make such referrals. I suggest that the way to avoid confusion is to inform me of any advice that sounds reasonable and logical to the family. I tell them that if I know anything about it, I will discuss it with them, and if I do not, I will investigate it and report back promptly. In dealing with cancer patients now for more than a quarter of a century, I have lost only two patients to cancer quacks, and one of these returned. I think if I had been more specific with the families earlier, both of these tragic circumstances could have been avoided.

It used to be said in World War II that there were no atheists in fox holes. I have found that there are very few atheists among the parents of dying children. This is a time when religious faith can see a family through the most trying circumstances. I think it is well to work closely with the family's clergyman, if this is their wish, and very commonly one finds that such a minister will accompany the family upon their second or third visit to the hospital after knowing of their child's diagnosis.

Again in line with being all things to all men, at a time like this, I can speak from the standpoint of my own faith, and when I am asked such questions as "Why did God do this to my child?" or "What have we done to be punished like this?" or when I hear statements such as "All we can do is hope and pray," I attempt to meet the family on some compatible ground that will not be argumentative, but might be reassuring. I have found that most commonly, people who ask these questions are reassured by the fact that the God they question is sovereign and does not act capriciously. I am certain that it helps many times for the family to hear me say that if I did not believe in the sovereignty of God, I would find it most difficult, if not impossible, to be caring for their child. If the family requests you to talk to their minister, do so. If they want you to talk to their relatives now that the first awful crisis is past, this is reasonable. If they ask you to pray with them, pray with them. About the only thing you cannot do, much as you might want to, is cry with them. Hospital chaplains can be invaluable at times, yet parents appreciate nonprofessional help from their doctors.

There probably has never been a conception nor a parent-child relationship in which, under stress, the parent could not find cause for guilt. These guilt feelings very commonly become serious reactions around the grave illness or death of a child. So frequently do parents, particularly mothers, consider the affliction of their child to be punishment from God that it is commonly openly expressed. No matter what one's theological doctrine on punishment might be, parents benefit by the statement that such an affliction of a child and punishment of a parent would be evil, and that no evil comes from the hand of God.

It is inevitable in a medical center, particularly one well staffed with physicians, residents, and fellows, that all of the discussions around a child's illness will not conform to the statements made by the physician in charge. It is well to point out that if any questions arise because of variations in advice, that the surgeon's door is always open to try to answer questions. At the same time, it is well to train a house staff that in these stressful situations we have to be of one mind and one goal. High on the list of priorities is the admonition never to make a promise that cannot be fulfilled.

ANSWERING PARENTS' QUESTIONS

Parents inevitably ask, "How long?", "Will he be well again before he dies?", "Can he go back to school?", "Will he suffer?"

These questions should be faced head-on and answered from the physician's experience to the advantage of this particular family. Frequently one must say that the youngster will be so well for a time that the parents will doubt the diagnosis and prognosis. The question of school must be individualized, but in general, if a child feels well, it is probably best for him to go to school. Even if his life expectancy is limited, it is very difficult for a family to have what amounts to a "death watch" around a seemingly well child. When he begins to falter and school becomes difficult physically, mentally, or emotionally, he probably should stay at home. In some instances, half-day schooling is good for morale all around.

The promise to alleviate suffering can always be made—but it should then be kept. There a number of pain-killers and sedatives for the night that should be made available, even if these are narcotics for pain that cannot otherwise be controlled. Families should not be promised this sort of help unless the surgeon and his medical colleagues are determined to deliver on that promise.

The most difficult question, the one concerning the time of death, cannot be definitely answered, but there are some pitfalls to avoid. Do not be specific; the course of the disease is too variable. Do not encourage Christmas in October for the child who may die in November; it takes its toll on the family, the community, and frequently on the child, out of all proportions to the associated reward.

Parents are helped by the statement that the physician will keep no secrets from them and that when he is reasonably assured concerning timing, that information will be shared.

In any circumstance where there is even the most remote possibility of a genetic factor in the illness of the seriously ill or dying child, the family should have the assurance that genetic counseling will be made available to them as soon as they wish it.

DEALING WITH THE SICK AND DYING CHILD HIMSELF

As in any relationship with children, something akin to honesty is probably best. Few children really inquire if they are dying; some ask if they are ever going to get better. To the latter question, I frequently say something like, "Of course you're going to get better, but it is also true that I think you will probably feel worse before you start to feel better."

If the physician is one who banters with his patient, such is the way to relate to the child throughout his illness, but avoid the bantering if it is reserved only for the severely ill child—usually out of embarrassment. Youngsters can detect a phony.

I am convinced that many more children have known they were dying than shared that information with me. Some knew it and kept it from their family; with a few I have discussed death, at their request. I have not seen a child upset by this. With many, I have talked about close calls—after the fact. One can only gently feel his way along this uncharted path, and be guided by the child.

In an institution where there is an aggregation of patients of poor prognosis, such as a chemotherapy ward for cancer, a neurosurgical ward for brain tumors, an intensive care unit where the mortality is higher than elsewhere in the hospital, there is a recognizable chain of events which repeats itself. Student nurses inevitably look forward to pediatrics because of their mental image of holding a rosy-cheeked baby in their laps for feeding. Instead of this, they are frequently ushered into a pediatric environment involving unconscious neurosurgical patients, ecchymotic leukemics, and neuroblastoma patients with bulging eyes. The high concentration of these, particularly in any one area, leads to depression, emotional upset, or frank hysterics, and occasionally to inability to continue an assignment. Charge nurses, familiar with this "syndrome" are, as a rule, very capable in handling it, but after they have handled a certain number of these situations, they too begin to feel the depression and frustration of high mortality; and they too lean on someone else, who in turn leans on someone else. In most hospitals there is one individual where the buck stops. If that individual's sense of prophylaxis is as good as his sense of therapy, he can frequently avoid such breakdown by conferences to which cured children are brought for review, by tumor conferences where student and staff are invited to see the progress of disease and its suppression, and by encouraging relationships with parents who have had happy experiences with successfully treated disease of poor prognosis.

PALLIATION WITHOUT CURE

In the field of cancer management today, there are a number of modalities of therapy which can prolong life, but rarely cure the underlying disease. In the process of prolonging life, we sometimes produce undesirable situations, including pain and the necessity for transfusion of blood or blood components. Regardless of where one stands philosophically about doing everything or doing nothing, the physician must be on guard so that he never puts a family who has lost a child in the position of being able to say, "We didn't do all we could for our boy," or worse than that, "You wouldn't do so and so for him when you could have." The physician can do a great deal while establishing his rapport with the family in guiding their thinking along these lines long before the occasion for decision arises. I happen to believe that the terminal patient with neuroblastoma and extensive bone metastases, for example, should be permitted to die as quietly and in as dignified a manner as possible rather than to use every conceivable combination of chemotherapeutic agents for the prolongation of life without the alleviation of the disease. Seldom does the family fail to go along with this thinking if they are properly introduced to it in advance. Sometimes these decisions are difficult, particularly in an academic environment where legalism sometimes prevails in therapy. For example, the youngster with cancer approaching his terminal phase may be quite subdued, quite comfortable, and of minimal emotional hazard to his family, while his hemoglobin is, say, 6 gm. per 100 ml. The "legalist" transfuses to 11 gm., whereupon all of his sensoria are activated; he now perceives his pain more acutely, he is fretful, and his family is put through another period of stress.

HEREDITARY DISEASE

The family whose child is dying of hereditary disease must be handled with special care. Not only does the family carry the guilt of transmission, but they have great questions about future pregnancies and the occurrence of similar conditions in other children. Families whose children have died from accidental causes in the presence of hemophilia, children with cystic fibrosis and perhaps meconium ileus, youngsters with neurofibromatosis, etc., should have genetic counseling, and should be encouraged to talk about their own feelings. There are few family situations more pitiful than the silent father with obvious Von Recklinghausen's disease whose child is dying of neurofibrosarcoma in the presence of the same malady. His guilt about his child's condition and his self-reproach before his wife can frequently be talked out satisfactorily, so that these problems are not added to the impending grief of the loss of the child.

THE TERMINAL PHASE OF ILLNESS

As the terminal phase of chronic illness approaches, the physician frequently has the choice of choosing a hospital or the family's home for the final days. There are no flat rules of procedure about this. Some people feel that a youngster should not die in a home where there are other children. I have known this to work out very satisfactorily with a family understanding the situation extremely well and salvaging a happy family relationship—perhaps because of it rather than in spite of it.

The family should always know that there will be a place in the hospital for quiet refuge as the end approaches and that this facility will be for the family's convenience rather than for the patient's treatment. If such a facility is eventually used, the family should be permitted free access to the youngster's room. It should be a room not shared by others, if possible. It should be at a quiet end of a hospital corridor, and the usual disturbing observations of pulse, temperature, blood pressure, etc., should be eliminated. The child's comfort should be the primary goal of the hospital team, and if this is followed, the family's needs will be automatically taken care of for the moment. If the physician chooses to have a youngster's terminal days passed at home, he should visit that home and assess the situation at first hand.

AUTOPSY PERMISSION

The ability of the physician to obtain permission for an autopsy is dependent largely upon the rapport he has established beforehand, and I think that under most circumstances success is more likely if this is handled by the physician in charge rather than by a member of his house staff, unless that individual has had a particular role to play in which he has acted as his chief's surrogate.

As with the breaking of the news of impending death, autopsy permission is the business of the mother and father and not of the entire family. It is well to obtain it early, rather than after relatives have talked to the grieved parents and convinced them that "their child has suffered enough."

If the parents have consented to an autopsy, they are entitled to know what the major findings were, and this should become part of the physician's obligation. I make it a point to write a letter to the family of each child who has died, assuring them that they did all that was possible in providing care for their youngster, pointing out the inevitablity of his death with our present state of knowledge, and assuring them of my availability should any questions arise. Some weeks later, I send them a nondetailed but nevertheless informative summary of the autopsy findings.

Do not avoid the family of the child who has died. There is nothing more disheartening to parents than to have lived through a trying time and given permission for an autopsy, only to realize that the physician who cared for their youngster has come to the end of his obligation. Particularly with children, relatives ask questions long after death. It is frequently very difficult for a family to come back to the same hospital and to the same doctor's office where they once heard the first inkling of the fact that their youngster was going to die. The physician should be aware of this, and if it is impossible for him to meet in another building, he should at least find a different area in his hospital or office accommodations to meet with parents and answer their late questions.

The willingness of a family to come back to the scene of their previous tragedy is about the highest compliment that can be paid to the hospital and the medical team that cared for the dying child.

HOW HOSPICES COPE

The word "hospice" is reminiscent of the Middle Ages when hundreds of hospices were dotted all over Europe, where travellers found food, refuge and spiritual encouragement to fit them for the journey ahead. Mary Aikenhead applied this name to terminal hospitals because she saw them as fulfilling a parallel purpose, death to her being a thoroughfare, not a terminus.

For many years nuns and other Christian groups have run terminal homes on both sides of the Atlantic, and in 1952 the Marie Curie Foundation opened the first of its homes. It should be pointed out that in these homes, as well as caring for people dying of cancer, they also rehabilitate patients whose cancers have been cured. With 410 beds in 12 homes this is the largest voluntary organization in the field. Within the National Health Service are St. Luke's, Bayswater and St. Columba's, Hampstead. Most of the hospices, however, are independent charities, often working with support from the Department of Health and Social Security, though the Hostel of God in Clapham is completely independent of State support.

HISTORY

To St. Luke's Hospital and St. Joseph's Hospice, Hackney, goes the honour of being the first to put the care of the dying on a firm scientific footing. In the nineteen fifties purpose-built wards were opened at St. Joseph's. The building has bays of six beds with a spacious central day-room. As the windows reach almost to the floor, a patient in bed can see across the gardens and into a busy thoroughfare. Consequently he is not cut off from day to day events, but can still enjoy the turmoil of the traffic and fire engines and fights of the East End in which he has always lived. To put someone in a window bed is the best cure for depression at St. Joseph's. In contrast to this, patients at Ardenlea Marie Curie Home in Ilkley told me how wonderful it was to look out over their beloved Yorkshire Moors.

Hospices usually provide room for visitors to stay all day, so that they can share in looking after the patients if they wish to. Gardens are a great asset, especially if the patient's beds can be wheeled into them. In the wards, the televisions are silent with lightweight earphones on every bed for any patient who wants to listen.[1]

Earlier in this century hospices were mainly concerned with people dying of tuberculosis, but now cancer holds the stage. Indeed the Marie Curie Homes are exclusively for cancer patients. The Irish Sisters of Charity have hospices in Eire, Britain and Australia. Other recent foundations not run by religious orders are in New Haven, U.S.A.; Manchester, Brighton, Thornton, Sheffield, Worthing and Stoke in Britain; and Kalorama in Holland. Jospice International has several homes in S. America and Pakistan. The idea is meeting with enthusiasm everywhere, and those who are planning new hospices are turning to those already established.

From the outset Mary Aikenhead linked the care of dying patients in the wards with community care and the support of the sick in their homes. This lady's genius set the pattern which the new hospices are still adopting today.

Most of these institutions are religious in essence, working in close co-operation with the clergy of all faiths. All have a remarkably peaceful and—dare I say it?—distinctly joyful atmosphere. They are thus establishing a rather different reputation from the municipal homes for the elderly described by Peter Townsend.[2] Many of these are grim ex-workhouses where regimentation drains away the individuality and happiness of the inmates. As Professor Hinton said in his Pelican book *Dying,*

> To choose between a below-standard hospital for the chronic sick and a poor home is a painful dilemma. Many dying people or their relatives have to do this, some in ignorance and some with painful awareness of the implications.

The opening of hospices in every community will make available to all men as they die the benefit of the skills and experience now being developed.

Let us examine some of these skills more closely.

TEACHING

Care of the dying is best learnt by practice. A film or lecture can be stimulating, but it is no substitute for personal experience. For this reason hospices welcome visits from groups of students, nurses and anyone else who is professionally interested. Ward rounds and discussions are useful, but it may be more helpful for a student to be introduced to the patient and left to see what he can learn from this encounter. From the patient's point of view another interested visitor is usually welcome; and for the student—here is life in all its unpredictable wonder. Such a breath of fresh air after all the books!

These ward rounds are becoming more popular as a gap in medical education is recognized. Medical students in Sheffield receive instruction in St. Luke's Home[3] and in Sydenham St. Christopher's Hospice now has a new teaching centre, where individual tutorials and small discussion groups are the mainstay of the teaching. Medical students and ordinands do holiday work and gain valuable first hand experience in the wards of both these hospices. As more hospices open it is this —more than any theoretical teaching—which will bring up a new generation able and ready to cope with the proper care of the dying both in general hospitals and in their own homes.

There is also a duty to educate the general public. Books, articles,[4] letters in newspapers[5] and hospice open days[6] all contribute to help the community to a calmer, less fearful approach to dying. Soon people will cease to associate serious illness and death with inevitable pain, but rather will actually expect to have a joyful death. The Marie Curie Foundation publishes an excellent series of leaflets to educate the public on the prophylaxis and management of cancer, stressing the high proportion of cures now possible.

MEDICAL SKILLS

The principles of symptomatic treatment with drugs are simple. The first secret lies in realising that when we give people drugs, it is not like feeding data into a machine. People respond differently to any one drug. And the second secret is that symptoms should be anticipated.

Why should patients with terminal illness—notably cancer—have to suffer so much pain when the knowledge of effective pain control is now so widespread? While many doctors may have encountered a confounding case where nothing they could do with drugs, surgery or radiation, was able to control the pain, such cases are very rare. Usually all that is required is someone who cares enough.[7] Caring is such an effort, isn't it? In an age of disposable everythings, "just heat and eat," "labour saver—just spray it on," taking care is less and less exercised, and becomes unfashionable.

One sometimes hears odd comments about pain which prompt doubts about our whole way of life:

"All right, I'll let Doctor know it's hurting again, but we just have to bathe you now."

"Mr. Smith keeps saying he's in pain, but I doubt it: he's always demanding attention."

You can tell if a man is in pain simply by looking and listening. A wrinkled brow, tense fingers and cautious breathing may betray underlying pain even in an unresponsive patient. It has been noted that these signs can even be removed in some unconscious patients by the administration of analgesics. But in order to notice these signs, and to feel inclined to do something about them, it is necessary really to look, and to care.

Each kind of pain has its distinctive treatment. For minor pains there are many effective agents, particularly variations on the aspirin theme. These may be sufficient by themselves, but if they do not control pain adequately, one can progress to a number of more powerful drugs which are available as tablets (Fortral, Dieconal and Narphen are popular examples). For severe pain, however, the strong narcotic analgesics may eventually be needed (for example morphine, diamorphine and physeptone). Fearing that the patient may become addicted, doctors are often reluctant to use adequate doses of these drugs. Given by mouth, often mixed with a little gin and cocaine in one of the variations of the so-called "Brompton cocktail," these drugs do not have to be given in the ever-increasing doses dreaded by those unaccustomed to their use. Of course, if an inadequate dose is given, by injection, so that by the time of the next medicine-round the patient has pain again and is longing for the relief that the injection brings, then the scene is perfectly set for the development of physical and psychological dependence.

Most people can cope with short-term pain, but what we most fear is pain which lasts for months. This constant pain will need constant control with analgesics, and if the control is to be sustained the drug must obviously be given regularly, day and night. Pain severe enough to require large doses of narcotics is rare. The usual starting dose in one hospice which uses diamorphine is five or ten milligrams, given by mouth every four hours. This may be increased, to reach double that dose before the patient dies. In one series, only 13% of patients ever needed more than a thirty milligram dose, which is a small quantity by any standards. If tolerance (a lessening of effectiveness of the drug because the patient's body is compensating for it) is developing, then there is a substance called amiphenazole (Daptazole) which appears to arrest the process.

It should, however, be noted that for a dying man there is no maximum dose of a pain-killer. If his pain really needs five times the normal quantity (presumably because some measure of tolerance is present) then that is his correct dose. The severer pains may need injections to keep them below the horizon. When they are given by injection, the actual dose of narcotic analgesics should be halved, not kept the same as when given by mouth, because not all of the drug is absorbed from the gut. In short, by carefully observing the individual's response, the doctor can *titrate* his drugs against the patient's pain.[8]

It has been suggested that larger doses of narcotics, because of their inhibitory effect on a patient's breathing, may shorten his life. My experience has been quite the contrary. By easing the sense of breathlessness as well as the pain, these drugs relieve the distress which can exhaust the dying. Being able to rest, they live longer if anything. The popular idea is an utter myth.

Excitement or depression also contributes to pain, perhaps by lowering a man's resistance—his "pain threshold" as the physiologist calls it, and so tranquilizers and anti-depressants have their place in pain relief. For not all pain is physical. . . .

Continuing for a while, however, to consider the physical methods of easing pain, there are many other techniques in the doctor's arsenal. Gardham wrote a paper, for instance, on the use of surgery just for the relief of symptoms, without hoping to effect a cure.[9] The neurosurgeon may be able to help by cutting the pain-carrying nerves, or the anaesthetist by paralysing them. Radiotherapy may cause shrinkage of large tumors which are exerting painful pressure on surrounding parts of the body, and so may some hormones and "cytotoxic" drugs. The ingenuity of modern medicine is quite wonderful, but as death approaches, many of these techniques give steadily diminishing returns. Most of them anyway, may have unpleasant side-effects. There comes a time when these measures should neither be initiated nor continued. All that is necessary is that the doctor should pause and ask himself Sir Stanford Cade's famous question "What is the relative value of the various available forms of treatment *in this particular patient?*"[10]

Vomiting can usually be controlled by anti-emetic drugs and it is worthwhile to try several different ones to see which works for the patient without making him drowsy. If vomiting is due to an actual blockage of the stomach or bowel (which is rare), then a stomach tube can be passed through the nose to suck out the contents of the stomach before they are vomited. Thereafter his fluid intake will have to be by rectal infusions, with ice lollies to suck to keep his mouth moist. Such use of tubes is very seldom indicated, but when these very unusual circumstances arise, they can bring comfort to the patient. They are not intended to extend his life.

Hiccups usually stop if carbon dioxide is inhaled, so the patient should be told to breath in and out of a paper bag for a few minutes. If this measure fails, an injection of chlorpromazine (Largactil) may help.

Inevitably the doctor will be using a number of different drugs—one for each symptom—and their use should be explained to the patient.

"Did the tablet help your breathing?"

"Oh, I thought it was for the bowels." No comment.

It may be necessary to experiment with different remedies to find what suits each patient, but each doctor gradually fills his box of tricks. Drugs for headaches, nausea, anxiety, loss of appetite,[11] breathlessness, diarrhoea, constipation, coughs and cramps. The list is endless. And drugs are not all. Raising the head or foot of the bed, draining off excesses of fluid collecting in the body cavities or bladder, or pumping fluid away from a swollen hand or leg, can all be of help to some patients. Honey taken after food can stop the unpleasant waterbrash in people with cancer of the gullet, and can be used to disinfect bedsores. Oxygen may, rarely, help breathlessness though open windows are better. Alcohol helps almost everything.

Not least, the doctor's own confidence in his remedies can be transmitted to the patient. Nowadays he can meet his patients with the assurance that he can bring comfort. Why, even the "death rattle" itself can be quietened by an injection of a mixture of belladona and a narcotic. It is due to secretions in the throat which a dying person cannot cough up, and drugs of the belladonna family dry up the production of these secretions.

Certainly our drugs are marvellous, and great fun, but their use is only chemistry at best, and the physics and chemistry are only the deadest part of a man. To know which drugs are needed and which are not, and to know how to relieve distress, we need to look at the patient, and to care. Used in the right way and by those who retain their sensitivity to pain and discomfort, they will be of immense help in the last stages of life.

NURSING SKILLS

Some aspects of nursing are intensified in caring for the dying, and some fade into the background.[12] There arises, quite naturally, a certain reverence for the patients. This includes unresponsive patients, who must always be handled gently, and treated as if fully aware. Careless conversations over an apparently unconscious person are sometimes clearly heard by that person. It is usually considered that hearing is the last of the senses to fade, and many religions have accordingly provided special prayers to be read quietly into the ear of the dying man.

Routine procedures such as taking the temperature and

pulse need not disturb the patient now as they are of no further practical use. On the other hand, attention to the patient's appearance preserves his dignity. The men should still be shaved regularly, and the ladies should have their hair done.

When a new patient arrives at a hospice he is welcomed by name while still in the ambulance, and his future ward sister or staff nurse accompanies him to the ward. It is important that the relatives should also be welcomed, because henceforth treatment will be directed towards the whole family. Suffering will not be confined to the patient himself: everyone who loves him will to some extent be a patient of the hospice.

When his pain is controlled, the patient may be well enough to get up, or even to go home for a few weeks. Many will spend part of the morning in the dayroom where they may watch television, develop a new skill in occupational therapy or chat with friends. One hospice has a sitting room in which patients who are mobile enough can entertain their friends and take tea provided by voluntary workers.

All the ancillary aid possible must be maintained for the patients at this stage,[13] as I will discuss in the next section of this chapter. But as time passes the patient will feel weaker and will want to spend more time in bed, needing ever more intensive nursing. This can be very heavy work for the nurses, and the full complement of nurses to a ward should be the same as for an acute medical ward—namely at least one nurse to one patient* quite apart from ward orderlies and voluntary workers.

It is at this stage that the work of the nurse earns profound admiration. Gradually she has to take over more and more of the patient's activities for him. He will have to be lifted and turned, washed and fed, and all without impinging on his dignity. One girl who recently died of motor neurone disease, and whose only means of communication was by blinking in Morse Code, dictated the following to a friend:

> Possibly I am particularly sensitive, but I hate to be fed. Nevertheless it makes an enormous difference to one's enjoyment of a meal if the person helping takes a real interest in what she is doing. I know that it must re-

*i.e. including day and night nurses, on or off duty.

quire infinite patience, but there are some
people who will go to endless trouble to keep
the food hot, and make it as tasty as possible.
They also give the impression that there is
nothing they would rather be doing at that
particular time. Others, however, will carry on
an animated conversation with another, whilst
holding an appetising forkful—just out of reach!
—or stare out of the window, in deep thought,
while one watches the food get cold.

The person in whom I have most confidence
is the one who goes about her work slowly and
deliberately, telling what she is about to do,
giving me the opportunity to indicate if anything is wrong. She seems to get through her
work just as quickly as the one who exercises a
more forceful approach.

The rest of this essay is equally valuable reading, particularly for nurses or physiotherapists.[14]

Our techniques must be good, but we must also give ourselves to the patients. It can be very lonely in hospital, and
no amount of science will alleviate that. But one gentle cheerful nurse can. She need not be a Socrates—it is not the profundity of her understanding which is of value—but the fact
that she cares enough to try. A nurse who was dying wrote
about this as follows:

I know, you feel insecure, don't know what to
say, don't know what to do. But please believe
me, if you care, you can't go wrong. Just admit
that you care. That is really for what we search.
We may ask for why's and wherefores, but we
don't really expect answers. Don't run away . . .
wait . . . all I want to know is that there will be
someone to hold my hand when I need it. I am
afraid. Death may get to be a routine to you,
but it is new to me. You may not see me as
unique, but I've never died before, to me, once
is pretty unique!

You whisper about my youth, but when one
is dying, is he really so young any more? I have
lots I wish we could talk about. It really would
not take much of your time because you are in
here quite a bit anyway.

If only we could be honest, both admit our
fears, touch one another. If you really care,

would you lose so much of your valuable profes-
sionalism if you even cried with me? Just person to person? Then, it might not be so hard to
die . . . in a hospital . . . with friends close by.[15]

A number of techniques and methods have been developed
in hospices which are worth describing because they may be
used at home or in hospital, and bring great relief.

Medicines must be given regularly, every four hours being
the best timing, day and night. They should never be inacces-
sible, for once a patient needs help, there should be no delay.
The senior nurses often exercise discretion with drugs. Pain
killers and tranquillizers, for instance, are prescribed with a
range of doses. The sister can then give the exactly appropriate quantity herself, and thus learn to use the drugs accurately.

Many different methods can be used for avoiding bedsores, but if they do occur this is not a sign of bad nursing—
they may sometimes be inevitable. Then one must try at least
to render them painless. They arise because of continuous
pressure on one patch of the skin of a patient who cannot
move about, the places to watch being the heels and base of
the spine.

Ripple mattresses with inflatable ribs which are alternately filled and deflated by an electric pump can help by
shifting the points on which the person's weight is borne.
Some Local Authorities have these for hire. For a slightly
mobile patient who is not incontinent, a sheepskin can help to
spread the weight. The usual method is just to turn the patient regularly from one side to the other. With this method
one should watch that sores do not develop on the hips, and
that the sheet does not rub against the skin as the person is
being turned. This procedure should be repeated every two to
four hours. This need only continue throughout the night if
the patient is very sore. All lumps and wrinkles should be
smoothed out of the bedding under the patient. If the pressure areas become red, the skin should be gently massaged
with a mixture of surgical spirit and olive oil, or just pow-
dered to keep it dry. When a patient is incontinent there
should be a rubber or plastic drawsheet, covered by a twill
one which can be moved or changed when soiled. Every time
this sheet is changed, a barrier cream should be applied to the
affected area.

If the skin breaks in spite of all these measures, the sore

should be dressed with a disinfectant and a local anaesthetic cream. Cicatrin powder or honey are excellent disinfectants to use. When any slough forming in the floor of the ulcer has been removed, the cavity should be cleaned with hydrogen peroxide ten volumes solution which produces an oxygen-rich foam, killing gangrene germs. (Care should be taken not to splash this solution in the eyes.) The edges of the sore should be gently massaged. Some doctors find that zinc sulphate capsules (220 milligrams, thrice daily) help healing to take place provided they do not cause vomiting. Deep bedsores should be packed with gauze soaked in Eusol and paraffin every six hours to keep them free from infection. Many other forms of treatment are favoured in different hospitals, but the one I have described could also be carried out at home.

To prevent the skin of an incontinent patient becoming soggy it is always worth while to insert a catheter which drains urine from the bladder into a bag. Infection of a catheter can be prevented by a once-weekly dose of a long-acting sulphonamide tablet or some similar drug. If he is still mobile, the patient could have the urine bag strapped to his leg, suspended from his pyjama cord under the dressing gown or, for the ladies, carried in a little crocheted hand-bag. Male patients who are not confused can use a condom attachment for the urine tube. One of the best is a Stille Uridom, held on with Warne skin adhesive.

Adequate care of the mouth is essential. It pays to have ill-fitting dentures refashioned as long as the person can eat. Chewing gum may freshen up the mouth and help the patient to make saliva.[16] Thrush in the mouth—like flecks of milk curd stuck to the gums and palate, each surrounded by a red inflamed flare—is a constant nuisance to debilitated patients. It is important to be on the lookout for this, because it is extremely uncomfortable but easy to treat. When a patient becomes very weak, mouthwashes every four hours are essential. The mouth may drop open and become dry. Water should be given in frequent small quantities as long as the person can swallow. A gauze wick with one end in ice water and the other in the mouth for the patient to suck has been recommended. Ice wrapped in gauze may be placed inside the cheek to melt gradually, replacing saliva. On the other hand if there is too much saliva, it may be absorbed by wads of gauze placed between the cheek and gums. The patient should be turned on his side so that fluid does not trickle down his windpipe making him cough.

A considerable problem—indeed one of the greatest—is constipation, especially when pain-killing drugs are in use. If laxatives do not work, suppositories may, and an enema may be tried on the third or fourth day. It is worth while to proceed quickly to the most active measures because they make the person feel so much better. A good intake of drinks is a great help, and the motions can be softened by medicines like "Dioctyl." Sometimes bowel blockage produces distension. The doctor can deflate this, for a dying patient, by puncturing the distended loop of bowel with a large hypodermic needle and letting out the gas. The procedure is painless.

If his breathing is laboured, the patient should be turned slightly on his side, and propped up on pillows with his head well supported. To prevent him sliding back down, a "bed donkey" can be inserted on which to rest his feet. A cushion rolled in a sheet which is tucked in at both sides of the bed will do.

Moving an unconscious or semi-conscious person who cannot co-operate is a job for two people, one on each side, linking their hands under him and co-ordinating their efforts by saying "one, two, three, Lift." This requires knowledge of exactly where to place the hands and how to grasp the wrists of the other helper. When the balance and position are exactly right, even heavy people are easy to move. This technique cannot be taught, it comes from practice, bearing in mind the comfort of the patient.[17] Full attention is required, so social conversation at the time should be avoided.

Above all, a dying man needs company. There is usually nothing to do but hold his hand. Hospices have a rule that no one shall die alone: if no relatives can be present, then a nurse or any other sympathetic helper should be with him, day or night.

Once a patient has been declared incurable, those not accustomed to treating the dying tend to forget him, to withdraw quickly and leave him alone. The sense of desolation and loneliness to which this often gives rise has been called a state of being "socially dead."[18] The patient becomes depressed and introverted. He may exhibit resentment and aggression, or just an overwhelming hopelessness. He sleeps most of the time, withdrawing from the world into a dark and haunted cavern of dreams and drifting imaginings. This is real suffering.

At this point, the more members of the team who can be

interested in the patient, the better.[19] Of course, later on when he is moribund, the need is for the more discreet presence of only one or two trusted friends in an atmosphere of peace and confidence. But as long as the patient can be encouraged to be bright and alert, the less he will suffer. What hope has morphia if the patient is not happy?

One expects to find social workers, physiotherapists, occupational therapists and chaplains in the hospice setting; but also important are the visiting dentist and optician, the family doctor who visits to show he is still concerned, the chiropodist and the hairdresser. Voluntary workers of all kinds can bring their own special abilities and listening ears. They can help in the wards, run the patients' libraries, mobile shops and social functions, as well as launch fund-raising programmes.

PATIENTS AND STAFF

The magic in life springs from our relationships with other people. In a hospice which cares for the dying what happens to the patient's outlook? What happens to the staff?

So often I have heard it said "Terminal care? I couldn't do that, it must be awfully depressing." That this popular picture of a hospice as a gloomy house full of agonized corpse-like people is not accurate, is a tribute to the quality of the nursing. Although extreme illness is treated with horror and people avoid even looking at it,[20] it is often a positive force, binding people together and bringing out the best in them.[21] It is not a question of getting hardened to suffering—one always remains vulnerable. If one person is to receive comfort, someone else has to give it up. Merely staying beside someone who is struggling with physical deterioration and mental anguish can be very painful. But this pain can be a rewarding experience, because of the comfort such fellowship brings to the patient. Although some patients are in the hospice for only a few days, others may spend much longer in the ward. To benefit fully from the care a hospice gives, some patients need to be there for several weeks. Inevitably the staff will make friends with them, so that a series of bereavements for the staff cannot be avoided. If a much loved patient dies, there is a cloud over the whole ward for a while. To support the staff and to develop their own insight, group meetings are held to discuss these matters. For one person alone it might well prove too much, but with the strength of a whole caring community, it is easy. This is the main reason why specialist hospices are needed: the individual's confidence can be sustained by the group which will also guide his attitude to his work.

The patient's hope of recovery should never be completely extinguished. He should never be spoken of as if he were as good as dead, nor should a wholly pessimistic prognosis be given. The staff should always remember that miracles do happen—as I shall recount in a later chapter—in fact, the miraculous is quite commonplace.

I had the honour of helping to care for a lady whose story illustrates several of these points: When she arrived in February Mrs. P. said her cancer had been cured, so she could not think what was wrong with her breast now. She turned off completely, keeping the curtains shut and the bed covers over her head. Having told the psychiatrist that she should have died long ago, she dismissed him by saying she found it hard to open up to people. Gradually Mrs. P.'s depression lifted, and by April she was able to discuss her family problems at length with the doctors and became much easier to nurse. Though she still produced many untreatable symptoms and vague complaints, she did so with a perverse impishness which betrayed growing insight. Occasionally her barriers fell away, and one day she met the psychiatrist with "You don't think you are going to beat me, do you?" He replied, "I thought we were both on the same side." After a brief tirade she suddenly smiled mischievously and squeezed his hand. By June she was able to ask the doctor "Am I dying? Now come on, be honest." She then asked him to read her notes to her, showing much interest, but no distress. When she died, the nurses had all grown very fond of her.

To watch someone coming to terms, in his own special way, with an unbearable situation, is a very great privilege. Here more than anywhere else a good nurse can give valuable help. On their death beds many men mature wonderfully. Priorities fall into place, tolerance and courage may grow in the most unlikely soil and more amazing still is the serenity which so often comes to one from the dying.

Much of the work of those caring for the dying is to prevent anything arising which may hinder this growth in the patient's being. He must be free from pain, but still alert; he must be told as much of the truth about his condition as he can cope with, but no more; he must be encouraged to turn his attention away from himself, and must be given a clean example of real service.[22]

When a man's responsibilities drop away, either by reason of physical weakness or of senile dementia, there remains a great beauty which has been covered by busy-ness—or laziness—for many a year. Death removes the covers: this unmasking can be a thrilling revelation.

When people say that they would find the care of the dying depressing, I wonder whether they are not denying expression to that very part of their nature which could give the most to others. Nurses or doctors who get elated or depressed with their patients are not considering what the patients may need from them. It follows that such feelings must be self-centered. This kind of "involvement" may well render a person useless. For instance, a nurse who vomits when cleaning up an incontinent patient has all her attention on herself, instead of on the needs of the patient. Just so she who grieves with him, suffers with him, "feels for him" or does anything but serve him.[23]

To see a man's needs and to minister to them efficiently and considerately requires a measure of detachment. This is not—as is commonly supposed—a cold thing. Far from it!—it is an indispensable pre-requisite of love. Surges of emotion take your attention off the person in need on to yourself. However, if some situation is very moving another trap is to try to conceal your feelings. When you consider it, such suppression is untruthful. It is better to keep a level head if you can, but if you cannot, at least do not be dishonest about it!

I remember one family who were overwhelmed with gratitude because the nurse who imparted bad news to them also cried with them. "How wonderful," they said afterwards, "that she cared so much." The significant thing, however, was that she *stayed* with them in spite of her own sorrow and embarrassment.

This love is essential in caring for the dying. In a general ward, there is usually so much one can do for the patients[24] that the duty to be with them and the pure giving entailed in listening to them, can be dismissed as an encumbrance. But to provide the dying with masses of hospital equipment and drugs, and no love, is like offering a pot of gold to a starving man buried in sovereigns.

The right attitude to the dying, then, is neither that of a vivisector, nor that of an indulgent granny, but is one of esteem, of reverence, of loving kindness. This is a tall order, certainly, but it is a worthy aim. In this setting one hopes the patient may be able to approach death like the Chinese poet Po Chu-i, who wrote:

Within my breast no sorrows can abide,
I feel the great world's spirit through me thrill
And as a cloud I drift before the wind,
Or with the random swallow take my will.

As underneath the mulberry tree I dream,
The water-clock drips on, and dawn appears:
A new day shines o'er wrinkles and white hair,
The symbols of the fullness of my years.

If I depart, I cast no look behind:
If still alive, I still am free from care.
Since life and death in cycles come and go,
Of little moment are the days to spare.

Thus strong in faith I wait and long to be
One with the pulsings of Eternity.
                    Poems transcribed by L. Cranmer-Byng[25]

THE PATIENT DIES

The vigil of relatives and friends, or just one of the hospice staff, must be discreetly supervised to prevent its being a traumatic experience. People feel helpless beside the dying because they do not realize that what counts is their presence, not their activity. They may feel guilty because the mind plays with irrelevant thoughts, taking attention off the dying person. They should be encouraged to touch the patient—hold his hand for instance—for this will be one of his last channels of reassurance. To the last he can be assumed to hear all that is said. Often a flicker of a smile or a faint squeeze of a finger will confirm that the message has been received. In searching for the appropriate message, people commonly turn to the traditional prayers and scriptures of the Church; the *Nunc Dimittis* for instance:

> Lord, now lettest thou thy servant depart in peace, according to thy word: For mine eyes have seen thy salvation, which thou has prepared before the face of all people.
>
> Luke 2:29-31.

Distress in the last hour is rare and fear of it is a morbid twist in our culture. The idea of suffering may well be projected on to a person by distressed spectators who are in fact dreading their own imminent bereavement. There is, on the contrary, almost always a rather beautiful giving-in. The person withdraws serenely and willingly, as gently as an ocean liner slips away from the quayside. Sometimes there may be a brief period of complete lucidity, as in the case of Mr. B. who, when I went to say good-bye, suddenly opened his eyes and said to me "I'm joining your flock now, Doctor. I hope the coffin is ready. Cheerio!"

In the last few hours dying patients will usually prefer being somewhat propped up, with the head well supported to the side. Restlessness probably indicates discomfort so they should be moved frequently but gently. They dislike feeling closed in, so bedclothes should be kept to a minimum. Sunlight, fresh air and flowers are needed. Profuse sweating often occurs necessitating sponging them down and changing the bedclothes. Cold and clammy hands and feet do not usually mean that the patient feels cold. The nostrils can be kept moist and free from crusts with vaseline, and if the mouth is very dry a little fluid can be given in a medicine dropper. More than this will make them choke. In her booklet *Care of the Dying* (see bibliography), Dr. Cicely Saunders wrote,

> Some have said to me that they hoped "it would be in their sleep," and this is something we can promise with little fear that we will be wrong. We must be ready to use sedation for the occasional patient who feels that he is choking or suffocating but almost always unconsciousness precedes death.

Even if a body is dead, it is still the most magnificent set of tools yet to have arisen on this earth. And this is not the only reason why it is worthy of respect, for it is still the symbol of a man. His loved ones will refer to it as if it were still the person. When the idea of a post-mortem examination is mentioned by the doctor, his request is often met with a look of anguish and a question such as "Does that mean they'll cut him open?" "Haven't they messed him about enough?" or "Please let him rest now: I don't want that." For this reason academic interest is not, in my view, an adequate excuse for an autopsy[26] and coroners also might stay their hand whenever no obvious benefit will be gained.

Whatever we do outwardly, it is the *inner* respect that matters. I asked a nurse to tell me about the last washing of a body, and what she wrote shows this respect very clearly:

"To nurse the dying was for me one of the most rewarding types of nursing. I was afraid of death when I first began and therefore chose to do orthopaedic nursing to avoid meeting it. In my general training hospital we were gently introduced to death. If a patient died, an experienced senior nurse would take a junior and teach her very gently how to do the last wash. The atmosphere of the room, the beauty of the ritual and reverence of the washing and the Presence in the room, removed from me this fear of death.

"The last wash was done in two parts, and between the two parts the priest came and said some prayers. At first when I became attached to a patient who was dying, I did not want to be there to see him die or to perform the last wash, but later it was the opposite. To be able to perform that last act of service was important to me and when I became the senior nurse I was very careful to be gentle with the new junior who was meeting death for the first time."

1. Saunders, C.M., "St. Christopher's Hospice," *British Hospital Journal and Social Service Review,* 10th November, 1967.

2. Townsend, P., *The Last Refuge* (Routledge & Kegan Paul, 1962).

3. Wilkes, E., "Where to Die," *B.M.J.,* 1973, vol. 1, p. 32.

4. *Hackney Gazette,* "Introducing St. Joseph's Hospice" (30th June, 1972).

5. *Sunday Times,* "Death and the Doctor's Duty" (20th August, 1972).

6. Kentish Times, *What's "Different" about St. Christopher's?* (Sidcup, 8th September, 1972).

7. MacMillan, S., "Margaret—A Study in Perception," *Nursing Times,* 28th December, 1972.

8. Saunders, C.M., "The Symptomatic Treatment of Incurable Malignant Disease," *Prescribers' Journal,* 1964, vol. 4, p. 68.

9. Gardham, J., *Palliative Surgery* (Royal Society of Medicine, 1964, vol. 57, p. 123).

10. Cade, S., *Cancer: the Patient's Viewpoint and the Clinician's Problems* (Proceedings of Royal Society of Medicine, 1963, vol. 56, p. 1).

11. Twycross, R.G., "How Steriods Can Help Terminal Cancer Patients," *General Practitioner,* 18th August, 1972.

12. Wallace, L., "The Needs of the Dying," *Nursing Times,* 13th November, 1969.

13. Downie, P.A., "Persistent Cancer," *Nursing Mirror,* 29th September, 1972.

14. Moreton, V., "At St. Christopher's Hospice," *Physiotherapy,* June 1969.

15. Anon. "Death in the First Person," *American Journal of Nursing,* February, 1970, p. 335.

16. Ogilvie, H., "Journey's End," *Practitioner,* 1957, vol. 179, p. 584.

17. MacMillan, S., "Margaret—A Study in Perception," *Nursing Times,* 28th December, 1972.

18. Miller, E.J. and Gwynne, G.V., *Dependence, Independence and Counter-Dependence in Residential Institutions for Incurables* (Tavistock Institute of Human Relations, Belsize Lane, London N.W.3).

19. Downie, P.A., "The Physiotherapist and the Patient with Cancer," *Physiotherapy,* March, 1971, p. 117.

20. Kastenbaum, R., "Death and Responsibility," *Psychiatric Opinion,* 1966, vol. 3, pp. 5, 35.

21. Le Shan, L.L., "The World of the Patient in Severe Pain of Long Duration," *Journal of Chronic Diseases,* 1964, vol. 17, p. 119.

22. Nightingale, F., *The Art of Nursing* (London, 1859), ch. 13.

23. McNulty, B.J., "The Needs of the Dying" (St. Christopher's Hospice, Lawrie Park Road, London, S.E.26).

24. Kubik, M.M., and Das Gupta, P.K., "Survival After 195 Defibrillations," *B.M.J.,* 1969, vol. 4, p. 432.

25. Giles, L., *Musings of a Chinese Mystic* (Murray, London, 1955), p. 32.

26. Page, I.H., "Death and the Practitioner," *Modern Medicine,* July, 1970.

VI.
Legalized
Euthanasia:
Social Attitudes
and
Governmental
Policies.

MEDICAL SCIENCE UNDER DICTATORSHIP

LEO ALEXANDER

Science under dictatorship becomes subordinated to the guiding philosophy of the dictatorship. Irrespective of other ideologic trappings, the guiding philosophic principle of recent dictatorships, including that of the Nazis, has been Hegelian in that what has been considered "rational utility" and corresponding doctrine and planning has replaced moral, ethical and religious values. Nazi propaganda was highly effective in perverting public opinion and public conscience, in a remarkably short time. In the medical profession this expressed itself in a rapid decline in standards of professional ethics. Medical science in Nazi Germany collaborated with this Hegelian trend particularly in the following enterprises: the mass extermination of the chronically sick in the interest of saving "useless" expenses to the community as a whole; the mass extermination of those considered socially disturbing or racially and ideologically unwanted; the individual, inconspicuous extermination of those considered disloyal within the ruling group; and the ruthless use of "human experimental material" for medicomilitary research.

This paper discusses the origins of these activities, as well as their consequences upon the body social, and the motivation of those participating in them.

PREPARATORY PROPAGANDA

Even before the Nazis took open charge in Germany, a propaganda barrage was directed against the traditional compassionate nineteenth century attitudes toward the chronically ill, and for the adoption of a utilitarian, Hegelian point of view. Sterilization and euthanasia of persons with chronic mental illnesses was discussed at a meeting of Bavarian psychiatrists in 1931.[1] By 1936 extermination of the physically or socially unfit was so openly accepted that its practice was mentioned incidentally in an article published in an official German medical journal.[2]

Lay opinion was not neglected in this campaign. Adults were propagandized by motion pictures, one of which, entitled "I Accuse," deals entirely with euthanasia. This film depicts the life history of a woman suffering from multiple sclerosis; in it her husband, a doctor, finally kills her to the accompaniment of soft piano music rendered by a sympathetic colleague in an adjoining room. Acceptance of this ideology was implanted in the children. A widely used high school mathematics text, *Mathematics in the Service of National Political Education*,[3] includes problems stated in distorted terms of the cost of caring for and rehabilitating the chronically sick and crippled. One of the problems asked, for instance, how many new housing units could be built and how many marriage-allowance loans could be given to newly wedded couples for the amount of money it cost the state to care for "the crippled, the criminal and the insane."

EUTHANASIA

The first direct order for euthanasia was issued by Hitler on September 1, 1939, and an organization was set up to execute the program. Dr. Karl Brandt headed the medical section, and Phillip Bouhler the administrative section. All state institutions were required to report on patients who had been ill five years or more and who were unable to work, by filling out questionnaires giving name, race, marital status, nationality, next of kin, whether regularly visited and by whom, who bore financial responsibility and so forth. The decision regarding which patients should be killed was made entirely on the basis of this brief information by expert consultants, most of whom were professors of psychiatry in the key universities. These consultants never saw the patients themselves. The thoroughness of their scrutiny can be appraised by the work of one expert, who between November 14 and December 1, 1940, evaluated 2109 questionnaires.

These questionnaires were collected by a "Realm's Work Committee of Institutions for Cure and Care."[4] A parallel organization devoted exclusively to the killing of children was known by the similarly euphemistic name of "Realm's Committee for Scientific Approach to Severe Illness Due to Heredity and Constitution." The "Charitable Transport Company for the Sick" transported patients to the killing centers, and the "Charitable Foundation for Institutional Care" was in charge of collecting the cost of the killings from the relatives, without, however, informing them what the charges were for; in the death certificates the cause of death was falsified.

What these activities meant to the population at large was well expressed by a few hardy souls who dared to protest. A member of the court of appeals at Frankfurt-am-Main wrote in December, 1939:

> There is constant discussion of the question of the destruction of socially unfit life—in the places where there are mental institutions, in neighboring towns, sometimes over a large area, throughout the Rhineland, for example. The people have come to recognize the vehicles in which the patients are taken from their original institution and from there to the liquidation institution. I am told that when they see these buses even the children call out: "They're taking some more people to be gassed." From Limburg it is reported that every day from one to three buses with shades drawn pass through on the way from Weilmunster to Hadamar, delivering inmates to the liquidation institution there. According to the stories the arrivals are immediately stripped to the skin, dressed in paper shirts, and forthwith taken to a gas chamber, where they are liquidated with hydrocyanic acid gas and an added anesthetic. The bodies are reported to be moved to a combustion chamber by means of a conveyor belt, six bodies to a furnace. The resulting ashes are then distributed into six urns which are shipped to the families. The heavy smoke from the crematory building is said to be visible over Hadamar every day. There is talk, furthermore, that in some cases heads and other portions of the body are removed for anatomical examination. The people working at this liquidation job in the institu-

tions are said to be assigned from other areas and are shunned completely by the populace. This personnel is described as frequenting the bars at night and drinking heavily. Quite apart from these overt incidents that exercise the imagination of the people, they are disquieted by the question of whether old folk who have worked hard all their lives and may merely have come into their dotage are also being liquidated. There is talk that the homes for the aged are to be cleaned out too. The people are said to be waiting for legislative regulation providing some orderly method that will insure especially that the aged feebleminded are not included in the program.

Here one sees what "euthanasia" means in actual practice. According to the records, 275,000 people were put to death in these killing centers. Ghastly as this seems, it should be realized that this program was merely the entering wedge for exterminations of far greater scope in the political program for the genocide of conquered nations and the racially unwanted. The methods used and personnel trained in the killing centers for the chronically sick became the nucleus of the much larger centers in the East, where the plan was to kill all Jews and Poles and to cut down the Russian population by 30,000,000.

The original program developed by Nazi hotheads included also the genocide of the English, with the provision that the English males were to be used as laborers in the vacated territories in the East, there to be worked to death, whereas the English females were to be brought into Germany to improve the qualities of the German race. (This was indeed a peculiar admission on the part of the German eugenists.)

In Germany the exterminations included the mentally defective, psychotics (particularly schizophrenics), epileptics and patients suffering from infirmities of old age and from various organic neurologic disorders such as infantile paralysis, Parkinsonism, multiple sclerosis and brain tumors. The technical arrangements, methods and training of the killer personnel were under the direction of a committee of physicians and other experts headed by Dr. Karl Brandt. The mass killings were first carried out with carbon monoxide gas, but later cyanide gas ("cyclon B") was found to be more effective. The idea of camouflaging the gas chambers as shower baths was developed by Brack, who testified before Judge Sebring that the patients walked in calmly, deposited their towels and stood with their little pieces of soap under the shower outlets waiting for the water to start running. This statement was ample rebuttal of his claim that only the most severely regressed patients among the mentally sick and only the moribund ones among the physically sick were exterminated. In truth, all those unable to work and considered nonrehabilitable were killed.

All but their squeal was utilized. However, the programs grew so big that even scientists who hoped to benefit from the treasure of material supplied by this totalitarian method were disappointed. A neuropathologist, Dr. Hallervorden, who had obtained 500 brains from the killing centers for the insane, gave me a vivid firsthand account.[5] The Charitable Transport Company for the Sick brought the brains in batches of 150 to 250 at a time. Hallervorden stated:

> There was wonderful material among those brains, beautiful mental defectives, malformations and early infantile diseases. I accepted those brains of course. Where they came from and how they came to me was really none of my business.

In addition to the material he wanted, all kinds of other cases were mixed in, such as patients suffering from various kinds of Parkinsonism, simple depressions, involuntary depressions and brain tumors, and all kinds of other illnesses, including psychopathy that had been difficult to handle:

> These were selected from the various wards of the institutions according to an excessively simple and quick method. Most institutions did not have enough physicians, and what physicians there were were either too busy or did not care, and they delegated the selection to the nurses and attendants. Whoever looked sick or was otherwise a problem was put on a list and was transported to the killing center. The worst thing about this business was that it produced a certain brutalization of the nursing personnel. They got to simply picking out those whom they did not like, and the doctors had so many patients that they did not even know them, and put their names on the list.

Of the patients thus killed, only the brains were sent to Dr. Hallervorden; they were killed in such large numbers that autopsies of the bodies were not feasible. That, in Dr. Hallervorden's opinion, greatly reduced the scientific value of the material. The brains, however, were always well fixed and suspended in formalin, exactly according to his instructions. He thinks that the cause of psychiatry was permanently injured by these activities, and that psychiatrists have lost the respect of the German people forever. Dr. Hallervorden concluded: "Still, there were interesting cases in this material."

In general only previously hospitalized patients were exterminated for reasons of illness. An exception is a program carried out in a northwestern district of Poland, the "Warthegau," where a health survey of the entire population was made by an "S.S. X-Ray Battalion" headed by Professor Hohlfelder, radiologist of the University of Frankfurt-am-Main. Persons found to be infected with tuberculosis were carted off to special extermination centers.

It is rather significant that the German people were considered by their Nazi leaders more ready to accept the exterminations of the sick than those for political reasons. It was for that reason that the first exterminations of the latter group were carried out under the guise of sickness. So-called "psychiatric experts" were dispatched to survey the inmates of camps with the specific order to pick out members of racial minorities and political offenders from occupied territories and to dispatch them to killing centers with specially made diagnoses such as that of "inveterate German hater" applied to a number of prisoners who had been active in the Czech underground.

Certain classes of patients with mental diseases who were capable of performing labor, particularly members of the armed forces suffering from psychopathy or neurosis, were sent to concentration camps to be worked to death, or to be reassigned to punishment battalions and to be exterminated in the process of removal of mine fields.[6]

A large number of those marked for death for political or racial reasons were made available for "medical" experiments involving the use of involuntary human subjects. From 1942 on, such experiments carried out in concentration camps were openly presented at medical meetings. This program included "terminal human experiments," a term introduced by Dr. Rascher to denote an experiment so designed that its successful conclusion depended upon the test person's being put to death.

THE SCIENCE OF ANNIHILATION

A large part of this research was devoted to the science of destroying and preventing life, for which I have proposed the term "ktenology," the science of killing.[7,8,9] In the course of this ktenologic research, methods of mass killing and mass sterilization were investigated and developed for use against non-German peoples or Germans who were considered useless.

Sterilization methods were widely investigated, but proved impractical in experiments conducted in concentration camps. A rapid method developed for sterilization of females, which could be accomplished in the course of a regular health examination, was the intrauterine injection of various chemicals. Numerous mixtures were tried, some with iodopine and others containing barium; another was most likely silver nitrate with iodized oil, because the result could be ascertained by X-ray examination. The injections were extremely painful, and a number of women died in the course of the experiments. Professor Karl Clauberg reported that he had developed a method at the Auschwitz concentration camp by which he could sterilize 1000 women in one day.

Another method of sterilization, or rather castration, was proposed by Viktor Brack especially for conquered populations. His idea was that X-ray machinery could be built into desks at which people would have to sit, ostensibly to fill out a questionnaire requiring five minutes; they would be sterilized without being aware of it. This method failed because experiments carried out on 100 male prisoners brought out the fact that severe X-ray burns were produced on all subjects. In the course of this research, which was carried out by Dr. Horst Schuman, the testicles of the victims were removed for histologic examination two weeks later. I myself examined four castrated survivors of this ghastly experiment. Three had extensive necrosis of the skin near the genitalia, and the other an extensive necrosis of the urethra. Other experiments in sterilization used an extract of the plant *Caladium seguinum,* which had been shown in animal studies by Madaus and his co-workers[10,11] to cause selective necrosis of the germinal cells of the testicles as well as the ovary.

The development of methods for rapid and inconspicuous individual execution was the objective of another large part of the ktenologic research. These methods were to be applied to members of the ruling group, including the SS itself, who were suspected of disloyalty. This, of course, is an essential requirement in a dictatorship, in which "cutthroat competition" becomes a grim reality, and any hint of faint-heartedness or lack of enthusiam for the methods of totalitarian rule is considered a threat to the entire group.

Poisons were the subject of many of these experiments. A research team at the Buchenwald concentration camp, consisting of Drs. Joachim Mrugowsky, Erwin Ding-Schuler and Waldemar Hoven, developed the most widely used means of individual execution under the guise of medical treatment— namely, the intravenous injection of phenol or gasoline. Several alkaloids were also investigated, among them aconitine, which was used by Dr. Hoven to kill several imprisoned former fellow SS men who were potential witnesses against the camp commander Koch, then under investigation by the SS. At the Dachau concentration camp Dr. Rascher developed the standard cyanide capsules, which could be easily bitten through, either deliberately or accidentally, if mixed with certain foods, and which, ironically enough, later became the means with which Himmler and Goering killed themselves. In connection with these poison experiments there is an interesting incident of characteristic sociologic significance. When Dr. Hoven was under trial by the SS the investigating SS judge, Dr. Morgen, proved Hoven's guilt by feeding the poison found in Dr. Hoven's possession to a number of Russian prisoners of war; these men died with the same symptoms as the SS men murdered by Dr. Hoven. This worthy judge was rather proud of this efficient method of proving Dr. Hoven's guilt and appeared entirely unaware of the fact that in the process he had committed murder himself.

Poisons, however, proved too obvious or detectable to be used for the elimination of high-ranking Nazi party personnel who had come into disfavor, or of prominent prisoners whose deaths should appear to stem from natural causes. Phenol or gasoline, for instance, left a telltale odor with the corpse. For this reason a number of more subtle methods were devised. One of these was artificial production of septicemia. An intramuscular injection of 1 cc. of pus, containing numerous chains of streptococci, was the first step. The site of injection was usually the inside of the thigh, close to the adductor canal. When an abscess formed it was tapped, and 3 cc. of the creamy pus removed was injected intravenously into the patient's opposite arm. If the patient then died from septicemia, the autopsy proved that death was caused by the same organism that had caused the abscess. These experiments were carried out at many concentration camps. At the Dachau camp the subjects were almost exclusively Polish Catholic priests. However, since this method did not always cause death, sometimes resulting merely in a local abscess, it was considered inefficient, and research was continued with other means but along the same lines.

The final triumph on the part of ktenologic research aimed at finding a method of inconspicuous execution that would produce autopsy findings indicative of death from natural causes was the development of repeated intravenous injections of suspensions of live tubercle bacilli, which brought on acute miliary tuberculosis within a few weeks. This method was produced by Professor Dr. Heissmeyer, who was one of Dr. Gebhardt's associates at the SS hospital of Hohenlychen. As a means of further camouflage, so that the SS at large would not suspect the purpose of these experiments, the preliminary tests for the efficacy of this method were performed exclusively on children imprisoned in the Neuengamme concentration camp.

For use in "medical" executions of prisoners and of members of the SS and other branches of the German armed forces the use of simple lethal injections, particularly phenol injections, remained the instrument of choice. Whatever methods he used, the physician gradually became the unofficial executioner, for the sake of convenience, informality and relative secrecy. Even on German submarines it was the physician's duty to execute the troublemakers among the crew by lethal injections.

Medical science has for some time been an instrument of military power in that it preserved the health and fighting efficiency of troops. This essentially defensive purpose is not inconsistent with the ethical principles of medicine. In World War I the German empire had enlisted medical science as an instrument of aggressive military power by putting it to use in the development of gas warfare. It was left to the Nazi dictatorship to make medical science into an instrument of political power—a formidable, essential tool in the complete and effective manipulation of totalitarian control. This should be a warning to all civilized nations, and particularly to individuals who are blinded by the "efficiency" of a totalitarian rule, under whatever name.

This entire body of research as reported so far served the master crime to which the Nazi dictatorship was committed— namely, the genocide of non-German peoples and the elimination by killing, in groups or singly, of Germans who were considered useless or disloyal. In effecting the two parts of this program, Himmler demanded and received the cooperation of physicians and of German medical science. The result was a significant advance in the science of killing, or ktenology.

MEDICOMILITARY RESEARCH

Another chapter in Nazi scientific research was that aimed to aid the military forces. Many of these ideas originated with Himmler, who fancied himself a scientist.

When Himmler learned that the cause of death of most SS men on the battlefield was hemorrhage, he instructed Dr. Sigmund Rascher to search for a blood coagulant that might be given before the men went into action. Rascher tested this coagulant when it was developed by clocking the number of drops emanating from freshly cut amputation stumps of living and conscious prisoners at the crematorium of Dachau concentration camp and by shooting Russian prisoners of war through the spleen.

Live dissections were a feature of another experimental study designed to show the effects of explosive decompression.[12,13,14] A mobile decompression chamber was used. It was found that when subjects were made to descend from altitudes of 40,000 to 60,000 feet without oxygen, severe symptoms of cerebral dysfunction occurred—at first convulsions, then unconsciousness in which the body was hanging limp and later, after wakening, temporary blindness, paralysis or severe confusional twilight states. Rascher, who wanted to find out whether these symptoms were due to anoxic changes or to other causes, did what appeared to him the most simple thing: he placed the subjects of the experiment under water and dissected them while the heart was still beating, demonstrating air embolism in the blood vessels of the heart, liver, chest wall and brain.

Another part of Dr. Rascher's research, carried out in collaboration with Holzloehner and Finke, concerned shock from exposure to cold.[15] It was known that military personnel generally did not survive immersion in the North Sea for more than sixty to a hundred minutes. Rascher therefore attempted to duplicate these conditions at Dachau concentration camp and used about 300 prisoners in experiments on shock from exposure to cold; of these 80 or 90 were killed. (The figures do not include persons killed during mass experiments on exposure to cold outdoors.) In one report on this work Rascher asked permission to shift these experiments from Dachau to Auschwitz, a larger camp where they might cause less disturbance because the subjects shrieked from pain when their extremities froze white. The results, like so many of those obtained in the Nazi research program, are not dependable. In his report Rascher stated that it took from fifty-three to a hundred minutes to kill a human being by immersion in ice water—a time closely in agreement with the known survival period in the North Sea. Inspection of his own experimental records and statements made to me by his close associates showed that it actually took from eighty minutes to five or six hours to kill an undressed person in such a manner, whereas a man in full aviator's dress took six or seven hours to kill. Obviously, Rascher dressed up his findings to forestall criticism, although any scientific man should have known that during actual exposure many other factors, including greater convection of heat due to the motion of water, would affect the time of survival.

Another series of experiments gave results that might have been an important medical contribution if an important lead had not been ignored. The efficacy of various vaccines and drugs against typhus was tested at the Buchenwald and Natzweiler concentration camps. Prevaccinated persons and non-vaccinated controls were injected with live typhus rickettsias, and the death rates of the two series compared. After a certain number of passages, the Matelska strain of typhus rickettsia proved to become avirulent for man. Instead of seizing upon this as a possibility to develop a live vaccine, the experimenters, including the chief consultant, Professor Gerhard Rose, who should have known better, were merely annoyed at the fact that the controls did not die either, discarded this strain and continued testing their relatively ineffective dead vaccines against a new virulent strain. This incident shows that the basic unconscious motivation and attitude has a great influence in determining the scientist's awareness of the phenomena that pass through his vision.

Sometimes human subjects were used for tests that were totally unnecessary, or whose results could have been predicted by simple chemical experiments. For example, 90 gypsies were given unaltered sea water and sea water whose taste was camouflaged as their sole source of fluid, apparently to test the well-known fact that such hypertonic saline solutions given as the only source of supply of fluid will cause severe physical disturbance or death within six or twelve days. These persons were subjected to the tortures of the damned, with death resulting in at least two cases.

Heteroplastic transplantation experiments were carried out by Professor Dr. Karl Gebhardt at Himmler's suggestion. Whole limbs—shoulder, arm or leg—were amputated from live prisoners at Ravensbrueck concentration camp, wrapped in sterile moist dressings and sent by automobile to the SS hospital at Hohenlychen, where Professor Gebhardt busied himself with a futile attempt at heteroplastic transplantation. In the meantime the prisoners deprived of a limb were usually killed by lethal injection.

One would not be dealing with German science if one did not run into manifestations of the collector's spirit. By February, 1942, it was assumed in German scientific circles that the Jewish race was about to be completely exterminated, and alarm was expressed over the fact that only very few specimens of skulls and skeletons of Jews were at the disposal of science. It was therefore proposed that a collection of 150 body casts and skeletons of Jews be preserved for perusal by future students of anthropology. Dr. August Hirt, professor of anatomy at the University of Strassburg, declared himself interested in establishing such a collection at his anatomic institute. He suggested that captured Jewish officers of the Russian armed forces be included, as well as females from Auschwitz concentration camp; that they be brought alive to Natzweiler concentration camp near Strassburg; and that after "their subsequently induced death—care should be taken that the heads not be damaged [sic]" the bodies be turned over to him at the anatomic institute of the University of Strassburg. This was done. The entire collection of bodies and the correspondence pertaining to it fell into the hands of the United States Army.

One of the most revolting experiments was the testing of sulfonamides against gas gangrene by Professor Gebhardt and his collaborators, for which young women captured from the Polish Resistance Movement served as subjects. Necrosis was produced in a muscle of the leg by ligation and the wound was infected with various types of gas-gangrene bacilli; frequently, dirt, pieces of wood and glass splinters were added to the wound. Some of these victims died, and others sustained severe mutilating deformities of the leg.

MOTIVATION

An important feature of the experiments performed in concentration camps is the fact that they not only represented a ruthless and callous pursuit of legitimate scientific goals but also were motivated by rather sinister practical ulterior political and personal purposes, arising out of the requirements and problems of the administration of totalitarian rule.

Why did men like professor Gebhardt lend themselves to such experiments? The reasons are fairly simple and practical, no surprise to anyone familiar with the evidence of fear, hostility, suspicion, rivalry and intrigue, the fratricidal struggle euphemistically termed the "self-selection of leaders," that went on within the ranks of the ruling Nazi party and the SS. The answer was fairly simple and logical. Dr. Gebhardt performed these experiments to clear himself of the suspicion that he had been contributing to the death of SS General Reinhard ("The Hangman") Heydrich, either negligently or deliberately, by failing to treat his wound infection with sulfonamides. After Heydrich died from gas gangrene, Himmler himself told Dr. Gebhardt that the only way in which he could prove that Heydrich's death was "fate determined" was by carrying out a "large-scale experiment" in prisoners which would prove or disprove that people died from gas gangrene irrespective of whether they were treated with sulfonamides or not.

Dr. Sigmund Rascher did not become the notorious vivisectionist of Dachau concentration camp and the willing tool of Himmler's research interests until he had been forbidden to use the facilities of the Pathological Institute of the University of Munich because he was suspected of having Communist sympathies. Then he was ready to go all out and do anything merely to regain acceptance by the Nazi party and the SS.

These cases illustrated a method consciously and methodically used in the SS, an age-old method used by criminal gangs everywhere: that of making suspects of disloyalty clear themselves by participation in a crime that would definitely and irrevocably tie them to the organization. In the SS this process of reinforcement of group cohesion was called *"Blutkitt"* (blood-cement), a term Hitler himself is said to have obtained from a book on Genghis Khan in which this technic was emphasized.

The important lesson here is that this motivation, with which one is familiar in ordinary crimes, applies also to war crimes and to ideologically conditioned crimes against humanity—namely, that fear and cowardice, especially fear of punishment or of ostracism by the group, are often more important motives than simple ferocity or aggressiveness.

THE EARLY CHANGE IN MEDICAL ATTITUDES

Whatever proportions these crimes finally assumed, it became evident to all who investigated them that they had started from small beginnings. The beginnings at first were merely a subtle shift in emphasis in the basic attitude of the physicians. It started with the acceptance of the attitude, basic in the euthanasia movement, that there is such a thing as life not worthy to be lived. This attitude in its early stages concerned itself merely with the severely and chronically sick. Gradually the sphere of those to be included in this category was enlarged to encompass the socially unproductive, the ideologically unwanted and finally all non-Germans. But it is important to realize that the infinitely small wedged-in lever from which this entire trend of mind received its impetus was the attitude toward the nonrehabilitable sick.

It is, therefore, this subtle shift in emphasis of the physicians' attitude that one must thoroughly investigate. It is a recent significant trend in medicine, including psychiatry, to regard prevention as more important than cure. Observation and recognition of early signs and symptoms have become the basis for prevention of further advance of disease.[8]

In looking for these early signs one may well retrace the early steps of propaganda on the part of the Nazis in Germany as well as in the countries that they overran and in which they attempted to gain supporters by means of indoctrination, seduction and propaganda.

THE EXAMPLE OF SUCCESSFUL RESISTANCE BY THE PHYSICIANS OF THE NETHERLANDS

There is no doubt that in Germany itself the first and most effective step of propaganda within the medical profession was the propaganda barrage against the useless, incurably sick described above. Similar, even more subtle efforts were made in some of the occupied countries. It is to the everlasting honor of the medical profession of Holland that they recognized the earliest and most subtle phases of this attempt and rejected it. When Seiss-Inquart, Reich Commissar for the Occupied Netherlands Territories, wanted to draw the Dutch physicians into the orbit of the activities of the German medical profession, he did not tell them "You must send your chronic patients to death factories" or "You must give lethal injections at Government request in your offices," but he couched his order in most careful and superficially acceptable terms. One of the paragraphs in the order of the Reich Commissar of the Netherlands Territories concerning the Netherlands doctors of 19 December 1941 reads as follows:

> It is the duty of the doctor, through advice and effort, conscientiously and to his best ability, to assist as helper the person entrusted to his care in the maintenance, improvement, and re-establishment of his vitality, physical efficiency and health. The accomplishment of this duty is a public task.[16]

The physicians of Holland rejected this order unanimously because they saw what it actually meant—namely, the concentration of their efforts on mere rehabilitation of the sick for useful labor, and abolition of medical secrecy. Although on the surface the new order appeared not too grossly unacceptable, the Dutch physicians decided that it is the first, although slight, step away from principle that is the most important one. The Dutch physicians declared that they would not obey this order. When Seiss-Inquart threatened them with the revocation of their licenses, they returned their licenses, removed their shingles and, while seeing their own patients secretly, no longer wrote birth or death certificates. Seiss-Inquart retraced his steps and tried to cajole them— still to no effect. Then he arrested 100 Dutch physicians and sent them to concentration camps. The medical profession remained adamant and quietly took care of their widows and orphans, but would not give in. Thus it came about that not a single euthanasia or non-therapeutic sterilization was recommended or participated in by any Dutch physician. They had the foresight to resist before the first step was taken, and they acted unanimously and won out in the end. It is obvious that if the medical profession of a small nation under the conqueror's heel could resist so effectively, the German medical profession could likewise have resisted had they not taken the fatal first step. It is the first seemingly innocent step away from principle that frequently decides a career of crime. Corrosion begins in microscopic proportions.

THE SITUATION IN THE UNITED STATES

The question that this fact prompts is whether there are any danger signs that American physicians have also been infected with Hegelian, cold-blooded, utilitarian philosophy and whether early traces of it can be detected in their medical thinking that may make them vulnerable to departures of the type that occurred in Germany. Basic attitudes must be examined dispassionately. The original concept of medicine and nursing was not based on any rational or feasible likelihood that they could actually cure and restore but rather on an essentially maternal or religious idea. The Good Samaritan had not thought of nor did he actually care whether he could restore working capacity. He was merely motivated by the compassion in alleviating suffering. Bernal[17] states that prior to the advent of scientific medicine, the physician's main function was to give hope to the patient and to relieve his relatives of responsibility. Gradually, in all civilized countries, medicine has moved away from this position, strangely enough in direct proportion to man's actual ability to perform feats that would have been plain miracles in days of old. However, with this increased efficiency based on scientific development went a subtle change in attitude. Physicians have become dangerously close to being mere technicians of rehabilitation. This essentially Hegelian rational attitude has led them to make certain distinctions in the handling of acute and chronic diseases. The patient with the latter carries an obvious stigma as the one less likely to be fully rehabilitable for social usefulness. In an increasingly utilitarian society these patients are being looked down upon with increasing definiteness as unwanted ballast. A certain amount of rather open contempt for the people who cannot be rehabilitated with present knowledge has developed. This is probably due to a good deal of unconscious hostility, because these people for whom there seem to be no effective remedies have become a threat to newly acquired delusions of omnipotence.

Hospitals like to limit themselves to the care of patients who can be fully rehabilitated, and the patient whose full rehabilitation is unlikely finds himself, at least in the best and most advanced centers of healing, as a second-class patient faced with a reluctance on the part of both the visiting and the house staff to suggest and apply therapeutic procedures that are not likely to bring about immediately striking results in terms of recovery. I wish to emphasize that this point of view did not arise primarily within the medical profession which has always been outstanding in a highly competitive economic society for giving freely and unstintingly of its time and efforts, but was imposed by the shortage of funds available, both private and public. From the attitude of easing patients with chronic diseases away from the doors of the best types of treatment facilities available to the actual dispatching of such patients to killing centers is a long but nevertheless logical step. Resources for the so-called incurable patient have recently become practically unavailable.

There has never in history been a shortage of money for the development and manufacture of weapons of war; there is and should be none now. The disproportion of monetary support for war and that available for healing and care is an anachronism in an era that has been described as the "enlightened age of the common man" by some observers. The comparable cost of jet planes and hospital beds is too obvious for any excuse to be found for a shortage of the latter. I trust that these remarks will not be misunderstood. I believe that armament, including jet planes, is vital for the security of the republic, but adequate maintenance of standards of health and alleviation of suffering are equally vital, both from a practical point of view and from that of morale. All who took part in induction-board examinations during the war realize that the maintenance and development of national health is of as vital importance as the maintenance and development of armament.

The trend of development in the facilities available for the chronically ill outlined above will not necessarily be altered by public or state medicine. With provision of public funds in any setting of public activity the question is bound to come up, "Is it worth while to spend a certain amount of effort to restore a certain type of patient?" This rationalistic point of view has insidiously crept into the motivation of medical effort, supplanting the old Hippocratic point of view. In emergency situations, military or otherwise, such grading of effort may be pardonable. But doctors must beware lest such attitudes creep into the civilian public administration of medicine entirely outside emergency situations, because once such considerations are at all admitted, the more often and the more definitely the question is going to be asked, "Is it worth while to do this or that for this type of patient?" Evidence of the existence of such an attitude stared at me from a report on the activities of a leading public hospital unit, which stated rather proudly that certain treatments were given only when they appeared promising:

> Our facilities are such that a case load of 20 patients is regularly carried . . . in selecting cases for treatment careful consideration is given to the prognostic criteria, and in no instance have we instituted treatment merely to satisfy relatives or our own consciences.

If only those whose treatment is worthwhile in terms of prognosis are to be treated, what about the other ones? The doubtful patients are the ones whose recovery appears unlikely, but frequently if treated energetically, they surprise the best prognosticators. And what shall be done during that long time lag after the disease has been called incurable and the time of death and autopsy? It is that period during which it is most difficult to find hospitals and other therapeutic organizations for the welfare and alleviation of suffering of the patient.

Under all forms of dictatorship the dictating bodies or individuals claim that all that is done is being done for the best of the people as a whole, and that for that reason they look at health merely in terms of utility, efficiency and productivity. It is natural in such a setting that eventually Hegel's principle that "what is useful is good" wins out completely. The killing center is the *reductio ad absurdum* of all health planning based only on rational principles and economy and not on humane compassion and divine law. To be sure, American physicians are still far from the point of thinking of killing centers, but they have arrived at a danger point in thinking, at which likelihood of full rehabilitation is considered a factor that should determine the amount of time, effort and cost to be devoted to a particular type of patient on the part of the social body upon which this decision rests. At this point Americans should remember that the enormity of a euthanasia movement is present in their own midst. To the psychiatrist it is obvious that this represents the eruption of unconscious aggression on the part of certain administrators alluded to above, as well as on the part of relatives who have been understandably frustrated by the tragedy of illness in its close interaction upon their own lives. The hostility of a father erupting against his feebleminded son is understandable and should be considered from the psychiatric point of view, but it certainly should not influence social thinking. The development of effective analgesics and pain-relieving operations has taken even the last rationalization away from the supporters of euthanasia.

The case, therefore, that I should like to make is that American medicine must realize where it stands in its fundamental premises. There can be no doubt that in a subtle way the Hegelian premise of "what is useful is right" has infected society, including the medical portion. Physicians must return to the older premises, which were the emotional foundation and driving force of an amazingly successful quest to increase powers of healing and which are bound to carry them still farther if they are not held down to earth by the pernicious attitudes of an overdone practical realism.

What occurred in Germany may have been the inexorable historic progression that the Greek historians have described as the law of the fall of civilizations and that Toynbee[18] has convincingly confirmed—namely, that there is a logical sequence from Koros to Hybris to Ate, which means from surfeit to disdainful arrogance to disaster, the surfeit being increased scientific and practical accomplishments, which, however, brought about an inclination to throw away the old motivations and values by disdainful arrogant pride in practical efficiency. Moral and physical disaster is the inevitable consequence.

Fortunately, there are developments in this democratic society that counteract these trends. Notable among them are the societies of patients afflicted with various chronic diseases that have sprung up and are dedicating themselves to guidance and information for the fellow sufferers and for the support and stimulation of medical research. Among the earliest was the mental hygiene movement, founded by a former patient with mental disease. Then came the National Foundation for Infantile Paralysis, the tuberculosis societies, the American Epilepsy League, the National Association to Control Epilepsy, the American Cancer Society, the American Heart Association, "Alcoholics Anonymous" and, most recently, the National Multiple Sclerosis Society. All these societies, which are coordinated with special medical societies and which receive inspiration and guidance from outstanding physicians, are having an extremely wholesome effect in introducing fresh motivating power into the ivory towers of academic medicine. It is indeed interesting and an assertion of democratic vitality that these societies are activated by and for people suffering from illnesses who, under certain dictatorships, would have been slated for euthanasia.

It is thus that these new societies have taken over one of the ancient functions of medicine—namely, to give hope to the patient and to relieve his relatives. These societies need the wholehearted support of the medical profession. Unfortunately, this support is by no means yet unanimous. A distinguished physician, investigator and teacher at an outstanding university recently told me that he was opposed to these special societies and clinics because they had nothing to offer to the patient. It would be better to wait until someone made a discovery accidentally and then start clinics. It is my opinion, however, that one cannot wait for that. The stimulus supplied by these societies is necessary to give stimulus both to public demand and to academic medicine, which at times grows stale and unproductive even in its most outstanding centers, and whose existence did nothing to prevent the executioner from having logic on his side in Germany.

Another element of this free democratic society and enterprise that has been a stimulus to new developments is the pharmaceutical industry, which, with great vision, has invested considerable effort in the sponsorship of new research.

Dictatorships can be indeed defined as systems in which there is a prevalence of thinking in destructive, rather than in ameliorative terms in dealing with social problems. The ease with which destruction of life is advocated for those considered either socially useless or socially disturbing instead of educational or ameliorative measures may be the first danger sign of loss of creative liberty in thinking, which is the hallmark of democratic society. All destructiveness ultimately leads to self-destruction; the fate of the SS and of Nazi Germany is an eloquent example. The destructive principle, once unleashed, is bound to engulf the whole personality and to occupy all its relationships. Destructive urges and destructive concepts arising therefrom cannot remain limited or focused upon one subject or several subjects alone, but must inevitably spread and be directed against one's entire surrounding world, including one's own group and ultimately the self. The ameliorative point of view maintained in relation to all others is the only real means of self-preservation.

A most important need in this country is for the development of active and alert hospital centers for the treatment of chronic illnesses. They must have active staffs similar to those of the hospitals for acute illnesses, and these hospitals must be fundamentally different from the custodial repositories for derelicts, of which there are too many in existence today. Only thus can one give the right answer to divine scrutiny: Yes, we are our brothers' keepers.

1. Bumke, O. Discussion of Faltlhauser, K. Zur Frage der Sterilisierung geistig Abnormer. *Allg. Ztschr. f. Psychiat.*, 96:372, 1932.

2. Dierichs, R. Beitrag zur psychischen Anstaltsbehandlung Tuberkuloser. *Ztschr. f. Tuberk.*, 74:21-8, 1936.

3. Dorner, A. *Mathematik in Dienste der Nationalpolitischen Erziehung: Ein Handbuch für Lehrer; herausgegeben in Auftrage des Reichsverbandes Deutscher mathematischer Gesellschaften und Vereine.* Moritz Diesterweg, Frankfurt, 1935, pp. 1-118. Second edition (revised). 1936, pp. 1-118, Third edition (revised).

4. Alexander, L. *Public Mental Health Practices in Germany, Sterilization and Execution of Patients Suffering from Nervous or Mental Disease.* Combined Intelligence Objectives Subcommittee, Item No. 24, File No. XXVIII-50, Aug. 1945, pp. 1-173.

5. _____. *Neuropathology and Neurophysiology, Including Electro-Encephalography in War-time Germany.* Combined Intelligence Objectives Sub-committee, Item No. 24, File No. XXVII-1, July 1945, pp. 1-65.

6. _____. *German Military Neuropsychiatry and Neurosurgery.* Combined Intelligence Objectives Subcommittee. Item No. 24, File No. XXVIII-49, Aug. 1945, pp. 1-138.

7. _____. Sociopsychologic Structure of SS: Psychiatric Report of Nuremberg Trials for War Crimes. *Arch. Neurol. & Psychiat.* 69:622-34, 1948.

8. _____. War Crimes: Their Social-Psychological Aspects. *Amer. J. Psychiat.*, 105:170-7, 1948.

9. _____. War Crimes and Their Motivation: Socio-Psychological Structure of SS and Criminalization of Society. *J. Crim. Law & Criminol.*, 39:298-326, 1948.

10. Madaus, G., and Koch, F. Tierexperimentelle Studien zur Frage der Medikamentosen Sterilisierung (durch Caladium seguinum) (Dieffenbachia seguina). *Ztschr. f. d. ges. exper. Med.*, 109:68-87, 1941.

11. Madaus, G. Zauberpflanzen im Lichte experimenteller Forschung, Das Schweigrohr — Caladium seguinum. *Umschau*, 24:600-2, 1941.

12. Alexander, L. *Miscellaneous Aviation Medical Matters.* Combined Intelligence Objectives Subcommittee, Item No. 24, File No. XXIX-21, Aug. 1945, pp. 1-163.

13. Document 1971 a PS.

14. Document NO 220.

15. Alexander, L. *Treatment of Shock from Prolonged Exposure to Cold, Especially in Water.* Combined Intelligence Objectives Subcommittee, Item No. 24, File No. XXVI-37. July 1945, pp. 1-228.

16. Seiss-Inquart. *Order of the Reich Commissar for the Occupied Netherlands Doctors.* (Gazette containing the orders for the Occupied Netherlands Territories), Dec. 1941, pp. 1004-26.

17. Bernal, J. D. *The Social Function of Science.* George Routledge & Sons, London, 1946. 482 pp. Sixth edition.

18. Toynbee, A. J. *A Study of History.* Abridgement of Vol. I-VI. By D. C. Somervell. Oxford Univ. Press, New York and London, 1947, pp. 617.

DEATH AND THE MECHANIZATION OF MAN

MARSHALL McLUHAN

The Waste Land of T.S. Eliot is a compressed vision of
the contemporary Life-in Death and Death-in Life. He sees
the Christian role as a dying unto the self as the means to
life; whereas the people in his drama are typically engaged in
living a life-in-death. Early in the "play" one of the "jet set"
is "staying at the Arch-duke's my cousin's," and goes out on
a sled in the high hills and states the rootless creed: "In the
mountains there you feel free/I read, much of the night, and
go south for the winter." Later, one of the lowly victims of
metropolitan existence is socializing at a pub, and her friend
comments, with worldly scorn: "Well, if Albert won't leave
you alone, there it is, I said/What you get married for if you
don't want children?" In a world of perpetual motion and
high mobility there can be no community, since by definition,
all we really have in common is the mobility; and the one
thing we depend upon is change. The mobility itself is insep-
arable from our new affluent technologies which demand that
we become servo-mechanisms.

Wordsworth's quaint lament in the early nineteenth century that "the world is too much with us," serves at least to
remind us that the power and scope of the world has increased
considerably since his time. When Sputnik put the entire
planet inside a man-made environment of information, the
world may have seemed to become much smaller, but it also
became much more obsessive and demanding. The power of
the world to invade every feature of our personal lives has
been given a kind of medieval Morality Play treatment by the
Watergate episode. It is almost as if we had revived "for real"
the popular medieval narratives of the Falls of Princes. As the
world manifests its credentials and rewards in ever more the-
atrical terms, it becomes ever more difficult for some to resist

the world, while for others it becomes easier and easier to reject its sinister and shallow pretentions. Like our money, which is a "promise to pay," our advertising and P.R. only promise to pay promises.

Even theatrically speaking, the drama of the world has become more and more a mockery of merely human satisfactions, when it is quite evident that the richest people in the world have to become "hotel hermits" for security reasons, and when the most powerful people in the world lead lives of frantic uncertainty. The story of why many people choose life-in-death (the merely human and secular way of the world) is stated in an unexpected way by Siegfried Giedion in his classic work *Mechanization Takes Command* (New York: Oxford U.P., 1948). It is a lovingly and artistically studied account of how man has come to do more and more with less and less at the expense of robotizing his existence. There is a long and careful account of the mechanizing of agriculture, on the one hand, and of the making of bread, on the other hand. (He does not look at the wine process.) But the most telling pages are those in which Giedion minutely scrutinizes the Mechanization of Death in his study of the meat packers. The universal awareness of mankind has until now held to a ritual sense of death, even the death of animals. By the simple procedure of ever-diminishing fragmentation of processes, however, it is possible to eliminate all pain and ritual and meaning in death. Belsen, and Buchenwald, and Auschwitz testify to the inevitability of gradualness and to the power of cleanly bureaucratic efficiency in the administration of death.

It is probably a mistake to isolate the abortion mills of current death programs from the seamless fabric of our worldly lives, which have become invaded by the death principle of minute attrition *via* fragmentation. The situation suggests that no mere disapproval of abortion practises could avail an iota against the technological movement of life towards a way-of-death. Let us consider for the moment one of our conquerors, the TV image itself. This image is constituted by innumerable pulsations of bits of light. What makes the image so enthralling and compelling is precisely the intervals or gaps between these pulsations. It is in these intervals, which people feel urged to fill, that their involvement with the action of the image occurs. Just as the action is in the *play* between a wheel and an axle, so it is in our psychic and social lives.

As long as there is the interval of "play" between man and his world, there is action and life; but when the interval between the spirit and the world closes, there is no more play but the fusion of stasis and death. Those who merge with the *mores* of the world lose this power to play and to laugh at the world and its pretentions.

When the human spirit feels drawn into the mesh of the man-made images of the electric world, it sacrifices its identity. Part of the process of transforming life into a way-of-death is to involve mankind in the universal surround of resonating intervals which turns the whole environment of existence into a kind of irresistable TV image. A consequence of this total involvement in the man-made environment is the loss of private identity. With this loss comes the sense of unreality and of irresponisibility towards our own and other lives. As people have become more deeply involved in each other technologically, they have acquired the "mass" or crowd mind, with its irresistible demand for sensation and thrill and death. Against this tide, the Church alone can prevail.

EUTHANASIA: THE THREE-IN-ONE ISSUE

Thomas St. Martin*

Since the beginning of the abortion controversy (and before if we are to include pro-euthanasia agitation between about 1930 and 1950), Americans have been involved in a euthanasia debate. Especially since the January 22, 1973 Supreme Court abortion decision, euthanasia has become a widely, and sometimes intensely, discussed topic. Yet few recognize the complexities and ramifications of the euthanasia issue; they tend to forget that euthanasia is a euphemistic term which has come to cover a constellation of ideas and attitudes. The term itself is of Greek origin and means "good death" (eu-thanatos). However, in modern usage it has been stretched to encompass three quite different concepts as follows:

(1) *Death with dignity.* When used in this sense, "euthanasia" means allowing a patient to die a truly human death; it means freeing the dying person from the loneliness and alienation brought about by the application of "extraordinary" medical technology. It means, in short, letting the terminally ill die "naturally," letting death come as a deliverer to those for whom there is no hope for continuation of life. It means avoiding the kind of mechanized desperation which, by trying to hold back the inevitable, often turns death into an inhumane ordeal.

This is not to imply or to urge neglect of the dying patient. The dying person, like any other human being, is entitled to medical care which is reasonable and prudent under the circumstances involved. We must, in short, care for the dying; we must humanize death by "being present" with the dying patient.

(2) *Mercy Killing.* As opposed to death with dignity (which permits the dying to die naturally), mercy killing entails the intentional use of medical technology in such a way as to induce or hasten death. This type of euthanasia can include giving a terminally ill patient a dosage of a lethal drug with the express intention of causing death. Or it can include abandonment (or withdrawal) of "ordinary," reasonable and prudent medical care (e.g. "allowing" Mongoloid children to die of pneumonia). The advocates of mercy killing, ostensibly, base their case on pity. The suffering of incurably or painfully ill (and/or defective) persons should not be "inhumanely" prolonged, they argue.

(3) *Death Selection.* Whatever one might believe to be the real motives of the advocates of mercy killing, we must at least accept their

---

*Past President, Minnesota Citizens Concerned for Life.

concern for the alleviation of individual human suffering. It is this intention or concern which distinguishes "mercy killing" from death selection (or, to use a more revealing term, from managerial euthanasia). Death selection/managerial euthanasia involves the deliberate termination of lives which are no longer considered "socially useful" (i.e. which are considered to be a burden on society). And because it is rooted in a hard core utilitarianism which sees no value beyond social utility, managerial euthanasia poses a threat to a wide range of people: the "habitual" criminal, the aged, the seriously mentally ill, the retarded, etc. In the death selection scenario, people become "human resources" to be manipulated in the accomplishment of "planned" social objectives and to be discarded when no longer useful. At the moment, managerial euthanasia is the "sleeper" in the euthanasia debate. Although some social engineering ideologues are quite open in advocating killing for utilitarian reasons, most euthanasia advocates, for the moment at least, stop with "mercy killing." Consequently, it is unclear as to exactly how the managerial elite proposes to practice managerial or eliminative medicine. Certainly, overt killing would have its place in their program. It is more likely, however, that more subtle methods would be used: withdrawal or withholding of ordinary, preventive and/or restorative medical care for certain categories of people; "prioritizing" use of health care resources so as to favor those who are considered more socially useful (for example, putting the young, "bright" scientist in a higher priority group than the middle-aged heart attack victim); and curtailing, or limiting, health research and developmental efforts in low priority health program areas, e.g., geriatric medicine.

Death with dignity, mercy killing and death selection/managerial euthanasia are used, then, because they promise to be more helpful than more common and conventional categories: negative and positive euthanasia, voluntary and involuntary euthanasia, etc. This is true insofar as the three-tiered breakdown provides a good to bad, better to worse arrangement of possible euthanasia practices. More significantly, however, it focuses attention on the intentions or the world view of those who promote one or more variations of euthanasia. This, in turn, makes it easier to determine who the proponents of euthanasia really are. It places the emphasis on the principles involved rather than on the methods (positive or negative) or the circumstances (voluntary or involuntary).

Terms such as "negative" and "positive" euthanasia, "extraordinary" means, and "ordinary" means are highly confusing. And to make matters worse, these terms are often used in a misleading way by euthanasia advocates. For example, many people have come to think of "positive" euthanasia (or overt killing) as a bad thing and "negative" euthanasia (allowing a patient to die) as an acceptable thing. However, negative euthanasia can encompass such practices as the withholding of routine intestinal surgery from "unwanted" mongoloid children (with a resulting "natural" death by starvation). In fact, much managerial killing could easily be categorized as "negative" euthanasia. The same concerns apply, generally, to the concept of "extraordinary" means. People who have given the matter any thought at all usually identify withholding of extraordinary means with "death with dignity." In a general way, this is an accurate identification: human death can be, and often is, robbed of its dignity by over-technization of the dying process. Regrettably, however, "extraordinary" (when used in the context of the euthanasia controversy) is an extremely slippery term. What is "extraordinary" and what is "ordinary"? Can anyone develop a general definition of "extraordinary"? Or must we rely on the physician's judgment of what is "extraordinary" in any given, unique situation? These are extremely difficult but highly pertinent questions. And, although they are questions to which no one, in good conscience, can give glib or easy answers, careless use of terminology will prevent us from even formulating coherent questions. Accordingly, we must always insist on a sharp line of demarcation between death with dignity on the one hand and mercy killing and death selection on the other. One involves medical and community ethics relative to the dying. The others are concerned, in one way or another, with shortening life; whether out of a misguided sympathy or out of a calculating utilitarian attitude.

Underlying all of this is the fact that, for some time now, our society has tried to sweep death under the rug. Modern man cannot accept death. The knowledge that men and women must die is too humiliating —too final—to be accepted by men who feel that they are masters of themselves and of the universe. Consequently, we try to avoid death. We treat it as being unimportant or we push it from our conscious world. Or we engage in desperate measures designed to "conquer" death. This heroic struggle against death goes a long way toward explaining the zeal of modern medicine and public health. Such zeal may allow us to accomplish human miracles but it can also lead us to excesses. Among these excesses is the almost desperate application of modern technology in the death bed. The result is often a separation of the dying patient from his friends, his family, his community and, above all, from his own death.

And how can one be alienated from one's own death? Modern man's alienation from his own death has to do, I think, with the objectification of death. In our efforts to control and subdue death, we turn death into a problem to be solved. Thus we cast death out from, or away from, our own existence. Death becomes something which will happen in the impersonal future: something which must be banished from our day-to-day awareness. Unfortunately, however, the problem of death cannot be so easily "solved." In reality, death is a mystery which we cannot banish; in fact, cannot even fully understand. It is part and parcel of our very being. It is our constant companion for in the midst of life we are in death.

Thus, when we flee from death, we are, in a very real sense, fleeing from ourselves. A part of our own personhood is denied. It follows from this that the desperate application of medical machinery often turns dying into a last ditch effort to assert modern man's illusion that he—and he alone—is master of the gods of life and death, and the master, to the bitter end, of that "thing" which he calls his body.

Curiously, the objections to mercy killing rest on the same general premises as the objection to the use of extraordinary or high powered medical technology to prolong dying. Mercy killing is but another manifestation of man's desire to subdue death—or, at the least, to force death to meet man on his own terms. In other words, the mercy killers arrogate to themselves the prerogative to decide who is to die and when. They treat the dying or suffering patient as an object whose pain and suffering can be turned off like a light bulb. This means, again, that one's death is no longer one's own: it is "something" to be manipulated by a physician, a relative or by the patient himself. There is little difference, on these grounds, between a desperate attempt to keep someone alive and a decision to hasten death. Both are examples of what is popularly referred to as "man trying to play God"—man's attempt to shape and subdue his own being.

Mercy killing, particularly in its "voluntary" form, also stems from the widely held opinion that one "owns" or "controls" one's own body (witness the effectiveness of the pro-abortion rhetoric on this point). If one owns one's body, in much the same way as one owns a house or a car, then one can dispose of that body in much the same way as any piece of property. This view, of course, presupposes a profound dualism: a mind-spirit-subject acting upon or controlling a mechanized mass of clay. But, apart from a rejection of dualism, there are other arguments against voluntary or requested self-destruction. Simply put, these arguments say that life has value even when the individual involved places no value on it. Although I may feel "worthless," I must recognize—or society must recognize—that my being has an objective value which transcends my feelings of the moment. Of course, all of this presumes that life is a gift and that life has supreme value in the eye of the giver. It presumes that the value of the gift somehow transcends the value which the recipient might place upon it.

We all know, however, that the "life as a gift" philosophy has been deeply eroded in our time. The combination of dualism and a humanism which insists that man must seize and shape his own destiny has fostered the idea that one has absolute control over one's body and that life is something which man has a "right" to shape and to manipulate at will. Given this kind of intellectual and moral climate, the struggle against mercy killing, particularly the voluntary kind, is not going to be easy.

Moreover, it is likely that the mercy killing debate is little more than a preliminary to the death selection debate. Just as abortion on demand always provided the clandestine motivation behind abortion for rape and incest, death selection provides the clandestine (or latent) motivation behind the current, but limited, euthanasia debate. In short, the real programme of the euthanasia forces is probably only partially articulated. But the hints and the innuendoes provide the clues of things to come.

Accordingly, I think that we should see some form of death selection as the ultimate goal of the pro-euthanasia movement. Mercy killing provides a kind of opening skirmish. But it will not provide the ground for the last battle.

What, then, might we expect the ultimate battlefield to look like? First, I think that we will see increasing attempts to categorize the senile, the hopelessly ill, the severely retarded and others as non-persons. As in the abortion movement, we will see increasing use of the socio-logical definition of "person": that is "a human being who is conscious of his social relations to other human beings toward whom he acts." Clearly, this definition of person leaves out the unborn. It could also leave out the newborn, the severely retarded and lots of others.

Second, I think that we will see an increasing tendency to apply some sort of "triage" concept in the field of health care. Triage is, of course, a concept taken largely from military medicine. It entails a utilitarian prioritizing of battlefield medical care in terms of military usefulness. Applied throughout the medical community, this system would obviously favor patients considered to be the most socially useful; patients who would be most likely to benefit from medical care. Presumably, some sort of cost-benefit analysis might be applied, whether to individual patients or groups of patients. And scarce medical resources could be diverted to those individuals, or groups, promising the highest return on the investment involved. This could mean that low priority groups would become targets for medical neglect; that is they would be denied reasonable and prudent medical care (e.g. the withholding of antibiotics from mentally retarded children with pneumonia). Low priority groups might very well also become targets of a kind of eliminative medicine. Certain categories of people might be selected for active or positive euthanasia; selected not out of any humanitarian desire to eliminate pain and suffering but selected out of a calculated utilitarian desire to rid society of useless lives.

To many, such a state of affairs may seem to be an impossible Orwellian nightmare. I submit that it is not. First, we have already manifested a profound indifference to human life. Abortion on demand, after all, is a serious denigration of life. Second, medicine is becoming increasingly bureaucratized. The medical community is increasingly coming under the influence of health managers or health planners; professionals whose role is one of planning and allocating the use of medical resources. This, combined with increasing governmental control of medicine, will tend to bring about a unified, disciplined and utilitarian medical community. We could easily find ourselves confronted by a bureaucratically regimented medical community concerned, almost exclusively, with medical care which dispenses the "greatest good for the greatest number." Further, any such trend toward managerial medicine could be accelerated by continued economic decline and/or by an increasing proportion of older people in the population. It is the latter factor which has already put a state like Florida into the forefront of the euthanasia controversy.

And what can be done about all of this? Laws, to the extent that they shape and control community or individual behavior, are important. Education is important. But the euthanasia issue goes beyond the scope of legislation and education. What is really required is a transformation of the human spirit. Our society is increasingly controlled, or managed, by men and women who are utilitarian to the core. For many, God is dead as man is dead. Life, to an alarming degree, has become meaningless. Man is only a functionary. A cog in a machine. A bundle of skills. A complex of behaviors and social relationships. For men in this predicament, death is welcome. Such men are not likely to resist euthanasia even when their own lives are threatened. Men and women who see no value in life can easily arrange to have their burdens lifted by the physician with the needle. People who have never really lived will never really know how to die. Push button death: This is the simple solution offered by the advocates of mercy killing and death selection.

The response to this challenge can only be a rekindling of our sense of humanity. We must re-assert the mystery and dignity of human life and human death. We must rouse some sense of what Alexander Sholzhenitsyn has called the image of eternity with which each person comes into the world.

THE GERANIUM IN THE WINDOW
The "Euthanasia" Murders

FREDRIC WERTHAM

If the physician presumes to take into consideration in his work whether a life has value or not, the consequences are boundless and the physician becomes the most dangerous man in the state.

—DR. CHRISTOPH HUFELAND
(1762-1836)

If we want to understand violence as a whole, we cannot leave any of its major manifestations in a fog of half-knowledge. But this is exactly what has happened with an unprecedented occurrence of mass violence, the deliberate killing of large numbers of mental patients, for which psychiatrists were directly responsible. To both the general public and the psychiatric profession, the details and the background are still imperfectly known. This is not only a chapter in the history of violence; it is also a chapter in the history of psychiatry. Silence does not wipe it out, minimizing it does not expunge it. It must be faced. We must try to understand and resolve it.

It should be kept in mind at the outset that it is a great achievement of psychiatry to have brought about the scientific and humane treatment of mental patients after centuries of struggles against great obstacles. In this progress, as is universally acknowledged, German psychiatrists played a prominent part. And German public psychiatric hospitals had been among the best and most humane in the world.

In the latter part of 1939, four men, in the presence of a whole group of physicians and an expert chemist, were purposely killed (with carbon monoxide gas). They had done nothing wrong, had caused no disturbance, and were trusting and cooperative. They were ordinary mental patients of a state psychiatric hospital which was—or should have been—responsible for their welfare. This successful experiment led to the installation of gas chambers in a number of psychiatric hospitals (Grafeneck, Brandenburg, Hartheim, Sonnenstein, Hadamar, Bernburg).

Let us visualize a historical scene. Dr. Max de Crinis is professor of psychiatry at Berlin University and director of the psychiatric department of the Charité, one of the most famous hospitals of Europe. He is one of the top scientists and organizers of the mass destruction of mental patients. Dr. de Crinis visits the psychiatric institution Sonnenstein, near Dresden, to supervise the working of his organization. He wants to see how the plans are carried out. Sonnenstein is a state hospital with an old tradition of scientific psychiatry and humaneness. In the company of psychiatrists of the institution, Dr. de Crinis now inspects the latest installation, a shower-roomlike chamber. Through a small peephole in an adjoining room he watches twenty nude men being led into the chamber and the door closed. They are not disturbed patients, just quiet and cooperative ones. Carbon monoxide is released into the chamber. The men get weaker and weaker; they try frantically to breathe, totter, and finally drop down. Minutes later their suffering is over and they are all dead. This is a scene repeated many, many times throughout the program. A psychiatrist or staff physician turns on the gas, waits briefly, and then looks over the dead patients afterward, men, women, and children.

HOURGLASS OF DEATH

The mass killing of mental patients was a large project. It was organized as well as any modern community psychiatric project, and better than most. It began with a careful preparatory and planning stage. Then came the detailed working out of methods, the formation of agencies for transporting patients, their registration and similar tasks (there were three main agencies with impressive bureaucratic names), the installing of crematory furnaces at the psychiatric institutions, and finally the action. It all went like clockwork, the clock being the hourglass of death. The organization comprised a whole chain of mental hospitals and institutions, university professors of psychiatry, and directors and staff members of mental hospitals. Psychiatrists completely reversed their historical role and passed death sentences. It became a matter of routine. These psychiatrists, without coercion, acted not figuratively but literally in line with the slogan of one of the most notorious concentration-camp commanders, Koch, the husband of Ilse Koch: "There are no sick men in my camp. They are either well or dead."

The whole undertaking went by different designations: "help for the dying," "mercy deaths," "mercy killings," "destruction of life devoid of value," "mercy action"—or, more briefly, the "action." They all became fused in the sonorous and misleading term "euthanasia." Strangely enough—or perhaps not so strangely—the name has persisted. We hear and read of the "euthanasia program," "euthanasia experiments," "euthanasia campaign," "euthanasia action," "euthanasia trials." In reality, these mass killings had nothing whatever to do with euthanasia. These were not mercy deaths but merciless murders. It was the merciless destruction of helpless people by those who were supposed to help them. There was nothing individual about it; it was a systematic, planned, massive killing operation. The whole proceeding was characterized by the complete absence of any compassion, mercy, or pity for the individual. What a physician does or should do with a special individual patient under special circumstances had absolutely nothing to do with those mass exterminations.

The greatest mistake we can make is to assume or believe that there was a morally, medically, or socially legitimate program and that all that was wrong was merely the excesses. There were no excesses. Rarely has a civil social action been planned, organized, and carried through with such precision. It was not a "good" death, as the term "euthanasia" implies (from *eu,* "well," and *thanatos,* "death"), but a bad death; not a euthanasia but what may be called a dysthanasia. Often it took up to five minutes of suffocation and suffering before the patients died. If we minimize the cruelty involved (or believe those who minimize it), these patients are betrayed a second time. It was often a slow, terrible death for them. For example, a male nurse of one of the state mental hospitals described the routine he saw through the peephole of the gas chamber: "One after the other the patients sagged and finally fell all over each other." Others have reported that the dead gassed victims were found with their lips pushed outward, the tip of the tongue stuck out between them, clearly showing that they had been gasping for breath.

The false term "euthanasia" was used by those who planned, organized, and carried out the action, and it is still being used now by those who do not know, or do not want to know, what really happened.

The ancients meant by euthanasia the art and discipline of dying in peace and dignity. The only legitimate medico-social extension of this meaning is *help* toward that end, with special emphasis on relief from pain and suffering. Euthanasia in this sense is the mitigation and relief of pain and suffering of the death agony by medication or other medical means. For the physician, that means a careful diagnosis, prognosis, and consequent action in relation to a special clinical state. As in any other medical procedures, this may involve a certain risk which requires the physician's best responsible judgment in the individual case. Whatever problems this may represent, they have no relation whatsoever to this massacre of mental patients. To confuse the two means to confuse humanity with inhumanity.

When Dr. Hans Hoff, professor of psychiatry at the University of Vienna, begins his introduction to the recent book, *Euthanasia and Destruction of Life Devoid of Value* like this: "As long as there are incurable, suffering and painfully dying people, the problem of euthanasia will be open to discussion," he is adding to the confusion and concealment, as does the author of this whitewashing book. These victims were not dying, they were not in pain, they were not suffering, and most of them were not incurable.

From the very beginning—that is, before the outbreak of war and before any written expression by Hitler—it was officially known to leading professors of psychiatry and directors of mental hospitals that under the designation of "euthanasia" a program was about to be carried through by them and with their help to kill mental patients in the whole of Germany. The object was "the destruction of life devoid of value." That definition was flexible enough for a summary proceeding of extermination of patients.

VIOLENCE SET IN SOCIAL THINKING

The term "euthanasia" was deliberately used to conceal the actual purpose of the project. But there is also a real confusion about the term that reaches into many quarters. In the *American College Dictionary*, for example, "euthanasia" is defined as "the putting of a person to death painlessly." That is not euthanasia; it is homicide. If you "put a person to death," that is, deliberately kill him, you are committing murder. If it is done painlessly, it is still murder. Many murders, just like suicides, are committed without inflicting pain. In similar fashion, a widely used recent dictionary of psychological and psychoanalytical terms defines "euthanasia" as "the practice of ending life painlessly." Criminology is familiar with cases of mass murderers who made it a practice to do just that. For example, the man who over a considerable period of time lured good-looking young boys into the woods and put them to sleep, a sleep from which they never woke up. They were found, partly undressed, with peaceful expressions on their faces. That was not euthanasia, however; it was mass murder. The fact that such confused and confusing definitions are given in standard dictionaries is another documentation of my thesis that violence is much more solidly and insidiously set in our social thinking than is generally believed.

Just as the designation has been left in ambiguity, so also has the number of victims. We read about "thousands" or "tens of thousands" or "almost a hundred thousand." But how many were there? One would think that this fact would be indispensible for understanding not only the history of violence but even that of psychiatry and of modern civilization in general. Yet in none of the publications, books, or news reports of recent years is a more-or-less-correct figure given. It is characteristic that without exception all the figures that are mentioned are far below the reality. The individual psychiatric hospitals were not so squeamish about the number of patients put to death while the program lasted. For example, in 1941 the psychiatric institution Hadamar celebrated the cremation of the ten thousandth mental patient in a special ceremony. Psychiatrists, nurses, attendants, and secretaries all participated. Everybody received a bottle of beer for the occasion.

We can get an idea of the proportional numbers involved by studying some partial but exact statistics referring to a special locality. From 1939 to 1945 the number of patients in the psychiatric hospitals of Berlin dropped to one-fourth of the original total. As the cause of this drop the official statistics give "evacuations." That is a euphemistic expression for the fact that three-fourths of the patients were transported to other institutions and killed. Sometimes patients slated for murder were not sent directly to the hospitals that had the proper installations, but went first temporarily to so-called intermediate institutions. In 1938 the psychiatric institutions of the province of Brandenburg had 16,295 mental patients of the city of Berlin. In 1945 only 2,379 were left. Almost 14,000 were destroyed. In the institution Berlin-Buch, of 2,500 patients, 500 survived; in the hospital of Kaufbeuren in Bavaria, of 2,000 patients, 200 were left. Many institutions, even big ones, i.e., in Berlin, in Silesia, in Baden, in Saxony, in Austria, were closed entirely because all the patients had been liquidated.

In the special killing institutions the turnover was fast. The psychiatric institution Grafeneck normally had 100 beds. Early in the "action," within thirty-three days 594 patients died (i.e., were killed). A while later, within forty-seven days 2,019 inmates were written off. Eventually the crematorium of Grafeneck smoked incessantly.

In 1939 about 300,000 mental patients (according to some figures it was 320,000) were in psychiatric hospitals, institutions, or clinics. In 1946 their number was 40,000. It was discussed during the project that 300,000 hospital beds would be made available by getting rid of mental patients.

The most reliable estimates of the number of psychiatric patients killed are at least 275,000. We have to realize particularly that the largest proportion of them were not "incurable," as is often lightly stated. Even if "euthanasia" is defined, as it falsely is, as "the killing of incurable mentally diseased persons," that is not at all what happened. According to the best established psychiatric knowledge, about 50 percent of them either would have improved to such an extent that they could have been discharged and lived a social life outside a hospital or would have gotten completely well.

Another misconception widely credited is that these patients had hereditary diseases. Even publications completely condemning the "euthanasia" action fall into this error. However, in the largest number of patients the hereditary factor played either no role at all or only the slightest (and that not well established scientifically). The whole number comprises both curable and incurable conditions, psychopathic personalities, epileptics, encephalitics, neurological cases, mental defectives of both severe and mild degree, arteriosclerotics, deaf-mutes, patients with all kinds of nervous diseases, handicapped patients who had lost a limb in the First World War and were in a state hospital, "cripples" of every description, *et al.*

The indications became wider and wider and eventually included as criteria "superfluous people," the unfit, the unproductive, any "useless eaters," misfits, undesirables. The over-all picture is best understood as the identification and elimination of the weak.

CURSORY EXAMINATION

A considerable percentage of the whole number were senile cases, including people who had no senile psychosis but were merely aged and infirm. Many of the old people included in the program were not in institutions but were living at home, in good health, with their families. A psychiatrist would go to these homes and give the aged people a cursory examination. Of course, it is easy, if you confront a very old person with a lot of psychological questions, to make it appear that something is mentally wrong with him. The psychiatrist would then suggest that such people be placed under guardianship and sent to an institution for a while. From there they were quickly put into gas chambers. It is difficult to conceive that thousands of normal men and women would permit their parents or grandparents to be disposed of in this way without more protest, but that is what happened. As early as September, 1939, word had gotten about among the population in Berlin that inmates of homes for the aged had been exterminated and that it was planned to kill all aged invalids as quickly as possible.

During the first phase of the program, Jewish mental patients, old and young, were strictly spared and excluded. The reason given was that they did not deserve the "benefit" of psychiatric euthanasia. This lasted up to the second half of 1940. Eventually they were all rounded up, however, and by 1941, practically without exception, were exterminated.

Thousands of children were disposed of. A special agency existed for them, consisting of a commission of three experts: one a psychiatrist and director of a state hospital, the other two prominent pediatricians. The children came from psychiatric hospitals, institutions for mental defectives, children's homes, university pediatric clinics, children's hospitals, pediatricians, et al. They were killed in both psychiatric institutions and pediatric clinics. Especially in the latter a number of woman physicians were actively involved in the murders. Among these children were those with mental diseases, mental defectives—even those with only slightly retarded intelligence—handicapped children, children with neurological conditions, and mongoloid children (even with minimal mental defects). Also in this number were children in training schools or reformatories. Admission to such child-care institutions occurs often on a social indication and not for any intrinsic personality difficulties of the child. One physician who killed such training-school boys and girls with intravenous injections of morphia stated in court to explain his actions: "I see today that it was not right. . . . I was always told that the responsibility lies with the professors from Berlin."

The chief of the mental institution Hadamar was responsible for the murder of "over a thousand patients." He personally opened the containers of gas and watched through the peephole the death agonies of the patients, including the children. He stated:

> I was of course torn this way and that. It reassured me to learn what eminent scientists partook in the action: Professor Carl Schneider, Professor Heyde, Professor Nitsche.

This, of course, is not an excuse either legally or morally, but it is a causal factor which has to be taken into account. And when Dr. Karl Brandt, the medical chief of the euthanasia project, defended himself for his leading role in the action, he stated that he had asked for the "most critical" evaluation of who was mentally incurable. And he added: "Were not the regular professors of the universities with the program? Who could there be who was better qualified than they?"

"LIFE DEVOID OF VALUE"

These statements that leading psychiatrists supplied the rationalization for these cruelties and took a responsible part in them are true. We must ask ourselves what was the pre-history, in the pre-violence phase, of their ideas. Historically there were tendencies in psychiatry (and not only in German psychiatry) to pronounce value judgments not only on individuals, on medical grounds, but on whole groups, on medico-sociological grounds. What was (and still is) widely regarded as scientific writing prepared the way. Most influential was the book *The Release of the Destruction of Life Devoid of Value*, published in Leipzig in 1920. Its popularity is attested by the fact that two years later a second edition became necessary. The book advocated that the killing of "worthless people" be released from penalty and legally permitted. It was written by two prominent scientists, the jurist Karl Binding and the psychiatrist Alfred Hoche. The concept of "life devoid of value" or "life not worth living" was not a Nazi invention, as is often thought. It derives from this book.

Binding and Hoche speak of "absolutely worthless human beings"; they plead for "the killing of those who cannot be rescued and whose death is urgently necessary"; they refer to those who are below the level of beasts and who have "neither the will to live nor to die"; they write about those who are "mentally completely dead" and who "represent a foreign body in human society." It is noteworthy that among the arguments adduced for killing, the economic factor is stressed, namely, the cost of keeping these patients alive and caring for them. The psychiatrist author decries any show of sympathy in such cases, because it would be based on "erroneous thinking." The jurist author recognizes that errors in diagnosis and execution might be made. But he dismisses that like this: "Humanity loses so many members through error that one more or less really hardly makes any difference." In the beginning of the book we read about the feeling of "pity" for the patient. But in the bulk of the text the question of pity does not come up any more. It gets completely lost. Instead, both authors enlarge on the economic factor, the waste of money and labor in the care of the retarded. Both extol "heroism" and a "heroic attitude" which our time is supposed to have lost.

SLOGAN LAUNCHED

These ideas were expressed in 1920. Surely Hoche and Binding had not heard of Hitler at that time, nor did Hitler read this book. It is not without significance that at this time, when Hitler was just starting his career, the "life devoid of value" slogan was launched from a different source. Evidently there is such a thing as a spirit of the times which emanates from the depths of economic-historical processes.

This little book influenced—or at any rate crystallized—the thinking of a whole generation. Considering how violence-stimulating the ideas in it are, it is significant that both authors were eminent men who played a role as intellectual leaders in a special historical period. This illustrates the proposition that violence does not usually come from the uncontrolled instincts of the undereducated, but frequently is a rationalized policy from above. Hoche was professor of psychiatry and director of the psychiatric clinic at Freiburg from 1902 to 1934. He made valuable contributions to neuropsychiatry. In his clinic a number of eminent specialists were trained—for example, Dr. Robert Wartenberg, who later became one of the outstanding and most popular teachers of neurology in California. Hoche's sound views on classification of mental diseases had considerable influence on American psychiatry, especially through Adolph Meyer, professor of psychiatry at Johns Hopkins.

Wherever his work touched on the social field, however, he had illiberal tendencies. For example, in a series of monographs which he edited, he published and gave wide currency to a book which tried to prove women intellectually inferior to men. In his work on forensic psychiatry, he exhibited a punitive, legalistic attitude with regard to sexual deviations. He was a reactionary opponent of psychoanalysis, not recognizing even Freud's well-established clinical observations. He regarded his book on the destruction of "life devoid of value" as one of his "more important" works.

The other author, Karl Binding, was professor of jurisprudence at the University of Leipzig. He was the chief representative of the retribution theory in criminal law. He combatted the idea that the protection of society is the purpose of punishment and that the personality of the criminal has to be taken into account. He taught that for every criminal deed there has to be full retribution. His son Rudolph G. Binding was also a jurist, and a recognized poet as well. When Romain Rolland in 1933 warned against Nazi violence and pleaded for humaneness, Rudolph G. Binding answered in a "Letter to the World." He advocated fanaticism on the part of everybody and called for "fanatics big and small, down to the children."

Another intellectual stream that contributed to the final massacre of mental patients was the exaggeration of the influence of heredity on mental disorders. The chief representative of this trend was Ernest Ruedin. Ruedin was professor of psychiatry at the universities of Basel, in Switzerland, and Munich. Some of his studies on heredity, and those of his pupils and associates (like Eugen Kahn, who later became professor of psychiatry at Yale), were undoubtedly valuable. This was widely recognized. He participated in the First International Congress for Mental Hygiene in Washington, D.C. But it was he who supplied the "scientific" reasons according to which mass sterilizations of all kinds of physically and mentally handicapped people took place. He was the chief architect of the compulsory sterilization law of 1933. This law was so vigorously formulated and interpreted (by Reudin in 1934) that, for example, any young man with a harmless phimosis was forced to be sterilized. The summary official explanation for this was that he would be "incapable of achieving extraordinary performances in sport, in life, in war, or in overcoming dangers." The results of enforced castrations in the period from 1933 to 1945 are still quoted in current psychiatric literature without any critique of their inhumanity.

The compulsory sterilization law was the forerunner of the mass killing of psychiatric patients, which was organized and carried out with Ruedin's full knowledge. He expressly warned psychiatrists against the "excessive compassion and love of one's neighbor characteristic of the past centuries."

GUIDED BY PSYCHIATRISTS

Against this theoretical-intellectual background, mental patients were sacrificed in psychiatric institutions and in the name of psychiatry. From its very inception the "euthanasia" program was guided in all important matters, including concrete details, by psychiatrists. The administrative sector was handled by bureaucrats who dealt merely with executive, management, and formal questions such as the transport of patients, cremation, notification of relatives, and so on. Even the false death certificates were signed by psychiatrists. The psychiatrists made the decisions. For these physicians, as the physical chemist Professor Robert Havemann expressed it, denouncing the "euthanasia" murders,

> . . . the patient is no longer a human being needing help, but merely an object whose value is measured according to whether his life or his destruction is more expedient for the nation. The physicians took over the function of judge over life and death. . . . They made themselves into infallible gods.

How matter-of-factly they considered this role is illustrated by the replies of the veteran director of one of the biggest and formerly most well-administered psychiatric hospitals during an interrogation:

> Q. To how many children have you applied euthanasia in your hospital?
> A. I couldn't tell you exactly . . .
> Q. To how many have you done that? 200? 500? 1,000?
> A. For God's sake, I really don't remember how many there were. I really don't know whether there were a hundred or more.
> Q. Do you know when euthanasia was practiced on the last child in your hospital?
> A. I don't know exactly. But Dr.———says that until a short time before the arrival of the Americans [the American Army], children were still subjected to euthanasia.
> Q. For how long have you practiced the euthanasia of children?
> A. After so much time, I can't remember the dates exactly.
> Q. When did the extermination of these children stop?
> A. The extermination of these children never stopped until the end. I never received an order [to stop it].
> Q. To how many adults did you apply euthanasia in your institution?
> A. I don't know any more.

Q. How many adults have you submitted to
euthanasia in your institution?
A. That didn't happen in my institution. I
contented myself with transferring the patients
[to other institutions where they were killed].

It has been stated that the psychiatrists were merely following a law or were being forced to obey an order. Again and
again we read—as if it were a historical fact—of Hitler's secret order to exterminate those suffering from severe mental
defect or disease. Those who hold the one-man theory of history (sometimes called the great-man theory of history), according to which important developments, for good or evil,
are to be explained by the wish and will of one individual person, favor the illusion that such an order was the entire cause
of the extermination of psychiatric patients. According to
this view, everything was fine until that order was given and
became fine again when the order was revoked. The reality
was very different. There was no law and no such order. The
tragedy is that the psychiatrists did not have to have an order.
They acted on their own. They were not carrying out a death
sentence pronounced by somebody else. They were the legislators who laid down the rules for deciding who was to die;
they were the administrators who worked out the procedures,
provided the patients and places, and decided the methods of
killing; they pronounced a sentence of life or death in every
individual case; they were the executioners who carried the
sentences out or—without being coerced to do so—surrendered their patients to be killed in other institutions; they
supervised and often watched the slow deaths.

The evidence is very clear on this. The psychiatrists did
not have to work in these hospitals; they did so voluntarily,
were able to resign if they wished, and could refuse to do special tasks. For example, the psychiatrist Dr. F. Hoelzel was
asked by the psychiatric director of the mental institution
Eglfing-Haar to head a children's division in which many
handicapped and disturbed children were killed (right up to
1945). He refused in a pathetic letter saying that his "temperament was not suited to this task," that he was "too soft."

Hitler gave no order to kill mental patients indiscrimin-
ately. As late as mid-1940 (when thousands of patients had
been killed in psychiatric institutions), Minister of Justice
Guertner wrote to Minister Hans Lammers: "The Fuehrer
has declined to enact a law [for putting mental patients to

death]." There was no legal sanction for it. All we have is one note, not on official stationery but on Hitler's own private paper, written in October, 1939, and predated September 1, 1939. Meetings of psychiatrists working out the "euthanasia" program had taken place long before that. Hitler's note is addressed to Philipp Bouhler, chief of Hitler's chancellery, and to Dr. Karl Brandt, Hitler's personal physician at the time and Reich Commissioner for Health. (Bouhler committed suicide; Dr. Brandt was sentenced to death and executed.) The note reads as follows:

> Reichleader Bouhler and
> Dr. Med. Brandt
>   are responsibly commissioned to extend the authority of physicians, to be designated by name, so that a mercy death may be granted to patients who according to human judgment are incurably ill according to the most critical evaluation of the state of their disease.
>   (Signed) Adolf Hitler

To kill patients (Hitler does not speak of mental patients), even if one were sure that they are incurable, is bad enough. But even if his wish, as the note clearly expresses it, had been executed, the number of victims would have been infinitely smaller and the whole proceeding could not have been carried out in the way in which it was carried out. Referring to this note, anyone could have refused to do what was later actually done. The note does not give the order to kill, but the *power* to kill. That is something very different. The physicians made use of this power extensively, ruthlessly, cruelly. The note is not a command but an assignment of authority and responsibility to a particular group of persons, namely, physicians, psychiatrists, and pediatricians. This assignment, far from ordering it, did not even give psychiatrists offical permission to do what they did on a grand scale, *i.e.*, kill all kinds of people who were not at all incurable or even mentally ill, making no attempt even to examine them first. The assignment gives to the psychiatrist the widest leeway for "human judgment" and a "most critical evaluation." It certainly cannot be construed as an order to kill people with no serious disease or with no disease at all.

SCIENTIFIC RATIONALIZATION

Even if the note was not meant to be taken literally, it was a formal concession to ethics and offered a loophole for contradiction or at least question. The psychiatrists in authority did not take advantage of this. Instead they initiated the most extreme measures and cloaked them in scientific terminology and academic respectability. No mental patients were killed without psychiatrists being involved. Without the scientific rationalization which they supplied from the very beginning and without their mobilization of their own psychiatric hospitals and facilities, the whole proceeding could not have taken the shape it did. They were responsible for their own judgments, their own decisions, their own acts. It helps us to understand the wide social ramifications of violence if we realize that from the highest echelons down, the psychiatrists acted spontaneously, without being forced.

A court in Coblenz probed this question most carefully in the case of three hospital psychiatrists who were charged with "aid to murder in an indefinite number of cases":

> They have taken this task upon themselves voluntarily, just as altogether the collaboration in the "action" was voluntary throughout.

This is borne out by a letter from Himmler, chief of the SS, in response to an inquiry by a high judge:

> What happens in the place in question [a psychiatric institution] is carried out by a commission of physicians. . . . The SS furnish only help in vehicles, cars, etc. The medical specialist, expert and responsible, is the one who gives the orders.

In this connection the statement of Dr. Hans Hefelmann, an agronomist who was a highly placed bureaucrat in the "euthanasia" program, is significant. He made it in the abortive "euthanasia" trial at Limburg in 1964: "No doctor was ever ordered to participate in the euthanasia program; they came of their own volition." Other evidence confirms this.

What psychiatrists did made even members of the Nazi Party weep. When patients were transferred from their regular institution to one where they were to be killed, they were usually told that it was only a regular normal transfer from one hospital to another or that it was a change to a better place. Sometimes a glimpse of the truth would become known to patients, and scenes worthy of Callot or Goya would follow. Here is such a (true) scene. In the sleepy little town of Absberg, two large autobuses (belonging to the central transport agency of the "euthanasia" program) are parked on the street near an institution where there are several hundred mental patients. Some time before, twenty-five patients had been fetched by such a bus. Of these twenty-five, twenty-four "died" and one woman patient returned. The other patients in the institution learned what had happened, as did the inhabitants of the town. As the patients leave the institution to enter the buses, they are afraid, they refuse and remonstrate. Force is used by the personnel, and each patient is shoved violently into a bus. A large group of bystanders has assembled. They are so moved that they break into tears. The whole operation is presided over by an experienced psychiatrist from the big state hospital Erlangen. Among those spectators who cried openly at this pitiful spectacle were—as the official Nazi report states—"even members of the Nazi Party." There is no mention anywhere that doctors had any tears in their eyes.

To place causal responsibility on the physician does not in any way diminish the responsibility of the high and low Nazi officials and bureaucrats involved. But by the same token, placing full responsibility on these officials does not in the slightest diminish the role of the psychiatrist in the slaughter. In order to get the proper focus, we must think in terms of causal factors. If it takes two to plan and commit deliberate murder, that does not mean that only one is guilty. Even if the psychiatrists had been under orders, which they were not, it is noteworthy that their complete mobilization for killing patients went as speedily as the military mobilization of soldiers to fight the enemy.

PREPOSTEROUS ASSUMPTION

Two "extenuating" circumstances, often claimed, have to be seriously weighed. One is that the psychiatrists did not know; the other is that very few were involved. In the very beginning, some psychiatrists may not have known what happened to their patients when they were transferred en masse in buses to other, unnamed institutions. But it is preposterous to assume that this ignorance could last after tens of thousands had been killed. The claim that only a few psychiatrists were involved is equally invalid. The lowest estimate is that there were "perhaps fifty" who participated. Even if this were a correct number (which it is not), among them were some of the most renowned and distinguished academic and hospital figures. Actually, the extent of the operation makes it inevitable that there were many more involved in Germany and Austria, perhaps three or four times that many (not to speak of the many psychiatric nurses acting under the instructions of psychiatrists). Of course, the degree of participation varied. For example, in the internationally famous hospital of Gütersloh, the director and his staff did not "select" patients for annihilation. But they delivered the patients, without resistance or protest, to the guards and escorts who drove up for them in trucks. That is participating in murder too.

In July, 1939, several months before Hitler's note was written, a conference took place in Berlin in which the program to kill mental patients in the whole of Germany was outlined in concrete, final form. Present and ready to participate were the regular professors of psychiatry and chairmen of the departments of psychiatry of the leading universities and medical schools of Germany: Berlin, Heidelberg, Bonn, Würzburg. Historians of medicine and sociologists will have a lot of work to do to explain this. So far they have not stated the problem or even noted the fact. At a conference in Dresden in March, 1940, Professor de Crinis, of Berlin University, talked over the program with the chief psychiatrists of large public mental hospitals (state hospitals). The classification of mental disorders on which devoted physicians in all countries had worked for centuries was reduced to a simple formula: patients "not worthy to live" and patients "worthy to be helped." There was no opposition on the part of the physicians, every one of whom held a responsible position in the state-hospital system. Questions of ethics or the juridical aspects were not even mentioned. The only questions raised by the participants at the conference were how the project could be carried through most "practically and cheaply." For example, the transfer of patients from their original institution to one where they were to be killed was called "impractical" because it meant "wasting of gasoline." Mass graves, to be leveled later, were recommended as being an economical procedure.

For several years during the time of the program, psychiatrists held meetings every three months in Heidelberg under the chairmanship of the professor of psychiatry at the University of Heidelberg. At these conferences the ways to conduct the extermination action were studied, and suitable measures were suggested to assure its efficacy.

DEATH CANDIDATES

The whole project is a model of the most bureaucratic mass murder in history. It functioned as follows. In the preparatory meetings the chief psychiatric experts of the project worked out the criteria by which patients should be selected. Questionnaires were prepared with questions as to diagnosis, duration of stay in the institution; and so on. In October, 1939, the first questionnaires went out to state hospitals and other public and private institutions where mental patients, epileptics, the mentally retarded, and other handicapped persons were taken care of. Copies of each filled-out questionnaire were sent to four psychiatric experts, who indicated with a + or − their opinion about whether the patient was to live or die. (No expert gave an opinion on questionnaires filled out for patients in his own institution, but only on those of other institutions. Therefore he had no personal knowledge whatsoever of the patients.) This typical correspondence shows that the psychiatric experts worked very hard.

Letter from the "euthanasia" central office in Berlin to Member of the Commission of Experts dated November 25, 1940:

> Enclosed I am sending you 300 report sheets [questionnaires] from the institution Lüneburg with the request for your expert opinion.
>
> (Signed)

Answering letter from the Member of the Commission of Experts to the central office in Berlin, dated November 29, 1940:

> Enclosed I am sending you the 107th batch of report sheets, namely, 300 sheets complete with my expert opinion.
>
> (Signed)

This rapid selection and certification of death candidates is not a record or by any means exceptional. The same expert formed his opinion on 2,190 questionnaires in two weeks and on 258 in two days.

The questionnaires with expert opinions indicated by the + or the − were then sent to a chief expert, who passed the final judgment. Beginning in January, 1940, the patients marked for death were transferred, directly or via intermediate stations, to the six psychiatric institutions in which gas chambers had been installed for the program. In these lethal institutions the patients were dealt with summarily and quickly, as this typical letter shows, from the social-welfare association Swabia to the director of the state hospital Kaufbeuren:

> I have the honor to inform you that the female patients transferred from your hospital on November 8, 1940, all died in the month of November in the institutions Grafeneck, Bernburg, Sonnenstein, and Hartheim.
>
> (Signed)

In some institutions, like Hartheim in Austria, things went so fast sometimes that it took only four hours from the time a patient was admitted till he left "through the chimney."

PROMINENT PROFESSORS, NOT PUPPETS

The backbone of the whole project was the experts. It was their decision which sealed the fate of every victim. Who were these men? That is the most remarkable part of the story —and the most important one for the future of violence and, I believe, of mankind. They were not nonentities or outsiders. Most of them had all the hallmarks of civic and scientific respectability. They were not Nazi puppets, but had made their careers and reputations as psychiatrists long before Hitler came to power. Among them were more than twelve full professors at universities. Most of their names read like a roster of prominent psychiatrists. They have made valuable contributions to scientific psychiatry. They are still quoted in international psychiatric literature, which testifies to their scientific stature. The bibliography of their papers, monographs, and books—not to mention their graduate and post-graduate lectures and their editorial work on leading psychiatric journals—would fill a whole brochure. We must make ourselves familiar with the caliber of these men if we want to comprehend the full meaning of this historical occurrence.

Dr. Max de Crinis was professor of psychiatry at the University of Berlin and director of the psychiatric department of the famous Charité Hospital. He was originally chief physician at the psychiatric clinic at the University of Graz. Those who knew him personally describe him as a "charming Austrian." He has many scientific studies to his credit, on alcoholism, epilepsy, war neuroses, pathology of the central nervous system (brain edema and brain swelling), etc. He was especially interested in the bodily concomitants of mental disorders—for instance, malfunction of the liver. Textbooks, including recent ones, refer to some of his scientific work as authoritative. In 1944, he published an interesting book on the somatic foundations of emotions which is still quoted in the scientific literature today. It is not easy to understand—but is important to know—how such a man could deliberately and personally, from his own department in the university hospital, send a thirteen-year-old boy afflicted with mongolism, with only minor mental impairment, to one of the murder institutions—the children's division of Goerden—to be killed. In 1945, when his car could not get through the Russian encirclement of Berlin, Dr. de Crinis committed suicide with a government-supplied capsule of cyanide.

One of the most distinguished (and most unexpected) members of the team of experts which was the heart of the whole killing operation was Werner Villinger, who at the time was professor of psychiatry at the University of Breslau. Prior to that he was head of the department of child psychiatry at Tuebingen and then psychiatric director at Bethel, a world-famous institution for epileptics and mentally and physically disabled persons founded in 1867. From 1946 to 1956 he was professor of psychiatry at the University of Marburg. His clinical research on the outbreak of an acute psychosis after the commitment of a violent crime became well known. He wrote especially on the psychological and social difficulties of children and youths, on child guidance, group therapy, juvenile delinquency, and similar subjects. He has been decorated by the West German government. In 1950 he was invited to participate in the White House Conference on Children and Youth and did so.

DIFFICULT TO UNDERSTAND

His name alone, quite apart from his activity in it, gave a great boost to the "euthanasia" project. For his name suggested to others, especially younger psychiatrists, that there could be nothing wrong with the "action." It is difficult to understand how a man with concern for youths could not only consent to but actively participate in projects of killing them, but we may find some slight hints in his previous writings. Two years before Hitler came to power, Villinger advocated the sterilization of patients with hereditary diseases. Writing about the "limits of educability," he stated that "the deepest roots of what we call temperment and character are deep in the inherited constitution." Contrary to our modern point of view, he regarded the chances for the rehabilitation of juvenile delinquents with definite emotional difficulties as very poor.

During the preparation of the "euthanasia" trial in Limburg, Dr. Villinger was questioned by the prosecutor in three sessions. At about the same period, it became publicly known that he was implicated in the "euthanasia" murders in a leading active role. He went to the mountains near Innsbruck and committed suicide. An attempt was made later to make this appear an accident, but there is no doubt about what happened.

To find Dr. Carl Schneider as a leading member of a wholesale murder project is also unexpected. For twelve years he was professor of psychiatry at the University of Heidelberg. As such he held the same important position as Emil Kraepelin a generation before. And Kraepelin was the founder of modern clinical psychiatry. In a recent textbook, Schneider's scientific work is referred to eleven times. In some of the most recent publications on the course of mental diseases and on the effect of tranquilizers, his clinical subdivisions are taken as a basis. He made clinical investigations of mental disorders in organic brain diseases and in pernicious anemia. He wrote on abnormal personalities in relation to diminished legal responsibility. Since experimental psychoses are currently much investigated, it is of interest that more than thirty years ago he induced an experimental psychosis in himself with mescaline. He described it in his monograph on hallucinations. One of his monographs deals with "The Treatment and

Prevention of Mental Disorders." He studied epilepsy and expressed modern views about it, and his research on that subject is still quoted. He wrote two books on schizophrenia. The first, *The Psychology of Schizophrenia*, is considered a landmark of this type of clinical study. Originally more interested in subtle psychological analyses, he stressed more and more the hereditary factor.

Carl Schneider was very active in all phases of the program. He served as expert for the processing of death questionnaires, participated in the frequent conferences, and regularly instructed younger psychiatrists in the methods and procedures of the project. Perhaps the most extraordinary part of his story is that before going to Heidelberg, he, like Werner Villinger, had held the highly respected position of chief physician at the universally recognized institution Bethel. Ten years later, when he was professor at Heidelberg, he appeared with an SS commission at Bethel, went over the questionnaires, ordered the personnel to present patients to him, and personally selected the candidates for extermination. When, after the defeat of the Nazi regime, Dr. Schneider was to be put on trial, he committed suicide.

Another psychiatrist with an international reputation is Professor Paul Nitsche. He was successively director of several state hospitals, including the tradition-rich Sonnenstein in Saxony, which was the first psychiatric state hospital in Germany. In the authoritative *Handbook of Psychiatry* (1925-1932), he wrote the section on "Therapy of Mental Diseases," based on his own vast experience. He was one of the editors of the German *Journal for Mental Hygiene*. He wrote understandingly on modern psychotherapeutic measures in mental hospitals. He was interested in psychoses in prisoners (prison psychoses), and his book on the subject appeared in the best American monograph series on nervous and mental diseases. In the killing project he held a top position. He functioned as a representative of Dr. Brandt, the "leader" of the medical sector (as opposed to the strictly administrative bureau). He did his work of organizing and selecting death candidates so well that during the project he was advanced from expert to chief expert.

"EXCEPTIONALLY GOOD PSYCHIATRIST"

Nitsche presents perhaps the most remarkable psychological enigma. Colleagues of his who knew him well and who condemn him for his "euthanasia" work nevertheless say of him that he was "an exceptionally good psychiatrist, especially kind to his patients and concerned about them day and night." So can a false fanatical social orientation play havoc with a man's character. Here we come up against a contradiction which plays a great role in modern violence: the contrast in the same individual between the private, intimate, spontaneous personality and the corporate, public, official personality.

After the Nazi regime ended, Dr. Nitsche was tried in Dresden for the murder of mental patients and was sentenced to death. In 1947 he was executed.

PROBLEM FOR HISTORIAN

Perhaps the greatest break with the humane traditions of psychiatry is connected with the name of Dr. Werner Heyde. Heyde was professor of psychiatry at the University of Würzburg and director of the psychiatric clinic there. Few places in the world can look back on such a long history of successful care of mental patients. The clinic grew out of a division of a general hospital where mental patients were admitted and kindly treated as early as the last decades of the sixteenth century. It is interesting that exactly contemporary with the extant case histories of this hospital are the descriptions by Cervantes in *Don Quixote* (first chapter of the second part) of the mental institution in Seville (around 1600). Cervantes' stories of the inmates show that this institution (*casa de los locos*) was humanely administered. In other words, in two geographically widely separated and different localities, Seville and Würzburg, pioneer work was done that long ago in treating the mentally afflicted as human beings and as medical patients. It is certainly a problem for the historian of culture, as it is for the student of violence, that in the same place where mental patients were treated most humanely in 1583, they were doomed to be killed in 1940. In the later nineteenth and in the twentieth century, the Wurzburg psychiatric clinic played a prominent role in scientific research. A number of outstanding psychiatrists got their training there. The first intelligence test was devised there in 1888. One of the earliest clinical observations and descriptions of what was later called schizophrenia came from that clinic.

Dr. Heyde's reputation as a scientific psychiatrist was excellent. He worked for several years in the clinic, became director of the outpatient department, and began his teaching there in 1932.

One of Heyde's predecessors as head of the Würzburg clinic, Conrad Rieger, who studied especially the history of psychiatry, wrote, almost prophetically, in his autobiography in 1929 (ten years before the start of the extermination program):

> Whether it is deliberate or through negligence, it is wrong to kill human beings and to deprive them of care. On the contrary, we must care for them and protect them, well and humanely. This care and protection is needed in the same measure for the so-called curable and the so-called incurable.

We do not know whether Heyde ever read this statement, which he so completely reversed. Heyde was a key figure in the program. When carbon monoxide was suggested as a method for killing, this proposal had to be submitted first to him for evaluation. He approved the method and directed the idea into the proper administrative channels for its practical realization. He was the head of one of the agencies of the project, the Reich Society for Mental Institutions (state hospitals). In his office the data from these institutions were collected and the last word pronounced about the patients to be sent to the special extermination hospitals. He played the leading role in the preparatory and organizing conferences (before Hitler's private note), helped in working out the questionnaires, functioned as chief expert, and selected the younger psychiatrists for the program and instructed them in their task.

From the beginning, he personally inspected the death institutions and the installation of the gas chambers, to make sure that everything functioned expeditiously. In addition, far from being told what to do, he gave lectures before high officials in the Nazi ministries to promote and explain the weeding out of those "not worthy to live." For example, on

April 23, 1941, in the Department of Justice, he gave a lecture on "The Euthanasia Program" before high officials, judges, and prosecutors. The most important person was the president of the highest court, the Reich Court, Judge Erwin Bumke. Bumke had been appointed to his office in 1929, during the democratic Weimar Republic. He raised no objection to the mass killing after this lecture, and the doom—the legal doom—of the mental patients was sealed. Psychiatry and law had met in the spirit of violence.

"WANTED FOR MURDER . . ."

After the collapse of the Nazi regime, Heyde was arrested, but he escaped from custody. A warrant for his arrest (Wanted for Murder . . ."), with his picture on it, was sent out. It is said that he was probably working as a physician. For 12 years he lived a charmed existence under a different name. He was employed by a state insurance agency, again as chief expert. He did a great deal of work for courts. During this time his wife was receiving a widow's pension, and from money earned in his new career she bought a beautiful house on Lake Starnberg, near Munich. Many private persons—judges, prosecutors, physicians, university professors, and high state officials—knew his real identity. There was a certain solidarity in protecting this secret of violence. When his identity did come out, almost by accident, he surrendered to the authorities. His trial at Limburg was delayed for four years for preliminary investigation. He made another attempt to escape, which failed. When he was left unguarded in his cell five days before the trial was due to start, he committed suicide.

This trial, which would have been the most important "euthanasia" trial, delayed overlong, never took place. One day before Dr. Heyde's suicide, his co-defendant, Dr. Friedrich Tillman, who from 1934 to 1945 was director of orphanages in Cologne and who has been called a "bookkeeper of death," jumped or was pushed from a tenth-story window. Another defendant, Dr. Gerhard Bohne, escaped from jail to South America. And the fourth defendant, Dr. Hefelmann, was declared not able to stand trial because of illness. The widely held belief that there was great pressure against this trial's taking place seems to be not without foundation.

Among other outstanding professors of psychiatry who were involved in the program were the following:

NOT ONLY DEATH CROSSES

Dr. Berthold Kihn was the professor of psychiatry at the famous University of Jena, where Hegel, Fichte, Schiller, and Haeckel taught, where Karl Marx got his doctor's degree and the composer Schumann an honorary doctorate. He contributed chapters to several authoritative textbooks—for example, on neurosyphilis, on peripheral nerves, and on disorders of old age. He did research on the microscopic study of brain tissues. Kihn not only was busy making the death crosses on questionnaires, but also personally supervised the selection of patients for extermination in various institutions. He and Dr. Carl Schneider were among the charter members of one of the main project agencies.

Dr. Friedrich Mauz was professor of psychiatry at Koenigsburg from 1939 to 1945 and has held the same position at the University of Münster since 1953. A good deal of his scientific work became generally acknowledged: his studies on hysteria and epilepsy, with interesting clinical observations; on psychoses in juveniles; on the physical constitution in mental disorders. From him comes the term "schizophrenic catastrophe," for the most severe progressive types of the disease. In 1948 he participated as one of three official delegates from Germany at an international mental hygiene meeting in London. At that congress, the World Federation for Mental Health was founded, its purpose being the "furthering of good human relations."

Dr. Mauz excused himself later, without any condemnation of the "euthanasia" project, by saying that his invitation to a "euthanasia" conference in Berlin was "harmlessly formulated" and that as late as the autumn of 1940 (when tens of thousands of patients from all over Germany had been killed and whole hospitals closed because all the patients had been evacuated to death institutions), he, who held a responsible and administrative position in psychiatry, did not know anything about any "carrying through of the euthanasia program."

This list is far from complete.

In the whole "euthanasia" matter the universities, including the psychiatric and pediatric departments, wrapped themselves in silence. How easy it would have been (and riskless) to refuse, had anyone been so minded, is shown by the case of Gottfried Ewald, professor of psychiatry in Göttingen. He was invited to a conference at the central office in Berlin under the chairmanship of Heyde and was asked to join the program. He refused and left the conference. He remained unmolested and had no disadvantage on account of his complete refusal.

There is an interesting sidelight on his exceptional behavior. Among those whom the experts marked on the questionnaires or report sheets as "unworthy to live," and who were consequently killed, were veterans who had lost an arm or leg in the war. The records are clear about that. For example, among a group of male patients transferred from the state hospital Rottenmuenster to a death institution was one whose "euthanasia" questionnaire said: "Receives war pension. Handicapped for work through loss of an arm." Professor Ewald had lost his left arm in World War I and referred to it occasionally in his lectures. Maybe that made it easier for him to identify with the victims.

A young German psychiatrist of much lower rank, Dr. Theo Lang, made a serious attempt to stem the whole program. He was at that time in Germany and later became chief physician of the institution Herisau in Switzerland. On January 20, 1941, he obtained an interview with Dr. M.H. Goering at the German Institute for Psychological Research and Psychotherapy. His plan was to get Dr. Goering to sign a declaration against the extermination of mental patients. When he tried to tell Dr. Goering the whole story of the program, which at that time had been going on for more than a year, he found that Dr. Goering knew all about it and confirmed its truth. However, he refused to sign the declaration, and so nothing came of this *demarche*.

In taking this step—and for this reason his name should not be forgotten—Dr. Lang showed extraordinary courage. In going to Dr. Goering, he knew that he was approaching the very seats of Nazi power, both political and psychiatric. Dr. Goering was a cousin of Marshal Hermann Goering, with whom he was in personal contact. And his close collaborator and coeditor for the Nazi-coordinated *Journal for Psychotherapy* for several years was Dr. C.G. Jung. Dr. Jung, in the words of the then State Secretary for Health, Dr. Conti, "represented German psychiatry under the Nazis." So Dr. Lang could not reach any higher with his plea for mercy and decency.

PARALLEL PHENOMENA

In addition to the professors of psychiatry, the experts included directors of large and well-known state hospitals from different parts of Germany, like Buch, near Berlin, and Eglfing, near Munich. They were also busy making the death crosses on the questionnaires and helping in other ways. These experts were not new appointees of the Nazi regime, but had had long and honorable careers. They were by no means products of Nazism, but were parallel phenomena. Their thinking was similar: the attacking of a social problem by violence. However well disguised by high-sounding terms like "eugenics" and "euthanasia," the problem was essentially economic and sociopolitical, namely, the cost of care for the temporarily "unproductive" and the prosperity and glory of the nation.

It is important to keep in mind that among those in responsible positions and most actively engaged in the killing were psychiatrists of ability. For example, Dr. Valentin Falthauser, director of a state hospital, was sentenced to three years in prison for practices that contributed to the death of three hundred hospital inmates. He was coauthor of an important book *Home Care in Psychiatry and Allied Fields,* which contains ideas which are still of great actuality for current community psychiatry.

The special agency for child "euthanasia," the Reich Commission for the Scientific Registration of Hereditary and Constitutional Severe Disorders, had as its most prominent expert Dr. Werner Catel, who was subsequently professor of pediatrics at the University of Kiel until the sixties. This was a commission of experts, psychiatric and pediatric, that decided—entirely on its own—which children should be killed as being mentally below par or handicapped or physically malformed. Dr. Catel still defends and advocates his type of "euthanasia" today—for instance, in his book *Borderline Situations of Life* (1962). It is a noteworthy fact for the recognition of the violence content of a democratic society that the head of a child-killing organization with thousands of victims should become the professor of pediatrics and head of a pediatric clinic at a renowned university.

CHILDREN'S DIVISIONS

The children slated for death were sent to special "children's divisions," first Goerden, then Eichberg, Idstein, Steinhof (near Vienna), and Eglfing. They were killed mostly by increasing doses of Luminal or other drugs either spoon-fed as medicine or mixed with their food. Their dying lasted for days, sometimes for weeks. In actual practice, the indications for killing eventually became wider and wider. Included were children who had "badly modeled ears," who were bed wetters, or who were perfectly healthy but designated as "difficult to educate." The children coming under the authority of the Reich Commission were originally mostly infants. The age was then increased from three years to seventeen years. Later, in 1944 and 1945, the work of the commission also included adults.

A further method of "child euthanasia" was deliberately and literally starving children to death in the "children's divisions." This happened to very many children. In most instances, these deaths were recorded as normal or natural deaths. But many people knew about the fact itself. As early as autumn 1939, a student of psychology, later a public-school teacher, Ludwig Lehner, was permitted with other visitors to go through the state hospital Eglfing-Haar. He went there as part of his studies in psychology. In the children's ward were some twenty-five half-starved children ranging in age from one to five years. The director of the institution, Dr. Pfannmueller, explained the routine. We don't do it, he said, with poisons or injections. "Our method is much simpler and more natural." With these words, the fat and smiling doctor lifted an emaciated, whimpering child from his little bed, holding him up like a dead rabbit. He went on to explain that food is not withdrawn all at once, but the rations are gradually decreased. "With this child," he added, "it will taken another two or three days."

Surely this is a scene worse than Dante. But the punishment was anything but Dantesque. In 1948, Dr. Pfannmueller was specifically charged in court with having ordered the killing of at least 120 children and having killed some himself. It was testified that he had personally killed some of the children with injections. He was sentenced to six years in jail, of which he served two years. That makes about six days per killed child.

How great the professional moral confusion can become is evident from this sidelight. Professor Julius Hallervorden, a well-known neuropathologist, after whom a special brain disease is named (Hallervorden-Spatz disease), asked the central office of the program to send him the brains of "euthanasia" victims for his microscopic studies. While the victims were still alive, he gave instructions about how the brains should be removed, preserved, and shipped to him. Altogether he got from the psychiatric death institutions no less than six hundred brains of adults and children. It evidently did not occur to him, or to anybody else, that this of course involved him seriously in the whole proceeding. An American professor of psychiatry at a well-known medical school told a national magazine that there was no ethical problem involved here and that Dr. Hallervorden "merely took advantage of an opportunity.

MURDER SCHOOLS

By the middle of 1941, at least four of the death hospitals in Germany and Austria not only killed patients but became regular murder schools: Grafeneck, in Brandenburg; Hadamar, near Limburg; Sonnenstein, in Saxony; and Hartheim, near Linz. They gave a comprehensive course in lethal institutional psychiatry. Personnel were trained in the methods of assembly-line killing. They were taught the mass-killing techniques, "gassing," cremation, and so on. It was called basic training in "mercy killing." The "material" for all this training was mental hospital patients. On them the methods were tried out and tested before they were applied later to Jewish and other civilian populations of the occupied countries. Technical experience first gained with killing psychiatric patients was utilized later for the destruction of millions. The psychiatric murders came first. It is a revealing detail that a man named Gomerski, who was engaged in mass killing in the death camps of Sobibor and Treblinka, was nicknamed the Doctor because of his "euthanasia" training in the psychiatric hospital Hadamar.

The method of taking out gold fillings and gold teeth from victims was first tried, worked out, and routinely used on the mental-hospital patients killed. Only after that was it practiced on concentration-camp inmates. The patients had to open their mouths and a number was stamped on their chests. From this number the personnel knew which patients had gold teeth, so that they could be removed later. The first human-derived ingots of gold for the Reichsbank were made from the mouths of these mental patients. According to sworn testimony, several grams of gold meant several thousand people killed. In Berlin there was a special office, the Central Accounting Office, to keep track of the proceeds from killed mental patients. How to take gold teeth from the dead was taught as a special skill. For example, in the institution Hadamar, a man named Loeding had learned this "breaking of teeth," as it was called. Later he was transferred for this purpose to the institution Eichberg. All this was done in the name of euthanasia. Later it was applied to millions of people.

Toward the end of 1941 the gas chambers in the death institutions were dismantled, transported to the east, and there freshly erected for their new tasks in concentration camps. Meanwhile the killing of mental patients went on with other methods, with injections, for instance. "Only" a few thousand were now being killed each month.

Some of the same psychiatrists who selected patients in hospitals went to concentration camps and selected death candidates there. Himmler had the idea of having the inmates of these camps examined "to comb out" those to be eliminated. He needed suitable physicians. So the central bureau of the "euthanasia" program supplied him with "experienced psychiatrists." In practice, this worked out as follows. In 1941 a commission of five went to the concentration camp Dachau to select prisoners to be transferred to Mauthausen to be killed. All five men were psychiatrists, and their chief was a professor of psychiatry of the University of Berlin. As they sat at tables put up between two barracks, the inmates had to file past while the doctors looked at their records. The criteria for selection were set by two chief experts in psychiatry. They consisted in (a) ability to work and (b) political reports. Several hundred of the so-selected prisoners were sent to Mauthausen and destroyed there.

The director of the state hospital Eichberg, Dr. Fritz Mennecke, who went to concentration camps as expert to select death candidates, was asked in court about the two types of cases he had judged interchangeably, the mental patients on medical grounds and the camp prisoners on political grounds. "One cannot separate them," he answered. "They were not subdivided and neatly separated from each other."

The typical case of Dr. Adolf Wahlmann, psychiatrist at the state hospital Hadamar, shows how easy the change was for some psychiatrists from killing mental patients to killing foreign civilians. He was not a Nazi and not a sadist. He had had a good medical education in the universities of Giessen, Marburg, Erlangen, and Kiel and had worked for years in responsible psychiatric posts in different institutions. In the Hadamar institution, thousands of mental patients were killed. In 1944 shipments of Polish and Russian men, women, and children from other institutions and work camps in occupied territories were sent to Hadamar. They were killed by lethal injections which he prescribed, exactly as he had done before with mental patients.

PERSISTENT MYTH

There is a persistent myth about the whole "euthanasia project which serves to ease the conscience of the civilized world. It is entirely false. According to this myth, Hitler stopped the program after about a year (when "only" some 70,000 patients had been killed) because of protests and pressure from the churches and the public. The "euthanasia" killing was *not* stopped. It went on until 1945, to the end of the Hitler regime—and in some places, e.g., Bavaria, even a few days longer. There is no evidence that it was stopped; all the evidence is that it continued. It did not end; it merely changed its outer form. It did not even get less cruel but in many cases was more cruel. The killing was not done as before, in the form of conspicuous big actions, but was carried out in a more cautious form and at a slower pace. From 1941 on, instead of the gas chambers (which had been transferred), other methods were used. Without any formal procedure and without any norm, it was carried out by individual institutions and individual doctors. They selected, decided, and acted. The end effect was the same. The methods employed were deliberate withdrawal of food, poisoning, or in many cases a combination of both. The poisoning was done by injections of overdoses of drugs. Patients screaming from hunger were not unusual. If it got too bad, they were given injections which quieted them and made them apathetic, or killed them. This was called euthanasia too. "Euthanasia" by starvation. Such methods had the advantage of more discretion: patients who were destroyed in this way could more easily be counted as "natural deaths." It was the occupation by the Allied armies both in the north and the south which freed the remaining patients from the psychiatrists.

Examples of continued general "mercy killings" after their alleged end in the summer of 1941 exist for every year thereafter, until 1945. At the end of 1942, at a conference of state officials and the directors of state hospitals, there was a discussion of the "excellent" method of making the "useless eaters" (i.e., patients) die by "slow starvation." A hospital employee has reported that in 1940 she worked in one of the death-dealing hospitals; then she was transferred to another, there the patients were not killed with gas but with injections and overdoses of drugs; she worked there until 1943; she was sent to a third hospital, where the same procedures were used until the overthrow of the regime in 1945. The chief male nurse of one mental hospital described the progression. In 1940 the program started when mental patients were gassed to death and then burned. In 1941 the gassing was discontinued. Beginning in 1942 the patients were killed with lethal doses of morphine, scopolamine, Veronal, and chloral. In 1944 foreign slave laborers from the camp were also admitted to the hospital and killed in the same way. This account is entirely uncontested testimony and is typical for the whole project. In 1944 patients were still being transported from the hospitals to "special institutions" (to be killed) under the pretext that it was a regular routine transfer from one hospital to another.

With respect to children, the legend of the 1941 ending of "mercy deaths" does not have even a semblance of truth. The child-killing agency functioned openly and efficiently till the collapse of the regime in 1945. Nobody has claimed that it ended before. Under its auspices, the mass murder of children continued routinely all over Germany and Austria. In Vienna, for example—the golden Viennese heart notwithstanding—children were killed in the children's division of the famous institution Steinhof and the municipal children's institution Spiegelgrund until the end of the war. Professor I.A. Caruso, now well known for his book *Existential Psychology*, who as a young psychologist witnessed some of this himself, says of the Reich Commission that its "murderous activity" was "massive." It was also, as one writer put it, unbelievably cruel.

As for the Hitler "order" for the alleged termination of the project, no document existed, not even a private note as at the outset of the "action." What happened was that in the late summer of 1941 in his General Headquarters, in a conversation with his physician, Dr. Karl Brandt, Hitler asked for the "provisional cessation of the euthanasia action on a large scale." This was purely verbal and was not written. It was an organizational change. It was clearly foreshadowed in a previous statement by Gestapo chief Himmler that there were "faults in the practical procedures." (The killing with the gas installations was too conspicuous.) Soon after Hitler's talk with Dr. Brandt, the chief expert, Professor Heyde, made it very plain in a written communication that the change was merely a "technical matter." Indeed, the gas chambers were moved, but the killing in the mental institutions in Germany continued with other methods.

NOT ENOUGH

As for the resistance of the churches, the fact that the killing did continue shows that it was not so strong or so persistent as to be effective. It was not enough. Dr. Karl Brandt stated that it was Hitler's opinion (which proved right) that resistance to the "euthanasia" killings on the part of the churches would under the circumstances not play a great role. The efforts were sporadic, isolated, and fragmentary. At certain levels the attitude was for a long time so passive and ambiguous that a top bureaucrat in the mercy killings, Hans Hefelmann, could state truthfully in court in Limburg that it had been his understanding that the church "was willing to tolerate such killings [at the time] under certain conditions."

What clergymen did was sixfold. They first protested about the transfer and eventual killing of patients in institutions under their jurisdiction. They wrote to the government and submitted evidence. They protested against the project from the pulpit. In some, but not all, institutions where religious sisters worked as nurses, the clergy made the further work of the sisters dependent on the assurance that they did not *have* to "participate" in any way in any part of the project. They reported instances to local juridical authorities as punishable crimes. (This was of no effect, because all complaints relating to the "action" were forwarded to Berlin and disregarded.) Finally we know of at least one occasion when a prominent clergyman achieved a long personal interview with one of the officials of the program and pleaded with him. A highly respected pastor, Fritz von Bodelschwingh, the chief of the Bethel institution, invited Dr. Karl Brandt to visit Bethel. Dr. Brandt accepted and the two men conferred for three hours.

It was a memorable event. Dr. Karl Brandt was a complex personality. He knew Dr. Albert Schweitzer well, was impressed with his theory of "reverence for life" and interested in his philanthropic work. As a young doctor he had planned to work with him as an assistant in Lambaréné in Africa. The only reason why that did not come about was that Brandt was born in Alsace and the French would have called him up in Lambaréné for military service. We can speculate that his whole career might have been different—in fact, might have taken just the opposite direction—if social preparation for war and violence had not prevented it. From what Pastor Bodelschwingh related later of their talk, Dr. Brandt tried to explain that the "euthanasia" project was necessary to save the nation. Bodelschwingh's position was that nobody has the right to be inhuman to his fellowmen. It seems that as a result of this discussion the liquidation of the "not worthy to live" inmates of Bethel was at least postponed and it may have helped many to escape this fate.

On March 8, 1941, the Catholic bishop Clemens von Galen of Münster, in Westphalia, spoke from the pulpit against the "euthanasia" action. He said:

> These unfortunate patients must die because according to the judgment of some doctor or the expert opinion of some commission they have become "unworthy to live" and because

> according to these experts they belong to the
> category of "unproductive" citizens. Who, then,
> from now on could still have confidence in a
> physician?

This sermon helped to inform the public further but it had no
lasting effect. For it was only a one-shot condemnation, not
followed up by the bishop, not reinforced by higher dignitaries
of the church, and not backed by Rome. (Von Galen died a
Cardinal in 1946.) The forces of destruction and propaganda
had become so entrenched that the public could no longer do
anything about it anyhow.

Why then, in 1941 was the program changed in methods,
speed and conspicuousness? From the historical context of
events and opinions, it is abundantly clear why Hitler interfered. He was concerned, and rightly so, with military morale.
Would the spirit of the troops hold out to see the war through?
It was late summer of 1941. Soldiers were learning that at
home Germans were killing Germans. They were afraid that
the wounded with head injuries would be sent to the gas chambers—and this might well happen to them. So the gas chambers were conspicuously dismantled. Moreover, going home
on leave they might find that a grandparent or other aged
relative had disappeared. Morale became affected, so it was
more or less officially given out that the program was stopped.
In reality it continued, but less blatantly than before.

In June, 1945, the American Military Government,
through its Public Health and Security officers, investigated
the psychiatric institution Eglfing-Haar, on the outskirts of
Munich. In this hospital, some 300 children, from six months
to sixteen years old, and about 2,000 adult patients had been
killed on a thoroughly organized basis. This went on until the
American occupation. Some of the adult patients had not
been killed in the place itself but had been sent to an institution at Linz for killing and cremation. There were, at the very
minimum, thirty such hospitals in Germany with "special
departments" for destroying patients.

In Eglfing-Haar, which had had an excellent reputation
as a psychiatric hospital, there was a children's division with
a capacity of about 150 children called the *Kinderhaus*. This
division had a "special department" with twenty-five beds
and cribs for the children about to be exterminated. In June,
1945, it was still occupied by twenty children. They were saved
by the American Army. In the children's "special department"

there was a small room. It was bare except for a small white-tiled table. At the window was a geranium plant which was always carefully watered. Four or five times a month a psychiatrist and a nurse took a child to this little room. A little while later they came out, alone.

The killing of children was carried out by different methods. One was overdoses of Luminal given either by injection or as a powder sprinkled over food. Another method was injection of a drug called modiscope, a combination of morphine, dionine, and scopolamine. Some children were given iodine injections with the result that they died in convulsions. Among the victims were retarded children who could have been taught and have led well-adjusted lives. Some were emotionally disturbed children who could not play well with other children and were regarded as "antisocial." The brains of the murdered children were sent to a psychiatric research institution for scientific microscopic studies.

The killing of adults was done almost entirely by deliberate starvation. The patients were given only vegetables and water until they died. They never got bread or meat or anything else. In this "special department," until the American Military Government took over, no patient got any treatment whatsoever, mental or physical. If he cut himself, he was not bandaged and was allowed to bleed. The selection of the patients to be put into this "special department" was largely in the hands of the staff psychiatrists and was a matter of routine. One criterion for selection was the length of stay in the institution. The whole procedure was known to all the hospital personnel.

SOCIAL FORGETFULNESS

We are still in the postviolence phase of the "euthanasia" murders. That is perhaps one of the darkest spots of the story. For the whole action has been minimized and left in a cloud of obfuscation, concealment, and social forgetfulness. We read about errors where there really was precision, about excesses where there were regular procedures, about dictates where there was all too ready compliance, about "misunderstood humaneness" where there was routine inhumanity. This happens not only in popular literature, but also in the writings of leading professional men.

To some extent, the courts have contributed to the confusion, which in its turn breeds indifference. For what were identical or very similar crimes, the sentences were of the greatest imaginable variety. A very few of those involved were sentenced to death and either executed or given death sentences which were commuted to life imprisonment and then reduced further; many were pardoned; in a number of cases, the courts decided that there was no case and no occasion for a trial; many were acquitted or received relatively short jail sentences; most remained entirely unmolested by the law and continued their professional or academic careers.

In some instances, the courts have made general statements about the project which tend to minimize its wrongfulness. For example, a court in Munich decided that "the extermination of mental patients was not murder, but manslaughter." In this summary form, which has been quoted in newspapers and magazines, the statement might give some people the dangerous idea that killing one person may be murder, but killing many is just manslaughter.

The reasons the courts have given for leniency or acquittal are revealing:

A court in Cologne, in acquitting one of the physicians, spoke of the victims, the patients, as "burned-out human husks." In another court opinion, the patients are called "poor, miserable creatures."

The director of a psychiatric hospital which served as an "intermediate institution" had accepted patients and then sent them on to death institutions with full knowledge of their eventual fate. The court gave as one reason for his acquittal that his role "does not represent an acceleration of the process of destruction, but a delay, and therefore a gain of time [for the patients]."

The director of a state hospital was acquitted on the ground that the many patients in whose death he was instrumental would have perished anyhow.

In a number of cases, the courts acted as if to kill or not to kill was a metaphysical question, like "to be or not to be." They quote the "ethics of Plato and Seneca" or speak of a "tragic conflict of duties" (acquittal in both cases).

Classic is the judgment of a Frankfurt court about a psychiatrist who not only killed many patients—adults and children—personally, but also watched their death agonies through the peep window of the gas chambers. "We deal," said the court, "with a certain human weakness which does not as yet deserve moral condemnation."

In the same way, in the case of a pediatric clinic in Hamburg where many children were deliberately killed ruthlessly, a medical organization proclaimed that the "actions of the inculpated female and male physicians in the years from 1941 to 1943 under the circumstances obtaining at that time did not represent any serious moral transgressions." And a medical journal stated that no professional action was indicated (such as depriving the physicians of their right to practice or to work in hospitals) because after the murders "their work in their profession was beyond reproach."

VIOLENCE UNRESOLVED

There has been—and still is—a great reluctance to face the whole "euthanasia" project as what it really was. We are concerned that the truth may damage the image of psychiatry (and pediatrics). But is not the substance more important than the image? A successful effort has been made to hush the whole thing up, in a cloud of silence, distortion, abstract speculations about life and death, irrelevant discussions of the duties of the doctor, and wholly irrelevant misuse of the term "euthanasia." In a recent book by a physician, Professor de Crinis is praised as a "courageous and energetic physician." The book *Euthanasia and Destruction of Life Devoid of Value* (1965), by the present professor of forensic and social psychiatry at the University of Marburg, speaks of the "comparatively few [sic] mental patients" killed. (This book is highly recommended in a recent number of an American psychiatric journal.)

In 1950 the then director of the state hospital Bernburg wrote an article in a scientific psychiatric journal in celebration of the seventy-fifth anniversary of that institution's beginning. In Bernberg more than 60,000 people had been murdered, the psychiatric director during that time having been a willing tool of the "euthanasia" project. The anniversary article speaks three times of the "reputation of the institution" as if that were the main point and calls the period of the mass killing an "episode and a step backwards" comparable to the (unavoidable) disruption of the service in the First World War.

This is violence unresolved. The psychiatric profession, to the limited extent that it has spoken at all, claims that the "euthanasia" murders were "ordered" by the Nazis. The record shows that is not true. But even supposing it were true, can we accept the position that if a political party "orders" the psychiatric profession to murder most of its patients, it is justified in doing so?

A recent trial in Munich throws light on several aspects of both the action phase and the postviolence phase of the "euthanasia" murders. What was established there was entirely typical. Tried for participation in murder were fourteen nurses of the psychiatric state hospital Obrawalde-Meseritz in which at least 8,000 mental patients (including children) were killed. This killing went on until 1945. The nurses gave lethal doses of drugs to the patients. The staff psychiatrists, male and female, selected the patients who were to be killed, prescribed the lethal doses and ordered the killing. Once, in the beginning, when a nurse refused to give a deadly dose of Veronal (barbitol) to a woman patient, the female chief psychiatrist gave her a "big bawling out." The defense of the nurses was that "we had to bow to the orders of physicians." Routinely two or three patients were killed every day; in 1945 the number was increased to four a day. On the weekends there was no killing; it was a matter of "never on Sunday." After the end of the Nazi regime, most of the fourteen nurses continued in their regular professional work in hospitals as before. Three were working as nurses in hospitals at the time of the trial. All fourteen were acquitted. It was a triumph for the Goddess of Violence.

We are not dealing here with just the behavior of individual practitioners or professors or with just an accident in the practice of a science. What confront us are crucial problems in the relation of science and medicine to society and politics, of the value of human life versus national and social policy. We can learn what Dr. Richard Madden, a physician and social historian of "fanaticism," wrote a hundred years ago, that behind all the veneer there is still "a great deal of savagery in the heart's core of civilization."

ON EUTHANASIA

Eugene Ionesco
translated by
Joseph J. Tomasek

In Switzerland, France and England they continue to speak more so than ever of the case of Doctor Haemmerli who permitted the sick, the too old, at any rate the incurable, to die of hunger. The fact remains we are all condemned to die. Why not immediately commit suicide? What is the probable duration of our life-times in a future which would permit us to care for ourselves? Twenty years? Two years? Six months would doubtlessly be too short.

The well-known historian, Leon Poliakov, in his book *Breviary of Hate*, speaks to us of euthanasia practiced in Germany at the time of Hitler yet before the war. Before applying their techniques of extermination to the Jews, the German politicians and doctors first tried them on Germans of pure-race themselves. "The mentally ill of Germany were a trial run for the Jews of Europe." The doctors and psychologists presented the tests to several people suspected of being mentally ill. If the tests were negative, they exterminated the insane person. What is an insane person? What is insanity? Holderlin? Artaud? Nerval? Baudelaire? Perhaps the asocial personality which would encompass those personages who had to be asocial for their respective times since they failed to conform to then contemporary social morality. Marx for example. So many revolutionaries and inventors as well as Galileo were themselves also considered insane by their contemporaries. Yet at the time of Hitler who was not insane: Hitler himself, the Hitlerites, Stalin, the mad murderer of Beria.

Madness can have reasons superior to reason itself.* Yet does reason exist, does insanity? We have equally set about to eliminate deformed, handicapped children. Among those maybe there was a hunchbacked Aesop.

In any event, the conscience of the world at the time was horrified. The taste of slaughter expanding, they exterminated, as we are aware, several million Jews, Gypsies, and Slavs. When the unknowing masses learned of it there was a universal cry of horror.

Hitler has won. Morality is overthrown, subverted. Not only is abortion permitted for some "humanitarian" reasons, to protect the woman since it is often for worthy motives that some crimes are committed, but now we shift to other issues. Public opinion has been prepared for the legislation of abortion by a number of women and doctors who confessed publicly to having practiced this type of surgical intervention. Today, in Switzerland and elsewhere, millions of letters are being received by newspapers defending Doctor Haemmerli. We know that euthanasia was practiced and that medical personnel were often requested to perform it by the sons and daughters who could symbolically, yet no longer effectively, deal with their Oedipus and Electra complexes. Today I encounter some doctors at their homes or on the street who confess to having perpetrated some assassinations by euthanasia at least two or three times in their careers. Euthanasia is going to be sanctioned by the law. It does not have to do with justifying such or such a case. What we would have to do would be to leave this issue untouched since no one knows where it can lead us. A Swiss newspaper speaks not only of the elimination of handicapped children but also of the dying who suffer intolerably and would themselves, perhaps, prefer to die. This newspaper declares itself favorable to the "elimination" of certain old people.

In a book by Jean Pasqualini, *Prisoner of Mao*, recently published by Gallimard, the author recounts to us his sojourn spent in a Chinese prison and afterward in a work camp. As the Swiss doctor did for his patients, the concentration camp supervisors of Popular China reduced, even abolished, the

---

* Trans. note: Is this a reference to Pascal's famous proverb: *"La coeur a ses raisons que la raison ne connait point"*? (The heart has its reasons that reason knoweth not.) Blaise Pascal, *Pensees.*

rations of prisoners who had no longer the strength to work. Only those who are useful to society therefore can live. What sort of usefulness? Is such a society now being formed? A monstrous and diabolic Moloch which is created only to destroy its children and constituents.

It is that which must be emphasized. Abortion, the elimination of the dying and of handicapped children all comprise a segment of the ensemble of a new mentality. Yet that is not the complete picture: school children in Israel are going to die at the hands of commandos in an effort to exterminate a race. The genocide contrived by Hitler rages in the world. The taking of hostages was considered one of the most shameful crimes that man could ever commit. These methods are considered entirely normal by political terrorists as well as by bandits who steal or kidnap. I should say that all these acts do not surprise me and that evil will take possession of the world to a greater degree. I understood that immediately after the last war. The man of peace, of love, of non-violence, Mahatma Gandhi, was assassinated in the street. I understood immediately that the war had not exorcised the demons and that they would recommence their penetration with renewed fervor. We plainly see how that happens, how it all had been prepared and how one could arrive at that point. The majority of idiotic philosophers today, French, German, and Italian, theorize about violence in the service of a just cause. But there is not a just cause. It would serve no purpose to present the names of these "thinkers." You would have, perhaps, then a desire to buy their books.

* * *

I am not defending the bourgeois class. I am familiar with the egotism, cynicism, cruelty, and inhumanity of the wealthy. Several serious economists tell us it is possible to redistribute the riches of the affluent countries among those nations less favorably endowed. That would be relatively easy to arrange if there were no egotism and if men did not all detest one another. This treacherous, egotistical nature, resulting in the scenario of man against man, had already been pointed out by Jung and Freud who thought it would lead to the total annihilation of humanity. So much the worse.

I ought to add that the bourgeois social order, in the light of several "realizations" and revolutionary regimes, now seems to us like a dream, yet, not quite so. One hears talk in a socialist country that from the dawn of bourgeois society man has exploited his fellow-man. Fortunately, in the socialist world of today it is the contrary.

* * *

My friend B. is a young Algerian. He writes songs. He is unable to sell them. I ask him why he does not go live in Algeria. He first answers me that it is to avoid the military service. Military service lasts two years and is difficult. Improved condition, objections, protests, all of that is not possible nor even conceivable. Any breach of discipline is punished by military prison or death. And why perform these two years of military service at all? What is the point of it? There is, he tells me, a sad and pitiless way of life which only prolongs the army barracks. He tells me that since we won independence we have lost our liberty. Iron discipline. Radical French journalists know that tyranny reigns in Algeria. They utter not a word of it. They also know that on the African continent there are dictatorships, repressions, oppressions, and murderous civil wars among the recently born nations. They will never tell of this. In quite a few African states large-scale hangings and torture of victims take place publicly. Two or three years ago, you could have seen them on Parisian television reports. These massacres were performed before the camera with the approval of the nation's leaders who thought it perfectly natural to massacre prisoners. Such events no longer enjoy television coverage. The African leaders have understood that such performances were not proper and would discredit them in the eyes of Westerners of whom they have and will continue to yet have need.

* * *

The sympathy and even love and admiration that so many Europeans harbour for Russia and her prisons, for China and her forced communal state, for the cruel, despotic and enslaving African and Asian states, a little while ago, still seemed to me astonishing. I am less surprised now. Western civilization as humanistic as it was, was but a bet, a lost wager, man is not a "humanist." Love of one's neighbor, in reality, is an aberration. Christianity has not changed man.

It was in the name of Christianity that the pre-Columbian peoples were assassinated. They have become weakened and decadent. They are neither charitable nor can they attain the heights of spiritual perfection.

Today one can no longer kill but in the name of either communism, Mohammedanism, or international revolution. The Christian has truly become almost human. He is displaced. Furthermore, the Christian can no longer prevent his countrymen from returning to what Christianity did not want them to be: beasts and savages. Consciously or not, Occidentals want not only to destroy bourgeois or any such other society, they want to eradicate civilization itself. A number of philosophers speak to us of the need for the explosion of desire, the interdiction of interdicting (there is no civilization without interdiction) and for orgiastic feast. What some desire is the return to irrational forces and telluric powers which in fact is conceivable. Civilization has never been, if I may say, 100% civilized. I understand the savage appetite.

Other Occidentals find in repression and authoritarianism the fulfillment of their tendancies, either masochistic or sadistic. This is also comprehensible: it is a temptation to become an object or an instrument without the obligation to choose. The taste for liberty is not felt during periods of liberty in liberal countries. We need oppression. Hoorah! Let's call the oppression "liberation," "independence," or "liberty." As for myself, I would be delighted to be able to oppress certain people, in fact, quite a few people. For example . . .

DEATH AND THE RHETORIC OF UNKNOWING*

DAVID MALL

*In order to arrive at what you do not know
You must go by a way which is the way of ignorance.*

T.S. Eliot

Positive and negative theology have their counterparts in rhetoric. On a metaphysical level, the distinction can be most clearly seen in the rhetoric of social movements, particularly those which proceed from definition.[1] In the following pages I will attempt to explore this distinction with respect to the pro-life movement and emphasize the persuasive campaign to gain public acceptance of euthanasia.

THE WAY OF UNKNOWING

It is said that man is a mystery to himself and that the human personality is the profoundest mystery of nature. The psalmist gave voice to this idea when he formalized the equation, *Abyssus abyssum invocat*—The deep calls to the deep."

While those who study theology emphasize one side of this equation, those who study man emphasize the other, with both striving for insight in a never ending search for meaning. One approach is to proceed by affirmation and a contrary approach is to proceed by denial.[2] Orthodox theologians consider the second approach to be superior. They first ascertain what God is *not* to gain a limited understanding of what God *is*. In short, it is only by a process of unknowing that one can begin to develop a true knowledge of God (and man).[3]

At the outset it should be made clear that the rhetoric I will be discussing is not the radical denial so characteristic of Orthodox Christianity but rather a milder form useful in categorizing representative persuasive materials. A negative rhetoric is a convenient label used to describe a particular stance or mode of thought. It is used to describe a position or strategy in the attempt to define what it is to be human. Regarding the abortion debate, a classic expression of this genre would be "I don't know when life begins, but surely we can't exclude the moment of conception." Such a rhetoric affirms by denial.

Any attempt to measure the boundaries of human nature has immediate social ramifications. Berdyaev, in fact, asserts that the maintenance of human freedom demands a negative sociology. A significant element of his thesis is that since values tend to become absolutized, totalitarian social structures must employ an affirmative approach to defining the individual's relationship to that structure. Given the antinomial tension between the individual and society, the latter tends to use man as an instrument for purely social ends. Man is defined by the social structure as an object to be manipulated and is assimilated by it accordingly. He is forced to accommodate to this objectifying demand and thereby loses his freedom.[4]

That a negative approach to human understanding has rhetorical significance cannot be gainsaid. Any denial of a value absolute is in some way communicated and the communication can in some way be analyzed. Admittedly, we are not dealing here with pure denial but with a general tendency toward negative discourse. The former leads to religious mysticism while the latter produces a better grasp of social reality. Negative discourse can be an instrument for defining God or man and rhetoric is its social expression.

Before proceeding with the analysis, I would like to direct the reader's attention to some preliminary considerations involving materials and methodology.

An effective way to observe the development of an ideology is by the comprehensive inspection of a nation's print media. The gradual unfolding of a point-of-view can be detected with exceptional clarity by reading daily what is said in those print sources most frequently encountered by the average citizen.

Contrary to the belief that prevails in certain literary circles, the bulk of a nation's print media is more than so much superficial trash hurriedly read on its way to the garbage can. Even as an obviously imperfect artifact of culture, it helps to reflect and mold a nation's thinking. The major issues of the day are covered by journalists, most of whom try to be sensitive to what is troubling a nation's conscience.

Anyone monitoring a nation's print media will experience lived argument as it reaches a nation's consciousness. Apart from the questionable practice of advocacy journalism, even straight unbiased reporting can have a persuasive effect as the slogans and leading arguments for a point-of-view are mentioned. In fact, the line between information and persuasion is difficult to detect, if it actually exists.

As vehicles for shaping opinion, the print and broadcast media are unexcelled at catching the propaganda consumer unawares. Since propaganda favors the unguarded moment when most psychological defenses are in a weakened condition, straight news stories are prime locations for material which is cleverly designed to manipulate. By its very nature, propaganda is an inextricable part of the media and those who conspire to modify human behavior must carefully analyze its characteristics.

A print media monitoring capability is a basic instrument of propaganda analysis. Most ideas confined to the pages of obscure scholarly journals are relatively innocuous compared to those seen by millions. Whoever champions a cause must do more than succeed in the political arena, for unless the thinking of a substantial portion of the population can be taught to accept the designated innovation, any institutional gains will be of short duration.

For approximately eighteen months (from June, 1973 to December, 1974) I edited a print media monitoring service for the American pro-life movement. Its purpose was to provide the movement with arguments pro and con as they actually appeared in print. It was assumed that an argument seen in its natural habitat would probably be a more accurate reflection than otherwise of how this argument would be encountered in real debating situations. In short, speakers inexperienced with the subject could be appraised of what to expect and also be kept generally informed about any shifting nuances.

Over 15,000 print sources were monitored every day by this service.[5] If anything appeared in these sources on certain carefully selected subjects, it was clipped by a national clipping bureau and mailed to our headquarters. Most of the news items to be mentioned herein were obtained from these clipping bureau mailings. Euthanasia was one of the subjects investigated.

An apologist for any ideological position would be hard pressed to match the unvarnished rendering of live argument as it appears in a nation's press. The power of a print media monitoring service is such that one who presides over it has an opportunity to peer into a nation's soul and watch the play of ideologies as they ceaselessly contend. Moreover, it gives one a sense of completeness when realizing that most of what is said in print on a given subject has come to your attention.[6]

Having kept careful watch on the peculiarities of pro-abortion rhetoric for many years, it is easy to recognize its close relationship to pro-euthanasia rhetoric. Apart from the fact that both movements have the same ideologue-activists (Joseph Fletcher and the two late M.D.'s Walter Alvarez and Alan Guttmacher),[7] their strongest kinship is a common philosophical origin. The best evidence for this is found in the middle of the Hippocratic Oath which forbids both practices in two juxtaposed sentences. "I will neither give a deadly drug to anybody if asked for it, nor will I make a suggestion to this effect. Similarly, I will not give to a woman an abortive remedy."[8] A more extensive philosophical explication has been published elsewhere and further treatment here is unnecessary.[9]

The many similarities between the drive for abortion and euthanasia are clearly apparent and can be seen by comparing the arguments advanced for the two issues. By design or happenstance, a number of rhetorical strategies are used for both. The most prominent are 1) divisioning, 2) incrementalism, and 3) linguistic displacement. Within the American cultural setting, the affirmative or absolutist, objectifying tendency of the rhetoric thus becomes manifest. Our task now is to consider each strategy by way of analogue.

Divisioning

Advocates of both abortion and euthanasia emphasize the religious dimension of these questions. One of the facts frequently pressed upon the public consciousness is that those who oppose abortion and euthanasia must necessarily be Catholics. In fact those pro-life spokesmen who happen to be Catholic generally feel that in communicating within the American pluralistic environment their religious affiliation is a definite handicap.

It is no secret that non-Catholic spokesmen, too numerous to mention, have assumed highly visible positions in the American pro-life movement and that this visibility has been promoted and encouraged. The Catholic rank and file who easily constitute the largest number of pro-life activists, realized from the earliest beginnings of the movement that their voices would be more readily heard on the national level if they were filtered through non-Catholic spokesmen. While this was certainly an overcompensating defensive reaction to the sensitivity of the "religious connection" which later became unnecessary, one way of demonstrating the fundamental unity of Judeo-Christian belief is to have a variety of non-Catholic message senders.[10]

The body of persuasive literature generated by the pro-life movement contains numerous tracts which stress the ideological commonality of the many divergent doctrinal elements within the Judeo-Christian cultural heritage. Any efficiently run pro-life educational organization, particularly those which are interfaith or denominationally oriented, will have a large supply.[11] Many of these tracts are of ancient vintage while others are being produced as of this writing. They demonstrate a commonality of belief and represent a rhetoric of unity.

On the other hand, when one inspects the body of persuasive materials produced by those who favor abortion and euthanasia, quite the opposite is found. Here the tendency is to show a disunity of belief through a tripartite divisioning. First, the issue is made to appear as predominantly Catholic, with the clear implication that other elements in the Judeo-Christian tradition believe otherwise.[12] Second, it is stressed that Catholics themselves are actually divided on the issue with the laity and clergy not of one mind. And finally, the Catholic clerical leadership itself is shown to be confused.[13]

While there does not appear to be an invariant sequence to this divisioning strategy, the net result is to create uncertainty within the Catholic community. The authentic church position becomes fractionated and any concerted opposing efforts are thereby diluted. Thus, the old antagonisms between Catholics and non-Catholics are reanimated.

Specifically regarding the question of euthanasia, the same divisioning occurs but in a more attenuated fashion. In the writer's judgment, this attenuation is mainly caused by the fact that early in the controversy a significant part of all subsequent pro-euthanasia appeals had been stripped of their potency through the clarification Pope Pius XII gave in 1957 to the official Catholic position. In a statement which has since received considerable scholarly attention, the Pope said:

> Natural reason and Christian morals say that man (and whoever is entrusted with the task of taking care of his fellow man) has the right and the duty in case of serious illness to take the necessary treatment for the preservation of life and health. This duty that one has toward himself, toward God, toward the human community, and in most cases toward certain determined persons, derives from well ordered charity, from submission to the Creator, from social justice and even from strict justice, as well as from devotion to one's family.
>
> But normally one is held to use only ordinary means—according to circumstances of persons, places, times, and culture—that is to say, means that do not involve any grave burden for oneself or another. A more strict obligation would be too burdensome for most men and would render the attainment of the higher, more important good too difficult. Life, health, all temporal activities are in fact subordinated to spiritual ends. On the other hand, one is not forbidden to take more than the strictly necessary steps to preserve life and health, as long as he does not fail in some more serious duty.[14]

The Pope's statement is included here because it represents, so to speak, a starting point or formulation of the boundaries within which the debate on euthanasia is taking place. References to it are frequently made in the nation's print media so that what reasonableness it may contain is brought to the attention of those who are to be persuaded. No such timely formulation has been able to help arbitrate the abortion controversy which may in part account for the increasing social acceptance of abortion. In passing, the writer is tempted to observe that the ecclesiastical delineation of the argumentative boundaries of euthanasia is a modern version of the Pope's ancient practice of arbitrating disputes among the European sovereigns.

A possible consequence of the early clarification of the Catholic position on euthanasia by the Pope is that severe antagonisms within the Judeo-Christian religious elements do not seem to have materialized or at least have not been reflected in the nation's print media. That tensions do exist is a safe assumption, but the divisioning strategy has not been noticeable.

Disagreements over euthanasia between Catholic clergy and laity seem to be more easily exploited than any differences among the sects. Dr. Walter W. Sackett, Jr., M.D., the Florida state legislator who is one of the more politically active euthanasia proponents, has stated publicly in regard to a piece of legislation he sponsored that "the priests and the bishops are against this bill but the down to earth Catholics favor it."[15] Such assertions are typical of the divisioning strategy.

The clearest example of the rhetorical exploitation of organizational differences can be seen in the print media coverage of theological dissent. The controversy surrounding Catholic theologians McCormick and McGuire are significant cases in point.

Reaction to McCormick's views in the nation's press helped to create the impression that respected Catholic moral theologians were able to justify the killing of defective offspring. One newspaper article was headlined "Priest Offers Guideline for Letting Malformed Babies Die."[16] Another article was suggestively titled "Jesuit's Plea to Let Infant 'Vegetables' Die (has) Generally Positive Reaction." This latter article described McCormick's opinions as "possibly the first time a Catholic theologian has taken such a liberal position" and as receiving "strongly negative reaction" in certain conservative Catholic periodicals. The article displayed his academic credentials in an imposing manner and gave him what could be interpreted as a public relations build-up. The authors of the article apparently intended the reader to take McCormick's views seriously.[17]

McGuire's views, which also received considerable national publicity, advocated in a less ambiguous fashion positive acts to bring on death. In one newspaper interview he said he thought it significant "that I'm not the only Catholic moral theologian advocating mercy death by positive means."[18] Again, the impression is created in the public mind that the views of certain dissident theologians have equal stature with the official church position. Showing dissention in theological ranks may be legitimately newsworthy but its divisiveness is also a natural consequence.

Incrementalism[19]

When abortion first imposed itself upon the public consciousness and was discussed at length in various state legislatures, the solution most frequently encountered was a proposal of the American Law Institute which advocated selective abortion for such things as rape and incest, fetal defects and psychiatric complications.[20] This Model Penal Code was an attempt to produce a compromise solution appealing to a desire for law and order. At the time, it appeared to be all the nation would accept and, with the exception of California and New York and, possibly Alaska and Hawaii, no state legislature exceeded its provisions until the Supreme Court decision in *Roe* v. *Wade* struck down all state laws regulating abortion.

It seems accurate to say that in the early stages of the pro-abortion campaign there was a general tendency to deny that abortion-on-demand was the ultimate objective. Pro-abortion rhetoric emphasized extreme cases which fell mainly within the purview of the "ALI Proposal." Horrible examples of botched illegal abortions prompted by alleged rape and incest and cases of severe maternal psychiatric instability abounded in pro-abortion literature. Equally horrible examples of defective offspring, complete with pictures, were also promulgated. This veritable chamber-of-horrors provided the emotional impetus for a limited modification of the then existing law.

With respect to euthanasia rhetoric the same incrementalism is clearly apparent, although the campaign at the time of this writing is at a less mature stage of development. Already, a legalistic approach has been stressed which masks the movement's ultimate purpose, and the California "Natural Death Act" so called is a prime example.[21] If permitted to fulfill itself that purpose, it is felt, would actualize a death program that is active, direct and involuntary.

A good example of euthanasia incrementalism can be found in the legislative maneuverings of state representative Sackett of Florida. In the spring of 1974 the Florida legislature considered a bill which contained three provisions. The first enabled a competent person 18 years or older to sign a document requesting the attending physician to discontinue medical treatment when a terminal stage of illness or injury had been reached. The second granted the right to make this decision to a spouse or a majority of the person's family when two licensed physicians determined that the patient was physically or mentally incapacitated. The third gave three doctors authority to decide in the event no person of kinship could be found within 30 days. What is important for our analysis here is that the last two parts were eventually deleted to accommodate legislative realities. In speeches delivered in the fall of 1973 Sackett was quoted as saying "I'd like to see all of them passed, but it looks like I'm going to have them a step at a time."[22]

As with abortion, so also with euthanasia, the case for change included more than a limited solution could possibly deliver. This is to say that the reasons given for a change in the law were often beyond the efficacy of the answer. Several years before the decision in *Roe v. Wade,* for example, when pro-abortion literature was not officially recognizing abortion-on-demand as an ultimate goal, the need for eliminating unwanted pregnancies was nevertheless advanced. The "ALI Proposal" obviously could not provide a satisfactory solution for such a problem, so a woman's right to do whatever she wanted with her own body became the new emphasis, a "woman's right to choose" the new slogan, and a woman's right to privacy the new legal justification.

Our print media abound in pro-euthanasia stories of deep emotional impact. Hardly a month goes by that the public is not given another gruesome sample of terminal suffering. Major medical dilemmas are posed and suggestions made to turn off respirators and let nature prevail. The result is often the creation of a cause célèbre.[23]

Through pro-euthanasia rhetoric the public is led to believe that death is only allowed and never induced. The phenomenon of the living will, for example, stresses euthanasia which is largely passive, indirect, and voluntary. Yet, while these may seem much more acceptable than their opposites, the fact remains that in order to solve some of the problems typically presented in pro-euthanasia literature (e.g., the severely retarded or physically incapacitated) it would be necessary to step beyond the provisions of currently proposed legislation and sanction deliberate killing of those who have accidentally become a burden to others.

"Not more than what the traffic will bear" is more than just a simple commercial strategy; it also has application to the rhetoric of social movements. Ideology can sometimes be given in only small doses, particularly when deeply entrenched social values are involved. Such a strategy shows moderation and helps create an image of reasonableness and respectability. In general, it shows good audience adaptation and can, as one writer puts it, "gain entry into decision centers."[24]

Linguistic Displacement

Language is one of the first casualties in any controversy over fundamental human values. The abuse of words often gives justification for acts previously regarded as inhuman. Thucydides noted this phenomenon when he wrote his account of the Peloponnesian War many centuries ago. "To fit in with the change of events," he wrote, "words, too, had to change their usual meanings." And in explanation of this he observed:

> What used to be described as a thoughtless act of aggression was now regarded as the courage one would expect to find in a party member; to think of the future and wait was merely another way of saying one was a coward; any idea of moderation was just an attempt to disguise one's unmanly character; ability to understand a question from all sides meant that one was totally unfitted for action.[25]

Thucydides thought such debasement of language was an indication of moral breakdown; correct usage therefore became a moral imperative.[26]

In a similar spirit, Merton has lamented the denatured prose of our own day in which action is stifled and identity threatened.[27] When vagueness enters the linguistic domain, words begin to lose their meanings. There is a general degradation of accustomed usage or, for want of a better term, linguistic slippage.

An interested reader will observe in the rhetoric of euthanasia a lack of consistency in the use of descriptive terminology. Eighteen months of reading the nation's print media yielded no clear or consistent definition of "euthanasia" itself nor of "mercy killing" nor "death with dignity." There seems to be a sliding scale of euphony and euphemism with "mercy killing," the least desirable, at one end and "death with dignity," the most desirable, at the other. "Euthanasia" is then placed somewhere between.

Even such a careful observer of death and dying as Kübler-Ross has struggled with the semantic problem. She writes:

> We should also find a new definition for "euthanasia" since it is used for "good death" (e.g., the patient's own natural death without prolonging his dying process unduly), and for mercy killing, which has nothing to do with the original intent of the word euthanasia. To me this is the difference between allowing someone to die his own death or killing him. I am naturally in favor of the former and opposed to the latter.[28]

Scattered throughout her books are occasional, though indirect, laments to language's imprecision.

Apropos of what was said previously about a strategy of disunity, the non-use of extraordinary means in a dying situation is often equated in euthanasia rhetoric with the slogan "death with dignity." This, of course, would make Pius XII a supporter of the American Euthanasia Foundation. An impression difficult to refute is that both sides would like dignified death, notwithstanding Ramsey's scholarly corrective.[29]

If language were the only factor determining the future of the euthanasia debate, there could hardly be a happy outcome. In truth, the extent of the semantic confusion seems almost beyond the pale of human efficacy, as though language were inherently incapable of reflecting rational thought. Consider the headline "Euthanasia: Is It Mercy or Killing" and the follow-up commentary "does stopping treating constitute euthanasia—called mercy killing by some, death with dignity by others, the 'good death' by some others?"[30] The balance of the article, although well intentioned, gave no answer.

The search for semantic rigor has led some authorities to devise alternate terminology. A doctor speaks of "paraeuthanasia," a clergyman of "dysthanasia," and an educator of "benemortasia." While such neologisms have no discernible print media impact, they are nonetheless healthy attempts to make necessary distinctions. Whether they are sufficient remains to be seen. The *is* of journalism and the *ought* of moral education seem at times irreconcilable.

Verbal distinctions are particularly important in value controversies. Failure to agree on basic terminology leads to a blurring of the battlelines and, carrying the military metaphor one step further, to what might be called a type of guerrilla warfare in which combatants are confused with non-combatants. Who stands for what is a legitimate question for any concerned citizen to ask and the answers should be given unambiguously.

Failure to define terms contributes to poor debating and, more importantly, provides an opportunity for the use of propaganda techniques. One such technique, found in both the abortion and euthanasia controversies, is the bandwagon. Public opinion surveys thrive on it. An unscrupulous propagandist can elicit a desired trend response by asking a question with key terms left undefined. If, for example, "death with dignity" is left undefined, it becomes confused with mercy-killing or euthanasia or, as an umbrella term, can be used to promote them. Similarly, the euthanasia-suicide interface becomes an arena of philosophical maneuvering and subtle linguistic contention.

Few distinctions regarding euthanasia are drawn in the nation's print media. In an advice column in a large Eastern daily, a doctor considers suicide to be distantly related to passive euthanasia without specifying the degree of kinship.[31] A letter-to-the-editor considers euthanasia to be aptly called "mercy-killing"[32] while an editorial from a Southern paper contends that "active euthanasia, as with active rape, is not to be confused with passive euthanasia any more than is passive rape a truly definable entity."[33]

Although truly thoughtful pieces are seldom read by the masses,[34] even seasoned writers appear to have trouble making distinctions. Hendin links voluntary euthanasia with death with dignity.[35] Alsop holds that "the theory of euthanasia permits a doctor to kill a patient, or let him or her die, without the patient's conscious consent (which) is . . . a euphemism for murder."[36] The guileless reader may legitimately ask "what am I supposed to believe" or "how am I supposed to act?" The print media gives no answer.

HUMAN OBJECTIFICATION

In sifting through the nation's print media what one does find is an obvious tendency toward human objectification. It would be difficult and perhaps unfair to blame the pro-euthanasia movement exclusively for this objectification, since there might well be a basic objectifying tendency of all language or at least languages exposed for so long to Cartesian dualism. While science profited immensely through objectifying the universe, this same objectification, when applied to man, can easily become distorted and dangerous. The response of the pro-life movement is simply that man is not a thing to be manipulated.

To objectify is to dehumanize and to dehumanize is to maltreat. The sequence may not be inevitable but the ingredients are combined more often than not. What lies at the heart of pro-life rhetoric and the theme expressed in this essay is the belief that perceiving a person as less than human is the first step toward his eventual abuse.

In a very real sense, the objectifying language of the pro-euthanasia movement is an extension of the linguistic tendency, noted by Erik Erikson, which governs the outlook of in-groups to out-groups. This process is known as "pseudo-speciation" and, according to one commentator is "a process of clearly defining an enemy or prey as different from members of the in-group, and finally coming to an implicit decision that the members of the out-group are not really human and may be killed without any of the inhibitions (as expressed by laws governing homicide, for example) against killing one's own kind."[37]

The phenomenon, which appears to be universal, is often quite subtle. In certain primitive languages, for example, the terms for in-groups and out-groups reflect such a humanizing and dehumanizing process. The *Handbook of American Indians North of Mexico* indicates that Athapascan, the most widely distributed of all North American Indian linguistic families, uses a word which in various forms means "people" to describe nearly every tribe of the Athapascan stock.[38] Algonquian, the most populous North American Indian linguistic family, provided the names for two neighboring families known later to European settlers as the Sioux and the Iroquois. In this regard, a revealing passage from the *Handbook* gives further evidence of Erikson's pseudospeciation:

> Dakota ("allies"). The largest division of the Siouan family, known commonly as Sioux, according to Hewitt a French-Canadian abbreviation of the Chippewa *Nadowe-is-iw*, a diminutive of *nadowe*, "an adder," hence "an enemy." *Nadoweisiw-eg* is the diminutive plural. The diminutive singular and plural were applied by the Chippewa to the Dakota, and to the Huron to distinguish them from the Iroquois proper, the true "adders" or "enemies."[39]

Thus, by metaphor, a word signifying "snake" stands for an out-group of fellow humans.

Disdaining subtlety, however, a more obvious example of pseudospeciation would be the institution of slavery and ultra rigid caste structures. And even perhaps more pertinently, a bellicose Communist China has called American allies "running dogs of American imperialism," while Americans still refer to victims of Down's syndrome as Mongoloids. The latter designation, of course, makes a whole class of defectives into an out-group from some strange and hostile land.

While Lorenz considers pseudospeciation to be a perfectly normal process and under certain conditions even desirable (as when group isolation produces quick cultural development) he maintains that it has a very serious negative side which leads to war.[40] He is particularly disturbed by the thought that "today's younger generation is beginning to treat the older one as an alien pseudospecies."[41] The growing generation gap experienced in many industrialized nations, and especially noticeable in America, is manifested by a heavy accent on youth. Carried to an extreme, this accent would transform nursing homes into an exotic territory where divergent generations dwell. Labels like "senior citizens" help to set old people apart and create a differentiated cultural grouping.

In terms of our discussion, by applying a non-human label to a potential victim, euthanasia becomes more palatable culturally since, it is reasoned, the victim was not really human in the first place. Print media news stories abound in examples of this practice and the pro-euthanasia ideologues quoted in them are usually the most imaginative practitioners.

The following were taken from news items dealing with euthanasia: "a hopeless, helpless vegetable," "a living mummy," "a parasite," "a living cabbage," "human wrecks praying for death," "living cadavers," "grotesques," "living shells," "geeks and gorks." The litany is long and includes specimens from both plant and animal kingdoms. Says Vincent F. Sullivan, executive director of the American Euthanasia Foundation: "I just hope we bring some measure of relief to these suffering veterans leading a hopeless vegetable existence."[42] Says Doctor Sackett: "Unfortunately, rehabilitative folks have taken over for doctors. They clamor to keep them (the hopelessly ill) alive to the point that they can grunt or sit on a potty."[43]

Those who treat the dying person as a human being inject an essential reciprocity into a relationship that is oftentimes in danger of deteriorating. The process is much discussed by Buber who on a theoretical level describes the tendency to objectify as a failure in human relating to human. He in fact states that the undiluted meaning of relation is to be found in reciprocity and renders a judgment concerning man's objectification: "Now I can again abstract from him the color of his hair, of his speech, of his graciousness; but as long as I can do that he is my You no longer and not yet again."[44] "But as soon as a You becomes an It, the world-wideness of the relationship appears as an injustice against the world, and its exclusiveness as an exclusion of the universe."[45]

As a corrective to this dehumanization, the response of the pro-life movement has been to formulate positive alternatives to abortion and euthanasia. In the former case the work of Mecklenburg[46] and service organizations like Birthright and Alternatives to Abortion are exemplary; in the latter case the work of Lamerton and the hospice movement.[47] These responses directed at each end of the life continuum are attempts to promote interpersonal activity designed to revivify weakened human relationships. Life whether germinating or dying is treated with utmost respect.

CONCLUSION

This, in a manner of speaking, has been an eyewitness account of a persuasive campaign. I attempted by analogue to gain a deeper understanding of the euthanasia debate from data gathered primarily from the American print media. Although my main emphasis has been upon a rhetoric of unknowing, there are, of course, other emphases not considered here. Also, it should be stressed that any generalizations made herein are with respect to the American cultural setting only and do not preclude characteristics which may exist at other times in other places.

Like its pro-abortion analogue, pro-euthanasia rhetoric is characterized by a strategy of disunity, a masking of ultimate purpose, and a language of ambiguity. Unlike pro-abortion rhetoric however, it seems that the promotion of euthanasia may well be hampered by a disadvantageous debating position arising from a more clearly defined debating perimeter.

Yet, while the term strategy has often been used to describe certain rhetorical phenomena, perhaps what has been observed in the final analysis is the way opposing ideologies naturally relate to one another within the context of fundamental social change. These ideologies may well be engaged in functional activities the details of which are still largely unknown.

In broadest terms, the pro-life movement takes a dynamic view of man and defines him in terms of what he is not. It denies that man is completely knowable and rejects society's tendency to make an object of him. Pro-life rhetoric assumes that man is an essential mystery. Man is defined in terms of possibility and becoming and not within the fixity of a static determinism.

It is in the pro-life movement where rhetoric can be said to approach the mystical for, ultimately, in treating man as an end rather than a means, we are faced with the eternal question posed in the riddle of the Sphinx—What is this creature called man?

*Preparation for the actual writing of this essay began in a classroom and ended on a picket line. The original motivation came from a promise to lecture on the rhetoric of social movements. I wish, therefore, to thank Joanne Seiser of the University of Illinois (Chicago Circle) for the opportunity, in the Spring of 1974, to interact with one of her classes to help clarify my initial thinking on the relationship between abortion and euthanasia. Ideas first expressed then have been incorporated herein. Also, in the Summer of 1975, the final disposition of my thinking was helped by a chance conversation with two Greek Orthodox priests who, together with a number of other Chicago area residents, had staged a demonstration before the State of Illinois Building in the Loop to urge the governor to sign HB 1851, a measure supported by state and local pro-life organizations. To Fathers James Carellas and John Chakos I owe a clearer understanding of certain theological concepts pertaining to rhetoric and I wish to thank them.

1. For a rhetorical analysis of movements proceeding from definition, see David Mall, "Stalemate of Rhetoric and Philosophy," in *Abortion and Social Justice*, eds. Thomas W. Hilgers and Dennis J. Horan (New York: Sheed and Ward, 1972), p. 207.

2. The technical terms for these approaches are cataphasis (affirmation) and apophasis (denial).

3. The idea is presaged in neo-Platonism and Aquinas attempted to synthesize the two approaches by using negative theology as a complement to positive theology. For a comprehensive treatment of the subject, see Vladimir Lossky, *The Mystical Theology of the Eastern Church*, trans. by the Fellowship of St. Alban and St. Sergius (London: James Clarke and Co., 1957).

4. See Jean-Luis Segundo, Berdiaeff: *Une Réflexion Chrétienne sur la Personne* (Paris: Aubier, 1963), pp. 129-176.

5. In round numbers, 1,900 dailies, 9,000 weeklies, and 4,200 trade publications and consumer magazines.

6. The national clipping bureau used, which at the time was generally acknowledged to be the largest in the country, claimed to have a retrieval capability for most topics of well over 50 percent of what had actually been printed. This claim was made by a Chicago based representative of the bureau in private conversation with the writer.

7. For a description of the bonds between abortion and euthanasia, see Paul Marx, *Death without Dignity* (Collegeville: The Liturgical Press, 1975), pp. 11-13.

8. Ludwig Edelstein, *The Hippocratic Oath*, Supplements to the Bulletin of the History of Medicine, ed. Henry E. Sigerist, No. 1 (Baltimore: The Johns Hopkins Press, 1943), pp. 2-3. For a more recent analysis of the oath, see Herbert Ratner, "The Oath I. Why" *Child and Family*, IX, No. 4 (1970), pp. 290-91. This is the beginning of a series of articles which continues for seven consecutive issues.

9. See Mall, *op. cit.*, p. 202.

10. Professor Harold O.J. Brown, Congregational minister and prominent non-Catholic pro-life spokesman, summarized and placed the matter in perspective. "The Roman Catholics may be more aggressive . . ., but they are not alone." See Letter-to-the-Editor, *Chicago Tribune*, Dec. 24, 1975, Sec. 1, p. 8. Also, in another context it is worth noting that in the earliest days of Gandhi's experiment with non-violence in South Africa, he specifically utilized the abilities of Indian Christian youth, "in whom he had recognized the best educated and potentially the most activist segment of the Indian population." See Erik H. Erikson, *Gandhi's Truth* (New York: W.W. Norton and Co. 1969) p. 172.

11. A few of the more prominent pro-life groups with strong interfaith or denominational structures are American Citizens Concerned for Life, Americans Against Abortion, Americans United for Life, Baptists for Life, the Christian Action Council, and ForLIFE, Inc. These organizations are national in scope and attempt primarily to reach non-Catholic audiences.

12. To realize the extent of intersect antagonisms, see the chapter titled "The Aftermath of Abortion Reform: The Seeds of Religious Warfare" in Arlene Carmen and Howard Moody, *Abortion Counseling and Social Change* (Valley Forge: Judson Press, 1973), pp. 107-120.

13. Divisions among Catholic clergy and laity on abortion were described in the American press during the 1976 presidential campaign, although the strategy was probably used more to justify a party platform than to promote the abortion ideology. The following wire service account is noteworthy:

> The friction between Carter and the Catholics has been evident since Archbishop Bernardin (Joseph L. Bernardin of Cincinnati) called the abortion plank of the party's platform "irresponsible" and "morally offensive" giving rise to a rejoinder by Carter's issues adviser, Stuart Eizenstat, that Archbishop Bernardin did not speak for the Catholic community.
>
> Bishop James S. Rausch, general secretary of the NCCB (National Conference of Catholic Bishops), wired Eizenstat that he was "seriously misinformed" and that Archbishop Bernardin's views of the Democrats' abortion position "have the unqualified support of the bishops of the United States as well as being shared by millions of other Americans." See "Carter in Talks with Top Catholics" *The Chicago Tribune*, September 1, 1976, p. 1.

14. This passage is taken from an address to an International Congress of Anesthesiologists, November 24, 1957. For a transcript see "The Prolongation of Life," *The Pope Speaks*, IV, No. 4 (Spring, 1958), pp. 393-98.

15. Quoted in David Schultz, "Florida Physician Fights to Give Hopelessly Ill 'Death with Dignity,'" *Evening Globe* (Boston), May 20, 1973, p. 66. Earlier, before a congressional committee, Sackett said much the same thing. See U.S. Congress, Senate, Special Committee on Aging, *Death with Dignity: An Inquiry into Related Public Issues*, 92nd Cong., 2nd sess., August 7, 1972, Part 1, p. 38.

16. By Julian DeVries in *The Arizona Republic* (Phoenix), July 10, 1974. For the McCormick statement to which the headline refers, see Richard A. McCormick, "To Save or Let Die," *Journal of the American Medical Association*, CCXXIX, No. 2 (July 8, 1974), pp. 172-76.

17. By J.P. and L.K. in the *Globe* (Arlington, Va.) September 19, 1974. This article appeared in several papers from the Washington D.C. suburban area. The initials L.K. stand for the Rev. Lester Kinsolving, an outspoken abortion advocate.

18. Quoted in Alicia Armstrong, "Should Sufferers Always Be Kept Alive?" *Milwaukee Journal*, November 10, 1974, Sec. Accent on the News, p. 1.

19. The term refers to piecemeal decision-making which occurs over a period of time. It is usually considered the opposite of "comprehensivism" or decision-making of a more sweeping nature which occurs all at once. Although originally applied to economic and political decision-making, the term has found application in the field of jurisprudence. See Charles E. Lindblom, *The Intelligence of Democracy* (New York: The Free Press, 1965) and Martin Shapiro "Stability and Change in Judicial Decision-Making: Incrementalism or Stare Decisis?" *Law in Transition Quarterly*, II, No. 3 (Summer, 1965), pp. 134-57.

20. For a copy of the proposal, see Appendix B in *Doe v. Bolton*, 410 U.S. 179 (1973).

21. See Les Ledbetter, "California Grants Terminally Ill Right to Put an End to Treatment," *The New York Times,* October 2, 1976, p.1.

22. Quoted in Jim Durham, "A Nation Watches Some Vital Signs," *Tallahassee Democrat,* April 21, 1974, sec. E, p. 1.

23. During the writing of this essay the most controversial case to be argued in the American print and broadcast media was that of Karen Quinlan, a young New Jersey woman who lapsed into coma and some of whose vital functions had to be maintained artificially. For authoritative details, see the opinion of Judge Robert Muir, Jr., Superior Court of New Jersey, Chancery Division, Morris County, November 10, 1975. For an example of the print media treatment, see "A Right to Die?" *Newsweek,* LXXXVI, No. 18 (November 3, 1975), pp. 58-69.

24. Herbert W. Simons, "Requirements, Problems, and Strategies: A Theory of Persuasion for Social Movements," *Quarterly Journal of Speech,* LVI, No. 1 (February, 1970), 8.

25. Thucydides, *History of the Peloponnesian War,* trans. by Rex Warner (Baltimore: Penguin Books, Inc., 1975), p. 242.

26. For a helpful description of the background of Thucydides' moral thinking, see Moses I. Finley, *Aspects of Antiquity* (New York: The Viking Press, 1968), pp. 44-57.

27. Thomas Merton, "War and the Crisis of Language," in *The Critique of War,* ed. by Robert Ginsberg (Chicago: Henry Regnery Co., 1969), p. 99.

28. Elisabeth Kübler-Ross, *Questions and Answers on Death and Dying* (New York: MacMillan Publishing Co., 1974), p. 75.

29. See Paul Ramsey, "The Indignity of 'Death with Dignity'," *Hastings Center Studies,* II, No. 2 (May, 1974), pp. 47-62.

30. Quoted in Gordon Slovut, "Euthanasia: Is it Mercy or Killing?" *Minneapolis Star,* August 26, 1974, p. 1.

31. Theodore R. Van Dellen, M.D., "Euthanasia: Active, Passive Forms," *Daily News* (New York), August 30, 1974.

32. "Abortion and Euthanasia," *News American* (Baltimore), May 29, 1973.

33. Editorial, *Iberian* (New Iberia, La.), October 2, 1973.

34. See, for example, Thomas St. Martin, "Euthanasia: The Three-In-One Issue," *Baylor Law Review,* XXVII, No. 1 (Winter, 1975), pp. 62-67.

35. David Hendin, "Should the Law Look the Other Way?" *News Tribune* (Woodbridge, N.J.), February 25, 1974. See also his *Death As a Fact of Life* (New York: W.W. Norton and Co., 1973).

36. Stewart Alsop, "The Right to Die with Dignity," *Good Housekeeping,* CLXXIX, No. 2 (August, 1974), 130.

37. Lionel Tiger, *Men in Groups,* Vintage Books (New York: Random House, 1969), p. 213. See Erikson's published work for the heuristic richness of this term.

38. Frederick W. Hodge, ed. *Handbook of American Indians North of Mexico* (2 vols.; New York: Rowman and Littlefield, 1971), II, 41.

39. *Ibid.,* I, 376.

40. Konrad Lorenz, "The Enmity between Generations," in *Play and Development,* ed. by Maria W. Piers (New York: W.W. Norton, 1972), p. 93.

41. Konrad Lorenz, *Civilized Man's Eight Deadly Sins,* trans. by Marjorie Kerr Wilson (New York: Harcourt Brace Jovanovich, 1974), p. 66.

42. Quoted in Paul Travis, "Death with Dignity Urged for Vets," *Fort Lauderdale News,* September 16, 1974.

43. Quoted in Jim Durham, "Dr. Sackett Says Retardation Folks 'Have Taken

Over'," *Tallahassee Democrat,* April 21, 1974, sec. E, p. 1.

44. Martin Buber, *I and Thou,* trans. by Walter Kaufmann (New York: Charles Scribner's Sons, 1970), p. 69.

45. *Ibid.,* p. 127.

46. See the testimony of Marjory Mecklenburg, President of American Citizens Concerned for Life, in U.S. Congress, Senate, Committee on the Judiciary, *Abortion Hearings,* before the Subcommittee on Constitutional Amendments, on S.J. Ress. 6, 10, 11 and 91, 94th Cong., 1st sess. June 19, 1975, Part 4, pp. 643-63.

47. See Richard Lamerton, *Care of the Dying* (London: Priory Press Ltd., 1973).

VII.
Suicide
and the
Patient's
Right
to Reject
Medical
Treatment.

SUICIDE

KAREN LEBACQZ, PH.D.
AND
H. TRISTRAM ENGELHARDT, JR. PH.D., M.D.

I. THE PROBLEM

Voluntary euthanasia has been dubbed "assisted suicide" (Gillon, 1969:181). The morality of euthanasia is thus inextricably linked to that of suicide. It is the purpose of this essay to examine the morality of suicide.

We will make a modest argument in favor of the right of persons to dispose of their own lives. We say "modest" argument because we will also argue that this right is usually overridden by duties to other persons. In making this case, we will first examine a typology of arguments against suicide in order to show that arguments in principle against suicide do not succeed. To take this approach is to suggest that suicide should be considered acceptable unless sufficient reason can be found why it is not. It is, therefore, to put the burden of proof on those who oppose suicide, rather than on those who defend it. As Flew suggests (1969:32), "It is up to any person and any institution wanting to prevent anyone from doing anything(s) he wishes to do . . . to provide positive good reason to justify that interference." The fundamental principle of liberty is taken as constitutive of human life and meaning.

Since arguments in principle against suicide do not succeed, there is a *prima facie* right to kill oneself. The question of suicide thus becomes a question of distributive justice—of balancing this right against the legitimate claims of others. We propose that duties to others often override the *prima facie* right to suicide. However, there are certain limited circumstances in which the right to suicide is not contravened by such duties to others; thus suicide is not always wrong.

Accordingly, there are some circumstances in which others may have a duty to assist in carrying out a suicide. Nonetheless, we conclude that there is a general duty both to reduce the tendency to suicide and to provide procedural safeguards against the coercion of vulnerable persons or the irrational exercise of the *prima facie* right to kill oneself.

II. DEFINITION

A preliminary problem that must be addressed is that of defining "suicide." If I smoke heavily, knowing the risk to my health and yet persisting in what is obviously a self-destructive course, is that suicide? If I wade out over my head in deep rushing water, knowing that I cannot swim, is that suicide? If I refuse life-saving medical treatment, is that suicide? Analyses of the morality of suicide are dependent at least in part on the definition of suicide.[1]

Kluge (1975) suggests that "suicide" proper can be distinguished from a "suicidal act." An action is a "suicidal act" if (a) it will, with reasonable certainty, lead to the death of the actor, and (b) the actor knows that it will do so. A suicidal act becomes suicide proper only when a third condition is added: namely, (c) "the actor must engage in that action for the express purpose of bringing about (her) own death." Thus, heavy smoking, wading beyond one's own depth, and refusing life-saving medical treatment are *suicidal acts*, but they become *acts of suicide* only when they are done with the express intent of ending one's life and not for some other purpose—e.g., for the enjoyment of smoking, in order to throw a life line to someone else, or in order to spare one's family unbearable economic burden. What makes an action "suicide," then, is the *intent* of the actor. If it is done in order to kill oneself, it is suicide. If it is done for some other purpose, even though one's death results, it is not "suicide" proper.[2]

This definition is not without problems, however. The concept of "intention" is a particularly tricky one. In general, our "intention" in acting can be said to include our *objective* (what we hope to *achieve* by doing X), our *action per se* (what we really *are doing* in doing X), and the *known consequences* of our action (what we know will *result* from our doing X) (Anscombe, 1957). The *intention* with which we act includes therefore not only our primary objective but also such aspects and results of the action as we know accompany what we do.

Thus, for example, in ceasing life-saving therapy our *primary* objective may be to avoid extreme pain. But we know that our death will result, and therefore death must be said to be in some way part of our "intention" in acting. We can therefore distinguish between *direct* intention and *oblique* intention (Engelhardt, 1975:190).

Further, the question of intention in suicide is problematic because even where one may be said to intend one's own death directly, this is rarely if ever the *only* intention in the act. Suicide rarely if ever has as its end *simply* the destruction of the self; one kills oneself in order to bring about some other state of affairs—for example, in order to avoid great pain in the future, or in order to benefit or hurt someone else. Thus, in killing oneself one may *also* relieve one's family of great financial burden. The relief from burden is as much a part of the act as is the destruction of oneself, and thus the "intention" of the act is not simply to do "A" (to kill oneself), but also to do "B" (to relieve one's family). Indeed, we may say that the true intention of the act was to relieve one's family of a burden, and that the destruction of oneself was only a means to achieve that end. As a means to the end, it is also *intended*, but it is not the overriding intention.[3]

While suicide may thus be defined as the "intentional taking of one's own life" (Funk and Wagnalls, 1930), any elaboration of this definition becomes problematic. Actors are ordinarily presumed to intend the natural consequences of their actions (Cantor, 1972:255). Thus it makes sense to think of the act of refusing life-saving therapy as in some sense also an act of "suicide"—i.e., an act with the intention of killing oneself. Since we know that death will result, we must "intend" that death in some oblique sense.

Yet consider the case of a woman who wades out into deep rushing water to save her child, knowing that she cannot swim. She "knows" that she will die, and yet we are loath to say that she "intended" to die and that her act was therefore an act of suicide. Instead, we are inclined to say that her intention was to save the child and that she sacrificed herself without in any way directly intending her own death.

But suppose someone will say: in this case the woman does not know *for certain* that she will die; she only takes a *risk* of death. Thus her death is not a *necessary means* to save the child. Only if it were a necessary means to save the child could she be said to "intend" her death. Consider then the following case: a woman offers her life in place of her friend who is about to be hanged. In this case, her *intention* is to save her friend, but her death is a necessary means to achieve that end. Thus she must will or intend her own death at the same time. Is this a case of suicide?

It seems reasonable, following Kluge's distinction, to call this a suicidal act, not an act of suicide, because the woman does not substitute her life for her friend in order that she might die, but in order to have her friend live. In short, suicidal acts, given this distinction, would include those acts done without clear knowledge of their suicidal character (e.g., a heavy smoker who represses all thought of the danger of smoking), and those that are done with such knowledge (e.g., being a stand-in for a hanging). It is worth noting that the woman substituting her life for another does not actually kill herself to save the other. If she had, she would have engaged in an act of suicide.[4] The definition of "suicide," therefore, includes both direct *intention* to die and the notion of *self-agency* of the act which effects that result. If the woman in this example had shot herself so that her friend would be freed, that would be suicide.

III. DESCRIPTION

Problems in defining suicide are paralleled by problems in describing suicide. Here our everyday language may be hazardous to ethical clarity. Common usage employs the phrase "to commit suicide"—as in "she committed suicide by jumping off the Golden Gate Bridge." Several commentators have noted that such usage portrays suicide as a "crime" to be "committed" as is, for example, murder.[5] Thus the use of language is itself not neutral. It suggests, in a loose sense, a criminal act.

Unfortunately, this usage is so deeply embedded in modern consciousness that other constructions seem awkward: "she did suicide," "she performed suicide," and so on have a sterile and cumbersome ring.[6] We shall avoid use of the term "commit suicide" by substituting the phrase "kill oneself" in hopes that this term will have a more neutral ring. The use of a more neutral phrase is not intended to obscure the question of criminality but only to avoid pre-judging it.

Finally, a word must be said about the use of the phrase "a suicide" or "the suicide" in reference to the person who kills herself. This usage is also to be rejected on grounds that it is judgmental and biased—it suggests that the total person can be defined in terms of one action.[7] We shall use instead the phrase "a person who has killed herself," recognizing that a person who kills herself is also a person who does many other things and that the person cannot be confined to a single act.[8]

With these caveats in mind, we proceed to analyze arguments against suicide.

IV. TELEOLOGICAL ARGUMENTS

The first set of arguments proffered against suicide may be called "teleological" arguments. They assert that suicide is wrong because it has adverse consequences.

Three such arguments are examined here. All three rest on the same basic mode of reasoning—a syllogism which goes something like this:

(1) Actions are right if they tend to maximize good, wrong if they tend to maximize evil.

(2) Suicide tends to maximize evil.

(3) Therefore, suicide is wrong.

All three arguments claim that suicide tends to maximize evil and is therefore wrong; they differ in the definition of evil and of the scope of consequences to be considered.

They also differ as to what good or goods are held to be decisive. One should here imagine *a person with an act utilitarian ethic in conflict with an absolutist with a religious ethic.* The first would argue that each act should be decided in terms of whether it tends to increase the sum of good redounding to the greatest number of persons. The absolutist in contrast may only be concerned with how things please God: *Placeat deo*

pereat mundus. One must determine what goods are significant goods (including a weighing of goods, a hierarchy of
values) and for whom they are significant in order to determine the direction of teleological arguments.

1.   Suicide results in eternal damnation.

The first argument claims that suicide results in eternal
damnation of the soul and that therefore to kill oneself or to
assist another to kill herself is to cause the most adverse possible consequences for the individual concerned, (cf. Flew,
1969) or to displease the deity. In either case the scope of concern is somewhat restricted: the individual to be damned, the
displeased deity, or both. The status of the pleasure or good redounding to other persons is left unexamined.

There are two problems with this argument: first, it rests
on an unexamined premise which requires further substantia-
tion; second, it recognizes only one agent for whom the consequences of the action may be morally significant.[9]

With respect to the first problem, it is clear that the supposition that suicide results in eternal damnation rests on the
following kind of syllogism:

(1) Heinous acts result in eternal damnation and/or dis-
    please the deity.

(2) Suicide is a heinous act.

(3) Therefore, suicide results in eternal damnation and/or
    displeases the deity.

On the assumption, then, that eternal damnation or displeas-
ing the deity is an evil, and that acts which result in evil are
wrong, suicide is clearly wrong.

However, what is the basis for the assertion that suicide
is a heinous act? Clearly, it would be circular to assert that
suicide is heinous because it results in damnation or displeases
the deity and then assert that suicide results in damnation or
displeases the deity because it is heinous! Some other *reason*
must therefore be proffered why suicide is heinous.

Of course, evidence for suicide being a damnable or a
deity-displeasing act may simply derive from its being asserted to be such by a deity—that is, reported to be such in scripture. However, there is no explicit condemnation of suicide in
the Old or New Testament (cf. Baelz, 1972:244). One must

suppose, therefore, that if suicide is taken to be heinous it is because it violates other prescriptions of the Old or New Testament—such as the commandment against killing—or because it violates the meaning and purpose of human life.[10] Such arguments will be examined below; if they are shown not to hold, then the argument that suicide is heinous collapses and with it this particular argument against suicide. The conclusion that suicide results in eternal damnation or displeases the deity must therefore await further analysis of the character of suicide as an act.

But a second objection might be raised to this argument as well. The argument as it stands considers only consequences to the individual. Even if the consequence to the individual is eternal damnation, other teleologists might argue that this consequence is not the only one to be considered in deciding whether an action maximizes good. Suppose that A's suicide brings harm to A (eternal damnation), but great benefit to B, C, and D (e.g., causes them to be saved rather than damned). In order to determine whether suicide maximizes good or evil, *all* these consequences must be considered.[11]

2. Suicide is harmful to family and friends.

Perhaps a more compelling argument against suicide, therefore, is the argument that it is not only (or not even) harmful to the self but to others. Suicide creates emotional trauma for family and friends and often brings economic hardship as well (for example, when the one who kills herself is the wage earner of the family). Surely, then, suicide is wrong because it produces these detrimental consequences.

No doubt this is one of the strongest arguments against suicide.[12] The "wrongness" of leaving a heartbroken and destitute family seems almost painfully self-evident. Yet the argument bears closer examination.

The first thing we notice about this argument is that if it is the harm done to family and friends that makes suicide wrong, then presumably suicide would not be wrong if one had no family and friends!

Alternatively, if the consequences to family and friends are what makes suicide right or wrong, then suicide would be right (and possibly even mandatory) if it would benefit one's family and friends rather than burden them! Thus the argument that suicide is wrong because it hurts family and friends presupposes a mode of reasoning in which suicide would be right if it helped rather than hurt others.

But suppose someone will say that one's family and friends are never benefitted by suicide, since they always feel the grief or loss.[13] In that case suicide would always be wrong because it always causes pain to someone. But here, we have a problem: suppose that the suicide results in great pain of loss to the family, but even greater financial benefit. Has it not then maximized the good? And if it is responded that the pain of grief can never be quantified and measured in economic terms, then surely we can never know whether the pain produced by an act of suicide is great enough to make that action wrong, all things considered.

Moreover, the pain caused for family and friends may have to be weighed not only against possible benefits to them, but also against possible benefits to others and to society at large. Suppose, for example, that "A" is very ill with an incurable disease that costs a considerable sum every year. A's family may not want her to die, and her suicide might indeed cause them great pain, but it might also benefit other patients who need the resources of the hospital which currently go into her care. One could argue, then, that in order to decide whether suicide maximizes evil or maximizes good, the consequences to a wider range of persons and a wider range of goods must be considered.[14] Where an act of suicide produces more good than evil for society as a whole, it would be right and not wrong.

3.   Suicide is harmful to society at large.

But just as some would argue that suicide always harms family and friends, so it can be argued that suicide always harms society. Notice that the argument here is not that a given case of suicide can be shown to produce more harm than good for society at large; to make such an argument is to allow room for the possibility that another act of suicide would produce more good than harm and would therefore be right. The argument under consideration here is one of a general prohibition of suicide on grounds that suicide *always* produces more harm than good—that is, *every* act of suicide does so and is therefore wrong.[15]

This argument can take one of two forms, which are sometimes confused with each other. It is important to keep these forms separate, since one is less vulnerable to criticism than the other.

The first form is usually called the "edge of the wedge" (or "camel's nose under the tent") argument. This argument runs essentially as follows:

(1) Action A is similar to action B in morally relevant ways;

(2) To do A is therefore to establish a precedent for (or remove a precedent against) B;

(3) Once A has been done, there will be sufficient forces operative to ensure that B will follow (i.e., that the precedent will be utilized in action)

(4) Action B is undesirable;

(5) Therefore, A has undesirable consequences.

If then, an action is wrong if it has undesirable consequences, action A (suicide) will be wrong.

It must be noted here that the argument is not that A is wrong *in itself*, but only that it leads to B, which is evil. If it can be shown, therefore, that A does *not* lead to B, then the argument collapses.[16] This is moreover a characteristic of teleological arguments generally. They concern ends, not means, and thus whether or not a particular act is evil will turn on whether it is conducive to the good sought.

There are two ways in which it might be argued that A does not result in B. First, it may be argued that action B is not similar to action A in morally relevant ways and thus that no precedent for B is established in doing A. This argument will be addressed further below. Second, it may be argued that there are not sufficient forces operative to ensure that action B will indeed follow upon action A. For example, suppose it is argued that once suicide is permitted and the prohibition against killing removed, wide-scale enforced suicide of the elderly will follow; if this is considered an undesirable consequence, then it is wrong to permit suicide in the first place. To counter this argument, one need only show that there are not in fact sufficient forces operative so that wide-scale enforced suicide of the elderly will follow (e.g., one might point to the existence of the Grey Panthers and other lobby groups which defend the elderly).

The "edge of the wedge" argument is therefore always vulnerable to the charge that it cannot demonstrate the presence of sufficient forces to bring about the undesired consequence.

The second form of this argument is not vulnerable to this criticism. This is the "argument from precedent." This argument accepts premises (1), (2) and (4) of the previous argument, but does not require that action B *will result* from the establishment of the precedent. It merely argues that taking action A establishes a precedent such that action B *could* logically be done; it does not assert that action B *will* necessarily be done. The "undesirable consequence" established here, therefore, is not a particular action B, but the presence of a precedent which would allow for other undesirable actions (possibly B, C, and D) if forces arose to pursue those actions.

Clearly, one might counter this argument by asking why it is wrong to establish a precedent *per se*, provided no particular undesirable consequences do in fact follow. That is, it hardly seems that the establishment of a precedent can be considered an undesirable consequence *in itself*; surely what is undesirable about the establishment of a precedent are the adverse consequences that do follow. If no adverse consequences follow, the precedent hardly seems undesirable.

Yet this response is a bit too hasty. The threat of adverse consequences which might follow, and the knowledge that a precedent has been established which would allow for them at any time, does seem an undesirable state of affairs. We also note that arguments from precedent underlie much of our legal structure and have been the basis for much advancement in the area of civil rights. It does not appear, therefore, that the argument from precedent can be refuted altogether convincingly.

However, a problem remains as to exactly when a precedent is established. Action A establishes a precedent for action B only if action B is similar to action A in morally relevant ways. What are the actions that are similar to suicide in morally relevant ways such that allowing suicide would establish a precedent for these other actions?

Some would argue that since suicide is a form of killing human life, it is similar in morally relevant ways to all other forms of killing human life. Thus to allow suicide is to open the door for voluntary and involuntary euthanasia, infanticide, and other forms of destruction of human life which may be considered to be undesirable.[17]

But are all these other actions really similar to suicide in morally relevant ways? Suicide is the *voluntary* taking of *one's own* life. Infanticide is the *involuntary* taking of *another's* life. Infanticide thus differs from suicide in two ways which may be morally relevant. If so, then allowing suicide would not establish a precedent for infanticide.

Perhaps the form of destruction of human life most similar to suicide is voluntary euthanasia. In that it is voluntary, it may be seen as a kind of "assisted" suicide. Even here, however, one might argue that the involvement of another agent is morally relevant, and thus that allowing suicide would not establish a precedent for voluntary euthanasia.

If certain characteristics of actions are taken to be morally relevant, therefore, many of those actions thought to be akin to suicide are not. If the *voluntariness* of the action and the identity of the *agent* are relevant considerations, then suicide stands in a class by itself and does not establish a precedent for other forms of destruction of human life.[18]

But perhaps it could be argued that to allow *some* instances of suicide is to establish a general precedent for *suicide* and thus to open the door to a variety of suicides, some undesirable.[19] To this argument, we would respond that to allow suicide in some limited cases is not necessarily to open the door to other cases of suicide. Just as there may be morally relevant differences between suicide and other forms of destruction of human life, so there may be morally relevant differences between cases or types of suicide. Thus once again, the question becomes what characteristics are taken as morally relevant.

Here we propose that morally relevant features of an action include the *reasons* that support it and the *circumstances* that surround it. For example: to hold that suicide of an 80-year-old woman in failing health is morally permissible is not necessarily to establish a precedent for allowing suicide in a 20-year-old healthy woman, although it may establish a precedent for allowing suicide in other elderly people whose health is failing. The individual's life *circumstances* are morally relevant considerations.

Similarly, the *reasoning* used to support the action is relevant to the establishment of a precedent. In proposing that suicide in an 80-year-old woman in failing health is different from suicide in a healthy young woman, we are not suggesting that a simple criterion of "quality of life" justifies the destruction of life. If this criterion alone is employed, then the practice of suicide does indeed open the way to other practices. For example, Kluge (1975:132) suggests that suicide is justifiable as an act "of alleviating the unbearable and inescapably unalterable suffering of a person."[20]

If suicide is justified as a form of relieving suffering of "*a person*" [emphasis ours], a different precedent is established than would be the case if suicide is justified as a form of relieving the suffering of *oneself*. In Kluge's formulation, the notion of freedom over oneself has been dropped in favor of a strict "quality of life" approach. If the only criterion for taking a human life is the quality of that life, then the life that is taken need not be one's own.[21]

But if both reasoning and life circumstances are morally relevant features, then a decision to allow suicide in some cases does not necessarily open the flood gates either to other forms of suicide or to other forms of destruction of human life. Thus the argument that suicide is *always* harmful to society in establishing dangerous precedents may be refuted.

None of the teleological arguments examined, therefore, provides sufficient grounds for the conclusion that suicide is always wrong. On the basis of teleological reasoning, any suicide that results in more good than harm is right, not wrong. The argument that any suicide is wrong because it establishes a dangerous precedent does not withstand closer examination of the nature of precedents. Thus we are not yet convinced that suicide is always wrong. To say this is not to deny that suicide may be wrong in a particular case in which it produces more harm than good; surely the consequences of the act are *one* criterion to be taken seriously in deciding whether the act is right or wrong. But no argument from consequences alone has proven that suicide is *always* wrong.

If an argument is to be developed which would absolutely forbid suicide, it must turn on suicide being intrinsically a violation of a duty, which cannot be overridden by other duties or the pursuit of other goods. That is, one would need an argument that did not turn on consequences, and all teleological arguments turn on consequences. As a result, deontological arguments offer the possibility of a more stringent resolution of the issue of suicide.

V. DEONTOLOGICAL ARGUMENTS

Deontological arguments assert that suicide is wrong not because it produces adverse consequences but because in itself it violates the meaning and purpose of human life and destroys the dignity of human nature. According to this kind of argument, it is not the results of the action that make it wrong, but something about its very nature.

There are a large number of such arguments brought to bear against suicide. Some of them overlap. We shall attempt to deal with the major arguments of this kind that have been presented.

1.   Suicide is "unnatural."

A classical argument against suicide is that it is contrary to inclinations of self-preservation. It is therefore to be condemned as violating human nature and the natural law. As St. Thomas put it, "To the natural law belongs everything to which a man is inclined according to his nature" (Pegis, 1945: 750). Suicide is against this nature: "[E]verything naturally loves itself. . . . Wherefore suicide is contrary to the inclination of nature, and to charity whereby every man should love himself" (Brandt, 1975b:66).

Clearly, suicide is not always contrary to inclination, since it occurs and indeed is prevalent.[22] However, St. Thomas and others have distinguished between true and fallen nature. Suicide may be an expression of fallen humanity, but it is not an expression of the true purposes of humankind. Suicide violates *true* human inclinations.

The moral relevance of inclinations—whether "true" or fallen—is not clear. To place the issue in a more contemporary context, Freudian psychology suggests that humans have a death instinct as well as an instinct for self-preservation. Yet the presence of such a "death instinct" does not in itself justify suicide, any more than the presence of an aggressive instinct justifies murder. As one observer astutely put it, "It is not easy to see how moral judgments are to be derived from the presence or absence of instincts" (Baelz, 1972:240). The fact that suicide is contrary to *some* human inclinations is not, therefore, enough to show that it violates human nature and is wrong in itself. The argument does not stand.[23]

2.   Suicide is cowardly.

Suicide is often thought to be cowardly. But is suicide always cowardly? For example, a mother may take her own life
rather than leave her family destitute from providing her medical care. While we might deplore the conditions that led to
such destitution and perhaps even judge the action wrong, it
hardly seems to be an example of cowardice. The ardent opponent of suicide, Immanual Kant, rejected the argument that
suicide is cowardly: "Even right-thinking people declaim
against suicide on wrong lines. They say that it is arrogant
cowardice. But instances of suicide of great heroism exist."
(1963:152). If by "cowardice" is meant moral cowardice—that
is, shirking one's duties and responsibilities—then not all
acts of suicide appear to be cowardly. To condemn all acts of
suicide as cowardly would then prejudge what should only be
judged in each individual case. "Significant judgment can be
passed on the specific event only after an analysis has been
carried out in the same terms of our ethical vocabulary as we
use for other events" (Hook, 1975:61). Acts of suicide will be
right or wrong in accordance with ordinary standards for judging the rightness and wrongness of human action; they are not
to be prejudged as a class.

Finally, to judge suicide as cowardly is really to judge the
character of the actor, not the action itself. By implication, the
action would not be wrong if it were not done out of cowardice.[24] Strictly speaking, assessment of the character of the
actor is relevant to judgments about moral *blameworthiness*
i.e., when to assign blame or guilt—but not about the *rightness* of the act. An act may be *wrong* but the actor not *blameworthy*—for example, if there is some excusing condition or
extenuating circumstance to explain why the actor did what
she did. The assessment that an act was done out of cowardice does not, therefore, render the act *wrong*.[25]

Clearly, therefore, this argument does not suffice to show
that suicide is always wrong.

3.   Suicide is irrevocable.

Another argument is that suicide is intrinsically wrong
because it is irrevocable and an individual who kills herself at
one time in her life might have been happy and wanted to live

at a later time (cf. Baelz, 1972:242). Such arguments are often paternalistic and are framed in terms of protecting the long-range best interests of the persons involved through short-term coercion as, for example, occurs in policies which prevent persons from selling themselves into slavery. But the wrongness of the irrevocable acts which are wrong (and it is surely not the case that all irrevocable acts are wrong) is not at once clear, and involves at least two issues which bear on the morality of suicide.

First, it may be that suicide is wrong because it forecloses all possible future options and deprives the individual of any future freedom. In that case, it would be irrevocable *loss of freedom* which is central. Thus, for example, we speak of liberty as a right which is "inalienable"—i.e., which the individual cannot alienate or give away. The first possible meaning to this argument, therefore, really hinges on our understanding of human freedom. This question will be addressed below.

The second possible meaning to this argument is that suicide makes a premature judgment, since the individual might have changed her mind had she lived. In this form, the argument reflects the regret that is felt at premature or hasty suicide—it reflects our assessment that a person who is depressed at one point in her life would have been happier later and might have learned to adjust to adversities. But to suggest that an action is wrong because we can never know all future possibilities is not to take seriously the context of all human action. Every action is based on probabilities and forecloses possibilities for the future. Yet this alone is not sufficient to suggest that we should never act at all! Assessments of the situation and of the "right" thing to do must be made here as elsewhere—on the basis of the best reasonable calculation as to future prospects. We cannot know for sure the future state of any individual; as Flew (1969:40) suggests, therefore, "it is only necessary and it is only possible to insist on ordinarily exacting rather than obsessional criteria of what is beyond reasonable doubt."

When an action is irrevocable, it may be wise to institute safeguards to protect against precipitous exercise of that action.[26] But the fact that it is irrevocable does not, in itself, render the action wrong. Thus the fact that suicide is irrevocable is not enough to establish that it is always wrong.[27] Moreover, in special cases where suicide occurs in the imminence of death, the argument concerning irrevocability fails since there will not be a significant future within which freedom would be lost, or regret possible.

4.   Suicide is self-contradictory, and cannot be universalized.

Kant argued that suicide is a contradiction, because one destroys the very self that one wishes to save from pain or suffering. Kant held that humans ought to act freely and rationally and that to take one's life subverts human freedom and thus the possibility of acting according to the moral law. That is, since suicide is logically contradictory, it cannot be willed as a universal law or maxim for human action[28] and thus fails the first test for the morality of human action—that one must be willing to have the maxim of one's action become a universal law.[29]

But is suicide logically contradictory, in that one destroys the very self one is trying to relieve from some burden? Brandt (1975b:67) suggests that what Kant finds contradictory is that "the motive of self-love (interest in one's own long-range welfare) should sometimes lead one to struggle to preserve one's life, but at other times to end it." To this Brandt replies "But where is the contradiction?" It does not seem contradictory to say that one's interest in oneself can include an interest in dying at a certain time or in a certain fashion. To argue that one should stop one's existence before it takes on a disvalue is not to argue that one does not value oneself.

Consider the point this way: In killing oneself, one acts in order to preclude certain future states or events. If there were another way to preclude those events, one would choose it. Thus in killing oneself, one is not willing (or intending) to destroy the self, which one would keep if possible. One intends only to preclude certain undesirable states of affairs for oneself. However, it happens that the only way to achieve this end is to destroy the self that would experience those states of affairs. In suicide, the act of preventing such future states is materially identical with the act of destroying one's own self. But they are not logically identical, and they differ clearly as two distinguishable objects of intention.

Thus, whether the person considering suicide is justified in her action or not, she does appear vindicated against Kant's charge of being self-contradictory in virtue of being self-destructive. In short, the position of the person seeking suicide could at least on this point meet Kant's test of universalizability.[30]

5. Life is a gift from God, and therefore not at the disposal of humans.

It is argued that life is a gift from God and that therefore since God has given it only God may take it away. As Kant (1963:154) expressed it, "Human beings are sentinels on earth and may not leave their posts until relieved by another beneficent hand." To kill oneself is therefore to act against God's purposes for human life, and in this way to violate the meaning of human life.

This argument underscores a basic attitude of reverence for life. Nonetheless, as a specific injunction against suicide, it becomes rather problematic. As Baelz (1972:245f) points out, the "givenness" of life does not settle the question of what we are to do with the gift. Not only life but also human freedom are gifts from God. In the absence of specific injunctions, therefore, it is not clear that the giftedness of life *per se* constitutes an argument against suicide. Indeed, a radical approach to the "givenness" of life would require that humans take *no* interventions in the course of human life—either to destroy or save life.

6. Suicide violates the commandment not to kill.

If a specific injunction from God is needed in order to show that suicide is wrong, it is sometimes thought that the sixth commandment—"Thou shalt not kill"—provides such an injunction. Suicide is always wrong, therefore, because it violates a specific commandment from God.

Two responses can be made to this argument. The first is that there are recorded instances of suicide in the Bible which do not appear to have been censured by God—for example, the case of Samson (Kluge, 1975: 104). It seems strange that these cases would not have been disapproved by God if they are indeed contrary to one of the commandments.

However, Augustine and others argued that in these cases there was a specific injunction from God superseding the general commandment though not explicitly recorded in the Bible (see Baelz, 1972:244). Thus it is claimed that the Sixth Commandment holds as a general prohibition of suicide in the absence of a contrary order from God.

To this, one may respond, second, that the interpretation of the Sixth Commandment given here is erroneous. Biblical scholars agree that the Commandment is more accurately interpreted "Thou shalt do no murder," where "murder" is not simply "killing" but "wrongful killing" (Baelz, 1972:244). The question then becomes whether suicide is to count as murder, or wrongful killing. None of the arguments examined thus far have sufficed to prove that suicide is always wrongful killing.

7.   Suicide is self-murder.

Some opponents of suicide do argue that suicide is murder and thus the wrongful killing of an innocent human life. They argue that it is "self-murder."

Clearly, this definition of suicide as murder will stand only if "murder" is defined as the direct and intentional killing of any (innocent[31]) human life independently of any consideration of what makes murder wrong to begin with and whether, therefore, the taking of human life may in some circumstances be justified. If the evil in murder is the radical subversion of another's freedom, then it is morally significant when the actor and the "victim" are the same—i.e., when no one's freedom is being subverted. In short, what holds *prima facie* in the case of taking the life of another may not hold in the case of taking one's own life. As Flew (1969:43) sarcastically puts it, if suicide is murder then "by parity of reasoning, marriage is really adultery—'own-wife' adultery."

Kluge takes a somewhat different approach. He rejects the notion that the identity of the agent *per se* is central, but he argues that the definition of murder has been misconstrued. Murder is not simply the *destruction* of human life (simple "killing," even if direct and intentional), but it is the violation of a person's *right to life*. In suicide, there is no violation of someone's right to life, because the act is not against the victim's will. Thus suicide is not murder.[32]

8. There is a duty to oneself to preserve one's life.

But perhaps it could be argued that even if suicide is not self-murder but only self-destruction, it is nonetheless wrong because it violates a duty to oneself to preserve one's life. This is an argument one finds, for example, in Kant. For Kant, the fundamental duty is to treat persons as ends and never merely as means to an end. One has duties to oneself in virtue of being a person; thus one has a duty to oneself not to use oneself as a means only. On the basis of this argument, Kant held that transplantation of organs would be wrong since the donor would be using herself as a means merely (Kant's example was that of donating a tooth). Suicide was simply a more radical case: "If [s]he destroys [herself] in order to escape from painful circumstances, [s]he uses a person merely as *a means* . . ." (Kant, 1973:47).

The sense of such duties to oneself is hard to clarify. As Singer (1954) has argued, the concept of a duty to oneself is problematic because it is awkward if not impossible to speak of a duty to oneself in the same way in which we normally speak of duties. First, "duties" imply "rights": my duty to pay a debt is paralleled by my creditor's right to be paid. Yet it hardly makes sense to speak of a right against oneself in virtue of which one has a duty. Second, one can be released from a duty by the person to whom it is owed. Yet we do not normally think that individuals can release themselves from their obligations. And if they can, then one could release oneself from the duty to preserve one's life!

Singer suggests (1954:204), therefore, that a distinction needs to be made between "the person *to whom* one is under an obligation and the person *regarding whom* one is under the obligation." Those things which we have tended to call duties *to* oneself may actually be duties *to* others *regarding* oneself. Thus, for example, I may have a duty to others to preserve my life, but not a duty to myself to preserve it: "Hence, if it really is a duty to preserve one's life, this can be regarded as a duty to mankind generally" (Singer, 1954:204).

9.   There is a general duty to preserve life.

Clearly, then, the next argument that suicide is always wrong rests on the general duty to preserve human life. The prohibition of suicide is derivative from this general duty. The four preceding arguments are all in some sense attempts to condemn suicide as the destruction of human life. One can claim that the sanctity of human life is such that it should never be directly taken, whether by self or by others. Suicide is wrong, therefore, because it violates the sanctity of human life.

Logically, of course, to take such a position commits one to oppose all direct forms of destruction of human life, including capital punishment and "just war." Most opponents of suicide do not take an exceptionless stand. "But as soon as any exceptions or qualifications are admitted, it becomes excessively difficult to find any presentable principle upon which these can be admitted while still excluding suicide . . ." (Flew, 1969:44). Unless the destruction of human life is to be condemned altogether, any principle by which some destruction of human life is permitted is likely to make room for at least *some* cases of suicide.

But what of the argument, then, that *all* destruction of human life is wrong? One could claim that the requirement of consistency, far from proving that suicide is right because other forms of destruction of human life are acceptable proves instead that these other forms are also wrong and should not be accepted. There may not be many persons who adhere to such an absolutist position, but it is a logical and strong stance.

There is no easy answer to this claim. To respond requires a philosophical and theological debate about the relative value of human life and human freedom. This issue will be addressed directly below. At this point, we simply note that unless one takes an absolutist stand on this issue and accepts the logical consequences of that stand—i.e., a condemnation of *all* destruction of human life—it must be acknowledged that a limited case might be found for suicide. Arguments about the value of life do not *per se* rule out all possible instances of suicide.

VI. LIFE, FREEDOM, AND JUSTICE

At a fundamental level, questions of the ethical acceptability of suicide are questions of the value of life and the dignity of freedom. The authors have already indicated their bias toward a fundamental libertarian principle that puts the burden of proof on those who would deprive persons of freedom over their bodies and lives.

Our argument is simply this: that which gives humans their unique worth is the fact that they can be respected, blamed or praised for their actions because they are rational free agents.[00] Respect for persons as free moral agents should entail that they be allowed to choose that which endows their lives with meaning as long as such choice will not seriously affect the freedoms of others or violate prior agreements between persons. That is, persons have a *prima facie* right to seek out their own values. The right is a *"prima facie"* one in this sense: persons are to be held to have that right until there is evidence to the contrary—e.g., covenants by which they cede some liberty.

With respect to suicide, therefore, we hold that persons are the best judges of the proper balance of values in their lives. An element of respecting others is respecting their right to take their lives in the absence of any contravening duties. Persons should be permitted to take their own lives when they have chosen to do so freely and rationally and when there are no other duties which would override this freedom.

There is thus nothing in principle morally wrong with suicide. But to say that one has a *prima facie* right to take one's own life is not to say that it is always morally justifiable to do so. It means rather that one has a right to take one's life until a contravening moral obligation obtains. The question of suicide is therefore at root a question of distributive justice—of the proper distribution of benefits and burdens, the proper balancing of personal good and social obligation.

As human beings, we exist in mutual relationships of responsibility. Perhaps the strongest reason that can be given in opposition to suicide is that it violates our covenantal obligations to others. It breaks through the faithfulness we owe to those around us. A critic might agree with us, therefore, that there is a *prima facie* right to kill oneself, but might argue that the right to suicide is nonetheless always defeated by the claims of others.

This argument does not turn on whether bad consequences follow from the act of suicide. It is not a consequentialist or teleological argument such as those discussed above. Rather, the argument is that suicide is wrong because it violates certain *prima facie* duties of covenant-fidelity—such as gratitude, promise-keeping, and reparations. For example, parents choosing to have children make an implicit promise to provide for them, just as children who are provided for have obligations of gratitude to their parents. Suicide destroys the possibility of keeping the promise to care or the obligation of showing gratitude. Insofar as it violates these duties the right to suicide is overriden.[34] Suicide is wrong when it violates obligations of covenant-fidelity.

If suicide is wrong when it violates obligations of covenant-fidelity, then it may be right when it does not violate such obligations. We propose that there are at least three circumstances in which suicide may be right.

1.   Voluntary Euthanasia.

There are circumstances in which normal obligations of covenant-fidelity cease because their fulfillment is impossible (Ross, 1939:109). Under certain life circumstances, such as terminal illness accompanied by great pain, it may be impossible to fulfill normal covenant obligations to one's family and friends. If so, these obligations cease and thus the right to dispose of one's own life is not contravened by any restraining duties. In these circumstances, the right to suicide cannot be defeated because the circumstances themselves defeat the possibility of fulfilling any obligation to others.[35]

2.   "Covenantal" Suicide.

If the first instance in which suicide is morally justifiable is that in which covenantal obligations cease to exist, the second is that where the suicide itself fosters rather than violates covenantal obligations. Suicide need not be covenant-breaking; it can be covenant-affirming.

There are two types of covenant-affirming suicide. The

first is the "suicide pact" or joint suicide in which marriage partners, close friends, or others who live in covenantal rela- tionship bind themselves "even unto death." The second is the "self-sacrificial" suicide of one who chooses to die rather than to burden her family or friends.[36] (For example, one who kills herself rather than deplete family resources with expensive medical treatment affirms the covenant with her family in so doing.)

Whether any particular instance of "covenantal" suicide is justifiable depends on the extent to which it fulfills rather than violates other covenantal obligations. An act of suicide which fosters some covenants at the expense of others might still be wrong. But in cases where the act does not violate the *prima facie* duty of covenant-fidelity, it is not *prima facie* wrong.

3.   "Symbolic Protest."

In the first two instances of justifiable suicide, the suicide was not judged to be wrong either because the duty of covenant-fidelity ceased or because it was supported by suicide. But are there any cases where the suicide appears to violate covenants but may yet be justifiable? We propose that there is at least one such case: that of suicide as "symbolic protest." Suicide is occasionally used as an act of symbolic protest against great evil and injustice—e.g., against war or imprisonment—and is meant to support in a radical fashion respect for persons generally.[37]

In such cases, suicide appears to violate one's immediate obligations of covenant-fidelity, since family and friends may be abandoned in order to make symbolic protest. However, the intention of the act is to protest those institutions and structures which undermine the very conditions that make human life and covenant-fidelity possible. When suicide as symbolic protest provides a significant contribution to the struggle against forces which would destroy the freedom of others, taking one's own life can be at root an affirmation of the dignity of persons.[38] We might say that in this form of suicide, the individual aligns herself with more basic loyalties than those to family and friends—namely the community of moral agents. The need to struggle for justice may in circumstances be more compelling than obligations to one's immediate family and friends.[39]

Viewed within the perspective of justice, therefore, there are at least three instances in which suicide may be right: Those in which *prima facie* obligations of covenant-fidelity cease to exist, those in which the suicide fulfills *prima facie* obligations of covenant-fidelity, and those in which obligations of covenant-fidelity are superseded by demands of justice on a larger scale.[40]

VII. SUICIDE AND SOCIETY

If suicide is not always wrong but may be right on occasion, then we must ask what are the obligations of others to one who attempts or desires suicide.

The "rightness" of suicide depends upon two balances required by justice: the balancing of values for the individual, and the balancing of that individual's free choice against the legitimate claims of others. Each of these balances has ramifications for the rights of others to interfere or to assist in the suicide.

We have argued that only the individual can decide what balance of freedom and life constitutes the best choices for her.[41] Clearly, in making this argument, we have assumed that the individual is competent to decide—that is, that she is a rational adult capable of exercising free choice. If the individual is not competent by reason of age or insanity, then she may be presumed not to be able to choose freely the proper balance of values in her life. In this case others have a right and may indeed have a duty to interfere in order to protect her interests.

A difficulty arises, of course, in deciding what constitutes insanity or sufficient impairment of rational choice so as to justify interference. We suggest that in general certain safeguards such as the requirement of a waiting period are acceptable in order to ensure that the individual is indeed rational.[42] However, we also caution against *assuming* that a person is irrational just because she has chosen to kill herself; the intention to die is not *per se* irrational. A person must be shown not to be competent, or there must be good evidence that she is incompetent, before intervention is justified on grounds of protecting her interests.[43]

Where a person is competent and has freely chosen to kill herself, the rights and obligations of others depend upon the balance of justice claims between that individual and those around her. Many if not most of the persons in the last stages of dying from a debilitating disease are not only unable to fulfill their covenant obligations but are also often in great pain and suffering. In such cases, suicide not only does not violate the demands of justice, it may be that we may say that she "needs" suicide. If a person who needs suicide is unable to effect it herself, although she would choose freely to do so if she could, we may have a duty to assist her based on our general duty to assist those in need if no one else is available to give assistance.[44] It would surely be an obligation in cases where the person in need of assistance and the person who can render assistance are bound by covenantal relationships of mutual support. However, we note that this obligation holds only where the decision for suicide is "right" (cf. Brandt, 1975b:73)—that is, where the demands of justice are not violated, as in cases of illness in which pain and debility prevents the discharge of any duties on the part of the person needing suicide.

Finally, we must ask about those cases in which a competent adult chooses to die, but others have reason to think that the demands of justice would be violated by the suicide (i.e., that it is wrong and that the person seeking suicide is not relieved of her obligations because illness prevents their discharge). In such circumstances, persons have a right to intervene to prevent the act in order to protect their rights or the rights of others. It is important to keep clear here the distinction between this case and the one above in which the individual is judged not competent to decide her own best interests; in this case, the individual is judged competent, but the claims of others are assessed to be sufficiently strong to override her interests. It is also important to note that this does not mean that others may interfere simply because they disagree with the decisions made; rather, they must have reason to think that it is a wrong decision.

In short, where the individual contemplating suicide is competent and the demands of justice would not be violated by the suicide, others have no right to intervene.[45] The right to intervene to prevent suicide grows out of the demands of justice in one of two circumstances: first, when the individual *cannot* make a rational choice regarding her own life values; or second, when there are legitimate overriding claims of others. The duty to assist in effecting suicide grows out of the "rightness" of the act (i.e., it does not violate the requirements of justice) coupled with the *need* for assistance and one's covenantal relations with the person in need.

This analysis suggests that a legal framework must allow for the possibility of justifiable suicide. Neither suicide nor assisted suicide (voluntary euthanasia) should be illegal in cases such as those described above.[46] Safeguards may be needed to ensure that the decision for suicide is rational; the presumption should be given to saving life when there is doubt (e.g., when someone is found lying in a coma). Nonetheless, room must be made for cases of justifiable suicide.

While suicide should be legal and there may even be instances in which it is the *duty* of others to assist in the suicide, there are also broader responsibilities incumbent upon all persons to work for the conditions which would make the inclination towards suicide less frequent by supporting conditions of justice. The high rate of suicide attempts by women and blacks (Stengel, 1973:90f; Hendin, 1969:150f) is a sign that the present conditions of society are not just and do not foster conditions in which life, liberty, and happiness are mutually supportive for all persons.[47] Suicide is often symbolic of unresolved racism and sexism. To view suicide under the rubric of the demands of justice is to remind us that these basic problems of society are the responsibility of all.

Suicide, therefore, is not simply a matter of individual responsibility; it is a matter of social responsibility. The choice of freedom over life is a choice made in the context of social demands and expectations.[48] While we have argued above that limited cases of suicide such as those involved in voluntary euthanasia are justifiable, we are also concerned lest there be coercion of vulnerable persons in pain and distress. Those who do not want to, should never be coerced to take their lives. Towards this end, a euthanasia bill introduced in Britain requires a request in writing thirty days in advance and the certification by two physicians that the patient is indeed suffering from a terminal condition (Downing, 1969:197f). Such provisions are intended to restrict "assisted suicide" to considered action in the limited case of terminal illness where it is clear that obligations of covenant-fidelity cannot be fulfilled. There are other and quite serious procedural issues of providing for sufficient safeguards to assure the ability of the

person or patient to change her mind any time after an initial
decision for suicide.

But the issues concerning coercion are difficult, for how
are patients and others in distress to be prevented from being
bullied into taking their lives or requesting assistance to do
so? When overwhelmed by illness and pain and confronted by
the "duty" not to burden one's family with costly, non-pro-
ductive continued existence, a pattern of coercion may emerge.
Further, the pattern of coercion could be substantial apart
from any ambiguous cases where either the physician or the
family might have vested interests in the expeditious departure of the patient. Thus, procedural safeguards must convincingly protect against complex patterns of forces which
may be brought to bear upon patients and others contemplating suicide.

VIII. CONCLUSIONS

Conclusions with regard to suicide are, thus, difficult. On
the one hand, a general argument in principle against suicide
does not hold. The accent of this essay has been upon general
arguments. Yet these general arguments must be tempered
by the realities of covert coercion and the need for convincing
procedural safeguards, particularly in the realm of voluntary
euthanasia.

Our conclusions are thus in the end somewhat muted.
Although (1) arguments in principle against suicide do not
succeed and (2) persons have a *prima facie* right to take their
own lives, still (3) the duties persons have to others will often
override their right to take their own lives, and (4) procedural
safeguards are in order to protect vulnerable persons from
coercion. We have found three sets of circumstances when it
would be morally permissible to take one's own life: (1) when
it is impossible to discharge one's duties, (2) when suicide
supports rather than violates obligations of covenant-fidelity,
and (3) when the intention of the suicide is to support the
general good of persons and the conditions which make covenant-fidelity possible. This way of viewing suicide leads us
to hold that persons have a right to intervene when another
intends suicide (1) if that person is not able to choose freely

and rationally, or (2) if that person is defaulting on obligations to others. But persons have no right to intervene, absent these two circumstances, and may have a duty in some cases to assist. How these general conclusions can be worked out in particular circumstances depends on the respect and support given to freedom and to covenant-fidelity in society at large.

REFERENCES

Alvarez, Walter C. 1972. "The Right to Die." in Maurice B. Visscher (ed.), *Humanistic Perspectives in Medical Ethics.* Buffalo: Prometheus.

Anscombe, G.E.M. 1963. *Intention.* (2nd edition) Ithaca, N.Y.: Cornell University Press.

Baelz, P.R. 1972. "Voluntary Euthanasia: Some Theological Reflections." *Theology* 75:238, May.

Bandman, Bertram and Elsie. 1975. "Rights, Justice and Euthanasia." in Kohl.

Barrington, Mary Rose. 1969. "Apologia for Suicide." in Downing.

Beeson, T. 1974. "Sacrificial Suicides." *Christian Century* 91:836, 18 Sept.

Brandt, Richard B. 1975a. "A Moral Principle About Killing." in Kohl.

Brandt, Richard B. 1975b. "The Morality and Rationality of Suicide." in Perlin.

Cantor, Norman L. 1972. "A Patient's Decision to Decline Life-Saving Medical Treatment: Bodily Integrity Versus the Preservation of Life." *Rutgers Law Review* 26:228, Winter.

Close, H.T. 1973. "Suicide: A Theological Perspective." *J. Pastoral Care* 27:18, Mr.

Derrett, J.D.M. 1970. "St. Thomas More and the Would-Be Suicide." *Downside Review* 88:372, Oct.

Dorpat, Theodre L. and Boswell, John W. 1963. "An Evaluation of Suicidal Intent in Suicide Attempts." *Comprehensive Psychiatry* 4:117, April.

Downing, A.B. (ed.) 1969. *Euthanasia and the Right to Death.* Los Angeles: Nash Publ.

Engelhardt, Jr., H. Tristram. 1975. "Ethical Issues in Aiding the Death of Young Children." in Kohl.

Fletcher, Joseph. 1969. "The Patient's Right to Die." in Downing.

Flew, Anthony. 1969. "The Principle of Euthanasia." in Downing.

Gillon, Raanan. 1969. "Suicide and Voluntary Euthanasia: Historical Perspective." in Downing.

Grollman, Earl A. 1971. *Suicide: Prevention, Intervention, Postvention.* Boston: Beacon Press.

Lendin, Herbert. 1969. *Black Suicide.* New York: Harper and Row.

Hook, Sidney. 1975. "The Ethics of Suicide." in Kohl.

Kamisar, Yale. 1969. "Euthanasia Legislation: Some Non-Religious Objections." in Downing.

Kant, Immanuel. 1873. "Fundamental Principles of the Metaphysic of Morals," in Kant's *Critique of Practical Reason and Other Works on the Theory of Ethics,* trans. Thomas K. Abbott. London: Longmans, Green and Co. *Akademie Ausgabe,* IV.

Kant, Immanuel. 1963. *Lectures on Ethics.* New York: Harper and Row.

Kohl, Marvin (ed.) 1975. *Beneficent Euthanasia.* Buffalo, New York: Prometheus Books.

La Fontaine, Jean. 1975. "Anthropology." in Perlin.

McCaughey, J.D. 1967. "Suicide: Some Theological Considerations." *Theology* 70:63, Feb.

McConnell, T.A. 1968. "Suicide Ethics in Cross-Disciplinary Perspective." *J. Religion and Health* 7:7, Jan.

Neale, R.E. 1972. "Call Us Ishmael: Suicide in Contemporary Society." *Christianity and Crisis* 32:260, 27 Nov.

Nelson, James B. 1973. *Human Medicine: Ethical Perspectives on New Medical Issues.* Minneapolis: Augsburg.

Pegis, Anton C. (ed.) 1945. *Basic Writings of St. Thomas Aquinas.* New York: Random House.

Perlin, Seymour. 1975. *A Handbood for the Study of Suicide.* New York: Oxford University Press.

Ramsey, Paul. 1970. *The Patient as Person.* New Haven: Yale University Press.

Richardson, Herbert W. 1968. "What is the Value of Life?" in Donald Cutler (ed.) *Updating Life and Death.* Boston: Beacon Press.

Rose, K. Daniel and Rosow, Irving. 1973. "Physicians Who Kill Themselves." *Archives of General Psychiatry* 29:800, Dec.

Ross, Sir William David. 1939. *Foundations of Ethics.* London: Oxford University Press.

Ruitenbeek, Hendrik M. (ed.) 1969. *Death: Interpretations.* New York: Dell Publ.

Singer, Marcus G. 1954. "On Duties to Oneself." *Ethics* 69: 202.

Sprott, S.E. 1961. *The English Debate on Suicide.* LaSalle, Ill: Open Court.

Stein, E.V. 1971. "Faith, Hope and Suicide." *J. Religion and Health* 10:214, July.

Stengel, Erwin. 1973. *Suicide and Attempted Suicide.* London: Penguin Books.

Szasz, Thomas S. 1971. "The Ethics of Suicide." *Intellectual Digest,* October.

Trowell, Hugh. 1973. *The Unfinished Debate on Euthanasia.* London: SCM Press Ltd.

Van Der Horst, P.W. 1971. "A Pagan Platonist and a Christian Platonist on Suicide." *Vigilae Christianae* 25:282.

Walzer, Michael. 1975. "Consenting to One's Own Death: The Case of Brutus." in Kohl.

Williams, Glanville. 1969. "Euthanasia Legislation: A Rejoinder to the Non-Religious Objections." in Downing.

Wilson, Jerry B. 1975. *Death By Decision: The Medical, Moral, and Legal Dilemmas of Euthanasia.* Philadelphia: Westminster Press.

1. Conversely, we suspect that definitions of "suicide" are sometimes dependent upon prior judgments about its justifiability. Some observers classify acts of self-sacrifice as "suicide"; some do not. While technically the distinction may be said to turn on the "intent" of the actor, one suspects that those who refuse to classify self-sacrificial actions as suicide do so at least in part because of a prior judgment about the wrongness of suicide; thus actions which seem more ethically acceptable are not classified as "suicide" because it has already been determined that "suicide" is wrong.

1. Cf., Kant [1963:150] "A man who shortens his life by intemperance is guilty of imprudence and indirectly of his own death; but his guilt is not direct; . . . we cannot say of him that he is a suicide. What constitutes suicide is the intention to destroy oneself."

3. Anscombe [1957:46] explains: "So there is one action with four descriptions, each dependent on wider circumstances, and each related to the next as description of means to end; which means that we can speak equally well of *four* corresponding intentions, or of *one* intention—the last term that we have brought in in the series. By making it the last term so far brought in, we have given it the character of being the intention . . . *with* which the act in its other descriptions was done . . . [T]his intention so to speak swallows up all the preceding intentions . . ." e.g., if one pulls the trigger of a gun in order to kill oneself in order to spare one's family, the sparing of one's family is the intention *with* which the act was done. The act may be variously described as "pulling the trigger of a gun," "killing oneself," or "sparing one's family of a burden," and in some sense each of these descriptions also has a corresponding intention, (i.e., one intended to pull the trigger of the gun), but it is the *last* description that gives the overriding intention (in this case: the sparing of one's family).

4. For those who hold there is no moral distinction between acting and refraining, one could agree that in some cases the two acts may be morally equivalent (i.e., an act of suicide and a suicidal act), though they remain in other respects distinguishable.

5. Flew [1969] says: "If you believe, as I do, that suicide is not always and as such wrong, it is inappropriate to speak of 'committing suicide'." Barrington [1969] calls the phrase "commit suicide" a "tendentious expression . . . calculated to poison the unsuspecting mind."

6. Flew (1969) suggests the expression "suiciding oneself." The awkwardness of this phrase serves to illustrate the problems attendant upon the lack of a verb form for "suicide."

7. The use of such an expression does, of course, indicate the *definitiveness* of the action of suicide. Not only is it the *last* action a person takes in her life; it also seems to overshadow other actions; thus the expression "a suicide" in reference to the person reflects the particular weight of the action of suicide.

8. Throughout this essay, we shall use the feminine form as the inclusive language form; thus when we say "a person who kills herself" it is to be understood as "a person who kills her or himself." If this use of language seems strange to the reader, it should serve to make her aware of the importance of language for defining the reality in which we live.

9. We ignore here the obvious problem that "eternal damnation" or the concept of an everlasting hell after death is probably alien to most Christians today.

10. The ardent opponent of suicide, Immanuel Kant, said of the religious argument against suicide: "[S]uicide is not inadmissible and abominable because God has forbidden it; God has forbidden it because it is abominable . . ." [1963: 154] Kant's arguments will be examined below.

11. We leave aside the problem of measuring "temporal" benefits such as economic gain against presumed "eternal" burdens such as damnation. One might also question whether an action that produced great benefits for others is *really* likely to result in eternal damnation for the self.

12. Hook[1975:63] says: "Consideration for the peace of mind of one's friends and family is the most powerful deterrent to suicide."

13. We might, of course, suggest that not all family members do feel grief of loss., To this, the opponents of suicide will no doubt reply that those who do not feel grief will feel guilt over not feeling grief; thus there is always some adverse feeling created by the act of suicide. We doubt that their point can be strictly supported; however, it does point to a significant psychological reality associated with suicide, which is the guilt and/or grief of the survivors.

14. Indeed, one might argue that where my suicide does more good than evil on the whole, my family ought *not* to feel pain but rather joy at my action. If the action is *right*, then no *injury* has been done to one's family. (An analogy here would be the young adult who moves out of the parent's home; while they will feel pain of loss and loneliness, we would not generally say that they had been *injured* by the action.)

15. A variant form of this argument would be a rule-utilitarian approach, in which actions are judged to be right or wrong in accordance with *rules* chosen so as to maximize the good. In this kind of argument, it need not be shown that every act of suicide produces more harm than good, but only that the *practice* of suicide *generally* produces more harm than good. Thus a rule prohibiting the practice is established, and the action judged wrong in accordance with the rule.

16. The problem with this approach, however, is that it must account for the instance in which the *particular* act would appear to maximize good even though the *general practice* does not. Thus there will be cases in which the good is maximized by having a rule against action A in general, but where the particular action A_1 would do more good than harm. If the rightness of actions depends on maximizing the good, then it appears that action A_1 should be allowed in spite of the rule. But if action A_1 is allowed, then it hardly makes sense to have the rule in the first place, and the act-utilitarian approach would appear to make more sense.

17. We shall not take up here the question whether these other forms of destruction of human life are *in fact* undesirable. At this point, our concern is only to question whether they are similar to suicide in morally relevant ways so that allowing suicide would establish a precedent for these other actions.

18. Debates will, of course, arise as to which characteristics of actions are morally relevant. The two suggested here—the aspect of volition and the identity of the agent—would generally be considered morally relevant.

19. For example, Brandt [1975b] suggests that it might be better for society to *think* that suicide is wrong in order to prevent hasty suicide and the loss of valuable life. This form of rule-utilitarianism has been discussed above.

20. He therefore classifies suicide as a form of euthanasia rather than vice versa.

21. And, indeed, Kluge does find permissible cases of euthanasia, both voluntary and involuntary.

22. In 1972, suicide ranked tenth on the scale of top killers in the U.S., with approximately 22,000 suicides reported—or one every half hour. Further, Neale [1972:260] points out that these are recorded suicides, and that many suicides may be recorded under other "causes of death"—e.g., traffic accident, drowning, etc.

23. However, the argument is not without value for other purposes. Sociological studies have shown that the incidence of suicide tends to rise in socially disruptive circumstances [see Dubos, 1959; Durkheim, 1951]. In this sense suicide can be understood as "contrary to nature," for it would not occur with such frequency in the "natural" setting of the organism. It is often a signal of psychological or sociological upheaval; therefore, while suicide is not always "contrary to nature," it often suggests that socially disruptive forces are at work. We shall return to this point below.

24. Baelz [1972] suggests that "cowardice" is an evaluative term that implies "running away when one ought not to"; by implication, there would be situations in which "running away" would be acceptable.

25. Brandt [1975b:62] suggests that "X is morally blameworthy on account of A" can be understood to mean "X did A, and X would not have done A had not his character been in some respect below standard; and in view of this it is fitting or justified for X to have some disapproving attitudes including remorse toward himself, and for some other persons Y to have some disapproving attitudes toward X . . ." It is the suggestion that X "would not have done A" had not his character been in some respect below standard that lends support to the notion that suicide may be a wrong act because it is done out of cowardice. A distinction needs to be made here between the *rightness* of the act and its moral worth: where the motive of the actor appears to be in some sense reprehensible, we would not call the act a morally *good* act; however, it may still be the *right* act. I can do the right things out of good or bad motives; the motives do not determine the rightness of the act. Thus, assessment of motivation is irrelevant for our purposes here.

26. Cantor [1974:256] argues that governmental interventions into suicide attempts are justified in order to secure help for the individual, since many suicides are the "product of rash, unbalanced, or confused judgments." The intervention of the government will save some who wish to be saved and will only postpone the death of those who are determined to die.

27. And as Kluge [1972:242] suggests, there may be cases in which the individual would *not* be happy later and would regret not having killed herself earlier.

28. "Now we see at once that a system of nature of which it should be a law to destroy life by means of the very feeling whose special nature it is to impel to the improvement of life would contradict itself, and therefore could not exist as a system of nature; hence, that maxim cannot possibly exist as a universal law of nature, and consequently would be wholly inconsistent with the supreme principle of all duty." [Kant, 1873:39]

29. "Act as if the maxim of thy action were to become by thy will a universal law of nature." [Kant, 1873:39]

30. We might point out here that once again this is a place where the definition of the action in question becomes important. The test of universalizability does *not* require that "if I can do A (e.g., kill myself), anybody can do A"; it requires only that "if I can do A for reasons X in circumstances Y, then anybody can do A for reasons X in circumstances Y. Kant's test of universalizability does *not* require that any action taken become a universal law, but that the *maxim* on which one acts become a universal law.

31. The concept of "innocence" in this context is intriguing. Kant [1963:152] suggests that "he who is prepared to take his own life is no longer worthy to live at all." One might ask whether the intention to take an innocent life does not render one "not innocent"; if so, then the person who kills herself is no longer "innocent," and suicide is not the destruction of innocent human life.

32. Kluge's approach seems to us more accurate than Flew's. The identity of the agent alone is not sufficient to settle the moral question of whether murder occurs. For example, take the case of one who kills herself under duress; this act we would not call suicide, but murder, for although agent and victim are the same person, agent acted under duress and thus her right to life was violated. What is at stake is not simply the physical identity of the actor and victim but whether the agent is at one with her act (i.e., to kill herself) or that act being performed upon her (e.g., assisted suicide).

33. To say this is not to deny the value of human life *per se* but to suggest that the meaning of human life goes beyond mere physical existence. We take moral agency and covenant-fidelity as central to the meaning of human life. [c.f., Ramsey, 1970:xii: "covenant-fidelity is the inner meaning and purpose of our creation as human beings."]

34. It is for this reason that Brandt [1975b:69] suggests that suicide is not simply a choice of one's own future but a choice of "world" futures. In choosing to foreclose certain future states for oneself, one also chooses to alter the nature of one's covenantal relationships. Suicide therefore points to the nature of human relationships. The central theological problem raised by suicide is not death *per se*, but abandonment, or breach of covenant-fidelity.

35. Our position here stands in sharp contradistinction to that of Kluge [1975: 121], who claims that suicide is morally justifiable only when the life of the individual is, in her own eyes, "unwanted and unliveable." To say, as we do here, that one's situation is such that one cannot fulfill covenant obligations is not to say that life has ceased altogether to have value or that the remaining life of the individual is "not worth living." An individual may affirm the value of her life and yet choose freely to end it provided that there are no restraining duties.

36. Because of the importance of convenant-fidelity, however, we would agree with Walzer [1975:104] that the concurrence of friends and others with whom one stands in covenantal relationship should be sought.

37. Such acts of symbolic protest should not be labelled irrational: "The broad evidence suggests that those who go on hunger strikes [in jail] are well aware of what they are doing and in fact pursue their course even to the point of death in order to exert pressure on their captors and to witness to something they believe to be important." [Beeson, 1974:836]

38. McCaughey [1967:68] argues that Christians should be cautious about suicide because as Christians they are called to affirm life and resurrections over death and destruction. The kind of suicide described here is precisely such an affirmation. Not all suicide, therefore, is a denial of faith. [Cf., Stein, 1971:216]

39. Though it may be permissible to take one's life in such circumstances, it does not follow that it is obligatory. It is one thing to hold that one always has a right to contribute to the general good of moral agents, but it is not obligatory to give one's life as a contribution. Giving one's life is generally regarded as an act of supererogation not of obligation.

40. Our position is more restrictive than that proposed by Bertram and Elsie Bandman [1975]. They argue that rational persons have the right to decide to live or die, and that only another's right to live outweighs one's right to decide to die. Thus suicide is wrong *only* if another is dependent on one for life itself. This prohibition of suicide is very limited: There are very few instances in which others are dependent on oneself *alone* for their continued existence. The prima facie obligation of covenant-fidelity proposed here encompasses more than the physical survival of one's dependents, and thus the requirements of distributive justice are more restrictive than those proposed by the Bandmans.

41. Thus the argument presented here in no way countenances involuntary euthanasia. For the views of the authors on this subject, see Engelhardt [1975].

42. For example, when a person chooses not to continue renal dialysis, the precaution of one more cleansing of the blood "in to make sure that it is the person and not the uremia talking" is an acceptable precaution against irrational suicide.

43. There is of course a presumption that children are incompetent and thus that intervention is justified. A difficult question is that of deciding when a child or young adult may be considered competent for purposes of making such a decision.

44. Cf., Brandt [1975b:73]: "The moral obligation of other persons toward one who is contemplating suicide is an instance of a general obligation to render aid to those in serious distress . . ." Brandt suggests that this principle is so widely accepted that it can simply be assumed as a premise.

45. It is important to stress here that general beneficence does not constitute a demand of justice for purposes of making this decision. The general welfare of society does not present a claim which can legitimately override the individual's free choice. Just as the needs of society are not sufficient to require that one kill herself, so they are not sufficient to prevent one from doing so.

46. The authors would like to emphasize that this moral obligation is in direct conflict with legal statutes of every state in the United States. American law makes aiding and abetting suicide a felony. It is worth noting that until recently aiding and abetting suicide was not a crime in the state of Texas, see *Sanders* v. *State*, 112 S.W. 68 (Cr App 1908). The authors, after some search, have not been able to find any case indicating an abuse of this freedom. The conflict between moral obligation to at times assist others in committing suicide versus the legal proscription of giving such assistance, indicates the need for the reform of such laws.

47. While we have argued that suicide is not always wrong, we do note that it points to situations in which persons do not find life, liberty and happiness to be mutually supportive. Even the most justifiable cases of suicide, therefore, are *regrettable* insofar as they reflect a departure from the ideal situation in which one would choose freely to live.

48. Perhaps the most obvious exception would be cases of voluntary euthanasia, in which the suicide appears to be a response not to the social environment but to physical distress. Even here, however, the work of Cicely Saunders suggests that for many if not most dying persons, life, happiness, and freedom can be mutually supportive.

COMPULSORY LIFESAVING TREATMENT
FOR THE COMPETENT ADULT

ROBERT M. BYRN*

I. INTRODUCTION

A SIGNIFICANT problem in any discussion of sensitive medical-legal issues is the marked, perhaps unconscious, tendency of many to distort what the law is in pursuit of an exposition of what they would like the law to be. Nowhere is this barrier to the intelligent resolution of legal controversies more obstructive than in the debate over patient rights at the end of life. Judicial refusals to order lifesaving treatment in the face of contrary claims of bodily self-determination or free religious exercise are too often cited in support of a preconceived "right to die," even though the patients, wanting to live, have claimed no such right. Conversely, the assertion of a religious or other objection to lifesaving treatment is at times condemned as attempted suicide, even though suicide means something quite different in the law.

The purpose of this Article is to elucidate the present law and the current trends concerning the question of whether a competent, unwilling adult may be required to undergo lifesaving medical treatment. I begin with a consideration of five cases typical of the situations wherein courts, deferring to rights implicit in the American concept of personal liberty, have given priority to patient choice. In discussing these cases, I have not attempted in this first section of the Article to carry them beyond their facts and the exact language of the courts. Quite the contrary, my goal has been to provide a detailed, rigorous, and conservative critique for it is impossible to project the full sweep of the patient's right to forego lifesaving treatment without a close scrutiny of the situations in which courts have ordered the treatment.

The second section of the Article examines five decisions in which various governmental and private interests have been found sufficiently compelling to overbalance patient choice. Obviously, to the extent that these limiting decisions are valid, they define the extent of patient rights.[1]

---

* Professor of Law, Fordham University School of Law.

1. Since the matter at hand always involves patients who are indisputably alive, the problem of defining death is irrelevant. See Friloux, Death, When Does it Occur?, 27 Baylor L. Rev. 10 (1975); Note, The Time of Death—A Legal, Ethical and Medical Dilemma, 18 Catholic Law. 243 (1972). Also beyond the scope of this Article is the established right of a court of equity to order lifesaving treatment for a minor over parental objection. See People ex rel. Wallace v. Labrenz, 411 Ill. 618, 104 N.E.2d 769, cert. denied, 344 U.S. 824 (1952); State v. Perricone, 37 N.J. 463, 181 A.2d 751, cert. denied, 371 U.S. 890 (1962); In re Vasko, 238 App. Div. 128, 263 N.Y.S. 552 (2d Dep't 1933).

II. THE PARAMOUNTCY OF PATIENT CHOICE: FIVE MODELS

A. *The Right of Bodily Control in a Non-emergency–Prognosis: Poor Without the Treatment*

In *Erickson v. Dilgard,*[2] a competent, conscious adult patient was admitted to a county hospital, suffering from intestinal bleeding. An operation was suggested, including a transfusion to replace lost blood. The transfusion was deemed necessary "to offer the best chance of recovery," in that "there was a very great chance that the patient would have little opportunity to recover without the blood."[3] The patient consented to the operation but refused the transfusion. The superintendent of the hospital, in seeking an order to compel the transfusion, stated that the refusal "represented the patient's calculated decision."[4] Although the patient's refusal was based on religious grounds,[5] the court chose another avenue for its decision:

> The County argues that it is in violation of the Penal Law to take one's own life and that as a practical matter the patient's decision not to accept blood is just about the taking of his own life. The court [does not] agree . . . because it is always a question of judgment whether the medical decision is correct. . . . [I]t is the individual who is the subject of a medical decision who has the final say . . . . [T]his must necessarily be so in a system of government which gives the greatest possible protection to the individual in the furtherance of his own desires.[6]

Erickson has certain distinguishing characteristics. While the odds for surviving the operation were good with a transfusion and poor without it, there is no clear indication in the case of a present threat to life. There was testimony that "an operation was necessary to tie off the bleeding site," but no testimony—at least, the court referred to none—of imminent danger of death.[7] Implicit in the court's opinion is a conclusion that the patient was not *in extremis,* and conceivably might not become so even without the treatment.[8] Furthermore, though the odds for survival were poor, the operation might have proceeded successfully without the transfusion. Whether these conclu-

---

Mandated medical treatment for mental incompetents will be discussed only in so far as it is necessary to distinguish the competent from the incompetent adult patient.

2. 44 Misc. 2d 27, 252 N.Y.S.2d 705 (Sup. Ct. 1962).

3. Id. at 28, 252 N.Y.S.2d at 706.

4. Id.

5. See 33 Fordham L. Rev. 513 (1965).

6. 44 Misc. 2d at 28, 252 N.Y.S.2d at 706.

7. Some have advocated limiting the term "terminal illness" to imminent death because of unexpected remissions. Note, Informed Consent and the Dying Patient, 83 Yale L.J. 1632 n.1 (1974).

8. See also United States v. George, 239 F. Supp. 752 (D. Conn. 1965) where the court contrasted a "precarious" condition with a "critical" one. Id. at 752-53.

sions of the court were medically correct is irrelevant. They are the premises of the opinion.

In the absence of an emergency, the suicide analogy was inapposite. The court was guided by the settled principle that a competent, conscious adult patient has "the final say" on whether to submit to medical treatment. Courts have long and uniformly held that "[e]very human being of adult years and sound mind has a right to determine what shall be done with his own body; and a surgeon who performs an operation without his patient's consent, commits an assault . . . ."[9] The *Erickson* court obviously regarded this right as fundamental—as "necessarily so" in a system of government oriented toward personal freedom.[10]

A natural corollary to *Erickson* is *In re Nemser*,[11] wherein the court refused to order the amputation of the leg of an elderly woman when there was conflicting medical opinion as to whether the amputation would kill, cure, or merely lead to further surgery. Mrs. Nemser's competency was in doubt, but it is clear that if a court will not override patient choice to order relatively minor treatment, such as a blood transfusion, in the face of a poor prognosis, it will not order radical surgery in the face of conflicting prognoses, especially where there is evidence of substantial hazard to the patient.[12]

B. *The Right of Privacy in a Non-emergency—Prognosis: Death Without the Treatment*

In re Yetter[13] presents a case where death was perhaps inevitable, but not imminent. Mrs. Yetter, a sixty year old inmate of a state mental institution, was discovered to have a breast discharge, indicating the possible presence of a carcinoma. A biopsy with corrective surgery, if necessary, was recommended. Mrs. Yetter refused, because she felt that the death of her aunt had been caused by such surgery. "[I]t was her own body and she did not desire the operation."[14] Her brother petitioned for appointment as her guardian so as to consent to the surgery. At the hearing Mrs. Yetter stated that she was afraid of surgery,

---

9.   Schloendorff v. Society of the N.Y. Hosp., 211 N.Y. 125, 129-30, 105 N.E. 92, 93 (1914); accord, Canterbury v. Spence, 464 F.2d 772, 780 (D.C. Cir.), cert. denied, 409 U.S. 1064 (1972); Natanson v. Kline, 186 Kan. 393, 406-07, 350 P.2d 1093, 1104 (1960); Mohr v. Williams, 95 Minn. 261, 268-69, 104 N.W. 12, 14-15 (1905).

10.   See Union Pac. Ry. v. Botsford, 141 U.S. 250, 251 (1891).

11.   51 Misc. 2d 616, 273 N.Y.S.2d 624 (Sup. Ct. 1966).

12.   Erickson is frequently and erroneously cited as authority for the proposition that a patient in extremis will not be compelled to undergo lifesaving medical treatment. But the patient's condition was not critical. In so far as Erickson is concerned, that question remains open.

13.   62 Pa. D. & C.2d 619 (C.P., Northampton County Ct. 1973).

14.   Id. at 621.

that it "might hasten the spread of the disease and do further harm" and that "she would die if surgery were performed."[15]

In fact, her aunt had died from unrelated causes fifteen years after breast surgery, and Mrs. Yetter, after her initial refusal, suffered from delusions concerning her problem. The court, however, found her competent, at the time of her original refusal, to understand and decide the question of the proposed surgery, and concluded that her subsequent delusions were not the primary reason for her rejection of the treatment.[16]

Citing the Supreme Court abortion case, *Roe v. Wade*,[17] the court held:

[T]he constitutional right of privacy includes the right of a mature competent adult to refuse to accept medical recommendations that may prolong one's life and which, to a third person at least, appear to be in his best interests; in short, that the right of privacy includes a right to die with which the State should not interfere where there are no minor or unborn children and no clear and present danger to public health, welfare or morals. If the person was competent while being presented with the decision and in making the decision which she did, the court should not interfere even though her decision might be considered unwise, foolish or ridiculous.

. . . .

There is no indication that Mrs. Yetter's condition is critical or that she is in the waning hours of life . . . . Upon reflection, balancing the risk involved in our refusal to act in favor of compulsory treatment against giving the greatest possible protection to the individual in furtherance of his own desires, we are unwilling now to overrule Mrs. Yetter's original irrational but competent decison.[18]

The reasoning of the *Yetter* court is cloudy in several respects. First of all, although the opinion states as a general proposition that "the right of privacy includes a right to die," subject to circumstances external to the patient which might create a compelling state interest in preventing death, this broad statement is limited by the finding that Mrs. Yetter's condition was not critical. We do not know what the court would have decided in a different case—for example, where a patient in critical condition could be saved by relatively minor treatment. The court recognized that, as a matter of common knowledge, "[t]he ordinary person's refusal to accept medical advice [may be] based upon fear . . . ."[19] The court was prepared to accept, and defer to, this phenomenon. But if the patient were *in extremis,* fear of death from treatment would not ordinarily be a factor in his refusal, for instance, of a blood transfusion which would otherwise save his life.

---

15. Id. at 622.
16. Id.
17. 410 U.S. 113 (1973).
18. 62 Pa. D. & C.2d at 623, 624 (footnote omitted).
19. Id. at 624.

A second and puzzling aspect of the court's opinion is the reliance on "a right to die." Mrs. Yetter did not assert any such right but rather claimed, "it was her own body and she did not desire the operation"—a claim of right not different from that recognized in *Erickson*.[20] In fact, Mrs. Yetter refused treatment precisely because she feared she would die from it. The court may have meant no more by "a right to die" than in the absence of external circumstances establishing a compelling state interest, a competent adult patient is free to reject radical surgery to cure a disease which at some time may prove fatal—particularly when the refusal is based on fear of death, a "commonly known" phenomenon.

The final confusing aspect of *Yetter* is the court's resort to a right of privacy to justify a refusal of medical treatment. This same result could have been reached by invocation of the traditional right of an individual to decide what shall be done with his body, as demonstrated by the numerous tort cases which hold that a patient has a cause of action against medical personnel who perform an operation that the patient has forbidden.[21]

I have elsewhere set forth my opinion on the merits of the Supreme Court's abortion decisions.[22] The specific issue of abortion is not relevant to the discussion here, but because there has been a tendency to expand the right of privacy, expounded in the abortion decisions, into other areas of the law, it is necessary to spend some time discussing the implications of these decisions on compulsory lifesaving treatment. In this context, the discussion is most enlightening when it is directed toward a comparison of the right of privacy with the right to determine what shall be done with one's body.

Probably the most frequently cited statement of the right to control one's body is from *Union Pacific Railway v. Botsford*,[23] where the Court held: "No right is . . . more sacred, or is more carefully guarded, by

---

20. See notes 9-10 supra and accompanying text.

21. Schloendorff v. Society of the N.Y. Hosp., 211 N.Y. 125, 105 N.E. 92 (1914) (operation to remove a tumor, after the patient had specifically forbidden the operation, was an "assault"); Garzione v. Vassar Bros. Hosp., 36 App. Div. 2d 390, 320 N.Y.S.2d 830 (1st Dep't 1971), aff'd, 30 N.Y.2d 857, 286 N.E.2d 731, 335 N.Y.S.2d 293 (1972) (amputation without consent held an assault); Pearl v. Lesnick, 20 App. Div. 2d 761, 247 N.Y.S.2d 561 (1st Dep't 1964), aff'd, 19 N.Y.2d 590, 224 N.E.2d 739, 278 N.Y.S.2d 237 (1967) (radical mastectomy alleged to be an assault); accord, Natanson v. Kline, 186 Kan. 393, 350 P.2d 1093 (1960) (dictum); Woods v. Brumlop, 71 N.M. 221, 377 P.2d 520 (1962) (dictum). Not one of these cases was premised on a right of privacy.

22. See Byrn, An American Tragedy: The Supreme Court on Abortion, 41 Fordham L. Rev. 807 (1973); Byrn, The Abortion Amendments: Policy in the Light of Precedent, 18 St. Louis L.J. 380 (1974).

23. 141 U.S. 250 (1891).

the common law, than the right of every individual to the possession and control of his own person, free from all restraint or interference of others, unless by clear and unquestionable authority of law."[24] But even *Botsford* recognized an exception for the intimate physical examination of a condemned woman to determine if she is pregnant so as "to guard against the taking of the life of an unborn child for the crime of the mother."[25] There are other instances of limitation on bodily inviolability. A stop and frisk may be reasonable though it constitutes "a severe, though brief, intrusion upon cherished personal security."[26] Similarly a person may be required to submit to a vaccination,[27] or a blood sample may be extracted forcibly from the body of an individual arrested for drunken driving.[28]

Neither the right to privacy nor the right to bodily self-determination is absolute. Both give way to more compelling governmental interests. As the Court said in *Jacobson v. Massachusetts*,[29] "[r]eal liberty for all could not exist under the operation of a principle which recognizes the right of each individual person to use his own, whether in respect of his person or his property, regardless of the injury that may be done to others."[30] The right to determine what shall be done with one's own body is limited by the potential of harm to others.

The right of privacy is similarly circumscribed. As already noted, *Yetter* premised its thesis that "the right of privacy includes a right to die" upon the Supreme Court's abortion decision.[31] To the various

---

24. Id. at 251.

25. Id. at 253.

26. Terry v. Ohio, 392 U.S. 1, 24-25 (1968).

27. Jacobson v. Massachusetts, 197 U.S. 11 (1905).

28. Schmerber v. California, 384 U.S. 757 (1966).

29. 197 U.S. 11 (1905).

30. Id. at 26.

31. In Roe v. Wade, 410 U.S. 113 (1973), and the companion case of Doe v. Bolton, 410 U.S. 179 (1973), the Court was faced with constitutional challenges to restrictive state abortion laws. In striking down the laws the Court held, "that the right of privacy, however based, is broad enough to cover the abortion decision; that the right, nonetheless, is not absolute and is subject to some limitations; and that at some point the state interests as to protection of health, medical standards, and prenatal life, become dominant." 410 U.S. at 155. Since the right of privacy is "fundamental," any regulation limiting the exercise of the right must be justified by a "compelling state interest." Id. But some regulation is permitted, and the Court rejected any theory of an absolute right of a woman to terminate her pregnancy "at whatever time, in whatever way, and for whatever reason she alone chooses." Id. at 153. The Court stated, "[i]n fact, it is not clear to us that the claim asserted by some amici that one has an unlimited right to do with one's body as one pleases bears a close relationship to the right of privacy previously articulated in the Court's decisions. The Court has refused to recognize an unlimited right of this kind in the past. Jacobson v. Massachusetts, 197 U.S. 11 (1905) (vaccination); Buck v. Bell, 274 U.S. 200 (1927) (sterilization)." Id. at 154.

compelling state interests centering on the protection of others in society, *Wade* added a paternalistic interest in the protection of an individual against himself or herself. That is to say, the state may forbid an individual to engage in conduct which is hazardous to that individual's life or health. Before examining the specific holding in *Wade* concerning such state power, it is well to note that even this limitation on personal liberty is not without precedent. Statutes requiring motorcyclists to wear crash helmets come most readily to mind. The courts are split on the constitutionality of these statutes and one of the frequently litigated issues is whether a state may enact penal legislation designed not to promote or protect the welfare and safety of others, but to prevent competent adults from engaging in hazardous activities when the adults themselves are fully aware of and completely willing to assume any attendant risks. At least some courts have held such enactments to be a reasonable and valid exercise of the police power.[32] There are other precedents for paternalism in the exercise of the police power. In a case upholding the constitutionality of a statute forbidding the use or handling of snakes in religious rituals, a state court opined, "that the Federal Constitution does not preclude a state from enacting a law prohibiting the practice of a religious rite which endangers the lives, health or safety *of the participants,* or other persons."[33] Similarly in the polygamous marriage case, the Supreme Court in dictum asked rhetorically, "[I]f a wife religiously believed it was her duty to burn herself upon the funeral pile of her dead husband, would it be beyond the power of the civil government to prevent her carrying her belief into practice?"[34]

Given that the Court had decided to create a new "zone of privacy," the citation to Jacobson was to be anticipated. But Buck v. Bell, which upheld the constitutionality of a state statute providing for compulsory sterilization of mental defectives, had been cast in doubt by strong dicta in Skinner v. Oklahoma, 316 U.S. 535 (1942), which struck down as invidiously discriminatory a state statute providing for punishment by sterilization of some, but not all, theft offenders. The Wade Court's revival of Buck is somewhat surprising. Nevertheless both Buck and Jacobson have traditionally been thought of as limitations on the right of bodily self-determination. As a result of Wade, they also are now cast as limitations on the right of privacy indicating that the state's interest in limiting the exercise of both rights for the protection of others in society becomes compelling at the same point and for the same reasons.

32. See Annot., 32 A.L.R.3d 1270 (1970).

33. Lawson v. Commonwealth, 291 Ky. 437, 441-42, 164 S.W.2d 972, 974 (1942) (emphasis added).

34. Reynolds v. United States, 98 U.S. 145, 166 (1878). But see Morrison v. State, 252 S.W.2d 97, 103 (Mo. 1952) ("A religious zealot may have the right to fast until death in the sincere belief that, by so doing, God will be influenced to act positively on behalf of a sinful world . . . ."). More recently, in an obscenity case, the Supreme Court stated, "[o]ur Constitution establishes a broad range of conditions on the exercise of power by the state, but for us to say that our Constitution incorporates the proposition that conduct involving consenting adults only is

There is at least some authority, therefore, for the proposition that personal liberty (whether it be bodily self-determination, privacy, or free religious exercise) is not violated by penal legislation designed to protect individuals from activities which are hazardous to life and limb despite their desire to engage in the activities with full knowledge of the risks. In this respect the *Wade* Court held that protecting the pregnant woman's own health and safety is a sufficiently compelling state interest to justify regulation of abortion after the first trimester, when the danger increases. The Court gave, as examples of appropriate regulation, those dealing with qualification and licensure of medical personnel and abortion facilities.[35] Does the state interest extend further? In taking cognizance of the contention that restrictive abortion laws were enacted originally to protect women, the Court did not assert that these laws were unconstitutional when enacted or that a state may not today bar a dangerous medical procedure. To the contrary, the Court stated, "[t]o restrict the legality of the abortion to the situation where it was deemed necessary, in medical judgment, for the preservation of the woman's life was only a natural conclusion in the exercise of the legislative judgment [that abortion was hazardous to the woman] of that time. A State is not to be reproached . . . for a past judgmental determination made in the light of then-existing medical knowledge."[36] Given its compelling interest in the preservation of the life and health of its people, a state is free to bar an elective medical procedure which is dangerous to life even though, by so doing, the state prevents competent, informed adults from choosing to run the risks of the procedure. Thus, a patient's right of privacy is subordinated in some instances, at least, to the state's paternalistic and compelling interest in preserving his life. The broad statement in *Yetter* that the right of privacy includes the right to die[37] must be read in the light of this state interest.

On the other hand, the crash helmet and snake-handlers cases and the Supreme Court's statements in the polygamous marriage and obscenity decisions[38]—while they colorably support a paternalistic exercise of the police power—are all, nevertheless, couched in a negative way: hazardous conduct may be forbidden or regulated. The cases were not concerned with coercing a competent adult either actively to engage in conduct or to submit to conduct by others in

---

always beyond State regulation, is a step we are unable to take." Paris Adult Theatre I v. Slaton, 413 U.S. 49, 68 n. 15 (1973) (citing such "constitutionally unchallenged laws" as those against suicide and self-mutilation).

35. 410 U.S. at 149-50, 163, 164.
36. Doe v. Bolton, 410 U.S. 179, 190 (1973); see Roe v. Wade, 410 U.S. at 149.
37. See notes 13-21 supra and accompanying text.
38. See notes 32-34 supra and accompanying text.

order to neutralize an existing condition which is a hazard to none but the adult. Indeed, the common law has always been hesitant to impose liability for inaction as opposed to action.[39] And one detects in constitutional decisions in a variety of contexts a sense of uneasiness, an intuition, that a compulsion to act contrary to individual judgment is undesirable when there is no external, compelling state interest to be served and no conflicting private right to be protected.[40]

Wade spoke in terms of prohibiting or regulating action—more specifically the performance of a hazardous medical procedure. The Court did not consider whether the state's interest extended to forcing an unwilling, competent adult to undergo lifesaving treatment for his or her own good. The abortion cases are not determinative of that issue. It cannot be said that the traditional right to control one's body has been subsumed in toto under the right of privacy. The law of compulsory medical treatment is not controlled by *Wade*.

Given that the abortion decisions do not bear on the question, the court in *Yetter* would have been better advised to avoid any reference to them. The governing principle might more aptly have been stated by holding that the traditional right to determine what shall be done with one's body includes the right to refuse lifesaving treatment in a non-emergency, even when the condition may ultimately prove fatal, provided there are no facts in the particular case establishing an external compelling state interest in the continuance of the patient's life.

With the principle so stated, *Yetter* has a certain resemblance to *Erickson*. In both cases the court, deferring to the fundamental right to determine what shall be done with one's own body, gave priority to patient judgment although a reasonable patient might have chosen differently. Each opinion reflects a distrust of medical paternalism.[41] The major distinction in the cases is, of course, the poor prognosis in *Erickson* as opposed to the assumed inevitability of death, albeit remote, in *Yetter*.

The right of bodily self-determination includes the right to reject medical treatment even though the patient's choice means death at

---

39. Binavince, The Ethical Foundation of Criminal Liability, 33 Fordham L. Rev. 1, 11 (1964).

40. E.g., Papachristou v. City of Jacksonville, 405 U.S. 156, 164-65, 170-71 (1972); Board of Educ. v. Barnette, 319 U.S. 624, 640-41 (1943); Fenster v. Leary, 20 N.Y.2d 309, 314-15, 229 N.E.2d 426, 429-30, 282 N.Y.S.2d 739, 744-45 (1967); cf. Union Pac. Ry. v. Botsford, 141 U.S. 250, 251-52 (1891).

41. A reaction against medical paternalism may also be seen in the informed consent cases, e.g., Canterbury v. Spence, 464 F.2d 772, 789 (D.C. Cir.), cert. denied, 409 U.S. 1064 (1972); see Note, Informed Consent and the Dying Patient, 83 Yale L.J. 1632, 1636-39 (1974).

some time in the future. In the next case death was not a remote inevitability. It was an imminent certainty.

C. *The Right of Free Religious Exercise in an Emergency— Prognosis: Death Without the Treatment*

In *In re Estate of Brooks*,[42] the court formulated the following question:

When approaching death has so weakened the mental and physical faculties of a theretofore competent adult without minor children that she may properly be said to be incompetent, may she be judicially compelled to accept treatment of a nature which will probably preserve her life, but which is forbidden by her religious convictions, and which she has previously steadfastly refused to accept, knowing death would result from such refusal?[43]

The recommended treatment was a blood transfusion. For two years Mrs. Brooks had repeatedly informed the physician who was treating her for a peptic ulcer that her "religious and medical convictions" precluded her from receiving blood transfusions and she had gone as far as to release the doctor from liability for failing to give a transfusion. Although she was disoriented when she entered the hospital, the court obviously presumed that her prior competent refusal continued up to the point where the situation became urgent.[44]

Upon petition of her doctor, the state and the county public guardian, a lower court had appointed a conservator (guardian) of the person of Mrs. Brooks and the transfusion was performed before the appeal reached the Illinois Supreme Court. Finding a substantial public interest in a resolution of the controversy despite its mootness, the court held that there was no showing that Mrs. Brooks' exercise of her religious belief "endangers, clearly and presently, the public health, welfare or morals."[45] Lacking such endangerment, the right of free religious exercise predominated. Nor would the court inquire into the reasonableness of the belief underlying the conduct.

Like the right of bodily self-determination, the right of free exercise of religion is not absolute. It gives way to a compelling state interest. But "only those interests of the highest order and those not otherwise served can overbalance legitimate claims to the free exercise of religion."[46]

---

42. 32 Ill. 2d 361, 205 N.E.2d 435 (1965).

43. Id. at 365-66, 205 N.E.2d at 438.

44. Thus, the case is to be distinguished from situations where a present emergency justifies treatment of an unconscious adult under a theory of implied consent, absent evidence that the adult would have refused the treatment if conscious and aware of impending death. See note 64 infra.

45. 32 Ill. 2d at 372, 205 N.E.2d at 441.

46. Wisconsin v. Yoder, 406 U.S. 205, 215 (1972). Although Brooks has been criticized for

Again, however, the distinction must be made between forbidding one from engaging in a dangerous or fatal religious ritual (snake handling or self-destruction) and requiring one to engage in conduct or submit to conduct by others (medical treatment) in violation of religious principles, where the only interest at stake is the health and welfare of the coerced individual. "[W]e must not confuse the issue of governmental power to regulate or prohibit conduct *motivated by religious beliefs* with the quite different problem of governmental authority to compel behavior *offensive to religious principles*."[47] The *Brooks* case, in the view of the court, involved the latter problem, and the court could find no authority in government to compel the behavior.

The *Brooks* principle speaks to emergency situations, but the *Brooks* facts were such that the emergency was over because the patient had already been transfused. The life or death of the patient did not immediately hinge upon the decision of the court. Will a court react differently under such an onus?

On November 14, 1968, the New York Times reported the case of Mrs. Betty Jackson, a twenty-four year old mother of three, who suffered multiple injuries and internal bleeding following an automobile accident.[48] She was admitted to a Long Island hospital at 11:30 a.m., but despite the pleas of her doctors, her husband refused to allow a blood transfusion because both his and his wife's religion forbade it. At 4:30 p.m., a New York State Supreme Court judge denied the hospital administrator's petition for an order compelling the transfusion. Mrs. Jackson died at 6:30 p.m. No doubt the judge was tormented by the knowledge that Mrs. Jackson would most certainly die in a matter of hours without the transfusion—an agony the *Brooks* court did not have to endure. Yet he reached the same result.[49]

Other courts have reacted differently when faced with the same life and death dilemma. In *Powell v. Columbian Presbyterian Medical Center,*[50] Mrs. Powell was dying. She had refused a blood transfusion

---

employing a "clear and present danger" rather than a "compelling state interest" test, 44 Texas L. Rev. 190, 192-93 (1965), it is difficult to imagine that the result would have been different. See Prince v. Massachusetts, 321 U.S. 158, 166-67 (1944). Even the paternalistic interest of the state in the safety of the individual may be a sufficiently compelling interest to support a limitation on the individual's free exercise of religion. See notes 33-34 supra and accompanying text.

47. Abington School Dist. v. Schempp, 374 U.S. 203, 250 (1963) (Brennan, J., concurring) (emphasis in original).

48. N.Y. Times, Nov. 14, 1968, at 23, col. 1.

49. A like decision, with the same fatal consequences, was rendered in Milwaukee in 1972. In re Phelps, No. 459-207 (Milwaukee County Ct., filed July 11, 1972), discussed in Sullivan, The Dying Person—His Plight and His Right, 8 New England L. Rev. 197, 198-200 (1973).

50. 49 Misc. 2d 215, 267 N.Y.S.2d 450 (Sup. Ct. 1965).

that would save her life, for reasons of religious belief, and "[t]here was danger that at any moment such refusal might result in her death."[51] Her husband petitioned for an order compelling the transfusion. The court's agony of decision is apparent:

Never before had my judicial robe weighed so heavily on my shoulders.
. . . .

I knew that no release—no legalistic absolution—would absolve me or the court from responsibility if I, speaking for the court, answered "No" to the question "Am I my brother's keeper?" This woman wanted to live. I could not let her die![52]

The court found a way around the assertion of free exercise of religion by distinguishing between compulsion to act and compulsion to submit to the act of another. "[T]he crux of the problem lay, not in Mrs. Powell's religious convictions, but in her refusal to sign a prior written authorization for the transfusion of blood. She did not object to receiving the treatment involved—she would not, however, direct its use."[53] The court ordered the transfusion. In *Application of President & Directors of Georgetown College, Inc.,*[54] the court went through a similar agony of decision, and arrived at the same conclusion, using, *inter alia*, the argument that the patient objected to consenting to the transfusion—not to the transfusion itself.[55]

Brooks can be profitably compared to *Erickson* and *Yetter*. While *Brooks* was premised on free exercise of religion, *Erickson* and *Yetter* expounded rights of bodily self-determination (mislabeled personal pri-

---

51. Id. at 215, 267 N.Y.S.2d at 451.
52. Id. at 216, 267 N.Y.S.2d at 451, 452.
53. Id. at 216, 267 N.Y.S.2d at 451.
54. 331 F.2d 1000 (D.C. Cir.), cert. denied, 377 U.S. 978 (1964).
55. Id. at 1009. The patients in Powell and Georgetown College, like the patient in Brooks, were Jehovah's Witnesses, a religion which believes that blood transfusions fall within the proscription of several scriptural passages forbidding the "eating of blood."10 Vill. L. Rev. 140 n.1 (1964). The conscientious Jehovah's Witness must refuse a transfusion and resist a court order by all proper and convenient means, but not by violence. If he has done this and done all in his power to nullify the court order, he has not offended God. Id. at 140 n.3. To the extent that Powell and Georgetown College conclude that the respective patients, if transfused, would be guilty of no sin within the tenets of their faith, they seem to be theologically correct. But see In re Osborne, 294 A.2d 372 (D.C. Ct. App. 1972), wherein the Jehovah's Witness patient maintained that he would suffer "a loss of everlasting life" even if the transfusions were forced upon him. Id. at 375. To the extent that these decisions view the plaintiff's lack of spiritual culpability as a valid basis for compelling the transfusion, they are open to question. To interpret the nonviolence of Jehovah's Witnesses as acquiescence is wrong. Not only do they object to consenting to the transfusion, they challenge the right of a court to order it. See United States v. George, 239 F. Supp. 752, 753 (D. Conn. 1965). As Judge Burger intimated in his dissent to the denial of a petition for rehearing in Georgetown College, it may well be that the Georgetown College medical dilemma places in the hands of courts and medical personnel the power to emasculate the right of free exercise by the simple expedient of removing the onus of decision-making from the individual who asserts the right. 331 F.2d at 1017-18 (dissenting opinion).

vacy in *Yetter*) without regard to any underlying religious belief. As in *Erickson*, the objectionable procedure in *Brooks*, though not free from hazard, was relatively simple—unlike the radical surgery in *Yetter*. In neither *Erickson* nor *Yetter* was the situation urgent. Although in *Yetter* the court assumed that death was inevitable without treatment, nevertheless, the court hedged its opinion by noting that Mrs. Yetter's condition was not critical, nor was she in the waning hours of life.

The trend in the law favors *Brooks*. When there are no circumstances establishing a compelling interest in preserving the life of a competent adult patient for the welfare and safety of others, a court will not invade the religious conscience of the patient in compelling submission to medical treatment—even though the patient is in imminent danger of death and the lifesaving treatment is relatively simple and safe.[56]

The *Brooks* decision speaks of free religious exercise in the context of a medical emergency. In the next case, death was imminent, and the patient's objection to treatment was not based on any religious principle.

D. *The Right to Acquiesce in Imminent and Inevitable Death— Prognosis: Death Despite the Treatment*

Mrs. Carmen Martinez, a 72 year old Miami resident suffering from terminal hemolytic anemia, refused "cut down" transfusions and the removal of her spleen. Death was certain without treatment, but she "begged her family not to 'torture me any more' with further surgery."[57] The medical procedures might have prolonged her life, but there was no hope of a cure. In *Palm Springs General Hospital Inc. v. Martinez*,[58] her physician sought guidance as to his obligation to administer the treatment, lest he be accused of "in effect helping her to die."[59] The court ruled that Mrs. Martinez could not be forced to undergo the surgery. She died in less than a day.

Religious objections played no part in the patient's refusal of treatment. She apparently wanted to be left in peace, knowing full well that the disease from which she suffered would inevitably cause death. The court honored her decision, competently made. In so doing,

---

56.   See notes 48-49 supra and accompanying text. See also Holmes v. Silver Cross Hosp., 340 F. Supp. 125 (N.D. Ill. 1972); In re Osborne, 294 A.2d 372, 374 (D.C. Ct. App. 1972). Contra, United States v. George, 239 F. Supp. 752, 753 (D. Conn. 1965); John F. Kennedy Mem. Hosp. v. Heston, 58 N.J. 576, 584, 279 A.2d 670, 674 (1971).

57.   Wash. Post, Jul. 5, 1971, at A10, col. 1.

58.   Palm Springs Gen. Hosp., Inc. v. Martinez, Civil No. 71-12687 (Dade County Cir. Ct., filed July 2, 1971).

59.   Wash. Post, Jul. 5, 1971, at A10, col. 2.

the court confirmed accepted medical practice. As a matter of course, valuable hospital and medical resources are not expended upon a terminal patient who no longer desires arduous life-prolonging treatment which offers, at best, a brief reprieve from death.[60]

It remains to determine what right Mrs. Martinez was asserting when she refused further treatment. The answer is implicit in the language of the court:

> Based upon [her] debilitated physical condition . . . and the fact that performance of surgery . . . and administration of further blood transfusions would only result in the painful extension of her life for a short period of time, it is not in the interest of justice for this Court of Equity to order that she be kept alive against her will. A conscious adult patient who is mentally competent has the right to refuse medical treatment, even when the best medical opinion deems it essential to save her life.[61]

Since the court expressly relied on *Erickson*, there is no doubt as to the right at issue. The right to acquiesce in imminent and inevitable death is no more than a corollary of the right to determine what shall be done with one's own body.

The carefully circumscribed language of the *Martinez* court is a caveat against overextension. The *Yetter* court was wrong in extrapolating a "right to die" from a combination of the irrelevant right of privacy and the relevant right to determine what shall be done with one's body. So too, would it be erroneous to expand the *Martinez* application of the right of bodily self-determination into a broad right to die by whatever means one may choose.

In *Erickson*, *Yetter*, and *Brooks*, the patients, although in varying degrees of danger and asserting different rights, all wanted to live and the recommended treatment promised a cure for their ills. Mrs. Martinez wanted to acquiesce in a death which no treatment could prevent. Next we consider a case in which the patient presumably wanted the treatment which would save his life but another objected.

E. Patient-Implied Consent vs. Next of Kin Nonconsent in an Emergency—Prognosis: Death Without the Treatment

Last November, newspapers in New York City reported the case of one Harry Murray, a critically wounded, unconscious adult, awaiting "a desperately needed operation" while two women argued over which was his wife. One woman consented to the operation and the other

---

60. Sharpe & Hargest, Lifesaving Treatment for Unwilling Patients, 36 Fordham L. Rev. 695, 700 (1968). In accord with Martinez, see In re Raasch, No. 455-996 (Milwaukee County Ct., filed Jan. 25, 1972), discussed Sullivan, The Dying Person—His Plight and His Right, 8 New England L. Rev. 197, 198, 205 (1973).

61. Palm Springs Gen. Hosp., Inc. v. Martinez, No. 71-12687 (Dade County Cir. Ct., filed July 2, 1971), citing Erickson v. Dilgard, 44 Misc. 2d 27, 252 N.Y.S.2d 705 (Sup. Ct. 1962).

refused.[62] Unanimous consent was finally obtained after the hospital sought court permission for the procedure.[63] It is difficult to understand why the consent of the spouse is necessary in such situations.[64] The relationship of husband and wife, without more, does not confer authority to make a binding decision on the administration of emergency lifesaving treatment.[65]

A different question arises when the spouse's refusal to consent expresses the wishes of the unconscious patient. If there is a barrier to treatment, it is the patient's nonconsent, not the refusal of his spouse.[66] Mr. Murray presumably wanted to live and desired the treatment that would heal the condition which threatened him. No third party had a right to interfere.

F. The Five Models: In Sum

The five models are not exhaustive of all situations where the validity of compulsory lifesaving medical treatment for a competent adult may come into issue. They do typify the five situations in which the issue has been raised and in which courts, in the absence of an overbalancing state interest, have given priority to patient choice. The relevant fundamental patient rights—all concomitants of the American

---

62. N.Y. Post, Nov. 19, 1974, at 13, col. 1.

63. Id.

64. There is a universally accepted principle that a present emergency justifies treatment of an unconscious, but previously competent adult, under a theory of implied consent, at least when there is no evidence that the adult would have refused the treatment if conscious and aware of impending death. See W. Prosser, Torts § 18, at 103 (4th ed. 1971); Restatement (Second) of Torts § 62, Illustration 3 (1965); N.Y. Pub. Health Law § 2504(3) (McKinney Supp. 1974).

65. Karp v. Cooley, 493 F.2d 408, 421 (5th Cir.), cert. denied, 419 U.S. 845 (1974); Application of Pres. & Dirs. of Georgetown College, Inc., 331 F.2d 1000, 1008 (D.C. Cir.), cert. denied, 377 U.S. 978 (1964).

66. In Collins v. Davis, 44 Misc. 2d 622, 254 N.Y.S.2d 666 (Sup. Ct. 1964), a wife refused to consent to an operation deemed immediately necessary to save her comatose husband's life. There were no religious objections to the procedure nor was there any indication that the wife's decision was evidentiary of the patient's choice, although the court did distinguish Erickson on the ground that the patient there was at all times conscious. The Collins court, in ordering treatment, made no comment on the efficacy of the wife's refusal but instead stressed the hospital's legal dilemma. See notes 145-61 infra and accompanying text.

N.Y. Pub. Health Law § 2504(3) (McKinney Supp. 1974) provides: "Medical, dental, health and hospital services may be rendered to persons of any age without the consent of a parent or legal guardian when, in the physician's judgment an emergency exists and the person is in immediate need of medical attention and an attempt to secure consent would result in delay of treatment which would increase the risk to the person's life or health." The clear inference is that consent of a third person is required for lifesaving treatment only if the patient is a minor or has a "legal guardian," and even then, only if there is time. No mention is made of a spouse. Unless a spouse's refusal to consent is based on the unconscious patient's own previously expressed desires, it would seem to be irrelevant in emergency situations.

concept of personal liberty—are: (1) the right to determine what shall be done with one's body in *Erickson*, *Yetter* and *Murray*, and its corollary, the right to acquiesce in imminent and inevitable death, as in *Martinez*; and (2) the right of free exercise of religion, in *Brooks*. As we have seen, it is misleading to characterize any of these as a right to die.

As a general rule the exercise of any right may be limited if it conflicts with compelling state interests, at least where there are no less drastic means available to accomplish the state purpose. A consideration of the cases in which a state interest has been held to overbalance the competent adult's decision to forego medical treatment will facilitate a projection, beyond the five models presented, of a more comprehensive set of situations wherein patient choice should be paramount.

III. The Subordination of Patient Choice: Five Models

A. *The State Interest in Preventing Suicide*

Since ignominious burial and forfeiture of goods have been abolished as forms of punishment in the United States, suicide, not being punishable, is not strictly speaking a crime. In some American jurisdictions attempted suicide remains criminal.[67] Even in those states that no longer punish attempted suicide, there is a recognized privilege to use reasonable force to prevent another from committing suicide or inflicting serious harm upon himself.[68] Is it possible to analogize the refusal of lifesaving treatment to an attempt at suicide or self-inflicted injury so that saving action by another is justified?

The answer requires some examination of the common law. From the earliest times, the law of suicide dealt with cases in which an individual *(felo de se)* purposefully set in motion a death-producing agent with the specific intent of effecting his own destruction or, at least, serious injury. Suicide was *malum in se,* the equivalent of murder.[69]

Thus, "in legal acceptation and in popular use, the word suicide is employed to characterize . . . . 'the act of designedly destroying one's

---

67. See W. LaFave & A. Scott, Criminal Law 568-69 (1972). In New York and many states, aiding and abetting a suicide or an attempt is a crime. E.g., N.Y. Penal Law §§ 120.30, 120.35, 125.15(3), 125.25(1)(b) (McKinney 1975); see W. LaFave & A. Scott, supra, at 570-71.

68. See, e.g., Conn. Gen. Stat. Ann. § 53a-18(4) (Ann. 1972); N.Y. Penal Law § 35.10(4) (McKinney 1975); Model Penal Code § 3.07(5) (1962); Comment, Unauthorized Rendition of Lifesaving Medical Treatment, 53 Calif. L. Rev. 860, 869 (1965).

69. Mikell, Is Suicide Murder?, 3 Colum. L. Rev. 379 (1903). "[A]s to the quality of the offence . . . it is in a degree of murder, and not of homicide or manslaughter, for homicide is the killing a man feloniously without malice prepense. . . . And here the killing of himself was prepensed and resolved in his mind before the act was done." Hales v. Petit, 75 Eng. Rep. 387, 399 (C.B. 1562).

own life, committed by a person of years of discretion and of sound mind.' "[70]

When an individual actively inflicts injuries upon himself in an attempt to take his own life, a justification for coerced medical treatment may be that the patient's refusal is an extension of the suicide attempt, and the medical procedures a privileged interference with the attempt.[71] Otherwise, given its elements of active causation and specific intent to end life, suicide would seem to have little application to a competent adult's refusal of lifesaving medical treatment. The confusion of the two probably had its genesis in Emile Durkheim's nineteenth century non-legal definition of suicide, which was predicated on the assumption that an "objective" analysis of ethical and social phenomena could take no account of so "intimate a thing" as specific intent.[72] Durkheim defined suicide as "all cases of death resulting directly or indirectly from a positive or negative act of the victim himself, which he knows will produce this result."[73] Obviously this is not the common law definition. Yet it was the one unwittingly adopted by the court in *John F. Kennedy Memorial Hospital v. Heston*.[74]

Delores Heston, aged 22 and unmarried, was severely injured in an automobile accident. She was taken to the plaintiff hospital where it was determined that surgery and a blood transfusion would be necessary to save her life. She was disoriented and incoherent, but her mother informed the hospital that the patient and the family, as Jehovah's Witnesses, were opposed to the transfusion, but not to the surgery. Upon petition of the hospital, a guardian was appointed to consent to the transfusion. Surgery was performed and the patient recovered.

As in *Brooks*,[75] the highest court of the state rendered its opinion after the transfusion had been administered. In affirming the denial of a motion to vacate the guardianship order, the court observed:

[T]here is no constitutional right to choose to die. Attempted suicide was a crime at common law . . . . It is now denounced [in New Jersey] as a disorderly persons offense.

Nor is constitutional right established by adding that one's religious faith ordains his death.[76]

---

70. Connecticut Mut. Life Ins. Co. v. Groom, 86 Pa. 92, 97 (1878). See also 83 C.J.S. Suicide § 1 (1953).

71. Cf. Myer v. Supreme Lodge, 178 N.Y. 63, 70 N.E. 111 (1904), aff'd, 198 U.S. 508 (1905).

72. E. Durkheim, Suicide 42-43 (1951).

73. Id. at 44 (emphasis omitted).

74. 58 N.J. 576, 279 A.2d 670 (1971).

75. See notes 42-47 supra and accompanying text.

76. 58 N.J. at 580, 279 A.2d at 672.

The answer, of course, is that suicide at common law required a specific intent to die. Miss Heston did not want to die; she did not "claim a right to choose to die," nor did her religious faith "ordain" her death. Had the court resorted to the genuine common law test of specific intent, rather than unwittingly espousing Durkheim's theory, it would have perceived that an indispensable element of common law suicide was lacking.

Having set up the strawman of a "right to die," the court proceeded to knock it down: "Appellant suggests there is a difference between passively submitting to death and actively seeking it. The distinction may be merely verbal, as it would be if an adult sought death by starvation instead of a drug. If the State may interrupt one mode of self-destruction, it may with equal authority interfere with the other."[77] Not only did the court impute a purpose to Miss Heston which she did not have ("an adult sought death"), it also failed to appreciate the second component of common law suicide—that the individual has purposefully set in motion the death-producing agent. Whether in other areas of law his conduct be called misfeasance or nonfeasance, the person who starts out to starve himself to death has no doubt deliberately set in motion the agency of his own destruction. Miss Heston had not. For this reason too her conduct cannot be called attempted suicide.[78]

The court in *Application of President & Directors of Georgetown College, Inc.,*[79] made a mistake similar to that of the *Heston* court. In *Georgetown College* it was said that in states where attempted suicide is not unlawful by statute, the refusal of necessary medical aid is lawful; whereas in states where attempted suicide is unlawful, lifesaving medical assistance may be compelled. "Only quibbles about the distinction between misfeasance and nonfeasance, or the specific intent necessary to be guilty of attempted suicide, could be raised against this latter conclusion."[80] As to the first proposition, the failure to outlaw attempted suicide does not make it lawful in the sense that a right has been conferred. The existence of a privilege to prevent the suicide attempt is conclusive on that point. As to the second proposition, the well-established elements of attempted suicide should not be dismissed by pejoratives like "quibbles" in order to accommodate a non-legal definition.

Both *Heston* and *Georgetown College* are *contra* to *Brooks,* but

---

77. Id. at 581-82, 279 A.2d at 672-73.

78. See generally Ford, Refusal of Blood Transfusions by Jehovah's Witnesses, 10 Catholic Law. 212, 214-16 (1964).

79. 331 F.2d 1000 (D.C. Cir.), cert. denied, 377 U.S. 978 (1964).

80. Id. at 1009.

Brooks represents the trend in the law. In all three cases, the patient undoubtedly wanted to live, and the distinction from suicide—especially considering the patient's religious motivation—is clear. Suicide was also not a problem in either *Erickson,*[81] where the patient wanted to live and the prognosis, though poor, was not of death, or in *Yetter,*[82] where the patient refused treatment because she believed it would cause her death. The active causation and specific intent components of suicide were absent in each case. In *Murray*[83] the patient presumably wanted the treatment. And in *Martinez,*[84] the patient, though willing to acquiesce in the inevitability of early death, did not set in motion the death-producing agency with the specific intent of causing her own death, nor could she have prevented her death by submitting to treatment.

More complex problems arise when one combines and permutes the facts of the five models. Consider the following hypothetical examples:

Patient *A,* an otherwise healthy athlete, requires a leg amputation. Without it he will die, perhaps immediately or at some later time, distinguishing the merely poor prognosis in *Erickson.* The amputation will cure completely the condition that threatens to cause his death, distinguishing *Martinez. A* does not fear the surgery itself, distinguishing *Yetter,* nor does he have religious objections, distinguishing *Brooks.* Nevertheless, he refuses, distinguishing *Murray,* because "I came into life with two legs and I'm going out with two legs."

Patient *B* is paralyzed or otherwise seriously incapacitated by a disease or injury which threatens to cause *B*'s death at some time unless he consents to medical treatment. The treatment will neutralize the condition but will not restore *B* to health. He refuses for no other reason than "I would rather die than live like this."

Patient *C* has a chronic and ultimately fatal disease. Medical treatment will enable him to live and function normally for an unpredictable period of time, but death from the existing condition is inevitable. Knowing that he is doomed by the disease, *C* refuses the treatment solely because, "I would rather go now than live in dread."

Patient *D* is elderly and in a debilitated condition. He suffers from a disease or injury which will cause death sooner or later unless cured or controlled by arduous medical treatment. Although he is a "good risk," *D* refuses treatment because, "I'm too old for all that trouble and it's too expensive for my family."

It may be argued that *A, B, C* and *D* all have chosen to die and

81. See notes 2-10 supra and accompanying text.
82. See notes 13-21 supra and accompanying text.
83. See notes 62-66 supra and accompanying text.
84. See notes 57-61 supra and accompanying text.

that in rejecting treatment, they have, by analogy to the doctrine of avoidable consequences in tort law, become intervening active causes of their own prospective deaths; hence they are attempting suicide.[85] It is submitted that an examination of the rationale of the common law crime of suicide rebuts the argument.

In *Hales v. Petit*,[86] Justice Dyer listed four objections to suicide. First, suicide is "[a]gainst nature, because it is contrary to the rules of self-preservation . . . and then to destroy one's self is contrary to nature, and a thing most horrible."[87] In a modern, right-oriented society, the "unnatural" quality of suicide is translatable into the apparent contradiction inherent in a claim of right to destroy the life from which all rights flow.[88] But it must be apparent that A, B, C and D have not set out to "destroy" or "extinguish" their lives or to "execute" themselves. They do not claim a right of affirmative self-destruction but a right, in a sense, to allow "nature" to take its course. It is not they, but the natural progress of their ills, which will destroy their lives. Their conduct manifests a kind of pacifism, a fatalistic attitude far removed from the "extreme forms of aggression"[89] of the suicidal person who makes war on his own life. Where there is no claim of a right positively to extinguish that from which all rights flow, nor a right to kill *contra* to nature, their conduct is essentially different from suicide.

Secondly, suicide is "[a]gainst God, in that it is a breach of His commandment, *thou shalt not kill.*"[90] In modern law, the commandment finds a modified, secular counterpart in the value placed upon the life of a human being, *qua* human, no matter how burdensome or burdened that life may be.[91] It may be argued, with at least some validity, that actively killing oneself disvalues human life, *qua* human, because it constitutes aggression against life. Suicide treats human life as property which may be destroyed or alienated at the will of the "owner," contrary to the

---

85. "Psychiatric reports indicated the patient showed a lack of concern for life, and a somewhat fatalistic attitude about his condition was described as 'a variant of suicide.' " United States v. George, 239 F. Supp. 752, 753 (D. Conn. 1965).

86. 75 Eng. Rep. 387 (C.B. 1562).

87. Id. at 400.

88. "An executed person has indeed 'lost the right to have rights.' " Furman v. Georgia, 408 U.S. 238, 290 (1972) (Brennan, J., concurring). At the other end of life, the contradiction has been noted in actions brought by a child for "wrongful birth." See Gleitman v. Cosgrove, 49 N.J. 22, 227 A.2d 689 (1967); Williams v. State, 18 N.Y.2d 481, 223 N.E.2d 343, 276 N.Y.S.2d 885 (1966).

89. A. Henry & J. Short, Suicide and Homicide 13 (Free Press ed. 1964).

90. 75 Eng. Rep. at 400.

91. See e.g., In re Weberlist, 79 Misc. 2d 753, 757, 360 N.Y.S.2d 783, 787 (Sup. Ct. 1974); Long Island Jewish-Hillside Medical Center v. Levitt, 73 Misc. 2d 395, 396-97, 342 N.Y.S.2d 356, 358-59 (Sup. Ct. 1973); Blackburn v. State, 23 Ohio St. 146, 163 (1872).

principle that since life is unalienable, one may not be allowed to cause or consent to his own destruction.[92]

Some would argue that refusal of lifesaving treatment cheapens life in the same way, and is indistinguishable from suicide.[93] But *A, B, C* and *D* are not engaged in aggression against life; they are not treating their lives as private property which may be alienated or destroyed at will. Quite the contrary, their claim is to passivity so that life may run its own course. They defer to the vagaries of life. We may disagree with the morality or wisdom of what they choose to do (or more accurately, not do), but it is wrong to say that their conduct undermines society's concept of the inalienability of life. A court, in ordering a lifesaving amputation for an eighty-four year old incompetent, may wisely opine that the concern we express for human life affects the very structure of society. At the same time it can consistently assert that the operation could not have been performed had the patient been competent and unwilling to undergo it.[94]

Thirdly, suicide is "[a]gainst the King in that hereby he has lost a subject . . . one of his mystical members."[95] The common law prerogative of the King has been transformed in American law into an inherent function of goverment. "[T]he care of human life and happiness, and not their destruction, is the first and only legitimate object of good government."[96] As a result, "[t]he life of every human being is under the protection of the law, and cannot be lawfully taken by himself, or by another with his consent, except by legal authority."[97] However, as so expressed, the governmental function of caring for life, and the corollary obligation of protecting it, extend only so far as preventing the active destruction of life.[98] *A, B, C* and *D* are not engaged in actively destroying or taking their own lives.

---

92. Martin v. Commonwealth, 184 Va. 1009, 37 S.E.2d 43 (1946). And this is so whether the act of self-destruction is prompted by the pain of mortal illness or the hurt of emotional despair. Each life, as life, is equally valued. Otherwise, can we assuredly say that recognition of a "right" actively to destroy (devalue) one's own life because it is burdened, will not provide for others, to whom the life is burdensome, a rationalization for its destruction to improve the quality of their own lives?

93. Note, Unauthorized Rendition of Lifesaving Medical Treatment, 53 Calif. L. Rev. 860, 867 (1965); Note, Compulsory Medical Treatment and the Free Exercise of Religion, 42 Indiana L.J. 386, 399-401 (1967).

94. See Long Island Jewish-Hillside Medical Center v. Levitt, 73 Misc. 2d 395, 342 N.Y.S.2d 356 (Sup. Ct. 1974).

95. 75 Eng. Rep. at 400.

96. 16 Writings of Thomas Jefferson 310 (Lipscomb & Bergh 1903).

97. Commonwealth v. Mink, 123 Mass. 422, 425 (1877).

98. See Ford, Refusal of Blood Transfusions by Jehovah's Witnesses, 10 Catholic Law. 212, 225 (1964).

Finally, suicide is also an offense against the King, in that "the King, who has the government of the people, [takes] care that no evil example be given them . . . ."[99] Certainly it remains within the power of government to bar conduct which will encourage suicide.[100] To the extent that any killing invites imitation, active self-destruction may serve as an "evil example" to other susceptible members of society. But it is difficult to conceive how the individual judgments of A, B, C and D to let their lives run their courses will persuade others to seek death. In the experience of one surgeon, a seriously ill patient typically "clings to life."[101] One person's refusal of treatment will not spur others to do the same.

Neither the actual patients in the models in Part II, above, nor the hypothetical patients A, B, C and D were attempting suicide as that term should be properly understood. Nor can interference in the competent adult's decision to forego lifesaving treatment be justified as a paternalistic exercise of the police power. Paternalism, in this respect, should be limited to preventing hazardous or fatal acts.[102]

Because the prevention of suicide and the paternalistic exercise of the police power do not, in general, appear to provide bases for compelling a competent adult to undergo lifesaving medical treatment, we are required to re-examine the breadth and application of the rights which underpin the models in Part II, above. Various questions may be asked. Which right has the patient asserted? Does he want to live or would he rather accept death? Is the risk of death immediate? Is the proposed treatment simple or arduous, hazardous or non-hazardous? Will the treatment merely postpone inevitable death? Will the patient be, or remain incapacitated or mutilated after treatment? Despite the numerous possibilities, the principle is easily stated: Assuming no other external, compelling state interest, a patient's decision to reject treatment ought to prevail in every case, including: (a) where the prognosis is poor although life is not immediately threatened (*Erickson*); (b) where the patient wants to live, although his reasons for rejecting treatment are unreasonable (*Yetter* and *Brooks*); (c) where death is inevitable despite treatment (*Martinez* and patient *C*); and (d) where the treatment is particularly hazardous or arduous, or where the patient

---

99. 75 Eng. Rep. at 400.

100. See Ritter v. Mutual Life Ins. Co., 169 U.S. 139, 154 (1898) (against public policy to include suicide within life insurance coverage).

101. W. Nolen, The Making of a Surgeon 215 (1972). "Resigning oneself to fate is not the same as seeking death. No one I've ever cared for has actually sought death, at least not openly." W. Nolen, A Surgeon's World 280 (1972).

102. See notes 13-56 supra and accompanying text.

will remain seriously incapacitated or mutilated after treatment (patient *D,* patients *A* and *B*).

What then is left? The one situation not covered involves the patient who can be treated relatively easily and inexpensively, without discomfort or hazard, in such a way that the threat of death from his condition will be eliminated, and the patient will not be incapacitated or mutilated. This patient rejects treatment only because he wants to die. Given all the factors, one might argue that the individual has technically become the active cause of his own impending death—like the person who sets out to starve himself to death. It has been said, for example, that the diabetic who refuses to take insulin is attempting suicide.[103] The assertion may be technically correct, but there are substantial practical problems in so labelling the conduct. How do we determine the patient's real motives? Does he truly want to die or is his conduct traceable to some other, albeit unreasonable, motivation like that of Mrs. Yetter? Is he old, debilitated and resigned to an early death, or young, healthy and seeking death? Should we distinguish the two? At what point may the law properly intervene—early or when the situation becomes critical?

Perhaps it is the difficulty of resolving these questions, or the rarity of the case, or both, that have persuaded some judges to make sweeping statements like, "[a]s to an adult (except possibly in the case of a contagious disease which would affect the health of others) I think there is no power to prescribe what medical treatment he shall receive, and . . . he is entitled to follow his own election, whether that election be dictated by religious belief or other considerations."[104]

It is impossible to predict how a court would deal with the last situation. It might never come to judicial attention. Because of the rarity of the case and the overwhelming difficulties of proof, it ought not give us further pause. We can therefore formulate a rule of general application, beyond the specifics of the five models in Part II. I would state it as follows: aside from the individual with self-inflicted injuries resulting from a suicide attempt, a competent adult is free to reject lifesaving medical treatment unless some other compelling state interest overbalances his claim of right. It is as much an error to distort this freedom to include a right to commit suicide, as it is to condemn its exercise as an attempt at suicide. Rejection of lifesaving therapy

---

103. Perr, Suicide Responsibility of Hospital and Psychiatrist, 9 Clev.-Mar. L. Rev. 427, 433 (1960).

104. People v. Pierson, 176 N.Y. 201, 212, 68 N.E. 243, 247 (1903) (Cullen, J., concurring); accord, In re Osborne, 294 A.2d 372, 376 (D.C. Ct. App. 1972) (Yeagley, J., concurring).

and attempted suicide are, and should be, as different in law as the proverbial apples and oranges.

B. *The State Interest in Protecting Incompetents*

In *Long Island Jewish-Hillside Medical Center v. Levitt,*[105] an eighty-four year old man was admitted to plaintiff hospital with a gangrenous leg which, if not amputated, would cause his death. He was a good surgical risk, but vascular disease disabled him from making judgments and decisions concerning his own health. Emphasizing the value of the life of every human being and the necessity of maintaining society's concern for human life, the court ordered the amputation. The decision is reflective of judicial concern that the lives of the elderly, the ill, and the burdensome not be devalued. The state, as *parens patriae,* has a special duty to help the person who is mentally incompetent to make such vital decisions as whether to submit to necessary treatment.[106] This concern for life, along with recognition of the state's duty, has persuaded courts to order substantial surgery under circumstances where, as the court pointed out in *Levitt,* a competent adult's refusal of treatment would be binding.[107]

By definition, an incompetent lacks the ability to choose, so that court-ordered lifesaving treatment is not the subordination of patient choice to a compelling state interest. Nevertheless, *Levitt* is appropriate for consideration of the efficacy of patient choice because it exemplifies the solicitude of the law for the right to live of the helpless. This commendable attitude sometimes unduly influences the position of the court and the medical community when an unconscious or disoriented patient is brought to a hospital in need of emergency lifesaving treatment, and the medical personnel are informed of a prior decision by the individual to forego treatment should an emergency

---

105. 73 Misc. 2d 395, 342 N.Y.S.2d 356 (Sup. Ct. 1973).

106. In re Weberlist, 79 Misc. 2d 753, 360 N.Y.S.2d 783 (Sup. Ct. 1974).

107. When the patient (unlike Levitt) has been adjudicated an incompetent, the obligation of providing necessary medical care falls upon his committee, and the consent of the committee must be obtained. Dale v. State, 44 App. Div. 2d 384, 355 N.Y.S.2d 485 (3d Dep't 1974). If the committee were arbitrarily to refuse to consent, a court, upon application, would undoubtedly order the necessary procedures, using as authority decisions overriding parental rejection of treatment for minors.

Commitment to an institution does not constitute an adjudication of incompetency. If the committed person is factually capable of making a judgment on recommended therapy, courts will treat the patient's decision as one competently made. See Winters v. Miller, 446 F.2d 65 (2d Cir.), cert. denied, 404 U.S. 985 (1971); New York City Health & Hosps. Corp. v. Stein, 70 Misc. 2d 944, 335 N.Y.S.2d 461 (Sup. Ct. 1972). The capability of making this judgment has been defined as "capacity to know and understand the nature and extent of her illness and the consequences of her refusal to consent to . . . treatment. . . ." Id. at 946, 335 N.Y.S.2d at 464.

occur. A conflict exists between the patient's right to reject treatment and the court's *parens patriae* concern for the lives of incompetents, given the usual implication of consent in an emergency,[108] and the fact that the patient's previously expressed objections were not voiced in the face of a real hazard of imminent death.

Since the choice belongs ultimately to the patient, the implication of consent is the key. It is a fiction based not on any conduct of the patient, but on an estimate of how a reasonable man would react under the circumstances.[109] Is the implication destroyed by a previously expressed objection to treatment?

Relevant to this question is the decision in *Application of President & Directors of Georgetown College, Inc.*[110] In *Georgetown College,* Mrs. Jesse Jones, a twenty-five year old woman, was brought to the hospital in imminent danger of death from the loss of two-thirds of her body blood due to a ruptured ulcer. After a district court judge refused to order a transfusion, a circuit judge visited Mrs. Jones in the hospital and told her that she would die without the blood, but that there was a better than fifty percent chance of survival with it. "The only audible reply I could hear was 'Against my will.' "[111] The court concluded, "Mrs. Jones was *in extremis* and hardly *compos mentis* at the time in question; she was as little able competently to decide for herself as any child would be. Under the circumstances, it may well be the duty of a court . . . to assume the responsibility of guardianship for her, as for a child, at least to the extent of authorizing treatment to save her life."[112] Incompetency became another basis for ordering the treatment. It is possible to challenge the court's finding of fact of incompetence since Mrs. Jones' reply to the court's question was entirely consistent with her long-held beliefs as a Jehovah's Witness.[113] But this aside, the court's decision is some authority for the proposition that the previously expressed sentiments of a patient are irrelevant when the patient has become disoriented or unconscious prior to being informed that rejection of treatment will bring imminent death.

Given the patient's fundamental right to reject treatment, the sole function of a court in this situation is to make a good faith finding with respect to what the desires of the patient would have been had he been conscious and competent.[114] Insofar as *Georgetown College* may be

---

108. See note 64 supra.

109. W. Prosser, Torts § 18, at 103 (4th ed. 1971).

110. 331 F.2d 1000 (D.C. Cir.), cert. denied, 377 U.S. 978 (1964).

111. Id. at 1007.

112. Id. at 1008 (footnote omitted).

113. See 113 U. Pa. L. Rev. 290, 294 (1964).

114. See Cantor, A Patient's Decision to Decline Life-Saving Medical Treatment: Bodily Integrity Versus the Preservation of Life, 26 Rutgers L. Rev. 228, 231-32 n.15 (1973).

read to mean that previously articulated beliefs are irrelevant, it would be considered in error. Where: (a) the objections to a particular kind of treatment (for instance, blood transfusion in the case of Jehovah's Witnesses) or to any treatment at all (for example the faith-healing sects)[115] are religiously motivated, (b) the evidence indicates a strong adherence to the tenets of the sect, and (c) there is no countervailing evidence of irresolution, I would urge that the usual implication of consent is destroyed, and the patient's right to reject lifesaving treatment should prevail. In other situations it would be more difficult for the court to determine the desires of the patient. Such variables as the basis, profundity and longevity of the patient's objections, his age and usual state of health, the nature and risks of the treatment, and the likelihood of medical success and return to health will all, no doubt, enter into the court's calculations. Because life hangs in the balance, it seems probable that a court, properly aware of the incalculable value of even the most burdened life, will more frequently decide in favor of the treatment. In any event, the decision must be ad hoc.

A related problem arises when an irreversibly dying patient lapses into unconsciousness. May life-prolonging medical treatment be terminated prior to actual death? *Martinez*[116] does not govern because Mrs. Martinez was competent and capable of personally rejecting the proposed treatment. *Murray*[117] is factually distinguishable because death could be avoided by proper treatment. Yet the two cases do offer some clue to the answer.

Regardless of her objections to further treatment, it seems likely that Mrs. Martinez did not want to be neglected completely. If she were thirsty or hungry or uncomfortable or experienced any of the other usual needs of life, she would expect to be cared for. Neglect would degrade her, and would manifest an inhumane disregard for life on the part of medical personnel.[118] All else aside, to have failed to provide for Mrs. Martinez' routine needs would have been inexcusable. The conclusion should be the same in the case of the unconscious patient.

Mr. Murray presumably wanted to live, but his implied consent is only half of the doctor-patient relationship. The other half is the doctor's duty of reasonable care once he undertakes treatment. What can the irreversibly dying and unconscious patient reasonably expect of the doctor?

115. See Cawley, Criminal Liability in Faith Healing, 39 Minn. L. Rev. 48 (1954).
116. See notes 57-61 supra and accompanying text.
117. See notes 62-66 supra and accompanying text.
118. It is possible that some jurisdictions would find such conduct sufficiently outrageous to give rise to a cause of action for the mental distress caused to grieving relatives. See Rockhill v. Pollard, 259 Ore. 54, 485 P.2d 28 (1971) (en banc); Grimsby v. Samson, 85 Wash. 2d 52, 530 P.2d 291 (1975) (en banc).

Clearly the patient has no right to anticipate the continuation of therapy which will not even prolong life. Blood transfusions in the case of massive, unyielding hemorrhaging may accomplish nothing.[119] There can be no obligation to do that which does not even buy time for the patient. Take the situation one step backwards. Patient E, in the last stages of a fatal and incurable disease, contracts pneumonia. Penicillin might be effective, but it is not administered—"why prolong the agony?"[120] Patient F has had a severe heart attack; his kidneys have ceased to function—an early death is inevitable. After consultation with F's family, F's doctor turns off the kidney machine.

The lives of both E and F might have been prolonged for a short period. Since the legal relationship is between the patient and the doctor, F's family's consent appears to be irrelevant. Further the two cases are somewhat distinguishable in that E's doctor negatively withheld treatment while F's affirmatively turned off the machine. Finally the law presumes a will to live, and the law is particularly solicitous of the helpless. These are the arguments against the physicians' conduct. They are unpersuasive. The majority and best opinion is that the doctors breached no duty, either to the patients (civil liability) or to society (criminal liability) when they ceased treatment of E and F.

It is true, of course, that a doctor or hospital that undertakes the care of a patient may not abandon him.[121] There are several reasons for distinguishing the conduct toward E and F from culpable abandonment.

It has been said that the physician's duty continues so long as the case requires;[122] it is unlikely, under this standard, that discontinuance of life-prolonging measures for E and F would be held a breach of duty because the cases no longer "require" the physician's services.

In addition the physician is held to a duty of ordinary care. To require him to continue futile treatment goes beyond the demands of ordinary care. He is not required to exert his skill or expend his resources in vain. The conduct of E's and F's doctors is properly viewed as an omission to exert skill or expend resources involving no breach of duty because there was no want of ordinary care.[123]

---

119. See W. Nolen, The Making of a Surgeon 270-71 (1972).

120. See id. at 271-72.

121. 1 D. Louisell & H. Williams, Medical Malpractice ¶ 8.08 (1973) [hereinafter cited as Louisell & Williams].

122. Survey, Euthanasia: Criminal, Tort, Constitutional and Legislative Considerations, 48 Notre Dame Law. 1202, 1208 (1973).

123. Editorial, When Do We Let the Patient Die?, 68 Annals of Internal Medicine 695, 696-97 (1968).

Doctors also commonly understand that they are not required to do that which is useless.[124] As a result, it cannot be said that *E*'s and *F*'s doctors' conduct violated the usual standards of good medical practice.[125]

Finally, futile life-prolonging measures sometimes proceed from motives not entirely admirable. One critic alleges that some patients have been kept alive in order to gain experience in the intensive-care treatment of their diseases.[126] The patient becomes a test subject while his family's depleting finances are subtly extorted by the experimenters. An unscrupulous doctor may continue to treat a hopeless case just to earn a fee.[127]

In sum, moralists are generally agreed that there is no obligation to continue lifesaving efforts in a hopeless case, and no decision has been found holding a doctor liable for ceasing treatment under these circumstances.[128] All these factors compel the conclusion that *E*'s and *F*'s doctors did not culpably abandon their patients. It was the disease or injury—not their omissions—which caused death.[129]

---

124. Ayd, Voluntary Euthanasia: The Right to be Killed—Con, Medical Counterpoint, June, 1970, at 12.

125. Louisell, Euthanasia and Biathanasia: On Dying and Killing, 22 Catholic U. L. Rev. 723, 736-37 (1973).

126. Ayd, Voluntary Euthanasia: The Right to be Killed—Con, Medical Counterpoint, June, 1970, at 16.

127. W. Nolen, The Making of a Surgeon 201-02 (1972).

128. Survey, Euthanasia: Criminal, Tort, Constitutional and Legislative Considerations, 48 Notre Dame Law. 1202, 1208-09 (1973).

129. See Fletcher, Prolonging Life, 42 Wash. L. Rev. 999, 1004-16 (1967). Lest this conclusion be misunderstood, let us make some crucial distinctions. First, absent contrary evidence of the patient's own wishes, the medical profession has no right to terminate treatment when the patient's life can be saved. See The Citation, June 1, 1974, at 49 (recounting a decision in Maine ordering medical treatment for a newborn infant who was left to die). Secondly, there is a wide chasm between allowing the irreversibly dying patient to die and killing him. The duty of ordinary care does not require a doctor to engage in an exercise in futility. By the same token, it does not confer a license to kill. "Discontinuing the intravenous feedings and antibiotics, taking away the supports we use to prop up a life, is one thing; doing something to shorten a life is quite another. I have no hesitation about the first; the second is beyond me." W. Nolen, A Surgeon's World 279-80 (1972). The House of Delegates of the American Medical Association adopted the following statement on December 4, 1973: "The intentional termination of the life of one human being by another . . . is contrary to that for which the medical profession stands and is contrary to the policy of the American Medical Association.

"The cessation of the employment of extraordinary means to prolong the life of the body when there is irrefutable evidence that biological death is imminent is the decision of the patient and/or his immediate family. The advice and judgment of the physician should be freely available to the patient and/or his immediate family." Medical-Moral Newsletter, May, 1975, at 17.

C. *The State Interest in Protecting the Medical Profession; the Medical Profession's Interest in Protecting Itself*

In *United States v. George,*[130] the court ordered transfusions for a thirty-nine year old Jehovah's Witness, the father of four, who had refused the transfusions for religious reasons while lucid but in a physically critical condition from a bleeding ulcer. The court adopted "where applicable"[131] the rationale of *Georgetown College,*[132] various aspects of which have already been discussed, and added a further reason:

> In addition to the factors weighed by Judge Wright one consideration is added to the scale. In the difficult realm of religious liberty it is often assumed only the religious conscience is imperiled. Here, however, the doctor's conscience and professional oath must also be respected. In the present case the patient voluntarily submitted himself to and insisted upon medical care. Simultaneously he sought to dictate to treating physicians a course of treatment amounting to medical malpractice. To require these doctors to ignore the mandates of their own conscience, even in the name of free religious exercise, cannot be justified under these circumstances. The patient may knowingly decline treatment, but he may not demand mistreatment.[133]

Certainly there is nothing in professional ethics or plain logic which should require congruence between the doctor's conscience and the patient's choice. By this I do not mean that the doctor is bound by the patient's choice to do something contrary to the doctor's conscience. That is discussed below. I do mean that the patient is not bound by the doctor's conscience to do something contrary to the patient's choice, and consequently the doctor may have the right and choice to do nothing.

The law of informed consent[134] would be rendered meaningless if patient choice were subservient to conscientious medical judgment. Tort cases condemning unauthorized medical treatment as a battery,[135] or, in some instances, if there has been state action, as an invasion of constitutional rights,[136] would have to be overruled. The rule of the supremacy of the "doctor's conscience" finds no real support in law.[137]

---

130. 239 F. Supp. 752 (D. Conn. 1965).

131. Id. at 754.

132. 331 F.2d 1000 (D.C. Cir.), cert. denied, 377 U.S. 978 (1964). See notes 110-15 supra and accompanying text.

133. 239 F. Supp. at 754.

134. See Plante, An Analysis of "Informed Consent," 36 Fordham L. Rev. 639 (1968).

135. See note 21 supra.

136. See Winters v. Miller, 446 F.2d 65 (2d Cir.), cert. denied, 404 U.S. 985 (1971); Holmes v. Silver Cross Hosp., 340 F. Supp. 125 (N.D. Ill. 1972).

137. One would hope, on the other hand, that the ethics of medical practice remain life-oriented, and that the day will not arrive when doctors are forced to destroy life.

Much more difficult is the problem raised by the court's reference to "a course of treatment amounting to medical malpractice."[138] A doctor is not bound to undertake treatment of a patient even in an emergency.[139] Once treatment is undertaken, the doctor owes his patient a duty of reasonable care,[140] which is breached by abandoning the patient.[141] In *Yetter,* it will be recalled that Mrs. Yetter was confined in a mental institution. The court mentioned as a factor in its decision that "the present case does not involve a patient who sought medical attention from a hospital and then attempted to restrict the institution and physicians from rendering proper medical care."[142] But the involuntarily confined are also owed a duty of reasonable medical care.[143] And they may, if competent adults, reject medical treatment unless the demands of institutional security require otherwise.[144] If the duty of care owed by the medical profession to a competent adult patient, in combination with the adult's subsequent rejection of treatment, creates a legal dilemma it is the same dilemma whether the patient is involuntarily confined, or voluntarily seeks medical aid, or is unconscious when brought to the hospital and thereafter becomes lucid.

The dilemma arises in the following way. If unauthorized treatment is administered, the patient has an action for battery or, perhaps, for invasion of his constitutional rights. On the other hand, if the doctor and the hospital fail to treat the patient, they may be civilly liable for abandoning him. Further, a person under a duty to provide medical treatment, whose unreasonable failure to do so causes death, may also be criminally liable.[145] Taking the middle course is also hazardous. The doctor and the hospital might subject themselves to a claim of negligence were they to defer to patient wishes and refrain

---

138. 239 F. Supp. at 754. See Application of Pres. & Dirs. of Georgetown College, Inc., 331 F.2d 1000, 1009 (D.C. Cir.), cert. denied, 377 U.S. 978 (1964); Collins v. Davis, 44 Misc. 2d 622, 254 N.Y.S.2d 666 (Sup. Ct. 1964).

139. Hurley v. Eddingfield, 156 Ind. 416, 59 N.E. 1058 (1901). In the absence of statute or regulation, e.g., N.Y. Pub. Health Law § 2805-b (McKinney Supp. 1974), neither is a hospital, although it has been held that the opening of an emergency facility may be an undertaking to treat those for whose benefit it has been established and who rely on its existence. Annot., 35 A.L.R.3d 841, 846-47 (1971).

140. See 1 Louisell & Williams, supra note 121, ¶ 8.08. If there are no problems of charitable immunity, the hospital may also be liable. C. Kramer, Medical Malpractice 21-27 (rev. ed. 1965).

141. 1 Louisell & Williams, supra note 121, ¶ 8.08, at 217-20.

142. In re Yetter, 62 Pa. D. & C.2d 619, 623 (C.P. Northampton County Ct. 1973). See notes 13-21 supra and accompanying text.

143. Fischer v. City of Elmira, 75 Misc. 2d 510, 347 N.Y.S.2d 770 (Sup. Ct. 1973); O'Neil v. State, 66 Misc. 2d 936, 323 N.Y.S.2d 56 (Ct. Cl. 1971).

144. Runnels v. Rosendale, 499 F.2d 733 (9th Cir. 1974).

145. Application of Pres. & Dirs. of Georgetown College, Inc., 331 U.S. 1000, 1009 n.18 (D.C. Cir.), cert. denied, 377 U.S. 978 (1964). See Annot., 100 A.L.R.2d 483 (1965).

from the forbidden treatment, for example, a blood transfusion, while performing another procedure, surgery, which is rendered more dangerous by the absence of the forbidden treatment, with consequent ill effects to the patient. A release given by the patient in this situation might be questioned on the ground that the patient was not competent at the time,[146] or that the release does not protect against criminal prosecution,[147] or that the release is against public policy.[148]

The conclusions already reached can be of assistance in finding a way out of the dilemma. Since a competent adult has a comprehensive right to reject lifesaving treatment, the liability of the treating institution and the responsible medical personnel is narrowly circumscribed. If the patient rejects treatment entirely, the problem is simplified. His instructions prevail provided that he is competent, or if he is not, that the objections of others truly reflect his wishes and beliefs, so long as there are no compelling state interests which outbalance the patient's rights to the extent that coerced treatment is justified. If there be doubt on these questions, the doctor and the hospital must seek judicial direction on how to proceed in order to protect themselves against liability.[149] Full disclosure must be made, with notice to next of kin who have information on the patient's wishes, lest there be a question of fraud upon the court.[150] Treatment will be administered or omitted as the court directs, and the court's order protects the hospital and the doctor from liability.[151]

Additional and more vexing problems arise when the patient bars only part of the treatment. Must the doctor, on demand of his patient, operate on a ruptured ulcer and, at the same time, withhold necessary blood transfusions? It must be evident that neither a court nor a patient can dictate treatment contrary to reasonable and good faith medical judgment. Even in *Roe v. Wade,* the Court, while holding abortion to be a fundamental right, agreed that "the abortion decision and its effectuation *must be left to the medical judgment of the pregnant woman's attending physician.*"[152] Conversely, the general rule is that the patient's rejection of reasonable treatment relieves the doctor of liability for damages due to the failure to treat.[153] In sum,

---

146. United States v. George, 239 F. Supp. 752 (D. Conn. 1965).

147. Application of Pres. & Dirs. of Georgetown College, Inc., 331 F.2d 1000, 1009 n.18 (D.C. Cir.), cert. denied, 377 U.S. 978 (1964).

148. Cf. 11 U.C.L.A.L. Rev. 639 (1964).

149. See Sharpe & Hargest, Lifesaving Treatment for Unwilling Patients, 36 Fordham L. Rev. 695, 696-97 (1968) (discussing the doubtfully competent patient).

150. Holmes v. Silver Cross Hosp., 340 F. Supp. 125, 131 (N.D. Ill. 1972).

151. W. Prosser, Torts § 18, at 102 (4th ed. 1971).

152. 410 U.S. at 164 (emphasis added). See note 31 supra.

153. Peterson v. Branton, 137 Minn. 74, 162 N.W. 895 (1917); Steele v. Woods, 327 S.W.2d 187, 196 (Mo. 1959)

the doctor cannot be forced to treat contrary to prudent medical judgment and the patient is bound, at risk of relieving the doctor of future liability, to accept reasonable medical treatment; it follows that the doctor ought to be able to withdraw from the case without liability. It has been held that a patient's refusal to follow the reasonable instructions of his doctor is a defense to a claim of abandonment.[154]

What of the hospital's liability in these circumstances? The hospital's duties are, in general, "to furnish the patient with diligent and skillful care, competent attendants and safe equipment."[155] Even if the patient's doctor is not a hospital employee, the hospital may be liable to the patient if aware of conduct by the doctor which is clearly contradictory to normal practice.[156] But since the patient has rejected the reasonable recommendations of a competent doctor, it cannot be said that the hospital has breached any of these duties. However, if the patient is in a precarious condition, he ought not be discharged by the hospital lest the discharge become a contributing factor to subsequent death or injury.[157] The conclusion from all the above is that neither the doctor nor the hospital is required to undertake a course of treatment contrary to good medical judgment. The surgeon need not operate on the bleeding ulcer if the patient rejects the necessary transfusion.

But suppose the surgeon does operate? He may decide that because the patient will certainly die without surgery, he ought to proceed even without the transfusion. Under these circumstances the additional risks must be explained to the patient. If the patient consents, he assumes the risk.[158] If the patient becomes disoriented or unconscious prior to the explanation being given, he cannot, of course, assume the risk. As suggested above, doubts as to competency must be resolved judicially.

The medical dilemma is a real one only in so far as it requires

---

154. Roberts v. Woods, 206 F. Supp. 579, 584-85 (S.D. Ala. 1962). Indeed, the patient may be deemed contributorily negligent for failing to follow instructions. 1 Louisell & Williams, supra note 121, ¶ 9.03, at 246 n.25.

155. C. Kramer, Medical Malpractice 24-25 (rev. ed. 1965). In those jurisdictions which no longer distinguish between "medical" and "administrative" acts of hospital employees, the hospital will be liable for the malpractice of its employees under a respondeat superior theory. Id. at 23-44.

156. Fiorentino v. Wenger, 19 N.Y.2d 407, 414-15, 227 N.E.2d 296, 299-300, 280 N.Y.S.2d 373, 377-79 (1967).

157. C. Kramer, Medical Malpractice 25 (rev. ed. 1965). Patients, apparently in extremis, have been known to recover even without the recommended treatment when the hospital continues with indicated supportive treatment. See, e.g., In re Osborne, 294 A.2d 372, 376 n.6 (D.C. Ct. App. 1972).

158. 1 Louisell & Williams, supra note 121, ¶ 9.02 (1973).

judicial resolution of such possibly disputed questions as competency or the existence of some overbalancing state interest, and only to the extent that some courts yet fail to appreciate that a competent adult has a right to reject lifesaving treatment, and that neither the doctor nor the hospital is required by even a dying patient's choice to act contrary to reasonable medical judgment.

In view of the numerous possibilities for liability, doctors and hospitals will, and prudently should, continue to seek judicial determination of their duties whenever a patient in precarious condition refuses lifesaving treatment—with the possible exception of a *Martinez* situation[159] where honoring the patient's wishes is fairly well-accepted in principle and adhered to in practice. Criticism of the medical profession for resorting to the courts[160] is unfair. If there is an issue of competence the court is best equipped to resolve it. If the patient's right to refuse treatment, and his willingness to sign a release, render the controversy nonjusticiable for lack of any danger of liability, let the court say so.[161]

When all is said and done, the medical dilemma is a problem of judicial fact-finding and resolution of doubts, not a substantive reason for disregarding patient choice.

D. *The State Interest in Protecting Minor Children*

In *Georgetown College,*[162] the court gave as a further reason for ordering the transfusion: "[t]he patient, 25 years old, was the mother of a seven-month-old child. The state, as *parens patriae,* will not allow a parent to abandon a child, and so it should not allow this most ultimate of voluntary abandonments. The patient had a responsibility to the community to care for her infant. Thus, the people had an interest in preserving the life of this mother."[163]

One author found two separate alleged state interests in this statement: (a) prevention of psychic harm to the child by loss of the parent and (b) prevention of economic harm to the state by the child's becoming a public charge.[164] It has been held that a pregnant woman

---

159. See notes 57-61 supra and accompanying text.

160. E.g., In re Nemser, 51 Misc. 2d 616, 273 N.Y.S.2d 624 (Sup. Ct. 1966).

161. See Application of Pres. & Dirs. of Georgetown College, Inc., 331 F.2d 1000, 1015 (D.C. Cir.) (Burger, J., dissenting on denial of rehearing), cert. denied, 377 U.S. 978 (1964). Effective mechanisms are available for an expeditious and thorough inquiry and resolution. See, e.g., In re Osborne, 294 A.2d 372 (D.C. Ct. App. 1972).

162. 331 F.2d 1000 (D.C. Cir.), cert. denied, 377 U.S. 978 (1964). See notes 110-15 supra and accompanying text.

163. 331 F.2d at 1008.

164. Cantor, A Patient's Decision to Decline Life-Saving Medical Treatment: Bodily Integrity Versus the Preservation of Life, 26 Rutgers L. Rev. 228, 251-54 (1973).

may be compelled to submit to a blood transfusion, contrary to her religious beliefs, when the transfusion is necessary to perserve the life of her unborn child.[165] In *Yetter*[166] and *Brooks*[167] the courts were careful to point out that no minor children were involved. In *George,*[168] the court adopted *Georgetown College*.

Without disputing *Georgetown College*, a few courts have modified it. It has been argued: "[a]t best the State's interest in preserving two spouses to care for their children instead of one seems attenuated; one wonders if it would be a stronger interest if a sole surviving parent's life were at stake, so that public guardianship of the minors became an imminent reality."[169]

The state's interest is even more in doubt, it has been urged, when the surviving parent is in accord with the patient's decision and willing to provide for the child alone.[170] Perhaps this reasoning persuaded a court to decline to order lifesaving transfusions for a twenty-four year old mother of three whose husband conveyed to the court the family's religious objection to such treatment.[171]

At least within these limitations it would seem that the "minor child" interest of the state does limit the right of a competent adult to reject lifesaving treatment. Whether the rule will survive remains to be seen. It will, perhaps, be put to its ultimate test if the *parens patriae* interest is asserted in a situation wherein it is the disability, rather

---

165. See Byrn, An American Tragedy: The Supreme Court on Abortion, 41 Fordham L. Rev. 807, 844-49 (1973). It may be true that it is a quantum leap from this situation to Georgetown College. It may also be true that the economic justification is somewhat undermined by a case like Montgomery v. Board of Retirement, 33 Cal. App. 3d 447, 109 Cal. Rptr. 181 (5th Dist. 1973) wherein it was held that disability benefits may not be denied a recipient who refuses, for religious reasons, to undergo corrective surgery. Finally, some might agree that the dangers of psychic harm to the child and depletion of the public fisc are, respectively, speculative and de minimis. Nevertheless, no court has directly taken issue with the Georgetown College parens patriae approach.

166. See notes 13-21 supra and accompanying text.

167. See notes 42-47 supra and accompanying text.

168. See notes 130-33 supra and accompanying text.

169. Sharpe & Hargest, Lifesaving Treatment for Unwilling Patients, 36 Fordham L. Rev. 695, 697 (1968).

170. 113 U. Pa. L. Rev. 290, 294 (1964).

171. See N.Y. Times, Nov. 14, 1968, at 23, col. 1. In In re Osborne, 294 A.2d 372 (D.C. Ct. App. 1972), the court refused to order a transfusion of a thirty-four year old man whose wife agreed with his decision and "who had, through material provision and family and spiritual bonds, provided for the future well-being of his two children." Id. at 375. In Holmes v. Silver Cross Hosp., 340 F. Supp. 125 (N.D. Ill. 1972), the court denied a motion to dismiss a complaint for violation of constitutional rights in the administration of a blood transfusion under color of law. The patient had a wife and young child, but "we presently do not have sufficient information on the status of these dependents, whether their sole support came from the decedent [patient] . . . ." Id. at 130.

than the death of the parent that is threatened, or where the unwilling patient, asserting a religious objection to lifesaving treatment, does not share the Jehovah's Witnesses' abhorrence of physical resistance to the mandated procedure.

E. The State Interest in Protecting Public Health

Jacobson v. Massachusetts[172] involved a challenge to the validity of a conviction under a state statute authorizing a fine for an adult who "refuses or neglects" to be vaccinated as required by the statute.[173] The court found defendant's claim of an "inherent right of every freeman to care for his own body"[174] to be overbalanced by the interest of the state in the protection of its inhabitants from a dangerous, contagious disease.[175]

The state interest in protecting the health of others in the community clearly justifies compulsory medical procedures to neutralize the danger of contagion from potential carriers of disease. In an unusual case the treatment may also save the life of one already infected and in danger of death. The purpose, however, is not to save the patient's life but to prevent the spread of the disease. Very little controversy surrounds the power of the state to compel lifesaving treatment in such cases.

F. The Five Models: In Sum

It would seem that only the state interests in the welfare of the minor child,[176] and the protection of the public from communicable disease[177] may be said, with colorable legal basis, to impinge upon the competent adult's freedom to reject lifesaving medical treatment.[178]

IV. CONCLUSION

This Article is not a morality play. By no means did I set out to judge whether, in the scenario of a particular case, the patient's choice to forego treatment was ethically defensible. I have attempted only to

---

172. 197 U.S. 11 (1905).

173. Id. at 12.

174. Id. at 26.

175. Id. at 24-31. "The right to practice religion freely does not include liberty to expose the community . . . to communicable disease . . . ." Prince v. Massachusetts, 321 U.S. 158, 166-67 (1944) (dictum). The state interest in preventing or arresting an epidemic must not, however, be confused with unauthorized human experimentation on the victim of the disease.

176. See notes 162-71 supra and accompanying text.

177. See notes 172-75 supra and accompanying text.

178. In a particular disciplinary setting, such as jail custody, it is possible that patient choice to forego lifesaving treatment might validly be subordinated to custodial authority. "Allegations that prison medical personnel performed major surgical procedures upon the body of an inmate, without his consent and over his known objections, that were not required to preserve his life or further a compelling interest of imprisonment or prison security, may foreshadow proof of conduct violative of rights under the Fourteenth Amendment sufficient to justify judgment under the Civil Rights Act." Runnels v. Rosendale, 499 F.2d 733, 735 (9th Cir. 1974).

discover the law and its trends. From an examination of these I deduce the following:

First: Every competent adult is free to reject lifesaving medical treatment. This freedom is grounded, depending upon the patient's claim, either on the right to determine what shall be done with one's body or the right of free religious exercise—both fundamental rights in the American scheme of personal liberty. There is no "zone of privacy" involved.

Second: The patient's freedom of choice, like all fundamental freedoms, may be subordinated to a compelling state interest at least when there are no less drastic means available to effectuate the interest.

Third: Interference with the patient's right cannot be justified either by a claimed state interest in preventing suicide or by a paternalistic exercise of the police power. Rejection of lifesaving medical treatment, except for injuries self-inflicted in an active attempt by an individual to destroy his own life, is not an attempt at suicide. However, one cannot extrapolate a right to commit suicide from the patient's freedom to reject lifesaving medical treatment. For this reason alone it is misleading to characterize the patient's freedom as a "right to die."

Fourth: The state has a *parens patriae* interest in protecting incompetents. But the disorientation of a patient ought not be used as an excuse to thwart his objection to, and rejection of, medical treatment.

Fifth: The "medical dilemma" is neither a substantive state interest justifying coerced medical treatment nor a problem of balancing conflicting personal rights. It is merely a matter of judicial resolution of doubts on such issues as patient competency. Protection of the medical community against liability requires that doctors and hospitals have free access to the courts and expeditious direction on how to proceed whenever a patient in precarious condition rejects lifesaving treatment. But under no circumstances may medical personnel be required to engage in procedures which are contradicted by reasonable medical judgment.

Sixth: In the present state of the law, lifesaving medical treatment may be compelled to further governmental interests in preventing the spread of communicable disease and in protecting the spiritual and material welfare of minor children. As to the latter, it is possible that the interest becomes attenuated when one parent would survive and is willing to care for the child, or where the child's needs have otherwise been provided for.

Reported cases on compulsory treatment are relatively rare. Newspaper accounts of such cases are frequent enough to indicate that the problem, if not pressing, at least requires clarification. Such has been the end and aim of this Article.

SUICIDE AND EUTHANASIA

Germain Grisez

1. INTRODUCTION

Many attacks upon the moral permissibility of suicide and the legalization of euthanasia involve assumptions which are easily rejected. For example, sometimes a religious believer attacks these practices on the authority of his own religious tradition; a nonbeliever can brush aside such an argument. However, one can oppose suicide and euthanasia on strictly philosophical grounds.

One can argue that suicide is morally wrong simply because one should not directly destroy the basic human good of the life of a person, and that euthanasia should not be legalized, because even voluntary euthanasia is morally wrong and there are good reasons why *this sort* of morally wrong act should be a crime.

Those who defend the moral permissibility of suicide and the legalization of euthanasia must answer such a philosophical argument with an argument of their own. They admit that the life of a person ordinarily is a basic human good; there is a *prima facie* moral rule against killing people.

However, they claim that there are several generally accepted exceptions to this rule. Most people admit that one may bring about one's own death by laying down one's life in testimony to one's faith (martyrdom) or by acting courageously to save another from death (heroism). No one holds that people are morally obliged to use every possible means to prolong life; if one omits or discontinues the use of an available means one surely contributes to the causation of one's death. Most people admit that one may bring about another's death in some cases of individual self-defense and also in certain cases of social self-defense (capital punishment and war).

Killing oneself or another—the argument in defense of suicide and euthanasia proceeds—is justified in such unusual cases provided that the act of killing is rationally necessary. Killing is rationally necessary if it is the lesser of two or more evils, or if the act of killing brings about some good which outweighs the evil of death. More stringent moral requirements thus can override the *prima facie* obligation to respect human life. To deny this position would be to claim that life must be treated as the highest good, a good so great that the evil of its destruction is worse than any other evil.

However—proceeds the argument of those who defend suicide and euthanasia—even if human life is a basic good, mere life is not an absolute good. Life is a necessary condition for consciousness in which personal and interpersonal values are realized. But mere biological life is only a condition for what is truly personal in a human being. If respect for life is allowed to interfere with the protection or attainment of personal goods, then right order is upset. The merely instrumental good of life should not block action for the intrinsic values of the person.

Moral responsibility—the argument continues—requires one to take into account all factors in the situation in which one acts, and to do what is best all things considered. If one is inhibited in acting by some moral absolute, and if due to this inhibition one produces a state of affairs less good than one could produce, then one is morally at fault.

The argument in defense of the moral permissibility of suicide concludes that it is sometimes morally permissible and even rationally necessary to kill oneself in order to preserve and foster intrinsic personal values. Since suicide can be morally right, one can have a moral obligation to assist another who desires to die.

Voluntary euthanasia—its proponents argue—can violate no one's right to life, for a right is not violated if the person who has the right willingly gives up what the right protects. Then too, if it is morally right that a person's life be terminated, such a person has no right to life which can be violated. Society must foster life, but it also must respect other rights and promote the common welfare.

Besides—those who urge the legalization of euthanasia argue—it is cruel to compel persons who are suffering greatly and who would freely choose death to go on living simply to maintain an absolute legal prohibition of homicide. It is a sound, general libertarian principle that the freedom of all members of society to do what they believe right in their own affairs ought to be respected. Furthermore, many physicians now break the letter of the law and will go on doing so if it is not amended to permit what is becoming a more and more widely accepted practice. The freedom of physicians also ought to be respected.

Then too, there is a class of individuals, including but not necessarily limited to severely defective infants, whose lives seem to many proponents of euthanasia to lack the quality which alone makes life worth living.

The argument for the legalization of euthanasia concludes that society ought not to interfere with the right of individuals to end their own lives or with the duty of others to aid them in this good deed.

In what follows, I argue that suicide is immoral and that euthanasia should not be legalized. In my argument, I deal with the case just summarized for the position which I reject.

In section two, I define the act of committing suicide in a way which distinguishes it from other acts by which one brings about one's death. In section three, I argue that the claim that other goods sometimes outweigh the good of life is meaningless. In section four, I argue that the good of human life is an intrinsic good of the person, not merely an instrumental good. In section five, I argue that it is always wrong to act against such goods intrinsic to persons. In section six, I argue that although not every immoral act should be a crime, euthanasia ought to be a crime.

2. DEFINITION OF SUICIDE

Most people do admit that martyrs and heroes can bring death upon themselves without thereby committing suicide. Also, most people do admit that sometimes individuals may blamelessly contribute to the causation of their own deaths by omitting the use of available means to prolong life. Those who argue for the moral permissibility of suicide think these admissions amount to exceptions to a *prima facie* moral rule against killing. Assuming that the rule already has several exceptions, why not make additional exceptions?

A clear definition of the moral act of committing suicide will not answer this argument, but it will help to answer it. Most people who consider suicide immoral do not classify as suicides martyrs, heroes, and those who draw a reasonable line beyond which they will not carry efforts to prolong life.[1] A proponent of the permissibility of suicide might argue that such cases are not classed as suicides simply because "suicide" means "the wrongful killing of oneself." But this is not so. A definition of the moral act of committing suicide will make clear that many suicides are not morally wrong, because they are not moral acts at all, while some self-destructive acts other than suicide surely are morally wrong.

The reluctance of most people to call "suicide" every act which brings about one's death is not arbitrary nor is it based upon a moral dividing line. This . eluctance rather reflects the insight that suicide is a human act, and that as such it is defined by what one is *doing*, not simply by what one is *causing*.

One does a moral act of suicide if and only if one brings about one's own death by an action which one chooses as a means to an end which one expects will be served by one's dying or by one's being dead.

In this definition, the expression "moral act" does not mean an act which is morally *good*, but an act which is morally *significant*—that is, an act which counts morally as good or as bad.

An end is served by an action if a desired good is realized or its realization promoted—for example, by being rendered more probable—or if a feared evil is forestalled or mitigated. The relation of one's action to the end need not obtain in reality; it is sufficient that the agent expect that his act will serve the end he has in view. The suicidal act always is chosen as a means; no one regards dying or the condition of being dead as an end in itself.

The suicidal act need not be a deed; it can be an omission if the omission is proposed as a method of killing oneself.

If one does not succeed in bringing about one's own death, one does not commit suicide. If the other conditions are given for a moral act of suicide but one accidentally fails to bring about one's death, one has attempted to commit suicide.

The action by which one brings about one's own death can be consent to a deadly deed upon oneself by another; if the other conditions are given, such consent is sufficient for suicide, and the act can be called "assisted suicide."

The definition I have proposed of the moral act of suicide will be clarified further by the following considerations bearing upon the meaning of "an action which one chooses." One chooses an action only if one deliberates about what one could do, and in the course of deliberation proposes to oneself two or more alternative possible deeds and/or omissions between or among which one settles upon a single deed or omission as the possibility to be carried out.

Deliberation begins when the spontaneous course of behavior is blocked. One is aware of a conflict. One could act this way or that, but any possible course of action will be unsatisfactory in some respects in which an alternative would be satisfactory. One's interests or purposes have incompatible implications; no possible course of action which one can think of will be entirely satisfying. One is aware that one must consider each of the two or more possible courses of action which suggest themselves, and then make up one's own mind what one will do. The consideration of possibilities is *deliberation*; the making up of one's mind which terminates deliberation is *choosing a course of action.*

As one deliberates, one takes into account many sorts of facts. One is aware of one's own powers and their limits. One also is aware of the states of affairs apart from oneself which facilitate but also limit what one can do. One is aware not only of the relevant present, but also of the relevant and likely future. For example, one thinks about some of the consequences which are likely to follow from the carrying out of each alternative one is considering. Taking facts into account is part of the process of deliberation, but not its distinctive feature. Statements about these facts are *descriptive* statements. One might consider these facts in a merely *theoretical* frame of mind.

What is distinctive about deliberation is that factual observations take on a more than theoretical interest as they are organized by their relevance to practical *proposals*. One proposes to oneself the possible courses of action from which one will choose what one will do.

In the case of suicide, the proposal to kill oneself is among the proposals one considers in deliberation and this proposal is settled upon by the choice which terminates deliberation.

For example, a person who for some reason is suffering greatly might think: "I wish I no longer had to suffer as I am now suffering. If I were dead, my suffering would be ended. But I am not likely to die soon. However, *I could kill myself.* But I also want to live. *I could put up with my misery* for a while longer, and perhaps find another way out." One thinking in this way is deliberating. In saying to oneself "I could kill myself," one proposes suicide. If the alternative thus proposed is chosen and carried out, one commits suicide.

In saying to oneself "I *could* kill myself," one is not merely observing a possibility which might or might not be realized. "Could" here means more than causal contingency. It does express one's capacity to cause one's own death. But it also expresses the practical possibility of using this capacity; it projects the use of this capacity in a context in which one thinks its use requires only one's own choice to use it. "I could kill myself" is a *proposal* that one should act in a certain definite way. If one adopts this proposal by choice and executes the choice by action, then one's action is in reality precisely what one proposed in deliberation.

One can propose to kill oneself without saying to oneself "I could kill myself." One might say something *which one would accept* as equivalent in meaning: "I could destroy myself," "I could rub myself out," "I could end it all," "I could put myself to sleep permanently," or something of the sort. Again, one might say something *which one would accept* as amounting to "I could kill myself" although not equivalent in meaning to it, such as "I could shoot myself" when what one has in mind is shooting oneself in the head and thereby causing death, not merely shooting oneself in the leg and causing a wound. In a more subtle case, an individual might propose an omission, such as "I could refuse to accept this medical treatment," and if it were pointed out: "By refusing this treatment, you will be killing yourself," might reply: "That is precisely what I have in mind."

This last example begins to bring out the subtlety of defining suicide in terms of suicidal choice and clarifying the latter in terms of what one *proposes* in deliberation. If a proposal to kill oneself is adopted by choice and this choice is successfully executed, many people would say that one's bringing about of death, one's dying, and one's being dead are "deliberate," "voluntary," and "intentional." Hence, such language often is used in defining "suicide" in an effort to distinguish the moral action of committing suicide from actions of other kinds which also make some causal contribution to one's own death.

There is a sense of such expressions in which they might be used to define the moral act of committing suicide. For example, there is a sense in which what one intends when one chooses a course of action is precisely what one proposed to do when in deliberating one articulated the possibility which one adopts by choice. However, words such as "deliberate," "voluntary," and "intentional" have various meanings; in most of their uses, as a few examples will show, they do not clearly mark out the relevant distinctions.

An individual who has had several operations for cancer and who is not hopeful about the possibilities of greatly prolonging his life by additional surgery, upon noting the recurrence of symptoms which suggest that he should see his physician, might deliberate and articulate the following possibility: "I would like to avoid further painful treatment. *I could ignore these symptoms.* If they indicate a recurrence of the disease, it is of course likely to kill me sooner than if I seek further treatment at once. But my agony would be prolonged by any further attempt to extend my life." Such an individual *observes* the probable consequence of omitting to go to the doctor: that he is likely to die sooner than if he does go.

Because of this observation, many people would say that if he chooses to omit further treatment, he is deliberately, voluntarily, or intentionally contributing to the causation of his own death. But such an individual is not unreasonable if he thinks that his adoption of the proposal to ignore the symptoms is not a choice to kill himself, for *as he understands this proposal* it is neither equivalent in meaning to nor does it amount to "I could kill myself."

The preceding example suggests a clarification of the distinction drawn in Roman Catholic moral teaching between "ordinary" and "extraordinary" means of medical care. This distinction is not descriptive.[2] It need have nothing to do, for example, with the distinction between the natural and the artificial. Nor is this distinction reducible to the one physicians make between what is required by the common standards of medical practice and what exceeds these standards.[3]

I think that a means should be called "ordinary" in a moral sense if one who is deliberating in a reasonable and careful way would take a proposal to omit this means as amounting to a proposal to kill the person in need of care. Thus, if it is always wrong to adopt a proposal to kill a person, it is by definition always wrong to neglect ordinary means of care. It can also be wrong to neglect extraordinary means of care if this neglect is understood as a way of killing or of carrying out some other wrongful proposal.

The concept of "deliberating in a reasonable and careful way," used in the preceding paragraph, is too complex to explore fully here, but it certainly requires that rationalization and self-deception be excluded, that facts be considered, that advice which would throw light on the facts be sought, that logical fallacies be avoided, that so far as possible ways of thinking which generally lead to truth be followed, and that an effort be made to find alternatives besides those which come easily to mind.

Another example of a kind of action which contributes to the causation of an individual's death but which is not an act of suicide is the typical martyr's laying down of his or her life. Such a person—of whom St. Thomas More is a good example—reasons as follows: "I would like to please everyone and I would like to stay alive. But they are demanding that I do something I believe to be absolutely wrong, something which would involve compromising a principle which should not be compromised. So I propose to refuse to do what is demanded. Of course, they are likely to kill me." Such a person proposes only to refuse to do what he believes is wrong.

Others, especially if they do not understand his reasoning, are likely to say that the martyr is deliberately, voluntarily, or intentionally bringing an end to his own life. However, he does not propose to kill himself. He is on firm ground in thinking that what he does propose—to refuse to do what he believes wrong—is not equivalent to and does not amount to a proposal to kill himself. The first persons for whom the martyr bears witness to his belief are his persecutors; they are free to accept this testimony and in the martyr's view they ought to accept it. Thus, the martyr's refusal to give in does not *bring about* the act of his persecutors, which results in the martyr's death. The martyr only fails to win over his persecutors and thus to forestall their deadly deed.

The case of the typical martyr must be contrasted with that of a person who does propose to kill himself or herself as a means of serving some end in view. A virgin, for example, might propose to kill herself in order to forestall violation. The adoption of such a proposal clearly is a suicidal choice.

Similarly, a war-protestor might propose: "I wish to make clear the horror of this war. *I could* douse myself with gasoline and *set myself afire.*" An individual considering this proposal might well admit that it amounts to a proposal to kill himself. If so, the execution of the choice would be a moral act of suicide. If the individual did not admit the proposed demonstration to be suicide, the reasonableness of his deliberation could be questioned.

For example, if someone claimed this sort of demonstration would not amount to self-destruction but only to an emphatic communication similar to that of the typical martyr, it would be fair to ask whether a like communication could not be made without this deadly deed. If so, why was this proposal adopted? Is it not precisely the horror *of such a manner of dying* which is expected to make the desired point? If so, the proposal is to kill oneself in the service of peace.

The definition which I have given of the moral act of suicide will help not only to clarify why certain self-destructive acts are not suicidal but also why many suicidal acts are not regarded as morally wrong even by those who maintain that a moral act of suicide is never morally justifiable. Many suicidal acts are not moral acts of suicide either because they are not moral acts at all, or because they are moral acts which execute some choice other than a suicidal choice.

A person who is suffering psychological stress—even though not mentally ill—can reach a point at which deliberation and choice become impossible. Perhaps the thought of suicide has recurred over and over again, and the proposal has been rejected each time it has come to mind. But at some point the possibility of a deadly deed against oneself can become obsessive. Without one's own choice, every other possibility is excluded from awareness. One can think only: "*I will kill myself.*" A person in such a state is not necessarily insane and in some sense can be said to be acting "deliberately," "voluntarily," and "intentionally." But the deadly deed executes no choice; such a person acts without adopting a proposal to treat his life as an expendable means to some other end.

Someone with an intimate knowledge of suicidal thinking —whether that knowledge is based upon introspective experience or upon close study of others—is likely to object that the foregoing vastly oversimplifies the confusion in the mind of an individual who is about to commit suicide. I agree. But my purpose here is not to describe the complex phenomena of suicidal thought and action.[4]

Perhaps unconscious determinants of behavior play as large a role as conscious ones in the genesis of the deadly deed. Certainly, people often engage in behavior which has self-destructive potential without being conscious of it. Moreover, even when one is conscious of what one is doing, one's action can be ambiguous. For example, an individual who proposes "I could take the pills" might not be sure whether the pills are deadly or not, and might not be clear whether the proposal amounts to "I could kill myself" or only to "I could make them see how desperate I am."

None of this complexity and confusion is excluded by the definition of suicide which I have given. The function of a definition is to show what is involved in a paradigm case, and to indicate how borderline cases arise and how they are to be understood. My definition of the moral act of suicide and my distinction of such an act from a suicidal act which does not execute a choice apply to clear-cut cases. By calling attention to what is involved in these cases, I also try to clarify why so many cases of suicide are existentially ambiguous and to suggest how ambiguous cases are to be understood—namely, by reference to what the one performing the deadly deed *proposed and adopted* (in morally significant acts) or *projected and executed* (in suicidal acts wholly determined by factors other than one's own choice).

Some suicidal acts execute choices which are not suicidal choices. One might believe that some fundamental principle to which one is already committed demands that one here and now kill oneself; one might have integrated this principle so completely that one proceeds without deliberation and choice to do what seems necessary. For example, a person who believes in God might be convinced that God is commanding that he kill himself. Given a sufficiently blind faith, such an individual might not think of disobeying. Similarly, persons in some cultures in which ritual self-destruction is expected in certain situations perhaps carry out the ritual without considering any alternative to compliance with received customs. In cases like these, the morally relevant choice is not in respect to suicide, concerning which no choice is made at all, but is a commitment to the fundamental principle—for example, the religion or the culture—which now requires such behavior.

Certain nonsuicidal acts which bring about one's own death would be held to be morally wrong by most people, including many who think that a moral act of committing suicide can be morally right. For example, a daredevil might accept very high risks of death carrying out deeds which do not involve great skill or other noble qualities. He might do this simply in order to create a sensation by pandering to morbid curiosity, hoping in this way to acquire considerable wealth with little effort. He might very much desire to survive to enjoy his wealth. If he dies, he has not committed suicide. But I think that most people would regard such risk-taking as immoral.

Actions of this sort must be distinguished from moral acts of committing suicide which are executed by means which have a limited probability of success. For example, the proposal to play Russian Roulette is a proposal to kill oneself conditioned only upon something—which chamber the bullet is in—wholly outside one's knowledge and control. Simply because the bullet *happens* not to be in the chamber, the Russian Roulette player cannot claim that the proposal to play did not entail a proposal to kill himself. The daredevil differs in that he accepts *risk* to his life for the sake of an end which will be served only if he survives.

Finally, even if one neglects to obtain or refuses to accept medical treatment upon a proposal which does not amount to one's killing oneself, still such neglect or refusal could be morally wrong. For example, an individual who has a special and very great obligation to prolong his life might be morally blameworthy if he refused to use available means, even though he might refuse those means only to avoid the pain of the treatment itself, not to kill himself. In a case of this sort, those who use the terminology of "ordinary" and "extraordinary" means might say that the patient has an obligation to use extraordinary means.

In sum. A moral act of committing suicide involves the execution of a suicidal choice, and a suicidal choice is the adoption of a proposal to kill oneself or of a more specific proposal which amounts to this. This definition is not simply a reflection of the received moral judgment upon suicide. However, the definition does make clear why most people wish to distinguish between suicidal acts and other sorts of acts which contribute to the causation of one's own death. Thus, the clarifications I have provided in this section show that there is no inevitable inconsistency or arbitrariness in the position of those who maintain that the moral act of suicide is always wrong, and yet who admit the permissibility of certain deeds and omissions which in fact contribute to bringing about one's own death.

3. CAN OTHER GOODS OUTWEIGH LIFE?

No one holds that the continuation of a person's life—on any terms and under any conditions is the supreme human good. This is evident because no one holds that every human life must be prolonged as much as possible, no matter what the cost; likewise, no one holds that every other good must be subordinated to bare survival. Thus, even those who maintain that every act of committing suicide which is morally significant at all is morally evil agree that it can be right to act—as do martyrs, heroes, and those who draw a reasonable line beyond which they will not go in efforts to prolong life—for other goods to the detriment of the good of life.

From these facts those who argue in defense of the moral permissibility of suicide draw what they think is a logical conclusion: The good of human life can be outweighed by other goods of the person, goods such as the quality of life, personal dignity, well-being, and happiness. The good of human life, they add, can be outweighed by other goods even in some cases in which one is deliberating about a proposal to kill oneself. In such cases, they conclude, the moral act of suicide is permissible and even indicated.

Further, those who defend the moral permissibility of suicide argue that those who hold that suicide is always wrong are unreasonable. Absolute opponents of suicide, they assert, must defend one of two implausible theses: (1) the value of mere human life always outweighs the personal values involved in any alternative to a proposal to kill oneself, or (2) the adoption of such a proposal remains wrong even when it involves a lesser personal evil or yields a greater net personal value than any alternative. The first of these theses is implausible because it seems to imply that life—which admittedly is not the supreme good in cases where self-sacrifice and letting oneself die are permissible—suddenly becomes the supreme good in every case which would require the adoption of a proposal to kill oneself. The second of these theses is implausible because it seems to imply that human values, which are the goods of persons, must be subordinated to an impersonal moral rule prohibiting suicide. But, the defenders of suicide argue, it cannot be wrong to choose the alternative which would be most fruitful in personal goods.

I hold that the moral act of committing suicide is always wrong. I do not hold that "mere life" is the supreme human good. I do not say that the good of life always—*or ever*—outweighs other personal goods. Nor do I defend the second implausible thesis, which pits morality against the good of persons. In my view, which I sketch out in section five, human goods do ground the norms by which a morally upright person acts. How, then, do I avoid the conclusion that suicide is justified when the good of life is outweighed by other goods? I avoid this conclusion by denying the assumption that various human goods *are measurable and commensurable,* that they *can be weighed and balanced against one another.*

The defense of the moral permissibility of committing suicide rests on a general theory of moral judgment. This theory, which I call "consequentialism," claims that the truth of a moral judgment is its conformity to a fact. For example, the truth of the moral judgment that one ought to commit suicide in a given case might be said by a consequentialist to rest upon the fact that a greater net human value will be achieved or preserved in that difficult situation if one adopts the proposal to commit suicide than if one adopts any alternative proposal.[5]

In general, consequentialists maintain that a moral judgment refers to the comparative value in a state of affairs which can be achieved or preserved by means of human acts.

Some versions of consequentialism are direct; they locate the preponderance of value which justifies an action in each particular act and its consequences. Other versions of consequentialism are indirect; they look to the consequences of accepting some rule or other principle by which particular acts will be judged. Again, some versions of consequentialism are pure; they admit no moral obligation which cannot be justified by consequentialist arguments alone. Other versions of consequentialism are mixed; they hold that some moral obligations can be justified only by using some nonconsequentialist principles.

All versions of consequentialism fail in the same way. But for the sake of simplicity, in what follows I do not mention indirect and mixed consequentialism. The interested reader will be able to apply what I say about direct and pure consequentialism—which often is called "act consequentialism" or "act utilitarianism"—to more complex versions of this theory.

Likewise, I will use expressions such as "preponderance of value" and "greater good" to refer to any outcome of the weighing and measuring of values and disvalues which any version of consequentialism considers sufficient to justify a choice. Thus "greater good" includes "lesser evil," and refers as well to any other comparative value which any consequentialist proposes as the truth-condition of moral judgment.

Given these clarifications, the defense of the moral permissibility of suicide can be restated as follows. When one is making a moral choice, one ought to choose that alternative by which one expects to bring about the greater good. The choice and execution of the proposal to kill oneself can be expected to bring about the greater good in certain difficult situations—for example, if the only alternative is a slow, miserable, and undignified process of dying. Hence, in such cases one ought to commit suicide.

I contend that this argument suffers from a concealed logical fallacy. Either "greater good" is used in different senses in the two premises or it is not. If it is, then the argument is invalid because of equivocation. If it is used in the same sense in both premises, then "greater good" either is used in a sense which presupposes and includes *moral* goodness, or it is used in a sense which can be specified without invoking prior moral principles, *or it is used ambiguously in both premises*.

If "greater good" is taken in both premises in a moral sense, then everyone will agree with the truism that one ought to do what is morally good. But only those who defend the moral permissibility of suicide will grant that this act is at times good. In other words, understood in this way, the argument is question-begging.

This brings us to the second possibility: "Greater good" in the premises of the argument must be taken in a sense which can be specified without invoking prior moral principles. As a matter of fact, those who use this argument usually accept this alternative. They hold that "greater good" is defined in terms of human goods such as quality of life, personal dignity, well-being, and happiness. They claim that these goods—which they regard as the ultimate goods of human persons and communities—can be defined apart from moral considerations. They regard these goods as pre-moral or nonmoral goods, not as inferior to moral goods but rather as superior to them. For the consequentialist, the goods on which all morality depends must be like moral goods in being human and personal but must be prior to moral goods, for the latter only lead to and serve these ultimate values.

I grant that "greater good" can be used meaningfully in extramoral contexts provided that one is interested in measuring the relative value of means to a specific, nonmoral objective. Some mouse-traps are better than others for catching mice. Some routes are better than others for getting to a specific destination. For carrying out any specific task, some techniques are better than others. Some generals are better than others at winning wars, and some politicians are better than others at achieving any particular, peacetime goal. But in all such cases, the *moral* rightness or wrongness of adopting the particular objective as one's own remains an open question. A better H-bomb is not necessarily a weapon for which there is any morally acceptable use whatsoever.

The consequentialist proposes to draw an ethical conclusion from premises in which "greater good" can have only a nonmoral or premoral sense. Logically, as I shall show more fully below, the consequentialist cannot succeed. He is trying to deduce a moral "ought" from a comparison of values which is a mere "is" so far as morality is concerned. He is trying to derive prescriptions for acts from descriptions of facts.

There remains only one possibility: The consequentialist is committing a logical fallacy, but one which is concealed. It is concealed by equivocation upon "greater good." This equivocation is not between one premise and the other in a consequentialist argument. Rather, "greater good" in consequentialist arguments must bear two incompatible meanings *at the same time*. Such arguments appear valid because the ambiguity is the same throughout. However, a consequentialist argument's exigence that "greater good" bear at once two incompatible meanings altogether deprives the expression of meaning.

If I can establish this thesis, it has the following relevance to the argument about suicide. If I am right in thinking that "greater good" in the consequentialist argument for suicide loses all meaning, then when I argue that suicide is always wrong I need maintain neither that life is man's supreme good nor that morality requires one to subordinate a greater to a lesser personal good.

The consequentialist simply takes for granted what I maintain to be impossible: that one can balance nonmoral goods against one another and that one can make an estimate of preponderant value which is relevant to moral judgment.

The consequentialist is assuming that if one maintains that the good of human life may not be subordinated to other personal goods, then one must maintain that the good of "mere" life is the *highest* human good. But if "greater good" is meaningless, this assumption is false.

My rejection of the consequentialist's assumption rests not only on the maxim that "ought" cannot be derived validly from "is," but also on the following considerations which make clear the sense of this maxim and its relevance in the present argument.

I agree with consequentialists on one very important point. Moral judgments primarily bear upon possible courses of action and direct one to adopt some proposals rather than others. One makes a moral judgment as to what one ought to do when one is considering what one could do. Thus, moral judgments can shape one's action only when one is deliberating.

Deliberation begins when one experiences a conflict of desires or interests.[6] One is aware of incompatible possibilities, such as either acting or refraining from action. Something in oneself draws one to each of the alternatives. The conflict makes one stop and think. Each alternative is somehow attractive, but none promises complete satisfaction: If only one had some previously established principle which clearly dictated that one alternative had to be carried out, one would have no need to make a choice. But when one is aware of no such unquestionable assumption, one feels that a choice must be made. One finds oneself in a practical impasse; deliberation is a quest for a way out. One deliberates, considering the advantages and disadvantages which probably would follow from the adoption of each proposal.

While one is deliberating, one regards alternative proposals as genuine possibilities. Any of the proposals under consideration could be adopted. One expresses this possibility by saying to oneself: "I could adopt this alternative, and then again I could adopt that one." As I explained in section two, this "could" expresses a *practical* possibility. One is projecting a use of one's capacity in a context in which one thinks its use requires only one's choice to use it. Thus, a person who deliberates is aware of alternative proposals for action and he thinks that he can and must settle among these alternatives. "The choice is mine and I must make it," one says to oneself.

If some possibility did not appear good in any respect at all, that possibility would be of merely theoretical interest. Only what seems good can become a practical proposal which must be chosen or rejected. The proposal which is adopted at the end of deliberation is chosen precisely for the sake of the good which kept it in the running to the end. Hence, when one has made a choice, one always can give a reason for one's choice by citing the good for the sake of which one adopted this alternative.

Now, the consequentialist holds that the goods involved in each alternative are commensurable, and that a person ought to adopt that proposal which promises the greater good. But this "ought" is vacuous if it is impossible to choose any other alternative. Let us suppose that a person makes a consequentialist moral judgment and acts upon it. By hypothesis, such a person *does* adopt the proposal which promises the greater good, but he *could* instead have adopted an alternative proposal promising measurably less good. The question is: How could anyone knowingly choose the lesser good?

Whether or not one is a consequentialist, a choice by a person of an alternative known to promise a lesser good would be puzzling indeed. One might suppose that the wrong choice is made by mistake. But this supposition does not help the consequentialist, for he holds that the morality of one's actions is determined by one's conformity to one's actual appraisal; moral evil is not merely an honest error in computation. One also might suppose that the wrong choice is made due to the influence of unconscious factors upon choice. However, this supposition also is no help to the consequentialist, for he offers his theory as a method of intelligent adjudication between values and disvalues which he claims can be rationally measured and compared in deliberation.

Therefore, the consequentialist must maintain that one *could* purposely adopt a proposal which promises less good than an alternative proposal which one *should* adopt. But there is never any reason for choosing the alternative which one does choose except the good it promises. If one alternative promises a measurably greater good than any other, a person who is deliberating has all the reason for choosing the alternative promising the measurable greater good that he has for choosing any other, and he has the further reason for choosing the former provided by the extra good it promises.

Thus, given the commensurability demanded by the consequentialist's theory of moral oughtness, no one can purposely prefer the lesser good. The reason for choosing the greater good would be not merely a good reason but a sufficient reason. Hence, one *could not* purposely adopt any proposal other than that which the consequentialist says one *should* adopt. But this implies that no one can do moral evil. Yet consequentialism is advanced as a theory of moral judgment, and a theory of moral judgment must leave open the *possibility* of wrong choices.

Someone might object that the foregoing argument presupposes that choices are free, and that this supposition is question-begging against consequentialists, who can reject free choice and defend some form of determinism or compatibilism. As a matter of historical fact, many famous consequentialists have rejected the libertarian conception of choice; Bentham, Mill, and Sidgwick are examples, and others easily come to mind. Many such consequentialists base their determinism on a psychological theory of motivation according to which one always chooses in accord with the stronger motive. This theory involves the same assumption as consequentialism: that prospective goods are commensurable. Psychological determinists and consequentialists often use the same analogy—that of the balance scale. The greater good or the stronger motive tilts the balance to one side.

I do think that people can make free choices.[7] However, my present argument does not presuppose *freedom* of choice. All I need for the present argument are the *phenomena* of deliberation and choice. Someone like Mill who is both a psychological determinist and a consequentialist holds both that one necessarily chooses the greater good and that one ought to do so. The two positions are incompatible. If the goods promised by alternative proposals were commensurable, then one could pursue the greater, but one would have no choice about it, and so it would be senseless to say that one ought to choose the greater good.

In fact, choices are possible, for "greater good" has no definite meaning *antecedent to* the choice which ends the perplexity which gave rise to deliberation. The goods promised by different proposals are diverse and incommensurable. Thus one can and must choose, and the consequentialist's advice to adopt the proposal which promises the "greater good" is meaningless; anyone who is deliberating is uncertain where the "greater good" lies. Even if one's practical perplexity, one's belief that one can and must resolve such perplexity by choice, and one's feeling that one chooses freely are all illusions caused by determining conditions of which one is not aware, still the two requirements—that one be able to know the greater good and that one be able to choose the lesser—cannot be simultaneously met. But both of these requirements are essential to consequentialism for they are implicit in saying that one *ought* to choose the greater good.

Someone might object that it must be possible to know what is better and yet choose what is worse, for such perverse choice is at the heart of immorality on any account of it, non-consequentialist as well as consequentialist. I grant that one can know what is morally *better* yet do *what is* morally worse. What is bad from a moral point of view can be good—and a greater good—from some other perspective. Moral goodness and the good one is tempted to prefer to it simply are incommensurable, until one renders them commensurable after choosing one or the other, by stipulating as one's standard the mode of goodness which rendered interesting and eligible the proposal one adopted.

When the consequentialist argues for the moral permissibility of suicide—or of any other kind of action—in certain situations, he considers the possibilities in the light of his own prior commitments. These prior commitments need not have involved adopting any proposal for his own conduct, but might have involved condoning the act of another. Moreover, these prior commitments need have had nothing directly to do with suicide, but they have had sufficient bearing upon the various goods involved in the proposal to kill oneself and its alternatives that the consequentialist has assigned a definite weight to each of these goods allowing him to compare them one with another.

Thus the consequentialist is confident that he knows what is the "greater good." But "greater good" here means only the "good which anyone with my commitments would prefer." Nevertheless, the consequentialist wishes his judgment to be a *moral* one, to express an objective criterion which any reasonable person should accept. So while the consequentialist means by "greater good" the good anyone like him would prefer, he also wishes this expression to mean the "good which any unprejudiced person ought to prefer."[8]

In sum. The consequentialist aspires to provide an objective norm of morality. But he succeeds in proposing a merely subjective standard. A moral standard is required only when choice is possible. But whenever a choice is possible, "greater good" is meaningless unless one good is stipulated to be greater than another. Whenever "greater good" does have a definite meaning, one for whom it has this meaning has no choice to make. If he tells someone else who does have a choice that he ought to choose the greater good, this advice fails to convey any intelligible guidance, for it can mean no more than "Choose as I would choose."

That consequentialism is not really a workable method of moral judgment is confirmed by several familiar objections against it.[9] If consequentialism were meaningful, one making a moral judgment as it directs would need a way of defining and measuring human goods. He also would need an objective way of delimiting possibilities, of drawing the line in the investigation of consequences, and of determining whose interests should be considered.

A consequentialist talks in vague language of the "quality of life," "personal dignity," "well-being," "happiness," and the like. Such expressions are well suited to commend one's own preferences, but they hardly lend themselves to the measurement suggested by the analogies of weighing and computing, which are implicit in "greater good." In the mouth of a consequentialist, "quality of life" means whatever he is ready to accept as sufficient to justify an attack upon "mere" life. It is notorious in ethical theory that no one ever has produced a workable method of computing so-called "utilities," such as enjoyments or desire-fulfillments. Still, this insoluble problem is treated as if it were a mere technical difficulty. Commensurability is held as an article of consequentialist faith.

Similarly, only prior commitments delimit the possible alternatives to be considered and the extent to which inquiry into consequences is to be pressed. Very often, the consequentialist considers no alternative to the action he seeks to justify except not acting at all. Ordinarily, he considers consequences only up to the point at which his view seems to gain some intuitive plausibility.

For example, a consequentialist defending the moral permissibility of assisted suicide in order to assure "death with dignity" discusses none of the range of choices open even to a dying person—to curse, to pray, to jest, to moan, to think of this or that. Nor does he discuss the much wider set of alternatives open to the individual who proposes to serve "dignity" by doing the deadly deed. Instead, the only possibilities seriously entertained are to kill or not to kill. And usually only one consequence of omitting to kill is considered: "useless suffering and the prolongation of *mere* life."

In considering whose interests are to count, the consequentialist usually opts for absolute impartiality. An egoistic option obviously would lack objectivity; impartiality between egoism and altruism (in theological consequentialists, "Christian love") gives consequentialism an appearance of moral objectivity. However, absolute impartiality is no better a moral standard than is egoism.

With respect to suicide, the implications of complete impartiality are serious. For if the consequentialist thinks that it is morally permissible to take one's life for the sake of one's own greater good, the logic of his method compels him to hold that it can be morally obligatory to take one's life for the sake of the greater good of another or of society at large. The inference from permissibility to obligation follows on consequentialist principles because the only right choice is the one which adopts the proposal which will yield the greater good; any other choice is not merely a less admirable moral option but a morally wrong option. The inference from one's own greater good to the greater good of another or of society at large follows on consequentialist principles because impartiality (or "Christian love") excludes as immoral any general preference of one's own interests to the interests of others.

In sum. The consequentialist who defends the moral permissibility of suicide in some situations seeks to justify this choice, but in his attempted justification the consequentialist adopts a perspective in which one will seem to have no choice but to take this course of action. The consequentialist says that sometimes the greater good is promised by the proposal to kill oneself, and that in such a case one *ought* to adopt this proposal. But no one can rationally choose what is measurably less good, and so if the consequentialist were correct about the "greater good," one could not help choosing as he says one ought to choose.

4. IS HUMAN LIFE AN INTRINSIC GOOD OF THE PERSON?

Those who defend the moral permissibility of suicide might admit that consequentialism is meaningless and that goods are incommensurable. Still, they will object, any ethical theory must admit a radical distinction between those fundamental goods which are intrinsic to persons and those goods which are merely instrumental—for example, all the things money can buy. Such instrumental goods, in due measure, are necessary for the flourishing of persons. But wealth and property must serve persons; persons must not become slaves of their possessions. Likewise, the objection concludes, mere human life is only an instrumental good.

If "mere" life is only an instrumental good, then no doubt it should be subordinated to the goods intrinsic to persons. But I maintain that the life which is destroyed when one kills oneself is not only a necessary condition for consciousness but also one of the intrinsic goods of a person.

In saying that human life is *not only* a necessary condition for consciousness, I do not deny that life *is* a necessary condition for consciousness. Like other personal goods, such as theoretical truth and genuine friendship, human life is prized for its indirect as well as for its direct contribution to the flourishing of persons. But life can be and often is valued for its own sake, without reference to other personal goods. The same cannot be said of merely instrumental values.

Most people fear death; very few ever deliberately adopt a proposal to kill themselves. The ordinary person is perplexed if he is asked why he fears death or why he does not kill himself. The goodness of life and the evil of death are too obvious to need explanation or to be susceptible to it. The great masses of people throughout history, and probably the majority of people today, devote most of their energy and concern to the simple project of maintaining their own lives and the lives of their children. Only a few of us enjoy a degree of affluence such that we can take "mere" life for granted.

But if life is threatened by an accident or an illness, we quickly return to fundamentals: "If only my loved one survives"; "I would give anything to regain my health."

Jews and Christians traditionally endorsed and reinforced the common human valuation of life. Life and death are the great symbols of good and evil; the hope of salvation is for life and more abundant life; the wages of sin are mortality and eternal death.[10] Jews and Christians did not consider human life is a mere extrinsic condition of personal goods, for they believed the human person to be a *living body*. Commenting upon St. Paul's teaching on the resurrection of the body, St. Thomas Aquinas expressed the common Judeo-Christian view:

> . . . man naturally desires his own salvation. Now since the soul is part of the body of a man, it is not the whole man, and my soul is not my self. Hence even if the soul attains salvation in another life, yet *I* do not, nor does any man.[11]

According to this view, the self does not survive death. Death not merely takes away one's most useful instrument or most valued possession, but utterly destroys one's self. The only hope of salvation for the human person is in his descendants or in personal resurrection to a new, bodily life.

Classical modern philosophy substituted a radical dualism for the Judeo-Christian concept of man. Descartes set in opposition the thinking subject and material objects of thought. The thinker's own body was placed among objects of thought in the material world. For Hume, the "mind" theoretically is merely a bundle of impressions and ideas, and one's own body like any other object is part of this bundle. But in practice Hume treats the mind as a receptive and active center, and places the body among other contents processed by the mind. For Kant, the person is identified with the autonomous self—an extraempirical reality which alone is the principle of moral life and human dignity—while the body is consigned to the purely factual world of nature, from which all value is banished. For Hegel, the human mind brings about the self-realization of Absolute Spirit, but any particular human body is a merely contingent datum with no ultimate meaning or value.

Philosophers since Hegel have tried to restore the unity of the human person, but they have not succeeded in doing so. Some call man an "incarnate spirit"; they use a theological adjective to modify a substantive description of the person as a reality to which bodiliness is alien. Others struggle to reinsert spirit into the world, but find that the bodily person is permanently displaced in the categories of existential phenomenology, for one's body is neither the-being-which-is-in-the-world nor the-world-in-which-being-there-is.

Even Marxists and pragmatists, who exclude any reality beyond the dialectic of nature or the interaction of organism with environment, separate the center of praxis or the problem-solving intelligence from the bodily self. For both Marxists and pragmatists, the living human body is part of nature and is a tool for transforming the whole of nature, including human nature itself. But the transforming agent *looks forward to abiding in* a future more suited to itself. Despite their struggle to overcome dualism, the user and the used must be diverse, and this diversity, taken as metaphysically fundamental by Marxists and pragmatists, leads them inexorably back to dualism.

Few contemporary philosophers would defend an explicit dualistic theory of the person. Such a theory would frankly state that a person owns and uses a body, but that a person is *not* a body. Hardly anyone defends a dualistic theory of the person because there are well-known, conclusive objections against such a position. It renders inexplicable human thought and action, for these involve the living body not merely as tool and as material, but as a mode of personal reality presupposed by one's taking account or making use of anything whatsoever. The bodiliness of human persons is especially evident in the phenomenon of communication among persons. If our bodies were not really our *selves*, we would be literally *out of touch* with the world and one another.[12]

Yet dualism remains implicit in many theories of the person, and it becomes explicit in ethical discussions. Classical utilitarianism, for example, locates value in conscious experience. For practical purposes, the person is nothing but the conscious subject, which has experiences of pleasure and pain, and which calculates, manipulates the world including the body itself, and receives a pay-off in pleasurable experience. Since one is not one's body, the destruction of the living body is not a direct attack upon any intrinsic personal value.

A very clear example of the influence of dualism on ethics is the following statement by Joseph Fletcher:

> Physical nature—the body and its members, our organs and their functions—all of these *things* are a part of "what is over against us," and if we live by the rules and conditions set in physiology or any other *it* we are not men, we are not *thou*. When we discussed the problem of giving life to new creatures, and the authority of natural processes as over against the human values of responsibility and self-preservation (when nature and they are at cross-purposes), we remarked that spiritual reality and moral integrity belong to man alone, in whatever degree we may possess them as made *imago Dei*. Freedom, knowledge, choice, responsibility —all these things of personal or moral stature are in us, not *out there*. Physical nature is what is over against us, out there. It represents the world of *its*. Only men and God are *thou;* they only are persons.[13]

For Fletcher, the body and its members, our organs and their functions, belong to physical nature; physical nature is not the person; everything of moral significance is located exclusively *within* the person. Thus, Fletcher argues in another work:

> The right of spiritual beings to use intelligent control over physical nature, rather than submit beastlike to its blind workings, is the heart of many crucial questions. Birth control, artificial insemination, sterilization, and abortion are all medically discovered ways of fulfilling and protecting human values and hopes in spite of nature's failures or foolishnesses. Death control, like birth control, is a matter of human dignity. Without it persons become puppets. To perceive this is to grasp the error lurking in the notion—widespread in medical circles—that life as such is the highest good. This kind of vitalism seduces its victims into being more loyal to the physical spark of mere biological life than to the personality values of self-possession and human integrity. The beauty and spiritual depths of human stature are what should be preserved and conserved in our value system, with the flesh as the means rather than the end.[14]

For Fletcher, the living human body is a pure means. Anything which is done to a person's body, in Fletcher's view, takes its whole ethical significance from "things of personal or moral stature" which are "in us, not *out there.*"

A sound understanding of moral principles cannot be based upon assumptions which are indefensible. Since the living human body is not extrinsic to the person, human life of itself is personal. Therefore, the practical dualism which underlies typical arguments in defense of the moral permissibility of suicide ought to be rejected. Whatever value human life has, this value is not merely instrumental and infrapersonal as Fletcher and others would have it be.

Those who defend suicide often argue that a person is justified in taking his own life, because one's body is *one's own*, and one has a right to dispose as one wishes of what is one's own. But one's body is not one's property. This is not to say that it is someone else's property. A living human body does not belong to anyone, not even to God.

Ownership is a moral power over parts of the environment which are somehow joined to one's body and thus assimilated to one's bodily self. One's body is too immediate to be a possession, for one's bodily self is necessarily presupposed by all possessions. As for God—as Jews and Christians conceive of him—his dominion over human life must be understood on the model of the care of a kingly leader or of a father, not on the model of a property holder such as a slave owner.

Someone might object that in killing a person, one does not destroy the person as a whole. Life is only part of the person. Perhaps it is *intrinsic* to the person, but other parts of the person are more properly personal, more specifically human. Even carrots live, and those who argue for the permissibility of suicide often argue that a person who is barely alive is little more than a vegetable.

Those who take this view look upon the life of a living human body as if such life were merely a generic property common to persons and to other organisms. Growth, nutrition, and reproduction are vital functions. Thus, it seems that life is nothing but this set of functions. Biology, the science of life, studies these functions. Biology does not study the person as person. And so, it seems, life is at most an inferior part of the human person, a part shared with other animals and even with carrots.

But this objection neglects a very important fact: Life permeates the person and every aspect of personal reality. Existence is not merely one characteristic among other characteristics of existing things. Neither is life merely one characteristic among other characteristics of organic entities. Life is the existence of the living being.

Even from a biological point of view, growth, nutrition, and reproduction are not really *common* functions of all organisms. As an abstract generality, all organisms do have such functions. But in concrete reality, what is involved in the growth, nutrition, and reproduction of human persons is not precisely what is involved in the growth, nutrition, and reproduction of any other kind of organism. *Human* physiology is a special story which could not be told if one limited the account to "common" biological functions.

Moreover, although living things have some generically common functions, it does not follow that the life of a human person is nothing more than a collection of organic functions. The organism is a unity; the functions of each part are exercised for the sake of the whole. In saying this, I do not embrace the metaphysical theory that there is a vital principle apart from all of the functions; such a theory is itself a dualistic philosophy of organic life. Rather, I embrace a theory of organic individuals—especially of living, bodily persons—which regards them as substantial unities.

From the modest metaphysical premise that a human person really is *this some-thing*—which is *some-one*—it follows that the life of a person is more than each of the organic functions, more even than all of these organic functions together. The exercise of these functions is the realization of certain possible aspects of a person. If all organic functions cease, there is no life, no organism, no person. Yet the unified life of the whole person embraces the multiplicity of his vital functions. The *one* life of the person cannot be identical with his *many* functions.

Furthermore, growth, nutrition, and reproduction are not the only vital functions. Sensation and anticipation, memory and emotion, and other functions belong to certain species of organisms. Thinking and choosing and using are functions characteristic of the human species. It is dualism to divide organic functions from so-called "personal" functions, and to define "mere life" in terms of the former. The life which is terminated when a human person is killed is not merely a set of organic functions. If I take my life, I do not merely stop *my* heartbeat, *my* breathing, and *my* brain waves, I eliminate at one stroke the single principle of these and also of *my* knowing, *my* choosing, and *my* responsibility. If something of myself nevertheless survives and somehow acts, that something is only the ghostly remains of me, and is no more *I* than my corpse—my bodily remains—is *I*.

Dualistic conceptions of the human person, which are often concealed in ethical arguments, lead to a falsely atomistic or monadic notion of human life. In reality, bodily life transcends individuals; it unites persons with one another and living human bodies with the natural environment. Sexual reproduction unites at least three persons in a vital, personal bond; this link is the foundation for all community. Nutrition and respiration unite persons with the environment. Suicide is the ultimate step in a process of alienation between one's "autonomous" agent self and one's dependent bodily reality.

Those who fail to see that human life is an intrinsic personal good, who regard "mere life" as a good only instrumental to the goods of the person, not only presuppose a theoretically indefensible dualism. They also accept an opinion which is at odds with experience. Common sense knows better, as is clear whenever ordinary men and women celebrate the hope and joy of new life, the anxiety and grief of death. In concrete experience, a person whom one loves and the life of such a person are the same.

5. IS SUICIDE EVER MORALLY PERMISSIBLE?

In section two, I defined the moral act of suicide and carefully distinguished this act both from the suicidal deed which is not morally significant inasmuch as it does not carry out a choice at all, and from the moral act which leads to one's death but which carries out a choice other than that carried out by a moral act of suicide. A moral act of suicide carries out a choice by which one adopts a proposal to kill oneself or a proposal which amounts to this. (In what follows, I refer to the moral act of suicide simply as "suicide.") In the present section, I argue that suicide is always wrong.

If consequentialism were correct, it would be pointless to consider the morality of suicide as defined in section two, precisely because this definition distinguishes cases in which one adopts a proposal to kill oneself from cases in which one adopts a proposal to do something else which will have the same result. For example, a consequentialist naturally resists making any morally significant distinction between killing oneself and letting oneself die.

In my view, suicide is not the only morally blameworthy deed which results in one's own death; moreover, malign neglect *can be a method* of committing suicide. Nevertheless, if consequentialism is indeed meaningless—as I have argued in section three—the distinctions built into the definition of suicide need not be nugatory. For on a nonconsequentialist theory of moral judgment, such as the one I am about to sketch out, moral good and evil do not depend upon the expected results of one's choices, although probable results must be taken into account.

Those who defend the moral permissibility of suicide by using a consequentialist ethics usually assume that the only alternative to consequentialism is a morality of duty. Such a morality, they argue, enslaves persons to a set of impersonal, absolute moral rules. Consequentialism, by contrast, they say, grounds morality in the good of persons.

I agree that morality must be grounded in human goods which constitute the flourishing of persons, as individuals and in communities. Yet I regard consequentialism as meaningless. I hold suicide always wrong precisely because I consider it to be an attack upon human life, which is an intrinsic good of persons. I shall now propose a nonconsequentialist way of grounding moral judgments in the basic human goods which contribute intrinsically to the flourishing of persons.

Consequentialism and many other ethical theories fail to account for the origin of the moral "ought." This "ought" cannot be derived from the "is" of facts about premoral human goods.

Many philosophers have held that the only way to maintain the truth-value of moral judgments is to regard propositions about the moral quality of various kinds of acts as statements about so-called "moral facts," which are supposedly known by moral intuition. But this view involves many difficulties, not the least of which is that it precludes rational argument about these "facts." The question of the morality of suicide, for example, would have to be left to moral intuition, and arguments about the question would be excluded as useless.

However, there is another possibility. The propositions about the moral quality of various kinds of acts can be regarded as practical precepts, which are derived from basic principles of practical reasoning. On this view, practical precepts are not true by conforming to any special sort of fact, but by articulating the necessary conditions for fully rational human action. Intuition of a sort is required, but this intuition grasps basic principles rather than specific moral precepts. Because these precepts articulate intrinsic conditions for human action, they are not extrinsic commandments, nor are they imperatives issued by one part of oneself to another. Rather, practical reasoning shapes human action from within and shapes it in the form of moral goodness if arbitrariness in choice-making does not interfere.[15]

On this approach, reason is not theoretical by nature and practical only by some additional factor. To be practical is natural to human reason. Reason is doing its own work when it guides action just as when it leads to theoretical truth. "Ought" requires no special act legitimating it; the "ought" of the principles of practical thinking is not derived from any "is," although practical principles do involve an action-oriented interpretation of certain data.

The principles of practical thinking establish the minimal conditions without which no human act is possible. No one chooses except in view of an intelligible good; no one acts except for an end. Thus the first principle of practical reason is that good is to be promoted and protected, and that what interferes with or threatens good is to be avoided or opposed.[16]

This primary principle does not *exclude* any good accessible to a person by action. The "is to be" is not yet an "ought" of moral obligation. The first principle provides only a framework which makes deliberation possible. Every proposal which is considered in deliberation, even if it is an immoral proposal, is articulated within this framework, just as every logically coherent proposition which can be entertained is articulated within the framework for meaningful discourse provided by the principle of noncontradiction.

The framework provided by the first principle of practical reason must be given content by the various modes of human good for which one can act. The goods promised by each proposal considered in deliberation provide reasons for adopting it.

The reason for any particular choice is revealed when one asks: "Why did I choose *that*?" or "Why is he doing *that*?" The answer must be given in terms of the good one sees in it. Each choice aims at some good. This good was not compelling in deliberation to the exclusion of alternative proposals, or one would not have had a choice to make. Each proposal offered its own limited and incommensurable good, and the good promised by each proposal was sufficient to make possible one's adoption of it.

The immediate good sought in a particular choice often is subordinate to some ulterior good. One works for wages in order to buy food, and one buys food in order to satisfy hunger. A chain of purposes quickly comes to a purpose beyond which there is no further end in view. A good which is intrinsic to oneself or to another person or persons whom one loves is perceived as a self-sufficient end which extrinsic goods serve.

If one considers from a psychological point of view the ultimate goods for which people act, one can distinguish various categories of basic human needs. These are broader than the specific objects of physiological drives which in other animals are satisfied by instinctive behavior. People are interested not only in satisfying hunger and thirst, in avoiding specific threats, and so on, but in preserving their lives, cultivating health, promoting safety and security.[17] Moreover, human needs include thirst not only for water but also for truth, hunger not only for food by also for justice.

Considering *all* of man's basic needs in this way, we discern *all* of the goods for which a person *can* act. One can act only by choice; one can choose only by adopting an interesting proposal; one can formulate proposals only in the light of an understanding of what they promise as goods to be pursued.

By experience one is aware of one's tendencies or inclinations and of what satisfies them. One's own longings, frustrations, and delights are data, which one observes as one observes other facts. But one is aware of *possible* objects of one's tendencies in a practical way when one understands the data with an orientation to action—that is, when one considers the possible, in the framework of the first practical principle, as a good-to-be-done.

I call these various modes of human good, which provide content for the first principle of practical thinking, "basic human goods." For my present purpose it is not necessary to try to make a list of all the basic human goods. Such a list might include the following goods, all of which are intrinsic to persons and all of which can be sought for their own sake: life and health, play, esthetic experience, theoretical truth, inner peace, truth to oneself, justice, friendship, and holiness. Many other candidates for such a list would have to be critically examined, and either rejected or given a place on it: enjoyment, freedom, self-fulfillment, success, honor, patriotism, quality of life, a sense of dignity, and so on. For the present argument, I do not need to exclude candidates from the list of basic human goods; I only need assume what I argued for in section four: Human life is one of the basic goods, which contribute not merely instrumentally but intrinsically to the flourishing of persons.

The basic human goods, understood as practical principles, provide possible grounds for adopting various proposals considered in deliberation. But even before deliberation can begin, they give the possibilities open to one the form of intelligible proposals. For example, it is only because one assumes that play is a good to be pursued, that the possibility of engaging in some recreational activity presents itself as a proposal worth considering as one completes or finds oneself blocked in some other activity.

Thus, when one deliberates one sees in each alternative an attractive, practical possibility—a "live option" as William James calls it. Something about each proposal makes it appealing; it calls out to be adopted and realized. The principles underlying this practical mode of thinking usually are taken for granted. For example, in arguments about public policies, if a certain proposal would lead to a loss of human life, this fact is taken at once as relevant and as a reason—even if not decisive—for rejecting the proposal. An adverse effect on human life has such immediate relevance in deliberation only because a principle too obvious to require explicit formulation is taken for granted: Human life is a good to be protected, and what damages it is to be avoided.

But the gerundive force—the "is to be"—of such a practical principle is not yet a moral "ought." The basic human goods described thus far underlie *every* proposal a person can consider, whether that proposal be morally good or bad. When one deliberates, the moral goodness of some choices and the moral badness of others is a factor one is aware of, but moral goodness is not necessarily a compelling factor. Just as the basic goods are incommensurable with one another, so moral goodness is incommensurable with various modes of premoral human good. In other words, there are *intelligible* alternatives to what one morally ought to do; immoral action is not sheerly irrational behavior. If this were not the case, one could not choose contrary to moral judgment.

It is at this point that the consequentialist suggests his solution: The right act is the one which of available alternatives realizes as fully as possible the concrete result—human well-being or the whole circle of possible human goods—indicated by all the practical principles together. As I explained in section three, this suggested solution is unworkable, because alternative proposals cannot be evaluated by the standard of the "greater good"—that is, by the "as fully as possible" of the preceding formulation.

Another solution is necessary. But any solution must be consistent with the fact that not every choice is morally evil, and yet every choice responds to the appeal of the human goods promised by one proposal and leaves unanswered the appeal of the equally basic and incommensurable human goods promised by one or more other proposals. Thus the principles which underlie deliberation are not moral norms merely by being practical principles. The underlying assumption that human life is to be preserved does not of itself dictate that no one is ever to be killed.

The distinction between moral good and evil is primarily a distinction between ways in which proposals are related to the principles of practical thinking. Some proposals are *consistent with all* of the principles of practical thinking, although they *promise only some participation in some* of the basic human goods towards which these principles direct action. Other proposals are *consistent with some* of the principles of practical thinking—those which direct action to the goods promised by these proposals—but *inconsistent with at least one* principle of practical thinking. Proposals of the former sort are morally good, while those of the latter sort are morally bad.

A morally bad proposal is intelligible because of the good it promises. It can be adopted if one is prepared to regard the good with which it is inconsistent as a lesser good than the good it promises. It is possible to regard one basic human good as a lesser good than another precisely because the goods are incommensurable, and so any of them can appear to be a lesser good if it is judged by a standard of goodness specified by a competing mode of goodness.

However, it also is unreasonable to regard any basic human good as a lesser good than another precisely because the goods are incommensurable. If a person cares for all of them insofar as they are goods, not insofar as they are particular modes of goodness toward which he has a special bias, he never judges one of them by a standard of goodness specified by another.

One who is about to choose in the morally right way respects equally all of the basic goods and listens equally to all of the appeals they make through the principles of practical thinking. Because of the incompatibility of practical alternatives—in other words, since one cannot do everything at once—a choice is necessary. No single good, nothing promised by any one proposal, exhausts human possibilities, realizes the whole potentiality for mankind's flourishing. However, just as two propositions having no common terms are not inconsistent with each other, so also a proposal is consistent with those principles of practical thinking to which it is merely irrelevant.

Thus, one can adopt a proposal which promises certain goods and is irrelevant to other goods promised by an alternative proposal without violating the practical principle which directs action to these other goods. In this case, one remains open to these other goods. One does not adopt a restrictive standard of good. One's understanding of the various goods, one's appreciation of their special potential contribution to the flourishing of persons, remains the same after choice as before.

One who is about to choose in the morally wrong way does not respect equally all of the basic human goods and does not listen equally to all of the appeals they make through the principles of practical thinking. The proposal which one is about to adopt involves detriment to some human good. One is tempted to accept this detriment for the sake of the service accepting it will render to another good—that is, to another instance of some basic human good. Such a proposal is based upon at least one principle of practical thinking and it might be merely irrelevant to—and so consistent with—some others,

but it is relevant to and inconsistent with the principle which
directs action to promote and respect the good to which the
proposed action will be detrimental. Yet the principle which is
to be violated is as basic as the one upon which the proposal
is based; the good which is going to be served is no more
basic than the one which is going to be harmed.

A person who adopts such a proposal cannot remain open
to the good promised by alternatives, for this good is going to
be violated. In choosing to accept this violation, one implicitly adopts a restrictive standard of good. One's understanding
of the various goods is affected by the choice. The good which
is violated is no longer regarded as equally basic and incommensurable with the good to which it is sacrificed. The good
which is violated now becomes a "lesser good," and the good
to which it is sacrificed becomes a "greater good." The choice,
which is partially irrational insofar as it conflicts with some
principle of practical thinking, is rationalized by reducing to
the extent necessary a basic human good from the status of
an end to that of a means.

The unfolding of the complete ethical theory implicit in
this way of distinguishing between moral good and evil is an
extensive project.[18] But from the basic distinction there follows directly a relevant ethical principle: *While one cannot
always promote and protect every basic human good in all of
one's actions, one ought never to adopt a proposal to serve
one or more of the basic goods intrinsic to persons by acting
in a way detrimental to one or more of these same goods.* This
ethical principle articulates the classical maxim that evil may
not be done that good might follow therefrom.[19] It also is expressed, though more loosely, in the saying that the end does
not justify the means.[20]

The morality of respect for persons which Kant attempts
to articulate in one of the versions of his categorical imperative also is based upon the same insight. Kant's ethical theory is deficient because of his formalistic conception of practical reasoning, but he comes very close to an accurate expression of the relevant ethical principle when he says: "Act so
that you treat humanity, whether in your own person or in
that of another, always as an end and never as a means only."[21]

The basic human goods against which one ought not to
act are not impersonal; the moral norms forbidding violation
of these goods are not mere legalistic rules. These goods make
an intrinsic contribution to the flourishing of human persons.

They do not transcend persons by subordinating their good to some "higher," nonhuman purpose. The goods only transcend persons as they are by drawing them toward what they are not yet, but still can come to be by their creative effort.

The absolute negative norms which demand unconditional respect for these basic goods of persons are not restrictions imposed to limit the flourishing of persons, but rather exclusions of the arbitrary limits which are implicitly placed upon the principles of human action by the adoption of any proposal to act against a basic human good. To diminish in no way the full scope of these basic principles is to maintain an indispensable condition for human flourishing, for it is to keep open all the possibilities of actions which might promote this flourishing.

Beyond one's immediate choice, there always remains an unlimited and unforeseeable possibility of "something more," of human goods still to be realized in oneself and in others. This something more will unfold as it should only if people in choosing remain creatively faithful to it, and such faithfulness demands unconditional respect for the principles which ground its very possibility.

A consequentialist, observing that any choice is relevant to two or more human goods, proposes that morality be determined by reference to all of the goods involved. However, consequentialism focuses only on the goods as they are concretized in limited, prospective good results, and confines the person within the limits of measurable goods, reduced to one mode of goodness by the standard adopted arbitrarily for the occasion. Thus, a consequentialist attitude not only demotes the "lesser good" from its proper status as end to the status of a mere means, but also demotes the "greater good" from its proper status as an inexhaustible aspect of potential human flourishing to the status of an attainable goal, an objective to be achieved and then replaced by some new objective.

A sound ethical theory also proposes that morality be determined by reference to all of the goods involved, but respects the complexity and richness of human goods and maintains openness to human flourishing beyond the present situation, beyond any measure even conceivable at a given moment in a person's life and in the life of mankind. Moral norms limit a person only from limiting himself more narrowly than is inevitable for a limited being.

A proposal to kill oneself is a proposal to act against one's life as a means to some other good. Human life is an intrinsic good of persons. One ought not to act in a manner detrimental to such a good. Therefore, one ought not to commit suicide. If one does commit suicide, one reduces the good of human life in oneself to the status of a mere means, one regards one's life as if it were a measurable good which may be disposed of in the service of some other, "greater good."[22]

As I pointed out at the beginning of this section, "suicide" here means the moral act of suicide, as defined in section two.

In arguing that suicide is wrong and in admitting no exception to this proposition, I make no judgment on individuals who choose to kill themselves. Not everyone who commits suicide acts with full moral responsibility. Various circumstances can diminish the evil of the act and mitigate responsibility for it to an extent no one can judge. Moreover, it is not for us to judge one another's moral guilt.

Rather it is for us to regard one another with a compassion which never condones the evil act but which always communicates love to warm the chilled heart and hope to encourage the faint heart. Perhaps most of us can recall occasions upon which fear alone rather than good will restrained us from an attempt upon ourselves; probably all of us at some time in the future will need the compassion of others. But when that time comes, our hearts will need to be warmed and lifted up, not merely anesthetized by the sentimental insensitivity of others to the evil of the act we have done.

The fundamental principle of moral goodness—the consistency of a proposal with *all* of the principles of practical thinking—has implications for one's existential attitudes toward oneself, toward other human persons, and toward God.

In reference to oneself, respect for all the basic human goods means that one will always strive to promote one's own good and will never willingly restrict or cut off one's own possibilities. In reference to other human persons, respect for all the basic human goods means that one will strive to contribute to their flourishing and will never willingly limit or break off community with them. In reference to God, respect for all the basic human goods means that one will recognize that these goods have an objective validity whether people respect them or not, and that in difficult cases there is a real ground for confidence that absolute respect for human goods is not irrational.

Considered from each of these points of view, suicide can be seen to be wrong, apart from any impossible weighing of good or bad consequences. I next briefly articulate these considerations. They do not stand alone; they build upon the preceding argument and manifest its existential significance.

Those who argue for the moral permissibility of suicide often point out that one who kills himself does not violate the right to life, since a person has no rights against himself. Moreover, at least in some cases one who kills himself does not thereby fail to fulfill any duty, for duties bear only upon one's relationship with others, and in some cases an individual who kills himself is incapable of serving others in any significant way.

The trouble with this argument is that rights and duties themselves are derivative moral principles, grounded in the basic human goods. Consequently, not all morality is a matter of rights and duties. An individual who decides not to develop his talents, because he prefers trivial satisfactions to the goods he could promote if he made the effort, does what is wrong, although he violates no one's rights. The basic principle is to do what is good, and this principle excludes as immoral the wasting of one's life. This is so even if one has no specific duty to others and even if one excludes, as I would, the concept of duty to oneself. Fundamental moral obligations are too profound to be analyzed in terms of rights and duties alone.

Considered in this perspective, the claim that one may commit suicide if he wishes, because one may do as he pleases if he violates no one's rights, seems to undermine morality even more radically than does the defense of an injustice. Perhaps this point is what Wittgenstein—who was himself tormented by the temptation to commit suicide—had in mind when he wrote that if suicide is allowed then everything is allowed, and added: "This throws a light on the nature of ethics, for suicide is, so to speak, the elementary sin."[23]

Suicide is an elementary sin because one who commits it implicitly rejects as meaningless the most fundamental question about morality—"Why should I be moral?" He removes himself permanently from the range of the primal demand *to do what one can*, to serve human goods, to communicate human meaning to every aspect of life and of the world.

Even if suicide in some cases does not conflict with any specific duty which a person has to others, it does terminate one's capacity for community. A person who separates himself from his own bodily life takes the last step in what is usually a long process of withdrawal from intimate communion with the world and with other persons. One who commits suicide breaks off relations definitively; he does not go gently and reluctantly from our midst, but leaves willingly, as it were slamming the door as he departs. The shock is bound to upset those who are left behind.

Moreover, each individual who willingly abandons the project of human life in community makes it more difficult for others to carry on. This is especially so for others who also are discouraged. Each fresh example of self-destruction compels many sensitive people to think once more about the unthinkable. Thus, one who commits suicide bequeaths his own misery to others and intensifies their suffering.

Furthermore, one who commits suicide is taking an irreversible step into darkness. He does not *know* where this path leads; he gambles on the unsure supposition that he cannot be worse off than he is. Religious beliefs regarding a divine commandment and a threat of punishment in an afterlife are not decisive for nonbelievers. However, nonbelief does not eliminate Hamlet's *perhaps*—"perhaps to dream."

Moreover, philosophical arguments which are independent of religious faith can be proposed for thinking that there is a creator whose intelligence and goodness stand behind the meaning and value of human life, and whose plan of creation ensures that human faithfulness to moral goodness will not prove vain. Even for a believer, the possibility of offending God is not a possibility of either hurting or enraging him. Rather, to offend God is to love the Good which he is less than some other good. Since one who loved Goodness Itself would love every human good, which is an image of divine goodness, as wholeheartedly as it can and should be loved, one who offends against any of the intrinsic goods of human persons does not love God and does offend him. This is why Christians believed that love of one's neighbor and of oneself spontaneously follow from love of God.

Someone who defends the moral permissibility of suicide is likely to be unimpressed by such considerations offered to manifest its existential significance. He will propose a case in which an individual has minimal future possibilities, because his useful life is at an end, and the only remaining alternatives are a quick and painless death or prolonged and useless suffering. Such an individual might kill himself quietly, and even take care to make his death appear accidental. Arguments for the reality of God and for the possibility of an afterlife might be dismissed as theoretical, weak, and thus negligible in practice. Surely, it will be argued, such an individual's suicidal act is not evil in any important sense.

Undoubtedly, if one grants all the suppositions of this counterexample, it is impossible to point to any harm likely to result from the suicidal act. However, since consequentialism is not true, measurable harm is not the criterion of moral evil. The counterexample helps to make clear—if one grants all its suppositions—that there can be cases in which it makes no difference ulterior to the act itself whether one does moral good or moral evil. However, even if there can be such cases, this does not show that suicide is sometimes morally permissible. It only shows that—under these suppositions—its moral wrongness could be irrelevant to anything else.

Many recent arguments in defense of assisted suicide for those suffering from serious illnesses refer to such suicide as "death by choice" and "death with dignity." Undoubtedly, there is a certain dignity in a person's morally significant action, even if it be evil action, which is not present in the passivity of suffering, in being overcome by accident or disease and carried unwillingly by natural forces to one's death. Psychological thinking has highlighted this motivation as one reason for suicide; one who kills himself perhaps feels that he "cheats death" as a condemned person cheats the hangman or a defeated general cheats the enemy who would humiliate him.[24]

But one who kills himself merely in order to avoid suffering a natural death obviously does not *cheat death.* He is more like the man who is never fired because he always quits when his current employer is about to fire him. More important, the dignity which belongs to human action as such is infinitely less precious than the dignity which belongs to moral goodness. It is better to be an innocent infant than a vicious adult, better to suffer injustice than to do it. And so it is better to suffer anything, however degrading, than to do what is morally wrong. Of course, the comparison of values here is made from a moral point of view.

Furthermore, an individual who voluntarily endures suffering rather than avoid it by committing suicide also does a morally significant act. He chooses to dispose of his power to kill himself by not doing so, out of respect for the good of human life. This attitude also manifests dignity and it is far more to be respected than is the attitude of one willing to take his own life in order that it might not be taken from him.

Oddly enough, arguments for "death with dignity" often couple this appeal with one drawn from a quite different perspective—that of the humane termination of animal suffering. "They shoot horses, don't they?" puts this argument simply and bluntly. This argument clearly rests upon a rejection of the status of *human* life as a basic good intrinsic to persons. The justification for killing animals is that their life is not a good which human action must respect. Thus, if it is useless to humans that an animal live and in accord with human feelings that it die, there is nothing wrong with satisfying the human impulse to kill it.

But apart from the fact that the life of other animals is only an instrumental good for humans, the killing of suffering animals and of suffering persons differ in another important respect. No other animal can dispose of its own life, and so horses cannot voluntarily endure their own suffering. Thus the dignity immanent in a resolute choice not to kill oneself not only is overlooked in the appeal to "death with dignity," but also is overlooked in the appeal to humane treatment of animals as a model for the treatment of dying persons.

Furthermore, arguments using the slogan "death with dignity" often use examples of esthetically unpleasant and emotionally repulsive events and conditions which sometimes accompany terminal illnesses. The use of such examples manifests confusion between the dignity of persons and dignified appearances. Surely everything within reason should be done —and often far too little is done—to support the composure, maintain the comfort, and protect the privacy of persons who are dying. But no one loses his dignity merely because he loses control of his bodily functions. The idea that the human body lacks decency unless it is fully under the control of reason is merely another aspect of the dualism which has no room for the true dignity of bodily persons. The false sense of decency is probably a vestige of Victorian evasiveness about the bodily reality of persons; it is of a piece with the attitude that sexual ecstasy as such is filthy and degrading.

The consequentialist, attending only to the prospective results of choices, denies that there is any difference in one's responsibility for one's death whether one commits suicide or adopts some other proposal with the same result. I call this line of argument the "no-difference objection."

As I explained in section two, one *can* propose to kill oneself by omission, and other things being the same such an omission is morally the same as a deed. Also, potentially self-destructive behavior which is not suicidal—that of the daredevil—can be immoral. The cases of the martyr and the hero are complicated by the fact that the expected results presuppose that their proposal is *not* to kill themselves. The same can be said for cases in which individuals kill themselves without choosing to do so, but act by an earlier choice to carry out the demands of some much more general proposal—for example, a proposal to carry out unquestioningly the commands of God or the usages of one's culture.

The sort of case on which the consequentialist can build his most plausible no-difference objection is none of the preceding, but rather is one in which an individual might be justified in omitting or refusing medical treatment, although he expects this act will hasten his death, and yet would be guilty of suicide if he adopted a proposal to kill himself. Here, if anywhere, the consequentialist seems right in saying that it makes no difference whether one commits suicide or not.

The first point to be noticed in answer to this objection is that even in a case in which an individual would be justified in adopting a proposal to omit or refuse treatment, his adoption instead of a proposal to kill himself ordinarily does make some difference. I do not merely mean that there are certain other consequences which can lead the consequentialist to prefer suicide in such cases, nor that the nonsuicidal choice will result in a slightly longer lifespan than its suicidal alternative. Rather, I mean that the existential considerations outlined above with respect to the significance of suicide for oneself, for other human persons, and for one's relation to God do indicate that even in this case there is an important human difference between killing and letting die.

But there is a further point to be made in answer to the no-difference objection. Moral acts not only affect the realization of goods apart from the acts themselves, they also affect the realization of certain goods in which a human person shares precisely insofar as he is a moral agent. A person who adopts—or who is prepared to adopt—a suicidal proposal is a different sort of person from one who remains unwilling to kill himself.

One who is prepared to adopt a suicidal proposal accepts the character of killer; his moral identity is different from one who adopts a nonsuicidal proposal to omit or refuse care. One prepared to kill himself cannot regard the lives of human persons generally as a basic and intrinsic personal good, never to be violated. One who adopts a nonsuicidal proposal, even knowing that it will hasten his own death, can maintain the identity and attitudes of one who respects human life, who does not reduce it to the status of means, who does not regard it as a merely measurable good, and who *thus holds fast to the principle* on which alone it makes sense to regard the lives of other persons as *absolutely* inviolable.

The bearing of one's readiness to kill oneself upon one's own character is especially important when euthanasia is in question. For individuals might make—in fact, some are making—choices in favor of suicide under certain possible conditions long before these conditions arise. A moral commitment in this matter is more than a mere theoretical judgment. To adopt a proposal that one will seek assisted suicide is to accept the character of killer, to reduce human life generally to the status of mere means, to regard it as a measurable good, and implicitly to hold that the lives of others also may be violated under appropriate conditions.

Someone might object that even if a proposal is not precisely to kill a person, but only to do something which will contribute to the causation of a person's death, still the adoption of such a proposal is just as relevant to the good of life and inconsistent with this good as is the adoption of a proposal to kill a person or of a proposal which amounts to this. For, it might be argued, one who foresees the deadly result of his deed yet does not forebear to do the deed must be willing that the result occur, and so must be ready and willing to violate the good of life, since his deed is *in fact* detrimental to an instance of this good.

I grant that in *general* one who foresees detriment to a basic human good resulting from his deed or omission but nevertheless adopts a proposal to do such an act despite the foreseen detriment acts against the good he harms even though the proposal he adopts neither is nor amounts to a proposal to harm this good. However, in some cases it seems that one is morally obliged to adopt a proposal which cannot be carried out without contributing to the causation of a person's death, although the proposal is in itself consistent with all basic human goods.

The theoretical question of how such moral obligations can arise is one which cannot be discussed here, for an adequate discussion would require an examination of all of the modes of responsibility by which moral obligations are generated. But the predicament of the martyr is an example, for such an individual thinks both that it would be wrong to adopt the proposal to do what is demanded of him and that he will be killed if he refuses to adopt this proposal. Clearly, the martyr is willing to die rather than to do what is in itself wrong. In this sense and only in this sense, he is willing that the foreseen result of his refusal—namely, his death—should occur. However, this willingness is imposed upon the martyr by another's readiness to violate a basic human good. It is not conditioned upon the martyr's *setting himself against* the good of life, but is rather conditioned upon his *unwillingness to do what he believes is wrong.* Hence the martyr is not willing to violate the good of human life. If he were willing to violate this good, he would cease to be a martyr and would instead become a fanatic.

From the example of the martyr one can draw a general principle: A proposal is not inconsistent with any of the principles of practical thinking even if the act or omission which will execute the proposal has a detrimental effect upon some basic human good, provided that the proposal meets two conditions: (1) it is not in itself inconsistent with one or more of the principles of practical thinking, even apart from the detrimental effect, and (2) there is no morally good alternative to the proposal—that is to say, no alternative consistent with all of one's responsibilities grounded in various ways in a morally good attitude of openness to all the basic human goods.

Anyone who does not admit that one ought never to adopt a proposal to kill a human individual is likely to feel that my answer to the no-difference objection is unconvincing. If there is no afterlife and if an individual only considers the possibility of killing himself when he discovers that he has an incurable and painful disease, then it makes no great difference to his character whether he decides to kill himself or to endure a slower and more painful death. Hence, a consideration of effects upon one's character does not show that the choice to kill oneself in such a situation is always wrong.

However, my answer to the no-difference objection is not meant to show that suicide is always wrong. Rather, I assume the success of my argument against suicide based upon the inconsistency of such a choice with the principle of practical thinking which directs action to respect human life. In answering the no-difference objection, I merely try to show that there is no inconsistency between considering suicide always wrong and considering sometimes justified the adoption of some other proposal which by its effects contributes to the causation of one's own death. For a consequentialist to demand that his nonconsequentialist opponent demonstrate in consequentialist fashion the difference made by every significant distinction a nonconsequentialist draws, is for the consequentialist to beg the question. For a nonconsequentialist to attempt to meet such a demand is not only for him to surrender his own position but also for him to undertake a pointless effort, since nothing whatsoever can be demonstrated in consequentialist fashion, because the terms of every consequentialist argument are meaningless.

A defender of the moral permissibility of suicide will raise another objection against the consistency of those who hold it is always wrong to kill oneself: Is it not equally wrong to kill others? Yet in the Judeo-Christian tradition, the condemnation of other killing has been accompanied by the justification of capital punishment and of killing in a just war. One who holds the traditional view of all these matters will answer that the prohibition of killing does not extend to these cases, for the life which is inviolable is innocent life: "Do not slay the innocent and righteous" (Exodus 23:7).

One thing is clear in this matter. Those whose grasp of the morality of killing was conditioned by the belief that divine law permits and even enjoins capital punishment and war in the cause of justice undoubtedly might have engaged in such acts of killing without setting themselves against the basic good of human life. Their proposal might have been only this: to do justice in obedience to God. If so, the peculiar ritualistic character of capital punishment and of much military combat becomes intelligible, and so does the claim that killing in capital punishment and warfare was justified insofar as it was authorized by public authority acting in accord with law, for public authority and just law were considered by both Jews and Christians to be instruments of God's governance of his people.

But it is a different question whether this traditional view of the morality of killing is correct. Personally, I do not believe that it is. Anyone today who carefully studies the Old

Testament texts relevant to capital punishment and warfare —even a person who accepts the Bible as a communication from God—is unlikely to find in these texts the last word on justifiable homicide.[25] The New Testament offers no clear justification of killing as capital punishment and in war, and some Christians have regarded the adoption of any proposal to kill another person as incompatible with the law of the Gospel.[26] On this view, human life does not lose its inviolability because of the wrongful behavior of the person who bears this life, and God does not will men to adopt any proposal to kill one another.

Still, just as one might justifiably adopt a proposal consistent with all the basic human goods which nevertheless by its effects contributes to the causation of one's own death, so one might justifiably bring about the death of another without adopting a proposal to kill him. Thomas Aquinas tried to justify killing in self-defense in this way.[27] However, a like analysis of capital punishment hardly seems possible. As for acts of war, it is clear that many of them do precisely propose the death of the enemy. The language adopted by government officials in talking about the Vietnam war—for example, "search and destroy operation," "body count," and "cost per kill"—as well as the whole strategy of that war made clear that the proposal was to kill as a means of breaking the enemy's will. Nuclear deterrent strategy involves the same willingness and readiness to kill as a way of influencing the behavior of others; in this respect the present balance of terror is an extension of the policy of obliteration bombing in World War II, which culminated in the atomic bombing of Japan. In all of these cases, consequentialist rationalizations were offered for murderous policies.

It is a complex question, which I have discussed elsewhere, whether any other deadly deed, in warfare or not, can be justified along the lines of the justification of self defense.[28] For my part, if anyone thinks no deadly deed of war can be morally justified, my sympathies are with him, although I think that some proposals which are not proposals to kill might be justified even though the acts which execute them will contribute by their effects to the death of persons. If I were persuaded that no such proposal really is consistent with uncompromising respect for the basic good of the lives of persons, then I would not approve the adoption of such a proposal to do a deadly deed even as a means to secure justice, to preserve freedom, or to serve any other human good whatsoever.

Many current arguments for euthanasia stress that morally speaking fully voluntary euthanasia must be regarded as assisted suicide. I grant this point. It is important to notice that unlike some other self-destructive acts, voluntary euthanasia must be called "suicide" in the full sense in which I am using the word here, for the individual precisely adopts a proposal that he be killed, and thus the choice bears upon the good of human life and is purposely destructive of this good. It follows that voluntary euthanasia is always wrong for the same reason that any other suicide is.

However, since suicide is always immoral, voluntary euthanasia always adds another and specific evil to that of unassisted suicide: the involvement of at least one other person, and perhaps of many other persons, in the wrongful act. What I have said above about the existential implications of suicide and about the significance of readiness and willingness to violate the basic good of the life of a human person extends to all who cooperate in suicide and other wrongful killing. One who asks another to kill him invites the other to share his character as killer.

Of course, just as a person might kill himself without committing suicide—for the deed might lack moral significance or have some significance other than that of suicide—so a person might kill another without assuming the moral character of one ready and willing to kill people. Moreover, in some cases of intense distress and emotional turmoil—for example, when a close relative kills someone suffering greatly at the suffering person's own repeated request—whatever guilt there is can be greatly mitigated, and such a killer might be quite unready to kill anyone else.

Freudian theories point to the interchangeability of inwardly and outwardly directed aggression as aspects of the death instinct. Suicide and murder often are associated in fact, and perhaps more often in potentiality.[29] Whatever one thinks of the psychodynamic theory of behavior hostile to human life, it seems safe to say the theory is more relevant to subconscious determinants of behavior than to the morally relevant determinants consciously present in deliberation, in choice, and in the distortion of one's attitude toward basic goods characteristic of morally wrong choices.

However, the phenomenon of aggression is not to be explained wholly by a given, unconscious force, such as the so-called death instinct. Aggression also has a moral significance. Here, too, there is likely to be some degree of indifference about whose life is to be destroyed. For if human life is not inviolable as such, it is not absolutely inviolable in any particular instance.

There may be cultural factors, psychological conditions, or concern for certain goods at stake in particular cases which will prevent an individual who in general is ready to kill from being willing to kill in these cases. Even professional killers are selective about their victims. Hence, one cannot make predictions that an individual ready and willing to kill himself or ready and willing to cooperate in voluntary euthanasia will be ready and willing to kill in other circumstances. Nevertheless, any such individual's attitude toward human life renders it impossible that killing people should any longer be unthinkable for him. For him, killing is a proposal to think about whenever it occurs to him as a possible solution to some problem. One who is ready and willing to kill anyone at all, even if only himself, is inconsistent if he does not regard the proposal to kill as a live option.

6. SHOULD VOLUNTARY EUTHANASIA BE LEGALIZED?

Those who argue for the legalization of euthanasia usually assume that suicide is not always wrong. They then argue that in a case in which suicide is morally permissible an individual has a right to kill himself. Assisted suicide—voluntary euthanasia—would violate no one's right to life. The legalization of euthanasia would merely permit individuals to help others in the project of killing themselves. Such help is a form of beneficence which the law should encourage, not interfere with.

I have tried to show that suicide, when it is morally significant at all, is never morally permissible. A proponent of euthanasia will argue that even if suicide is immoral, it need not be prohibited by criminal law. In many jurisdictions, in fact, neither suicide nor attempted suicide is any longer regarded as a crime. Why, then, should voluntary euthanasia, which is assisted suicide, continue to be regarded as a crime? The prohibition of voluntary euthanasia means that individuals who are burdened with severe suffering and who desire death are legally prevented from having their desire fulfilled. Is it not cruel and inhumane to require such individuals to continue suffering? Cannot the law be altered to help them?

No one will deny that the law ought to promote practices other than euthanasia which will ease the suffering of the sick and the dying. Such practices include the careful use of pain-relieving drugs as needed, even if such remedies also incidentally shorten life. Moreover, other methods of relieving pain— for example, the blocking or cutting of nerves—should be available to all who can be helped by them.

The easing of the suffering of the sick and dying also demands an effort to relieve unpleasant conditions other than pain. As part of its duty to promote the general welfare, society should support research to seek ways to minimize the suffering of the dying, should provide facilities to care for the chronically ill, and should cushion the impact of terminal illness upon the estates of those who need expensive care to ease their dying. The conditions under which people die often are horrible not because better conditions *cannot* be provided, but because health-care personnel and society at large fail to do what *could* and *should* be done.

Moreover, the dying of the mortally ill is eased considerably if a reasonable limit is placed upon efforts to prolong life. Proponents of the legalization of euthanasia usually classify a person's omission or refusal of medical treatment as "suicide" and classify any limitation by physicians upon efforts to prolong life as "euthanasia." These classifications are arbitrary; they lack foundation in morality and law.

The only reason for making them is that everyone grants the moral permissibility in many cases and the legal right of any person to omit or to refuse medical treatment provided that he does not adopt a proposal to kill himself. Likewise, everyone admits the legal right of any physician to limit efforts to prolong life provided that he does what is required by the common standards of medical practice. Moreover, a physician is not held to care for a patient who refuses to cooperate in treatment.[30] Proponents of the legalization of euthanasia wish to class as euthanasia what everyone admits to be permissible and legitimate, precisely in order to justify and legitimate acts which until now have been rejected as immoral and illegal.

It is often argued that with advancing medical techniques, it will become possible to keep alive indefinitely many comatose patients and individuals suffering from senile dementia.[31] However, the medical profession through its own associations and governing bodies can define standards of medical practice to limit measures which would prolong life.

The reasonable point at which to draw the line is not easily decided; it depends in part upon complex technical considerations. Medical standards ought to take into account factors such as the cost of further measures to prolong life to the patient both in money and in suffering, the degree of probability that these measures will help a patient keep or regain consciousness and a coherent state of mind, and the competing demand for health-care facilities from patients with better prospects of recovery.

Medical standards can take such factors into account, provided that no one adopts a proposal that a patient be killed either by deed or by omission. The medical profession can and should regulate the professional activities of its members in accord with respect for all the basic human goods, and sometimes such respect demands that treatment go no further. Moreover, the medical profession can and should see to it that health-care facilities are used as efficiently as possible in view of the objective of the medical art, which is to promote the life and health of everyone. Thus, sometimes these resources must be withdrawn from certain patients if others with a better prognosis are to be fairly served.

If the medical profession fails to set reasonable limits upon measures which prolong life, public authority might justly require the profession to deal with this problem. However, if medical standards are within tolerable bounds and if they do not condone omitting care as a method of killing patients, public authority would be most unwise to attempt to legislate in so complex and technical an area. But it is equally unwise for the medical profession to allow standards of care to be altered by evolving practice and custom alone.

By acting in an organized way, the profession can ensure that ample consideration be given to all aspects of the problem, and to the opinions of the public at large. Then the profession can clarify its own standards, and in doing so define the legal liability of its members. Individual physicians will thus be able to omit or discontinue measures which stretch out dying at a point which seems reasonable, and to continue to exercise such judgments without undue fear of incurring criminal or civil liability.

One thing is clear. The problem of drawing a line in active treatment is a distinct question from euthanasia. Even if voluntary euthanasia were legal under certain conditions for certain cases, physicians still would be legally responsible in all other cases for judging the point at which to omit or discontinue medical treatment. Therefore, the legalization of euthanasia would not resolve the problem of the proper limits of active treatment.

If the question of limiting active treatment is set aside, the jurisprudential issue about voluntary euthanasia is reduced to the question whether criminal law should be amended to permit someone to kill a consenting person—specifically, whether one person should be legally permitted to help another to commit suicide. Homicide in general is severely prohibited by criminal law because it violates the right to life of a member of society. Homicide upon a consenting person does not violate the right to life. Indeed, the prohibition of such homicide interferes with the liberal ideal that an individual be permitted to do as he pleases provided that he harms no one but himself. Even if suicide is immoral, the law should not attempt to prevent every immoral act. Hence, it seems to some people that voluntary euthanasia should be legalized.

I grant that not every immoral act should be regarded as a crime. Many sorts of immoral activity should be ignored by criminal law. But voluntary euthanasia is one kind of act criminal law should not ignore.

An immoral act ought not to be treated as a crime unless it violates one of the goods to which political society is directed. For example, those acts which only violate holiness ought not to be treated as crimes, because political society is not directed toward this good. But this society is directed toward justice, and so unjust acts which are likely to cause serious harm should be crimes. It is an error to suppose, however, that justice is the only good which should be protected by criminal law. Political society also is concerned with peace, including domestic peace; the general welfare; liberty; and the life, health, and safety of persons within its jurisdiction. Under appropriate conditions, acts which violate any of these goods, even if they do not violate justice, are reasonably treated as crimes.

What are the "appropriate conditions"? At least that there be a fair prospect that the law will protect and promote the good to which it is directed and that it not be itself unjust. A criminal law against the manufacture and sale of alcoholic beverages, even if it met other conditions, might be ruled out on the ground that there is little prospect that it will protect and promote the goods to which it is directed. A criminal law which was retroactive, or which arbitrarily exempted some members of the society, or which seriously violated some guaranteed right such as freedom of religion would be unjust in itself.

Suicide—that is, the moral act of suicide as defined in section two—is immoral. However, such an act is not easily distinguished from many suicidal acts which fall short of moral significance. The only good always violated by suicide is the human life of the agent himself; the act does not always violate justice and usually it has little detrimental effect upon other goods in which society has an interest. If suicide is forbidden by law, there obviously is no prospect that such a law will protect the good of life. If attempted suicide is forbidden, there is hardly a better prospect for effective protection of the good at stake. Indeed, if criminal laws against suicide attempts were enforced, the criminal process probably would inhibit reporting of suicide attempts, prompt care for those who have attempted suicide, and treatment by medical and other means of nonrational, suicidal persons. For these reasons, it is reasonable that suicide and attempted suicide be exempt from criminal liability.

In practice, this is the legal policy in English-speaking countries, although in some jurisdictions the letter of the law still regards suicide or attempted suicide as criminal. Even in jurisdictions in which there is no criminal statute directly bearing on suicide, however, public policy discourages the act. One who forcibly prevents another from committing suicide is never charged with assault, as he might be if he prevented the same person from going about other legitimate business.[32]

Moreover, police officers and other public officials regularly use force to interfere with suicide attempts. No doubt it is often assumed that the person attempting suicide is not acting by rational choice, and in many cases this assumption is correct. However, so far as I know, no effort is made anywhere to protect from the interference of others those who make a rational choice to commit suicide.

Thus, public policy recognizes a general right to prevent suicide, and even imposes a duty in this regard upon certain individuals. This state of affairs is perfectly intelligible, even though attempted suicide is not regarded as criminal, since suicide does violate the good of life, in which society has an interest. It simply is not the case that individuals have a legal right to do whatever the law does not prohibit them from doing. An unrelated example is the collection of gambling debts; the law need recognize no right to collect such debts even if it does not prohibit their collection. Thus, in some cases, public policy may discourage what criminal law ought not to prohibit.

Proponents of the legalization of euthanasia also often claim that the practice already is widespread, and urge that the law be altered to conform with this practice. Undoubtedly, there is a widespread practice of limiting active medical treatment. But, as already explained, this practice—which is not fairly classed as euthanasia—does not violate existing law so long as the treatment meets the common standards of medical practice.

Again, some physicians admit that they have violated existing standards of medical practice and have purposely killed patients, sometimes by deed and sometimes by omission, sometimes at the patient's request and sometimes without it.

The claim that the criminal law of homicide ought to be altered to conform to existing practice, taken as a general proposition, is absurd. Not only certain physicians but also certain members of the Mafia and of the CIA seem to regard their behavior as exempt from regulation by the criminal law of homicide.

But proponents of euthanasia point out that physicians are members of a respectable profession and that they are particularly competent in the matter of life and death. The premise of this argument also is absurd. Public officials too are members of a respectable profession and they are particularly competent in the matter of dispensing public funds, but it does not follow that even the beneficient dispensing of public funds for purposes other than those authorized by law ought to be legalized, although this sort of beneficence now occurs in some cases.

Some who *oppose* the legalization of euthanasia suggest that the law need not be altered to permit it because physicians now do it and will continue to do it in "appropriate" cases even though this practice is "outside the letter of the law." I regard this suggestion as vicious, however well-intentioned might be those who offer it. There ought not to be any elite group exempt from criminal law, particularly in a matter as serious as homicide. Especially in a democratic society, justice demands that everyone from the highest official to the humblest citizen be equally subject to the enforcement of the criminal law when he chooses to violate it. Anyone who encourages physicians to violate the law of homicide, moreover, encourages the whole spectrum of present violations. According to their own testimony, some physicians have killed patients without their consent.

Those who *support* the legalization of what physicians are now doing also approve the whole spectrum of present violations, including homicide without the patient's consent.

If proponents of legalization say they seek only a legal clarification to explicitly permit present practices which are at the borderline of legality, this demand still is unreasonable. On the one hand, physicians are not being prosecuted for what they are now doing. Moreover, as explained above, any problems with regard to the proper cut-off point for treatment can and must be dealt with by the medical profession itself. On the other hand, any amendment to the law which would admit some borderline practice will only move the line, not eliminate it.

To a great extent, borderline cases arise because criminal liability extends only as far as a crime *can be proved*. Whereever criminal law draws its line, there always will be cases— ones further along the spectrum of practices now engaged in by physicians who take it upon themselves to violate the law of homicide—in which the boundary is violated but admissible evidence is not available to prove this fact beyond a reasonable doubt. If the law is altered to permit an act previously forbidden in such cases, a new class of cases arises in which the same situation obtains. The initial relaxations in abortion laws which purportedly only clarified the law as to a few borderline cases illustrate how such amendments to a criminal statute relocate the boundary rather than mark it more clearly.

The central argument proposed in favor of legalizing voluntary euthanasia is along the following lines. The criminal law of homicide, to the extent that it prohibits voluntary euthanasia, violates the *liberty* of the patient and of the physician, because there is no *compelling* public interest which justifies legal interference in this matter. According to this argument, the individual who seeks euthanasia is not acting in an arbitrary way, but has a legitimate interest in avoiding suffering. Unless there is a *compelling* public interest which would justify interference, the frustration of a suffering individual's desire to escape is cruel and unjustified. Even if others regard this mode of escape as immoral, this judgment should not be imposed by law upon those who do not agree with it.[33]

Clearly, if there were no public interest at all, it would be cruel to require individuals to undergo avoidable suffering, and it would violate liberty to forbid patients and physicians to follow their own judgment in this matter. However, if suicide does violate the good of life and if there is a public interest in this good, then the only question about the justification for a legal prohibition of voluntary euthanasia is whether the public interest ought or ought not to take precedence over the interest of individuals in avoiding suffering and their claim of liberty.

To answer this question, one must consider what possible ways there might be to amend the criminal law of homicide to permit euthanasia. Amendments could take either of two forms. One approach would be to entrust the decision to physicians with few formal safeguards; the other approach would be to provide formal safeguards and a legal process to ensure that legally established conditions had been met before the deadly deed was carried out.

Glanville Williams spells out the essential content of a bill which would leave the matter of euthanasia to the judgment of physicians:

> It would provide that no medical practitioner should be guilty of an offence in respect of an act done intentionally to accelerate the death of a patient who is seriously ill, unless it is proved that the act was not done in good faith with the consent of the patient and for the purpose of saving him from severe pain in an illness believed to be of an incurable and fatal character. Under this formula it would be for the physician, if charged, to show that the patient was seriously ill, but for the prosecution to prove that the physician acted from some motive other than the humanitarian one allowed to him by law.[34]

Thus, Williams would leave the matter of euthanasia to the discretion of the physician.

This means that every physician—general practitioner or specialist, young or old, experienced or inexperienced, most competent or least competent, drunk or sober, chosen by the patient or assigned by someone in charge of an emergency room, well-informed about a patient's condition or misinformed about it, on the basis of a thorough study of tests and careful consultation or on the basis of one superficial examination, primarily concerned to serve individuals or primarily concerned to serve his own or someone else's conception of the public welfare, inclined to fight losing battles or eager to have a record of never losing a patient who did not consent to "accelerated" death, honestly dedicated to saving life or venally interested in terminating it—for example, having been paid by an individual's prospective heirs or enemies—*every physician* would have a license to kill any seriously ill patient.

Once the physician could show that the patient was indeed "seriously ill"—whatever that might mean—the physician could claim that the patient did give consent and then the physician would be free of criminal liability unless the prosecution could prove *beyond reasonable doubt* that he did not act *in good faith* or that he did not *intend* to save the patient from pain or that he did not *believe* the illness to be incurable or fatal. However, once the patient was dead, the prosecution could not disprove *beyond reasonable doubt* the physician's *good faith* or his *intent* or his *belief* or his *claim* that the patient had indeed consented. Once the patient was dead, it would hardly be possible to evaluate the worth of his consent, whether it was truly voluntary or extorted, whether the patient was competent or incompetent at the time of consent. Unless a physician committed a homicide entirely outside the course of medical practice—for example, while engaged in an armed robbery—it would be impossible to rebut the presumption in his favor established by so lax an amendment to the law of homicide. Anyone who proposed to murder someone who was seriously ill would need only find a cooperative medical practitioner in order to execute the murderous purpose.

If euthanasia is to be left so completely to the judgment of physicians, it is clear that there is a *compelling* public interest in the life of an individual who voluntarily consents to his own death in order to avoid suffering. The life of such an individual is *in practice* indistinguishable from the lives of many potential victims of murder. It also is worth bearing in mind that most individuals who are seriously ill and who genuinely desire their own death to avoid pain and suffering can fulfill their desire without endangering anyone else by committing suicide without the assistance of another person.[35]

Therefore, one who, like Williams, wants euthanasia legalized by entrusting the matter to the discretion of physicians is ready to accept a serious risk to the lives of many who do not desire to be killed for the sake of easing the deaths of a few who wish help in committing suicide. Moreover, one who adopts this approach to legalizing euthanasia is ready to add to the anxiety most people already feel—because of the terrorism and violence so widespread today—the further cause for anxiety that some physician, acting in malicious conspiracy or in honest error, might "accelerate" their death.

A safer approach would be to provide formal safeguards and a legal process to ensure that legally established conditions had been met before the deadly deed was executed.

Conditions could be set to ensure the fact and the competence of the patient's consent; these conditions surely would include disinterested witnesses and a waiting period, and probably should include a judicial hearing and court certification, analogous to the probating of a will. Care would be needed to assure that if consent had been given before the illness began, it was not subsequently revoked, and if consent was given during the illness, it was fully informed and not conditioned by a state of mind abnormal because of transient suffering or the psychic effect of remedies. It is hardly unreasonable that as much care be taken in disposing of a person's life as will be taken in disposing of his property. Even if a probate process were not required in every instance of euthanasia, legal processes surely would be necessary to settle cases in which there were disputes—for example, between the physician and a member of the patient's family—about the patient's true wishes.

Because of the danger that an individual physician might act precipitately or incompetently or even maliciously, consultation and independent confirmation of the diagnosis would be indispensible. Thus a safe law would have to establish a committee system or a public medical board empowered to make the medical judgment which would inform the patient's consent or certify that the conditions under which that patient previously declared his desire to be killed were in fact fulfilled.

Similar committees in the matter of abortion did not work very satisfactorily, but the problem was eliminated by the elimination of laws forbidding abortion. In the case of euthanasia, there can be no question of eliminating the problems by eliminating the relevant criminal law, for it is the law prohibiting homicide, and no society can exist without some restriction on homicide.

The legalization of euthanasia would not merely permit the practice for those who felt morally free or morally bound to engage in it. Euthanasia, if legal, would become an ordinary medical operation.[36] Physicians would be expected to perform it, nurses to participate in it, hospitals to permit it, and private health plans and medicare to pay for it.

The argument that euthanasia be legalized out of respect for personal liberties is modeled upon a similar argument which was made in regard to abortion. However, once the asserted right of pregnant women to abortion was given legal force by the decision of the United States Supreme Court, cases were pressed by purported advocates of civil liberties to compel public and private hospitals to facilitate abortion, and to mandate the use of public funds to pay for abortions.[37]

If euthanasia is to be regulated so carefully by legal process and integrated so completely into important public institutions, the public interest in the life of each individual—even one who voluntarily consents to his own death—becomes *compelling*. For if voluntary euthanasia cannot be legalized without being legally regulated and institutionalized, then the amendment of the criminal law to permit such homicide will deeply involve the state and many of its members in a practice repugnant to the convictions of many citizens. This repugnance is a reasonable one—even if the conviction that suicide is morally wrong has roots in religious tradition—for purely philosophical arguments, such as those outlined in previous sections of this paper, support it.

In regulating and institutionalizing euthanasia, the state not only would respect the liberty of patients and physicians who wish to engage in this practice but also would infringe the liberty of citizens who wish to remain clear of involvement in it. When the state acts officially, all citizens are involved in its action; when a practice is institutionalized, all who participate in the relevant institution are pressed to cooperate in the practice. Those who advocate the legalization of euthanasia with ample safeguards evidence little respect for the right of those who consider this practice murder to keep their society and themselves clear of it.[38]

Those who favor what they call "liberalization" of criminal law to permit killing in some cases frequently use the example of sexual activities involving only consenting adults in private as a model for analyzing the jurisprudential problems raised by their proposals with regard to killing. I submit that this model is hardly relevant. Society can officially ignore what Doe and Roe do sexually with each other in private, provided that they are adults, that they both consent, and that they do not cause each other lasting bodily harm.

However, if Doe and Roe engage in sadistic practices upon Oe, even with her consent, such that her life in endangered or her body seriously injured, then the situation is more like voluntary euthanasia. If the state, to protect persons who are not masochists, as Oe is, must regulate and institutionalize the consensual practices of Doe, Roe, and Oe—for example, by issuing licenses to certain public houses in which these practices will be permitted and by requiring that there be legal certification of the consent of Oe—then a jurisprudential problem arises closely analogous to that involved in legally regulated and institutionalized assisted suicide. If these practices are to be carried on, not in public houses reserved for the purpose, but in existing institutions which were created for quite a different purpose, many of the present members of which abhor such practices, then the analogy is still more precise.

Does the public have a right to remain clear of involvement in sado-masochism? I submit that the public does have such a right, and that such practices could not be safely legalized without public involvement, by way of legal regulation and institutionalization, which would violate the right to remain clear. Similarly, the public has a right to remain clear of the killing of human beings, and even voluntary euthanasia cannot be safely legalized without public involvement which would violate the right of the public to remain clear. There is nothing liberal in a policy which would facilitate the exercise of the liberty of some citizens to act against the good of life, in which there is some public interest, by involving in activities repugnant to many citizens the legal processes and institutions in which all citizens participate willy-nilly.

In the matter of euthanasia as in some other matters, many who regard themselves as liberals seem to be intent upon creating a society in which they and those who agree with them can live and die most comfortably, even if this supposedly liberal society must be one from which those who do not wish to share the character of killer must find themselves profoundly alienated. The moral justification of euthanasia is part of a worldview; some people believe in this worldview and are committed to putting it into practice so far as possible in their own lives. Society can respect this worldview as a secular religious belief; the law might go so far as to forbid interference in suicide attempts by those who adhere to this form of belief.

However, proponents of this worldview are not satisfied with the legal status of their belief as one of many religions to which anyone is free to adhere or not. They wish to have their worldview accepted as a secular, established religion. In the name of liberty, they press society to adapt itself to the rites of their religion, which include the killing of human beings.

It should be noticed that a compromise between voluntary euthanasia at the discretion of the physician and legally regulated and institutionalized voluntary euthanasia would not mitigate the difficulty involved in the alternatives. Just to the extent that euthanasia is not legally regulated and institutionalized, it will be difficult to distinguish from homicide without consent; just to the extent that euthanasia is legally regulated and institutionalized, it will require the involvement of the people—through their participation willy-nilly in the law and other public institutions—in practices to which many have a reasonable repugnance.[39]

In arguing against the legalization of euthanasia, Yale Kamisar criticized Glanville Williams' proposal that the matter be left to the discretion of physicians. Kamisar then went on to point out that adequate safeguards would make euthanasia anything but quick and easy, and that such safeguards are repulsive even to many who sympathize with the movement.[40] Kamisar did not offer the line of argument I am proposing with regard to the involvement of unwilling persons in euthanasia, but his argument was forceful even without this consideration and, I believe, sound within its limits.

In responding to Kamisar, Williams argued that the problem posed by the alternatives of intolerable formalities and a dangerous lack of formalities is not an "ordinary logical dilemma." Williams proposes a parable to clarify what he believes to be the fallacy in Kamisar's argument. The parable concerns a mythical state of Ruritania from which citizens are not permitted to emigrate. A proposal is made to permit emigration, but its proponent "is aware of the power of traditional opinion, and so seeks to word his proposal in a modest way," including many safeguards. (The phrasing suggests the significance of any modesty in Williams' proposal for legalizing euthanasia.) An opponent attacks the safeguards as an intolerable imposition upon a free Ruritanian citizen who wishes to emigrate. Williams suggests that this attack is only legitimate if the opponent of the safeguards is willing to go farther in permitting emigration than the original proponent of legalization of emigration was willing to go.[41]

Williams' effort to rebut Kamisar's dilemma fails. By using the analogy of euthanasia to emigration, Williams begs the question, since the moral and legal acceptability of emigration is unquestioned while the acceptability of euthanasia is precisely what is in question. Also, in the parable, the only reason for the safeguards is to protect those who wish to emigrate, whereas the real necessity for safeguards is to protect those who do not wish to be killed. Moreover, Williams assumes that the only objection to safeguards is their interference with the liberty of the person who wishes to emigrate, while I have pointed out that safeguards required for legalized euthanasia are objectionable because they draw into the killing of human beings people who do not wish to be involved in such killing. Williams says: ". . . it is better to be allowed to emigrate on condition of form-filling than not to be allowed to emigrate at all."[42] He simply ignores the rights of those who do not wish to be killed and who do not wish to participate by way of their legal processes and institutions in killing others, even if those who are killed desire it.

Apart from the dilemma posed by the problem of regulation, the legalization of voluntary euthanasia can be attacked on another ground: danger to the *right* to life of those who do not volunteer to be killed. This danger will arise from the increase with the legalization of euthanasia of the number of persons sharing in the character of killer and from the intensification of readiness to take human life in many persons who already share in this character. Glanville Williams tries to deal with this sort of argument, phrased as the danger that legalization of euthanasia will lead "to a general disrespect for the sanctity of life." Williams answers the argument by pointing out that the murder rate in England did not significantly differ after World War II from what it was in 1939. He concludes:

> It is clear that if war had any effect on the murder rate, it was infinitesimal. In other words, active encouragement to slaughter on an immense scale does not diminish respect for the sanctity of life outside the area permitted. It is inconceivable that permission to put an end to the existence of the comparatively small number of suffering patients who positively wish for death would bring about any widespread decline in the value attached to human life and well-being. On the contrary, it would express that value.[43]

Williams and others undoubtedly would respond in a similar way to the danger I suggest is involved in encouraging greater numbers of people to a deeper readiness to take human life.

What exactly is the danger I foresee? The danger is not that people will develop some sort of mechanical habit of killing others or lose their inhibitions about violating the criminal law of homicide in general. Rather, the danger is that the public acceptance of voluntary euthanasia and involvement in it would alter people's perception of the value of human life. This altered perception would facilitate a variety of acts which can be rational only if human life is a merely instrumental good. These acts would include, but not be limited to, acts of homicide similar in some ways to voluntary euthanasia, such as the killing of infants who become unwanted after they are born and it is too late to abort them.

I see the danger arising not only in respect to physicians who would administer voluntary euthanasia, but also in respect to persons who would consent to it, perhaps years before the occasion arose to act upon this consent, and even in respect to persons who would in any way cooperate in or condone this practice.

In arguing that encouragement of soldiers in World War II to slaughter did not increase the murder rate in England, Williams points out one case in which a correlation is lacking. I think there are other cases in which there is a correlation; there also are reasons why the correlation should not be expected in the case Williams cites.

If it were not impossible to prove due to lack of hard evidence, it would be interesting to consider whether the training of soldiers during World War II did not affect their readiness to kill noncombatants in the war zone but off the field of battle or on the margins of that field. Soldiers returning from World War II often told stories of unauthorized killing which did not contribute to the attainment of military objectives. Among these stories were accounts of cases in which the victim was an unpopular fellow soldier or officer.

Apart from killings, other acts of unauthorized violence against persons, such as forcible rapes, did occur under war conditions.

The terroristic use of bombing during World War II, culminating in the atomic bombing of Japan, did pave the way for the nuclear deterrent strategy and the balance of terror in which the great powers are now locked. Public acceptance of and involvement in this strategy perhaps partly explains the increase of terrorism and other violence in recent years. Furthermore, there is ample evidence of atrocities against noncombatants in the war in Vietnam and in some other wars since World War II, in which terrorism has become common.

As I explained at the end of section five, an individual who is in general willing to kill may be inhibited from doing so in any particular case. Those encouraged to slaughter on an immense scale during World War II, even if they assumed the character of killer, probably were inhibited by social restraints from acting upon their altered perception of the value of human life when they returned to the very different conditions of their normal world.

But what is more helpful in explaining the lack of correlation to which Williams points is the distinction between outward behavior and the proposal which is executed by that behavior if it is a morally significant action. Soldiers in World War II brought about many deaths. But, reasonably or not, many if not almost all of these soldiers acted not on a proposal to kill, but on a more basic proposal to do one's duty as a citizen by going into combat; once in combat, many if not almost all soldiers acted on a proposal to preserve their own lives by stopping the enemy's action. The allied nations surrounded the war with a mystique which was generally reinforced by all of the institutions of society; this mystique created an illusion, at least, of justification which made it possible for many persons to do deadly deeds without assuming the character of killer.

Persons who accept voluntary euthanasia and become existentially involved in it perhaps will never have occasion to kill anyone. However, the proposal in this case clearly and precisely is to destroy human lives as a means to serve other goods. The way such persons perceive the good of human life cannot fail to be affected by their choices inconsistent with this good. For this reason, such persons are likely to proceed from voluntary euthanasia to nonvoluntary euthanasia, much as persons who were involved in terror bombing during World War II proceeded to construct the present balance of terror and to direct the atrocities of Vietnam.

Proponents of the legalization of voluntary euthanasia regularly respond to any argument which refers to its relationship to nonvoluntary euthanasia by classifying the argument as a fallacy. Arguments variously called "the wedge" or "the slippery slope" or "the camel's nose under the tentflap" are discussed in many works on fallacies. However, those who classify any argument as fallacious bear the burden of proof of showing that it does involve the fallacy they claim it does. How well do proponents of voluntary euthanasia fulfill their responsibility in this regard?

Kamisar devoted part of his article to developing an argument which he himself called a "wedge principle." He suggests the likelihood that voluntary euthanasia will lead to nonvoluntary euthanasia, and points to the precedent of Nazi Germany as supporting evidence. Kamisar also points out that defenders of civil liberties frequently appeal to the wedge principle to resist even slight, technical violations of civil liberties in cases in which there is little otherwise to be said against the violation.[44]

Williams responded to this argument: "C.M. Cornford put the argument in its place when he said that the wedge objection means this, that you should not act justly today, for fear that you may be asked to act still more justly tomorrow."[45] Obviously, this response begs the question, for Kamisar had argued that voluntary euthanasia is undesirable in itself and that it leads to even worse consequences. Williams assumes that the likelihood that voluntary euthanasia will pave the way for nonvoluntary euthanasia is no argument against his position because he himself already concedes the principle at issue— *Williams advocates nonvoluntary euthanasia* for "hopelessly defective infants."[46] Moreover, Williams is prepared to think about nonvoluntary euthanasia for the elderly, although he does not propose it in today's society.[47]

In this paper I have been dealing with suicide and with voluntary euthanasia insofar as it is assisted suicide. I assume that an argument against nonvoluntary euthanasia is easier than an argument against voluntary euthanasia. If the killing is not voluntary, it not only violates the *good* of life but also violates the *right* to life. Both in morality and in law, it is easier to show the wrongfulness of an act which violates a right than it is to show the wrongfulness of an act contrary only to goods other than justice. Hence, in pointing out that the legalization of voluntary euthanasia is likely to lead to the legalization of nonvoluntary euthanasia, I am arguing that we should not adopt a bad public policy today in part—*but only in part*—for fear that we shall be asked to adopt an unjust policy tomorrow.

In the legal domain, the lines between voluntary and nonvoluntary are not sharply drawn, for any program of voluntary euthanasia would raise the problem of the validity of consent by a parent or guardian for the killing of a noncompetent minor or adult.[48] If consent on behalf of the noncompetent is permitted, nonvoluntary euthanasia is a fact. The next step would be involuntary euthanasia. Individuals who refused to consent might be ruled incompetent if those around them did not care to sustain them, and if a judge or other public official designated for the purpose decided that the refusal was irrational. Then the guardian of the incompetent individual could consent on his behalf to the termination of his miserable and useless life.

Among proponents of euthanasia, Williams is by no means alone in being willing to go beyond voluntary euthanasia to nonvoluntary euthanasia, at least in the case of infants. Kamisar documents the extent of this thrust in the pro-euthanasia movement.[49] He shows that nonvoluntary euthanasia is an important part of the declared objectives of leaders of the movement. He also shows—and this point is a very telling one—that homicide without the victim's consent is the sort of killing which has occurred in many of the "mercy killings"used as illustrations by proponents of euthanasia. Obviously, if the true objective of the movement were voluntary euthanasia alone, the use of such inappropriate examples would be avoided with great care, for they would misrepresent the objective in a very serious way.

In this situation, it is disingenuous to contend that voluntary euthanasia and nonvoluntary euthanasia are unrelated matters, and that acceptance of the first no more paves the way for the second than training to kill in war paves the way for murder on the homefront after the war. In the present situation, the public ought to realize that the legalization of euthanasia in any set of cases will lead to its legalization in a very broad range of cases, just as the legalization of abortion in a few cases led to unrestricted abortion.

Of course, there are differences. One of them is that no one who was able to think about the abortion issue was in danger of being included among the victims if abortion was made completely legal, as it eventually was. Some now thinking about the euthanasia issue are in danger of being included among the victims if nonvoluntary euthanasia becomes legal.

The analogue of unrestricted abortion for those already born would, however, be unrestricted homicide. The law cannot go so far, since the lives of those who can fight to protect themselves and the lives of those who have strong protectors must be guaranteed by law if any sort of social order is to be preserved. However, if only such lives are guaranteed by law, no principle of equal justice before the law would remain. Among citizens of such a society as among nations in today's world, justice would be little more than a word; in reality all relationships would be based upon power rather than upon any ideal principle.

The legalization of voluntary euthanasia would deprive unwanted infants of their last line of defense. Their first line of defense was that the killing of the innocent without their consent violates the right to life. But abortion breached this line. Their second line of defense is that the killing of persons with or without their consent violates the good of life, in which there is a public interest implemented in part by the existing law of homicide. But voluntary euthanasia will breach this line. After that, there will remain only the technical obstacle of using the consent of a parent or guardian to extend to the unwanted infant the same right to "death with dignity" granted to anyone competent to consent on his own behalf. Since there is no clear dividing line between seriously defective infants and normal infants and since being unwanted is certain to be regarded as a serious defect in itself, there is no reason to suppose that the killing of infants with the sanction of law would be limited to the killing of some few suffering from the most serious defects.

In some societies, birth was regarded as a magical dividing line, at which human individuals became persons and members of society. But we know too much about unborn children to believe that birth is a very important dividing line. And our technical society has little regard for magical lines in any case.

Joseph Fletcher, writing with his usual bluntness, assumes that abortion is justified and argues from this assumption that the killing of infants afflicted with Down's syndrome (mongolism) also is justified.

> Now, then, if through ignorance or neglect or sheer chance (like the forty-seventh chromosome) the damage has not been ended prenatally, why should it not be ended neonatally? To have given birth innocently to a Down's case, when we would not have done so if we had known the truth, does not of itself justify our extending the tragedy. By stubbornly persisting we only compound the evil; we make ourselves "accessories" after the fact of a monstrous accident. We cannot be blamed for what we did not know, but we can be blamed when we do know.
>
> The only difference between the fetus and the infant is that the infant breathes with its lungs. Does this make any significant difference morally or from the point of view of values? Surely not. Life and human *being* is a process, not an event; a continuum, not an episode. It is purely superstitious to assert that life "occurs" at fertilization or nidation or embryonic formation or fetal animation (movement) or birth or at school or voting age.[50]

Thus Fletcher makes clear that no one's life in inviolable unless the individual meets Fletcher's criteria of personhood. Fletcher says that no one having Down's syndrome meets these criteria: "True guilt arises only from an offense against a person, and a Down's is not a person."[51]

This statement is brutal. What is an individual who has Down's syndrome and who can read to think when he reads what Fletcher says about such individuals? *There are individuals with Down's syndrome who could read and understand what Fletcher says about them.*[52] Fletcher obviously lacks Glanville Williams' inhibitions about causing anxiety in potential victims of nonvoluntary euthanasia.

It also is worth noticing that Fletcher is not satisfied to claim that the killing of infants having Down's syndrome might be morally permissible. He holds blameworthy parents who love such children. He says that such parents "compound the evil" and he refers to them as "accessories." In Fletcher's view, any parent who cherishes a child whom Fletcher has decided is a nonperson is morally blameworthy.

Proponents of the legalization of euthanasia dismiss the Nazi example as irrelevant. The Nazi regime had its own absurd ideology, which is unlikely to appear again. No one today is pressing to send Jews or some other ethnic group to death camps. This dismissal of the Nazi precedent is an important part of the argument that the oppositon to voluntary euthanasia on the basis of its relationship to nonvoluntary euthanasia is fallacious.

Perhaps the Nazi precedent is not precisely relevant. However, certain elements of *liberal* ideology together with a consequentialist jurisprudence can lead to an equally horrible final solution.

The liberal ideology contains two factors which can come together with explosive political force: an individualistic conception of rights and a very high regard for personal property and money.

Harriet F. Pilpel, testifying in 1966 on behalf of the New York Civil Liberties Union before a New York State Assembly committee considering the partial legalization of abortion, gave first place in her attack upon the existing statute to the tremendous social cost of illegitimacy. While admitting that it would be simplistic and callous to view the problem merely in monetary terms, she first presented the claim that the nationwide cost of supporting the "unwanted children" born during a single year could run to a public expense of seventeen-and-one-half billion dollars over a seventeen year period. She also argued that women have a right to abortion and that the foetus' competing interest in life might be regarded as "highly insignificant."[53] When the United States Supreme Court decided the abortion issue, the decision justified abortion as a woman's right, but it mentioned very obliquely other considerations in claiming that the decision was consistent "with the demands of the profound problems of the present day."[54] The combination of rights with economics seems to have been effective.

Consequentialism, as I explained in section three, has a logical dynamism to move from admitting an act as morally permissible to claiming it to be rationally necessary and obligatory, and from admitting an act as justified by an individual's own interest to considering it to be a duty to society. Joseph Fletcher's condemnatory attitude toward the parents of "Down's cases" who do not kill their children illustrates this dynamism. The permissible becomes obligatory because any alternative which promises a lesser good is condemned by the consequentialist as morally wrong. What is justified by self-interest becomes justified by the interest of society because the consequentialist seeks impartiality as a solution to the opposition between egoism and altruism.

Thus, whenever consequentialist arguments are used, one can expect that today's arguments to recognize an individual right will be followed tomorrow by arguments to establish a social duty in the same matter. And if it is once agreed that some individuals have a duty to society to consent to their own deaths, then it will be argued that those who fail to do their duty must be required by law to do it.

Mrs. Pilpel's testimony as the authorized representative of the New York Civil Liberties Union before the New York State Assembly committee in 1966 followed very closely a working paper she and William Kopit prepared about a year earlier. This working paper, considered by the New York Civil Liberties Union Board of Directors on April 20, 1965, claimed that most people do not regard a fetus of twenty-six or less weeks a living child, and then added with emphasis a very significant sentence: *"Moreover, acceptance of a utilitarian philosophy requires that we recognize that no person has an absolute right to life."*[55] In legalizing abortion, the United States Supreme Court did not adopt this utilitarian principle —at least, they did not explicitly adopt it. They simply held that the law has not recognized the unborn "as persons in the whole sense" and that the law must not protect the unborn individual before birth until it is viable outside the uterus, for until then it lacks "the capability of meaningful life."[56]

If liberal ideology and the implications of consequentialism are considered together, it becomes clear that no legalization of euthanasia can stop at voluntary euthanasia, or even at the nonvoluntary euthanasia of defective infants. The hesitation of Glanville Williams about the anxiety of those who feel insanity coming on and about the shocking aspects of the idea of disposing of the elderly is hardly likely to block the juggernaut of the pro-death movement.[57]

The final solution in the United States and other western societies will be unlike the final solution in Nazi Germany in its details, but not unlike it in its horror. And I fear that some who now live will experience this final solution. They will live to see the day they will be killed.

They will be killed, but not because they are Jews. They will be killed because the quality of their lives has declined to the point that such lives are judged not to be worth living.

They will be killed, but not to create a master-race. They will be killed to promote the general welfare, to reduce the social cost of maintaining individuals whose lives are judged to be without redeeming social value, to meet the demands of the profound problems of the day, to protect the right of individuals to pursue happiness without the burden of unwanted grandparents, parents, spouses, siblings, children, and other relatives.

They will be killed, but not on the authority of a secret, dictatorial decree. They will be killed to vindicate their right to die. This right will be discovered in one or several amendments to the United States Constitution, or perhaps discerned by the sharp insight of some Justice in the penumbra of the right to life. Or, perhaps, they will be killed by the fiat of the Supreme Court, which in disregard of every legal precedent will declare that they are not persons and that people like them never have been persons in the whole sense. Or, perhaps, they will be killed both to protect their rights and because they are not persons with rights to protect.

They will be killed, but not with poison gas in a shower room; their bodies will be disposed of, but not in incinerators. Technological progress surely will find a better, a more efficient, a less ugly way to do the job—a way which will not cause air pollution. How, then, will they be killed? Nobody can forecast the technical details. But one thing is certain. They will be killed with "dignity."

1. See David Daube, "The Linguistics of Suicide," *Philosophy and Public Affairs*, 1 (1971-1972), pp. 387-437, especially 433-437, for the limits of "suicide" and related expressions in several languages.

2. Pius XII, "The Prolongation of Life," *The Pope Speaks*, 4 (1957-1958), pp. 395-396 (*AAS*, 49 [1957], pp. 1027-1033 at 1030), perhaps regarded the distinction between ordinary and extraordinary means as descriptive. His language in the original French—"Mais il n'oblige habituellement qu'à l'emploi des moyens ordinaires (suivant les circonstances de personnes, de lieux, d'époques, de culture), c'est-à-dire des moyens qui n'imposent aucune charge extraordinaire pour soi-même ou pour un autre."—seems to hover between the purely descriptive and the frankly moral. His formulation does imply that one is obliged in every case to use "ordinary" means and can be obliged to use "extraordinary" means. I do not think any explication of the distinction which is independent of ethical criteria is likely to fit the moral judgments agreed upon by those who use the distinction, unless the descriptive explication were vague (as Pius XII's is with its use of circumstantial considerations) or circular (as Pius XII's is with its definition of "moyens ordinaires" by means of "charge extraordinaire") and so useless in practice.

3. Cf. Paul Ramsey, *The Patient as Person* (New Haven and London: 1970), pp. 118-132, for confirmation that the moral distinction does not coincide with *these* descriptive distinctions. Ramsey points out how the concept of *benefit to the patient* came to be built into the articulation of the distinction. If this concept is not to suffer the difficulties I point out in consequentialism in section three, then it must be moral, not descriptive, in its sense.

4. Edwin S. Shneidman, Norman L. Farberow, and Robert E. Litman, *The Psychology of Suicide* (New York: 1970), pp. 3-93, 227-304, and *passim*, extensively illustrate the phenomena and provide an introduction to much similar literature.

5. For an early version of a consequentialist argument for suicide, see John Donne, *Biathanatos: A Declaration of that Paradox or Thesis that Self-homicide is not so naturally Sin that it may never be otherwise* (London: n.d. [c. 1646]), especially pp. 170-176, where Donne deals with Romans 3.8. For a recent version, see R. B. Brandt, "The Morality and Rationality of Suicide," in Seymour Perlin, ed., *A Handbook for the Study of Suicide* (New York, London, Toronto: 1975), pp. 61-76, especially pp. 69-70. Leading proponents of suicide and assisted suicide (euthanasia) take the same consequentialist approach; for example, Glanville Williams, *The Sanctity of Life and the Criminal Law* (New York: 1957) pp. 248-350; Joseph Fletcher, *Morals and Medicine* (Boston: 1960), pp. 172-210. Consequentialism also is at the heart of the most extensive defense of euthanasia published up to now by a Catholic moralist: Daniel C. Maguire, *Death by Choice* (Garden City, N. Y.: 1974), especially pp. 126-129.

6. This summary of the experience of deliberation and choice owes much to Yves R. Simon, *Freedom of Choice*, ed. Peter Wolff (New York: 1969), pp. 75-127; Richard Taylor, *Action and Purpose* (Englewood Cliffs, N.J.: 1966), pp. 153-257; Paul Ricoeur, *Freedom and Nature: The Voluntary and the Involuntary*, trans. Erazim V. Kohak (Evanston, Ill.: 1966).

7. Moreover, I think this point has been established. See Joseph M. Boyle, Jr., Germain Grisez, and Olaf Tollefsen, *Free Choice: A Self-Referential Argument* (Notre Dame, Ind.: 1976).

8. R. M. Hare has attempted in various works to articulate an ethical theory which would systematically combine arbitrariness and the willingness to universalize in the genesis of moral principles. Hare's theory has been criticized—I believe conclusively—by several other philosophers. See, for example, H. J. McCloskey, *Meta-Ethics and Normative Ethics* (The Hague: 1969), pp. 66-80;

Henry B. Veatch, *For an Ontology of Morals* (Evanston, Ill.: 1971), pp. 26-36. One can put the essential difficulty in Hare's prescriptivism in terms of the is/ought fallacy: Hare tries to derive a moral "ought" from the "is" of a combination of facts—facts about premoral desires, facts about linguistic usage, and facts about decisions.

9. Dan W. Brock, "Recent Work in Utilitarianism," *American Philosophical Quarterly*, 10 (1973), pp. 241-276, examines many recent efforts to solve the problem of commensuration and the other difficulties I note, and concludes: "In my view, recent work in general strongly supports the conclusion that utilitarianism is an unacceptable moral theory." The difficulties with utilitarianism he is considering equally afflict any consequentialist theory.

10. See especially Dt. 30.15-20, Jn. 10.9-10, 11.25-26, 1 Cor. 15.12-26.

11. S. Thomae Aquinatis, *Super primam epistolam ad Corinthos lectura*, XV, lect. ii: ". . . homo naturaliter desiderat salutem sui ipsius, anima autem cum sit pars corporis hominis, non est totus homo, et anima mea non est ego; unde licet anima consequatur salutem in alia vita, non tamen ego vel quilibet homo."

12. See P. F. Strawson, "Persons," in G. N. A. Vesey, ed., *Body and Mind* (London: 1964), pp. 403-424; Gabriel Marcel, *The Mystery of Being*, vol. 1, *Reflection and Mystery* (Chicago: 1960), pp. 127-153.

13. Fletcher, *op. cit.*, p. 211 (emphasis his). Fletcher, who quotes Martin Buber, although Buber's attitude toward the body was quite different, goes on (pp. 212-213) to compare the relationship between "man" and his own "physical frame" to a partnership, but admits that this analogy fails and suggests instead that one's body is like the materials used by an artist.

14. Joseph Fletcher, *Moral Responsibility: Situation Ethics at Work* (Philadelphia: 1967), pp. 151-152.

15. A very common, but misleading, notion of moral norms is that developed on the analogy of rules of activities such as games. Such a conception misses the point that moral norms shape action from within. A helpful critique of this mistaken notion of moral norms has been provided by B. J. Diggs, "Rules and Utilitarianism," *American Philosophical Quarterly*, 1 (1964), pp. 32-44.

16. In my article, "The First Principle of Practical Reason: A Commentary on the *Summa theologiae*, 1-2, Question 94, Article 2," *Natural Law Forum*, 10 (1965), pp. 168-201, I explain at length and defend the view of practical reason and its first principle which I summarize here. Several other studies on the subject also are mentioned and/or discussed in the article.

17. Cf. Morris Ginsberg, *On the Diversity of Morals* (London: 1962), pp. 134-135. Robert H. Lowie, *An Introduction to Cultural Anthropology*, new and enlarged ed. (New York: 1940), has chapter headings which correspond to basic human inclinations; this reflects the fact that basic human goods are categories always *presupposed* by any anthropological study.

18. Germain Grisez and Russell Shaw, *Beyond the New Morality: The Responsibilities of Freedom* (Notre Dame, Ind.: 1974), pp. 76-149, is an attempt, written for nonphilosophers, at such a project.

19. The maxim is derived from Romans 3.8, where St. Paul rejects the contradictory. Christians, he says, were accused of justifying evil-doing. It is noteworthy that this point is in the context of a discussion of the ways of divine providence; God permits evil for a greater good. If both consequentialism and the theistic conception of providence were accepted, one would have a simple ethics: If in doubt as to the morality of some act, try it! Since on the theistic conception of providence, God permits no evil from which he does not draw a greater good, every act would be justified, if consequentialism were correct, by its ultimate good consequences. So Paul rejects consequentialism. Contemporary Christians, other than those who have adopted the "new morality," continue to reject it. See,

for example, Ronald Lawler, O.F.M.Cap., Donald W. Wuerl, and Thomas Comerford Lawler, eds., *The Teaching of Christ: A Catholic Catechism for Adults* (Huntington, Ind.: 1976), pp. 299-300, 314-321.

20. Joseph Fletcher, *Moral Responsibility*, pp. 21-23, as well as in other works, rejects the principle in this formulation, which he regards as an absolutization of Paul's "remark." However, Fletcher never takes the trouble to clarify the traditional meaning of the maxim that evil may not be done, that good might follow therefrom, and he takes the saying that the end does not justify the means as if it meant—what is absurd—that one can act without any end in view.

21. Immanuel Kant, *Foundations of the Metaphysics of Morals*, trans. Lewis White Beck (Indianapolis, New York, Kansas City: 1959), p. 47 (vol. 4, p. 429 in the Akademie edition).

22. *Ibid.*, Kant immediately follows his enunciation of the principle of respect for persons as ends with an argument intended to exemplify the principle: ". . . he who contemplates suicide will ask himself whether his action can be consistent with the idea of humanity as an end in itself. If, in order to escape from burdensome circumstances, he destroys himself, he uses a person merely as a means to maintain a tolerable condition up to the end of life. Man, however, is not a thing, and thus not something to be used merely as a means; he must always be regarded in all his actions as an end in himself. Therefore, I cannot dispose of man in my own person so as to mutilate, corrupt, or kill him." I think Kant's insight here is correct, although his formalism and his use of the misleading concept of "duty to oneself" detract very seriously from his articulation of this insight.

23. Ludwig Wittgenstein, *Notebooks, 1914-1916*, trans. G. E. M. Anscombe (New York and Evanston: 1961), p. 91e. For Wittgenstein, there might be ethics even if there were only a single person (p. 79e), for "I am my world" (p. 84e), and so I have a responsibility for the meaning I confer or fail to confer on the world. I think Wittgenstein was influenced in these remarks by Kant, who puts the treatment of suicide *in first place* in his most mature work in normative ethics, *The Metaphysical Principles of Virtue: Part II of the Metaphysics of Morals*, trans. James Ellington (Indianapolis, New York: 1964), pp. 82-85 (vol. 6, pp. 421-424 in the Akademie edition). The most relevant paragraph in Kant's argument is: "Man cannot deprive himself of his personality so long as one speaks of duties, thus so long as he lives. That man ought to have the authorization to withdraw himself from all obligation, i.e., to be free to act as if no authorization at all were required for this withdrawal, involves a contradiction. To destroy the subject of morality in his own person is tantamount to obliterating from the world, as far as he can, the very existence of morality itself; but morality is, nevertheless, an end in itself. Accordingly, to dispose of oneself as a mere means to some end of one's own liking is to degrade humanity in one's person (*homo noumenon*), which, after all, was entrusted to man (*homo phenomenon*) to preserve." The trouble with this argument is that Kant makes morality, not life, the good which is violated; he is transposing an ethics of the will of God into an ethics of human autonomy, and in doing so fails to solve the question of the relationship between moral requirements (commands of God/imperatives of one's own reason) and human goods.

24. Cf. Seymour Perlin and Chester W. Schmidt, Jr., "Psychiatry," in Perlin, ed., *op. cit.*, pp. 149-150; also see David Bakan, "Suicide and Immortality," in Edwin S. Shneidman, ed., *On the Nature of Suicide* (San Francisco: 1969), pp. 120-128, who regards this will to dominate death and life as the key to suicide in general.

25. A person guilty of accidental manslaughter could be executed (Nm. 35.26-28, 32); a family or city as a whole could be destroyed under the penalty of the ban (Ex. 22.19-20, Lv. 20.2-5, Dt. 13.13-18, Jos. 7.10-26); a victim of rape in a city or a bride discovered not to be a virgin was presumed guilty of unchastity and could be executed (Dt. 22.20-24); wars and executions based upon religion make up an important part of the Old Testament.

26. Many Christians appeal to Rm. 13.4 to justify capital punishment and killing in war. Speaking of capital punishment, Pius XII insisted upon the legitimacy of vindicative punishment imposed by public authority, but stated ("Crime and Punishment," *The Catholic Mind*, 53 [1955], p. 381; *AAS*, 47 [1955], p. 81): ". . . the words of the sources and of the living teaching power do not refer to the specific content of the individual juridical prescriptions or rules of action (cf. particularly, Rm. 13.4), but rather to the essential foundation itself of penal power and of its immanent finality." This remark seems to endorse the view that Rm. 13.4, despite mention of the sword, need not be taken as referring to the death penalty; on this view, the sword is mentioned here as a symbol of the general authority of legitimate rulers, an authority which comes from God. See also Franziskus Stratmann, O.P., *The Church and War: A Catholic Study* (London: 1928), pp. 52-80, for a discussion of the development and weakening of the just-war theology; he also traces (pp. 110-134) Christian theories of peace.

27. *Summa theologiae*, 2-2, question 64, article 7, response.

28. Germain Grisez, "Toward a Consistent Natural-Law Ethics of Killing," *The American Journal of Jurisprudence*, 15 (1970), pp. 64-96. Thomas Nagel, "War and Massacre," *Philosophy and Public Affairs*, 1 (1971-1972), pp. 123-144, offers a defense of what he called an "absolutist" position. His attempt to articulate this position (especially on pp. 133-141 and note 11 on p. 141) comes close to my own view of what *might possibly* be justifiable in war. Thomas Aquinas (*Summa theologiae*, 2-2, question 40, article 1, response) quotes and agrees with St. Augustine who condemns "the desire to harm, the cruelty of revenge, a vindictive spirit, the rage of self-defense, the lust of power, and such like" as incompatible with an upright intention in the conduct of war. It seems to me that *if desire to harm is excluded, only acts which neither are nor amount to the execution of a proposal to kill are permissible.*

29. See Perlin and Schmidt, in Perlin, ed., *op cit.*, pp. 148-149; D. J. West, *Murder Followed by Suicide* (Cambridge, Mass.: 1966).

30. See Robert M. Byrn, "Compulsory Lifesaving Treatment for the Competent Adult," *Fordham Law Review*, 44 (1975), pp. 29-36.

31. For example, by Glanville Williams, " 'Mercy-Killing' Legislation—A Rejoinder," *Minnesota Law Review*, 43 (1958), p. 11; "It is not impossible that, in the foreseeable future, medical men will be able to preserve the mindless body until the age, say, of 1000, while the mind itself will have lasted only a tenth of that time. What will mankind do then? It is hardly possible to imagine that we shall establish huge hospital-mausolea where the aged are kept in a kind of living death. Even if it is desired to do this, the cost of the undertaking may make it impossible."

32. See Byrn, *op. cit.*, pp. 16-24.

33. Williams argues along this line, briefly in " 'Mercy-Killing' Legislation—A Rejoinder," pp. 1-2.

34. Williams, *Sanctity of Life and the Criminal Law*, p. 340.

35. The truth in this matter of the saying, "Where there's a will, there's a way," is borne out by data—for instance, Norman L. Farberow, Edwin S. Shneidman, and Calista V. Leonard, "Suicide among Patients with Malignant Neoplasms," in Shneidman, Farberow, and Litman, eds., *op. cit.*, pp. 325-344.

36. Williams," 'Mercy-Killing' Legislation—A Rejoinder," p.7, already insisted on characterizing euthanasia as a medical operation, although he professed to expect ridicule for so doing.

37. And cases have succeeded with respect to a public hospital (*Nyberg* v. *City of Virginia*, 495 F. 2d 1342 [8th Cir. 1974]), a private hospital (*Doe* v. *Charleston Area Medical Center, Inc.*, . . . F. 2d . . . [4th Cir. 1975] decided Nov. 6, 1975 #75-1161), and the mandating of the use of public funds to pay for abortions (*Klein* v. *Nassau County Medical Center*, 347 F. Supp. 496 [E.D. N.Y. 1972]).

38. Indeed, I suspect that an important motivation, perhaps unconscious, of those who urge the legalization of euthanasia is precisely to generalize public cooperation in the deadly deeds of those who have assumed the character of killer. Generalizing participation not only serves the practical purpose of ensuring social acceptance of killing, but also serves the psychological purpose of establishing solidarity in guilt. In other words, just as some criminal organizations demand that new members commit a serious crime as part of the rite of initiation, so the proponents of legalized killing perhaps wish to abolish innocence, because when none is innocent, none is blameworthy.

39. An example of a compromise is the British Voluntary Euthanasia Bill (1969) which leaves a heavy presumption in favor of a physician or nurse who "acting in *good faith*, causes euthanasia to be administered to a qualified patient in accordance with what the person so acting *believes to be* the patient's declaration," but which also involves public officials in regulating declarations of desire to be killed and appointing physicians to do or supervise the killing. (The text of this bill is included in O. Ruth Russell, *Freedom to Die: Moral and Legal Aspects of Euthanasia* [New York: 1975], pp. 291-293).

40. Yale Kamisar, "Some Non-Religious Views against Proposed 'Mercy-Killing' Legislation," *Minnesota Law Review*, 42 (1958), pp. 978-985.

41. Williams, " 'Mercy-Killing' Legislation—A Rejoinder," pp. 3-4.

42. *Ibid.*, p. 4.

43. Glanville Williams, "Euthanasia and Abortion," *University of Colorado Law Review*, 38 (1966), p. 181.

44. Kamisar, *op. cit.*, pp. 1030-1041.

45. Williams, " 'Mercy-Killing' Legislation—A Rejoinder," p. 9.

46. Williams, *Sanctity of Life and the Criminal Law*, pp. 349-350.

47. Williams, " 'Mercy-Killing' Legislation—A Rejoinder," pp. 11-12; however, "Euthanasia and Abortion," pp. 178-187, seems more favorable toward such a proposal.

48. See David W. Louisell, "Euthanasia and Biathanasia: On Dying and Killing," *Catholic University Law Review*, 22 (1973), pp. 723-734.

49. Kamisar, *op cit.*, pp. 1014-1030. The same thrust still is part of the pro-euthanasia movement; see, for example, Russell, *op cit.*, pp. 236-247.

50. Joseph Fletcher, "The Right to Die: A Theologian Comments," *Atlantic*, 221 (April, 1968), p. 63.

51. *Ibid.*, p. 64.

52. One case of mongolism, admittedly unusual, was a girl of normal intelligence: Frank R. Ford, *Diseases of the Nervous System in Infancy, Childhood, and Adolescence*, 5 ed. (Springfield, Ill.: 1966), p. 182; another was a boy who attained the linguistic ability of a seventh-grade student, and who was anything but lacking in personal quality: May V. Seagoe, *Yesterday Was Tuesday, All Day and All Night* (Boston and Toronto: 1964).

53. Testimony of Harriet F. Pilpel on behalf of the New York Civil Liberties Union before the Committee on Health, New York State Assembly, March 7, 1966 (mimeograph).

54. *Roe* v. *Wade* 410 U.S. 165 (1973).

55. William Kopit and Harriet F. Pilpel, *Abortion and the New York Penal Laws*, directed as a memorandum to the Due Process Committee of the American Civil Liberties Union, December 7, 1966, with a note, "Working Paper (originally considered by the NYCLU Board of Directors, April 20, 1965" (mimeograph), p. 7.

A footnote to the paragraph denying the absolute right to life cites Glanville Williams, *Sanctity of Life and the Criminal Law*, p. 198, as an authority for the claim that even "Catholic dogma" agrees by sanctioning killing in self-defence and during a just war!

56. *Roe* v. *Wade* 410 U.S. 162-163 (1973).

57. Williams, "Euthanasia and Abortion," p. 187, speaks of care for the aged: "To provide this assistance commensurate with the need may be beyond our resources, particularly if medical science continues to become more skillful in aggravating the problem by increasing the numbers of the aged and senile. Thus we still need to consider the help that could be given by a different solution, requiring not a social reorganization but a change in our philosophical attitudes." In other words, we can avoid changing society to provide justice for the elderly by changing our attitudes to provide death for them.

List of Contributors

Alexander, Leo
> *Lecturer in Psychiatry, School of Medicine, Tufts University.*

Byrn, Robert M.
> *Attorney and Professor of Law, School of Law, Fordham University.*

Campbell, Alexander George Macpherson
> *Director of the Newborn Service, Yale-New Haven Hospital.*

Capron, Alexander Morgan
> *Assistant Professor of Law, School of Law, University of Pennsylvania.*

Cass, Leon R.
> *Executive Secretary of the Committee on the Life Sciences and Social Policy, National Research Council, National Academy of Sciences.*

Collins, Vincent Joseph
> *Chairman of the Division of Anesthesiology, Cook County Hospital, Chicago.*

Diamond, Eugene F.
> *Assistant Chairman, Department of Pediatrics, Stritch School of Medicine, Loyola University of Chicago.*

Duff, Raymond Stanley
> *Associate Professor of Pediatrics, School of Medicine, Yale University.*

Dyck, Arthur J.
> *Mary B. Saltonstall Professor of Population Ethics, School of Public Health, Harvard University.*

Engelhardt, H. Tristram, Jr.
> *Associate Professor, Institute for the Medical Humanities and Department of Preventive Medicine and Community Health, University of Texas Medical Branch, Galveston.*

Fletcher, Joseph
Emeritus Professor of Social Ethics and Moral Theology, Episcopal Theological School and Visiting Professor of Biomedical Ethics, School of Medicine, University of Virginia.

Friloux, C. Anthony, Jr.
Attorney and Dean of the National College of Criminal Defense Lawyers and Public Defenders.

Grisez, Germain
Professor of Philosophy, Campion College, University of Regina.

Gustafson, James M.
University Professor of Theological Ethics, University of Chicago.

Hauerwas, Stanley Martin
Associate Professor of Theology and Director of Graduate Studies, Department of Theology, University of Notre Dame.

Horan, Dennis J.
Attorney and Instructor, School of Law, University of Chicago; Chairman, ABA Right-to-Live/Right-to-Die Committee.

Hughes, Richard
Chief Justice, Supreme Court of New Jersey.

Ionesco, Eugene
Playwright and Member of the French Academy.

Jakobovits, Immanuel
Chief Rabbi of the United Hebrew Congregations of the British Commonwealth of Nations.

Kamisar, Yale
Professor of Law, School of Law, University of Michigan.

Koop, C. Everett
Professor of Pediatric Surgery, School of Medicine, University of Pennsylvania and Surgeon-in-Chief, Children's Hospital of Philadelphia.

Lamerton, Richard
Director of St. Joseph's Hospice, Hackney, England.

Lebacqz, Karen A.
Assistant Professor of Christian Ethics, Pacific School of Religion.

Louisell, David W.
Elizabeth Josselyn Boalt Professor of Law, School of Law, University of California, Berkeley.

Mall, David
Teacher of Rhetoric and Executive Director of Americans United for Life, Inc.

McLuhan, Herbert Marshall
Director of the Centre for Culture and Technology, University of Toronto.

O'Rourke, Kevin D.
Director of Medical Moral Affairs, Catholic Hospital Association.

Ramsey, Paul
Harrington Spear Paine Professor of Religion, Department of Religion, Princeton University.

Robertson, John A.
Assistant Professor of Law, School of Law, University of Wisconsin.

St. Martin, Thomas
Specialist in Educational Administration, Minnesota Department of Education.

Shaw, Anthony
Specialist in Pediatric Surgery, University of Virginia Medical Center.

Tomasek, Joseph J.
Student of International Law and Graduate of the University of Strasbourg.

Wertham, Frederic
Consulting Psychiatrist, Queens Hospital Center, New York.

Williams, Glanville
Fellow of Jesus College, Cambridge University.

Index

Table of Cases

State Statutes